1st Joint SLTU and CCURL Workshop (SLTU-CCURL 2020)

Marseille, France
11-16 May 2020

Editors:

Dorothee Beermann
Laurent Besacier
Sakriani Sakti
Claudia Soria

ISBN: 978-1-7138-1277-7

LREC 2020 Workshop
Language Resources and Evaluation Conference
11–16 May 2020

**1st Joint SLTU and CCURL Workshop
(SLTU-CCURL 2020)**

PROCEEDINGS

Editors:
Dorothee Beermann, Laurent Besacier, Sakriani Sakti, and Claudia Soria

Proceedings of the LREC 2020
1st Joint SLTU and CCURL Workshop
(SLTU-CCURL 2020)

Edited by: Dorothee Beermann, Laurent Besacier, Sakriani Sakti, Claudia Soria

For more information:
European Language Resources Association (ELRA)
9 rue des Cordelières
75013, Paris
France
http://www.elra.info
Email: lrec@elda.org

Introduction

Created in April 2017, SIGUL (http://www.elra.info/en/sig/sigul/) is a joint Special Interest Group of the European Language Resources Association (ELRA) and of the International Speech Communication Association (ISCA). SIGUL intends to bring together a number of professionals involved in the development of language resources and technologies for under-resourced languages. Its main objective is to build a community that not only supports linguistic diversity through technology and ICT but also commits to increase the lesser-resourced languages (regional, minority, or endangered) chances to survive the digital world through language and speech technology.

Before the creation of SIGUL, two workshops addressed language technologies for low resource languages: there have been 6 editions of SLTU (Spoken Language Technologies for Under-resourced languages) which started in 2008; and 3 editions of CCURL (Collaboration and Computing for Under-Resourced Languages) which started in 2014. For 2020, and as a satellite event of LREC, SIGUL board decided to organize the 1st Joint Workshop of SLTU (Spoken Language Technologies for Under-resourced languages) and CCURL (Collaboration and Computing for Under-Resourced Languages) (SLTU-CCURL 2020).

We solicited papers related to all areas of natural language processing, speech and computational linguistics, as well as those at the intersection with digital humanities and documentary linguistics, provided that they address less-resourced languages. One goal of this workshop was to offer a venue where researchers in different disciplines and from varied backgrounds can fruitfully explore new areas of intellectual and practical development while honoring their common interest of sustaining less-resourced languages.

Our programme committee comprised 60 experts in natural language processing and spoken language processing from 19 countries. Each of the 64 submitted papers was reviewed by 3 committee members. We finally accepted 54 papers for the proceedings. We would like to express our sincere thanks to all members of this committee (who worked hard despite the difficult conditions associated with the pandemic) and authors for their great work in making this event a scientifically recognised international Workshop. We would also like to extend our thanks to all our sponsors: Google as platinum sponsor; ELRA, ISCA and ACL/SIGEL for endorsing this event.

Unfortunately, as a consequence of the COVID-19 pandemic, LREC 2020 has been canceled and - as a satellite event of the Conference - SLTU-CCURL 2020 has been canceled as well. We nevertheless hope that you will find these workshop proceedings relevant and stimulating for your own research. We are looking forward to see you soon for future events organised by SIGUL.

SLTU-CCURL-2020 Workshop co-chairs:

Dorothee Beermann (NTNU, Norway)
Laurent Besacier (LIG – Université Grenoble Alpes, France)
Sakriani Sakti (NAIST, Japan)
Claudia Soria (CNR-ILC, Italy)

Organizers

Dorothee Beermann (NTNU, Norway)
Laurent Besacier (LIG – Université Grenoble Alpes, France)
Sakriani Sakti (NAIST, Japan)
Claudia Soria (CNR-ILC, Italy)

Program Committee:

Adrian Doyle (University of Galway, Ireland)
Alexey Karpov (SPIIRAS, Russian Federation)
Alexis Palmer (University of North Texas, USA)
Amir Aharoni (Wikimedia Foundation)
Andras Kornai (Hungarian Academy of Sciences, Hungary)
Angelo Mario Del Grosso (CNR-ILC, Italy)
Antti Arppe (University of Alberta, Canada)
Atticus Harrigan (University of Alberta, Canada)
Charl Van Heerden (Saigen, South Africa)
Daan Van Esch (Google)
Dafydd Gibbon (Bielefeld University, Germany)
Delyth Prys (Bangor University, UK)
Dewi Bryn Jones (Bangor University, UK)
Dorothee Beermann (NTNU, Norway)
Emily Le Chen (University of Illinois, USA)
Federico Boschetti (CNR-ILC, Italy)
Francis Tyers (Indiana University, USA)
Gerard Bailly (GIPSA Lab, CNRS)
Gilles Adda (LIMSI/IMMI CNRS, France)
Heysem Kaya (Utrecht University, The Netherlands)
Hyunji "Hayley" Park (University of Illinois at Urbana-Champaign, USA)
Irina Kipyatkova (SPIIRAS, Russia)
Jeff Good (University at Buffalo, USA)
Jelske Dijkstra (Fryske Akademy, The Netherlands)
John Judge (ADAPT DCU, Ireland)
John Philip McCrae (National University of Ireland Galway, Ireland)
Jonas Fromseier Mortensen (Google)
Jordan Lachler (University of Alberta, Canada)
Joseph Mariani (LIMSI-CNRS, France)
Katherine Schmirler (University of Alberta, Canada)
Kepa Sarasola (University of the Basque Country, Spain)
Kevin Scannell (Saint Louis University, Missouri, USA)
Klara Ceberio (Elhuyar, Spain)
Lane Schwartz (University of Illinois at Urbana-Champaign, USA)
Lars Hellan (NTNU, Norway)
Lars Steinert (University of Bremen, Germany)
Laurent Besacier (LIG-IMAG, France)
Maite Melero (Barcelona Supercomputing Center, Spain)

Marcely Zanon Boito (LIG-IMAG, France)
Mathieu Mangeot-Nagata (LIG-IMAG, France)
Matt Coler (University of Groningen, The Netherlands)
Mohammad A. M. Abushariah (The University of Jordan, Jordan)
Nick Thieberger (University of Melbourne / ARC Centre of Excellence for the Dynamics of Language, Australia)
Omar Farooq (AMU, India)
Pierric Sans (Google)
Pradip K Das (IIT, India)
Richard Littauer (University of Saarland, Germany)
Sahar Ghannay (LIMSI, CNRS, France)
Sakriani Sakti (NAIST, Japan)
Satoshi Nakamura (NAIST, Japan)
Sebastian Stüker (KIT, Germany)
Shyam S Agrawal (KIIT, India)
Sjur Moshagen (UiT The Arctic University of Norway, Norway)
Solomon Teferra Abate (Addis Ababa University, Ethiopia)
Steven Bird (Charles Darwin University, Australia)
Tanja Schultz (Uni-Bremen, Germany)
Thang Vu (Uni-Stuttgart, Germany)
Teresa Lynn (ADAPT Centre, Ireland)
Trond Trosterud (Tromsø University, Norway)
Win Pa Pa (UCS Yangon, Myanmar)

Table of Contents

Proceedings of the 1st Joint SLTU and CCURL Workshop (SLTU-CCURL 2020), pages 1–8
Language Resources and Evaluation Conference (LREC 2020), Marseille, 11–16 May 2020
© European Language Resources Association (ELRA), licensed under CC-BY-NC

Neural Models for Predicting Celtic Mutations

Kevin P. Scannell

Department of Computer Science
Saint Louis University
St. Louis, Missouri, USA 63103
kscanne@gmail.com

Abstract

The Celtic languages share a common linguistic phenomenon known as *initial mutations*; these consist of pronunciation and spelling changes that occur at the beginning of some words, triggered in certain semantic or syntactic contexts. Initial mutations occur quite frequently and all non-trivial NLP systems for the Celtic languages must learn to handle them properly. In this paper we describe and evaluate neural network models for predicting mutations in two of the six Celtic languages: Irish and Scottish Gaelic. We also discuss applications of these models to grammatical error detection and language modeling.

Keywords: Celtic languages, initial mutations, Irish, Scottish Gaelic, language modeling, neural networks

1. Introduction

The Insular Celtic language family consists of two branches, the Goidelic (or Q-Celtic) branch, comprised of Irish, Manx, and Scottish Gaelic, and the Brythonic (or P-Celtic) branch, comprised of Welsh, Breton, and Cornish. All six languages are under-resourced in terms of language technology, although substantial progress has been made in recent years, especially for Irish and Welsh (Judge et al., 2012; Evas, 2013).

The Celtic languages share a linguistic phenomenon known as *initial mutations*. These are pronunciation and spelling changes that occur at the beginning of certain words based on the grammatical context. For example, the Irish word *bád* ('a boat') undergoes an initial mutation known as *lenition* when preceded by the first person singular possessive adjective *mo*, hence *mo bhád* ('my boat'). Each Celtic language has multiple mutation types, each one governed by sometimes-complicated rules that can be challenging for learners and native speakers alike. Initial mutations are quite common (occurring, for example, in about 15% of tokens in typical Irish corpora), and so all NLP technologies for the Celtic languages must handle them correctly.

Our goal in this paper is to describe and evaluate several neural network models for predicting Celtic mutations. We restrict ourselves to Irish and Scottish Gaelic for reasons we will make clear in §2.2 below.

We have two primary applications in mind for this work. First, mutation errors are among the most common made by learners of the Celtic languages, and a sufficiently accurate predictive model can be used as part of a system for detecting and correcting grammatical errors. We address this application in §4.1. The second application is to language modeling, the idea being to separately predict the probability of a demutated token given its history followed by the probability of a given mutation on that token. We show in §4.2 that the resulting factored language model (Bilmes and Kirchhoff, 2003) yields a decrease in perplexity over a baseline 5-gram model. This language model can in turn be incorporated into end-user technologies like machine translation engines, reducing the number of mutation errors output by such systems.

The current research landscape in NLP is dominated by work on English, and algorithms or architectures that give state-of-the-art results on English are often applied without modification to other languages. We hope that the results of this paper show that one can improve upon language-independent approaches by incorporating linguistic knowledge specific to a given language or language family.

The outline of the remainder of the paper is as follows. We begin in §2 with an overview of the initial mutations that occur in Irish and Scottish Gaelic, and we explore the information-theoretic content of the mutation system. In §3 we define and evaluate our neural network models for predicting mutations. The final section §4 discusses the applications of these models to Irish grammar checking and language modeling.

2. Celtic Initial Mutations

2.1. Definitions and Examples

We begin with descriptions of the initial mutations that occur in Irish and Scottish Gaelic: lenition, t-prothesis, h-prothesis, and eclipsis.

- **Lenition** is a "softening" of the initial consonants *b*, *c*, *d*, *f*, *g*, *m*, *p*, *s*, and *t*, that occurs in both languages in certain contexts. It is indicated in the modern orthographies by the insertion of an *h* after the initial consonant. For example, adjectives following a feminine noun are lenited: *beag* ('small'), but *bean bheag* ('small woman'). (This example works in both languages).

- **T-prothesis**. In both languages a *t-* is prefixed to a masculine noun beginning with a vowel in the nominative singular when preceded by the definite article. There is a similar (but distinct) phenomenon triggered by the definite article that occurs for some nouns beginning with *s*. This is represented as a prefixed *t-* in Scottish Gaelic orthography, so *slat* ('a stick') becomes *an t-slat* ('the stick'), but is written without the hyphen in Irish (*an tslat*). For the purposes of our models these are treated as a single type of mutation.

- **H-prothesis**. An *h* (modern Irish) or *h-* (Scottish Gaelic and older Irish orthographies) is prefixed to some words having an initial vowel, e.g. nouns preceded by the third person feminine possessive adjective *a* ('her'), hence *aisling* ('dream') becomes *a haisling* ('her dream', Irish), or *a h-aisling* (Scottish Gaelic).

- **Eclipsis**. Roughly speaking, eclipsis causes voiceless stops to become voiced and voiced stops to become nasal. The full set of orthographic changes is given in the following section as part of Algorithm 1. Eclipsis occurs in both languages but is usually not realized orthographically as an initial mutation in Scottish Gaelic. One example that does occur in both languages is eclipsis of an initial vowel after the first person plural possessive adjective, so *athair* ('father') becomes *ár n-athair* ('our father', Irish) and *ar n-athair* (Scottish Gaelic).

We define a set of labels $\mathcal{M} = \{\mathbf{L}, \mathbf{T}, \mathbf{H}, \mathbf{E}, \mathbf{N}\}$ where $\mathbf{L}$, $\mathbf{T}$, $\mathbf{H}$, and $\mathbf{E}$ correspond to the four mutations above, and the label $\mathbf{N}$ is used for tokens having no mutation.

There are dozens of rules governing exactly when each mutation occurs, and we make no attempt to cover them all here, instead referring the interested reader to (Tithe an Oireachtais, 2016) and (Bauer, 2011) for Irish and Scottish Gaelic respectively. The rules can be quite challenging for language learners, and there is even significant variation in how the mutations are used among native speakers, based primarily on dialect.

A rule-based system for predicting Irish mutations has been implemented in previous work of the author.[1] But this approach relies at minimum on a rich lexicon and accurate part-of-speech tagging, and fails to implement certain rules that would require deeper syntactic or semantic analysis. The resulting system suffers from the brittleness that plagues many rule-based NLP systems. The pure machine learning approach we propose in this paper aims to overcome these shortcomings.

2.2. Orthographic Transparency and Demutation

All of the initial mutations in Scottish Gaelic are orthographically transparent, by which we mean that they can be trivially and algorithmically removed whenever they occur. With a single exception that we will describe momentarily, the same is true for Irish. This means that we can produce unlimited amounts of training data labeled with the correct mutations for either language, starting from plain text corpora. This is in contrast with the other four Celtic languages where mutations are generally *not* algorithmically removable,[2] and so the approach of this paper does not apply directly to Manx Gaelic, Cornish, Breton, or Welsh.

For Irish, lenition, eclipsis, and t-prothesis can be removed algorithmically, but h-prothesis cannot be, because, unlike

Scottish Gaelic, it is written without a hyphen in the standard orthography. Therefore, without making use of a comprehensive lexicon one cannot be certain if a given initial *h* represents h-prothesis or if it is instead an integral part of the word, e.g. *hidrigin* ('hydrogen'). Even a dictionary-based approached is doomed because of ambiguities like *aiste* ('an essay') vs. *haiste* ('a hatch'), and because of new or non-standard words that will always be missing from a dictionary. Instead, we will take a brute force approach and define every initial *h* in Irish to be an example of h-prothesis.

Let $\mathcal{V}$ be the set of legal tokens. In our experiments we will assume all tokens have been lowercased which simplifies the model and the rules below. The goal of Algorithm 1 is to define two functions; the first $\sigma : \mathcal{V} \to \mathcal{V}$ strips mutations and the second $\mu : \mathcal{V} \to \mathcal{M}$ maps a token to its mutation label.

Algorithm 1. Given a token w, this algorithm returns the demutated token $\sigma(w)$ and the mutation label $\mu(w) \in \mathcal{M}$.

1. If a token w begins with *bhf*, set $\mu(w) = \mathbf{E}$, and remove the *bh* to obtain $\sigma(w)$.

2. Otherwise, if the second letter of a token w is an *h*, set $\mu(w) = \mathbf{L}$, and remove the *h* to obtain $\sigma(w)$.

3. Otherwise, if a token w begins with *h-*, set $\mu(w) = \mathbf{H}$, and remove the *h-* to obtain $\sigma(w)$.

4. (Irish only) Otherwise, if a token w begins with *h*, set $\mu(w) = \mathbf{H}$, and remove the *h* to obtain $\sigma(w)$.

5. Otherwise, if a token w begins with *t-*, set $\mu(w) = \mathbf{T}$, and remove the *t-* to obtain $\sigma(w)$.

6. Otherwise, if a token w begins with *ts*, set $\mu(w) = \mathbf{T}$, and remove the initial *t* to obtain $\sigma(w)$.

7. Otherwise, if a token w begins with *n-*, set $\mu(w) = \mathbf{E}$, and remove the *n-* to obtain $\sigma(w)$.

8. (Irish only) Otherwise, if a token w begins with *mb*, *gc*, *nd*, *ng*, *bp*, or *dt*, set $\mu(w) = \mathbf{E}$, and remove the first letter to obtain $\sigma(w)$.

9. Otherwise, set $\mu(w) = \mathbf{N}$ and $\sigma(w) = w$.

Note that we have defined slightly different functions for the two languages, but in what follows we will abuse notation and write them simply as σ and μ, understanding that the additional rules for Irish will be applied only in the Irish experiments.

Since we are trying to explore the learnability of the mutation system from raw text, it is important to note that neither function definition encodes any information about the lexicon or the grammatical context in which these mutations occur; they are simply defined in terms of the orthographic changes in question. In the case of lenition, for example, we do not even encode the knowledge that lenition only applies to consonants. This means that σ and μ sometimes do the "wrong thing" linguistically, as in the case of Irish h-prothesis noted above ($\sigma(hidrigin) = idrigin$), or when applied to English words embedded in otherwise Gaelic

---

[1] See `https://cadhan.com/gramadoir/`.

[2] Consider for example the surface form *vea* in Manx Gaelic, which can be a lenited form of the noun *bea* ('life') as in *my vea* ('my life'), or else an eclipsed form of *fea* ('quiet, rest') as in *gow-jee nyn vea* ('take your (pl.) rest', cf. Matthew 14:41).

texts, e.g $\sigma(Chaucer) = Caucer$ or $\mu(tsunami) = \mathbf{T}$. There are also more subtle cases one could quibble over, for example lenited Irish words like *cheana* or *chugat* for which the unlenited form does not exist in the lexicon. Again, all of this is fine for our purposes: we have simply defined a task in which our labels differ in rare cases from the linguistically-correct ones. In theory, this complicates the learning process since examples like these can occur in contexts where one would not expect to see the corresponding mutation. But as we will see in the sections that follow, there was no practical impact on the neural networks we trained; they simply learned to predict, for example, a (very) high probability for the label $\mathbf{H}$ given a "demutated" token like *idrigin*, or for the label $\mathbf{L}$ given examples like *ceana*, *cugat*, or *Caucer*.

2.3. Mutations as Low-Entropy Features

Celtic mutations carry very little information. Informally speaking, if one were to remove all of the mutations from a text, a native speaker would be able to restore almost all of them correctly and unambiguously. One of our goals in this section is to make this notion more precise, and assign a numerical value (in units of bits per token) to the information content of initial mutations.

We will write P for a model that produces the probability of a mutation given the demutated target word and preceding context. More precisely, let $w_1, \ldots, w_N$ be a sequence of tokens, and let $\mathbf{m} \in \mathcal{M}$. For $k \in \{1, \ldots, N\}$, we write $P(\mathbf{m}|\sigma(w_1)\ldots\sigma(w_k))$ for the probability that $\mu(w_k) = \mathbf{m}$ given the demutated token $\sigma(w_k)$ and the history $\sigma(w_1)\ldots\sigma(w_{k-1})$. Conditioning our predictions on *demutated* words to the *left* of the target word will allow us to incorporate P into a full language model; see §4.2. for details.

We write the average log loss Λ of this model as

$$\Lambda = -\frac{1}{N}\sum_{i=1}^{N}\log_2 P(\mu(w_i)|\sigma(w_1)\ldots\sigma(w_i)) \quad (1)$$

with units of bits per token. This gives an estimate of the information content of initial mutations based on the given model P and test corpus $w_1, \ldots, w_N$.

Our claim is that Celtic mutations are "low-entropy" linguistic features, by which we mean that the quantity Λ will be close to zero given a sufficiently accurate model P. We will demonstrate this experimentally in the next section. This claim will come as no surprise to readers familiar with the rules for Irish and Scottish Gaelic initial mutations, since the mutations are often completely determined by the surrounding context, often the previous one or two words along with the initial letter of the target word.

There are, however, some well-known exceptions where mutations appear to carry important information. One example is the Irish third person possessive *a* which can mean "his", "her", or "their", with the correct sense sometimes being determined by the mutation on the possessed noun: *a bád* ('her boat', no mutation), *a bhád* ('his boat', lenited), *a mbád* ('their boat', eclipsed). Of course in many cases the correct sense can also be reliably guessed from the surrounding context (necessarily so in cases where the pos-

sessed noun does not admit an initial mutation), but sometimes this is challenging, especially for sentences in isolation, and the mutation does convey non-trivial information. Another well-known example is a difference in mutations that occurs between Irish dialects in the dative case. In the Ulster dialect, speakers usually lenite a noun in the dative, e.g. *ar an bhád* ('on the boat'), while in the other major dialects the noun is eclipsed (*ar an mbád*) and so the mutation conveys information about the dialect of the speaker or writer. We will return to the question of which mutations carry the most information in a data-driven way in §3.3.

3. Neural Networks for Mutation Prediction

3.1. Design and Implementation

The goal of this section is to define a number of models which predict probabilities of initial mutations. All models are evaluated according to their (base 2) log loss Λ as defined in Equation 1 above. Because we plan to incorporate these into full language models, it is important that the predictions be conditioned only on the demutated target word and any preceding words. See §4.2 below for further details.

Because five-fold classification problems evaluated via log loss are not particularly common in the literature, we will define and evaluate a few very simple baselines to help frame the problem. For each model, we assume we have seen a history of demutated tokens $\sigma(w_1)\ldots\sigma(w_k)$ and want to predict the probability that mutation $\mathbf{m} \in \mathcal{M}$ occurs on w_k. We denote the tokens in the training corpus by $t_1 \ldots t_N$.

- **Label priors.** The unmutated label $\mathbf{N}$ is by far the most common, so we do reasonably well by simply assigning to every token the prior probability of $\mathbf{m}$ as seen in training:

$$P(\mathbf{m}|\sigma(w_1)\ldots\sigma(w_k)) = \frac{1}{N}\sum_{\mu(t_i)=\mathbf{m}} 1$$

- **First letter.** Certain initial letters are incompatible with certain mutations. We take this into account in this baseline by assigning the maximal likelihood probability of $\mathbf{m}$ as estimated from training tokens t_i such that $\sigma(t_i)$ and $\sigma(w_k)$ have the same first character.

- **Unigram model.** This baseline assigns the probability

$$P(\mathbf{m}|\sigma(w_1)\ldots\sigma(w_k)) = \frac{\sum_{\mu(t_i)=\mathbf{m},\sigma(t_i)=\sigma(w_k)} 1}{\sum_{\sigma(t_i)=\sigma(w_k)} 1},$$

but smoothed using add-α smoothing with the parameter α tuned on the development set.

- **Trigram model.** This model is analogous to the unigram but computes the maximal likelihood estimate of $\mathbf{m}$ based on trigrams (t_{i-2}, t_{i-1}, t_i) seen in training such that $(\sigma(t_{i-2}), \sigma(t_{i-1}), \sigma(t_i)) = (\sigma(w_{k-2}), \sigma(w_{k-1}), \sigma(w_k))$. In case of zero counts, we back off to a bigram estimate, and then to the unigram model above.

The trigram model gives a reasonably strong baseline, which is not surprising given the fact that mutations can often be predicted from the previous word or two. Improving the trigram to be competitive with our best neural models would require a more sophisticated backoff strategy along the lines of the generalized parallel backoff proposed in (Bilmes and Kirchhoff, 2003), and perhaps incorporating some linguistic knowledge. To see this, consider a prepositional phrase like the Irish *ar an mbád* ('on the boat') with eclipsis on the noun *bád* ('boat'). Were this trigram not seen in training, a naive backoff strategy would estimate the probability of eclipsis by backing off to the bigram *an bád*, and for this and most other nouns the counts would be dominated by nominative examples where eclipsis is highly unlikely.[3]

Next we will describe our three neural network models, beginning with definitions of the layers that are used in more than one model.

All three models use character embeddings; for this, we fixed a vocabulary $\mathcal{C}$ consisting of the most common 32 characters seen in training, and the models learn an embedding $\chi : \mathcal{C} \to \mathbb{R}^{10}$.

The second and third models make use of a trainable token embedding layer. Here we fix a "demutated vocabulary" $\mathcal{V}_\sigma$ consisting of the 100,000 most common tokens in training after removing mutations, and then this layer learns a mapping $\psi : \mathcal{V}_\sigma \to \mathbb{R}^{200}$.

The latter two models also make use of a character-level bidirectional LSTM (Graves and Schmidhuber, 2005) which provides a second embedding of each input token as a fixed-length vector, in this case one that hopefully captures internal orthographic or morphological features relevant to the mutation system. The character embedding χ is used to convert the characters in a demutated token into a sequence of vectors in $\mathbb{R}^{10}$ which is in turn input into a BiLSTM layer with 75 cells in each direction. The two unidirectional outputs are concatenated, defining a mapping $\beta : \mathcal{V}_\sigma \to \mathbb{R}^{150}$.

The top two (output) layers are the same across all three models: first, a dense layer with 100 cells and reLU activation, followed by a softmax layer that outputs a probability distribution over the set of five labels $\mathcal{M}$.

With this notation established, we define our three neural networks as follows:

- **Character LSTM.** In this model, we rejoin the full token history $\sigma(w_1), \ldots, \sigma(w_k)$ into one long string separated by spaces, and then extract the final 20 characters of the resulting string. The character embedding χ is then applied to produce a sequence of 20 vectors in $\mathbb{R}^{10}$ which are passed into an LSTM with 150 cells and recurrent dropout of 0.4. The final state vector output by the LSTM is fed into the dense and softmax output layers where the loss is computed.

- **Trigram and character BiLSTM.** Since mutations are usually triggered by one or two preceding words,

we wanted to define a strong baseline that only considers the target token $\sigma(w_k)$ (for which we are predicting the mutation) and the two previous tokens $\sigma(w_{k-2})$ and $\sigma(w_{k-1})$. For $i \in \{0, 1, 2\}$ we embed $\sigma(w_{k-i})$ by concatenating the token embedding $\psi(\sigma(w_{k-i}))$ and the BiLSTM embedding $\beta(\sigma(w_{k-i}))$. The three resulting vectors are concatenated and fed directly into the dense and softmax output layers.

- **Token LSTM and character BiLSTM.** The idea here is to use an LSTM to encode a longer token history as a fixed-length vector, hopefully enabling the model to make better predictions in subtle cases (e.g. words preceded by third person possessive adjectives where anaphora resolution is needed). We fix a window size of L tokens. For $i \in \{0, \ldots, L-1\}$ we again embed $\sigma(w_{k-i})$ by concatenating the token embedding $\psi(\sigma(w_{k-i}))$ and the BiLSTM embedding $\beta(\sigma(w_{k-i}))$. The resulting sequence of L vectors is input into an LSTM with 500 cells and recurrent dropout of 0.25. The final state vector output by the LSTM is fed into the dense and softmax output layers; see Figure 1.

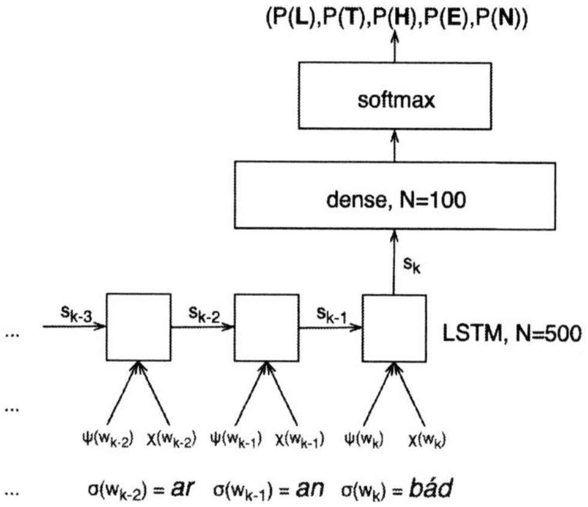

Figure 1: Architecture of the Token LSTM and character BiLSTM model

3.2. Training and Evaluation

The training, development, and test corpora for both languages were assembled by crawling the web (Scannell, 2007). The corpora are sentence-shuffled,[4] tokenized, and then lowercased.

It is important to take note of a subtlety when lowercasing Irish and Scottish Gaelic that involves initial mutations. When t-prothesis or eclipsis occurs with a capitalized vowel-initial word in Irish, the prefixed letter is written without a hyphen, e.g. *ár nAthair* ('our Father').

---

[3]We conjecture that this is the cause of many of the mutation errors seen in the output of machine translation engines that use n-gram language models.

[4]By shuffling sentences, we greatly increase the size of the corpora that can be freely distributed, with the tradeoff that it becomes impossible for the model to learn contextual clues across sentences, as is sometimes required for correct prediction.

Therefore, when lowercasing, the hyphen must be reinserted: *ár n-athair* and not *ár nathair* which would mean something completely different ('our snake'). We do the same thing when lowercasing Scottish Gaelic as well (where the hyphen is sometimes omitted), and additionally for h-prothesis, so *Pàrlamaid na hAlba* lowercases to *pàrlamaid na h-alba*.

The Scottish Gaelic training corpus contains 8 million tokens, and the development and test sets have 500k tokens each. There is substantially more Irish than Scottish Gaelic available online and so the corpora are much bigger: 50 million tokens of Irish for training, and 1 million tokens each for development and testing.

In performing error analysis on the Irish model (see §3.3), it became clear that a significant portion of the loss exhibited by our models came from grammatical errors in the test corpus rather than flaws in the model. For this reason, we created a second test set from a corpus of well-edited articles from the online Irish news service Tuairisc.ie. The full corpus consists of about 7.7 million tokens from which we extracted a 1 million token test set, disjoint from the training corpus, which was shuffled, tokenized, and lowercased as above.

The neural network models were implemented in TensorFlow (Abadi et al., 2016) and each was trained for 20 epochs, checkpointing and saving the models with smallest loss on the development set. The test losses for all models are reported in Table 1 in units of bits per token, and columns are labeled with ISO 639-1 language codes ("ga" for Irish and "gd" for Scottish Gaelic).[5]

Model	Test (ga)	Clean (ga)	Test (gd)
Label priors	0.75917	0.79581	0.66670
First letter	0.52064	0.54242	0.40187
Unigram model	0.40571	0.39485	0.31835
Trigram model	0.10710	0.07995	0.10205
Char LSTM	0.10336	0.08531	0.08598
3-gram+BiLSTM	0.08051	0.05949	0.07662
LSTM+BiLSTM	**0.06949**	**0.04719**	**0.07222**

Table 1: Test loss in bits per token for best-performing models

3.3. Error Analysis

We performed an error analysis by applying the best neural network model to a 10000-token subset of the Irish development set. The total loss in bits per token over this subset was 0.07254, slightly larger than the test loss of 0.06949. The ground truth label was assigned a probability of at least 0.5 for 9833 of the 10000 tokens. In many cases we see that the model has successfully generalized to forms not seen directly in training. For example, no form of the word *ubhal* (a pre-standard spelling of *úll* 'apple') was seen in training, but the model correctly predicts t-prothesis for *an t-ubhal* ('the apple') in the development set. Similarly, the model correctly predicts lenition on the conditional verb *mhaoinfeadh* ('would fund') despite not having seen this word in training, presumably based on other conditional verbs ending in *feadh*.

The remaining 167 tokens (for which the predicted probability of the ground truth label was less than 0.5) account for the great majority (77.24%) of the total loss; we manually examined and classified these tokens into *ad hoc* categories as reported in Table 2.

Classification	Count	Loss (bpt)	% Loss
Error in dev set	61	4.25447	35.78
Right-context needed	30	2.95675	12.23
Non-standard form	23	3.30608	10.48
Possessive *a, ina, …*	16	2.73679	6.04
Dialect in dative	9	3.18118	3.95
Non-Irish words	7	3.55753	3.43
Others $P < 0.5$	21	1.84388	5.34
All $P \geq 0.5$	9833	0.01651	22.76
TOTAL	10000	0.07254	100.00

Table 2: Breakdown of the total loss on a 10000 token subset of the Irish development set

The greatest part of the loss was contributed by grammatical errors in the development set. In fact, the five tokens with the smallest predicted probability for the ground truth label all correspond to obvious errors. This provides evidence of the usefulness of our model for grammatical error detection and correction, which we report on below in §4.1. Quite a few of the bad predictions stem from our self-imposed restriction that the model only use context to the left. A fluent speaker (and, most likely, a sufficiently strong neural network model) could predict most of these mutations given context on both sides, while failing to do so given only the left context. We can therefore view these particular mutations as conveying information about what comes next in the sentence. Common examples of this type include:

- confusion between imperative (unlenited) and past tense (lenited) verbs at the beginning of a sentence;

- the words *dá* ('if') and *dhá* ('two');

- the preposition *idir* in the sense 'both' (lenition) vs. 'between' (no mutation); and

- the direct vs. indirect relativizing particles, both written as *a*, but distinguished in part by lenition or eclipsis of the following verb.

These and all similar examples are classified as "Right-context needed" in the table.

In our analysis we distinguished true errors from examples that are correct but that do not follow the Official Standard for Irish; the latter are labeled "Non-standard forms" in Table 2. An example would be lenition of the prepositional pronouns *dom*, *duit*, etc., which is common in the spoken language for certain dialects, but is not part of the official orthography.

---

[5]N.B. TensorFlow uses natural logs, and so the losses shown in training are smaller by a factor of ln(2) than those reported in Table 1.

The next two rows in Table 2 correspond to the mutations noted in §2.3 as (sometimes) carrying information; namely, the possessive *a* along with its various forms fused with prepositions (*ina*, *faoina*, *dá*, etc.), and the choice of lenition or eclipsis on nouns in the dative case based on dialect (both choices being permitted in the Official Standard).

The final class consists of non-Irish (mostly English) words which do not follow Irish spelling conventions and therefore confuse the model.

3.4. Model Introspection

The two best neural network models learn 200-dimensional embeddings for all tokens in the vocabulary. By visualizing these embeddings we can verify that the model is learning various linguistic properties that we know *a priori* to be important in the mutation system.

For example, Figure 2 is a two-dimensional projection of the embedding space (using tSNE) in which we have plotted 7242 Irish nouns (nominative forms only) according to their gender: blue dots are feminine and red dots are masculine. At the most basic level, it is encouraging that words of each gender tend to cluster together since gender plays a key role in determining the correct mutation on nouns and on the adjectives that modify them.

Interestingly, the visualization reveals additional regularities that the model learns at the character level. For example, there are subclusters visible within each gender; these are made up of words whose initial letters behave similarly with respect to mutations. Words with initial vowels form a tight subcluster within each gender, for example, as do nouns with initial *l*, *n*, *r*, *sc*, *sm*, or *sp* (none of which mutate). Similarly, there are subclusters of nouns with initial *b*, *c*, *f*, *g*, *p* (consonants that admit lenition and eclipsis in the same contexts), and another consisting of nouns with initial *d* or *t* (which also admit lenition and eclipsis, but not following certain words like the definite article *an*).

4. Applications

4.1. Grammar Checking

In this section we evaluate the ability of the best-performing model to detect grammatical errors in Irish.

There is an active community of Irish speakers on Twitter, with more than 3.3 million Irish language tweets posted through the end of October 2019.[6] The informal nature of social media combined with the presence of many language learners makes Twitter an excellent resource for creating a corpus of grammatical errors. To this end, we examined a random sample of about 80,000 Irish language tweets for mutation errors, and from these selected a gold-standard corpus of 895 tweets containing 1029 mutation errors.[7] The tweets were lowercased and tokenized in the same way as our training corpora in §3, yielding 14406 tokens. Tokens beginning with @ (representing Twitter usernames) were

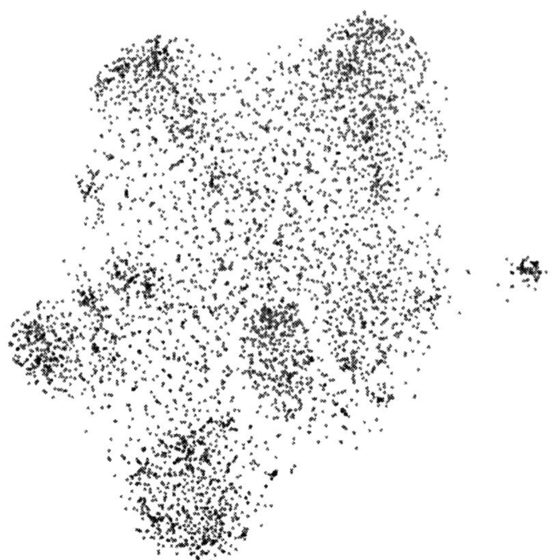

Figure 2: 2D projection of word vectors for 7242 Irish nouns in their nominative form; blue are feminine and red are masculine.

preserved, but were all converted to a single token (*@twitter*) as a way of partially anonymizing the corpus. We did *not* correct any of the errors, but simply flagged all tokens for which we believe the "ground truth" mutation label to be an error.

Then, for various probability cutoff values $0 < C < 1$, we apply the LSTM+BiLSTM model to the corpus and instruct the model to report an error any time it assigns a probability less than C to the ground truth label. The precision, recall, and F-scores for detecting mutation errors are given in Table 3 at cutoff increments of 0.1, and plotted as a precision-recall curve at increments of 0.05 in Figure 3.

$P < C$	Precision	Recall	F-score
0.1	0.93	0.66	0.771
0.2	0.91	0.80	0.853
0.3	0.90	0.87	0.885
0.4	0.87	0.90	0.887
0.5	0.85	0.93	0.889
0.6	0.82	0.94	0.880
0.7	0.80	0.96	0.868
0.8	0.75	0.96	0.844
0.9	0.66	0.97	0.781

Table 3: Precision, recall, and F-scores for mutation error detection at given probability cutoffs

The lowest cutoff used in our experiments was probability C=0.05, and in this case there were 38 false positives reported. For many of these, the model was led astray by informal language found in tweets that is not well-represented in our training corpora. For example, 10 of the 38 false positives are exclamations written according to English con-

---

[6]See http://indigenoustweets.com/ga/.

[7]Available from https://github.com/kscanne/gramadoir/blob/master/ga/corpas.json. Mutations that are acceptable in at least one dialect were *not* included in the error corpus, despite not conforming to the Official Standard in some cases.

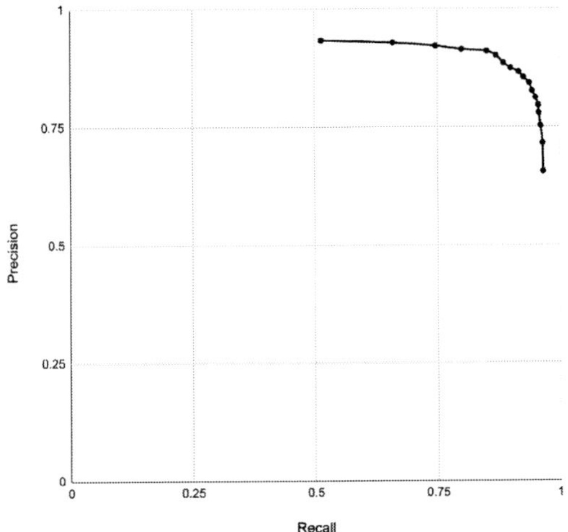

Figure 3: Precision/Recall curve for error detection

ventions (*ah, hi, oh, ha*), and several others are caused by misspellings that distorted a word enough to confuse the model, e.g. *bhanada* for *bhanda* ('band', lenited) or *Ghàidlig* for *Ghàidhlig* (the autonym for Scottish Gaelic, lenited).

We remind the reader again that our neural network makes its predictions based only on the left context, whereas a typical batch-style grammar checking application would be able to make use of both left and right context. Therefore it is likely that a model tailored to this particular application could improve upon the results in this section.

4.2. Language Modeling

Given a vocabulary $\mathcal{V}$ of tokens, a language model assigns a probability $P(v_1 \ldots v_N)$ to any sequence $v_1, \ldots, v_N \in \mathcal{V}$. These are usually computed as a product of token probabilities conditioned on their histories:

$$P(v_1 \ldots v_N) = \prod_{i=1}^{N} P(v_i | v_1 \ldots v_{i-1}) \qquad (2)$$

Given a test corpus $\mathbb{T} = w_1 \ldots w_N$, a language model can be evaluated using the per-token cross entropy $h(P, \mathbb{T})$ (cf. Equation 1):

$$h(P, \mathbb{T}) = -\frac{1}{N} \sum_{i=1}^{N} \log_2 P(w_i | w_1 \ldots w_{i-1}), \qquad (3)$$

or, more commonly, the perplexity:

$$PPL = 2^{h(P, \mathbb{T})} = \left[\prod_{i=1}^{N} P(w_i | w_1 \ldots w_{i-1}) \right]^{-\frac{1}{N}} \qquad (4)$$

This paper arose, more or less, from the following simple observation. A 5-gram language model with modified Kneser-Ney smoothing (Chen and Goodman, 1999) trained on *demutated* Irish text gives a better than 6% improvement in perplexity over the same model trained on raw text, "for free". That we see some improvement should come as no surprise since demutation allows the model to learn generalizations across words in the training set that would otherwise differ; e.g. an important collocation like *bád seoil* can be learned or strengthened even from mutated training examples like *mo bhád seoil* ('my sailboat', lenited) or *ár mbád seoil* ('our sailboat', eclipsed).

The idea then is that a sufficiently accurate model for predicting mutations allows us to realize most of this 6% improvement in a language model on the original corpus, without demutation. We achieve this by means of a *factored language model*, following (Bilmes and Kirchhoff, 2003). In our setup, we would like to model each surface token w as a pair of features, its unmutated form $f_1 = \sigma(w)$ and its mutation $f_2 = \mu(w)$. Given a sequence of tokens $w_1 \ldots w_k$, we factor the probability $P(w_k | w_1 \ldots w_{k-1})$ as follows:

$$P(w_k | w_1 \ldots w_{k-1}) = P(\sigma(w_k) | w_1 \ldots w_{k-1}) \cdot$$
$$P(\mu(w_k) | w_1 \ldots w_{k-1} \sigma(w_k))$$
$$\approx P(\sigma(w_k) | \sigma(w_1) \ldots \sigma(w_{k-1})) \cdot$$
$$P(\mu(w_k) | \sigma(w_1) \ldots \sigma(w_k))$$

The first factor here is simply a language model trained on demutated text, while the second term is a mutation model of exactly the type developed in §3.

We experiment only on Irish, making use of the clean Tuairisc.ie corpus described in §3.2 upon which the mutation model works the best. We hold out development and test sets containing 750k tokens each, and use the remaining 6.2M tokens for training. The n-gram models were trained and evaluated with the MITLM toolkit (Hsu and Glass, 2008) using modified Kneser-Ney smoothing. We used the full training vocabulary (95905 tokens in the base corpus and 75902 in the demutated corpus) and tuned parameters to minimize perplexity on the development set. The results are presented in Table 4.

Model	PPL (dev)	PPL (test)
KN 5-grams (raw)	75.04	74.10
KN 5-grams (demutated)	70.28	69.53
Factored LM	72.81	72.03

Table 4: Perplexities of Irish language models

The drop in perplexity from 74.10 for the baseline model to 69.53 for the demutated model is the roughly 6% improvement noted above, occurring presumably because the latter model is able to learn generalizations across words differing only in mutations. The perplexity of 72.03 for the factored language model shows that an accurate model for mutation prediction allows a good chunk of this improvement to be realized in a language model on the original corpus. With further improvements to the mutation prediction model, we would expect the perplexity of the factored language model to move even closer to the perplexity of the demutated model.

There is nothing special about the 5-gram language model as far as the formal setup; it is possible to similarly factor out initial mutations with state-of-the-art neural language models. It remains to be seen whether a comparable perplexity improvement is achievable in that case, since a character-aware neural model may be able to learn to predict initial mutations effectively despite not being explicitly trained to do so. We will return to this question in forthcoming work in which we evaluate a wide variety of neural language models for the Celtic languages.

5. Acknowledgements

This work was completed while visiting Acadamh na hOllscolaíochta Gaeilge in Carna, Co. Galway, Ireland as a Fulbright Senior Scholar. I am grateful to the Fulbright Commission in Ireland and the staff of the Acadamh, especially Séamas Ó Concheanainn, for their hospitality and for making the visit possible. I would also like to thank Mícheál Ó Meachair, Brian Ó Conchubhair, Cathal Convery, Teresa Lynn, and Michael Goldwasser for their help and encouragement during the Fulbright application process.

6. Bibliographical References

Abadi, M., Barham, P., Chen, J., Chen, Z., Davis, A., Dean, J., Devin, M., Ghemawat, S., Irving, G., Isard, M., et al. (2016). TensorFlow: A system for large-scale machine learning. In *12th USENIX Symposium on Operating Systems Design and Implementation (OSDI '16)*, pages 265–283.

Bauer, M. (2011). *Blas na Gàidhlig: The Practical Guide to Gaelic Pronunciation*. Akerbeltz, Glasgow.

Bilmes, J. A. and Kirchhoff, K. (2003). Factored language models and generalized parallel backoff. In *Proceedings of the 2003 Conference of the North American Chapter of the Association for Computational Linguistics on Human Language Technology: companion volume of the Proceedings of HLT-NAACL 2003–short papers-Volume 2*, pages 4–6. Association for Computational Linguistics.

Chen, S. F. and Goodman, J. (1999). An empirical study of smoothing techniques for language modeling. *Computer Speech & Language*, 13(4):359–394.

Evas, J. (2013). *The Welsh Language in the Digital Age / Y Gymraeg yn yr Oes Ddigidol*. Springer.

Graves, A. and Schmidhuber, J. (2005). Framewise phoneme classification with bidirectional LSTM and other neural network architectures. *Neural Networks*, 18(5–6):602–610.

Hsu, B.-J. and Glass, J. (2008). Iterative language model estimation: efficient data structure & algorithms. In *Ninth Annual Conference of the International Speech Communication Association*.

Judge, J., Ní Chasaide, A., Ní Dhubhda, R., Uí Dhonnchadha, E., and Scannell, K. P. (2012). *The Irish Language in the Digital Age / An Ghaeilge sa Ré Dhigiteach*. Springer.

Scannell, K. P. (2007). The Crúbadán Project: Corpus building for under-resourced languages. In *Building and Exploring Web Corpora: Proceedings of the 3rd Web as Corpus Workshop*, volume 4, pages 5–15.

Tithe an Oireachtais. (2016). *Gramadach na Gaeilge: An Caighdeán Oifigiúil*. Baile Átha Cliath.

Proceedings of the 1st Joint SLTU and CCURL Workshop (SLTU-CCURL 2020), pages 9–20
Language Resources and Evaluation Conference (LREC 2020), Marseille, 11–16 May 2020
© European Language Resources Association (ELRA), licensed under CC-BY-NC

Eidos: An Open-Source Auditory Periphery Modeling Toolkit and Evaluation of Cross-Lingual Phonemic Contrasts

Alexander Gutkin

Google Research

6 Pancras Square, London, N1C 4AG, United Kingdom

agutkin@google.com

Abstract

Many analytical models that mimic, in varying degree of detail, the basic auditory processes involved in human hearing have been developed over the past decades. While the auditory periphery mechanisms responsible for transducing the sound pressure wave into the auditory nerve discharge are relatively well understood, the models that describe them are usually very complex because they try to faithfully simulate the behavior of several functionally distinct biological units involved in hearing. Because of this, there is a relative scarcity of toolkits that support combining publicly-available auditory models from multiple sources. We address this shortcoming by presenting an open-source auditory toolkit that integrates multiple models of various stages of human auditory processing into a simple and easily configurable pipeline, which supports easy switching between ten available models. The auditory representations that the pipeline produces can serve as machine learning features and provide analytical benchmark for comparing against auditory filters learned from the data. Given a low- and high-resource language pair, we evaluate several auditory representations on a simple multilingual phonemic contrast task to determine whether contrasts that are meaningful within a language are also empirically robust across languages.

Keywords: open-source, auditory perception, features, software, phonology

1. Introduction

The science of hearing is an interdisciplinary field that studies the perception of sound (Schnupp et al., 2011), including speech (Moore, 2007; Young, 2007). It places a particular emphasis on studying the function of the auditory periphery, defined between the point where the sound pressure wave meets the ear and the auditory nerve (AN). This region is thought to be of critical importance because it converts continuous analog signal into discrete all-or-nothing nerve action potentials. A simplified description of this mechanism consists of several complex processing stages: the pressure wave causes vibration of the eardrum, which is passed to the cochlea. Inside the cochlea the basilar membrane (BM) responds with tuned vibrations that are further modified by the cochlear amplification feedback mechanism provided by the outer hair cells (OHCs) (LeMasurier and Gillespie, 2005). The BM motion is detected by inner hair cells (IHCs) that transduce it into electric receptor potentials that control the generation of action potentials in the AN fibers converging on the IHCs through the release of a neurotransmitter into the AN synaptic cleft (Meddis et al., 2010; Manley et al., 2017).

Many models that approximate the functioning of the human auditory periphery to varying degrees of detail have been developed over the decades. Comprehensive reviews of the most popular ones are provided in (Lopez-Poveda, 2005; Rudnicki et al., 2015; Saremi et al., 2016; Verhulst et al., 2018). The models range from phenomenological models that reproduce the overall auditory input-output relation by employing filterbanks (Meddis et al., 2010; Lyon, 2017), often implemented in hardware (Freedman et al., 2013), or transmission lines (Verhulst et al., 2012), to detailed biophysical models (Bell, 2012; Corey et al., 2017). Among many applications, such as cochlear implants (Tabibi et al., 2017), the phenomenological models of human auditory periphery were shown to benefit the

automatic speech recognition (ASR) systems in noisy conditions (Hemmert et al., 2004; Harczos et al., 2007; Tjandra et al., 2015; Li and Príncipe, 2018; Pan et al., 2018), improve neural network-based speech enhancement (Baby and Verhulst, 2018) and provide high-quality text-to-speech vocoding (Irino et al., 2006).

The success of the end-to-end approaches to ASR (Tjandra et al., 2017; Zeyer et al., 2018; Zeghidour et al., 2018) was facilitated by the observation that traditional fixed front-ends can be replaced by the feature extractors learned from data by joint optimization with the rest of the deep network architecture (Sainath et al., 2015; Ghahremani et al., 2016). The learned representations outperform the traditional fixed features on many tasks (Zeghidour, 2019). This led some to question the relevance of traditional approaches that handcraft valuable prior knowledge (Trigeorgis et al., 2016). However, the properties of the band pass-like filters learned by deep networks roughly correspond to human audio-biological distribution (Tüske et al., 2014) and the recent study by Ondel et al. (2019) demonstrates that human auditory processing and data-driven methods are not necessarily as divergent as they would often appear. In a machine learning context, this observation leads us to believe that the powerful analytical models developed by hearing science, including the ones provided by the toolkit described in this paper, are still very useful for informing model design and explaining the structure of the representations learned by black box-like data-driven approaches. Moreover, analytical models of human hearing may provide useful insights in low and zero-resource speech and language learning scenarios (Dupoux, 2018), where the data scarcity can potentially be alleviated by employing models incorporating rich prior knowledge.

This paper describes EIDOS, an open-source toolkit[1] con-

---

[1] https://github.com/google/eidos-audition

Name	Period	Language
Auditory Toolbox	1982–1993	MATLAB
HUTear	1991–1998	MATLAB, C/MEX
DSAM	1986–2007	C
AMToolbox	1979–2017	MATLAB, C/MEX
Brian Hears	1987–2003	Python
Cochlea	2007–2014	Python, Cython
UR EAR	2004–2018	MATLAB, C/MEX

Table 1: Auditory model collections.

taining the collection of various auditory perception models developed over the years by hearing scientists. The original models were developed by diverse research groups using different programming languages and software design approaches. In this work the models have been reimplemented entirely in modern C++ and integrated into a single easily configurable and simple to use pipeline that represents all critical stages of the auditory periphery from the BM to the AN. The pipeline produces auditory representations that are easy to integrate with the popular Python machine learning toolkits (Abadi et al., 2016; Paszke et al., 2019).

We evaluate the quality of several auditory representations offered by our toolkit on a cross-lingual phonemic contrast detection task recently introduced by Johny et al. (2019). The method involves training separate binary neural classifiers for several phonological contrasts, defined in terms of phonological features, in audio spans centered on particular segments within continuous speech. To assess cross-linguistic consistency, these classifiers are evaluated on held-out languages and classification quality is reported. More often than not, phoneme inventories and their corresponding phonemic featurizations are provided by cross-linguistic typological ontologies, such as PHOIBLE (Moran et al., 2014). This approach can be used to test how accurately such phoneme inventories for low- or zero-resource languages describe the speech data at hand.

This paper is organized as follows: various auditory toolkits developed over the years are presented in Section 2. Section 3 provides an overview of the auditory models currently supported by our software. The core library design features and basic usage examples are presented in Section 4. In Section 5 we evaluate and discuss several audio representations on the phonemic contrast task. Section 6 concludes the paper.

2. Related Work

Several collections of auditory models have been developed over the years. The list of such collections that we review below is in no way complete, but covers some of the most popular and widely used pipelines for auditory processing that support combining models from various sources. This review does not cover the initiatives undertaken in specialized areas of auditory perception, such as binaural processing, for which excellent reviews exist (Dietz et al., 2018).

The list of the auditory model collections of interest is shown in Table 1 where, along with the name of each toolbox, the years when the models were published are shown along with the programming language(s) used to implement them. The toolboxes vary among several dimensions. One dimension is the year when the models were first published,

with the Auditory Toolbox being the oldest among toolkits covered. An additional dimension is the number of supported models, with the AMToolbox and DSAM being the most comprehensive in the list. A further dimension reflects the design philosophy, with some of the toolboxes focusing of reproducibility (AMToolbox and Cochlea), others designed for efficiency (Brian Hears and DSAM), or both.

Auditory Toolbox One of the earliest and arguably the most widely used collections of auditory models is the Auditory Toolbox by Slaney (1998). The toolbox is a MATLAB (Pärt-Enander et al., 1996; Moore, 2017) reimplementation of the earlier package (Slaney, 1988) written in Mathematica (Wolfram, 1999) and includes public-domain implementations of several classical machine perception algorithms from the early days of the field: the cochlear model by Lyon (1982) that combines a series of filters that model traveling pressure waves with Half Wave Rectifiers (HWR) to detect the energy in the signal and several stages of Automatic Gain Control (AGC), the cochlear model by Seneff (1988) that combines a critical band filterbank with models of detection and AGC, and the original hair cell model by Meddis (1986) using the physiological AN parameters from Meddis et al. (1990). Finally, the toolbox includes the implementation of gammatone filterbank (Johannesma, 1972) – a model of psychoacoustic filtering (Moore and Glasberg, 1983; Glasberg and Moore, 1990) based on critical bands originally proposed by Roy Patterson (Patterson, 1986; Slaney, 1993). Most of these implementations have been widely used in many auditory processing scenarios, reimplemented in various programming languages and have made their way into other software.

HUTear This toolbox was developed in the Laboratory of Acoustics and Audio Signal Processing at Helsinki University of Technology (Härmä and Palomäki, 2000). It is implemented in MATLAB with the performance critical algorithms written in C/MEX. In addition to some popular algorithms from the Auditory Toolbox, such as the Meddis IHC model, the toolbox provides the original implementations, such as the quantitative signal preprocessing and detector model by Dau et al. (1996) and an auditory model by Karajalainen (1996). This software is distributed under an attribution license.

DSAM The Development System for Auditory Modelling (DSAM) is a computational library designed specifically for producing time-sampled auditory system simulations. It was originally developed by Lowel P. O'Mard from the Centre for the Neural Basis of Hearing (CNBH) as a joint collaboration between University of Essex and University of Cambridge (O'Mard, 2010). Implemented entirely in C programming language, this library brings together many established auditory models under a flexible programming platform. The latest DSAM version includes eight BM response models, such as gammatone filterbank and the dual-resonance nonlinear (DRNL) filter by Lopez-Poveda and Meddis (2001), seven hair cell models, such as the IHC synaptic model by Carney (1993), AN spike generation and neuron firing models, such as the cochlear nucleus neuron model by Arle and Kim (1991), many utility and analysis facilities, multi-threading, as well as the support for most sound file formats. DSAM provides implementations for most of the algorithms from the Auditory Toolbox by Slaney (1998) described above and is licensed under the version 3 of GNU General Public License (GPL).

AMToolbox The Auditory Modeling Toolbox (AMToolbox) is likely the largest model collection for representing various stages of auditory perception (Søndergaard and Majdak, 2013). Implemented in MATLAB/Octave this toolbox is intended to serve as a common ground for reproducible research in auditory modeling. Similar to DSAM, AMToolbox is not just the collection of models, all the models are implemented using strict requirements on model interfaces. Unlike DSAM, AMToolbox also provides a comprehensive testsuite and verification guidelines to ensure that the implementations produce the results that match the results reported in the literature. Furthermore, the toolbox provides published human data and model demonstrations. The AMToolbox is maintained by Acoustic Research Institute (ARI) of Austrian Academy of Sciences, with project being supported by multiple universities across Europe and the United States. The toolbox incorporates 29 algorithms which, unlike the other software described so far, also puts an emphasis on models of binaural and spatial perception, although other types of models, such as the cochlear model of the auditory periphery by Verhulst et al. (2012), are provided as well. The toolbox is distributed under the version 3 of GNU General Public License (GPL).

Brian Hears This package is an auditory toolbox (Fontaine et al., 2011) developed in the Python programming language for the spiking neural network simulator framework called "Brian" (Goodman and Brette, 2009). Integration with Brian makes it possible to model the auditory neurons higher up in the auditory perception chain. The salient feature of the design is vectorization, an algorithmic strategy that consists in grouping identical operations operating on different data. In the context of auditory modeling, vectorization happens over the frequency channels, which makes it possible to take advantage of heavily parallel architecture of auditory models that exclusively rely on filterbanks. This greatly improves the efficiency of the implementation which otherwise relies on an interpretable language. The toolbox supports several filterbank-based models, such as gammatone, DRNL, gammachirp filter by Irino and Patterson (1997) and middle ear model by Tan and Carney (2003). In addition, modular filter design allows multiple filters to be combined efficiently to form new models. The package is distributed under CeCILL (from "CEA CNRS INRIA Logiciel Libre") Free Software License.

Cochlea This Python package contains a small collection of models of auditory periphery created by Rudnicki and Hemmert (2014). The package allows researchers to run and analyze a selection of three inner ear models, such as the algorithm by Holmberg et al. (2007), which generate AN spike trains from arbitrary sound signals. The design rationale for this package is similar to AMToolbox in that it makes it easy to run different models and to analyze and compare them with the same methods (Rudnicki et al., 2015). The package is distributed under the version 3 of GNU General Public License (GPL).

Model	Auditory Stage			
	BM	HC	Synapse	Spikes
GAMMATONE-SLANEY	✓			
GAMMATONE-COOKE	✓			
MEDDIS1986			✓	
BAUMGARTE	✓	✓		
SUMNER2002			✓	
CARFAC	✓	✓	✓	
ZILANY2014		✓		
BRUCE2018			✓	✓
ZHANG2001				✓
JACKSON				✓

Table 2: Supported auditory models and their estimates.

UR EAR "University of Rochester: Envisioning Auditory Responses" (UR EAR) is a MATLAB package with a graphical user interface designed to run various AN models and the higher-level auditory pathway models, such as inferior colliculus (IC), developed over the years by researchers in the University of Rochester, McMaster University and their collaborators (Farhadi and Carney, 2019). Computation intensive models, such as the IHC and the AN models by Bruce et al. (2018), are implemented in MEX, which is an environment for interoperability between the C functions and MATLAB. Models provided by this package are replaced whenever a new research finding results in a revised version of the existing model.

3. Overview of Supported Models

The list of auditory models currently supported by the toolkit is shown in Table 2. The models come from miscellaneous sources and differ along several dimensions, the primary of which is the stage of auditory perception that each model estimates: the BM, the hair cells (HC) and the synapse between the IHC and the AN. In addition, several models provide the estimates of AN discharge (also known as spike generation). Some models, such as CARFAC, produce estimates for several auditory stages, while others are highly detailed and focused on a single stage only.

Gammatone Filterbanks Historically, the gammatone filterbanks have perhaps been the most widely used abstractions for modeling the human auditory system. They are often used as a front-end component of the cochlear models, decomposing the stimulus into multi-channel components mimicking the function of human cochlea. The output of each filter in a filterbank estimates the BM frequency response at a particular place corresponding to the center frequency of the filter.

The gammatone function is defined in time domain by its impulse response that is a product of a gamma distribution and periodic tone (Johannesma, 1972). The gammatone implementation GAMMATONE-SLANEY provided by this toolbox follows the original version developed in (Slaney, 1998), which uses the findings of Patterson et al. (1992) who showed that the fourth-order gammatone function produces an impulse response that provides a good fit to the human auditory filter shapes proposed by Patterson (1986). Gammatone filterbank is a collection of gammatone filter functions where the filters are designed in such a way that their center frequencies are distributed across frequency range in proportion to their bandwidth according to the Equivalent Rectangular Bandwidth (ERB) scale described in (Moore and Glasberg, 1983; Glasberg and Moore, 1990). Our implementation uses the ERB approximation from Glasberg and Moore (1990). The second gammatone filterbank GAMMATONE-COOKE provided by this toolbox derives from the implementation by Ma et al. (2007) of the original idea of Cooke (1993), also mentioned in (Slaney, 1993), who used base-band impulse invariant transformations to dramatically improve the speed efficiency of the original gammatone filterbank algorithm.

MEDDIS1986 The model proposed by Meddis (1986) represents one of the most popular models of mechanical-to-neural transduction that is performed between the HCs and the AN synapse. The model MEDDIS1986 is specified in terms of the production, movement, and dissipation of a transmitter substance in the region between the HC and the AN fiber synapse (Meddis, 1988). Briefly, the HC contains a quantity of the "free transmitter" $q(t)$, which leaks through a permeable membrane into the synaptic cleft. The permeability $k(t)$ fluctuates as a function of the instantaneous amplitude of the mechanical stimulation $s(t)$, provided by the BM model, such as GAMMATONE-SLANEY. The synaptic cleft contains a fluctuating amount of transmitter substance $c(t)$, part of it being continuously being returned to the cell and part of it continuously being lost. The cleft transmitter level $c(t)$ relates to the free transmitter quantity $q(t)$ and permeability $k(t)$ via a system of differential equations. The constant model parameters (such as replenishment rate) corresponding to physiological observations are provided in (Meddis et al., 1990). In this model, there is a linear relationship between the instantaneous value of the transmitter quanta $c(t)$ and the postsynaptic excitation potential: the greater the quantity of the transmitter, the higher the probability of a spike.

BAUMGARTE While historically the gammatone filterbanks have provided a reasonable tradeoff between computation efficiency and physiological accuracy, alternative, more detailed models of peripheral sound processing were developed as well. The BAUMGARTE is a peripheral ear model proposed by Baumgarte (2000) which originates from the hardware analog model of Zwicker (1986) and its extensions provided by Peisl (Peisl, 1990; Zwicker and Peisl, 1990). This model includes components that model the outer, middle and inner ear structures. Both outer and middle ears are treated as reasonably simple linear filters. The inner ear model involves nonlinear mechanical filtering, which simulates the passive cochlear hydromechanics enhanced by the feedback from active OHCs providing cochlear amplification. The implementation is a one-dimensional macromechanical model, in which the length of a BM is divided into sections of equal length on a Bark scale (Zwicker, 1961) and described by a system of coupled differential equations, one equation per section. Each equation also integrates an amplifier with nonlinear feedback that models the effect of OHCs. The parallel resonance of each section is tuned to the BM resonance at the location represented by that section (Baumgarte, 1997). The system of coupled differential equations is internally represented as a collection of equivalent electrical circuits which are simulated in the time domain by a system of wave digi-

tal filters (WDF) (Fettweis, 1986). The model is capable of outputting the estimates (represented in terms of voltage) of local transverse velocity of the BM as well as the excitation of the IHCs located along its length.

SUMNER2002 This computational model of the IHC and the AN complex (Sumner et al., 2002) is a modernized version of the earlier IHC models, such as MEDDIS1986 model described above. According to the authors, the purpose of this model was to generate an accurate representation of the input–output characteristics of the HC for arbitrary stimuli. The main differences of this model with MEDDIS1986 are as follows: First, the model proposed by Sumner et al. (2002) takes into account populations of medium (MSR) and low (LSR) spontaneous rate fibers in addition to high (HSR) spontaneous rate ones traditionally considered by the earlier models.[2] Second, the model incorporates a modified version of the transduction of BM motion into receptor potentials originally developed by Shamma et al. (1986). In addition, the transmitter release rate, or permeability, $k(t)$ of the original MEDDIS1986 model is made more sophisticated by taking into account the model of calcium concentration. Finally, in SUMNER2002 model the release of transmitter into the cleft is described by a random process $N(n, \rho)$ describing probabilistic transport of transmitter quanta. Each of n possible events has an equal probability, ρdt, of occurring in a single simulation epoch (Sumner et al., 2003).

CARFAC The cascade of asymmetric resonators with fast-acting compression (CARFAC) model is based on a pole–zero filter cascade (PZFC) model of auditory filtering combined with a multi-time-scale coupled automatic gain control (AGC) network (Lyon, 2011). The model differs from other cochlear models in its application of cascaded, rather than parallel, filterbank which is well suited for modeling the traveling waves in the cochlea. In a PZFC filterbank, each filter stage models a segment of a non-uniform distributed system corresponding to a single section along the cochlear partition. The stage transfer function is a pole–zero approximation to the transfer function corresponding to the local complex wavenumber (Lyon, 2011; Lyon, 2017). The PZFC stages provide a variable peak gain via a variable pole damping. The pole damping is adjusted by slowly varying feedback control signals from the automatic gain control (AGC) smoothing network that mimics the feedback from the OHCs. The overall architecture is very efficient, with several existing hardware implementations (Thakur et al., 2014; Singh et al., 2018; Xu et al., 2018). Our implementation provides a facade over an existing open-source CARFAC library (Lyon, 2011). The model is capable of producing estimates of BM displacements, OHC control signals and neural activity patterns (NAPs). According to Lyon (2017), the NAPs can be used as an estimate of average instantaneous AN firing rates.

ZILANY2014 This particular model is derived from a model of the auditory periphery developed by Zilany et al. (2014), which is a more physiologically accurate version of the earlier phenomenological models of the synapse between the IHC and AN developed by the researchers at

---

[2]Our implementation only supports HSR fibers at the moment.

McMaster and Rochester Universities (Zilany et al., 2009; Ibrahim and Bruce, 2010; Zilany et al., 2013). In this toolbox, ZILANY2014 provides the component that forms the front-end of the original model corresponding to the models of the middle ear (ME) and the IHC originally described by Zilany et al. (2009). The input to the ME is an instantaneous pressure waveform of the stimulus (in pascals) sampled at 100 kHz. The ME filter is followed by three parallel filter paths: with $C1$ and $C2$ filters in the signal path and a broad-band filter in the control-path. The combined response of the two transduction functions following the $C1$ and $C2$ filters provides the input to a IHC low-pass filter the output of which can drive the IHC-AN models. The parameters of the filters used in ZILANY2014 are adjusted according to the BM tuning values described by Ibrahim and Bruce (2010) and parameters for fitting the model to the human data based on (Glasberg and Moore, 1990; Greenwood, 1990; Pascal et al., 1998; Shera et al., 2002) are provided as well.

BRUCE2018 A phenomenological model of the synapse between the IHC and the AN by Bruce et al. (2018) retains the ZILANY2014 model described above as the peripheral front-end that drives the synapse. The synapse and the spike generation model provided by the BRUCE2018 model improves upon the original approach described in (Zilany et al., 2009; Zilany et al., 2014). The first component in the model is a gently saturating nonlinearity followed by a model of power-law dynamics using two parallel paths, fast and slow. Power-law adaptation describes an adaptation process of the AN fibers to the varying stimuli that continues to adapt no matter the length of the stimulus rather than having fixed time constants (Drew and Abbott, 2006). This presynaptic adaptation portion of the model also includes the fractional Gaussian noise (fGn) model by Jackson and Carney (2005) that takes into account the observation that the spiking probability fluctuates over time and depends on the long-term history of spike times. The synaptic portion of the model includes a detailed adaptive model of neurotransmitter release and replenishment at the four synaptic vesicle docking sites, described in detail by Bruce et al. (2018), who report this model to be a more accurate fit for the available physiological data and describe the improvements in several measures of AN fiber spiking statistics.

Spike Generation In addition to the BRUCE2018 synaptic model described above that includes a spike generation component, this toolbox supports two further spike generation algorithms. The first spike generation algorithm ZHANG2001 is part of a phenomenological model for the responses of AN fibers developed by Zhang et al. (2001). In this model the discharge times are produced by a renewal process that simulates a nonhomogeneous Poisson process driven by the output from the synapse. The time-dependent arrival rate of the Poisson process $R(t)$ is defined via the synapse output $s(t)$ and the synapse discharge history $H(t)$, modeled by two exponentials, per Westerman and Smith (1988). The parameters for refractoriness and other constants were adjusted by the authors to fit the physiological data. The other spike generator JACKSON provided by this toolbox is derived from the original implementation by Jackson (2007). In terms of its function this generator is very similar to the ZHANG2001 discharge model but is significantly more computational efficient due to two main performance improvements: the use of the time-transformation method for simulating a nonhomogeneous Poisson process, as described by Jackson and Carney (2005), and avoiding the computation of the relative refractory ratio from scratch at each time bin by using running approximations to the differential equations of which the exponentials in the relative refractory equation are solutions (Jackson, 2007).

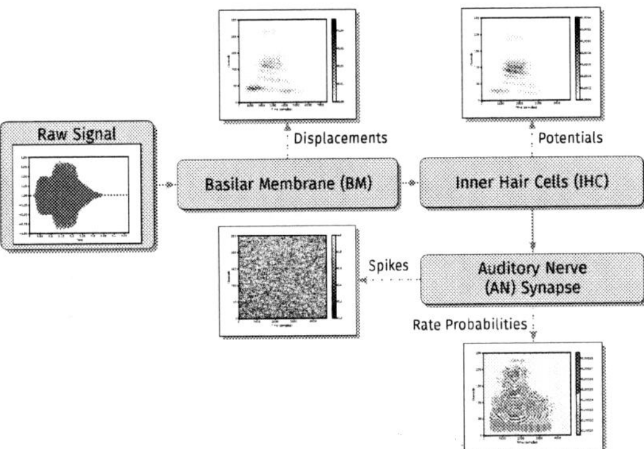

Figure 1: Schematic depiction of an auditory pipeline.

4. Design Features and Usage

Our toolkit consists of an engine and the corresponding tools for running the auditory pipeline over the supplied stimulus, storing the response (we refer to this process as *feature extraction*) and visualizing it. The engine and feature extraction are written in C++, while the visualization component is implemented in Python.

The engine defines the necessary interfaces for implementing the auditory pipeline which can be thought of as a sequence of auditory stages, or models, shown in Table 2. Each model is capable of outputting responses of one or more types and the implementation logic ensures that each model can receive the inputs of the valid type from the previous stage in the pipeline. For example, the BM displacements can be used to estimate the transmembrane potentials across the IHC, but not the other way around. A simplified depiction of the auditory pipeline, with the outputs of each stage visualized, is shown in Figure 1. The models used in this pipeline include BAUMGARTE model for estimating the BM displacements and IHC response, the SUMNER2002 model for the AN synapse rate probabilities and the spike discharge estimates from 2000 HSR fibers from the ZHANG2001 model.

The toolbox is structured along simple lines depicted in Figure 2. There are three main directories. The directory `build` contains the necessary scaffolding for building and testing the dependencies. The directory `audition` contains the pipeline and configuration parser implementations, as well as main tools and model tests. In addition, this directory contains the CARFAC model (denoted by a blue oval shape in Figure 2). Finally, the `third_party` directory houses most of the auditory model implementations.

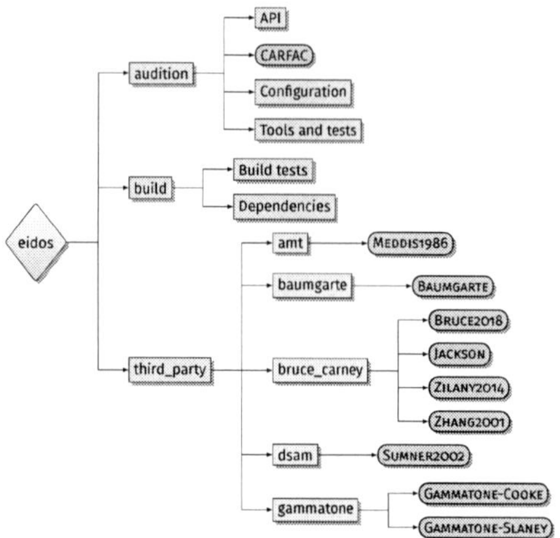

Figure 2: Toolbox directory layout.

```
1   # Download the toolbox.
2   git clone https://github.com/google/eidos-audition.git
3   cd eidos-audition
4   # Build the libraries, tools and tests.
5   bazel build -c opt ...
6   # Run the tests.
7   bazel test -c opt ...
```

Table 3: Setting up the toolbox.

It contains five subdirectories, whose names correspond to either the original name of an author, the university lab or name of the toolkit where the original implementation is found. For example, the MEDDIS1986 model is located under the `amt` directory which stands for Auditory Modeling Toolbox, while the subdirectory `bruce_carney` houses several models developed by Ian Bruce, Laurel Carney and their colleagues in their respective university labs. In addition to the code, each subdirectory contains the `LICENSE` file that contains the license for the original implementation from which our code derives. Further information about the models can be found in `README` files accompanying the code.

The toolbox is hosted on GitHub open-source repository that uses Git version control system (Blischak et al., 2016). The toolbox uses the flexible Bazel framework (Google, 2019) for building its dependencies, libraries, and tools in both C++ and Python. Bazel is also used to build and invoke the unit and integration tests which are implemented using Google Testing and Mocking Framework (Google, 2010). The sequence of steps for fetching the toolbox, building it and running the provided unit and integration tests is shown in Table 3.

As was mentioned above, the toolbox consists of three functional components: the pipeline, the feature extractor and the visualizer. The auditory pipeline is implemented using Google Protocol Buffers, which is a platform and language-neutral framework for serializing structured data (Google, 2008). The added benefit of using the protocol buffers is a simple and flexible configuration language and the built-in parser for instantiating the pipeline from its textual specification. Given the auditory stimulus (in PCM RIFF format) and a pipeline configuration provided

```
1    # Compute BM response.
2    DIR=eidos/audition
3    cd eidos-audition
4    bazel-bin/${DIR}/auditory_feature_extractor --helpshort
5    bazel-bin/${DIR}/auditory_feature_extractor \
6        --waveform_file test.wav \
7        --config_proto_file ${DIR}/configs/bm_carfac.textproto \
8        --output_file bm.npy --num_channels 251
9    # Visualize the response.
10   bazel-bin/${DIR}/visualize_auditory_signals \
11       --input_signal_file bm.npy --color_map gray_r
```

Table 4: Example: Computing the BM response.

as a simple string list of model names or in a protocol buffer format, the `auditory_feature_extractor` utility can be used to instantiate the pipeline and process the provided stimulus, storing the outputs in NumPy numeric format (Van der Walt et al., 2011) suitable for processing by various machine learning toolkits in Python (Pedregosa et al., 2011; Abadi et al., 2016; Paszke et al., 2019). An output of the last stage only can be saved by providing the `npy` extension for the output file name. The outputs from all auditory stages in the pipeline can be saved by providing the `npz` extension. Finally, the outputs can be visualized using the `visualize_auditory_signals` utility. This process is demonstrated in Table 4, where a stimulus provided in `test.wav` is processed using the pipeline in `bm_carfac.textproto` consisting of a single CARFAC model configured to provide the BM response only.

Since this toolkit provides different front-end models for processing the audio stimuli for converting them into the estimates of BM displacement, these implementations impose different requirements on the input signal. The CARFAC and GAMMATONE models can process signals at 16 kHz sampling rate and above, while the BAUMGARTE model requires a signal with a sampling rate of 100 kHz. The ZHANG2001 model can produce accurate middle-ear estimates for sampling rates between 100 kHz and 500 kHz. Providing an input at the sampling rate that a model cannot process will result in an error message, as the current version of the toolkit does not support automatic resampling.

Licensing Because the toolkit contains work derived from the original implementations available under different licenses, we chose to distribute the software under open-source version 3 of GNU General Public License (GPL), which is the most restrictive (in terms of commercial use) license among the original algorithms.

5. Experiments

Previously, we introduced the methodology for evaluating the cross-lingual consistency of phonological features in a multilingual setting (Johny et al., 2019). Whether grounded in acoustic, articulatory or phonological process properties, phonological features are the recurrent elementary components that form the sound systems of world's languages and describe the individual phonemes in a succinct way (Clements, 2009). We hypothesized that in order to consider a phonemic contrast to be consistent or robust across languages, it needs to be easily predicted on held-out languages. We performed classification experiments on a wide range of phonemic contrasts in multiple languages. Here, we focus on similar experiments on a smaller number of tasks on different data, but using a much wider range of acoustic features provided by our toolkit.

Problem Formulation A particular phonemic contrast is presented as a binary classification problem. An instance of this problem consists of a span of a speech signal (e.g. a vowel in surrounding context) and a positive or negative label (e.g. front vowel vs. back vowel). We train a classifier on a (possibly multi-speaker) dataset for one language and hold out another language. We then evaluate the trained classifier on the held-out data and report its quality in terms of Area Under (resp. Over) the receiver operating characteristic Curve (AUC, resp. AOC). If the binary contrast in question is cross-linguistically consistent, we expect it to be readily predictable on a held-out language (Johny et al., 2019).

We focus our experiments on the Bengali and Spanish language pair that demonstrates really well the subtle confounding factor, which is due to well-known mismatches in how different languages group allophones under different phonemes. The aspiration is contrastive in Bengali, but not in Spanish. In Bengali, the phoneme /p/ (unaspirated) contrasts with an aspirated phoneme, which has [p^h] and [f] as allophones (our Bengali corpus uses /f/ as the phoneme label). In Spanish, the phoneme /p/ is unmarked for aspiration and could be realized as [p^h], which contrasts with the phoneme /f/. That means in a given multilingual dataset we may find [f] and [p^h] sounds labeled differently depending on language, because we are working with phonemic rather than phonetic transcriptions.

The first experiment, denoted P-F, deals with classifying the phonemic contrast between the labial phonemes /p/ (positive class) and /f/ (negative class) across Bengali and Spanish. This experiment is interesting because it validates the robustness of phonemic labels /p/ and /f/ in the presence of conflicting allophone [p^h] mentioned above. The second experiment, denoted VOICED, deals with classifying the voicing contrast between the labial sets { /p/, /f/ } (positive class) and their voiced counterparts { /b/, /b^h/ } (negative class). Each experiment has four possible configurations: training and testing on disjoint sets of the same language (bn–bn and es–es), and training on one language while testing on a heldout language (bn–es and es–bn).

Corpora Details For our experiments, we used a proprietary high-quality corpus of Castilian Spanish from a single female speaker that consists of around 20,000 utterances and a crowd-sourced multi-speaker corpus of Bengali (as spoken in India) that includes around 8,000 utterances from 23 female volunteer speakers. The original audio for both languages was recorded at 48 kHz. The speech data was downsampled to 16 kHz and then parameterized into HTK-style Mel Frequency Cepstral Coefficients (MFCCs) (Ganchev et al., 2005) using a 10 ms frame shift. The dimension of the MFCC parameters is 39 (13 static + Δ + $\Delta\Delta$ coefficients). To determine the phoneme time boundaries, the MFCCs were force-aligned with the corresponding transcriptions independently for each language (Young et al., 2006).

Acoustic Representations We chose four auditory representations provided by our toolkit for the experiments:

the two BM displacement measurements provided by CAR-FAC and GAMMATONE-SLANEY models, and the measurements of the IHC transmembrane potentials provided by BAUMGARTE and ZILANY2014 models that were introduced in Section 3. We compare the performance of acoustic features derived from these models against two baselines: the MFCC parameters, described above, and the mel-frequency filterbank features, denoted MEL-FBANK, that are often preferred to MFCCs, which are strongly decorrelated because their computation includes an additional discrete cosine transform (DCT) (Ahmed et al., 1974). The dimension of MEL-FBANKs is 120 (40 static + Δ + $\Delta\Delta$ coefficients). The four auditory representations provide frequency-selective features at the full sampling rate of the stimulus, which is computationally expensive. Similar to the approach taken by Hemmert et al. (2004), we temporally integrated the root-mean-square energy of each channel using a Hann window (25 ms width) advanced in 10 ms steps in order to obtain the same number of frames as for the baselines. For CARFAC and GAMMATONE-SLANEY models, the analysis is performed at 16 kHz. For BAUMGARTE and ZILANY2014, the analysis was performed at 112 kHz, hence downsampling to 16 kHz was required prior to temporal integration. No spectral integration across channels was performed, instead a simple decimation was applied to reduce the frequency resolution, when required.

Experiment Setup A single training example consists of 40 frames. It is constructed by stacking the frames corresponding to the particular phoneme plus its right and left context frames, possibly padding with zeros if the context is too short. Phonemes longer than 40 frames are ignored.

The training and evaluation sets in our experiments always consist of disjoint sets of languages and speakers. For each dataset we limit the number of training examples to 50,000 and evaluation examples to 10,000. In order to keep the overall set of training labels balanced, with equal number of positive and negative examples, we employ a simple under-sampling approach (Japkowicz and Stephen, 2002; Krawczyk, 2016). If enough examples are available, we sample equal number of them from every language in the training set. Conversely, an imbalance in a language is preferred over the lack of training examples. It is important to note that we do not guarantee that the number of training examples is the same across speakers of a language. We use mean and standard deviation computed over the training set input features to scale the training as well as evaluation sets.

Model Architectures We employ vanilla feed-forward Deep Neural Network (DNN) binary classifier from TensorFlow (Abadi et al., 2016), further tuning the model hyperparameters for maximizing the AUC. A simple two-layer architecture with 200 Softplus (Zheng et al., 2015) units in each layer, dropout probability of 0.2 (Srivastava et al., 2014), Adadelta optimizer (Zeiler, 2012) and the decaying learning rate of 0.6 with a large batch size of 6000 (Smith et al., 2017) were found to perform well across our experiments.

We also used a Convolutional Neural Network (CNN) (Abdel-Hamid et al., 2014) architecture. The network has two CNN layers, where each layer consists of

Features	Channels	Model	P - F					VOICED				
			bn–bn	bn–es	es–bn	es–es	avg	bn–bn	bn–es	es–bn	es–es	avg
MFCC	39	CNN	1.17	0.16	6.02	0.00	1.84	0.85	1.31	2.38	0.11	1.16
		DNN	2.11	**0.07**	**3.70**	0.00	**1.47**	0.71	1.90	2.55	0.04	1.30
MEL-FBANK	120	CNN	**0.05**	0.52	7.70	0.00	2.07	0.48	1.11	2.92	0.03	1.14
		DNN	1.82	0.04	7.08	0.00	2.24	0.63	1.82	3.02	0.06	1.38
GAMMATONE-SLANEY	64	CNN	1.14	0.40	9.04	0.06	2.66	0.88	0.85	2.89	0.09	1.18
		DNN	3.22	1.71	12.64	0.11	4.42	0.54	3.58	4.85	0.05	2.26
	32	CNN	2.34	0.31	9.65	0.00	3.08	0.44	**0.51**	2.23	0.11	0.82
		DNN	2.87	0.47	10.05	0.06	3.36	0.68	1.67	1.68	0.27	1.08
BAUMGARTE	83	CNN	0.81	0.19	8.11	0.00	2.28	**0.37**	0.67	2.70	0.09	0.96
		DNN	0.59	0.26	8.41	0.00	2.32	0.52	2.80	1.80	0.02	1.29
	50	CNN	1.98	0.40	7.98	0.00	2.59	0.59	0.74	1.33	0.06	**0.68**
		DNN	2.30	0.22	8.21	0.00	2.68	0.70	2.47	**1.32**	0.03	1.13
CARFAC	65	CNN	2.54	0.51	7.83	0.00	2.72	0.69	0.99	2.64	**0.02**	1.09
		DNN	4.39	0.80	9.11	0.00	3.57	0.57	1.96	2.14	0.14	1.20
ZILANY2014	64	CNN	2.44	0.15	13.29	0.00	3.97	0.50	0.77	3.88	0.08	1.31
		DNN	7.72	0.75	16.63	0.06	6.29	0.44	2.10	4.03	0.04	1.65
	32	CNN	1.11	0.17	13.81	0.00	3.77	0.65	1.15	2.56	0.13	1.12
		DNN	6.69	0.77	14.73	0.01	5.55	0.57	2.42	1.86	0.02	1.22

Table 5: Bengali–Spanish phoneme asymmetry experiments evaluated using AOC metric.

two-dimensional convolution layer (Abdel-Hamid et al., 2013) with 32 filters with receptive field of 3×3, followed by a max-pooling layer with a pooling region of 2×2 and a stride of 2. The CNN layers are followed by a dense layer with 200 ReLU (Zeiler et al., 2013) units. Batch normalization was applied after each layer in the network (Ioffe and Szegedy, 2015). Similar hyperparameters to DNN were used, with a smaller batch size of 400 and a decaying learning rate of 0.4.

Evaluation Results and Discussion Each classification experiment is repeated three times and the results are averaged. For each classification, we measure the area under the ROC curve (AUC) numbers for every pair of training and evaluation languages, including a language against itself. Since AUC values are generally high, we instead report Area Over the Curve (AOC) values for better readability. Classification results for cross-linguistic consistency of the two contrasts P-F and VOICED are shown in Table 5 for each of the six acoustic feature types. The averages over all four language combinations for each contrast are shown in avg columns. For some of the acoustic representations we produced the acoustic features at two frequency resolutions (shown as the number of channels in the second column). The third column shows the type of the binary classifier that we trained. Best classification results are shown in bold.

The P-F contrast only distinguishes between the phonemic labels /p/ and /f/. Both languages have phonemes that are labeled /f/ and /p/, but as discussed earlier [p^h] is an allophone of /f/ in Bengali and an allophone of /p/ in Spanish. As can be seen from Table 5, this contrast is only truly robust between Bengali and Spanish (despite the conflicting status of the allophone [p^h]) with the DNN model trained on MFCC acoustic features. This confirms the previous findings by Johny et al. (2019), who only used this type of features in their experiments. For all other acoustic configurations, the AOC values are relatively too high when predicting Bengali from the Spanish data (es-bn). It is worth noting that for this experiment, none of the sophisticated auditory configurations outperform the baseline features, although the CNN models trained on the 50-channel BAUMGARTE features and the 65-channel CARFAC features perform slightly worse than the MEL-FBANK baseline.

The VOICED contrast distinguishes between voiced and unvoiced labial sets ({ /b/, /b^h/ } and { /p/, /f/ }). As can be seen from Table 5, this contrast is generally robust and is predicted consistently by all the configurations. Furthermore, in this experiment there is at least one configuration corresponding to each of the four auditory representations that outperforms the MFCC and MEL-FBANK baselines, although not by a big margin. It is interesting to note that there is no clear "winning" representation, although the CNN architecture trained on the 50-channel BAUMGARTE features performs the best according to the average of the four corresponding AOC metrics. Moreover, the four ZILANY2014 configurations, which have the worst performance in resolving the P-F contrast, can detect the VOICED contrast reliably.

6. Conclusion and Future Work

We presented an auditory modeling toolkit designed for easy combination of various models of human auditory periphery in a flexible processing pipeline. Ten models of auditory periphery are currently supported. These range from the popular GAMMATONE filterbanks, also provided by software similar to ours, to the less frequently used peripheral BAUMGARTE model. Some models are highly specialized to model one particular biological mechanism, such as SUMNER2002, while others, such as CARFAC provide simulations for most of the critical mechanisms active in the auditory periphery. The toolkit supports some interesting, and to the best of our knowledge not explored in the literature, combinations of models in a single pipeline, such as combining the BAUMGARTE estimates of IHC transmembrane potentials with BRUCE2018 synaptic model. We demonstrated the effectiveness of the resulting auditory representations on a simple phonemic contrast detection task, where they often outperform the baselines.

Future work will focus on supporting more auditory models. In addition, no special effort was undertaken to finetune various model combinations, which can be problematic because different models sometimes require their inputs to be scaled appropriately. Finally, we plan to broaden the scope of experiments to evaluate more phonemic contrasts on languages less-resourced than Bengali.

7. Bibliographical References

Abadi, M., Barham, P., Chen, J., Chen, Z., Davis, A., Dean, J., Devin, M., Ghemawat, S., Irving, G., Isard, M., et al. (2016). TensorFlow: A System for Large-Scale Machine Learning. In *Proc. 12th USENIX Symposium on Operating Systems Design and Implementation (OSDI '16)*, pages 265–283.

Abdel-Hamid, O., Deng, L., and Yu, D. (2013). Exploring convolutional neural network structures and optimization techniques for speech recognition. In *Proc. of Interspeech*, volume 2013, pages 1173–1175, Lyon, France. ISCA.

Abdel-Hamid, O., Mohamed, A., Jiang, H., Deng, L., Penn, G., and Yu, D. (2014). Convolutional Neural Networks for Speech Recognition. *IEEE/ACM Transactions on Audio, Speech, and Language Processing*, 22(10):1533–1545.

Ahmed, N., Natarajan, T., and Rao, K. R. (1974). Discrete Cosine Transform. *IEEE transactions on Computers*, 100(1):90–93.

Arle, J. and Kim, D. O. (1991). Neural modeling of intrinsic and spike-discharge properties of cochlear nucleus neurons. *Biological Cybernetics*, 64(4):273–283.

Baby, D. and Verhulst, S. (2018). Biophysically-inspired features improve the generalizability of neural network-based speech enhancement systems. In *Proc. of Interspeech*, pages 3264–3268, Hyderabad, India. ISCA.

Baumgarte, F. (1997). A physiological ear model for specific loudness and masking. In *Proc. Workshop on Applications of Signal Processing to Audio and Acoustics*, page 4, New York. IEEE.

Baumgarte, F. (2000). *Ein psychophysiologisches Gehörmodell zur Nachbildung von Wahrnehmungsschwellen für die Audiocodierung*. Ph.D. thesis, Universität Hannover, Germany, October. In German.

Bell, A. (2012). A Resonance Approach to Cochlear Mechanics. *PloS One*, 7(11):e47918.

Blischak, J. D., Davenport, E. R., and Wilson, G. (2016). A quick introduction to version control with Git and GitHub. *PLoS Computational Biology*, 12(1):e1004668.

Bruce, I. C., Erfani, Y., and Zilany, M. S. A. (2018). A phenomenological model of the synapse between the inner hair cell and auditory nerve: Implications of limited neurotransmitter release sites. *Hearing Research*, 360:40–54.

Carney, L. H. (1993). A model for the responses of low-frequency auditory-nerve fibers in cat. *The Journal of the Acoustical Society of America*, 93(1):401–417.

Clements, G. N. (2009). *Contemporary Views on Architecture and Representations in Phonology*, volume 48 of *Current Studies in Linguistics*. MIT Press.

Cooke, M. (1993). *Modelling Auditory Processing and Organisation*. Distinguished Dissertations in Computer Science. Cambridge University Press.

Corey, D. P., Maoiléidigh, D. Ó., and Ashmore, J. F. (2017). Mechanical Transduction Processes in the Hair Cell. In Geoffrey A Manley, et al., editors, *Understanding the Cochlea*, pages 75–111. Springer.

Dau, T., Püschel, D., and Kohlrausch, A. (1996). A quantitative model of the "effective" signal processing in the auditory system. I. Model structure. *The Journal of the Acoustical Society of America*, 99(6):3615–3622.

Dietz, M., Lestang, J.-H., Majdak, P., Stern, R. M., Marquardt, T., Ewert, S. D., Hartmann, W. M., and Goodman, D. F. M. (2018). A framework for testing and comparing binaural models. *Hearing Research*, 360:92–106.

Drew, P. J. and Abbott, L. F. (2006). Models and Properties of Power-Law Adaptation in Neural Systems. *Journal of Neurophysiology*, 96(2):826–833.

Dupoux, E. (2018). Cognitive science in the era of artificial intelligence: A roadmap for reverse-engineering the infant language-learner. *Cognition*, 173:43–59.

Farhadi, A. and Carney, L. H. (2019). UR EAR – University of Rochester Envisioning Auditory Responses (Version 2.1). `https://www.urmc.rochester.edu/Med iaLibraries/URMCMedia/labs/carney-lab/co des/UR_EAR_v2_1.zip`.

Fettweis, A. (1986). Wave digital filters: Theory and practice. *Proceedings of the IEEE*, 74(2):270–327.

Fontaine, B., Goodman, D. F. M., Benichoux, V., and Brette, R. (2011). Brian hears: online auditory processing using vectorization over channels. *Frontiers in Neuroinformatics*, 5:9, July. Available from: `https: //github.com/brian-team/brian2hears`.

Freedman, D. S., Cohen, H. I., Deligeorges, S., Karl, C., and Hubbard, A. E. (2013). An analog VLSI implementation of the inner hair cell and auditory nerve using a dual AGC model. *IEEE Transactions on Biomedical Circuits and Systems*, 8(2):240–256.

Ganchev, T., Fakotakis, N., and Kokkinakis, G. (2005). Comparative Evaluation of Various MFCC Implementations on the Speaker Verification Task. In *Proc. of SPECOM*, volume 1, pages 191–194, Patras, Greece.

Ghahremani, P., Manohar, V., Povey, D., and Khudanpur, S. (2016). Acoustic Modelling from the Signal Domain Using CNNs. In *Proc. of Interspeech*, pages 3434–3438, San Francisco. ISCA.

Glasberg, B. R. and Moore, B. C. J. (1990). Derivation of auditory filter shapes from notched-noise data. *Hearing Research*, 47(1-2):103–138.

Goodman, D. F. M. and Brette, R. (2009). The Brian simulator. *Frontiers in Neuroscience*, 3:26. Available from: `http://briansimulator.org/`.

Google. (2008). Protocol Buffers. Google's Data Interchange Format. `https://developers.google.co m/protocol-buffers/`. [Online], Accessed: 2019-12-2.

Google. (2010). Google Test – Google Testing and Mocking Framework. `https://github.com/google/go ogletest`. [Online], Accessed: 2019-12-2.

Google. (2019). Bazel. `http://bazel.build`. [Online], Accessed: 2019-12-2.

Greenwood, D. D. (1990). A cochlear frequency-position function for several species – 29 years later. *The Journal of the Acoustical Society of America*, 87(6):2592–2605.

Harczos, T., Szepannek, G., and Klefenz, F. (2007). Towards automatic speech recognition based on cochlear traveling wave delay trajectories. In *Proc. Interna-*

tional Symposium on Auditory and Audiological Research (ISAAR), volume 1, pages 83–92.

Härmä, A. and Palomäki, K. (2000). HUTear – a free Matlab toolbox for modeling of human auditory system. In *Proc. Matlab Digital Signal Processing (DSP) Conference*, pages 96–99, Espoo, Finland, November. Available from: http://legacy.spa.aalto.fi/software/HUTear/.

Hemmert, W., Holmberg, M., and Gelbart, D. (2004). Auditory-based Automatic Speech Recognition. In *ISCA Tutorial and Research Workshop (ITRW) on Statistical and Perceptual Audio Processing*, Jeju, Korea.

Holmberg, M., Gelbart, D., and Hemmert, W. (2007). Speech encoding in a model of peripheral auditory processing: Quantitative assessment by means of automatic speech recognition. *Speech Communication*, 49(12):917–932.

Ibrahim, R. A. and Bruce, I. C. (2010). Effects of Peripheral Tuning on the Auditory Nerve's Representation of Speech Envelope and Temporal Fine Structure Cues. In Enrique Lopez-Poveda, et al., editors, *The neurophysiological bases of auditory perception*, pages 429–438. Springer.

Ioffe, S. and Szegedy, C. (2015). Batch normalization: Accelerating deep network training by reducing internal covariate shift. *arXiv preprint arXiv:1502.03167*.

Irino, T. and Patterson, R. D. (1997). A time-domain, level-dependent auditory filter: The gammachirp. *The Journal of the Acoustical Society of America*, 101(1):412–419.

Irino, T., Patterson, R. D., and Kawahara, H. (2006). Speech segregation using an auditory vocoder with event-synchronous enhancements. *IEEE Transactions on Audio, Speech, and Language Processing*, 14(6):2212–2221.

Jackson, B. S. and Carney, L. H. (2005). The spontaneous-rate histogram of the auditory nerve can be explained by only two or three spontaneous rates and long-range dependence. *Journal of the Association for Research in Otolaryngology*, 6(2):148–159.

Jackson, B. S. (2007). The SGfast Mex Function. https://www.urmc.rochester.edu/MediaLibraries/URMCMedia/labs/carney-lab/documents/articles/Jackson-SGfast-2003.pdf. Department of Neurobiology and Behavior, Cornell University.

Japkowicz, N. and Stephen, S. (2002). The class imbalance problem: A systematic study. *Intelligent data analysis*, 6(5):429–449.

Johannesma, P. I. M. (1972). The Pre-response Stimulus Ensemble of Neurons in the Cochlear Nucleus. In *Proc. IPO Symposium on Hearing Theory*, pages 58–69, Eindhoven, Netherlands.

Johny, C., Gutkin, A., and Jansche, M. (2019). Cross-Lingual Consistency of Phonological Features: An Empirical Study. In *Proc. of Interspeech*, pages 1741–1745, Graz, Austria. ISCA.

Karajalainen, M. (1996). A binaural auditory model for sound quality measurements and spatial hearing studies. In *Proc. International Conference on Acoustics, Speech, and Signal Processing Conference (ICASSP)*, volume 2, pages 985–988, Atlanta, USA. IEEE.

Krawczyk, B. (2016). Learning from imbalanced data: open challenges and future directions. *Progress in Artificial Intelligence*, 5(4):221–232.

LeMasurier, M. and Gillespie, P. G. (2005). Hair-Cell Mechanotransduction and Cochlear Amplification. *Neuron*, 48(3):403–415.

Li, K. and Príncipe, J. C. (2018). Biologically-Inspired Spike-Based Automatic Speech Recognition of Isolated Digits Over a Reproducing Kernel Hilbert Space. *Frontiers in Neuroscience*, 12:194.

Lopez-Poveda, E. A. and Meddis, R. (2001). A human nonlinear cochlear filterbank. *The Journal of the Acoustical Society of America*, 110(6):3107–3118.

Lopez-Poveda, E. A. (2005). Spectral processing by the peripheral auditory system: facts and models. *International Review of Neurobiology*, 70:7–48.

Lyon, R. (1982). A computational model of filtering, detection, and compression in the cochlea. In *Proc. International Conference on Acoustics, Speech, and Signal Processing (ICASSP)*, volume 7, pages 1282–1285, Paris, France. IEEE.

Lyon, R. F. (2011). Using a Cascade of Asymmetric Resonators with Fast-Acting Compression as a Cochlear Model for Machine-Hearing Applications. In *Proc. Autumn Meeting of the Acoustical Society of Japan*, pages 509–512. Available from: https://github.com/google/carfac.

Lyon, R. F. (2017). *Human and Machine Hearing: Extracting Meaning from Sound.* Cambridge University Press, United Kingdom.

Ma, N., Green, P., Barker, J., and Coy, A. (2007). Exploiting correlogram structure for robust speech recognition with multiple speech sources. *Speech Communication*, 49(12):874–891. Available from: https://staffwww.dcs.shef.ac.uk/people/N.Ma/resources/gammatone/#Pat1986.

Manley, G. A., Gummer, A. W., Popper, A. N., and Fay, R. R. (2017). *Understanding the Cochlea*, volume 62 of *Springer Handbook of Auditory Research*. Springer.

Meddis, R., Hewitt, M. J., and Shackleton, T. M. (1990). Implementation details of a computation model of the inner hair-cell auditory-nerve synapse. *The Journal of the Acoustical Society of America*, 87(4):1813–1816.

Meddis, R., Lopez-Poveda, E. A., Fay, R. R., and Popper, A. N. (2010). *Computational Models of the Auditory System*, volume 35 of *Springer Handbook of Auditory Research*. Springer.

Meddis, R. (1986). Simulation of mechanical to neural transduction in the auditory receptor. *The Journal of the Acoustical Society of America*, 79(3):702–711.

Meddis, R. (1988). Simulation of auditory–neural transduction: Further studies. *The Journal of the Acoustical Society of America*, 83(3):1056–1063.

Moore, B. C. J. and Glasberg, B. R. (1983). Suggested formulae for calculating auditory-filter bandwidths and excitation patterns. *The Journal of the Acoustical Society of America*, 74(3):750–753.

Moore, B. C. J. (2007). Basic auditory processes involved in the analysis of speech sounds. *Philosophical Transactions of the Royal Society B: Biological Sciences*, 363(1493):947–963.

Moore, H. (2017). *MATLAB for Engineers*. Pearson.

Moran, S., McCloy, D., and Wright, R. (2014). *PHOIBLE Online*. Max Planck Institute for Evolutionary Anthropology, Leipzig. Available from: http://phoible.org/.

O'Mard, L. P. (2010). Development System for Auditory Modelling (DSAM). http://dsam.org.uk. Centre for the Neural Basis of Hearing (CNBH), Version 2.8.44.

Ondel, L., Li, R., Sell, G., and Hermansky, H. (2019). Deriving Spectro-Temporal Properties of Hearing from Speech Data. In *Proc. IEEE Intl. Conference on Acoustics, Speech and Signal Processing (ICASSP)*, pages 411–415, Brighton, UK. IEEE.

Pan, Z., Li, H., Wu, J., and Chua, Y. (2018). An Event-Based Cochlear Filter Temporal Encoding Scheme for Speech Signals. In *Proc. Int. Joint Conference on Neural Networks (IJCNN)*, pages 1–8, Rio de Janeiro, Brazil. IEEE.

Pärt-Enander, E., Sjöberg, A., Melin, B., and Isaksson, P. (1996). *The MATLAB Handbook*. Addison-Wesley Harlow.

Pascal, J., Bourgeade, A., Lagier, M., and Legros, C. (1998). Linear and nonlinear model of the human middle ear. *The Journal of the Acoustical Society of America*, 104(3):1509–1516.

Paszke, A., Gross, S., Massa, F., Lerer, A., Bradbury, J., Chanan, G., Killeen, T., Lin, Z., Gimelshein, N., Antiga, L., et al. (2019). PyTorch: An imperative style, high-performance deep learning library. In *Advances in Neural Information Processing Systems*, pages 8024–8035.

Patterson, R. D., Robinson, K., Holdsworth, J., McKeown, D., Zhang, C., and Allerhand, M. (1992). Complex Sounds and Auditory Images. In Y Cazals, et al., editors, *Auditory Physiology and Perception: Proc. 9th International Symposium on Hearing*, pages 429–446. Elsevier.

Patterson, R. D. (1986). Auditory filters and excitation patterns as representations of frequency resolution. *Frequency Selectivity in Hearing*.

Pedregosa, F., Varoquaux, G., Gramfort, A., Michel, V., Thirion, B., Grisel, O., Blondel, M., Prettenhofer, P., Weiss, R., Dubourg, V., et al. (2011). Scikit-learn: Machine learning in Python. *Journal of Machine Learning Research*, 12(Oct):2825–2830.

Peisl, W. (1990). *Beschreibung aktiver nichtlinearer Effekte der peripheren Schallverarbeitung des Gehörs durch ein Rechnermodell*. Ph.D. thesis, Technische Universität München, Germany. In German.

Rudnicki, M. and Hemmert, W. (2014). Cochlea: inner ear models in Python. https://github.com/mrkrd/cochlea.

Rudnicki, M., Schoppe, O., Isik, M., Völk, F., and Hemmert, W. (2015). Modeling auditory coding: from sound to spikes. *Cell and Tissue Research*, 361(1):159–175.

Sainath, T. N., Weiss, R. J., Senior, A., Wilson, K. W., and Vinyals, O. (2015). Learning the speech front-end with raw waveform CLDNNs. In *Proc. of Interspeech*, pages 1–5, Dresden, Germany. ISCA.

Saremi, A., Beutelmann, R., Dietz, M., Ashida, G., Kretzberg, J., and Verhulst, S. (2016). A comparative study of seven human cochlear filter models. *The Journal of the Acoustical Society of America*, 140(3):1618–1634.

Schnupp, J., Nelken, I., and King, A. (2011). *Auditory Neuroscience: Making Sense of Sound*. MIT Press.

Seneff, S. (1988). A joint synchrony/mean-rate model of auditory speech processing. *Journal of Phonetics*, 16(1):55–76.

Shamma, S. A., Chadwick, R. S., Wilbur, W. J., Morrish, K. A., and Rinzel, J. (1986). A biophysical model of cochlear processing: Intensity dependence of pure tone responses. *The Journal of the Acoustical Society of America*, 80(1):133–145.

Shera, C. A., Guinan, J. J., and Oxenham, A. J. (2002). Revised estimates of human cochlear tuning from otoacoustic and behavioral measurements. *Proc. National Academy of Sciences*, 99(5):3318–3323.

Singh, R. K., Xu, Y., Wang, R., Hamilton, T. J., van Schaik, A., and Denham, S. L. (2018). CAR-lite: A multi-rate cochlea model on FPGA. In *Proc. IEEE International Symposium on Circuits and Systems (ISCAS)*, pages 1–5, Florence, Italy. IEEE.

Slaney, M. (1988). Lyon's Cochlear Model. Technical Report 13, Apple Computer, Advanced Technology Group.

Slaney, M. (1993). An Efficient Implementation of the Patterson-Holdsworth Auditory Filter Bank. Tech. Rep. 35, Apple Computer, Inc. Perception Group.

Slaney, M. (1998). Auditory Toolbox: Version 2. Technical Report #1998-010, Interval Research Corporation. Available from: https://engineering.purdue.edu/~malcolm/interval/1998-010.

Smith, S. L., Kindermans, P.-J., Ying, C., and Le, Q. V. (2017). Don't decay the learning rate, increase the batch size. *arXiv preprint arXiv:1711.00489*.

Søndergaard, P. L. and Majdak, P. (2013). The Auditory Modeling Toolbox. In Jens Blauert, editor, *The Technology of Binaural Listening*, Modern Acoustics and Signal Processing, pages 33–56. Springer. Available from: http://amtoolbox.sourceforge.net/.

Srivastava, N., Hinton, G. E., Krizhevsky, A., Sutskever, I., and Salakhutdinov, R. (2014). Dropout: a simple way to prevent neural networks from overfitting. *Journal of Machine Learning Research*, 15(1):1929–1958.

Sumner, C. J., Lopez-Poveda, E. A., O'Mard, L. P., and Meddis, R. (2002). A revised model of the inner-hair cell and auditory-nerve complex. *The Journal of the Acoustical Society of America*, 111(5):2178–2188.

Sumner, C. J., Lopez-Poveda, E. A., O'Mard, L. P., and Meddis, R. (2003). Adaptation in a revised inner-hair cell model. *The Journal of the Acoustical Society of America*, 113(2):893–901.

Tabibi, S., Kegel, A., Lai, W. K., and Dillier, N. (2017). Investigating the use of a Gammatone filterbank for a cochlear implant coding strategy. *Journal of Neuroscience Methods*, 277:63–74.

Tan, Q. and Carney, L. H. (2003). A phenomenological

model for the responses of auditory-nerve fibers. II. Nonlinear tuning with a frequency glide. *The Journal of the Acoustical Society of America*, 114(4):2007–2020.

Thakur, C. S., Hamilton, T. J., Tapson, J., van Schaik, A., and Lyon, R. F. (2014). FPGA Implementation of the CAR Model of the Cochlea. In *Proc. IEEE International Symposium on Circuits and Systems (ISCAS)*, pages 1853–1856, Melbourne, Australia. IEEE.

Tjandra, A., Sakti, S., Neubig, G., Toda, T., Adriani, M., and Nakamura, S. (2015). Combination of two-dimensional cochleogram and spectrogram features for deep learning-based ASR. In *Proc. IEEE Int. Conf. on Acoustics, Speech and Signal Processing (ICASSP)*, pages 4525–4529, South Brisbane, Australia. IEEE.

Tjandra, A., Sakti, S., and Nakamura, S. (2017). Attention-based wav2text with feature transfer learning. In *2017 IEEE Automatic Speech Recognition and Understanding Workshop (ASRU)*, pages 309–315. IEEE.

Trigeorgis, G., Ringeval, F., Brueckner, R., Marchi, E., Nicolaou, M. A., Schuller, B., and Zafeiriou, S. (2016). Adieu features? End-to-End Speech Emotion Recognition Using a Deep Convolutional Recurrent Network. In *Proc. IEEE Intl. Conference on Acoustics, Speech and Signal Processing (ICASSP)*, pages 5200–5204, Shanghai, China. IEEE.

Tüske, Z., Golik, P., Schlüter, R., and Ney, H. (2014). Acoustic modeling with deep neural networks using raw time signal for LVCSR. In *Proc. of Interspeech*, pages 1420–1424, Singapore. ISCA.

Van der Walt, S., Colbert, S. C., and Varoquaux, G. (2011). The NumPy array: a structure for efficient numerical computation. *Computing in Science & Engineering*, 13(2):22. Online: `https://numpy.org/`.

Verhulst, S., Dau, T., and Shera, C. A. (2012). Nonlinear time-domain cochlear model for transient stimulation and human otoacoustic emission. *The Journal of the Acoustical Society of America*, 132(6):3842–3848.

Verhulst, S., Altoe, A., and Vasilkov, V. (2018). Computational modeling of the human auditory periphery: Auditory-nerve responses, evoked potentials and hearing loss. *Hearing Research*, 360:55–75.

Westerman, L. A. and Smith, R. L. (1988). A diffusion model of the transient response of the cochlear inner hair cell synapse. *The Journal of the Acoustical Society of America*, 83(6):2266–2276.

Wolfram, S. (1999). The mathematica book. *Assembly Automation*.

Xu, Y., Thakur, C. S., Singh, R. K., Hamilton, T. J., Wang, R. M., and van Schaik, A. (2018). A FPGA implementation of the CAR-FAC cochlear model. *Frontiers in Neuroscience*, 12:198.

Young, S., Evermann, G., Gales, M., Hain, T., Kershaw, D., Liu, X., Moore, G., Odell, J., Ollason, D., Povey, D., Valtchev, V., and Woodland, P. (2006). *The HTK Book*. Cambridge University Engineering Department.

Young, E. D. (2007). Neural representation of spectral and temporal information in speech. *Philosophical Transactions of the Royal Society B: Biological Sciences*, 363(1493):923–945.

Zeghidour, N., Usunier, N., Synnaeve, G., Collobert, R., and Dupoux, E. (2018). End-to-End Speech Recognition From the Raw Waveform. *arXiv preprint arXiv:1806.07098.*

Zeghidour, N. (2019). *Learning Representations of Speech from the Raw Waveform*. Ph.D. thesis, Paris Sciences et Lettres (PSL), Paris, March.

Zeiler, M. D., Ranzato, M., Monga, R., Mao, M., Yang, K., Le, Q. V., Nguyen, P., Senior, A., Vanhoucke, V., Dean, J., and Hinton, G. (2013). On rectified linear units for speech processing. In *Proc. ICASSP 2013*, pages 3517–3521, Vancouver, Canada, May. IEEE.

Zeiler, M. D. (2012). Adadelta: An adaptive learning rate method. *CoRR*, abs/1212.5701.

Zeyer, A., Irie, K., Schlüter, R., and Ney, H. (2018). Improved training of end-to-end attention models for speech recognition. *arXiv preprint arXiv:1805.03294.*

Zhang, X., Heinz, M. G., Bruce, I. C., and Carney, L. H. (2001). A phenomenological model for the responses of auditory-nerve fibers: I. Nonlinear tuning with compression and suppression. *The Journal of the Acoustical Society of America*, 109(2):648–670.

Zheng, H., Yang, Z., Liu, W., Liang, J., and Li, Y. (2015). Improving deep neural networks using softplus units. In *2015 International Joint Conference on Neural Networks (IJCNN)*, pages 1–4, Budapest, Hungary. IEEE.

Zilany, M. S. A., Bruce, I. C., Nelson, P. C., and Carney, L. H. (2009). A phenomenological model of the synapse between the inner hair cell and auditory nerve: long-term adaptation with power-law dynamics. *The Journal of the Acoustical Society of America*, 126(5):2390–2412.

Zilany, M. S. A., Bruce, I. C., Ibrahim, R. A., and Carney, L. H. (2013). Improved parameters and expanded simulation options for a model of the auditory periphery. In *Proc. Association for Research in Otolaryngology (ARO) Midwinter Research Meeting*, pages 440–441, Baltimore, MD.

Zilany, M. S. A., Bruce, I. C., and Carney, L. H. (2014). Updated parameters and expanded simulation options for a model of the auditory periphery. *The Journal of the Acoustical Society of America*, 135(1):283–286.

Zwicker, E. and Peisl, W. (1990). Cochlear preprocessing in analog models, in digital models and in human inner ear. *Hearing Research*, 44(2-3):209–216.

Zwicker, E. (1961). Subdivision of the audible frequency range into critical bands (Frequenzgruppen). *The Journal of the Acoustical Society of America*, 33(2):248–248.

Zwicker, E. (1986). A hardware cochlear nonlinear preprocessing model with active feedback. *The Journal of the Acoustical Society of America*, 80(1):146–153.

Proceedings of the 1st Joint SLTU and CCURL Workshop (SLTU-CCURL 2020), pages 21–27
Language Resources and Evaluation Conference (LREC 2020), Marseille, 11–16 May 2020
ⓒ European Language Resources Association (ELRA), licensed under CC-BY-NC

Open-Source High Quality Speech Datasets for Basque, Catalan and Galician

Oddur Kjartansson, Alexander Gutkin, Alena Butryna, Işın Demirşahin, Clara Rivera

Google Research
United Kingdom and United States
{oddur, agutkin, alenab, isin, rivera}@google.com

Abstract

This paper introduces new open speech datasets for three of the languages of Spain: Basque, Catalan and Galician. Catalan is furthermore the official language of the Principality of Andorra. The datasets consist of high-quality multi-speaker recordings of the three languages along with the associated transcriptions. The resulting corpora include over 33 hours of crowd-sourced recordings of 132 male and female native speakers. The recording scripts also include material for elicitation of global and local place names, personal and business names. The datasets are released under a permissive license and are available for free download for commercial, academic and personal use. The high-quality annotated speech datasets described in this paper can be used to, among other things, build text-to-speech systems, serve as adaptation data in automatic speech recognition and provide useful phonetic and phonological insights in corpus linguistics.

Keywords: Speech Corpora, Open Source, Basque, Catalan, Galician

1. Introduction

Castilian Spanish is the official language of entire Spain. In addition, Basque, Catalan and Galician are the official languages of the three respective autonomous communities of the Basque Country, Catalonia and Galicia (Hoffmann, 1996; Lasagabaster, 2011). Catalan is also spoken in Valencia, Balearic Islands, Andorra, French Catalonia, and a small region of Sardinia. Basque is also spoken in Navarre and the French Basque Country. According to Ethnologue (2019), Basque has close to 800,000 native (first language or L1) speakers, Catalan around 4 million native speakers and Galician around 1.5 million native speakers. Out of the three languages, UNESCO considers Basque to be endangered (Moseley, 2010).

Since the 1980s there has been a resurgence of these languages due to democratization of the central government's cultural and language policies towards the regions (Ferrer, 2000; O'Rourke and Ramallo, 2013; Gorter et al., 2014). As part of this process, considerable work has gone into building speech and language technologies for these languages, especially since late 1990s (López de Ipiña et al., 1995; Villarrubia et al., 1998). Despite evident progress, the availability of speech and language technology in these languages is still not on par with Castilian Spanish and the scarcity of linguistic resources available for building competitive systems, especially in Basque and Galician, has often been pointed out by the researchers (Agić et al., 2016; Vania et al., 2019).

Building language resources is expensive. It can be time consuming to set up the recording logistics, collect and analyze the data. In the case of low-resource languages, finding linguistic experts can become an added factor of complexity. When collecting high-quality speech resources for applications such as text-to-speech, further complications arise as one needs to secure a location for the recording, as well as find an adequate voice talent. Our work relies on several methods that were proposed to mitigate some of these issues. In case of the recording script preparation, freely available text resources such as Wikipedia are used. In addition, using templates which are automatically filled out to cover local place names, important holidays and prominent figures help reduce the time required for recording script design (Wibawa et al., 2018). Finally, to mitigate the cost of professional voice talents, multiple volunteer speakers are used instead of relying on one person (Gutkin et al., 2016).

In this paper we present open high-quality speech resources for three languages, Basque (Google, 2019a), Catalan (Google, 2019b) and Galician (Google, 2019c). The corpora are distributed under a "Creative Commons Attribution-ShareAlike" (CC BY-SA 4.0) license (Creative Commons, 2019) and are freely available for download from Open Speech and Language Resources (OpenSLR) repository (Povey, 2019). Similar speech resources for these three minority languages of Spain have been developed in the past. These resources, however, vary in either availability (academic-only or unclear licensing terms, non-free distribution) or quality (low quality, e.g. 16kHz, recordings), and sometimes both. The main contribution of the work described in this paper is the corpora that is both free for commercial and academic use, and is of sufficiently high-quality to be used in state-of-the-art speech applications, such as multilingual multi-speaker text-to-speech (Chen et al., 2019). To the best of our knowledge, based on the review of existing databases provided in the next section, our three datasets are among the very first truly free resources available online for public use.

The rest of this paper is organized as follows: Section 2 provides an overview of related corpora. Brief linguistic introduction into the languages in question is given in Section 3. The details of the recording script design, the recording process and corpora details are provided in Section 4. Section 5 concludes the paper.

2. Related Corpora

Considerable effort has gone into developing speech resources for Basque, Catalan and Galician in the past. Among the databases that cover multiple minority languages, Rodriguez-Fuentes et al. (2012) describe a large TV Broadcast database developed for automatic speech recognition (ASR) of Basque, Catalan and Galician in clean and noisy environments. The licensing terms are negotiable with the authors.

Basque Basque is included as part of the open-source CMU Wilderness Multilingual Speech Dataset (Black, 2019) containing Bible translation for over 700 languages. Sainz et al. (2012) introduced a high-quality text-to-speech (TTS) database of Basque containing six hours of speech recorded by 11 speakers, with the availability of the corpus being unclear. The database was used by the authors to successfully build statistical parametric speech synthesis system based on Hidden Markov Models (HMMs) using their prior work (Erro et al., 2010). One of the earliest attempts to develop a parallel corpus of Basque and Spanish was undertaken by Pérez et al. (2006), who developed a weather forecast corpus consisting of 28 months of spoken daily weather forecast reports in Spanish and Basque, which were used in speech-to-speech translation (Pérez et al., 2008), language identification (Guijarrubia and Torres, 2010) and ASR (Guijarrubia et al., 2009). Pérez et al. (2012) later described a more sophisticated parallel corpus of Spanish and Basque that includes both text and speech data and consists of the proceedings of the Basque Parliament. The speech portion of the corpus contains 189 hours of speech from 81 speakers. The licensing of this corpus appears unclear and it cannot be located online. The other, more specialized, corpora developed for Basque include the Emotional Speech Database for corpus-based speech synthesis by Saratxaga et al. (2006) that consists of approximately 20 hours of high-quality recordings, evaluated in detail by Sainz et al. (2008), and a smaller 1.5 hour-long multimodal audiovisual database of emotional speech developed by Navas et al. (2004) for prosody studies. Further Basque speech resources are hopefully going to be developed as part of the BerbaTek project, an joint effort by various academic and commercial organizations in the Basque Autonomous Community to increase the availability of speech and language technologies (Arrieta et al., 2008; Leturia et al., 2018).

Catalan Bonafonte et al. (1997) from Universitat Politècnica de Catalunya (UPC) describe one of the earliest datasets of Catalan developed for bilingual Spanish-Catalan unit selection TTS, detailed in (Bonafonte et al., 1998). Additional small corpus of Catalan consisting of 3,600 short utterances was recorded at UPC for prosodic modeling (Febrer et al., 1998). Around the same time Hernando and Nadeu (1999) from UPC developed SpeechDat – a Catalan speech database that contains recordings of 2,000 speakers (each uttering around 50 sentences) over fixed telephone lines. The database is primarily intended for ASR systems (Mariño et al., 2000; Padrell and Mariño, 2002) and is distributed by ELRA under the restricted license. The lack of emotional speech database for Catalan was first noticed by Iriondo et al. (2004), who built emotional HMM-based TTS piggybacking on the existing corpus of Castilian Spanish. Bonafonte et al. (2008) describe a Catalan text-to-speech database consisting of 10 hours of

single male and female speaker recordings. This resource is free for academic and commercial use, but it does not seem to be available online. This database was used by the authors to produce HMM-based TTS voices (Bonafonte et al., 2009). The most recent development is the open ASR database described by Külebi and Öktem (2018) consisting of 240 hours of transcribed Catalan TV broadcasts that is freely available online. A slightly outdated work by Moreno et al. (2006) and Schulz et al. (2008) provides reviews of existing programs for Catalan and a roadmap for constructing speech and language applications.

Galician There has been a reasonably late focus on speech applications in Galician, with one of the earliest efforts undertaken by Dieguez-Tirado et al. (2005), who built a bilingual ASR system for Galician and Spanish based on corpus of TV shows, and by González et al. (2008), who outlined the challenges of the language, such as homograph disambiguation (Mourín et al., 2009), for speech processing. Proprietary database of Galician was used by Microsoft to build HMM TTS system (Braga et al., 2010). This effort was a joint collaboration with University of Vigo that resulted in a speech database consisting of 10,000 utterances (Campillo et al., 2010). Among recent work is the large high-quality corpus of spoken Galician annotated on multiple linguistic levels (García-Mateo et al., 2014) that consists of 98 hours of recordings and the corresponding transcriptions. The corpus is mostly intended for corpus linguistic studies and sociolinguists as it contains recordings of Galician in various styles and dialects over a long period of time starting in 1960s and may not be suitable for building speech applications. Similar to Basque, there is a growing awareness of the need to increase the availability of Galician language resources (Mateo and Rodríguez, 2012).

3. Overview of the Languages

There is a general consensus that Basque is a language isolate with no known relatives and uncertain origins (Hualde et al., 1996; Etxeberria, 2008; Trask, 2013). Basque is an inflectional and agglutinative language (Hualde and de Urbina, 2003; King, 2012), its grammatical relations between components within a clause are represented by suffixes, and many words consist of compounded morphemes. Among several uses, the suffixes are used to mark over a dozen cases and four definite determiners (Albizu, 2002; King, 2012). This markedly distinguishes Basque from its neighbouring Romance languages. Although the traditional phonology of Basque is noticeably different from Spanish (Hualde, 1991; Bengtson, 2003), Hualde (2015) mentions the acceleration in the processes of convergence between pronunciations of the two languages, whereby "for many speakers of the younger generations there are not many phonological or phonetic differences between their Basque and their Spanish, if any".

Catalan is an Indo-European language of the Romance family sharing many traits with the neighbouring Romance languages from Ibero- and Gallo-Romance groups (Posner, 1996; Hualde, 2013), yet differing from them in several respects, such as phonology, which places the language roughly between Spanish, French and Italian (Wheeler,

| Language | Gender | Lines | Tokens | | | | | Chars | | | Speakers | Audio Duration | |
			min	max	avg	Total	Unique	min	max	avg		Total [h:m:s]	Average[s]
Basque	F	3,858	1	20	8.0	30,901	8,583	17	156	58.1	29	7:26:36	6.77
	M	3,278	1	18	8.0	26,383	8,030	23	129	58.3	23	6:36:00	7.25
Catalan	F	2,321	2	24	10.5	24,385	6,568	17	142	59.5	20	5:24:00	8.38
	M	1,919	2	29	10.6	20,261	6,514	28	141	60.8	16	4:01:12	7.53
Galician	F	4,264	3	28	11.6	49,674	6,530	18	174	68.3	34	7:40:12	6.48
	M	1,324	4	28	11.7	15,462	4,336	20	186	69.4	10	2:38:24	7.19
Total	–	**16,963**	–	–	–	167,066	–	–	–	–	132	33:35:19	–

Table 1: Details of the recording script lines and the audio properties of the corpora.

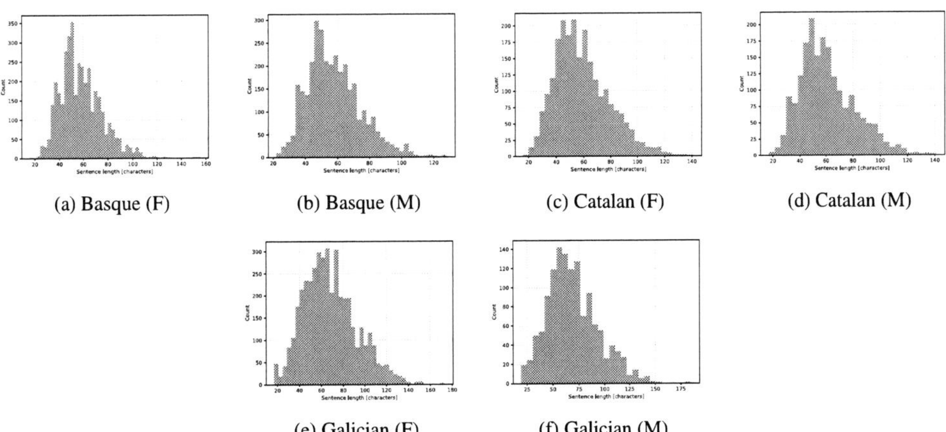

(a) Basque (F)   (b) Basque (M)   (c) Catalan (F)   (d) Catalan (M)

(e) Galician (F)   (f) Galician (M)

Figure 1: Histograms of the utterance length (in characters) by language and gender (x-axis shows the lengths, y-axis the frequency).

2005). Some of these differences from Spanish are manifest in greater complexity in terms of syllable structure types (Prieto et al., 2012), the existence of vowel reduction (Cabré, 2009) and dissimilar vowel and consonant inventories, such as the existence of three more vowels and voiced fricatives (Pallier et al., 2001).

According to an areal classification Galician belongs to the Ibero-Romance family together with Spanish and Portuguese. Galician shares strong similarities with Portuguese, such as possible use of inflectional endings in infinitive forms, both languages descending from the same medieval ancestor deriving from Vulgar Latin (Holt, 2016; Martìnez-Gil, 2020). However, similar to Vulgar Latin and Italian, Galician distinguishes seven vowels, which differs it from modern Portuguese that has two extra vowels and Spanish with its five vowels (Kabatek and Pusch, 2011; Gibson and Gil, 2019). In other respects, such as phonotactics, the language is more similar to Spanish (Harris, 1983).

4. Corpus Design and Overview

Script Design Recording scripts were generated by native speakers using a mixture of Wikipedia and template sentences. The templates were filled in using local and global entity names including businesses, places and people. Examples of such templates include sentences of the form "*person* traveled from *place$_A$* to *place$_B$* at *time*" and "*event* is celebrated in *place* on *date*", where the variable template slots are denoted by italics. Using a template method makes it relatively easy to automatically generate sentences for the script. However, the applicability of this method is language-dependent. In the case of morphologically rich languages, such as Basque, the template wording might need to be changed depending on grammatical context. Using this process we generated up to 5,000 sentences for each of the languages, which were then proofread and hand-tuned (if necessary) by the native speakers. Even though transcriptions mostly contain sequences of natural language words, because they have not been text normalized they also contain non-standard word (NSW) expressions, such as numbers (Sproat et al., 2001). Therefore, here and below we refer to the constituent space-separated elements of transcriptions as "tokens" rather than words. The total number of script lines, the minimum, maximum and average number of tokens and characters (including spaces) per sentence for each language and gender are shown in the first nine columns of Table 1. Please note, some sentences may contain a single token, such as telephone number (e.g., Basque "*zortzi-zazpi-bi-bederatzi-zazpi-bost-zero-zero-zero*"). The corresponding distributions of sentence lengths per language and per gender are represented as histograms in Figure 1. The distribution shapes and the modes for all the datasets are roughly similar, with Galician having the longest orthographic representation if sentences of over 120 characters are considered. According to Table 1, Galician also has the highest average number of characters per sentence.

Recording Process The recordings took place in three different locations in Spain. Catalan was recorded in Barcelona, Basque was recorded in Bilbao and Galician

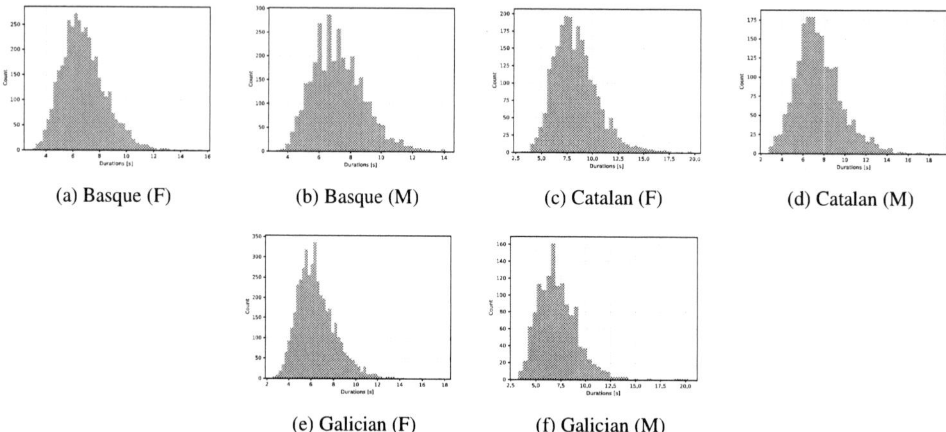

(a) Basque (F)   (b) Basque (M)   (c) Catalan (F)   (d) Catalan (M)

(e) Galician (F)   (f) Galician (M)

Figure 2: Histograms of the utterance durations (in seconds) by language and gender (x-axis shows duration, y-axis the frequency).

was recorded in Santiago de Compostela. Instead of renting professional recording studios, sound insulated rooms were used in each location. Volunteer amateur native speakers were sourced with the help from local groups in each area and represent a variety of local accents.

The audio was recorded using a Neuman KM184 diaphragm condenser cardioid microphone, a Blue ICICLE XLR to USB analogue to digital (A/D) converter, which also provides power to the microphone. The USB A/D converter was connected to an Asus Zenbook fanless laptop, which the participants used to control the recordings. The microphone was put on a microphone stand, and adjusted for each volunteer. The microphone was kept at a distance of 30 cm from the mouth of the volunteer, slightly off center and pointing either down towards or up towards the volunteer (approximately 5 degrees off the center on both axes). A proprietary Web-based recording software was used for the recordings. The setup is designed for self-service, so that the speaker both records and controls the recordings. Using a self-serve model eliminates the need for an extra person to control the recordings. Quality of the audio can be monitored from another computer, once the volunteer has saved the recordings. Most speakers were able to record about 150 sentences in the span of an hour, which included a short break about half way through the recordings. A few minutes were needed to familiarize them with the recording software, and the volunteers then took over the process. The volunteers were instructed to keep their voice neutral, and speak clearly.

All the recordings went through a quality control process performed by trained native speakers to ensure that each recording matched the corresponding script, had consistent volume, was noise-free and consisted of fluent speech without unnatural pauses or mispronunciations. Problematic lines that could not be re-recorded were dropped.

Corpora Overview The last three columns of Table 1 show various properties of the resulting corpora that include the total number of speakers, the total duration of each dataset and the average utterance duration for each gender for each language. The corresponding distributions of utterance durations (measured in seconds) for each language and gender are shown in Figure 2. As can be seen from the figure, Catalan has the highest number of long utterances (over 10 seconds long) among the three languages and also has the longest average audio duration (as shown in Table 1).

Each language is distributed in two ZIP archives, one for each gender. The audio is stored in a single channel 48kHz 16-bit signed integer PCM RIFF audio format. No post-processing was performed on the audio files. The file naming scheme of the audio files consists of a three letter code denoting the language and gender (e.g., `caf` represents Catalan female), a 5 digit speaker identifier, followed by an 11 digits number identifying the utterance. All components are separated by underscores (e.g., `caf_00195_00047731813.wav`). The transcriptions for the audio files are stored in a single textual index file (`line_index.tsv`).

5. Conclusion

In this paper, we presented free high quality multi-speaker speech corpora for three official languages of Spain: Basque, Catalan and Galician. The corpora has been designed with speech applications in mind, such as multi-speaker TTS and ASR speaker adaptation. We described the details of the process used to construct the corpora. The data is released with an open-source license with no limitations on academic or commercial use. We hope that this data will contribute to research and development of speech applications for these important languages.

6. Acknowledgments

The authors would like to thank following entities for supporting this work by finding volunteers, recording environment and their help with script generation: Bilboko Udala, Eusko Jaurlaritza and Euskaltzaindia (Basque), Direcció General de Política Lingüística del Departament de Cultura, Generalitat de Catalunya (Catalan) and Secretaría Xeral de Política Lingüística da Consellería de Cultura e Turismo, Xunta de Galicia (Galician).

7. Bibliographical References

Agić, Ž., Johannsen, A., Plank, B., Martínez Alonso, H., Schluter, N., and Søgaard, A. (2016). Multilingual projection for parsing truly low-resource languages. *Transactions of the Association for Computational Linguistics*, 4:301–312.

Albizu, P. (2002). Basque Verbal Morphology: Redefining Cases. *Anuario del Seminario de Filología Vasca" Julio de Urquijo"*, pages 1–19.

Arrieta, K., Leturia, I., Iturraspe, U., De Ilarraza, A. D., Sarasola, K., Hernáez, I., and Navas, E. (2008). AnHitz, development and integration of language, speech and visual technologies for Basque. In *2008 Second International Symposium on Universal Communication*, pages 338–343. IEEE.

Bengtson, J. D. (2003). Notes on Basque Comparative Phonology. *Mother Tongue*, 8:23–39.

Black, A. W. (2019). CMU Wilderness Multilingual Speech Dataset. In *Proc. of IEEE International Conference on Acoustics, Speech and Signal Processing (ICASSP)*, pages 5971–5975. IEEE.

Bonafonte, A., Esquerra Llucià, I., Febrer Godayol, A., and Vallverdú Bayés, S. (1997). A bilingual text-to-speech system in Spanish and Catalan. In *Proc. of EUROSPEECH'97*, pages 2455–2458, Rhodes, Greece.

Bonafonte, A., Esquerra, I., Febrer, A., Fonollosa, J. A., and Vallverdú, F. (1998). The UPC text-to-speech system for Spanish and Catalan. In *Fifth International Conference on Spoken Language Processing*.

Bonafonte, A., Adell, J., Esquerra, I., Gallego, S., Moreno, A., and Pérez, J. (2008). Corpus and Voices for Catalan Speech Synthesis. In *Proc. Language Resources and Evaluation Conference (LREC)*.

Bonafonte, A., Aguilar, L., Esquerra, I., Oller, S., and Moreno, A. (2009). Recent work on the FESTCAT database for speech synthesis. *Proc. SLTECH*, pages 131–132.

Braga, D., Silva, P., Ribeiro, M., Dias, M. S., Campillo, F., and Garcia-Mateo, C. (2010). Hélia, Heloısa and Helena: new HTS systems in European Portuguese, Brazilian Portuguese and Galician. In *PROPOR: 2010 - International Conference on Computational Processing of the Portuguese Language*, pages 27–30.

Cabré, T. (2009). Vowel reduction and vowel harmony in Eastern Catalan loanword phonology. In Sónia Frota Marina Vigário et al., editors, *Phonetics and Phonology: Interactions and interrelations*, pages 267–285.

Campillo, F., Braga, D., Mourín, A. B., García-Mateo, C., Silva, P., Dias, M. S., and Méndez, F. (2010). Building high quality databases for minority languages such as Galician. In *Proc. Language Resources and Evaluation Conference (LREC)*, Valetta, Malta.

Chen, M., Chen, M., Liang, S., Ma, J., Chen, L., Wang, S., and Xiao, J. (2019). Cross-Lingual, Multi-Speaker Text-to-Speech Synthesis Using Neural Speaker Embedding. pages 2105–2109, Graz, Austria.

Creative Commons. (2019). Attribution-ShareAlike 4.0 International (CC BY-SA 4.0). `http://creativecommons.org/licenses/by-sa/4.0/deed.en`.

Dieguez-Tirado, J., Garcia-Mateo, C., Docio-Fernandez, L., and Cardenal-Lopez, A. (2005). Adaptation strategies for the acoustic and language models in bilingual speech transcription. In *Proc. IEEE International Conference on Acoustics, Speech, and Signal Processing (ICASSP)*, volume 1, pages I–833. IEEE.

Erro, D., Sainz, I., Luengo, I., Odriozola, I., Sánchez, J., Saratxaga, I., Navas, E., and Hernáez, I. (2010). HMM-based speech synthesis in Basque language using HTS. *Proc. FALA*, pages 67–70.

Ethnologue. (2019). Ethnologue. SIL International: `https://www.ethnologue.com`. Accessed: 2020-01-20.

Etxeberria, U. (2008). On Basque Quantification and on How Some Languages Restrict their Quantificational Domain Overtly. In Lisa Matthewson, editor, *Quantification: A Cross-Linguistic Perspective*, volume 64 of *North-Holland Linguistic Series: Linguistic Variation*. Emerald.

Febrer, A., Padrell, J., and Bonafonte, A. (1998). Modeling phone duration: Application to Catalan TTS. In *The Third ESCA/COCOSDA Workshop (ETRW) on Speech Synthesis*.

Ferrer, F. (2000). Languages, minorities and education in Spain: the case of Catalonia. *Comparative Education*, 36(2):187–197.

García-Mateo, C., López, A. C., Regueira, X. L., Rei, E. F., Martinez, M., Seara, R., Varela, R., and Basanta, N. (2014). CORILGA: a Galician Multilevel Annotated Speech Corpus for Linguistic Analysis. In *Proc. Language Resources and Evaluation Conference (LREC)*, pages 2653–2657.

Gibson, M. and Gil, J. (2019). *Romance Phonetics and Phonology*. Oxford University Press.

González, M. G., Banga, E. R., Díaz, F. C., Pazó, F. M., Liñares, L. R., and Iglesias, G. I. (2008). Specific features of the Galician language and implications for speech technology development. *Speech Communication*, 50(11-12):874–887.

Gorter, D., Zenotz, V., Etxague, X., and Cenoz, J. (2014). Multilingualism and European minority languages: The case of Basque. In *Minority Languages and Multilingual Education*, pages 201–220. Springer.

Guijarrubia, V. G. and Torres, M. I. (2010). Text-and speech-based phonotactic models for spoken language identification of Basque and Spanish. *Pattern Recognition Letters*, 31(6):523–532.

Guijarrubia, V. G., Torres, M. I., and Justo, R. (2009). Morpheme-based automatic speech recognition of Basque. In *Proc. Iberian Conference on Pattern Recognition and Image Analysis*, pages 386–393. Springer.

Gutkin, A., Ha, L., Jansche, M., Kjartansson, O., Pipatsrisawat, K., and Sproat, R. (2016). Building Statistical Parametric Multi-Speaker Synthesis for Bangladeshi Bangla. In *5th Workshop on Spoken Language Technolo-*

gies for Under-Resourced Languages (SLTU '16), pages 194–200.

Harris, J. W. (1983). *Syllable structure and stress in Spanish. A nonlinear analysis*. Number 8 in Linguistic Inquiry Monographs. MIT Press, Cambridge, MA.

Hernando, J. and Nadeu, C. (1999). SpeechDat. Catalan Database for the Fixed Telephone Network. *Corpus Design Technical Report, TALP-UPC*.

Hoffmann, C. (1996). Language Planning at the Crossroads: the Case of Contemporary Spain. In Charlotte Hoffmann, editor, *Language, Culture and Communication in Contemporary Europe*, pages 93–110. Multilingual Matters Clevedon.

Holt, D. E. (2016). From Latin to Portuguese: Main Phonological Changes. In W. Leo Wetzels, et al., editors, *The Handbook of Portuguese Linguistics*, pages 457–470. Wiley-Blackwell, UK.

Hualde, J. I. and de Urbina, J. O. (2003). *A Grammar of Basque*. Mouton de Gruyter, Berlin.

Hualde, J. I., Lakarra, J. A., and Trask, R. L. (1996). *Towards a History of the Basque Language*, volume 131. John Benjamins Publishing.

Hualde, J. I. (1991). *Basque Phonology*. Routledge, United Kingdom.

Hualde, J. I. (2013). *Catalan*. Routledge.

Hualde, J. I. (2015). Basque as an Extinct Language. In *Ibon Sarasola, Gorazarre. Homenatge, Homenaje*, pages 319–326. Bilbao: University of the Basque Country.

Iriondo, I., Alías, F., Melenchón, J., and Llorca, M. A. (2004). Modeling and synthesizing emotional speech for Catalan text-to-speech synthesis. In *Tutorial and research workshop on affective dialogue systems*, pages 197–208. Springer.

Kabatek, J. and Pusch, C. D. (2011). The Romance Languages. In Bernd Kortmann et al., editors, *The Languages and Linguistics of Europe: A Comprehensive Guide*, volume 1, pages 69–96. Walter de Gruyter, Berlin.

King, A. R. (2012). *The Basque Language: A Practical Introduction*. University of Nevada Press.

Külebi, B. and Öktem, A. (2018). Building an Open Source Automatic Speech Recognition System for Catalan. In *Proc. IberSPEECH*, pages 25–29.

Lasagabaster, D. (2011). Language policy in Spain: The coexistence of small and big languages. In Catrin Norrby et al., editors, *Uniformity and Diversity in Language Policy. Global Perspectives*, pages 109–125. Multilingual Matters Clevedon.

Leturia, I., Sarasola, K., Arregi, X., de Ilarraza, A. D., Navas, E., Sainz, I., del Pozo, A., Baranda, D., and Iturraspe, U. (2018). The BerbaTek project for Basque: Promoting a less-resourced language via language technology for translation, content management and learning. *Language Technologies for a Multilingual Europe*, 4:181.

López de Ipiña, M., Torres, M., and Oñederra, M. (1995). Design of a phonetic corpus for Automatic Speech Recognition in Basque Language. In *Proc. EUROSPEECH*, volume 95, pages 851–854.

Mariño, J. B., Padrell, J., Moreno Bilbao, M. A., and Nadeu Camprubí, C. (2000). Monolingual and bilingual Spanish-Catalan speech recognizers developed from SpeechDat databases. In *Proc. XLDB-Very Large Telephone Speech Databases*, pages 57–61. C. Draxler.

Martìnez-Gil, F. (2020). Galician. In Christoph Gabriel, et al., editors, *Manual of Romance Phonetics and Phonology*, volume 27 of *Manuals of Romance Linguistics*, pages 1–46. Walter de Gruyter, Berlin.

Mateo, C. G. and Rodríguez, M. A. (2012). Language Technology Support for Galician. In *The Galician Language in the Digital Age*, pages 50–67. Springer.

Moreno, A., Febrer, A., and Márquez, L. (2006). Generation of Language Resources for the Development of Speech Technologies in Catalan. In *Proc. LREC*, Genoa, Italy, May. European Language Resources Association (ELRA).

Moseley, C. (2010). *Atlas of the world's languages in danger*. UNESCO Publishing, Paris, 3 edition. http://www.unesco.org/culture/en/endangeredlanguages/atlas.

Mourín, A., Braga, D., Coelho, L., García-Mateo, C., Campillo, F., and Dias, M. (2009). Homograph Disambiguation in Galician TTS Systems. In *IX Congreso Internacional da Asociación Internacional de Estudos Galegos, A Coruña-Santiago de Compostela-Vigo*.

Navas, E., Castelruiz, A., Luengo, I., Sánchez, J., and Hernáez, I. (2004). Designing and Recording an Audiovisual Database of Emotional Speech in Basque. In *Proc. Language Resources and Evaluation Conference (LREC)*.

O'Rourke, B. and Ramallo, F. (2013). Competing ideologies of linguistic authority amongst new speakers in contemporary Galicia. *Language in Society*, 42(3):287–305.

Padrell, J. and Mariño, J. B. (2002). Taking Advantage of Spanish Speech Resources to Improve Catalan Acoustic HMMs. *Co-operating Organisation*, page 67.

Pallier, C., Colomé, A., and Sebastián-Gallés, N. (2001). The influence of native-language phonology on lexical access: Exemplar-based versus abstract lexical entries. *Psychological Science*, 12(6):445–449.

Pérez, A., Torres, I., Casacuberta, F., and Guijarrubia, V. (2006). A Spanish-Basque Weather Forecast Corpus for Probabilistic Speech Translation. In *Proc. 5th SALT-MIL Workshop on Minority Languages*, pages 99–101, Genoa, Italy.

Pérez, A., Torres, M. I., and Casacuberta, F. (2008). Joining linguistic and statistical methods for Spanish-to-Basque speech translation. *Speech Communication*, 50(11-12):1021–1033.

Pérez, A., Alcaide, J. M., and Torres, M.-I. (2012). EuskoParl: a speech and text Spanish-Basque parallel corpus. In *Proc. Interspeech*, pages 2362–2365, Portland, Oregon.

Posner, R. (1996). *The Romance Languages*. Cambridge University Press.

Povey, D. (2019). Open Speech and Language Resources (OpenSLR). http://www.openslr.org/resources.php. Accessed: 2019-03-30.

Prieto, P., del Mar Vanrell, M., Astruc, L., Payne, E., and Post, B. (2012). Phonotactic and phrasal properties of speech rhythm. Evidence from Catalan, English, and Spanish. *Speech Communication*, 54(6):681–702.

Rodriguez-Fuentes, L. J., Penagarikano, M., Varona, A., Diez, M., and Bordel, G. (2012). KALAKA-2: a TV Broadcast Speech Database for the Recognition of Iberian Languages in Clean and Noisy Environments. In *Proc. Language Resources and Evaluation Conference (LREC)*, pages 99–105.

Sainz, I., Saratxaga, I., Navas, E., Hernáez, I., Sanchez, J., Luengo, I., Odriozola, I., and Madariaga, I. (2008). Subjective Evaluation of an Emotional Speech Database for Basque. In *Proc. Language Resources and Evaluation Conference (LREC)*.

Sainz, I., Erro, D., Navas, E., Hernáez, I., Sanchez, J., Saratxaga, I., and Odriozola, I. (2012). Versatile Speech Databases for High Quality Synthesis for Basque. In *Proc. Language Resources and Evaluation Conference (LREC)*, pages 3308–3312.

Saratxaga, I., Navas, E., Hernáez, I., and Luengo, I. (2006). Designing and Recording an Emotional Speech Database for Corpus Based Synthesis in Basque. In *Proc. Language Resources and Evaluation Conference (LREC)*, pages 2126–2129.

Schulz, H., Costa-Juss, M. R., and Fonollosa, J. A. (2008). TECNOPARLA – Speech technologies for Catalan and its application to Speech-to-speech Translation. *Procesamiento del lenguaje Natural*, 41.

Sproat, R., Black, A. W., Chen, S., Kumar, S., Ostendorf, M., and Richards, C. (2001). Normalization of Non-Standard Words. *Computer Speech and Language*, 15(3):287–333, July.

Trask, R. L. (2013). *The History of Basque*. Routledge.

Vania, C., Kementchedjhieva, Y., Søgaard, A., and Lopez, A. (2019). A systematic comparison of methods for low-resource dependency parsing on genuinely low-resource languages. *arXiv preprint arXiv:1909.02857*.

Villarrubia, L., León, P., Hernández, L., Elvira, J., Nadeu, C., Esquerra, I., Hernando, J., Garcia-Mateo, C., and Docio, L. (1998). VOCATEL and VOGATEL: Two telephone speech databases of Spanish minority languages (Catalan and Galician). In *Proc. of the Workshop on Language Resources for European Minority Languages, LREC*.

Wheeler, M. W. (2005). *The Phonology of Catalan*. Oxford University Press.

Wibawa, J. A. E., Sarin, S., Li, C., Pipatsrisawat, K., Sodimana, K., Kjartansson, O., Gutkin, A., Jansche, M., and Ha, L. (2018). Building Open Javanese and Sundanese Corpora for Multilingual Text-to-Speech. In *Proc. of the 11th International Conference on Language Resources and Evaluation (LREC)*, pages 1610–1614, Miyazaki, Japan, May.

8. Language Resource References

Google. (2019a). *Crowd-sourced high-quality Basque speech data set by Google*. Google, distributed by Open Speech and Language Resources (OpenSLR), `http://www.openslr.org/76`, Google crowd-sourced speech and language resources, 1.0, ISLRN 490-901-445-079-2.

Google. (2019b). *Crowd-sourced high-quality Catalan speech data set by Google*. Google, distributed by Open Speech and Language Resources (OpenSLR), `http://www.openslr.org/69`, Google crowd-sourced speech and language resources, 1.0, ISLRN 993-764-975-949-2.

Google. (2019c). *Crowd-sourced high-quality Galician speech data set by Google*. Google, distributed by Open Speech and Language Resources (OpenSLR), `http://www.openslr.org/77`, Google crowd-sourced speech and language resources, 1.0, ISLRN 799-821-375-475-5.

Proceedings of the 1st Joint SLTU and CCURL Workshop (SLTU-CCURL 2020), pages 28–35
Language Resources and Evaluation Conference (LREC 2020), Marseille, 11–16 May 2020
© European Language Resources Association (ELRA), licensed under CC-BY-NC

Two LRL & Distractor Corpora from Web Information Retrieval and a Small Case Study in Language Identification without Training Corpora

Armin Hoenen, Cemre Koc, Marc Rahn
Goethe University Frankfurt
Empirical Linguistiscs, Juridicum, Senckenberganlage 29, 60325 Frankfurt
hoenen@em.uni-frankfurt.de, cem_koc@icloud.com, marc.rahn@venturerebels.de

Abstract

In recent years, low resource languages (LRLs) have seen a surge in interest after certain tasks have been solved for larger ones and as they present various challenges (data sparsity, sparsity of experts and expertise, unusual structural properties etc.). For a larger number of them in the wake of this interest resources and technologies have been created. However, there are very small languages for which this has not yet led to a significant change. We focus here one such language (Nogai) and one larger small language (Māori). Since especially smaller languages often face the situation of having very similar siblings or a larger small sister language which is more accessible, the rate of noise in data gathered on them so far is often high. Therefore, we present small corpora for our 2 case study languages which we obtained through web information retrieval and likewise for their noise inducing distractor languages and conduct a small language identification experiment where we identify documents in a boolean way as either belonging or not to the target language. We release our test corpora for two such scenarios in the format of the An Crúbadán project (Scannell, 2007) and a tool for unsupervised language identification using writing system and toponym information.

Keywords: similar languages, less resourced languages, language identification, distractor languages, Māori, Nogai

1. Introduction

For Less Resourced Languages (LRLs), it may be especially hard to obtain data. The smaller the LRL is, the harder this will tendentially be (apart from some very well described small languages). The level and degree of possible expertise and the number of linguistic descriptions decreases. Thus, labelling and obtaining labelled data for these cases is especially hard and often unrealistic. Language Identification (LI) on the other hand uses mainly supervised methods with training corpora for which the language/s or variety/ies is/are known. This extends to the Discrimination between Similar Languages (DSL) task. In Web Information Retrieval (WIR) for LRLs LI can be part of a pipeline, be it in manual or automatic extraction. A retrieved document must be classified as relevant or not for an LRL corpus. Since labelled data is often not a priori available for the training of LI classifiers, in this paper, we present a very simple approach which leans only on resources which are relatively easily obtainable.

The paper is organized as follows: Section 2. recounts briefly the large body of related work. Section 3. then describes in detail how to define similar language scenarios (in WIR and beyond) by using linguistic criteria, before a classifier and its features are presented along the test scenario corpora. Section 4. summarizes the results of the main experiment, which are discussed alongside some detail on toponyms in Section 5. Finally, Section 6. briefly summarizes the achievements and concludes.

2. Related Work

In order to compose a noise-free corpus even for very small languages for which expertise (and thus the capacity of noise recognition in the face of similar sister languages) is very limited, we need a method to discriminate between the target language and what we want to call *distractors*. We understand this step as crucial for corpus generation.

This paper draws from two subfields, the first one being DSL as closely related to LI and the second one WIR. The task of LI precedes that of DSL, which has come up after standard language identification had been shown to work less well for similar languages (see for instance Padró and Padró (2004), Martins and Silva (2005),Ljubesic et al. (2007)). Tiedemann and Ljubešić (2012) developed methods for the efficient discrimination between Croatian, Serbian, Slovenian and Bosnian, Ranaivo-Malançon (2006) for Malay and Indonesian. In 2014, the first DSL shared task has been conducted (Zampieri et al., 2014) which has since been run so far until 2018 (Zampieri et al., 2018). Approaches to language identification and similar language discrimination have been plenty and Jauhiainen et al. (2019) give a recent overview. The large majority of these has used supervised techniques trained and tested on labeled data. As for unsupervised scenarios, clustering and other approaches have been used.

Our method is based on intersections of grapheme inventories. Henrich (1989) already use knowledge on peculiar letters in alphabets. Some other researchers also employed them in language identification in various ways (Giguet, 1995; Hanif et al., 2007; Samih and Kallmeyer, 2017; Hasimu and Silamu, 2017). Our binary intersection approach is to our best knowledge new as is the combination with place names. As for place names, for instance Chen and Maison (2003) have shown that place names can be successfully used in person name LI since their ngrams are more typical than those extracted from normal text.

WIR is a constantly active field since the seminal paper of *Web as Corpus* (Kilgarriff and Grefenstette, 2001). For LRLs, several works have been published (Biemann et al., 2007; Scannell, 2007) partly releasing publicly available repositories such as the Leipzig Corpora Collection. The retrieval of LRL content on the web is complicated by the fact that large parts of the web consist of content in the largest languages[1] and that those matter most for the business models of large search engines. Scannell (2007) consequently speaks of 'polluting languages' when characterising unwanted results in LRL queries. We draw from such aspects of these studies as well as from general linguistic literature on language genealogy and contact phenomena (see for instance (Cysouw, 2013; Thomason, 2001)).

3. Method

In order to facilitate WIR in particular for LRLs, we present an approach to rigorously define similar language scenarios and implement a binary classifier for each pair *target language-distractor language* using writing system related and toponymic information.

3.1. Defining Distractors

Ljubesic et al. (2007) in her first paper discriminated Croatian, Serbian and Slovenian, then in a follow-up, the variety of Bosnian was included (Tiedemann and Ljubešić, 2012). This variety had only recently become ever more recognized as a language in the aftermath of the civil war in former Jugoslavia. However, as this example shows, apart from the fuzzy border between what can count as language and what as dialect (Barfield, 1998, p.85), other factors such as availability of labelled data or the official status of a variety may play a role when deciding which languages to include in a particular DSL task. Here, we advocate a linguistically informed uniform approach towards the definition of what we'd like to call *distractor languages*. We propose to take into account the following three types of target languages:

- language isolates without known relatives,

- pidgin and creole laguages, and

- all other languages.

Departing from this distinction, now distractors are languages which share confusingly many features with a target language. In the case of language isolates, fortunately there are no linguistically closely related sister languages, so only a language which has intense contact can be potentially confusing. This language (languages) can usually be identified by an analysis of language geography and history as well as loanwords. In WIR, we would argue that one should include this language in the distractors since it will often be a very ubiquitous web language, but for evaluating LI tasks alone, depending on the amount of loaning and the degree of orthographic adaptation this might not always be necessary.

For creoles obviously the superstrate language[2] is the most obvious distractor coming to mind. In case of English and

French based creoles (which should be the most numerous)[3] however much orthographic simplification may apply rendering them somewhat less confusable with the superstrate. This however depends on the nature of the superstrate's writing system, which for English is especially deep (Katz and Frost, 1992). This can not be presupposed for the general case. Some linguists have hypothesized a universality of certain features of creoles such as double negation (Déprez and Henri, 2018) which would render them similar amongst each other apart from the often parallel simplification of the superstrate. Their common vocabulary will render them similar, too. So far, we have not found a DSL on the discrimination between creoles of the same superstrate although this could be a challenging task. However, for creoles, also the substrate language contributes fewer or more lexemes and should thus be considered on a case by case basis as possible distractor.

For all other languages, the most probably similar languages are closely related sister languages (written in the same script), where the degree of similarity correlates with the degree of relatedness (Cysouw, 2013). For those languages, one should thus adhere to a language genealogy, such as the ones provided by the WALS (Dryer and Haspelmath, 2013) or Ethnologue[4] and define those languages as distractors which are most closely related. In another experiment (Hoenen et al., 2020), we found that computing the overlap of most frequent words can provide useful hints to which languages from the same family (or sprachbund) should be included. We found in a scenario for Galician that Spanish and Portuguese clearly showed most lexical overlap followed by Italian with approximately a quarter of the similarity, then followed with a large gap indistinguishably by other Romance, Germanic and other languages. Historical stages of the target language – even in case it is an isolate – should always count as distractors.

For WIR, there might also be paralinguistic distractors such as badly OCRed text, written glossolalia, program code, cryptographic cyphers or other artifacts. Summarizing the approach to defining similar language discrimination scenarios:

- language isolates: contact languages (orthography, loanword sources)

- pidgin and creole laguages: other creoles based on the same superstrate language, superstrate language, substrate language

- all other languages: closely related languages, contact languages

Thresholds for similarity must be chosen according to the scenario on a case by case basis, since context (here WIR, writing systems), number of relatives and interrelatedness (if there are only 2 close relatives one may want to include

---

[1]As one can see from statistics on pages such as `https://w3techs.com/technologies/overview/content_language` or `https://www.internetworldstats.com/stats7.htm`, both last accessed on 30-03-2020.

[2]This is for instance the language of the former colonial power from which the creole has then inherited its vocabulary.

[3]A hint towards this is found when searching language names for the word 'creole' in Glottologue (`https://glottolog.org/`, last accessed on 30-03-2020), where of the 35 results 14 include English, 8 French in their name. Of course, Spanish, Portuguese, Dutch, Russian, Arabic, Hindi and others also have creoles based on them.

[4]ethnologue.com

them even though the second is a little less similar) may crucially differ.

3.2. Two Scenarios

We describe two LRL scenarios. One with the target language of Nogai[5], a Turkic language of Russia and one with Māori[6], an Austronesian language of New Zealand. The choice of these languages was determined by several factors, a) their alphabets contain few to no special characters which make them difficult scenarios for our classifier, b) they exhibit a number of differences such as alphabet, location, primary lingua franca, language family, typological profile etc. and finally they were accessible to us through previous work, (Hoenen et al., 2020). We defined distractors according to the above logic and criteria.

Language	Distractors(Type), C=Contact, R=Related
Nogai	Russian(C), Kumyk(R), Bashkir(R), Karachai(R), Kazakh(R)
Māori	English(C), Indonesian(R), Tahitian(R), Tongan(R), Samoan(R)

Table 1: The similar languages chosen as distractors for two unrelated LRLs

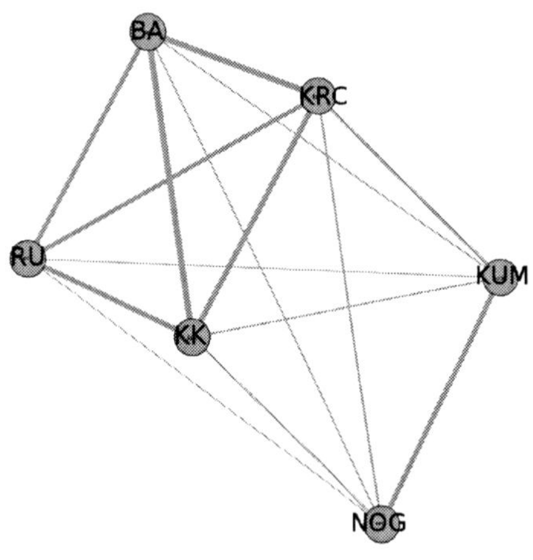

Figure 1: Fully connected graph with token similarities.

Table 1 shows the target languages alongside their distractors. We computed the lexical overlap of the top $10,000$ most frequent tokens in the Nogai subcorpora and produced some visualizations from the concurrent similarity matrix and will briefly discuss them to give a deeper exemplary insight into one of our corpora.

The matrix can be rendered as a fully connected graph,

Figure 2: An unrooted neighbor joining tree from the corpus word list similarity data (left) and the genealogy according to Glottologue (right).

see Figure 1, produced with the R library *igraph*.[7] We see some overlap between Russian, Karachai, Bashkir and Kazakh, while also Nogai and Kumyk share some items. Both Kumyk and Nogai are spoken very close to each other but we did not go furher into this since random patterns may arise in such corpora naturally. An important question is if the data is very noisy. One could imagine that the pattern observed is due to longer sections of Russian in the other languages. However, by means of a language identification heuristic, we had tried to remove longer Russian sections (not single loans) before computing similarity.

Using the Neighbour Joining (Saitou and Nei, 1987) implementation in the R library *phangorn*[8], we generated the unrooted tree in Figure 2 to see if genealogy is instead reflected, which it was not. We display genealogy as in Glottologue[9] building on linguistic sources and considered also (Johanson and Csató, 2015) and (Dryer and Haspelmath, 2013). Indeed, this tree is interesting in respect to its relation to both genealogy and the composition of the respective alphabets.

In order to approach both the shape of this tree and the amount of noise from Russian in the other languages, apart from thorough manual inspection[10], we intersected each language in the corpus with the $20,000$ most frequent words from the Russian National Corpus[11]. We found that the percentages of frequent Russian words was in all cases fairly low. Bashkir and Kazakh, which interestingly also have the alphabets most different from standard Russian,

---

[5]http://olac.ldc.upenn.edu/language/nog
[6]http://olac.ldc.upenn.edu/language/mri

[7]https://cran.r-project.org/web/packages/igraph/index.html

[8]https://cran.r-project.org/web/packages/phangorn/index.html

[9]https://glottolog.org/resource/languoid/id/noga1249, accessed on 30-03-2020.

[10]Partly, we used machine translation (MT), where we pasted whole subcorpus sections of non-Russian text into online MT APIs such as *DeepL* and *Google Translate* for the automatic translation of Russian to English spotting where the English translation was readable. For the other languages, purity was checked linguistically.

[11]http://ruscorpora.ru/new/ via https://en.wiktionary.org/wiki/Appendix:Frequency_dictionary_of_the_modern_Russian_language_(the_Russian_National_Corpus), accessed on 30-03-2020

adding most letters, showed the lowest rates of overlap with
1.7 % for Bashkir and 2.7% for Kazakh. Karachai had
4.2%, Nogai 4.3% and Kumyk showed the largest overlap with 5.9%. The amounts of frequent Russian words for
the group of Nogai, Kumyk and Karachai seem to correlate
with the tree. If Kazakh and Bashkir in comparison to the
other languages are less likely to loan Russian words un-
altered because of their enhanced alphabets this could further explain some of the data. However, the amounts of
most frequent Russian words and the similarity were rather
incongruent, Russian and Kumyk for instance shared least
of their top $10,000$ most frequent words in the corpus, for
Kumyk, Karachai shared second most tokens. In summary,
whilst being quite pure, the across similarity patterns seem
to be influenced by some random factors such as alphabet
composition, areal contact and others more than by genealogy. In the other corpus the similarity data reflected genealogy to a much larger degree.

3.3. Writing System

A distractor is only a formidable distractor if it uses
the same writing system for otherwise the discrimination
can be achieved on first sight without any technical aids.
Transliterations especially into the Latin alphabet exist but
are generally less standardized than the main writing system. Some languages use more than one writing system.
We suggest to split LI into subtasks each concerned with a
single writing system if necessary since comparisons across
writing systems, for instance of ngrams make little sense.
Thus, some distractors can be dismissed immediately.[12]
More often than not, languages use special letters or diacritics or letter combinations in their writing systems (orthographies) distinguishing them even from closely related
languages. The case that a pair of languages has a 100%
congruent grapheme inventory is rare and an exception
rather than the rule. Furthermore, the combination of characters forms a highly significant set. To this end, Wikipedia
features a page[13] with a sample of different languages summarizing their use of special characters. Although the information is partly inconcrete, looking at the subset of roughly
50 languages there, which use the Latin alphabet, only 6 of
them use only the basic 26 letters, furthermore, Danish with
Norwegian and Croatian with Bosnian and Serbian use the
same extension. This entails that we have 34 pairs which
are indistinguishable qua writing system, thereof only 10
are probable to be present in distractor scenarios (for instance Malay-Indonesian but not Zulu-Norwegian or Zulu-
Latin). Taking all possible pairs for 50 languages, we have
2450 possible language pairs and only 10 are possibly un-
derinformative for a classifier, which corresponds to 0.4
percent. There is good reason to believe that the general
statistical lesson holds also for other LRLs.
We thus extracted the information on each of the target languages writing systems in Table 1 from Wikipedia which

hosts very accurate accounts which we verified and intersected those sets for each pair *target language-distractor
language* in our datasets. We use the so obtained sets of
exclusive letters later as simple features for classification.
Finding a description of the writing system a language uses
is much simpler for most LRLs than compiling a corpus
of labeled data in order to train statistical LI. Generating
pairwise lists allows for maximal information since a more
global intersection would result in much fewer features.
Likewise, extracting from the to be classified texts in the
test set all used letters may be misleading since foreign
named entities especially in the contact language may accidentally enhance the document letter sets at hand. Extracting letter sets from training data only may therefore not be
able to distinguish between the linguistic core graphemes
of a writing system and sporadically occuring foreign characters. Frequency alone may be very low for some core
characters such as <x> in many languages which use the
Latin alphabet.

3.4. Toponyms

Since, even if this is an exception, some grapheme inventories of writing systems overlap entirely, we use a second source of information both slightly more complex and
slighlty less straightforward. The basic idea is that more
often than not, a place name is mentioned by texts (in documents) in the main language of that exact place. Especially
smaller towns and villages might not be talked of in other
languages. Thus the presence is a strong positive hint for
LI while the absence does not help to conclude anything.
Here, however, more subtleties have to be taken into account. Factors which can influence how probably the mention of a certain place indicates a certain language are:

- the international renown of a place (government, pil-
  grimage, war, ...)

- mixed populations and languages (in towns languages
  could be more homogeneous)

- patchwork pattern of different language settlements

- place names which occur multiple times in the world

- etc.

The factor of population size of a settlement subtly plays
into many of those factors but by itself may or may not
be a priori decisive as to whether a place name is a good
candidate. These factors will thus be analyzed as to their
occurrence in the data of the target languages and their distractors.
Note that often local toponyms have a different spelling or
name in the local and the dominant language (sometimes
similar, sometimes calques, sometimes entirely different;
for instance Christchruch in Māori is Ōtautahi, an entirely
different lexeme) or generally in other languages (compare
Venice, originally Venezia, Venedig in German, Venise in
French ...). This should, of course, be taken into account
compiling language specific toponym lists.
Bootstrapping lists of toponyms is relatively straightforward and we used two different strategies, the first one being the use of place name lists from Wikipedia for Māori,

---

[12]In fact, some languages as the LRL Yi in China have an exclusive or almost exclusive writing system, where LI simply can
use the Unicode Code Block information.

[13]https://en.wikipedia.org/wiki/Wikipedia:
Language_recognition_chart: last accessed on
18.11.2019

the second the Google Maps Crawler BotSol[14] which allows to extract place names in a variety of languages from manually assigned polygons for Nogai.

3.5. Writing a Classifier

The classifier is a binary classifier. We intend to use it in connection with WIR, which is why the contact languages are especially important.[15] Our prospective task is the build up of an LRL corpus from Web Resources supposing that results of automatic tools such as BootCat (Baroni and Bernardini, 2004) if input were available have to be post-processed from noise through LI. When intending to build a corpus on language X, we are not interested in whether a document which is not in language X is in language Y or Z, hence the set-up as a sequence of binary scenarios is sufficient. For each pair *target-distractor*, we collect lists of

- the exclusive letters (one file per language). If $L1 = \{a, b, c, ...\}$; $L2 = \{a, b, c, ..\}$, exclusive lettersets are for instance the set of all letters l_i where $i = 1..|L1|$, where $l_i \in L1$ and $l_i \notin L2$

- some letter combinations as mentioned as characteristic according to the sources

- a list of toponyms extracted as described above; for the large contact languages we leave this list empty

For each text in our testsets, we classify the text for each binary scenario simply counting the sum of occurrences (points) of each of the exclusive letters ($P_{L1}(l)$), of the exclusive letter combinations ($P_{L1}(c)$) and of the typical toponyms ($P_{L1}(t)$) per language as an independent language indicator LI_{L1} and LI_{L2}, $LI_{LX} = P_{LX}(l) + P_{LX}(c) + P_{LX}(t)$. We output a decision based on the number of points as probability (here for L1):

$$p(D = L1) = \frac{LI_{L1}}{LI_{L1} + LI_{L2}} \qquad (1)$$

. We chain all binary classification scenarios and use a simple majority threshold for the decision of whether to include our document into the corpus or not. We call our classifier LCT-maj (letters, combinations, toponyms - majority vote). So for instance a document D from the testset will be classified as 5 times binarily: Nogai/Kumyk, Nogai/Karachai, Nogai/Russian, Nogai/Kazakh, Nogai/Bashkir so as to end with a vote vector (nog, krc, nog, nog, ba). If there is a nog-majority in the vote vector, we accept the document.

Since our classifier is a binary one, for each pair *target language - distractor*, a number of files (6) have to be produced. If we assume the maximum realistic number of distractors to range between 1 and 11, maximally around 60 files are needed. Whilst this seems a lot, the target language place name file is redundant. In fact, with 11 languages (10

binary pairs) this reduces the number of needed files to actually 51 or $4(n - 1) + n$. Whilst this still seems a lot, many of them can and should be produced automatically. Each language pair needs as input a) two files of exclusive letters, b) two files of exclusive letter combinations[16] and c) two files of toponyms. Exclusive letters are those which occur in a languages core grapheme inventory, but which do not occur in the other of the two languages' core grapheme inventory. Given one file with one letter per line for the core grapheme inventories of all languages in the corpus, it is very straightforward to write a small programm to produce all of those files. For the toponyms, we have outlined the use of BotSol above. Producing the files of letter combinations may require some n-Gram extraction or linguistically curated resources. The classifier works also if files are empty out of necessity or lack of information.

3.6. Corpora, Testsets

Language	Number of Tokens	Number of Sites	Size of Wordlist	Size of Placelist
Nogai	57,477	3	15,321	92
Russian	794,603	1	125,509	0
Kumyk	68,347	2	17,191	20
Bashkir	877,827	1	70,116	19
Karachai	269,651	1	49,251	18
Kazakh	973,927	1	130,574	20
Māori	473,375	1	16,882	1,858
English	1,170,472	1	55,373	0
Indonesian	805,072	1	59,250	94
Hawaiian	352,003	1	17,599	146
Tahitian	22,253	1	2,965	18
Tongan	101,847	1	10,265	423
Samoan	129,317	1	12,628	185

Table 2: The corpora and some characteristics. We used a simple space tokenizer first splitting off the usual punctuation marks. Source was most often the Wikipedia.

Table 2 summarizes the two corpora we provide in the same format as the An Crúbadán project (for copyright reasons) albeit adding our place name lists. This includes also source URL information. Additionally, we make our classifier as executable jar available in a generic version and provide the exclusive letter and letter combination lists we used for classification in the binary scenarios.[17] Our two corpora are corpora manually devised from web sources, where as many Wikipedias were extracted as possible by using the tool WikiExtractor[18]. In case of the large languages, we used only the initial section of the Wikipedia (Russian, Indonesian) whereas in English we used the Brown corpus' (Francis and Kucera, 1979) text content (without tags). For Nogai, no Wikipedia was available, so the corpus is manually devised.

The corpora are diverse in terms of size and text types which could be a certain challenge for the training of statistical approaches. For comparison, we used two supervised state-of-the-art tools. The first is langID, (Lui and Baldwin, 2012) which classifies through n-gram statistics and comes with a pretrained model currently recognizing 97 languages. The second is a language identification tool re-

---

[14] http://www.botsol.com/Products/ GoogleMapsCrawler, 18.11.2019

[15] They are usually larger (e.g. the governing states main language or the language of former colonial administration) and their content will appear in mixed documents and as results to queries designed to retrieve content only in our target languages. There is more content in these languages on the web.

[16] Inspiring the current approach, for distinguishing Irish and Scottish Gaelic this Youtube user describes an approach using under more diacritics and letter combinations https://www. youtube.com/watch?v=adg5Ds_9zCA.

[17] https://github.com/ArminHoenen/URLCoFi

[18] https://github.com/attardi/wikiextractor

leased through the fasttext website[19] featuring a pretrained model with 176 languages, it operates with embedding vectors internally, see also (Joulin et al., 2016). Both technologies allow to train an own model which we did separately for the two above described corpora. In addition to the corpora, we manually composed testsets with a larger number of documents in the target language and one document per distractor.

We classified each of the documents in the test sets with

- LCT-maj

- langID with the large pretrained model and langID with a model trained on our corpora

- fastText with the large pretrained model and fastText with a model trained on our corpora

Additionally, we used only toponyms for classification and intersected all toponyms with all corpora (of one scenario) in order to see how exclusively the places occurred.

4. Results

Classifier	Accuracy	Failures	Comments
LCT-maj Nogai	$\frac{18}{18}$	-	binary, no non nogai doc had more than $\frac{2}{5}$ nog votes, all nogai docs solely nog votes
fastText (pretrained)	$\frac{3}{18}$	15	model aware of Russian (ru), Kazakh (kk), Bashkir (ba) and Karachai (krc); ru, kk & ba correct krc $\rightarrow$ ru, Nogai as Russian or Kirghiz
fastText own model	$\frac{18}{18}$	-	
langID (pretrained)	$\frac{2}{18}$	16	model aware of Russian, Kazakh ru, kk correct, Nogai mostly as Russian
langID own model	$\frac{18}{18}$	-	
LCT-maj Māori	$\frac{33}{34}$	1	binary, the rejected document (Māori) was short, loanwords and urls lead to a 3:3 vote
fastText (pretrained)	$\frac{2}{34}$	32	model aware of English and Indonesian no systematic confusion, often English, also Latvian, Welsh, Portuguese etc.
fastText own model	$\frac{34}{34}$	-	
langID (pretrained)	$\frac{2}{34}$	32	model aware of English and Indonesian rather systematic confusion of Māori with Swedish
langID own model	$\frac{32}{34}$	2	same problematic document as in LCT-maj as well as one other Māori $\rightarrow$ Tahitian

Table 3: Classification of independent test set, which consisted of 18 documents for Nogai, 34 in Māori, one in each distractor. Size chosen for interpretability and availability.

One can see in Table 3 is that the considerably differently composed pretrained models (97 languages for langID, 176 for fastText), which are aware of only a small subset of the required languages in both our scenarios are not useful in our context. But, both individually trained classifiers are extremely accurate and the pronounced differences in sizes of the training corpora do not affect performance of either in our scenarios. The performance of LCT-maj is also on par. Looking into those documents which have been partly classified as another language by either of the classifiers, we found them to contain code-switching or (large) amounts of noise. Thus, rejecting them will lead to a cleaner corpus.

[19]https://fasttext.cc/blog/2017/10/02/blog-post.html

5. Discussion

The results show, that with a very simple input (grapheme inventories, toponyms) which could be bootstrapped relatively easily in our cases, we achieved a statisfactory solution to target language identification for WIR for our LRLs which can compete with state-of-the-art supervised techniques albeit only solving the binary question whether or not a given document is written in a certain LRL and not which other language it is written in. We suspect that this method is applicable to most other smaller languages and especially in WIR for LRL where ressources may be so scarce that acquiring enough training data for any statistical LI approach may be impossible. Furthermore the option might be the only one if part of a Web Corpus Retrieval Pipeline which starts from zero. For larger languages, especially English, the procedure is not applicable as is since there are other languages using the exact same set of letters; also the larger settlement area with placenames appearing multiple times would require different strategies. Thus, the method presented here is primarily one for very small languages with restricted settlement areas and the more idiosyncratic the writing system, the better this is for the method.

Looking into some of the classification results, we note that the vote vectors are often uniform (all votes for Nogai in a Nogai document) for the target language and fully heterogeneous for distractor documents. For some comparisons, the alphabets were very similar and thus uninformative making the system rely more on toponyms. Toponym lists were slightly imbalanced in size (sometimes inevitably so due to the difference in size of the surface area of the settlement areas of the speakers of a language pair). In all, the difference between characters and toponyms as features of a classification helped the system gain robustness.

As to the place names, which were overwhelmingly city and village names, we analyzed them a posteriori and identified those which had most often lead to a misclassification. In all, using only place names was not informative for some documents which simply lacked them (22% of documents for Nogai, 32% for Māori) but classified the others largely correctly for Nogai and Māori. It lead to one false positive in Māori, because the document contained a capitalized noun at a sentence start (where it is indistinguishable from a named entity) which accidentally matched a Māori place. In Nogai, 3 Nogai documents were falsely rejected and 1 Karachai document was identified as Nogai because Nogai places had been talked about. In both cases, the majority of documents was classified correctly. However, here more research is necessary before being able to claim generalizability. To this end, we looked at all mismatched places and ordered them for frequency of mismatch and mismatch (vs. match) ratio (mismatches divided by matches plus mismatches of that place across binary scenarios).

Table 4 shows some example places and reasons for their mismatches. We looked at characteristics of those places such as popularity, population etc. The goal was to define general rules which can be applied a priori to a toponym list in order to exclude items which can deteriorate performance. We found that

Place	Mismatch	Count	Mismatch Types	Reason
Maitai	1	5	MR → th (5)	homograph in Tahitian
Kihikihi	1	2	MR → tg (2)	homograph in Tongan
Puhi	0.99	474	mr(473), HW(3), tg(1)	Māori place name part
Kereta	0.83	10	MR(2), id(10)	homograph in Indonesian
Stawropol	0.67	33	NOG → ba, kum, krc	administrative seed
Kisliar	1	20	NOG → ba, kum, krc	media coverage

Table 4: Examples of mismatched cities (the city was a cue in the list for the capitalized language but appeared in another corpus). Russian transliterated.

- size

- government/administrative seeds

- accidental (more) frequent lexical homograph in distractor language

- famous places, pilgrimages

- places inhabited by more than one of the concurrent language communities

- place names which are not unique

were such deteriorating factors and some can be excluded a priori.

For the Māori scenario with many languages that have a relatively simple syllable structure and phoneme inventory, the problem with accidental homographs was more pronounced than for Nogai. This suggests a better performance of places for languages with more complex syllable structures and phoneme inventories. English names which appeared as place names in Māori were constantly confused. Of course for different scenarios weighting to the terms, letters and letter combinations could be introduced depending on such factors. Summarizing, despite the very heterogenous sizes of place name lists, the overall results were good for both scenarios.

6. Conclusions

Recently neural architectures have become popular. In one of the DSL tasks however they performed rather poorly in comparison to other techniques (Malmasi et al., 2016). This shows that statistically sophisticated architectures often but not always represent the most successful approaches. Our approach here of course could be interpreted or implemented in a statistical way using unigram frequencies and highly feature selected tokens (toponyms). But, the binary set-up identifying divergences between grapheme inventories of writing systems would not be equally captured since unigrams would include special characters which occur out of the rule (for instance in loanwords) in the training or test documents. Furthermore, a feature selection scheme ending up with only toponyms (and filtered ones), would be hard to construct. We thus believe that our approach involving hand-picked features, maybe because the task at hand is -compared to others in NLP- relatively simple (even in the face of similar languages) is reasonable even apart from the advantage of using relatively few input data. Furthermore, we believe that our two chosen scenarios are to be interpreted in a hermeneutical way. In hermeneutics sometimes one single example is enough to dismiss the validity of a certain hypothesis. Looking at writing systems in the world, we find languages which have exclusive systems such as Yi. Other writing systems are used for comparatively few languages such as the Georgian letters. Within writing systems, languages (often upon introduction of script) maintain their own letters (often for phonemes not shared with the writing system donor) or in comparison to all other languages using the same writing system a unique combination of letters (or diacritics). Comparing languages only to the set of their distractors further increases uniqueness. This makes it plausible that what we have shown for our two examples extends to many more smaller languages. We have demonstrated a simple classifier for LI in WIR for LRLs based on writing systems and toponyms. The classifier can compete with state-of-the-art supervised technologies in our case study. It is applicable for scenarios where no labelled data is available (not statistically supervised as it draws only from linguistic descriptions such as graphematic system descriptions and toponyms), but answers only to the binary question whether a document is or is not written in a respective LRL. We provide two corpora including testsets and a customizable binary LI tool for WIR for LRLs. Also, we confirmed the positive capacity of toponyms for LI and identified some rules for a priori exclusion of certain toponyms so as to increase their effect.

7. Acknowledgements

We would like to thank studiumdigitale, the central eLearning authority at Goethe University Frankfurt for their financial support and our reviewers who significantly contributed to improving the content of the paper.

8. Bibliographical References

Barfield, T. (1998). *The Dictionary of Anthropology*. Wiley.

Baroni, M. and Bernardini, S. (2004). Bootcat: Bootstrapping corpora and terms from the web. In *LREC*, page 1313.

Biemann, C., Heyer, G., Quasthoff, U., and Richter, M. (2007). The leipzig corpora collection-monolingual corpora of standard size. *Proceedings of Corpus Linguistic*, 2007.

Chen, S. F. and Maison, B. (2003). Using place name data to train language identification models. In *Eighth European Conference on Speech Communication and Technology*.

Cysouw, M. (2013). Disentangling geography from genealogy. In Peter Auer, et al., editors, *Space in Language and Linguistics: Geographical, Interactional, and Cognitive Perspectives*, pages 21–37, Berlin. De Gruyter Mouton.

Matthew S. Dryer et al., editors. (2013). *WALS Online*. Max Planck Institute for Evolutionary Anthropology, Leipzig.

Viviane Déprez et al., editors. (2018). *Negation and Negative Concord: The view from Creoles*. John Benjamins.

Giguet, E. (1995). Categorization according to language: A step toward combining linguistic knowledge and statistic learning. In *Proceedings of the 4th International Workshop on Parsing Technologies (IWPT-1995), Prague, Czech Republic.*

Hanif, F., Latif, F., and Khiyal, M. S. H. (2007). Unicode aided language identification across multiple scripts and heterogeneous data. *Information Technology Journal*, 6(4):534–540.

Hasimu, M. and Silamu, W. (2017). Three-stage short text language identification algorithm. *Journal of Digital Information Management*, 15(6):354–371.

Henrich, P. (1989). Language identification for the automatic grapheme-to-phoneme conversion of foreign words in a german text-to-speech system. In *First European Conference on Speech Communication and Technology*.

Hoenen, A., Koc, C., and Rahn, M. (2020). A manual for web corpus crawling of low resource languages. *Umanistica Digitale*. forthcoming.

Jauhiainen, T. S., Lui, M., Zampieri, M., Baldwin, T., and Lindén, K. (2019). Automatic language identification in texts: A survey. *Journal of Artificial Intelligence Research*, 65:675–782.

Johanson, L. and Csató, É. (2015). *The Turkic Languages.* Routledge.

Joulin, A., Grave, E., Bojanowski, P., and Mikolov, T. (2016). Bag of tricks for efficient text classification. *CoRR*, abs/1607.01759.

Katz, L. and Frost, R. (1992). The reading process is different for different orthographies: The orthographic depth hypothesis. *Haskins Laboratories Status Report on Speech Research*, SR-111:147–160.

Kilgarriff, A. and Grefenstette, G. (2001). Web as corpus. In *Proceedings of Corpus Linguistics 2001*, pages 342–344. Corpus Linguistics. Readings in a Widening Discipline.

Ljubesic, N., Mikelic, N., and Boras, D. (2007). Language indentification: How to distinguish similar languages? In *2007 29th International Conference on Information Technology Interfaces*, pages 541–546. IEEE.

Lui, M. and Baldwin, T. (2012). langid.py: An off-the-shelf language identification tool. In *Proceedings of the ACL 2012 System Demonstrations*, pages 25–30, Jeju Island, Korea, July. Association for Computational Linguistics.

Malmasi, S., Zampieri, M., Ljubešić, N., Nakov, P., Ali, A., and Tiedemann, J. (2016). Discriminating between similar languages and Arabic dialect identification: A report on the third DSL shared task. In *Proceedings of the Third Workshop on NLP for Similar Languages, Varieties and Dialects (VarDial3)*, pages 1–14, Osaka, Japan, December. The COLING 2016 Organizing Committee.

Martins, B. and Silva, M. J. (2005). Language identification in web pages. In *Proceedings of the 2005 ACM symposium on Applied computing*, pages 764–768. ACM.

Padró, M. and Padró, L. (2004). Comparing methods for language identification. *Procesamiento del lenguaje natural*, 33.

Ranaivo-Malançon. (2006). Automatic identification of close languages – case study: Malay and indonesian.

ECTI Transactions on Computer and Information Technology, 2(2):126–134.

Saitou, N. and Nei, M. (1987). The neighbor-joining method: a new method for reconstructing phylogenetic trees. *Molecular biology and evolution*, 4(4):406–425.

Samih, Y. and Kallmeyer, L. (2017). *Dialectal Arabic processing Using Deep Learning*. Ph.D. thesis, Ph. D. thesis, Düsseldorf, Germany.

Scannell, K. P. (2007). The crúbadán project: Corpus building for under-resourced languages. In *Building and Exploring Web Corpora: Proceedings of the 3rd Web as Corpus Workshop*, volume 4, pages 5–15.

Thomason, S. G. (2001). *Language Contact.* Georgetown University Press.

Tiedemann, J. and Ljubešić, N. (2012). Efficient discrimination between closely related languages. In *Proceedings of COLING 2012*, pages 2619–2634.

Zampieri, M., Tan, L., Ljubešić, N., and Tiedemann, J. (2014). A report on the DSL shared task 2014. In *Proceedings of the First Workshop on Applying NLP Tools to Similar Languages, Varieties and Dialects*, pages 58–67, Dublin, Ireland, August. Association for Computational Linguistics and Dublin City University.

Zampieri, M., Malmasi, S., Nakov, P., Ali, A., Shon, S., Glass, J., Scherrer, Y., Samardžić, T., Ljubešić, N., Tiedemann, J., et al. (2018). Language identification and morphosyntactic tagging. the second vardial evaluation campaign.

9. Language Resource References

Francis, W. N. and Kucera, H. (1979). *Brown Corpus*. Department of Linguistics, Brown University, Providence, Rhode Island, US.

Proceedings of the 1st Joint SLTU and CCURL Workshop (SLTU-CCURL 2020), pages 36–40
Language Resources and Evaluation Conference (LREC 2020), Marseille, 11–16 May 2020
© European Language Resources Association (ELRA), licensed under CC-BY-NC

Morphological Disambiguation of South Sámi with FSTs and Neural Networks

Mika Hämäläinen, Linda Wiechetek

University of Helsinki, UiT The Arctic University of Norway

Finland, Norway

mika.hamalainen@helsinki.fi, linda.wiechetek@uit.no

Abstract

We present a method for conducting morphological disambiguation for South Sámi, which is an endangered language. Our method uses an FST-based morphological analyzer to produce an ambiguous set of morphological readings for each word in a sentence. These readings are disambiguated with a Bi-RNN model trained on the related North Sámi UD Treebank and some synthetically generated South Sámi data. The disambiguation is done on the level of morphological tags ignoring word forms and lemmas; this makes it possible to use North Sámi training data for South Sámi without the need for a bilingual dictionary or aligned word embeddings. Our approach requires only minimal resources for South Sámi, which makes it usable and applicable in the contexts of any other endangered language as well.

Keywords: Sámi languages, disambiguation, endangered languages

1. Introduction

Sámi languages are a part of the Uralic language family, and like many other Uralic languages they are endangered. The languages of this family are synthetic, meaning that they exhibit a great deal of inflectional and derivational morphology making their processing with computational means far from trivial.

In this paper, we present a method for morphological disambiguation of South Sámi (ISO 639-3 code sma) by using a morphological FST (finite-state transducer) analyzer and a Bi-RNN (bi-directional recurrent neural network) trained on North Sámi (ISO 639-3 code sme) data and synthetically generated South Sámi data. The disambiguation process takes in all the morphological readings produced by the FST and uses the neural network to pick the contextually correct disambiguated reading.

North and South are not direct neighbors in the dialect continuum, but share a big part of the lexicon and many grammatical features like an elaborate case system, non-finite clause constructions, a large amount of verbal and nominal derivations. However, they have a number of distinctions in lexicon, morphology and syntax.

One of the important differences is the omission of the copula verb in South Sámi, but not or less so in North Sámi. The typical word order is SOV (subject-object-verb) in South Sámi, and SVO (subject-verb-object) in North Sámi. The case system is slightly different as well. South Sámi distinguishes between inessive (place) and elative (source) case (Bergsland, 1994). In North Sámi, this is synthesized in one morpho-syntactic case, called locative case.

In addition to the aforementioned differences, also the homonymies are not the same. In North Sámi, regular noun homonymies are genitive/accusative and comitative singular/locative plural. In South Sámi, on the other hand, they are illative plural/accusative plural and essive (underspecified as regards number)/inessive plural/comitative singular. Even in the context of morphologically rich languages, a simple POS (part-of-speech) tagging is often not enough as it only reduces some of the ambiguity, and is not enough for lemmatization, for instance. Then again, without lemmati-

zation and the small amount of data available for these languages, modern NLP methods such as word embeddings cannot be as reliably used as in the case of majority languages.

South Sámi, with its estimated number of 500 speakers, is categorized as severely endangered by UNESCO (Moseley, 2010) and is spoken in Norway and Sweden. The language is spoken in Norway and Sweden and its bilingual users frequently face bigger challenges regarding literacy in the lesser used language than in the majority language due to reduced access to language arenas (Outakoski, 2013; Lindgren et al., 2016).

The central tools used for disambiguation of Sámi languages are *finite state transducers* and *Constraint Grammars*. Constraint Grammar is a rule-based formalism for writing disambiguation and syntactic annotation grammars (Karlsson, 1990; Karlsson et al., 1995). Constraint Grammar relies on a bottom-up analysis of running text. Possible but unlikely analyses are discarded step by step with the help of morpho-syntactic context. The *vislcg3* implementation[1] is used in particular.

South Sámi has several Constraint Grammars including a morpho-syntactic disambiguator, a shallow syntactic analyzer, and a dependency analyzer (Antonsen et al., 2010; Antonsen and Trosterud, 2011). Antonsen and Trosterud (2011) use a fairly small Constraint Grammar (115 rules) for South Sámi part of speech (POS) and lemma disambiguation, resulting in a precision of 0.87 and a recall of 0.98 for full morpho-syntactic disambiguation. While these are very good results with a comparatively small workload, they require the work of a linguist with knowledge of the language or a linguist and a language expert in addition. However, we want to show how grammatical tools can be built in the absence of these.

Whereas our paper deals with South Sámi disambiguation, the main purpose of this work is to demonstrate that a disambiguator can be built with relatively few resources based on a morpho-syntactically related language. This is

---

[1] `http://visl.sdu.dk/constraint_grammar.html` (accessed 2018-10-08), also (Didriksen, 2010)

Sentence	***Gos dáppe lea máddi?* 'Where is the South here?'**
FST output	['gos+Adv+Subqst', 'gos+Adv'], ['dáppe+Adv'], ['leat+V+IV+Ind+Prs+Sg3'], ['máddat+V+TV+Imprt+Du2', 'máddat+V+TV+PrsPrc', 'máddi+N+Sg+Nom'], [?+CLB]
Source sequence	Adv Subqst _ Adv _ IV Ind Prs Sg3 V _ Du2 Imprt N Nom PrsPc Sg TV V _ CLB
Target sequence	Adv _ Adv _ Mood=Ind Number=Sing Person=3 Tense=Pres VerbForm=Fin V _ Case=Nom Number=Sing N _ CLB

Table 1: An example of the training data

useful, not only in the wider context of Sámi languages, but also for other endangered languages as it provides the language community quickly with much-needed resources while there are children - the future speakers - learning the language. Our approach follows the previously established ideology for using FSTs together with neural networks to solve the problem of disambiguation (Ens et al., 2019).

2. Related Work

Parallel texts have been used to deal with morphological tagging in the context of low-resourced languages (Buys and Botha, 2016). They use aligned parallel sentences to train their their Wsabie-based model to tag the low-resource language based on the morphological tags of a more resourced language sentences in the training data. A limitation of this approach is that the morphological relatedness of the high-resource and low-resource languages has to be high.

Andrews et al. (Andrews et al., 2017) have proposed a method for POS (part of speech) tagging of low-resource languages. They use a bilingual dictionary between a low-resource and high-resource language. In addition, their system requires monolingual data for building cross-lingual word embeddings. The resulting POS tagger is trained on an LSTM neural network, and their approach performs consistently better than the other approaches on the benchmarks they report.

Lim et al. (Lim et al., 2018) present an approach for syntactic parsing of Komi-Zyrian and North Sámi data using multilingual word embeddings. They use pre-trained word-embeddings of two high-resource languages; Finnish and Russian. Then they train monolingual word-embeddings for the low-resource languages from small corpora. They project these individual word embeddings into a single space by using bilingual dictionaries for alignment. The parser was implemented as an LSTM based model, and its performance is higher for POS tagging than for syntactic parsing. The most important finding for our purposes is that including a related high-resource language improves the accuracy of their method.

DsDs (Plank and Agić, 2018) is a neural network based part-of-speech tagger intended to be used in the context of low-resource languages. Their core idea is to use a bi-LSTM model to project POS tags from one language to another with the help of lexical information and word embeddings. Their experiments in a low-resource setting reveal that including word embeddings can boost the model, but lexical information can also help to a smaller degree.

The scope of a great part of the related work is limited to POS tagging. Nevertheless, the morphologically rich

Uralic languages call for a more full blown morphological disambiguation than a mere POS tagging in order to make higher-level NLP tools usable for these languages. Moreover, our approach cannot count on the existence of high-quality bilingual dictionaries between morphologically similar languages nor aligned word embeddings, as such resources are not easily available for endangered languages.

3. Data and Tools

The training data for South Sámi disambiguation comes from the Universal Dependencies Treebank of the related North Sámi language (Sheyanova and Tyers, 2017). Out of all the Sámi languages, North Sámi has by and large the biggest amount of NLP resources available and therefore its use as a starting point for related languages makes perfect sense. The treebank consists of 26K tokens and comes pre-divided into a training and testing datasets.

In addition to the treebank, we use FSTs for both North Sámi and South Sámi with UralicNLP (Hämäläinen, 2019). These transducers are integrated in the open *GiellaLT* infrastructure (Moshagen et al., 2014) for Uralic languages. The FSTs take in a word in an inflectional form and produce all the possible morphological readings for it.

In order to evaluate our system, we use a small dataset for South Sámi that has been disambiguated automatically by a Constraint Grammar and checked manually. Currently, the dataset is not publicly available. The data consists of 1994 disambiguated sentences and we only use it for the evaluation.

	North Sámi	South Sámi
Average	3.1	1.8

Table 2: Average ambiguity

Table 2 shows the average morphological ambiguity in the North Sámi training set and South Sámi test set when the FSTs are used to produce all morphological readings for every word in the corpus. As we can see, North Sámi exhibits a much higher degree of morphological ambiguity than South Sámi.

For generating more data, we use the South Sámi lemmas from the South Sámi-Norwegian dictionary located in the *GiellaLT* infrastructure (Moshagen et al., 2014). The dictionary has 11,438 POS tagged South Sámi lemmas. We only use this dictionary for South Sámi words and omit all the Norwegian translations in our method.

Template	Target morphology
(N Sg Nom) (N Sg Ill) (V IV Ind Prs Sg3)	(N Case=Nom Number=Sing) (N Case=Ill Number=Sing) (V Mood=Ind Number=Sing Person=3 Tense=Pres VerbForm=Fin)
(N Sg Nom) (Adv) (V TV Ger)	(N Case=Nom Number=Sing) (Adv) (V VerbForm=Ger)
(N Sg Nom) (N Sg Ine)	(N Case=Nom Number=Sing) (N Case=Ine Number=Sing)
mannem (N Sg Acc) (V TV Ind Prs Sg1)	(Pron Case=Acc Number=Sing Person=1 PronType=Prs) (N Case=Acc Number=Sing) (V Mood=Ind Number=Sing Person=1 Tense=Pres VerbForm=Fin)
(N Sg Nom) (N Sg Ela) (V IV Ind Prs Sg3)	(N Case=Nom Number=Sing) (N Case=Ela Number=Sing) (V Mood=Ind Number=Sing Person=3 Tense=Pres VerbForm=Fin)
altemse (V TV Ind Prs Sg1) (N Ess)	(Pron Case=Acc Number=Sing Person=3 PronType=Prs) (V Mood=Ind Number=Sing Person=1 Tense=Pres VerbForm=Fin) (N Case=Ess)

Table 3: Templates for generating South Sámi data

4. Neural Disambiguation

We train a sequence-to-sequence Bi-RNN model using OpenNMT (Klein et al., 2017) with the default settings except for the encoder where we use a BRNN (bi-directional recurrent neural network) instead of the default RNN (recurrent neural network) as BRNN has been shown to provide a performance gain in a variety of tasks. We use the default of two layers for both the encoder and the decoder and the default attention model, which is the general global attention presented by Luong et al. (Luong et al., 2015).

We experiment with two models, one that is trained with the North Sámi Treebank only, and another one that is trained with South Sámi text generated by templates and the North Sámi data. Both models are trained for 60,000 training steps with the same random seed value.

The North Sámi data gives us the target sequence, that is the correct morphological tags and the POS tag. However, the source sequence has to be generated automatically before the training. For this, we use the North Sámi FST analyzer. We produce all the possible morphologies for each word in the Treebank. The training is done from a sorted list of homonymous readings for each word separated by a character indicating word boundary to the disambiguated set of homonymous readings from the UD (universal dependencies) TreeBank on a sentence level. In other words, the only thing the model sees are morphological tags on the source and the target side. Lemmas and words are dropped out so that the model can be used for South Sámi without the need of aligned word embeddings or dictionaries. This is illustrated in Table 1.

For producing synthetic data, we wrote six small templates that reflect some common morpho-syntactic differences between South Sámi and North Sámi. This is, for instance, the absence of elative and inessive case in North Sámi, both of which are merged into the single locative case. For each template, we produce 20 different ambiguous sentences by selecting words fitting to the template at random from the South Sámi dictionary and inflecting them accordingly with the FST. Once the words are inflected, we can analyze them to get the ambiguous reading. The templates can be seen in Table 3.

5. Results and Evaluation

We evaluate the models, the one trained only with the North Sámi Treebank and the one that had additional template generated training data, with the disambiguated gold standard that exists for South Sámi. As the South Sámi gold standard follows the *GiellaLT* FST tags, we converted the tags automatically into UD format, since the neural network is trained to output UD tags.

The evaluation results are shown in Table 4. The first column shows the percentage of sentences that have been fully disambiguated correctly, the second columns shows this on a word level i.e. how many words were fully correctly disambiguated and finally the last column shows the accuracy in POS tagging. The results indicate that adding the small synthetically generated data to the training boosted the results significantly.

	Fully correct sentences	Fully correct words	POS correct
N. Sámi only	12.0%	37.6%	59.7%
N. Sámi & templates	13.0%	42.2%	66.4%

Table 4: Evaluation results of the two different models on South Sámi data

As for the incorrectly disambiguated morphological readings, there is a degree to how incorrect they are. This is shown in Table 5, which shows the errors based on how many morphological tags were predicted wrong. In both cases, more than half of the wrongly disambiguated words only differ by one tag from the gold standard. The results for the model trained on the additional template data show that the errors the model makes are still closer to the correct reading.

Below, we are having a closer look at the actual sentences and their analyses, shedding some light on the shortcomings the neural network and suggesting improvements. In ex. (1), our system erroneously picks the nominal singular nominative instead of the adverb reading for *daelie*. The nominal reading, however, is very rare.

	1 tag	2 tags	3 tags	more tags
North Sámi only	58.4%	11.8%	15.8%	14.0%
North Sámi & templates	60.8%	12.1%	15.1%	12.0%

Table 5: Errors based on the number of erroneous morphological tags on a word level

(1)   Daelie   dle geajnam gaavnem!
        now;thenSG.NOM so street.ACC find.PRS.SG1
        'Then I find the street!'

Negation verbs pose a problem to the neural network. Of the 238 instances only very few negation verbs - despite not being homonymous with any other forms - are analyzed as such. In ex. (2), *im* 'I don't' is analyzed a an indicative past tense verb 1st person singular (the last of which is correct) despite the fact that *im* is not ambiguous.

(2)   Im   sïjhth   gåabph gih, men
        not.NEG.SG1 want.CONNEG anywhere then, but
        tjidtjie jeahta månnoeh.
        mother says us.DU1.NOM
        'I don't want anywhere then, but mother says us two will go.'

There are other difficulties related to negation in the system. In the following example, the neural network predicts more tokens than the sentence contains, i.e. a negative verb (correctly) and a connegative form (erroneously) usually preceded by the negative verb.

(3)   - Aellieh!
        - not.NEG.IMPRT.SG2
        '- Don't!'

6. Discussion and Conclusions

Uralic languages are highly ambiguous in terms of their morphology, and the linguistic resources such as annotated corpora for these languages are quite limited. This poses challenges in the use of modern NLP methods that have been successfully employed on high-resource languages. In order to overcome these limitations, we proposed a representation based on the ambiguous morphological tags of each word in a sentence.

We have presented a viable way of disambiguation for South Sámi based on an FST and training data on North Sámi with minimal templates needed to cover some of the morpho-syntactic differences of the two languages. The preliminary results look promising, especially since there are nine different Sámi languages. Not to mention similar situations for other endangered languages, where data for a similar language is available.

Our method is more of a hybrid pipeline of rule-based FSTs that produce the possible morphological readings and a neural network that does the disambiguation. This makes it possible to replace the FST with some other rule-based solution or a neural network based morphological analyzer, given that recent research has shown promising results for the use of neural networks in morphology of endangered languages (Schwartz et al., 2019; Silfverberg and Tyers, 2019).

Moreover, our pipeline can be further enhanced by rules. In our experiments, we had the neural network disambiguate out of all the possible morphological readings. Instead of doing that, it is possible to disambiguate first with a rule-based tool such as a Constraint Grammar, and use the neural network to disambiguate the remaining ambiguity. That way we do not need to guess what we already know. It is particularly important to make sure that if the morphology is known, the neural network would not be used to guess it again. This would allow for combining the best of the two worlds; the accuracy of the rule-based methods and the scalability of a neural network.

An interesting question for the future is how far one could get in disambiguation with our proposed method if one was only to train the model by using templates. As even a small number of templates was enough to improve the results noticeably, an entirely template based approach does not seem to be entirely out of the question. Especially if the templates were constructed with more generative freedom such as by following a formalism deriving from CFG (context-free grammar). The use of synthetically generated source data is known to improve NMT (neural machine translation) models when the target data is of a high quality (see (Sennrich et al., 2016)). Also, some promising work has been conducted in fully synthetically generated parallel data in NMT (Hämäläinen and Alnajjar, 2019).

This year has been particularly good for Uralic languages with small UD Treebanks recently published for Skolt Sámi, Karelian, Livvi, Komi-Permyak and Moksha. This means that in the future we can try different variations of our method with these languages as well with minimal modifications to the current approach as all of these languages have rule-based FSTs available in the *GiellaLT* infrastructure.

7. Acknowledgments

We would like to thank Lene Antonsen and Anja Regina Fjellheim Labj for their work on the South Sámi Constraint Grammar disambiguator within the *GiellaLT* infrastructure and for making their automatically annotated and manually corrected South Sámi corpus available to us.

8. Bibliographical References

Andrews, N., Dredze, M., Van Durme, B., and Eisner, J. (2017). Bayesian modeling of lexical resources for low-resource settings. In *Proceedings of the 55th Annual Meeting of the Association for Computational Linguistics (Volume 1: Long Papers)*, pages 1029–1039. Association for Computational Linguistics.

Antonsen, L. and Trosterud, T. (2011). Next to nothing – a cheap south saami disambiguator. pages 131–137, 05.

Antonsen, L., Wiechetek, L., and Trosterud, T. (2010). Reusing grammatical resources for new languages. In *Proceedings of the 7th International Conference on Language Resources and Evaluation (LREC 2010)*, pages 2782–2789, Stroudsburg. The Association for Computational Linguistics.

Bergsland. (1994). *Sydsamisk grammatikk*. Davvi Girji.

Buys, J. and Botha, J. A. (2016). Cross-lingual morphological tagging for low-resource languages. In *Proceedings of the 54th Annual Meeting of the Association for Computational Linguistics (Volume 1: Long Papers)*, pages 1954–1964. Association for Computational Linguistics.

Didriksen, T., (2010). *Constraint Grammar Manual: 3rd version of the CG formalism variant*. GrammarSoft ApS, Denmark.

Ens, J., Hämäläinen, M., Rueter, J., and Pasquier, P. (2019). Morphosyntactic disambiguation in an endangered language setting. In *Proceedings of the 22nd Nordic Conference on Computational Linguistics*, pages 345–349.

Hämäläinen, M. and Alnajjar, K. (2019). A template based approach for training nmt for low-resource uralic languages-a pilot with finnish. In *Proceedings of the 2019 2nd International Conference on Algorithms, Computing and Artificial Intelligence*, pages 520–525.

Karlsson, F., Voutilainen, A., Heikkilä, J., and Anttila, A. (1995). *Constraint Grammar: A Language-Independent System for Parsing Unrestricted Text*. Mouton de Gruyter, Berlin.

Karlsson, F. (1990). Constraint Grammar as a Framework for Parsing Running Text. In Hans Karlgren, editor, *Proceedings of the 13th Conference on Computational Linguistics (COLING 1990)*, volume 3, pages 168–173, Helsinki, Finland. Association for Computational Linguistics.

Klein, G., Kim, Y., Deng, Y., Senellart, J., and Rush, A. M. (2017). OpenNMT: Open-Source Toolkit for Neural Machine Translation. In *Proc. ACL*.

Lim, K., Partanen, N., and Poibeau, T. (2018). Multilingual dependency parsing for low-resource languages: Case studies on north saami and komi-zyrian. In *Proceedings of the Eleventh International Conference on Language Resources and Evaluation (LREC 2018)*.

Lindgren, E., Sullivan, K., Outakoski, H., and Westum, A. (2016). Researching literacy development in the globalised North: studying tri-lingual children's english writing in Finnish, Norwegian and Swedish Sápmi. In David R. Cole et al., editors, *Super Dimensions in Globalisation and Education*, Cultural Studies and Transdiciplinarity in Education, pages 55–68. Springer, Singapore.

Luong, M.-T., Pham, H., and Manning, C. D. (2015). Effective approaches to attention-based neural machine translation. *arXiv preprint arXiv:1508.04025*.

Christopher Moseley, editor. (2010). *Atlas of the World's Languages in Danger*. UNESCO Publishing, 3rd edition. Online version: http://www.unesco.org/languagesatlas/.

Outakoski, H. (2013). Davvisámegielat čálamáhtu konteaksta [The context of North Sámi literacy]. *Sámi diealaš áigečála*, 1/2015:29–59.

Plank, B. and Agić, Ž. (2018). Distant supervision from disparate sources for low-resource part-of-speech tagging. In *Proceedings of the 2018 Conference on Empirical Methods in Natural Language Processing*, pages 614–620. Association for Computational Linguistics.

Schwartz, L., Chen, E., Hunt, B., and Schreiner, S. L. (2019). Bootstrapping a neural morphological analyzer for st. lawrence island yupik from a finite-state transducer. In *Proceedings of the 3rd Workshop on the Use of Computational Methods in the Study of Endangered Languages Volume 1 (Papers)*, pages 87–96, Honolulu, February. Association for Computational Linguistics.

Sennrich, R., Haddow, B., and Birch, A. (2016). Improving neural machine translation models with monolingual data. In *Proceedings of the 54th Annual Meeting of the Association for Computational Linguistics (Volume 1: Long Papers)*, pages 86–96, Berlin, Germany, August. Association for Computational Linguistics.

Silfverberg, M. and Tyers, F. (2019). Data-driven morphological analysis for uralic languages. In *Proceedings of the Fifth International Workshop on Computational Linguistics for Uralic Languages*, pages 1–14, Tartu, Estonia, January. Association for Computational Linguistics.

9. Language Resource References

Hämäläinen, M. (2019). UralicNLP: An NLP library for Uralic languages. *Journal of Open Source Software*, 4(37):1345. 10.21105/joss.01345.

Moshagen, S., Rueter, J., Pirinen, T., Trosterud, T., and Tyers, F. M. (2014). Open-Source Infrastructures for Collaborative Work on Under-Resourced Languages. The LREC 2014 Workshop "CCURL 2014 - Collaboration and Computing for Under-Resourced Languages in the Linked Open Data Era".

Sheyanova, M. and Tyers, F. M. (2017). Annotation schemes in north sámi dependency parsing. In *Proceedings of the 3rd International Workshop for Computational Linguistics of Uralic Languages*, pages 66–75.

Proceedings of the 1st Joint SLTU and CCURL Workshop (SLTU-CCURL 2020), pages 41–45
Language Resources and Evaluation Conference (LREC 2020), Marseille, 11–16 May 2020
© European Language Resources Association (ELRA), licensed under CC-BY-NC

Effects of Language Relatedness for Cross-lingual Transfer Learning in Character-Based Language Models

Mittul Singh[*], **Peter Smit**[*‡], **Sami Virpioja**[†], **Mikko Kurimo**[*]

[*]Department of Signal Processing and Acoustics, Aalto University, Espoo, Finland
[†]Department of Digital Humanities, Helsinki University, Helsinki, Finland
[‡]Inscripta, Helsinki, Finland

`firstname.lastname@{aalto,helsinki}.fi`

Abstract

Character-based Neural Network Language Models (NNLM) have the advantage of smaller vocabulary and thus faster training times in comparison to NNLMs based on multi-character units. However, in low-resource scenarios, both the character and multi-character NNLMs suffer from data sparsity. In such scenarios, cross-lingual transfer has improved multi-character NNLM performance by allowing information transfer from a *source* to the *target* language. In the same vein, we propose to use cross-lingual transfer for character NNLMs applied to low-resource Automatic Speech Recognition (ASR). However, applying cross-lingual transfer to character NNLMs is not as straightforward. We observe that relatedness of the source language plays an important role in cross-lingual pretraining of character NNLMs. We evaluate this aspect on ASR tasks for two target languages: Finnish (with English and Estonian as source) and Swedish (with Danish, Norwegian, and English as source). Prior work has observed no difference between using the related or unrelated language for multi-character NNLMs. We, however, show that for character-based NNLMs, only pretraining with a related language improves the ASR performance, and using an unrelated language may deteriorate it. We also observe that the benefits are larger when there is much lesser target data than source data.

Keywords: Cross-lingual transfer, Character language models, Low-resource ASR

1. Introduction

Multilingual training of language models has successfully leveraged datasets from other languages to improve Neural Network Language Modeling (NNLM) performance in low-resource scenarios (Kim et al., 2019; Conneau and Lample, 2019; Conneau et al., 2019; Aharoni et al., 2019). One such method for training NNLM is the multi-task-based approach, where multiple language corpora train the model simultaneously (Aharoni et al., 2019). Another approach is cross-lingual pretraining, where the NNLM is trained on a set of *source* languages followed by fine-tuning on the *target* language (Kim et al., 2019; Conneau and Lample, 2019; Conneau et al., 2019). The second approach, explored in this work, is favorable when re-training with the large source data is time-consuming as an existing trained source model's weights can be transferred to the target model and then fine-tuned on the smaller target data.

Cross-lingually pretrained NNLMs have utilized multi-character units to construct large shared vocabulary to allow the positive transfer of information from source to target. Instead of multi-character units, we explore a single character as a modeling unit for applying cross-lingual pretraining. This choice has the advantage of reducing the vocabulary size by several orders of magnitude and providing a larger intersection of vocabulary terms than multi-character units. In this paper, we apply cross-lingual pretraining to character NNLMs. However, this off-the-shelf application is not trivial. For multi-character based NNLMs, cross-lingual pretraining works by sharing information across various source languages independent of relatedness to the target language in terms of closeness in the language family tree[1]. In contrast, for character-based NNLMs, a source language in the same family subtree as the target (related) affects the downstream performance positively than from an unrelated source language.

We experiment with available Finnish and Swedish Automatic Speech Recognition (ASR) systems in a simulated low-resource ASR scenario by limiting the language modeling resources. We apply pretraining with two source languages (Estonian and English) for Finnish ASR and three source languages (Danish, English, and Norwegian) for Swedish ASR. In our experiments, we observe perplexity and ASR performance improvements when pretraining NNLMs with related languages (i.e. Estonian for Finnish and Danish and Norwegian for Swedish), whereas pretraining NNLMs on English performs adversely.

We also study the impact on cross-lingual transfer due to the target data size and number of source model layers transferred. Relatively, smaller amounts of target language data than the source language data leads to more considerable ASR performance improvements. Moreover, we find that pretrained NNLMs perform best when we transfer only the parameters of the lowest layer of the source model.

2. Related Work

In our work, we follow the cross-lingual pretraining scheme utilizing a shared vocabulary as proposed by Zhuang et al. (Zhuang et al., 2017), where they transfer all the hidden layers except the final layer from the source model to the target model. For NNLMs, such an application does not obtain the best results. In sections 6. and 7., we present results to support this observation.

Concurrently, Lample and Conneau (Conneau and Lample, 2019) have also shown that cross-lingual pretraining can improve the performance of language models on intrinsic measures like perplexity. They train a multi-character

---

[1]`https://en.wikipedia.org/wiki/Language_family`

Language	Vocabulary	Train	Dev
Finnish ASR			
English (En)	232K	116M	107K
Estonian (Et)	1.7M	97M	33K
Finnish (Fi)	1.1M	17M	130K
Swedish ASR			
Danish (Da)	2.7M	365M	222K
English (En)	466K	366M	107K
Norwegian (No)	2.4M	381M	194K
Swedish (Sv)	936K	45M	158K

Thousands (K), Millions (M)

Table 1: The table reports the word vocabulary, training set (Train) and development set (Dev) sizes of the languages used in the experiments.

transformer-based language model with a masked language model training procedure for cross-lingual pretraining. In their model, multi-character units from both the source and target languages are combined to form one large vocabulary. This large shared vocabulary leads to a large output layer, which can be inefficient to train. The layer size can be reduced by shortlists and class-based models (Goodman, 2001; Le et al., 2011), or approximated by applying a hierarchical softmax (Morin and Bengio, 2005). Instead, we choose characters as the basic unit of modeling, which provides a more natural way of reducing the vocabulary size. Simultaneously, this choice supports the cross-lingual information transfer by providing a larger intersection of vocabulary terms than multi-character units.

For cross-lingual pretraining, language relatedness remains an unexplored factor, which becomes the focus of our work. Prior work has applied cross-lingual transfer by using several unrelated languages as a source. Using related language can be crucial in low-resource scenarios as we discover in Section 6. and 7. In our work, we limit cross-lingual transfer from one source language allowing a simpler setup for better analysis, in future, we would like to explore the impact of relatedness when the number of source languages is increased dramatically.

3. Datasets

We create two setups to evaluate cross-lingual pretraining for NNLMs. In the first setup, English (En) and Estonian (Et) are the high-resource sources of language modeling corpora, and Finnish (Fi) is the low-resource target language. In the second setup, Danish (Da), English, and Norwegian (No) are the high-resource source languages, and Swedish (Sv) is the low-resource target language.

Estonian and Finnish are contained in the Finnic language subtree, and Danish, Norwegian, and Swedish belong to the North Germanic language subtree. Thus, these source-target set of languages are considered as related languages. For both Finnish and Swedish, English, being part of the West Germanic language subtree, is considered as a more unrelated language. We also chose English as it has a large intersection for the character set, but is less mutually intelligible in comparison.

The English text is obtained from the training data of 2015 MGB Challenge (Bell et al., 2015) consists of BBC news transcripts. The Estonian corpus consists of web crawl text

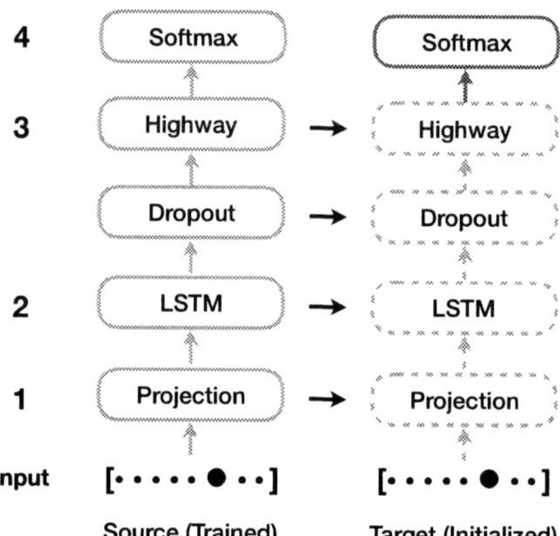

Figure 1: The figure displays the source and target NNLMs with the hidden layers used in our experiments. In cross-lingual pretraining, the source-language-trained hidden layers initialize parts (dotted lines) of the target-language network shown by the arrows. In contrast, the rest is randomly initialized (bold lines in the target network).

and spontaneous conversational transcripts from Meister et al. (2012) and has been used by Enarvi et al. (2017). The Finnish corpus is from Finnish Text Collection containing text from newspaper, books and novels (CSC - IT Center for Science, 1998) and has been used by Smit et al. (2017). The Swedish, Danish, and Norwegian corpora, containing newspaper articles, are downloaded from Språkbanken corpus[2] and have been used by Smit et al. (2018). For Finnish as the target, more data for English was available than for Estonian, so we extract only a portion of English dataset to allow for a similar average of words per line for both datasets. We list the corpora statistics for the various languages used in our experiments in Table 1.

4. Building Language Models

We train character NNLMs for our experiments and mark both the left and right ends of characters except when at the beginning or the end of a word (e.g., model = m+ +o+ +d+ +e+ +l) to achieve best results (Smit et al., 2017). With this marking scheme, we can differentiate the characters from a word into beginning (B), middle (M), end (E) and singleton units. This notation becomes relevant in Section 6., where analyze the differences in perplexity per word position.

We build Recurrent Neural Network Language Models (RNNLM) with a projection layer (200 neurons), an LSTM layer (1000 neurons), a highway layer (1000 neurons) and a softmax output layer (displayed in Figure 1). In our experiments, both the source- and target-language neural networks have the same architecture. We train the RNNLMs using TheanoLM (Enarvi and Kurimo, 2016), applying the adaptive gradient (Adagrad) algorithm to update the model parameters after processing a mini-batch of training examples. The mini-batch size for models was 64, with a sequence length of 100. We used an initial learning rate of 0.1 in all the experiments and a dropout of 0.2 was used to regularize the parameter learning.

---

[2] https://www.nb.no/sprakbanken

Finnish Test Set Perplexity			
Fi$_0$ (baseline)	3788		
l	4	3	2	1
En→Fi	4195	4617	5458	4211
Et→Fi	3402	3585	3901	**3009**
Swedish Test Set Perplexity			
Sv$_0$ (baseline)	311		
l	4	3	2	1
En→Sv	334	322	337	315
No→Sv	**285**	311	312	287
Da→Sv	291	292	317	291

Table 2: The table reports NNLM's test set perplexity for Finnish and Swedish using different cross-lingual initializations. For Finnish, English and Estonian are used as the source languages for pretraining. For Swedish, we use Danish, English and Norwegian as source languages. The best results in each category are marked in boldface.

5. Exploring Cross-Lingual Pretraining

Cross-lingual pretraining involves first training the neural network on a source language. Then, starting from the input layer, the source network's hidden layers initialize the target-language neural network partially or wholly. In a partial initialization, we initialize the uninitialized layers randomly. This initialization step is followed by training on the target language, also referred to as the fine-tuning step. In both the pretraining and the fine-tuning step, the output-layer vocabulary consists of character units from all the source languages and the target language. The pretraining step transfers coarser-level information from input to higher layers into the target model and during fine-tuning, the target model refines this transferred information to a more fine-grained level.

We study neural network models across three dimensions: **1)** the source language used for pretraining step; **2)** using the number of target-model hidden layers (l) initialized starting from the input layer; and **3)** the amount of target language data. We represent the LM pretrained using the source language y and fine-tuned using target language z as $y \rightarrow z$. We vary l from 1 to 4 for the architecture in Figure 1, which also shows an example for $l = 3$. Here $l = 1$ would refer to just initializing with the projection layer and $l = 4$ would refer to initializing with all the layers. We increase the amount of target data size to match the source data size. Varying these parameters allows us to understand their effect on transfer capacity of cross-lingual pretraining.

6. Perplexity Experiments

Table 2 presents the test set perplexity of Finnish and Swedish LMs. When using related source languages — like Estonian for Finnish, or Danish and Norwegian for Swedish — to pretrain the models, we obtain better perplexity than the baseline and when English (the unrelated source language) is used, which leads to a worse perplexity for all ls. Using related source languages, the pretrained target LMs outperform the baseline results for most values of l but, notably, when initialized with configurations $l = 1, 4$ of the source model. Here, we note that Finnish perplexity values are large due to long words and the domain mismatch be-

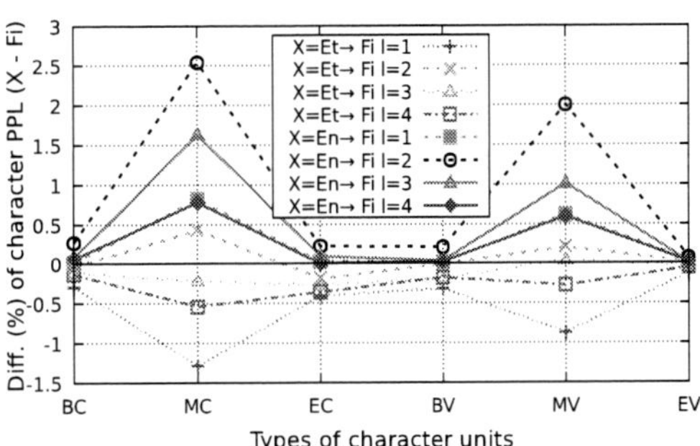

Figure 2: The figure shows the relative differences (%) in character perplexity (PPL) for three different types of character units of different Finnish NNLMs on the test set. These character units exist due to the marking scheme used here: beginning (B), middle (M) and end (E), which can further be classified into consonants (C) and vowels (V).

tween the training (books, newspaper articles and journals) and test (broadcast news) sets.

On characters, similar trends of perplexity improvement for related vs unrelated source language and different values of l are observed. Character perplexity differences for Finnish are presented in Figure 2 for different types of units, i.e., consonant (C) and vowels (V) dependent on their position in words beginning (B), middle (M) and end (E). In Figure 2, most perplexity improvements are obtained for middle consonants (MC) and middle vowels (MV), which are more frequent than other character units. For other character units, small but consistent improvements are obtained by Et→Fi ($l = 1$) LM over other baseline and other LMs.

For Swedish, similar improvements to Finnish results are observed for MC and MV, but some dips are seen for Danish-pretrained LMs on end consonants (EC). For brevity, we do not present this result in the paper. Overall, improvements from related-language pretraining impacts the different types of characters, enabled by a large intersection in the source-target character set.

We suspect that pretraining with a related language finds more useful information than with an unrelated one. To investigate this effect, we calculate the cosine similarity between pretrained and baseline LMs' output layer embeddings. We first find an affine transformation to align pretrained LM's embeddings with the baseline's embedding space, and then calculate the average similarity between the two sets. On Finnish, the English-pretrained embeddings have a higher average similarity (0.53) to the baseline embeddings than the Estonian-pretrained embeddings (0.51). On Swedish, similar results are observed with cosine similarity for the English-, Norwegian- and Danish-pretrained embeddings at 0.43, 0.42 and 0.42. They suggest that the related-language pretrained LMs have more conflicting information than the English-pretrained LMs. As they also perform better in terms of perplexity, the related-language pretraining seems to learn information that is complementary to the baseline LM.

7. Speech Recognition Experiments

For training the Finnish acoustic models, we used 1500 hours of Finnish audio from three different sources, namely,

Language	Baseline Architecture			
Fi_0 (baseline)	**16.44**			
l	4	3	2	1
En→Fi	16.70	16.90*	17.34*	16.56
Et→Fi	16.20	16.14*	16.61	**16.01***
Linear interpolations				
En→Fi + Fi_0	16.00*	16.24*	16.34	15.95*
Et→Fi + Fi_0	15.89*	15.87*	16.04*	**15.74***

Table 3: The table reports WER on Finnish ASR task using different cross-lingual initializations for RNNLMs used in rescoring. Here English and Estonian are used as the source languages for pretraining. Asterisks (*) denote statistical significance while comparing against Fi (16.44) using the matched pairs test with $p < 0.05$. The best results in each section are marked in boldface.

Language	Baseline Architecture			
Sv_0 (baseline)	**4.42**			
l	4	3	2	1
En → Sv	4.43	4.46	4.62	4.41
No → Sv	4.18	4.42	4.38	4.17*
Da → Sv	4.24	4.16*	4.39	**4.15***
Linear Interpolations				
En → Sv + Sv_0	4.15*	4.18*	4.20	4.15*
No → Sv + Sv_0	4.02*	4.40	4.35	4.00*
Da → Sv + Sv_0	4.01*	4.04*	4.15*	**3.98***

Table 4: The table reports WER on Swedish ASR task for different configurations of RNNLMs used in rescoring. Here Danish, English and Norwegian are used as the source languages for cross-lingual pretraining. Asterisks (*) denote statistical significance when comparing to Sv (4.41) using the matched pairs test with $p < 0.05$. The best results in each section are marked in boldface.

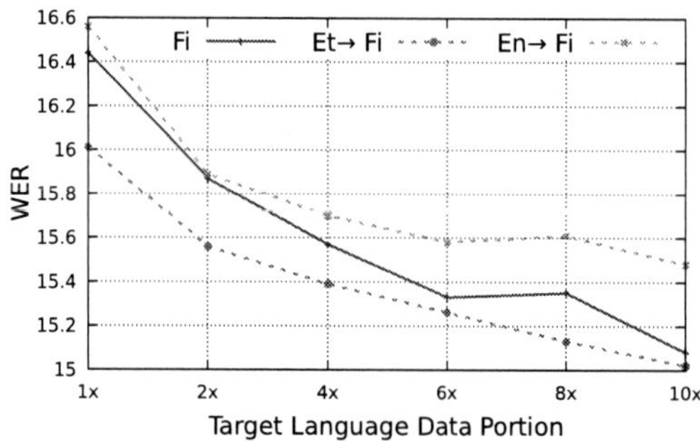

Figure 3: The figures display WERs on Finnish ASR measured when varying the amount of source language data and when varying the amount of target language data.

the Speecon corpus (Iskra et al., 2002), the Speechdat database (Rosti et al., 1998) and the parliament corpus (Mansikkaniemi et al., 2017). For testing, we used a broadcast news dataset from the Finnish national broadcaster (Yle) containing 5 hours of speech and 35k words (Mansikkaniemi et al., 2017). For training Swedish acoustic models, we used 354 hours of audio provided by the Språkbanken corpus. From the original evaluation set, we used a total of 9 hours for development and evaluation.

The acoustic models were trained with the Kaldi toolkit (Povey et al., 2011) with a similar recipe as (Smit et al., 2017). Instead of phonemes, we use grapheme-units, as this allows for a trivial lexicon that maps between the acoustic and language modeling units. We evaluate the ASR performance in terms of Word Error Rates (WER).

For the first-pass, we train a variable-length Kneser-Ney (Kneser and Ney, 1995) n-gram LM using the VariKN toolkit (Siivola et al., 2007). Then, RNNLMs, built in Section 4., are used to rescore the lattices. We also linearly interpolate cross-lingually pretrained NNLMs with target-only NNLM while optimizing the interpolation weight. We test the statistical significance of our results using the Matched Pairs Sentence Segment Word Error Test from NIST Scoring toolkit[3] to compare different systems. Ta-

[3]SCTK: http://www1.icsi.berkeley.edu/ Speech/docs/sctk-1.2/sctk.htm

bles 3 and 4 outline the performance of rescoring with RNNLMs (Section 4.) on a Finnish and a Swedish ASR task. The first row of both these tables displays the performance of target-only trained RNNLMs (baseline). The second part reports the performance of cross-lingually pretrained models (Section 5.) and the third part reports their linear interpolations with target-only baseline models.

Similar to the perplexity results (Section 6.), related source language pretraining improves the ASR performance over the baseline models and the unrelated source language pretraining degrades the performance. On Finnish ASR, English-pretrained RNNLM (En→Fi) lags behind the Estonian-pretrained RNNLM (Et→Fi), which also outperforms Finnish-only models. On Swedish ASR, Danish (Da→Sv) and Norwegian (No→Sv) pretrained models outperform the baseline and English pretrained models (En→Sv). In contrast with perplexity results, lower-layer ($l = 1$) based initialization shows the most benefit over the higher-layer ($l = 2, 3, 4$) initializations for both Finnish and Swedish ASR. We note that quite like perplexity results, ASR performance on Swedish is lower than Finnish as the Swedish task is easier than the Finnish one.

In Figure 3, we observe little performance increase by cross-lingual pretraining when we vary the target data size by increasing it to comparable sizes of source language data. At least for Estonian, increasing Finnish data (target) closes the gap between cross-lingual pretraining and target-only model. The cross-lingual transfer seems to work best with a larger number of resources for the related source language in comparison to the target language.

Furthermore, interpolations of the baseline model with the cross-lingually pretrained models improve over its constituent models. On both Finnish and Swedish ASR, cross-lingual pretraining with English combined with the baseline model can outperform the baseline model, unlike when used individually. This improvement can be attributed to the regularization effect of such an interpolation. Linear interpolations based on other source languages like Estonian, Danish and Norwegian further improve the results consistently across different initialization schemes. We hypothesize that this effect is due to the complementary information learned by these related-language models. Overall, the individual systems and the interpolations based on related source languages show a significant and the most substantial improvement in performance.

8. Concluding Remarks

We investigated cross-lingual transfer for character-based neural network language models in a low-resource scenario. Cross-lingual pretraining with related source language significantly improved (3-6% relative) over no pretraining, whereas pretraining with unrelated source language had adverse effects. At a character level, we suspect cross-lingual pretraining works for related languages as they share a large portion of the character set. The large shared vocabulary provides soft alignments between characters in related languages supporting the transfer of relevant information from source to target models. This information transfer is in contrast to multi-character units where the transfer is dependent on shared anchor tokens (like numbers, proper nouns). However, we still lack an empirical understanding of this phenomenon and in our future work, we hope to explore this phenomenon.

Additionally, transferring the lower layer information and having more source data than target data was significant for low-resource ASR. As a followup to our study, we investigate the effects of language relatedness for cross-lingual pretraining in transformer-based language models.

9. Bibliographical References

Aharoni, R., Johnson, M., and Firat, O. (2019). Massively multilingual neural machine translation. In *Proceedings of the 2019 Conference of the North American Chapter of the Association for Computational Linguistics: Human Language Technologies, Volume 1 (Long and Short Papers)*, pages 3874–3884, Minneapolis, Minnesota, June. Association for Computational Linguistics.

Bell, P., Gales, M. J., Hain, T., Kilgour, J., Lanchantin, P., Liu, X., McParland, A., Renals, S., Saz, O., Wester, M., et al. (2015). The mgb challenge: Evaluating multi-genre broadcast media recognition. In *2015 IEEE Workshop on Automatic Speech Recognition and Understanding (ASRU)*, pages 687–693.

Conneau, A. and Lample, G. (2019). Cross-lingual language model pretraining. In *Advances in Neural Information Processing Systems 32: Annual Conference on Neural Information Processing Systems 2019, NeurIPS 2019, 8-14 December 2019, Vancouver, BC, Canada*, pages 7057–7067.

Conneau, A., Khandelwal, K., Goyal, N., Chaudhary, V., Wenzek, G., Guzmán, F., Grave, E., Ott, M., Zettlemoyer, L., and Stoyanov, V. (2019). Unsupervised cross-lingual representation learning at scale. *CoRR*, abs/1911.02116.

CSC - IT Center for Science. (1998). The Helsinki Korp Version of the Finnish Text Collection.

Enarvi, S. and Kurimo, M. (2016). Theanolm - an extensible toolkit for neural network language modeling. In *INTERSPEECH*, pages 5; 3052–3056.

Enarvi, S., Smit, P., Virpioja, S., and Kurimo, M. (2017). Automatic speech recognition with very large conversational Finnish and Estonian vocabularies. *IEEE/ACM Transactions on Audio, Speech, and Language Processing*, 25(11):2085–2097.

Goodman, J. (2001). Classes for fast maximum entropy training. In *ICASSP*, pages 561–564.

Iskra, D. J., Grosskopf, B., Marasek, K., van den Heuvel, H., Diehl, F., and Kießling, A. (2002). Speecon - speech databases for consumer devices: Database specification and validation. In *LREC*. European Language Resources Association.

Kim, Y., Gao, Y., and Ney, H. (2019). Effective cross-lingual transfer of neural machine translation models without shared vocabularies. In *Proceedings of the 57th Conference of the Association for Computational Linguistics, ACL 2019, Florence, Italy, July 28- August 2, 2019, Volume 1: Long Papers*, pages 1246–1257. Association for Computational Linguistics.

Kneser, R. and Ney, H. (1995). Improved backing-off for m-gram language modeling. In *ICASSP*, volume 1, pages 181–184.

Le, H. S., Oparin, I., Messaoudi, A. K., Allauzen, A., Gauvain, J. L., and Yvon, F. (2011). Large vocabulary SOUL neural network language models. In *INTERSPEECH*, pages 1469–1472.

Mansikkaniemi, A., Smit, P., and Kurimo, M. (2017). Automatic construction of the Finnish parliament speech corpus. In *INTERSPEECH*, pages 3762–3766.

Meister, E., Meister, L., and Metsvahi, R. (2012). New speech corpora at IoC. In *XXVII Fonetiikan päivä — Phonetics Symposium*, pages 30–33.

Morin, F. and Bengio, Y. (2005). Hierarchical probabilistic neural network language model. In *AISTATS*.

Povey, D., Ghoshal, A., Boulianne, G., Burget, L., Glembek, O., Goel, N., Hannemann, M., Motlicek, P., Qian, Y., Schwarz, P., Silovsky, J., Stemmer, G., and Vesely, K. (2011). The kaldi speech recognition toolkit. In *ASRU*. IEEE Signal Processing Society, December.

Rosti, A., Rämö, A., Saarelainen, T., and Yli-Hietanen, J. (1998). Speechdat Finnish database for the fixed telephone network. Technical report, Tampere University of Technology.

Siivola, V., Hirsimaki, T., and Virpioja, S. (2007). On growing and pruning Kneser-Ney smoothed n-gram models. *IEEE Transactions on Audio, Speech, and Language Processing*, 15(5):1617–1624.

Smit, P., Gangireddy, S. R., Enarvi, S., Virpioja, S., and Kurimo, M. (2017). Character-based units for unlimited vocabulary continuous speech recognition. In *ASRU*, pages 149–156.

Smit, P., Virpioja, S., and Kurimo, M. (2018). Advances in subword-based hmm-dnn speech recognition across languages. Technical report, Aalto University.

Zhuang, X., Ghoshal, A., Rosti, A., Paulik, M., and Liu, D. (2017). Improving DNN bluetooth narrowband acoustic models by cross-bandwidth and cross-lingual initialization. In *INTERSPEECH*, pages 2148–2152.

Proceedings of the 1st Joint SLTU and CCURL Workshop (SLTU-CCURL 2020), pages 46–52
Language Resources and Evaluation Conference (LREC 2020), Marseille, 11–16 May 2020
© European Language Resources Association (ELRA), licensed under CC-BY-NC

Multilingual Graphemic Hybrid ASR with Massive Data Augmentation

Chunxi Liu, Qiaochu Zhang, Xiaohui Zhang, Kritika Singh, Yatharth Saraf, Geoffrey Zweig

Facebook AI

New York, NY, and Menlo Park, CA, USA

{chunxiliu,frankz,xiaohuizhang,skritika,ysaraf,gzweig}@fb.com

Abstract

Towards developing high-performing ASR for low-resource languages, approaches to address the lack of resources are to make use of data from multiple languages, and to augment the training data by creating acoustic variations. In this work we present a single grapheme-based ASR model learned on 7 geographically proximal languages, using standard hybrid BLSTM-HMM acoustic models with lattice-free MMI objective. We build the single ASR grapheme set via taking the union over each language-specific grapheme set, and we find such multilingual graphemic hybrid ASR model can perform language-independent recognition on all 7 languages, and substantially outperform each monolingual ASR model. Secondly, we evaluate the efficacy of multiple data augmentation alternatives within language, as well as their complementarity with multilingual modeling. Overall, we show that the proposed multilingual graphemic hybrid ASR with various data augmentation can not only recognize any within training set languages, but also provide large ASR performance improvements.

Keywords: Multilingual graphemic acoustic models, hybrid speech recognition, data augmentation

1. Introduction

It can be challenging to build high-accuracy automatic speech recognition (ASR) systems in the real world due to the vast language diversity and the requirement of extensive manual annotations on which the ASR algorithms are typically built. Series of research efforts have thus far been focused on guiding the ASR of a target language by using the supervised data from multiple languages.

Consider the standard hidden Markov models (HMM) based hybrid ASR system with a phonemic lexicon, where the vocabulary is specified by a pronunciation lexicon. One popular strategy is to make all languages share the same phonemic representations through a universal phonetic alphabet such as International Phonetic Alphabet (IPA) phone set (Lin et al., 2009; Liu et al., 2016; Pulugundla et al., 2018; Tong et al., 2019), or X-SAMPA phone set (Wells, 1995; Knill et al., 2013; Knill et al., 2014; Wiesner et al., 2018). In this case, multilingual joint training can be directly applied. Given the effective neural network based acoustic modeling, another line of research is to share the hidden layers across multiple languages while the softmax layers are language dependent (Huang et al., 2013; Heigold et al., 2013); such multitask learning procedure can improve ASR accuracies for both within training set languages, and also unseen languages after language-specific adaptation, i.e., cross-lingual transfer learning. Different nodes in hidden layers have been shown in response to distinct phonetic features (Nagamine et al., 2015), and hidden layers can be potentially transferable across languages. Note that the above works all assume the test language identity to be known at decoding time, and the language specific lexicon and language model applied.

In the absence of a phonetic lexicon, building graphemic systems has shown comparable performance to phonetic lexicon-based approaches in extensive monolingual evaluations (Kanthak and Ney, 2002; Gales et al., 2015; Trmal et al., 2017). Recent advances in end-to-end or sequence-to-sequence ASR models have attempted to take the union of multiple language-specific grapheme (i.e. orthographic character) sets, and use such union as a universal grapheme set for a single sequence-to-sequence ASR model (Watanabe et al., 2017; Toshniwal et al., 2018; Kim and Seltzer, 2018; Kannan et al., 2019). It allows for learning a grapheme-based model jointly on data from multiple languages, and performing ASR on within training set languages. In various cases it can produce performance gains over monolingual modeling that uses in-language data only.

Since HMM-based hybrid model remains a competitive ASR approach especially in low/medium-resource settings (Lüscher et al., 2019; Wang et al., 2020), in our work, we aim to examine the same approach above of building a multilingual graphemic lexicon, while using a hybrid ASR system – based on Bidirectional Long Short-Term Memory (BLSTM) and HMM – learned with lattice-free maximum mutual information (MMI) objective (Povey et al., 2016). Our initial attempt is on building a single cascade of an acoustic model, a phonetic decision tree, a graphemic lexicon and a language model – for 7 geographically proximal languages that have little overlap in their character sets. We evaluate it in a low resource context where each language has around 160 hours training data. We find that, despite the lack of explicit language identification (ID) guidance, our multilingual graphemic hybrid ASR model can accurately produce ASR transcripts in the correct test language scripts, and provide higher ASR accuracies than each language-specific ASR model. We further examine if using a subset of closely related languages – along language family or orthography – can achieve the same performance improvements as using all 7 languages.

Though extensive end-to-end or sequence-to-sequence ASR works have been built on multilingual graphemic models, to the best of our knowledge, there is no prior work in hybrid ASR that uses a single multilingual graphemic lexicon (rather than an IPA or X-SAMPA based phonetic lexicon) for multiple training languages. In this work, we show for the first time that multilingual graphemic hybrid ASR can provide large improvements across all training languages, even though almost each training language has distinct graphemic set.

We proceed with our investigation on various data augmentation techniques to overcome the lack of training data in the above low-resource setting. Given the highly scalable neural network acoustic modeling, extensive alternatives to increasing the amount or diversity of existing training data have been explored in prior works, e.g., applying vocal tract length perturbation and speed perturbation (Ko et al., 2015), volume perturbation and normalization (Peddinti et al., 2015), additive noises (Amodei et al., 2016), reverberation (Peddinti et al., 2015; Ko et al., 2017; Kim et al., 2017), and SpecAugment (Park et al., 2019). In this work we focus particularly on techniques that mostly apply to our wildly collected video datasets. In comparing their individual and complementary effects, we aim to answer: (i) if there is benefit in scaling the model training to significantly larger quantities, e.g., up to 9 times greater than the original training set size, and (ii) if any, is the data augmentation efficacy comparable or complementary with the above multilingual modeling.

Improving accessibility to videos "in the wild" such as automatic captioning on YouTube has been studied in (Liao et al., 2013; Soltau et al., 2017). While allowing for applications like video captions, indexing and retrieval, transcribing the heterogeneous social media videos of extensively diverse languages is highly challenging for ASR systems. On the whole, we present empirical studies in building a single multilingual graphemic hybrid ASR model capable of language-independent decoding on multiple languages, and in effective data augmentation techniques for video datasets.

2. Multilingual Graphemic Hybrid ASR

In this section we first briefly describe our deployed hybrid ASR architecture based on the weighted finite-state transducers (WFSTs) outlined in (Mohri et al., 2008). Then we present its extension to multilingual training. Lastly, we discuss its language-independent decoding and language-specific decoding.

2.1. Graphemic ASR with WFST

In the ASR framework of a hybrid BLSTM-HMM, the decoding graph can be interpreted as a composed WFST of cascade $H \circ C \circ L \circ G$. Acoustic models, i.e. BLSTMs, produce acoustic scores over context-dependent HMM (i.e. triphone) states. A WFST H, which represents the HMM set, maps the triphone states to context-dependent phones. While in graphemic ASR, the notion of phone is turned to grapheme, and we typically create the grapheme set via modeling each orthographic character as a separate grapheme. Then a WFST C maps each context-dependent grapheme, i.e. tri-grapheme, to an orthographic character. The lexicon L is specified where each word is mapped to a sequence of characters forming that word. G encodes either the transcript during training, or a language model during decoding.

2.2. A Single Multilingual ASR Model Using Lattice-Free MMI

To build a single grapheme-based acoustic model for multiple languages, a multilingual graphemic set is obtained by taking a union of each grapheme set from each language considered, each of which can be either overlapping or non-overlapping. In the multilingual graphemic lexicon, each word in any language is mapped to a sequence of characters in that language.

A context-dependent acoustic model is constructed using the decision tree clustering of tri-grapheme states, in the same fashion as the context dependent triphone state tying (Young et al., 1994). The graphemic-context decision tree is constructed over all the multilingual acoustic data including each language of interest. The optimal number of leaves for the multilingual model tends to be larger than for a monolingual neural network.

The acoustic model is a BLSTM network, using sequence discriminative training with lattice-free MMI objective (Povey et al., 2016). The BLSTM model is bootstrapped from a standard Gaussian mixture model (GMM)-HMM system. A multilingual n-gram language model is learned over the combined transcripts including each language considered.

2.3. Language-Independent and Language-Specific Decoding in the WFST Framework

Given the multilingual lexicon and language model, the multilingual ASR above can decode any within training set language, even though not explicitly given any information about language identity. We refer to it as language-independent decoding or multilingual decoding. Note that such ASR can thus far produce any word in the multilingual lexicon, and the hypothesized word can either be in the vocabulary of the considered test language, or out of test language vocabulary as a mismatched-language error.

We further consider applying language-specific decoding, assuming the test language identity to be known at decoding time. Again consider the decoding graph $H \circ C \circ L \circ G$, and H & C are thus multilingual while the lexicon L and language model G can include only the words in test language vocabulary. The multilingual acoustic model can therefore make use of multilingual training data, while its language-specific decoding operation only produces monolingual words matched with test language identity.

3. Data Augmentation

In this section, we consider 3 categories of data augmentation techniques that are effectively applicable to video datasets.

3.1. Speed and Volume Perturbation

Both speed and volume perturbation emulate mean shifts in spectrum (Ko et al., 2015; Peddinti et al., 2015). To perform speed perturbation of the training data, we produce three versions of each audio with speed factors 0.9, 1.0, and 1.1. The training data size is thus tripled. For volume perturbation, each audio is scaled with a random variable drawn from a uniform distribution $[0.125, 2]$.

3.2. Additive Noise

To further increase training data size and diversity, we can create new audios via superimposing each original audio with additional noisy audios in time domain. To obtain diverse noisy audios, we use AudioSet, which consists of 632 audio event classes and a collection of over 2 million manually-annotated 10-second sound clips from YouTube videos (Gemmeke et al., 2017).

Note that in our video datasets, video lengths vary between 10 seconds and 5 minutes, with an average duration of about 2 minutes. Rather than constantly repeating the 10-second sound clip to match the original minute-long audio, we superimpose each sound clip on the short utterances via audio segmentation. Specifically, we first use an initial bootstrap model to align each original long audio, and segment each audio into around 10-second utterances via word boundaries. Then for each utterance in the original train set, we can create a new noisy utterance by the steps:

1. Sample a sound clip from AudioSet.

2. Trim or repeat the sound clip as necessary to match the duration of the original utterance.

3. Sample a signal-to-noise ratio (SNR) from a Gaussian distribution with mean 10, and round the SNR up to 0 or down to 20 if the sample is beyond 0-20dB. Then scale the sound clip signal to obtain the target SNR.

4. Superimpose the original utterance signal with the scaled sound clip signal in time domain to create the resulting utterance.

Thus for each original utterance, we can create a variable number of new noisy utterances via sampling sound clips. We use a 3-fold augmentation that combines the original train set with two noisy copies.

3.3. SpecAugment

We consider applying the frequency and time masking techniques – which are shown to greatly improve the performance of end-to-end ASR models (Park et al., 2019) – to our hybrid systems. Similarly, they can be applied online during each epoch of LF-MMI training, while time warping requires the need for realignment and thus does not fit hybrid model training.

Consider each utterance (i.e. after the audio segmentation in Section 3.2.), and we compute its log mel spectrogram with ν dimension and τ time steps:

1. Frequency masking is applied m_F times, and each time the frequency bands $[f_0, f_0 + f)$ are masked, where f is sampled from $[0, F]$ and f_0 is sampled from $[0, \nu - f)$.

2. Time masking is optionally applied m_T times, and each time the time steps $[t_0, t_0 + t)$ are masked, where t is sampled from $[0, T]$ and t_0 is sampled from $[0, \tau - t)$.

As in (Park et al., 2019), we increase the training schedule accordingly, i.e., number of epochs.

4. Experiments

4.1. Data

Our multilingual ASR attempt was on 7 geographically proximal languages: Kannada, Malayalam, Sinhala, Tamil, Bengali, Hindi and Marathi. The datasets were a set of public social media videos, which were wildly collected and anonymized. We categorized them into four sets: `clean`, `noisy`, `extremeI` (`xtrmI`) and `extremeII`

Language	Train	Test			
		clean	noisy	xtrmI	xtrmII
Kannada	125.5	1.5	9.9	0.8	2.7
Malayalam	127.7	4.5	9.2	0.7	1.0
Sinhala	160.0	13.9	25.0	8.6	8.8
Tamil	176.9	2.8	16.4	0.5	0.7
Bengali	160.0	7.4	24.9	25.0	16.4
Hindi	160.0	22.2	21.5	19.4	19.8
Marathi	148.6	2.7	13.7	0.3	0.5

Table 1: The amounts of audio data in hours.

(`xtrmII`). `xtrmI` differed from `xtrmII` in chronological order, and were both more acoustically challenging than `clean` and `noisy` categories.

For each language, the train and test set size are described in Table 1, and most training data were of `noisy` category. On each language we also had a small validation set for model parameter tuning. Each monolingual ASR baseline was trained on language-specific data only.

To create the grapheme set, we consult the unicode character ranges of each language, and also include apostrophe, hyphen and zero width joiner in the final character sets. The character sets of these 7 languages have little overlap except that (i) they all include common basic Latin alphabet, and (ii) both Hindi and Marathi use Devanagari script. We took the union of 7 character sets therein as the multilingual grapheme set (Section 2.2.), which contained 432 characters. In addition, we deliberately split 7 languages into two groups, such that the languages within each group were more closely related in terms of language family, orthography or phonology. We thus built 3 multilingual ASR models trained on:

(i) all 7 languages, for 1059 training hours in total,

(ii) 4 languages – Kannada, Malayalam, Sinhala and Tamil – for 590 training hours,

(iii) 3 languages – Bengali, Hindi and Marathi – for 469 training hours,

which are referred to as *7lang*, *4lang*, and *3lang* respectively. Note that Kannada, Malayalam and Tamil are Dravidian languages, which have rich agglutinative inflectional morphology (Pulugundla et al., 2018) and resulted in around 10% OOV token rates on test sets (Hindi had the lowest OOV rate as 2-3%). Such experimental setup was designed to answer the questions:

(i) If a single graphemic ASR model could scale its language-independent recognition up to all 7 languages.

(ii) If including all 7 languages could yield better ASR performance than using a small subset of closely related languages.

4.2. Model Configurations

Each bootstrap model was a GMM-HMM based system with speaker adaptive training, implemented with Kaldi

Language	Model	clean	noisy	xtrmI	xtrmII	Average	% Gain
Kannada	monolingual	56.9	56.6	58.7	57.6	57.5	–
	monolingual + fm	53.3	54.8	56.9	56.4	55.4	3.7
	monolingual + sp	53.1	54.7	56.4	55.2	54.9	4.5
	monolingual + fm + sp	50.3	53.1	**54.8**	53.9	53.0	7.8
	monolingual + sp + noise	50.7	53.3	54.8	53.6	53.1	7.7
	monolingual + fm + sp + noise	**49.7**	**52.5**	54.9	**52.7**	**52.5**	**8.7**
	multilingual, *4lang*	50.2	**53.4**	55.7	**53.4**	**53.2**	**7.5**
	multilingual, *7lang*	**49.7**	53.5	**54.9**	55.6	53.4	7.1
	multilingual, *7lang* + *lang-specific decoding*	*49.4*	*52.5*	*54.6*	*53.7*	*52.5*	*8.7*
	multilingual, *7lang* + fm + sp + noise	**46.6**	**52.0**	**53.0**	**53.3**	**51.2**	**11.0**
Malayalam	monolingual	56.5	53.2	70.3	55.9	59.0	–
	multilingual, *4lang*	52.8	**51.6**	**65.8**	**53.4**	**55.9**	**5.3**
	multilingual, *7lang*	**52.1**	51.9	66.3	54.0	56.1	5.0
Sinhala	monolingual	45.4	39.5	62.7	51.8	49.9	–
	multilingual, *4lang*	**42.1**	38.4	59.7	50.3	47.6	4.6
	multilingual, *7lang*	42.9	**38.3**	**59.3**	**49.9**	**47.6**	**4.6**
Tamil	monolingual	44.2	44.4	49.0	52.7	47.6	–
	multilingual, *4lang*	40.7	42.8	46.6	**50.9**	45.2	5.0
	multilingual, *7lang*	**40.1**	**42.7**	**46.1**	51.7	**45.2**	**5.0**
Bengali	monolingual	53.4	50.8	68.2	58.0	57.6	–
	multilingual, *3lang*	**45.5**	**47.0**	**62.6**	**53.3**	**52.1**	**9.5**
	multilingual, *7lang*	45.7	48.1	63.9	54.7	53.1	7.8
Hindi	monolingual	36.9	38.2	58.4	45.0	44.6	–
	monolingual + fm	33.2	34.8	54.1	40.9	40.8	8.5
	monolingual + sp	33.6	34.9	55.0	41.1	41.2	7.6
	monolingual + fm + sp	32.1	33.4	52.7	39.5	39.4	11.7
	monolingual + sp + noise	32.0	33.5	52.6	39.5	39.4	11.7
	monolingual + fm + sp + noise	**30.9**	**32.2**	50.7	**38.2**	**38.0**	**14.8**
	multilingual, *3lang*	32.2	33.9	**53.5**	40.3	40.0	10.3
	multilingual, *7lang*	**31.9**	**33.8**	53.6	40.8	**40.0**	**10.3**
	multilingual, *7lang* + *lang-specific decoding*	*31.8*	*33.4*	*52.7*	*40.1*	*39.5*	*11.4*
	multilingual, *7lang* + fm + sp + noise	**28.5**	**30.8**	**49.6**	**36.7**	**36.4**	**18.4**
Marathi	monolingual	38.2	39.8	63.2	49.0	47.6	–
	multilingual, *3lang*	**34.9**	**37.4**	**56.4**	46.3	**43.7**	**8.2**
	multilingual, *7lang*	35.2	38.1	56.5	**46.1**	44.0	7.6

Table 2: WER results on each video dataset. Frequency masking is denoted by fm, speed perturbation by sp, and additive noise (Section 3.2.) by noise. 3lang, 4lang and 7lang denote the multilingual ASR models trained on 3, 4 and 7 languages, respectively, as in Section 4.1.. Lang-specific decoding denotes using multilingual acoustic model with language-specific lexicon and language model, as in Section 2.3.. Average is unweighted average WER across 4 video types. Gain (%) is the relative reduction in the Average WER over each monolingual baseline.

(Povey et al., 2011). Each neural network acoustic model was a latency-controlled BLSTM (Zhang et al., 2016), learned with lattice-free MMI objective and Adam optimizer (Kingma and Ba, 2015). All neural networks were implemented with Caffe2 (Hazelwood et al., 2018). Due to the production real time factor (RTF) requirements, we used the same model size in all cases – a 4 layer latency-controlled BLSTM network with 600 cells in each layer and direction – except that, the softmax dimensions, i.e. the optimal decision tree leaves, were determined through experiments on validation sets, varying within 7-30k. Input acoustic features were 80-dimensional log-mel filterbank coefficients. After lattice-free MMI training, the model with the best accuracy on validation set was used for evaluation on test set. We used standard 5-gram language models in all cases. Each multilingual 5-gram language model is learned simply via combining transcripts of each language.

4.3. Results with Multilingual ASR

ASR word error rate (WER%) results are shown in Table 2. We found that, although not explicitly given any information on test language identities, multilingual ASR with language-independent decoding (Section 2.3.) - trained on 3, 4, or 7 languages - substantially outperformed each monolingual ASR in all cases, and on average led to relative WER reductions between 4.6% (Sinhala) and 10.3% (Hindi).

Note that, in contrast to the multilingual phonetic hybrid ASR (i.e. using phonetic lexicons), it is intuitive to see ASR performance improve when different languages share the same phone set via IPA or X-SAMPA , since each phonetic modeling can use more training data than monolingual training. However, in our multilingual graphemic ASR, only 2 of 7 training languages overlapped in character sets; for the first time, we show that, such multilingual graphemic-context decision tree based hybrid ASR can still improve performance for all languages.

Also, the word hypotheses from language-independent decoding could be language mismatched, e.g., part of a Kannada utterance was decoded into Marathi words. So we counted how many word tokens in the decoding transcripts were not in the lexicon of corresponding test language. We found in general only 1-3% word tokens are language mismatched, indicating that the multilingual model was very effective in identifying the language implicitly and jointly recognizing the speech.

Consider the scenario that, test language identities are known likewise in each monolingual ASR, and we proceed with language-specific decoding (Section 2.3.) on Kannada and Hindi, via language-specific lexicon and language model at decoding time. We found that, the language-specific decoding provided only moderate gains, presumably as discussed above, the language-independent decoding had given the mismatched-language word token rates as sufficiently low as 1-3%.

Additionally, the multilingual ASR of *4lang* and *3lang* (Section 4.1.) achieved the same, or even slightly better performance as compared to the ASR of *7lang*, suggesting that incorporating closely related languages into multilingual training is most useful for improving ASR performance. However, the *7lang* ASR by itself still yields the advantage in language-independent recognition of more languages.

4.4. Results with Data Augmentation

First, we experimented with monolingual ASR on Kannada and Hindi, and performed comprehensive evaluations of the data augmentation techniques described in Section 3.. As in Table 2, the performance gains of using frequency masking were substantial and comparable to those of using speed perturbation, where $m_F = 2$ and $F = 15$ (Section 3.3.) worked best. In addition, combining both frequency masking and speed perturbation could provide further improvements. However, applying additional volume perturbation (Section 3.1.) or time masking (Section 3.3.) was not helpful in our monolingual experiments, and we omit showing the results in the table.

Note that after speed perturbation, the training data tripled, to which we could apply another 3-fold augmentation based on additive noise (Section 3.2.), and the final train set was thus 9 times the size of original train set. We found that all 3 techniques were complementary, and in combination led to large fusion gains over each monolingual baseline – relative WER reductions of 8.7% on Kannada, and 14.8% on Hindi. Secondly, we applied the 3 data augmentation techniques to the multilingual ASR of *7lang*, and tested their additive effects. We show the resulting WERs on Kannada and Hindi in Table 2. Note that on Kannada, we found around 7% OOV token rate on `clean` but around 10-11% on other 3 test sets, and we observed more gains on `clean` ; presumably because the improved acoustic model could only correct the in-vocabulary word errors, lower OOV rates therefore

left more room for improvements. Hindi had around 2.5% OOV rates on each test set, and we found incorporating data augmentation into multilingual ASR led to on average 9.0% relative WER reductions.

Overall, we demonstrated the multilingual hybrid ASR with massive data augmentation – via a single graphemic model even without the use of explicit language ID – allowed for relative WER reductions of 11.0% on Kannada and 18.4% on Hindi.

5. Conclusion

Multilingual training have been extensively studied in conventional phonetic hybrid ASR (Lin et al., 2009; Knill et al., 2013) and the recent end-to-end ASR (Watanabe et al., 2017; Toshniwal et al., 2018). In our work, for the first time, we demonstrate that a multilingual grapheme-based hybrid ASR model can effectively perform language-independent recognition on any within training set languages, and substantially outperform each monolingual ASR alternative. Various data augmentation techniques can yield further complementary improvements. Such single multilingual model can not only provide better ASR performance, but also serves as an alternative to a typical production deployment, which typically includes extensive monolingual ASR systems and a separate language ID model. The proposed approach of building a single multilingual graphemic hybrid ASR model without requiring individual language ID - while being especially competitive in low-resource settings - can greatly simplify the productionizing and maintenance process.

Additionally, as compared to the multilingual multitask learning plus monolingual fine-tuning methods in (Huang et al., 2013; Heigold et al., 2013), our preliminary experimentation shows that our proposed approach above can give comparable performance without requiring separate language ID guidance during decoding. We leave the detailed studies to the future work. Also, future work will expand the language coverage to include both geographically proximal and distant languages.

6. Acknowledgements

The authors would like to thank Duc Le, Ching-Feng Yeh and Siddharth Shah, all with Facebook, for their invaluable infrastructure assistance and technical discussions. We also thank Yifei Ding and Daniel McKinnon, also at Facebook, for coordinating the ASR language expansion efforts.

7. Bibliographical References

Amodei, D., Ananthanarayanan, S., Anubhai, R., Bai, J., Battenberg, E., Case, C., Casper, J., Catanzaro, B., Cheng, Q., Chen, G., et al. (2016). Deep speech 2: End-to-end speech recognition in English and Mandarin. In *International conference on machine learning*, pages 173–182.

Gales, M. J., Knill, K. M., and Ragni, A. (2015). Unicode-based graphemic systems for limited resource languages. In *Proc. ICASSP*.

Gemmeke, J. F., Ellis, D. P., Freedman, D., Jansen, A., Lawrence, W., Moore, R. C., Plakal, M., and Ritter, M. (2017). Audio set: An ontology and human-labeled dataset for audio events. In *Proc. ICASSP*.

Hazelwood, K., Bird, S., Brooks, D., Chintala, S., Diril, U., Dzhulgakov, D., Fawzy, M., Jia, B., Jia, Y., Kalro, A., et al. (2018). Applied machine learning at facebook: A datacenter infrastructure perspective. In *IEEE International Symposium on High Performance Computer Architecture (HPCA)*.

Heigold, G., Vanhoucke, V., Senior, A., Nguyen, P., Ranzato, M., Devin, M., and Dean, J. (2013). Multilingual acoustic models using distributed deep neural networks. In *Proc. ICASSP*.

Huang, J.-T., Li, J., Yu, D., Deng, L., and Gong, Y. (2013). Cross-language knowledge transfer using multilingual deep neural network with shared hidden layers. In *Proc. ICASSP*.

Kannan, A., Datta, A., Sainath, T. N., Weinstein, E., Ramabhadran, B., Wu, Y., Bapna, A., Chen, Z., and Lee, S. (2019). Large-scale multilingual speech recognition with a streaming end-to-end model.

Kanthak, S. and Ney, H. (2002). Context-dependent acoustic modeling using graphemes for large vocabulary speech recognition. In *Proc. ICASSP*.

Kim, S. and Seltzer, M. L. (2018). Towards language-universal end-to-end speech recognition. In *Proc. ICASSP*.

Kim, C., Misra, A., Chin, K., Hughes, T., Narayanan, A., Sainath, T., and Bacchiani, M. (2017). Generation of large-scale simulated utterances in virtual rooms to train deep-neural networks for far-field speech recognition in google home. In *Proc. Interspeech*.

Kingma, D. P. and Ba, J. (2015). Adam: A method for stochastic optimization. In *The International Conference on Learning Representations (ICLR)*.

Knill, K. M., Gales, M. J., Rath, S. P., Woodland, P. C., Zhang, C., and Zhang, S.-X. (2013). Investigation of multilingual deep neural networks for spoken term detection. In *Proc. ASRU*.

Knill, K. M., Gales, M. J., Ragni, A., and Rath, S. P. (2014). Language independent and unsupervised acoustic models for speech recognition and keyword spotting. In *Proc. Interspeech*.

Ko, T., Peddinti, V., Povey, D., and Khudanpur, S. (2015). Audio augmentation for speech recognition. In *Proc. Interspeech*.

Ko, T., Peddinti, V., Povey, D., Seltzer, M. L., and Khudanpur, S. (2017). A study on data augmentation of reverberant speech for robust speech recognition. In *Proc. ICASSP*.

Liao, H., McDermott, E., and Senior, A. (2013). Large scale deep neural network acoustic modeling with semi-supervised training data for YouTube video transcription. In *Proc. ASRU*.

Lin, H., Deng, L., Yu, D., Gong, Y.-f., Acero, A., and Lee, C.-H. (2009). A study on multilingual acoustic modeling for large vocabulary ASR. In *Proc. ICASSP*.

Liu, C., Jyothi, P., Tang, H., Manohar, V., Sloan, R., Kekona, T., Hasegawa-Johnson, M., and Khudanpur, S. (2016). Adapting ASR for under-resourced languages using mismatched transcriptions. In *Proc. ICASSP*.

Lüscher, C., Beck, E., Irie, K., Kitza, M., Michel, W., Zeyer, A., Schlüter, R., and Ney, H. (2019). RWTH ASR systems for librispeech: Hybrid vs attention-w/o data augmentation. In *Proc. Interspeech*.

Mohri, M., Pereira, F., and Riley, M. (2008). Speech recognition with weighted finite-state transducers. In *Springer Handbook of Speech Processing*, pages 559–584. Springer.

Nagamine, T., Seltzer, M. L., and Mesgarani, N. (2015). Exploring how deep neural networks form phonemic categories. In *Proc. Interspeech*.

Park, D. S., Chan, W., Zhang, Y., Chiu, C.-C., Zoph, B., Cubuk, E. D., and Le, Q. V. (2019). SpecAugment: A simple data augmentation method for automatic speech recognition. *arXiv preprint arXiv:1904.08779*.

Peddinti, V., Chen, G., Manohar, V., Ko, T., Povey, D., and Khudanpur, S. (2015). JHU ASPIRE system: Robust LVCSR with tdnns, ivector adaptation and RNN-LMs. In *Proc. ASRU*.

Povey, D., Ghoshal, A., Boulianne, G., Burget, L., Glembek, O., Goel, N., Hannemann, M., Motlíček, P., Qian, Y., Schwarz, P., et al. (2011). The Kaldi speech recognition toolkit. In *Proc. ASRU*.

Povey, D., Peddinti, V., Galvez, D., Ghahremani, P., Manohar, V., Na, X., Wang, Y., and Khudanpur, S. (2016). Purely sequence-trained neural networks for ASR based on lattice-free MMI. In *Proc. Interspeech*.

Pulugundla, B., Baskar, M. K., Kesiraju, S., Egorova, E., Karafiát, M., Burget, L., and Černocký, J. (2018). BUT system for low resource Indian language ASR. *Proc. Interspeech*.

Soltau, H., Liao, H., and Sak, H. (2017). Neural speech recognizer: Acoustic-to-word LSTM model for large vocabulary speech recognition. *Proc. Interspeech*.

Tong, S., Garner, P. N., and Bourlard, H. (2019). An investigation of multilingual ASR using end-to-end LF-MMI. In *Proc. ICASSP*.

Toshniwal, S., Sainath, T. N., Weiss, R. J., Li, B., Moreno, P., Weinstein, E., and Rao, K. (2018). Multilingual speech recognition with a single end-to-end model. In *Proc. ICASSP*.

Trmal, J., Wiesner, M., Peddinti, V., Zhang, X., Ghahremani, P., Wang, Y., Manohar, V., Xu, H., Povey, D., and Khudanpur, S. (2017). The Kaldi OpenKWS system: Improving low resource keyword search. In *Proc. Interspeech*.

Wang, Y., Mohamed, A., Le, D., Liu, C., Xiao, A., Mahadeokar, J., Huang, H., Tjandra, A., Zhang, X., Zhang, F., et al. (2020). Transformer-based acoustic modeling for hybrid speech recognition. In *Proc. ICASSP*.

Watanabe, S., Hori, T., and Hershey, J. R. (2017). Language independent end-to-end architecture for joint language identification and speech recognition. In *Proc. ASRU*.

Wells, J. C. (1995). Computer-coding the IPA: a proposed extension of SAMPA. *Revised draft*, 4(28):1995.

Wiesner, M., Liu, C., Ondel, L., Harman, C., Manohar, V., Trmal, J., Huang, Z., Dehak, N., and Khudanpur, S. (2018). Automatic speech recognition and topic identification for almost-zero-resource languages. In *Proc. Interspeech*.

Young, S. J., Odell, J. J., and Woodland, P. C. (1994). Tree-based state tying for high accuracy acoustic modelling. In *Proceedings of the workshop on Human Language Technology*, pages 307–312. Association for Computational Linguistics.

Zhang, Y., Chen, G., Yu, D., Yaco, K., Khudanpur, S., and Glass, J. (2016). Highway long short-term memory rnns for distant speech recognition. In *Proc. ICASSP*.

Proceedings of the 1st Joint SLTU and CCURL Workshop (SLTU-CCURL 2020), pages 53–60
Language Resources and Evaluation Conference (LREC 2020), Marseille, 11–16 May 2020
© European Language Resources Association (ELRA), licensed under CC-BY-NC

Neural Text-to-Speech Synthesis for an Under-Resourced Language in a Diglossic Environment: the Case of Gascon Occitan

**Ander Corral[1], Igor Leturia[1],
Aure Séguier[2], Michäel Barret[2], Benaset Dazéas[2],
Philippe Boula de Mareüil[3], Nicolas Quint[4]**

[1] Elhuyar Foundation
{a.corral, i.leturia}@elhuyar.eus
[2] Lo Congrès permanent de la lenga occitana
{a.seguier, m.barret, b.dazeas}@locongres.org
[3] Université Paris-Saclay, CNRS, LIMSI
philippe.boula.de.mareuil@limsi.fr
[4] Laboratoire Langage, Langues et Cultures d'Afrique (LLACAN - UMR 8135 - CNRS/INALCO/USPC)
nicolas.quint@cnrs.fr

Abstract

Occitan is a minority language spoken in Southern France, some Alpine Valleys of Italy, and the Val d'Aran in Spain, which only very recently started developing language and speech technologies. This paper describes the first project for designing a Text-to-Speech synthesis system for one of its main regional varieties, namely Gascon. We used a state-of-the-art deep neural network approach, the Tacotron2-WaveGlow system. However, we faced two additional difficulties or challenges: on the one hand, we wanted to test if it was possible to obtain good quality results with fewer recording hours than is usually reported for such systems; on the other hand, we needed to achieve a standard, non-Occitan pronunciation of French proper names, therefore we needed to record French words and test phoneme-based approaches. The evaluation carried out over the various developed systems and approaches shows promising results with near production-ready quality. It has also allowed us to detect the phenomena for which some flaws or fall of quality occur, pointing at the direction of future work to improve the quality of the actual system and for new systems for other language varieties and voices.

Keywords: TTS, Occitan, Gascon, Tacotron 2, WaveGlow

1. Introduction

1.1. The Occitan Language and the Gascon Variety

Occitan is a Romance language spoken in three states of the European Union (France, Spain and Italy) on an area of about 180,000 km^2. The Occitan language is co-official with Catalan and Spanish in Val d'Aran (in the Pyrenees). Although it has no public recognition elsewhere, several French territorial collectivities support it and it is one of the languages considered by the linguistic minorities protection law in Italy. As there are no officially imposed standards, Occitan may be described as a fairly dialectalised language. It is traditionally divided into six major varieties (Bec, 1986; Quint, 2014): Gascon, Languedocian, Provençal, Limousin, Auvergnat and Vivaro-Alpine. Gascon, the South-Western variety, displays many specific features (on both phonological and morphosyntactic levels), partly due to the Aquitanic substrate shared with Euskara (Basque). Perceptually, the presence of the [h] sound is particularly salient in the phonemic inventory: /p b t d k g n ɲ m f s z ʃ ʒ h r l ʎ i ɥ j w e ɛ a ɔ y u/.

1.2. Language Technologies for Occitan

Occitan being in a minorised language situation, it is also one of the many "under-resourced" or "poorly endowed" languages in the area of Natural Language Processing (NLP). However, NLP is a prioritary issue for its development and its diffusion. Hence, there was a need to develop a strategy according to the existing means, with planned goals as described in the Digital Language Survival Kit (Ceberio et al., 2018). The Occitan language benefits from some resources: text corpora such as Batelòc (Bras and Vergez-Couret, 2008) or Lo Congrès' one; online dictionaries or lexica such as dicod'Òc, tèrm'Òc, Lof lòc (Bras et al., 2017); a verb conjugator (vèrb'Òc), among others. Some tools have also been tested on Occitan: Talismane PoS tagger (Urieli, 2013), used within the framework of the ANR Restaure program (Bernhard et al., 2019), a spell checker, a predictive keyboard (Congrès, 2018a; Congrès, 2018b) and an automatic translator on the Apertium platform (Apertium, 2016).

These resources are mentioned in the Roadmap for Occitan Digital Develoment (Gurrutxaga and Leturia, 2014), a document for the planification of the development of Occitan NLP resources based on the Meta-Net method (Rehm and Uszkoreit, 2012). An Occitan text-to-speech (TTS) system is planned for 2019, also mentioned in the Inventory of linguistic resources for the languages of France (Leixa et al., 2014). In this report produced by the French Ministry of Culture (DGLFLF), the resources for Occitan are described as weak.

2. A Text-To-Speech System for Gascon

The recommendations for 2019 of the aforementioned Roadmap for Occitan Digital Develoment included building a Text-To-Speech (TTS) system. In accordance with these recommendations, work aiming at developing TTS technologies for Occitan took off. As a first approach, we decided to perform some experiments and evaluations with one variety and one voice. Once the desired results would be achieved (and therefore, the technology chosen, the process mastered and the sizes and features of the training datasets known), we would then expand the same methodology to other voices and varieties.

This first work was carried out for the Gascon variety with a female voice. However, there were some restrictions or preconditions to take into account in the experiments, which we will describe in the following subsections.

2.1. Deep Neural Network Technology

In recent years there has been a great change in the TTS area, whereby systems have progressively shifted from parametric or concatenative methods to deep neural network based ones. Naturally, this was due to the great improvement in quality and naturalness obtained by the latter technique.

The shift started with Google publishing the first WaveNet paper (Oord et al., 2016), a deep neural network model to implement the last steps of a TTS system, that is to say, the vocoder and acoustic modeling part (they produce the speech waves out of linguistic or acoustic features). WaveNet largely surpassed existing systems in terms of naturalness and quality. The paper was later followed by another one on Parallel WaveNet (Oord et al., 2018), a faster implementation of the same principle.

Tacotron (Wang et al., 2017) accelerated the shift. It was another neural network model to get spectrograms directly from text, instead of having the usual multiple steps chain (text analysis, duration modeling, acoustic feature modeling...) where errors tend to accumulate. Combined with a simple waveform synthesis technique, Tacotron outperformed production parametric systems in terms of naturalness. Tacotron 2 (Shen et al., 2018) put the final nail, proving that they could obtain a naturalness score almost as good as professionally recorded speech by generating mel spectrograms using the Tacotron approach and subsequently generating the speech waveform using a WaveNet model.

Also most of the other TTS systems that have come into scene in recent years, like Deep Voice (Arik et al., 2017) or Char2Wav (Sotelo et al., 2017) are also using deep learning approaches and improving the quality of previously used methods.

In view of the results of the Tacotron-WaveNet method, free software implementations of Tacotron and WaveNet have arisen, to allow researchers to perform experiments and developers to produce systems for other languages or situations. One of the most prominent is NVIDIA's, who have published under a free license a Tacotron 2 implementation (NVIDIA, 2018a) and WaveGlow (NVIDIA, 2018b), a system combining WaveNet and Glow (Kingma and Dhariwal, 2018) which, according to a paper they released (Prenger et al., 2019), delivers audio quality as good as the best publicly available WaveNet implementation. For these reasons, we chose NVIDIA's Tacotron 2 and WaveGlow combination as the software to perform our experiments with Gascon and, if successful, to put into production TTS systems for Occitan in general.

2.2. Few Recording Hours

Occitan being an under resourced language, audio recordings such as those needed for training TTS systems (good quality, one speaker, transcribed, aligned and in large quantities) are not available for Occitan. This means that recordings had to be made specifically for the project. And taking into account that TTS systems for many voices and varieties are planned to be developed in the future, we needed to adjust the recording hours to the minimum required. But since the amount of recording hours needed to obtain good quality cannot be known beforehand, we decided to start with a small amount of hours and evaluate the results obtained, and then make more recordings afterwards if necessary.

However, we needed a starting point of reference for the amount of recording hours. The Google experiments mentioned in the Tacotron and WaveNet papers use proprietary training datasets of at least 25 hours for each language (English and Chinese). The system mentioned in the WaveGlow paper uses the free LJ Speech dataset (Ito, 2017), which also represents 24 hours of audiobooks recorded in English. As we have already stated, our goal was to do it with much fewer hours if possible.

To our knowledge, the majority of research work using the deep neural Tacotron-WaveNet approach was based on the above referred training datasets, and there is not much work mentioning other datasets or languages. (Yasuda et al., 2019) have developed a system for Japanese, but they use a 47 hour dataset.

Some other works like Latorre et al. (2019) prove that, in the absence of many recording hours from a single speaker, a similar or better quality can be achieved with few hours from many speakers; but this does not help us, since there is not a corpus of this kind for Occitan anyway. And others like Tits et al. (2020) focus on developing new voices with few recordings, but this requires having already a multispeaker TTS system, which raises the same issue regarding Occitan. Finally, Chen et al. (2019) explore the development of a new voice with few hours using a TTS system developed for another language, with promising, albeit experimental, results.

One reference that could be of use for our work is the one described by Choi et al. (2018), where they made experiments with around 9 hours data. However, the Mean Opinion Score (MOS) they achieved is far below the levels reported in the rest of the above papers, which is not very promising. On the other hand, Podsiadło and Ungureanu (2018) prove that a quality dataset (phonetically balanced, professional quality recordings) of 10 hours can achieve almost as good MOS scores as a 23 hour dataset, and Liu et al. (2019) also achieve good MOS scores with 8 hours. So we decided to start with a similar number of hours, which was in principle affordable to us, as a first experiment, which we would forcibly enlarge if the experiment did not achieve good results.

2.3. Standard Pronunciation of French Proper Names

Due to the sociolinguistic situation of the region where Occitan is spoken, where there is a remarkable diglossia of Occitan with respect to French, many French words are included in Occitan oral and text production (notably proper names of people, streets, places, brands, titles, etc.). These words are usually pronounced as in French, and if they are pronounced following the traditional phonological rules of Occitan, the result is incomprehensible for the speakers themselves. Therefore, if an Occitan TTS would not take this into account and pronounce French names like "Beauvais" or "Jeanssins" with the Occitan pronunciation as [be/aw/'bajs] and [ʒe/an/'sis], rather than [/bo/'vɛ] and [/ʒã/'sɛ̃s], it would not be good for practical use with real texts.

This same problem had been detected in Iparrahotsa (Navas et al., 2014), a TTS system for the Navarro-Lapurdian variety of Basque, spoken in the French part of the Basque Country. The project is still ongoing, precisely due to that problem.

For this reason, in order to be properly developed, the TTS system for Occitan had to correctly pronounce French proper names following the French (vs. Occitan) phonological system, so we also needed to record French words, to test phoneme-based approaches and to develop language detection and text-to-phoneme conversion tools.

In the aforementioned work by Yasuda et al. (2019), they perform some experiments using phonemes as input. Other systems using phonemes or mixed input are mentioned in Kastner et al. (2019).

3. Experiments

3.1. Training Dataset

3.1.1. Text Corpus

We designed a relatively small Occitan corpus made up of literary works, press articles and Wikipedia pages. In order to maximise the recording time in terms of phoneme diversity, we sorted all its sentences according to a score indicating the *number of unique diphones/total number of diphones* ratio and the proximity to the average sentences length, inspired by the "Unique Unit Coverage Score" introduced by Arora et al. (2014).

The corpus aimed at including all diphones which might occur in an Occitan conversation mixed with French words: every possible combination of Occitan and French phonemes was therefore taken into account. We first picked up in the Occitan corpus all sentences showing a diphone that did not appear in the sentences already selected. Then, we manually added sentences containing diphones which did not occur in the corpus.

In addition, we used a list of phonetised French given names and family names (Boula de Mareüil et al., 2005) as an exception database (see Section 3.2.). Those proper names were then combined automatically to get a corpus with all diphones combining a French phoneme and a French or an Occitan phoneme (by "French phonemes" we mean the 10 vowels and consonants which do not belong to the standard Occitan phoneme inventory, such as nasal

vowels). We manually created sentences including proper names with diphones which did not occur in the resulting corpus. Sentences including diphones with the Spanish *jota* (/x/) (which does not belong to the phoneme inventories of Occitan and French) were added in order to account for Spanish loans, whose frequency is particularly significant in written texts produced in Aranese Occitan (a Gascon variety spoken alongside Spanish in the Val d'Aran).

As a result, we obtained a first "mandatory" corpus containing all possible diphones formed with Occitan and French phonemes (as well as the *jota*). Also, we manually added sentences which are likely to appear in systems using TTS synthesis, such as GPS or public transport (e.g., "Turn left"). Finally, we picked up sentences in our sorted Occitan corpus until we obtained a total of 100,000 words. We obtained a corpus of approximately 13,600 sentences: about 10,900 entirely Occitan sentences, around 2,700 sentences with French phonemes, 43 sentences with the Spanish jota. There were around 1,300 exclamatory sentences and 700 interrogative sentences.

3.1.2. Audio Recordings

We looked for Occitan speakers suited for the task, that is, speaking for hours in a "neutral tone", and we chose to hire a female radio news announcer. We recorded her in a studio usually dedicated to movies dubbing. Therefore, the sound engineer present in the studio was used to working with spoken material. The recordings lasted six days, with an average of seven hours work per day. Sentences were projected on a large screen about seven meters away from the speaker, in order to elicit a voice similar to that of someone speaking from a certain distance. After cleaning, we obtained a total of almost 7 hours of speech (without counting the pauses between sentences, which would otherwise add a few hours). We were, however, not able to record the whole written corpus.

We had to deal again with the internal great variability of the Occitan language, even within the Gascon domain. We wanted our TTS system to fit the regional standard as much as possible. However, we soon realized that it was impossible to have our speaker speak during hours with some pronunciations that were unnatural to her (e.g.: pronounce the j /ʒ/ instead of /j/). These pronunciation variations were rather few and were not pointed out during the quantitative evaluation. Still, we had to settle for compromises in favour of a less standard Occitan (Gascon): the result is still a reasonably standard accent, easily understandable by most Occitan speakers. Moreover, after the recording sessions, we spent a lot of time in post-processing to make adjustments. In particular, many sentences of our corpus were not written in the speaker's subvariety, and she pronounced them following her own speech habits. It was thus necessary to correct a number of written sentences to make them fit the recorded pronunciation. Also, we took advantage of this opportunity to correct the mispronounced words.

The size of the corpus is 6:52 hours, out of which 5:46 contained only Occitan words and another 1:06 hours contained sentences including French (or other languages) words. A total of 23 minutes were recordings of interrogative sentences and 36 minutes of exclamatory sentences.

The mean sentence length is around 2.5 seconds, with a standard deviation of around 1.8. However, some of the sentences were much longer. Those exceeding 10 seconds triggered memory errors on training, so we had to remove them (they accounted for fewer than 1% of the sentences).

3.2. Linguistic Tools

We created an expansion tool which cleans the input and expands Arabic numerals and most Roman numerals, e-mail addresses, website URLs, phone numbers, dates, hours, measurement units, currencies, some acronyms and abbreviations. A rule-based grapheme-to-phoneme conversion tool was developed, containing about 230 hand-written rules. It uses an exception base (including thousands of French proper names) as well as a syllabification tool composed of 40 rules, for lexical stress assignment. Occitan is a language in which stress is distinctive, and stress location may be predicted in most cases even in the absence of part-of-speech tagging — a component which has not yet been designed.

3.3. TTS Systems

3.3.1. The Tacotron Part

We devised three setups for our experiments, all of them using the NVIDIA's Tacotron 2 and WaveGlow above mentioned systems. The first one (hereinafter OccTxt) was trained with those sentences that only contain Occitan words, in their character-based version (with numbers, acronyms, etc. expanded using the tool described above). The second one (hereinafter OccPho) was also trained only with Occitan sentences, but these were converted to phonemes by the tool mentioned in the previous subsection. Finally, a third setup (AllPho) was prepared using all available sentences (including French proper names) converted to phonemes (the French words being transcribed according to their standard French pronunciation).

We are aware that Tacotron 2 can accept a mixed character-phoneme notation as an entry (the code includes the example "Turn left on {HH AW1 S S T AH0 N} Street") and that for the third setup we could have used such a notation with Occitan text in characters and only French words as phonemes. However, since the grapheme-to-phoneme conversion tool we developed could convert all the text to phonemes, we considered this to be a better option, because it reduced the symbol set (some of the French phonemes also exist in Occitan) and so we could expect better results. Tacotron 2 includes a list of the accepted letters and symbols (which are the English ones). We changed this list to also accept Occitan diacritics in the first setup, Occitan phonemes in the second and Occitan and French phonemes in the third. The list of characters and phonemes was obtained from the training corpus which, depending on the setup, was passed through the phonemizer or not.

OccTxt and OccPho were designed to test if an acceptable quality could be achieved in Occitan with a relatively small number of recording hours, although we did not expect them to work well with French proper names. AllPho would serve both to check (i) if French words were well pronounced, and (ii) if the inclusion of French words into the training set would impact the pronunciation of the Occitan words with respect to the other setups.

In all cases, we used as a starting point the models NVIDIA trained for English with their Tacotron 2 implementation using the LJ Speech dataset, which are both downloadable from their GitHub page (NVIDIA, 2017a). As the authors of these systems explain, "training using a pre-trained model can lead to faster convergence", which proved to be the case: in some experiments we carried out there was no noticeable difference between the results of a system trained on a random state and a system trained on the English model, with a much smaller training time for the latter. For the training phase, default parameters were used, with no hyperparameter optimization. Models were trained until no further improvement was obtained on the validation data.

3.3.2. The WaveGlow Part

Whatever the results might be, we did not expect a quality comparable to what was reported in the original Tacotron 2 - WaveNet paper, because of the much smaller amount of available hours of recordings. But it was interesting to see (i) if the effect of this reduced corpus could be more significant at the level of the production of mel spectrograms from text (the Tacotron part) or at the level of the production of the audio wave from the mel spectrograms (the WaveGlow part), and (ii) if we were able to improve the results by somehow intervening in one of those steps.

We observed that using a WaveGlow model trained for English with more hours -precisely, the one reported in the WaveGlow paper, trained with the 24 hours LJ Speech dataset and also downloadable from its GitHub page (NVIDIA, 2017b)- could also be used as vocoder with a relatively good quality for Occitan. This result may seem curious at first, but was in some way logical: mel spectrograms are nothing but frequency-based representations of a sound wave, and all that a system like WaveGlow or WaveNet does is learning to produce an audio wave from a mel spectrogram; therefore, if a system learns from a large dataset where many frequencies are represented, it should be able to decode mel spectrograms of other voices and languages quite efficiently, unless the new language and voice contain many frequencies both new and unknown to the system. In our case, both the LJ Speech dataset and the Occitan training dataset were female voices (and so supposedly relatively near from each other in the frequency spectrum), and the English model seemed to fit well for the Occitan spectrograms.

Therefore, for the WaveGlow step, in additon to the models trained on the Occitan audios (henceforth OccWav), we also tested a model produced from the English LJ Speech dataset (henceforth EngWav).

4. Evaluation and Results

For the evaluation, a corpus of 100 sentences was prepared, containing examples of all the phenomena we wanted to test, with the following distribution: 10 exclamations, 20 interrogations, 15 with rare diphones, 20 with at least one French noun, and the remaining 35 being affirmative sentences with only Occitan words. These sentences were all recorded by the speaker of the training set.

4.1. The Tacotron Part

In a first phase, evaluators were presented with these sentences both in (i) their recorded and (ii) their synthesized version produced using in turn the three Tacotron setups (OccTxt, OccPho and AllPho) with the EngWav model in the WaveGlow part, i.e. 400 audios, in a blind random way. For each of these, the evaluators were required to evaluate three points:

- If the sentence was correctly pronounced (in a scale from 1 to 5), which would allow us to detect pronunciation errors in French proper names, question intonations, rare diphones, etc.

- If the sentence was fluid and natural (in a scale from 1 to 5), so that we could have a MOS (Mean Opinion Score) of the voices' naturalness.

- If there was a major technical problem such as truncated sentence, blank, gibberish... (yes/no rating), because we observed that such things sometimes happened due to the small amount of recorded hours, the length of some sentences or other reasons.

The evaluations of the first phase were done by 8 Gascon-speakers over a period of ten days, which represents a total of 3,200 (= 8 x 400) evaluated sentences. The evaluators are professionals working with Occitan language in many fields (teaching, administration, linguistics, translation...). They were not familiar with TTS systems, but had occasionally heard synthesized speech in French (GPS, public transport...).

The MOS obtained for the pronunciation correctness by the three systems and compared to the human recordings can be seen in Figure 1. The system that scores best is AllPho, obtaining a score of 4.2, whereas the human recordings obtained 4.9. Besides, it has a difference of at least 0.3 with respect to the other two systems, which was somehow expected, since the other systems lacked the phoneme conversion or the recordings for French, which could only make them score lower in the sentences containing French proper names.

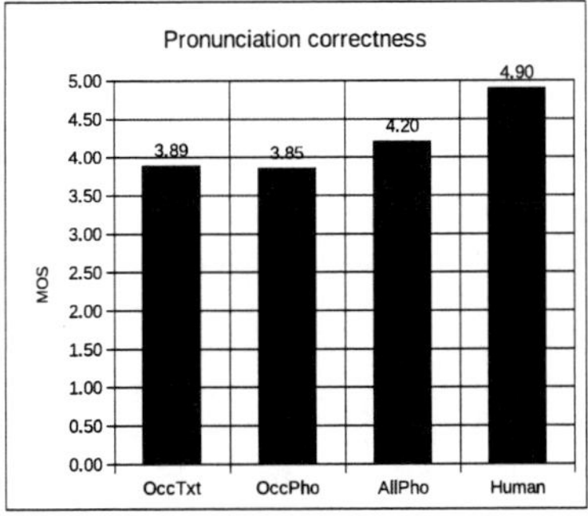

Figure 1: MOS for pronunciation correctness.

In fact, if we look at the scores obtained by each sentence type (Table 1), we can see that, although the AllPho setup scores best for every type of sentence, the improvement obtained is much larger for the sentences with French nouns (almost 0.5 points).

Sentence	System			Human
	OccTxt	OccPho	AllPho	
Normal	3.96	3.93	**4.23**	4.91
French	3.47	3.64	**4.08**	4.81
Interrogative	3.91	3.81	**4.10**	4.95
Exclamatory	4.53	4.04	**4.65**	4.93
Rare diphones	3.85	3.87	**4.17**	4.90
Average	3.89	3.85	**4.20**	4.90

Table 1: MOS for pronunciation correctness for each type of sentence.

The AllPho system is also the best one regarding fluidity and naturalness, as is shown in Figure 2. This can be the result of having 15% extra-time of recordings for training, because the sentences with French words also include Occitan text and therefore a larger audio corpus of Occitan was used. The score obtained can be considered as satisfactory, taking into account the relatively small number of training hours used.

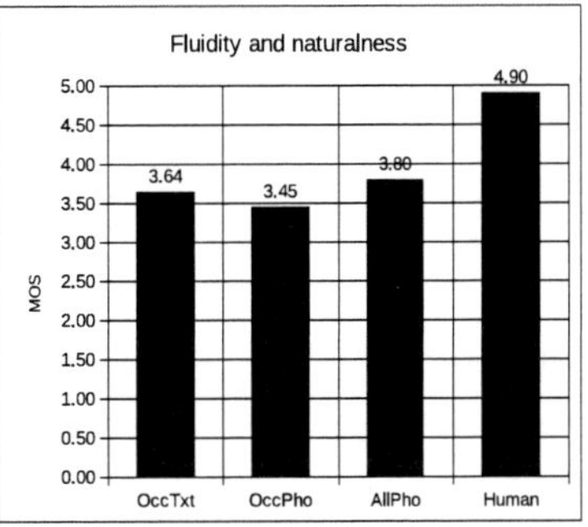

Figure 2: MOS for fluidity and naturalness.

Table 2 shows us that AllPho scores best in all types of sentences. This is a very important positive result, because it means that the inclusion of French phonemes in the recordings and the fact of basing the TTS system on phonemes instead of text characters does not impact negatively the voice quality; rather, it slightly improves it.

Sentence	System			Human
	OccTxt	OccPho	AllPho	
Normal	3.85	3.60	**3.93**	4.92
French	3.25	3.26	**3.63**	4.83
Interrogative	3.56	3.33	**3.60**	4.96
Exclamatory	4.15	3.60	**4.21**	4.88
Rare diphones	3.48	3.39	**3.68**	4.89
Average	3.64	3.45	**3.80**	4.90

Table 2: MOS for fluidity and naturalness for each type of sentence.

We can also observe in Tables 1 and 2 that exclamatory sentences obtain the highest score both in correctness and naturalness in all setups, with a significant difference with respect to the other types of sentence especially in the AllPho system. Interrogative sentences, on the other hand, get the lowest score in naturalness and the second lowest in correctness (very close to the lowest one, i.e. sentences containing French names) in the AllPho setup, with a difference of more than 0.5 points with respect to exclamatory sentences. This may be due to the fact that there are 56% more recordings of exclamatory sentences than interrogative sentences in the corpus (36 min. vs. 23 min., see Section 3.1.2.). Recording some extra interrogative sentences (just 13 more minutes) in order to have the same amount of recordings as available for exclamatory sentences might be a way to improve the synthesis of interrogative sentences. However, we cannot exclude that other factors (such as pragmatic saliency or cognitive aspects) may also account for this difference between the two sentence types.

Finally, regarding the third question (if the sentence presented some major technical error or problem), as can be seen in Table 3, there does not seem to be any significant difference among the three systems, although AllPho seems more reliable. All three systems seem to meet with similar difficulties in correctly synthesizing the same specific sentences.

Sentence	System			Human
	OccTxt	OccPho	AllPho	
Normal	49	45	**46**	4
French	36	38	**30**	3
Interrogative	24	25	**26**	3
Exclamatory	3	8	**3**	1
Rare diphones	19	16	**18**	1
Average	131	132	**123**	12

Table 3: Major technical problems or errors for each type of sentence.

4.2. The WaveGlow Part

In a second phase, we prepared an evaluation that would play the 100 sentences synthesized by the system that scored best in the first phase (AllPho) with the EngWav and OccWav WaveGlow vocoders, that is, 200 audios, again in blind and random conditions. In this case, the evaluators only had to evaluate the fluidity and naturalness and give it a score on a 1 to 5 scale. However, listening to just some few sentences was enough for the evaluators to clearly identify which ones were produced with the EngWav vocoder used in the first phase or with the new OccWav one. The evaluators reported that EngWav was by far better and more natural, and saw no point in going on with a tiring and costly evaluation.

4.3. Qualitative Evaluation

After finishing the quantitative evaluation, the evaluators were asked two questions about their qualitative impression on the systems developed:

- What was their global impression on the sentences they had heard.

- The type of technical or quality errors or problems they had encountered.

Globally speaking, the evaluators find that the synthesized sentences (they were usually distinguishable from the human recorded ones) were easy to understand and of good quality. Taking into account the fact that the evaluators did not know which system had produced each sentence, if they thought the synthesized sentences had a good average quality, we can suppose that the system which got the highest scores (AllPho) would be considered by the same evaluators still better.

Regarding the errors or problems, the evaluators mentioned occasional silences or missing words, noise (which they qualified as whistling, blowing, metallic..), artificiality, intonation problems and difficulties with specific words.

A more detailed analysis of the sentences marked by the evaluators as problematic enabled us to see the causes of some of these problems and devise possible solutions for a production system. For example, some of the silence and intonation problems are due to the fact that the systems implemented get confused when producing very long sentences (as mentioned earlier, we removed sentences longer than 10 seconds from the training datasets because they resulted in memory errors); therefore, to solve this problem, we divided long sentences at points where a comma was found, synthesized them as separate sentences and concatenated them; but this produced too long silences and intonation falls at commas (similar to those at the end of a sentence). We believe that if we cut some long sentences at commas from the training dataset, this problem can be relieved. This work is yet to be done. Likewise, it seems that by applying a filter to reduce the trebles by 10 dB, the whistling or metallic effect is reduced, although we have not yet tested this effect formally.

5. Conclusions

With the objective of obtaining a neural state-of-the-art TTS for Gascon Occitan with relatively few recording hours which would pronounce French proper names in a standard way, we have developed and evaluated different systems, all based on the NVIDIA Tacotron 2 - WaveGlow software, some of them text-based and others phoneme-based, some of them including recordings of French words and some not. The system based on phonemes which included the recordings of French words obtained a MOS of 4 out of 5 for correctness and naturalness, and evaluators and language experts consider it to be of a near production-ready quality.

Moreover, the evaluation results were useful to show which sentence types or phenomena may need improvements or adjustments and which types of sentence produce some major problems. Basing ourselves on these results, we will be able to decide if further recordings of some kinds of sentences must be done or if we should choose other technical solutions in order to solve the various problems encountered, with a view to putting into production a TTS system for Gascon Occitan and developing systems for other voices and other Occitan varieties such as Languedocian. The idea is to put these systems into production and to make them available for interested users, organizations and companies in the short term. The MOS of these systems might not be as high as that of systems trained with more hours, but it was considered to be of a satisfactory quality, especially if we take into account the fact that there are no TTS systems currently available for Occitan. At any rate, this Occitan TTS system will probably be better than many other systems produced for other languages with older technologies. However, it is important to note that the system we have chosen to put into production makes use of a vocoder model produced for English, because it sounds much better to the evaluators than the model trained specifically for Occitan. This means that the recording hours used in the project might not always be sufficient to train a WaveGlow system with a production-ready quality. Here a model trained for another language with more recording hours was useful, but it might not always be the case. For example, the model may not be useful for correctly synthesizing male voices due to a different frequency spectrum, since it was trained using recordings of a female speaker. Also, to our knowledge, there are no free WaveGlow models trained with large datasets of male voices. Thus, if we are faced with this problem in the future, we will have to try and train a model using free recorded datasets of male voices (if available), or maybe endeavour to expand our own set of recordings.

6. Acknowledgements

The research carried out in this project is part of the project "LINGUATEC: Development of cross-border cooperation and knowledge transfer in language technologies" (POCTEFA EFA227/16, ERDF), funded by the Ministry of Economy and Competitiveness of Spain and the European Regional Development Fund (ERDF).

7. Bibliographical References

Apertium. (2016). Apertium translation pair for Occitan and French. https://github.com/apertium/apertium-oci-fra.

Arik, S. O., Chrzanowski, M., Coates, A., Diamos, G., Gibiansky, A., Kang, Y., Li, X., Miller, J., Ng, A., Raiman, J., Sengupta, S., and Shoeybi, M. (2017). Deep Voice: Real-time Neural Text-to-Speech. In *Proceedings of the 34th International Conference on Machine Learning (ICML)*, Sidney, Australia, July.

Arora, K., Arora, S., Verma, K., and Agrawal, S. S. (2014). Automatic Extraction of Phonetically Rich Sentences from Large Text Corpus of Indian Languages. In *Proceedings of 8th International Conference on Spoken Language Processing (Interspeech 2004 - ICSLP)*, Jeju, Korea, October.

Bec, P. (1986). *La langue occitane*. Number 1059 in Que sais-je? Presses universitaires de France, Paris, 5th edition.

Bernhard, D., Bras, M., Erhart, P., Ligozat, A.-L., and Vergez-Couret, M. (2019). Language Technologies for Regional Languages of France: The RESTAURE Project. In *Proceedings of International Conference Language Technologies for All (LT4All): Enabling Linguistic Diversity and Multilingualism Worldwide*, Paris, France, December.

Boula de Mareüil, P., d'Alessandro, C., Bailly, G., Béchet, F., Garcia, M.-N., Morel, M., Prudon, R., and Véronis, J. (2005). Evaluating the Pronunciation of Proper Names by Four French Grapheme-to-Phoneme Converters. In *Proceedings of 9th European Conference on Speech Communication and Technology (Interspeech'2005 - Eurospeech)*, pages 1251–1254, Lisbon, Portugal, September.

Bras, M. and Vergez-Couret, M. (2008). BaTelÒc: A Text Base for the Occitan Language. *Language Documentation & Conservation*, Special Publication No. 9(Language Documentation and Conservation in Europe):133–149.

Bras, M., Vergez-Couret, M., Hathout, N., Sibille, J., Séguier, A., and Dazéas, B. (2017). Loflòc, lexic obèrt flechit occitan. In *Proceedings of the XIIn Congrès de l'Associacion internacionala d'estudis occitans*, Albi, France, July.

Ceberio, K., Gurrutxaga, A., Baroni, P., Hicks, D., Kruse, E., Quochi, V., Russo, I., Salonen, T., Sarhimaa, A., and Soria, C. (2018). Digital Language Survival Kit: The DLDP Recommendations to Improve Digital Vitality. Technical report, The Digital Language Diversity Project.

Chen, Y.-J., Tu, T., Yeh, C.-c., and Lee, H.-Y. (2019). End-to-End Text-to-Speech for Low-Resource Languages by Cross-Lingual Transfer Learning. In *Proceedings of Interspeech 2019*, pages 2075–2079, September.

Choi, Y., Jung, Y., Kim, Y., Suh, Y., and Kim, H. (2018). An end-to-end synthesis method for Korean text-to-speech systems. *Phonetics and Speech Sciences*, 10(1):39–48, March.

Congrès, L. (2018a). Occitan gascon pack for AnySoftKeyboard. https://play.google.com/store/apps/details?id=com.anysoftkeyboard.languagepack.gascon.

Congrès, L. (2018b). Occitan lengadocian pack for AnySoftKeyboard. https://play.google.com/store/apps/details?id=com.anysoftkeyboard.languagepack.lengadoc.

Gurrutxaga, A. and Leturia, I. (2014). Diagnostic et feuille de route pour le développement numérique de la langue occitane : 2015-2019. Technical report, Elhuyar Foundation, Media.kom, November.

Kastner, K., Santos, J. F., Bengio, Y., and Courville, A. (2019). Representation Mixing for TTS Synthesis. In *Proceedings of ICASSP 2019 - 2019 IEEE International Conference on Acoustics, Speech and Signal Processing (ICASSP)*, pages 5906–5910, Brighton, United Kingdom, May. IEEE.

Kingma, D. P. and Dhariwal, P. (2018). Glow: Generative Flow with Invertible 1x1 Convolutions. *arXiv:1807.03039 [cs, stat]*, July. arXiv: 1807.03039.

Latorre, J., Lachowicz, J., Lorenzo-Trueba, J., Merritt, T., Drugman, T., Ronanki, S., and Klimkov, V. (2019). Effect of Data Reduction on Sequence-to-sequence Neural TTS. In *Proceedings of ICASSP 2019 - 2019 IEEE International Conference on Acoustics, Speech and Signal Processing (ICASSP)*, pages 7075–7079, Brighton, United Kingdom, May.

Leixa, J., Mapelli, V., and Choukri, K. (2014). Inventaire des ressources linguistiques des langues de France. Technical Report ELDA/DGLFLF-2013A, ELDA, November.

Liu, B., Chen, Y., Yin, H., Li, Y., Lei, X., and Xie, L. (2019). The Mobvoi Text-To-Speech System for Blizzard Challenge 2019. In *Proceedings of The 10th ISCA Speech Synthesis Workshop (SSW10)*, Vienna, Austria, September.

Navas, E., Hernaez, I., Erro, D., Salaberria, J., Oyharçabal, B., and Padilla, M. (2014). Developing a Basque TTS for the Navarro-Lapurdian Dialect. In *Proceedings of IberSPEECH 2014*, volume 8854, pages 11–20, Las Palmas de Gran Canaria, Spain.

NVIDIA. (2018a). NVIDIA/tacotron2, May. https://github.com/NVIDIA/tacotron2.

NVIDIA. (2018b). NVIDIA/waveglow, November. https://github.com/NVIDIA/waveglow.

Oord, A. v. d., Dieleman, S., Zen, H., Simonyan, K., Vinyals, O., Graves, A., Kalchbrenner, N., Senior, A., and Kavukcuoglu, K. (2016). WaveNet: A Generative Model for Raw Audio. *arXiv:1609.03499 [cs]*, September. arXiv: 1609.03499.

Oord, A. v. d., Li, Y., Babuschkin, I., Simonyan, K., Vinyals, O., Kavukcuoglu, K., Driessche, G. v. d., Lockhart, E., Cobo, L. C., Stimberg, F., Casagrande, N., Grewe, D., Noury, S., Dieleman, S., Elsen, E., Kalchbrenner, N., Zen, H., Graves, A., King, H., Walters, T., Belov, D., and Hassabis, D. (2018). Parallel WaveNet: Fast High-Fidelity Speech Synthesis. In Jennifer Dy et al., editors, *Proceedings of 35th International Conference on Machine Learning*, volume 80, pages 3918–2926, Stockholm, Sweden, July. arXiv: 1711.10433.

Podsiadło, M. and Ungureanu, V. (2018). Experiments with Training Corpora for Statistical Text-to-speech Systems. In *Proceedings of Interspeech 2018*, pages 2002–2006, September.

Prenger, R., Valle, R., and Catanzaro, B. (2019). Waveglow: A Flow-based Generative Network for Speech Synthesis. In *Proceedings of ICASSP 2019 - 2019 IEEE International Conference on Acoustics, Speech and Signal Processing (ICASSP)*, pages 3617–3621, Brighton, United Kingdom, May.

Quint, N. (2014). *L'Occitan*. Assimil, Chennevières sur Marne, France.

Georg Rehm et al., editors. (2012). *META-NET White Paper Series: Europe's Languages in the digital age*. Springer, Heidelberg, Germany.

Shen, J., Pang, R., Weiss, R. J., Schuster, M., Jaitly, N., Yang, Z., Chen, Z., Zhang, Y., Wang, Y., Skerrv-Ryan, R., Saurous, R. A., Agiomvrgiannakis, Y., and Wu, Y. (2018). Natural TTS Synthesis by Conditioning Wavenet on MEL Spectrogram Predictions. In *Proceedings of IEEE International Conference on Acoustics, Speech and Signal Processing (ICASSP)*, pages 4779–4783, Calgary, Canada, April.

Sotelo, J., Mehri, S., Kumar, K., Santos, J. F., Kastner, K., Courville, A., and Bengio, Y. (2017). Char2Wav: End-to-End Speech Synthesis. In *Proceedings of the 5th International Conference on Learning Representations (ICLR)*, Toulon, France, April.

Tits, N., El Haddad, K., and Dutoit, T. (2020). Exploring Transfer Learning for Low Resource Emotional TTS. In Yaxin Bi, et al., editors, *Intelligent Systems and Applications*, volume 1037, pages 52–60. Springer International Publishing.

Urieli, A. (2013). *Robust French syntax analysis: reconciling statistical methods and linguistic knowledge in the Talismane toolkit*. Ph.D. thesis, Université Toulouse 2 Le Mirail, Toulouse, France, December.

Wang, Y., Skerry-Ryan, R., Stanton, D., Wu, Y., Weiss, R. J., Jaitly, N., Yang, Z., Xiao, Y., Chen, Z., Bengio, S., Le, Q., Agiomyrgiannakis, Y., Clark, R., and Saurous, R. A. (2017). Tacotron: Towards End-to-End Speech Synthesis. In *Proceedings of Interspeech 2017*, pages 4006–4010, Stockholm, Sweden, August. ISCA.

Yasuda, Y., Wang, X., Takaki, S., and Yamagishi, J. (2019). Investigation of enhanced Tacotron text-to-speech synthesis systems with self-attention for pitch accent language. In *Proceedings of ICASSP 2019*, pages 6905–6909, Brighton, UK, May. arXiv: 1810.11960.

8.   Language Resource References

Ito, K. (2017). The LJ Speech Dataset. https://keithito.com/LJ-Speech-Dataset.

NVIDIA. (2017a). Tacotron 2 model weights pre-trained on the LJ Speech dataset. https://drive.google.com/file/d/1c5ZTuT7J08wLUoVZ2KkUs_VdZuJ86ZqA/view.

NVIDIA. (2017b). WaveGlow model weights pre-trained on the LJ Speech dataset. https://ngc.nvidia.com/catalog/models/nvidia:waveglow_ljs_256channels.

Proceedings of the 1st Joint SLTU and CCURL Workshop (SLTU-CCURL 2020), pages 61–69
Language Resources and Evaluation Conference (LREC 2020), Marseille, 11–16 May 2020
© European Language Resources Association (ELRA), licensed under CC-BY-NC

Transfer Learning for Less-Resourced Semitic Languages Speech Recognition: the Case of Amharic

Yonas Woldemariam

Dept. Computing Science, Umeå University, Sweden
yonasd@cs.umu.se

Abstract

While building automatic speech recognition (ASR) requires a large amount of speech and text data, the problem gets worse for less-resourced languages. In this paper, we investigate a model adaptation method, namely transfer learning for a less-resourced Semitic language i.e., Amharic, to solve resource scarcity problems in speech recognition development and improve the Amharic ASR model. In our experiments, we transfer acoustic models trained on two different source languages (English and Mandarin) to Amharic using very limited resources. The experimental results show that a significant WER (Word Error Rate) reduction has been achieved by transferring the hidden layers of the trained source languages neural networks. In the best case scenario, the Amharic ASR model adapted from English yields the best WER reduction from 38.72% to 24.50% (an improvement of 14.22% absolute). Adapting the Mandarin model improves the baseline Amharic model with a WER reduction of 10.25% (absolute). Our analysis also reveals that, the speech recognition performance of the adapted acoustic model is highly influenced by the relatedness (in a relative sense) between the source and the target languages than other considered factors (e.g. the quality of source models). Furthermore, other Semitic as well as Afro-Asiatic languages could benefit from the methodology presented in this study.

Keywords: Less-resourced, Semitic languages, Amharic, Transfer learning, weight transfer, Automatic Speech Recognition

1. Introduction

Afro-Asiatic is one of the major language families widely spoken in north and west Africa. Semitic languages belong to Afro-Asiatic. Next to Arabic, Amharic is the second most spoken Semitic language. Moreover, Amharic is an official language of Ethiopia, spoken by over 22 million people, according to Central Statistical Agency of Ethiopia[1]. Amharic has its own unique orthographic representation containing 32 consonants and 7 vowels called **Amharic-Fidel**. The orthographic representation is also shared with Tigrinya, the other Semitic language of Ethiopia (also the main language of Eritrea). Amharic also shares several linguistic features (including morphological structure and vocabulary) with Arabic.

Although there is a large volume of Amharic content available on the web, searching and retrieving them is hard as they only exist in their raw form (not analyzed and indexed well). Therefore, building language specific tools that analyze and index, could potentially enhance the accessibility of Amharic web content. Particularly, automatic speech recognition highly improves the searchability of audio and video content due to its speech transcription support (Mezaris et al., 2010).

Existing Amharic ASR prototypes never seem to be used to perform even other common speech oriented tasks such as language learning (Farzad and Eva, 1998) or solve practical problems by integrating them in other large natural language processing systems such as machine-translation. This is mainly due to the requirement of a fairly large amount of annotated data (e.g., speech transcriptions, language models, lexicons) along with a reasonable degree of quality sufficient to train ASR models.

Compared to other well researched languages for which computational linguistic models have been developed,

Amharic is one of the less resourced languages due to a lack of research attention. Even though there are some growing efforts to build general multi-lingual ASR systems and resources (Karafiát et al., 2017; Rosenberg et al., 2017; Das et al., 2016) to support low resourced languages, some languages (including Semitic ones) require exclusive attention due to their unique linguistic nature.

There are also some studies (Abate et al., 2009; Tachbelie et al., 2014; Demeke and Hailemariam, 2012; Melese et al., 2017) on developing language-processing technologies for Amharic, but most of them are done with very limited resources (ELRA-W0074, 2014; Gauthier et al., 2016; HaBiT, 2016). They also do not consider re-using linguistic resources available for other languages. As a result they fail to achieve sufficient quality, especially for commercial use.

Developing good quality speech recognizers typically requires large amounts of transcribed speech and texts. Unfortunately, only small quantities of such data are available for Amharic. They are also limited for specific application domains (not diverse) and formatted to work on specific frameworks. Moreover, preparing data is expensive and time-consuming as it needs to be manually annotated. Therefore, in this study, we explore techniques that enable sharing and adapting existing resources available for other languages.

The most widely used approach to alleviate resource related problems is multilingual model training using pooled data from various languages (Ghoshal et al., 2013; Wang and Zheng, 2015; Karafiát et al., 2017), where under resourced languages get trained together with well-resourced ones. Then, the resulting model could serve to recognize inputs of any of these languages (Wang and Zheng, 2015; Feng and Lee, 2018). While multilingual training potentially improves the recognition performance of the under resourced languages, it demands a huge amount of multilingual re-

---

[1] https://www.csa.gov.et

sources including a universal (shared) phone set, speech-text corpora, language models and lexicons (Besacier et al., 2014; Wang and Zheng, 2015; Karafiát et al., 2018). In addition, the languages need to be somehow similar (related) to achieve a better outcome. It is often challenging to meet these requirements, especially for those languages that have never been investigated through this approach. Moreover, the problem gets worse when it comes to a language family where most of the member languages are under resourced. Semitic is such an example.

The alternative approach that relaxes these requirements is the transfer learning approach (Huang et al., 2013; Ghahremani et al., 2017; Manohar et al., 2017) (explained in Section 2). Once an acoustic model is trained solely on one of well resourced languages (source languages), the model could be adapted to baseline systems built for less-resourced ones (target languages) through transfer learning. Compared to multilingual training, transfer learning does not only eliminate the requirement for the shared phone set, the source and the target languages do not necessarily need to be related. Also, in terms of computing resources, training multiple languages simultaneously is more costly than training them sequentially.

In this paper, we investigate how well transfer learning is effective for improving the performance (regarding accuracy) of the selected under resourced Semitic language (Amharic) ASR. We aim to adapt pre-trained acoustic models built on two well resourced languages: English and Mandarin. In the speech recognition community, these source languages are considered to be widely accepted as resource rich languages for speech recognition research.

Among other Afro-Asiatic languages, Amharic is strongly related with other many Ethiopian and Eritrean Semitic (e.g., Tigrinya) and non-Semitic Afro-Asiatic (e.g., Afar) languages. Thus, the learning transfer methods achieved in this study could potentially be further transferred to several under resourced Ethiopian and Eritrean languages.

In this paper, we discuss related works in Section 2, transfer leaning in Section 3, the experimental setup in Section 4, the results and discussion in Section 5, the challenges and solutions in Section 6 and, finally, future work and conclusion in Section 7.

2. Related Work

Even though it seems to be difficult to find published articles on transfer learning that are targeted directly at Semitic languages, there are a number of studies (Abate et al., 2009; Yifiru, 2003; Tachbelie et al., 2014; Melese et al., 2017) on the development of ASR for Amharic using conventional methods. Also in (Karafiát et al., 2017; Huang et al., 2013; Rosenberg et al., 2017), some European and other low-resourced languages have been investigated using multilingual transfer learning.

A survey study can be found in (Abate et al., 2009), which summarizes the ASR research attempted for Amharic over the years (2001-2015). According to the survey, speech recognition systems ranging from syllable to sentence level detection, from speaker dependent to speaker independent speech recognition, are built. However, most studies only built proof-of-concept prototypes using quite limited data,

similar acoustic modeling techniques i.e. HMM (Hidden Markov Model) (Rabiner, 1989) and tools such as HTK (HMM Tool Kit). State of the art methods such as deep learning (neural methods) do not seem to be investigated yet for Amharic, while the survey was conducted.

Compared to other languages where ASR is being used in various speech technology applications, ASR research for Amharic is very young. There are, of course, a few attempts to integrate an Amharic ASR into different applications, for example, the Microsoft Word application to enable hands-free interactions and support speech commands. Also in (Woldemariam, 2018; Karafiát et al., 2017; Rosenberg et al., 2017) some effort has been made to build a deep neural network (DNN) based ASR for Amharic.

For instance authors in (Woldemariam, 2018) design an ASR-named entity recognition (NER) pipeline that serves as a meta-data extractor in a cross-media framework. The ASR-NER pipeline aims to generate speech transcriptions from audio/video content and tags words in the transcriptions with part-of-speech tags. That potentially helps index Amharic content with those tags and improves their searchability (Chang et al., 2005; Le et al., 2017). However, relatively the recognition quality of the ASR is low and needs to be improved further.

Among other alternative ways to improve the speech recognition accuracy such as increasing training data, improving the quality of language models and pronunciation dictionaries, adapting pre-trained acoustic models available for other languages seems to be more reasonable in terms of resource requirements and time. For example, Jui-Ting et al. in (Huang et al., 2013) experimented with neural net based ASR models transferring for European languages (French, German, Spanish and Italian) and achieved relative WER reductions up to 28%.

There are also some attempts (Manohar et al., 2017; Elmahdy et al., 2013) on adapting cross-lingual acoustic models for Arabic. However, the transfer learning methods used in these studies used to just solve speech recognition errors caused by out-domain-data problems. The authors in (Manohar et al., 2017) apply the transfer learning approach to acoustic models trained on a corpus of multi-dialect Arabic TV broadcast to the YouTube video corpus. In their experiments, all the hidden layers from the source model transferred to the target model and the target model gives an 11.35% absolute improvement over the baseline system. The authors in (Elmahdy et al., 2013) investigate the joint training adaptation approach to improve an acoustic model trained on one of the dialects of Arabic i.e, Qutari.

3. Transfer Learning for Less-Resourced Languages

One way of adapting models trained for one domain/language to another is through the transfer learning method (Wang and Zheng, 2015; Huang et al., 2013; Ghahremani et al., 2017). Parameters learned by a pre-trained deep neural net based model can be transferred to new domains/languages. These parameters are neural net weights estimated and computed during model training.

In natural language processing (NLP), this approach can be applied to transfer knowledge between models trained on data of different related languages. For example, Greg et al. in (Durrett et al., 2012) applies transfer learning in dependency parsing by using bilingual lexicons of two different languages, acting as source and target. The authors make syntactic analysis of parallel sentences of resource-rich and resource-poor languages, to transfer learned syntactic knowledge between words representing similar concepts. For instance, if there are two words (that mean the same thing) in English and German sentences, the contextual syntactic information of the word in English, could be transferred to the word belonging to German, though not always applicable (effective). In dependency parsing, that potentially used to determine lexical attachment choices during a syntactic tree construction. By using this idea, the authors in (Durrett et al., 2012) reported that significant gains have been achieved for some target languages.

Transfer learning has also been effectively used in speech recognition applications, to adapt acoustic models trained for resource-rich domains (or well-resourced languages) to under-resourced domains (or less-resourced languages).

The main advantages of the adaptation is to tackle resource scarcity and reduce the effort of preparing a huge amount data which is always a challenge in speech recognition research. Moreover, as is evident from some studies (Ghahremani et al., 2017; Yan et al., 2018; Zhuang et al., 2017; Feng and Lee, 2018), the resulting transfered acoustic models perform better as long as the source models perform well and are related with target languages/domains.

Unlike other adaptation methods such as multilingual training, transfer learning does not necessarily require a shared universal phone set across languages. Multilingual training performs multitasking training, that includes merging data from source and target languages, and build a shared acoustic model where each language has its own final (softmax) layer. On the other hand, transfer learning does not necessarily require phone set matching. That practical reason makes it preferable for less-resourced languages, particularly those whose phone set is very unique and hard to share with others.

Compared to other under resourced European languages where multilingual/cross-lingual model adaptation is quite applicable due to their relatedness, Semitic languages seem to have their own unique phone sets along with phonetic representations that are hard to map with other languages. Thus, employing the learning transfer approach seem to be a reasonable choice to serve under resourced Semitic languages.

Knowledge transfer in transfer learning can be achieved by sharing hidden layers of already trained neural net based models. While the input and final layers of pre-trained models are assumed to be language dependent, the hidden layers are regarded as language independent and transferable between languages.

During the learning transfer process, the final layer gets removed from the source models and replaced by the final layer of the model being trained for the corresponding target languages. Also, the input layer gets trained on the data of the target languages. Finally, the whole network is re-trained with the shared hidden layers and evaluated on the target language test set (Zhuang et al., 2017; Feng and Lee, 2018).

Generally speaking, transfer learning in speech recognition can be summarized with the four steps: building acoustic models on source languages, removing the final layers from the trained models, transferring hidden layers to target languages and re-train the models with new data.

In practice, however, several challenges may occur during the application of transfer learning, these include mismatching between source and target languages in many ways such as variations in extracted acoustic features. Unless properly handled, these mismatching potentially lead to a high speech recognition error.

4. Experimental Setup

Our experiments cover three different languages: Amharic, English and Chinese Mandarin. While Amharic is intended to be a target language, English and Chinese are source languages.

Kaldi (Povey et al., 2011) has been used as an open speech recognition toolkit for ASR prototypes development and evaluation. It has been configured with the CUDA toolkit to access the GPU card (GeForce GTX 1050 Ti) installed on our machine and train DNN models on the selected source and target languages.

4.1. Datasets

An Amharic corpus consists of read speech collected from 100 different Amharic native speakers of 20 hours for training and 2 hours for testing. Information regarding gender distributions across the speakers is not provided in the paper (Tachbelie et al., 2014) where the corpus with its lexicon is prepared as experimental data. As part of our study, we built different size n-gram language models (n=3 to 7) using the SRILM[2] language modeling toolkit.

An English corpus (Panayotov et al., 2015)] consists of two sets (100 and 360 hours) of read speech (the majority have the US English accent) prepared from audio books, collected from OpenSLR (open speech and language resources)[3]. The test set contains 5.4 hours of speech. We run two different experiments corresponding to the two sets of speech corpus and build acoustic models on each set. In order to assess how the amount of training data affects the result of transfer learning, the first experiment is done with the acoustic model trained on the 100 hours (English-1) set and the second one involves combining the two sets (English-2) together, (we refer English-1 to the 100 hours set and English-2 to the 460 hours set).

A Mandarin corpus (Bu et al., 2017)] contains 178 hours (of which 85% is for training and the remaining is for testing) of speech collected from 400 speakers, provided by Beijing Shell Technology[4] as an open source database. That is the largest Mandarin corpus available for ASR research (Bu et al., 2017) and can be found at OpenSLR[5].

---

[2]http://www.speech.sri.com/projects/srilm/

[3]http://www.openslr.org/12/

[4]http://www.aishelltech.com/kysjcp

[5]http://www.openslr.org/33/

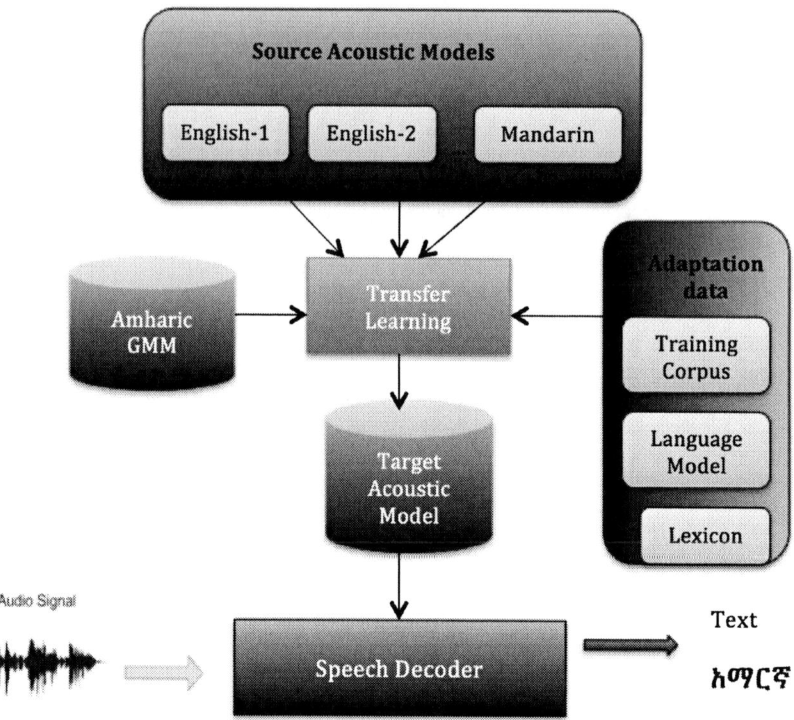

Figure 1: The transfer learning based architecture of the proposed Amharic ASR

4.2. Baseline Systems

A deep neural net baseline system has been built for each language and evaluated on their test sets (the results are summarized in Table 1) after the development of context dependent GMM-HMMs (Gaussian mixture model-hidden Markov model) acoustic models.

The GMM-HMM models are tri-phone based intermediate acoustic models, generated after mono-phone models training. And they are used for the purpose of doing initial alignment (speech with text) for the DNN training.

The DNN acoustic models trained on English and Mandarin, are used for as seed models to be adapted to Amharic. These models make use of a TDNN (time delay deep neural network) architecture (Peddinti et al., 2015) along with the ReLU (rectified linear unit) and 6 hidden layers, each layer has 1026 units. The TDNN architecture is capable of capturing wider context information, and is more efficient than other DNN architectures (e.g. recurrent neural networks).

During training, each frame of the input data is provided with 5 preceding and 5 succeeding frames as contextual information to the network. In order to optimize model parameters (weights and biases), the stochastic gradient descent algorithm is used and run iteratively over the development set. Prior to that, features required to train acoustic models are extracted from the speech corpus of each language. These include MFCC (Mel-Frequency Cepstrum Coefficients) and I-vector (George et al., 2013) features.

In addition, speaker independent features are extracted using LDA (Linear Discriminant Analysis) and MLLT (Maximum Likelihood Transform) techniques (Gales, 1998; Gopinath, 1998).

4.3. Transfered Models

Before the actual transfer learning process, we did feature dimension matching between the source languages and the target languages. That is achieved by taking the matrix of the source languages produced at the LDA stage, providing to the target language to re-train their LDA model. We also need to make sure that they have the same splicing settings which determine the context size of concatenated speech segments. For example, while the Chinese corpus uses the splicing options of "–left-context=5 –right-context=5", relatively Amharic uses narrow context i.e. "–left-context=3 –right-context=3".

Compared to the English model, preparing and adapting from the Mandarin model is quite difficult as it uses very different acoustic features and parameter settings than Amharic and English, due to its tonal nature, (discussed in detail in the challenges and solutions section).

Then we provided the transfer learning algorithm the two required inputs for generating transfered models: pre-trained acoustic models of the sources languages (English and Mandarin), and the adaptation data from the target language (Amharic) along with its GMM-HMM model (as illustrated in Figure 1). The adaptation data includes the speech and text corpus, the lexicon and the language model prepared for Amharic.

The learning algorithm, then takes each pre-trained acoustic model at a time and removes their final (softmax) layer and transfers all the hidden layers to the target Amharic model. Once the transfer has been made, the final layer of the target model gets trained on the adaptation data and added on top of the transferred layers. Also, the weights and biases of the resulting acoustic model is re-computed and fine-tuned with back-propagation. As part of the target model fine-tuning, a smaller learning rate (compared to the learning rate set to the source models) has been used. Among other hyper-parameters (e.g, batch size, number of transferred layers, and so on), lowering the learning rate seems to gives a better result (Ghahremani et al., 2017; Ghoshal et al., 2013). Finally, each version of the final transfered model has been evaluated on the Amharic test set. The results from the transfer learning algorithm have been summarized in Table 1.

5. Results and Discussions

As the experimental results shown in Table 1, the recognition performance of the baseline acoustic model trained for Amharic has been significantly improved through transfer learning. In the best case scenario, adapting from English-2 (with 460 hours), yields improvement over the baseline Amharic ASR with WER decreasing from 38.72% to 24.50% (14.22% absolute). Next, a significant (absolute) improvement is achieved by the model transferred from Engilsh-1 (with 100 hours) to Amharic by 13.66%. The Mandarin model gives a 10.25% absolute reduction over the baseline Amharic model.

Baseline Models	WER(%)
Amharic	38.72
English-1	8.06
English-2	**5.75**
Mandarin	14.65

Adapted Models		
Source Model	Target Model	WER%
English-1		25.06
English-2	Amharic	**24.50**
Mandarin		28.47

Table 1: Experimental results from the baseline and the adapted acoustic models

We attempt to analyze the results across three important parameters: the relatedness between the source and the target languages, the quality of the source models, the amount of the data used to train the source languages. We also consider other possible independent factors that potentially influence the performance of the adapted acoustic model and provide analysis on phonetic similarities/ differences of source-target models.

5.1. Impacts and Implications of Source-Target Models Relatedness over Speech Recognition

Basically, in transfer leaning there is a general intuitive assumption that, more or less, natural languages share similar characteristics and are guided by common linguistic principles (Wang and Zheng, 2015). That leads transfer learning to be carried out between two unrelated languages, though more effective when the source and the target languages are somehow similar.

When it comes to this study, assessing how the similarity of the source languages (English and Mandarin) with Amharic impacted the speech recognition performance of the resulting acoustic model is not easy, as there is no direct relationship between them in terms of phonology. While Amharic is one of the most phonetic languages, English and Mandarin are viewed as non-phonetic. That means, in the phonetic languages, a grapheme (alphabetic letters) always has the same sound regardless of its context, whereas in the non-phonetic languages, a single phoneme might have multiple phone realization (variants) depending on its context. Of course, some Amharic speech units have various orthographic representations, but such variations do not affect meanings of words.

Furthermore, there is not sufficient literature that clearly show that how the phonology of such languages associated with Amharic. Relatively speaking, while there are a few investigations (Gashaw, 2017; Yimam, 2000) on phonetic similarity between Amharic and English, there does not seem to exist any studies between Amharic and Mandarin. For instance, Judith et al. in (Judith et al., 2008) show Amharic incorporates several English loan words into its vocabulary, these words are mainly from medical and technology domains. That somehow increases the chance of shared medical or technological terms for being correctly recognized by the adapted acoustic models. In relation to that, however, the size of the Amharic lexicon used in this study is quite small (i.e., 65k), for example, compared to English (i.e., 130k).

Also, the grapheme-to-phoneme (letter-to-sound) rules used in the lexicon do not seem to capture complex syllabification phenomena (e.g., gemminnation, presence of the epenthetic vowel) that typically occur in the Amharic phonetics (Hailu and Hailemariam, 2012; Sebsibe et al., 2004; Demeke and Hailemariam, 2012). Obviously, that causes the OOV (out-of-vocabulary) words (new unseen words that do not belong to a lexicon) problem and increases the recognition error during decoding. As observed from the decoding results in Table 1, the performance of the acoustic models trained on such source languages have been impacted by their lexicon size and show differences over Amharic. So, increasing the Amharic lexicon's size could minimize the effect of the OOV words problem and reduce recognition errors. In addition to that, improving the quality of the lexicon using a grapheme-to-phoneme converter that better detects syllable structures of Amharic words might enhance the recognition performance of the Amharic acoustic models.

5.1.1. Phonetic Inventory Overlapping between Source and Target Models

One of the most important aspects of source-target models' relatedness is the similarity between them at the phone level, as the potential underlying reasons for speech recognition errors of the adapted acoustic models might be pretty much related with phonetic mismatching between the target and the source models (Wang and Zheng, 2015; Huang et al., 2013; Ghahremani et al., 2017). During weights (model parameters) transfer, the internal (transferable) DNN layers get trained on source models' phone sets. So, ideally having similar phone sets between source and target languages highly improves the quality of the target models. However, while that is not the case between Amharic and Mandarin, there is partial overlapping between Amharic and English (Gashaw, 2017). Baye in (Yimam, 2000) reveals some similarities between speech units (vowels and consonants) of Amharic and English including their articulation.

Further investigations and understanding of similarities (especially between Amharic and other tonal languages including Mandarin) at the phone level would be interesting as future directions to effectively benefit out of transfer learning.

Looking into the corpus structure used, and domains covered by English and Mandarin, while there are some similar features (e.g. sampling frequency and audio recordings quality) shared between them, the English corpus contains only read speech and the Mandarin corpus mixes both read and telephone speech. On the other hand, the Amharic speech corpus (Tachbelie et al., 2014) contains read speech. That might slightly cause bias towards English. Thus, these facts provide us important clues why adapting the English acoustic model to Amharic is more effective in reducing speech recognition errors.

5.2. Impacts and Implications of the Quality of Source Models over Speech Recognition

The other most important factor is the quality of the source acoustic models. However, considering that the two source models are evaluated on different test sets, it is hard to exactly measure the quality difference between them. Thus, we take the comparisons made between the quality of the acoustic models of English and Mandarin in a relative sense. As shown in Table 1, the baseline systems of English outperform the Mandarin model. As also observed from the WER results of the target models, the Amharic models transferred from English outperform the models transferred from Mandarin. That partially indicates how the quality of the source models affects the quality of the target model.

Probably, that is not always the case because tonal languages like Mandarin can be enhanced by using pitch features and those features have much less influence on nontonal target languages like Amharic. However, as very significant part of prosodic information (e.g., duration, intonation) of speech, adding the pitch features potentially helps for capturing emotions in speech for both the source and target languages. For instance, effectively detecting such information by acoustic models used, for instance in spoken dialog applications, leads to better decisions (Min and Shrikanth, 2005) during human-machine communications.

Therefore, different results might be obtained, if these features are included in both source and target languages.

5.3. Impacts and Implications of the Data Size of Source Models over Speech Recognition

In general, regardless of acoustic models adaptation, the quality of any ASR system is heavily dependent on the quantity of the training data. That is also true in case of transfer learning model adaptation. In our experiment, the model trained on a largest data i.e., English model, has the lowest WER, whereas, the model trained on the smallest data i.e., Amharic, has the highest WER. Also, the target model transfered from the source model trained on the largest dataset yields the best WER. However, the training data size of the Mandarin model is greater than the English-1 by 78 hours, yet the source model trained on English-1 outperforms the Mandarin one by a WER of 6.59%. Also, the transfered model from the Mandarin has slightly higher WER than English-1. This indicates that, the recognition performance of the target models seem to be more sensitive to the quality of the source models than the quantity of the data set where the source models are trained on.

5.4. Impacts and Implications of Other Independent Linguistic Factors over Speech Recognition

It is also worth considering other linguistic factors that are pertinent for understanding the cause of the target model recognition errors. Some of the factors are pretty much inherent to the linguistic and phonetic nature of Amharic, which also apply to other Semitic languages.

Morphologically, Amharic is highly inflectional and complex. That implies, a single Amharic word could appear in many alternative forms conveying various lexical meanings. Like any NLP systems, the Amharic ASR is affected by such morphological complexity. Moreover, as discussed above the Amharic lexicon used in this study is too limited to handle words coming in various derivations. That potentially leads to the OOV problem. To partially address such problem the text corpus containing speech transcriptions has been segmented into morphemes. Also the entries of the lexicon and the language model are made to be morpheme based. Although such approach helps achieve a reasonable performance improvement over word-based ASR, it still gets challenged with OOV words unless supported with a high quality morphology analyzer.

Among other speech sounds in Amharic that could affect the quality of acoustic models, possibly leads to speech recognition errors is the epenthetic vowel (i.e., /ix/) (Sebsibe et al., 2004). While being present in spoken words or utterances, mostly absent in the corresponding training transcriptions causes acoustic confusability. Effective handling of such vowel during acoustic models building takes a bit of research effort, particularly in the context of speech recognition.

6. Challenges and Solutions

In our experiments, compared to English models, adapting from Mandarin seems to be a bit complex and requires more effort due to the presence of extra dimensions (added to capture the tonal nature of Mandarin) in the trained acoustic network. Originally, the corpus is prepared to have 43 dimensions, that quite deviate from the standard followed to develop ASR for other languages. There are at least two alternative solutions: either adjusting the dimensionality of the adaptation data or reducing the dimensionality of the features by which the network trained on. Relatively the former seems to be difficult as it affects the target language and takes a bit of effort than the later option. We, therefore, took the later option in order to solve the problem and align with the dimension of the adaptation data used by Amharic. Investigating speech recognition methods, particularly transfer learning is very expensive in many ways. Because most of transfer learning related studies (Karafiát et al., 2017) are based on the proprietary speech corpora mostly purchase from LCD (Linguistic Data Consortium)[6]. Even worse, they released data for some selected languages. For instance, while it is possible to get LDC datasets for other low-resourced languages (e.g., Swahili) with a reasonable price, the separate Amharic datasets are not released yet. The one which is available (by the time this research has been conducted) in LDC is packed with other languages, and to buy the whole pack is really quite expensive.

Therefore, our study is limited to the data available from open source providers. For this reason, in our experiments, relatively well resourced Semitic languages e.g., Arabic, are not considered as source languages. Moreover, that affects the flexibility of our experiments, and experimenting with other variants of the transfered learning approach is quite difficult.

Although transfer learning seems to be a good alternative approach to deal with the problem of resource scarcity, it heavily depends on several pre-conditions that need to be met in advance. Satisfying these requirements, in turn, become challenging in terms of time and cost.

Apart from failing to tackle some mis-match conditions between source and target languages, the lack of deep neural net based computing resources (e.g., GPU) needed for extremely large matrix operations seriously affect the expected results. To meet such challenge and be able to run transfer learning experiments on our server, we took different actions, reducing the size of frames processed at a time, the number of training/decoding jobs and so on. Our experiments have been based on an exclusive use of a single GPU processor with limited memory. That is only able to run one job at a time. That affected the experiments in many ways, for example, limiting the training with certain parameter settings (instead of trying to use possible alternative parameters) and slowing down the training processes, in particularly training larger acoustic models (e.g, the English model with 460 hours takes about a week).

7. Conclusions and Future Work

We conducted transfer learning experiments with selected source and target languages. As a result, we demonstrate that transfer learning could improve the recognition performance of the selected Semitic language. We also attempted to assess the factors affecting the quality (speech recognition performance) of the results obtained from transfer

---

⁶https://www.ldc.upenn.edu/

learning. Our assessment partially reveals that, the relatedness (in a relative sense) of the source languages with the target language has high impact than other related factors discussed in Section 4. Due to this reason, the Amharic ASR models transfered from English outperform the model transfered from Mandarin. Also within English source models, the model trained on the larger data set gives better recognition performance.

According to our experimental results, transfer learning seems to be a very effective method as long as the pre-conditions discussed above are sufficiently met. However, most under-resourced Semitic languages did not take advantage of such recently introduced model adapting methods due to various reasons. We think that this research effort sheds light for investigating transfer learning for other related Semitic languages such as Tigrinya, Arabic, Hebrew and so on. Thus, in the future, it is very interesting to further explore how these languages benefit from the transfer learning approach. Moreover, we consider to investigate other model adaptation methods, in particular multilingual training with additional open source multilingual data and powerful computing resources.

It would also be interesting to evaluate how well the resulting acoustic models perform in various speech based applications such as machine translation, and media analysis frameworks.

8. Acknowledgments

We acknowledge the financial support from the Kempe foundation, Sweden.

9. Bibliographical References

Abate, S., Tachbelie, M., and Menze, W. (2009). Amharic speech recognition: Past present and future. In *In: Proceedings of the 16th International Conference of Ethiopian Studies*, pages 1391–1401.

Besacier, L., Barnard, E., Karpov, A., and Schultz, T. (2014). Automatic speech recognition for under-resourced languages. *Speech Communication*, 56:85–100.

Bu, H., Du, J., Na, X., Wu, B., and Zheng, H. (2017). Aishell-1: An open-source mandarin speech corpus and a speech recognition baseline. *2017 20th Conference of the Oriental Chapter of the International Coordinating Committee on Speech Databases and Speech I/O Systems and Assessment (O-COCOSDA)*, pages 1–5.

Chang, S.-F., Manmatha, R., and Chua, T.-S. (2005). Combining text and audio-visible features in video indexing. In *Acoustics, Speech, and Signal Processing*, pages 1005–1008.

Das, A., Jyothi, P., and Hasegawa-Johnson, M. (2016). Automatic speech recognition using probabilistic transcriptions in swahili, amharic, and dinka. In *INTERSPEECH*, pages 3524–3528.

Demeke, Y. and Hailemariam, S. (2012). Duration modeling of phonemes for amharic text to speech system. In *Proceedings of the International Conference on Management of Emergent Digital EcoSystems (MEDES)*, pages 1–7.

Durrett, G., Pauls, A., and Klein, D. (2012). Syntactic transfer using a bilingual lexicon. In *EMNLP-CoNLL*.

Elmahdy, M., Hasegawa-Johnson, M., and Mustafawi, E. (2013). A transfer learning approach for under-resourced arabic dialects speech recognition. In *Proceedings of the 6th Language and Technology Conference*, page 290â293.

Farzad, E. and Eva, K. (1998). Speech technology in computer-aided language learning: Strengths and limitations of a new call paradigm. *Language Learning & Technology*, 2(1):45–60.

Feng, S. and Lee, T. (2018). Improving cross-lingual knowledge transferability using multilingual tdnn-blstm with language-dependent pre-final layer. In *Interspeech*, pages 2439–2443.

Gales, M. (1998). Maximum likelihood linear transformations for hmm-based speech recognition. *Computer Science and Language*, 12:75–98.

Gashaw, A. (2017). Rhythm in ethiopian english: Implications for the teaching of english prosody. *International Journal of Education and Literacy Studies*, 5(1):13–19.

George, S., Hagen, S., David, N., and Michael, P. (2013). Speaker adaptation of neural network acoustic models using i-vectors. In *2013 IEEE Workshop on Automatic Speech Recognition and Understanding*, pages 55–59.

Ghahremani, P., Manohar, V., Hadian, H., Povey, D., and Khudanpur, S. (2017). Investigation of transfer learning for asr using lf-mmi trained neural networks. *2017 IEEE Automatic Speech Recognition and Understanding Workshop (ASRU)*, pages 279–286.

Ghoshal, A., Swietojanski, P., and Renals, S. (2013). Multilingual training of deep neural networks. *2013 IEEE International Conference on Acoustics Speech and Signal Processing*, pages 7319–7323.

Gopinath, R. (1998). Maximum likelihood modeling with gaussian distributions for classification. In *Proceedings of the 1998 IEEE International Conference on Acoustics, Speech and Signal Processing, ICASSP'98*, pages 661–664.

Hailu, N. and Hailemariam, S. (2012). Modeling improved syllabification algorithm for amharic. In *Proceedings of the International Conference on Management of Emergent Digital EcoSystems*, pages 16–21.

Huang, J.-T., Li, J., Yu, D., Deng, L., and Gong, Y. (2013). Cross-language knowledge transfer using multilingual deep neural network with shared hidden layers. *2013 IEEE International Conference on Acoustics Speech and Signal Processing*, pages 7304–7308.

Judith, R., Rotem, K., and MyiLibrary. (2008). *Globally speaking : motives for adopting English vocabulary in other languages*. Clevedon UK ; Buffalo [N.Y.] : Multilingual Matters, New York.

Karafiát, M., Baskar, M. K., Matejka, P., Veselý, K., Grézl, F., Burget, L., and Cernocký, J. (2017). 2016 but babel system: Multilingual blstm acoustic model with i-vector based adaptation. In *The Proceedings of INTERSPEECH 2017*, pages 719–723.

Karafiát, M., Baskar, M. K., Veselý, K., Grézl, F., Burget, L., and ernocký, J. (2018). Analysis of multilingual blstm acoustic model on low and high resource languages. *2018 IEEE International Conference on Acoustics, Speech and Signal Processing (ICASSP)*, pages 5789–5793.

Le, N., Bredin, H., Sargent, G., India, M., Lopez-Otero, P., Barras, C., Guinaudeau, C., Gravier, G., da Fonseca, G. B., Freire, I. L., do Patrocínio, Z. K. G., Guimarães, S. J. F., Martí, G., Morros, J. R., Hernando, J., Fernández, L. D., García-Mateo, C., Meignier, S., and Odobez, J.-M. (2017). Towards large scale multimedia indexing: A case study on person discovery in broadcast news. In *Proceedings of International Workshop on Content-Based Multimedia Retrieval*, pages 1–6.

Manohar, V., Povey, D., and Khudanpur, S. (2017). Jhu kaldi system for arabic mgb-3 asr challenge using diarization audio-transcript alignment and transfer learning. *2017 IEEE Automatic Speech Recognition and Understanding Workshop (ASRU)*, pages 346–352.

Melese, M., Besacier, L., and Meshesha, M. (2017). Amharic-english speech translation in tourism domain. In *SCNLP@EMNLP 2017*.

Mezaris, V., Gidaros, S., Papadopoulos, G. T., Kasper, W., Steffen, J., Ordelman, R., Huijbregts, M., de Jong, F., Kompatsiaris, Y., and Strintzis, M. G. (2010). A system for the semantic multimodal analysis of news audio-visual content. *EURASIP Journal on Advances in Signal Processing*, 2010:1–16.

Min, L. and Shrikanth, N. (2005). Toward detecting emotions in spoken dialogs. *IEEE transactions on speech and audio processing*, 13(2):293–303.

Peddinti, V., Povey, D., and Khudanpur, S. (2015). A time delay neural network architecture for efficient modeling of long temporal contexts. In *The Proceedings of INTERSPEECH 2015*, pages 3214–3218.

Povey, D., Ghoshal, A., Boulianne, G., Burget, L., Glembek, O., Goel, N. K., Hannemann, M., Motlícek, P., Qian, Y., Schwarz, P., Silovský, J., Stemmer, G., and Veselý, K. (2011). The Kaldi speech recognition toolkit. In *IEEE 2011 Workshop on Automatic Speech Recognition and Understanding*.

Rabiner, L. R. (1989). A tutorial on hidden Markov models and selected applications in speech recognition. *Proceedings of the IEEE*, 77(2):257–286.

Rosenberg, A., Audhkhasi, K., Sethy, A., Ramabhadran, B., and Picheny, M. (2017). End-to-end speech recognition and keyword search on low-resource languages. *2017 IEEE International Conference on Acoustics, Speech and Signal Processing (ICASSP)*, pages 5280–5284.

Sebsibe, H., Prahallad, K., Alan, B., Rohit, K., and Rajeev, S. (2004). Unit selection voice for amharic using festvox. In *Fifth ISCA Workshop on Speech Synthesis*, pages 103–107.

Tachbelie, M., Abate, S., and Besacier, L. (2014). Using different acoustic lexical and language modeling units for asr of an under-resourced language - amharic. *Speech Communication*, 56:181–194.

Wang, D. and Zheng, T. F. (2015). Transfer learning for speech and language processing. *2015 Asia-Pacific*

Signal and Information Processing Association Annual Summit and Conference (APSIPA), pages 1225–1237.

Woldemariam, Y. (2018). *Natural Language Processing in Cross-Media Analysis*. Licentiate thesis, Faculty of Science and Technology, Umeå University, Jun.

Yan, J., Yu, H., and Li, G. (2018). Tibetan acoustic model research based on tdnn. *2018 Asia-Pacific Signal and Information Processing Association Annual Summit and Conference (APSIPA ASC)*, pages 601–604.

Yifiru, M. (2003). Automatic amharic speech recognition system to command and control computers. Master's thesis, School of Information Studies for Africa, Addis Ababa University.

Yimam, B. (2000). *Amharic Grammar*. Eleni Publishing Ltd, Addis Ababa.

Zhuang, X., Ghoshal, A., Rosti, A.-V., Paulik, M., and Liu, D. (2017). Improving dnn bluetooth narrowband acoustic models by cross-bandwidth and cross-lingual initialization. In *INTERSPEECH*, pages 2148–2152.

10.   Language Resource References

Hui Bu and Jiayu Du and Xingyu Na and Bengu Wu and Hao Zheng. (2017). *Aishell ASR corpus.* provided by Beijing Shell Technology and distributed via OpenSLR, ISLRN SLR33.

ELRA-W0074. (2014). *Amharic-English bilingual corpus, distributed via ELRA,1.0.* distributed via ELRA,1.0, 1.0, ISLRN 590-255-335-719-0.

Elodie Gauthier and Laurent Besacier and Sylvie Voisin and Michael Melese and Uriel Pascal Elingui. (2016). *Collecting Resources in Sub-Saharan African Languages for Automatic Speech Recognition: a Case Study of Wolof.* European Language Resources Association (ELRA), Proceedings of the Tenth International Conference on Language Resources and Evaluation (LREC'16).

HaBiT. (2016). *Harvesting big text data for under-resourced languages.* distributed via Natural Language Processing Centre, Faculty of Informatics, Masaryk University.

Vassil Panayotov and Guoguo Chen and Daniel Povey and Sanjeev Khudanpur. (2015). *LibriSpeech ASR corpus.* distributed via OpenSLR, ISLRN SLR12.

Proceedings of the 1st Joint SLTU and CCURL Workshop (SLTU-CCURL 2020), pages 70–78
Language Resources and Evaluation Conference (LREC 2020), Marseille, 11–16 May 2020
© European Language Resources Association (ELRA), licensed under CC-BY-NC

Semi-supervised Acoustic Modelling for Five-lingual Code-switched ASR using Automatically-segmented Soap Opera Speech

Nick Wilkinson[1], Astik Biswas[1], Emre Yılmaz[2], Febe de Wet[1], Ewald van der Westhuizen[1], Thomas Niesler[1]

[1] Department of Electrical and Electronic Engineering, Stellenbosch University, South Africa
[2] Department of Electrical and Computer Engineering, National University of Singapore, Singapore
{nwilkinson, abiswas, fdw, ewaldvdw, trn}@sun.ac.za, emre@nus.edu.sg

Abstract

This paper considers the impact of automatic segmentation on the fully-automatic, semi-supervised training of automatic speech recognition (ASR) systems for five-lingual code-switched (CS) speech. Four automatic segmentation techniques were evaluated in terms of the recognition performance of an ASR system trained on the resulting segments in a semi-supervised manner. The systems' output was compared with the recognition rates achieved by a semi-supervised system trained on manually assigned segments. Three of the automatic techniques use a newly proposed convolutional neural network (CNN) model for framewise classification, and include a novel form of HMM smoothing of the CNN outputs. Automatic segmentation was applied in combination with automatic speaker diarization. The best-performing segmentation technique was also tested without speaker diarization. An evaluation based on 248 unsegmented soap opera episodes indicated that voice activity detection (VAD) based on a CNN followed by Gaussian mixture model-hidden Markov model smoothing (CNN-GMM-HMM) yields the best ASR performance. The semi-supervised system trained with the resulting segments achieved an overall WER improvement of 1.1% absolute over the system trained with manually created segments. Furthermore, we found that system performance improved even further when the automatic segmentation was used in conjunction with speaker diarization.

Keywords: code-switched speech, under-resourced languages, automatic segmentation, semi-supervised training

1. Introduction

Code-switching is the alternation between two or more languages by a single speaker during discourse, and is a common phenomenon in multilingual societies. In South Africa, for example, 11 official and geographically co-located languages are in use, including English which serves as the lingua franca. Here, speakers frequently code-switch between English, a highly-resourced language, and their Bantu mother tongue, which is in comparison highly under-resourced.

The automatic recognition of code-switched speech has become a topic of growing research interest, as reflected by the increasing number of language pairs that have recently been studied. While English-Mandarin has received extensive attention (Li and Fung, 2013; Zeng et al., 2018; Vu et al., 2012; Taneja et al., 2019), other language pairs such as Frisian-Dutch (Yılmaz et al., 2016; Yılmaz et al., 2018), Hindi-English (Pandey et al., 2018; Emond et al., 2018; Ganji et al., 2019), English-Malay (Ahmed and Tan, 2012), Japanese-English (Nakayama et al., 2018) and French-Arabic (Amazouz et al., 2017) have also attracted interest. We have introduced the first South African corpus of multilingual code-switched soap opera speech in (van der Westhuizen and Niesler, 2018).

For code-switched speech, the development of robust acoustic and language models that are able to extend across language switches is a challenging task. When one or more of the languages are under-resourced, as it is in our case, data sparsity limits modelling capacity and this challenge is amplified. Acoustic data that includes code-switching is extremely hard to find, because it usually does not occur in formal conversation, such as broadcast news, and also because it requires skilled multilingual language practitioners for its annotation. The result is that manually-prepared

datasets including code-switched speech in Africa are destined to remain rare and small.

In previous work, we have demonstrated that multilingual training using in-domain soap opera code-switched speech and poorly matched monolingual South African speech improves the performance of both bilingual and five-lingual automatic speech recognition (ASR) systems when the additional training data is from a closely-related language (Biswas et al., 2018a; Biswas et al., 2018b). Specifically, isiZulu, isiXhosa, Sesotho and Setswana belong to the same Bantu language family and were found to complement each other when combined into a multilingual training set for acoustic modelling. Hence, increasing the amount of in-domain code-switched speech data is a reliable way to achieve more robust ASR. However, the development of such in-domain data is a time-consuming and costly endeavour as it requires highly skilled human annotators and transcribers.

To address this lack of annotated data, automatically transcribed training material has been shown to be useful in under-resourced scenarios using semi-supervised training (Thomas et al., 2013; Yılmaz et al., 2018; Guo et al., 2018). This strategy was successfully implemented on South African code-switched speech to obtain bilingual and five-lingual ASR systems using 11.5 hours of manually segmented but untranscribed soap opera speech (Biswas et al., 2019). Recently a study has analyzed the performance of batch-wise semi-supervised training on South African code-switched ASR (Biswas et al., 2020). However, manual segmentation of the raw soap opera audio by skilled annotators was still required to identify the speech that is useful for ASR. Therefore, this approach is not fully automatic which remains an impediment in resource-scare settings.

In this study, we apply four automated approaches to the

segmentation of soap opera speech and investigate the effect on ASR performance. A conventional energy-based voiced activity detector (VAD) (Povey et al., 2011), as well as CNN-HHM and CNN-GMM-HMM systems that we have developed are used to distinguish between speech, music and noise. In addition, an X-vector DNN embedding system is used for speaker diarization to obtain speaker specific metadata for three of the segmentation approaches (Snyder et al., 2018). For the experiments, 248 complete soap opera episodes, each approximately 22 minutes in length, were used. It is important to note that we also have the manual segmentation (approximately 24 hours of speech) of these 248 episodes and can therefore perform a comparative evaluation with the automated approaches. Semi-supervised systems trained using the manually-segmented speech were used as baselines and compared with systems trained on speech identified by the automatic approaches.

Pseudo-labels or transcriptions of automatically segmented speech were generated using our best baseline systems trained on 21 hours manually transcribed speech and 11 hours of manually segmented but automatically transcribed speech. Given the multilingual nature of the data, the transcription systems must not only provide the orthography, but also the language(s) present at each location in each segment. To achieve this, each segment was presented to four individual code-switching systems as well as to a five-lingual system.

2. Data

For experimentation, we use a corpus of multilingual, code-switched speech compiled from South African soap opera episodes. This corpus contains both manually and automatically-annotated speech divided into four language pairs: English-isiZulu (EZ), English-isiXhosa (EX), English-Setswana (ET), and English-Sesotho (ES). Of the Bantu languages, isiZulu and isiXhosa belong to the Nguni language family while Setswana and Sesotho are Sotho-Tswana languages.

The corpus contains 8 275, 11 352, 6 169, 1 902 and 2 792 unique English, isiZulu, isiXhosa, Setswana and Sesotho words, respectively. IsiZulu and isiXhosa have relatively large vocabularies due their agglutinative nature and conjunctive writing system. Although Setswana and Sesotho are also agglutinative, they use disjunctive writing systems which result in smaller vocabularies than isiZulu and isiXhosa. The speech in the soap opera episodes is also typically fast and often expresses emotion. These aspects of the data in combination with the high prevalence of code-switching makes it a challenging corpus for conducting ASR experiments.

2.1. Manually Segmented and Transcribed Data (ManT)

Our first code-switching ASR systems were developed and evaluated on 14.3 hours of speech divided into four language-balanced sets, as described in (van der Westhuizen and Niesler, 2018). In addition to the language-balanced sets, approximately another nine hours of manually transcribed speech was available. This additional data

is dominated by English and was initially excluded from our training set to avoid bias. However, pilot experiments indicated that, counter to expectations, its inclusion enhanced recognition performance in all languages. The additional data was therefore merged with the balanced sets for the experiments described here. Of this, 21.1 hours is used as a training set, 48 minutes as a development set, and 1.3 hours as a test set. The composition of the unbalanced training set is shown in Table 1.

Language	Mono (m)	CS (m)	Total (h)	Total (%)	Word tokens	Word types
English	755.0	121.8	14.6	69.3	194 426	7 908
isiZulu	92.8	57.4	2.5	11.9	24 412	6 789
isiXhosa	65.1	23.8	1.5	7.0	13 825	5 630
Setswana	36.9	34.5	1.2	5.6	21 409	1 525
Sesotho	44.7	34.0	1.3	6.2	22 226	2 321
Total	994.5	271.5	21.1	100.0	276 290	24 170

Table 1: Duration in minutes (m) and hours (h) as well as word type and token counts for the unbalanced training set.

An overview of the composition of the development (Dev) and test (Test) sets for each language pair is given in Table 2. The table includes values for the total duration as well as the duration of the monolingual and code-switched segments. The test sets contain no monolingual data and a total of approximately 4 000 language switches (English-to-Bantu and Bantu-to-English).

	English-isiZulu				
	emdur	zmdur	ecdur	zcdur	**Total**
Dev	0.0	0.0	4.0	4.0	8.0
Test	0.0	0.0	12.8	17.9	30.4
	English-isiXhosa				
	emdur	xmdur	ecdur	xcdur	**Total**
Dev	2.9	6.5	2.2	2.1	13.7
Test	0.0	0.0	5.6	8.8	14.3
	English-Setswana				
	emdur	tmdur	ecdur	tcdur	**Total**
Dev	0.8	4.3	4.5	4.3	13.8
Test	0.0	0.0	8.9	9.0	17.8
	English-Sesotho				
	emdur	smdur	ecdur	scdur	**Total**
Dev	1.1	5.1	3.0	3.6	12.8
Test	0.0	0.0	7.8	7.7	15.5

Table 2: Duration (minutes) of English, isiZulu, isiXhosa, Sesotho, Setswana monolingual (mdur) and code-switched (cdur) segments in the code-switching development and test sets.

2.2. Manually Segmented Automatically Transcribed Data: Expert Segmentation (AutoT$_{Exp}$)

During corpus development, approximately 11 hours of manually segmented speech (representing 127 different speakers) was produced in addition to the manually transcribed data described in the previous section. Segmentation was performed manually by experienced language practitioners. This dataset (AutoT$_{\text{Exp}}$) was automatically transcribed during our initial investigations into semi-supervised acoustic model training, resulting in 7 951 EZ, 3 796 EX, 11 415 ES and 128 ET segments (Biswas et al., 2019).

2.3. Manually Segmented Automatically Transcribed Data: Non-expert Segmentation (AutoT$_{\text{NonE}}$)

A subsequent phase of corpus development, currently still underway, has produced manual segmentations for a further 248 soap opera episodes. These 248 episodes amount to 89 hours of audio data before segmentation, and 23 hours of speech data (AutoT$_{\text{NonE}}$) after segmentation. The segmentation was not performed by language experts and is therefore expected to be less accurate than that of the AutoT$_{\text{Exp}}$ data. Furthermore South African languages other than the five present in the transcribed data are known to occur in this batch, but to a limited extent.

This set of 248 episodes was used in the automatic segmentation experiments described in the next section because the manually assigned segment labels were available as a reference in the form of AutoT$_{\text{NonE}}$.

3. Automatic Segmentation

A number of automatic segmentation techniques were considered as alternatives to the labour-intensive process of manually segmenting the soap operas. Different voice activity detection (VAD) approaches were combined with the X-vector DNN embedding-based speaker diarization system introduced in (Snyder et al., 2018) to obtain speaker labels. In subsequent ASR experiments, the best performing VAD technique was also evaluated without speaker diarization.

3.1. VAD$_1$: Energy-based

In our first experiment, the X-vector diarization recipe provided in the Kaldi toolkit was applied using an X-vector DNN model pre-trained on wide-band VoxCeleb data (Povey et al., 2011; Nagrani et al., 2017; Chung et al., 2018). This system uses 24-dimensional filterbank features based on 25ms frames. Speech frames are identified using a simple energy threshold and are subsequently passed to the pre-trained DNN which extracts the X-vectors. Finally, probabilistic linear discriminant analysis (PLDA) is applied to the X-vectors, and agglomerative hierarchical clustering is used to assign speaker labels.

A difficulty observed when using this approach was that, while a simple energy VAD works reasonably well under low noise conditions where most frames are speech, it performs poorly when confronted with our soap opera data in which extensive non-speech segments containing music and other sounds are common. Post-diarization listening tests revealed that many non-speech segments were still present in the data classified as speech. Adjustment of the VAD threshold to more aggressively remove non-speech segments resulted in the loss of many speech segments.

3.2. VAD$_2$: CNN-HMM

At the time of writing, the X-vector based system achieved state-of-the-art performance in diarization tasks. However,

Layer	Kernels/Nodes	Activation Function
Convolutional_1	32 (3x3 kernel)	ReLU
Max_Pooling_2	-	-
Convolutional_3	64 (3x3 kernel)	ReLU
Max_Pooling_4	-	-
Convolutional_5	64 (3x3 kernel)	ReLU
Flatten_6	1024	-
Fully_Connected_7	64	ReLU
Fully_Connected_8	2	Sigmoid

Table 3: The CNN architecture used in the VAD systems.

the energy based VAD it uses limits performance. For this reason, efforts to improve automatic segmentation focused on developing improved VAD. Recently, CNNs have been successfully applied to the task of VAD (Thomas et al., 2014), and both large and small architectures have been found to perform well (Sehgal and Kehtarnavaz, 2018; Hershey et al., 2017). In our resource-constrained setting, computational efficiency is important since VAD will most likely occur on a mobile device.

We introduce a small CNN architecture ($\approx$120 000 parameters) implemented in Python, using Tensorflow (v2.0.0) and Keras (v2.2.4-tf), to create a fast, lightweight VAD system whose architecture is shown in Table 3. This system computes 32-dimensional log-mel filterbank energies using a frame length of 10ms and then stacks these over 320ms to form 32x32 spectrogram features as input to the CNN. The CNN was trained on the balanced subset ($\approx$ 53 hours) of Audio Set (Gemmeke et al., 2017) to classify frames as containing "speech" and/or "non-speech".

While our CNN on its own performs well at the VAD task, it fails to capture temporal patterns in the data and was observed to often mislabel single frames within extended sections of speech or non-speech. In an initial attempt to address this, we introduce a HMM for smoothing. The AVA-Speech dataset (Chaudhuri et al., 2018) was used to train our HMMs, and for testing of the final VAD. The full dataset contains $\approx$ 46 hours of densely labeled, multilingual movie data, with the following class labels: "NoSpeech","CleanSpeech", "Speech+Music" and "Speech+Noise". AVA-Speech (train), a randomly selected $\approx$ 23 hour subset of the dataset, was used to train the HMM. Table 4 provides a description of the dataset used for training and testing of the automatic segmentation systems.

For training the "CleanSpeech", "Speech+Music" and "Speech+Noise" classes were treated as a single "speech" class. A two state HMM was defined, with states representing ground truth "speech" and "no-speech" labels respectively. The HMM observations are the binary output of the "speech" neuron in the CNN, which indicates "speech" or "no-speech". Note, the "no-speech" label differs slightly from the "non-speech" label, since the "speech" and "non-speech" sounds can co-occur, whereas "no-speech" implies "speech" does not occur in the signal.

Transition and emission probabilities were trained in a supervised manner, by passing AVA-Speech (train) though the CNN, then using the labels predicted by the CNN and corresponding ground truth labels as observations and hid-

Dataset	Size (hours)	Use
Audio Set	≈ 53	CNN training
AVA-Speech (train)	≈ 23	HMM/GMM-HMM training
AVA-Speech (test)	≈ 23	VAD testing

Table 4: Datasets used for training and testing of automatic segmentation systems.

den state sequences respectively. Viterbi decoding was then used to find the most likely underlying label sequence, given CNN predicted labels. Finally the VAD segments are used as input to the X-vector diarization system.

3.3. VAD$_3$: CNN-GMM-HMM

While the CNN-HMM approach yields a large improvement over the energy-based VAD, it may be possible to improve it further by making use of the CNN soft label outputs, rather than the hard labels obtained by taking the argmax of the CNN outputs. In this case the HMM observation sequence is chosen to consist of the output probabilities computed by the CNN speech neuron, rather than the binary labels. Where the observations were previously modelled as repeated Bernoulli trials, they are now continuous and can therefore be modelled by a more complex distribution function. A 3-mixture GMM for each of the two HMM states was found to be an effective choice. Fewer mixtures led to deteriorated performance, while more mixtures did not result in further improvement. As before, the GMM-HMM is trained on AVA-Speech (train) in a supervised manner and the resulting segments used as input for the X-vector diarization system.

3.4. VAD$_4$: VAD$_3$ Without Speaker Diarization

While the X-vector diarization system is useful for obtaining speaker labels for each segment, it is computationally expensive and represents only a pre-processing step for downstream ASR. To determine its importance, our final experiment used the segments produced by our best performing VAD system directly, without diarization. Hence each segment was treated as being from a different speaker.

4. Automatic Transcription

Recent studies demonstrated that semi-supervised training can improve the performance of Frisian-Dutch code-switched ASR (Yılmaz et al., 2018) as well as South African code-switched ASR (Biswas et al., 2019). The approach taken in this study is illustrated in Figure 1. The figure shows the two phases of semi-supervised training for the parallel bilingual as well as five-lingual configurations: automatic transcription followed by bilingual semi-supervised acoustic model retraining. The five-lingual system was not retrained with the automatically transcribed data for this set of experiments as our primary motive was to study the effect of automatic segmented speech on bilingual semi-supervised ASR.

4.1. Parallel Bilingual Transcription

This system (System A) consists of four subsystems, each corresponding to a language pair for which code-switching

occurs. Acoustic models were trained on the manually segmented and transcribed soap opera data (ManT, described in Section 2.1) pooled with the manually segmented but automatically transcribed speech (AutoT$_{\text{Exp}}$, introduced in Section 2.2). Because the languages spoken in the untranscribed data were unknown, each segment was decoded in parallel by each of the bilingual decoders. The output with the highest confidence score provided both the transcription and a language pair label for each segment.

4.2. Five-lingual Transcription

Some of our previous experiments indicated that the automatic transcriptions generated by the five-lingual baseline model enhanced the performance of the bilingual semi-supervised systems (Biswas et al., 2019). Five-lingual transcriptions were therefore also included in this study. The five-lingual system (System H) is based on a single acoustic model trained on all five languages. It was trained on the same data as the bilingual systems, except for the fact that the AutoT$_{\text{Exp}}$ data was transcribed using a five-lingual baseline model.

Since the five-lingual system is not restricted to bilingual output, its output allows Bantu-to-Bantu language switching. Examples of such switches were indeed observed in the transcriptions. Moreover, the automatically generated transcriptions sometimes contained more than two languages. Although the use of more than two languages within a single segment is not common, we have observed such cases during the compilation of the manually transcribed dataset. For our fast, continuous speech, the automatically generated segments have been observed to produce longer segments than manual segmentation of the data. This increases the likelihood of multiple language switches within the segment. Unfortunately, since the automatic segments are generated from untranscribed data, the degree to which multiple languages occur within a single automatic segment is difficult to quantify.

5. Automatic Speech Recognition

5.1. Acoustic Modelling

All acoustic models were trained using the Kaldi ASR toolkit (Povey et al., 2011) and the data described in Section 2. The models were trained on a multilingual dataset that included all the data in Table 1. In addition, three-fold data augmentation (Ko et al., 2015) was applied prior to feature extraction. The feature set included standard 40-dimensional MFCCs (no derivatives), 3- dimensional pitch and 100 dimensional i-vectors.

The models were trained with lattice free MMI (Povey et al., 2016) using the standard Kaldi CNN-TDNN-F (Povey et al., 2018) Librispeech recipe (6 CNN layers and 10 time-delay layers followed by a rank reduction layer) and the default hyperparameters. All acoustic models consist of a single shared softmax layer for all languages, as in general there is more than one target language in a segment.

No phone merging was performed between languages and the acoustic models were all language dependent. For the bilingual experiments, the multilingual acoustic models were adapted to each of the four target language pairs.

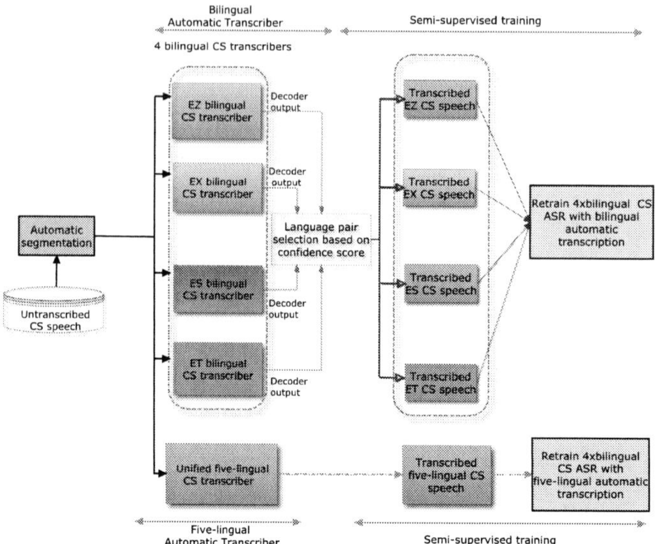

Figure 1: Semi-supervised training framework for bilingual code-switch (CS) ASR. EZ, EX, ES and ET refer to Engish-isiZulu, English-isiXhosa, English-Sesotho and English-Setswana language pairs respectively.

5.2.   Language Modelling

The EZ, EX, ES, ET vocabularies contained 11 292, 8 805, 4 233, 4 957 word types respectively and were closed with respect to the training, development and test sets. The vocabularies were closed since the small datasets and the agglutinative character of the Bantu languages would otherwise lead to very high out-of-vocabulary rates. The SRILM toolkit (Stolcke, 2002) was used to train and evaluate all language models (LMs).

Transcriptions of the balanced subset of the ManT dataset as well as monolingual English and Bantu out-of-domain text were used to develop trigram language models. Four bilingual and one five-lingual trigram language model were used for the transcription systems as well as for semi-supervised training (Yılmaz et al., 2018; Biswas et al., 2019). Table 5 summarises the development and test set perplexities for the bilingual LMs. Details on the monolingual and code-switch perplexities are only provided for the test set (columns 3 to 6 in Table 5). The test set perplexities of the five-lingual LM are 1007.1, 1881.8, 345.3, and 277.5 for EZ, EX, ES and ET respectively. Further details regarding the five-lingual perplexities can be found in (Biswas et al., 2019).

Much more monolingual English text was available for language model development than text in the Bantu languages (471M vs 8M words). Therefore, the monolingual perplexity (MPP) is much higher for the Bantu languages than for English for each language pair.

Code-switch perplexities (CPP) for language switches indicate the uncertainty of the first word following a language switch. EB corresponds to switches from English to a Bantu language and BE indicates a switch in the other direction. Table 5 shows that the CPP for switching from English to isiZulu and isiXhosa is much higher than switching from these languages to English. This can be ascribed to the much larger isiZulu and isiXhosa vocabularies, which

are, in turn, due to the high degree of agglutination and the use of conjunctive orthography in these languages. The CPP for switching from English to Sesotho and Setswana is found to be lower than switching from those languages to English. We believe that this difference is due to the much larger English training set. The CPP values are even higher for the five-lingual language model. This is because the five-lingual trigrams allow language switches not permitted by the bilingual models.

6.   Semi-supervised Training

For semi-supervised ASR, lattice-based supervision was combined with the lattice-free MMI objective function (Manohar et al., 2018; Carmantini et al., 2019). Conventionally, semi-supervised training only considers the best path while lattice-based supervision uses the entire decoding lattice. Hence, the latter approach allows the model to learn from alternative hypotheses when the best path is not accurate.

Table 6 gives an overview of the bilingual ASR systems that were trained using the manually segmented data (System B) as well as five different versions of the automatically segmented data (Systems C-G & I). In addition to manually-transcribed speech, ManT, the AutoT$_{\text{Exp}}$ data was also included in all the training sets.

Also defined in Table 6 are systems A and H, which are the bilingual and five-lingual baseline systems respectively, trained only on the ManT and AutoT$_{\text{Exp}}$ data. These baseline systems were used to obtain automatic transcriptions, AutoT$_{\text{A}}$ and AutoT$_{\text{H}}$, for each version of the additional data shown in Table 6. These automatic transcriptions were subsequently used to train new acoustic models.

VAD$_{\text{2Sub}}$ was included to enable a fair comparison between automatic and manual segmentation. This is a 21-hour, randomly selected subset of the VAD$_2$ data which is comparable in size to the manually-segmented dataset (AutoT$_{\text{NonE}}$).

	Dev	Test	all CPP	CPP_{EB}	CPP_{BE}	all MPP	MPP_E	MPP_B
EZ	425.8	601.7	3 291.9	3 835.0	2 865.4	358.1	121.1	777.8
EX	352.9	788.8	4 914.4	6 549.6	3 785.6	459.0	96.8	1 355.6
ES	151.5	180.5	959.0	208.6	4 059.1	121.2	126.9	117.8
ET	213.3	224.5	70.2	317.3	3 798.1	160.4	142.1	176.1

Table 5: Development and test set perplexities. CPP: code-switch perplexity. MPP: monolingual perplexity.

System	Type	AutoT$_{NonE}$ (23h)	VAD$_1$ (83.6h)	VAD$_2$ (47h)	VAD$_{2Sub}$ (20.9h)	VAD$_3$ (37.0h)	VAD$_4$ (45.63h)
A	Bilingual baseline						
B		✓					
C			✓				
D	Bilingual system trained with AutoT$_A$			✓			
E					✓		
F						✓	
G							✓
H	Five-lingual baseline						
I	Bilingual system trained with AutoT$_H$					✓	

Table 6: ASR systems trained on different versions of the automatically segmented data. The duration of each of these datasets is given in parentheses.

Model	True positive rate			
	Clean	Noise	Music	All
RTCvad	0.786	0.706	0.733	0.722
tiny320	0.965	0.826	0.623	0.810
resnet960	0.992	0.944	0.787	0.917
VAD$_1$	0.564	0.662	0.693	0.646
VAD$_2$	0.972	0.898	0.778	0.886
VAD$_3$	0.985	0.917	0.811	0.907

Table 7: The true positive rate reported at a false positive rate of 0.315 for various VAD systems tested on AVA-Speech. The first three systems are baselines from (Chaudhuri et al., 2018), tested on the full dataset. The final three systems are tested on a $\approx$ 23 hour test set split.

7. Results & Discussion

The next three subsections concern results of the systems described in Sections 3., 4. and 5. Finally, ASR results are presented for specific languages, as well as at code-switching points.

7.1. Automatic Segmentation

AVA-Speech (test), which is the $\approx$ 23 hour subset of AVA-Speech not used for HMM training, was used as a test set to evaluate VAD performance. This dataset provides similar conditions to our target domain of soap opera data, as well as dense voice activity labels. Furthermore, it is accompanied by baseline results for the WebRTC project VAD (WebRTC.org, 2011) as well as two CNN-based systems based on the architecture proposed in (Hershey et al., 2017). The smaller of these two CNN-based systems, *tiny320*, is similar in size to our CNN, also containing three convolutional layers, while the other, *resnet960*, is based on the much larger ResNet-50 architecture (He et al., 2016).

Frame-based true positive rates (TPR) for a fixed false positive rate (FPR), scored over 10ms frames are shown for all VAD systems in Table 7. To allow comparison, all VAD systems were tuned to achieve a FPR of 0.315, as described in (Chaudhuri et al., 2018). TPR is reported for each individual speech condition (clean speech, speech with noise and speech with music) as well as for all conditions combined.

As expected, VAD$_1$ performs poorly. However, it is interesting to note that it is the only system that performs better for the "Noise" and "Music" conditions than for the "Clean" condition. This is because noisy signals tend to have more energy than their clean counterparts, making noisy signals more likely to exceed an energy threshold.

A large performance improvement is seen for VAD$_2$ which uses the CNN-HMM. In particular, this system already outperforms *tiny320*. A smaller performance increase is reported for VAD$_3$ which uses the CNN-GMM-HMM. However, this increase brings its performance to a level comparable to the much larger *resnet960* system. In the case of "Music", VAD$_3$ outperforms *resnet960*, whilst for "All" the TPR of VAD$_3$ is within 1% absolute.

In terms of computational complexity, the energy VAD is about 30 times faster than the CNN based VADs. However, the speaker diarization system is two orders of magnitude slower than the slowest VAD, making the compute times of VAD$_1$, VAD$_2$ and VAD$_3$ are roughly equivalent. VAD$_4$, which removes the speaker diarization, is much faster.

7.2. Automatic Transcription

The automatic transcription outputs of the bilingual (System A) and five-lingual (System H) baseline systems are summarised in Table 8. The first five rows of the table correspond to segments that were classified as monolingual while the last row shows the number of segments that contain code-switching. The values in this row reveal a high number of code-switched segments in the additional data.

In terms of the number of segments per category, the output of the automatic segmentation systems agree with the manual segmentation process. The only exception is the number of English segments identified by the five-lingual system, which is higher than for the other systems. We believe that this is because the five-lingual language model was trained on more in-domain English text (Biswas et al., 2019).

The table also shows that including speaker diarization in the segmentation process produces smaller chunks of words than using only the VAD. Due to the varying duration of each set, comparisons are difficult to make. For this reason, the set VAD$_{2Sub}$ is included, which is of a similar duration to AutoT$_{NonE}$, allowing comparison between the non-expert manual segmentation and automatic segmentation. It

System	A: Bilingual						H: Five-lingual
Language	$\text{AutoT}_{\text{NonE}}$	VAD_1	VAD_2	$\text{VAD}_{2\text{Sub}}$	VAD_3	VAD_4	VAD_3
English	8 570	12 155	7 608	4 721	11 686	4 754	23 973
IsiZulu	5 955	4 084	3 583	2 065	7 995	2 122	7 315
IsiXhosa	302	154	116	57	443	236	831
Sesotho	1 317	2 267	1 695	759	3 457	719	1 942
Setswana	2 598	6 272	4 341	2 241	6 691	2 196	1 973
Code-switched	25 824	39 562	30 904	12 572	36 475	17 911	30 616

Table 8: Number of segments per language identified by the baseline bilingual (A) and baseline five-lingual (H) ASR systems for different segmentation approaches.

can be seen that for the same duration of data, the automatic segmentation produces fewer segments.

7.3. Automatic Speech Recognition

The performance of the ASR systems introduced in Table 6 were measured in terms of the word error rate (WER) achieved after semi-supervised training. Results for the different training configurations are reported in Table 9. The values in the table indicate that including the additional 23 hours of non-expert manually segmented data ($\text{AutoT}_{\text{NonE}}$) in the training set (System B) yields absolute improvements of 1.5% and 1.4% over the baseline (System A) for the development and test sets respectively.

The results for System C show that using 83 hours of automatically-segmented speech results in an absolute improvement of 1.7% and 1.6% for the development and test sets relative to System A. Although System C's performance is on par with that of System B, its training set was much larger which means that the computational cost of developing the system is also much higher.

According to Table 6, VAD_2 reduced the additional training data from 83.6 to 47 hours. Furthermore, including this reduced additional data in System D's training set resulted in lower WERs for both the development and test sets, when compared with Systems A, B and C.

The semi-supervised system trained on the 21-hour subset of VAD_2 (System E) achieved results that are comparable to those of System B. The two additional dataset seem to have had almost the same impact on the accuracy of the resulting acoustic models. This result seems to indicate that, in terms of ASR performance, manually and automatically-produced segmentations are equally well suited for system development. However, it should be kept in mind that the segment labels used by System B were not assigned by experts.

System F, trained on the segments generated by VAD_3, yielded better performance than system D, despite the fact that System D's training set contained 10 more hours of data. The improvement in WER was found to be statistically significant at the 95% confidence level using bootstrap interval estimation (Bisani and Ney, 2004).

The results for System G show that automatic segments that do not take speaker identity into account (VAD_4) do not achieve the accuracy levels as those that do (System F). Therefore, the inclusion of speaker diarization does tend to improve ASR performance.

The performance of System H (five-lingual baseline system) is included in Table 9 but should not be directly com-

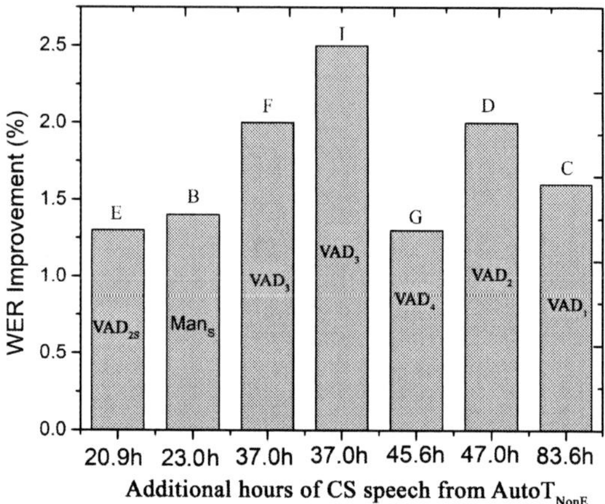

Figure 2: Improvement (% in comparison with the baseline) in test set WER for different semi-supervised systems incorporating additional soap opera training data.

pared with the bilingual systems because the recognition task is inherently more complex. However, as has been observed before (Biswas et al., 2019), the bilingual System I, trained on automatic transcriptions generated by System H, shows the best overall performance of all the evaluated systems. The improvement on the test set over its closest competitor (System F) is 0.5% absolute and this was found to be statistically significant above the 90% confidence level using bootstrap interval estimation. This improvement may be due to the ability of the five-lingual system to transcribe more than two languages, as well as Bantu-to-Bantu switches. The untranscribed soap opera speech is known to contain at least some segments that do not conform to the four considered bilingual language groupings. The degree to which such language switches do occur is unfortunately difficult to quantify without manual transcriptions. However, since the key difference between the bilingual and five-lingual systems is the ability to handle a greater variety of language switches, we speculate that this is a likely cause for the superior performance of System I.

The improvement in WER achieved by the semi-supervised ASR systems incorporating different versions of the additional data is summarised in Figure 2. The figure confirms that the largest gain in recognition accuracy was achieved by System I. It also affirms the observation that an equal amount of manually and automatically segmented

CS Pair	A (baseline)		B		C		D		E		F		G		H		I	
	Dev	Test	Dev	Test	Dev	Test	Dev	Test	Dev	Test	Dev	Test	Dev	Test	Dev	Test	Dev	Test
EZ	34.5	40.8	33.1	39.6	33.3	39.2	33.1	39.0	33.8	39.1	32.7	38.6	33.3	38.9	37.6	43.6	33.2	38.5
EX	35.8	42.7	35.3	42.0	34.8	41.9	34.7	41.8	35.2	42.1	34.7	41.4	34.7	42.3	40.6	54.5	33.8	41.0
ES	51.7	48.7	48.7	46.5	49.8	47.3	48.7	47.7	49.0	47.1	49.2	46.8	49.1	47.9	54.5	49.3	49.6	45.7
ET	44.3	41.3	42.7	39.7	41.1	38.9	40.7	38.5	41.7	40.0	40.1	38.7	40.8	39.3	47.2	43.9	39.9	38.4
Overall	41.5	**43.4**	40.0	**42.0**	39.8	**41.8**	39.3	**41.7**	39.9	**42.1**	39.2	**41.4**	39.5	**42.1**	46.5	**46.7**	39.1	**40.9**

Table 9: Mixed WERs (%) for the four code-switched language pairs.

System	English-isiZulu			English-isiXhosa			English-Sesotho			English-Setswana		
	E	Z	Bi_{CS}	E	X	Bi_{CS}	E	S	Bi_{CS}	E	T	Bi_{CS}
A (baseline)	37.9	48.7	33.3	37.8	54.5	25.8	43.7	61.4	25.2	36.2	51.8	35.6
B	32.3	45.2	36.8	32.7	49.1	32.1	32.9	57.2	33.7	28.1	48.3	40.5
F	31.6	43.9	37.8	31.5	48.3	34.2	32.5	56.8	33.8	27.4	46.4	42.2
I	31.7	43.7	37.3	31.6	47.6	34.4	32.0	56.4	34.2	26.8	45.7	42.0

Table 10: Language specific WER (%) (lowest is best) for English (E), isiZulu (Z), isiXhosa (X), Sesotho (S), Setswana (T) and code-switched bigram correct (Bi_{CS}) (%) (highest is best) for the test set.

data yields an equal improvement in recognition accuracy in a semi-supervised set-up.

7.4. Language Specific WER Analysis

For code-switched ASR, the performance of the recogniser at code-switch points is of particular interest. Language specific WERs and code-switched bigram correct (Bi_{CS}) values for the different semi-supervised systems are presented in Table 10. Code-switch bigram correct is defined as the percentage of words correctly recognised immediately after code-switch points. All values are percentages. The table reveals that both the English and Bantu WERs for all the semi-supervised systems are substantially lower than the corresponding values for the baseline system. The accuracy at the code-switch points is also substantially higher for the semi-supervised systems. Hence, adding the additional training data enhances system performance at code-switch points. Moreover, there are no substantial differences between the gains achieved by adding the manually (System B) or automatically (Systems F, I) segmented data.

8. Conclusions

In this study, we have evaluated the impact of using automatically-segmented instead of manually-segmented speech data for semi-supervised training of a code-switched automatic speech recognition system. Four different automatic segmentation approaches were evaluated, based respectively on simple energy thresholding with diarization, a CNN classification with two variants of HMM smoothing and diarization, and CNN classification with GMM-HMM smoothing and no diarization. It was found that applying our new CNN-GMM-HMM based VAD followed by X-vector speaker diarization resulted in the best ASR performance. The results also showed that the performance of systems that used automatically and manually-segmented data were comparable. We conclude that automatic-segmentation in combination with semi-supervised training is a viable approach to enhancing the recognition accuracy of a challenging five-language code-switched speech recognition task. This is a very positive outcome, since the difficulty in providing a manual segmentation of new broadcast material has remained an impediment to the development of speech technology in severely under resourced settings such as the one we describe. Future work will focus on improving the VAD and speaker diarization techniques as well as incorporating language identification into the automatic segmentation process.

9. Acknowledgements

We would like to thank the Department of Arts & Culture (DAC) of the South African government for funding this research. We are grateful to e.tv and Yula Quinn at Rhythm City, as well as the SABC and Human Stark at Generations: The Legacy, for assistance with data compilation. We also gratefully acknowledge the support of the NVIDIA corporation for the donation of GPU equipment.

10. Bibliographical References

Ahmed, B. H. and Tan, T.-P. (2012). Automatic speech recognition of code switching speech using 1-best rescoring. In *Proc. IALP*, Hanoi, Vietnam.

Amazouz, D., Adda-Decker, M., and Lamel, L. (2017). Addressing code-switching in French/Algerian Arabic speech. In *Proc. Interspeech*, Stockhom, Sweden.

Bisani, M. and Ney, H. (2004). Bootstrap estimates for confidence intervals in ASR performance evaluation. In *Proc. ICASSP*, Montreal, Canada.

Biswas, A., de Wet, F., van der Westhuizen, E., Yılmaz, E., and Niesler, T. R. (2018a). Multilingual neural network acoustic modelling for ASR of under-resourced English-isiZulu code-switched speech. In *Proc. Interspeech*, Hyderabad, India.

Biswas, A., van der Westhuizen, E., Niesler, T. R., and de Wet, F. (2018b). Improving ASR for code-switched speech in under-resourced languages using out-of-domain data. In *Proc. SLTU*, Gurugram, India.

Biswas, A., Yılmaz, E., de Wet, F., van der Westhuizen, E., and Niesler, T. R. (2019). Semi-supervised acoustic model training for five-lingual code-switched ASR. In *Proc. Interspeech*, Graz, Austria.

Biswas, A., Yılmaz, E., de Wet, F., van der Westhuizen, E., and Niesler, T. R. (2020). Semi-supervised development of ASR systems for multilingual code-switched speech in under-resourced languages. In *Proc. LREC*, Marseille, France.

Carmantini, A., Bell, P., and Renals, S. (2019). Untranscribed web audio for low resource speech recognition. In *Proc. Interspeech*, Graz, Austria.

Chaudhuri, S., Roth, J., Ellis, D., Gallagher, A. C., Kaver, L., Marvin, R., Pantofaru, C., Reale, N. C., Reid, L. G., Wilson, K., and Xi, Z. (2018). AVA-speech: A densely labeled dataset of speech activity in movies. In *Proc. Interspeech*, Hyderabad, India.

Chung, J. S., Nagrani, A., and Zisserman, A. (2018). Voxceleb2: Deep speaker recognition. In *Proc. Interspeech*, Hyderabad, India.

Emond, J., Ramabhadran, B., Roark, B., Moreno, P., and Ma, M. (2018). Transliteration based approaches to improve code-switched speech recognition performance. In *Proc. SLT*, Athens, Greece.

Ganji, S., Dhawan, K., and Sinha, R. (2019). IITG-HingCoS corpus: A Hinglish code-switching database for automatic speech recognition. *Speech Communication*, 110:76–89.

Gemmeke, J. F., Ellis, D. P. W., Freedman, D., Jansen, A., Lawrence, W., Moore, R. C., Plakal, M., and Ritter, M. (2017). Audio set: An ontology and human-labeled dataset for audio events. In *Proc. ICASSP*, New Orleans, USA.

Guo, P., Xu, H., Xie, L., and Chng, E. S. (2018). Study of semi-supervised approaches to improving English-Mandarin code-switching speech recognition. In *Proc. Interspeech*, Hyderabad, India.

He, K., Zhang, X., Ren, S., and Sun, J. (2016). Deep residual learning for image recognition. In *Proc. CVPR*, Las Vegas, USA.

Hershey, S., Chaudhuri, S., Ellis, D. P. W., Gemmeke, J. F., Jansen, A., Moore, R. C., Plakal, M., Platt, D., Saurous, R. A., Seybold, B., Slaney, M., Weiss, R. J., and Wilson, K. (2017). CNN architectures for large-scale audio classification. In *Proc. ICASSP*, New Orleans, USA.

Ko, T., Peddinti, V., Povey, D., and Khudanpur, S. (2015). Audio augmentation for speech recognition. In *Proc. Interspeech*, Dresden, Germany.

Li, Y. and Fung, P. (2013). Improved mixed language speech recognition using asymmetric acoustic model and language model with code-switch inversion constraints. In *Proc. ICASSP*, Vancouver, Canada.

Manohar, V., Hadian, H., Povey, D., and Khudanpur, S. (2018). Semi-supervised training of acoustic models using lattice-free MMI. In *Proc. ICASSP*, Calgary, Canada.

Nagrani, A., Chung, J. S., and Zisserman, A. (2017). Voxceleb: a large-scale speaker identification dataset. In *Proc. Interspeech*, Stockholm, Sweden.

Nakayama, S., Tjandra, A., Sakti, S., and Nakamura, S. (2018). Speech chain for semi-supervised learning of Japanese-English code-switching ASR and TTS. In *Proc. SLT*, Athens, Greece.

Pandey, A., Srivastava, B. M. L., Kumar, R., Nellore, B. T., Teja, K. S., and Gangashetty, S. V. (2018). Phonetically balanced code-mixed speech corpus for Hindi-English automatic speech recognition. In *Proc. LREC*, Miyazaki, Japan.

Povey, D., Ghoshal, A., Boulianne, G., Burget, L., Glembek, O., Goel, N., Hannemann, M., Motlicek, P., Qian, Y., Schwarz, P., et al. (2011). The Kaldi speech recognition toolkit. In *Proc. ASRU*, Hawaii.

Povey, D., Peddinti, V., Galvez, D., Ghahremani, P., Manohar, V., Na, X., Wang, Y., and Khudanpur, S. (2016). Purely sequence-trained neural networks for ASR based on lattice-free MMI. In *Proc. Interspeech*, San Francisco, USA.

Povey, D., Cheng, G., Wang, Y., Li, K., Xu, H., Yarmohammadi, M., and Khudanpur, S. (2018). Semi-orthogonal low-rank matrix factorization for deep neural networks. In *Proc. Interspeech*, Hyderabad, India.

Sehgal, A. and Kehtarnavaz, N. (2018). A convolutional neural network smartphone app for real-time voice activity detection. *IEEE Access*, 6:9017–9026.

Snyder, D., Garcia-Romero, D., Sell, G., Povey, D., and Khudanpur, S. (2018). X-vectors: Robust DNN embeddings for speaker recognition. In *Proc. ICASSP*, Calgary, Canada.

Stolcke, A. (2002). SRILM – An extensible language modeling toolkit. In *Proc. ICSLP*, Denver, USA.

Taneja, K., Guha, S., Jyothi, P., and Abraham, B. (2019). Exploiting monolingual speech corpora for code-mixed speech recognition. In *Proc. Interspeech*, Graz, Austria.

Thomas, S., Seltzer, M. L., Church, K., and Hermansky, H. (2013). Deep neural network features and semi-supervised training for low resource speech recognition. In *Proc. ICASSP*, Vancouver, Canada.

Thomas, S., Ganapathy, S., Saon, G., and Soltau, H. (2014). Analyzing convolutional neural networks for speech activity detection in mismatched acoustic conditions. In *Proc. ICASSP*, Florence, Italy.

van der Westhuizen, E. and Niesler, T. R. (2018). A first South African corpus of multilingual code-switched soap opera speech. In *Proc. LREC*, Miyazaki, Japan.

Vu, N. T., Lyu, D.-C., Weiner, J., Telaar, D., Schlippe, T., Blaicher, F., Chng, E.-S., Schultz, T., and Li, H. (2012). A first speech recognition system for Mandarin-English code-switch conversational speech. In *Proc. ICASSP*, Kyoto, Japan.

WebRTC.org. (2011). The WebRTC project. [Online]. Available: https://webrtc.org.

Yılmaz, E., van den Heuvel, H., and van Leeuwen, D. (2016). Investigating bilingual deep neural networks for automatic recognition of code-switching Frisian speech. *Procedia Computer Science*, 81:159–166.

Yılmaz, E., McLaren, M., van den Heuvel, H., and van Leeuwen, D. (2018). Semi-supervised acoustic model training for speech with code-switching. *Speech Communication*, 105:12–22.

Zeng, Z., Khassanov, Y., Pham, V. T., Xu, H., Chng, E. S., and Li, H. (2018). On the end-to-end solution to Mandarin-English code-switching speech recognition. *arXiv preprint arXiv:1811.00241*.

Proceedings of the 1st Joint SLTU and CCURL Workshop (SLTU-CCURL 2020), pages 79–87
Language Resources and Evaluation Conference (LREC 2020), Marseille, 11–16 May 2020
© European Language Resources Association (ELRA), licensed under CC-BY-NC

Investigating Language Impact in Bilingual Approaches for Computational Language Documentation

Marcely Zanon Boito[1], Aline Villavicencio[2,3], Laurent Besacier[1]

(1) Laboratoire d'Informatique de Grenoble (LIG), UGA, G-INP, CNRS, INRIA, France

(2) Department of Computer Science, University of Sheffield, England

(3) Institute of Informatics (INF), UFRGS, Brazil

contact: marcely.zanon-boito@univ-grenoble-alpes.fr

Abstract

For endangered languages, data collection campaigns have to accommodate the challenge that many of them are from oral tradition, and producing transcriptions is costly. Therefore, it is fundamental to translate them into a widely spoken language to ensure interpretability of the recordings. In this paper we investigate how the choice of translation language affects the posterior documentation work and potential automatic approaches which will work on top of the produced bilingual corpus. For answering this question, we use the MaSS multilingual speech corpus (Boito et al., 2020) for creating 56 bilingual pairs that we apply to the task of low-resource unsupervised word segmentation and alignment. Our results highlight that the choice of language for translation influences the word segmentation performance, and that different lexicons are learned by using different aligned translations. Lastly, this paper proposes a *hybrid* approach for bilingual word segmentation, combining *boundary clues* extracted from a non-parametric Bayesian model (Goldwater et al., 2009a) with the attentional word segmentation neural model from Godard et al. (2018). Our results suggest that incorporating these clues into the neural models' input representation increases their translation and alignment quality, specially for challenging language pairs.

Keywords: word segmentation, sequence-to-sequence models, computational language documentation, attention mechanism

1. Introduction

Computational Language Documentation (CLD) is an emerging research field whose focus lies on helping to automate the manual steps performed by linguists during language documentation. The need for this support is ever more crucial given predictions that more than 50% of all currently spoken languages will vanish before 2100 (Austin and Sallabank, 2011). For these very low-resource scenarios, transcription is very time-consuming: one minute of audio is estimated to take one hour and a half on average of a linguist's work (Austin and Sallabank, 2013).

This *transcription bottleneck* problem (Brinckmann, 2009), combined with a lack of human resources and time for documenting all these endangered languages, can be attenuated by translating into a widely spoken language to ensure subsequent interpretability of the collected recordings. Such parallel corpora have been recently created by aligning the collected audio with translations in a well-resourced language (Adda et al., 2016; Godard et al., 2017; Boito et al., 2018), and some linguists even suggested that more than one translation should be collected to capture deeper layers of meaning (Evans and Sasse, 2004). However, in this documentation scenario, the impact of the language chosen for translation rests understudied, and it is unclear if similarities among languages have a significant impact in the automatic bilingual methods used for information extraction (these include word segmentation, word alignment, and translation).

Recent work in CLD includes the use of aligned translation for improving transcription quality (Anastasopoulos and Chiang, 2018), and for obtaining bilingual-rooted word segmentation (Duong et al., 2016; Boito et al., 2017). There are pipelines for obtaining manual (Foley et al., 2018) and automatic (Michaud et al., 2018) transcriptions, and for

aligning transcription and audio (Strunk et al., 2014). Other examples are methods for low-resource segmentation (Lignos and Yang, 2010; Goldwater et al., 2009b), and for lexical unit discovery without textual resources (Bartels et al., 2016). Moreover, direct speech-to-speech (Tjandra et al., 2019) and speech-to-text (Besacier et al., 2006; Bérard et al., 2016) architectures could be an option for the lack of transcription, but there is no investigation yet about how exploitable these architectures can be in low-resource settings. Finally, previous work also showed that Neural Machine Translation models at the textual level are able to provide exploitable soft-alignments between sentences by using only 5,130 training examples (Boito et al., 2019).

In this work, we investigate the existence of language impact in bilingual approaches for CLD, tackling word segmentation,[1] one of the first tasks performed by linguists after data collection. More precisely, the task consists in detecting word boundaries in an unsegmented phoneme sequence in the language to document, supported by the translation available at the sentence-level. The phonemes in the language to document can be manually obtained, or produced automatically as in Godard et al. (2018).

For our experiments, we use the eight languages from the multilingual speech-to-speech MaSS dataset (Boito et al., 2020): Basque (EU), English (EN), Finnish (FI), French (FR), Hungarian (HU), Romanian (RO), Russian (RU) and Spanish (ES). We create 56 bilingual models, seven per language, simulating the documentation of each language supported by different sentence-level aligned translations. This setup allows us to investigate how having the same content, but translated in different languages, affects bilingual word segmentation. We highlight that in

---

[1]Here, word is defined as a sequence of phones that build a minimal unit of meaning.

this work we use a dataset of well-resourced languages due to the lack of multilingual resources in documentation languages that could be used to investigate this hypothesis. Thus, for keeping results coherent and generalizable for CLD, we down-sample our corpus, running our experiments using only 5k aligned sentences as a way to simulate a low-resource setting. We train bilingual models based on the segmentation and alignment method from Godard et al. (2018), investigating the language-related impact in the quality of segmentation, translation and alignment.

Our results confirm that the language chosen for translation has a significant impact on word segmentation performance, what aligns with Haspelmath (2011) who suggests that the notion of word cannot always be meaningfully defined cross-linguistically. We also verify that joint segmentation and alignment is not equally challenging across different languages: while we obtain good results for EN, the same method fails to segment the language-isolate EU. Moreover, we verify that the bilingual models trained with different aligned translations learn to focus on different structures, what suggests that having more than one translation could enrich computational approaches for language documentation. Lastly, the models' performance is improved by the introduction of a *hybrid* approach, which leverages the *boundary clues* obtained by a monolingual non-parametric Bayesian model (Goldwater et al., 2009b) into the bilingual models. This type of intermediate annotation is often produced by linguists during documentation, and its incorporation into the neural model can be seen as a form of validating word-hypotheses.

This paper is organized as follows. Section 2. presents the models investigated for performing word segmentation. Section 3. presents the experimental settings, and Section 4. the results and discussion. Section 5. concludes the work.

2. Models for Word Segmentation

2.1. Monolingual Bayesian Approach

Non-parametric Bayesian models (Goldwater, 2007; Johnson and Goldwater, 2009) are statistical approaches that can be used for word segmentation and morphological analysis, being known as very robust in low-resource settings (Godard et al., 2016; Goldwater et al., 2009a). In these monolingual models, words are generated by a uni or bigram model over a non-finite inventory, through the use of a Dirichlet process. Although providing reliable segmentation in low-resource settings, these monolingual models are incapable of automatically producing alignments with a foreign language, and therefore the discovered pseudo-word segments can be seen as "meaningless". Godard et al. (2018) also showed that dpseg[2] (Goldwater et al., 2006; Goldwater et al., 2009a) behaves poorly on pseudo-phone units discovered from speech, which limits its application. Here, we investigate its use as an intermediate monolingual-rooted segmentation system, whose discovered boundaries are used as clues by bilingual models.

---

²Available at `http://homepages.inf.ed.ac.uk/sgwater/resources.html`

2.2. Bilingual Attention-based Approach

We reproduce the approach from Godard et al. (2018) who train Neural Machine Translation (NMT) models between language pairs, using as source language the translation (word-level) and as target, the language to document (unsegmented phoneme sequence). Due to the attention mechanism present in these networks (Bahdanau et al., 2014), posterior to training, it is possible to retrieve *soft-alignment probability matrices* between source and target sentences.

The soft-alignment probability matrix for a given sentence pair is a collection of context vectors. Formally, a context vector for a decoder step t is computed using the set of source annotations H and the last state of the decoder network (s_{t-1}, the translation context). The attention is the result of the weighted sum of the source annotations H (with $H = h_1, ..., h_A$) and their α probabilities (Eq. 1). Finally, these are obtained through a feed-forward network $align$, jointly trained, and followed by a softmax operation (Eq. 2).

$$c_t = Att(H, s_{t-1}) = \sum_{i=1}^{A} \alpha_i^t h_i \qquad (1)$$

$$\alpha_i^t = \text{softmax}(align(h_i, s_{t-1})) \qquad (2)$$

The authors show that these soft-alignment probability matrices can be used to produce segmentation over phoneme (or grapheme) sequences. This is done by segmenting neighbor phonemes whose probability distribution (over the words in the aligned source translation) peaks at different words. The result is a pair of phoneme sequences and translation words, as illustrated on the bottom half of Figure 1. In this work we refer to this type of model simply as **neural model**.

2.3. Bilingual Hybrid Approach

The monolingual approach (§2.1.) has the disadvantage of not producing bilingual alignment, but it segments better than the bilingual approach (§2.2.) when the phonemic input is used (Godard et al., 2018). In this work we investigate a simple way of combining both approaches by creating a *hybrid* model which takes advantage of the Bayesian method's ability to correctly segment from small data while jointly producing translation alignments.

We augment the original unsegmented phoneme sequence with the `dpseg` output boundaries. In this augmented input representation, illustrated in Figure 1, a boundary is denoted by a special token which separates the words identified by `dpseg`. We call this *soft-boundary insertion*, since the `dpseg` boundaries inserted into the phoneme sequence can be ignored by the NMT model, and new boundaries can be inserted as well. For instance, in Figure 1 `aintrat` becomes `a intrat` (boundary insertion), and `urat debine` becomes `uratdebine` (soft-boundary removal).

3. Experimental Settings

Multilingual Dataset: For our experiments we use the MaSS dataset (Boito et al., 2020), a fully aligned and multilingual dataset containing 8,130 sentences extracted

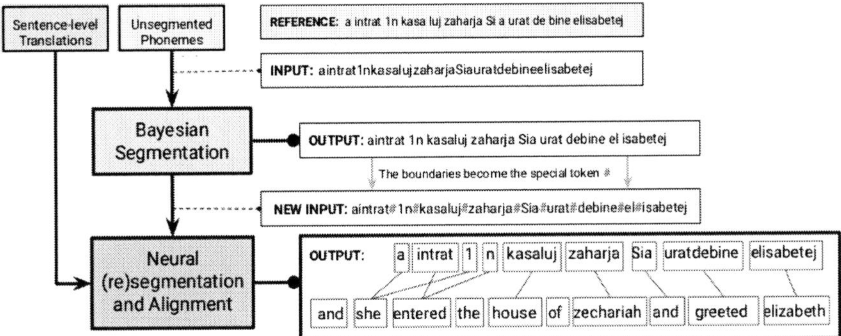

Figure 1: An illustration of the hybrid pipeline for the EN>RO language pair. The Bayesian model receives the unsegmented phonemes, outputting segmentation. The discovered boundaries are then replaced by a special token, and bilingual re-segmentation and alignment are jointly performed.

from the Bible. The dataset provides multilingual speech and text alignment between all the available languages: English (EN), Spanish (ES), Basque (EU), Finnish (FI), French (FR), Hungarian (HU), Romanian (RO), Russian (RU). As sentences in documentation settings tend to be short, we used RO as the pivot language for removing sentences longer (in terms of number of tokens) than 100 symbols. The resulting corpus contains 5,324 sentences, a size which is compatible with real language documentation scenarios. Table 1 presents some statistics. For the phonemic transcription of the speech (target side of the bilingual segmentation pipeline), we use the automatic phonemization from *Maus forced aligner* (Kisler et al., 2017), which results in an average vocabulary reduction of 835 types, the smallest being for RO (396), and the most expressive being for FR (1,708). This difference depends on the distance between phonemic and graphemic forms for each language. The phonemizations present an average number of unique phonemes of 42.5. Table 2 presents the statistic for the phonemic representation.

Training and Evaluation: For monolingual segmentation, we use `dpseg`'s unigram model with the same hyperparameters as Godard et al. (2016). The bilingual neural models were trained using a one-layer encoder (embeddings of 64), and a two-layers decoder (embeddings of 16). The remaining parameters come from Godard et al. (2018). From this work, we also reproduced the *multiple runs averaging*: for every language pair, we trained two networks, averaging the soft-alignment probability matrices produced. This averaging can be seen as *agreement* between the alignment learned with different parameters initialization. Regarding the data, 10% of the multilingual ids were randomly selected for validation, and the remaining were used for training. We report BLEU scores (Papineni et al., 2002) over the validation set for assessing translation quality. For hybrid setups, the soft-boundary special token is removed from the output before scoring, so results are comparable. Finally, for the reported word discovery results, the totality of the corpus is considered for evaluation.

	#Types	#Tokens	Token Length	Token/ Sentence
EN	5,232	90,716	3.98	17.04
ES	8,766	85,724	4.37	16.10
EU	11,048	67,012	5.91	12.59
FI	12,605	70,226	5.94	13.19
FR	7,226	94,527	4.12	17.75
HU	13,770	69,755	5.37	13.10
RO	7,191	88,512	4.06	16.63
RU	11,448	67,233	4.66	12.63

Table 1: Statistics for the textual portion of the corpus. The last two columns bring the average of the named metrics.

	#Types	#Tokens	Token Length	Phonemes/ Sentence
EN	4,730	90,657	3.86	56.18
ES	7,980	85,724	4.30	68.52
EU	9,880	67,012	6.94	71.13
FI	12,088	70,226	5.97	72.37
FR	5,518	93,038	3.21	52.86
HU	12,993	69,755	5.86	65.52
RO	6,795	84,613	4.50	68.04
RU	10,624	67,176	6.19	59.26

Table 2: Statistics for the phonemic portion of the corpus. The last two columns bring the average of the named metrics.

4. Bilingual Experiments

Word segmentation boundary F-scores are presented in Table 3. For the bilingual methods, Table 4 presents the averaged BLEU scores. We observe that, similar to the trend observed in Table 3, hybrid models are in average superior in terms of BLEU scores.[3] Moreover, we observe that segmentation and translation scores are strongly correlated for six of the eight languages, with an average ρ-value of 0.76

[3]We find an average BLEU scores difference between best hybrid and neural setups of 1.50 points after removing the outlier (RO). For this particular case, hybrid setups have inferior translation performance (average BLEU reduction of 11.44).

		EN	ES	EU	FI	FR	HU	RO	RU
neural	EN	-	51.8	36.1	53.8	**65.8**	47.7	57.5	50.3
	ES	60.1	-	**38.4**	46.3	63.4	45.9	53.5	46.3
	EU	48.3	44.2	-	42.5	46.4	41.2	44.7	41.8
	FI	60.0	46.8	36.5	-	53.7	**50.1**	51.5	**53.5**
	FR	**69.1**	**57.7**	37.0	53.7	-	47.4	**62.8**	49.8
	HU	53.3	46.0	36.5	52.9	48.7	-	48.7	49.8
	RO	60.9	51.5	37.9	51.1	63.9	47.6	-	51.6
	RU	58.7	47.6	35.6	**54.7**	54.0	49.3	53.9	-
hybrid	EN	-	57.9	43.5	57.5	**69.6**	52.9	64.2	58.1
	ES	66.4	-	**47.3**	54.3	68.8	51.7	63.4	56.1
	EU	58.6	53.1	-	50.1	58.1	49.2	55.1	50.1
	FI	66.5	55.6	45.7	-	62.7	**58.5**	60.7	**62.6**
	FR	**73.3**	**62.1**	45.6	56.9	-	54.2	**70.0**	59.5
	HU	62.6	54.2	45.0	59.7	60.0	-	58.8	59.3
	RO	68.2	57.6	46.9	56.2	69.3	53.8	-	60.1
	RU	66.8	56.1	44.6	**60.7**	63.0	55.3	63.6	-
dpseg		82.4	79.2	81.0	80.0	78.1	75.5	82.0	78.3

Table 3: Word Segmentation Boundary F-score results for neural (top), hybrid (middle) and dpseg (bottom). The columns represent the target of the segmentation, while the rows represented the translation language used. For bilingual models, darker squares represent higher scores. Better visualized in color.

		EN	ES	EU	FI	FR	HU	RO	RU
neural	EN	-	39.7	35.2	**45.1**	40.5	**36.0**	43.3	37.3
	ES	37.3	-	**37.7**	37.9	37.6	32.7	39.2	32.8
	EU	28.3	32.8	-	33.8	26.8	28.0	31.1	27.6
	FI	40.4	36.0	34.6	-	35.2	35.5	39.2	**37.5**
	FR	**45.7**	**42.2**	35.9	43.9	-	34.7	**50.8**	37.5
	HU	35.4	34.7	33.5	41.0	31.4	-	36.3	36.0
	RO	40.7	39.7	36.0	42.4	**44.3**	34.8	-	**37.8**
	RU	38.9	36.7	32.8	43.0	35.2	34.6	40.4	-
hybrid	EN	-	40.5	35.5	**47.0**	42.3	37.2	30.9	39.5
	ES	38.3	-	**38.4**	39.2	37.3	33.7	28.6	34.9
	EU	28.8	33.5	-	34.4	26.8	29.6	22.6	28.2
	FI	41.5	36.7	35.4	-	36.3	**37.4**	27.9	38.6
	FR	**46.6**	**43.6**	36.2	45.3	-	36.2	**34.9**	39.1
	HU	35.6	35.8	35.0	41.8	32.4	-	26.5	36.2
	RO	42.7	41.4	36.3	43.8	**46.1**	36.6	-	40.2
	RU	39.7	37.2	34.6	44.4	36.4	36.2	28.8	-

Table 4: BLEU 4 average results for neural (top) and hybrid (bottom) bilingual models. The columns represent the target of the segmentation. Darker squares represent higher scores. Better visualized in color.

	EN	ES	EU	FI	FR	HU	RO	RU
EN	-	36.0	32.5	37.1	**41.4**	34.2	36.6	36.6
ES	37.6	-	32.3	36.9	41.0	34.0	36.7	36.8
EU	35.5	36.1	-	38.0	38.8	34.5	36.2	**37.3**
FI	36.1	36.1	32.9	-	39.3	34.3	36.5	37.1
FR	**38.4**	**36.4**	32.2	36.4	-	33.9	**36.9**	36.5
HU	35.9	35.9	**33.0**	37.8	39.3	-	36.4	37.2
RO	37.6	36.3	32.6	36.8	40.9	34.0	-	36.8
RU	34.8	35.9	32.9	**38.5**	38.2	**34.8**	36.2	-

Table 5: Proportional segmentation results. The columns represent the target of the segmentation. Darker squares represent higher word boundary F-scores. Better visualized in color.

(significant to $p < 0.01$). The exceptions were EU (0.46) and RO (-0.06). While for EU we believe the general lack of performance of the systems could explain the results, the profile of RO hybrid setups was surprising. It highlights that the relationship between BLEU score and segmentation performance is not always clearly observed. In summary, we find that the addition of soft-boundaries will increase word segmentation results, but its impact to translation performance needs further investigation.

Looking at the segmentation results, we verify that, given the same amount of data and supervision, the segmentation performance for different target languages vary: EN seems to be the easiest to segment (neural: 69.1, hybrid: 73.3), while EU is the most challenging to segment with the neural approach (neural: 38.4, hybrid: 47.3). The following subsections will explore the relationship between segmentation, alignment performance and linguistic properties.

4.1. Source Language Impact

Bilingual Baseline Comparison: The results confirm that there is an impact related to using different source languages for generating the segmentations, and we identify interesting language pairs emerging as the most efficient, such as FI>HU (Uralic Family), FR>RO and FR>ES (Romance family).[4] In order to consolidate these results, we investigate if the language ranking obtained (in terms of *best translation languages for segmenting a target language*) is due to a similar profile of the source and target languages in terms of word length and tokens per sentence. Since translation words are used to cluster the phoneme se-

quences into words (bilingual-rooted word segmentation), having more or less translation words could be a determining aspect in the bilingual segmentation performed (more details about this in Section 4.3.). For this investigation, we use a naive bilingual baseline called proportional (Godard et al., 2018). It performs segmentation by distributing phonemes equally between the words of the aligned translation, insuring that words that have more letters, receive more phonemes (hence *proportional*). The average difference between the best hybrid (Table 3) and proportional (Table 5) results is of 25.92 points. This highlights not only the challenge of the task, but that the alignments learned by the bilingual models are not trivial.

We compute Pearson's correlation between bilingual hybrid and proportional segmentation scores, observing that no language presents a significant correlation for $p < 0.01$. However, when all languages pairs are considered together ($N = 56$), a significant positive correlation (0.74) is observed. Our interpretation is that the token ratio between the number of tokens in source and the number of tokens

---

[4]We denote L1>L2 as using L1 for segmenting L2. L1<>L2 means L1>L2 and L2>L1.

in target sentences have a significant impact on bilingual segmentation difficulty. However, it does not, by itself, dictates the best choice of translation language for a documentation scenario. For instance, the proportional baseline results indicate that EU is the best choice for segmenting RU. This choice is not only linguistically incoherent, but bilingual models reached their worst segmentation and translation results by using this language. This highlights that while statistical features might impact greatly low-resource alignment and should be taken into account, relying only on them might result in sub-optimal models.

Language Ranking: Looking into the quality of the segmentation results and their relationship with the language ranking, our intuition was that languages from the same family would perform the best. For instance, we expected ES<>FR, ES<>RO, FR<>RO (Romance family) and FI<>HU (Uralic family) to be strong language pairs. While some results confirm this hypothesis (FR>ES, FI>HU, FR>RO), the exceptions are: EN>FR, RU<>FI and ES>EU. For EN>FR, we argue that EN was ranked high for almost all languages, which could be due to some convenient statistic features. Table 1 shows that EN presents a very reduced vocabulary in comparison to the other languages. This could result in an easier language modeling scenario, which could then reflect in a better alignment capacity of the trained model. Moreover, for this and for RU<>FI scenarios, results seemed to reproduce the trend from the proportional baseline, in which these pairs were also found to be the best. This could be the result of a low syntactic divergence between languages of these pairs. Finally, the language isolate EU is not a good choice for segmenting any language (worst result for all languages). If we consider that this language has no relation to any other in this dataset, this result could be an indication that documentation should favor languages somehow related to the language they are trying to document. In fact, results for EU segmentation are both low (F-score and BLEU) and very close to the proportional baseline (average difference of 4.23 for neural and 13.10 for hybrid), which suggests that these models were not able to learn meaningful bilingual alignment.

4.2. Hybrid Setups

Looking at the hybrid results, we verify that the these models outperform their neural counterparts. Moreover, the impact of having the *soft-boundaries* is larger for the languages whose bilingual segmentation seems to be more challenging, hinting that the network is learning to leverage the *soft-boundaries* for generating a better-quality alignment between challenging language pairs. Table 6 presents the intersection between the correct types discovered by both monolingual and hybrid models. Results show that while the monolingual baseline *informs* the bilingual models, it is not completely responsible for the increase in performance. This hints that giving boundary clues to the network will not simply force some pre-established segmentation, but instead it will enrich the network's internal representation. Moreover, it is interesting to observe that the degree of overlap between the vocabulary generated will depend on the language target of segmentation,

	EN	ES	EU	FI	FR	HU	RO	RU
EN	-	0.60	0.74	0.64	0.68	0.59	0.69	0.51
ES	0.76	-	0.67	0.45	0.59	0.43	0.59	0.43
EU	0.81	0.57	-	0.49	0.70	0.48	0.68	0.50
FI	0.72	0.46	0.58	-	0.61	0.34	0.57	0.34
FR	0.72	0.44	0.68	0.48	-	0.48	0.56	0.41
HU	0.76	0.47	0.57	0.34	0.64	-	0.59	0.37
RO	0.76	0.56	0.70	0.51	0.62	0.48	-	0.43
RU	0.74	0.48	0.60	0.35	0.61	0.39	0.56	-

Table 6: Intersection between the correct types discovered by both monolingual and hybrid models. We notice that the target language of the segmentation (columns) has an impact in the acceptance of soft-boundaries by the neural model.

hinting that some languages might *accept* more easily the *soft-boundaries* proposed by the monolingual approach.

Nonetheless, compared to the monolingual segmentation (Table 3), even if the hybrid approach improves over the base neural one, it deteriorates considerably the performance with respect to dpseg (average difference of 16.54 points between the best hybrid result and its equivalent monolingual segmentation). However, this deterioration is necessary in order to discover semantically meaningful structures (joint bilingual segmentation and alignment), which is a harder task than monolingual segmentation. In this scenario, the monolingual results should be interpreted as an intermediate, good quality, segmentation/word-hypotheses created by linguists, which might be validated or not in light of the system's bilingual output.

4.3. Analysis of the Discovered Vocabulary

Next we study the characteristics of the vocabulary outputed by the bilingual models focusing on the impact caused by the aligned translation. For this investigation, we report results for hybrid models only, since their neural equivalents present the same trend. We refer as *token* the collection of phonemes segmented into word-like units. *Types* are defined as the set of distinct tokens. Table 7 brings the hybrid model's total number of types.

Looking at the rows, we see that EN, ES, FR, RO, which are all fusional languages, generated in average the smallest vocabularies. We also notice that HU and FI are the languages that tend to create the largest vocabularies when used as translation language. This could be due to both languages accepting a flexible word order, thus creating a difficult alignment scenario for low-resource settings. Moreover, these languages, together with EU, are agglutinative languages. This might be an explanation for the lack of performance in general for setups using these languages as target. In these conditions, the network must learn to align many translation words to the same structure in order to achieve the expected segmentation. However, sometimes over-segmentation might be the result of the network favoring alignment content instead of phoneme clustering.

Notwithstanding, the models for agglutinative languages are not the only ones over-segmenting. Looking at the average token length of the segmentations produced in Figure 2,

	EN	ES	EU	FI	FR	HU	RO	RU
EN	-	12,170	9,173	17,532	13,658	17,029	15,830	15,844
ES	13,732	-	13,249	12,965	10,984	13,283	13,073	13,247
EU	13,942	16,202	-	17,106	15,996	17,931	16,138	17,904
FI	16,201	18,349	16,540	-	17,478	19,993	17,470	17,938
FR	10,886	13,985	13,737	15,217	-	15,574	13,609	14,531
HU	17,086	18,398	17,218	21,097	18,472	-	18,861	18,728
RO	12,063	13,948	12,768	15,226	12,094	15,764	-	14,811
RU	14,973	16,856	16,027	18,805	16,515	18,349	16,595	-

Table 7: Number of types produced by the hybrid models.

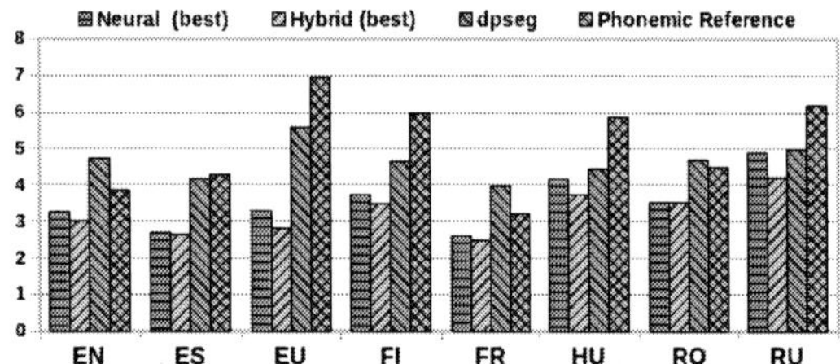

Figure 2: Average token length of the reference, monolingual `dpseg`, and best neural and hybrid setups from Table 3.

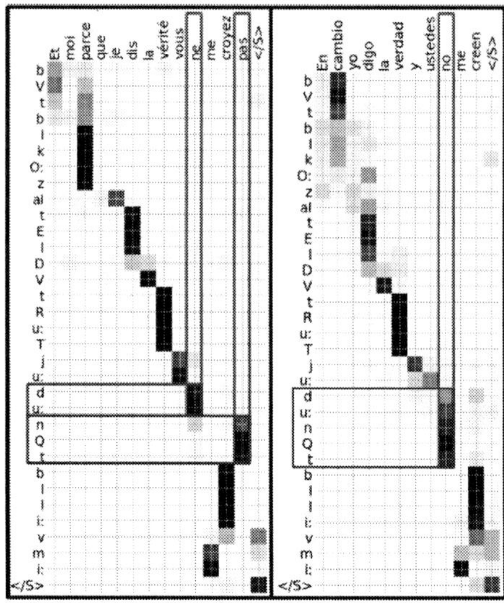

Figure 3: EN attention matrices generated by neural FR (left) and ES (right) bilingual models. The squares represent alignment probabilities (the darker the square, the higher the probability). The EN phonemization (rows) correspond to the following sentence: "But because I tell the truth, you do not believe me".

and supported by the size of the vocabularies, we verify that bilingual approaches tend to over-segment the output independent of the language targeted. This over-segmentation tends to be more accentuated in hybrid setups, with the exception of EN, FR and RO. This is probably due to the challenge of clustering the very long sequence of phonemes into the many available source words (see statistics for words and phonemes per sentence in Tables 1 and 2).

Furthermore, the very definition of a word might be difficult to define cross-linguistically, as discussed by Haspelmath (2011), and different languages might encourage a more fine-grained segmentation. For instance, in Figure 3 we see the EN alignment generated by the FR and ES neural models for the same sentence. Focusing at the *do not* (`du:nQt`) at the end of the sentence, we see that the ES model does not segment it, aligning everything to the ES translation `no`. Meanwhile the FR model segments the structure in order to align it to the translation `ne pas`. In both cases the discovered alignments are correct however, the ES segmentation is considered wrong. This highlights that the use of a segmentation task for evaluating the learned alignment might be sub-optimal, and that a more in-depth evaluation of source-to-target correspondences should be considered. In Section 4.4. we showcase a method for filtering the alignments generated by the bilingual models.

Concluding, in this work we study the alignment *implicitly* optimized by a neural model. An interesting direction would be the investigation of explicit alignment optimization for translation models, such as performed in Godard et al. (2019), where the authors consider the segmentation length generated by the bilingual alignments as part of their loss during training.

4.4. Alignment Confidence

The neural approach used here for bilingual-rooted word segmentation produces alignments between source and target languages. In this section we investigate how these alignments vary in models trained using different translation (source) languages. This extends the results from the previous section, that showed that models trained on different languages will present different lexicon sizes. We aim to show that this difference in segmentation behavior comes from the different alignments that are discovered by the models with access to different languages.

We use the approach from Boito et al. (2019) for extracting the alignments the bilingual models are more *confident about*. For performing such a task, *Average Normalized Entropy*, as defined in Boito et al. (2019), is computed for every (segmentation, aligned translation) pair. The scores are used for ranking the alignments in terms of confidence, with low-entropy scores representing the high-confidence automatically generated alignments. In previous work, we showed that this approach allow us to increase type retrieval scores by filtering the good from the bad quality alignments discovered. For this investigation, we chose to present results applied to the target language FR.

Table 8 presents the top 10 low-entropy (high-confidence) pairs from 3 different translation languages (from Table 3, FR column). The phoneme sequences are accompanied by their grapheme equivalents to increase readability, but all presented results were computed over phoneme sequences. The other translation languages were also omitted for readability purpose.

We observe a different set of discovered types depending on the language used, but all languages learn a fair amount

	EN			ES			RU		
1	Galates	galat	Galatians	N-A-W	Jo	Cordero	Jean	Za~	Иохан
2	Femmes	fam	Wives	Jeanne	Zan	Juana	les+huissiers	leHisie	Служители
3	Jude	Zyd	Jude	guéri	geRi	recuperará	Galates	galat	Галатам
4	Kaïnan	kaj	Cainan	Galates	galat	Gálatas	neuf	n2f	9
5	Philippiens	filipje~	Philippians	onze	?o~z	11	Marc	maRk	Марк
6	N-A-W	tR	treacherous	Hébreux	ebR2	Hebreos	Matthieu	matj2	Матай
7	Luc	lyk	Luke	manne	man	maná	sachez	saSe	Знайте
8	car	kaR	main	douze	duz	12	déclare	deklaR	Проповедуй
9	Seth	sEt	Seth	N-A-W	afliZ	afligidos	asa	aza	Аса
10	boue	bu	mud	treize	tREz	13	amis	ami	друзья

Table 8: Top low-entropy/high-confidence (graphemization, phonemic segmentation, aligned translation) results for EN, ES and RU models for segmenting FR. The output of the system is the phonemic segmentation, and graphemization is provided only for readability purpose. N-A-W identify unknown/incorrect generated types.

of biblical names and numbers, very frequent due to the nature of the dataset.[5] This highlights that very frequent types might be captured independently of the language used, but other structures might be more dependent on the chosen language. We also notice the presence of incorrect alignments (the word `car` (because) aligned to the word `main`), concatenations (the words `les huissiers` (the ushers) became a single word) and incorrect types (`N-A-W` in the table). This is to be expected, as these are automatic alignments.

Confirming the intuition that the models are focused on different information depending on the language they are trained on, we studied the vocabulary intersection of the FR bilingual models for the top 200 correct discovered types ranked by alignment confidence. We observed that the amount of shared lexicon for the sets is fairly small: the smallest intersection being of 20% (between EU and RO) and the largest one of 35.5% (between RU and FI). In other words, this means that the high-confidence alignments learned by distinct bilingual models differ considerably. Even for models that shared most structures, such as FI and RU (35.5%), and HU and RU (34%), this intersection is still limited. This shows that the bilingual models will discover different structures, depending on the supervision available. This is particularly interesting considering that the content of the aligned information remains the same, and the only difference between the bilingual models is the language in which the information is expressed. It highlights how collecting data in *multilingual settings* (that is, in more than one translation language) could enrich approaches for CLD. Lastly, we leave as future work a more generalizable study of the distinctions in the bilingual alignments, including the evaluation of the word-level alignments discovered by the models.

5. Conclusion

In language documentation scenarios, transcriptions are most of the time costly and difficult to obtain. In order to ensure the interpretability of the recordings, a popular solution is to replace manual transcriptions by translations of the recordings in well-resourced languages (Adda et al., 2016). However, while some work suggests that translations in multiple languages may capture deeper layers of meaning (Evans and Sasse, 2004), most of the produced corpora from documentation initiatives are bilingual. Also, there is a lack of discussion about the impact of the language chosen for these translations in posterior automatic methods.

In this paper we investigated the existence of language-dependent behavior in a bilingual method for unsupervised word segmentation, one of the first tasks performed in post-collection documentation settings. We simulated such a scenario by using the MaSS dataset (Boito et al., 2020) for training 56 bilingual models, the combination of all the available languages in the dataset. Our results show that in very low-resource scenarios (only 5,324 aligned sentences), the impact of language can be great, with a large margin between best and worst results for every target language. We also verify that the languages are not all equally difficult to segment. Moreover, while some of our *language rankings*, in terms of best translation languages for segmenting a target language, could be explained by the linguistic family of the languages (FR>ES, FI>HU, FR>RO), we found some surprising results such as ES>EU and EN>FR. We believe these are mostly due to the impact of existing statistic features (e.g. token length ratio between source and target sentences, and vocabulary size), related to the corpus, and not to the language features.

Additionally, we investigated providing a different form of supervision to the bilingual models. We used the monolingual-rooted segmentation generated by `dpseg` for augmenting the phoneme sequence representation that the neural models learn from at training time. We observed that the networks learned to leverage `dpseg`'s *soft-boundaries* as hints of alignment break (boundary insertion). Nonetheless, the networks are still robust enough to ignore this information when necessary. This suggests that, in a documentation scenario, `dpseg` could be replaced by early annotations of potential words done by a linguist, for instance. The linguist could then validate the output of the neural system, and review their word hypotheses considering the generated bilingual alignment.

In summary, our results highlight the existence of a relationship between language features and performance in

---

[5]The chapter names and numbers (e.g. "Revelation 2") are included in the dataset, totalizing 260 examples of *"name, number"*.

(neural) bilingual segmentation. We verify that languages close in phonology and linguistic family score better, while less similar languages yield lower scores. While we find that our results are rooted in linguistic features, we also believe there is a non-negligible relationship with corpus statistic features which can impact greatly neural approaches in low-resource settings.

6. Bibliographical References

Adda, G., Stüker, S., Adda-Decker, M., Ambouroue, O., Besacier, L., Blachon, D., Bonneau-Maynard, H., Godard, P., Hamlaoui, F., Idiatov, D., Kouarata, G.-N., Lamel, L., Makasso, E.-M., Rialland, A., de Velde, M. V., Yvon, F., and Zerbian, S. (2016). Breaking the unwritten language barrier: The BULB project. *Procedia Computer Science*, 81:8–14.

Anastasopoulos, A. and Chiang, D. (2018). Leveraging translations for speech transcription in low-resource settings. In *Proc. Interspeech 2018*, pages 1279–1283.

Austin, P. K. and Sallabank, J. (2011). *The Cambridge handbook of endangered languages*. Cambridge University Press.

Austin, P. K. and Sallabank, J. (2013). *Endangered languages*. Taylor & Francis.

Bahdanau, D., Cho, K., and Bengio, Y. (2014). Neural machine translation by jointly learning to align and translate. *arXiv preprint arXiv:1409.0473*.

Bartels, C., Wang, W., Mitra, V., Richey, C., Kathol, A., Vergyri, D., Bratt, H., and Hung, C. (2016). Toward human-assisted lexical unit discovery without text resources. In *Spoken Language Technology Workshop (SLT), 2016 IEEE*, pages 64–70. IEEE.

Bérard, A., Pietquin, O., Servan, C., and Besacier, L. (2016). Listen and translate: A proof of concept for end-to-end speech-to-text translation. *arXiv preprint arXiv:1612.01744*.

Besacier, L., Zhou, B., and Gao, Y. (2006). Towards speech translation of non written languages. In *Spoken Language Technology Workshop, 2006. IEEE*, pages 222–225. IEEE.

Boito, M. Z., Bérard, A., Villavicencio, A., and Besacier, L. (2017). Unwritten languages demand attention too! word discovery with encoder-decoder models. In *2017 IEEE Automatic Speech Recognition and Understanding Workshop (ASRU)*, pages 458–465. IEEE.

Boito, M. Z., Anastasopoulos, A., Lekakou, M., Villavicencio, A., and Besacier, L. (2018). A small griko-italian speech translation corpus. *arXiv preprint arXiv:1807.10740*.

Boito, M. Z., Villavicencio, A., and Besacier, L. (2019). Empirical evaluation of sequence-to-sequence models for word discovery in low-resource settings. *arXiv preprint arXiv:1907.00184*.

Boito, M. Z., Havard, W. N., Garnerin, M., Ferrand, É. L., and Besacier, L. (2020). Mass: A large and clean multilingual corpus of sentence-aligned spoken utterances extracted from the bible. *Language Resources and Evaluation Conference (LREC)*.

Brinckmann, C. (2009). Transcription bottleneck of speech corpus exploitation.

Duong, L., Anastasopoulos, A., Chiang, D., Bird, S., and Cohn, T. (2016). An attentional model for speech translation without transcription. In *Proceedings of the 2016 Conference of the North American Chapter of the Association for Computational Linguistics: Human Language Technologies*, pages 949–959.

Evans, N. and Sasse, H.-J. (2004). In *Searching for meaning in the Library of Babel: field semantics and problems of digital archiving*. Open Conference Systems, University of Sydney, Faculty of Arts.

Foley, B., Arnold, J. T., Coto-Solano, R., Durantin, G., Ellison, T. M., van Esch, D., Heath, S., Kratochvil, F., Maxwell-Smith, Z., Nash, D., et al. (2018). Building speech recognition systems for language documentation: The coedl endangered language pipeline and inference system (elpis). In *SLTU*, pages 205–209.

Godard, P., Adda, G., Adda-Decker, M., Allauzen, A., Besacier, L., Bonneau-Maynard, H., Kouarata, G.-N., Löser, K., Rialland, A., and Yvon, F. (2016). Preliminary experiments on unsupervised word discovery in mboshi. In *Proc. Interspeech*.

Godard, P., Adda, G., Adda-Decker, M., Benjumea, J., Besacier, L., Cooper-Leavitt, J., Kouarata, G.-N., Lamel, L., Maynard, H., Müller, M., et al. (2017). A very low resource language speech corpus for computational language documentation experiments. *arXiv preprint arXiv:1710.03501*.

Godard, P., Zanon Boito, M., Ondel, L., Berard, A., Yvon, F., Villavicencio, A., and Besacier, L. (2018). Unsupervised word segmentation from speech with attention. In *Interspeech*.

Godard, P., Besacier, L., and Yvon, F. (2019). Controlling utterance length in nmt-based word segmentation with attention. *arXiv preprint arXiv:1910.08418*.

Goldwater, S., Griffiths, T. L., and Johnson, M. (2006). Contextual dependencies in unsupervised word segmentation. In *Proc. International Conference on Computational Linguistics*, pages 673–680, Sydney, Australia.

Goldwater, S., Griffiths, T. L., and Johnson, M. (2009a). A Bayesian framework for word segmentation: Exploring the effects of context. *Cognition*, 112(1):21–54.

Goldwater, S., Griffiths, T. L., and Johnson, M. (2009b). A Bayesian framework for word segmentation: Exploring the effects of context. *Cognition*, 112(1):21–54.

Goldwater, S. J. (2007). *Nonparametric Bayesian models of lexical acquisition*. Ph.D. thesis, Citeseer.

Haspelmath, M. (2011). The indeterminacy of word segmentation and the nature of morphology and syntax. *Folia linguistica*, 45(1):31–80.

Johnson, M. and Goldwater, S. (2009). Improving nonparameteric bayesian inference: experiments on unsupervised word segmentation with adaptor grammars. In *Proc. NAACL-HLT*, pages 317–325. Association for Computational Linguistics.

Kisler, T., Reichel, U., and Schiel, F. (2017). Multilingual processing of speech via web services. *Computer Speech & Language*, 45:326 – 347.

Lignos, C. and Yang, C. (2010). Recession segmentation: simpler online word segmentation using limited resources. In *Proceedings of the fourteenth conference on computational natural language learning*, pages 88–97. Association for Computational Linguistics.

Michaud, A., Adams, O., Cohn, T. A., Neubig, G., and Guillaume, S. (2018). Integrating automatic transcription into the language documentation workflow: Experiments with na data and the persephone toolkit.

Papineni, K., Roukos, S., Ward, T., and Zhu, W.-J. (2002). Bleu: a method for automatic evaluation of machine translation. In *Proceedings of the 40th annual meeting on association for computational linguistics*, pages 311–318. Association for Computational Linguistics.

Strunk, J., Schiel, F., Seifart, F., et al. (2014). Untrained forced alignment of transcriptions and audio for language documentation corpora using webmaus. In *LREC*, pages 3940–3947.

Tjandra, A., Sakti, S., and Nakamura, S. (2019). Speech-to-speech translation between untranscribed unknown languages. *arXiv preprint arXiv:1910.00795*.

Proceedings of the 1st Joint SLTU and CCURL Workshop (SLTU-CCURL 2020), pages 88–96
Language Resources and Evaluation Conference (LREC 2020), Marseille, 11–16 May 2020
© European Language Resources Association (ELRA), licensed under CC-BY-NC

Design and Evaluation of a Smartphone Keyboard for Plains Cree Syllabics

Eddie Antonio Santos[*†], **Atticus G. Harrigan**[†]

[*]National Research Council Canada
Eddie.Santos@nrc-cnrc.gc.ca

[†]Alberta Language Technology Lab
University of Alberta
Edmonton, Alberta, Canada
· {easantos,Atticus.Harrigan}@ualberta.ca

Abstract

Plains Cree is a less-resourced language in Canada. To promote its usage online, we describe previous keyboard layouts for typing Plains Cree syllabics on smartphones. We describe our own solution whose development was guided by ergonomics research and corpus statistics. We then describe a case study in which three participants used a previous layout and our own, and we collected quantitative and qualitative data. We conclude that, despite observing accuracy improvements in user testing, introducing a brand new paradigm for typing Plains Cree syllabics may not be ideal for the community.

Keywords: cree, syllabics, smartphone

1. Introduction

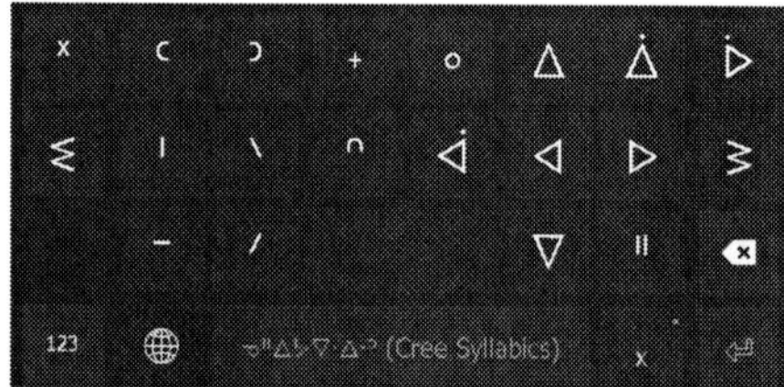

Figure 1: The virtual keyboard layout introduced in this paper for typing Plains Cree syllabics on iOS and Android smartphones.

To reclaim an minority language in the digital space, the language must be used and shared online. However, minority language users of new media often resort to a majority language when writing online (Keegan et al., 2015). There is a need for quality mobile support for minority languages (Cassels, 2019), such as Plains Cree. Having a good mobile keyboard enables the language to be used online, and encourages the language's use at home and in the classroom. There is no well-established keyboard layout for Plain Cree syllabics, although there have been plenty of alternatives for smartphones (First Peoples' Cultural Council, 2016; van Esch et al., 2019; Houle, 2018; Moshagen et al., 2016). In this paper, we explore the existing keyboard layouts, describe a few areas of improvement, and propose our own smartphone keyboard layout for writing in Plains Cree syllabics (Figure 1). We describe how we created our layout basing its key locations on ergonomics research and corpus statistics. We then describe a case study wherein we had participants use our keyboard and compared it to an existing solution. We conclude by discussing the preferences we learned from the case study.

2. nêhiyawêwin: the Cree Language

Plains Cree (ISO 639-3: crk) or its endonym, ᓀᐦᐃᔭᐍᐏᐣ (*nêhiyawêwin*) is a member of the Algonquian language family. It is the westernmost language of the Cree language continuum, and has been historically spoken by the *nêhiyawak* people in an area spanning present day north and central Alberta, central Saskatchewan, and the eastern edge of British Columbia. As with many Indigenous languages in Canada, the use of Plains Cree was actively suppressed by government and institutional efforts (The Truth and Reconciliation Commission of Canada, 2015).

Plains Cree is written primarily in two orthographies. The most commonly supported orthography by computers and smartphones is the **standard Roman orthography (SRO)**, an alphabet that borrows the consonants *ptkcshmnywrl* and vowels *êiao* from the Latin script (ISO 15924: Latn), and denotes long vowels with either macron (ē ī ō ā) or circumflex (ê î ô â) diacritics. Note that there is no short *e* vowel.

3. ᒐᐦᑭᐯᐦᐃᑲᓇ: Writing in Syllabics

Syllabics or ᒐᐦᑭᐯᐦᐃᑲᓇ (*cahkipêhikana*) (ISO 15924: Cans) is a writing system created in the 1800s to write the Swampy Cree language (Stevenson, 1999). Syllabics are used to write many Canadian Indigenous languages and often have different conventions language to language. Such languages include Inuktut, Eastern Cree dialects, and Dene languages, among others. Their use for Plains Cree will be the focus of this paper.

The syllabics writing system is similar to an **abugida**—its primary graphemes represent a **consonant-vowel pair**, with the **shape** of each grapheme indicating the consonant of the pair, and the **orientation** of the grapheme indicating the vowel of the pair.

For example, the graphemes ᐺ, ᐞ, ᐸ, ᐷ all have the same shape, which represents a syllable starting with the /p/ sound; these graphemes represent the syllables /pe/, /pɪ/, /po/, /pɐ/, respectively. The graphemes ᑯ, ᑦ, ᑕ, ᒐ are all oriented in the same way (the tips "point" to the southwest) which means they all contain the /ɐ/ vowel; these graphemes represent the syllables /kɐ/, /sɐ/, /t͡sɐ/, /mɐ/, respectively.

Syllables in Plains Cree have the general shape (C)(w)V-(C)(C), where C is a consonant and V is a vowel, and w is

Category	Elaboration	Example		
		Syllabic	IPA	SRO
V	Vowel	◁	/ɑ:/	â
wV	Syllable with /w/ as onset	◁·	/wɑ:/	wâ
CV	Syllable with consonant onset	Ṗ	/t͡si:/	cî
CwV	Syllable with consonant + /w/ onset	ȯ:	/nwɑ:/	nwâ
final	Coda	°	/w/	w

Table 1: The different syllabic categories used in this paper.

the /w/ sound[1] (Wolfart, 1996). Given that most syllables in Plains Cree are predominately CV or CwV, the syllabics writing system is particularly well-suited for writing Plains Cree. Further, the writing system is thought to be more Indigenous and authentic than using the borrowed Latin writing system, thus it holds greater cultural value.

3.1 Diacritics

The onset of a syllable, if present, is a consonant, or a consonant with an intervening /w/ sound. The /w/ sound is written in syllabics as a dot to the right-side of the (C)V syllabic. For example, ∪ represents the /te/ syllable; ∪·, with a dot to the right, represents the /twe/ syllable.

Long vowels are denoted by putting a dot on top of a syllabic; for example, given the short vowels Δ (/ɪ/), ▷ (/o/), ◁ (/ɐ/), adding a dot diacritic on top of these vowels yields the long vowels, Δ̇ (/i:/) ▷ (/o:/), and ◁ (/ɑ:/), respectively. Note: although ∇ (/e/) is considered to be a long vowel, it does not take a diacritic, as there is no short /e/ vowel.

3.2 Finals

Codas in Plains Cree, if present, are one or two consonants written using syllabics called *finals*. Finals appear anywhere in a word where a consonant cannot be paired with a vowel or an intervening /w/. For example, the word for horse, /mɪstɐtɪm/, is written as ⌐ᐁᑕᑎᶜ in syllabics. The finals correspond to /s/ and /m/ phonemes, respectively, and are the two consonants in the word that are *not* followed by a vowel or a /w/ + vowel pair. There are three special finals: ‖ for writing /h/ anywhere in a word; ° for words that end with /w/; and ˣ for words that end with /hk/; Every consonant in Plains Cree has a corresponding final syllabic, though these are not transparently related to their corresponding CV syllabic shape.

3.3 Categorizing Syllabics

In this paper, we define five categories for the Plains Cree syllabics: V, wV, CV, CwV, and final (Table 1). The keyboards described in this paper (Sections 4, 5) each have different methods of typing characters in each category.

4. Prior Work

We describe an existing solution to type Plains Cree syllabics on smartphones: the **FirstVoices Keyboards** app.

---

[1]This is an oversimplification of Plains Cree phonotactics. For a full explanation, see Wolfart (1996).

4.1 The FirstVoices Layout

Figure 2: The FirstVoices Plains Cree syllabics layout.

The ᐅ‖ᐃᕀᐁᐁᐧ (**Plains Cree**) keyboard layout (Figure 2) was created by the First Peoples' Cultural Council as part of their **FirstVoices Keyboards** app (2016). The FirstVoices Keyboards app is a suite of smartphone keyboard layouts that covers all Indigenous languages in Canada. The technology that allows the creation of many keyboard layouts is Keyman (2020), a keyboard creation engine. Keyman is embedded within the FirstVoices Keyboards app, and all of the keyboard layouts it provides—including ᐅ‖ᐃᕀᐁᐁᐧ (**Plains Cree**)—can be used standalone with the (separate) Keyman app. Throughout the rest of this paper, we will refer to this layout as the **FirstVoices** layout.

The FirstVoices layout uses a two *page* system: the initial page (Figure 2) displays all **V** and **CV** syllabics that have the underlying /ɐ/ and /ɪ/ vowel. Below the CV syllabics are all of the **finals**, with the exception of ˣ. Pressing the ⇧ key switches to the second page, which displays all **V** and **CV** syllabics that have the underlying /e/ and /o/ vowel, as well as keys for ᔕ (/l/), ᔥ (/r/), and ˣ.

To type a syllabic with a long vowel, the typist first types the **V** or **CV** syllabic with the corresponding short vowel. Then, the typist must press the ˙ key, which has the effect of adding a long vowel dot to the previously entered **V** or **CV** syllabic. To type a **wV** or **CwV** syllabic, one must first type the corresponding **V** or **CV** syllabic, including long vowel dot, and then press the ˙ key; this places a middle dot after the corresponding syllabic.

This layout has the advantage of having a shallow learning curve; All **V** and **CV** syllabics are one or two presses away. However, since there are 40 **V** and **CV** syllabics, plus 13 finals, this keyboard makes the decision to split them in half. Notably, syllables with the vowels /ɐ/ or /ɪ/ are more common in Plains Cree, so the keyboard made the right choice in prioritizing which syllabics are immediately selectable. That said, the keyboard is still cramped; on our test device, most keys on this layout are 5mm wide.

The FirstVoices layout produces dubious Unicode character output. The Unified Canadian Aboriginal Syllabics block of Unicode defines unique characters for all **V**, **wV**, **CV**, and **CwV** syllabics and includes finals specifically for use in Western Cree syllabics (The Unicode Consortium, 2019b). The FirstVoices layout does not produce precomposed characters for **CwV** syllabics; instead, it appends U+1427 CANADIAN SYLLABICS FINAL MIDDLE DOT to emulate a /w/ diacritic, despite the character actually encoding a final. Another oddity is that this layout sometimes opts to produce *look-alike* finals, instead of the characters specifically intended for Western Cree. Additionally, the keyboard has no key for the full-stop used in Plains Cree syllabics (namely: ×).

4.2 Other Layouts

The Gboard application (van Esch et al., 2019) has an Android-only Cree syllabics layout. The layout is "pan-Cree", aiming to cover all Cree dialects. Covering all dialects in one layout has the effect that, out of 48 syllabics keys immediately available to type on the primary page, 18 keys (37.5%) are *completely unused* in Plains Cree syllabics orthography. Given that the Gboard layout is Android-only, we will not discuss it further. To our knowledge, there are a few other smartphone keyboards for Cree syllabics (Houle, 2018; Moshagen et al., 2016), however, we were unable to install them as the system-wide keyboard on our test device. As such, they will also not be discussed any further.

5. Design and Development of the Keyboard

After studying the strengths and weaknesses of the layout presented in Section 4, we sought to make our own syllabics layout for smartphones with the following goals:

1. All syllabics must be **accessible on the primary page**.
2. Only keys used in **Plains Cree** should be on the primary page.
3. It must facilitate efficient **two-thumbed typing**.
4. Its Unicode output must produce **pre-composed** syllabic code points.

With these goals in mind, we present our method for developing this layout, which we will henceforth refer to as the **Keyman layout**. The **Keyman layout** is a "build-a-syllable" dynamic layout, designed specifically for use with the Plains Cree language.

5.1 Creating an Ergonomic, Two-handed Layout

Upon using the **FirstVoices** layout, the authors of this paper felt that, in order to facilitate fast and accurate typing, this layout could do better to improve the *placement* of the syllabic characters.

As such, we sought research in the ergonomics of thumbed-input on smartphones. We focused on two-thumbed input, as most smartphone keyboard layouts position the virtual keyboard at the very bottom of the screen, where one would hold the phone with either one or two hands, using one's thumbs to tap on the keyboard's keys.

Park and Han (2010) discuss the design and placement of touchscreen targets for *one-handed* interaction on a mobile phone. The authors tested the effects of 5mm, 7mm, and 10mm targets on a 5×5 grid on a smartphone display. They measured study participants' first transition time—how long it takes to go from a neutral position to any target on the screen; the task completion time—how long it takes to press the *correct* target on the screen; the number of errors made; and the pressing convenience—the participants' subjective opinion of how easy it is to press a target. We have calculated the median of all metrics measured in Park and Han (2010). We opted to use the 7mm grid, as it strikes a good balance between allowing for a great number of keys, and it is not as error-prone as smaller layouts. This

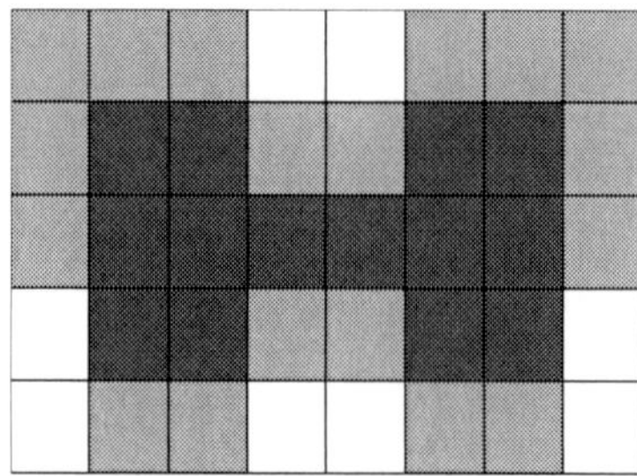

Figure 3: The superposition of the original right-handed grid and the mirrored left-handed grid. Lighter areas are worse places to assign keys, and darker areas are better places to assign keys.

indicated which 7mm targets are good places to assign keys, and which targets to avoid.

Now that we know which areas of the layout are easier and less error-prone to touch, and which areas are more error prone, and more difficult to touch, we can begin placing keys on the layout.

We decided, that in order to support **two-thumbed typing**, we would create a "build-a-syllable" keyboard, where **CV** syllabics would be assembled by typing a consonant final first, then followed by the appropriate vowel. We placed **consonants** and **vowels** on opposite side of the keyboard. This way, when typing **CV** syllable sequences, the typist alternates between thumbs, allowing simultaneous articulation of their thumbs. For example, while the left thumb is finishing the articulation of typing a consonant, the right thumb is starting the articulation of typing a vowel. This follows the design recommendations set by Norman and Fisher (1982), who state that a keyboard should equalize the load of both hands, maximizing sequences where keys are typed by alternating hands.

Since Park and Han (2010) only collected data for *right-handed* touches, we made the assumption that this figure can be mirrored horizontally to account for left-handed usage. We then determined the width of a grid of 7mm wide keys, with a 1mm gap between keys that would comfortably fit the width of a contemporary smartphone. Using a smartphone with a screen width of 68mm, we calculated $8 \times 7\text{mm} + 7 \times 1\text{mm} = 63\text{mm}$. Thus we determined that the grid should be 8 keys wide. We then superimposed both the original right-handed grid, and the mirrored left-handed grid, assuming that keys in the overlapping portion of the grid will take the median of measures from both the left-handed and right-handed button placements (Figure 3).

5.2 Placing Keys Based on Corpus Statistics

We wanted to place **frequent keys** in the darker areas in Figure 3, and **rare keys** in lighter areas. To get an idea of **key frequency**, we counted unigram and bigram frequency in the **Ahenakew-Wolfart corpus of Cree text** (Arppe et al., 2019).[2] This corpus is composed of a number of interviews and monologues recorded by Freda Ahenakew and H. C. Wolfart and includes roughly 73,000 Cree word tokens.

---

[2]The full results are available: https://gist.github.com/ eddieantonio/1b0f25f1c6d78e6dfb611f490a0822c7

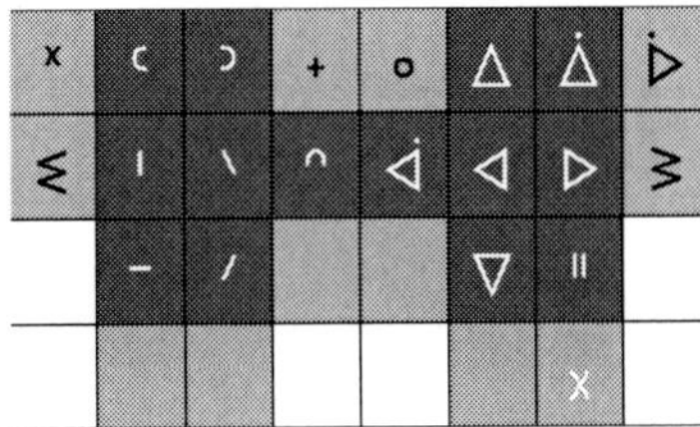

Figure 4: The grid of our placements with syllabics keys filled in. Lighter areas indicate harder-to-type keys; darker areas indicate easier-to-type keys.

Most texts in the corpus are some sort of narrative being told to the interviewer. The corpus is written entirely in SRO, but since the mapping between SRO and syllabics is (for the most part) straightforward, SRO letter frequencies are informative when creating a "build-a-syllable" keyboard.

First, we placed generic keys, such as the spacebar, the return key, the full-stop key (x) and the backspace key in areas that are frequent among QWERTY smartphone keyboard layouts. Then, we placed the most frequent consonant, ˋ (/k/) in the dark area on the left-hand side; then, we placed the most frequent vowel, ◁ (/ɛ/), in the right-hand area of the grid. We continued this by placing higher frequency keys in the darker areas of Figure 3, and then placing lower-frequency letters in lighter areas. Consonants were placed primarily on the left-hand side, while all 7 vowels were placed on the right-hand side. Most of the placement of the keys were based on the corpus statistics, however some keys were placed for aesthetic value. For example, the ≲ (/l/) and ≳ (/r/) were placed opposite of each other, since both are only used for loanwords from English and French. The <hk> digraph occurred 5414 times in the corpus; thus, <hk> is less frequent than <c>—so we placed it in a harder-to-type place. In total, we assigned 12 consonants, 7 vowels, and ˣ (/hk/), and for a total of 20 keys, requiring at least three rows of 8 keys per row. Since we only require three rows for syllabic characters, and an extra row for the spacebar and punctuation, we removed the top row from Figure 3; this row is reserved for presenting predictive text suggestions, however predictive text is not addressed in this paper. The final layout we obtained is in Figure 4.

Note that the hyphen occurred 14,740 times in the corpus; the hyphen is used in SRO as a *morpheme separator*, especially, to separate prefixes from the verb stem. Upon consultation with Cree syllabics writers (Wolvengrey, 2018; Ogg, 2018), we decided the equivalent to a hyphen in syllabics should be a **thin, non-breaking space**. For this we used U+202F NARROW NO-BREAK SPACE or the NNBSP. This follows the precedent set by Mongolian orthography, in which the NNBSP is used as a thinner space that separate affixes *without introducing a word break* (The Unicode Consortium, 2019a). The full-sized space is still used as a word separator.

To write the thinner, non-breaking space, we added a *secondary spacebar* above the regular spacebar. Much like the thinner space itself, the secondary spacebar is thinner than the regular spacebar. This key was positioned above the regular space, and centered horizontally.

5.3 Development with Keyman Developer

As its name suggests, we made the **Keyman** layout using the Keyman Developer software (2020).

To create a "build-a-syllable" *dynamic layout*—where some keys change based on the consonant just typed—we implemented the keyboard using several *layers*. "Layers" is the term that Keyman Developer refers to as *pages* in the rest of this paper; however, while a page in a layout such as FirstVoices consists of completely different keys, in the Keyman layout, we employed layers to implement *variations* of the primary page.

We created Keyman layers for the primary page (the *default* layer) and created layers for all possible **CV**, and **CwV** consonant "shapes". All of these layers were identical, except that the keys for the vowels were changed to reflect the previously typed consonant. For example, starting from the default layer (Figure 5a), typing the ˋ (/k/) final switches to the kV layer (Figure 5b), which swaps all of the vowel syllabics with all possible **kV** syllabics, namely, ꝗ, ꝓ, ꝺ, ꝷ, ꝓ̇, ꝺ̇, ꝷ̇. Pressing any of these keys replaces the ˋ with the indicated **kV** syllabic. If instead, one presses ○ (/w/), the keyboard switches to the kwV layer (Figure 5c), swapping all the vowels once again with all **kwV** syllabics—ꝗ·, ꝓ·, ꝺ·, ꝷ·, ꝓ̇·, ꝺ̇·, ꝷ̇·. Pressing a **kwV** syllabic replaces the ˋ○ with the appropriate syllabic. In this way, a syllabic is "built" by first typing a final, then optionally typing ○, and finally its corresponding vowel is selected.

Layer switching was accomplished using Keyman's next-layer directive for keys. In addition, each non-default layer visually highlights the keys that differ from the default layer, as well as highlighting which consonant keys have been pressed (Figures 5b, 5c).

In total, the keyboard contains 19 layers: the default layer, 9 **CV** layers, 8 **CwV** layers, and a *numeric* layer to type Arabic numerals and additional punctuation. Since duplicating the same layer several times with minor changes is an error-prone process, we wrote Python code to generate the .keyman-touch-layout file that defines the layout. The source code to generate the layout is open-source and can be found online.[3]

The **Keyman layout** can be installed on either iOS (iPhone) or Android smartphones by downloading the Keyman app,[4] and then then installing the nrc_crk_cans layout, either within the app, or online.[5] We have also written a short tutorial for using the layout on Keyman's website.[6]

6. Evaluation

In order to evaluate the Keyman layout, we opted to measure the accuracy, pleasantness, and general efficacy of both the FirstVoices and Keyman layouts. This evaluation was composed of two main components: quantitative data collected during controlled typing experiments (Section 6.2.1) and qualitative data collected by questionnaire

---

[3]https://github.com/eddieantonio/
plains-cree-touch-keyboard/tree/master/release/nrc/
nrc_crk_cans/extras

[4]https://keyman.com/downloads/

[5]https://keyman.com/keyboards/nrc_crk_cans

[6]https://help.keyman.com/keyboard/nrc_crk_cans/1.
0.1/nrc_crk_cans.php

(a) Default layer   (b) kV layer   (c) kwV layer

Figure 5: Switching layers in the Keyman layout. (Note: images have been scaled down).

(Section 6.2.2). The remainder of this section describes the demographics of participants and the methodologies of the quantitative and qualitative analyses.

6.1 Participants

For the purposes of this case study, we recruited three participants from the Edmonton, Alberta, Canada area. Participants were recruited through open calls at the University of Alberta and targeted recruitment of Plains Cree speakers with syllabics literacy. Participants ranged from 22–52 years of age (with a mean age of 32.67). Females composed two of the three participants, and all three participants identified as First Nations or Métis. Two of the three participants completed all parts of the study. Every participant had an extensive background in typing on smartphones, regularly communicated in Plains Cree, and used syllabics on a smartphone or computer at least multiple times a week. Given that testing focused on reproducing stimuli, fluency in Plains Cree was not a requirement, but familiarity with syllabics and smartphones was. Figure 6 provides basic demographic information for participants and their relationship to both Cree and syllabics on a 5-point Likert scale measuring how much they agreed with each statement.

Although no participants had made use of our Keyman layout previous to this study, Participants A and C both had prior experience using the FirstVoices layout. Participant B had no prior experience with either of the layouts studied. Although participants would have ideally had no knowledge of either layout tested, considering that there are only a few options available for typing syllabics on a smartphone, prior experience was unavoidable. Worth noting is that, despite being *able* to read and write syllabics, Participant B expressed discomfort in doing so.

6.2 Methodology

We invited each participant to a 90 minute study, conducted at the University of Alberta. The 90 minute study comprised of a typing study to collect quantitative data regarding the speed and accuracy of each keyboard layout, followed by a short questionnaire to collect qualitative data.

6.2.1 Quantitative Methodology

To collect quantitative data regarding the speed and accuracy of using both keyboard layouts, we had participants take part in a typing experiment. The typing experiment was facilitated by one of the authors.

Participants were given a Samsung A10 smartphone running the Android 9.0 operating system for the duration of the typing test. The Samsung A10 is 155.6mm tall, 75.6mm wide, and 7.9mm thick. It has a diagonal screen size of 6.2 inches (157mm). The typing experiment was presented using an ad hoc web application, running in standalone mode. We have posted the source code of this application online.[7] The following methodology was repeated twice—once for the FirstVoices layout, and then again for the Keyman layout. First, one of the two keyboard layouts was selected by the study facilitator. The study facilitator then left the room, giving participants a chance to **learn** and **practice** using the layout, privately, and at their own pace. We intentionally did not teach participants how to use the selected layout; instead, participants had to teach themselves how to use it. We presented 10 hand-picked words as prompts on a single screen. Participants were asked to type the prompts in a text box positioned directly underneath it. These prompts could be completed in any order. It was not mandatory for participants to type these prompts accurately; it was only mandatory that each prompt was attempted. No data were collected during this period.

After the practice period, the participants asked the study facilitator back into the room. Then, participants were given a chance to ask the facilitator how to type *specific* character sequences. The study facilitator would instruct in a rehearsed and structured form, for any question asked by the participant. Once satisfied, participants moved on to the typing task. The facilitator instructed participants to type each prompt as quickly and as accurately as possible. The facilitator left the room again to allow the participant to complete the typing task in private. We presented 30 sentences of Plains Cree syllabics to participants for each layout. We used a different set of 30 sentences for each layout, resulting in 60 different sentences presented in the study. Before seeing each stimulus, participants were allowed to take a break, if desired. The sentences used as stimuli were first prompted without a text box for 30 seconds to prime participants. This was to encourage participants to fully read the stimulus. After the 30 second priming period, a text box would appear, allowing participants to type the prompt. We manually constructed stimuli sentences to test the most common syllabics observed in the Ahenakew-Wolfart corpus (Arppe et al., 2019). This was chosen over directly pulling sentences from the mentioned corpus because the conversational nature of the sentences required excessive editing. Furthermore, many of the "clauses" in the corpus were defined by speech pauses, and include multiple clauses that made little sense without the requisite context. In order to capture behaviour as naturally as possible, participants

---

[7]https://github.com/eddieantonio/typing-test.

92

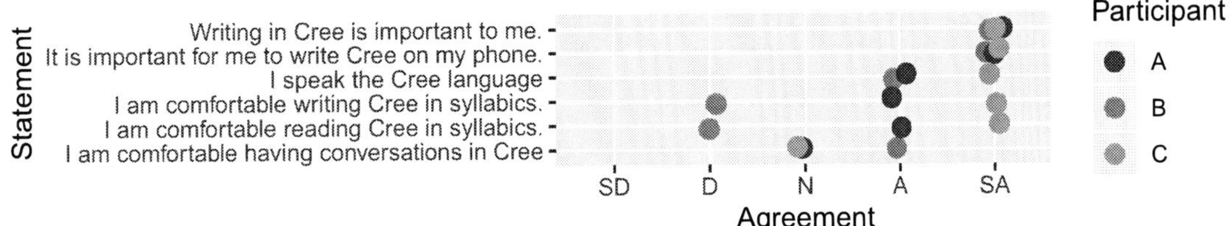

Figure 6: Likert scale responses for participant demographics. Responses from left-to-right are strongly disagree, disagree, neutral, agree, and strongly agree.

were not presented with individual words, but grammatical clauses or sentences. Sentences were constructed to be fully grammatical clauses that could be easily understood, even if incomplete (e.g. the English subordinate clause: *if I ever see him again...*). There are 95 individual syllabics used in this corpus. Because constructing a set that covers all 95 syllabics would require a large number of sentences, only those characters in the 90th percentile by frequency were tested. The remaining syllabics occurred fewer than 20 times in a corpus of over 200,000 characters. The number of sentences presented was capped at 30 per layout to maximize the number of syllabics tested without overly taxing participants, as participants took roughly 80 minutes to complete two sets of 30 sentences (60 sentences in total).

Data was collected starting when the participant tapped on the text box, issuing a *focus event*. Upon focusing the text box, the keyboard would pop-up, allowing the participant to type. We collected timing information for each key tapped by the participant, including the backspace key. Keystroke events were collected in JavaScript by registering an event handler on the HTML <textarea> used for the text box, listening on all input DOM events. Timestamps were collected by recording the return value of performance.now(), which yields timestamps with a 0.1 ms time resolution on Google Chrome 78 for Android (McIlroy and Kyöstilä, 2018). Input events were collected until the participant tapped the Done button, in the upper left-hand corner of the screen.

We measured the speed of each layout by determining the time intervals between the user starting (the *focus event*) and finishing each stimuli (pressing the Done button). We then divided these times by the number of characters in each of the presented stimuli to determine the average time-to-type per character for each sentence. We did this because not all stimuli sentence contained the same number of characters.

In addition to speed, we assessed the accuracy of each layout. To determine each layout's accuracy we compared stimuli and input data via ocreval (Santos, 2019). In addition to error rates, we reviewed the various errors and categorized them into distinct types.

6.2.2 Qualitative Methodology

Qualitative data was collected directly after the typing experiment via an online questionnaire administered on a laptop given to each participant. Qualitative assessments were measured in two ways: an open ended invitation for the participant to provide any general feedback on each layout, as well as a set of 5-point Likert scale agreement ratings (as described for participant demographics). These ratings were composed of the following seven statements:

1. I would use this keyboard again to type Cree syllabics.
2. I would recommend this keyboard to my friends, family, and/or students.
3. Overall, I like using this keyboard.
4. I can type quickly with this keyboard.
5. This keyboard was easy to use.
6. I can type on this keyboard without making mistakes.
7. I could find each syllabic easily on this keyboard.

Participants were also asked to give any feedback they had in a free-form response for each layout.

The results of both the qualitative and quantitative assessments are presented and described in the rest of this paper.

7. Results

This section details the quantitative results (i.e., accuracies and averages) and qualitative results (i.e., questionnaire responses) of this case study.

7.1 Quantitative Results

The foremost quantitative result that we have access to is the accuracy rate of each layout. Regardless of ease or enjoyability, a keyboard that is prone to mistakes is an inferior keyboard. Table 2 details the accuracies of each layout for each participant. Overall, the two keyboards layouts performed quite similarly, though the FirstVoices layout appears to have a very slight advantage, with a mean of 96.50% compared to the Keyman layout's 96.06%. Due to having a negative reaction to using the Keyman layout, Participant B declined to progess beyond the practice stage on this layout.

As shown in Table 2, there appears to be significant differences between participants. Participant A's FirstVoices results were 5% higher in accuracy than their Keyman layout's results. Conversely, Participant C's Keyman layout accuracy was roughly 1.5% higher than their FirstVoices results. Participant B's FirstVoices results were lower than both Participant A's and Participant C's results.

The actual types of errors for each layout generally took one of three forms: mis-orienting characters (typing $\vee$ instead of $\wedge$), errors with a w-dot (adding one where there was none, not typing one when prompted), and general insertions/deletions of completely incorrect characters. Interestingly, regardless of participant, the FirstVoices layout tended to have a larger variety of errors. Conversely,

	FirstVoices	Keyman
Participant A	98.88%	93.70%
Participant B	93.70%	N/A
Participant C	96.92%	98.42%
Mean	96.50%	96.06%

Table 2: Keyboard Accuracies

the Keyman layout errors were largely those of spacing:
the Keyman layout's novel feature— the thin, non-breaking
space—was never used by Participant A and was frequently
missed by Participant C. Spacing errors alone made up 31
out of 43 (72%) of the Keyman layout's errors. Since the
thin spaces are a feature of the Keyman layout alone, when
we disregard these errors, the overall accuracy of the Keyman layout rose to 98.8%, two percent points higher than
the FirstVoices keyboard.

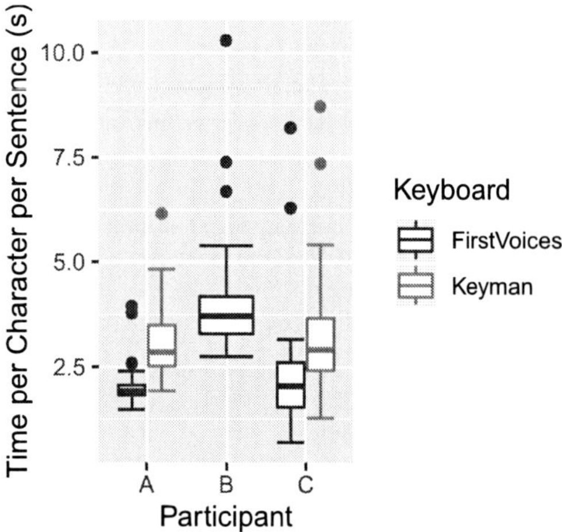

Figure 7: Average time-to-type per sentence (in seconds).

In addition to accuracy, we calculated the average time it
took to type each character for each stimuli sentence. Because the number of characters varied between stimuli sentences, we opted to divided the total time it took to type each
sentence by the number of characters in that sentence. This
measure, *time-to-type*, was used to evaluate how fast a participant was able to type on each layout. Figure 7 plots the
average time to type a character per stimuli sentence.

7.2 Qualitative Results

Participants as a whole preferred the FirstVoices layout.
Figure 8 plots participant responses to each of the questions
detailed in Section 6.2.2. The labels on the y-axes represent
abbreviated forms of the questions from Section 6.2.2.
All three participants generally agreed with all statements
for the FirstVoices layout, indicating positive attitudes toward the keyboard. The only negative ratings were from
Participants A and C who disagreed that the keyboard allowed for accurate typing. Participant A also reported a
neutral response toward the keyboard being quick to type
on. Notably, all participants agreed that they would recom-

mend the FirstVoices layout to friends and family, and that
they would use the keyboard again. Participant C reported
a strong agreement toward recommendation and regarding
the ease to find keys on the keyboard (henceforth *naviga-
bility*). Results for the Keyman layout were more varied.
Participant B *strongly disagreed* with all statements, suggesting a very negative impression of this layout. Participant C *disagreed* with all statements, except for describing
ease of use, a statement with which they agreed. Participant
A had mixed feelings: they disagreed that the Keyman layout was quick and navigable, were neutral as to how easy
the keyboard was to use and how likely they were to recommend it, and agreed that they would use the keyboard again,
liked the keyboard, and that the keyboard was accurate.
In freeform feedback for the keyboards, one participant reported issues with the FirstVoices spacebar being too small,
and that the ᐦ key was too close to the backspace key, causing accidental deletions throughout the session. Participant
A mentioned that they like the layout of the FirstVoices layout, and that once they realized each row contained syllabics
with the same vowel, it became easy to use.
Regarding the Keyman layout, one participant described
their issues as being that "This keyboard required too much
thinking, slowing down the typing process. I liked the idea
about it and its simplicity, but after a while I started not to
like it just because it took too long." Another participant
suggested that our layout was too rooted in English ideology, and that they did not think of syllabics of being proce-
durally generated first by a consonant to determine shape,
and then by a vowel to determine orientation. This participant further suggested adopting a keyboard layout reminis-
cent of the "star chart" layout as described in Houle (2018).
Although this layout is familiar to some, it is by no means
learned by the majority of syllabics users.
Both layouts were criticized for being too small by multiple
participants. They reported poor accuracy due to not being
able to read key labels. One participant noted that the ex-
clamation mark was unavailable on both layouts. In fact,
this symbol was available on the Keyman layout, but required a long press to be accessed and so went unnoticed by
this participant. Finally, one participant reported generally
"having issues" with both keyboards and wanting a solution for mobile typing of Plains Cree syllabics; they made it
clear, however, that the Keyman layout was not the solution
they were looking for.

8. Discussion

The results described above expressed a general preference
for the FirstVoices layout. On nearly every dimension, the
FirstVoices layout was preferred over the Keyman layout,
regardless of which participant was doing the ratings. It
is worth noting, however, that Participants A and C report
previous familiarity with the FirstVoices layout. Given their
extremely limited exposure to the Keyman layout, the lack
of confidence in using it is understandable. Accuracies were
comparable between keyboards, though the FirstVoices'
was slightly higher. However, most of the Keyman layout's errors were due to not using the non-breaking space,
a feature not found in the FirstVoices layout. When ignoring these errors, the Keyman layout proved *more accurate*

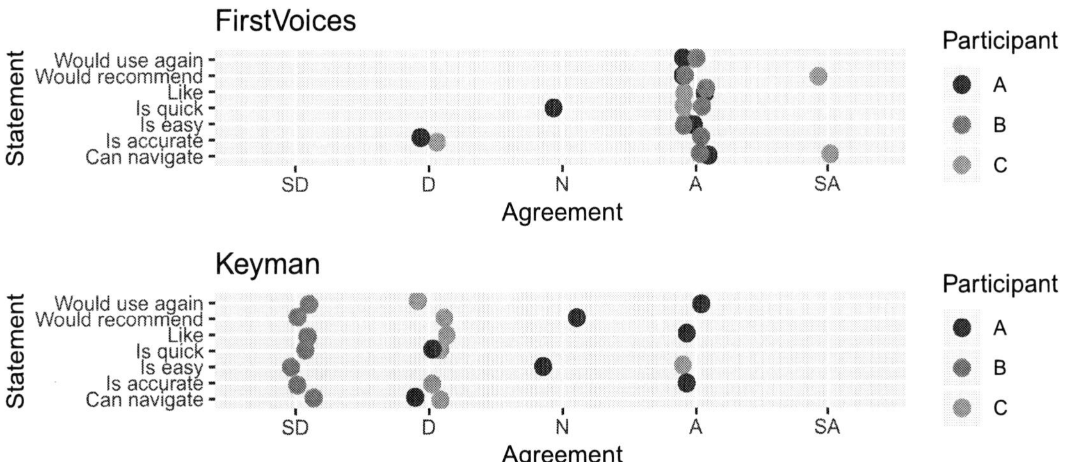

Figure 8: Responses to usage questionnaire about the layouts.

than FirstVoices keyboard. Further, the FirstVoices layout was observed to have a broader ranger of errors, though this may be due to the fact that it was the only keyboard used by Participant B, who exhibited a much higher error rate than the other two participants. The quantitative data suggest that despite being a more accurate keyboard, the Keyman layout was less pleasant to use.

In terms of qualitative assessments, all participants preferred the FirstVoices layout. Although some amount of preference is expected for a familiar keyboard layout, participants showed slower typing speeds on the Keyman layout and commented on the amount of effort it took to type on the Keyman layout. Although built from the ground up as a Cree-based keyboard, one that eschews European baggage, the Keyman layout supposed some amount of compositionally for the characters. Asking participants to first type a *final* version of a consonant and then presenting them with all syllabics using that consonant as an *onset* appeared to be unintuitive. Compared to the FirstVoices layout, which is a straightforward listing of all syllabics, participants had a harder time navigating through the keyboard to type the appropriate character. This in turn required a lot of thought. Considering that Plains Cree syllabic finals do not transparently map to the associated shape of their onset counterparts (e.g. ˋ and /k/ shares no similarities to the shape of syllabics with /k/ as an onset, like ᐸ), it is possible that participants struggled to quickly determine which *final* was needed for a given syllabic shape. This disconnect may have significantly contributed to the experience of using the keyboard.

In addition to mental effort, the Keyman layout required a lot of comfort and familiarity with syllabics. It is unsurprising that Participant B, who was least comfortable in syllabics, was completely unwilling to use the keyboard.

Efforts to improve the ergonomics seemed not to factor much into participants reviews. Despite community members disliking the current options available for typing Plains Cree—including the FirstVoices layout—participants struggled throughout the case study with the new Keyman layout. It remains unclear as to whether or not this is an effect of having little experience with the keyboard. It is plausible that, once participants familiarized themselves with the Keyman layout, their opinions could change. We intentionally avoided giving participants explicit training, but the Keyman layout proved unintuitive; however, it would be interesting to know the opinions of typists who have gained significant experience on the layout, rather than the 90 minute session presented in this paper. Future evaluation could require a longer timescale, allowing participants to learn and practice the layouts.

9. Conclusion

This paper has described an attempt to build a mobile keyboard for writing in Plains Cree syllabics. To address community calls for a Cree worldview based syllabics keyboard, we built a keyboard layout using the Keyman infrastructure. This keyboard required participants to first select the consonant of the syllabic they wished to type before presenting them with a set of syllabics using that consonant as an onset. As there is no English on this keyboard, participants had to choose a consonant value based on the consonant's final character. This keyboard was tested in a case study along side the existing FirstVoices layout for comparison. Although accuracy was higher on the Keyman layout, participants unanimously preferred the FirstVoices layout. The Keyman layout was reviewed as hard to use, requiring much mental effort, and being unpleasant, and slow. The results of this paper indicate that, while there is a desire for alternatives to the solutions that currently exists, there is a high cost in introducing an unfamiliar typing system and asking people to adapt to it.

10. Acknowledgements

Thanks to Marilyn Shirt for prompting this project. Thanks to Marc Durdin, Joshua Horton, and Darcy Wong for putting up with our constant bug reports. Thanks to Lorna Williams and David L. Rowe for helping us publish the keyboard on Keyman's website. Thanks to Anna Kazantseva and Roland Kuhn for their endless support. Thanks to the following people, in no particular order, for help with this paper: Aidan Pine, Antti Arppe, Delaney Lothian, Rebecca Knowles, and Katherine Schmirler. ᐸᖃᐊ᷎ᐣᑯᕐᓈᐅ᷎x

11. Bibliographical References

Arppe, A., Schmirler, K., Harrigan, A. G., and Wolvengrey, A. (2019). A morphosyntactically-tagged corpus for Plains Cree. In Maculay M. et al., editors, *Papers of the Forty-Ninth Algonquian Conference*, East Lansing. Michigan State University Press.

Cassels, M. (2019). Indigenous languages in new media: Opportunities and challenges for language revitalization. *Working Papers of the Linguistics Circle*, 29(1):25–43.

First Peoples' Cultural Council. (2016). FirstVoices apps. https://www.firstvoices.com/content/apps/, May. (Accessed on 02/03/2020).

Houle, J. R. (2018). ᒪᓯᓇᐦᐄᑫᔨᐣ ᐊᒑᐦᑭᐯᐦᐄᑲᓇ; masinatahikeyin acahkipehikana; typing syllabics. Master's thesis, University of Alberta, Edmonton, Alberta, Canada, September.

Keegan, T. T., Mato, P., and Ruru, S. (2015). Using Twitter in an Indigenous language: An analysis of Te Reo Māoria tweets. *AlterNative: An International Journal of Indigenous Peoples*, 11(1):59–75.

Keyman. (2020). Keyman | type to the world in your language. https://keyman.com/, January. (Accessed on 02/03/2020).

McIlroy, R. and Kyöstilä, S. (2018). Clamp performance.now() to 100us. https://chromium.googlesource.com/chromium/src/+/a77687fd89adc1bc2ce91921456e0b9b59388120%5E%21/, January. (Accessed on 02/06/2020).

Moshagen, S. N., Siewertsen, E., and Gaup, B. (2016). giellalt/keyboard-crk: Plains Cree keyboard layout. https://github.com/giellalt/keyboard-crk, May. (Accessed on 02/10/2020).

Norman, D. A. and Fisher, D. (1982). Why alphabetic keyboards are not easy to use: Keyboard layout doesn't much matter. *Human Factors*, 24(5):509–519.

Ogg, A. (2018). Private communication, September.

Park, Y. S. and Han, S. H. (2010). Touch key design for one-handed thumb interaction with a mobile phone: Effects of touch key size and touch key location. *International journal of industrial ergonomics*, 40(1):68–76.

Santos, E. A. (2019). OCR evaluation tools for the 21st century. In *Proceedings of the Workshop on Computational Methods for Endangered Languages*, volume 1, page 4.

Stevenson, W. (1999). Calling Badger and the Symbols of the Spirit Language: The Cree Origins of the Syllabic System. *Oral History Forum*, 19–20:19–24.

The Truth and Reconciliation Commission of Canada. (2015). What we have learned: Principles of truth and reconciliation. http://nctr.ca/assets/reports/Final%20Reports/Principles_English_Web.pdf.

The Unicode Consortium, (2019a). *The Unicode Standard, Version 12.1.0*, chapter 6, page 265. The Unicode Consortium, Mountain View, CA. http://www.unicode.org/versions/Unicode12.1.0/.

The Unicode Consortium. (2019b). Unified Canadian Aboriginal Syllabics range: 1400–167F. In *The Unicode Standard, Version 12.1.0*. The Unicode Consortium, Mountain View, CA. https://unicode.org/charts/PDF/U1400.pdf.

van Esch, D., Sarbar, E., Lucassen, T., O'Brien, J., Breiner, T., Prasad, M., Crew, E., Nguyen, C., and Beaufays, F. (2019). Writing across the world's languages: Deep internationalization for Gboard, the Google keyboard.

Wolfart, H. C. (1996). Sketch of Cree, an Algonquian language. In Ives Goddard, editor, *In Handbook of North American Indians*, volume 17, pages 390–439. Smithsonia Institution Washington, DC, USA.

Wolvengrey, A. (2018). Private communication, August.

Proceedings of the 1st Joint SLTU and CCURL Workshop (SLTU-CCURL 2020), pages 97–105
Language Resources and Evaluation Conference (LREC 2020), Marseille, 11–16 May 2020
© European Language Resources Association (ELRA), licensed under CC-BY-NC

MultiSeg: Parallel Data and Subword Information for Learning Bilingual Embeddings in Low Resource Scenarios

Efsun Sarioglu Kayi * , **Vishal Anand** * , **Smaranda Muresan**
Columbia University
Department of Computer Science, New York, NY, USA
{ek3050, va2361, sm761}@columbia.edu

Abstract

Distributed word embeddings have become ubiquitous in natural language processing as they have been shown to improve performance in many semantic and syntactic tasks. Popular models for learning cross-lingual word embeddings do not consider the morphology of words. We propose an approach to learn bilingual embeddings using parallel data and subword information that is expressed in various forms, i.e. character n-grams, morphemes obtained by unsupervised morphological segmentation and byte pair encoding. We report results for three low resource languages (Swahili, Tagalog, and Somali) and a high resource language (German) in a simulated a low-resource scenario. Our results show that our method that leverages subword information outperforms the model without subword information, both in intrinsic and extrinsic evaluations of the learned embeddings. Specifically, analogy reasoning results show that using subwords helps capture syntactic characteristics. Semantically, word similarity results and intrinsically, word translation scores demonstrate superior performance over existing methods. Finally, qualitative analysis also shows better-quality cross-lingual embeddings particularly for morphological variants in both languages.

Keywords: low resource languages, crosslingual embeddings, byte-pair encoding, morphological segmentation

1. Introduction

Considering the internal word structure when learning monolingual word embeddings has shown to produce better quality word representations, particularly for morphologically rich languages (Luong et al., 2013; Bojanowski and others, 2017). However, the most popular approaches for learning cross-lingual embeddings have yet to use subword information directly during learning in the cross-lingual space.

One of the most widely used approaches for monolingual embeddings (fastText) (Bojanowski and others, 2017) extends the continuous skip-gram model with negative sampling (SGNS) (Mikolov et al., 2013a) to learn subword information given as character n-grams and then representing words as the sum of the n-gram vectors. SGNS has also been used to learn bilingual embeddings using parallel data, the most notable approach being BiSkip (a.k.a, BiVec) (Luong et al., 2015a). This joint model learns bilingual word representations by exploiting both the context co-occurrence information through the monolingual component and the meaning equivalent signals from the bilingual constraint given by the parallel data.

We propose a combined approach that *integrates subword information directly when learning bilingual embeddings* leveraging the two extensions of the SGNS approach. Our model extends the BiSkip model that uses parallel data by learning representations of subwords and then representing words as the sum of the subword vectors (as was done in the monolingual case for character n-grams (Bojanowski and others, 2017)). As subwords, we consider character n-grams , morphemes obtained using a state-of-the-art unsupervised morphological segmentation approach (Eskander et al., 2018) and byte pair encoding (BPE) (Sennrich et al., 2016).

* Equal Contribution

We report results for learning bilingual embeddings for three low resource languages (Swahili-swa, Tagalog-tgl, and Somali-som) and a high resource language (German-deu), all of which are morphologically rich languages. For German, we simulate a low-resource learning scenario ($100K$ parallel data). Our results show that our method that leverages subword information outperforms the BiSkip approach, both in intrinsic and extrinsic evaluations of the learned embeddings (Section 3.). Specifically, analogy reasoning results show that using subwords helps capture syntactic characteristics. Qualitative and intrinsic analysis also shows better-quality cross-lingual embeddings particularly for morphological variants.

2. Methodology

Our proposed method to learn bilingual embeddings uses both parallel data and information about the internal structure of words in both languages during training. In SGNS, given a sequence of words $w_1, ..., w_T$, the objective is to maximize average log probability where c represents the context:

$$1/T \sum_{t=1}^{T} \sum_{c} logp(w_c|w_t), \qquad (1)$$

This probability can be calculated with a softmax function as below:

$$logp(w_c|w_t) = \frac{\sum e^{u_{w_t}^T v_{w_c}}}{\sum^{W} e^{u_{w_t}^T v_w}} \qquad (2)$$

where W is the size of the vocabulary, and u_{w_t} and v_{w_c} are the corresponding word vector representations for w_c and w_t in $\mathbb{R}$. BiSkip (Luong et al., 2015b) uses sentence-level aligned data (parallel data) to learn bilingual embeddings by extending the SGNS to predict the surrounding words in each language, using SGNS for both the monolingual and cross-lingual objective. In other words, given two languages l_1 and l_2, BiSkip model trains four SGNS models

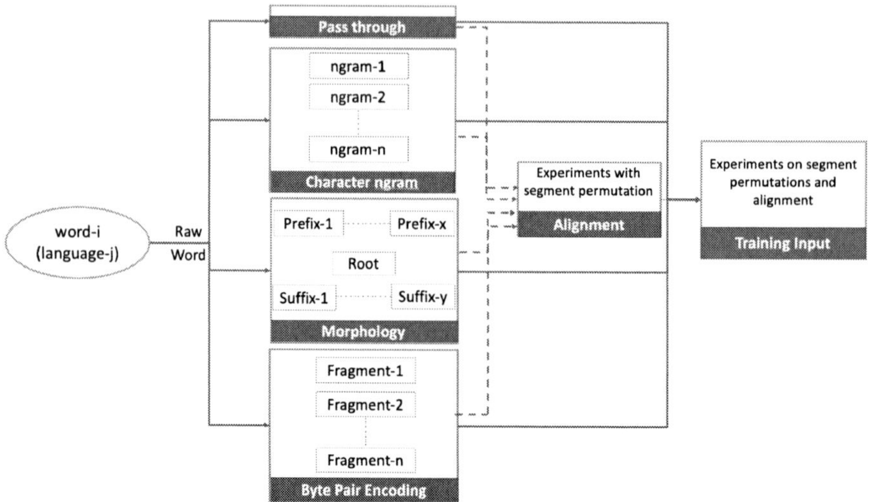

(a) Training and Alignment Schema for word w_i in language l_j

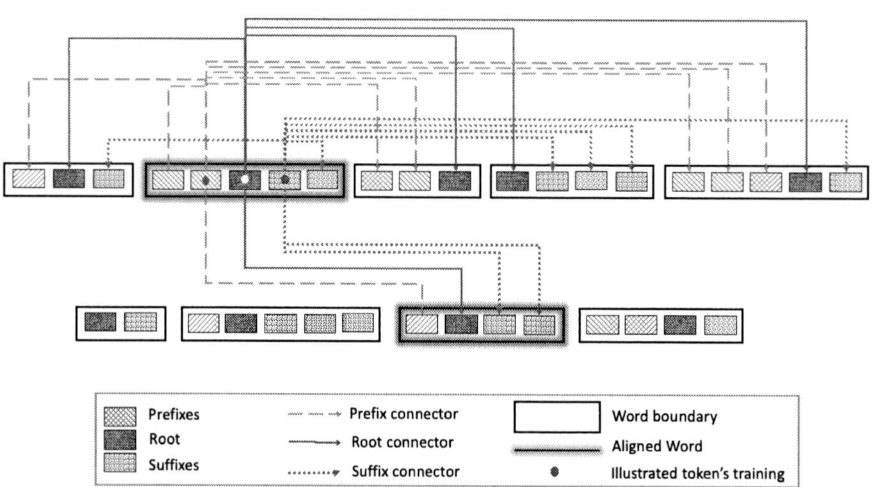

(b) MultiSeg model illustration for Morph$_{All}$ case

Figure 1: MultiSeg Architecture

	Somali	English
Word	Wax aanan si fiican umaqlin ayuu ku celceliyey .	he repeated something that I could not hear well .
Stem	Wax aan si fiic maql ayuu ku celcel .	he repeat someth that I could not hear well .
Alignment	Wax:something aanan:something aanan:I si:that si:could fiican:well umaqlin:hear ayuu:not ku:NA celceliyey:repeated	

Table 1: English-Somali Alignment

jointly which predict words between the following pairs of languages:

$$l_1 \rightarrow l_1, l_2 \rightarrow l_2, l_1 \rightarrow l_2, l_2 \rightarrow l_1 \tag{3}$$

However, in this model each word is assigned a distinct vector. To take into account the morphology of words in both languages, we extend BiSkip to include subword information during learning. The approach is based on the idea introduced by Bojanowski and others (2017) for the monololingual fastText embeddings, where the SGNS is extended to learn the representation of character n-grams and then represent the word as the sum of its n-gram vectors as in Equation 4 where N is set of character n-grams and c_n is the word embedding for n-gram n.

$$w = 1/|N| \sum_{n \in N} c_n \tag{4}$$

In our approach, which we call MultiSeg, we consider subwords as character n-grams (between *3* and *6* as in fast-Text), or as morphemes, or as byte pair encoding (BPE)

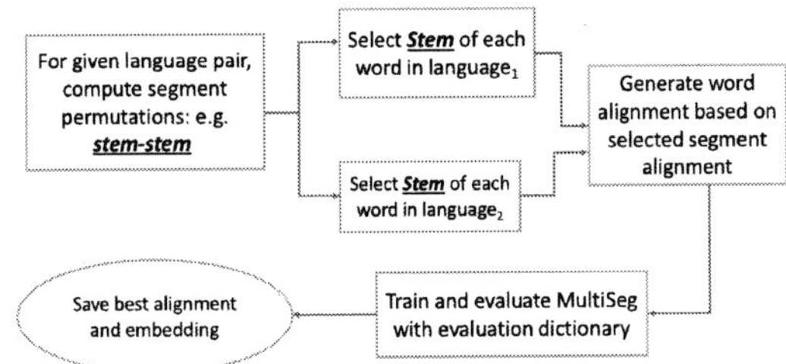

Figure 2: Alignment algorithm

that are computed by merging most frequent adjacent pairs of characters in the corpora. When considering morphemes as subwords, we either split the words into *prefix, stem* and *suffix*, or we consider all morphemes, that is the *stem* and all *affixes*. We use an unsupervised morphological segmentation approach (Eskander et al., 2018; Eskander et al., 2019) based on Adaptor Grammars that has been shown to produce state-of-the-art results for a variety of morphologically rich languages (e.g., Turkish, Arabic, and 4 Uto-Aztecan languages which are low resource and polysynthetic).

We denote our proposed method using each subword type as MultiSeg$_{CN}$ (uses char n-gram as representation during training), MultiSeg$_M$ (uses prefix, stem, suffix morphemes), MultiSeg$_{morph_{all}}$ (uses all morphemes), MultiSeg$_{BPE}$ (uses byte pair encondings), MultiSeg$_{All}$ (uses all subword types as representations during training). Figure 1a shows all possible segmentations for a given word in a language. Once best alignment is chosen, e.g. word-level or stem-level alignment, it is passed as input data to the training algorithm. As an example, Figure 1b shows subword structure i.e. morphological segmentation, of two parallel sentences, one in English and the other in low resource language. First sentence consists of five words and the corresponding aligned sentence consists of four words and internally, they are made up of various counts of segments i.e. one root and one or more prefixes and suffixes. For the current word in training (highlighted in the Figure 1b), corresponding aligned word in the other sentence is also highlighted and their internal alignment is shown. Similarly, within the same sentence, the current word's internal alignment with neighboring words in its context is shown. For aligning segments of the words, we consider several possibilities i.e. word and stem-based alignment and pick the best one as shown in Figure 2. Example Somali and English sentences and their stemmed output is shown in Table 1. In the case that alignment based on stem performs better than alignment based on words, word level alignment can still be constructed through stem-to-word connection.

Dataset	Parallel Sentences	Vocabulary	TD
Swahili	24,900	48,259	7,720
Tagalog	51,704	43,646	9,523
Somali	24,000	66,870	12,119
German	100,000	59,333	57,617

Table 2: Data Statistics (TD: Test Dictionary pairs)

2.1. Training of Bilingual Embeddings

This section describes the data used for training our bilingual word embeddings and our evaluation setup, including the evaluation datasets and measures.

We build bilingual embeddings for Swahili-English, Tagalog-English, Somali-English and German-English. For Swahili, Tagalog and Somali, we use parallel corpora provided by the IARPA MATERIAL program[1]. Data statistics for each language i.e. size of parallel corpora, vocabulary and dictionaries, are listed in Table 2. For German, we use the Europarl dataset (Koehn, 2005). Since the size of this parallel dataset is much larger than the others (1,908,920), we select a random subset of $100K$ parallel sentence to imitate a low-resource scenario. This is important as parallel corpora is more costly to obtain than other bilingual resources, such as dictionaries. For all the models, symmetric word alignments from parallel corpora are learned via the fast align tool (Dyer et al., 2013). For aligning segments of the words, we compute word and stem-based alignments and between the two, aligning based on stem performs better across all languages and dimensions. We train embeddings with different dimensions, $d = 40$ and $d = 300$, for 20 iterations. Our code for training Multi-Seg embeddings, pre-trained cross-lingual embeddings and evaluation scripts such as word translation score and coverage will be publicly available[2].

We evaluate our approach both intrinsically and extrinsically on various monolingual and cross-lingual tasks and compare the performance to the BiSkip baseline. Recall, that BiSkip does not use any subword information when training the bilingual embeddings.

2.1.1. Intrinsic Evaluation

Word Translation Task. An important intrinsic evaluation task for learning bilingual embeddings is the word translation task a.k.a. *bilingual dictionary induction* which assesses how good bilingual embeddings are at detecting word pairs that are semantically similar across languages by checking if translationally equivalent words in different languages are nearby in the embedding space. As our evaluation dictionaries, we use bilingual dictionaries derived from Wiktionary using *Wikt2Dict* tool (Acs et al., 2013) which has polysemous entries in both directions. We generate Swahili-English, Tagalog-English. Somali-English and German-English dictionaries (the sizes are given in Table 2). We argue that these dictionaries are more reliable as evaluation dictionaries compared to Google Translate dictionaries, which are generally used only for evaluation. We calculate precision at k, where $k = 1$ and $k = 10$) ($P@1$, $P@10$) for both source-to-target and target-to-source directions and take an average of these scores as the final accuracy. We take the definition of the task from (Ammar et al., 2016). In conjunction with $P@1$ and $P@10$, we also report coverage as in (Ammar et al., 2016), given as the total number of common word pairs (l_1, w_1), (l_2, w_2) that exist in both the test dictionary and the embedding, divided by size of the dictionary. The precision at 1 ($P@1$) score for

---

[1]MATERIAL is an acronym for Machine Translation for English Retrieval of Information in Any Language (Rubino, 2016)

[2]https://github.com/vishalanand/MultiSeg

| Model | Dimension | German | | Swahili | | Tagalog | | Somali | |
| | | Coverage: 0.159 | | Coverage: 0.212 | | Coverage: 0.116 | | Coverage: 0.195 | |
		P@1	P@10	P@1	P@10	P@1	P@10	P@1	P@10
BiSkip	40	0.278	0.379	0.528	0.666	0.554	0.698	0.404	0.630
	300	0.358	0.492	0.613	0.749	0.640	0.770	0.513	0.729
MultiSeg$_{CN}$	40	0.296	0.429	0.580	0.728	0.624	0.774	0.440	0.708
	300	0.376	**0.566**	**0.632**	0.749	0.666	**0.828**	0.525	**0.830**
MultiSeg$_{M}$	40	0.309	0.438	0.580	0.731	0.626	0.780	0.451	0.704
	300	**0.382**	0.559	**0.632**	0.788	0.673	0.818	0.532	0.815
MultiSeg$_{M_{all}}$	40	0.306	0.435	0.580	0.731	0.625	0.778	0.449	0.701
	300	0.380	0.556	0.631	0.784	**0.674**	0.822	**0.538**	0.813
MultiSeg$_{BPE}$	40	0.294	0.421	0.575	0.719	0.595	0.750	0.449	0.682
	300	0.373	0.541	0.626	0.776	0.656	0.809	0.534	0.791
MultiSeg$_{All}$	40	0.305	0.440	0.570	0.726	0.611	0.778	0.454	0.724
	300	0.367	0.556	0.620	**0.798**	0.665	0.825	0.531	0.829

Table 3: Word translation scores and coverage percentages for all languages

Language	English	Deu/Swa/Tgl/Som	BiSkip	MultiSeg$_{CN}$	MultiSeg$_{M}$	MultiSeg$_{M_{all}}$	MultiSeg$_{M_{BPE}}$
German	correct	berichtigen					x
	correction	berichtigung			x	x	x
Swahili	office	afisi		x			
	officer	afisa	x	x	x	x	x
Tagalog	mine	akin			x		
	my	aking	x	x	x	x	x
Somali	approve	ansixinta				x	
	approving	ansixiyay			x		

Table 4: Qualitative Analysis: x show if the method correctly learned the word translation

one word pair $(l_1, w_1), (l_2, w_2)$ both of which are covered by an embedding E is 1 if $cosine(E(l_1, w_1), E(l_2, w_2)) \geq cosine(E(l_1, w_1), E(l_2, w_2')) \ \forall w_2' \in G^{l_2}$ here G^{l_2} is the set of words of language l_2 in the evaluation dataset, and *cosine* is the cosine similarity function. Otherwise, the score is 0. The overall score is the average score for all word pairs covered by the embedding. Precision at 10 ($P@10$) is computed as the fraction of the entries (w_1, w_2) in the test dictionary, for which w_2 belongs to the top-10 neighbors of the word vector of w_1.

Analogy Reasoning Task. Analogy reasoning task consists of questions of the form if A is to B then what is C to D, where D must be predicted. Question is assumed to be correctly answered if the closest word to the vector is exactly the same as the correct word in the question. We use the datasets for English (Mikolov et al., 2013b) which consist of 8,869 semantic and 10,675 syntactic questions. Some of the example semantic categories are *Capital City*, *Currency*, *City-in-State* and *Man-Woman* and some of the example syntactic categories are *opposite, superlative, plural nouns* and *past tense*.

Word Similarity Task. Word similarity datasets contain word pairs which are assigned similarity ratings by humans. These rankings are then compared with cosine similarity between the word vectors based on the Spearman's rank correlation coefficient to estimate how well they capture semantic relatedness. In our evaluations, we use three word similarity datasets: WordSimilarity-353 (WS353) (Finkelstein et al., 2001), Stanford Rare Word (RW) similarity dataset (Luong et al., 2013), and Stanford's Contextual Word Similarities (SCWS) dataset (Huang et al., 2012).

2.1.2. Extrinsic Evaluation

As extrinsic evaluation of our embeddings in a downstream semantic task, we use Cross-Language Document Classification (CLDC)[3] (Klementiev et al., 2012). In this task, a document classifier is trained using the document representations derived from the cross-lingual embeddings for language l_1, and then the trained model is tested on documents from language l_2. The classifier is trained using the averaged perceptron algorithm and the document vectors are the averaged vector of words in the document weighted by their idf values. For this task, we only have dataset for German-English, and we report results where we train on $1,000$ documents and test on $5,000$ to be consistent with the original BiSkip setup.

3. Results

The performance on the *word translation task* for all languages is shown in Table 3, where the best scores are highlighted in red for dimension 40 and blue for dimension 300. MultiSeg methods outperform BiSkip for all languages both for $P@1$ and $P@10$. Among MultiSeg methods, across languages, morphological segmentation based models have the best scores followed by MultiSeg$_{All}$ especially for $P10$ and with 40 dimension. MultiSeg$_{CN}$ with 300 dimension also performs well across languages specifically for $P10$. Through an error analysis, we noticed that some of the performance gain for MultiSeg was due to the fact that these models were able to learn word translations of morphological variants of words. Table 4 lists some of

---

[3]CLDC code is provided by the authors.

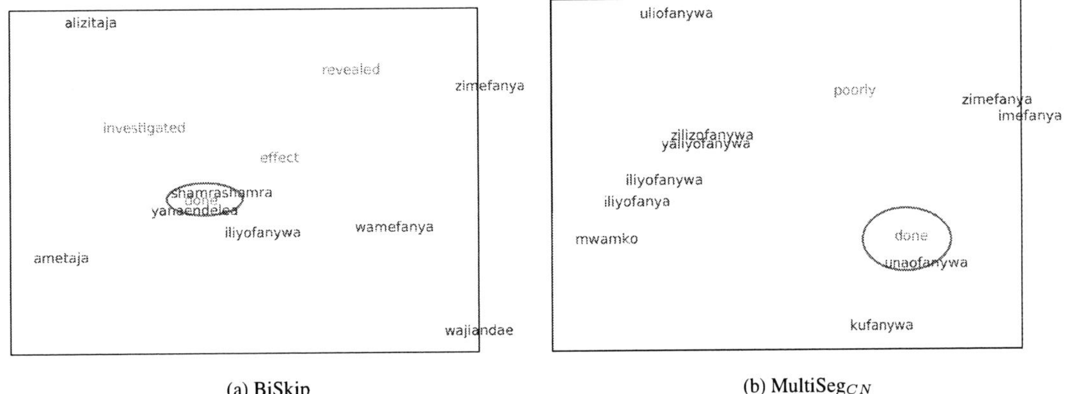

(a) BiSkip

(b) MultiSeg$_{CN}$

Figure 3: t-SNE visualization of English-Swahili vectors

(a) BiSkip

(b) MultiSeg$_{CN}$

Figure 4: t-SNE visualization for English-Tagalog vectors

the examples for the words from the test bilingual dictionaries and their morphological variants and show whether or not they are predicted correctly using each technique. For all of the languages, BiSkip is only able to predict zero or one form of the word correctly, whereas MultiSeg predict various forms of the words correctly in both English and other languages.

Qualitatively, two-dimensional visualizations of crosslingual word vectors are produced using t-Distributed Stochastic Neighbor Embedding (t-SNE) (van der Maaten and Hinton, 2008) dimensionality reduction method. Figures 3 and 4 show similar words related to the word *done* for Swahili and Tagalog respectively. It can be seen that MultiSeg$_{CN}$ learns better word representations than BiSkip by placing morphologically and semantically related words in both languages closer ($done - nagawa$, $did - ginawa$, $doing - ginagawa$). Similar graphs for Somali are provided in Figure 5 for all MultiSeg approaches. As an illustration, in Figure 5d, *qaranimo* is close to *togetherness* while the same (*nationhood*) is also shown in a coarser fashion in 5c, while other approaches could not capture this representation.

Word similarity, *analogy reasoning* and *CLDC* results for English and German are summarized in Table 5 where Spearman's rank correlation coefficients ($\rho * 100$) are reported for word similarity task and accuracy is reported for analogy reasoning task (as percentages) and for CLDC. MultiSeg approaches outperform BiSkip for all languages and for all tasks except semantic analogy. For syntactic and overall analogy reasoning scores, MultiSeg$_{All}$ performs the best which demonstrates that with better crosslingual embedding, a performance increase is seen in monolingual space, i.e. English. For CLDC task, morphological segmentation approaches, i.e. MultiSeg$_M$ and MultiSeg$_{MAll}$ perform the best. For word similarity task, overall MultiSeg$_{BPE}$ and MultiSeg$_{All}$ performs the best for English and MultiSeg$_{BPE}$ and MultiSeg$_{MAll}$ for German.

Word similarity and *analogy reasoning* results for English using low resource languages' cross-lingual embeddings are shown in Table 6. Again, MultiSeg approaches outperform BiSkip for all languages and for all tasks except for Somali semantic analogy and among them, MultiSeg$_{All}$ performs the best overall for all languages. A more detailed analysis of analogy reasoning task (Mikolov et al., 2013b) including breakdown of each semantic and syntactic cat-

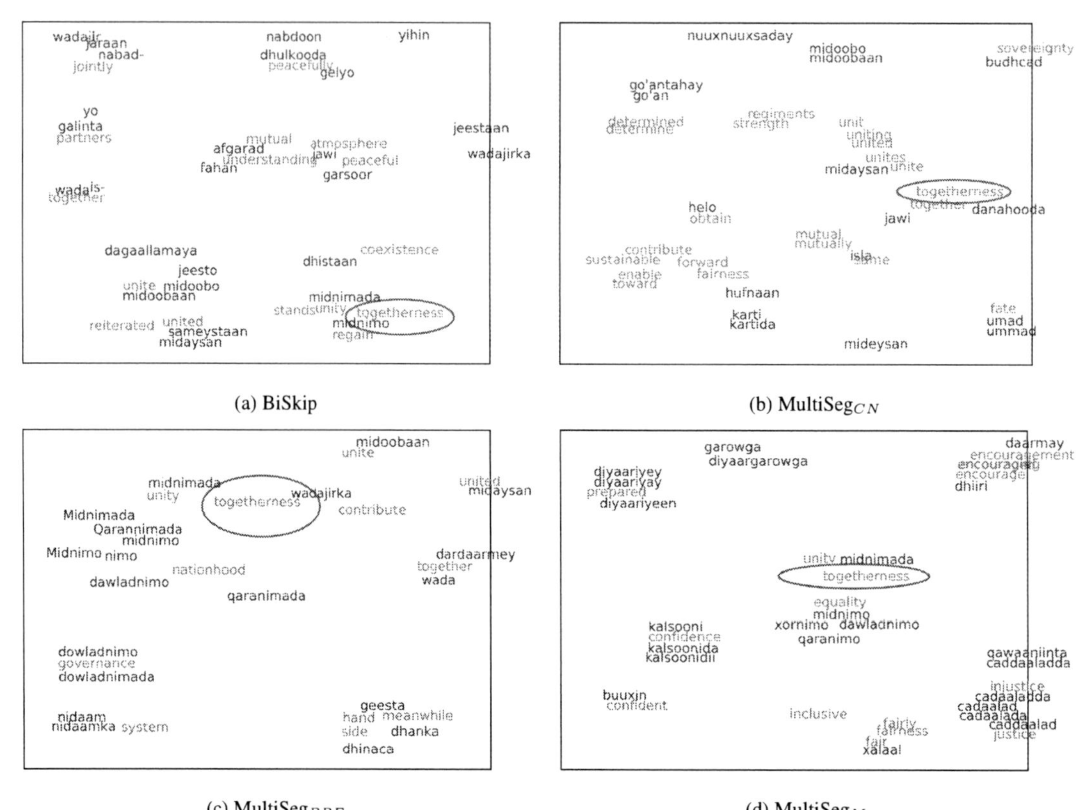

Figure 5: t-SNE visualization for English-Somali vectors

| Model | Dimension | Word Similarity | | | | Analogy Reasoning | | | CLDC | |
| | | German | English | | | English | | | | |
		WS353	WS353	SCWS	RW	Semantic	Syntactic	All	eng→deu	deu→eng
BiSkip	40	26.32	22.18	23.62	12.97	3.10	5.30	5.01	0.828	0.666
	300	25.40	22.65	21.65	8.30	**3.30**	7.74	7.16	0.839	0.667
MultiSeg$_{CN}$	40	27.60	25.77	25.91	13.64	1.20	27.56	24.11	0.814	0.662
	300	33.23	26.77	**28.68**	14.37	1.80	41.36	36.18	0.812	0.69
MultiSeg$_M$	40	31.10	28.48	25.61	16.44	2.80	21.64	19.18	0.841	0.710
	300	33.47	33.08	28.21	13.84	1.30	35.78	31.27	0.861	**0.734**
MultiSeg$_{M_{all}}$	40	31.35	30.14	26.85	16.60	2.80	22.15	19.62	0.836	0.724
	300	**36.00**	27.42	28.43	13.35	2.50	39.25	34.44	**0.864**	0.652
MultiSeg$_{BPE}$	40	32.03	33.83	25.51	15.11	1.70	11.28	10.03	0.812	0.720
	300	30.45	**33.64**	26.83	13.64	1.70	19.71	17.36	0.846	0.723
MultiSeg$_{All}$	40	26.97	28.59	26.86	16.82	1.20	34.80	30.41	0.822	0.631
	300	29.58	31.57	28.67	**15.52**	1.90	**48.95**	**42.79**	0.828	0.713

Table 5: German-English Monolingual and Cross-lingual Evaluation Results

egories can be seen in Figure 6 for Swahili.[4] Semantic analogy task consists of questions such as capital countries, currency, city-in-the-state and hence it does not necessarily benefit from our subword based approach. For German and Somali, BiSkip has the best performance in this category whereas for Swahili and Tagalog MultiSeg approaches perform the best. On the other hand, syntactic analogy consists of questions about base/comparative/superlative forms of adjectives, singular/plural and possessive/non-possessive forms of common nouns; and base, past and third person present tense forms of verbs. Accordingly, our representation is able to perform better for syntactical analogy questions where MultiSeg methods consistently outperform BiSkip in all of the categories. Among the MultiSeg representations, $MultiSeg_{CN}$ performs the best.

<hr>

[4]We obtained similar graphs for other languages.

Language	Model	Dimension	Word Similarity			Analogy Reasoning		
			WS353	SCWS	RW	Semantic	Syntactic	All
Swahili	BiSkip	40	13.41	9.31	15.97	9.94	2.05	2.85
		300	17.25	10.05	15.64	8.01	4.28	4.66
	MultiSeg$_{CN}$	40	25.05	20.87	17.05	9.67	18.82	17.89
		300	29.43	22.06	16.62	9.39	**30.91**	**28.71**
	MultiSeg$_{M}$	40	26.05	16.92	2.97	12.43	13.79	13.65
		300	29.16	18.64	2.73	**14.64**	23.29	22.41
	MultiSeg$_{M_{all}}$	40	27.79	16.92	1.81	13.54	13.22	13.25
		300	26.19	16.48	1.99	14.09	23.67	22.69
	MultiSeg$_{M_{BPE}}$	40	26.37	19.30	2.56	11.33	7.21	7.63
		300	30.38	17.69	3.86	14.09	13.98	13.99
	MultiSeg$_{All}$	40	27.48	21.99	18.24	9.94	20.74	19.64
		300	**31.85**	**23.66**	**17.23**	11.33	29.49	27.63
Tagalog	BiSkip	40	13.17	11.49	10.37	8.64	3.11	3.67
		300	11.38	13.19	11.00	15.64	5.75	6.75
	MultiSeg$_{CN}$	40	26.18	18.64	12.80	20.78	32.54	31.35
		300	29.59	19.96	16.13	18.72	36.76	34.93
	MultiSeg$_{M}$	40	18.51	16.62	-3.11	21.60	25.23	24.86
		300	17.63	14.98	-2.80	19.14	28.66	27.70
	MultiSeg$_{M_{all}}$	40	21.08	16.24	-1.19	26.13	25.05	25.16
		300	20.81	17.07	-1.57	17.49	28.71	27.57
	MultiSeg$_{M_{BPE}}$	40	17.24	15.67	-1.88	24.49	14.17	15.21
		300	18.66	15.24	-1.67	**21.81**	19.60	19.82
	MultiSeg$_{All}$	40	27.80	21.10	13.25	21.60	35.62	34.20
		300	28.95	23.21	14.73	20.16	**38.31**	**36.47**
Somali	BiSkip	40	8.04	7.06	10.48	12.82	1.87	2.48
		300	10.92	9.86	11.96	**10.26**	2.28	2.72
	MultiSeg$_{CN}$	40	20.39	17.65	14.94	4.49	12.28	11.85
		300	**26.41**	19.02	**13.98**	2.56	22.53	21.43
	MultiSeg$_{M}$	40	16.53	10.67	-1.26	8.97	11.90	11.74
		300	15.50	11.93	0.65	5.13	24.21	23.16
	MultiSeg$_{M_{all}}$	40	15.83	9.44	-1.55	5.77	13.21	12.80
		300	16.44	12.86	-0.72	3.21	27.66	26.31
	MultiSeg$_{M_{BPE}}$	40	21.63	10.12	1.96	3.21	2.47	2.51
		300	19.62	11.28	0.76	4.49	4.90	4.88
	MultiSeg$_{All}$	40	20.77	20.03	15.11	7.05	16.77	16.23
		300	25.35	**19.86**	13.88	1.92	**29.19**	**27.69**

Table 6: Monolingual English Evaluation of Low Resource Languages

4. Related Work

4.1. Monolingual Morphological Embeddings

There are several ways of incorporating morphological information into word embeddings. One approach adapted by fastText embeddings (Bojanowski and others, 2017) is to use character n-grams. In addition to whole words, several sizes of n-grams, i.e. three to six, are used during training of the skip-gram model. This approach is language-agnostic and can be adapted to new languages easily. Another approach is to have morphological segmentation as a preprocessing step before training the embeddings (Luong et al., 2013). Other techniques predict both the word and its morphological tag (Cotterell and Schütze, 2015) however, all these approaches are monolingual and work on one language at a time.

The most closely related work to ours is (Chaudhary et al., 2018) which uses the fastText (Bojanowski and others, 2017) approach to include morphological information when learning cross-lingual embeddings by combining the high-resource and low resource corpora and training using the skip-gram objective. Their evaluation is limited to named-entity-recognition and machine translation and requires detailed linguistically tagged words on a large monolingual corpus for related languages. Our approach incorporates supervision through small amount of parallel corpora while training on subwords for any two languages including unrelated ones.

4.2. Bilingual Embeddings

Bilingual word embeddings create shared semantic spaces in multi-lingual contexts and can be trained using different types of bilingual resources. Techniques such as BiSkip (Luong et al., 2015b) use sentence aligned parallel corpora, whereas BiCVM (Vulić and Moens, 2015) use document aligned comparable corpora. There are also techniques that map pre-trained monolingual embeddings into shared space via bilingual dictionaries (Lample et al., 2018b; Artetxe et al., 2018). Finally, there are semi-supervised and unsupervised methods that require little to none bilingual supervision (Lample et al., 2018a; Artetxe and others, 2018). Among these techniques, we adapted BiSkip to learn embeddings jointly. This eliminates the need for having pre-

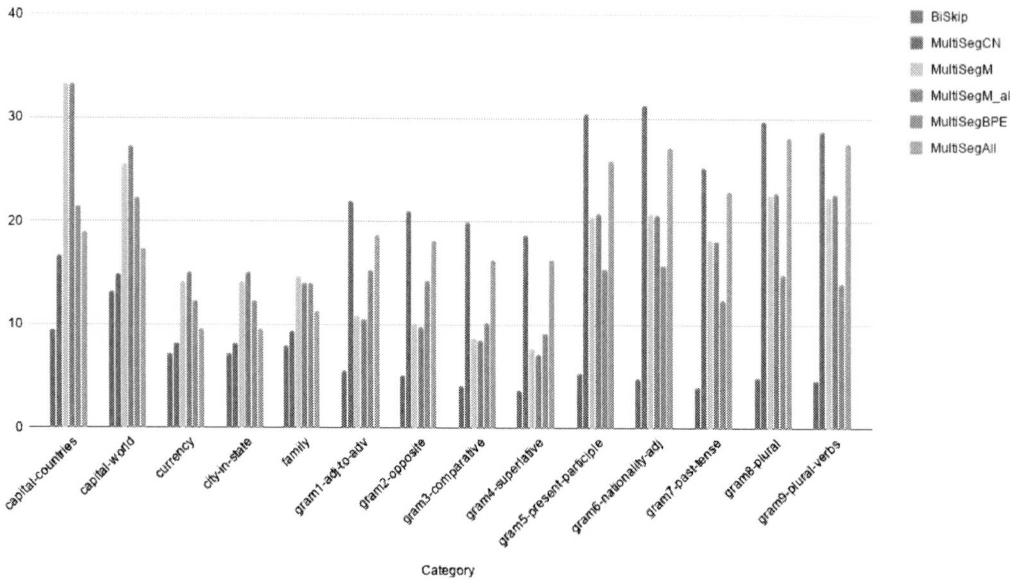

Figure 6: Swahili Analogy Reasoning Task Semantic and Syntactic Categories

trained monolingual embeddings and it has been shown to have better accuracy than comparable corpora based approaches (Upadhyay et al., 2016). In addition, our intrinsic evaluations of semi-supervised and unsupervised embeddings did not perform well.

Recently, pre-trained contextual embeddings have been extended to other languages, e.g. XLM (Lample and Conneau, 2019), cross-lingual ELMo (Schuster et al., 2019) and multilingual BERT (Devlin et al., 2019) shown to have promising results on a variety of tasks. However, they are not as amenable in low resource scenarios where they tend to overfit. They are also not good at fine-grained linguistic tasks (Liu et al., 2019) and geared toward sentence level tasks. In addition, if a pretrained model is not available, it requires lots of computing power and data to be trained from scratch. For instance, XLM model uses $200K$ for low resource and 18 million for German. For parallel data, they use $165K$ for Swahili and 9 million for German.

5. Conclusions and Future Work

We present a new cross-lingual embedding training method for low resource languages, MultiSeg, that incorporates subword information (given as character n-grams, morphemes, or BPEs) during training from parallel corpora. The morphemes are obtained from a state-of-the-art unsupervised morphological segmentation approach. We show that it consistently performs better than the BiSkip baseline, including on word similarity, syntactical analogy and word translation tasks across all languages. Extrinsically, cross-lingual document classification scores also outperform BiSkip. Finally, qualitative results show that our approach is able to learn better word-representations espe-

cially for morphologically related words in both source and target language. We plan to extend our technique to train on more than two languages from the same language family.

Acknowledgments

This research is based upon work supported by the Intelligence Advanced Research Projects Activity (IARPA) MATERIAL program, via contract FA8650-17-C-9117. The views and conclusions contained herein are those of the authors and should not be interpreted as necessarily representing the official policies, either expressed or implied, of IARPA or the U.S. Government. The U.S. Government is authorized to reproduce and distribute reprints for governmental purposes notwithstanding any copyright annotation therein.

6. Bibliographical References

Acs, J., Pajkossy, K., and Kornai, A. (2013). Building basic vocabulary across 40 languages. In *Proceedings of the Sixth Workshop on Building and Using Comparable Corpora*, pages 52–58.

Ammar, W., Mulcaire, G., Tsvetkov, Y., Lample, G., Dyer, C., and Smith, N. A. (2016). Massively multilingual word embeddings. *ArXiv*, abs/1602.01925.

Artetxe, M. et al. (2018). A robust self-learning method for fully unsupervised cross-lingual mappings of word embeddings. In *ACL*, pages 789–798.

Artetxe, M., Labaka, G., and Agirre, E. (2018). Generalizing and improving bilingual word embedding mappings with a multi-step framework of linear transformations.

Bojanowski, P. et al. (2017). Enriching word vectors with subword information. *TACL*, 5:135–146.

Chaudhary, A., Zhou, C., Levin, L., Neubig, G., Mortensen, D. R., and Carbonell, J. (2018). Adapting word embeddings to new languages with morphological and phonological subword representations. In *Proceedings of the 2018 Conference on Empirical Methods in Natural Language Processing*, pages 3285–3295.

Cotterell, R. and Schütze, H. (2015). Morphological word embeddings. In *Proceedings of the 2015 Conference of the North American Chapter of the Association for Computational Linguistics: Human Language Technologies*, pages 1287–1292.

Devlin, J., Chang, M.-W., Lee, K., and Toutanova, K. (2019). BERT: Pre-training of deep bidirectional transformers for language understanding. In *Proceedings of the 2019 Conference of the North American Chapter of the Association for Computational Linguistics: Human Language Technologies, Volume 1*, pages 4171–4186.

Dyer, C., Chahuneau, V., and Smith, N. A. (2013). A simple, fast, and effective reparameterization of ibm model 2. In *Proceedings of the 2013 Conference of the North American Chapter of the Association for Computational Linguistics: Human Language Technologies*.

Eskander, R., Rambow, O., and Muresan, S. (2018). Automatically tailoring unsupervised morphological segmentation to the language. In *Proceedings of the Fifteenth Workshop on Computational Research in Phonetics, Phonology, and Morphology*, pages 78–83.

Eskander, R., Klavans, J., and Muresan, S. (2019). Unsupervised morphological segmentation for low-resource polysynthetic languages. In *Proceedings of the 16th Workshop on Computational Research in Phonetics, Phonology, and Morphology*, pages 189–195.

Finkelstein, L., Gabrilovich, E., Matias, Y., Rivlin, E., Solan, Z., Wolfman, G., and Ruppin, E. (2001). Placing search in context: The concept revisited. In *Proceedings of the 10th International Conference on World Wide Web*, pages 406–414.

Huang, E., Socher, R., Manning, C., and Ng, A. (2012). Improving word representations via global context and multiple word prototypes. In *Proceedings of the 50th Annual Meeting of the Association for Computational Linguistics*, pages 873–882.

Klementiev, A., Titov, I., and Bhattarai, B. (2012). Inducing crosslingual distributed representations of words. In *Proceedings of COLING 2012*.

Koehn, P. (2005). Europarl: A Parallel Corpus for Statistical Machine Translation. In *Conference Proceedings: the tenth Machine Translation Summit*, pages 79–86.

Lample, G. and Conneau, A. (2019). Cross-lingual language model pretraining. *Advances in Neural Information Processing Systems (NeurIPS)*.

Lample, G., Conneau, A., Denoyer, L., and Ranzato, M. (2018a). Unsupervised machine translation using monolingual corpora only. In *International Conference on Learning Representations*.

Lample, G., Conneau, A., Ranzato, M., Denoyer, L., and JÃ©gou, H. (2018b). Word translation without parallel data. In *International Conference on Learning Representations*.

Liu, N. F., Gardner, M., Belinkov, Y., Peters, M. E., and Smith, N. A. (2019). Linguistic knowledge and transferability of contextual representations. In *Proceedings of the 2019 Conference of the North American Chapter of the Association for Computational Linguistics: Human Language Technologies, Volume 1*, pages 1073–1094.

Luong, T., Socher, R., and Manning, C. (2013). Better word representations with recursive neural networks for morphology. In *Proceedings of the Seventeenth Conference on Computational Natural Language Learning*, pages 104–113.

Luong, T., Pham, H., and Manning, C. D. (2015a). Bilingual word representations with monolingual quality in mind. In *Proceedings of the 1st Workshop on Vector Space Modeling for Natural Language Processing*, pages 151–159.

Luong, T., Pham, H., and Manning, C. D. (2015b). Bilingual word representations with monolingual quality in mind. In *Proceedings of the 1st Workshop on Vector Space Modeling for Natural Language Processing*, pages 151–159.

Mikolov, T., Sutskever, I., Chen, K., Corrado, G., and Dean, J. (2013a). Distributed representations of words and phrases and their compositionality. In *Proceedings of the 26th International Conference on Neural Information Processing Systems - Volume 2*, NIPS'13, pages 3111–3119.

Mikolov, T., Yih, W.-t., and Zweig, G. (2013b). Linguistic regularities in continuous space word representations. In *Proceedings of the 2013 Conference of the North American Chapter of the Association for Computational Linguistics: Human Language Technologies*, pages 746–751.

Rubino, C. (2016). Iarpa material program.

Schuster, T., Ram, O., Barzilay, R., and Globerson, A. (2019). Cross-lingual alignment of contextual word embeddings, with applications to zero-shot dependency parsing. In *Proceedings of the 2019 Conference of the North American Chapter of the Association for Computational Linguistics: Human Language Technologies, Volume 1*, pages 1599–1613.

Sennrich, R., Haddow, B., and Birch, A. (2016). Neural machine translation of rare words with subword units. In *Proceedings of the 54th Annual Meeting of the Association for Computational Linguistics*, pages 1715–1725.

Upadhyay, S., Faruqui, M., Dyer, C., and Roth, D. (2016). Cross-lingual models of word embeddings: An empirical comparison. In *Proceedings of the 54th Annual Meeting of the Association for Computational Linguistics*, pages 1661–1670.

van der Maaten, L. and Hinton, G. (2008). Visualizing data using t-SNE. *Journal of Machine Learning Research*, 9:2579–2605.

Vulić, I. and Moens, M.-F. (2015). Bilingual word embeddings from non-parallel document-aligned data applied to bilingual lexicon induction. In *Proceedings of the 53rd Annual Meeting of the Association for Computational Linguistics and the 7th International Joint Conference on Natural Language Processing*, pages 719–725.

Proceedings of the 1st Joint SLTU and CCURL Workshop (SLTU-CCURL 2020), pages 106–110
Language Resources and Evaluation Conference (LREC 2020), Marseille, 11–16 May 2020
© European Language Resources Association (ELRA), licensed under CC-BY-NC

Poio Text Prediction: Lessons on the Development and Sustainability of LTs for Endangered Languages

Vera Ferreira, Pedro Manha, Gema Zamora

Interdisciplinary Centre for Social and Language Documentation (CIDLeS)
Rua do Remexido, Loja 15, 2395-174 Minde, Portugal
vferreira@cidles.eu, pmanha@cidles.eu, gzamora@cidles.eu

Abstract

2019, the International Year of Indigenous Languages (IYIL), marked a crucial milestone for a diverse community united by a strong sense of urgency. In this presentation, we evaluate the impact of IYIL's outcomes in the development of LTs for endangered languages. We give a brief description of the field of Language Documentation, whose experts have led the research and data collection efforts surrounding endangered languages for the past 30 years. We introduce the work of the Interdisciplinary Centre for Social and Language Documentation and we look at Poio as an example of an LT developed specifically with speakers of endangered languages in mind. This example illustrates how the deeper systemic causes of language endangerment are reflected in the development of LTs. Additionally, we share some of the strategic decisions that have led the development of this project. Finally, we advocate the importance of bridging the divide between research and activism, pushing for the inclusion of threatened languages in the world of LTs, and doing so in close collaboration with the speaker community.

Keywords : Less-Resourced/Endangered Languages

1. Motivation

2019, the International Year of Indigenous Languages (henceforth IYIL) marked a crucial milestone for everyone involved in the cause of endangered languages, either as researchers, teachers, or activists. We are a diverse community of experts and implementers united by a strong sense of urgency and, although our immediate interests do not always coincide, we have gathered momentum and we must make the most out of it.

There are around 7000 languages spoken today but, at the current rate, it is estimated that half of them will vanish in the next one or two generations. UNESCO has taken on, for good or for bad, the responsibility of following up on these statistics and map the languages of the world to raise awareness around the issue of language endangerment and its impact on minority groups and their environment. Following this line of action that started in the 1990s, UNESCO and many partnering institutions celebrated language diversity in 2019 and called for the empowering of indigenous peoples through the strengthening of their languages. In November 2019, UNESCO released a strategic outcome document summarising conclusions and recommendations drawn from consultations carried out during the IYIL. The ambitious and optimistic tone of this document is indeed refreshing, especially since we are used to the media treating the issue of endangered languages with a rather melancholic contentment. Moreover, the document reaches to a wide variety of stakeholders and it addresses technology developers directly. In its conclusion V, UNESCO has called for LT developers to "develop advanced tools for collection and analysis of language data as well as for the transliteration and annotation of multi-modal content", "supply necessary tools for advanced translation", and "extend and refine current language technologies as well as designing new ones, and developing necessary algorithms, applications and systems to support indigenous peoples in their own use of the internet and social media networks" (UNESCO, 2019 pp16-17). Considering these recent developments, we present our experiences with the development of LTs for endangered languages with special attention to the Poio project. The aim of this paper is to encourage participation among endangered language experts that are not familiar with LTs, and to make explicit these technologies' potential for impact and innovation.

In section 2, we give a brief overview of the motivations and concerns of the field of Language Documentation and introduce the work of our institution. Section 3 describes Poio, one of our long-standing projects, and some aspects of its roadmap. Section 4 to 6 describe the challenges that the institution has faced regarding the development of LTs for endangered languages and provide examples of our team's strategic approach. Finally, we conclude the presentation by summarising the lessons we have learnt during the development of Poio and other tools, and giving the message that it is possible to create LTs for speakers of endangered languages that are sustainable in the long-term.

2. CIDLeS' Background and Roadmap

The Interdisciplinary Centre for Social and Language Documentation (CIDLeS) is a non-profit institution founded in January 2010 in Minde (Portugal) by a group of national and international researchers. From the moment of its foundation, CIDLeS aimed at improving and deepening research in two linguistic areas: language documentation and linguistic typology. Besides the documentation, study and dissemination of European endangered and minority languages, CIDLeS (CIDLeS Media Lab only until recently) is also engaged in the development of language technologies for scientific and didactic work on lesser-used languages.

Language Documentation was recognized and established as a linguistic discipline in the late 90s of the 20th century. However, the areas of interest as well as its subjects of study (e.g. description and classification of linguistic features from around the world) have been of interest to all linguists, especially to those who worked in the area of typology or anthropological lingusitics with a broad experience of fieldwork. It is in this context that CIDLeS was founded, and its work stands out for the application of language documentation methods to European languages (Minderico, A Fala or Bavarian are some examples), which tend to be overlooked in a discipline that draws many of its methods from anthropology and ethnography.

CIDLeS also stands out for its push for community-driven maintenance, and its investment in LTs. It is widely recognised that language documentation and language maintenance/revitalisation efforts could and should work in tandem. However, some practicalities such as funding availability or workload make this synergy more complex than it seems. While most linguists recognise their ethical responsibility towards the communities from which they collect data, they often lack the means to provide said community with resources that can help keep the language vital (Leonard, 2018). On the other hand, language revitalisation experts and activists might sometimes overlook the potential of documentation materials as resources for the speakers due to their theoretical inaccessibility. CIDLeS tries to bridge that divide by developing software for speakers of lesser-used languages that can re-use data originally collected for linguistic research.

We believe that bridging this gap ties closely with conclusion and goal V in UNESCO's recommendations as it "[…] allow[s] the development of technologies specifically adapted to the characteristics of indigenous languages, which in turn will strengthen and underpin the status of these languages" (UNESCO, 2019 pp16).

3. Poio API, Poio Corpus and Poio Text Prediction

We do not want to limit ourselves to developing the necessary LT tools for local and minor languages and language varieties as mere aids for communication. Our goal is to use successful technology to teach, revitalize and therefore boost the use of minority languages. People should not only be able to communicate in their natural, native tongue, but technology should also assist the renewal of local languages and cultures by allowing people to actively teach, learn, extend and spread their language in their community (Ferreira, 2016). We see language diversity and multilingualism as one building block to empower local communities and their cultural identity and thus realize their cultural and economic potential in a globalized world.

Poio is the name of a project, under the responsibility of Peter Bouda, with several open source subprojects which develop LTs (Bouda, Ferreira, and Lopes, 2012). Our aim is to give people the ability to use their mother tongue in everyday, electronic communication in the digital world, no matter where they are and whatever language they speak. Poio provides the technological basis to process language data from a wide range of sources (e.g. language documentation corpora, Wikipedia, retro-digitized and digital dictionaries, etc.) for applications and research workflows. This includes, for example, the possibility of extracting data from ELAN transcription files, which are widely used for transcribing language documentation recordings and creating multimodal corpora.

Poio consists of several subprojects that make possible to process and manage language data, to extract corpora from diverse data sources and to calculate language models for the online tools. At the basis of the Poio project are our two scientific Python packages, Poio API1 and Graf-python, which allow us to manage data from a wide range of sources (eg. ELAN, Toolbox. TypeCraft XML) and convert them into GrAF for interoperability and further analysis. An example of an straightforward application is the conversion from Toolbox to TypeCraft with the aid of a JSON mapping file. Once the annotations are in TypeCraft, it is possible to share and further annotate the data in a group and/or to create web-based applications.

The Poio Corpus is a collection of data in under-resourced languages extracted from Wikipedia, websites, and dictionaries. It is available for free download in ISO format. With this corpus at its foundation, the Pressagio library, also in Python, predicts text based on n-gram models.

The data management and text prediction functionalities of Poio API and Pressagio are available as the web service Poio Web API. Poio Text Prediction is its equivalent for end users, which can be accessed online2. This is nowadays the visible face of the Poio project and the arm of the project that we are presenting here as an example of an LT devised with the needs of speakers of endangered languages in mind.

The text prediction that Poio offers can be easily used on the desktop and on mobile phones and tablets. Users can write their texts by clicking on the offered prediction and copying the texts to their email editor or messaging app. Figures 1 and 2 show how the predictions are displayed differently on computers or mobile devices. When accessing the service on a computer, the user can select the appropriate prediction by clicking with their mouse or using the F keys. On mobile devices, however, the user taps on the prediction the same way they would do with their usual predictor in Portuguese.

Figure 1: Example of Poio Text Prediction in Minderico.

---

[1] Poio API's development was part of the curation project F-AG3 within CLARIN-D. The latest version is available for download at https://github.com/cidles/poio-api and the documentation with use examples is available at https://poio-api.readthedocs.io/en/latest/introduction.html .

[2] Service available at https://www.poio.eu/. Documentation available at https://poio.readthedocs.io

Figure 2: Example of Poio in a mobile device.

The need to communicate seamlessly on social media or via texts and to do so in the language of one's choice goes often beyond adding special characters or using symbols. The traditional predicting keyboards support major languages like English, Spanish, or Chinese. Thus, the users that belong to lesser-used and under-resourced language speaking communities are not able to use their native tongue in an easy and successful way. Furthermore, these keyboards may work against the user's own effort to remember a word in their language by giving a suggestion in the national language or "correcting" its spelling.

Currently, manufacturers of mobile devices and operating system owners are gradually opening their systems and devices to developers. This tendency is becoming more evident for instance in the domain of virtual keyboards used in current mobile operating systems, with the possibility of creating third party keyboards for use alongside the default one. Additionally, open-source or more customisable alternatives are increasingly available on the market. These factors make clear to us that the development of Poio Text Prediction and its enhancement for mobile devices have now more potential than ever.

For all of us who take the English or Portuguese (or any language of major communication) predictive text engines in our phones for granted, this might seem a minor change. However, it would have a great impact among all the users who do not feel confident enough to write in their own minority language, or that simply do not know they can do it. Predictive text is also practical for learners and semi-speakers of the language, because it can help finish a sentence or remember a word without having to force oneself to look it up on a dictionary or switch to another language.

Our next steps within the Poio project are 1) improving the text prediction system for the languages already supported, 2) increasing the number of languages supported, and 3) working on the development of an offline service stored on mobile devices and desktops to allow text entry in under-resourced languages in different technological contexts.

(To be able to use Poio, the user needs an active internet connection – one of the issues CIDLeS team is working on at the moment.)

At the moment of writing, Poio Writetyper is available in Afrikaans, Aragonese, Asturian, Basque, Bavarian, Chechen, Corsican, Ewe, Faroese, Friulian, Haitian, Irish, Ligurian, Lombard, Low German, Lower Sorbian, Luxembourgish, Manx, Minderico, Norther Frisian, Romansch, Saterfriesisch, Scottish Gaelic, Upper Sorbian, Venetian, Welsh, and Western Frisian.

There is a steady interest in Poio that has allowed the team to further its development for several years now, but sustainability is indeed the Achilles heel for many technology projects aimed at endangered languages or developed around one single community. In the following sections, we elaborate on the three main challenges that the team has faced since the early stages of development and some strategic decisions that we have decided to carry on to our future endeavours. We hope that CIDLeS and Poio's example can encourage more groups of experts to invest time in data mobilisation and that it can help others identify opportunities for interdisciplinary collaboration and community involvement.

4. Challenge I: Do LTs Have to Take a Back Seat to Research?

Since its conception in 2013, the development of Poio and other CIDLeS projects have encountered a series of challenges that we believe are common to most LTs for speakers of endangered languages. The decreasing number of users or insufficient literacy in some communities might seem the most apparent problems. However, these respond to deeper political and developmental problems and, in today's globalised economy, any innovative practice aimed at preventing loss of diversity faces similar challenges. Here, we would like to assess those issues that we developers and implementers face in the specific case of LTs for endangered languages.

The first challenge is the gap between current research trends in Linguistics and what the speaker community actually finds useful. While there is a growing interest in academia for automating certain aspects of the language documentation process and enhancing the analysis of endangered languages with digital methods (Michaud et al., 2018), the outputs of these projects (e.g. grammars, corpora, highly technical dictionaries, etc.) do not always benefit the speaker community or respond to their needs (Leonard, 2018). On the other hand, programmers and computer scientists working with linguists are able to produce sophisticated databases, mine data and aid the methodology of a given research project, but are rarely involved in the ethically-charged process of giving back to the community. This is not to say that academics are not doing enough, but that they cannot be expected to do everything.

In this scenario, LTs for speakers of endangered languages have little time and space for recognition and development as they are not necessarily useful to answer a research question. The Poio project itself was initially motivated by the need to find new methods to mine data for typological and morphological research. However, Poio Text Prediction has proved advantageous for its developers and the CIDLeS community in ways that we did not necessarily predict. First, being so easy to deploy and test makes it a good instrument for networking and a great conversation starter. As such, it gives visibility to its developers' work beyond the academic sphere. And most importantly, it has a tangible impact in the community in the form of digital presence. This is especially true for communities that have little to no representation online as they lack the computer literacy or the networks to foster the growth of their languages in places like Wikipedia or Twitter.

For example, because it is possible to use Poio API to process language corpora or archival collections, the transformation of these materials into a text prediction service makes these resources accessible to a wider public. Furthermore, it does it in a way that is coherent with the community's context and it has the potential to appeal the younger generations. The basic requirements to achieve this are: 1) the source material must cover a fairly varied range of topics collected from speakers of different ages and genders, 2) the source texts must be anonymised, and 3) the potential user community must already have an interest in writing in their language, and 4) the potential user community has steady access to the internet in order to use the service.

This is also an example of how the development of an LT can derivee naturally from language documentation efforts, making the most out of the funding available, easing the relationship between linguists and community members, and producing content that is automatically tailored to its users. Given the sense of urgency that currently dominates the fields of language and intangible cultural heritage documentation, we believe that finding ways to bridge data collection, analysis, and community engagement as seamlessly as possible should be a priority for developers and implementers. In the following section, we elaborate further on the issue of community engagement.

5. Challenge II : Are LTs the New « Holy Grail » of Language Maintenance ?

The second challenge is the political pressures that surround endangered languages and the often counterproductive belief that the way to maintain the language is making it official and institutionalise its learning. Schools, and in particular those located in rural areas or that serve marginalised communities, have very limited resources and are a biased battleground for the endangered language to compete against the national language or English. On the surface, teaching the language in school is a sign of prestige, but it does not guarantee the natural transmission of the language. In a similar way, LTs play a crucial role in giving a sense of prestige to the language, especially among the younger generations who are constantly exposed to technologies that compete for their time and attention. Games, online resources, and electronic teaching aids have gained prominence since the early 2000s (Eisenlohr, 2004). However, just like we know that school education alone does not necessarily guarantee the maintenance of an endangered language, we must be cautious not to attribute to technology the capability of keeping a language vital just on its own. LTs must be part of a cohesive effort for improving the social status of a language and foster its use.

Nowadays, given the highly competitive market that we live in, the social status of a given language (endangered or not) is often based on the answers you can give to questions such us "Which benefits can I access through this language?", "Can this language get me better employment opportunities?", "How does learning/speaking this language make me look in front of my friends?". While not even the most appealing, innovative LT can give positive answers to these questions on its own, at CIDLeS we are learning to uncover the skills used throughout the stages of data collection, corpus building, or LT development and re-package them in ways that may appeal to more members of the community. This approach was inspired by the young Minderico speakers and learners that interned at CIDLeS in its early days and for whom their experience working in the development of Poio has been an asset in their careers.

The practice of involving the speakers actively in a linguistic research project is not new; see Harvey (2019) for a recent example. Nevertheless, we believe that there is still a lot of work to be done even in Western and/or urban contexts. Coders and developers could find here a platform to become mentors and strengthen ties with the communities they serve.

The success of an LT for endangered languages will always depend on grassroots, socially oriented groundwork and the motivation of the speaker and learner community. On top of this, the development of such technology has to be culturally contextualised. Analysing and taking into account the speakers motivations and networks, not only at the beginning and end of the project as potential users, but throughout the development process as stakeholders is a strategic decision. While we understand that this decision might present other logistics challenges, especially when introducing new technologies, it lays the groundwork for fruitful collaborations long-term.

6. Challenge III: Funding is in an Uncomfortable Grey Area

Academics in the area are already working at their maximum capacity and, despite the best intended advocacy efforts of the international community, the attitudes towards endangered languages are still pessimistic. These are just two of the factors that contribute to the biggest hurdle in the development of LTs for endangered languages: funding for community-oriented projects is very limited and it rarely takes into account the long-term sustainability of the outcomes. Furthermore, the private sector sees little to no gain in supporting these initiatives as the general attitude towards endangered and minority languages is that they do not have marketable value.

As we mentioned in the introduction to this paper, UNESCO has made a rather ambitious call for researchers and developers to work on sophisticated LTs that support indigenous peoples on the use of their native language. They also recommend all stakeholders to "encourage collaboration between indigenous people, researchers, and industry" and to "make it an urgent priority to encourage the donor community, intergovernmental organizations, and other stakeholders towards mobilizing additional financial resources and establishing new funding mechanisms and incentives for activities and projects on indigenous language issues" (UNESCO, 2019 pp.18-19).

We believe that this collaboration is highly beneficial for all parties and that it will keep growing over time. However, whether the funding will be more evenly distributed, or if specially designated funding will be allocated is something that we have yet to see. In the meantime, and in case that the funding situation does not improve significantly, we are exploring two options: crowdfunding and funding opportunities with a focus on social entrepreneurship.

Small contributions in the form of annual or monthly subscriptions are a way of maintaining the Poio Text Prediction service online. The project responsible is currently piloting different tiers with a focus on expanding the languages available and the quality of the service.

Simultaneously, CIDLeS is exploring whether Poio and other LTs for under-resourced languages could fit in and be benefited from funding pools aimed at community development, compulsory education, and further education. This way, we seek to make the most out of the working relationships we have stablished with stakeholders from communities outside Minde and to design an LT project that has endangered language speakers at its core.

7. Conclusion

Throughout this paper we have outlined the challenges commonly faced when developing LTs for endangered languages. However, we wanted to present Poio as a success story, not only because we have been working with it for 7 years, but because its scope is clearly in line with UNESCO's recommendations. UNESCO's white paper is in this case an assertion of what we and many other experts have been doing right so far and, here, we have offered an overview of the strategic decisions that we have taken in the development of one of our most successful projects.

We are optimistic that this new push for recognition will mean a positive stimulus for LTs for under-resourced languages and that they will encourage a new generation of developers to take an interest in supporting endangered languages research and maintenance with their work. Experience has taught us that, as developers, we cannot ignore the factors that make endangered languages endangered, and that resources are way too limited to risk investing time in a language without proactively involving its speakers throughout the development process.

We have seen that, in the case of endangered languages, LTs fit almost awkwardly between research and community development, with no interest from the private sector. However, these LTs are far from isolated projects developed around single small languages. Instead, they are part of a larger effort and have the potential for big societal impact. While our main objective is to make solid technologies, we are also project managers and advocates, and the future success of these technologies depend on acknowledging and exploiting our role within the communities we serve.

If we want LTs for endangered languages to be successful and sustainable, we must continue our work with linguists in order to keep the quality of the documentation and data collection at the highest standards. Also, equally importantly, we must make the most out of these resources and use them to create technologies that empower their users to assert themselves in the language of their choice. As long as there is grassroots interest, there will always be room for endangered languages in LT development.

8. Bibliographical References

Bouda, P., Ferreira, V. and Lopes, A (2012). Poio API - An annotation framework to bridge Language Documentation and Natural Language Processing. In F. Mambrini, M. Passarotti and C. Sporleder (eds.). Proceedings of the Second Workshop on Annotation of Corpora for Research in the Humanities. Lisboa: Edições Colibri, 15-26

Eisenlohr, P. (2004). Language Revitalization and New Technologies. *Cultures of Electronic Mediation and the Refiguring of Communities. Annual Review of Anthropology.* 33. 21-45.

Ferreira, V . (2016). The importance of new technologies in the revitalization of Minderico. In J. Olko, T. Wicherkiewicz & R. Borges (eds.). *Integral Strategies for Language Revitalization.* Warsaw: University of Warsaw, pp565-580.

Harvey, A. (2019). Gorwaa (Tanzania) —Language Contexts. In P. K. Austin (ed.) *Language Documentation and Description, vol 16.* London: EL Publishing, pp127-168

Leonard, W. Y. (2018). Reflections on (de)colonialism in language documentation. In B. McDonnell, A. L. Berez-Kroeker, & G. Holton. (Eds.) *Reflections on Language Documentation 20 Years after Himmelmann 1998.* Language Documentation & Conservation Special Publication no.15. Honolulu: University of Hawai'i Press. pp55-65.

Michaud, A., Adams, O., Cohn T.A., Neubig, G., and Guillaume, S. (2018). Integrating Automatic Transcription into the Language Documentation Workflow: Experiments with Na Data and the Persephone Toolkit. *Language Documentation & Conservation* Vol. 12 pp393-429

UNESCO (2019). *Strategic Outcome Document of the 2019 International Year of Indigenous Languages.* Annex to General Conference 40th session. Paris.

Proceedings of the 1st Joint SLTU and CCURL Workshop (SLTU-CCURL 2020), pages 111–120
Language Resources and Evaluation Conference (LREC 2020), Marseille, 11–16 May 2020
© European Language Resources Association (ELRA), licensed under CC-BY-NC

Text Corpora and the Challenge of Newly Written Languages

Alice Millour*, Karën Fort*[†]

*Sorbonne Université / STIH, [†]Université de Lorraine, CNRS, Inria, LORIA
28, rue Serpente 75006 Paris, France, 54000 Nancy, France
alice.millour@etu.sorbonne-universite.fr, karen.fort@sorbonne-universite.fr

Abstract

Text corpora represent the foundation on which most natural language processing systems rely. However, for many languages, collecting or building a text corpus of a sufficient size still remains a complex issue, especially for corpora that are accessible and distributed under a clear license allowing modification (such as annotation) and further resharing. In this paper, we review the sources of text corpora usually called upon to fill the gap in low-resource contexts, and how crowdsourcing has been used to build linguistic resources. Then, we present our own experiments with crowdsourcing text corpora and an analysis of the obstacles we encountered. Although the results obtained in terms of participation are still unsatisfactory, we advocate that the effort towards a greater involvement of the speakers should be pursued, especially when the language of interest is newly written.

Keywords: text corpora, dialectal variants, spelling, crowdsourcing

1. Introduction

Speakers from various linguistic communities are increasingly writing their languages (Outinoff, 2012), and the Internet is increasingly multilingual.[1]

Many of these languages are less-resourced: these linguistic productions are not sufficiently documented, while there is an urge to provide tools that sustain their digital use. What is more, when a language is not standardized, we need to build adapted resources and tools that embrace its diversity.

Including these linguistic productions into natural language processing (NLP) pipelines hence requires efforts on two complementary fronts: (i) collecting or building resources that represent the use of the language, (ii) developing tools which can cope with the variation mechanisms.

In all cases, the very first resource that is needed for further processing is a text corpus.

After presenting the challenges related to the processing of oral languages when they come to be written, we introduce in Section 3. the existing multilingual sources that are commonly used to collect corpora, as well as their main shortcomings.

In Section 4., we show how crowdsourcing has been used in the past to involve the members of linguistic communities into collaboratively building resources for their languages. We argue that this method is all the more reasonable when it comes to collecting meaningful data for non-standardized languages.

In Section 5., we present the existing initiatives to crowdsource text corpora. Based on our own experiments and on the result of a survey regarding the digital use of a non-standardized language, we explain why collecting this particular type of resource is challenging.

2. The Need for Text Corpora

The rise in use of SMS, online chat and of social media in general has created a new space of expression for an increasing number of speakers (see for instance, the studies on specific languages carried by Rivron (2012) or Soria et al. (2018)). Although linguistic communities are being threatened all over the world, this represents a valuable opportunity to observe, document and equip with appropriate tools an increasing number of languages. These new spaces of written conversation have been taken over by linguistic communities which practice had been mainly oral until then (van Esch et al., 2019). When no orthography has been defined for a given language, or when one (or various) conventions exist but are not consistently used by the speakers, spellings may vary from one speaker to another. Indeed, when the spellings are not standardized by an arbitrary convention, speakers may transcribe the language based on how they *speak* it.

In fact, standardizing spelling does not confine to defining the orthography, as it usually also acts as a unification process of potential linguistic variants towards a sole written form. By contrast, the absence of such a standardization process authorizes the raw transcription of a multitude of linguistic variants of a given language. These variants being transcribed according to the spelling habits and linguistic backgrounds of each speaker, the Internet, especially in its conversational nature, has become a breeding ground for linguistic diversity expression and observation.

Situations of spelling variations observed on the Internet are documented in diverse linguistic contexts such as the ones of:

- The Zapotec and Chatino communities in Oaxaca, Mexico, as detailed in (Lillehaugen, 2016) in the context of the *Voces del Valle* program. During this program, speakers were encouraged to write tweets in their languages. They were provided with spelling guidance they were not compelled to follow. As stated by the author: *"The result was that, for the most part, the writers were non-systematic in their spelling decisions—but they were writing"*.

- Some of the communities speaking Tibetan dialects outside China, which develop a *"written form based*

---

[1]See, for instance, the reports provided by `w3tech` such as `https://w3techs.com/technologies/history_overview/content_language/ms/y`.

on the spoken language" independently of the Classical Literary Tibetan (Tournadre, 2014).

- The Eton ethnic group, in Cameroon, about which Rivron (2012) observes that Internet is the support of *"the extension of a mother tongue outside its habitual context and uses, and the correlated development of its graphic system"*.

- Speakers of Javanese dialects who *"have their own way of writing down the words they use according to the pronunciation they understand"*, regardless of the official spelling. Each dialect developing its own spelling, a dialect that was *"originally only recognizable through its oral narratives (pronunciation) is now easily recognizable through the spelling used in social media"* (Fauzi and Puspitorini, 2018).

- Communities using Arabizi to transcribe Arabic online: as reported by Tobaili et al. (2019), Arabizi allows multiple mappings between Arabic and Roman alphanumerical characters, and thus makes apparent dialectal variations usually hidden in the traditional writing.

- Communities transliterating Indian dialects with Roman alphabet without observing systematic conventions for transliteration (Shekhar et al., 2018).

- Regional European languages such as Alsatian, a continuum of Alemannic dialects, for which a great diversity of spellings is reported (Millour and Fort, 2019) even though a flexible spelling system, Orthal (Crévenat-Werner and Zeidler, 2008), has been developed.

In the following, we will refer to these proteiform languages as "multi-variant". The variation observed is indeed the result of (at least) two simultaneous mechanisms: the dialectal and scriptural variations. Both of these degrees of freedom may be impacted by the usual dimensions for variation (diachronic, diatopic, diastratic, and diamesic).

From a NLP perspective, these linguistic productions represent a challenge. In fact, they push us to deal with the issues that variation processes imply, either because these productions account for most of the written existence of a non-standardized language, or because they diverge from a standard language in an undeterministic fashion. Yet, for the endangered languages there is an urge to develop tools that match the actual linguistic practice of its end-users to sustain their digital use.

Even though less-resourced languages benefit from the current trends in NLP which tend towards less supervision (see, for instance (Lample et al., 2017; Grave et al., 2018)) and seek higher robustness to variation, processing technologies still highly rely on the availability of text corpora.

3. Existing Sources Used for Corpus Collection

Although there exist sources of text corpus readily available for numerous languages, these "opportunistic" corpora (McEnery and Hardie, 2011) present several shortcomings, including:

- an insufficient coverage to constitute the basis for further linguistic resources developments. These corpora are unlikely to be balanced in terms of representativeness of the existing practices.

- their nature and license sometimes require operations that result in a loss of information such as the metadata necessary to identify the languages or the structure of the document.

- using them requires additional linguistic resources (to perform language identification, for instance).

In the following, we first present the Wikipedia project, which, with 306 active Wikipedias distributed under Creative Commons licenses, undoubtedly provides the largest freely available multilingual corpus.

Second, we present how the Web can more generally be used as a source of text corpora. We focus on describing how Web crawling has been used to gather corpora for less-resourced languages, and briefly comment on the use of social networks-based corpora.

3.1. Wikipedia as a Corpus

Wikipedia is an online collaborative multilingual encyclopedia supported by the WIKIMEDIA FOUNDATION, a non-profit organization.

Along with providing structured information from which lexical semantic resources or ontologies can be derived, Wikipedia is an easily accessible source of text corpora widely used in the NLP community, and from which both well- and less-resourced languages benefit.

Its popularity and its collaborative structure make it the most natural environment to foster collaborative text production. We discuss in this section to which extent Wikipedia represents a valuable source of text corpora for less-resourced and non-standardized languages, in terms of further NLP processing.

After a short introduction on the size and quality of the existing Wikipedias, we describe how the issue of language identification and the purpose of Wikipedia prevent it to be the most appropriate virtual place to host dialectal and scriptural diversity.

3.1.1. Size and Quality of Wikipedias

There exist 306 active Wikipedias[2], 16 of them showcasing more than 1 million articles, 62 more than 100,000, 147 more than 10,000, and 81 between 1,000 and 10,000.

Even though observing the size of the Wikipedia in terms of article count gives a useful overview of the linguistic diversity of the project, size is not the best indicator to get a sense of the amount of quality data available in each Wikipedia. Instead, the `Depth` indicator[3] has been defined by WIKIMEDIA to get an estimate of the quality of a given Wikipedia based on the number of articles, but also edits, and proportion of "non-article" pages such as user

---

[2]See `https://meta.wikimedia.org/wiki/List_of_Wikipedias`, as of January 2020.

[3]See `https://meta.wikimedia.org/wiki/Wikipedia_article_depth`

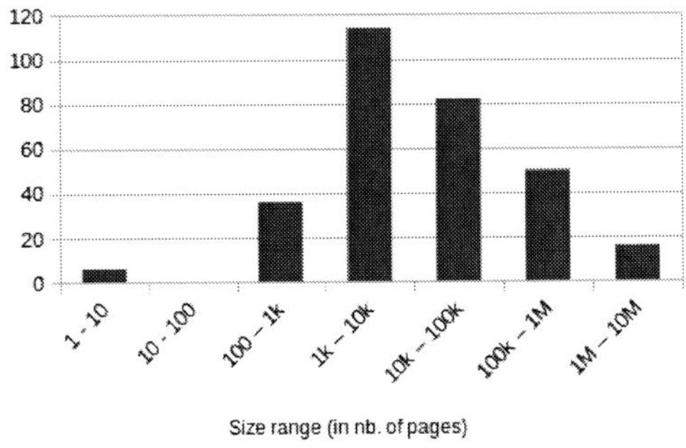

Figure 1: Number of Wikipedias per `size` range (log10 scale).

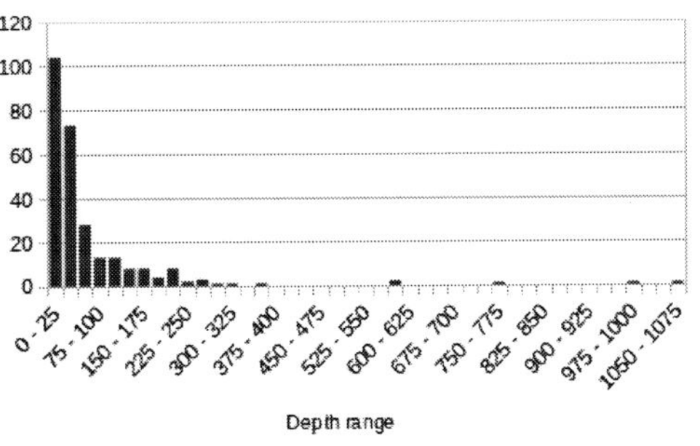

Figure 2: Number of Wikipedias per `depth` range.

pages, redirects etc. It ranges from 0 to 1,063 (Ripuarian Wikipedia). The English Wikipedia has a `depth` of 991. Figures 1 and 2 show the distribution of the Wikipedias according to their size and `depth`.

In fact, we can observe in table 3.1.1.[4] that three of the Top 10 Wikipedias in terms of page number show very poor `depth scores`. This might be explained by the use of translation or bots to produce pages (see, for instance the case of the Swedish Wikipedia (Guldbrandsson, 2013)). The table also shows that members of small linguistic communities such as the Aragonese or Vepsian ones have seized the opportunity offered by Wikipedia to develop their digital presence.

3.1.2. Identifying the Languages of the Wikipedias

In this section, we present the strategies and issues related to languages and spelling conventions identification in the Wikipedia projects. The examples that follow show that the Wikipedias host both dialectal and scriptural diversities.

Language Tag(s) In its `Language proposal policy`[5], WIKIMEDIA stipulates that each Wikipedia must correspond to a language with a valid ISO 639 1-3[6] code (or, in exceptional cases, a BCP 47 language tag[7] only). What is more :

> *"The language must be sufficiently unique that it could not coexist on a more general wiki. In most cases, this excludes regional dialects and different written forms of the same language."*

This definition of the accepted languages leads to Wikipedias containing articles written in closely-related dialects. This is the case, for instance, of the "Alemannischi Wikipedia" [8], that contains articles in *Schwyzerdütsch* (Swiss German), *Badisch* (Baden Alemannic), *Elsassisch* (Alsatian dialects), *Schwäbisch* (Swabian German) and *Vorarlbergisch* (Austrian dialect spoken in Vorarlberg). Each article of the Wikipedia is tagged with its corresponding linguistic `category`.

While there exist other examples of multi-dialectal Wikipedias (for instance the Bihari one, which covers more than ten dialects spoken in India and Nepal, or the Occitan one covering a continuum of roman dialects spoken in 4 countries), we have not identified any other Wikipedia in which the articles are explicitly tagged with their corresponding dialects.

Writing Convention(s) The spelling conventions are specific to each Wikipedia. We give here three examples of Wikipedias in which different rules are followed:

- The Alsatian section of the Alemannic Wikipedia contains pages written both in standardized and non-standardized spelling.

- Adversely, the Wikimedia Incubator for Mauritian Creole (ISO 639-3 code `mfe`)[9] displays this note on its front page:

  > "Please use the correct up-to-date standardized spelling of the Mauritian Creole language. Some pages have already been written in as "unstandardized" spelling which need to be replaced."

- The Egyptian Arabic edition (ISO 639-3 code `arz`) is written in Arabic script, yet one page makes the inventory of the articles written in Latin alphabet, intended for *"people who can speak Masry but can only write in the Latin alphabet"*[10].

3.1.3. The Encyclopedic Nature of Wikipedia

As a counterpart for the good quality of the Wikipedias (in terms of the well-formed, grammatical contents they host), contributing to a Wikipedia can be difficult.

---

[4]The statistics for each Wikipedia are provided by WIKIMEDIA (see `https://meta.wikimedia.org/wiki/List_of_Wikipedias`). The approximate number of speakers per language is the estimation provided by `ethnologue` or was found on the page of the language of the English Wikipedia.

[5]See `https://meta.wikimedia.org/wiki/Language_proposal_policy`.

[6]See `https://iso639-3.sil.org/`.

[7]See `https://tools.ietf.org/html/bcp47`

[8]See: `https://als.wikipedia.org/wiki/Wikipedia:Houptsyte`

[9]See `https://incubator.wikimedia.org/wiki/Wp/mfe/Main_Page`.

[10]See the `Introduction in English` page of the `https://arz.wikipedia.org`.

	Size rank	Size (Nb. articles)	Depth	Approx Nb of native speakers	Active users *
English	1	6,013,707	991	379M	137,409
Cebuano	2	5,378,563	2	15M	148
Swedish	3	3,738,252	7	10M	2,759
Waray-Waray	11	1,263,914	4	2.6M	65
Aragonese	100	36,706	63	10,000	76
Vepsian	167	6,369	39	1,500	23
Hawaiian	195	3,839	8	20,000	14

* "Active Users" are the registered users who have made at least one edit in the last thirty days.

Table 1: Comparison of 7 Wikipedias.

Before all, the Wikipedias are encyclopedias, and the text corpora they represent are a "side effect" of the participation.

The induced expected quality in terms of both content and form, as well as the structured and academic looking environment can represent a barrier for potential contributors.

In fact, encyclopedic articles may not be the most natural content to produce for linguistic communities with recent scriptural tradition.

What is more, as commented by Rémy Gerbert, coordinator of WIKIMEDIA FRANCE, developing Wikipedias for smaller languages faces the obstacle of sourcing the articles, since the sources required to support the article are unlikely to be available in the language of the Wikipedia (personal communication, November 2018).

Finally, it is hard for smaller Wikipedias to cope with the growth of the top ones, hence to be competitive in terms of interest for their users in bilingual contexts. This has for instance been reported in The Digital Language Diversity Project (2017) regarding the preference towards the Italian Wikipedia over the Sardinian one among Sardinian speakers.

There exist interesting initiatives to overcome this issue while taking advantage of existing articles written in a top language. This is for example the case of the experience presented in (Alegria et al., 2013), in which the authors use the Spanish and Basque Wikipedias as corpora, and associate machine translation techniques with human editing performed by volunteers to expand the Wikipedia semi-automatically while creating resources to improve the quality of machine translation.

3.2. The Web as a Corpus

3.2.1. Crawled Corpora for Less-Resourced Languages

One way to address the data bottleneck is to resort to Web crawling. Web crawling for multilingual corpus construction consists in gathering texts from the Web that are further curated and automatically classified by language. For instance, the An Crúbadán project (Scannell, 2007), first initiative of the kind to our knowledge, uses a combination of trigrams, automatically generated lexicons and lists of words specific to a given language, to identify on the Web contents written in 2,228 languages. Goldhahn et al. (2012) combine various techniques, including the bootstrap of corpora through search queries.

Whichever the method chosen to crawl the Web, it is nec-essary to perform language identification to classify the documents. Both works presented above indeed require statistical information on the distribution of characteristic patterns, such as trigrams, for each language. This kind of information is not always available, especially when it comes to multi-variant languages, composed of similar dialects (eg. the dialects of Occitan) or that can be written with competing orthographies (eg. Cornish).

What is more, the use of crawled corpora is questionable from the legal point of view, as many countries do not recognize the "fair use" applied in the English-speaking world. In order to circumvent the problem[11], some colleagues decided (i) to erase all metadata, and (ii) to scramble the documents[12]. Performing these operations causes a loss of information that results in at least two shortcomings:

- scrambling the documents of a multi-variant language results in building one heterogeneous resource;

- scrambling breaks the structure of the document, hence limiting further use to the sentence level.

Finally, there is no evidence that the best way of processing multi-variant languages is to use an heterogeneous corpus[13].

3.2.2. Social Media-Based Corpora

Social media are a widely used place of expression, hence they can be considered as a valuable source of text corpora. The contents produced on Twitter and Facebook are probably more representative of the conversational use, yet they are not sustainable. As for Facebook, the company does not allow for the free usage of the data and the consent of all the participants should be asked for.[14] Twitter presents different challenges, as Tweets are short texts, which could be considered as quotations and therefore more easily used. However, this does not apply to artistic creations, such as haikus, so the Tweets have to be manually scanned for these. More importantly, to avoid copyright issues the

---

[11]It is unclear to us to which extent this really solves the legal issue.

[12]See: `https://traces1.inria.fr/oscar/fr/`.

[13]In fact, our own experiments with Alsatian tend to show that training a tool with a small corpus of a given dialect yields to better results on this dialect than using a bigger multi-dialectal corpus.

[14]This has been made clear in a message on the CORPORA list by Eric Ringer, on October 27th, 2015.

Tweets are often referred to by their identifier, but they can be deleted or modified by their creators in the meantime, which generates discrepancies. Besides, the language still needs to be identified, as a user can write tweets in any language they feel is most appropriate to their communication goal.

The availability of linguistic resources being a prerequisite to their further re-usability and longevity, we do not investigate further these sources.

However, initiatives such as the `Nierika` project[15], which was presented at LT4ALL in December 2019, in Paris, could be a solution. This project aims at using social networks to collect linguistic data, while addressing the issue of consent and respecting privacy. As presented by its developer, `Nierika` is "a niche social network on development, which is founded on the objective to collaborate with and support the preservation of all the Mexican indigenous languages". To our knowledge, no result concerning the project has been published so far.

4. Motivations for Crowdsourcing

Crowdsourcing has been successfully used in NLP to compensate the lack of financial means and the unavailability of experts to produce linguistic resources, for example using games with a purpose (Chamberlain et al., 2013) or citizen science platforms, in particular the Language Arc, developed by the Linguistic Data Consorium (LDC)[16]. What is more, it has been repeatedly observed that the success of a crowdsourcing campaign of this kind relies on the openness of the call, that enables to get in touch with few active participants who eventually fulfill the bulk of the chosen task (Chamberlain et al., 2013; Fort et al., 2017; Millour and Fort, 2017).[17] This means that crowdsourcing is not necessarily about finding a way to recruit and motivate a "crowd", and in the context of NLP should not be kept for vast linguistic communities only.

That being said, commonly used microworking platforms such as `Amazon Mechanical Turk` are inadequate for getting in touch with smaller linguistic communities, unlikely to be represented among the microworkers. In fact, there may not exist off-the-shelf solutions to efficiently crowdsource linguistic resources among smaller communities, and such enterprise may lead us to the outer limits of crowdsourcing challenges.

Yet, in a context in which practices are evolving fast and there is probably no expert able to provide sufficient description and resources anyway, involving the speakers in the production of data for their language seems to be the only way out.

In the following, we first present the benefits of involving a variety of speakers to produce linguistic resources, we then detail how crowdsourcing has been successfully used to produce representative data in varied linguistic contexts.

4.1. Involving a Variety of Speakers to Produce Linguistic Resources

As multi-variant languages are by definition varied, we believe that the collection process should focus on gathering linguistic productions from a diversity of speakers. This can be observed in works on User Generated Content (UGC), which rely on corpora produced by many speakers to capture the diversity of linguistic practices in a setup where variation with respect to a norm can be observed. We believe a similar approach should be considered for multi-variant languages.

Using crowdsourcing as a way to produce text corpora solves the problem of language identification, since the language is constrained in the first place. Furthermore, the direct contact with participants enables the production of additional metadata such as the dialectal variant or the spelling habit in use. Although in some contexts the speakers may not be able to name the variant in use, they can be asked to point the geographical area on a map. Similarly, when the spelling convention is unknown, we may ask the speaker to indicate their preference towards a suggested spelling over another.

Moreover, crowdsourcing oral languages written by their own speakers allows to avoid the subjectivity of a transcription made by a (field)-linguist, for example. Transcription being an interpretation, we believe that in the context of corpus construction, we prefer having the interpretation of the speakers themselves.

In fact, building resources for endangered languages should focus on developing tools that are actually useful to empower the speakers to use their language.

We believe this cannot be done without collecting data that match today's practice. In fact, developing tools that would work on ancient or literary versions of the language is not what we aim at. Especially, content that may have entered into the public domain because it was published long ago is unlikely to be representative of the current practices. One such example is the corpus for Quechua described in (Monson et al., 2006), which is made of two literary texts first published at the beginning of the 20th century.

Although these corpora are valuable resources, they should not be considered as sufficient. What is more, if we want to be able to involve the speakers in participating into further linguistic processing such as annotation, translation etc., we need to provide them with contents they are comfortable with.

4.2. Crowdsourcing Variation

In this section, we survey how crowdsourcing has been successfully called upon to i) get in touch and involve a variety of speakers to collect data on linguistic variation, ii) collect real world linguistic productions in a controlled setup that matches specific needs and ensures further re-usability of the data.

4.2.1. Oral Data

Crowdsourcing is a common and successful practice when it comes to oral data collection, especially when the goal is to render and document the dialectal variability of a linguistic area. Examples of crowdsourcing of speech corpora

---

[15]See `https://vaniushar.github.io/about`.

[16]See: `https://languagearc.org/`.

[17]This phenomenon is observed on Wikipedia with for instance around 68K editors on the English Wikipedia, 1K on the Swedish one, 40 on the Cebuano one etc., see `https://stats.wikimedia.org`, figures from December 2019.

for less-resourced languages include works aiming at collecting the greatest possible variety such as, among others, the work of Cooper et al. (2019) for Welsh dialects (one orthography unifies six dialectal areas).

Such a trend is not surprising, especially considering the present need to document and process languages with a mainly oral tradition. This practice is, to our knowledge, less common when it comes to the collection of written data.

We hypothesize that this might be caused by the most official status taken by the written form over the oral form, even though in practice, spelling in any language is subjected to variations.

Because the transcription time makes the process too costly, and because transcribing crowdsourced oral data is different from crowdsourcing written data produced directly by speakers, we do not investigate further how such technique may be used.

4.2.2. Collaborative Lexicography

The involvement of speakers for collaborative lexicography is a well-studied field, especially when it comes to online dictionaries (Abel and Meyer, 2013).

In fact, there exist numerous projects involving the construction of lexical resources for regional languages and documentation of local variants, based on pre-existing documentation of the dialectal variation. For instance, the *Dictionnaire des mots de base du francoprovençal* uses a standardized supra-dialectal spelling for its entries (Stich et al., 2003).

Following another approach, the "Swiss Italian dialectal Lexicon" [18] has one entry per variant, each of them being linked to a head-term (*capolemma*). Although the designers of this online resource seem to work closely with local speakers, their actual contribution to enriching this resource is unclear (Zoli and Randaccio, 2016).

Duijff et al. (2016) provide feedback on the contribution of speakers for the construction of a Dutch-Frisian dialect dictionary, and especially underline their ability to fill the so-called "lexical-gaps".

These examples show that crowdsourcing can be used to involve a community into collaboratively producing linguistic resources.

5. Building Text Corpora with the Help of the Speakers

Compared to the strategies presented in Section 3., which rely on *collecting* and classifying existing content, we present here strategies developed to actively *build* corpora with the help of speakers.

Crowdsourcing has been used for a variety of tasks as exemplified in Section 4.2., showing that it is possible to involve small linguistic communities into collaboratively producing linguistic data. Yet, to our knowledge, there exists no initiative that aims at producing text corpora for multivariant languages.

In this Section we first present two works of interest with regard to their implicit strategies to collect text corpora.

Then, we present our ongoing work on crowdsourcing linguistic resources and more specifically text corpora for a non-standardized language. After describing the conditions and setup of this experiment, we present the challenges that were encountered as well as an analysis of their potential causes.

5.1. Eliciting Corpora

Crowdsourcing text corpora often resorts to eliciting techniques, such as asking for descriptions to inspire the contributors. In such cases, crowdsourcing can be described as *explicit*, meaning that the goal of the activity is expressed plainly to the participant.

Producing text corpora being a tedious task requiring time and effort, Niculae and Danescu-Niculescu-Mizil (2016) and Prys et al. (2016) have come up with original ideas to crowdource text corpora *implicitly*. The first article presents `Street Crowd`, an online game which objective is to identify the location where a picture was taken. This search towards the correct location is done collaboratively, with multiple participants giving their opinion and possibly debating the solution. The crowdsourced corpus is here composed of the conversations between the participants. The second article presents an online spell and grammar checker for Welsh, used as such by speakers. The corpus collected here is the input to be spellchecked. This strategy appears as particularly efficient to collect diverse data in terms both of form and content.

5.2. Crowdsourcing Cooking Recipes

We have focused in previous work on producing corpora collaboratively annotated with part-of-speech for under-resourced languages (Millour and Fort, 2018; Millour and Fort, 2019). Our experiments involved Alsatian, a continuum of Alemannic dialects spoken in Alsace, a diglossic French region, and Mauritian Creole, a French-based Creole spoken mostly in Mauritius. A flexible spelling system called Orthal has been developed for Alsatian (Crévenat-Werner and Zeidler, 2008) and a standardized spelling (*Lortograf Kreol Morisien*) is promoted by the Mauritian Creole Academy (*Akademi Kreol Morisien*) (Police-Michel et al., 2012) and supported by the Mauritian government. Although, to our knowledge, there exists no precise statistics on the use of these spelling recommendations, neither of them seem to be widespread among the Alsatian and Mauritian Creole speaking communities (Saarinen, 2016; Erhart, 2018). This lack of standardization translates into the coexistence of alternative spellings for many words, expressing both the dialectal and scriptural variations at stake.

For the sake of sustainability, we chose to provide the speakers with text corpora that was distributed under a clear license so that we would be able to share its annotated version.

Yet, in both cases, we were rapidly limited by the small size of the available corpora. Additionally, these annotating experiments confronted us with two issues:

1. The discomfort expressed by participants: some of them struggled annotating sentences that were not written accordingly to their own practice of the language, either in terms of dialect or spelling habit.

---

[18]*Lessico dialettale della Svizzera Italiana*, see `http://lsi.ti-edu.ch/lsi/`.

2. The unbalance in variants in our corpora, extracted from the Alemannic Wikipedia. The taggers trained on the crowdsourced annotated corpus were biased towards the over-represented variant (Millour and Fort, 2018).

This brought us to crowdsource additional text corpora. We chose to collect cooking recipes to elicit production. We found three benefits in involving the speakers into collaborative text corpus creation. First, text collection would naturally increase the size of the available corpora. Second, since the participants would annotate their own texts, they would not feel the discomfort expressed above. Third, involving speakers of various linguistic profiles would increase the representativeness of our corpus.

Along with the corpus collection, we added a feature called "I would have said it like that" which enabled the participants to suggest an alternative spelling for any word present on the crowdsourced corpus. This feature is exemplified in figure 3.

The corpus collection experiment did not yield the expected results, since less than 10 participants entered recipes. In fact, our first experiment with crowdsourcing, which was about annotating existing corpora with the universal part-of-speech tagset, was more successful than our second attempt, with more than 50 participants producing up to 19,000 annotations (Millour and Fort, 2018)

The hypothesis we had made that a "non-linguistic" task would be more attractive than an annotation task was not confirmed by our experiments, even though our second platform was designed with more attention, was publicized in the local newspaper and blogs, hence benefiting from better advertising. Actually, the advertising made on our second platform brought additional participants to the annotation task.

Interestingly, the feature aiming at collecting spelling alternatives on pre-existing words received more interest and 367 alternative spellings were provided for 148 words (Millour and Fort, 2019).

Overall, our experience in crowdsourcing linguistic material for Alsatian leads us to suspect that producing text corpora might be harder a task than we thought, and requires more careful design.

5.3. Why are the Speakers Reluctant to Participate?

To understand the unequal participation observed on our crowdsourcing platforms, we conducted online surveys. We were inspired by the `Digital Language Diversity Project` (DLDP), which, with the support[19] of WIKIMEDIA FRANCE, has conducted four surveys to understand how the digital presence of four "minority languages" could be developed. The languages which received attention were Breton (200 replies), Basque (428 replies), Karelian (156 replies), and Sardinian (596 replies) (Soria et al., 2018).

From our part, we have conducted, in parallel with the crowdsourcing experiments, two surveys to get a better insight on how the Alsatian and Mauritian Creole speaking communities felt about the use of their language online. A great majority of the members of both linguistic communities are at least bilingual with a language that is taught in school and standardized (like French or English).

To enable comparison with the surveys created by the DLDP, we kept most of their structure, to which we added a focus on:

- the relationship of the speakers with the written form of their language,

- their perception of dialectal and scriptural variety,

- their knowledge and use of the existing spelling standards.

The first survey, entitled "Alsatian, the Internet and you" [20] received 1,200 replies. The second is entitled "Mauritian Creole and its digital presence"[21] and received 144 replies. Both surveys were published in French, the Alsatian community (Huck et al., 2007) and 98% of the Mauritius population (Atchia-Emmerich, 2005) being bilingual with French.

Most of the respondents of the surveys led by DLDP are language activists, professionally involved with their language: 66% for Breton, 65.3% for Basque, 60.7% for Sardinian, 48.7% for Karelian (for which 69.9% of the respondents state they take part in either a revitalization or protection activity related to Karelian). As highlighted by the authors of these studies, this might introduce a strong bias.[22] In comparison, 25% of the Alsatian respondents and 18% of the Mauritian respondents to our surveys state they have either a professional or associative involvement with their language.

Note that there is no widely spread spelling standard for Alsatian, Mauritian Creole, Karelian and Sardinian, while there exist consensual orthographies for Breton (the Peurunvan orthography) and for Basque (*euskera batúa*, literally the "unified basque").

Interestingly, the survey led on Basque and Breton shows no difference between spoken and written self-evaluation. As for Mauritian Creole, 38% of the respondents had never heard of the spelling conventions defended by the Mauritian Creole Academy. Regarding Alsatian, 69% of the respondents claim they had never heard of the Orthal spelling system. Of the 73% who evaluate their oral proficiency as good, only 33% also evaluate their writing proficiency as good, while 49% evaluate it as medium, and 17% as weak.

---

[19]See `https://www.wikimedia.fr/2016/08/03/digital-language-diversity-project-et-wikimedia-france/`.

[20]In French *"L'alsacien, Internet et vous"*, available here: `https://framaforms.org/sondage-pratiques-linguistiques-en-ligne-1546808704`

[21]In French *"Le créole mauricien et sa présence en ligne"*, available here: `https://framaforms.org/sondage-le-creole-mauricien-et-sa-presence-en-ligne-1555054850`.

[22]"Language activists tend to be intentionally more assertive in their use of the language and, as a consequence, they can't represent average speakers." (Soria et al., 2018)

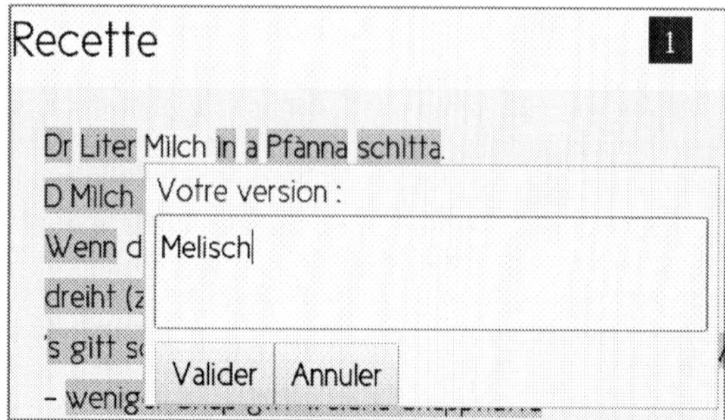

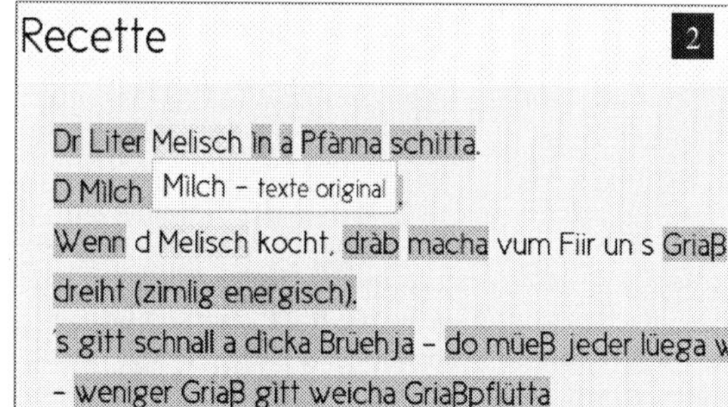

Figure 3: Spelling addition (1) and visualization (2) on a crowdsourced recipe in Alsatian (highlighted words present at least one additional variant).

It therefore seems that the average speakers –not the language activists– under-evaluate their ability to write their own language and might be reluctant to write it on a platform developed by researchers.

Depending on the strategy chosen to crowdsource (the task to perform can either be explicit, or hidden under another purpose, hence implicit), designers should bring an extra care to raising awareness about the urge to develop linguistic resources.

They also should make a pedagogical effort to convince the speakers that the way they write their language cannot be wrong and that we need their input to develop systems dealing with the language as it is used today.

6. Conclusions and Perspectives

Oral languages are more and more written by their speakers, especially on digital media. This is an opportunity for us, as researchers in linguistics and NLP, both in terms of needed applications (eg. word prediction) and collection of language resources.

In this context, and since very little research of this kind has been carried out, it is still unclear whether crowdsourcing to encourage data production is worth the effort. On the other hand, we have seen that the material spontaneously produced by the speakers and made available online is often insufficient to fulfill the NLP researchers needs, especially in the context of non-standardized languages. In fact, we believe that initiatives involving speakers are more likely to produce usable material.

During our experience with crowdsourcing, we have experimented that speakers seem to be reluctant to provide us with language data, as they feel like they do not know how to write their language properly. These psychological barriers should be addressed by researchers in order to overcome the lack of diversity in the freely available data we need.

A solution to this is to use a real game as support for crowdsourcing, so that the speakers "forget" that they are participating to a research experiment. We thus developed a prototype of a role-playing game (RPG), which aim is both to foster the inter-generational transmission of non-standardized languages and to collect lexicon (including multi-word expressions) and variants for the language (Millour et al., 2019). This game will be made freely available for translation and use in any language, so that, hopefully, kids will be proud to speak and write their family language.

7. Bibliographical References

Abel, A. and Meyer, C. M. (2013). The dynamics outside the paper: user contributions to online dictionaries. In *Proceedings of the 3rd eLex conference 'Electronic lexicography in the 21st century: thinking outside the paper*, pages 179–194.

Alegria, I., Cabezon, U., Fernández de Betoño, U., Labaka, G., Mayor, A., Sarasola, K., and Zubiaga, A., (2013). *Reciprocal Enrichment Between Basque Wikipedia and Machine Translation*, pages 101–118. 02.

Atchia-Emmerich, B. (2005). *La situation linguistique de l'île Maurice: Les developpements récents à la lumière d'une enquête empirique*. Ph.D. thesis, Universität Erlangen-Nürnberg, 03.

Chamberlain, J., Fort, K., Kruschwitz, U., Lafourcade, M., and Poesio, M. (2013). Using games to create language resources: Successes and limitations of the approach. In Iryna Gurevych et al., editors, *The People's Web Meets NLP*, Theory and Applications of Natural Language Processing, pages 3–44. Springer Berlin Heidelberg.

Cooper, S., Jones, D. B., and Prys, D. (2019). Crowdsourcing the paldaruo speech corpus of welsh for speech technology. *Information*, 10(8):247.

Crévenat-Werner, D. and Zeidler, E. (2008). *Orthographe alsacienne - Bien écrire l'alsacien de Wissembourg à Ferrette*. Jérôme Do Bentzinger.

Duijff, P., van der Kuip, F., Sijens, H., and Visser, W. (2016). User contributions in the online dutch-frisian dictionary. In *Proceedings of European Network of e-Lexicography (Enel) COST Action (WG1 meeting)*, Barcelona, Spain.

Erhart, P. (2018). Les émissions en dialecte de france 3 alsace : des programmes hors normes pour des parlers hors normes ? In *Les Cahiers du GEPE*. Strasbourg : Presses universitaires de Strasbourg.

Fauzi, A. I. and Puspitorini, D. (2018). Dialect and identity: A case study of javanese use in WhatsApp and line. *IOP Conference Series: Earth and Environmental Science*, 175:012111, jul.

Fort, K., Guillaume, B., and Lefèbvre, N. (2017). Who

wants to play Zombie? A survey of the players on ZOM-BILINGO. In *Games4NLP 2017 - Using Games and Gamification for Natural Language Processing*, Symposium Games4NLP, page 2, Valencia, Spain, April.

Goldhahn, D., Eckart, T., and Quasthoff, U. (2012). Building large monolingual dictionaries at the leipzig corpora collection: From 100 to 200 languages. In *Proceedings of the 8th International Conference on Language Resources and Evaluation (LREC'12)*, pages 759—765, Istanbul, Turkey. European Language Resources Association (ELRA).

Grave, E., Bojanowski, P., Gupta, P., Joulin, A., and Mikolov, T. (2018). Learning word vectors for 157 languages. *arXiv preprint arXiv:1802.06893*.

Guldbrandsson, L. (2013). Swedish wikipedia surpasses 1 million articles with aid of article creation bot. *Wikimedia blog*, 17.

Huck, D., Bothorel-Witz, A., and Geiger-Jaillet, A. (2007). *L'Alsace et ses langues. Éléments de description d'une situation sociolinguistique en zone frontalière*. Université de Strasbourg.

Lample, G., Conneau, A., Denoyer, L., and Ranzato, M. (2017). Unsupervised machine translation using monolingual corpora only.

Lillehaugen, B. D., (2016). *Why write in a language that (almost) no one can read? Twitter and the development of written literature*, volume 10, pages 356–393. University of Hawaii Press.

McEnery, T. and Hardie, A. (2011). *Corpus Linguistics: Method, Theory and Practice*. Cambridge Textbooks in Linguistics. Cambridge University Press.

Millour, A. and Fort, K. (2017). Why do we Need Games? Analysis of the Participation on a Crowdsourcing Annotation Platform. In *Games4NLP*, Valencia, Spain, April.

Millour, A. and Fort, K. (2018). Toward a Lightweight Solution for Less-resourced Languages: Creating a POS Tagger for Alsatian Using Voluntary Crowdsourcing. In *Proceedings of 11th International Conference on Language Resources and Evaluation (LREC'18)*, Miyazaki, Japan, May. European Language Resources Association (ELRA).

Millour, A. and Fort, K. (2019). À l'écoute des locuteurs : production participative de ressources langagières pour des langues non standardisées. In *Revue TAL : numéro spécial sur les langues peu dotées*, volume 59-3. Association pour le Traitement Automatique des Langues.

Millour, A., Grace Araneta, M., Lazić Konjik, I., Raffone, A., Pilatte, Y.-A., and Fort, K. (2019). Katana and Grand Guru: a Game of the Lost Words (DEMO). In *9th Language & Technology Conference: Human Language Technologies as a Challenge for Computer Science and Linguistics (LTC'19)*, Poznań, Poland, May.

Monson, C., Llitjós, A. F., Aranovich, R., Levin, L. M., Brown, R., Peterson, E., Carbonell, J. G., and Lavie, A. (2006). Building nlp systems for two resource-scarce indigenous languages : Mapudungun and quechua. In *Proceedings of 5th SALTMIL Workshop on Minority Languages*, pages 15–24, Genoa, Italy.

Niculae, V. and Danescu-Niculescu-Mizil, C. (2016). Conversational markers of constructive discussions. In *Proceedings of the 2016 Conference of the North American Chapter of the Association for Computational Linguistics: Human Language Technologies (NAACL-HLT'2016)*, pages 568–578, San Diego (CA), USA, June. Association for Computational Linguistics.

Outinoff, M. (2012). English won't be the internet's lingua franca. In *Towards the Multilingual Cyberspace*, pages 171–178. Vannini, Laurent and Le Crosnier, Hervé, c&f éditio edition.

Police-Michel, D., Carpooran, A., and Florigny, G. (2012). *Gramer Kreol Morisien*. Akademi Kreol Morisien, Ministry of Education and Human Resources.

Prys, D., Prys, G., and Jones, D. B. (2016). Cysill arlein: A corpus of written contemporary welsh compiled from an on-line spelling and grammar checker. In *Proceedings of the 10th International Conference on Language Resources and Evaluation (LREC'16)*, pages 3261–3264. Portorož, Slovenia, European Language Resources Association (ELRA), May.

Rivron, V. (2012). L'usage de Facebook chez les Éton du Cameroun. In *Net.lang Réussir le cyberespace multilingue*, pages 171–178. Vannini, Laurent and Le Crosnier, Hervé, c&f edition.

Saarinen, R. (2016). La distribution des fonctions des langues dans un contexte multilingue : cas de l'Île maurice. Master's thesis, Faculté des Lettres, Université de Turku, Turku, Finland.

Scannell, K. P. (2007). The crúbadán project: Corpus building for under-resourced languages. In *Proceedings of the 3rd Web as Corpus Workshop: Building and Exploring Web Corpora*, volume 4, pages 5–15, Louvain-la-Neuve, Belgium, September.

Shekhar, S., Sharma, D. K., and Beg, M. S. (2018). Hindi roman linguistic framework for retrieving transliteration variants using bootstrapping. *Procedia Computer Science*, 125:59–67.

Soria, C., Quochi, V., and Russo, I. (2018). The DLDP survey on digital use and usability of EU regional and minority languages. In *Proceedings of the 11th International Conference on Language Resources and Evaluation (LREC'2018)*, Miyazaki, Japan, May. European Language Resources Association (ELRA).

Stich, D., Gouvert, X., and Favre, A. (2003). *Dictionnaire des mots de base du francoprovençal : orthographe ORB supradialectale standardisée*. Le Carré.

The Digital Language Diversity Project. (2017). Sardinian — a digital language? In *Reports on Digital Language Diversity in Europe*. Editors: Claudia Soria, Irene Russo, Valeria Quoch.

Tobaili, T., Fernandez, M., Alani, H., Sharafeddine, S., Hajj, H., and Glavas, G. (2019). Senzi: A sentiment analysis lexicon for the latinised arabic (arabizi). in: International conference recent advances. In *Proceedings of Recent Advances in Natural Language Processing (RANLP'2019)*, Varna, Bulgaria, September.

Tournadre, N. (2014). The tibetic languages and their classification. In *Trans-Himalayan linguistics: Historical and descriptive linguistics of the Himalayan area*. Owen-

Smith, Thomas / Hill, Nathan.

van Esch, D., Sarbar, E., Lucassen, T., O'Brien, J., Breiner, T., Prasad, M., Crew, E., Nguyen, C., and Beaufays, F. (2019). Writing across the world's languages: Deep internationalization for gboard, the google keyboard. *arXiv preprint arXiv:1912.01218.*

Zoli, C. and Randaccio, S. (2016). The context of use of e-dictionaries for the minority languages of italy (case study). In *Proceedings of European Network of e-Lexicography (Enel) COST Action (WG3 meeting)*, Barcelona, Spain, March.

Proceedings of the 1st Joint SLTU and CCURL Workshop (SLTU-CCURL 2020), pages 121–125
Language Resources and Evaluation Conference (LREC 2020), Marseille, 11–16 May 2020

Scaling Language Data Import/Export with a Data Transformer Interface

Nicholas Buckeridge, Ben Foley
The University of Queensland
The Centre of Excellence for the Dynamics of Language
bucknich@gmail.com, b.foley@uq.edu.au

Abstract
This paper focuses on the technical improvement of Elpis, a language technology which assists people in the process of transcription, particularly for low-resource language documentation situations. To provide better support for the diversity of file formats encountered by people working to document the world's languages, a Data Transformer interface has been developed to abstract the complexities of designing individual data import scripts. This work took place as part of a larger project of code quality improvement and the publication of template code that can be used for development of other language technologies.

Keywords: language documentation, low-resource languages, automatic speech recognition, data conversion, Python, design patterns

1. Introduction

In the development of speech recognition language technologies, supporting the import and export of the wide range of language data formats currently in use presents a challenge. The tools available for language documentation, description and analysis produce many different formats, which makes it unfeasible to write individual import and export scripts for each format. This work aims to increase the range of corpora that tools such as Elpis (Foley et al., 2018) can feasibly import and export. To develop an understanding of the range of language data formats commonly used, archives including PARADISEC (Thieberger and Barwick, 2012), ELAR[1], OpenSLR[2] and Open Speech Corpora[3] were analysed. Existing technologies such as Salt and Pepper (Druskat et al., 2016) were reviewed to determine their suitability as a conversion engine for Elpis. For reasons of maintaining support for a commonly-used language documentation format, and concerns about increasing the complexity of the Elpis codebase, we developed a Python interface which simplifies the process of converting language data formats into an intermediate format. By identifying the design parameters of relating code structure to workflow processes, code simplicity and configuration flexibility, an "abstract factory" design pattern was determined as the architecture of the work. The development of Data Transformers, using abstract data manipulation factories, has given Elpis the capability to support importing a wide variety of transcription data formats.

2. Background

2.1. Transcription

There are many motivations for transcribing spoken language. Building collections of transcribed recordings is beneficial for language documentation as a multipurpose, lasting record of a language (Himmelmann, 2006). Transcription is currently a critical requirement for a spoken language to have a digital presence. Language technologies such as mobile keyboards, speech recognition (ASR) tools, translation systems, and text-to-speech require some degree of language in text format to train or develop the systems (van Esch, 2019).

Producing transcriptions is time-consuming; on average it takes 40 hours to transcribe one hour of audio (Foley et al., 2019). Given this "transcription bottleneck", most language workers will never get to transcribe all the speech that they have recorded (Bird, 2013; Brinckmann, 2009; McDonnell et al., 2018). The overwhelming effort required results in data graveyards, extensive collections of un-annotated audio data accumulating with limited use to anyone (Himmelmann, 2006). The lack of annotations also limits the use of the recordings in language technologies such as translation systems.

Software expertise and software literacy can hinder language community members from transcribing collections of recordings themselves, as the dominant tools used in transcription tend to involve a steep learning curve. Traditionally, transcription has been done by outsider language researchers, although this is a trend which is starting to see some change, with communities such as the Seneca language group using the Kaldi speech recognition toolkit to transcribe their own recordings (Jimerson et al., 2019).

2.2. Data Formats

The wide range of recording practises, technologies and software requirements used in language documentation and transcription activities have fostered a great variety of data formats. As an example, an analysis of the files in PARADISEC, an archive that supports work on endangered languages and cultures of the Pacific and the Australian region, shows >220,000 files with 43 file types, including approximately 20 media formats and eight formats generated by transcription software (refer to Table 1). Media files dominate, and ELAN files (.eaf) make up the most substantial portion of transcription file types (see Figure 1) . The variety of formats presents a challenge when designing language technologies which rely on importing files created or processed by other tools.

Standards have emerged to improve the interoperability of language tools. In recent years, there have been proposals to standardise formats such as XIGT (Goodman et al.,

---

[1] https://elar.soas.ac.uk
[2] https://www.openslr.org
[3] https://github.com/jrmeyer/open-speech-corpora

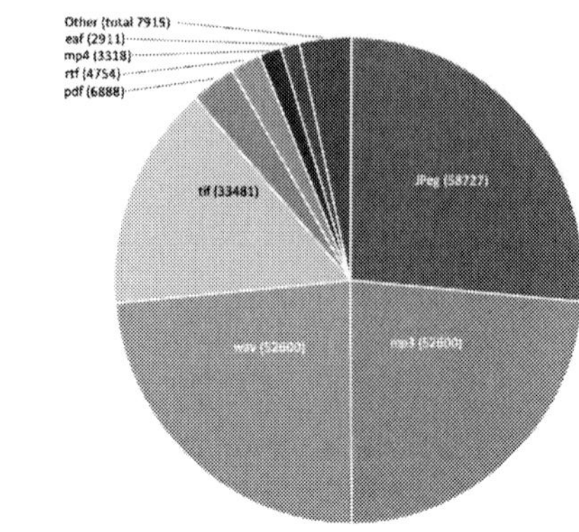

Figure 1: PARADISEC file types

File type	Number of files
jpg	58727
mp3	52600
wav	52600
tif	33481
pdf	6888
rtf	4754
mp4	3318
eaf	2911
mxf	2327
txt	1378
webm	1144
mov	880
JPG	597
tiff	355
xml	203
mpg	155
qua	140
trs	120
png	113
TextGrid	102
pfsx	76
flextext	60
docx	55
cha	39
tab	39
lbl	30
dv	21
csv	14
fwbackup	12
img	8
MP4	8
MTS	8
xlsx	7
avi	5
ixt	4
m4v	3
md5	3
TIF	3
kml	2
doc	1
EAF	1
mpeg	1
xhtml	1

Table 1: PARADISEC file formats

2015) for Interlinear Glossed Text; and to extend XML processing tools such as XPATH (Bird et al., 2006). Framework specifications such as EXMARaLDA span working with individual transcriptions through to corpus management (Schmidt and Wörner, 2009). Wider adoption of tools such as SayMore[4], and proposals like Holton and Thieberger's collections management tool, recently released as Digame[5] would make ingesting material into archives a more reliable and quicker process, and improve downstream processes such as ASR which rely on access to language corpora. Corpus conversion tools such as Salt and Pepper map between different language data formats using graph data structures (Druskat et al., 2016).

2.3. Corpus Formats

A selection of recording collections was sourced from archives and online repositories to facilitate the design of the Data Transformer interface. Source diversity was important to ensure that the interface design was generalised, rather than fitting too specifically to one archive. Smaller specialised repositories such as OpenSRL and Josh Meyer's Open Speech Corpora tended to publish files in simple structures, usually in one ZIP file, as opposed to large and highly organised repositories. These collections were typically internally organised for application with specific ASR tools, which can make pre-processing these corpora more complicated. Highly organised repositories such as PARADISEC or ELAR store copious amounts of data grouped into collections and tend to have more uniformity across the whole collection. Each file in these archives is paired with metadata and has permissions controls. Since some of the permissions restrictions do not allow open access, or use a request-for-access rule, these were more difficult to download. There are no single collection download mechanisms for these archives as sometimes permissions would differ per-file in the same collection.

2.4. Elpis

Elpis is being developed to provide an accessible interface to speech recognition tools, to accelerate the process of transcription (Foley et al., 2018). Early work focussed on writing a suite of Python scripts to assist in working with the Kaldi speech recognition toolkit. Scripts were writted to clean and normalise audio and text training data; prepare the intermediary file formats which Kaldi requires; to move files into the directories required by Kaldi; and to run a Kaldi recipe to train the ASR models. This early work was operated by typing instructions into a command-line interface to run the Python scripts, and supported working with ELAN, Transcriber and plain text file formats. Subsequent development resulted in the design and development

[4]https://software.sil.org/saymore
[5]https://go.coedl.net/digame

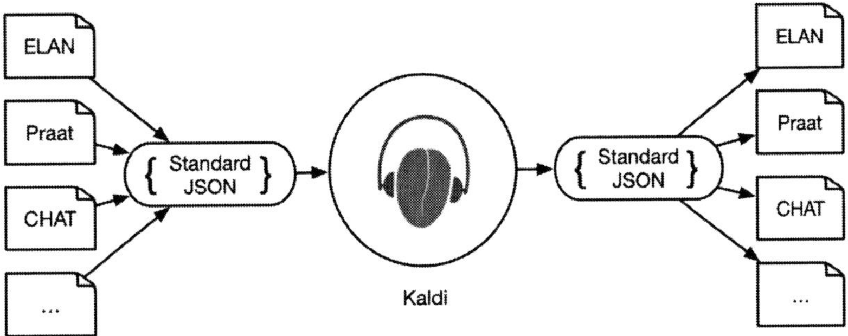

Figure 2: Data conversion mental model

of a graphical user interface (GUI) to provide a way of running Kaldi for people who had no experience with using command-line interfaces, however the GUI only imports ELAN files. Support of multiple file formats was lost due to limited development time preventing the implementation of import options.

3. Method

3.1. Approach

This work began by researching existing approaches to converting language data formats, and investigating methods which language tools use to import and export data. The initial plan to broaden Elpis' support for more file formats was to incorporate existing conversion technology, Salt and Pepper, into the Elpis pipeline. Two options were considered, firstly for Elpis to interact with Pepper via command-line calls; secondly to use a Python-to-Java bridge library for Elpis to interface with Pepper. Early tests showed that support for ELAN files with linked media was not complete[6]. Given that linked media in ELAN was commonly found in the language documentation contexts for which Elpis was originally designed, in addition to concerns about the complexity of writing wrappers around Pepper, a decision was made instead to develop a Data Transformer interface using Python. The mental model representing the data conversion process of inputs and outputs which Pepper uses was maintained in the design of the transformer interface, using Elpis' existing "Kaldi JSON" object structure as the intermediate data format (see Figure 2).

3.2. Data Analysis

After acquiring sample data sets, the data structures, formats and metadata were investigated to gain an understanding of the required features of each collection and data format. In general, collections from OpenSLR and Open ASR lacked standardisation. Another challenge facing these individual repositories was discerning the modalities of the data, with some corpora being collections of speech recordings and text, while others were image and text collections. Extreme cases of specialisation were found in the listings, including corpora that had been prepared for use directly in a machine learning toolkit. These over-specialised corpora (for example, most collections from OpenSRL) in-

cluded complex directory structures and configuration files that would be required for specific speech recognition tools.

3.3. Language Technology Architecture

Elpis is built according to an architecture of a sequence of software layers which interact via a programming interface (API). The API allows the user interface to be decoupled from the processing scripts and speech recognition toolkit, a design which enables the current speech recognition toolkit to be swapped out for another with minimal disruption to the user interface, or the development of different user interfaces for different user groups. A bare-bones version of these software layers has been published as an open-source project "Language Technology API pattern"[7], a template for other language technology projects.

3.4. Design

Designing the Data Transformer interface required adhering to the Elpis philosophy that the codebase and user interface should directly reflect the workflow process; that the code should be simple enough for a novice to understand; while allowing flexibility in configuration if necessary.

A key requirement for the transformer design was that the specification (or description) of a data format should be separate from its instantiation as a data transformer. To help implement this, "design patterns" were used. Design patterns are generic solutions to problems that match a pattern (Sommerville, 2011; Shvets, 2019). To choose a design pattern, the properties of a problem first need to be identified. For the design of the Data Transformer API, these were:

- there is one specification object per format;

- each specification can create multiple importers or exporters for that format; and

- each importer/exporter can be individually configured.

These properties fit the "abstract factory" creational design pattern. The purpose of an abstract factory is to provide an interface to create a family of related objects without specifying the concrete classes (Shvets, 2019). This pattern was implemented for the Data Transformer API.

---

[6]https://github.com/korpling/pepperModules-ElanModules

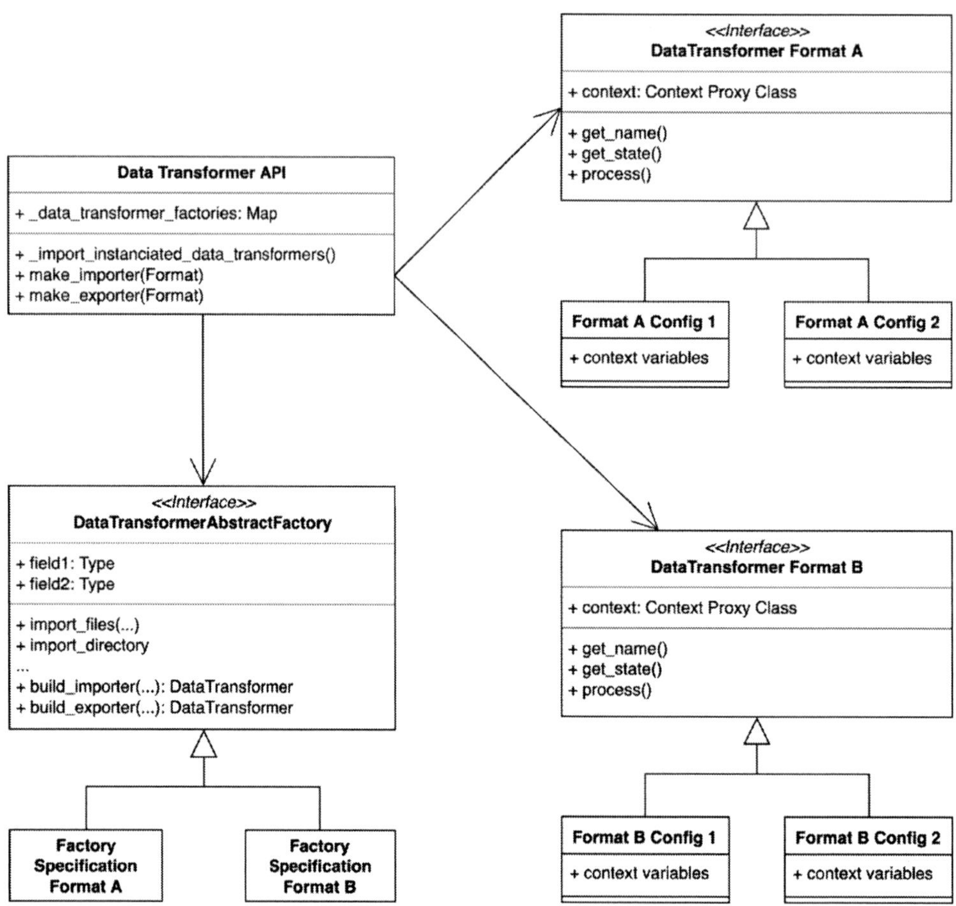

Figure 3: The transformer architecture

3.5. Data Transformer Architecture

The Data Transformer API component of the transformer architecture represents the Python *transformer* module. Import/export formats are specified by extending the *DataTransformerAbstractFactory*, represented here by Factory Specification Formats A and B. If two formats A and B are specified by extending the *DataTransformerAbstractFactory*, then as the properties indicate, concrete *DataTransformers* of the relevant format can be instantiated at any time.

When the API has a request to build a new data transformer, the API will attempt to find that format's factory if it exists. Then the factory uses a base *DataTransformer* class and in the build process, attaches the specification behaviour as per the factory's specification. The factory constructs a *process()* method specialised for the format. It also attaches the bound functions as a Python object attribute by name to the data transformer being built. This flexibility feature is in case an expert user wishes to call the bound function directly, but is not recommended for regular users.

7https://github.com/CoEDL/LT-API-pattern

```
from elpis.transformer import
    DataTransformerAbstractFactory
elan=DataTransformerAbstractFactory('Elan')
```

Example code 1: Elan factory

In Example code 1, the variable *elan* is a new factory. The factory constructor takes one argument, the name of the data transformer. *DataTransformerAbstractFactory* has informative methods that change the behaviour of the produced *DataTransformer* object. Building on the example shown in Figure 4, an implementer can inspect audio extension set, and import/export capabilities.

4. Future Work

4.1. Multi-threading Optimisation

During this work the observation was made that Elpis has limited support for multiprocessor computer resources. Performance optimization of Elpis hasn't been a high priority in its development, which has led to the sporadic use of multi-threading. Because of this, it was unclear if it was safe to include parallel-processing techniques into the design of the data transformers. Future work would improve Elpis' support for multi-threading and update the data transformer interface to make use of multiprocessor computer resources.

5. Conclusion

The development of Data Transformers, using abstract data manipulation factories, has given Elpis the capability to support importing a wide variety of transcription data formats. The software architecture uses "abstract factory" design patterns to ensure the implementation covers a range of known corpora and is scalable for unseen formats. Factory specification methods follow good design practice with extensive documentation and unit testing. A data transformer to import Elan files has been fully implemented to demonstrate the process of using the abstract factory methods. Through this work, Elpis is now in a position to be developed quickly to accommodate the requirements of more language workers and their diverse data formats.

6. Bibliographical References

Bird, S., Chen, Y., Davidson, S. B., Lee, H., and Zheng, Y. (2006). Designing and evaluating an XPath dialect for linguistic queries. In *22nd International Conference on Data Engineering (ICDE'06)*, pages 52–52. IEEE.

Bird, S. (2013). Androids in Amazonia: recording an endangered language. *The Conversation*, 21-May-2019, M. Ketchell.

Brinckmann, C. (2009). Transcription bottleneck of speech corpus exploitation.

Druskat, S., Gast, V., and Krause, T. (2016). An Interoperable Generic Software Tool Set for Multi-layer Linguistic Corpora. *Proceedings of the Tenth International Conference on Language Resources and Evaluation (LREC 2016)*.

Foley, B., Arnold, J. T., Coto-Solano, R., Durantin, G., Ellison, T. M., van Esch, D., Heath, S., Kratochvil, F., Maxwell-Smith, Z., Nash, D., et al. (2018). Building Speech Recognition Systems for Language Documentation: The CoEDL Endangered Language Pipeline and Inference System (ELPIS). In *The 6th Intl. Workshop on Spoken Language Technologies for Under-Resourced Languages*, pages 205–209.

Foley, B., Durantin, G., Ajayan, A., and Wiles, J. (2019). Transcription Survey.

Goodman, M. W., Crowgey, J., Xia, F., and Bender, E. M. (2015). Xigt: extensible interlinear glossed text for natural language processing. *Language Resources and Evaluation*, 49(2):455–485.

Himmelmann, N. P. (2006). Language documentation: What is it and what is it good for. *Essentials of language documentation*, 178(1).

Jimerson, R., Hatcher, R., Ptucha, R., and Prudhommeaux, E. (2019). Speech technology for supporting community-based endangered language documentation.

McDonnell, B., Berez-Kroeker, A. L., and Holton, G. (2018). Reflections on Language Documentation 20 Years after Himmelmann 1998.

Schmidt, T. and Wörner, K. (2009). EXMARaLDA–Creating, analysing and sharing spoken language corpora for pragmatic research. *Pragmatics. Quarterly Publication of the International Pragmatics Association (IPrA)*, 19(4):565–582.

Shvets, A. (2019). Dive Into Design Patterns.

Sommerville, I. (2011). *Software engineering*. Pearson, Boston, 9th ed., international ed.. edition.

Thieberger, N. and Barwick, L. (2012). Keeping records of language diversity in melanesia: the pacific and regional archive for digital sources in endangered cultures (PARADISEC). *Melanesian languages on the edge of Asia: Challenges for the 21st Century*, pages 239–53.

van Esch, D. (2019). Building Language Technologies for Everyone.

Proceedings of the 1st Joint SLTU and CCURL Workshop (SLTU-CCURL 2020), pages 126–130
Language Resources and Evaluation Conference (LREC 2020), Marseille, 11–16 May 2020
© European Language Resources Association (ELRA), licensed under CC-BY-NC

Fully Convolutional ASR for Less-Resourced Endangered Languages

Bao Thai[†], Robbie Jimerson[†], Ray Ptucha[†], Emily Prud'hommeaux[†‡]
[†]Rochester Institute of Technology, Rochester NY, USA
[‡]Boston College, Chestnut Hill MA, USA
{btt4530,rcj2772,rwpeec,emilypx}@rit.edu

Abstract

The application of deep learning to automatic speech recognition (ASR) has yielded dramatic accuracy increases for languages with abundant training data, but languages with limited training resources have yet to see accuracy improvements on this scale. In this paper, we compare a fully convolutional approach for acoustic modelling in ASR with a variety of established acoustic modeling approaches. We evaluate our method on Seneca, a low-resource endangered language spoken in North America. Our method yields word error rates up to 40% lower than those reported using both standard GMM-HMM approaches and established deep neural methods, with a substantial reduction in training time. These results show particular promise for languages like Seneca that are both endangered and lack extensive documentation.

Keywords: automatic speech recognition, endangered languages, indigenous languages

1. Introduction

Improvements and breakthroughs in deep learning for automatic speech recognition (ASR) have resulted in significant improvements in ASR performance in high-resource languages such as English and Mandarin (Hinton et al., 2012; Hannun et al., 2014; Chan et al., 2016; Audhkhasi et al., 2018; Chiu et al., 2018). Such methods, however, require very large volumes of labelled training data to achieve these notable results. Most languages of the world, even those with tens of millions of speakers, do not have the quantities of data required to train such systems. The data sparsity problem is even more dire for the many indigenous languages that have historically been undocumented for political or cultural reasons. Deep learning ASR systems for languages with truly limited labelled training data typically incorporate additional training resources such as cross-lingual acoustic models or in-domain synthetic acoustic data to begin to approach the word error rates found using traditional hidden Markov model (HMM) and Gaussian mixture model (GMM) frameworks.

While convolutional neural networks (CNNs) have demonstrated superior performance on vision tasks such as image classification, image segmentation, and object recognition, deep learning for ASR has relied heavily upon variants of recurrent neural networks (RNNs). In RNNs, information from timesteps before, and after in the case of bidirectional networks, is used in making the decision of the current timestep. CNNs are excellent at extracting regional patterns but typically require inputs to be of fixed size. However, as seen in object detection and image segmentation applications, fully convolutional variations can operate on multiple locations simultaneously and allow variable-size inputs.

In this paper, we present a convolutional acoustic model for ASR in low-resource conditions. We demonstrate our approach using a corpus of 10 hours of recordings of the Seneca language, a critically endangered, morphologically complex language spoken in the northeastern part of North America. Our model reduces the computational cost in terms of number of parameters while still capturing enough temporal dependencies to make accurate predictions. We find that our fully convolutional acoustic model yields significant accuracy improvements over both deep recurrent and HMM/GMM models. To demonstrate the robustness of our approach, we additionally apply our framework to Iban, an unrelated low-resource language with a phonetic inventory roughly the size of Seneca's but with a less complex morphology.

Our main contributions are as follows: 1) We introduce a deep convolutional architecture optimized for low-resource scenarios that captures feature-rich audio data over a broad temporal receptive field; 2) We utilize a fully convolutional framework for arbitrary length sequence processing; and 3) We show the effectiveness of utilizing transfer learning and data augmentation for further reducing word and character error rates.

2. Previous Work

When given sufficient in-domain monolingual training data, deep neural network methods for ASR often perform significantly better than traditional methods based on HMMs and GMMs (Hinton et al., 2012; Graves et al., 2013; Hannun et al., 2014; Amodei et al., 2016; Chan et al., 2016; Zhang et al., 2017; Chiu et al., 2018; Agenbag and Niesler, 2019). Common approaches for deep learning ASR rely on RNNs: sequence-to-sequence models like that in Chan et al. (2016) use RNNs to generate a latent representation of the utterance before decoding with RNNs, while DeepSpeech 1 and DeepSpeech 2 (Hannun et al., 2014; Amodei et al., 2016) use RNNs to capture temporal dependencies before making predictions for each timestep. Methods that produce characters, such as versions of DeepSpeech, currently use Connectionist Temporal Classification (CTC) (Graves et al., 2006) to reduce streams of characters to plausible words by combining consecutive similar characters and pauses during speech.

Convolutional architectures have achieved remarkable results in computer vision tasks such as image classification (Szegedy et al., 2015; Xie et al., 2017). Szegedy et al. (Szegedy et al., 2015) introduced the concept of an Inception block which consists of multiple filter sizes in a layer to capture different levels of regional dependencies. This concept can be applied to sequential data like speech by using filters with different widths to simultaneously capture different temporal dependencies. The Inception network introduces $1\times$ bottleneck filters to reduce the number of parameters in a model. Xie et al. (Xie et al., 2017) use Inception-like blocks but with similar filter sizes while adding skip connections similar to ResNet to allow for better gradient flow.

Previous experiments have shown that transfer learning from a model trained on resource-rich languages can improve the performance of ASR for low-resource languages (Gales et al., 2014; Imseng et al., 2014). Using synthetic data has also been found to yield improvements in true low-resource, artificially low-resource, and resource-rich conditions (Tüske et al., 2014; Billa, 2018; Wiesner et al., 2018). Carmantini et al. (Carmantini et al., 2019) introduced sample overgeneration during initialization for low-resource ASR for improved semi-supervised training on lattice-free maximum mutual information (LF-MMI) (Manohar et al., 2018). Malhotra el at. (Malhotra et al., 2019) selected samples with lower confidence in an active learning scenario for low-resource ASR.

Rosenberg et al. (Rosenberg et al., 2017) investigated the use of a CTC-based RNN and an RNN Encoder-Decoder network in character-based end-to-end ASR for low-resource languages. While recurrent-based models have demonstrated usefulness in ASR and other sequence modeling tasks, these models cannot easily take advantage of parallelization on modern hardware since the output of an RNN cell at each timestep depends on the results from the previous timestep. To mitigate this problem, Collobert et al. (Collobert et al., 2016) relies on convolution to capture temporal dependencies.

The fully convolutional, character-based architecture proposed by Collobert et al. (Collobert et al., 2016) still requires training models with large numbers of parameters. Additionally, these models have a high number of layers causing the models to converge more slowly. Our proposed model aims to reduce the complexity of the model without reducing performance by using bottleneck filters and skip connections. Additionally, instead of relying on different layers to capture different levels of temporal dependencies, we combine filters with different widths into one layer to reduce the number of layers in the model while still maintaining a wide context window. While transfer learning and data augmentation separately have both shown improvements, we explore the effectiveness of combining both concepts on low resource ASR, as well as a final fine-tuning step using only unaugmented data to prevent digital artifacts in augmented data from degrading performance.

3. Data

We conduct our experiments on Seneca, a morphologically complex and critically endangered language spoken by indigenous people in what is now Western New York State and Ontario. Although the language was still widely spoken in the Seneca community as recently as 75 years ago, Seneca children in the mid-twentieth century were typically required to attend state-run residential schools where they were punished or beaten for using their native language.

Today, roughly 50 elderly individuals speak Seneca as their first language, and a few hundred others are second language speakers. There are several ongoing efforts to revitalize the Seneca language, including language immersion programs for adults and children, but there are very few available Seneca recordings or texts, as many members of the Seneca community are reluctant to allow their speech to be recorded or transcribed. One motivation for developing a robust ASR system for Seneca is to accelerate efforts to document the language while there are living native speakers and to produce educational materials for the immersion programs that will train the next generation of speakers.

The available transcribed audio recordings consist of approximately 720 minutes of spontaneous, naturalistic speech produced by eleven adult speakers, eight male and three female. All speakers in the dataset are middle-aged or elderly first-language Seneca speakers whose second language is English. Recordings were made over many years primarily by Seneca language learners under a variety of conditions using various recording equipment, resulting in a diverse range of audio quality.

The recordings were transcribed using Seneca's current orthography, which uses 30 characters, and segmented at the utterance level by second-language Seneca speakers. Since Seneca orthography is quite reliably phonemic, with few ambiguous character-to-phone and phone-to-character mappings, we choose to treat characters (excluding punctuation) as phones. Using utterance boundaries provided in the reference transcripts, we randomly selected individual utterances from the full corpus of 720 minutes until we had obtained 600 minutes of audio for training. The remaining 120 minutes made up the test set. We deliberately selected utterances at random to maximize diversity in terms of gender, age, dialect, voice quality, and content (e.g. narrative vs. conversation) of both the train and test sets in order to avoid overfitting to any particular speaker or speaker characteristics. While this selection procedure lead to certain speakers appearing in both the testing and training sets, we were obliged to make this compromise due to the limited number of speakers of the language. In addition to the transcriptions of the recorded audio (roughly 35,000 words), we have available text data consisting of 6000 words of previously transcribed texts for which no corresponding audio is available.

To demonstrate the generalizability of our methods, we also conduct our experiments on Iban, a Malayic language spoken in Brunei and Malaysia. The publicly available dataset ((Juan et al., 2014)) consists of 479 minutes of professional recordings of broadcast news, partitioned into 408 minutes of training data and 71 minutes of testing data. There are 17 speakers (7 male, 10 female) in the training set and 6 speakers (2 male, 4 female) in the test set.

4. Methods

4.1. Acoustic Modeling

We utilize a fully convolutional acoustic model constructed from a family of one dimensional convolution layers. The model takes either 13 MFCCs and their first and second derivatives, or 80 log mel-filterbanks as input features. Both are obtained using 25ms windows with 10ms stride.

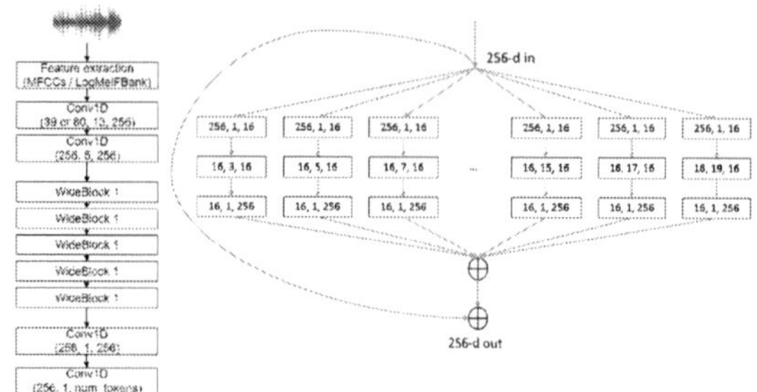

Figure 1: **Left:** The overall architecture of our convolutional approach. **Right:** A WideBlock consisting of 9 paths, each consisting of bottleneck filters centered by filters of different width to capture different levels of temporal dependencies. Each layer is shown as (# input channels, filter width, # output channels).

Figure 1 shows the overall network architecture and the architecture of a WideBlock, the main building block of our model. The details of each are described next.

WideBlock: The main building block of our architecture is the WideBlock (Figure 1), named for the high number of paths in each block. The architecture of the block, taking inspiration from ResNeXt blocks used in image classification (Xie et al., 2017), consists of several parallel streams, each consisting of bottleneck 1×1 convolution layers before and after a normal convolution layer. The bottleneck layers reduce the complexity of the model by reducing the number of parameters required by the middle convolution operation. Instead of keeping the same filter size for all paths, we draw inspiration from Inception networks and employ filters with different sizes in each layer. The filter widths are odd numbers between 3 and 19. This choice is suitable for speech-related tasks since temporal dependencies in audio typically have more variance than spatial dependencies in visual tasks. The different filter sizes allow the model to pick up both short-term and long-term temporal dependencies. The output from each path is then summed before being added to the input of each block, forming a skip connection.

Acoustic Model: Our acoustic model consists of two convolutional layers between the input feature vector and the first WideBlock (Figure 1). These embedding layers convert input audio features into a vector of desired depth and temporal content. The acoustic architecture continues with five WideBlocks, then two 1×1 convolution layers which act as fully-connected layers. The final layer outputs a vector with size corresponding to the number of tokens to be predicted. Batch normalization and ReLU are used after each convolution operation. To prevent overfitting due to limited data, dropout layers of 0.25 are added after each WideBlock. To train the network, the CTC loss function is used.

DeepSpeech: To compare the performance of our deep approach against recurrent-based ASR models, we also trained a DeepSpeech model. The DeepSpeech model consists of a five-layer recurrent neural network with Long-Short Term Memory cells. The first, second, third, and fifth layers of the neural network are fully connected, while the fourth layer is a bi-directional recurrent layer. All layers contain 2048 hidden units and are followed by a dropout layer of 0.2. The DeepSpeech model uses the same input features as our deep approach and also uses CTC loss.

Kaldi: We also compare the performance of our model against the traditional HMM/GMM framework provided by Kaldi (Povey et al., 2011) with a triphone acoustic model trained with the parameter settings described in the Kaldi tutorial and a word-level trigram language model. A second acoustic model was created using Kaldi's time-delay neural network (TDNN) architecture trained with the lattice-free maximum mutual information (LF-MMI) objective function (Peddinti et al., 2015).

4.2. Multistage Learning

Transfer learning has proven successful in deep learning tasks with limited domain data. We extend this concept with a multistage transfer learning strategy. In the first stage, we train an acoustic model on a 960-hour LibriSpeech English corpus for 100 epochs. In the second stage, weight initialization is from the model obtained in the first stage. The model was then trained on heavily augmented training data as per (Jimerson et al., 2018) for 100 epochs or until convergence. In the final stage, the weights of the model from the second stage were used to initialize a model which is trained only on unaugmented data. For this final stage, the learning rate is reduced by an order of magnitude.

5. Results

Table 1 shows the performance for Seneca across different acoustic models with different transfer learning and augmentation strategies. To evaluate the performance of each model, we use word error rate (WER) and character error rate (CER). WER is the minimum edit distance over a word alignment, aggregated across utterances and normalized by the total number of words in the reference transcript. CER is calculated by aggregating the character-level minimum edit distance over all utterances and normalizing by the total number of characters in the reference. We report results for decoding both with and without a trigram language model built on the transcripts of the 10 hours of acoustic training data using KenLM (Heafield, 2011) with modified Kneser-Ney smoothing and no pruning.

Table 1 shows that DeepSpeech (DS) with no transfer learning, augmentation, or language model yields little or no correct output. With a language model, the WER and CER for this model are reduced, but results are still mostly incorrect. Our deep approach shows slightly better performance than DeepSpeech without a language model and significantly lower WER when decoding with a trigram language model.

	DS (NO LM)		DS (w/LM)		Our CNN (NO LM)		Our CNN (w/LM)	
	WER	CER	WER	CER	WER	CER	WER	CER
No TL, no Aug (Baseline)	1.000	0.891	0.970	0.872	0.839	0.365	0.421	0.257
TL, no Aug (+TL)	0.859	0.436	0.727	0.409	0.785	0.328	0.337	0.199
TL + Aug (+TL,Aug)	1.000	0.716	0.975	0.698	0.730	0.303	0.319	0.194
TL + Aug + finetune (+TL,Aug,FT)	0.850	0.427	0.693	0.421	0.699	0.278	**0.299**	**0.175**

Table 1: Seneca WER and CER for various transfer learning (TL), augmentation (Aug), and fine-tuning (FT) strategies (rows) vs. DeepSpeech (DS) and our deep CNN architecture without (NO LM) and with (w/LM) a trigram language model.

	NO LM		w/LM	
	WER	CER	WER	CER
Baseline	0.784	0.307	0.369	0.197
+TL	0.768	0.309	0.302	0.172
+TL,Aug	0.758	0.324	0.307	0.187
+TL,Aug,FT	0.656	0.247	**0.243**	**0.130**

Table 2: Seneca WER and CER using our deep CNN approach with log mel-filterbank feature as input features with and without a trigram language model.

Acoustic Model	WER
Monophone GMM/HMM	0.608
Triphone GMM/HMM	0.524
TDNN LF-MMI	0.421

Table 3: Seneca WER for Kaldi HMM-GMM models and TDNN with LF-MMI.

	NO LM		w/LM	
	WER	CER	WER	CER
Baseline	0.856	0.463	0.487	0.286
+TL	0.668	0.287	0.413	0.257
+TL,Aug	0.665	0.226	0.420	0.286
+TL,Aug,FT	0.518	0.160	**0.266**	**0.116**

Table 4: Iban WER and CER for transfer learning and augmentation strategies within our architecture using with log mel-filterbanks as input features with and without trigram language model built using only the transcripts of the audio.

Acoustic Model	WER
Monophone GMM/HMM	0.372
Triphone GMM/HMM	0.265
TDNN LF-MMI	0.175

Table 5: Previously reported WER for Iban 2 HMM-GMM models and TDNN with LF-MMI, all decoded with a language model built on the full 2-million word text corpus.

Using transfer learning from a high resource language improves performance across all models and all language model settings. Training on augmented data after transfer learning from a high resource language degrades the performance of DeepSpeech models in terms of WER but improves CER. For our deep architecture, this configuration improves results across the board. In all configurations for Seneca, our deep approach substantially outperforms the corresponding DeepSpeech model.

Fine-tuning of the augmented model using only non-augmented data yields the best performance across all models, with a WER of 0.299 using our deep acoustic model. While fine-tuning after augmentation results in improvements, it yields much larger absolute and relative reductions in WER for the DeepSpeech model than for our deep architecture. Table 2 shows results of using log mel-filterbank features in place of MFCCs with modest improvement.

Table 3 shows three Kaldi results on this same dataset: two standard HMM/GMM models (monophone and triphone) and one deep architecture, TDNN with LF-MMI. For Seneca, our deep architecture substantially outperforms all three of these models, including the TDNN.
Demonstrating the efficacy and generalizability of our models on other low-resource datasets, Table 4 shows the performance of our deep method under different configurations for the Iban language. We see slightly higher but comparable error rates on this dataset, which had three fewer hours of acoustic training data.
Table 5 shows previously reported results [1] for the three Kaldi models for Iban. These results are noticeably lower than those we report using the same acoustic model training configurations for Seneca. In addition, the TDNN LF-MMMI model yields a lower error rate than our best deep model. We note that the language model used to decode with these Kaldi models was built on a 2-million word text corpus, while the results presented above in Table 4 for our own deep methods used a language model built using only the transcripts from the 7 hours of available audio data. We suspect that this accounts for much of this discrepancy. It is also possible that our framework is better suited to the lower-quality recordings typical in the Seneca dataset and less appropriate for the clean, professionally recorded Iban data. We also note that our model yields comparable WER error rates in both languages, which points to its superior ability to generalize to new datasets.

6. Conclusions

In this paper, we introduced a residual network with a very wide filter selection in a fully convolutional architecture for low-resource ASR acoustic modeling. We show that our acoustic model outperforms a typical recurrent-based deep neural network in all experimental settings while also being more compute-efficient. Our deep acoustic model, when combined with a trigram language model, outperforms the

---

[1]https://github.com/bagustris/id

traditional GMM/HMM model without the need for transfer learning or data augmentation. We also show that transfer learning from a high-resource language and data augmentation contribute to meaningful reductions in word error rate achieved by the model for two distinct low-resource languages. Our results point the way toward new, fast-training deep learning ASR methods for languages with extremely limited audio and textual training resources.

7. Acknowledgements

This material is based upon work supported by the National Science Foundation under Grant No. 1761562. We recognize the contributions of the team collecting and analyzing this dataset, including Morris Cooke, Richard Hatcher, Alex Jimerson, Mike Jones, Megan Kennedy, Whitney Nephew, Aryien Stevens, and Karin Michelson. We are grateful for the cooperation, support, generosity of the elders of the Seneca Nation of Indians.

8. Bibliographic References

Agenbag, W. and Niesler, T. (2019). Automatic sub-word unit discovery and pronunciation lexicon induction for asr with application to under-resourced languages. *Computer Speech & Language*, 57:20–40.

Amodei, D., Ananthanarayanan, S., Anubhai, R., Bai, J., Battenberg, E., Case, C., Casper, J., Catanzaro, B., Cheng, Q., and Chen, G. (2016). Deep Speech 2: End-to-end speech recognition in English and Mandarin. In *ICML*, pages 173–182.

Audhkhasi, K., Kingsbury, B., Ramabhadran, B., Saon, G., and Picheny, M. (2018). Building competitive direct acoustics-to-word models for english conversational speech recognition. In *ICASSP*, pages 4759–4763.

Billa, J. (2018). Isi asr system for the low resource speech recognition challenge for indian languages. *Interspeech*, pages 3207–3211.

Carmantini, A., Bell, P., and Renals, S. (2019). Untranscribed web audio for low resource speech recognition. *Interspeech*, pages 226–230.

Chan, W., Jaitly, N., Le, Q., and Vinyals, O. (2016). Listen, attend and spell: A neural network for large vocabulary conversational speech recognition. In *ICASSP*.

Chiu, C., Sainath, T. N., Wu, Y., Prabhavalkar, R., Nguyen, P., Chen, Z., Kannan, A., Weiss, R., Rao, K., Gonina, E., et al. (2018). State-of-the-art speech recognition with sequence-to-sequence models. In *ICASSP*.

Collobert, R., Puhrsch, C., and Synnaeve, G. (2016). Wav2letter: an end-to-end convnet-based speech recognition system. *arXiv preprint arXiv:1609.03193*.

Gales, M., Knill, K., Ragni, A., and Rath, S. (2014). Speech recognition and keyword spotting for low-resource languages: Babel project research at CUED. In *SLTU*, pages 16–23.

Graves, A., Fernández, S., Gomez, F., and Schmidhuber, J. (2006). Connectionist temporal classification: labelling unsegmented sequence data with recurrent neural networks. In *ICML*, pages 369–376.

Graves, A., Mohamed, A., and Hinton, G. (2013). Speech recognition with deep recurrent neural networks. In *ICASSP*, pages 6645–6649.

Hannun, A., Case, C., Casper, J., Catanzaro, B., Diamos, G., Elsen, E., Prenger, R., et al. (2014). Deep Speech: Scaling up end-to-end speech recognition. *arXiv preprint arXiv:1412.5567*.

Heafield, K. (2011). KenLM: Faster and smaller language model queries. In *SMT Workshop*, pages 187–197.

Hinton, G., Dahl, G., Mohamed, A., Jaitly, N., Senior, A., Vanhoucke, V., Kingsbury, B., and Sainath, T. (2012). Deep neural networks for acoustic modeling in speech recognition. *IEEE Signal Processing Magazine*, 29:82–97, November.

Imseng, D., Motlicek, P., Bourlard, H., and Garner, P. (2014). Using out-of-language data to improve an under-resourced speech recognizer. *Speech Communication*, 56:142–151.

Jimerson, R., Simha, K., Ptucha, R., and Prud'hommeaux, E. (2018). Improving ASR output for endangered language documentation. In *SLTU*, pages 182–186.

Juan, S., Besacier, L., and Rossato, S. (2014). Semi-supervised g2p bootstrapping and its application to asr for a very under-resourced language: Iban. In *SLTU*, May.

Malhotra, K., Bansal, S., and Ganapathy, S. (2019). Active learning methods for low resource end-to-end speech recognition. *Interspeech*, pages 2215–2219.

Manohar, V., Hadian, H., Povey, D., and Khudanpur, S. (2018). Semi-supervised training of acoustic models using lattice-free mmi. In *ICASSP*, pages 4844–4848.

Peddinti, V., Povey, D., and Khudanpur, S. (2015). A time delay neural network architecture for efficient modeling of long temporal contexts. In *Interspeech*.

Povey, D., Ghoshal, A., Boulianne, G., Burget, L., Glembek, O., Goel, N., Hannemann, M., Motlicek, P., Qian, Y., Schwarz, P., Silovsky, J., Stemmer, G., and Vesely, K. (2011). The Kaldi speech recognition toolkit. In *ASRU*.

Rosenberg, A., Audhkhasi, K., Sethy, A., Ramabhadran, B., and Picheny, M. (2017). End-to-end speech recognition and keyword search on low-resource languages. In *ICASSP*, pages 5280–5284.

Szegedy, C., Liu, W., Jia, Y., Sermanet, P., Reed, S., Anguelov, D., Erhan, D., Vanhoucke, V., and Rabinovich, A. (2015). Going deeper with convolutions. In *CVPR*, pages 1–9.

Tüske, Z., Golik, P., Nolden, D., Schlüter, R., and Ney, H. (2014). Data augmentation, feature combination, and multilingual neural networks to improve asr and kws performance for low-resource languages. In *Interspeech*.

Wiesner, M., Renduchintala, A., Watanabe, S., Liu, C., Dehak, N., and Khudanpur, S. (2018). Low resource multimodal data augmentation for end-to-end ASR. In *Interspeech*.

Xie, S., Girshick, R., Dollár, P., Tu, Z., and He, K. (2017). Aggregated residual transformations for deep neural networks. In *CVPR*, pages 1492–1500.

Zhang, Y., Chan, W., and Jaitly, N. (2017). Very deep convolutional networks for end-to-end speech recognition. In *ICASSP*, pages 4845–4849.

Proceedings of the 1st Joint SLTU and CCURL Workshop (SLTU-CCURL 2020), pages 131–138
Language Resources and Evaluation Conference (LREC 2020), Marseille, 11–16 May 2020

Cross-Lingual Machine Speech Chain for
Javanese, Sundanese, Balinese, and Bataks Speech Recognition and Synthesis

Sashi Novitasari[1], Andros Tjandra[1], Sakriani Sakti[1,2], Satoshi Nakamura[1,2]
[1]Nara Institute of Science and Technology, Japan
[2]RIKEN Center for Advanced Intelligence Project AIP, Japan
{sashi.novitasari.si3, tjandra.ai6, ssakti,s-nakamura}@is.naist.jp

Abstract

Even though over seven hundred ethnic languages are spoken in Indonesia, the available technology remains limited that could support communication within indigenous communities as well as with people outside the villages. As a result, indigenous communities still face isolation due to cultural barriers; languages continue to disappear. To accelerate communication, speech-to-speech translation (S2ST) technology is one approach that can overcome language barriers. However, S2ST systems require machine translation (MT), speech recognition (ASR), and synthesis (TTS) that rely heavily on supervised training and a broad set of language resources that can be difficult to collect from ethnic communities. Recently, a machine speech chain mechanism was proposed to enable ASR and TTS to assist each other in semi-supervised learning. The framework was initially implemented only for monolingual languages. In this study, we focus on developing speech recognition and synthesis for these Indonesian ethnic languages: Javanese, Sundanese, Balinese, and Bataks. We first separately train ASR and TTS of standard Indonesian in supervised training. We then develop ASR and TTS of ethnic languages by utilizing Indonesian ASR and TTS in a cross-lingual machine speech chain framework with only text or only speech data removing the need for paired speech-text data of those ethnic languages.

Keywords: Indonesian ethnic languages, cross-lingual approach, machine speech chain, speech recognition and synthesis.

1. Introduction

Indonesia, which has some of the world's most diverse religions, languages, and cultures (Abas, 1987; Bertand, 2003; Hoon, 2006), consists of approximately 17,500 islands with 300 ethnic groups and 726 native languages (Tan, 2004). Roughly ten percent of the world's languages are spoken in Indonesia, making it one of the most multilingual nations in the world. In the amidst of such a large number of local languages, *Bahasa Indonesia*, the national language, functions as a bridge that connects Indonesian people. *Bahasa Indonesia* is a unity language, which was coined by Indonesian nationalists in 1928 and became a symbol of national identity during the struggle for independence in 1945. Since then, the Indonesian language is increasingly being spoken as a second language by the majority of its population. The decision to choose Indonesian as a unity language is one great success story of national language policy (Sneddon, 2003; Paauw, 2009).

Worldwide globalization is encouraging people to learn and speak languages that are prominent in global communities. *Bahasa Indonesia* is now more commonly spoken as a first language. Some younger Indonesians are also speaking English as a second language. Although using *Bahasa Indonesia* as the unity language is helping them face globalization, multilingualism in Indonesia faces a catastrophe. The number of speakers of Indonesian ethnic languages is decreasing. It is predicted that Indonesia might shift from a multilingual nation to a monolingual society, threatening the existence of ethnic languages (Cohn and Ravindranath, 2014).

Among its 726 ethnic languages, only thirteen have more than a million speakers, accounting for about 70% of the total population in Indonesia. These ethnic languages include Javanese, Sundanese, Malay, Madurese, Minangk-

abau, Bataks, Bugisnese, Balinese, Acehnese, Sasak, Makasarese, Lampungese, and Rejang (Lauder, 2005). The remaining 713 languages have a total population of only 41.4 million speakers, and the majority of these have very small numbers of speakers (Riza, 2008). For example, 386 languages are spoken by 5,000 or less; 233 have 1,000 speakers or less; 169 languages have 500 speakers or less; and 52 have 100 or less (Gordon, 2005). These languages are facing various degrees of language endangerment (Crystal, 2000). Several attempts have addressed preserving ethnic languages, including national projects on the use of ethnic languages in schools. Unfortunately, the available technology that could support communication within indigenous communities as well as with people outside the villages is limited. Indigenous communities face the digital divide and isolation due to cultural barriers. Languages continue to be threatened.

Speech-to-speech translation (S2ST) technology (Nakamura, 2009; Sakti et al., 2013), which is innovative and essential, enables people to communicate in their native languages. S2ST recognized the speech of the source language into the text, translate the text to the target language, and synthesizes back to speech waveforms. This overall technology involves research in machine translation (MT), automatic speech recognition (ASR), and text-to-speech synthesis (TTS). However, the advanced development of these technologies relies heavily on supervised training and a broad set of language resources, including speech and corresponding transcriptions of the source and target languages. Unfortunately, the amount of available Indonesian ethnic language data is limited, and preparing a large amount of paired speech and text data is expensive.

Recently, a machine speech chain framework was proposed for the semi-supervised development of ASR and TTS systems (Tjandra et al., 2019b). This framework was motivated by the human speech chain mechanism (Denes et al., 1993), which is a feedback loop phenomenon between speech production and a hearing system that occurs when humans speak. In fact, humans do not separately learn to speak and listen using supervised training with a large amount of paired data. By simultaneously listening and speaking, they monitor their own volume and articulation and gradually improve their speaking capability, making it consistent with their intentions.

In the machine speech chain, both ASR and TTS components are pre-trained in supervised training using a limited amount of labeled data. By establishing a feedback closed-loop between the ASR (listening component) and the TTS (speaking component), both components can assist each other in unsupervised learning. Therefore, they can be trained without requiring a large number of speech-text paired data. Previous machine speech chain studies (Tjandra et al., 2019b; Tjandra et al., 2018; Tjandra et al., 2019a), however, only utilized the framework for monolingual model training and unsupervised training with a large number of unlabeled or unpaired data. The framework remains unutilized for a cross-lingual task with a limited number of unpaired data, such as ethnic languages.

In this work, we utilize the machine speech chain framework in a cross-lingual way to construct speech recognition and synthesis for the following four ethnic Indonesian languages: Javanese, Sundanese, Balinese, and Bataks. Although scant research has addressed the development of ASR for Indonesian ethnic languages, one study developed ASR for those languages using a statistical approach with a hidden Markov model and a Gaussian mixture model (HMM-GMM) (Sakti and Nakamura, 2014). However, no ASR construction with a sequence-to-sequence deep-learning approach has been made. Furthermore, no previous TTS study exists for Indonesian ethnic languages. The previous study also still requires paired speech and a corresponding transcription of the ethnic languages for supervised adaptation. In contrast, we develop both ASR and TTS of those ethnic languages based on sequence-to-sequence deep-learning architectures. We first separately train ASR and TTS of standard Indonesian in supervised training. We then train the ASR and TTS of those ethnic languages by utilizing Indonesian ASR and TTS in a cross-lingual machine speech chain framework with limited text or speech of those ethnic languages. This choice allows us to construct ASR and TTS for those languages, even without paired data for them.

2. Overview of Indonesian and Indonesian Ethnic Languages

Here, we briefly introduce the Indonesian and Indonesian ethnic languages.

2.1. Indonesian Language

The Indonesian language, *Bahasa Indonesia*, is derived from the Malay dialect, which was the lingua franca of Southeast Asia (Quinn, 2001). Bahasa Indonesia is closely related to the Malay spoken in Malaysia, Singapore, Brunei, and some other areas. It is the largest member of the Austronesian language family. The only difference is that Indonesia (a former Dutch colony) adopted the Van Ophuysen orthography in 1901; Malaysia (a former British colony) adopted the Wilkinson orthography in 1904. In 1972, the governments of Indonesia and Malaysia agreed to standardize "improved" spelling, which is now in effect on both sides. Even so, modern Indonesian and modern Malaysian are as different from one another as are Flemish and Dutch (Tan, 2004).

Many words in the Indonesian vocabulary reflect the historical influence of the various colonial cultures that occupied and influenced the archipelago. Indonesian words have borrowed heavily from Indian Sanskrit, Chinese, Arabic, Portuguese, Dutch, and English (Jones, 2007). Unlike Chinese, it is not a tonal language; it has no declensions or conjugations. It has no changes in nouns or adjectives for different gender, number, or case. Verbs do not take different forms to show number, person, or tense. A time adverb or question word can be placed at either the front or the end of sentences. Since plural is often expressed by reduplication, Indonesian sentences have reduplication words. It is also a member of the agglutinative language family, denoting a complex range of prefixes and suffixes that are attached to base words that can result in very long words (Sakti et al., 2004).

The standard Indonesian language is mostly used in such formal written settings as books, newspapers, and television/radio news broadcasts. Although the earliest records in Malay inscriptions are syllable-based and written in Arabic script, modern Indonesian is phonetic-based written in Roman script (Alwi et al., 2003). It only uses 26 letters, as in the English/Dutch alphabet.

2.2. Indonesian Ethnic Languages

In this study, we chose to work with four ethnic languages: Javanese, Sundanese, Balinese, and Bataks. Since a large number of the population speak them, the data collection of their native speakers remain possible to reach. However, despite their significant speech communities, the primary usage of these languages is gradually being subsumed by *Bahasa Indonesia*. The Javanese, Sundanese, Balinese, and Bataks languages also suffer from the inadequate intergenerational transmission, since they are often not being passed on to the next generation. It is pointed out that even such languages are at risk of language endangerment (Cohn and Ravindranath, 2014).

2.2.1. Javanese

Javanese is a member of Malayo-Polynesian, which is a branch of the Austronesian language family. It is spoken by Javanese people from the central and eastern parts of Java, which has almost 100 million native speakers (Cohn and Ravindranath, 2014) (more than 42% of Indonesia's population). It is also spoken in Suriname and New Caledonia to which it was originally brought by Javanese workers who were transferred from Indonesia by the Dutch. Javanese transcription is called *Aksara Hanacaraka*[1]. Aksara means transcription in Indonesia. It consists of 20 basic scripts

---

[1]The following is the official site of Aksara Jawa: http://hanacaraka.fateback.com/

or letters called *Carakan*. One *Carakan* stands for a syllable with a consonant and an inherent vowel. To create another sound with other Javanese vowels, an additional script called *Sandhangan* to define the vowel is need.

2.2.2. Sundanese

The Sundanese language, which is also a Malayo-Polynesian language spoken by the people who live on the western third of Java island, has almost 40 million native speakers who represent about 15% of Indonesia's population (Bauer, 2007). Modern Sunda transcription is called Aksara Sunda. Similar to Aksara Hanacaraka, Aksara Sunda also has a basic alphabet, vowels, and punctuation that change the phonemes and the basic punctuation[2].

2.2.3. Balinese

Balinese is the native language of Bali island. It is spoken by more than three million people and is also a member of the Malayo-Polynesian language family (Bauer, 2007). The Balinese script[3] is undoubtedly derived from the Devanagari and Pallava scripts from India. Its shape resembles southern Indian scripts like Tamil. However, most Balinese people only use the Balinese language for oral communication, often mixing it with Indonesian in their daily speech. In 2011, the Bali Cultural Agency estimates that the number of people still using Balinese does not exceed one million, which is only one-fourth of the total Bali population. Balinese is mostly spoken in social and cultural interactions; Indonesian, however, is increasingly the language of commerce, in schools and public places (Horstman, 2016).

2.2.4. Bataks

The Batak languages are a subgroup of the Austronesian languages spoken by the Batak people in the Indonesian province of North Sumatra and its surrounding areas (Bauer, 2007). The Batak tribes are descendants of a powerful Proto-Malayan people who mainly lived in the northern region of Sumatera Island. There are several subtribes and clans in Batak tribes. The Toba subtribe has the largest population, followed (in no particular order) by the Karo, Simalungun, Pakpak-Dairi, Angkola-Mandailing, and Nias (Niha) peoples. The Batak tribe has its own writing system, which dates back to the 13th century. The Batak people call their writing system *Surat Batak* (Surat = letters/writings)[4].

3. Speech and Text Data Resources

In this study, we utilized several data resources including Indonesian and Indonesian ethnic language corpora. The details are described below.

3.1. Indonesian Data Resources

The Indonesian speech dataset was developed by the R&D Division of an Indonesian telecommunications company (PT. Telekomunikasi Indonesia) in collaboration with ATR Japan under the Asia Pacific Telecommunity (APT) project (Sakti et al., 2004; Sakti et al., 2008). The corpus consists of 80.5 hours of speech spoken by multiple speakers. The following are its details of the data resources.

3.1.1. Text

The transcriptions in the Indonesian corpus were originally constructed from two sources: daily news passages and telephone services dialogs. The daily news sentences were compiled from the most widely read Indonesian newspapers: *Kompas* and *Tempo*. The text sentences from telephone service dialogs consist of language commonly required for such services as tele-home security, hotel reservations, billing information, e-Government status tracking, and hearing-impaired telecommunication (HITS) services. From the two sources, phonetically-balanced sentences were selected based on a greedy search algorithm (Zhang and Nakamura, 2003), resulting in 5,668 sentences of the total: 3,168 sentences from news passages and 2,500 sentences from telephone service dialogs.

3.1.2. Speech

The speech audio, which was recorded using the clean sentences of the above text data, was spoken by 400 speakers (200 males and 200 females) from various regions in Indonesia. The recording was conducted in parallel for both clean and telephone speech, recorded at a respective sampling frequency of 16 kHz and 8 kHz. However, in this study, only the speech utterances with 16 kHz sampling frequency were used. During the recording stage, all the speakers were instructed to speak in standard Indonesia without any ethnic accents. Each speaker spoke 110 sentences from the news passage, which resulted in 44,000 speech utterances (43.35 hours of speech), and 100 sentences from the telephone services dialogs, which resulted in 40,000 utterances (36.15 hours of speech). The size of the speech data was 84,000 utterances: around 80.5 hours of speech.

3.2. Indonesian Ethnic Data Resources

The Indonesian ethnic languages covered in this work include Javanese, Sundanese, Balinese, and Bataks, all of which were collected and recorded in a previous study (Sakti et al., 2013).

3.2.1. Text

The text data consist of 225 sentences selected from online newspapers and magazines in their ethnic languages: Pejabar-Semangat for Javanese[5], Sunda-News for Sundanese[6], Bali-Post for Balinese[7], and Halo-Moantondang for Bataks[8]. The sentences were selected by cleaning the raw text and limiting the sentences to those with a graphemically-balanced structure based on a greedy search algorithm (Zhang and Nakamura, 2003).

We also translated fifty Indonesian sentences from the ATR basic travel expression corpus (BTEC) (Kikui et al., 2003) dataset into these ethnic languages by native speakers of the corresponding language. We created 275 sentences for each ethnic language, comprised of 1,100 text transcriptions.

---

[2]http://en.wikipedia.org/wiki/Sundanese_alphabet
[3]http://en.wikipedia.org/wiki/Balinese_alphabet
[4]http://www.ancientscripts.comt

[5]www.penjebarsemangat.co.id
[6]sundanews.com
[7]www.balipost.co.id
[8]halomoantondang.wordpress.com

3.2.2. Speech

The speech data were recorded from ten native speakers (five males and five females) for each ethnic language. Each speaker spoke 225 graphemically balanced sentences and 100 Indonesian-ethnic language parallel sentences, which consist of 50 original Indonesian sentences and 50 that were translated into ethnic languages. However, in this study, we only used 275 sentences of the ethnic languages, and removed the 50 original Indonesian sentences. The speech was recorded at a 48-kHz sampling rate with 16-bit resolution. In the experiment, all the speech utterances were downsampled into 16 kHz. The speech data were composed of 2,750 utterances with ten speakers for each language, comprised of 11,000 speech utterances.

4. Speech Chain

4.1. Human Speech Chain

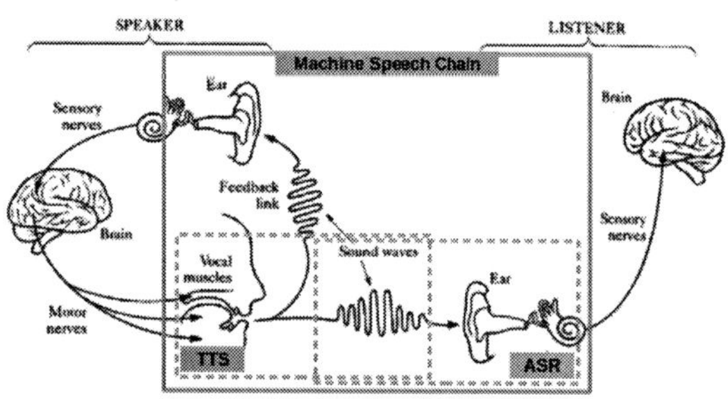

Figure 1: Human speech chain and corresponding components in machine speech chain (Denes et al., 1993).

The human speech chain was previously introduced (Denes et al., 1993) as a phenomenon in human communication (Fig. 1). In a conversation, the speaker's utterance is heard by the listener and also the speaker herself. A feedback chain is established among the speaker's hearing system, her brain, and the speech production system. When the speaker listens to her speech, she compares it to her intended quality and uses it to improve its quality in the next timestep. The speaking and listening processes occur simultaneously and are continually repeated until the end of the utterance.

4.2. Machine Speech Chain

Inspired by the human speech chain, a machine speech chain was proposed to jointly train ASR and TTS models in semi-supervised learning. An overview of the machine speech chain (Tjandra et al., 2019b) is shown in Fig. 2(a). The framework consists of a sequence-to-sequence ASR and a sequence-to-sequence TTS. Sequence-to-sequence networks are deep-learning architecture that include an encoder and a decoder with an attention mechanism. The machine speech chain establishes a loop that connects ASR to TTS and TTS to ASR. The components are trained with a semi-supervised approach that consists of two stages: supervised and unsupervised training.

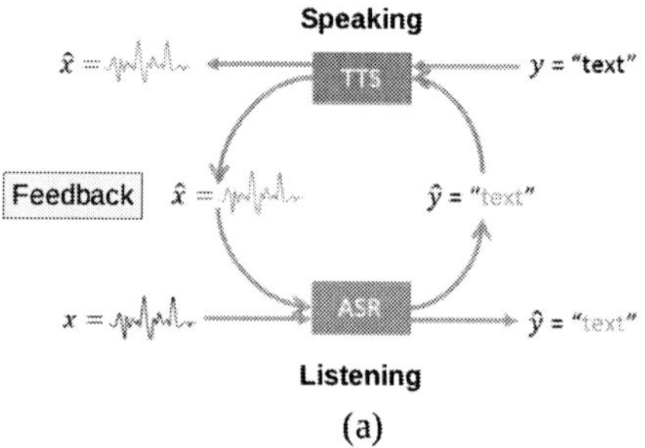

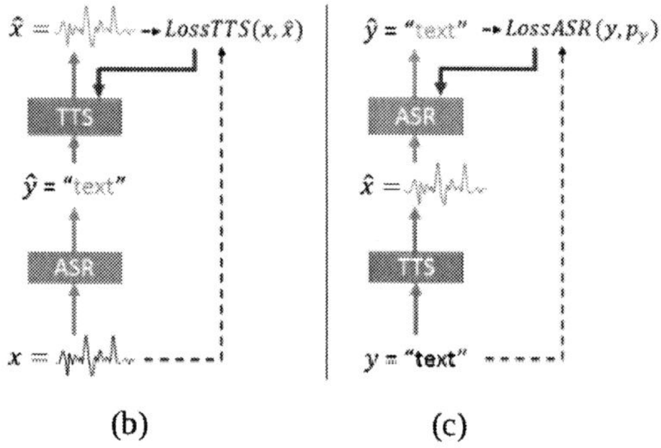

Figure 2: Overview of machine speech chain: (a) Feedback loop connects ASR and TTS based on concept of speaking while listening in human speech chain process. Loop can be unrolled into two processes: (b) from ASR to TTS and (c) from TTS to ASR (Tjandra et al., 2017).

4.2.1. Supervised Training

In the supervised training stage, both ASR and TTS are trained independently using labeled or speech-text paired data. Each model is trained by minimizing the loss between the predicted output sequence and the ground-truth sequence. Supervised training acts as knowledge initialization in each component.

4.2.2. Unsupervised Training

The unsupervised training stage utilizes models that have already been supervisedly pre-trained and further trained in the speech chain mechanism using unlabeled data (only speech or text). To learn from the unlabeled data, both ASR and TTS need to support each other, bypassing feedback through a loop that connects them. The loop consists of two unrolled processes: (1) given only speech data, the unrolled process performs from ASR to TTS; (2) given only text data, the unrolled process performs from TTS to ASR. The unrolled process from ASR to TTS is shown in Fig. 2(b). Given only speech feature sequences, ASR generates its transcription, and TTS reconstructs the speech based on ASR output. The loss is calculated by comparing the TTS-generated speech and the original speech. The unrolled process from TTS to ASR is shown in Fig. 2(c). Here given only text transcription, TTS synthesizes the speech from it, and ASR transcribes the speech from TTS. The loss is calculated by comparing the transcription from ASR and the original text.

5. Machine Speech Chain for Indonesian Ethnic Languages

Here we utilized the machine speech chain in a cross-lingual setting. Both the ASR output and the TTS input are represented as character sequences to avoid out-of-vocabulary words, especially during the unsupervised training phase. The ASR in this work does not utilize any language model. Below are the steps of the training process.

5.1. Step 1: Supervised training of standard Indonesian ASR and TTS

First, we supervisedly train the standard Indonesian ASR and TTS using Indonesian speech-text paired data (see Section 3.1.). Here the Indonesian language serves as prior knowledge for the system. In this stage, since Indonesian speech-text paired data are available, both the Indonesian ASR and TTS components are trained independently, as seen in Fig. 3. The ASR takes a sequence of Indonesian speech features $\mathbf{x}^{(IND)}$ and learns to transcribe it into text $\hat{\mathbf{y}}^{(IND)}$. The TTS takes Indonesian text sentence $\mathbf{y}^{(IND)}$ and learns to generate speech $\hat{\mathbf{x}}^{(IND)}$. The speech data here consist of multi-speaker speech. Therefore, the TTS input also includes speaker embedding vector $z = SPKREC(\mathbf{x}^{(IND)})$, and so the synthesized speech can be compared to the ground speech with appropriate voice characteristics, as proposed in a previous machine speech chain study (Tjandra et al., 2018).

5.2. Step 2: Unsupervised training of Javanese, Sundanese, Balinese, Bataks ASR and TTS

In this phase, we utilized the previously pre-trained Indonesian ASR and TTS in the speech-chain architecture to unsupervisedly train the ASR and TTS of Javanese, Sundanese, Balinese, and Bataks. Since the available data are minimal, we combined all the unlabeled data (only text or only speech) from the Javanese, Sundanese, Balinese, and Bataks corpus (see Section 3.2.). This phase is shown in Fig. 4, and the following are the details of the unrolled processes.

1. **Unsupervisedly train the system given only the text transcription of the Indonesian ethnic languages (Closed-loop from TTS to ASR)**: In this process, the provided ground information only consists of text data from the four ethnic languages. The TTS attempted to synthesize a sequence of speech features in particular ethnic language $\hat{\mathbf{x}}^{(ETH)}$, based on given text $\mathbf{y}^{(ETH)}$ and the speaker embedding vector. Speaker embedding vector $\hat{z}$ is generated based on speech sampled from the available speech data ($\tilde{\mathbf{x}}$). After the speech synthesis, ASR attempted to transcribe back ethnic language text $\hat{\mathbf{y}}^{(ETH)}$ based on the TTS output $\hat{\mathbf{x}}^{(ETH)}$. The loss is then calculated by comparing the original ethnic text transcription $\mathbf{y}^{(ETH)}$ and the ASR output $\hat{\mathbf{y}}^{(ETH)}$; and perform back-propagation to improve the ASR.

2. **Unsupervisedly train the system given only the speech utterances of the Indonesian ethnic languages (Closed-loop from ASR to TTS)**: This process uses only speech data from the four ethnic languages. First, ASR took original ethnic speech $\mathbf{x}^{(ETH)}$ and predicted its transcription $\hat{\mathbf{y}}^{(ETH)}$. The TTS then reconstructed ethnic language speech $\hat{\mathbf{x}}^{(ETH)}$ by processing the text generated by ASR and speaker embedding vector $z = SPKREC(\mathbf{x}^{(ETH)})$. The loss is calculated by comparing the original ethnic speech utterances $\mathbf{x}^{(ETH)}$ and the generated TTS speech output $\hat{\mathbf{x}}^{(ETH)}$; and perform back-propagation to improve the TTS.

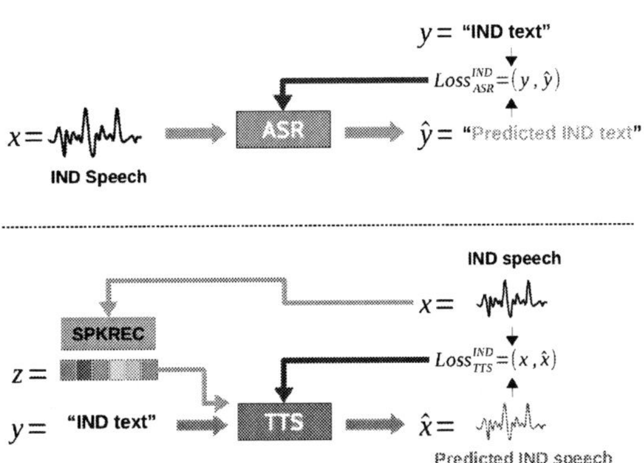

Figure 3: ASR and TTS supervised training using paired speech and text of Indonesian data. Both models were trained separately.

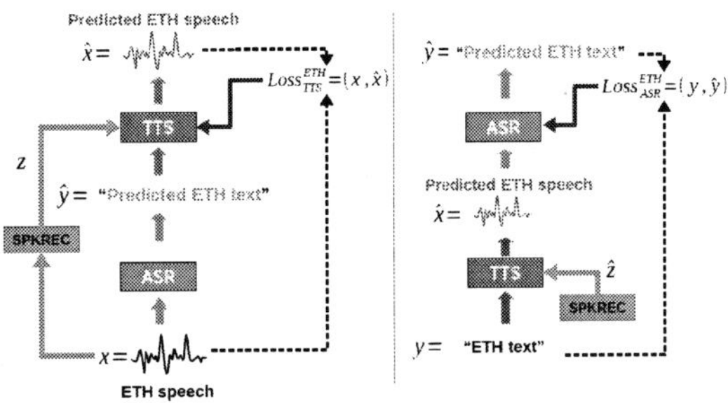

Figure 4: ASR and TTS unsupervised training using unpaired data of Indonesian ethnic languages: text only data (TTS-to-ASR process) and speech only data (ASR-to-TTS process). *ETH* is Indonesian ethnic language.

6. Experimental Set-Up

6.1. Training, Validation, and Test Datasets

For supervised training on both the ASR and TTS components of the Indonesian language, we chose 10% of the speech-text paired data with 40 speakers for testing. On the remaining speech-text paired data with 360 speakers, 20% of the data were randomly selected for validation or development sets, and 80% of the rest was used as a training set. For unsupervised training of both the ASR and TTS components of the Javanese, Sundanese, Balinese, and Bataks languages, we randomly chose 50 unpaired data from four speakers (200 speech utterances or text transcription only) of each language as a test set. On the remaining data of 225 speech or text unpaired data with six speakers (1350 speech utterances or text transcription only), 10% of the data were randomly selected for validation or development sets, and 90% of the rest was used for training.

6.2. Speech Features and Text Representation

We extracted two different sets of speech features. First, we applied pre-emphasis (0.97) on the raw waveform and then extracted the log-linear spectrogram with a 50-ms window, 12.5-ms steps, and a 2048-point short-time Fourier transform (STFT) with the Librosa package (McFee et al., 2017). Second, we extracted the log Mel-spectrogram with an 80 Mel-scale filterbank. For our TTS model, we used both log-linear and log-Mel spectrogram for the first and second outputs. For our ASR and speaker recognition components, we used the log-Mel spectrogram for the encoder input.

The text utterances were tokenized as Indonesian characters and mapped into a 33-character set: 26 alphabetic letters (a-z), three punctuation marks ('.-), and four special tags, $\langle$noise$\rangle$, $\langle$spc$\rangle$, $\langle$s$\rangle$, and $\langle$/s$\rangle$ as noise, space, start-of-sequence, and end-of-sequence tokens, respectively. Both the ASR input and the TTS output shared the same text representation in the training and inference stages.

6.3. ASR and TTS Systems

6.3.1. ASR Component

For the ASR system, we used a standard sequence-to-sequence model with an attention module. On the encoder sides, the input Mel-spectrogram features were projected by a fully connected layer with a 512 hidden units and LReLU function. Later, the results were processed by three bidirectional LSTMs (Bi-LSTM) with 256 hidden units for each LSTM (512 hidden units for Bi-LSTM). To reduce the memory consumption and processing time, we used hierarchical sub-sampling (Graves, 2012; Bahdanau et al., 2016) on all three Bi-LSTM layers and reduced the sequence length by a factor of 8. On the decoder sides, we projected one-hot encoding from the previous character into a 256-dims continuous vector with an embedding matrix, followed by a unidirectional LSTM with 512 hidden units. For the attention module, we used standard content-based attention (Bahdanau et al., 2014). In the decoding phase, the transcription was generated by beam-search decoding (size=5), and we normalized the log-likelihood score by dividing it by its own length to prevent the decoder from favoring shorter transcriptions.

6.3.2. TTS Component

For the TTS system, we followed the previously proposed TTS architecture (Tjandra et al., 2018), which is a modification from TTS Tacotron (Wang et al., 2017). The hyperparameters for the basic structure were generally identical as those of the original Tacotron, except ReLU is replaced with the LReLU ($\alpha = 0.01$) function. For the CBHG module, we used $K = 8$ filterbanks instead of 16 to reduce the GPU memory consumption. For the decoder sides, we deployed two LSTMs instead of a GRU with 256 hidden units. For each time-step, our model generated four consecutive frames to reduce the number of steps in the decoding process.

6.3.3. Speaker Recognition Component

For the speaker recognition system, we used the DeepSpeaker model (Li et al., 2017) and followed the original hyper-parameters in that previous paper. However, since data are often scarce in the Indonesian and Indonesian ethnic languages, we utilized a DeepSpeaker, which was already pre-trained on the Wall Street Journal CSR Corpus of English language (SI84 set with 83 unique speakers) (Paul and Baker, 1992). Thus, the model was expected to generalize effectively across all of the remaining unseen speakers to assist the TTS and speech chain training. We used the Adam optimizer with a learning rate of $5e - 4$ for the ASR and TTS models and $1e - 3$ for the DeepSpeaker model. All of our models in this paper were implemented with PyTorch (Paszke et al., 2017).

6.3.4. Systems Evaluation Metrics

We evaluated the ASR system performance based on the character error rate (CER) of the output. The CER calculation follows the Eq. 1.

$$CER = \frac{S + D + I}{N} \times 100\% \qquad (1)$$

S, D, and I denote the numbers of character substitutions, deletions, and insertions respectively, and N denotes the number of characters in the reference text. It is similar to the calculation of word error rate (WER), with a difference that WER is calculated based on word tokens, while CER is based on character tokens.

For the TTS system, we evaluated its performance by calculating the L2 norm-squared on log-Mel spectrogram of reference speech ($\mathbf{x}$) and TTS speech ($\hat{\mathbf{x}}$) using Eq. 2:

$$Loss_{TTS} = \frac{1}{T} \sum_{t=1}^{T} (x_t - \hat{x}_t)^2 \qquad (2)$$

where T is the length of speech.

7. Experimental Results

We separately evaluated the ASR and TTS using test sets of four ethnic languages: Javanese, Sundanese, Balinese, and Bataks.

7.1. ASR Evaluation

Table 1 shows the character error rate (CER (%)) performance of the ASR systems from multiple scenarios evaluated on those ethnic language test data. In the first block, we supervisedly trained our baseline system just using the speech-text paired data of the Indonesian language. Unfortunately, the number of errors (refer to $S + D + I$ in Eq. 1) in the recognition output exceeds the number of characters in the reference (N), resulting in a CER that above 100%. This indicates that directly using the Indonesian ASR is difficult for recognizing ethnic languages. In the second block, we showed our proposed approach that utilized cross-lingual speech-chain framework (see the training process in Section 5.). We utilized the previously pre-trained Indonesian ASR and TTS. We then develop ASR of those ethnic languages given only text or both text and speech (but unpaired). The results reveal that given only

Training		Testing				
ASR System	**Data**	**Javanese**	**Sundanese**	**Balinese**	**Bataks**	**Avr**
Baseline IND	Sup IND (Sp+Txt)	107.26	90.70	97.98	109.85	101.45
Proposed1 IND+ETH	Sup IND (Sp+Txt) + Unsup ETH (Txt Only)	63.73	63.04	70.80	72.79	67.59
Proposed2 IND+ETH	Sup IND (Sp+Txt) + Unsup ETH (Sp+Txt)	31.96	31.97	27.00	37.37	32.08
Topline IND+ETH	Sup IND (Sp+Txt) + Sup ETH (Sp+Txt)	20.20	17.89	15.41	26.69	20.05

Table 1: ASR performances by character error rate (CER (%)). Here, Indonesian language is denoted as *IND*, while Indonesian ethnic language is denoted as *ETH*. *Sup* is supervised learning and *Unsup* is unsupervised learning.

Training		Testing				
TTS System	**Data**	**Javanese**	**Sundanese**	**Balinese**	**Bataks**	**Avr**
Baseline IND	Sup IND (Sp+Txt)	1.016	1.247	1.129	1.254	1.162
Proposed IND+ETH	Sup IND (Sp+Txt) + Unsup ETH (Sp+Txt)	0.547	0.531	0.560	0.510	0.537
Topline IND+ETH	Sup IND (Sp+Txt) + Sup ETH (Sp+Txt)	0.415	0.470	0.478	0.399	0.441

Table 2: TTS performances in L2 norm-squared on log-Mel spectrogram. Here, Indonesian language is denoted as *IND*, while Indonesian ethnic language is denoted as *ETH*. *Sup* is supervised learning and *Unsup* is unsupervised learning.

text data, the proposed system improved the performance and reduced the average CER from 101.45% to 67.59%, which is 33.86% absolute reduction. If both text and speech data exist (but unpaired), we might further reduce the average CER to 32.08%, which is 69.37% absolute reduction from the baseline. In the last block, we showed the topline system in which the system was trained using both paired speech and the text of the Indonesian and Indonesian ethnic languages in a supervised manner. The system's performance achieved an average CER of 20.05%.

7.2. TTS Evaluation

Similar to the ASR evaluation, Table 2 shows the performance of the TTS systems from multiple scenarios evaluated on the ethnic language test data in L2 norm-squared error between the ground-truth and the predicted speech as a regression task. The baseline model was supervisedly trained using only the speech-text paired data of the Indonesian language, and the performance reached 1.162 of the L2 norm-squared on average. For the proposed system, we observed similar trends with the ASR results, where semi-supervised training with the speech chain method improved significantly over the baseline and achieved a L2 norm-squared reduction to 0.537 of L2 norm-squared on average. This performance is close to the upper-bound result, which is 0.441 of the L2 norm-squared on average.

8. Conclusion

We introduce a cross-lingual machine speech chain approach to construct an ASR and a TTS for the following Indonesian ethnic languages, Javanese, Sundanese, Balinese, and Bataks, when no paired speech or text data of those languages was available. We first pre-trained the ASR and TTS systems on the standard Indonesian language with parallel speech-text in a supervised manner. We then performed a speech chain mechanism with only limited text or limited speech of the Indonesian ethnic language (unsupervised learning). Experimental results revealed that our proposed speech-chain model achieved better ASR and TTS performances, indicating that such a closed-loop architecture enables ASR and TTS to teach each other and improved the performance even without any paired data. Note that although this study only focuses on the cross-lingual approach of the Indonesian language to Indonesian ethnic languages, the framework can be applied to any cross-lingual tasks without significant modification. In the future, we will investigate with other indigenous languages.

9. Acknowledgements

Part of this work was supported by JSPS KAKENHI Grant Numbers JP17H06101 and JP17K00237.

10. Bibliographical References

Abas, H. (1987). *Indonesian as a unifying language of wider communication: A historical and sociolinguistic perspective*. Pacific Linguistics, Canberra, Australia.

Alwi, H., Dardjowidjojo, S., Lapoliwa, H., and Moeliono, A. (2003). *Tata Bahasa Baku Bahasa Indonesia (Indonesian Grammar)*. Balai Pustaka, Jakarta, Indonesia.

Bahdanau, D., Cho, K., and Bengio, Y. (2014). Neural machine translation by jointly learning to align and translate. *arXiv preprint arXiv:1409.0473*.

Bahdanau, D., Chorowski, J., Serdyuk, D., Brakel, P., and Bengio, Y. (2016). End-to-end attention-based large vocabulary speech recognition. In *Proc. the IEEE International Conference on Acoustics, Speech and Signal Processing (ICASSP)*, pages 4945–4949. IEEE.

Bauer, L. (2007). *The Linguistics Student's Handbookr)*. Edinburgh University Press, Edinburgh, UK.

Bertand, J., (2003). *Language policy in Indonesia: The promotion of a national language amidst ethnic diversity*. MIT Press, Cambridge, MA, USA.

Cohn, A. and Ravindranath, M. (2014). Local languages in Indonesia: Language maintenance or language shift. *Masyarakat Linguistik Indonesia*.

Crystal, D. (2000). *Language Death*. Cambridge University Press, Cambridge, UK.

Denes, P., Denes, P., and Pinson, E. (1993). *The Speech Chain*. Anchor books. Worth Publishers.

Gordon, G. (2005). *Ethnologue: Languages of the World*. SIL International, Dallas, Texas, USA.

Graves, A. (2012). Supervised sequence labelling. In *Supervised Sequence Labelling with Recurrent Neural Networks*, pages 5–13. Springer.

Hoon, C.-Y. (2006). Assimilation, multiculturalism, hybridity: The dilemmas of the ethnic chinese in post-suharto indonesia. *Asian Ethnicity*, 7(2):149–166.

Horstman, R. (2016). Preserving the balinese language for generations to come. https://indonesiaexpat.biz/lifestyle/preserving-the-balinese-language-for-generations-to-come/.

Jones, R. (2007). *Loan-Words in Indonesian and Malay*. KITLV Press, Leiden, Netherland.

Lauder, M. M. (2005). *Language Treasures in Indonesia*. Prentice Hall, Clevedon, England.

Li, C., Ma, X., Jiang, B., Li, X., Zhang, X., Liu, X., Cao, Y., Kannan, A., and Zhu, Z. (2017). Deep speaker: an end-to-end neural speaker embedding system. *arXiv preprint arXiv:1705.02304*.

McFee, B., McVicar, M., Nieto, O., Balke, S., Thome, C., Liang, D., Battenberg, E., Moore, J., Bittner, R., Yamamoto, R., and et al. (2017). librosa 0.5.0. Feb.

Nakamura, S. (2009). Overcoming the language barrier with speech translation technology. *Science and Technology Trends*, (31):36–49.

Paauw, S. (2009). One land, one nation, one language: An analysis of indonesia's national language policy. *H. Lehnert-LeHouillier and A.B. Fine*, 5(1):2–16.

Paszke, A., Gross, S., Chintala, S., Chanan, G., Yang, E., DeVito, Z., Lin, Z., Desmaison, A., Antiga, L., and Lerer, A. (2017). Automatic differentiation in pytorch. In *Proc. the 31st Conference on Neural Information Processing Systems (NIPS)*.

Quinn, G. (2001). *The Learners Dictionary of todays Indonesian*. Allen and Unwin.

Riza, H. (2008). Indigenous languages of indonesia: Creating language resources for language preservation. In *Proc. IJCNLP*.

Sakti, S. and Nakamura, S. (2014). Recent progress in developing grapheme-based speech recognition for indonesian ethnic languages: Javanese, sundanese, balinese and bataks. In *Proc. SLTU*.

Sakti, S., Hutagaol, P., Arman, A., and Nakamura, S. (2004). Indonesian speech recognition for hearing and speaking impaired people. In *Proc. ICSLP*.

Sakti, S., Paul, M., Finch, A., Sakai, S., Vu, T.-T., Kimura, N., Hori, C., Sumita, E., Nakamura, S., Park, J., Wutiwiwatchai, C., Xu, B., Riza, H., Arora, K., Luong, C.-M., and Li, H. (2013). A-STAR: Toward translating asian spoken languages. *Computer Speech and Language Journal (Elsevier)*, 27(2):509–527.

Sneddon, J. (2003). *The Indonesian Language: Its History and Role in Modern Society*. UNSW Press.

Tan, J. (2004). Bahasa indonesia: Between faqs and facts. http://www.indotransnet.com/article1.html.

Tjandra, A., Sakti, S., and Nakamura, S. (2018). Machine speech chain with one-shot speaker adaptation. In *Proc. INTERSPEECH*.

Tjandra, A., Sakti, S., and Nakamura, S. (2019a). End-to-end feedback loss in speech chain framework via straight-through estimator. In *Proc. the IEEE International Conference on Acoustics, Speech and Signal Processing (ICASSP)*, pages 6281–6285.

Tjandra, A., Sakti, S., and Nakamura, S. (2019b). Listening while speaking: Speech chain by deep learning. In *Proc. the IEEE Automatic Speech Recognition and Understanding (ASRU)*, pages 301–308.

Wang, Y., Skerry-Ryan, R., Stanton, D., Wu, Y., Weiss, R. J., Jaitly, N., Yang, Z., Xiao, Y., Chen, Z., Bengio, S., et al. (2017). Tacotron: A fully end-to-end text-to-speech synthesis model. *arXiv preprint arXiv:1703.10135*.

Zhang, J. and Nakamura, S. (2003). An efficient algorithm to search for a minimum sentence set for collecting speech database. In *Proc. ICPhS*, pages 3145–3148, Barcelona, Spain.

11. Language Resource References

Kikui, G. and Sumita, E. and Takezawa, T. and Yamamoto, S. (2003). *Creating corpora for speech-to-speech translation*. EUROSPEECH.

Paul, Douglas B and Baker, Janet M. (1992). *The design for the Wall Street Journal-based CSR corpus*. Proceedings of the workshop on Speech and Natural Language.

Sakti, S. and Nakamura, S. (2013). *Towards Language Preservation: Design and Collection of Graphemically Balanced and Parallel Speech Corpora of Indonesian Ethnic Languages*. Oriental COCOSDA.

Sakti, S. and Arman, A.A. and Nakamura, S. and Hutagaol, P. (2004). *Indonesian speech recognition for hearing and speaking impaired people*. Eighth International Conference on Spoken Language Processing.

Sakti, S. and Kelana, E. and Riza, H. and Sakai, S. and Markov, K. and Nakamura, S. (2008). *Recent Progress in Developing Indonesian Large-vocabulary Corpora and LVCSR System*. MALINDO.

Proceedings of the 1st Joint SLTU and CCURL Workshop (SLTU-CCURL 2020), pages 139–143
Language Resources and Evaluation Conference (LREC 2020), Marseille, 11–16 May 2020
ⓒ European Language Resources Association (ELRA), licensed under CC-BY-NC

Automatic Myanmar Image Captioning using CNN and LSTM-Based Language Model

San Pa Pa Aung†, Win Pa Pa†, Tin Lay Nwe‡
†Natural Language Processing Lab, University of Computer Studies, Yangon, Myanmar
‡Visual Intelligence Department, Institute for Infocomm Research, Singapore
{sanpapaaung, winpapa}@ucsy.edu.mm, tlnma@i2r.a-star.edu.sg

Abstract

An image captioning system involves modules on computer vision as well as natural language processing. Computer vision module is for detecting salient objects or extracting features of images and Natural Language Processing (NLP) module is for generating correct syntactic and semantic image captions. Although many image caption datasets such as Flickr8k, Flickr30k and MSCOCO are publicly available, most of the datasets are captioned in English language. There is no image caption corpus for Myanmar language. Myanmar image caption corpus is manually built as part of the Flickr8k dataset in this current work. Furthermore, a generative merge model based on Convolutional Neural Network (CNN) and Long-Short Term Memory (LSTM) is applied especially for Myanmar image captioning. Next, two conventional feature extraction models Visual Geometry Group (VGG) OxfordNet 16-layer and 19-layer are compared. The performance of this system is evaluated on Myanmar image caption corpus using BLEU scores and 10-fold cross validation.

Keywords: Convolutional Neural Network, Long-Short Term Memory, Visual Geometry Group.

1. Introduction

An image consists of several information such as the objects, attributes, scenes and activities. Humans are capable of generating captions for images with much less difficulty. However, automatic caption generation for a given image is a very challenging task for machine (Yang et al., 2018). Automatic image caption generation involves two tasks: 1) recognizing and understanding significant objects in an image and 2) describing the proper relationship between these objects. To perform these two tasks, image captioning uses a combination of two sub-networks, CNN for salient object detection in images and LSTM for understanding relationship objects and decoding into sentences (Shiru et al., 2017).

With the availability of extremely large numbers of images in internet nowadays, image captioning becomes more and more popular for retrieving images by Google search engines or newspaper companies (Huda et al., 2018). In addition, image captioning is useful for description of images for visually impaired persons, teaching concepts for children and social media network like Facebook and Twitter can directly generate captions from images (Zakir et al., 2018).

Myanmar language is morphologically complex and scarcity of annotated resources than English. Therefore, it is necessary to build a corpus which is large enough to get the accurate caption for Myanmar automatic image captioning. Example of an image and five different Myanmar captions can be seen at Figure 1.

In this paper, we used the combination of two sub-network: deep Convolutional Neural Network for image feature extraction and Long Short Term Memory for sentences generations. These two sub-networks communicate with each other in a merge layer to predict the next word of the sentences and then generate the caption for the specific image (Huda et al., 2018).

This paper is organized as follows: the related work is discussed in Section 2. Methodology is proposed in Section 3. In Section 4, experiments details and evaluation results are explained. Finally, the concluding remarks and future work are summarized in Section 5.

(1) ပန်းရောင် အင်္ကျီ နဲ့ ကလေးငယ် က အိမ် ထဲကို ဝင် နေတယ်.
(2) မိန်းကလေးငယ် က သစ်သား အိမ် ထဲကို ဝင် နေတယ်.
(3) ကလေးငယ် က အိမ် ထဲကို ဝင် နေတယ်.
(4) ကလေးငယ် က အိမ် ပေါ်ကို လှေကားထစ် မှ တက် နေတယ်.
(5) ပန်းရောင် အင်္ကျီ နဲ့ ကလေးငယ် က သစ်သားအိမ် ထဲကို ဝင် နေတယ်.

Figure 1 : Example of an image and its Myanmar descriptions.

2. Related Work

The restriction of image caption corpora for morphological complex language rather than English is an issue to get the accurate results.

The image caption generation is mainly split in retrievable-based approaches and constructive-based approaches. The first category is used in the earlier attempts to solve image captioning which has the problem as a retrieval task. A database is constructed based on image features extraction and caption generation for given images and then the most appropriate sentence is extracted (Jacob et al., 2015). This approach is not effective to describe novel captions and the caption generation is restricted to the features size of the images and the database size. Therefore, retrieval-based approach is not appropriate for today's demand.

Recently, constructive-based approaches become popular due to recent progress in automatic image caption generation and neural machine translation. A constructed-based approach gradually constructs a novel caption for each image (Chetan and Vaishli, 2018 ; Yajurv et al., 2019) . The authors (Parth et al., 2017) used this approach that can be further divided into two phrases as deep convolutional neural network for encoding image attributes and Long Short Term Memory network for decoding to generate a syntactically correct caption.

The authors (Huda et al., 2018) implemented automatic image captioning in Arabic by using Deep Learning Technique. MSCOCO and Flickr8k dataset are used and Arabic image captions corpus is built using a professional English-Arabic translator and Google translator.

In this paper, we used constructive-based approaches and Myanmar images caption corpus is built so that the generated image captions are more accurate and relevant with each other. Furthermore, two different feature extraction models are compared in this paper.

3.   Methodology

Figure 2 shows the Architecture of CNN-LSTM-based image captioning system. The architecture involves two main modules. The first one is image understanding module using CNN and the second one is text understanding module using LSTM. Each module is described in details in the following subsections.

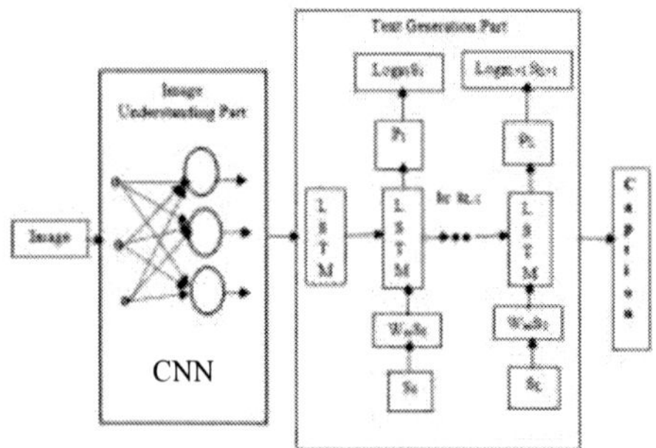

Figure 2 : Architecture of CNN-LSTM-based Image Captioning.

3.1   Convolutional Neural Network(CNN)

For image caption generation task, CNN is widely used because it has solved successfully for image annotation problems with high accuracy (Aditya et al., 2019). We have trained and tested two different models for feature extraction of images datasets. The two models have different capabilities in extracting features of images and the input image size of both models are 224× 224× 3 and the convolutional feature size of VGG is 4096.

VGG16: is a pre-trained model on ImageNet dataset based on Visual Geometry Group (VGG) OxfordNet 16-layer CNN (Rahul and Aayush, 2018 ; Lakshminarasimhan et al., 2018). The VGG16 neural network is used for image classification. Output of VGG16 is probability of individual classes that the classification system has to classify. We remove the last layer of the VGG16 and use the output from second last layer as feature parameters for each image. We extract 4096 parameters for each image, which are further processed by a Dense layer to produce a

256 element representation of an image (Micah et al., 2013).

VGG19: We also used a fully convolutional neural network based on Visual Geometry Group (VGG) OxfordNet 19-layer to extract features of each image. VGG16 and VGG19 networks have the total number of weight layers 16 and 19 respectively. VGG19 has 3 more convolutional layers than VGG16.

3.2   Long-Short Term Memory (LSTM)

LSTM can maintain information in memory for long periods of time and retrieve sequential information through time (Yang et al., 2018). The text understanding part produces words or phrases based on the word embedding vector of previous part. The language generation model is trained to predict each word in the caption after it has seen both image and all previous words. For any given sentence in Myanmar corpus we add two extra symbols for start word and stop word which designates the start and end of the sentence. Whenever stop word is found it halts generating caption and it denotes end of the sentence.

Sequence Processor is a word embedding layer to handle the input text and then followed by a Long Short-Term Memory (LSTM) recurrent neural network layer (Shiru et al., 2017). The proposed model is defined by the input sequences length (21 words) which are fed into an Embedding layer and then uses a mask to ignore padded values and followed by an LSTM layer with 256 memory units (Parth et al., 2017).

Both input models produced a 256 element vector and used regularization of 50% dropout to reduce over fitting during the training. In decoding, the model combined the vectors from both input models by using an addition operation and then fed to a Dense 256 neuron layer to   make a softmax prediction over the whole output vocabulary for the next word in the sentence.

Loss function for both models are evaluated as,

$$L\,(I,\,S) = -\sum_{t=1}^{N} \log p_t(S_t) \qquad (1)$$

Where I is input image and S is generated sentence, N is the length of generated caption. p_t and S_t are probability and predict word at time t respectively. During the training process we have tried to reduce this loss function.

4.   Experiments

4.1   Myanmar Image Captions Corpus Construction

The Flickr8k[1] dataset (Khumaisu et al., 2018 ; Micah et al., 2013) is applied in the first Myanmar Image Captioning task. It contains 8092 images and five annotated English captions for each image. Due to the limited time, we selected only 3k images of the Flickr8k dataset with five annotated Myanmar captions for each image. We constructed Myanmar image captions corpus in two different ways: 1) Automatic translation from English descriptions and 2) Direct image descriptions with Myanmar language.

---

[1]https://github.com/jbrownlee/Datasets/releases/download/Flickr8k/Flickr8k_Dataset.zip

4.1.1 Translation from English to Myanmar Captions without Images

Firstly, we translated the English image description of the Flickr8k dataset to Myanmar sentences without the image itself by using English to Myanmar Machine Translation. Attention based Neural Machine Translation model from English to Myanmar language (Yi et al., 2019), trained on UCSY Corpus that has 220k English Myanmar Parallel sentence, is applied in this stage. Due to the domain of the training data is general and influenced by News and conversations, the translation accuracy on 3k images of Flickr8k dataset is 13.93 multi-BLEU. Although the translation accuracy is low, the translated sentences help to reduce manual captioning time.

4.1.2 Direct Construction Myanmar Captions from Images

In this stage, we manually checked and corrected the translation of Myanmar captions by looking at the image and creating sentence descriptions correspond to the pictures. We have written our own natural language expressions based on our perception of the image without utilizing English descriptions. The total Myanmar captions for 3k images are 15,000 sentences with a vocabulary size of 3,138. The length of longest sentence is 21 words. The experiment was set as 2500 images for training, 300 images for validation and 200 images for testing.

4.2 Experiments Details

We conducted experiments to observe the different components of the image captioning system, and we evaluated the experiment results. The two different models are trained on K80 GPU machine using Keras API library with TensorFlow backend that are used for creating and training deep neural networks. The large amount of training data are given, the models fit the 10 epoch. After the 4th epoch both models stabilized and save the loss for each fold. The smallest value of loss on the training dataset is 2.097 and the validation loss on the development dataset is 2.513 in 10 folds cross validation setting using VGG16 with LSTM. And, the smallest loss on the training dataset is 2.114 and the validation loss on the development dataset is 2.513 when we used VGG19 with LSTM. As we can see the smallest validation loss for both models with 10 folds cross validation settings are the same. Figure 3 and 4 show the variation of training and validation loss using two different models.

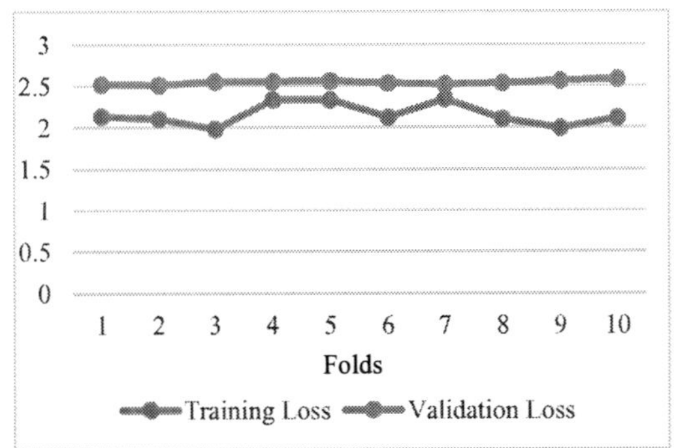

Figure 3 : Variation of training and validation loss in 10 folds using VGG16 with LSTM.

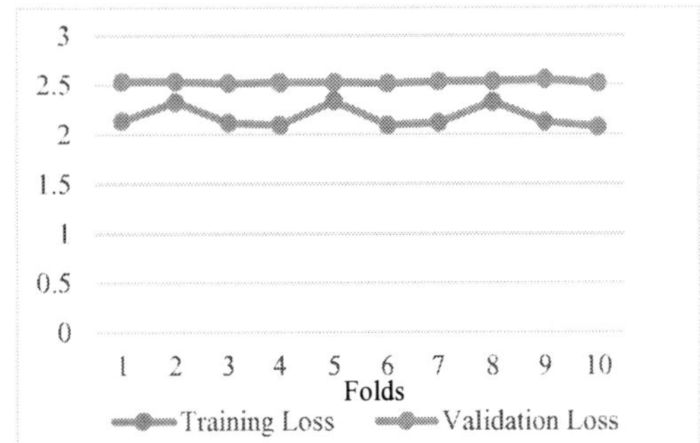

Figure 4 : Variation of training and validation loss in 10 folds using VGG19 with LSTM.

4.3 Evaluation Metric

BLEU (Bilingual Evaluation Understudy) is a metric that is used to compute the quality of machine translated texts (Zakir et al., 2018). The generated captions for each model are evaluated using BLEU to get the quality of machine translated texts (Shiru et al., 2017). BLEU score values range from 0 to 1 and higher values indicate the best score between the reference caption and machine generated captions. BLEU evaluates the modified precision of n-grams (Parth et al., 2017). In our experiment, BLEU scores are calculated as in equation 2:

$$\text{BLEU} = \min\left(1, \frac{output\_length}{reference\_length}\right) \left(\prod_{i=1}^{4} precision_i\right)^{1/4} \quad (2)$$

Where output_length is the output caption length and reference_length is the reference caption length.

4.4 10-Fold Cross Validation

This paper used 10-fold cross validation to compute predictive models by partitioning the original dataset into a training dataset to train the model and a test dataset to evaluate performance. In 10-fold cross validation, the original dataset is randomly partitioned into 10 equal subsets. Among these 10 subsets, one set is used as the validation data for testing the model, and the rest of 9 sets are used for training data. The cross-validation process repeated 10 times (the fold), with each of the subsets used exactly once for the validation data. We compute the average accuracy over all the folds to produce a single estimation. In table 1 and table 2, we show the BLEU scores of each fold with different testing datasets. Figure 5 shows the comparison of VGG16 with LSTM and VGG19 with LSTM average BLEU scores.

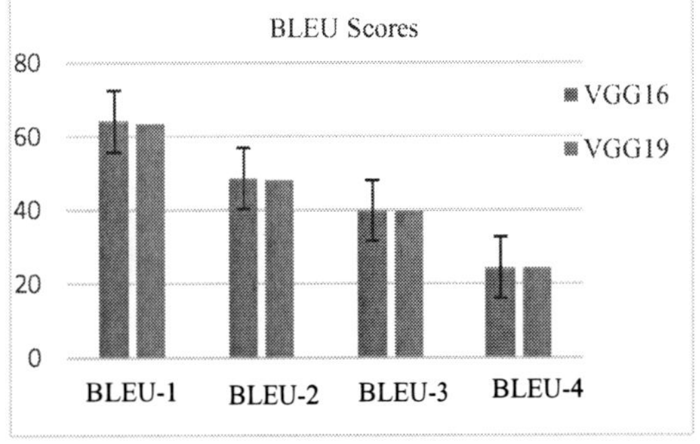

Figure 5 : Comparison of VGG16 and VGG19.

Training Times	BLEU-1	BLEU-2	BLEU-3	BLEU-4
Fold 1	61.5	47.6	40.3	25.9
Fold 2	62.4	46.4	37.1	22.2
Fold 3	64.8	49.3	40.5	23.8
Fold 4	65.6	49.8	41.2	26.0
Fold 5	66.2	50.8	41.6	25.2
Fold 6	64.3	48.7	40.5	25.6
Fold 7	62.5	46.4	36.9	21.4
Fold 8	63.1	46.8	37.9	22.8
Fold 9	64.9	50.2	42.4	26.8
Fold 10	66.1	49.8	40.2	24.1
Total	641.4	485.8	398.6	243.8
Average	**64.14**	**48.58**	**39.86**	**24.38**

Table 1 : 10-Fold Cross Validation for VGG16

Training Times	BLEU-1	BLEU-2	BLEU-3	BLEU-4
Fold 1	65.1	50.6	42.7	28.0
Fold 2	60.6	44.7	36.4	20.9
Fold 3	58.8	44.1	36.3	21.2
Fold 4	65.6	49.3	39.2	22.7
Fold 5	67.0	51.1	41.5	24.9
Fold 6	65.9	50.0	41.0	25.4
Fold 7	54.6	40.7	34.2	21.3
Fold 8	65.5	49.2	40.1	24.6
Fold 9	65.4	51.4	43.6	28.2
Fold 10	66.6	50.1	40.5	24.6
Total	635.1	481.2	395.5	241.8
Average	**63.51**	**48.12**	**39.55**	**24.18**

Table2 : 10-Fold Cross Validation for VGG19

4.5 Experiments Results

The captions generated from VGG16 and VGG19 are approximately similar and do not provide any qualitative difference. Therefore, in this section, we mainly focused on the results generated from VGG16 with LSTM. In figure 6(a), the model accurately generated the major features in the image such as "ကောင်လေး က ရေကူးကန် ထဲမှာ ရေကူး နေတယ်" ("The boy is swimming in the swimming pool") and the relationship between these features of image also describes accurately. In figure 6(b), the generated caption: "ကလေး များ က ရေကူးကန် ထဲမှာ ကစား နေ ကြ တယ်" ("Children are playing in the swimming pool") and in figure 6(c), the generated caption: "ခွေး နှစ် ကောင် က မြက်ခင်းစိမ်း ထဲမှာ ကစား နေ ကြ တယ်" ("Two dogs are playing in the green grass"). If we look at figure 6(b) and 6(c), the significant features of the images are captured accurately and grammatically correct. Nonetheless, we can see at figure 6(d) for random image, the model captures the major feature which is လူ တစ်ယောက် (a person) and ထိုင် နေတယ် (sitting) but fails to depict the minor features and incorrectly captures like နံရံ (wall) it is actually ခုံတန်းရှည် (bench). Finally, it is the limitations of our model and we would like to highlight the necessity for future work regarding the model. We are confident that larger datasets can be used to resolve these issues, and our models can accurately generate the relationship between images and its captions even for random images. All of the figures 6(a), 6(b), 6(c) and 6(d) are captioned automatically with Myanmar Language without any human interference.

(a) In English: The boy is swimming in the swimming pool

(b) In English: Children are playing in the swimming pool

(c) In English: Two dogs are playing in the green grass

(d) In English: A person is sitting on the wall

Figure 6 : Example of Myanmar image captioning results (a,b,c,d).

5. Conclusion

We created the first corpus of image captioning for Myanmar language, and manually checked and built the descriptions in detail to match captions and images. Convolutional Neural Network based on Visual Geometry Group (VGG) OxfordNet CNN and single hidden layer LSTM model were applied for Myanmar automatic image caption generation in this work. The experimental results showed that applying CNN and LSTM based image captioning trained on our corpus can give acceptable performance.

This tiny corpus will help building large corpora for Myanmar Image Captioning. Moreover, the other image feature extraction models of CNN will be applied for future research.

6. Bibliographical References

Aditya, A. N., Anditya, A. and Suyanto, (2019). "Generating Image Description on Indonesian Language using Convolutional Neural Network and Gated Recurrent Unit", 7th International Conference on Information and Communication Technology (ICoICT).

Chetan, A. and Vaishli, J. (2018). "Image Caption Generation using Deep Learning Technique", Fourth International Conference on Computing Communication Control andd Automation (ICCUBEA).

Huda A. Al-muzaini, Tasniem N. and Hafida B. (2018) "Automatic Arabic Image Captioning using RNN-LSTM-Based Language Model and CNN", International Journal of Advanced Computer Science and Applications (IJACSA), Vol. 9, No.6.

Jacob, D., Saurabh, G. and Ross, G. (2015). "Exploring Nearest Neighbor Approaches for Image Captioning", arXiv: 1505.04467.

Khumaisu, N., Johanes, E., Sakriani, S., Mirna, A. and Satoshi, N. (2018). "Corpus Construction and Semantic Analysis of Indonesian Image Description", The 6th Intl. Workshop on Spoken Language Technologies for Under-Resourced Languages, Gurugram, India.

Lakshminarasimhan, S. , Dinesh, S. and Amutha, A. (2018). "Image Captioning - A Deep Learning Approach", International Journal of Applied Engineering Research ISSN 0973-4562 Volume 13.

Micah, H., Peter, Y. and Julia, H. (2013) "Framing image description as a ranking task: Data, models and

evaluation metrics", Journal of Artificial Intelligence Research, Vol. 47, pp. 853-899, May.

Parth, S., Vishvajit, B. and Supriya, P. (2017). "Image Captioning using Deep Neural Architectures", International Conference on Innovations in information Embedded and Communication Systems (ICIIECS).

Rahul, S. and Aayush, S. (2018). "Image Captioning using Deep Neural networks".

Shiru, Q., Yuling, X and Songtao, D. (2017). "Visual Attention Based on Long-Short Term Memory Model for Image Caption Generation", 29th Chinese Control and Decision Conference (CCDC).

Sreela, S. R. and Sumam, M. I. (2018). "AIDGenS: An Automatic Image Description System using Residual Neural Network", International Conference on Data Science and Engineering (ICDSE).

Shuang, L., Liang, B. and Yanming, (2018). "Reference Based on Adaptive Attention Mechanism for Image Captioning", 2018 IEEE Fourth International Conference on Multimedia Big Data (BigMM).

Xinwei, H., Yang, Y. and Baoguang S. (2018). "VD-SAN: Visual-Densely Semantic Attention Network for Image Caption Generation", Neurocomputing.

Yajurv, B., Aman, B., Deepanshu, R. and Himanshu, M. (2019). "Image Captioning using Google's Inception-resnetv2 and Recurrent Neural Network",IEEE.

Yang, F., Jungang, X., Yingfei,S. and Ben, H. (2018). "Long-term Recurrent Merge Network Model for Image Captioning", IEEE 30th International Conference on Tools with Artificial Intelligence.

Yi, M. S. S., Win, P. P. and Khin, M. S. (2019). "UCSYNLP-Lab Machine Translation Systems for WAT 2019", Proceedings of the 6th Workshop on Asian Translation.

Zakir, H., Ferdous S., and Mohd F. S. (2018). "A Comprehensive Survey of Deep Learning for Image Captioning", ACM Computing Surveys.

Proceedings of the 1st Joint SLTU and CCURL Workshop (SLTU-CCURL 2020), pages 144–152
Language Resources and Evaluation Conference (LREC 2020), Marseille, 11–16 May 2020

Phoneme Boundary Analysis using Multiway Geometric Properties of Waveform Trajectories

Parabattina Bhagath, Pradip K. Das
Department of Computer Science and Engineering
Indian Institute of Technology Guwahati, Assam state, India
bhagath.2014, pkdas @ iitg.ac.in

Abstract

Automatic phoneme segmentation is an important problem in speech processing. It helps in improving the recognition quality by providing a proper segmentation information of phonemes or phonetic units. Inappropriate segmentation may lead to recognition accuracy falloff. The problem is essential not only for recognition but also for annotation purpose. In general, segmentation algorithms rely on large datasets for training where data is observed to find the patterns among them. But this process is not straight forward for languages that are under resourced because of less availability of datasets. In this paper, we propose a method that uses geometrical properties of waveform trajectory where intra signal variations are studied and used for segmentation. The method does not rely on large datasets for training. The geometric properties are extracted as linear structural changes in a raw waveform. The methods and findings of the study are presented.

Keywords:
Phoneme boundary,
Peak attributes,
Valley attributes,
Geometrical properties,
CCA.

1. Introduction

Speech recognition is a well-known area that deals with the understanding of spoken units (words, sentences) that has been spoken. It is fair to say that a speech recognition system should be equipped with a good segmentation procedure. A segmentation algorithm essentially identifies the boundaries between two consecutive phonemes in a word or sentence. For an input signal $S[n]$, a segmentation algorithm provides a set of points $b_0, b_1, ..., b_n$ such that the regions separated by these points belong to different phonemes. Phoneme segmentation has to be looked carefully to improve recognition accuracy. This problem has been studied by researchers in different ways.

A conventional segmentation procedure relies on features that can help to understand the changes in speech signals. This information is further processed by any modeling technique of choice to identify the required boundaries. So it is a common practice that a boundary detection involves some feature extraction methods. In literature, a variety of these techniques have been used for this purpose. They are generally categorized as temporal and spectral. Temporal features (Ali et al., 1999) like energy, ZCR (Zero Crossing Rate), Pitch period, LPCCs (Linear Predictive Cepstral Coefficients) are useful in understanding temporal changes in a speech signal. Spectral features like MFCCs (Mel Frequency Cepstral Coefficients), formants, etc. are used to analyze frequency components in a signal. In addition to these, phonetic studies are proven to be helpful in the segmentation task. Research has shown that HMM based systems alone are not sufficient to understand the temporal changes effectively (Yan et al., 2006). It is understood from the studies that structural processing methods are superior to conventional methods in capturing temporal patterns of the signals (Deng and Strik, 2007). Modeling speech trajec-

tory properties are useful to capture the temporal dynamics over the signal which can help to develop dynamic speech models (Liu and Sim, 2012). Even though these methods are effective in capturing temporal dynamics, computational cost and the need for a vast dataset are not relaxed. The present work aimed to develop a reasonable method for phoneme segmentation by incorporating the structural properties of a waveform which can work well on small-sized datasets. The proposed method uses attributes of waveform trajectories to identify the appropriate boundary points using Canonical Correlation Analysis (CCA).

The paper is organized as follows: The next section describes trajectory methods that were used for pattern analysis. Section 3 gives an overview of the CCA method. Section 4 explains the proposed approach for segmentation. The data and experimental setup is described in Section 5. Section 6 explains the results found in the study and Section 7 concludes the paper.

2. Trajectories for Pattern Analysis

In an Euclidean space, a trajectory is defined as a curve that is formed by the observation of the path that a moving object makes. The points in the path are characterized as ordered positional points. Trajectories that were initially known as Linear Trajectory Segmental Models (LTSMs) have been used to analyze speech signals for past 3 decades (Russell and Holmes, 1997). The need for LTSMs point back to the independence assumption in HMM systems. The basic underlying idea in these systems is understanding and equipping models with the knowledge of temporal patterns across segments of a signal. These dynamic features help in overcoming the problem of independence assumption in HMM systems. In LTSMs, each segment is treated as a homogeneous unit that helps in capturing the inter-segmental dependencies too (Yifan Gong, 1997). Trajectories are suitable in pattern analysis for two reasons (Siohan and Yifan Gong, 1996):

1. A speech trajectory is also influenced by the context

2. Trajectories formed by different phonetic units can create independent clusters based on the contextual information

However the models that are based on HMM are suitable for large vocabulary speech recognition (Mitra et al., 2013). Trajectories are not only used for speech signal analysis, but also for pattern analysis in different areas like road network (Atev et al., 2010), databases (Jeung et al., 2008), traffic management, etc.

In general, a trajectory contains vital information like spatiality and temporal patterns of an object. There can be different ways of treating trajectories as segments sequence and points sequence. The similarities in these entities can contribute to crucial knowledge. The similarity metrics to measure the affinity vary on the kind of trajectory. The effectiveness of the comparison method depends on the underlying components that the trajectory represents. Huanhuan et al. proposed a fusion based similarity method for traffic flow patterns (Li et al., 2018). The method combines different techniques like Merge Distance (MD), Multi Dimensional Scaling (MDS) and Density Based Spatial Clustering of applications with noise (DBSCAN) to identify traffic flow patterns and customary routes from vehicle movements. One of the fusion techniques is given by Equation 1.

$$MMTD(t_1, t_2) = 1 - (w_1, w_2) \begin{pmatrix} dist_1(t_1, t_2) \\ dist_2(t_1, t_2) \end{pmatrix} \quad (1)$$

where $dist_1$ and $dist_2$ are different similarity measurements and each measure is treated with unequal weightages. MMTD is maximum-minimum trajectory distance (Xiao et al., 2019) (Lin et al., 2019). The present work uses CCA as measurement metric which is described in the next section.

3. Canonical Correlation Analysis (CCA)

Canonical correlation analysis (CCA) was introduced by Hoteling for multi-variate analysis. It helps to find the relation between multiple variables simultaneously that makes analysis easy. The fundamental step in CCA is to find a set of transforming variables that can transform variables such that the transformation in the corresponding new coordinates is maximally correlated. In the process, a set of variables called as canonical weights are used. The solution to this is computationally expensive and time consuming. Therefore, it is convenient to solve the problem as an eigen value problem. The objective function to solve CCA for two variables x and y can be expressed by Equation 2:

$$C = \begin{pmatrix} 0 & C_{xy} \\ C_{yx} & 0 \end{pmatrix} \begin{pmatrix} a \\ b \end{pmatrix} = \rho^2 \begin{pmatrix} C_{xx} & 0 \\ 0 & C_{xx} \end{pmatrix} \quad (2)$$

where C_{xy} and C_{yx} are the covariances between variables x and y where as C_{xx}, C_{yy} are auto covariances of variables x and y respectively. There are various applications for CCA in the signal processing domain. It has been useful in finding relations which can help for multi-view learning (Liu et al., 2018). Heycem et.al. applied the technique for feature selection for the problem of depression recognition from speech signals (Kaya et al., 2014). Wang et.al. used CCA to learn acoustic features that can improve phonetic recognition (Wang et al., 2015). Apart from the above mentioned applications, CCA is also useful in areas like Blind Source Separation (BSS). The problem aims to recover the original signal when an unknown linear mixture of statistically independent signals are available (Borga and Knutsson, 2001). Another approach based on CCA focuses to improve the signal to noise ratio (SNR) in EEG data that is recorded from multiple channels (de Cheveigné et al., 2019).

In the present work, knowledge from a set of multiple features is used to detect boundary points in a word. The complete procedure is explained in Section 4..

4. Proposed Approach for Segmentation

The proposed method uses cumulative knowledge of multiple geometric features and use that to form a multi-view trajectory feature vector. The feature vector is then analyzed dynamically to extract the phonetic boundaries. There are

1. Basic feature set (τ)

2. Derived features (τ_D)

3. Multi-view boundary detection algorithm

Each component is explained in next subsequent subsections. Basic and derived features are defined in the next subsection. The segmentation algorithm is explained in Section 4.2.

4.1. Trajectory Features

A speech signal records the nature of vibrations when the vocal chord moves for uttering a sound. The resultant waveform consists of peaks and valleys which helps to understand salient features of the spoken unit and person who has uttered. Thus the waveform records different acoustic events which can be used for various purposes like classification, segmentation, etc. One of the crucial properties of a trajectory is its shape. Each event that is recorded in a speech signal can be distinct in structure. The structural properties of phonetic units have become an interesting area of study (Minematsu, 2005). The reason for this is that the features corresponds to phonetic characteristics with variations in a lucid way. And also the structural properties of waveform trajectories are useful in understanding the dynamic nature of different phonetic units. In the present work, a set of geometric features are proposed to capture the transitional behavior of the waveform that can be further used in identifying boundary points between different phonetic units. The feature set as a whole contains two different classes i.e. primitive and derived properties. The primitive properties are those characteristics that are inherent in a waveform. They are listed as follows:

1. Peak

2. Valley

3. Peak position

4. Valley position

In the second stage, the aforementioned features are transformed further to obtain derived attributes. This set contains the following elements:

1. Peak width

2. Valley width

3. Slope of peaks and valleys

4. Disparity of peaks and valleys

For a segment of speech signal $S[n]$ with size m, the terms are defined in Definitions 1 to 8.

Definition 1 A data point p_i is said to be as **peak** if $p_{i-1} < p_i > p_{i+1}$ where $\forall i \in \mathbb{Z}$

Definition 2 A data point p_i is said to be a **valley** if $p_{i-1} > p_i < p_{i+1}$ where $\forall i \in \mathbb{Z}$

Definition 3 **Peak position** is any integer k, such that $0 < k < m$ where peak is found at k^{th} location

Definition 4 **Valley position** is any integer k, such that $0 < k < m$ where valley is found at k^{th} location

Definition 5 The data point p_k being a peak point between the valleys v_q and v_r, the difference $r - q$ is defined as **peak width** for the peak p_k $\forall k, q, r \in \mathbb{Z}$ and $q < k < r$

Definition 6 The data point v_k being a valley point between two peaks p_q and p_r, the difference $r - q$ is defined as **Valley width** of valley v_k $\forall k, q, r \in \mathbb{Z}$ and $q < k < r$

Definition 7 The **slope** between two points $x = (x_1, y_1)$ and $y = (x_2, y_2)$ is defined by Equation 3.

$$Slope(x, y) = \frac{y_2 - y_1}{x_2 - x_1} \quad (3)$$

Definition 8 The **Disparity** between two points p_i and p_k is given by Equation 4.

$$Disparity(p_i, p_k) = \sqrt{(p_i - p_k)^2}, \forall i, k \in \mathbb{Z} \quad (4)$$

To understand the terms, let us consider Figure 1. In the figure, peaks and valleys are indicated as P_i and V_i respectively where i represents the sequence in which they occur in a waveform. The next term, peak-width is the width of the curve in a waveform between two valley positions. In the same way, valley width is the distance between two peaks in which a valley is present. Slope is the general gradient between two points in a geometric space. The points that are considered here are a pair of peaks (or valleys). This feature gives information of two adjacent peaks (or valleys). In the segmentation algorithm, the average slope between peaks (and valleys) of each frame in the source signal is studied. Finally, the property 'Disparity' between two points (peaks or valleys) is the continuous variation between the heights of peaks and depth of valleys. The property 'slope' considers the position at which the peaks (or valleys) occur whereas 'Disparity' does not regard this property. The derived features of the word "Zero" are shown in Figure 2. Figure 2-a shows the normalized source signal, Figure 2-b and Figure 2-c give slope and disparity of peaks respectively. Slope and disparity of valleys are shown in Figure 2-d and Figure 2-e respectively. The procedure used for segmentation is explained in next subsection.

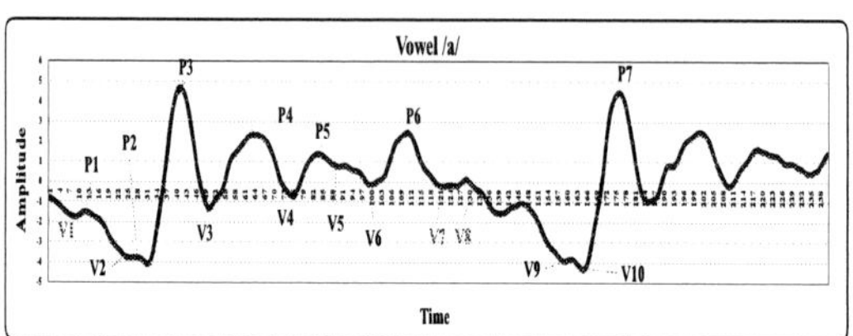

Figure 1: Peaks and valleys of a speech segment

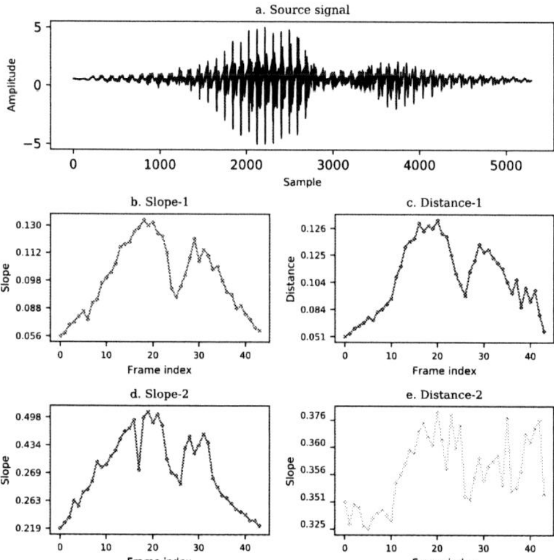

Figure 2: Peak attributes for the word "zero"

4.2. Multi-View Boundary Detection Algorithm

The features that are described in the previous section are analyzed to understand the boundaries of the phonetic units. The algorithm observes the dynamic changes of the waveform over the entire signal by capturing the variations with the extracted features. First, the given speech signal is divided into equal-sized frames and a set of basic features (τ) are extracted from each signal. From the basic features, a set of derived features are drawn. Thus the complete feature set is a matrix in which each set of derived features are present. This is a multi-view representation of the waveform trajectory features that will be processed to find the segmentation points.

The segmentation procedure comprises of two stages: In the first stage, the feature matrix is analyzed by the CCA procedure which will give a set of coefficients for each feature set simultaneously. These coefficients represent the correlation between the subsets of each feature set which will be used next. In the second stage, a pair of sequential frames that are adjacent will be used to generate correlation coefficients. Finally, the coefficients generated in first and second stages are then compared to get the variance between them. The crucial steps in the segmentation procedure can be summarized as follows:

1. The input signal $S[n]$ is divided into a set of frames $f_0, f_1, ..., f_n$ of equal size.

2. Each frame is then transformed to a set of primitive features : S_p, S_v, S_{pi}, V_{vi}, where:

   - S_p is set of peaks
   - S_v is set of valleys
   - S_{pi} is set of integers that represent peak positions
   - V_{vi} is set of integers that represent valley positions

3. The features obtained in Step 2 are then transformed to a set of trajectory features $\tau = \tau_{sv}, \tau_{sp}, \tau_{dpv}, \tau_{dp}$.

4. The feature sets τ are analyzed using CCA which gives a set of coefficients represented by CCA_τ.

5. The features sets belonging to subsequent frames are correlated to get the new coefficients. Each set consists of features belonging to 3 adjacent frames. The number of frames is empirically chosen so that variations can be captured in the corresponding CCA coefficients.

6. Variance between coefficients computed in Step 4 and Step 5 are compared. The peaks in this set forms the boundary points. Thus the peaks in each set are combined to identify the boundary points using the CCA_τ computed by Equation 5.

$$B_p = \{CCA_{\tau_{dp}} \cup CCA_{\tau_{dpv}} \cup CCA_{\tau_{sp}} \cup CCA_{\tau_{sv}}\} \tag{5}$$

The final variances obtained for each derived feature set are shown in Figure 3. From the diagram, it can be observed that the changes needed for identifying the phonemic variations are recorded in as peak points in the final variances. But different varieties of variations can be seen separately from features. Therefore it is required to combine the points obtained from each features to get the final boundary points. The detailed algorithm and the flowchart are given in Algorithm 1 and Figure 4 respectively. In the next section, the background setup used for the experiments is described.

5. Experimental Setup

The algorithms were implemented using Python platform. The CCA implementation that is available in Pyrcca (Bilenko and Gallant, 2016) library was used in the algorithm. The data used in present work is English digits belong to the Indian accent. The speakers belong to different regions (states) in India. They include male and female speakers. We used 50 speakers data in the analysis. Each English digit was recorded 15 times for all speakers. The digits were recorded using the Cool Edit software with 16KHz sampling rate, mono channel and 16 bits resolution. The behaviour of the algorithm for different cases are discussed in the next section.

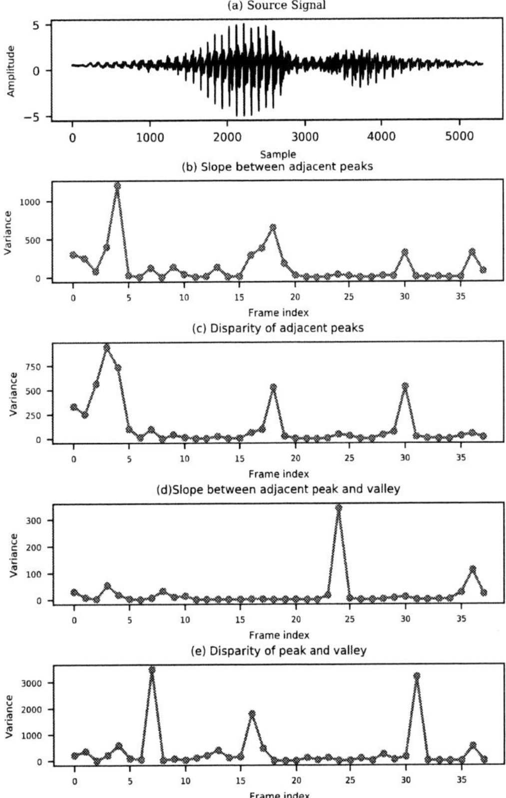

Figure 3: CCA of different features for the word "zero"

6. Results and Analysis

In the present study, a set of trajectory features are considered to be useful after conducting experiments on various properties. The properties that were observed are shown in Table 1. Figure 5 gives an idea of the nature of these features. They were not used as part of feature set in the segmentation process rather they are useful in understanding the characteristics of regions belonging to different phonetic units. Some observations are presented in each subsequent subsections separately. The analysis of the algorithm's nature for peaks and valleys are presented separately in subsequent subsections.

6.1. Peak Attributes Analysis

To understand meaningful cues from speech, an analysis of the nature of peaks in different classes of sounds like vowels, fricatives and stops are done. These clues are further used to find the boundaries of phonemes. It is helpful to know the regions where changes are occurring corresponding to the behaviour of attributes. Peaks can be classified into different types based on height and width. Vowels like /i/ and /e/ have the regions with higher peaks and vowels /a/, /o/ and /u/ have wider peaks. Figure 5 shows different statistics of peaks. We can understand that the vowel regions have comparatively more wider peaks than non-vowel regions. The analysis of slope was carried in two ways:

Algorithm 1: Boundary_detection algorithm

Input:

S[n]: Speech segment of length n
k: Size of the frame

Output:

BP: Boundary points of phonetic units

1 **begin**
2   **Step 1:** Normalize S[n]
3   **Step 2:** Divide S[n] into frames with equal size k
4   **Step 3:** Let F_n be number of frames
5   **for** $i \leftarrow 0$ **to** F_n **do**
6   Step 3.1: Find peaks using Definition 1
7   Step 3.2: Find valleys using Definition 2
8   **Step 4: for** $i \leftarrow 0$ **to** F_n **do**
9   **for** $j \leftarrow 0$ **to** $Max(n_{peaks}, n_{valleys})$ **do**
10   **Step 4.1**
11             $T_{sp} \leftarrow Slope(peaks_j, peaks_{j+1})$
12   **Step 4.2**
               $T_{sv} \leftarrow Slope(valleys_j, valleys_{j+1})$
13   **Step 4.3**
               $T_{dp} \leftarrow Disparity(peaks_j, peaks_{j+1})$
14   **Step 4.4**
               $T_{dv} \leftarrow Disparity(valleys_j, valleys_{j+1})$
15         $\tau_i \leftarrow \{T_{sp_i}, T_{sv_i}, T_{dp_i}, T_{dv_i}\}$
16   **Step 5:**
17   **for** $i \leftarrow 0$ **to** F_n **do**
18   canonicalcoef$_i \leftarrow CCA(\tau_i)$
19   **Step 6:**
20   **for** $i \leftarrow 0$ **to** F_n **do**
21   coeffnew$_i \leftarrow$
            $CCA_{validate}((\tau_i, ..., \tau_{i+3}), (\tau_{i+3}, ..., \tau_{i+6}))$
22         $variance_i \leftarrow$
            $CCA_{Variance}($canonicalcoef$_i,$ coeffnew$_i)$
23   **Step 7:** BP$\leftarrow$
        $peaks(variance_{sp}) \cup peaks(variance_{sv}) \cup$
        $peaks(variance_{dp}) \cup peaks(variance_{dv})$
24   return BP

S.No.	Attribute
1	Peak
2	Peak width
3	Peak position
4	Average difference between adjacent peak values
5	Average slope between adjacent peak values
6	Valley
7	Valley width
8	Valley position
9	Average difference between adjacent valley values
10	Average slope between adjacent valley values

Table 1: Attributes used for analysis

1. Slope between adjacent peaks in the same frame

2. Slope between peaks of adjacent frames

This attribute is used for understanding structural significance at phoneme boundaries. Slope between adjacent peaks in the same frame does not have much variations. The

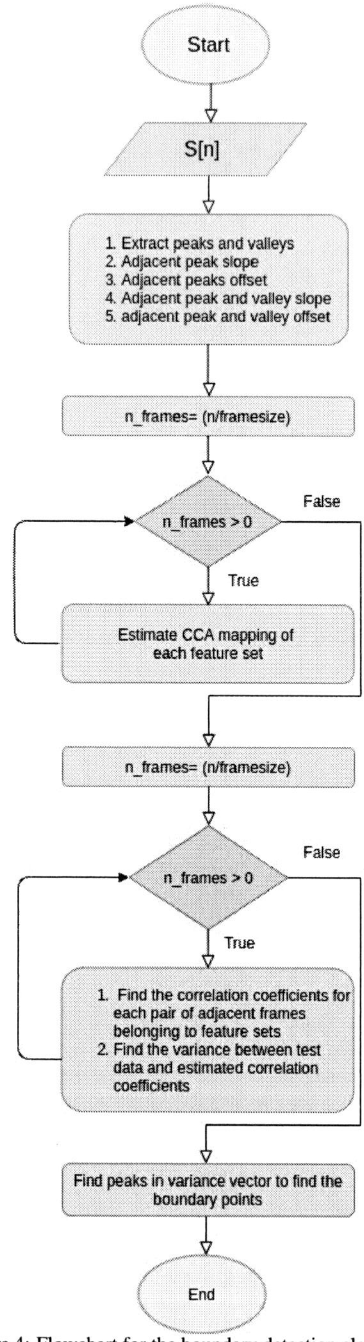

Figure 4: Flowchart for the boundary detection algorithm

difference between frames belonging to the same phonetic unit is small. But it is observed that this value is more at the phoneme boundaries. Slope between peaks of vowel regions and non-vowel regions give enough variations that helps in understanding the boundary points. Figure 6 and Figure 7 show slope and disparity between peaks of adjacent frames for the words "Zero" to "Nine". It can be observed that the changes in the wave forms are evident so that structural clues can be captured by features. There has been

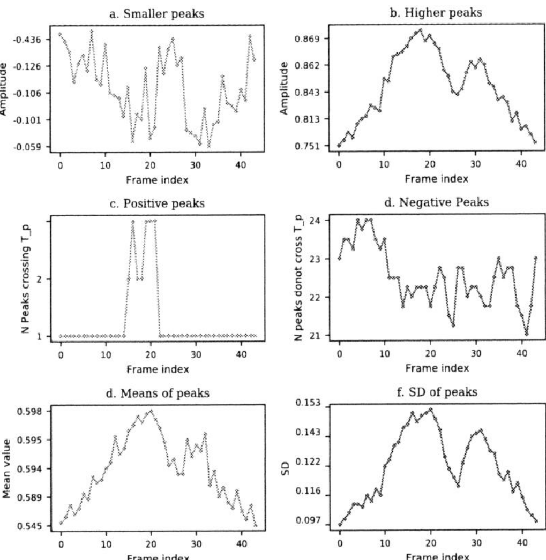

Figure 5: Peak statistics of the word "zero"

an interesting phenomena observed especially in vowel regions. There is a linear growth of the slope and disparity at the beginning of the vowel region and they start decaying at the middle part and continuing till the boundary is reached. This nature is observed both in intra-frame and inter-frame situations. There is a sudden increase in the slope value at the boundaries of different phonemes.

The average disparity between peaks within vowel region is more than non-vowel regions. Figure 7 shows the disparity between peaks for the word "Zero". We can observe that there are prominent changes at boundary frames. The distance between inter frame analysis is to understand the nature of the peak values with their neighbouring frames. This distance is more at the phoneme boundaries when compared to interior regions of phonemes. Anyhow this value is high in vowel regions similar to intra-frame difference. The difference between two frames is stable in the regions belonging to the same phoneme. Therefore it is inferred that intra-frame difference can be used to identify the syllable boundaries whereas inter frame difference is useful in identifying phoneme boundaries. Figure 12 shows distance between peaks in adjacent frames for the word "Zero". It also shows that changes can be observed clearly at boundary frames of phoneme or syllable.

6.2. Valley Attributes Analysis

The second crucial feature of waveform in the framework is valley attributes. In this class, the nature of valley was studied by understanding the properties of deeper valleys, higher valleys, positive valleys, negative valleys, etc. Figure 10 shows the statistics of these attributes. The mean and standard deviation of these properties of valleys are shown in each sub figure. These graphs suggest that there is a temporal variation across the frames in these statistics which implies that the properties are significant for phoneme boundary analysis. We can understand variations in valleys for different segments of the speech sub-units. Useful observations from the analysis are listed below:

1. Deeper valleys and shallow over valleys are found more in vowel regions than non-vowel regions.

2. Valleys in vowels are wide.

3. Standard deviation in vowel regions are comparatively higher than non-vowel regions.

These qualities mean that the structural variation can be achieved from valley features also. For example, vowels /i/ and /o/ have differences in the properties in terms of valleys. Vowel /i/ has deeper valleys compared to vowel /o/. It shows that there is more deviation between vowel and non-vowel regions. These statistics suggest that it is meaningful to use valley properties for understanding structural significance. The two properties Slope and disparity of the words "Zero" to "Nine" are shown in Figure 8 and Figure 9 respectively. We can see the structural consistency in different utterances of the same digit for a speaker.

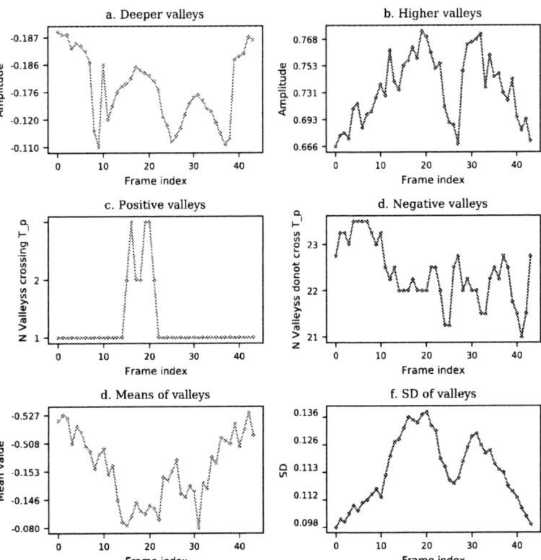

Figure 6: Valley statistics for the word "zero"

6.3. Characteristics of Method in Noisy Conditions

The method was also evaluated in the presence of noise in input signals. Here, the white noise up to 20dB SNR was considered. Figure 11 shows a source speech signal along with the CCA coefficients of each feature vector. A comparison between Figure 3 and Figure 11 helps in understanding the nature of the algorithm in noisy signals. The first point to understand is that there is a variation in structure of same feature vectors. In this example, the disparity vector differs in variance of CCA coefficients. The noise presence makes the adjacent frames belonging to two different phonetic units much higher in their variation that is reflected in the CCA coefficients. The multi-view analysis enables the method to learn necessary clues from different vectors. Therefore, the failure of capturing the boundary points in one case does not influence much in the final boundary points. So the results suggest that the proposed approach can be effective in noise conditions also.

6.4. Performance of the Algorithm

The proposed approach is successful in identifying the boundary points in 90% of the cases. The mis-identification of boundary points are influenced by speaker's characteristics in failure cases. This include accent, pauses between the phonetic units, etc. The time complexity of the approach includes two major parts including feature extraction step and CCA. Time complexities of different steps are as follows:

1. Peak and valley computation: $\mathcal{O}(n)$.

2. Finding the trajectory properties need constant time $\mathcal{O}(1)$ for each elementary operation which constitutes a linear time complexity $\mathcal{O}(n)$ for n samples.

3. Lastly, CCA algorithm requires $\mathcal{O}(n^3)$ time complexity equivalent to eigen value decomposition method (Uurtio et al., 2017).

Therefore total time complexity of the approach works out to $[\ \mathcal{O}(n) + 4 \times \mathcal{O}(n) + 2 \times \mathcal{O}(n^3)]$. The run time requirement of the method is approximately 470 milli seconds. The method was tested on a system with the following configuration:

- Processor : i5 (3.20 GHz)

- Memory : 8 GB

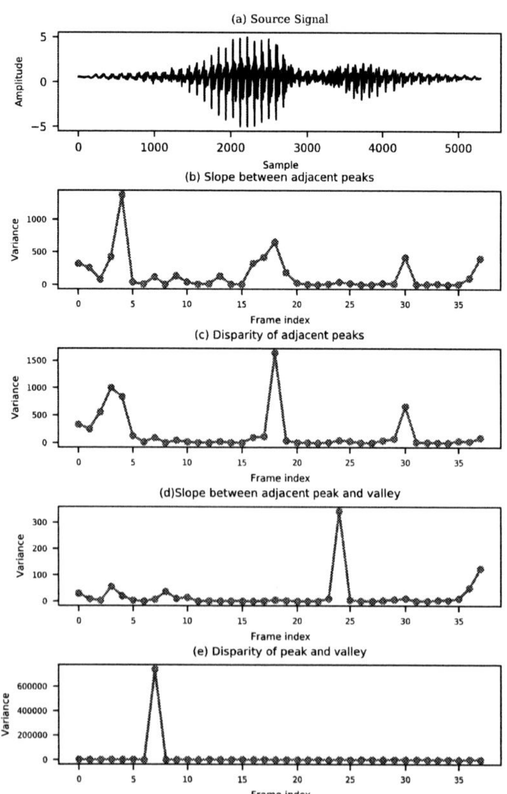

Figure 7: CCA of different features for the word "zero" (Noisy signal)

7. Conclusions and Future Work

In this paper, a phoneme segmentation approach based on multi-view geometrical features is proposed. The structural properties of speech trajectories are used to find the boundaries between phonetic units using the CCA method. The dissimilarities in geometrical features across a speech trajectory are used as parameters to identify boundary points. To prove the approach, Indian accented spoken English digits data was used in the experiments. The experiments gave reasonable results from which we can infer that the method is effective in identifying the boundary points. Since the approach does not require a training process, the requirement of large data sets are dispensed with. Also as the complexity of the method is reasonable, the run time is less and hence the method is very suitable for low or zero resource languages. The dataset is shared in [1] for the future use of the researchers. The method is being studied at the sentence level for the Hindi language that is spoken in India.

8. Bibliographical References

Ali, A. A., Van der Spiegel, J., Mueller, P., Haentjens, G., and Berman, J. (1999). An acoustic-phonetic feature-based system for automatic phoneme recognition in continuous speech. In *Circuits and Systems, 1999. ISCAS'99. Proceedings of the 1999 IEEE International Symposium on*, volume 3, pages 118–121. IEEE.

Atev, S., Miller, G., and Papanikolopoulos, N. P. (2010). Clustering of vehicle trajectories. *IEEE Transactions on Intelligent Transportation Systems*, 11(3):647–657, Sep.

Bilenko, N. Y. and Gallant, J. L. (2016). Pyrcca: regularized kernel canonical correlation analysis in python and its applications to neuroimaging. *Frontiers in neuroinformatics*, 10:49.

Borga, M. and Knutsson, H. (2001). A canonical correlation approach to blind source separation. *Report LiU-IMT-EX-0062 Department of Biomedical Engineering, Linkping University*.

de Cheveigné, A., Liberto, G. M. D., Arzounian, D., Wong, D. D., Hjortkjær, J., Fuglsang, S., and Parra, L. C. (2019). Multiway canonical correlation analysis of brain data. *NeuroImage*, 186:728 – 740.

Deng, L. and Strik, H. (2007). Structure-based and template-based automatic speech recognition - comparing parametric and non-parametric approaches. In *INTERSPEECH*.

Jeung, H., Shen, H. T., and Zhou, X. (2008). Convoy queries in spatio-temporal databases. In *2008 IEEE 24th International Conference on Data Engineering*, pages 1457–1459, April.

Kaya, H., Eyben, F., Salah, A. A., and Schuller, B. (2014). Cca based feature selection with application to continuous depression recognition from acoustic speech features. In *2014 IEEE International Conference on Acoustics, Speech and Signal Processing (ICASSP)*, pages 3729–3733. IEEE.

Li, H., Liu, J., Wu, K., Yang, Z., Liu, R. W., and Xiong, N. (2018). Spatio-temporal vessel trajectory cluster-

---

[1] IITG DIGITS: https://drive.google.com/drive/folders/1px1p2p5QRNNvFvLJT9hgkA93N7$_U$twzs

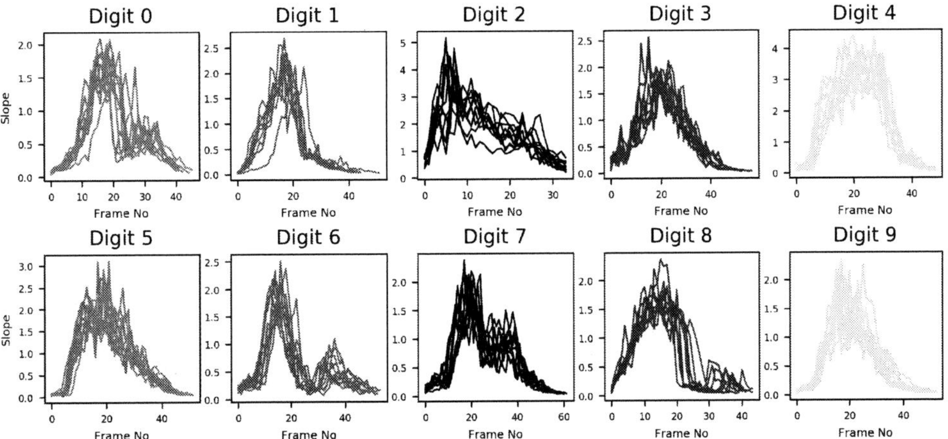

Figure 8: Slope between peaks of the words "Zero" to "Nine" for a speaker

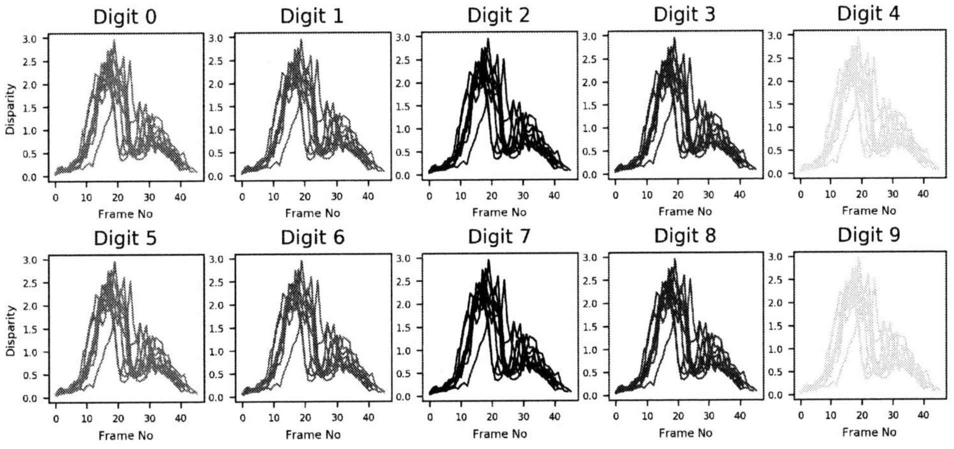

Figure 9: Disparity between peaks of the words "Zero" to "Nine" for a speaker

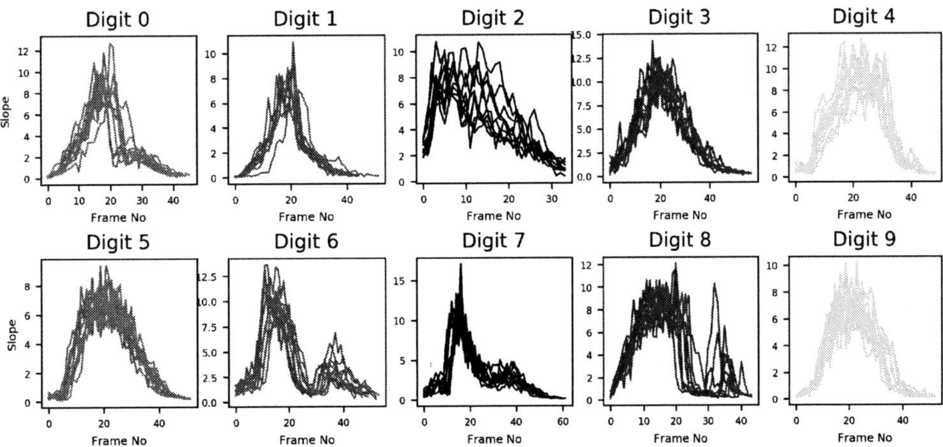

Figure 10: Slope between valleys of the words "Zero" to "Nine" for a speaker

ing based on data mapping and density. *IEEE Access*, 6:58939–58954.

Lin, Z., Zeng, Q., Duan, H., Liu, C., and Lu, F. (2019). A semantic user distance metric using gps trajectory data.

IEEE Access, 7:30185–30196.

Liu, S. and Sim, K. C. (2012). Implicit trajectory modelling using temporally varying weight regression for automatic speech recognition. In *2012 IEEE International*

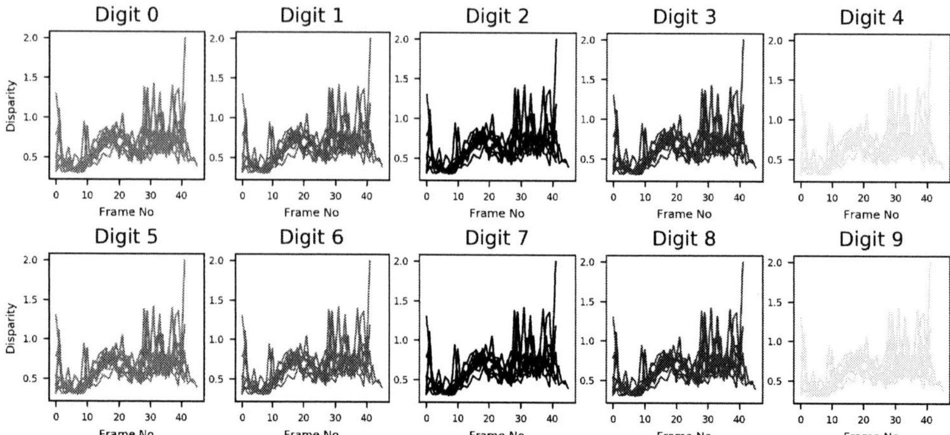

Figure 11: Disparity between valleys of the words "Zero" to "Nine" for a speaker

Conference on Acoustics, Speech and Signal Processing (ICASSP), pages 4761–4764, March.

Liu, Y., Li, Y., and Yuan, Y.-H. (2018). A complete canonical correlation analysis for multiview learning. In *2018 25th IEEE International Conference on Image Processing (ICIP)*, pages 3254–3258. IEEE.

Minematsu, N. (2005). Mathematical evidence of the acoustic universal structure in speech. In *Proceedings. (ICASSP '05). IEEE International Conference on Acoustics, Speech, and Signal Processing, 2005.*, volume 1, pages I/889–I/892 Vol. 1, March.

Mitra, V., Wang, W., Stolcke, A., Nam, H., Richey, C., Yuan, J., and Liberman, M. (2013). Articulatory trajectories for large-vocabulary speech recognition. In *2013 IEEE International Conference on Acoustics, Speech and Signal Processing*, pages 7145–7149, May.

Russell, M. J. and Holmes, W. J. (1997). Linear trajectory segmental hmms. *IEEE Signal Processing Letters*, 4(3):72–74, March.

Siohan, O. and Yifan Gong. (1996). A semi-continuous stochastic trajectory model for phoneme-based continuous speech recognition. In *1996 IEEE International Conference on Acoustics, Speech, and Signal Processing Conference Proceedings*, volume 1, pages 471–474 vol. 1, May.

Uurtio, V., Monteiro, J. M., Kandola, J., Shawe-Taylor, J., Fernandez-Reyes, D., and Rousu, J. (2017). A tutorial on canonical correlation methods. *ACM Computing Surveys (CSUR)*, 50(6):1–33.

Wang, W., Arora, R., Livescu, K., and Bilmes, J. A. (2015). Unsupervised learning of acoustic features via deep canonical correlation analysis. In *2015 IEEE International Conference on Acoustics, Speech and Signal Processing (ICASSP)*, pages 4590–4594, April.

Xiao, P., Ang, M., Jiawei, Z., and Lei, W. (2019). Approximate similarity measurements on multi-attributes trajectories data. *IEEE Access*, 7:10905–10915.

Yan, R., Zu, Y., and Zhu, Y. (2006). Automatic speech segmentation combining an hmm-based approach and recurrence trend analysis. In *Acoustics, Speech and Signal Processing, 2006. ICASSP 2006 Proceedings. 2006 IEEE International Conference on*, volume 1, pages I–I. IEEE.

Yifan Gong. (1997). Stochastic trajectory modeling and sentence searching for continuous speech recognition. *IEEE Transactions on Speech and Audio Processing*, 5(1):33–44, Jan.

Proceedings of the 1st Joint SLTU and CCURL Workshop (SLTU-CCURL 2020), pages 153–158
Language Resources and Evaluation Conference (LREC 2020), Marseille, 11–16 May 2020
© European Language Resources Association (ELRA), licensed under CC-BY-NC

Natural Language Processing Chains Inside a Cross-lingual Event-Centric Knowledge Pipeline for European Union Under-resourced Languages

Diego Alves, Gaurish Thakkar, Marko Tadić

University of Zagreb, Faculty of Humanities and Social Sciences
Ivana Lučića 3, 10000 Zagreb, Croatia
dfvalio@ffzg.hr, gthakkar@m.ffzg.hr, marko.tadic@ffzg.hr

Abstract
This article presents the strategy for developing a platform containing Language Processing Chains for European Union languages, consisting of Tokenization to Parsing, also including Named Entity recognition and with addition of Sentiment Analysis. These chains are part of the first step of an event-centric knowledge processing pipeline whose aim is to process multilingual media information about major events that can cause an impact in Europe and the rest of the world. Due to the differences in terms of availability of language resources for each language, we have built this strategy in three steps, starting with processing chains for the well-resourced languages and finishing with the development of new modules for the under-resourced ones. In order to classify all European Union official languages in terms of resources, we have analysed the size of annotated corpora as well as the existence of pre-trained models in mainstream Language Processing tools, and we have combined this information with the proposed classification published at META-NET whitepaper series.

Keywords: language processing chains, under-resourced languages, European languages resources.

1. Introduction

It is indisputable that major events such as Brexit and the recent migration crisis affect countries inside the European Union (EU) in several different ways. Due to the impact of major events inside local communities, with different languages, an enormous amount of event-centric multilingual information is available from different media sources. This diversity reflects community-specific aspects, opinions, sentiments, and bias (Annex 1 to the Grant Agreement of Cleopatra – 812997).

This multicultural data is potentially useful for a great variety of stakeholders, including digital humanities researchers, memory institutions, media monitoring companies, and journalists. However, in order to provide all the presented information in a valuable way, it must undergo first through a sequence of automatic processing: effective interlinking, verification, and analytics. The aim of CLEOPATRA[1] MSC Innovative Training Network (ITN) is to address these needs by bringing the cross-lingual event-centric information analytics technology to a higher level.

To achieve its objective, CLEOPATRA initiative focuses on three main dimensions:

- Alignment, validation, and contextualization of event-centric multilingual information across heterogeneous sources for all twenty-four EU official languages.
- Development of new interactive user access models to cross-lingual information to optimize the way to interact with the diverse data at different levels.
- Development of models that describe cross-cultural information propagation in a data-driven, application-centric manner.

The European Union (EU) has around 513 million inhabitants (Eurostat[2], 2020) and twenty-four official languages: Bulgarian, Croatian, Czech, Danish, Dutch, English, Estonian, Finnish, French, German, Greek, Hungarian, Irish, Italian, Latvian, Lithuanian, Maltese, Polish, Portuguese, Romanian, Slovak, Slovene, Spanish

and Swedish (European Union[3], 2020). One of the main challenges of CLEOPATRA ITN is the discrepancy of available data and resources between EU languages. This difference has an impact on the automatic extraction and processing of the information coming from different sources in different languages. Therefore, enhancing tools and resources for under-resourced language is in the core of this initiative activities.

The aim of this article is to present this project focusing on the main strategy behind the development of new resources for under-resourced EU languages in terms of Language Processing Chains (LPC's). The paper is organized as follows: the core CLEOPATRA Knowledge Processing Pipeline (CKPP) will be presented in section 2. In section 3, the role of NLP treatments through LPC's will be described, while the section 4 will encompass a brief analysis of the state of the art of basic tools for under-resourced EU languages. In section 5, the strategy for building enhanced LPC's will be detailed, while the Section 6 will come up with the conclusion and possible future steps

2. CLEOPATRA Knowledge Processing Pipeline (CKPP)

The Cleopatra Knowledge Processing Pipeline is composed of four steps as presented in Figure 1 and it comprises the whole event-centric analytics multilingual processing.

The first step refers to the extraction and alignment of event-related information from the varied multilingual media sources to obtain data providing enough linguistic information that will allow further analytics. It concerns the main Language Processing Chains that include tasks from tokenization to parsing and Named Entity Recognition and Classification.

Validation and contextualization of extracted data are part of the second step. For this, textual and visual information will be used to provide fact validation, relation between text and image and sentiment analysis.

---

[1] CLEOPATRA is the acronym for "Cross-lingual Event-centric Open Analytics Research Academy". Website: http://cleopatra-project.eu/

[2] https://ec.europa.eu/eurostat/home?
[3] https://europa.eu/european-union/about-eu/eu-languages_en

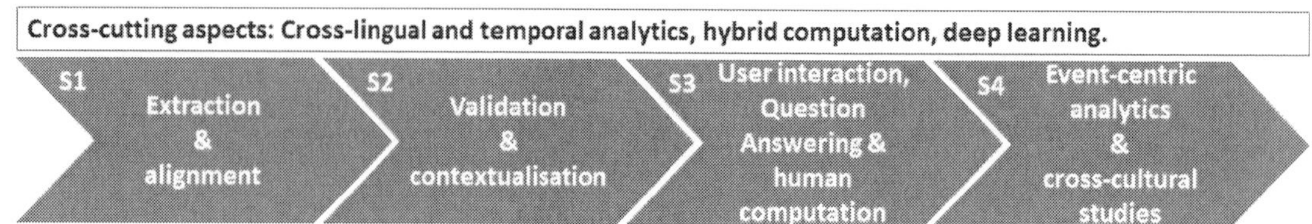

Figure 1: Steps of the Cleopatra Knowledge Processing Pipeline.

The third step involves user interaction with multilingual information to provide an efficient and intuitive search engine relying on the extracted information. Question Answering methods will also be developed to guarantee an effective cross-lingual analysis.

The aim of the fourth and final step of the CKPP is to provide examples of several analytics applications of the pipeline with respect to information propagation and bias, to conduct case studies in politics and sports topical areas, and to analyse community created data sources.

This article will focus on the Language Processing Chains inside steps one and two, which will be responsible for enriching the multilingual data with linguistic information.

3.   LPCs inside the CKPP

3.1   From Tokenisation to Parsing and Named Entity Recognition and Classification

The main NLP tasks that will be considered are: Sentence splitting, Tokenisation, Lemmatisation, Part-of-Speech and Morphosyntactic tagging, Parsing and NERC. The idea is to provide an online multilingual platform with different tools and pre-trained models that will allow to analyse raw texts from the twenty-four official languages of the European Union.

The platform will contain, for each language, enhanced LPC composed by different existing and newly modules, combining different NLP strategies and methods for different languages aligned with the BLARK (Basic LAnguage Resource Kit)/ELARK (Extended LAnguage Resource Kit) concept defined by ELRA and CLARIN (Krauwer 1998, Maegaard et al. 2005, Arppe et al. 2010). Such an example of NLP online platform is the Web-based Linguistic Chaining Tool (WebLicht) website[4] developed by the German partners in the CLARIN-ERIC, proposing different NLP pre-trained modules that can be combined to annotate texts from forty-one different world-wide languages. Our platform will differ from WebLicht as we aim to propose enhanced processing chains focusing on event-centric media data and to offer new optimized tools using deep learning for under-resourced languages.

For the tasks concerning tokenisation to parsing, in terms of reliable and homogeneous linguistic information to be used as training, development and test data, we will rely mostly on the corpora provided by the Universal Dependencies[5] framework (UD) and use the CoNLL-U format.

All twenty-four official EU languages have available corpora inside UD, however, the amount of data varies enormously between them. This will be analysed further in this article.

For the evaluation of the different LPC's in order to determine the most optimized one, we will follow the standard metrics described in the CoNLL 2018 Shared Task.

The proposed metrics concern each task of the chain individually but also include some combined metrics such as MLAS and BLEX (Straka et al., 2016).

The task of NERC does not have an equivalent framework to the Universal Dependencies one. Instead, many different tools propose different corpora and different types of classification schemes with different complexity in levels and number of predefined categories. However, to guarantee some homogeneity inside the platform to be created, in the beginning, we will base our annotations according to the guidelines of the Seventh Message Understanding Conference (MUC-7) as presented in Mikheev et al. (1997), while the proposal for Universal NER (UNER) scheme is presented in Alves et al. (in press).

3.2   Cross-lingual Sentiment Analysis

For the CKPP, we would like to associate sentiment values with the entities playing pivotal roles in the event. The aim is to process text using the various tools defined in the previous section and perform subjective analysis of the same.

We plan to run this process in two levels of granularities. The first cycle would be sentence-level sentiment analysis and second would be aspect/concept-based sentiment analysis. We assume 3-class (positive, neutral and negative) and 5 class (very-negative, negative, neutral, positive and very positive) classification schemes for sentence-based and aspect-based respectively. The former is easier to begin with and less-prone to phenomena like class-imbalance.

The main Sentiment Analysis tasks that will be considered are: Subjectivity Detection and Subjectivity Classification. For aspect-based sentiment analysis additional detection steps for Opinion Target/s (Aspects/Entities), Opinion Holders, Sentiment Phrase and its classification are foreseen.

Since not all the languages under study have uniform distribution for training data, our main focus in this study would be to employ cross-lingual knowledge transfer

---

methods that have shown good performance on some NLP tasks (Chen et al., 2018; Chidambaram et al., 2019). The creation of resources via the means of crowd-sourcing (implicit as well as explicit) (Nakov et al., 2016) is another viable option in the absence of annotated resources. The systems will be reported in terms of Accuracy, Precision-Recall, and F-Score.

4.   Under-resourced European Union Languages

As previously mentioned, one of the main challenges when proposing enhanced and robust LPC's in a multilingual platform is the different status of each language in terms of language resources.

According to the META-NET Language Whitepaper series[6] (META-NET LWS 2012), which described a state of the art of NLP development for 31 European languages, there is an enormous discrepancy between them concerning the availability of languages resources and processing tools.

In the following subsections, META-NET Classification will be presented as well as other State of the Art information that allows us to identify the languages that can be considered as under-resourced ones between the EU official languages.

4.1   META-NET White Book Series

In the META-NET White Book series (Rehm et al. 2012) a classification of 30 European languages in four different aspects of the development of the respective language technologies was proposed:

- Machine Translation.
- Speech Processing.
- Text Analysis (tools).
- Speech and text resources (data).

For each aspect languages were sorted into five different levels:

- Excellent.
- Good.
- Moderate.
- Fragmentary.
- Weak / No Support.

For CLEOPATRA ITN, the most relevant META-NET categories are "Text Analysis" and "Speech and Text resources". Therefore, considering as under-resourced the languages that are classified as "Fragmentary" or "Weak / No Support" in at least one of these two aspects, the under-resourced EU languages are: Bulgarian, Croatian, Czech, Danish, Estonian, Finnish, Greek, Hungarian, Irish, Latvian, Lithuanian, Maltese, Polish, Portuguese, Romanian, Slovak, Slovenian, Swedish. Eighteen out of twenty-four EU languages.

It is important to mention, however, that this whitepaper series has been published in 2012 and since then some progress has been made in most of these languages. Therefore, an additional contribution of this work will also be an update of META-NET white-papers series information for the selected languages.

Additionally, these two levels actually encompass a wider range of development of language technologies since both, Czech and Maltese appear there although their developments are quite distinct.

4.2   Universal Dependencies Corpora

As Universal Dependencies Corpora will be used as a reference for our project, it is also crucial to analyse the languages in terms of the quantity and size of UD corpora. The following table presents a list of all EU languages and the size of the available data in number of tokens.

Language	Size (Number of tokens)
Irish	40,572
Hungarian	42,032
Maltese	44,162
Greek	61,773
Lithuanian	75,403
Danish	100,733
Slovak	106,043
Bulgarian	156,149
Slovenian	170,158
Croatian	199,409
Swedish	206,903
Latvian	220,536
Dutch	306,764
Finnish	377,334
Estonian	465,055
Polish	496,682
Portuguese	530,327
Romanian	551,932
English	620,511
Italian	759,457
Spanish	993,848
French	1,124,269
Czech	2,217,119
German	3,748,466

Table 1: EU Languages and the size of their available UD Corpora (version 2.5)[7].

It is possible to notice that while some languages such as German, Czech and French have more than one million tokens corpora, some under-resourced ones have less than fifty thousand tokens datasets. It is the case for Maltese, Hungarian and Irish.

Considering as under-resourced languages the ones with less than five hundred thousand tokens corpora, sixteen can be classified as such: Irish, Hungarian, Maltese, Greek, Lithuanian, Danish, Slovak, Bulgarian, Slovenian, Croatian, Swedish, Latvian, Dutch, Estonian, Finnish, Polish.

---

[6] http://www.meta-net.eu/whitepapers/overview

[7] https://universaldependencies.org/

In comparison with META-NET information, Portuguese and Romanian are classified differently as they have considerable UD corpora.

An important point to consider when using UD datasets is that while the framework proposes stable and homogeneous guidelines, still, it is possible to identify some heterogeneity comparing different UD corpora of the same language: different number of tags used especially for morphological features but also for part-of-speech and dependency relations and different tokenisation strategies for treating contracted words.

4.3 Mainstream NLP tools

For this article, a tool is considered mainstream if it proposes pre-trained models for numerous EU languages concerning multiple NLP tasks (mainly from raw text to dependency parsing).

The selected tools that were tested are: Stanford NLP (Manning et al. 2014), UDPipe (Straka et al. 2016), NLP-Cube (Boros et al. 2018), Freeling (Padró & Staniloysky 2012), OpenNLP and spaCy[8].

Only UDPipe have pre-trained models for all EU languages. StandfordNLP and NLP-Cube do not propose downloadable models for Lithuanian or Maltese. The other tools are more limited in terms of multilingual coverage.

Considering the listed tools and their published results and concerning the evaluation metrics of their available models, it is possible to observe that the official results tend to be quite favorable in most of the cases for tasks before parsing. UAS and LAS metrics show more disparity and, thus, will be used here as a criterion for identifying under-resourced languages. If we consider as well-resourced languages the ones with at least one case where UAS is upper than 90, then, we have the following list of nine under-resourced EU languages: Danish, Estonian, Hungarian, Irish, Latvian, Lithuanian, Maltese, Slovak and Swedish.

Comparing UAS values with UD data size information, it is possible to observe that in almost all cases of language with corpora size below one hundred and fifty thousand tokens, UAS values are lower than 90. The only exception being Greek (low size dataset but UAS higher than 90) and Estonian (higher corpora size but low UAS).

All these criteria used to identify EU under-resourced languages were relevant to define the campaign strategy that will be used to build the LPC's and which will be presented in section 5.

4.4 Sentiment Analysis

Unlike the other tasks defined in the LPC's, there exist no open-source tools that handle multilingual sentiment analysis for under-resourced languages. The very essential resources required for performing sentiment analysis are sentiment lexicons, which are composed of words and/or multi-word expressions tagged with sentiment scores. Sentiment lexicon alone cannot achieve state of the art as the presence or the absence of intensifier, negations and sarcasm phenomenon can completely modify the expressed sentiment. Hence this type of resource is necessary but not sufficient. However, there have been various attempts in using Machine Translation (MT) as the core tool in generating or aiding the sentiment analysis process. Nevertheless, these MT systems are also prone to inducing translation errors and semantic shift in the translated text. The data (in-domain and out-domain) used for cross-lingual knowledge transfer play a major role in the final performance due to the inherent divergence present (Demirtas et al. 2013). Hence it would be interesting to study the cross-domain, cross-lingual setup for solving the task of sentiment analysis using the LPCs.

5. Campaign Strategy

The strategy that will be adopted can be divided in three parts that will be described in the following subsection. First, the idea is to start by developing LPCs for well-resourced languages, secondly, add gradually new processing chains for languages with lesser available data, and, finally, work on the development of modules for most under-resourced languages and integrate them in the platform.

5.1 NLP for Well-resourced Languages

In the first phase of the development of the online LPC platform, the focus will be on languages considered well-resourced ones. Taking into consideration the information presented in the previous section, these languages rich in resources and tools are: Dutch, English, French, German, Italian, Spanish.

Considering the existing tools and datasets, the objective is to analyse how all available resources, with different algorithms and methods, can be combined to optimise the processing of event-centric information.

By focusing on existing tools and models trained with sufficient data, our aim is to understand how well different methods work for different tasks and to identify possible synergies between them.

During this phase, the first processing chains will be shared with future CLEOPATRA users so that the possible enhancements concerning formats and interface will be identified.

5.2 Deployment to other Languages

In the second step, the idea is to use all the knowledge acquired during the first phase and apply it wisely in the development of LPC's for languages with less resources than the ones listed in the previous section but which are not considered as the most under-resourced ones: Bulgarian, Croatian, Czech, Finnish, Greek, Polish, Portuguese, Romanian and Slovenian.

Existing tools and data will be used and combined in order to achieve the best possible metrics throughout the whole processing chain.

5.3 Development of New Modules for Under-resourced Languages

During the last phase, besides testing existing tools, new models based on different deep learning techniques will be developed to all remaining languages, the ones conditionally considered as the most under-resourced ones

---

[8] https://spacy.io/

in the EU: Danish, Estonian, Hungarian, Irish, Latvian, Lithuanian, Maltese, Slovak and Swedish. The results obtained in this step will allow us to compare all techniques and decide which methodology will prevail, not just for particular module design, but for the whole LPCs.

All the results obtained will also allow for a deeper understanding of how different deep learning or statistical approaches deal with specific linguistic phenomena of the listed languages.

6. Conclusions and Future Directions

The development of robust and effective multilingual Language Processing Chains is crucial for achieving the main objective of CLEOPATRA ITN as text processing is inside the first step of its Knowledge Processing Pipeline. However, due to the difference in available resources of twenty-four official EU languages, an effective strategy must be put in place. Although there is no exact and unique way of classifying a language as under-resourced, we have proposed the division of EU languages into three different clusters, from languages having a good number of resources and tools to languages that could be called the most under-resourced ones in the EU.

This classification is important in our strategy for the development of LPC's as our idea is to start working with very well-resourced languages in the first step, following by the ones with less amount of language resources and finally, in a final phase, take advantage of all the learnings collected in the previous steps together with testing different machine learning methods to create the optimal LPC's for the languages with the lowest number and size of available resources.

Although this work is, primarily, focused on official European Union languages, the main findings could possibly be applied, in further steps, to other under-resources languages in Europe and worldwide.

7. Acknowledgements

The work presented in this paper has received funding from the European Union's Horizon 2020 research and innovation program under the Marie Kłodowska-Curie grant agreement no. 812997 and under the name CLEOPATRA (Cross-lingual Event-centric Open Analytics Research Academy).

8. Bibliographical References

Alves, D., Kuculo, T., Amaral, G., Thakkar, G., Tadić, M. (in press) UNER: Universal Named-Entity Recognition Framework, In Proceedings of the 1st international workshop on cross-lingual, event-centric open analytics, European Semantic Web Conference (ESWC2020).

Arppe, A., Beck, K., Branco, A., Camilleri, V., Caselli, T., Cristea, D., Hinrichs, E., Liin, K., Nissinen, M., Parra, C., Rosner, M. Schuurman, I., Skadina, I., Quochi, V., van Uytvanck, D., Vogel, I., "Description of the BLARK, the Situation of Individual Languages", *CLARIN deliverable D5C-4*, [https://office.clarin.eu/pp/D5C-4.pdf, accessed 2020-02-13].

Chen, X., Sun, Y., Athiwaratkun, B., Cardie, C., Weinberger, K. "Adversarial deep averaging networks for cross-lingual sentiment classification." *Transactions of the Association for Computational Linguistics 6*, p. 557-570, 2018.

Chidambaram, M., Yang, Y., Cer, D., Yuan, S., Sung, Y., Strope, B., & Kurzweil, R. (2019, August). Learning Cross-Lingual Sentence Representations via a Multi-task Dual-Encoder Model. In Proceedings of the 4th Workshop on Representation Learning for NLP (RepL4NLP-2019) (pp. 250-259).

Chinchor, A. "Overview of MUC-7". Proceedings of the Seventh Message Understanding Conference (MUC-7). 1998.

Demirtas, Erkin, and Mykola Pechenizkiy. "Cross-lingual polarity detection with machine translation." In *Proceedings of the Second International Workshop on Issues of Sentiment Discovery and Opinion Mining*, pp. 1-8. 2013.

European Union. Retrieved from: https://europa.eu/european-union/about-eu/eu-languages_en. Last visited on 13/02/2020.

Eurostat - Your key to European Statistics. Retrieved from: https://ec.europa.eu/eurostat/web/products-press-releases/-/3-10072019-BP. Last visited on 13/02/2020.

Krauwer S., "ELSNET and ELRA: A Common Past and a Common Future". *ELRA Newsletter*, vol. 3, n. 2, 1998.

Maegaard, B., Choukri, K., Calzolari, N., Odijk, J., "ELRA – European Language Resources Association-Background, Recent Developments and Future Perspectives", *Language Resources and Evaluation*, v. 39, p. 9-23, 2005.

Manning, C. D., Surdeanu, M., Bauer, J., Finkel, J., Bethard, S. J., McClosky, D., "The Stanford CoreNLP Natural Language Processing Toolkit", *Proceedings of the 52nd Annual Meeting of the Association for Computational Linguistics: System Demonstrations*, p. 55-60, 2014.

METANET Language Whitepaper series. (2012) Retrieved from: http://www.meta-net.eu/whitepapers/overview. Last visited on 10/02/2020.

Padró, L., Stanilovsky, E., "FreeLing 3.0: Towards Wider Multilinguality", *Proceedings of the Language Resources and Evaluation Conference (LREC 2012) ELRA*, 2012.

Speecon Consortium. Dutch Speecon Database. Speecon Project, distributed via ELRA, Speecon resources, 1.0, 2014.

Straka, M., Hajič, J., Straková, J., "UDPipe: Trainable Pipeline for Processing CoNLL-U Files Performing Tokenization, Morphological Analysis, POS Tagging and Parsing", *Proceedings of the Tenth International Conference on Language Resources and Evaluation (LREC 2016)*, Slovenia, 2016.

Zeman, D., Hajič, J., Popel, M., Potthtyersast, M., Straka, M., Ginter, F., Nivre, J., and Petrov, S. "Conll 2018 shared task: Multilingual parsing from raw text to universal dependencies". *Proceedings of the CoNLL 2018 Shared Task: Multilingual Parsing from Raw Text to Universal Dependencies*. Association for Computational Linguistics, pp. 1–21, 2018.

Nakov, Preslav, Alan Ritter, Sara Rosenthal, Fabrizio Sebastiani, and Veselin Stoyanov. "SemEval-2016 Task 4: Sentiment Analysis in Twitter." In Proceedings of the 10th International Workshop on Semantic Evaluation (SemEval-2016), pp. 1-18. 2016

9. Language Resource References

Speecon Consortium. Dutch Speecon Database. Speecon Project, distributed via ELRA, Speecon resources, 1.0, 2014.

Universal Dependencies. Retrieved from: https://universaldependencies.org/. Last visited on 24/09/2019.

WebLicht. Retrieved from: https://weblicht.sfs.uni-tuebingen.de/weblichtwiki/index.php/Main_Page .

Proceedings of the 1st Joint SLTU and CCURL Workshop (SLTU-CCURL 2020), pages 159–166
Language Resources and Evaluation Conference (LREC 2020), Marseille, 11–16 May 2020
© European Language Resources Association (ELRA), licensed under CC-BY-NC

Component Analysis of Adjectives in Luxembourgish for Detecting Sentiments

Joshgun Sirajzade[1], Daniela Gierschek[2], Christoph Schommer[1]
[1]MINE Lab, Computer Science, Université du Luxembourg
[2]Institute of Luxembourgish Linguistics and Literatures, Université du Luxembourg
{joshgun.sirajzade, daniela.gierschek, christoph.schommer}@uni.lu

Abstract

The aim of this paper is to investigate the role of Luxembourgish adjectives in expressing sentiments in user comments written at the web presence of rtl.lu (RTL is the abbreviation for Radio Television Lëtzebuerg). Alongside many textual features or representations, adjectives could be used in order to detect sentiment, even on a sentence or comment level. In fact, they are also by themselves one of the best ways to describe a sentiment, despite the fact that other word classes such as nouns, verbs, adverbs or conjunctions can also be utilized for this purpose. The empirical part of this study focuses on a list of adjectives which were extracted from an annotated corpus. The corpus contains the part of speech tags of individual words and sentiment annotation on the adjective, sentence and comment level. Suffixes of Luxembourgish adjectives like *-esch*, *-eg*, *-lech*, *-al*, *-el*, *-iv*, *-ent*, *-los*, *-bar* and the prefix *on-* were explicitly investigated, especially by paying attention to their role in regards to building a model by applying classical machine learning techniques. We also considered the interaction of adjectives with other grammatical means, especially other part of speeches, e.g. negations, which can completely reverse the meaning, thus the sentiment of an utterance.

Keywords: Opinion Mining / Sentiment Analisys, Corpus (Creation, Annotaton, etc.), Grammar and Syntax

1. Introduction

Detecting the sentiment of an utterance has been dealt with in numerous publications and using different machine learning techniques. A lot of the tools were built for languages with a large number of speakers such as English, French and German. For smaller languages like Luxembourgish, well-trained and established tools are still rather scarce. We utilize a large Luxembourgish corpus and extract a subset that we annotated for sentiment on comment, sentence and adjective level. The aim of the paper is to leverage this data source in order to explore feature combinations other than semantic similarity representations for detecting sentiment, primarily by analyzing adjectives and their components. As Luxembourgish is a low-resource language, no resources for sentiment detection have been built so far. Intuitively, adjectives carry a high amount of sentiment. Examining them and their components in our data subset could therefore provide important insights into how much they could potentially help to improve our system's performance. This paper first gives an overview over existing resources and research in sentiment analysis and over the Luxembourgish language. We then portray our annotation process and dig deeper into our corpus to look at the adjectives and their suffixes that we subsequently use for our experiments. To conclude, we discuss future work that could further help research on the importance of adjectives for sentiment analysis.

1.1. Research and Resources in Sentiment Analysis

Sentiment analysis has been seen for a long time as a pure text classification problem (Pang et al., 2002) whereas recent research in the area has brought light to many details and other forms of it. Placing it as a part of mining of opinions and emotions, it was shown that sentiment analysis can have different levels, e.g. sentence level vs. aspect based sentiment analysis (Liu, 2015). While classification, espe-

cially deep classification, still gives the best results, there are attempts to customize the text classification problem to the needs of sentiment analysis, e.g. by creating sentiment specific word embeddings (Tang et al., 2014). Word embeddings, alongside other bag of words techniques for text representation like Latent Semantic Analysis utilize the so called distributional similarity, in other words they calculate the semantic similarity of words based on their distribution in text data (Levy et al., 2015). This approach touches the semantics from a linguistic point of view, yet the usage of other levels of language are still to be investigated. Other methods for detecting sentiment include lexical approaches that use manually or automatically constructed dictionaries containing positive and negative words and sometimes even more granular description of sentiment, e.g. the strength of the polarity. Those dictionaries are then used to calculate the overall sentiment of the unseen data (Taboada, 2016). An example for a lexical resource is SentiWordNet (Esuli and Sebastiani, 2006) which was built for English and assigns either positive, negative or objective to synsets[1] of WordNet. For Luxembourgish, no resource of this kind exists yet which brings special difficulties to be tackled for implementing such an approach for this language.

Despite a large number of publications dealing with sentiment analysis and its different aspects, challenges that need to be solved still remain. Attempts have been made to use automatically translated data (Balahur and Turchi, 2012) or to (semi-)automatically create a sentiment corpus querying Twitter data for certain emojis (Pak and Paroubek, 2010). Very often however, sentiment detection systems are based on the manual labeling task of one or more annotators. Those annotators need to be recruited, trained and provided with adequate guidelines which makes this part of the

---

[1]Synsets are unordered sets of synonym words that denote the same concept and are interchangeable in many contexts, see https://wordnet.princeton.edu.

system construction time and resource intensive. Creating labels for sentiment very much depends on the guidelines given, as it is not as simple as just giving a positive, negative or neutral score to an entity and not always easy for an annotator to stay consistent in his/her annotation. Therefore, clear and simple instructions are crucial for ensuring the best annotation possible (Mohammad, 2016). One big challenge is that words can have very different meanings depending on their context (Mohammad, 2016). If we look at the adjective *stolz* [proud] for example, it conveys a very different sense in those two contexts: *Ech sinn stolz drop.* [I am proud of that.] vs. *Do bass du stolz drop???* [You are proud of that???]. These two different meanings would probably be impossible to catch in a lexical approach where an annotator would annotate *stolz* isolated from its context. Also, a sentiment can be directed towards the reader, the speaker or the writer of an utterance (Mohammad, 2016). It therefore has to be clearly stated in the annotation guidelines how the annotation is supposed to be undertaken. In this paper, we focus on the role of adjectives in sentiment analysis as they carry a lot of the subjective aspects of a text (Taboada, 2016) and thus bear a high sentiment content. More precisely, we focus not only on adjectives but especially on some specific suffixes and one prefix of adjectives in Luxembourgish and how those might have an impact on detecting the sentiment of sentences.

1.2. Luxembourgish Language

Luxembourgish is mainly spoken in the Grand Duchy of Luxembourg, a multilingual country with roughly 590,000 inhabitants (Gilles, in press). Despite Luxembourg having three official languages, i.e. French, German and Luxembourgish, only the latter was recognized as the unique national language of the country in 1984 and has become an important symbol for national identity (Gilles, in press) since. It developed out of a Central Franconian dialect and is thus related to German. However, Luxembourgish today is perceived as an independent language by the speech community (Gilles, 2015). The language plays an important role in spoken and written conversation. If all participants of a discussion are capable of using this language, Luxembourgish can be used in any formal or informal situation and code-switching to another language would be unimaginable (Gilles, in press). The importance of fostering the Luxembourgish language can be seen in several projects across the country. One prominent example is the *Schnëssen* app which was developed at the Institute of Luxembourgish Linguistics and Literatures to preserve the current varieties and ways of speaking Luxembourgish. Crowdsourcing techniques are leveraged for recording as many spoken examples of Luxembourgish as possible. Those are then used to portray the speakers' variation on different linguistic levels (Entringer et al., 2018).

On an NLP level, the LuNa Open Toolbox (Sirajzade and Schommer, 2019) was implemented as a rule-based part-of-speech tagger and tokenizer especially designed for dealing with Luxembourgish texts and their linguistic characteristics. LuNa is essential for working with Luxembourgish texts as it is the only tool so far that was built for processing and dealing with the special challenges related to this low-ressource language. Texts in digital media, such as user comments that we will investigate in this paper or text messages, are almost exclusively produced in Luxembourgish. This is remarkable, as the educational system mainly focuses on German and French and not that much on the orthographic rules of Luxembourgish (Gilles, 2015). Not focusing on Luxembourgish spelling in school results in high orthographic variation in texts such as our corpus data. Variation in spelling is a great challenge for our project. A lot of written data in Luxembourgish exists, but a big part of it is not spelled according to the official spelling rules. Using a lexical approach for Luxembourgish sentiment analysis would therefore be very labor-intensive because no tool that captures every kind of possible variation of Luxembourgish spelling has been built yet.

2. Annotation of the Data Source

For our project, we have obtained the database of rtl.lu (Radio Télévision Lëtzebuerg), a popular news website that mostly publishes in Luxembourgish (RTL Luxembourg, 2019). It consists of over 180,000 news articles from 1999 to 2018 and over 500,000 user comments from 2008 to 2018. More precisely, our corpus comprises more than 30 million running tokens for the news articles part and over 35 million running tokens for the comments part.

2.1. Corpus Creation

In a first step, we tokenized our whole corpus (Sirajzade and Schommer, 2019) and also undertook part-of-speech tagging and sentence splitting. We then used part of our database and asked one annotator to annotate this subcorpus on document (comment), sentence and word (adjective) level. The guideline was to annotate from the perspective of the author (Abdul-Mageed and Diab, 2011) and to use the labels *positive, negative* and *neutral*. Comments were randomly chosen to ensure that the training corpus would not just consist of sentiments towards a single topic. The sentences and adjectives in those comments were then also tagged with their sentiment value. Our data is stored in *XML*. During the annotation process, two new tags were introduced: *<comment>* and *<sentence>*. The annotator also included an attribute *value* into those two new tags and for the adjectives. Furthermore, she provided the attribute with its respective sentiment value, i. e. *positive, negative* or *neutral*. Figure 1 shows an example of an annotated user comment in our corpus in *XML*. Considering that we only had one annotator, no inter-annotator agreement was calculated. The dataset we used for our analysis is discussed in more detail in the following section.

2.2. Subcorpus

The annotated subcorpus that we use for our investigation in this paper is composed of 431 comments, 2050 sentences and 1339 adjectives. 132 comments were marked as positive, 208 as negative and 91 as neutral. On sentence level, the annotator perceived 499 as positive, 833 as negative and 718 as neutral. 574 adjectives of the ones annotated were tagged with a positive, 327 with a negative and 438 with a neutral value. Our special focus for this analysis lies on the annotated adjectives that we extracted from the

```xml
<comment value ="positive">
...
  <sentence value = "neutral">
    <w id="36" pos="P">Hien</w>
    <w id="37" pos="AUX">huet</w>
    <w id="38" pos="AV">do</w>
    <w id="39" pos="D">e</w>
    <w id="40" pos="N">grouse</w>
    <w id="41" pos="ADJ" value="neutral">perséinleche</w>
    <w id="42" pos="N">Konflikt</w>
    <c id="43" pos="$">,</c>
    <w id="44" pos="APPR">op</w>
    <w id="45" pos="P">hien</w>
    <w id="46" pos="D">sengem</w>
    <w id="47" pos="N">Gewëssen</w>
    <w id="48" pos="KO">oder</w>
    <w id="49" pos="D">senger</w>
    <w id="50" pos="N">Flicht</w>
    <w id="51" pos="KO">als</w>
    <w id="52" pos="N">Staatschef</w>
    <w id="53" pos="V">follegt</w>
    <c id="54" pos="$">.</c>
  </sentence>
</comment>
```

Figure 1: Example of an annotated user comment from the RTL corpus in *XML*

corpus for further fine-grained analysis. Using 1339 adjectives is likely too small to draw conclusions for all adjectives present in the Luxembourgish language. However, we expect to gain a first intuition concerning the impact of leveraging adjectives as features. Figure 1 shows an example of the extracted data from our corpus, which later serve as data instances for our machine learning experiments. It is important to note that the adjectives were annotated in their context and therefore do not always carry the same sentiment for all times they were annotated. For instance, *typesch* [typical] (see figure 2) was annotated three times whereas it was negative in two and positive in one case.

3. Distribution of Grammatical Properties

As a first step of setting up our experiment, we looked at the adjectives and counted all suffixes and prefixes that were annotated in our data. We then also investigated the occurrence of negation in the corpus. This information is essential for getting a better understanding of our data for the experiments we undertook.

3.1. The Distribution of Adjectives in Sentiments

Even though certain adjectives can utter different sentiments depending on the pragmatic or syntactic context, it can be observed that several adjectives have a tendency towards a certain sentiment. Tables 2 and 3 show the ten most frequent adjectives once by their own sentiment and once by the sentiment of the sentences they were used in. The ambiguity of adjectives in expressing the sentiment of the sentences becomes especially clear in the words *richteg*

Luxembourgish	English	Sentiment	Sentence Sentiment	Comment Sentence
sarkastesch	sarcastic	negative	negative	neutral
chinesesch	Chinese	neutral	neutral	neutral
europäesch	European	neutral	neutral	neutral
historesch	historical	neutral	negative	neutral
praktesch	practical	positive	negative	positive
komesch	strange	negative	negative	neutral
demokratesch	democratic	positive	negative	positive
pornografesch	pornographic	negative	neutral	neutral
gigantesch	gigantic	negative	negative	negative
typesch	typical	negative	positive	negative

Figure 2: Luxembourgish adjectives with the suffix *-esch* and their sentiments & sentiments of the respective sentence and comment

[right], *besser* [better] and *einfach* [simple]. They occur almost the same amount of time in both the positive and the negative categories. This phenomenon stretches, as mentioned before, from the pragmatic level, where the sentiment of the adjective in itself can be ambiguous depending on the intention of the author (which can be for example sarcastic) up to the syntactic structure of the utterance through combination with negation, which can instantly change the sentiment. The next step is to investigate the internal structure of the adjectives – their suffixes and prefixes and to look if using them as features can lead to some important generalization.

3.2. Suffixes and Prefixes

For this paper, we extracted some of the most important suffixes and one prefix of the adjectives in our corpus in order to study their importance for sentiment detection. More precisely, we used the suffixes *-esch*, *-eg*, *-lech*, *-al*, *-ent*, *-el*, *-iv*, *-los*, *-bar* and the prefix *on-* for this analysis. We chose those five suffixes and one prefix, because they are prominent for word formation processes in Luxembourgish language (Sirajzade, 2018). However, we need to keep in mind that word formation elements are generally not that frequently distributed and out of the 1339 adjectives in our corpus only 289 have one of these elements (see table 4). We will use those adjectives for our analysis. Besides looking at them individually, we also noticed what the sentiment of the sentence and comment they were found in was. In table 5 the relationship between the suffix of a particular adjective and the sentiment of the sentence are shown. The suffix *-esch* is mostly present in neutral adjectives such as *komesch* [funny], but builds rather negative sentences and comments. More positive adjectives are assembled using the suffix *-eg*, like for example in *spaasseg* [amusing]. As stated in section 3.3., those adjectives usually occur in negative sentences and comments which can be seen as a strong indication of the importance of negation in those contexts. The suffix *-lech*, like in *ënnerschiddlech* [different], mostly appears in neutral adjectives whereas sentences or comments are often positive or negative. *-bar* is a suffix which seems to have a strong tendency towards positivity. Adjectives like *tragbar* [portable] were mostly annotated as positive or neutral and so were sentences and comments that were almost exclusively perceived as positive. The last suffix we examined, *-los* like in *skrupellos* [unscrupulous], has a tendency towards negativity. We only found very few positive sentences or comments that included an adjective with this suffix. Most adjectives, sentences and comments were annotated as negative. The prefix *on-* that we examined is mostly used for negative adjectives such as *onfair* [unfair] and also negative sentences and comments. This is not surprising however as *un-* in itself reverses the meaning of an adjective to some extend (see section 3.3.).

3.3. Negation

There is only little evidence of negation in our small subcorpus that we have created for this experiment. Out of the 1339 sentences which contain adjectives, only 337 appear in the context of some sort of negation. We considered the negation particle *net*[not] and indefinite pronoun *kee(n)*[no]

	Adjective	Suffix	Negation	Adjective's Sentiment	Sentence's Sentiment
1	richteg [right]	-eg	/	positive	positive
2	flexibel [flexible]	-el	/	positive	neutral
3	héich [high]	/	net	positive	negative
4	illegal [illegal]	-al	/	negative	negative
5	diktatoresch [dictatorial]	-esch	net	negative	negative
6	eenzel [single]	-el	net	neutral	negative
7	domm [stupid]	/	net	negative	negative
8	perséinlech [personal]	-lech	/	neutral	negative
9	anonym [anonymous]	/	/	neutral	positive
10	éierlech [honest]	-lech	/	positive	positive

Table 1: The features adjective, its suffix, its sentiment and the sentiment of the sentence it is used in in the experiments

positive	Frequency	negative	Frequency	neutral	Frequency
besser [better]	23	schlecht [bad]	18	laang [long]	23
gudd [good]	23	falsch [wrong]	12	perséinlech [personal]	7
richteg [right]	21	deier [expensive]	9	kleng [small]	6
einfach [easy]	15	lues [slow]	7	grouss [big]	5
gutt [good]	13	traureg [sad]	7	groussen [big]	5
wichteg [important]	12	laang [long]	6	lang [long]	5
grouss [big]	9	blöd [stupid]	5	krank [sick]	4
kloer [clear]	8	domm [stupid]	5	normal [normal]	4
genau [exact]	7	egal [same]	4	nächst [next]	4
gudden [good]	7	komesch [strange]	4	nächsten [next]	4

Table 2: The 10 most frequent positive, negative and neutral adjectives

in our analysis. Nevertheless, we could make two interesting observations that should be examined further in future experiments. First of all, adjectives with the suffix *-eg* like in *wichteg* [important] were mostly annotated as positive, but very often occur in negative sentences. Negation thus seems to play an important role for expressing negativity in combination with an adjective that carries the suffix *-eg*. Adjectives with the prefix *on-* like in *onwichteg* [unimportant] were mostly annotated as negative and did not occur with negation in a sentence. This is interesting as *on-* already carries negativity and can reverse the sentiment of an adjective to negative. For instance, ommitting the prefix *on-* from the adjective "onwichteg" [unimportant] would result in the positive adjective "wichteg" [important]. It is therefore not surprising that we did not find any kind of double negation in sentences with *on-* adjectives.

4. Experiment

After having looked into our data, we explore different supervised machine learning settings using a combination of different features. The goal of the experiments will be to examine the role of adjectives and their suffixes in the overall sentiment of a sentence it appears in.

4.1. Setup of the Experiment

We build different kinds of scenarios in order to investigate the role of adjectives in the building of the sentiment of a sentence. We have a total of four features and one label, which we combine in different ways. The features (more precisely feature groups) are the adjective (ADJ), its suffix

(SUFF), negation in the sentence (NEG), and the adjective's sentiment (ADJ-SEN). The label is the sentiment of the sentence in which it is used (SENT-SEN). We decided not to include prefixes as a feature, as we only found one, i.e. *on-*, in our data and do not consider this sufficient for representing Luxembourgish prefixes in general. This structure is shown with the first ten instances of the data in table 1. We created one-hot vectors from ADJs, SUFFs and NEGs, so each adjective, suffix or negation particle is a feature in itself. Note that we did not use the TF-IDF vectorizer (except for comparison purposes in the eleventh scenario) or any other similar technique for this particular experiment, because the setup assumes that only certain part of speeches e.g. the adjectives and negation within the sentences are known. Because of the fact that a sentence in our dataset contains in average one and only seldomly two or more adjectives, we do not count their occurrences. Furthermore, we assume that by just seeing one adjective, it is possible to determine the sentiment of the sentence, so every adjective is considered as its own instance. For our experiments, we used the *scikit-learn (0.21.2)* library in *Python* (Pedregosa et al., 2011) and *WEKA (3.8.2)* (Hall et al., 2009). Both environments have implementations of many commonly known machine learning algorithms which can be applied in sentiment analysis. With some differences, which was the reason why we experimented with both of them, they are very suitable for testing purposes. We used 10-fold cross validation and optimized the gamma and the c value for SVM by using the Radial Basis Function (RBF) kernel.

positive	Frequency	negative	Frequency	neutral	Frequency
gudd [good]	12	laang [long]	14	grouss [big]	7
einfach [easy]	10	schlecht [bad]	13	laang [long]	7
richteg [right]	10	richteg [right]	10	wichteg [important]	7
besser [better]	9	besser [better]	9	besser [better]	5
laang [long]	9	einfach [easy]	9	gudd [good]	5
groussen [big]	5	gudd [good]	7	lang [long]	5
gutt [good]	5	lues [slow]	7	falsch [wrong]	4
kleng [small]	5	deier [expensive]	6	groussen [big]	4
wichteg [important]	5	grouss [big]	6	gutt [good]	4
falsch [wrong]	4	spéit [late]	6	kloer [clear]	4

Table 3: The 10 most frequent positive, negative and neutral adjectives by their sentence sentiment

The results of the experiments are presented in table 6. We carried out experiments in 11 different scenarios. For each scenario we used Decision Tree (DT), Support Vector Machine (SVM) and Complement Naive Bayes (CNB) from *scikit-learn* and Bayes Net (BN) from *WEKA*. We included DT in our experiment, because our data with the adjectives has a more categorical or nominal character and it is easy to interpret. SVM has been a standard algorithm for sentiment analysis for a long time. It is very suitable and effective in a high dimensional space which we have after vectorizing our data. We experimented with CNB and BN because we additionally wanted to test a predictive model which in the case of BN can also capture Markov states throughout our features. To examine the performance of each algorithm, we then calculated the weighted average of precision, recall and F1 score. Weighted F1 score is calculated as

$$\frac{1}{\sum_{l \in L} |\hat{y}_l|} \sum_{l \in L} |\hat{y}_l| \, F(y_l, \hat{y}_l),$$

where y_l is the subset of predicted labels, $\hat{y}$ the subset of true labels and L the set of labels. Precision and recall are then calculated in the same manner as described in (scikit-learn, 2019). Table 6 uses the commonly known machine learning notation X for describing the features used for a scenario and y for the label that was to be classified. The first scenario is the simplest one; there are only one feature (group) and one label. Those are the adjective and the sentiment of the sentences in which it is used. More precisely, this scenario classifies the sentiment of a sentence only by looking at the adjective that is contained in this sentence. Note that it is not the sentiment of the adjective itself, but of the sentence in which it was used. This approach was already tried on many languages, but was never implemented for the Luxembourgish language before. The weak point of this method is the fact that despite the big role that adjectives play in the building of sentiment of the utterance, there are some other language elements which can change or reverse the sentiment of the adjective. Those are, for instance, grammatical negation or the intentional use of sarcasm. For this reason, we first look at the role of the adjective in determining the sentiment of a sentence. Then we consequently add supplementary information, beginning with the suffix, the sentiment of the adjective itself and the negation. Those scenarios are shown in rows one to five in table 6. In the third scenario, we look for example at the adjective and its own sentiment as feature. This is directly connected to the semantics of the adjective and often different than the sentiment of the sentences it is used in. As mentioned before, the sentiment of words can be easily changed by some grammatical and pragmatical means. This change of sentiment was important for the annotation process described in 2.2. In the second, fourth and fifth scenarios we use the above mentioned suffixes as an additional feature, if the respective adjective contains one. Beginning in the sixth scenario, we try to determine if suffixes of adjectives play a role in the building of sentiments

	Suffix	Frequency	positive	negative	neutral
1	-eg	117	61	33	23
2	-lech	89	37	15	37
3	-esch	61	8	20	33
4	-al	36	9	11	16
5	-el	17	8	3	6
6	-ent	14	6	6	2
7	-iv	14	11	0	3
8	-bar	6	2	1	3
9	-los	3	0	3	0
	Prefix				
1	on-	22	0	19	3

Table 4: Suffixes, prefixes and their frequency according to the sentiment of the adjective

	Suffix	Frequency	positive	negative	neutral
1	-eg	117	35	55	27
2	-lech	89	27	40	22
3	-esch	61	11	32	18
4	-al	36	14	15	7
5	-el	17	4	10	3
6	-ent	14	4	7	3
7	-iv	14	6	4	4
8	-bar	6	4	1	1
9	-los	3	1	2	0
	Prefix				
1	on-	22	0	16	6

Table 5: Suffixes, prefixes and their frequency according to the sentiment of the sentence

	Scenario	Algorithm	Precision	Recall	F1 score
1	X = ADJ y = SENT-SEN	DT	0.617	0.403	0.465
		SVM	1.0	0.421	0.592
		CNB	0.533	0.353	0.382
		BN	NaN	0.427	NaN
2	X = ADJ, SUFF y = SENT-SEN	DT	0.538	0.374	0.425
		SVM	1.0	0.421	0.592
		CNB	0.444	0.363	0.374
		BN	NaN	0.427	NaN
3	X = ADJ, ADJ-SEN y = SENT-SEN	DT	0.51	0.511	0.51
		SVM	1.0	0.421	0.592
		CNB	0.509	0.511	0.509
		BN	0.552	0.508	0.506
4	X = ADJ, SUFF, ADJ-SEN y = SENT-SEN	DT	0.501	0.5	0.5
		SVM	1.0	0.421	0.592
		CNB	0.512	0.514	0.513
		BN	0.552	0.508	0.506
5	X = ADJ, SUFF, NEG y = SENT-SEN	DT	0.671	0.41	0.484
		SVM	1.0	0.421	0.592
		CNB	0.375	0.317	0.324
		BN	NaN	0.427	NaN
6	X = SUFF y = SENT-SEN	DT	1.0	0.421	0.592
		SVM	1.0	0.421	0.592
		CNB	0.672	0.342	0.397
		BN	NaN	0.427	NaN
7	X = SUFF, NEG y = SENT-SEN	DT	0.978	0.424	0.585
		SVM	1.0	0.421	0.592
		CNB	0.49	0.317	0.348
		BN	NaN	0.427	NaN
8	X = SUFF, ADJ-SEN y = SENT-SEN	DT	0.52	0.514	0.512
		SVM	0.541	0.529	0.527
		CNB	0.541	0.529	0.527
		BN	0.552	0.508	0.506
9	X = SUFF, NEG, ADJ-SEN y = SENT-SEN	DT	0.515	0.511	0.512
		SVM	0.541	0.529	0.527
		CNB	0.532	0.522	0.519
		BN	0.552	0.508	0.506
10	X = ADJ, SUFF, NEG, ADJ-SEN y = SENT-SEN	DT	0.509	0.5	0.503
		SVM	1.0	0.421	0.592
		CNB	0.502	0.504	0.502
		BN	0.552	0.508	0.506
11	X = tf-idf vectors from sentences y = SENT-SEN	DT	0.436	0.376	0.39
		SVM	1.0	0.362	0.531
		CNB	0.631	0.388	0.445
		BN	0.371	0.397	0.301

Table 6: Different scenarios of determining the sentiment with the help of adjectives with different algorithms

of sentences. Our tenth scenario uses all the available features, the adjective, its suffix, negation and the sentiment of the adjective to determine the sentiment of the sentence. The last scenario is a special one. For this we indeed created separately tf-idf vectors from the training text without considering any part of speeches. This is a classical way of how a text classification would be done and should serve as a comparison baseline.

4.2. Results of the Experiment

Table 6 shows the precision, recall and F1 score we achieved for our experimental setups using *scikit-learn* or *WEKA*. When looking at the results produced by BN, a couple of NaNs can be seen. Those signify that the corresponding value could not be calculated due to a denominator of 0. There is no best performing result for all scenarios, different algorithms react differently to the change of features. Interestingly, the first thing to notice is that all the scenarios perform similar or better than the 11th scenario with tf-idf vectorization. The reason for this is the small size of the data. SVM and BN seem to be the most resistant against change in the features. CNB is the algorithm that profits the most from the additional number of features. The most important observation however lies in the fact that the results in the sixth up to ninth scenarios do not drop substantially although the number of features are drastically reduced by removing adjectives and replacing them with suffixes from 1388 to around 15 depending on the scenario (10 endings, 2 negation particles, 3 adjective sentiments). Using adjectives and their suffixes together has mostly a negative influence on DT and CBN, because they both contain basically the same information, with suffixes being artificially withdrawn from the adjectives but presenting the information in a more general way. The tenth setup uses all possible features, i.e. the adjective, its sentiment, its suffix and the negation for determining the sentiment of a sentence. All algorithms perform relatively well in this scenario. An additional interesting point in the results lies in the fact that using a lexical approach indeed gives better results than using tf-idf values when dealing with a small amount of data. This could be useful especially in the case of low-resource languages.

To sum up, our results show that leveraging suffixes as an additional feature does not necessarily improve the performance of the classification system. Comparing the scenarios after the sixth to the previous ones demonstrates though that suffixes as features can replace adjectives while the algorithms give similar and comparable results. Especially DT delivers a good performance when using suffixes as an only feature to classify the sentiment of a sentence. Replacing adjectives with its suffixes results in a huge feature reduction, which is easy to maintain and can be very useful in the case of a low-resource language. However, the amount of annotated adjectives, as seen in 3.2., is rather small. In future work, we will have to annotate more data to explore whether or not the amount and diversity of suffixes available has an impact on the performance of our system or not.

5. Future Work and Outlook

We showed the importance of word formation elements for detecting the sentiment of adjectives in this paper. They can supply the same or similar amount of information as the adjectives themselves. The same should be done for other word classes, especially for the ones with more complex morphology like verbs and nouns. Using morphological information could give the same performance as using words without a need for a large annotated corpus. It is in a way a generalization which could be used for unseen words. That is why we propose a hybrid system for the Luxembourgish language which works combining language rules and machine learning techniques. However, we only worked on a relatively small sample. In the near future, we will annotate more word classes and include more suffixes and prefixes to investigate whether this can improve the performance of our system even further. We plan to integrate more annotators with the help of crowdsourcing and investigate the inter-annotator agreement. As we only annotated the prefix *on-* in our data, we will focus particularly on including a variety of prefixes (Luxembourgish verbs, for instance,

have more of them.) for further experiments. Additionally, we would like to compare it to a deep learning version of our experiments in order to investigate whether or not that kind of approach can lead to promising results. Similar approaches have been implemented for deep learning, e.g. fastText (Bojanowski et al., 2016), which can also include sub-word information using n-grams. Nevertheless, in this technology the information is again repeated by creating the n-grams. Additionally, these are still not hybrid approaches and do not use linguistic rules, but rather try to learn it from the data, which could be insufficient in the case of a low-resource language. So far we have used various feature and label combinations. When working with a low-resource language such as Luxembourgish, it is important to not forget to plan enough time for studying its syntax and for the annotation process. Despite it being time consuming, we believe that it is better than translating already existing resources from other languages, as e.g. adjectives can carry different sentiments in different cultures and languages. As described in section 1.2., Luxembourgish texts usually contain lots of spelling variation, which is also very typical for low-resource languages. When dealing with this kind of data, an intensive preprocessing step could be useful.

6. Acknowledgements

This study is part of *STRIPS - A Semantic Search Toolbox for the Retrieve of Similar Patterns in Luxembourgish Documents*, an interdisciplinary project between the MINE Lab and the Institute of Luxembourgish Linguistics and Literatures at the University of Luxembourg. The aim of the project is to develop a toolbox of semantic search algorithms for texts written in Luxembourgish with a special focus on detecting sentiment (Gilles et al., 2019). The project combines machine learning techniques with linguistic knowledge for its work.

7. Bibliographical References

Abdul-Mageed, M. and Diab, M. (2011). Linguistically-motivated subjectivity and sentiment annotation and tagging of Modern Standard Arabic. *International Journal on Social Media MMM: Monitoring, Measurement, and Mining*.

Balahur, A. and Turchi, M. (2012). Multilingual sentiment analysis using machine translation? In *Proceedings of the 3rd Workshop in Computational Approaches to Subjectivity and Sentiment Analysis*, pages 52–60, 07.

Bojanowski, P., Grave, E., Joulin, A., and Mikolov, T. (2016). Enriching Word Vectors with Subword Information. *arXiv preprint arXiv:1607.04606*.

Entringer, N., Gilles, P., Martin, S., and Purschke, C. (2018). Schnëssen-App - Är Sprooch fir d'Fuerschung.

Esuli, A. and Sebastiani, F. (2006). Sentiwordnet: A publicly available lexical resource for opinion mining. In *LREC*, volume 6, pages 417–422. Citeseer.

Gilles, P., Schommer, C., Sirajzade, J., Purschke, C., and Gierschek, D. (2019). STRIPS - A Semantic Search Toolbox for the Retrieve of Similar Patterns in Luxembourgish Documents.

Gilles, P. (2015). From status to corpus: Codification and implementation of spelling norms in Luxembourgish. *In W., Davies and E., Ziegler (Eds.), Macro and micro language planning (pp. 128-149). London: Palgrave Macmillan (2015).*

Gilles, P. (in press). Luxembourgish. *In P., Maitz, H. C., Boas (Ed.), A., Deumert (Ed.) and M., Louden (Ed.), Varieties of German Worldwide. Oxford: Oxford University Press.*

Hall, M., Frank, E., Holmes, G., Pfahringer, B., Reutemann, P., and Witten, I. H. (2009). The WEKA data mining software: an update. *SIGKDD Explorations*, 11(1):10–18.

Levy, O., Goldberg, Y., and Dagan, I. (2015). Improving Distributional Similarity with Lessons Learned from Word Embeddings. *Transactions of the Association for Computational Linguistics*, 3:211–225, 12.

Liu, B. (2015). *Opinions, Sentiment, and Emotion in Text*. Sentiment Analysis: Mining Opinions, Sentiments, and Emotions. Cambridge University Press.

Mohammad, S. M. (2016). Challenges in Sentiment Analysis. In *A Practical Guide to Sentiment Analysis*. Springer.

Pak, A. and Paroubek, P. (2010). Twitter as a Corpus for Sentiment Analysis and Opinion Mining. In *Proceedings of LREC*, volume 10, 01.

Pang, B., Lee, L., and Vaithyanathan, S. (2002). Thumbs Up?: Sentiment Classification Using Machine Learning Techniques. In *Proceedings of the ACL-02 Conference on Empirical Methods in Natural Language Processing - Volume 10*, EMNLP '02, pages 79–86, Stroudsburg, PA, USA. Association for Computational Linguistics.

Pedregosa, F., Varoquaux, G., Gramfort, A., Michel, V., Thirion, B., Grisel, O., Blondel, M., Prettenhofer, P., Weiss, R., Dubourg, V., Vanderplas, J., Passos, A., Cournapeau, D., Brucher, M., Perrot, M., and Duchesnay, E. (2011). Scikit-learn: Machine Learning in Python. *Journal of Machine Learning Research*, 12:2825–2830.

RTL Luxembourg. (2019). https://www.rtl.lu/. Accessed: 2020-01-20.

scikit-learn. (2019). https://scikit-learn.org/. Accessed: 2020-01-22.

Sirajzade, J. and Schommer, C. (2019). The LuNa Open Toolbox for the Luxembourgish Language. *In Petra Perner (Ed.), 19th Industrial Conference, ICDM 2019 New York, USA, July 17 to July 21 2019, Poster Proceedings 2019, Advances in Data Mining, Applications and Theoretical Aspects.*

Sirajzade, J. (2018). Korpusbasierte Untersuchung der Wortbildungsaffixe im Luxemburgischen. Technische Herausforderungen und linguistische Analyse am Beispiel der Produktivität. *Zeitschrift für Wortbildung = Journal of Word Formation*, 1:195–216.

Taboada, M. (2016). Sentiment Analysis: An Overview from Linguistics. *Annual Review of Linguistics*, 2(1):325–347.

Tang, D., Wei, F., Yang, N., Zhou, M., Liu, T., and Qin, B. (2014). Learning sentiment-specific word embedding for twitter sentiment classification. In *Proceedings of the 52nd Annual Meeting of the Association for Computational Linguistics (Volume 1: Long Papers)*, volume 1, pages 1555–1565.

Proceedings of the 1st Joint SLTU and CCURL Workshop (SLTU-CCURL 2020), pages 167–171
Language Resources and Evaluation Conference (LREC 2020), Marseille, 11–16 May 2020
© European Language Resources Association (ELRA), licensed under CC-BY-NC

Acoustic-Phonetic Approach for ASR of Less Resourced Languages Using Monolingual and Cross Lingual Information

Shweta Bansal, Shweta Sinha, Shyam S. Agrawal

KIIT College of Engineering, Amity University, KIIT College of Engineering
Gurugram, India
bansalshwe@gmail.com, shwetakant.sinha@gmail.com, ss_agrawal@hotmail.com

Abstract

The exploration of speech processing for endangered languages has substantially increased in the past epoch of time. In this paper, we present the acoustic-phonetic approach for automatic speech recognition (ASR) using monolingual and cross-lingual information with application to under-resourced Indian languages, Punjabi, Nepali and Hindi. The challenging task while developing the ASR was the collection of the acoustic corpus for under-resourced languages. We have described here, in brief, the strategies used for designing the corpus and also highlighted the issues pertaining while collecting data for these languages. The bootstrap GMM-UBM based approach is used, which integrates pronunciation lexicon, language model and acoustic-phonetic model. Mel Frequency Cepstral Coefficients were used for extracting the acoustic signal features for training in monolingual and cross-lingual settings. The experimental result shows the overall performance of ASR for cross lingual and monolingual. The phone substitution plays key role for the cross lingual as well as monolingual recognition. The result obtained by cross-lingual recognition compared with other baseline system and it has been found that the performance of the recognition system is based on phonemic units. The recognition rate of cross-lingual generally declines as compared with the monolingual.

Keywords : Cross-lingual, Mono-lingual, ASR

1. Introduction

Due to an increase in the demand for the speech recognition systems in various languages, the advancement of multilingual systems also increases. For developing the robust multilingual system, it is good to combine the phonetic inventory of the multiple languages to be identified into a single universal acoustic model because of the subsequent merits:

❖ The complication of the system gets reduced due to decrease in the size of the parameters by combining the parameters across the languages.

❖ The recognition of the new language is possible in the fast and efficient manner even if the existing quantity of training data is not sufficient((Schultz et al.,2013).

For merging the acoustic models of the different languages require the clarity of the speech sounds of a particular language. Former multilingual recognition systems with shared acoustic-phonetic models were restricted to context-independent modeling ((Stuker et al., 2003). In the case of monolingual, it is already verified that the recognition rate has been increased by context-dependent modeling (Partha Lal and Simon King, 2012). We used here context-dependent model to construct the robust and efficient multilingual models and develop a common system which shares their parameters by applying the clustering procedure based on decision tree and analyze the subsequent decision tree.

For conducting the experiments, we have created our multilingual database which is briefly described in the first section of this paper. In the second section, we explain the procedure to design the monolingual system. The experimental sections give results for the monolingual and crosslingual tests based on the systems designed.

2. Design for Text and Acoustic Corpus

For designing ASR in virtue of under-resourced languages, text and acoustic data collection is a predominantly difficult task. The corpus has been designed in following phases:

A. Extraction of Phonetically rich sentences

The process starts with collection of text corpus. This has been done by crawling the web for text corpus. As the corpus on web contains lots of clatter, it required cleaning and filtering. Once the clean corpus is built then phonetically rich sentences are extracted from it. Finally, text prompt sheet for each language were designed. Each prompt sheet consists of 300 meaningful phonetically rich sentences. The sentence length in the text corpus varies from 5 to 12 words.

B. Cleaning and filtering of corpus

Identification of improper syntax e.g. existence of invalid bigrams/character combinations has been done. Sentences with foreign word are filtered so as to have a good quality monolingual corpus. Inadequate sized sentences and words are identified and removed. Duplicate sentences along with duplicate punctuations are also removed.

C. Collection of Speech data

The corpus is recorded using 100 native speakers (60 male and 40 female) for each of the three languages. The age group of all the native speakers were 18 to 55 years and had at least 10 years of formal education in their respective language. Each speaker has to read 300 continuous sentences in one session. The total number of utterances in the corpus is (300 sentences × 3 languages) × 100 speakers = 9000. Nearly 1.20 h of read speech samples are obtained from each speaker. We apportion the recorded dataset into training and testing sets, with an 80-20 split. All recording was done using a single microphone in the office environment. The recorded signals were sampled at 16 kHz using the software GoldWave and are represented as 16 bit number.

LANGUAGES	UTTERANCES	SPEAKERS	
		MALE	FEMALE
HINDI	3000	60	40
PUNJABI	3000	60	40
NEPALI	3000	60	40

Table1: Detail of the Collected Speech Corpus

3. Phone Switching

The phonetic units of every language have peculiar characteristics. The correlation among the acoustic inventory of the prescribed languages must be discovered for performing the monolingual and cross-lingual speech recognition (T. Schultz and A. Waibel,1997). This section will describe the approaches to determine resemblance among sounds of the different languages. In monolingual and cross-lingual speech recognition, usually phonemes are used for the representation of the words. A phoneme may be realized by different phones, for example the phones /sh/ and /s/ can be represented by the same phoneme. The relation between the phones and phonemes of a language differs across languages. For example in Nepali, no difference between /kʂ /,/ ʂ/,/ ʃ/, / ʃrə/ and /s/ and they would belong to the same phoneme class in that language. In other languages, however they represent each a phoneme class on their own. As Punjabi is a tonal language, it was observed that Punjabi speakers used to pronounce the phonemes with tones which change the perception of that particular phoneme. It has been observed that the sound of some phonemes changed according to the positions of phoneme by Punjabi speakers. For example, 'घ/g^h/ is heard as 'घ/g^h / only when it is in the initial position of the word, however, sound as 'ग/g/ when /g^h/ lies at middle and final positions of any word. Similarly sound of /b^h / in Punjabi changes according to the position in a particular word. /bh/sounds like /b/ when occurring at the initial and final position of any word. This type of phone switching can affect the recognition rate of a particular language.

4. Monolingual Speech Recognition

For this work, we have developed three monolingual speech recognition baseline systems for Hindi, Punjabi and Nepali by applying the bootstrap HMM technique for initializing the acoustic models of the mentioned languages. the resultant monolingual system comprises of an entirely continuous 3-state HMM system for each involved language (R.K. Aggarwal, M. Dave,2012). The obtained monolingual system for each language is context-dependent and each HMM state having 1000 polyphone models. Modeling of each state is done by the use of a common codebook which consists of 32 Gaussian mixture distributions along with 24-dimensional feature space. The features of the acoustic signal were extracted by using Mel Frequency Cepstral Coefficients for monolingual speech recognition. The input speech sampled at 16 kHz was used to calculate the first and second derivative of power and 16 cepstra and then the process of Mean subtraction is employed. The word error rates (WER in percentage) and sentence error rate (SER) obtained by each of the monolingual system is shown in table 2. The performance

for the Punjabi system is experienced the lower accuracy rate due to the use of morpheme-based units.

LANGUAGES	HINDI	NEPALI	PUNJABI
WER	12%	10.9%	20.6%
SER	8.1%	7.1%	11.2%

Table 2: WER & SER (in %) for Hindi Nepali & Punjabi

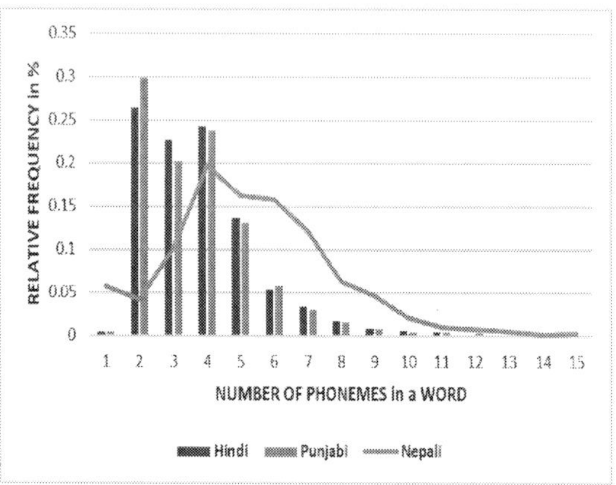

Figure 1: Plot of Number of Phonemes in a word vs Relative Frequency (%)

The total number of phonemes in a word along with their relative frequency in the training corpus was calculated as shown in figure 1. It has been observed from the plot that the Nepali language tends to have long words with phoneme 5,6,7, 10 or 15 which might make it easier to differentiate Nepali words with each other and results in a high accuracy rate. It is also be seen that in Punjabi data 30% of the words having only two phonemes which result in high confusability in recognition of these words. Therefore, the recognition rate of Punjabi is poor than others as shown in table 3.

LANGUAGES	HINDI-HINDI	NEPALI-NEPALI	PUNJABI-PUNJABI
Recognition Rate	88.05%	89.12%	79.4%

Table 3: Recognition rate of Hindi, Nepali & Punjabi

5. Cross-lingual Speech Recognition

In the experiment of Cross-lingual speech recognition, one language(L1) is used for training purpose and unknown language(L2) is used for testing (B. G. Nagaraja and H. S. Jayanna,2012). In this work, we need to integrate the acoustic models of the same sounds across languages into a common phone set. Moreover, the material which was used for the training of L1 is used for the estimation of parameters for developing the recognizer for the second language(L2). The effect of L1 on the recognizer of L2 is shown in Figure 2.

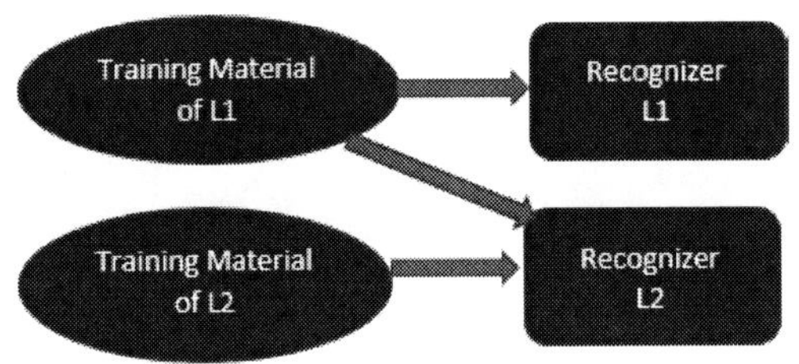

Figure 2: Setup for Cross – lingual recognition

All the sounds of each language were classified based on phonetic information and documented by using Indian Language Speech sound label set (ILSL) popularly known as "common phoneme set" as shown in Table 5. The common phone set comprises of 80 different phonemes including silence. On the basis of these 80 phonemes in the prescribed set, we developed cross-lingual recognizer for three languages, in which we share language and acoustic models across languages. Each phoneme gets initialized by the single mixture of 16 Gaussian distribution.

Following three cases were considered for performing the cross-lingual experiment for speech recognition:

- ❖ Training with Hindi language and testing with Nepali and Punjabi
- ❖ Training with Nepali language and testing with Hindi and Punjabi
- ❖ Training with Hindi language and testing with Punjabi and Nepali

In the current experiment, GMM is employed as a classifier which integrates EM optimization technique. The selection of the number of Gaussians is based on the amount of training material. In this test, a range of Gaussians components from 64 to 256 per state have been found convenient. As mentioned above, for cross-lingual recognition three cases are considered. In the first case, the system is trained with Hindi (HI) and Punjabi (PU) Language and tested with Nepali (NE) language. The success rate of the cross-lingual system for varying number of Gaussians is shown in Table 4:

Language (Tr/Te)*	SIZE OF GAUSSIANS					Average Success Rate
	32	64	128	256	512	
HI/PU	28	33.5	42.3	45	45.2	**38.7**
HI/NE	34.5	39.8	41	50	50.3	**43.1**
NE/PU	22	25	32.6	36.3	36.5	30.5
NE/HI	35	36.7	43.6	48.9	48.9	**42.6**
PU/NE	29	31.5	33.7	33.7	33.7	32.2
PU/HI	31	33	37	41.6	41.6	36.8

(*Tr-Training, Te- Testing)

Table 4: Rate of Performance (%) for Cross- lingual

The cross-lingual speech recognition system gives the excellent performance when the system gets trained by the Hindi (HI) language and tested by the Nepali(NE) language followed by NE(Tr)/HI(TE), HI(Tr)/PU(Te) whereas the performance of PU(Tr)/NE(Te) was not appreciable. It has also been observed that the performance rate does not affect very much by increasing the number of Gaussians from 256 to 512. As observed, the performance rate of HI(Tr)/NE(Te) was the highest among the other language combination. This may be due to the similarity in the script of both the languages as the writing style of Hindi and Nepali is the same as both the languages use the Devanagari script for the representation and Hindi use as secondary language in Nepal. It is also evident that the phonemes क्ष(kʂ),ष(ʂ),श(ʃ),ऋ(rə) of the Devanagari script get confused by स (s) in Nepal. On the other hand, the performance of PU/NE, NE/PU was the poorest among others. As Punjabi is tonal language (Dua et al.,2012), it was observed that Punjabi speakers used to pronounce the phonemes with tones which change the perception of that particular phoneme. Due to difference in the speaking style of Punjabi speakers the performance of the system gets deprived. This phenomena has also been outlined by Yogesh et al.(2017).

Phone Label	IPA	Hindi/Nepali	Punjabi
ac	/ə/	अ	ਅ
a	/ɔ/	औ	ਔ
aq	/ɑ/	आ	ਆ
i	/i/	ई	ਈ
ic	/ɪ/	इ	ਇ
u	/u/	ऊ	ਊ
uc	/ʊ/	उ	ੳ
e	/e/	ए	ਏ
ae	/ɛ/	ऐ	ਐ
o	/o/	ओ	ੲ
k	/k/	क	ਕ
kh	/kʰ/	ख	ਖ
g	/g/	ग	ਗ
gq	/ɣ/	ग़	ਗ਼
gh	/gʰ/	घ	
ng	/ŋ/	ङ	ਙ
c	/tʃ/	च	ਚ
ch	/tʃʰ/	छ	ਛ
j	/dʒ/	ज	ਜ

jh	/dʒʰ /	झ	
nj	/ɲ/	ञ	ਞ
t:	/ʈ/	ट	ਟ
t:h	/ʈʰ /	ठ	ਠ
d:	/ɖ/	ड	ਡ
d:h	/ɖʰ /	ढ	
n:	/ɳ/	ण	ਣ
t	/t̪/	त	ਤ
th	/t̪ʰ/	थ	ਥ
d	/d̪/	द	ਦ
dh	/d̪ʰ /	ध	
n	/n/	न	ਨ
p	/p/	प	ਪ
ph	/pʰ /	फ	ਫ
b	/b/	ब	ਬ
bh	/bʰ /	भ	
m	/m/	म	ਮ
y	/j/	य	ਯ
r	/r/	र	
l	/l/	ल	ਲ
x	/x/	ख़	ਖ਼
v	/ʋ/	व	ਵ
sh	/ʃ/	श	ਸ਼
s	/s/	स	ਸ
h	/h/	ह	ਹ
z	/z/	ज़	ਜ਼
l:	l	ळ	ਲ਼
r:	ɽ	ड़	

f	/f/	फ़	ਡ਼
rq	/r/		ਰ
SIL			

Table 5: List of Common Phone set for Hindi, Nepali and Punjabi

6. Conclusion

In the present paper, the Monolingual and Cross-lingual speech recognition systems were developed for Hindi, Punjabi and Nepali languages. It has been observed that in the mono-lingual study the performance of Nepali language was better than the other two languages. Furthermore, we also observed in a cross-lingual study that the Nepali language for training & testing with the Hindi language have good success rate. From table 4, it may be seen that 256 number of Gaussians gives optimum performance in all combinations of cross lingual recognition. Their performance may be ranked as HI/NE, NE/HI, HI/PU, PU/HI, NE/PU and PU/NE. The experimental results can be improved by employing more language-specific features and the latest modeling techniques in both Monolingual and Cross-lingual speech recognition system. In order to design the robust speech recognition system, the large text and speech data size is required.

7. Acknowledgement

The authors would like to acknowledge the suggestions and help received from Mr. Shambhu Sharan in analysis of the speech samples collected from speakers of different linguistic backgrounds. Our special thanks to Dr. Harsh Vardhan Kamrah and Mrs. Neelima Kamrah for their support and encouragement.

8. References

B. G. Nagaraja and H. S. Jayanna, "Mono and Cross lingual speaker identification with the constraint of limited data," *International Conference on Pattern Recognition, Informatics and Medical Engineering (PRIME-2012)*, Salem, Tamilnadu, 2012, pp. 439-443.

Dua, Mohit, et al. "Punjabi automatic speech recognition using HTK." International Journal of Computer Science Issues (IJCSI) 9.4 (2012): 359.

Hemant A. Patil, Sunayana Sitaram, and Esha Sharma, "DA-IICT Cross-lingual and Multilingual Corpora for Speaker Recognition", Proc.IEEE, pp. 187–190, 2009.

Partha Lal and Simon King "Cross-Lingual Automatic Speech Recognition Using Tandem Features" IEEE Transactions on Audio, Speech, And Language Processing, Vol. 21, No. 12, December 2013.

R.K. Aggarwal, M. Dave, " Integration of Multiple Acoustic and Language Models for improved Hindi Speech Recognition System". International Journal of Speech Technol ogy, Published Online, 3 Feb 2012.

Stuker, Sebastian /Metze, Florian / Schultz, Tanja / Waibel, Alex (2003): "Integrating multilingual articulatory features into speech recognition", In EUROSPEECH-2003, 1033-1036.

T. Schultz, N. T. Vu, and T. Schlippe, "Globalphone: A multilingual text & speech database in 20 languages," in Proc. IEEE Int. Conf. Acoust., Speech, Signal Process., 2013, pp. 8126–8130.

T. Schultz and A. Waibel "Fast Bootstrapping of LVCSR Systems with Multilingual Phoneme Setsin" Proc. Eurospeech, pp. 371-374, Rhodes 1997.

Yogesh Kumar et al. "An automatic speech recognition system for spontaneous Punjabi speech corpus," International Journal of Speech Technology volume 20, pages 297–303, 2017

Proceedings of the 1st Joint SLTU and CCURL Workshop (SLTU-CCURL 2020), pages 172–176
Language Resources and Evaluation Conference (LREC 2020), Marseille, 11–16 May 2020
© European Language Resources Association (ELRA), licensed under CC-BY-NC

An Annotation Framework for Luxembourgish Sentiment Analysis

Joshgun Sirajzade[1], Daniela Gierschek[2], Christoph Schommer[1]
[1]MINE Lab, Computer Science, Université du Luxembourg
[2]Institute of Luxemburgish Linguistics and Literatures, Université du Luxembourg
{joshgun.sirajzade, daniela.gierschek, christoph.schommer}@uni.lu

Abstract

The aim of this paper is to present a framework developed for crowdsourcing sentiment annotation for the low-resource language Luxembourgish. Our tool is easily accessible through a web interface and facilitates sentence-level annotation of several annotators in parallel. In the heart of our framework is an XML database, which serves as central part linking several components. The corpus in the database consists of news articles and user comments. One of the components is LuNa, a tool for linguistic preprocessing of the data set. It tokenizes the text, splits it into sentences and assigns POS-tags to the tokens. After that, the preprocessed text is stored in XML format into the database. The Sentiment Annotation Tool, which is a browser-based tool, then enables the annotation of split sentences from the database. The Sentiment Engine, a separate module, is trained with this material in order to annotate the whole data set and analyze the sentiment of the comments over time and in relationship to the news articles. The gained knowledge can again be used to improve the sentiment classification on the one hand and on the other hand to understand the sentiment phenomenon from the linguistic point of view.

Keywords: Opinion Mining / Sentiment Analysis, Corpus (Creation, Annotation, etc.), Crowdsourcing

1. Introduction

Dealing with a low-resource language like Luxembourgish comes with special challenges. Especially in the case of sentiment analysis, one is faced with the scarcity of resources. Neither sufficient amount of pre-labeled data, like Twitter data sets for English or several other languages, nor lexical resources such as SentiWordNet (Baccianella et al., 2010) exist for Luxembourgish. Nevertheless, doing research on sentiment detection for this language is important. First, it is a technical and scientific challenge for the algorithms. They need to be adapted to a scarce data set. The state-of-the-art NLP algorithms, especially those used in deep learning, require a lot of data. Many attempts have been made to adjust them to low-resource languages. Leveraging more information from the data, like the usage of subword units, is one of those attempts. Second, it is important to study these languages, because they play a crucial role in the political, economic and social lives of their speakers. For these reasons, we have decided to build an infrastructure for the Luxembourgish language which is freely accessible over the web using data from RTL Luxembourg (Radio Télévision Lëtzebuerg).

2. Luxembourgish Language

Luxembourgish, French and German are the three official languages of the Grand Duchy of Luxembourg, a European country with about 590,000 inhabitants (Gilles, in press). In 1984, the Luxembourgish language, which arised out of a Central Franconian dialect, was allocated the status of the only national language of the country and is an essential symbol for national identity today. Despite being related to German due to its history, Luxembourgish is perceived as an independent language by the speech community. If all people taking part in the conversation speak Luxembourgish, code-switching to another language would be unthinkable regardless of the formality or informality of the situation ((Gilles, in press); (Gilles, 2015)). One big challenge of implementing a natural language processing task with texts written in Luxembourgish is that a big part of it is not written following the official spelling rules of the language. This characteristic results from the educational system mainly focusing on French and German and not that much on Luxembourgish (Gilles, 2015).

3. Sentiment Analysis

The research field of sentiment analysis, or opinion mining, deals with analyzing people's opinions towards certain entities (Liu, 2012). There are two different main approaches to solving sentiment analysis tasks, i.e. lexical and machine learning methods. Lexical approaches leverage automatically or manually developed dictionaries containing the sentiment of specific words to calculate the overall sentiment score of an entity. Those dictionaries can consist of different words and their positivity or negativity while sometimes adding even the degree of this (Taboada, 2016). On the machine learning side, sentiment analysis was for a long time treated as a simple text classification task (Pang et al., 2002). Recent research however shows that sentiment analysis can be performed on different levels, such as on a sentence or aspect based level (Liu, 2015). Besides, efforts to adapt text representations needed for text classification to sentiment analysis have been made. For instance, sentiment specific word embeddings were trained that incorporate the sentiment information in the continuous representation of words (Tang et al., 2014).

Also, attempts to use transfer learning for implementing sentiment analysis for situations in which data is scarce have been made (Bataa and Wu, 2019). Big data sets for pretraining a Luxembourgish language model before finetuning on sentiment data do not exist yet. Since we believe that the expression of sentiment is culture and language-dependent, pretraining on a large dataset from a related language such as German is not an option. The morphosyntactical system of Luxembourgish and Standard German are very different and for some features, Luxembourgish has developed new grammatical structures that do not ex-

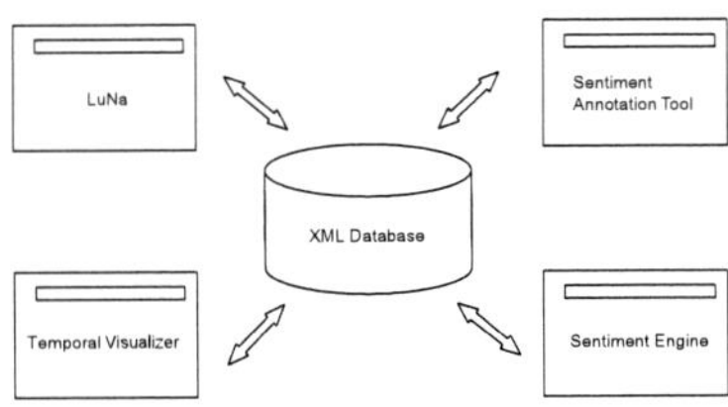

Figure 1: The architecture of our temporal text data warehouse

Figure 2: The GUI of the annotation tool

ist in Standard German (Gilles, in press) which make the two languages quite distinct from each other. Leveraging a lexical method for sentiment analysis is currently also not feasible due to a significant amount of spelling variation in Luxembourgish (see section 2.). An intensive amount of preprocessing is needed to remove all of this diversity and no such tool that captures all of the variation present in the Luxembourgish language has been built yet. In order to best fulfil the demand for a culture and language specific sentiment analysis setting, we have built our own tool for crowdsourcing Luxembourgish specific sentence level sentiment annotations.

4. Technical Implementation

4.1. A Database – Temporal Warehouse

We have set up a Temporal Warehouse for our project that acts as a data backbone to separate the data itself from the various applications that are linked to it. Users can access the Temporal Warehouse either by retrieving data using XQuery commands or by loading such data into the warehouse. For the database itself, we leverage the eXist-db infrastructure (Siegel and Retter, 2014). Each data entry in our database is of textual form and possesses both a time and a sentiment stamp. All texts in our warehouse are in XML format (Gierschek et al., 2019). If needed, the Temporal Warehouse can easily be reproduced from its data sources following an Extract-Transform-Load (ETL) pipeline (Kimball and Ross, 2013) which is, at present, facilitated by various Python and Java scripts. In order to provide textual data that can be loaded into our Temporal Warehouse, we can use two different tools. One is the LuNa Open Toolbox for the Luxembourgish Language which we used for tokenization, sentence splitting and part-of-speech tagging of the data (Sirajzade and Schommer, 2019). The other one is the annotation tool that we propose in this paper. We have decided to incorporate this as part of our database structure, as it allows for new annotations to be gathered with little additional effort. The data loaded into the Temporal Warehouse through the annotation tool or the LuNa Open Toolbox for the Luxembourgish Language is crucial as training data for further analyses that can be done using the Temporal Visualizer and the Sentiment Engine to detect sentiment changes over time.

4.2. Sentiment Annotation Tool

As mentioned before, the power of our Temporal Warehouse as a linguistic resource lies in its well-structured annotation. Being accessible as database it is possible to gather new annotation with little additional effort. The Sentiment Annotation Tool is a separate component of this warehouse. More precisely, it is a web application written in the programming language PHP. It connects to our eXist database, retrieves sentences from the user comments of our corpus and offers the annotator the possibility to annotate them with the labels *negativ* [negative], *neutral* [neutral] or *positiv* [positive]. If unsure how to label the instance, the button *iwwersprangen* [skip] might be clicked or the user can go back to the *Uleedung* [instruction] page. The sentences are presented in random order to the annotator to cover the whole time period of our text collection, i.e. from 2008 to 2018. To give a bit of context, one sentence before and one sentence after the sentence to be annotated are also shown. A counter returns the number of items already provided with a sentiment value as a motivational incentive. Figure 2 shows the graphical user interface [GUI] of our Sentiment Annotation Tool.

Label	Amount
negativ [negative]	1854 sentences
neutral [neutral]	1417 sentences
positiv [positive]	942 sentences
iwwersprangen [skip]	11 sentences

Table 1: Annotated sentences

5. Experiments

5.1. Data Set

The large data set leveraged for collecting sentiment annotations was provided by our project partner RTL Luxembourg (RTL Luxembourg, 2019a). It comprises over 180,000 news articles written between 1999 and 2018 and over 500,000 user comments to those articles. Most of those texts were published in Luxembourgish with only little occurence of publications in the other two official languages, i.e. German and French. The comments were recorded between 2008 and 2018 and include over 35 million running tokens whereas the news articles part amounts to about 30 million running tokens.

We carried out several preprocessing steps on this data to prepare our corpus for retrieval in the annotation tool. More precisely, we leveraged the LuNa Open Toolbox for the

```
<sentence id="7ep">
<w id="84" pos="P" sen="7" tagger="0,26">Mir</w>
<w id="85" pos="V" sen="7" tagger="0,27">ziichten</w>
<w id="86" pos="D" sen="7" tagger="0,19">eng</w>
<w id="87" pos="N" sen="7" tagger="0,24">imposeiert</w>
<w id="88" pos="N" sen="7" tagger="0,52">Meenung</w>
<c id="89" pos="$" sen="7" tagger="0,31">.</c>
</sentence>
```

Figure 3: Example of a sentence in our data set

Luxembourgish Language to tokenize, split the sentencces and to include part-of-speech codes in our data (Sirajzade and Schommer, 2019). Figure 3 illustrates a preprocessed sentence from our data.

5.2. Annotation Process

The annotators were recruited through crowdsourcing techniques. A call for participation was posted on the RTL Luxembourg website (RTL Luxembourg, 2019b) and in Luxembourgish schools. In total, we recruited 26 annotators. They annotated 4,206 sentences, as shown in table 1. The annotation guidelines were very open to avoid influencing the annotator during the decision making process. We simply asked the users to annotate from the perspective of the author (Abdul-Mageed and Diab, 2011). 637 sentences of our corpus were annotated three times, 1302 two times and 2274 one time. The amount of data annotated by an annotator varied greatly, from one annotation to almost 600. We will use those sentences annotated three times to calculate the inter-annotator agreement.

5.3. Inter-Annotator Agreement

We measured the inter-annotator agreement for the 637 sentences that were annotated by three of the 26 annotators we recruited. For those calculations, we chose Fleiss' kappa and Krippendorff's alpha as both allow the calculation of reliability for multiple annotators. Fleiss' kappa assumes that the coders' distributions are independent from one another (Artstein and Poesio, 2008). Krippendorff's alpha is a reliability measure able to determine the agreement for any number of observers, categories and even if some values are missing (Krippendorff, 2011). The calculation of expected agreement is done by looking at the overall distribution of the different judgments, no matter which annotator provided them (Artstein and Poesio, 2008). An α value of 0 means the absence of reliability, whereas a value of 1 would be a perfect score (Krippendorff, 2011). For kappa, a value of 1 denotes perfect agreement and 0 pure chance agreement (Artstein and Poesio, 2008). Table 2 shows the calculated Fleiss' kappa and Krippendorff's alpha for our annotation setup. Both scores are close to zero. Our annotated data set thus shows low agreement. One reason for this might be that giving two sentences as context is too short to infer sentiment. Also, the annotation guidelines might be too open and therefore might make the annotators unsure in case of doubtful cases where sentiment is not clearly expressed. Note, however, that our Sentiment Annotation Tool is still open to new annotations and annotators. We therefore will recalculate Fleiss' kappa and Krippendorff's alpha in the future and compare those results with the ones presented here.

Annotation measure	Result
Fleiss kappa	-0.018
Krippendorff's alpha	0.19

Table 2: Inter-annotator agreement

5.4. Sentiment Engine

We created our Sentiment Engine with deeplearning4j, an easy to use Java library for building ANNs. We use the word2vec algorithm (Mikolov et al., 2013) for constructing vectors that are used for the input layer of our network. More precisely, we first train our embedding model with over 100 million tokens of text written in Luxembourgish that were gathered at the Institute of Luxembourgish Linguistics and Literatures and include the comments and news articles from our RTL corpus. The word embeddings have 100 dimensions. Our network has a very simple RNN design. It has four layers: one input, two hidden and one output layer. As an activation function for the hidden layers we used hyperbolic tangent (tanh), which is an S-shaped function transforming the values x into the range $[-1, 1]$. The output layer gets softmax as its activation function, because we wanted to see the probability like values at the end of the classification. The first three layers have 256 neurons and the last one only three, corresponding to our labels. Word vector inputs created from the sentences are mostly padded and if there should be more than 256, it is truncated. The data set has a 80%/20% split and the network gives an accuracy score of 80%. We subsequently use the trained model to tag all sentences in our comments for the whole time span of 2008 until 2018 in order to see and to investigate the temporal patterns in our data.

5.5. Visualization

The setup of our Search Engine is similar to the architecture of the annotation tool. We built the engine using PHP and the XML database eXist-db to visualize the results of the performance of the Sentiment Engine. Figure 4 shows the functionality of it. The Search Engine makes it possible to search for words in our database and returns those words in their context. The sentences found are shown in the colors corresponding to their sentiment. Green is used for displaying positive, red for negative and grey for neutral sentences. We also developed a module which can present the change in sentiment over time. Figure 5 shows the absolute frequencies of positive/negative/neutral sentences per month in the period of 2008-2018 for the search word "Autobunn" [interstate].

6. Future Work

We have presented an annotation setup for collecting sentiment annotated data for the low-resourced language Luxembourgish. Our total of annotated data results to 4,206 sentences from 26 different annotators. In order to study the quality of the annotations gathered through crowdsourcing, we calculated Fleiss' kappa and Krippendorff's alpha. The results of our calculation of Fleiss' kappa and Krippendorff's alpha show that annotation for sentiment, especially

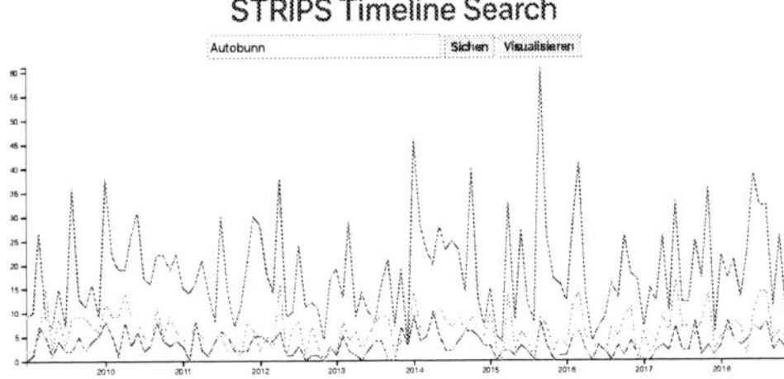

Figure 4: The GUI of our Search Engine

Figure 5: The change in sentiment over time in the example of the word Autobunn [interstate]

sentence-level annotation with open annotation guidelines, is a challenging task. Future work will include a further examination of the (open) annotation guidelines provided and the setup of crowdsourcing annotations. A possibility would be to carry out annotations with trained annotators, proving them with more detailed guidelines and then to compare the agreement to the one achieved with our crowdsourced annotators. We also plan to compare the data annotated by humans with the automatic annotations of our Sentiment Engine and to further improve our neural network. Future experiments will include the improvement of the training process by using all sentences where at least two of the three annotators agree for sentiment. This will increase the amount of training data. Furthermore, we would like to leverage annotated sentences with three different sentiments as well. By incorporating them into our training corpus with a smaller weight than the sentences annotated with the same sentiment by three or two users, we could increase the training set even more.

7. Acknowledgements

The annotation tool presented in this article is part of the STRIPS (A Semantic Search Toolbox for the Retrieve of Similar Patterns in Luxembourgish Documents) project, a 3-year project (02/18-01/21) that aims at developing a semantic search toolbox for the retrieval of similar patterns in documents written in Luxembourgish. STRIPS is an interdisciplinary project between the University of Luxembourg's MINE Lab and the Institute for Luxembourgish Linguistics & Literatures. RTL (Radio Télévision Lëtzebuerg) is the project partner providing their online news and corresponding user comments (2008-2018) for the retrieval of similar patterns over different time spans.

8. Bibliographical References

Abdul-Mageed, M. and Diab, M. (2011). Linguistically-motivated subjectivity and sentiment annotation and tagging of Modern Standard Arabic. *International Journal on Social Media MMM: Monitoring, Measurement, and Mining.*

Artstein, R. and Poesio, M. (2008). Inter-Coder Agreement for Computational Linguistics. *Computational Linguistics*, 34(4):555–596.

Baccianella, S., Esuli, A., and Sebastiani, F. (2010). SentiWordNet 3.0: An Enhanced Lexical Resource for Sentiment Analysis and Opinion Mining. In Nicoletta Calzolari, et al., editors, *LREC*. European Language Resources Association.

Bataa, E. and Wu, J. C. K. (2019). An Investigation of Transfer Learning-Based Sentiment Analysis in Japanese. In *Proceedings of the 57th Annual Meeting of the Association for Computational Linguistics*, page 4652–4657.

Gierschek, D., Gilles, P., Purschke, C., Schommer, C., and Sirajzade, J. (2019). A Temporal Warehouse for Modern Luxembourgish Text Collections.

Gilles, P. (2015). From status to corpus: Codification and implementation of spelling norms in Luxembourgish. *In W., Davies and E., Ziegler (Eds.), Macro and micro language planning (pp. 128-149). London: Palgrave Macmillan (2015).*

Gilles, P. (in press). Luxembourgish. *In P., Maitz, H. C., Boas (Ed.), A., Deumert (Ed.) and M., Louden (Ed.), Varieties of German Worldwide. Oxford: Oxford University Press (in press).*

Kimball, R. and Ross, M. (2013). *The Data Warehouse Toolkit: The Complete Guide to Dimensional Modeling.* John Wiley & Sons, Inc., New York, NY, USA, 3rd edition.

Krippendorff, K. (2011). Computing Krippendorff 's Alpha-Reliability.

Liu, B. (2012). *Sentiment Analysis and Opinion Mining.* Morgan & Claypool Publishers.

Liu, B. (2015). *Opinions, Sentiment, and Emotion in Text.* Sentiment Analysis: Mining Opinions, Sentiments, and Emotions. Cambridge University Press.

Mikolov, T., Sutskever, I., Chen, K., Corrado, G., and Dean, J. (2013). Distributed Representations of Words and Phrases and their Compositionality. *CoRR*, abs/1310.4546.

Pang, B., Lee, L., and Vaithyanathan, S. (2002). Thumbs Up?: Sentiment Classification Using Machine Learning Techniques. In *Proceedings of the ACL-02 Conference on Empirical Methods in Natural Language Processing - Volume 10*, EMNLP '02, pages 79–86, Stroudsburg, PA, USA. Association for Computational Linguistics.

RTL Luxembourg. (2019a). RTL. `https://www.rtl.lu/`. Accessed: 2019-09-05.

RTL Luxembourg. (2019b). Wéi si se geduecht: Positiv? Negativ? Neutral? `https://www.rtl.lu/kultur/news/a/1445783.html`. Accessed: 2020-02-08.

Siegel, E. and Retter, A. (2014). *eXist: A NoSQL Docu-*

ment Database and Application Platform. O'Reilly Media.

Sirajzade, J. and Schommer, C. (2019). The LuNa Open Toolbox for the Luxembourgish Language. *In Petra Perner (Ed.), 19th Industrial Conference, ICDM 2019 New York, USA, July 17 to July 21 2019, Poster Proceedings 2019, Advances in Data Mining, Applications and Theoretical Aspects*.

Taboada, M. (2016). Sentiment Analysis: An Overview from Linguistics. *Annual Review of Linguistics*, 2(1):325–347.

Tang, D., Wei, F., Yang, N., Zhou, M., Liu, T., and Qin, B. (2014). Learning sentiment-specific word embedding for twitter sentiment classification. In *Proceedings of the 52nd Annual Meeting of the Association for Computational Linguistics (Volume 1: Long Papers)*, pages 1555–1565.

Proceedings of the 1st Joint SLTU and CCURL Workshop (SLTU-CCURL 2020), pages 177–184
Language Resources and Evaluation Conference (LREC 2020), Marseille, 11–16 May 2020
© European Language Resources Association (ELRA), licensed under CC-BY-NC

A Sentiment Analysis Dataset for Code-Mixed Malayalam-English

Bharathi Raja Chakravarthi[1]**, Navya Jose**[2]**, Shardul Suryawanshi**[1]**,
Elizabeth Sherly**[2]**, John P. McCrae**[1]

[1]Insight SFI Research Centre for Data Analytics, Data Science Institute, National University of Ireland Galway
{bharathi.raja,shardul.suryawanshi, john.mccrae}@insight-centre.org
[2]Indian Institute of Information Technology and Management-Kerala
{navya.mi3, sherly}@iiitmk.ac.in

Abstract

There is an increasing demand for sentiment analysis of text from social media which are mostly code-mixed. Systems trained on monolingual data fail for code-mixed data due to the complexity of mixing at different levels of the text. However, very few resources are available for code-mixed data to create models specific for this data. Although much research in multilingual and cross-lingual sentiment analysis has used semi-supervised or unsupervised methods, supervised methods still performs better. Only a few datasets for popular languages such as English-Spanish, English-Hindi, and English-Chinese are available. There are no resources available for Malayalam-English code-mixed data. This paper presents a new gold standard corpus for sentiment analysis of code-mixed text in Malayalam-English annotated by voluntary annotators. This gold standard corpus obtained a Krippendorff's alpha above 0.8 for the dataset. We use this new corpus to provide the benchmark for sentiment analysis in Malayalam-English code-mixed texts.

Keywords: code-mixing, Malayalam, dataset, sentiment analysis

1. Introduction

The Internet gave users the opportunities to express an opinion on any topic in the form of user reviews or comments. The comments are usually of an informal style, mostly in social media forums such as Youtube, Facebook, and Twitter, which opens up the ground for mixing languages in the same conversation for multilingual communities. Some people with different linguistic backgrounds and cultures mark their impressions about a subject with the individual feeling in mixed language as not all are comfortable with a single language alone (Scotton, 1982; Tay, 1989; Suryawanshi et al., 2020b). This unplanned switching between more than one language in the same conversation for the speaker's convenience is referred to as *code-mixing* (Androutsopoulos, 2013; Chakravarthi et al., 2019a; Chakravarthi et al., 2020). Even though many languages have their own scripts, social media users use non-native script, usually Roman script, (Saint-Jacques, 1987; Rosowsky, 2010) for convenience in some part of the world, like India. This causes difficulties in finding the languages involved and also makes it hard to execute various existing natural language processing tasks, as these were developed for a single language (Bali et al., 2014; Diab et al., 2014; Solorio et al., 2014).

Malayalam is one of the Dravidian languages spoken in the southern region of India with nearly 38 million Malayalam speakers in India and other countries (Thottingal, 2019). Malayalam is a deeply agglutinating language (Sreelekha and Bhattacharyya, 2018). The Malayalam script is the Vatteluttu alphabet extended with symbols from the Grantha alphabet. It is an alphasyllabary (abugida), a writing system that is partially "alphabetic" and partially syllable-based (Krishnamurti, 2003; Lalitha Devi, 2019; Chakravarthi et al., 2019c). Still, social media users use Roman script for typing due to it being easier to input. There is a lot of code-mixed data between Malayalam and English among

the YouTube comments we surveyed. Monolingual datasets are available for Indian languages for various research aims (Agrawal et al., 2018). However, there are few attempts to make datasets for Malayalam code-mixed text. Thus traditional NLP tasks fail in this scenario due to the absence of a proper dataset. To create resources for a Malayalam-English code-mixed scenario, we collected comments of various Malayalam movie trailers from YouTube. Malayalam code-mixed sample text from the proposed dataset is shown below with the corresponding English glosses.

- Malayalam-English: *Innaleyaaane kandath super Padam.....ellarum familyaaayi poyi kananam super abinayam*

  English: "Watched yesterday only this super movie... everyone go and watch the movie with the family..super acting..".

The English words 'super' and 'family' intra-sententially code mixed (Barman et al., 2014) with the Malayalam language. Also, the word 'familyaayi' is a new word combining both English and Malayalam, which is another kind of code-mixing called Intra-word switching that happens at the word level (Das and Gambäck, 2014). In this case, 'with family' is together said as a single word following Malayalam morphology. Although the main word 'family' is in English and as the sentence is in Malayalam, the new word takes Malayalam morphology. This comment can be considered as a positive comment from the viewer of the trailer of a Malayalam movie as it is clear that he enjoyed the movie and also recommend that movie to other viewers of the trailer.

- Malayalam-English: *enthu oola trailer aanu ithu. poor dialogue delivery.*

  English: "What a useless trailer is this? Poor dialogue delivery."

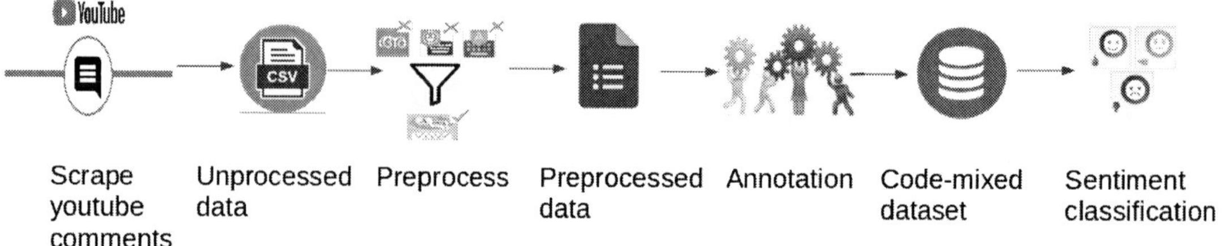

Figure 1: Data collection process.

This is an example of inter-sentential code-mixing (Barman et al., 2014). 'Oola' a slang word for 'useless' which is popular among the youth of Kerala.The viewer expressed strong dislike against the whole trailer and one aspect is 'poor dialogue delivery'. This comment has been marked as a negative comment as the disapproval of the trailer is evident.

Sentiment analysis is a topic of greater interest recently since business strategies can be enhanced with insights obtained from the opinion about the product or subject of interest from the users (Balage Filho et al., 2012; Suryawanshi et al., 2020a). As mentioned earlier, the greater part of comments in social media are code-mixed. The conducive nature of such platforms invits all users from different stratus of society to express their opinion about a subject with their own feeling. Hence it is true that the real sentiments about the subject can be extracted from the analysis of code-mixed data. Even with this massive enthusiasm for user-opinions, there is not much effort taken to analyse the sentiment of code-mixed content in under-resourced languages. The contribution of this paper is that we release the gold-standard code-mixed dataset for Malayalam-English annotated for sentiment analysis and provide comprehensive results on popular classification methods. To the best of our knowledge, this is the first code-mixed dataset for Malayalam sentiment analysis. Our code implementing these models along with the dataset is available freely for research purposes[1].

2. Related Work

The sentiment analysis task has become increasingly important due to the explosion of social media, and extensive research has been done for sentiment analysis of monolingual corpora such as English (Hu and Liu, 2004; Wiebe et al., 2005; Jiang et al., 2019), Russian (Rogers et al., 2018), German (Cieliebak et al., 2017), Norwegian (Mæhlum et al., 2019) and Indian languages (Agrawal et al., 2018; Rani et al., 2020).

There have been two traditional approaches to solve sentiment analysis problem such as lexicon-based, and machine learning approaches (Habimana et al., 2019). With the increasing popularity of lexicons in the field of sentiment analysis since 1966, new lexicons namely Word-Net (Fellbaum, 1998), WordNet-Affect (Valitutti, 2004; Chakravarthi et al., 2018; Chakravarthi et al., 2019b), Sen-

tiNet (Poria et al., 2012), and SentiWordNet (Esuli and Sebastiani, 2006) were primarily used. Although being famous for their simplicity, both traditional machine learning and lexicon-based approaches are not efficient when applied on user-generated data, due to the dynamic nature of such data. This is where deep learning approaches take the spotlight for being efficient in adapting to dynamic user-generated data. In the advent of transfer learning, GloVe (Pennington et al., 2014), Word2Vec (Mikolov et al., 2013b), fastText (Bojanowski et al., 2017a) comes with their pros and cons.

Malayalam (Nair et al., 2014; Sarkar and Chakraborty, 2015; Se et al., 2015; Se et al., 2016; Mouthami et al., 2013) has official status in India and other countries. Several research activities on sentiment analysis and events are focused on Malayalam due to their population and use of this language. However, sentiment analysis on Malayalam-English is very low, and data are not easily available for the research. Code-mixed data contains informal language with numerous accidental, deliberate errors, mixing of language and grammatical mixing, which makes previous corpora and methods less suitable to train a model for sentiment analysis in code-mixed data.

In the past few years, there have been increasing efforts on a variety of task using code-mixed text. However, the number of a freely available code-mixed dataset (Ranjan et al., 2016; Jose et al., 2020) are still limited in number, size, availability. For few languages, such as English-Hindi (Joshi et al., 2016; Patra et al., 2018; Priyadharshini et al., 2020), English-Spanish (Solorio et al., 2014) , Chinese-English (Lee and Wang, 2015), and English-Bengali (Patra et al., 2018) datasets are available for research. There are no dataset for Malayalam-English, so inspired by Severyn et al. (2014) we collected and created a code-mixed dataset from YouTube. We provided a use case of the code-mixed Malayalam-English dataset by laying down the baselines which make the use of state of the art techniques such as Dynamic Meta-Embeddings DME (Kiela et al., 2018), Contextualized DME CDME (Kiela et al., 2018), 1D Dimensional Convolution 1DConv (Zhou et al., 2016), and Bidirectional Encoder Representations for Transformers BERT (Devlin et al., 2018).

3. Corpus Creation and Annotation

Our goal was to create a code-mixed dataset for Malayalam-English and to ensure that enough data are available for research purposes. We used *youtube-*

---

[1]https://github.com/bharathichezhiyan/MalayalamMixSentiment

comment-scraper tool [2] to download the comments from YouTube. First, we collected 116,711 sentences for Malayalam from YouTube post comments. We collect the comments from the movie trailers of 2019 based on the YouTube search results for keyword "Malayalam movie 2019". Many of the comments that we downloaded were either fully in English or mixed. Therefore, we filtered out non-code-mixed corpus bases on language identification at comment level with the *langdect library* [3]. That is if the comment is fully in one language than we discarded that comment since monolingual resources are available for these languages. Comments in Malayalam script was also discarded. We preprocessed the comments by removing the emoji's, and sentence length longer than 15 or less than 5 words since sentence more than 15 words will be difficult for annotators. After cleaning, we got 6,738 sentences for Malayalam-English code-mixed post comments.

3.1. Annotation Setup

For annotation, we adopted the approach taken by Mohammad (2016) and each sentence was annotated by a minimum of three annotators according to the following schema:

- **Positive state:** There is an explicit or implicit clue in the text suggesting that the speaker is in a positive state, i.e., happy, admiring, relaxed, and forgiving.

- **Negative state:** There is an explicit or implicit clue in the text suggesting that the speaker is in a negative state, i.e., sad, angry, anxious, and violent.

- **Mixed feelings:** There is an explicit or implicit clue in the text suggesting that the speaker is experiencing both positive and negative feeling: Comparing two movies

- **Neutral state:** There is no explicit or implicit indicator of the speaker's emotional state: Examples are asking for like or subscription or questions about the release date or movie dialogue. This state can be considered as a neutral state.

- **Not in intended language:** For Malayalam if the sentence does not contain Malayalam then it is not Malayalam.

We anonymized sensitive elements that may result in the problem of confidentiality in the YouTube comments. We created Google Forms, in which we collected the annotator's email so the annotator can annotate only once. We collected gender, education and medium of schooling information to know the diversity of the annotators, and we informed the annotators about the use of the data for finding the diversity of annotators. The annotators were given a choice to quit the annotation whenever they are uncomfortable with annotation. Each Google Form has to set contain a maximum of 100 sentences. The annotation of each corpus was performed in three phases. First, each sentence was annotated by two annotators. The second step, the data

---

		Malayalam
Gender	Male	2
	Female	4
Highest Education	Undegraduate	0
	Graduate	0
	Postgraduate	6
Medium of Schooling	English	5
	Native	1
Total		6

Table 1: Annotators

were collected if both annotators agreed, in the case of conflict, a third annotator annotated the sentence. In the third step, if all the three annotators did not agree, then two more annotators annotated the sentences.

3.2. Annotators

Once the Google form was ready, we sent it out to an equal number of male and females to annotate. In the end, six annotators volunteered to annotate all of who are Malayalam-English bilingual proficiency and ready to take up the task seriously. From Table 1, we can see that four female and two male voluntarily annotated our forms. All of them were postgraduates. Though among the annotators only one did schooling in native (Malayalam) medium and others in English medium, we ensured it would not affect the task as all of them are fully proficient at using this language.

3.3. Corpus Statistics

Table 2 shows the corpus statistics of Malayalam-English code-mixed dataset. As is shown, this huge corpus at the end has 70,075 tokens, where 19,992 are unique. There are 6,739 comments and 7,743 distinct sentences in our code-mixed sentiment dataset. On average, there are ten tokens per sentence, and there is at least one sentence per post.

As mentioned before, the whole data has been categorized into five groups viz: positive, negative, neutral, mixed feeling, non-Malayalam. The distribution of data each category is detailed in Table 3. Out of 6,739 posts, 2,811 comments have a positive polarity which is the most frequent category here. If there is no indication of the speaker's emotional state about the subject in the post, the post belongs to a neutral state which is the second-largest category with 1,903 posts here. This may be due to the increasing trend of asking for likes to their comments by the users. We split the corpus retaining 20 percentage that is 1,348 for test, 10 percentage for validation that is 674 for validation, and remaining for training.

3.4. Inter Annotator Agreement

While labelling, the corpus linguist has to decide independently to which category the comment to be added following the guidelines provided strictly. It could be inferred that the guidelines for annotation were clearly understood by all the annotators if they made the same annotations freely. Because of this existence of more than one annotator to label the same set of data, it is necessary to have a metric to compare those annotation qualities. This motivates the use of

---

Language pair	Malayalam-English
Number of Tokens	70,075
Vocabulary Size	19,992
Number of Posts	6,739
Number of Sentences	7,743
Average Sentence Length	10
Average number of sentences per post	1

Table 2: Corpus statistic of Malayalam-English Data

Class	Malayalam-English
Positive	2,811
Negative	738
Mixed feelings	403
Neutral state	1,903
Non-Malayalam	884
Total	6,739

Table 3: Data Distribution

inter-annotator agreement which says how good the annotation decisions made by those multiple annotators on the same dataset are. A high score on this statistical metric does not mean the annotations are accurate, but it shows the homogeneity of agreement among the corpus linguists about the category. In other words, high inter-annotator agreement implies guidelines are clear, and interpretations are correct.

Though computationally complex, we used **Krippendorff's alpha** (α) a prominent method among the numerous approaches developed to measure the degree of agreement between annotators. Krippendorff's alpha (α) is more relevant in our case as it is not affected by missing data, takes care of varying sample sizes, categories, numbers of raters and can also be employed to any measurement levels like nominal, ordinal, interval, ratio. Since more than two people have done the annotation task here and the same peoples annotate not all sentences, Krippendorff's alpha (α) fits here more. We used *nltk*[4] for calculating Krippendorff's alpha (α). Our annotation produced an agreement of 0.890 using nominal metric and 0.911 using interval metric.

4. Difficult Examples

While annotating, a few of the comments were ambiguous about sensing the right feelings from the viewers. Hence the task of annotation for sentiment analysis seemed difficult. The problems include **the comparison of the movie with movies of same or other industries, expression of opinion of different aspects of the movie in the same sentence**. Below shows a few examples of such comments and detailed how we resolved those issues.

- *Kanditt Amala Paul Aadai Tamil mattoru version aanu ennu thonnunu*

"It looks like another version of amala paul's Tamil movie aadai".

Here the viewer doubts the Malayalam movie 'Helen' is similar to the Tamil movie 'Aadai'.Though that movie 'Aadai' was a positively reviewed movie by viewers and critics, we cannot generalize and assume this comment also as positive only because of this comparison. Hence we add it to the category of 'mixed feeling'.

- *Evideo oru Hollywood story varunnilleee. Oru DBT.*

"Somewhere there is a Hollywood storyline...one doubt."

This is also a comparison comment of that same movie 'Helen' mentioned above. Nevertheless, here the difference is that it is compared with the whole Hollywood standard, which is accepted worldwide. Hence it is marked as a positive comment.

- *Trailer pole nalla story undayal mathiyarinu.*

"It was good enough to have a good story like the trailer".

Here viewer mentioned about two aspects of that movie viz: 'trailer' and 'story'. He appreciates the trailer but at the same time doubt about the story. This comment we considered as a positive comment as it is clear that he enjoyed the trailer and also shows strong optimism for that particular movie.

5. Benchark Systems

Traditional machine learning algorithm such as Logistic regression (LR), Support vector machine (SVM), Decision tree (DT), Random Forest (RF), Multinomial Naive Bayes (MNB), K-nearest neighbours (KNN) have been used on the newly annotated English-Malayalam dataset to show the insights about the dataset. The input features are the Term Frequency Inverse Document Frequency (TF-IDF). This approach makes these models trained only on this dataset without taking any pre-trained embeddings.

We also show the result in the deep learning-based models. This is due to the dynamic nature of the data as it is hard to derive a pattern just by using the handcrafted features, which later could be feed inside the algorithms such as logistic regression (LR), support vector machines (SVM). To provide a simple baseline, we implemented four models, which includes Dynamic Meta-Embeddings DME (Kiela et al., 2018), Contextualized DME CDME (Kiela et al.,

---

[4]https://www.nltk.org/

	LR				SVM			
	Precision	Recall	f1-score	support	Precision	Recall	f1-score	support
Mixed feelings	0.59	0.23	0.33	70	0.00	0.00	0.00	70
Negative	0.70	0.45	0.55	138	0.00	0.00	0.00	138
Positive	0.68	0.83	0.75	565	0.00	0.00	0.00	565
Non-Malayalam	0.69	0.58	0.63	177	0.13	1.00	0.23	177
Neutral	0.65	0.65	0.65	398	0.00	0.00	0.00	398
macro avg	**0.66**	0.55	0.58	1348	0.03	0.20	0.05	1348
weighted avg	0.67	0.67	0.66	1348	0.02	0.13	0.03	1348
	DT				RF			
Mixed feelings	0.21	0.19	0.20	70	0.50	0.03	0.05	70
Negative	0.60	0.44	0.51	138	0.75	0.37	0.50	138
Positive	0.62	0.67	0.65	565	0.62	0.83	0.71	565
Non-Malayalam	0.42	0.57	0.49	177	0.61	0.60	0.61	177
Neutral	0.56	0.46	0.51	398	0.64	0.56	0.60	398
macro avg	0.48	0.47	0.47	1348	0.62	0.48	0.49	1348
weighted avg	0.55	0.55	0.55	1348	0.63	0.63	0.61	1348
	MNB				KNN			
Mixed feelings	0.00	0.00	0.00	70	0.50	0.01	0.03	70
Negative	0.93	0.10	0.18	138	0.75	0.02	0.04	138
Positive	0.54	0.93	0.68	565	0.73	0.11	0.19	565
Non-Malayalam	0.84	0.21	0.34	177	0.16	0.63	0.25	177
Neutral	0.66	0.52	0.58	398	0.34	0.47	0.39	398
macro avg	0.60	0.35	0.36	1348	0.50	0.25	0.18	1348
weighted avg	0.63	0.58	0.52	1348	0.53	0.27	0.23	1348
	DME				CDME			
Mixed feelings	0.11	0.06	0.07	70	0.08	0.11	0.10	70
Negative	0.20	0.12	0.15	138	0.24	0.12	0.16	138
Positive	0.59	0.44	0.50	565	0.57	0.52	0.54	565
Non-Malayalam	0.23	0.62	0.34	177	0.29	0.76	0.42	177
Neutral	0.52	0.44	0.47	398	0.67	0.35	0.46	398
macro avg	0.33	0.33	0.31	1348	0.37	0.37	0.34	1348
weighted avg	0.45	0.41	0.41	1348	0.51	0.44	0.44	1348
	1DConv				BERT			
Mixed feelings	0.26	0.26	0.26	70	0.00	0.00	0.00	70
Negative	0.56	0.33	0.41	138	0.57	0.55	0.56	138
Positive	0.70	0.74	0.72	565	0.83	0.87	0.85	565
Non-Malayalam	0.62	0.75	0.68	177	0.87	0.93	0.90	177
Neutral	0.61	0.60	0.61	398	0.73	0.79	0.76	398
macro avg	0.55	0.54	0.54	1348	0.60	**0.63**	**0.61**	1348
weighted avg	0.63	0.63	0.63	1348	**0.73**	**0.78**	**0.75**	1348

Table 4: Precision, recall, F1-score and support for Logistic regression (LR), Support vector machine (SVM), Decision tree (DT), Random Forest (RF), Multinomial Naive Bayes (MNB), K-nearest neighbours (KNN), DME, CDME, 1DConv, BERT.

2018), 1D Dimensional Convolution 1DConv (Zhou et al., 2016), Bidirectional Encoder Representations for Transformers BERT (Devlin et al., 2018).
We evaluated our dataset based on the precision, recall and F-score of these baselines. We used *sklearn* [5], the micro average is calculated globally by counting the total true positives, false negative and false positive. The macro average compute the metric independently for each class and then take the unweighted mean. The macro average does not take imbalance into account. A weighted average calculated for each label like macro, and find their average weighted by support. For our test, there are 2,075 positive examples, 424 negative, 173 neutral, 377 mixed feelings, and 100 non-Malayalam examples. This is a variation of macro to include label imbalance. This may cause F-score not be between precision and recall.

We combined fastText (Bojanowski et al., 2017b) and word2vec (Mikolov et al., 2013a) in DME and CDME baselines. The fastText and word2vec were trained on our code-switched dataset. In DME, we are combining the mentioned embeddings by doing a weighted sum. On the otherhand CDME is using self-attention based mechanism on top of DME to make the embeddings context-dependent. 1DConv makes use of a 1D convolution filter to represent each word with the context of the neighbouring word in the range of the kernel. In this convolutional neural network (CNN) (Kalchbrenner et al., 2014) approach, we are trying to capture the standout features from the text. BERT makes use of encoder-decoder architecture with an attention mechanism which increases the flexibility to read sequence both (left to right and vice versa) ways.

From the results shown in the Table 4, all the machine learning algorithms succeed in classifying all the classes except SVM. A recall of 1.00 and precision around 0.13 for non-Malayalam class shows that all the classes have been labelled as non-Malayalam irrespectively. Other than SVM, LR, DT, RF shows considerable macro average score for precision, recall and F1-score. However, MNB and KNN achieve higher macro-averaged precision at the expense of the lower recall values. As mentioned earlier, deep learning models are using pre-trained embeddings. The use of fastText in combination with word2vec for DME and CDME gives both local as well as global context. 1DConv shows the better macro-averaged score in precision, recall and F1-score, BERT, on the other hand, fails to identify "Mixed feeling" class. However, DME and CDME succeed in identifying all the classes.

6. Conclusion

In this paper, we have presented the Malayalam-English corpus a code-mixed corpus of YouTube comments annotated for sentiment analysis. This annotation project aims to allow researches to enable research on code-mixed sentiment analysis, as well as provide useful data for code-mixed research. We also provide an inter-annotator agreement score in terms of Kripendorff's alpha and baseline results, as well as making the corpus available to the research community.

7. Acknowledgments

This publication has emanated from research supported in part by a research grant from Science Foundation Ireland (SFI) under Grant Number SFI/12/RC/2289 (Insight), SFI/12/RC/2289_P2 (Insight_2), co-funded by the European Regional Development Fund as well as by the EU H2020 programme under grant agreements 731015 (ELEXIS-European Lexical Infrastructure), 825182 (Prêt-à-LLOD), and Irish Research Council grant IRCLA/2017/129 (CARDAMOM-Comparative Deep Models of Language for Minority and Historical Languages).

8. Bibliographical References

Agrawal, R., Chenthil Kumar, V., Muralidharan, V., and Sharma, D. (2018). No more beating about the bush : A step towards idiom handling for Indian language NLP. In *Proceedings of the Eleventh International Conference on Language Resources and Evaluation (LREC 2018)*, Miyazaki, Japan, May. European Language Resources Association (ELRA).

Androutsopoulos, J. (2013). Code-switching in computer-mediated communication. *Pragmatics of computer-mediated communication*, pages 667–694.

Balage Filho, P. P., Brun, C., and Rondeau, G. (2012). A graphical user interface for feature-based opinion mining. In *Proceedings of the Demonstration Session at the Conference of the North American Chapter of the Association for Computational Linguistics: Human Language Technologies*, pages 5–8, Montréal, Canada, June. Association for Computational Linguistics.

Bali, K., Sharma, J., Choudhury, M., and Vyas, Y. (2014). "I am borrowing ya mixing ?" an analysis of English-Hindi code mixing in Facebook. In *Proceedings of the First Workshop on Computational Approaches to Code Switching*, pages 116–126, Doha, Qatar, October. Association for Computational Linguistics.

Barman, U., Das, A., Wagner, J., and Foster, J. (2014). Code mixing: A challenge for language identification in the language of social media. In *Proceedings of the First Workshop on Computational Approaches to Code Switching*, pages 13–23, Doha, Qatar, October. Association for Computational Linguistics.

Bojanowski, P., Grave, E., Joulin, A., and Mikolov, T. (2017a). Enriching word vectors with subword information. *Transactions of the Association for Computational Linguistics*, 5:135–146.

Bojanowski, P., Grave, E., Joulin, A., and Mikolov, T. (2017b). Enriching word vectors with subword information. *Transactions of the Association for Computational Linguistics*, 5:135–146.

Chakravarthi, B. R., Arcan, M., and McCrae, J. P. (2018). Improving Wordnets for Under-Resourced Languages Using Machine Translation. In *Proceedings of the 9th Global WordNet Conference*. The Global WordNet Conference 2018 Committee.

Chakravarthi, B. R., Arcan, M., and McCrae, J. P. (2019a). Comparison of different orthographies for machine translation of under-resourced dravidian languages. In *2nd Conference on Language, Data and Knowledge (LDK 2019)*. Schloss Dagstuhl-Leibniz-Zentrum fuer Informatik.

Chakravarthi, B. R., Arcan, M., and McCrae, J. P. (2019b). WordNet gloss translation for under-resourced languages using multilingual neural machine translation. In *Proceedings of the Second Workshop on Multilingualism at the Intersection of Knowledge Bases and Machine Translation*, pages 1–7, Dublin, Ireland, August. European Association for Machine Translation.

Chakravarthi, B. R., Priyadharshini, R., Stearns, B., Jayapal, A., S, S., Arcan, M., Zarrouk, M., and McCrae, J. P. (2019c). Multilingual multimodal machine translation for Dravidian languages utilizing phonetic transcription. In *Proceedings of the 2nd Workshop on Technologies for MT of Low Resource Languages*, pages 56–63, Dublin, Ireland, 20 August. European Association for Machine Translation.

Chakravarthi, B. R., Muralidaran, V., Priyadharshini, R., and McCrae, J. P. (2020). Corpus creation for sentiment analysis in code-mixed Tamil-English text. In *Proceedings of the 1st Joint Workshop of SLTU (Spoken Language Technologies for Under-resourced languages) and CCURL (Collaboration and Computing for Under-Resourced Languages) (SLTU-CCURL 2020)*, Marseille,

France, May. European Language Resources Association (ELRA).

Cieliebak, M., Deriu, J. M., Egger, D., and Uzdilli, F. (2017). A Twitter corpus and benchmark resources for German sentiment analysis. In *Proceedings of the Fifth International Workshop on Natural Language Processing for Social Media*, pages 45–51, Valencia, Spain, April. Association for Computational Linguistics.

Das, A. and Gambäck, B. (2014). Identifying languages at the word level in code-mixed Indian social media text. In *Proceedings of the 11th International Conference on Natural Language Processing*, pages 378–387, Goa, India, December. NLP Association of India.

Devlin, J., Chang, M.-W., Lee, K., and Toutanova, K. (2018). BERT: Pre-training of deep bidirectional transformers for language understanding. *arXiv preprint arXiv:1810.04805*.

Mona Diab, et al., editors. (2014). *Proceedings of the First Workshop on Computational Approaches to Code Switching*, Doha, Qatar, October. Association for Computational Linguistics.

Esuli, A. and Sebastiani, F. (2006). Sentiwordnet: A publicly available lexical resource for opinion mining. In *In Proceedings of the 5th Conference on Language Resources and Evaluation (LREC'06*, pages 417–422.

Fellbaum, C. (1998). *WordNet: An Electronic Lexical Database*. Bradford Books.

Habimana, O., Li, Y., Li, R., Gu, X., and Yu, G. (2019). Sentiment analysis using deep learning approaches: an overview. *Science China Information Sciences*, 63(1):111102, Dec.

Hu, M. and Liu, B. (2004). Mining and summarizing customer reviews. In *Proceedings of the Tenth ACM SIGKDD International Conference on Knowledge Discovery and Data Mining*, KDD '04, page 168–177, New York, NY, USA. Association for Computing Machinery.

Jiang, Q., Chen, L., Xu, R., Ao, X., and Yang, M. (2019). A challenge dataset and effective models for aspect-based sentiment analysis. In *Proceedings of the 2019 Conference on Empirical Methods in Natural Language Processing and the 9th International Joint Conference on Natural Language Processing (EMNLP-IJCNLP)*, pages 6279–6284, Hong Kong, China, November. Association for Computational Linguistics.

Jose, N., Chakravarthi, B. R., Suryawanshi, S., Sherly, E., and McCrae, J. P. (2020). A survey of current datasets for code-switching research. In *2020 6th International Conference on Advanced Computing & Communication Systems (ICACCS)*.

Joshi, A., Prabhu, A., Shrivastava, M., and Varma, V. (2016). Towards sub-word level compositions for sentiment analysis of Hindi-English code mixed text. In *Proceedings of COLING 2016, the 26th International Conference on Computational Linguistics: Technical Papers*, pages 2482–2491, Osaka, Japan, December. The COLING 2016 Organizing Committee.

Kalchbrenner, N., Grefenstette, E., and Blunsom, P. (2014). A convolutional neural network for modelling sentences. In *Proceedings of the 52nd Annual Meeting of the Association for Computational Linguistics (Volume 1: Long Papers)*, pages 655–665, Baltimore, Maryland, June. Association for Computational Linguistics.

Kiela, D., Wang, C., and Cho, K. (2018). Dynamic meta-embeddings for improved sentence representations. In *Proceedings of the 2018 Conference on Empirical Methods in Natural Language Processing*, pages 1466–1477, Brussels, Belgium, October-November. Association for Computational Linguistics.

Krishnamurti, B. (2003). *The Dravidian Languages*. Cambridge University Press.

Lalitha Devi, S. (2019). Resolving pronouns for a resource-poor language, Malayalam using resource-rich language, Tamil. In *Proceedings of the International Conference on Recent Advances in Natural Language Processing (RANLP 2019)*, pages 611–618, Varna, Bulgaria, September. INCOMA Ltd.

Lee, S. and Wang, Z. (2015). Emotion in code-switching texts: Corpus construction and analysis. In *Proceedings of the Eighth SIGHAN Workshop on Chinese Language Processing*, pages 91–99, Beijing, China, July. Association for Computational Linguistics.

Mæhlum, P., Barnes, J., Øvrelid, L., and Velldal, E. (2019). Annotating evaluative sentences for sentiment analysis: a dataset for Norwegian. In *Proceedings of the 22nd Nordic Conference on Computational Linguistics*, pages 121–130, Turku, Finland, September–October. Linköping University Electronic Press.

Mikolov, T., Chen, K., Corrado, G., and Dean, J. (2013a). Efficient estimation of word representations in vector space. *arXiv preprint arXiv:1301.3781*.

Mikolov, T., Sutskever, I., Chen, K., Corrado, G. S., and Dean, J. (2013b). Distributed representations of words and phrases and their compositionality. In C. J. C. Burges, et al., editors, *Advances in Neural Information Processing Systems 26*, pages 3111–3119. Curran Associates, Inc.

Mohammad, S. (2016). A practical guide to sentiment annotation: Challenges and solutions. In *Proceedings of the 7th Workshop on Computational Approaches to Subjectivity, Sentiment and Social Media Analysis*, pages 174–179, San Diego, California, June. Association for Computational Linguistics.

Mouthami, K., Devi, K. N., and Bhaskaran, V. M. (2013). Sentiment analysis and classification based on textual reviews. In *2013 international conference on Information communication and embedded systems (ICICES)*, pages 271–276. IEEE.

Nair, D. S., Jayan, J. P., Sherly, E., et al. (2014). Sentima-sentiment extraction for Malayalam. In *2014 International Conference on Advances in Computing, Communications and Informatics (ICACCI)*, pages 1719–1723. IEEE.

Patra, B. G., Das, D., and Das, A. (2018). Sentiment analysis of code-mixed indian languages: An overview of sail_code-mixed shared task@ icon-2017. *arXiv preprint arXiv:1803.06745*.

Pennington, J., Socher, R., and Manning, C. D. (2014). Glove: Global vectors for word representation. In

EMNLP, volume 14, pages 1532–1543.

Poria, S., Gelbukh, A., Cambria, E., Yang, P., Hussain, A., and Durrani, T. (2012). Merging SenticNet and WordNet-Affect emotion lists for sentiment analysis. In *2012 IEEE 11th International Conference on Signal Processing*, volume 2, pages 1251–1255, Oct.

Priyadharshini, R., Chakravarthi, B. R., Vegupatti, M., and McCrae, J. P. (2020). Named entity recognition for code-mixed Indian corpus using meta embedding. In *2020 6th International Conference on Advanced Computing & Communication Systems (ICACCS)*.

Rani, P., Suryawanshi, S., Goswami, K., Chakravarthi, B. R., Fransen, T., and McCrae, J. P. (2020). A comparative study of different state-of-the-art hate speech detection methods for Hindi-English code-mixed data. In *Proceedings of the Second Workshop on Trolling, Aggression and Cyberbullying*, Marseille, France, May. European Language Resources Association (ELRA).

Ranjan, P., Raja, B., Priyadharshini, R., and Balabantaray, R. C. (2016). A comparative study on code-mixed data of Indian social media vs formal text. In *2016 2nd International Conference on Contemporary Computing and Informatics (IC3I)*, pages 608–611, Dec.

Rogers, A., Romanov, A., Rumshisky, A., Volkova, S., Gronas, M., and Gribov, A. (2018). RuSentiment: An enriched sentiment analysis dataset for social media in Russian. In *Proceedings of the 27th International Conference on Computational Linguistics*, pages 755–763, Santa Fe, New Mexico, USA, August. Association for Computational Linguistics.

Rosowsky, A. (2010). 'writing it in english': script choices among young multilingual muslims in the uk. *Journal of Multilingual and Multicultural Development*, 31(2):163–179.

Saint-Jacques, B. (1987). The roman alphabet in the japanese writing system. *Visible Language*, 21(1):88.

Sarkar, K. and Chakraborty, S. (2015). A sentiment analysis system for indian language tweets. In *International Conference on Mining Intelligence and Knowledge Exploration*, pages 694–702. Springer.

Scotton, C. M. (1982). The possibility of code-switching: motivation for maintaining multilingualism. *Anthropological linguistics*, pages 432–444.

Se, S., Vinayakumar, R., Kumar, M. A., and Soman, K. (2015). AMRITA-CEN@ SAIL2015: sentiment analysis in Indian languages. In *International Conference on Mining Intelligence and Knowledge Exploration*, pages 703–710. Springer.

Se, S., Vinayakumar, R., Kumar, M. A., and Soman, K. (2016). Predicting the sentimental reviews in Tamil movie using machine learning algorithms. *Indian Journal of Science and Technology*, 9(45).

Severyn, A., Moschitti, A., Uryupina, O., Plank, B., and Filippova, K. (2014). Opinion mining on YouTube. In *Proceedings of the 52nd Annual Meeting of the Association for Computational Linguistics (Volume 1: Long Papers)*, pages 1252–1261, Baltimore, Maryland, June. Association for Computational Linguistics.

Solorio, T., Blair, E., Maharjan, S., Bethard, S., Diab, M.,

Ghoneim, M., Hawwari, A., AlGhamdi, F., Hirschberg, J., Chang, A., and Fung, P. (2014). Overview for the first shared task on language identification in code-switched data. In *Proceedings of the First Workshop on Computational Approaches to Code Switching*, pages 62–72, Doha, Qatar, October. Association for Computational Linguistics.

Sreelekha, S. and Bhattacharyya, P. (2018). Morphology Injection for English-Malayalam Statistical Machine Translation. In Nicoletta Calzolari (Conference chair), et al., editors, *Proceedings of the Eleventh International Conference on Language Resources and Evaluation (LREC 2018)*, Miyazaki, Japan, May 7-12, 2018. European Language Resources Association (ELRA).

Suryawanshi, S., Chakravarthi, B. R., Arcan, M., and Buitelaar, P. (2020a). Multimodal meme dataset (MultiOFF) for identifying offensive content in image and text. In *Proceedings of the Second Workshop on Trolling, Aggression and Cyberbullying*, Marseille, France, May. European Language Resources Association (ELRA).

Suryawanshi, S., Chakravarthi, B. R., Verma, P., Arcan, M., McCrae, J. P., and Buitelaar, P. (2020b). A dataset for troll classification of Tamil memes. In *Proceedings of the 5th Workshop on Indian Language Data Resource and Evaluation (WILDRE-5)*, Marseille, France, May. European Language Resources Association (ELRA).

Tay, M. W. (1989). Code switching and code mixing as a communicative strategy in multilingual discourse. *World Englishes*, 8(3):407–417.

Thottingal, S. (2019). Finite state transducer based morphology analysis for Malayalam language. In *Proceedings of the 2nd Workshop on Technologies for MT of Low Resource Languages*, pages 1–5, Dublin, Ireland, August. European Association for Machine Translation.

Valitutti, R. (2004). WordNet-Affect: an affective extension of wordnet. In *In Proceedings of the 4th International Conference on Language Resources and Evaluation*, pages 1083–1086.

Wiebe, J., Wilson, T., and Cardie, C. (2005). Annotating expressions of opinions and emotions in language. *Language Resources and Evaluation*, 39(2):165–210, May.

Zhou, P., Qi, Z., Zheng, S., Xu, J., Bao, H., and Xu, B. (2016). Text classification improved by integrating bidirectional lstm with two-dimensional max pooling. *arXiv preprint arXiv:1611.06639*.

Proceedings of the 1st Joint SLTU and CCURL Workshop (SLTU-CCURL 2020), pages 185–193
Language Resources and Evaluation Conference (LREC 2020), Marseille, 11–16 May 2020
© European Language Resources Association (ELRA), licensed under CC-BY-NC

Speech-Emotion Detection in an Indonesian Movie

Fahmi, Meganingrum Arista Jiwanggi, Mirna Adriani
Faculty of Computer Science, Universitas Indonesia
Universitas Indonesia
fahmi51@ui.ac.id, meganingrum@cs.ui.ac.id, mirna@cs.ui.ac.id

Abstract

The growing demand to develop an automatic emotion recognition system for the Human-Computer Interaction field had pushed some research in speech emotion detection. Although it is growing, there is still little research about automatic speech emotion detection in Bahasa Indonesia. Another issue is the lack of standard corpus for this research area in Bahasa Indonesia. This study proposed several approaches to detect speech-emotion in the dialogs of an Indonesian movie by classifying them into 4 different emotion classes i.e. happiness, sadness, anger, and neutral. There are two different speech data representations used in this study i.e. statistical and temporal/sequence representations. This study used Artificial Neural Network (ANN), Recurrent Neural Network (RNN) with Long Short Term Memory (LSTM) variation, word embedding, and also the hybrid of three to perform the classification task. The best accuracies given by one-vs-rest scenario for each emotion class with speech-transcript pairs using hybrid of non-temporal and embedding approach are 1) happiness: 76.31%; 2) sadness: 86.46%; 3) anger: 82.14%; and 4) neutral: 68.51%. The multiclass classification resulted in 64.66% of precision, 66.79% of recall, and 64.83% of F1-score.

Keywords: Speech, Emotion Detection, Bahasa Indonesia, Artificial Neural Network (ANN), Recurrent Neural Network (RNN), Long Short Term Memory (LSTM), Word Embedding

1. Introduction

The growth of studies about speech emotion detection began to be applied in various fields of computing, especially in the field of Human-Computer Interaction (HCI). A good HCI system is said to not only be able to capture important information but also to detect emotions from users, so the system will give more appropriate responses (Wunarso and Soelistio, 2017). Some examples of the useful application of emotion detection in HCI systems are the automated call center system or personal assistant application in which such a system might provide the more natural interaction when emotions are involved to generate users' responses (Lubis et al., 2014).

The commonly used emotion grouping model is the valence-arousal model by Barrett and Russell (1999). Valence-arousal model states that emotions can be decomposed in 2 aspects i.e. the valence aspect which expresses the sentiment of emotions and the arousal/intensity aspect which states the intensity in expressing those emotions. Valence-arousal models are built-in 2-dimensional planes with the horizontal axis is valence and the vertical axis is intensity. Then each emotional class is measured in degrees of intensity and valence and mapped in the 2-dimensional plane. For example, anger can be seen as a class of emotions that have negative sentiments and are overflowed with a high enough intensity, then the valence-arousal model of angry emotions will be mapped to the high-intensity quadrant and negative valence. Valence-arousal models provide information that emotional classes that are in one quadrant have high similarity and are difficult to distinguish by humans (Barret and Russel, 1999). Generally, research on speech emotion considers the issue of choosing emotional classes.

One of the earliest studies about speech emotion is a study by Yu et al. (2001) that developed a speech classification model for 4 classes of emotion using pitch as its feature. For the following years, the leading studies in the field of speech emotion began to adapt Mel-scaled Frequency Cepstral Coefficient (MFCC) as the feature to improve the system performance, e.g. the research by Ko et al. (2017) that built a speech classification model for anger, sad, happiness, disgusted, shocked, scared, and neutral.

The research about speech in Bahasa Indonesia has also been beginning to grow in the past few years. The topics include speech-language identification (Safitri et al., 2016), speech synthesis (Vania and Adriani, 2011), and speech recognition (Wanagiri and Adriani, 2012). However, there are still a few numbers of research about speech emotion conducted in Bahasa Indonesia, whereas research on speech emotion has been done in other languages such as English (Livingstone and Russo, 2018), German (Burkhardt et al., 2005) and Language Persia (Keshtiari, 2015). The other issue is the lack of standard corpus in Bahasa Indonesia to be used for the experiments in automatic speech-emotion detection.

We also learn from the previous studies that although usually the speech data is transformed into statistical representations, the temporal speech data representation may address some issues on the previous well-known representation. However, the research that views speech data as temporal data was still hardly found. Also, studies of speech emotion were rarely utilizing textual information. To address the above problems, this research aims to develop the speech-emotion detection model for Bahasa Indonesia by transforming speech data into temporal representation as to the acoustic feature and also by adding textual information from speech as the lexical feature. Based on the valence-arousal model, we choose 4 emotion classes for this study i.e. happiness, sadness, anger, and neutral that comes from different quadrants in the model to improve the ability of the system to distinguish the emotion.

This paper structure is as follows: the Introduction section describes briefly about the background of this research. The second section of Related Works summaries the previous researches in a particular area. The Methodology section explains briefly about the steps run to do the research. The Results and Analysis sums up the result of our experiments and also the summary of our analysis behind the results. Lastly, the Conclusion wraps up the content of this paper and describes the possible future works.

2. Related Works

2.1 Research on Detecting Emotions in Speech Data

There were several prior studies related to speech-emotion detection. The research group that will be reviewed first used statistical representations such as averages, standard deviations, medians, minimums, and maximums as features in speech data. Previously, the audio data features are generally in the form of sequences that depends on to the duration and the majority of classification algorithms cannot process data of different sizes. The statistical view is one of the solutions to the above problems and was adopted in research conducted by Yu et al. (2001), Lubis et al.(2014), and Wunarso and Soelistio (2017).

The first study about speech emotion using the statistical feature was conducted by Yu et al. (2001). This study aimed to build a model of speech-emotion classification in 4 classes (anger, sadness, happiness, and neutral) using the corpus built from the television series. The features used in this study focus on the use of pitch and rhythm such as smoothed pitch, derivative pitch, and speaking rate. The results of this process are 16 features. This study used Artificial Neural Network (ANN) algorithm, K-Nearest Neighbor (KNN), and Support Vector Machine (SVM). The experimental results show that SVM resulted in the most accurate predictions of up to 77% for anger, 65% for happiness, 83% for neutral, and 70% for sadness.

The second study on the statistical feature group is the speech emotion research by Wunarso and Soelistio (2017) that builds a model of speech emotion classification for anger, sadness, and happiness using the corpus built by collecting voice recordings from 38 volunteers and producing around 3420 speech data. The study only used 3 features i.e. the average amplitude, average wavelet, and duration of the speech. The classification algorithms are ANN and SVM where SVM resulted in 76% accuracy and ANN reached only 66% accuracy.

The third study is the speech emotion research by Lubis et al. (2014) that builds a model of speech emotional classification for anger, sadness, happiness, and neutral using the corpus built by collecting speech from the talk show. The study used various features i.e. Mel-scaled Frequency Cepstral Coefficient (MFCC), spectral features, energy, and pitch with SVM as the classification algorithm. The average accuracy obtained is around 80% using SVM.

The second group of researchers used temporal representations as to the speech data features. It means, the sequence of features directly feeds into the algorithms without worrying about dimensional differences. As explained, the different duration of audio data can be a problem because there are not many algorithms that are able to handle these problems, but the studies below adopt algorithms that can accept sequence inputs such as the Hidden Markov Model (HMM) in research by Ko et al. (2017) and Recurrent Neural Network (RNN) in a study by Basu et al. (2017).

The first study using the temporal feature is the study of speech emotion by Ko et al. (2017) that aimed to build a speech emotion classification model in anger, pleasure, sadness, neutral, disgust, surprise, and fear. They build a corpus from drama and films with around 454 speech data with a fairly even distribution for each class. The 39 features were collected and the classification was performed with the Hidden Markov Model (HMM) resulting in an average accuracy of around 78%.

Another study using the temporal feature performed by (Basu et al., 2017) build a speech emotion classification model for anger, pleasure, boredom, neutral, anxiety, disgust, and fear. The speech corpus was the same as the research by Burkhardt et al. (2005) and they used 13 channels from MFCC as the features. The classification model uses a combination of Convolutional Neural Network and Recurring Neural Network (CNN-RNN). The accuracy of the combination model was up to 80%.

2.2 Research on Detecting Emotions in Text Data

Unlike the studies in speech data, research on emotion detection in Bahasa Indonesia for the text data has been done by various methods. Several prior studies will be discussed in this section including the research by The et al. (2015) which focuses on emotional tweets, and research by Muljono et al. (2016) which focuses on fairytale scripts, and research by Savigny and Purwarianti (2017) which focuses on YouTube comments.

The research conducted by The et al. (2015) aims to build a classification model of emotions in the text using 5 classes i.e. happy, love, anger, fear, and sadness. The text corpus was crawled from Indonesian-language tweets. The feature extraction includes various types of features i.e. N-Gram features such as Bigram and Unigram, linguistic features such as Part-Of-Speech (POS) Tagging, semantic features such as sentiments in the Indonesian lexicon, and orthographic features such as punctuations. The experiments were held in two stages. In the first stage, the tweets with emotion and without emotion were separated, then in the next stage, the classification model only works on the tweets with emotions. This study used several classification algorithms such as Maximum Entropy (ME) and Support Vector Machine (SVM). The evaluation results found that ME performance is superior to SVM with 72% accuracy.

The second study was conducted by Muljono et al. (2016) with the aim to build a classification model of emotions into six classes i.e. anger, sadness, joy, surprise, disgust, and fear. The corpus was obtained from a collection of fairy tales that are labeled manually with about 1200 data in the corpus. The pre-processing steps were stemming, stopword removal, and normalizing the data. Then the data is mapped into the feature vector using one-hot encoding with TF-IDF weighting. The machine learning model used is Naïve Bayes, Decision Tree J48, Support Vector Machine, and K-Nearest Neighbor. The experimental results show that SVM provides the best performance with an average accuracy of 85%.

The last study to be discussed was conducted by Savigny & Purwarianti (2017) with the aim of building a model of the classification of emotional emotions in 7 classes i.e anger, sadness, joy, surprise, disgust, fear and neutral. The text corpus was obtained from Indonesian-language comments on YouTube.The total data obtained was around 3000 comments with a relatively even distribution for each emotional class. The preprocessing methods were applied such as deleting duplicate characters, deleting numerical characters, and translating emoticons in the appropriate words. Next, each data in the corpus is changed in the vector representation using the word embedding algorithm with Continous Bag-Of-Words (CBOW) and Skip-Gram architecture. The classification methods used are vector averages, vector averages with Term Frequency - Inverse Document Frequency (TF-IDF) weighting, and Convolutional Neural Network (CNN). The results of the experiment show that CNN provides the best performance with an accuracy of around 73%.

3. Methodology

3.1 Data Collection

The dataset used for this study is collected from Indonesian widescreen movies because the dialogues in the movie mostly well-structured and rarely overlap. Moreover, the audio quality of the big screen movie is also very good given the clear voice and intonation of the actors in which the background noise is also rarely found.

The Indonesian movie selected in this study titled "Cek Toko Sebelah". The reason for choosing only one movie to build our dataset is to limit the variations in our audio data such as the variation of speakers (actors), the variations of the speaker's accents, and the variations caused by the difference of sound recording technique in the different movie. Ideally, the dataset is built with a limited number of variations with limited sentences as well, e.g. the research by Burkhardt et al. (2005) used a dataset using 5 actors and 5 actresses where each actor/actress can 10 different sentences in 7 emotional classes. However, the efforts to limit the number of films used have an impact on the amount of data that can be collected.

3.2 Initial Processing

The initial processing steps include audio and its respected transcript extraction, audio segmentation, and transcript tokenization. First, we did audio and transcript extraction from the film since the focus of the research was limited to speech and transcript data. The audio data has 1 hour and 44 minutes duration with a 48 kHz sampling rate along with the transcript data of 1776 sentences.

Before segmenting audio data, any particular segment of speech data must meet the set of standard eligibility conditions to be used in research i.e.

1. The sentences spoken in a segment of speech must be complete, uninterrupted in the middle or not an unfinished sentence;
2. Speech data must be properly spoken by 1 speaker, no other speaker may cut the sentence spoken in one segment of speech data
3. Speech data must be free from/minimally interrupted by background songs/noise that disturbs resulting in cannot be clearly heard.

Next, we performed segmentation by cutting the extracted audio data into pieces of speech data. At this stage, the transcript data is also used to help the segmentation process. Transcript data stores information about the start and end time of one particular speech that is accurate to milliseconds. By utilizing this information, the audio

segmentation can be done automatically and accurately. The segmentation results are 1776 speech pieces and transcripts.

However, the errors may occur from the automatic segmentation process e.g. when the start or end time in the transcript data is inaccurate. Therefore, it needs to be checked manually. After a manual check, 965 pieces of speech are valid and ready to be labeled. Then, we tokenized the transcript of 965 speech data from the previous process. The transcript tokenization includes lowercasing all letters and removing all the special symbols such as periods, commas and numerical symbols.

3.3 Labeling

At this stage, 965 collected speech data and transcripts were labeled. The labeling process involves two annotators i.e. a 20-year-old man student and a 40-year-old woman who works as a tailor. Each annotator labeled the pairs of speech data and the respected transcript following some annotation guidelines as follows:

1. Play speech audio, focusing on aspects of actor/actress pronunciation such as intonation, rhythm, pauses, and speech emphasis.
2. Read the speech transcript, focus on the meaning of the sentence spoken by the speaker.
3. Determine the emotion class that is most appropriate for the pronunciation of the speech and the meaning of the sentence. For example, the sentence "This is very funny huh" which is spoken in high intonation indicates happiness.
4. Give labels according to the emotional class captured, the following is a list of labels used i.e. a) Label "0" is for happiness, b) Label "1" is for sadness, c) Label "2" is for anger, d) Label "3" is for neutral.

Then, both annotators did the annotation process for each pair of speech data and its transcript. We only include the data that is annotated with the same class by two annotators in our dataset while the remaining data will be discarded. At this stage, there are 775 data with the number of samples for each class shown in Table 1 below.

Happiness	Sadness	Anger	Neutral
186	181	138	270

Table 1: The Number of Samples per Emotion Class

3.4 Feature Extraction

We conducted two steps of feature extraction, i.e. feature extraction for speech data and feature extraction for transcript data. For speech data, the features used are Mel-scaled Frequency Cepstral Coefficient (MFCC), pitch, and Root Mean Squared Energy (RMSE). As for the transcript data, the feature used is the dense word vector representation with the word embedding approach. In addition, statistical computing is also performed on the MFCC, PITT, and RMSE features so that it can be used on non-temporal models.

3.4.1 Feature Extraction in Speech Data

The first feature taken from speech data is the MFCC feature. The MFCC maps sound signals on a Mel scale that is compatible with the human hearing system. The MFCC feature of the sound signal has a dimensionality between 13 to 26 dimensions for each frame, but in this study, a more general variation with 13 dimensions for each frame was used. The second feature taken from speech data is the RMSE feature. RMSE provides cumulative energy information on speech. RMSE is used to measure the loudness of a sound signal. The RMSE feature is a 1-dimensional vector for each frame. The last feature taken from speech data is the pitch feature. The pitch feature represents the characteristics of the sound from a frequency perspective so that it is good to answer questions such as "what is the average frequency of an angry man's voice?" or "what is the average frequency of a woman's voice that is sad?". Pitch features are 1-dimensional vectors for each frame.

3.4.2 Feature Extraction in Transcript Data

Transcript data is represented in the dense word vector using the word embedding algorithm Continuous Bag-Of-Words (CBOW) with Word2Vec. To convert sentences into word vectors, it is necessary to develop a word embedding model based on data with similar characteristics. Therefore, 5,572 additional transcripts from other Indonesian big-screen films were also collected to build the Word2Vec model. Then, we will extract the vector representation for each word in the transcript sentence. Each word vector in one sentence will be calculated on average or we may call it the average word vector. The calculation of averages also considers the TF-IDF scores for each word.

3.4.3 Statistics Features on Speech Data

Features in speech data need to be represented in statistical measures so that they can be used by non-temporal models. Therefore, it is necessary to transform the speech data features which were originally in the form of sequences into a numerical value following certain statistical measures. In this study, the statistical measures that will be used are the average and standard deviations.

3.5 Model Development

The models used include non-temporal and temporal models for speech data and embedding models for transcript data. Also, a joint model will be discussed that can receive speech data input as well as transcript data.

3.5.1 Development of Non-Temporal Models

The algorithm used in the model is the Artificial Neural Network (ANN). ANN is composed of one layer for input and one activation layer in the form of a sigmoid function for output. The model will accept statistical representations (averages and standard deviations) of each feature (MFCC, pitch, and RMSE). In this study, hyperparameter tuning will be performed on the number of neurons in the input layer. We also performed feature selection by finding the best combination of the features above. The architectural detail used can be seen in Figure 1. The dense_25 represents the input layer that accepts a vector with dimension 30 and returns a vector with dimension 64 and dense_26 represents the sigmoid layer that receives a vector with dimension 64 and returns the numeric value in the form of the predicted emotional class probability.

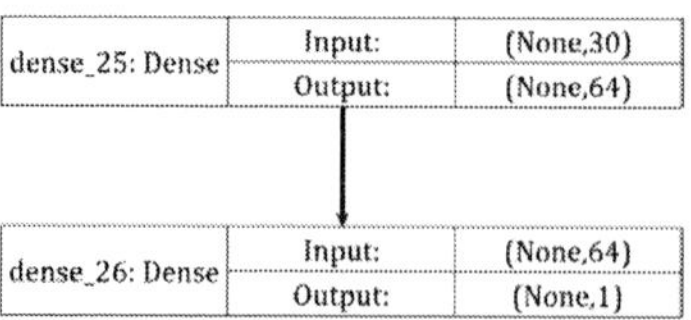

Figure 1: The Architecture of The Non-Temporal Model

3.5.2 Development of the Temporal Model

The algorithm used in the model is the Recurrent Neural Network (RNN) variation of Long Short Term Memory (LSTM). The model for the temporal model has a hidden layer as the addition to the input and activation layer. So, the model is composed of one LSTM layer for input, one hidden layer, and one activation layer in the form of a sigmoid function for output. The model will receive a temporal representation (sequence) of each feature. In this study, hyperparameter tuning will be carried out on the number of neurons in the input layer and hidden layer. We also performed feature selection by finding the best combination of the features above.

Figure 2 shows the detailed architecture. The lstm_50 is the LSTM input layer that accepts sequences of 300 vectors with each vector of dimension 15 and returns vectors with dimensions 128. The dense_99 is a hidden layer that accepts input vectors with dimensions 128 and returns vectors with dimensions 64. The dense_100 is a sigmoid layer that accepts a vector with dimension 64 and returns the probability of the predicted emotion class.

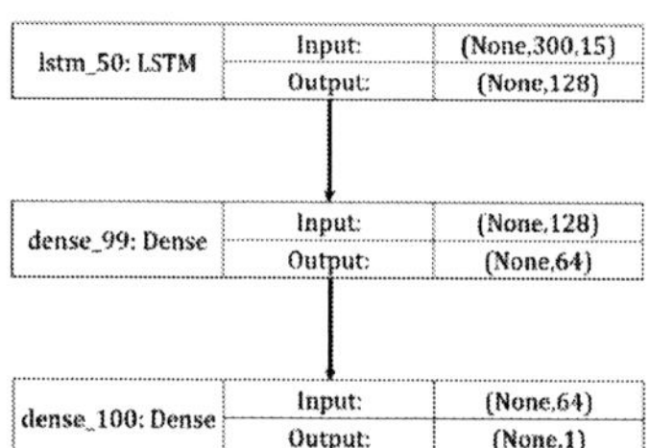

Figure 2: The Architecture of The Temporal Model

3.5.3 Embedding Model Development

The third model built is an embedding model for transcript data. The algorithm used in the model is ANN. ANN accepts average word vector input by weighting TF-IDF from the previous stage. ANN is composed of one input layer and an activation layer in the form of a sigmoid function as the output. In this study, hyperparameter tuning will be performed on the number of neurons in ANN. The detailed architecture used can be seen in Figure 3. The dense_5 represents the input layer which accepts a vector with a dimension of 150 and returns a vector with a dimension of 64. The dense_6 represents the sigmoid layer that receives a vector with dimension 64 and returns the probability of the predicted emotional class.

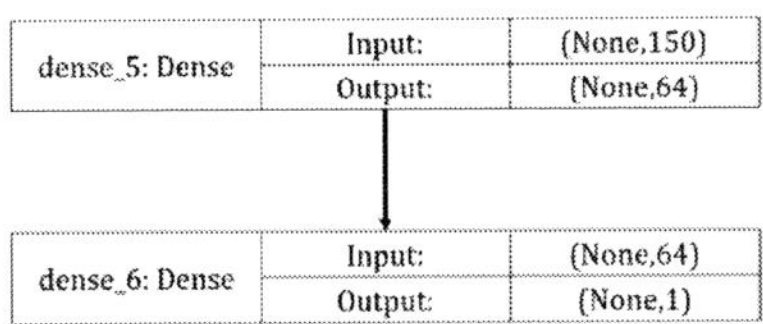

Figure 3: The Architecture of The Embedding Model

3.5.4 Building a Combined Model

The last model was built as a joint model. The purpose of building this model is to utilize both the features of the speech and the features of the transcript in one model. The combined model was built in 2 variations, namely: (1) a combination of non-temporal models and embedding models and (2) a combination of temporal models and embedding models.

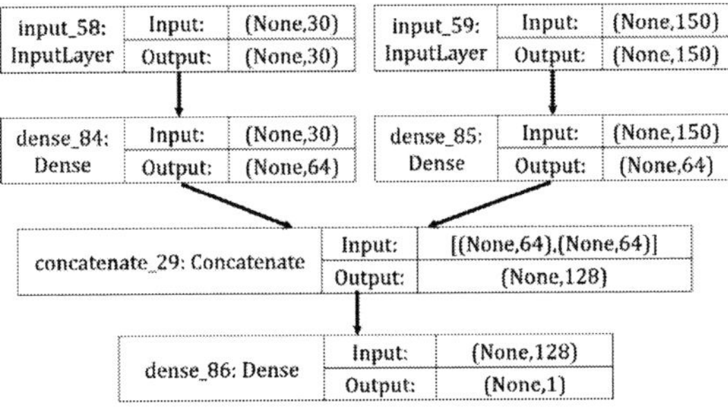

Figure 4: The Architecture of The Combined Model I (Non-Temporal and Embedding Model)

Figure 4 shows the detail of the combined model of non-temporal and embedding. input_58 states the input layer that receives a vector of speech data with a dimension of 30. input_59 expresses an input layer that accepts a vector of transcript data with a dimension of 150. dense_84 is the hidden layer that receives the inputs from the input_58 layer and returns a vector with dimension 64. dense_85 is a hidden layer that receives a vector from the input_59 layer and returns a vector with dimension 64. concatenate_29 accepts two output vectors from dense_84 and dense_85 and returns a concatenated vector with a dimension of 128. dense_86 is a sigmoid layer that receives a vector with dimensions 128 and returns the probability of the predicted emotion class.

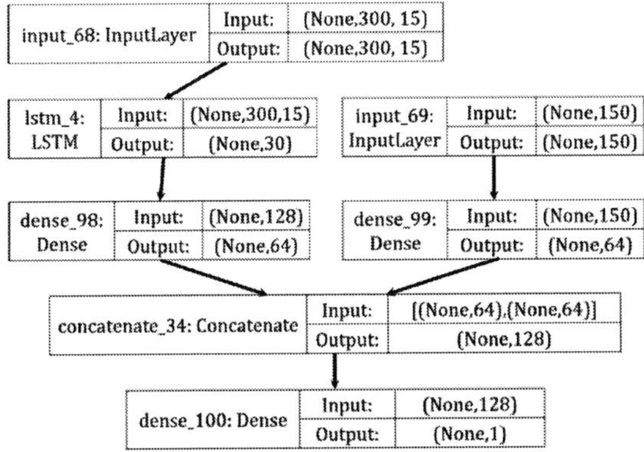

Figure 5: The Architecture of The Combined Model II (Temporal and Embedding Model)

Figure 5 describes the detail for the architectural model of the combination of temporal and embedding. input_68 states the input layer which receives a sequence of 300 vectors, each of which has dimension 15 of speech data. input_69 states the input layer that receives a vector with the dimension of 150 from the transcript data. lstm_4 is an LSTM layer that receives input sequences from the input_68 layer and returns a vector with a dimension of 128. dense_98 is the hidden layer that receives vector from layer lstm_4 and returns a vector with a dimension of 64. dense_99 is the hidden layer that receives vector from input_69 layer and returns a vector with the dimension of 64. concatenate_34 accepts two output vectors from dense_98 and dense_99 and returns a vector with a dimension of 128. Finally, dense_100 represents the sigmoid layer that receives a vector with a dimension of 128 and returns the probability of the predicted emotion class.

3.6 Design of Training Scenarios

According to Yu et al. (2001), it would be difficult to build a good model of each emotional class with only 200 data, thus the recommended alternative is to use a one-vs-rest scenario. The one-vs-rest scenario will divide the dataset into 2 classes, i.e. the class you want to study and the other class. For example to build a model to recognize anger, 130 data from anger classes and 130 data from other classes (labeled as "others") are prepared. With the one-vs rest scenario, the model can learn the characteristics of each emotional class deeper and the model is expected to provide better results. In addition, training parameters such as loss and activation functions need to be defined. The study will use the Binary Cross-entropy function for loss function and Root Mean Square Propagation (RMSProp) function for the activation function.

3.7 Design of Testing Scenarios

The research will involve two testing scenarios i.e. the testing scenario for each one-vs-rest model and the testing scenario for classification which directly recognizes the four classes of emotions. For the testing scenario of each model, the metric used to measure performance is accuracy. Accuracy provides information related to the proportion of correct predictions by the model of the testing data. For testing scenarios that can directly recognize the four emotions following the following mechanism, each test data will be run on the four one-vs-rest models and the emotional class is chosen which gives the highest probability as a label of the test data. The one-vs-rest model chosen for each emotion class is the best variation according to the one-vs-rest model testing scenario that was run before. The metrics used were precision, recall, and F1-score.

4. Results and Analysis

We describe the result of our experiments into two different sections i.e: non-temporal models and temporal models. For each section, we will explain the result of experiments in feature selection and hyperparameter tuning.

4.1 Non-Temporal Models

4.1.1 Feature Selection

The development of non-temporal models begins with feature selection. First, we trained the model for each possible feature subset of the 3 main research features i.e. MFCC, pitch, and RMSE. Then each model will be compared in performance through the accuracy metric. The subset of features of the model with the best accuracy will be taken and used as model candidates for tuning. The results of feature selection experiments can be seen in Figure 6. The accuracy shown is the accuracy of the test set.

According to Figure 6, the combination of the three features (MFCC, pitch, and RMSE) has the best accuracy for each model. The combination of the three features provides more information so that the model is able to classify more accurately. Furthermore, we can see that the MFCC feature alone gives a fairly high accuracy when compared to the pitch or RMSE features due to the MFCC feature consisting of 13 channels compared to the other two features which only consist of 1 channel. The combination of features with the best accuracy proceed to the tuning stage.

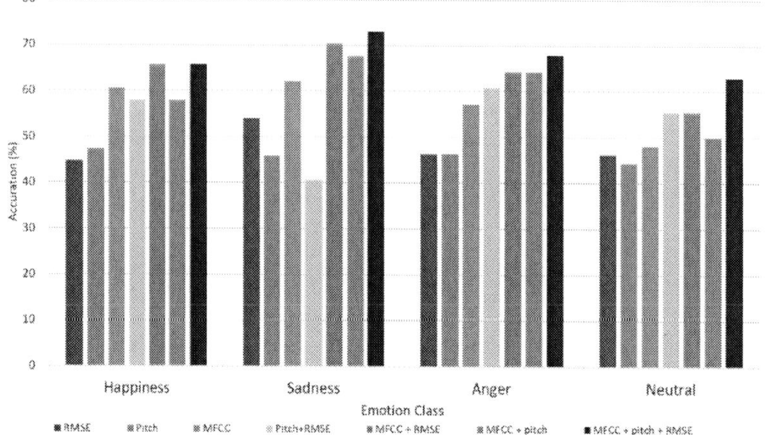

Figure 6: The Experiment Results on the Feature Selection of Non-Temporal Models

4.1.2 Hyperparameter Tuning

We performed tuning to the number of neurons. The numbers of neurons used in this experiment are 32, 64, 128, 256, and 512. After conducting several experiments, the best number of neurons for models in happiness is 64, sadness is 128, anger is 256, and neutral is 64. For neurons 512, the accuracy of each model variation tends to decrease. Goodfellow et al. (2016) say that a model with a high capacity (number of neurons) will be able to solve more complex problems, but a higher capacity than the problem needs can lead to overfitting. The best accuracy falls on the sadness model with an accuracy of 72.97% in the test set.

4.2 Temporal Models

4.2.1 Feature Selection

The feature selection method is the same as in the non-temporal model which testing each feature subset of 3 main features (MFCC, pitch, and RMSE) using the one-vs-rest model for each emotional class. The results of feature selection experiments can be seen in Figure 7.

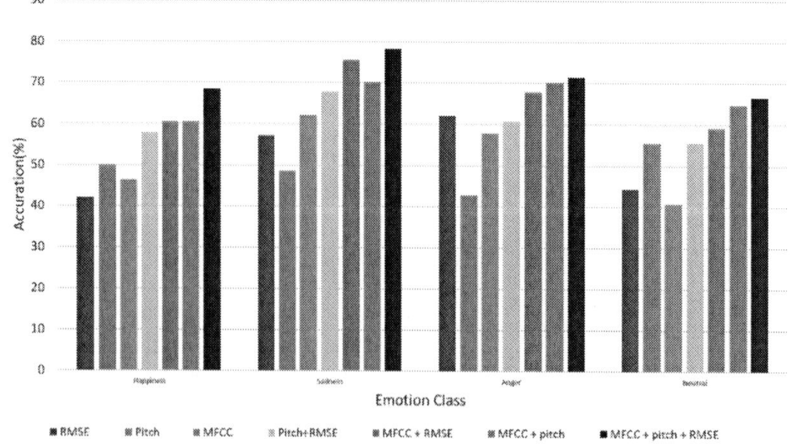

Figure 7: The Experiment Results on the Feature Selection of Temporal Models

The results of the experiments are also not much different from the non-temporal model where the combination of all three features provides the best performance on all variations of the model. Each model also only needs around

12 to 20 iterations to be converged according to the early stopping mechanism, meaning that in 12 to 20 iterations, the accuracy of the model in the validation set does not change significantly and the model starts showing signs of overfitting so the training process is stopped. Then, the most accurate model variations enter the hyperparameter tuning step by tuning of the number of neurons.

4.2.2 Hyperparameter Tuning

The most accurate model variations enter the hyperparameter tuning step by tuning of the number of neurons. Variations in the number of neurons used are 32, 64, 128, 256, and 512. The best number of neurons for the happiness is 64, sadness is 128, anger is 128, and neutral is 64. The highest accuracy is achieved by sadness class which is around 81.08% for test set accuracy.

4.3 Embedding Models

The next experiments are to build the embedding model. Embedding model experiments only involve the hyperparameter tuning process considering the features used are only one type i.e. average word vector with TF-IDF weighting. Variations in the number of neurons are 32, 64, 128, 256, and 512. The best number of neurons for happiness is 128, sadness is 256, anger is 256, and neutral is 64. The best accuracy is obtained for anger with the accuracy of 60, 71% in the test set.

4.4 Combined Models

The last experiments in model development are to build a combined model that only involves the tuning process and does not involve the selection of features considering the results of non-temporal and temporal experiments show that optimal results are obtained using all three features and the embedding model has only one feature representation. Tuning is performed on the number of neurons in both sub-models (non-temporal, temporal, and embedding). The best accuracy in the combined model I (non-temporal & embedding model) for the happiness is 76.31%, for the sadness is 78.37%, for the anger is 75.00%, and for the neutral is 64.81%. For the combined model II (temporal & embedding), the best accuracy is 71.05% for happiness, 86.46% for sadness, 82.14% for anger, and 68.51% for neutral.

4.5 Summary of Results and Analysis

Model	Accuracy (%)			
	Happiness	Sadness	Anger	Neutral
Non-temporal	65.78	72.97	71.42	62.96
Temporal	68.42	81.08	78.57	66.66
Embedding	60.52	56.75	60.71	48.14
Combined model I (non-temporal + embedding)	76.31	78.37	75.00	64.81
Combined model II (temporal + embedding)	71.05	86.46	82.14	68.51

Table 2: Summary of Experimental Results

The summary of our experimental results from the 5 variations of the model can be seen in Table 2. There is also another testing scenario mentioned in Section 3.7 to measure the accuracy of the classification which directly recognizes the four classes of emotions. This scenario obtained a precision of 64.66%, a recall of 66.79%, and an F1-score of 64.83%. The confusion matrix in Table 3 shows the detail evaluation of this direct classification scenario.

Prediction / Actual	Happiness	Sadness	Anger	Neutral
Happiness	15	4	3	2
Sadness	1	11	0	3
Anger	2	1	14	1
Neutral	4	5	4	15

Table 3: Confusion Matrix of The Direct Classification

From the results of our experiments, we formulate the following analysis:

- The accuracy of each emotional class in the temporal model is always higher than the non-temporal model. This shows that the sequence representation is better than using statistical measures to represent the audio. Furthermore, since RNN can capture temporal relations, the model does not only classify each frame independently but also learn the relationship between frames in the sequence.

- The accuracy of embedding models is lower compared to temporal or non-temporal models. This shows that emotions are easier to detect in speech than in transcripts. Linking it to the valence-arousal model (Barrett and Russell, 1999), emotions in speech are more easily mapped on by analyzing the intensity of the speaker's speech. While on the transcript data, emotions can only be captured by understanding the correlation of words with the emotional class and the context of the transcripts.

- The accuracy of the combined model is relatively higher compared to a single model (non-temporal, temporal, or embedding only). This phenomenon proves that the combined information from transcript data and speech data synergizes with each other to provide information about the emotion.

- In the happiness model, misclassification generally falls on the class of anger and sadness. It was found that misclassification which fell on the anger class was generally due to the delivery of high intensity as in one of the speeches with the transcript "Hooray! we won! Our shop wins!" which is blurted out. Another mistake arises from the use of words with a negative sentiment as in the word "dies" from the transcript "Cockroach, you see! When it dies, it is upside down, haha". Even though the main context of the transcript is intended as a joke. The misclassification that falls on sad emotions is due to the pronunciation with the intensity that is too low as in one of the speech data with the transcript "Hey, long time no see, where are you going? Let's go with me" said in a friendly tone so that the model mistakenly captures its emotion as sadness.

- In the sadness model, misclassification most often falls on neutral emotions. Most of the data that was incorrectly classified as having a unique pattern of sadness is emphasized on the semantics of the transcript by using flat-pitched pronunciation. However, from the experimental results, the model tends to utilize information from speech as the main consideration because it provides the best overall performance so that the model gives a higher "weight" to a flat pronunciation rather than the semantics of the transcript. For example in the transcript "But that's because of the last memories of my mom ... which I can hold ..." with a relatively flat delivery, the model considers the data to have neutrality emotions even though the real meaning of the transcript is expressing sadness.
- In the anger emotions model, misclassification tends to fall on happiness emotions. The inspection of the misclassified data shows that the speech is delivered with an intensity that is not as high as other speech data showing anger emotions. Besides, the data does not use groups of words that generally appear on anger emotions such as swear words or words with other negative connotations. For example in the speech data with the transcript "You are fired!" with a delivery that is not loud enough has a resemblance in terms of pronunciation with our previous example that shows happiness ("We won! Our store won!"). This expression also does not contain words with negative connotations so the model assumes that the data contains happiness.
- In the neutral emotion model, misclassification most commonly occurs in either one-vs-rest scenarios or direct classification scenarios. Through listening to the speech data and reading the transcript data from the neutral class, it was found that a lot of data in the neutral class is still ambiguous. For example, there are speech data with a neutral emotion but at the beginning of the speech spoken in a high tone so that it is classified as anger or speech data with a low intensity so that it is classified as sad emotions. In terms of transcripts, the data in the neutral class do not have certain words that imply neutrality. It is in fact in contrast to the happiness class that usually is expressed using the words of praise or gratitude, or in the anger class that is closely related to swearing words.

5.   Conclusion and Future Works

This research has aimed to develop the speech emotion detection model in Bahasa Indonesia. Our main objectives are to understand how to represent speech data into features to obtain the best model and use speech transcripts to improve model performance. Thus, we experimented with our dataset using five model variations for the 4 emotional classes i.e. happiness, sadness, anger, and neutral.

The best experimental results for each emotion are described as follows: (1) the best accuracy for the class of happiness is 68.42% using speech data only with a temporal approach and 76.31% using speech data and transcripts with a combined non-temporal and embedding approach; (2) the best accuracy for the class of sadness is 81.08% using speech data only with the temporal approach and 86.46% using speech data and transcripts with a combined temporal and embedding approach; (3) the best accuracy for the class of anger is 78.57% using speech data only with the temporal approach and 82.14% using speech data and transcripts with a combined temporal and embedding approach; (4) the best accuracy for the class of neutral emotion classes 66.66% using speech data only with the temporal approach and 68.51% use speech data and transcripts with a combined temporal and embedding approach. In addition, experiments were also carried out for direct classification in four classes of emotions and the precision results were 64.66%, recall of 66.79%, and the f1-score was 64.83%.

The conclusion we may draw from our results is that the temporal representations provide better accuracy than statistical representations. The experimental results also exhibit the impact of the combined model using speech data as well as transcript data as a feature to improve the model performance because the model gets information from two different perspectives.

There is still a lot of potential for the development of the use of RNN such as by trying variations of the Gated Recurrence Unit (GRU) or LSTM bidirectional variations. Other suggestions are aimed at the stage of building models that can be explored more deeply. Furthermore, the use of additional layers such as the dropout layer for regularization can be applied to models to avoid overfitting and obtain models with better generalization capabilities.

6.   Bibliographical References

Barrett, L. F., & Russell, J. A. (1999). The Structure of Current Affect: Controversies and Emerging Consensus. Current Directions in Psychological Science. SAGE Publishing.

Basu ,S., Chakraborty, J., & Aftabuddin, M. (2017). Emotion recognition from speech using convolutional neural network with recurrent neural network architecture. 2nd International Conference on Communication and Electronics Systems (ICCES) (hal. 333-336). IEEE.

Burkhardt, F., Paeschke, A., Rolfes, M.A., Sendlmeier, W.F., & Weiss, B. (2005). A database of German emotional speech. INTERSPEECH. Semantic Scholar

Goodfellow, I., Bengio, Y., & Courville, A. (2016). Deep Learning. MIT Press.

Keshtiari, Niloofar. (2015). Recognizing emotional speech in Persian: a validated database of Persian emotional speech (Persian ESD). Behavior Research Method. Springer.

Ko, Y., Hong, I., Shin, H., & Kim, Y. (2017). Construction of a database of emotional speech using emotion sounds from movies and dramas. International Conference on Information and Communications (ICIC) (page 266-267). IEEE.

Livingstone, S. R. & Russo, F. A. (2018). The Ryerson Audio-Visual Database of Emotional Speech and Song (RAVDESS): A dynamic, multimodal set of facial and vocal expressions in North American English. Public Library of Science (PLOS).

Lubis, N., Lestari, D., Purwarianti, A., Sakti, S., & Nakamura, S. (2014). Emotion recognition on Indonesian television talk shows. IEEE Spoken

Language Technology Workshop (SLT) (page 466-471). IEEE.

Muljono, Winarsih, N. A. S., & Supriyanto, C. (2016). Evaluation of classification methods for Indonesian text emotion detection. International Seminar on Application for Technology of Information and Communication (ISemantic) (hal. 130-133). IEEE.

Safitri, N. E., Zahra, A., & Adriani, M. (2016). Spoken Language Indentification Using Phonotactic Methods on Minangkabau, Sundanese, and Javanese. 5th Workshop on Spoken Language Technologies for Under-resourced Languages (SLTU) (page 182-187). Science Direct.

Savigny, J., & Purwarianti, A. (2017). Emotion classification on youtube comments using word embedding. International Conference on Advanced Informatics, Concepts, Theory, and Applications (ICAICTA) (hal. 1-5). IEEE.

The, J. E., Wicaksono, A. F., & Adriani, M. (2015). A two-stage emotion detection on Indonesian tweets. International Conference on Advanced Computer Science and Information Systems (ICACSIS) (hal. 143-146). IEEE.

Vania, C. & Adriani, M. (2011). The effect of syllable and word stress on the quality of Indonesian HMM-based speech synthesis system. International Conference on Advanced Computer Science and Information Systems (ICASIS) (hal. 413-418). IEEE.

Wanagiri, M. Z. & Adriani, M. (2012). Developing and Analyzing ASR System for Accented Indonesian Speech. The 15th Oriental COCOSDA Conference. IEEE.

Wunarso, N. B., & Soelistio, Y. E. (2017). Towards Indonesian speech-emotion automatic recognition (I-SpEAR). 4th International Conference on New Media Studies (CONMEDIA) (page 98-101). IEEE

Yu, F., Chang, E., Xu, Y. Q., & Shum, H. Y. (2001). Emotion Detection from Speech to Enrich Multimedia Content. Lecture Notes in Computer Science (LNCS) (hal. 550-557). Springer.

Proceedings of the 1st Joint SLTU and CCURL Workshop (SLTU-CCURL 2020), pages 194–201
Language Resources and Evaluation Conference (LREC 2020), Marseille, 11–16 May 2020
© European Language Resources Association (ELRA), licensed under CC-BY-NC

Macsen: A Voice Assistant for Speakers of a Lesser Resourced Language

Dewi Bryn Jones
Language Technologies Unit
Bangor University, Wales
d.b.jones@bangor.ac.uk

Abstract

This paper reports on the development of a voice assistant mobile app for speakers of a lesser resourced language – Welsh. An assistant with a smaller set of effective but useful skills is both desirable and urgent for the wider Welsh speaking community. Descriptions of the app's skills, architecture, design decisions and user interface is provided before elaborating on the most recent research and activities in open source speech technology for Welsh. The paper reports on the progress to date on crowdsourcing Welsh speech data in Mozilla Common Voice and of its suitability for training Mozilla's DeepSpeech speech recognition for a voice assistant application according to conventional and transfer learning methods. We demonstrate that with smaller datasets of speech data, transfer learning and a domain specific language model, acceptable speech recognition is achievable that facilitates, as confirmed by beta users, a practical and useful voice assistant for Welsh speakers. We hope that this work informs and serves as a model to researchers and developers in other lesser-resourced linguistic communities and helps bring into being voice assistant apps for their languages.

Keywords: Welsh, voice assistants, Mozilla Common Voice, Mozilla DeepSpeech, speech recognition, transfer learning

1. Introduction

Research and development of language technologies for lesser-spoken languages is characterised by not only a lack of data and human resources but also a lack of useful end user applications that address the technological needs and expectations of speakers as well as better mitigate linguistic digital extinction. In recent years the increasing popularity and capabilities of voice assistants such as Google Assistant, Alexa, Siri and Cortana for larger languages such as English have increased the urgency for language technologies and similar applications to serve speakers of other languages, in particular lesser resourced languages. (Evans, 2018)

This paper reports on the ongoing work for developing a useful voice assistant for Welsh speakers. This work builds on a series of previous short term projects which had crowdsourced Welsh speech corpora (Cooper et. al., 2019) (Prys et. al., 2018(1)) and developed a prototype voice assistant (Jones et. al., 2016) that could run on Raspberry Pis. Our initial prototype assistant was capable of responding to a very limited collection of questions regarding time, weather, news and a small set of article titles from the Welsh language Wikipedia. These 'skills' however were not fully implemented, and therefore not very useful due to the need to devote time and priorities towards speech recognition capabilities, to the neglect of other constituent components such as intent parsing, third party API service integration and generation of natural language answers. Despite attempts to make the Welsh voice assistant's implementation accessible[1] to an audience of developers not expert in language technologies, factors such as the complexity of speech recognition development kits, lack of simple documentation, hardware limitations and licensing restrictions collectively undermined

stimulating wider development of voice based applications and services for the Welsh speaking community by other developers.

Fortunately, progress in open source speech technology, machine learning and software development tools has accelerated in recent months and years to provide new opportunities for empowering lesser resourced language communities to develop their own improved voice assistants and other applications. (Jones, 2019)

2. A Welsh Voice Assistant Application

We have developed our own Welsh language voice assistant mobile application and have named it Macsen.

Some existing open source digital assistants' projects and products, such as MyCroft[2], support localization, allowing its software and supported skills to be translated into Welsh. A functionally complete and fully localized assistant is not feasible however if the underlying language technology components, in particular speech recognition and text-to-speech, are not yet as capable as English counterparts. MyCroft also requires specialised hardware, including Raspberry Pi, as a prerequisite for end users to use the software. We had observed from our previous projects that there was limited knowledge and usage of such equipment by the Welsh speaking community at large. Installations of any localized versions would thus be very limited.

Mobile devices however are very prevalent. Developing an assistant for such devices is a very obvious choice of platform for providing voice assistant functionality as easily and as wide as possible to the wider Welsh speaking community.

---

[1] Our website at https://projectmacsen.github.io/ provided easy to follow information on how to setup and create your own (limited) Welsh voice assistant on Raspberry Pi equipment.

[2] MyCroft – an open source voice assistant:
https://mycroft.ai

We designed the Macsen app with the following objectives in mind:

- It must be able to run on Android and iOS phones (and possibly other platforms in the future)
- It must provide complete and useful skills that users will want to use
- Communication should be in as natural as possible language
- Users should be able to easily ascertain what skills and questions the assistant supports
- If the app is not able to recognise the user's speech, then it must
  - still be usable as a text-based (chatbot) assistant
  - provide opportunities for users to contribute to improve its abilities
- It must be easy to add new skills with as few updates as possible
- It must provide freedom to the user and respect privacy
- The entire solution should be open source, be easy to integrate in part or as a whole into other solutions and permissively licensed.
- It must be helpful to the research of language technologies for lesser-resourced languages.

We have succeeded in developing the Macsen app for the two mobile platforms from more or less a single code base by using Flutter[3] by Google, an open source toolkit for building mobile, desktop and web applications. Platform specific code that access underlining OS services or integrate third-party SDK libraries is very limited but include:

- geolocation detection for the weather skill
- creating scheduled notifications for the alarm skill
- Spotify Android/iOS SDK integration[4]

The source code can be found on GitHub[5]. The app is available on Apple AppStore[6] and on Google Play[7].

The skills we anticipated being most useful and popular with end users were:

<u>tywydd</u> (*weather*) – provides the latest weather forecast for today and tomorrow at device's geo-location. Conditions are retrieved from the OpenWeatherMap API.

<u>newyddion</u> (*news)* – reads frontpage or category news headlines from RSS feeds provided by the Golwg360 Welsh language news website.

<u>amser</u> (*time*) – ask the app what time it is. TimeZoneDB API was used so as to get the time for the app's geo coordinates.

<u>larwm</u> (*alarm)* – ask the app to ring an alarm at a particular time later in the next 24 hours.

<u>spotify</u> – ask the app to play music by a particular Welsh musical artist on the device's Spotify app. Most popular artists were selected and whose names are challenging for English language assistants.

<u>wicipedia</u> – the assistant reads the first two sentences from the requested subject's Welsh language Wikipedia article.

For ease of implementation, components providing speech recognition, intent parsing, natural language generation and text-to-speech functionality are provided externally and are accessed by the app over the internet via specially crafted APIs. Separation of the key language technology components to hosted servers provides a more modular and flexible architecture. Such an architecture however might alarm users concerned with privacy. The app therefore provides reassurance with a page that states the privacy policy, explains what information the server uses and assures that no data is retained.

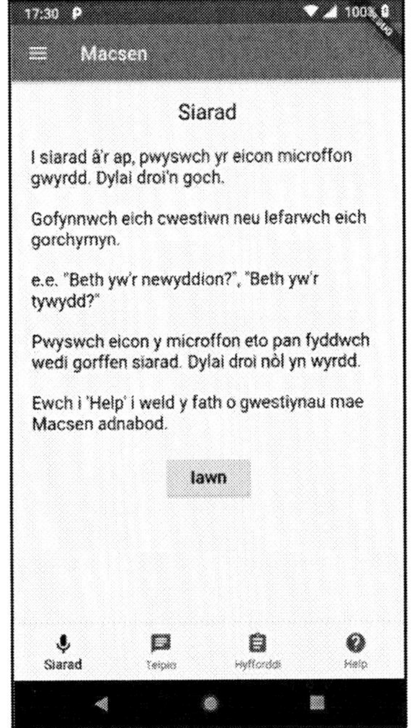

Figure 1 - Screenshot of Macsen upon opening

Figure 1 shows the first screen presented to the user upon opening the app. Four tabs at the bottom provides the user with four ways to interact with the assistant. 'Siarad' *(Speak),* the first and primary tab, allows the user to speak to the app. The 'Teipio' (*Typing*) tab allows users to type in their command or question in case the user's speech has perhaps not been recognized. With the use of predictive text keyboards, frequently typed questions can be quickly learnt and gradually become less cumbersome. The 'Hyfforddiant' (*Training*) tab meanwhile allows the user to contribute recordings for aiding in improving the

---

³ Flutter: https://flutter.dev/
⁴ Spotify for Developers: https://developer.spotify.com
⁵ Source code for the app can be found on GitHub at: https://github.com/techiaith/macsen-flutter

⁶ Macsen on Apple AppStore : https://apps.apple.com/gb/app/macsen/id1489915663
⁷ Macsen on Google Play : https://play.google.com/store/apps/details?id=cymru.techi aith.flutter.macsen

assistant's speech recognition. Finally the 'Help' tab provides the user with information on the skills and questions the app can respond to. The app also contains a burger menu on the top left, where further information can be found about Macsen, Privacy, server configuration and the Mozilla Common Voice project.

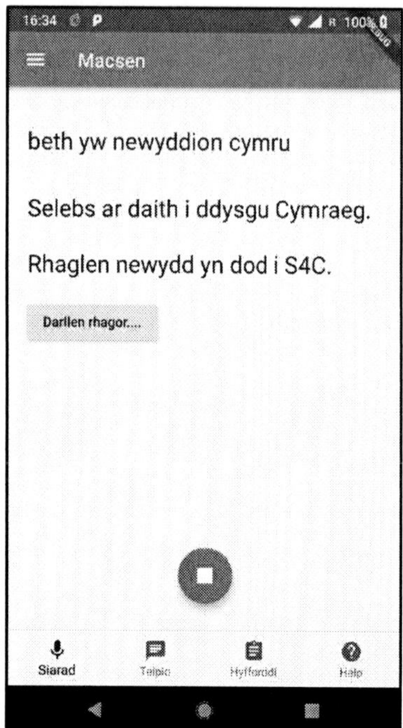

Figure 2- Example result from asking : "What's the news in Wales?"

Similar to other mobile based assistants, such as Siri and Alexa, speech interaction with Macsen is initiated by pressing a microphone button to start listening and then again to stop listening. It does not rely on a wake word which aids ease of implementation and improves privacy. The first opening screen shown in Figure 1 explains the operation of the microphone button and also recommends some initial questions for users to try (e.g. *What is the news?*). First impressions are important and so these recommended questions are easier for the speech recognition to recognize and provide very useful and dynamic information in their responses.

Figure 2 shows a screenshot of the app having responded to a more detailed question "What's the news in Wales?" This response is typical of a question and answering type skills (such as time, Wicipedia and weather). The recognised question is displayed first and above the text currently being uttered by the text-to-speech. A button may also be provided for each utterance that activates any hyperlinks to further related content. For example to the associated full news article or Wicipedia page. Displaying the uttered text is useful and probably necessary for the user to comprehend the speech produced from a simple

MaryTTS based Welsh voice that may not yet be every time sufficiently naturally sounding and intelligible.

Further example usages are showcased in videos online[8].

As mentioned, the assistant's language technology components are hosted externally to the app and are accessible via cloud based APIs.

Text to speech APIs from previous work in a project on providing online Welsh language text-to-speech services (Lleisiwr, 2019) was available and thus did not require further effort. Speech recognition required newly trained models and are described in subsequent sections.

Particular effort was required to implement intent parsing and the generation of natural language responses. We decided that utilising an existing library for intent parsing would limit development time and increase reusability in other projects and products. A number of chatbot platforms incorporate intent parsing, but we opted for the padatious[9] library developed by the MyCroft project.

Padatious is a very simple and fast neural network intent parser that is able to recognise the intent in a sentence and therefore identify the encompassing skill. Each intent is trained from example sentences generated from templates decorated with lists of associated entities. The entire collection of generated sentences[10] serves other purposes in the construction of our voice assistant, including as will be elaborated later in this paper, language modelling and transcripts for recording.

For example, the intent to trigger playing music by certain artist can be trained by the following template sentences:

```
Chwaraea gerddoriaeth {artist}
Chwaraea fiwsig gan {artist}
...
```

and an associated entities file containing all supported `{artist}` names (one per line):

```
Bryn Fôn
Lleuwen
Y Cyrff
Anhrefn
Sibrydion
Bwncath
Alffa
. . .
```

Especially crafted code in still required to handle each recognized intent and to construct natural language responses from further templates sentences decorated with the results from consuming third party APIs. Some API

196

services do not provide their results in Welsh, therefore extra effort was required to translate data items. For example, our weather skill handler uses our localization of the weather conditions[11] such as 'windy', 'raining', 'sunny' returned from the OpenWeatherMap API.

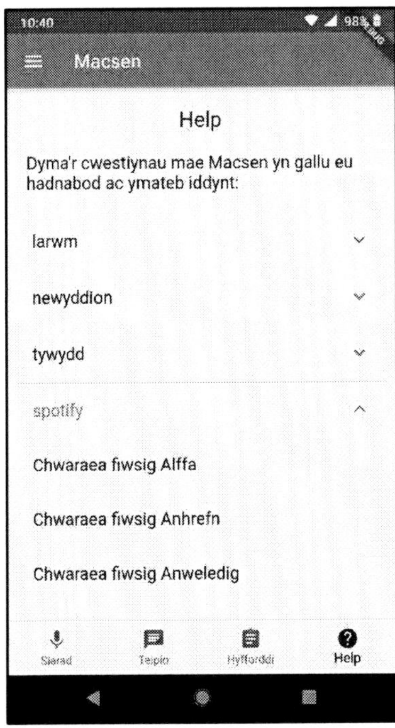

Figure 3- Help tab displaying the sentences Macsen recognizes for each skill

Figure 3 shows the app's 'Help' tab which consists of a collapsible tree like structure populated with the padatious intent parser with the skills and their generated sentences. This helps inform the user of Macsen's skills and of the sentences they can speak.

Finally, figure 4 shows the app's 'Hyfforddiant' (*Training*) tab which consists of a very simple interface for crowdsourcing recordings of Macsen sentences from users. A random sentence is selected from all the sentences generated by the intent parser and is presented for recording. The user uses the same microphone button operation to start and stop recording. Upon stopping the microphone, the recording is uploaded whilst the app presents the next random sentence. Before recording their first sentence, users have been presented with a disclaimer explaining the purpose of recording with assurances that no personal information is collected. Users have to confirm they consent to the sharing their recordings according to open and permissive licensing before recording can begin. Thus users are contributing their voices to an in-domain collection of speech data that, as can be seen in the next

section, serves as the test set for evaluating the voice assistant's speech recognition component.

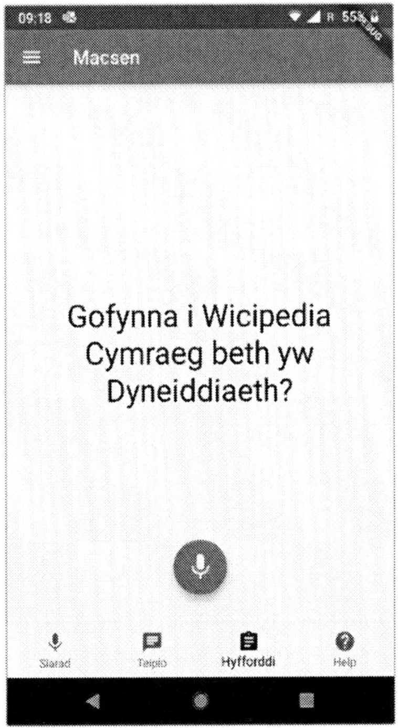

Figure 4- Simple interface for crowdsourcing recordings of Macsen domain sentences from users. "Ask Welsh Wikipedia what is humanism?"

3. Data Collection and Analysis

The data we used for training our assistant's speech recognition engine was sourced from a number of open speech and textual resources.

The primary speech data resource was the Welsh language data from Mozilla's Common Voice multilingual speech corpus (Ardila et. al., 2019). Having made previous attempts at crowdsourcing speech corpora (Cooper S. et. al., 2019), the Welsh community, consisting of our university research unit[12] and members of Welsh open source community[13] were ideally placed to enact Welsh as one of the first languages in the multilingual expansion of Common Voice in June 2018. (Henretty M., 2018).

Table 2 shows how Welsh has progressed through each Common Voice release since June 2018.

In comparison to previous efforts at crowdsourcing Welsh speech data, and relative to some larger languages in Common Voice, 77 hours of speech data for Welsh is a significant achievement and is evidence of the hard work done by Welsh open source volunteers in successfully promoting and attracting the wider Welsh language

---

[11] Our translations for OpenWeatherMap API weather status can be found at:
https://github.com/techiaith/macsen-

sgwrsfot/blob/master/online-
api/assistant/skills/tywydd/owm/status.cy

[13] http://www.meddal.com

speaking community to contribute their voices to the Mozilla Common Voice project.

	Published	**Recordings**	**Duration (hrs)**
CV1	Feb 2, 2019	19403	21
CV2	June 11, 2019	38001	47
CV3	June 24, 2019	38628	48
CV4	Dec 10, 2019	61235	77

Table 1 - Welsh data in Common Voice releases

Each Common Voice language specific release publishes its crowdsourced recordings with transcripts in six datasets. Tables 3 and 4 shows the details of each subset for Welsh in each Common Voice release to date.

	validated (hrs)	**invalidated (hrs)**	**other (hrs)**
CV1	21	0.7	0
CV2	40	2	5
CV3	42	2	4
CV4	59	3	15

Table 2 - Datasets contained within Welsh Common Voice data

While the number of validated speech (i.e. volunteers who have listened to a recording and have confirmed it is a valid recording of the transcript) has increased, so too has the number of hours of recordings not yet reviewed. This is an indication of the Welsh speaking community's enthusiasm for recording their voices. Hopefully by the fifth release, after a period of appealing for help in validating recordings, the number of 'other' hours can be brought down.

	train (mins)	**dev (mins)**	**test (mins)**
CV1	34	35	37
CV2	37	37	40
CV3	37	36	41
CV4	66	55	59

Table 3- Mozilla prescribed datasets within each Welsh Common Voice release

Table 4 shows the other three datasets. These datasets are recommended by Mozilla as the most suitable as training, development and training sets for creating Mozilla DeepSpeech models. They are very small in comparison to the entire Welsh data size, and have not increased much during 2019. Mozilla's explanation and justification[14] is that DeepSpeech models may exhibit bias towards recognizing sentences that have been recorded multiple times and therefore would not be as optimal as a general purpose speech recognition engine.

Figure 5 shows that the Welsh data in Common Voice contains just over 2000 sentence and therefore a significant proportion have been recorded many tens of times (one sentence having been recorded 69 times) by multiple speakers. During releases CV1, CV2 and CV3 all sentences were being recorded 10, then 20, then 30 times on average. The number of sentences available for recording increased by version CV4, thanks to efforts that began in August

2019 to add significant amounts of new sentences via the Mozilla Sentence Collector website[15]. Sentences were sourced from various public domain collections (Gutenburg, OCRed out of copyright books), donations of portions of copyrighted works and other corpora resources at the disposal of our research unit (Prys et. al., 2016). Since each sentence has to follow in the Mozilla Sentence Collector website a review process to confirm its suitability for reading and training speech recognition models, progress on adding to Common Voice has been slow. We aim to continue our co-ordinated efforts to submit and review sentences at a rate that is at least up with or ahead of the rate of new recordings.

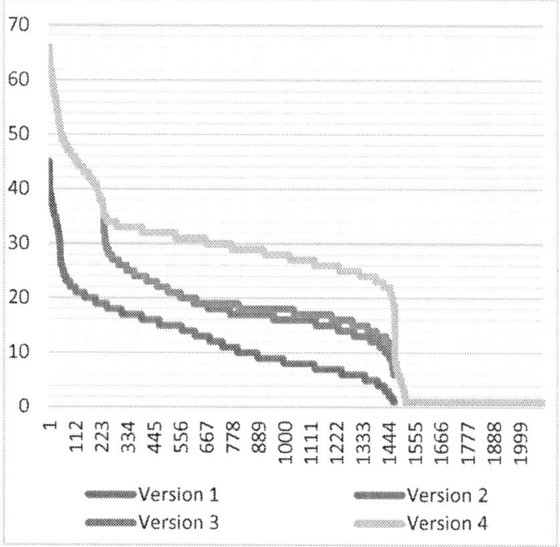

Figure 5- Repeat recordings in each Welsh Common Voice release (validated recordings)
(x – no. of sentences, y – no of recordings)

In the meantime, despite containing repeat recordings, the number of hours provided in Common Voice's validated (and 'other') datasets represent a high number of hours of speech data for a lesser resourced language such as Welsh, which cannot be dismissed and must be evaluated for training a speech recognition engine for a simple voice assistant.

In our speech recognition experiments we formed the following training sets:

SET_1: Mozilla's recommended training set

SET_2: the validated set

SET_3: the validated and other sets combined.

SET_4: Mozilla's recommended training, dev and test set.

The 'Hyfforddiant' (*Training*) from our Macsen voice assistant app, as described in section 2, has provided an

---

[14] "Why train.tsv includes few files (just 3% of validated set)?": https://discourse.mozilla.org/t/why-train-tsv-includes-a-few-files-just-3-of-validated-set/36471

[15] Mozilla Sentence Collector : https://common-voice.github.io/sentence-collector/#/

additional speech dataset[16] which to date contains 433 recordings, totalling approximately 20 minutes, from 19 beta testers. Each recording has been validated internally and can be used as an in-domain test set. In the presentation of experiment results in section 4, this dataset is denoted by the label 'MACSEN'.

The entire collection of sentences generated for training intent parser training also serves as a text corpus for training a domain specific language model. Consisting of 1033 sentences with 570 unique tokens/words, the language model is denoted in the experiment results in section 4 with the label LM_MACSEN.

We have also trained and used in our experiments a general purpose language model using Welsh texts sourced from the OSCAR multilingual corpus (Suárez et. al., 2019), which is derived from the CommonCrawl[17] corpus. Segments containing any illegal characters such as numbers were excluded and so reduced the training corpus word count from 37 million to 11 million. In the results in section 4, the usage of the OSCAR based language model is denoted by the label LM_OSCAR.

4. Speech Recognition Effectiveness

We decided to evaluate and use Mozilla DeepSpeech (Mozilla) for our assistant's speech recognition engine. Other speech recognition kits, such as Kaldi (Povey, 2011), may also perform sufficiently. Mozilla DeepSpeech however has the advantage of being much easier to use, is very developer friendly and easy to integrate into projects implemented in a wide range of programming languages and technologies.

Mozilla DeepSpeech is based on Tensorflow and is end-to-end neural network architecture which maps audio features directly to characters in words. While the general underlying architecture of DeepSpeech is language independent, the alphabet of possible output characters may be language specific, as is the case with Welsh. The following shows the alphabet used in our experiments:

<space>,a,b,c,d,e,f,g,h,i,j,k,l,m,n,o,p,r,s,t,u,v,w,y,z,á,â,ä,é, ê,ë,î,ï,ô,ö,ô,û,ŵ,ŷ,'

In our experiments we have evaluated the effectiveness of speech recognition for our assistant with two versions of DeepSpeech, each supporting two approaches of machine learning. First the conventional learning approach with the latest release of DeepSpeech (0.6.1[18]). Secondly, a branched work from DeepSpeech 0.5.1 that implements transfer learning[19].

Transfer learning provides a mechanism to exploit models trained on much larger collections of data from a larger language in the training of a new model for new and lesser resourced language. Typically, the bottom layers of a model trained with English language data are kept while a number of top layers are replaced by training with data from a lesser resourced language such as Welsh. Through initial trials and experimentation we found that the optimal number of top layers to drop (our value for the `--drop_source_layers` flag) was 2. The English model provided by Mozilla for DeepSpeech 0.5.1 was used as the source model.

ID	Training	Dev	Test
Training Method : Transfer Learning Language Model : LM_OSCAR			
TL 1	CV1_SET_1	CV1_DEV	CV1_TEST
TL 2	CV3_SET_1	CV3_DEV	CV3_TEST
TL 3	CV4_SET_1	CV4_DEV	CV4_TEST
TL 4	CV4_SET_1	10 epochs	MACSEN
TL 5	CV4_SET_2	10 epochs	MACSEN
TL 6	CV4_SET_3	10 epochs	MACSEN
Training Method : Transfer Learning Language Model : LM_MACSEN			
TL 7	CV4_SET_1	10 epochs	MACSEN
TL 8	CV4_SET_2	10 epochs	MACSEN
TL 9	CV4_SET_3	10 epochs	MACSEN
Training Method : Transfer Learning (with kfold devset) Language Model : LM_MACSEN			
TL 10	CV4_SET_3	MACSEN	MACSEN
TL 11	CV4_SET_4	MACSEN	MACSEN
Training Method : Conventional (no transfer learning) Language Model : LM_MACSEN			
N 1	CV4_SET_1	10 epochs	MACSEN
N 2	CV4_SET_2	10 epochs	MACSEN
N 3	CV4_SET_3	10 epochs	MACSEN
Training Method : Conventional (with kfold devset) Language Model : LM_MACSEN			
N 4	CV4_SET_3	MACSEN	MACSEN
N 5	CV4_SET_4	MACSEN	MACSEN

Table 4 - Experiments for Speech Recognition Evaluation

ID	WER	CER
TL 1	60.54	35.13
TL 2	92.17	68.45
TL 3	62.28	34.23
TL 4	69.16	34.74
TL 5	41.78	17.43
TL 6	41.83	17.84
TL 7	26.01	16.11
TL 8	17.27	9.27
TL 9	15.97	8.42
TL 10 (kfold)	**18.23**	**10.24**
TL 11 (kfold)	25.75	16.71
N 1	100	100
N 2	30.03	15.32
N 3	25.21	13.37
N 4 (kfold)	**25.50**	**13.91**
N 5 (kfold)	96.37	93.47

Table 5 - Speech recognition evaluation results

---

[16] Macsen test set data is available at http://techiaith.cymru/deepspeech/macsen/datasets/
[17] https://commoncrawl.org
[18] Mozilla DeepSpeech 0.6.1 release : https://github.com/mozilla/DeepSpeech/releases/tag/v0.6.

[19] Mozilla DeepSpeech transfer learning forked branch : https://github.com/mozilla/DeepSpeech/tree/transfer-learning2

Default values for flags affecting learning rate and dimensions were used in all experiments. The results are shown in Table 6. After initial experimenting with Mozilla's recommended train, dev and train (first three rows in Table 6) we observed that 10 epochs would suffice for experiments where a development set was not possible or appropriate.

Our training setup consisted of a single workstation containing two NVIDIA GTX 1080Ti graphics cards operated by our own crafted scripts[20] that made full use of Dockerfiles provided in each Mozilla DeepSpeech release. Training times ranged from a couple of minutes for SET_1 based experiments to approximately an hour for SET_3.

In Table 6, the k-fold cross validation (k=10) evaluation method (shown in bold), a commonly used resampling procedure to evaluate with a limited data set, was used as a means for reliably confirming the optimal model training configuration for each approach. Thus, the best WER scores are achieved by utilising as much speech data as possible (even if not yet validated by Common Voice volunteers) with transfer learning machine learning approach and a domain specific language model.

We learn from contrasting experiment N1 (WER 100%) with its corresponding transfer learning experiment – TL7 (WER 26.01%) in table 6 that transfer learning with only one hour of training speech data (CV4_SET_1) can provide an immediate and drastic reduction in WER. When we utilise all of Mozilla's recommended data sets of non-repeated recordings (CV4_SET_4, approximately 3 hours) and contrast results between experiments N5 and TL11, we observe there is no significant reduction in WER from the transfer learning method – 0.26% - compared to a 3.63% reduction achieved in the WER for conventional machine learning approach. Additional hours of training data brings down the conventional learning method's WER to a best score of 25.21% in N3. The same amount of data however brings the transfer learning method in TL9 to its lowest WER at 15.97%.

We can also observe also from these results that a domain specific language model aids significantly in reducing the WER. Experiment TL6 shows that running a DeepSpeech decoder, trained with transfer learning and with an OSCAR based language model only achieves a WER of 41.83% for the Macsen voice assistant domain. When using instead a domain specific language model, as in TL9, a WER of 15.97% is achieved.

These results reinforce that for a lesser resourced language, transfer learning and domain specific language models provide the best and only feasible means at present to achieve effective speech recognition capability for voice assistants.

5. Conclusion

This paper has reported on a project to develop a Welsh language voice assistant app for Apple iOS and Android mobile devices as well present how Mozilla's Common

Voice and DeepSpeech projects were exploited to provide an effective speech recognition engine component.

Our speech recognition engine still has a WER above 10 whereas a score of below 10 – as is regularly reported for engines for larger languages – may be considered as a prerequisite. We believe however that our speech recognition engine is sufficiently practical and effective in a voice assistant application setting. As the output from speech recognition in a voice assistant provides the input to the intent parser, the intent parser's tolerance and flexibility on sentence variations may mitigate any issues arising from less than perfect recognition results.

Initial user feedback has informed us that the Macsen voice assistant app is able to recognize and respond to nearly all of their questions and commands. The Spotify skill is particularly popular. Users also commented that they routinely ask for and obtain the latest news and weather from Macsen.

We aim to continue analysing and improving the Welsh data in Mozilla Common Voice in collaboration with Mozilla and the Welsh open source volunteer community. Analysis in this paper has highlighted the scale of repeated recordings and so an immediate task for further training of Welsh speech recognition is to understand and mitigate any bias.

We also aim to continue working on Macsen by adding more skills and making it more useful as a resource to the developer community. A particular ambition is for Macsen to be useful for researchers and developers in other lesser resourced language communities to bootstrap voice assistants for their languages. In this regard, the app's user interface is easily localizable with Flutter's i18n support. Crucially however, this evaluation of Mozilla's DeepSpeech suggests that, even with as little as an hour of speech data from the Mozilla Common Voice project, utilising a transfer learning approach to training, along with possibly a reduced number of skills, and therefore a smaller language model and possibly a smaller alphabet, an effective and reliable speech recognition component for a voice assistant is achievable and can enable the more immediate availability of voice assistant apps for other lesser resourced languages.

9. Acknowledgements

We thank all the volunteers who have recorded and contributed their voices to the Welsh Common Voice effort. We in particular thank Rhoslyn Prys who has given a great deal of his time and energy in a volunteer capacity to initially translate the Common Voice website to Welsh and subsequently to promoting the project relentlessly. Recruitment campaigns have been supported by the Welsh Government, Welsh Language Commissioner, large public organisations in Wales as well as coverage by local media.

We thank also Mozilla for the opportunities it has provided via its Common Voice and DeepSpeech projects, as open and decentralized speech technologies, to empower lesser

---

[20] Our scripts and information for reproducing our experiments can be found on GitHub at
https://github.com/techiaith/docker-deepspeech-cy

resourced language communities to develop their own applications such as voice assistants.

The work on developing the Macsen app was made possible with financial support from the Welsh government.

6. Bibliographical References

Cooper,S. Jones, D.B. and Prys, D. (2019) Crowdsourcing the Paldaruo Speech Corpus of Welsh for Speech Technology. *Information,* 10(8), p.247. Available at: http://dx.doi.org/10.3390/info10080247

Evans, J. (2018) Report on language equality in the digital age. *European Parliament Report 2018/2028 INI.* Available at http://www.europarl.europa.eu/doceo/document/A-8-2018-0228_EN.pdf

Henretty, M. (2018) More Common Voices. https://medium.com/mozilla-open-innovation/more-common-voices-24a80c879944 [Accessed Feb 5, 2020]

Jones, A. (2019) Voice recognition project offers big opportunity to Welsh language. https://nation.cymru/news/voice-recognition-project-offers-big-opportunity-to-welsh-language/ [Accessed Feb 5, 2020]

Jones,D.B. Cooper,S. (2016) Building Intelligent Digitial Assistants for Speakers of a Lesser-Resourced Language. *Proceedings of LREC 2016 Workshop "CCURL 2016 – Towards an Alliance for Digital Language Diversity" p.74.* Claudia Soria et. al. (eds). Available at: http://www.lrec-conf.org/proceedings/lrec2016/workshops/LREC2016 Workshop-CCURL2016_Proceedings.pdf

Lleisiwr (2019) Synthetic voices for patients that are about to loose their ability to speak as a result of diseases such as Motor Neurone Disease or throat cancer. Available at: https://lleisiwr.techiaith.cymru/?lang=en [Accessed: Feb 5, 2020]

Mozilla (n.d.). A TensorFlow implementation of Baidu's DeepSpeech architecture. Available at https://github.com/mozilla/DeepSpeech [Accessed: Feb 5, 2020].

Povey, D., Ghoshal, A., Boulianne, G., Burget, L., Glem, Qian,Y., Schwarz, P., Silovský, J., Stemmer, G., and Veselý,K. (2011). The Kaldi speech recognition toolkit. *In IEEE Workshop on Automatic Speech Recognition and Understanding (ASRU).* Waikoloa, HI, USA

Prys, D., Prys, G., Jones, D.B. (2016). Cysill Ar-lein Corpus: A corpus of written contemporary Welsh compiled from an online spelling and grammar checker. *Proceedings of the Tenth International Conference on Language Resources and Evaluation (LREC 2016). Protoroz, Slovenia*

Prys,D. Jones, D.B. (2018(1)). Gathering Data for Speech Technology in the Welsh Language: A Case Study. *Proceedings of the LREC 2018 Workshop "CCURL 2018 – Sustaining Knowledge Diversity in the Digital Age", p.56.* Claudia Soria, Laurent Besacier and Laurette Pretorius (eds.). Available at: http://lrec-conf.org/workshops/lrec2018/W26/pdf/book_of_proceedings.pdf

Prys, D., Jones D.B. (2018(2)) National Language Technologies Portals for LRLs: A Case Study. *In: Vetulani Z., Mariani J., Kubis M. (eds) Human Language Technology. Challenges for Computer Science and Linguistics.* LTC 2015. Lecture Notes in Computer Science, vol 10930. Springer, Cham

7. Language Resource References

Ardila R., Branson M., Davis K., Henretty M., Kohler M., Meyer J., Morais R., Saunders L., Tyers F., Weber G. (2019) Common Voice: A Massively-Multilingual Speech Corpus. *arXiv:1912.06670v1 [cs.CL]*

Suárez, P.J.O., Sagot,B., Romary, L. (2019) Asynchronous Pipeline for Processing Huge Corpora on Medium to Low Resource Infrastructures. *7th Workshop on the Challenges in the Management of Large Corpora (CMLC-7),* Jul 2019, Cardiff, United Kingdom. (hal-02148693)

Proceedings of the 1st Joint SLTU and CCURL Workshop (SLTU-CCURL 2020), pages 202–210
Language Resources and Evaluation Conference (LREC 2020), Marseille, 11–16 May 2020
© European Language Resources Association (ELRA), licensed under CC-BY-NC

Corpus Creation for Sentiment Analysis in Code-Mixed Tamil-English Text

Bharathi Raja Chakravarthi[1],Vigneshwaran Muralidaran[2],
Ruba Priyadharshini[3], John P. McCrae[1]
[1]Insight SFI Research Centre for Data Analytics, Data Science Institute,
National University of Ireland Galway, {bharathi.raja, john.mccrae}@insight-centre.org
[2]School of English, Communication and Philosophy, Cardiff University, muralidaranV@cardiff.ac.uk
[3]Saraswathi Narayanan College, Madurai, India, rubapriyadharshini.a@gmail.com

Abstract

Understanding the sentiment of a comment from a video or an image is an essential task in many applications. Sentiment analysis of a text can be useful for various decision-making processes. One such application is to analyse the popular sentiments of videos on social media based on viewer comments. However, comments from social media do not follow strict rules of grammar, and they contain mixing of more than one language, often written in non-native scripts. Non-availability of annotated code-mixed data for a low-resourced language like Tamil also adds difficulty to this problem. To overcome this, we created a gold standard Tamil-English code-switched, sentiment-annotated corpus containing 15,744 comment posts from YouTube. In this paper, we describe the process of creating the corpus and assigning polarities. We present inter-annotator agreement and show the results of sentiment analysis trained on this corpus as a benchmark.

Keywords: code mixed, Tamil, sentiment, corpus, dataset

1. Introduction

Sentiment analysis has become important in social media research (Yang and Eisenstein, 2017). Until recently these applications were created for high-resourced languages which analysed monolingual utterances. But social media in multilingual communities contains more code-mixed text (Barman et al., 2014; Chanda et al., 2016; Pratapa et al., 2018a; Winata et al., 2019a). Our study focuses on sentiment analysis in Tamil, which has little annotated data for code-mixed scenarios (Phani et al., 2016; Jose et al., 2020). Features based on the lexical properties such as a dictionary of words and parts of speech tagging have less performance compared to the supervised learning (Kannan et al., 2016) approaches using annotated data. However, an annotated corpus developed for monolingual data cannot deal with code-mixed usage and therefore it fails to yield good results (AlGhamdi et al., 2016; Aguilar et al., 2018) due to mixture of languages at different levels of linguistic analysis.

Code-mixing is common among speakers in a bilingual speech community. As English is seen as the language of prestige and education, the influence of lexicon, connectives and phrases from English language is common in spoken Tamil. It is largely observed in educated speakers although not completely absent amongst less educated and uneducated speakers (Krishnasamy, 2015). Due to their pervasiveness of English online, code-mixed Tamil-English (Tanglish) sentences are often typed in Roman script (Suryawanshi et al., 2020a; Suryawanshi et al., 2020b).

We present TamilMixSentiment [1], a dataset of YouTube video comments in Tanglish. TamilMixSentiment was developed with guidelines following the work of Mohammad

(2016) and without annotating the word level language tag. The instructions enabled light and speedy annotation while maintaining consistency. The overall inter-annotator agreement in terms of Kripendorffs's α (Krippendorff, 1970) stands at 0.6. In total, 15,744 comments were annotated; this makes the largest general domain sentiment dataset for this relatively low-resource language with code-mixing phenomenon.

We observed all the three types of code-mixed sentences - - Inter-Sentential switch, Intra-Sentential switch and Tag switching. Most comments were written in Roman script with either Tamil grammar with English lexicon or English grammar with Tamil lexicon. Some comments were written in Tamil script with English expressions in between. The following examples illustrate the point.

- **Intha padam vantha piragu yellarum Thala ya kondaduvanga.** - *After the movie release, everybody will celebrate the hero.* Tamil words written in Roman script with no English switch.

- **Trailer late ah parthavanga like podunga.** - *Those who watched the trailer late, please like it.* Tag switching with English words.

- **Omg .. use head phones. Enna bgm da saami ..** - - *OMG! Use your headphones. Good Lord, What a background score!* Inter-sentential switch

- **I think sivakarthickku hero getup set aagala.** - *I think the hero role does not suit Sivakarthick.* Intra-sentential switch between clauses.

In this work we present our dataset, annotation scheme and investigate the properties and statistics of the dataset and information about the annotators. We also present baseline classification results on the new dataset with ten

---

[1]https://github.com/bharathichezhiyan/TamilMixSentiment

models to establish a baseline for future comparisons. The best results were achieved with models that use logistic regression and random forest.

The contribution of this paper is two-fold:

1. We present the first gold standard code-mixed Tamil-English dataset annotated for sentiment analysis.

2. We provide an experimental analysis of logistic regression, naive Bayes, decision tree, random forest, SVM, dynamic meta-embedding, contextualized dynamic meta-embedding, 1DConv-LSTM and BERT on our code-mixed data for sentiment classification.

2. Related Work

Recently, there has been a considerable amount of work and effort to collect resources for code-switched text. However, code-switched datasets and lexicons for sentiment analysis are still limited in number, size and availability. For monolingual analysis, there exist various corpora for English (Hu and Liu, 2004; Wiebe et al., 2005; Jiang et al., 2019), Russian (Rogers et al., 2018), German (Cieliebak et al., 2017), Norwegian (Mæhlum et al., 2019) and Indian languages (Agrawal et al., 2018; Rani et al., 2020).

When it comes to code-mixing, an English-Hindi corpus was created by (Sitaram et al., 2015; Joshi et al., 2016; Patra et al., 2018), an English-Spanish corpus was introduced by (Solorio et al., 2014; Vilares et al., 2015; Vilares et al., 2016), and a Chinese-English one (Lee and Wang, 2015) was collected from Weibo.com and English-Bengali data were released by Patra et al. (Patra et al., 2018).

Tamil is a Dravidian language spoken by Tamil people in India, Sri Lanka and by the Tamil diaspora around the world, with official recognition in India, Sri Lanka and Singapore (Chakravarthi et al., 2018; Chakravarthi et al., 2019a; Chakravarthi et al., 2019b; Chakravarthi et al., 2019c). Several research activities on sentiment analysis in Tamil (Padmamala and Prema, 2017) and other Indian languages (Ranjan et al., 2016; Das and Bandyopadhyay, 2010; A.R. et al., 2012; Phani et al., 2016; Prasad et al., 2016; Priyadharshini et al., 2020; Chakravarthi et al., 2020) are happening because the sheer number of native speakers are a potential market for commercial NLP applications. However, sentiment analysis on Tamil-English code-mixed data (Patra et al., 2018) is under-developed and data tare not readily available for research.

Until recently, word-level annotations were used for research in code-mixed corpora. Almost all the previous systems proposed were based on data annotated at the word-level. This is not only time-consuming but also expensive to create. However, neural networks and meta-embeddings (Kiela et al., 2018) have shown great promise in code-switched research without the need for word-level annotation. In particular, work by Winata et al. (2019a) learns to utilise information from pre-trained embeddings without explicit word-level language tags. A recent work by Winata et al. (2019b) utilised the subword-level information from closely related languages to improve the performance on the code-mixed text.

As there was no previous dataset available for Tamil-English (Tanglish) sentiment annotation, we create a sentiment dataset for Tanglish with voluntary annotators. We also show the baseline results with a few models explained in Section 5.

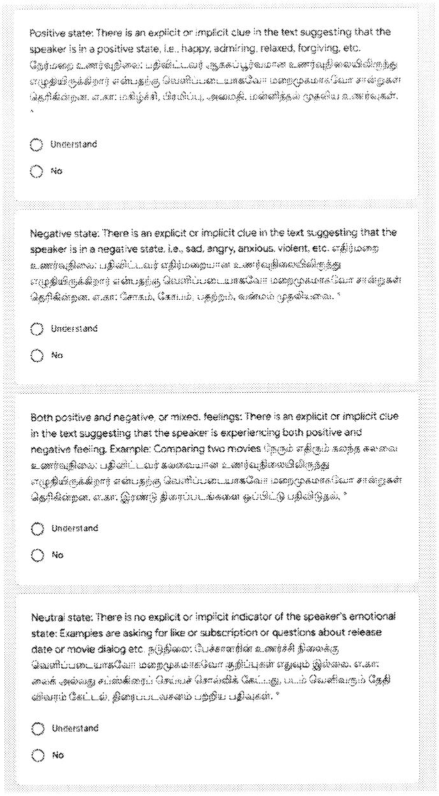

(a) Example 1

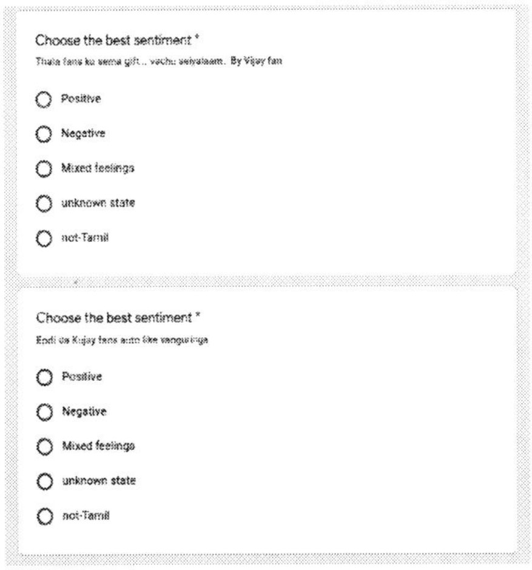

(b) Example 2

Figure 1: Examples of Google Form.

203

3. Corpus Creation and Annotation

Our goal was to create a code-mixed dataset for Tamil to ensure that enough data are available for research purposes. We used the *YouTube Comment Scraper tool*[2] and collected 184,573 sentences for Tamil from YouTube comments. We collected the comments from the trailers of a movies released in 2019. Many of the them contained sentences that were either entirely written in English or code-mixed Tamil-English or fully written in Tamil. So we filtered out a non-code-mixed corpus based on language identification at comment level using the *langdetect library* [3]. Thus if the comment is written fully in Tamil or English, we discarded that comment since monolingual resources are available for these languages. We also identified if the sentences were written in other languages such as Hindi, Malayalam, Urdu, Telugu, and Kannada. We preprocessed the comments by removing the emoticons and applying a sentence length filter. We want to create a code-mixed corpus of reasonable size with sentences that have fairly defined sentiments which will be useful for future research. Thus our filter removed sentences with less than five words and more than 15 words after cleaning the data. In the end we got 15,744 Tanglish sentences.

3.1. Annotation Setup

For annotation, we adopted the approach taken by Mohammad (2016), and a minimum of three annotators annotated each sentence in the dataset according to the following schema shown in the Figure 1. We added new category **Other language:** If the sentence is written in some other language other than Tamil or English. Examples for this are the comments written in other Indian languages using the Roman script. The annotation guidelines are given in English and Tamil.

As we have collected data from YouTube we anonymized to keep the privacy of the users who commented on it. As the voluntary annotators' personal information were collected to know about the them, this gives rise to both ethical, privacy and legal concerns. Therefore, the annotators were informed in the beginning that their data is being recorded and they can choose to withdraw from the process at any stage of annotation. The annotators should actively agree to being recorded. We created Google Forms in which we collected the annotators' email addresses which we used to ensure that an annotator was allowed to label a given sentence only once. We collected the information on gender, education and medium of instruction in school to know the diversity of annotators. Each Google form has been set to contain a maximum of 100 sentences. Example of the Google form is given in the Figure 1. The annotators have to agree that they understood the scheme; otherwise, they cannot proceed further. Three steps complete the annotation setup. First, each sentence was annotated by two people. In the second step, the data were collected if both of them agreed. In the case of conflict, a third person annotated the sentence. In the third step, if all the three of

them did not agree, then two more annotators annotated the sentences.

Gender	Male	9
	Female	2
Higher Education	Undegraduate	2
	Graduate	2
	Postgraduate	7
Medium of Schooling	English	6
	Tamil	5
Total		11

Table 1: Annotators

3.2. Annotators

To control the quality of annotation, we removed the annotator who did not annotate well in the first form. For example, if the annotators showed unreasonable delay in responding or if they labelled all sentences with the same sentiment or if more than fifty annotations in a form were wrong, we removed those contributions. Eleven volunteers were involved in the process. All of them were native speakers of Tamil with diversity in gender, educational level and medium of instruction in their school education. Table 1 shows information about the annotators. The volunteers were instructed to fill up the Google form, and 100 sentences were sent to them. If an annotator offers to volunteer more, the next Google form is sent to them with another set of 100 sentences and in this way each volunteer chooses to annotate as many sentences from the corpus as they want. We send the forms to an equal number of male and female annotators. However, from Table 1, we can see that only two female annotators volunteered to contribute.

3.3. Corpus Statistics

Corpus statistics is given in the Table 2. The distribution of released data is shown in Table 3. The entire dataset of 15,744 sentences was randomly shuffled and split into three parts as follows: 11,335 sentences were used for training, 1,260 sentences form the validation set and 3,149 sentences were used for testing. The machine learning models were applied to this subset of data rather than k-fold cross validation. The only other code-mixed dataset of reasonable size that we could find was an earlier work by Remmiya Devi et al. (2016) on code-mix entity extraction for Hindi-English and Tamil-English tweets, released as a part of the shared task in FIRE 2016. The dataset consisted of 3,200 Tanglish tweets used for training and 1,376 tweets for testing.

3.4. Inter Annotator Agreement

We used **Krippendorff's alpha** (α) (Krippendorff, 1970) to measure inter-annotator agreement because of the nature of our annotation setup. This is a robust statistical measure that accounts for incomplete data and, therefore, does not require every annotator to annotate every sentence. It is also a measure that takes into account the degree of disagreement between the predicted classes, which is crucial in our annotation scheme. For instance, if the annotators disagree

---

[2]https://github.com/philbot9/youtube-comment-scraper
[3]https://pypi.org/project/langdetect/

Language pair	Tamil-English
Number of Tokens	169,833
Vocabulary Size	30,898
Number of Posts	15,744
Number of Sentences	17,926
Average number of Tokens per post	10
Average number of sentences per post	1

Table 2: Corpus statistic of and Tamil-English

Class	Tamil-English
Positive	10,559
Negative	2,037
Mixed feelings	1,801
Neutral	850
Other language	497
Total	15,744

Table 3: Data Distribution

between **Positive** and **Negative** class, this disagreement is more serious than when they disagree between **Mixed feelings** and **Neutral**. α can handle such disagreements. α is defined as:

$$\alpha = 1 - \frac{D_o}{D_e} \tag{1}$$

D_o is the observed disagreement between sentiment labels by the annotators and D_e is the disagreement expected when the coding of sentiments can be attributed to chance rather than due to the inherent property of the sentiment itself.

$$D_o = \frac{1}{n} \sum_c \sum_k o_{ck\ metric}\ \delta_{ck}^2 \tag{2}$$

$$D_e = \frac{1}{n(n-1)} \sum_c \sum_k n_c \cdot n_{k\ metric}\ \delta_{ck}^2 \tag{3}$$

Here $o_{ck}\ n_c\ n_k$ and n refer to the frequencies of values in coincidence matrices and $metric$ refers to any metric or level of measurement such as nominal, ordinal, interval, ratio and others. Krippendorff's alpha applies to all these metrics. We used nominal and interval metric to calculate annotator agreement. The range of α is between 0 and 1, $1 \geq \alpha \geq 0$. When α is 1 there is perfect agreement between annotators and when 0 the agreement is entirely due to chance. Our annotation produced an agreement of 0.6585 using nominal metric and 0.6799 using interval metric.

4. Difficult Examples

In this section we talk about some examples that were difficult to annotate.

1. **Enakku iru mugan trailer gnabagam than varuthu** - *All it reminds me of is the trailer of the movie Irumugan*. Not sure whether the speaker enjoyed Irumugan trailer or disliked it or simply observed the similarities between the two trailers.

2. **Rajini ah vida akshay mass ah irukane** - *Akshay looks more amazing than Rajini*. Difficult to decide if it is a disappointment that the villain looks better than the hero or a positive appreciation for the villain actor.

3. **Ada dei nama sambatha da dei** - *I wonder, Is this our sampath? Hey!*. Conflict between neutral and positive.

4. **Lokesh kanagaraj movie naalae.... English Rap....Song vandurum** - *If it is a movie of Lokesh kanagaraj, it always has an English rap song*. Ambiguous sentiment.

According to the instructions, questions about music director, movie release date and remarks about when the speaker is watching the video should be treated as neutral. However the above examples show that some comments about the actors and movies can be ambiguously interpreted as neutral or positive or negative. We found annotator disagreements in such sentences.

5. Benchmark Systems

In order to provide a simple baseline, we applied various machine learning algorithms for determining the sentiments of YouTube posts in code-mixed Tamil-English language.

5.1. Experimental Settings

5.1.1. Logistic Regression (LR):
We evaluate the Logistic Regression model with L2 regularization. The input features are the Term Frequency Inverse Document Frequency (TF-IDF) values of up to 3 grams.

5.1.2. Support Vector Machine (SVM):
We evaluate the SVM model with L2 regularization. The features are the same as in LR. The purpose of SVM classification algorithm is to define optimal hyperplane in N dimensional space to separate the data points from each other.

5.1.3. K-Nearest Neighbour (K-NN):
We use KNN for classification with 3,4,5,and 9 neighbours by applying uniform weights.

5.1.4. Decision Tree (DT):
Decision trees have been previously used in NLP tasks for classification. In decision tree, the prediction is done by splitting the root training set into subsets as nodes, and each node contains output of the decision, label or condition. After sequentially choosing alternative decisions, each node

Classifier	Positive	Negative	Neutral	Mixed	Other language	Micro Avg	Macro Avg	Weighted Avg
KNN	0.70	0.23	0.35	0.16	0.06	0.45	0.30	0.53
Decision Tree	0.71	0.30	0.24	0.17	0.60	0.61	0.40	0.56
Random Forest	0.69	0.51	0.80	0.41	0.68	0.68	0.62	0.63
Logistic Regression	0.68	0.56	0.61	0.36	0.76	0.68	0.59	0.62
Naive Bayes	0.66	0.62	0.00	0.40	0.69	0.66	0.48	0.59
SVM	0.66	0.00	0.00	0.00	0.00	0.66	0.13	0.43
1DConv-LSTM	0.71	0.30	0.00	0.14	0.67	0.63	0.36	0.54
DME	0.68	0.34	0.31	0.29	0.71	0.67	0.46	0.57
CDME	0.67	0.56	0.56	0.20	0.68	0.67	0.53	0.59
BERT Multilingual	0.67	0.00	0.00	0.00	0.64	0.67	0.26	0.46

Table 4: Precision

Classifier	Positive	Negative	Neutral	Mixed	Other language	Micro Avg	Macro Avg	Weighted Avg
KNN	0.63	0.04	0.10	0.02	0.61	0.45	0.28	0.45
Decision Tree	0.83	0.21	0.13	0.12	0.54	0.61	0.36	0.61
Random Forest	0.98	0.18	0.09	0.04	0.55	0.68	0.32	0.68
Logistic Regression	0.98	0.13	0.06	0.01	0.32	0.68	0.30	0.68
Naive Bayes	1.00	0.01	0.00	0.01	0.18	0.66	0.24	0.67
SVM	1.00	0.00	0.00	0.00	0.00	0.66	0.20	0.66
1DConv-LSTM	0.91	0.11	0.00	0.10	0.28	0.63	0.28	0.63
DME	0.99	0.03	0.02	0.01	0.49	0.67	0.31	0.57
CDME	0.99	0.01	0.03	0.00	0.52	0.67	0.31	0.67
BERT Multilingual	0.99	0.00	0.00	0.00	0.58	0.67	0.31	0.46

Table 5: Recall

Classifier	Positive	Negative	Neutral	Mixed	Other language	Micro Avg	Macro Avg	Weighted Avg
KNN	0.66	0.06	0.15	0.04	0.10	0.45	0.29	0.50
Decision Tree	0.77	0.24	0.17	0.14	0.54	0.61	0.38	0.58
Random Forest	0.81	0.18	0.09	0.04	0.55	0.68	0.42	0.65
Logistic Regression	0.81	0.21	0.12	0.03	0.45	0.68	0.40	0.64
Naive Bayes	0.80	0.02	0.00	0.01	0.29	0.66	0.32	0.63
SVM	0.79	0.00	0.00	0.00	0.00	0.66	0.16	0.52
1DConv-LSTM	0.80	0.16	0.00	0.12	0.39	0.63	0.31	0.58
DME	0.80	0.05	0.04	0.01	0.58	0.67	0.37	0.57
CDME	0.80	0.02	0.05	0.01	0.59	0.67	0.39	0.63
BERT Multilingual	0.80	0.00	0.00	0.00	0.61	0.67	0.28	0.46

Table 6: F-score

recursively is split again and finally the classifier defines some rules to predict the result. We used it to classify the sentiments for baseline. Maximum depth was 800 and minimum sample splits were 5 for DT. The criterion were Gini and entropy.

5.1.5. Random Forest (RF):

In random forest, the classifier randomly generates trees without defining rules. We evaluate the RF model with same features as in DT.

5.1.6. Multinominal Naive Bayes (MNB):

Naive-Bayes classifier is a probabilistic model, which is derived from Bayes Theorem that finds the probability of hypothesis activity to the given evidence activity. We evaluate the MNB model with our data using $\alpha=1$ with TF-IDF vectors.

5.1.7. 1DConv-LSTM:

The model we evaluated consists of Embedding layer, Dropout, 1DConv with activation ReLU, Max-pooling and LSTM. The embeddings are randomly initialized.

5.1.8. BERT-Multilingual:

Devlin et al. (2019) introduced a language representation model which is Bidirectional Encoder Representation from Transforms. It is designed to pre-train from unlabelled text and can be fine-tuned by adding last layer. BERT has been used for many text classification tasks (Tayyar Madabushi et al., 2019; Ma et al., 2019; Cohan et al., 2019). We explore classification of a code-mixed data into their corresponding sentiment categories.

5.1.9. DME and CDME:

We also implemented the Dynamic Meta Embedding (Kiela et al., 2018) to evaluate our model. As a first step, we used Word2Vec and FastText to train from our dataset since dynamic meta-embedding is an effective method for the supervised learning of embedding ensembles.

5.2. Experiment Results and Discussion

The experimental results of the sentiment classification task using different methods are shown in terms of precision in Table 4, recall in Table 5, and F-score in Table 6. We used *sklearn* [4] for evaluation. The micro-average is calculated by aggregating the contributions of all classes to compute the average metric. In a multi-class classification setup, micro-average is preferable if there are class imbalances. For instance in our data, we have many more examples of positive classes than other classes. A macro-average will compute the metrics (precision, recall, F-score) independently for each class and then take the average. Thus this metric treats all classes equally and it does not take imbalance into account. A weighted average takes the metrics from each class just like macro but the contribution of each class to the average is weighted by the number of examples available for it. For our test, positive is 2,075, negative is 424, neutral is 173, mixed feelings are 377, and non-Tamil is 100.

As shown in the tables, all the classification algorithms perform poorly on the code-mixed dataset. Logistic regression, random forest classifiers and decision trees were the ones that fared comparatively better across all sentiment classes. Surprisingly, the classification result by the SVM model has much worse diversity than the other methods. Applying deep learning methods also does not lead to higher scores on the three automatic metrics. We think this stems from the characteristics of the dataset. The classification scores for different sentiment classes appear to be in line with the distribution of sentiments in the dataset.

The dataset is not a balanced distribution. Table 3 shows that out of total 15,744 sentences 67% belong to *Positive* class while the other sentiment classes share 13%, 5% and 3% respectively. The precision, recall and F-measure scores are higher for the *Positive* class while the scores for *Neutral* and *Mixed feeling* classes were disastrous. Apart from their low distribution in the dataset, these two classes are difficult to annotate for even human annotators as discussed in Section 4. In comparison, the *Negative* and *Other language* classes were better. We suspect this is due to more explicit clues for negative and non-Tamil words and due to relatively higher distribution of negative comments in the data.

Since we collected the post from movie trailers, we got more positive sentiment than others as the people who watch trailers are more likely to be interested in movies and this skews the overall distribution. However, as the code-mixing phenomenon is not incorporated in the earlier models, this resource could be taken as a starting point for further research. There is significant room for improvement in code-mixed research with our dataset. In our experiments, we only utilized the machine learning methods,

but more information such as linguistic information or hierarchical meta-embedding can be utilized. This dataset can be used to create a multilingual embedding for code-mixed data (Pratapa et al., 2018b).

6. Conclusion

We presented, to the best of our knowledge, the most substantial corpus for under-resourced code-mixed Tanglish with annotations for sentiment polarity. We achieved a high inter-annotator agreement in terms of Krippendorff α from voluntary annotators on contributions collected using Google form. We created baselines with gold standard annotated data and presented our results for each class in Precision, Recall, and F-Score. We expect this resource will enable the researchers to address new and exciting problems in code-mixed research.

7. Acknowledgments

This publication has emanated from research supported in part by a research grant from Science Foundation Ireland (SFI) under Grant Number SFI/12/RC/2289 (Insight), SFI/12/RC/2289_P2 (Insight_2), co-funded by the European Regional Development Fund as well as by the EU H2020 programme under grant agreements 731015 (ELEXIS-European Lexical Infrastructure), 825182 (Prêt-à-LLOD), and Irish Research Council grant IRCLA/2017/129 (CARDAMOM-Comparative Deep Models of Language for Minority and Historical Languages).

8. Bibliographical References

Agrawal, R., Chenthil Kumar, V., Muralidharan, V., and Sharma, D. (2018). No more beating about the bush : A step towards idiom handling for Indian language NLP. In *Proceedings of the Eleventh International Conference on Language Resources and Evaluation (LREC 2018)*, Miyazaki, Japan, May. European Language Resources Association (ELRA).

Gustavo Aguilar, et al., editors. (2018). *Proceedings of the Third Workshop on Computational Approaches to Linguistic Code-Switching*, Melbourne, Australia, July. Association for Computational Linguistics.

AlGhamdi, F., Molina, G., Diab, M., Solorio, T., Hawwari, A., Soto, V., and Hirschberg, J. (2016). Part of speech tagging for code switched data. In *Proceedings of the Second Workshop on Computational Approaches to Code Switching*, pages 98–107, Austin, Texas, November. Association for Computational Linguistics.

A.R., B., Joshi, A., and Bhattacharyya, P. (2012). Cross-lingual sentiment analysis for Indian languages using linked WordNets. In *Proceedings of COLING 2012: Posters*, pages 73–82, Mumbai, India, December. The COLING 2012 Organizing Committee.

Barman, U., Das, A., Wagner, J., and Foster, J. (2014). Code mixing: A challenge for language identification in the language of social media. In *Proceedings of the First Workshop on Computational Approaches to Code Switching*, pages 13–23, Doha, Qatar, October. Association for Computational Linguistics.

---

[4]https://scikit-learn.org/

Chakravarthi, B. R., Arcan, M., and McCrae, J. P. (2018). Improving wordnets for under-resourced languages using machine translation. In *Proceedings of the 9th Global WordNet Conference (GWC 2018)*, page 78.

Chakravarthi, B. R., Arcan, M., and McCrae, J. P. (2019a). Comparison of different orthographies for machine translation of under-resourced dravidian languages. In *2nd Conference on Language, Data and Knowledge (LDK 2019)*. Schloss Dagstuhl-Leibniz-Zentrum fuer Informatik.

Chakravarthi, B. R., Arcan, M., and McCrae, J. P. (2019b). WordNet gloss translation for under-resourced languages using multilingual neural machine translation. In *Proceedings of the Second Workshop on Multilingualism at the Intersection of Knowledge Bases and Machine Translation*, pages 1–7, Dublin, Ireland, 19 August. European Association for Machine Translation.

Chakravarthi, B. R., Priyadharshini, R., Stearns, B., Jayapal, A., S, S., Arcan, M., Zarrouk, M., and McCrae, J. P. (2019c). Multilingual multimodal machine translation for Dravidian languages utilizing phonetic transcription. In *Proceedings of the 2nd Workshop on Technologies for MT of Low Resource Languages*, pages 56–63, Dublin, Ireland, 20 August. European Association for Machine Translation.

Chakravarthi, B. R., Jose, N., Suryawanshi, S., Sherly, E., and McCrae, J. P. (2020). A sentiment analysis dataset for code-mixed Malayalam-English. In *Proceedings of the 1st Joint Workshop of SLTU (Spoken Language Technologies for Under-resourced languages) and CCURL (Collaboration and Computing for Under-Resourced Languages) (SLTU-CCURL 2020)*, Marseille, France, May. European Language Resources Association (ELRA).

Chanda, A., Das, D., and Mazumdar, C. (2016). Unraveling the English-Bengali code-mixing phenomenon. In *Proceedings of the Second Workshop on Computational Approaches to Code Switching*, pages 80–89, Austin, Texas, November. Association for Computational Linguistics.

Cieliebak, M., Deriu, J. M., Egger, D., and Uzdilli, F. (2017). A Twitter corpus and benchmark resources for German sentiment analysis. In *Proceedings of the Fifth International Workshop on Natural Language Processing for Social Media*, pages 45–51, Valencia, Spain, April. Association for Computational Linguistics.

Cohan, A., Beltagy, I., King, D., Dalvi, B., and Weld, D. (2019). Pretrained language models for sequential sentence classification. In *Proceedings of the 2019 Conference on Empirical Methods in Natural Language Processing and the 9th International Joint Conference on Natural Language Processing (EMNLP-IJCNLP)*, pages 3693–3699, Hong Kong, China, November. Association for Computational Linguistics.

Das, A. and Bandyopadhyay, S. (2010). SentiWordNet for Indian languages. In *Proceedings of the Eighth Workshop on Asian Language Resouces*, pages 56–63, Beijing, China, August. Coling 2010 Organizing Committee.

Devlin, J., Chang, M.-W., Lee, K., and Toutanova, K. (2019). BERT: Pre-training of deep bidirectional transformers for language understanding. In *Proceedings of the 2019 Conference of the North American Chapter of the Association for Computational Linguistics: Human Language Technologies, Volume 1 (Long and Short Papers)*, pages 4171–4186, Minneapolis, Minnesota, June. Association for Computational Linguistics.

Hu, M. and Liu, B. (2004). Mining and summarizing customer reviews. In *Proceedings of the Tenth ACM SIGKDD International Conference on Knowledge Discovery and Data Mining*, KDD '04, page 168–177, New York, NY, USA. Association for Computing Machinery.

Jiang, Q., Chen, L., Xu, R., Ao, X., and Yang, M. (2019). A challenge dataset and effective models for aspect-based sentiment analysis. In *Proceedings of the 2019 Conference on Empirical Methods in Natural Language Processing and the 9th International Joint Conference on Natural Language Processing (EMNLP-IJCNLP)*, pages 6279–6284, Hong Kong, China, November. Association for Computational Linguistics.

Jose, N., Chakravarthi, B. R., Suryawanshi, S., Sherly, E., and McCrae, J. P. (2020). A survey of current datasets for code-switching research. In *2020 6th International Conference on Advanced Computing & Communication Systems (ICACCS)*.

Joshi, A., Prabhu, A., Shrivastava, M., and Varma, V. (2016). Towards sub-word level compositions for sentiment analysis of Hindi-English code mixed text. In *Proceedings of COLING 2016, the 26th International Conference on Computational Linguistics: Technical Papers*, pages 2482–2491, Osaka, Japan, December. The COLING 2016 Organizing Committee.

Kannan, A., Mohanty, G., and Mamidi, R. (2016). Towards building a SentiWordNet for Tamil. In *Proceedings of the 13th International Conference on Natural Language Processing*, pages 30–35, Varanasi, India, December. NLP Association of India.

Kiela, D., Wang, C., and Cho, K. (2018). Dynamic meta-embeddings for improved sentence representations. In *Proceedings of the 2018 Conference on Empirical Methods in Natural Language Processing*, pages 1466–1477, Brussels, Belgium, October-November. Association for Computational Linguistics.

Krippendorff, K. (1970). Estimating the reliability, systematic error and random error of interval data. *Educational and Psychological Measurement*, 30(1):61–70.

Krishnasamy, K. (2015). Code mixing among Tamil-English bilingual children. *International Journal of Social Science and Humanity*, 5(9):788.

Lee, S. and Wang, Z. (2015). Emotion in code-switching texts: Corpus construction and analysis. In *Proceedings of the Eighth SIGHAN Workshop on Chinese Language Processing*, pages 91–99, Beijing, China, July. Association for Computational Linguistics.

Ma, X., Xu, P., Wang, Z., Nallapati, R., and Xiang, B. (2019). Domain adaptation with BERT-based domain classification and data selection. In *Proceedings of the 2nd Workshop on Deep Learning Approaches for Low-Resource NLP (DeepLo 2019)*, pages 76–83, Hong

Kong, China, November. Association for Computational Linguistics.

Mæhlum, P., Barnes, J., Øvrelid, L., and Velldal, E. (2019). Annotating evaluative sentences for sentiment analysis: a dataset for Norwegian. In *Proceedings of the 22nd Nordic Conference on Computational Linguistics*, pages 121–130, Turku, Finland, September–October. Linköping University Electronic Press.

Mohammad, S. (2016). A practical guide to sentiment annotation: Challenges and solutions. In *Proceedings of the 7th Workshop on Computational Approaches to Subjectivity, Sentiment and Social Media Analysis*, pages 174–179, San Diego, California, June. Association for Computational Linguistics.

Padmamala, R. and Prema, V. (2017). Sentiment analysis of online Tamil contents using recursive neural network models approach for Tamil language. In *2017 IEEE International Conference on Smart Technologies and Management for Computing, Communication, Controls, Energy and Materials (ICSTM)*, pages 28–31, Aug.

Patra, B. G., Das, D., and Das, A. (2018). Sentiment analysis of code-mixed indian languages: An overview of sail_code-mixed shared task@ icon-2017. *arXiv preprint arXiv:1803.06745*.

Phani, S., Lahiri, S., and Biswas, A. (2016). Sentiment analysis of Tweets in three Indian languages. In *Proceedings of the 6th Workshop on South and Southeast Asian Natural Language Processing (WSSANLP2016)*, pages 93–102, Osaka, Japan, December. The COLING 2016 Organizing Committee.

Prasad, S. S., Kumar, J., Prabhakar, D. K., and Tripathi, S. (2016). Sentiment mining: An approach for Bengali and Tamil tweets. In *2016 Ninth International Conference on Contemporary Computing (IC3)*, pages 1–4, Aug.

Pratapa, A., Bhat, G., Choudhury, M., Sitaram, S., Dandapat, S., and Bali, K. (2018a). Language modeling for code-mixing: The role of linguistic theory based synthetic data. In *Proceedings of the 56th Annual Meeting of the Association for Computational Linguistics (Volume 1: Long Papers)*, pages 1543–1553, Melbourne, Australia, July. Association for Computational Linguistics.

Pratapa, A., Choudhury, M., and Sitaram, S. (2018b). Word embeddings for code-mixed language processing. In *Proceedings of the 2018 Conference on Empirical Methods in Natural Language Processing*, pages 3067–3072, Brussels, Belgium, October-November. Association for Computational Linguistics.

Priyadharshini, R., Chakravarthi, B. R., Vegupatti, M., and McCrae, J. P. (2020). Named entity recognition for code-mixed Indian corpus using meta embedding. In *2020 6th International Conference on Advanced Computing & Communication Systems (ICACCS)*.

Rani, P., Suryawanshi, S., Goswami, K., Chakravarthi, B. R., Fransen, T., and McCrae, J. P. (2020). A comparative study of different state-of-the-art hate speech detection methods for Hindi-English code-mixed data. In *Proceedings of the Second Workshop on Trolling, Aggression and Cyberbullying*, Marseille, France, May. European Language Resources Association (ELRA).

Ranjan, P., Raja, B., Priyadharshini, R., and Balabantaray, R. C. (2016). A comparative study on code-mixed data of Indian social media vs formal text. In *2016 2nd International Conference on Contemporary Computing and Informatics (IC3I)*, pages 608–611.

Remmiya Devi, G., Veena, P., Anand Kumar, M., and Soman, K. (2016). Amrita-cen@ fire 2016: Code-mix entity extraction for Hindi-English and Tamil-English tweets. In *CEUR workshop proceedings*, volume 1737, pages 304–308.

Rogers, A., Romanov, A., Rumshisky, A., Volkova, S., Gronas, M., and Gribov, A. (2018). RuSentiment: An enriched sentiment analysis dataset for social media in Russian. In *Proceedings of the 27th International Conference on Computational Linguistics*, pages 755–763, Santa Fe, New Mexico, USA, August. Association for Computational Linguistics.

Sitaram, D., Murthy, S., Ray, D., Sharma, D., and Dhar, K. (2015). Sentiment analysis of mixed language employing hindi-english code switching. In *2015 International Conference on Machine Learning and Cybernetics (ICMLC)*, volume 1, pages 271–276, July.

Solorio, T., Blair, E., Maharjan, S., Bethard, S., Diab, M., Ghoneim, M., Hawwari, A., AlGhamdi, F., Hirschberg, J., Chang, A., and Fung, P. (2014). Overview for the first shared task on language identification in code-switched data. In *Proceedings of the First Workshop on Computational Approaches to Code Switching*, pages 62–72, Doha, Qatar, October. Association for Computational Linguistics.

Suryawanshi, S., Chakravarthi, B. R., Arcan, M., and Buitelaar, P. (2020a). Multimodal meme dataset (MultiOFF) for identifying offensive content in image and text. In *Proceedings of the Second Workshop on Trolling, Aggression and Cyberbullying*, Marseille, France, May. European Language Resources Association (ELRA).

Suryawanshi, S., Chakravarthi, B. R., Verma, P., Arcan, M., McCrae, J. P., and Buitelaar, P. (2020b). A dataset for troll classification of Tamil memes. In *Proceedings of the 5th Workshop on Indian Language Data Resource and Evaluation (WILDRE-5)*, Marseille, France, May. European Language Resources Association (ELRA).

Tayyar Madabushi, H., Kochkina, E., and Castelle, M. (2019). Cost-sensitive BERT for generalisable sentence classification on imbalanced data. In *Proceedings of the Second Workshop on Natural Language Processing for Internet Freedom: Censorship, Disinformation, and Propaganda*, pages 125–134, Hong Kong, China, November. Association for Computational Linguistics.

Vilares, D., Alonso, M. A., and Gómez-Rodríguez, C. (2015). Sentiment analysis on monolingual, multilingual and code-switching Twitter corpora. In *Proceedings of the 6th Workshop on Computational Approaches to Subjectivity, Sentiment and Social Media Analysis*, pages 2–8, Lisboa, Portugal, September. Association for Computational Linguistics.

Vilares, D., Alonso, M. A., and Gómez-Rodríguez, C. (2016). En-es-cs: An English-Spanish code-switching twitter corpus for multilingual sentiment analysis. In Nicoletta Calzolari (Conference Chair), et al., editors, *Proceedings of the Tenth International Conference on Language Resources and Evaluation (LREC 2016)*, Paris, France, may. European Language Resources Association (ELRA).

Wiebe, J., Wilson, T., and Cardie, C. (2005). Annotating expressions of opinions and emotions in language. *Language Resources and Evaluation*, 39(2):165–210, May.

Winata, G. I., Lin, Z., and Fung, P. (2019a). Learning multilingual meta-embeddings for code-switching named entity recognition. In *Proceedings of the 4th Workshop on Representation Learning for NLP (RepL4NLP-2019)*, pages 181–186, Florence, Italy, August. Association for Computational Linguistics.

Winata, G. I., Lin, Z., Shin, J., Liu, Z., and Fung, P. (2019b). Hierarchical meta-embeddings for code-switching named entity recognition. In *Proceedings of the 2019 Conference on Empirical Methods in Natural Language Processing and the 9th International Joint Conference on Natural Language Processing (EMNLP-IJCNLP)*, pages 3532–3538, Hong Kong, China, November. Association for Computational Linguistics.

Yang, Y. and Eisenstein, J. (2017). Overcoming language variation in sentiment analysis with social attention. *Transactions of the Association for Computational Linguistics*, 5:295–307.

Proceedings of the 1st Joint SLTU and CCURL Workshop (SLTU-CCURL 2020), pages 211–217
Language Resources and Evaluation Conference (LREC 2020), Marseille, 11–16 May 2020
ⓒ European Language Resources Association (ELRA), licensed under CC-BY-NC

Gender Detection from Human Voice Using Tensor Analysis

Prasanta Roy, Parabattina Bhagath and Pradip K. Das
Computer Science and Engineering Department, Indian Institute of Technology Guwahati
Guwahati, Assam, India
roy174101001@iitg.ac.in, bhagath.2014@iitg.ac.in, pkdas@iitg.ac.in

Abstract

Speech-based communication is one of the most preferred modes of communication for humans. The human voice contains several important information and clues that help in interpreting the voice message. The gender of the speaker can be accurately guessed by a person based on the received voice of a speaker. The knowledge of the speaker's gender can be a great aid to design accurate speech recognition systems. GMM based classifier is a popular choice used for gender detection. In this paper, we propose a Tensor-based approach for detecting the gender of a speaker and discuss its implementation details for low resourceful languages. Experiments were conducted using the TIMIT and SHRUTI dataset. An average gender detection accuracy of 91% is recorded. Analysis of the results with the proposed method is presented in this paper.

Keywords: speaker gender detection, tensor decomposition, method of moments, tensor power method, MFCCs

1. Introduction

Gender detection is one of the important problems in speaker and speech recognition domains. It has got significance because of the gain in popularity of voice-based systems like Alexa, Google Assistant, Cortana, Siri, etc. One of the applications of this is helping companies to provide better solutions. In speech recognition, it helps in improving the accuracy of recognition. It also has importance in sub-problems like age detection, emotion detection, speaker identification, etc. Research on the gender detection problem started in the early '90s. The problem was studied by using features like Linear Predictive Cepstral Coefficients (LPCCs), energy, Mel Frequency Cepstral Coefficients (MFCCs), etc. Konig and Morgan (Konig and Morgan, 1992) used LPCCs in their work to address this problem. In the system that was proposed, a multi-layer perceptron was employed for the classification of gender. As a result, this system achieved an accuracy of 84% on DARPA resource management database.

Neti (Neti and Roukos, 1997) proposed a GMM (Gaussian Mixture Model) based gender classification approach for an Air Travel Information System (ATIS) corpus. It was reported that 95% accuracy was obtained. This was an improvement over a simple pattern matching approach. MFCCs have widely accepted features in speaker characterization. They play an important role in GMM based systems that deal with gender recognition task. Tzanetakis (Tzanetakis and Cook, 2002) proposed a system that uses the above- mentioned features. The system was developed with gender classification and sports announcement facilities. Along with the techniques that are discussed, there are papers available on the same problem. In these systems, the pitch was used as a crucial feature. Several studies agree that modeling techniques like Convolutional Neural Networks (CNNs) (Doukhan et al., 2018), Expectation-Maximization (EM) (Yücesoy and Nabiyev, 2013), Hidden Markov Models (HMMs) (Parris and Carey, 1996), Support Vector Machine (SVM) classifiers (Jo et al., 2008) are successful in this area of research.

GMM-based classifiers and Expectation-Maximization (EM) have been used predominantly for modeling and parameter estimation, respectively. Most of the methods for estimating parameters of GMM are based on Maximum Likelihood Estimation (MLE), which has a drawback of getting stuck in a local optimum. So it needs to restart indefinitely to search for global optimum, and sometimes it may not find global optimum at all. As a result, the whole process of parameter estimation becomes very time-consuming.

In this paper, we have proposed an eigenvector-based approach to detect the gender from human voice using tensor analysis. We have used MFCCs as feature vector to form the feature vector space. Method of moments is used to build the tensor structure from the feature vector space for each gender. The tensor power method is applied to compute the eigenvectors from that tensor structure (Anandkumar et al., 2014). The proposed approach does not require multiple restarts but still provides 91% accuracy using Euclidean distance for evaluations.

2. Basic Understanding of Tensors

In this section, we will go through the basics of Tensors and related multi-linear algebra that are essential concepts to understand the tensor power method (Anandkumar et al., 2017) and its usefulness in parameter estimation of latent variable models. A comprehensive study about tensor is available in the work of Kolda (Kolda and Bader, 2009) and Sidiropoulos (Sidiropoulos et al., 2017), whereas a multi-linear map and its notations can be found in the work of Lim (Lek-Heng Lim, 2005).

2.1. Tensor Preliminaries

Tensor is a multiway collection of numbers or an extension of a matrix in higher order. Vectors and Matrices are first-order and second-order tensors, respectively. In general, a pth order tensor is an object that can be interpreted as a p-dimensional array of numbers. *Tensor order* is the number of dimensions of the tensor. Though the tensor can be of any order, we will describe tensor as a 3rd order tensor structure in our experiments. For discussion, an N-way tensor is the same as N-order tensor or vice versa. In terms of notation, a scalar is denoted by lower case letters $a \in \mathbb{R}$, vectors by bold lower case letter $a \in \mathbb{R}^{I_1}$, matrices by upper case bold letter $A \in \mathbb{R}^{I_1 \times I_2}$ and for higher order tensor calligraphic letters are used $\mathcal{A} \in \mathbb{R}^{I_1 \times I_2 \times \ldots \times I_N}$.

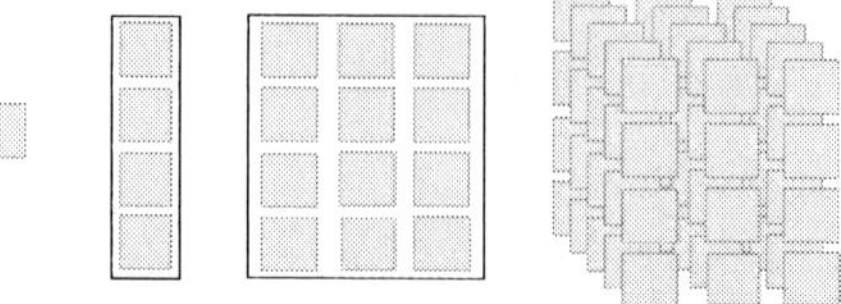

Figure 1: Zeroth Order Tensor ($a \in \mathbb{R}$, First Order Tensor ($a \in \mathbb{R}^4$), Second Order Tensor ($A \in \mathbb{R}^{4 \times 3}$), Third Order Tensor ($\mathcal{A} \in \mathbb{R}^{4 \times 3 \times 5}$).

2.1.1. Outer Product and Inner Product

Vector outer product is the element-wise product of two vectors. The outer product of two vectors produces a Matrix, which is a second-order tensor. In this discussion, the outer product will be denoted by $\odot$ symbol. For instance, if a and b are two n-sized vectors then their outer product will produce a matrix A as follows:

$$A = a \odot b = ab^T \tag{1}$$

Similarly, the outer product of three vectors will generate 3rd order tensor, which will be relevant to our topic of discussion. In general, the outer product of n vectors creates n-order tensor.

$$\mathcal{A} = a^{(1)} \odot a^{(2)} \odot a^{(3)} \ldots \odot a^{(n)} \tag{2}$$

In contrast to this, the inner product of two m-sized vectors will generate a scalar.

$$a = a^T b = \sum_{i=1}^{m} a_i b_i \tag{3}$$

2.1.2. Tensor Rank

Tensor rank is one of the important properties of a tensor. Before going to tensor rank, we will discuss about Rank-1 tensor. If an N-order tensor is strictly decomposed as an outer product of N vectors, then the N-order tensor is a Rank-1 tensor. So a Rank-1 matrix (2-way tensor) can be written as $A = a \odot b$. Similarly a Rank-1- third-order tensor can be represented as $\mathcal{A} = a \odot b \odot c$.

Minimum number of rank-1 N order tensors required that can sum up as N order tensor is called the rank of the N-order tensor. A rank-R third-order tensor can be represented as $\mathcal{A} = \sum_{i=1}^{R} \lambda_i a_i \odot b_i \odot c_i$. Here the λ is used to represent the weighting factor during normalization of matrices, which are the other factors of the resultant tensor.

2.2. Tensor Decomposition

In Mathematics, it is fundamental to decompose an object into some simpler and easy-to-handle objects. Matrix decomposition techniques are significant in the field of Mathematics in their application to solve linear equation systems and the implementation of numerical algorithms efficiently.

In the following part, we have discussed the non-uniqueness of general matrix decomposition and the uniqueness of tensor decomposition with much-relaxed conditions.

2.2.1. Matrix Decomposition and Rotational Problem

In our discussion on matrix decomposition, we focus on matrix rank decomposition, which is an information extraction technique. It can be expressed by the following equation:

$$A = BC^T \tag{4}$$

where $A \in \mathbb{R}^{n \times m}, B \in \mathbb{R}^{n \times r}, C \in \mathbb{R}^{m \times r}$ and r is rank of the decomposition.

Similar work was carried out by Charles Spearman, a British Psychologist in 1904, which is popularly known as Spearman's Hypothesis.

However Equation 4 is not unique. By using another invertible matrix R, we can create another decomposition. Absorbing R on the left with B and R^{-1} on the right of C we can generate matrix $\dot{B}$ and $\dot{C}$ respectively which can be used to reconstruct A.

$$A = BC^T = BRR^{-1}C^T = (BR)(R^{-1}C^T) = \dot{B}\dot{C} \tag{5}$$

We can see that matrix rank-decomposition is non-unique generally. Though some decomposition techniques provide unique decomposition over some conditions such as orthogonality for Singular Value Decomposition (SVD), tensor decomposition is unique under much milder conditions.

2.2.2. Tensor Uniqueness and Rigidness

Tensor decomposition is unique only if there is one type of rank-1 tensor that sums up to our main tensor with a certain scaling factor. It means we cannot construct a different arrangement of rank-1 tensors that can sum up to our desired main tensor. The uniqueness of tensor decomposition is under much milder conditions than matrix decomposition. Let's consider a slice of a tensor $\mathcal{A}$ which can be represented as follows:

$$A_k = \sum_{i=1}^{R} (a_i \odot b_i) c_{ki} \tag{6}$$

Here k represents the kth slice which is also a low-rank matrix. Therefore a tensor is not just a low-rank collection of these slices, there is an interrelation among them. If we observe, each slice is a differently scaled representation of the same matrix. This constraint helps us to address the rotational problem of a matrix that is faced during matrix decomposition.

To determine the factors that capture the underlying structure of a tensor, we subtract the scaled matrix formed by those factors. For matrices, there are multiple possibilities of finding those factors. But for tensors, these factors have to satisfy all the slices, thus making a strong interconnection between the slices, which further makes the tensor more rigid.

2.3. Tensor Decomposition Algorithms

Tensor Decomposition is one of the most studied topics of tensors. There are two different families of tensor decomposition techniques as follows:

1. Canonical Polyadic Decomposition (CPD)

2. Tucker Decomposition

CPD is mainly used for latent parameter estimation, and Tucker is used for compression, dimensionality reduction, estimation of subspace, etc.

In the following subsections, first, we have discussed the basic understanding of CPD and Tucker decomposition, followed by the tensor power method, which is a special kind of CPD decomposition. The tensor power method is used in our proposed approach.

2.3.1. Canonical Polyadic Decomposition

A rank decomposition is a way to express a tensor as a sum of rank-1 tensors of finite numbers. Rank decomposition has been discovered differently in different knowledge domains in many forms. Parallel Factors (PARAFAC) and Canonical Decomposition (CANDECOMP) is the most popular among them. The basic principle is the same for them. We will refer to this as CANDECOMP/PARAFAC or Canonical polyadic decomposition.

CPD for a 3-way Tensor($\mathcal{A}$) can be expressed as

$$\min_{\hat{\mathcal{A}}} \|\mathcal{A} - \hat{\mathcal{A}}\|$$

where

$$\hat{\mathcal{A}} = \sum_{i=1}^{R} \boldsymbol{a}_i \odot \boldsymbol{b}_i \odot \boldsymbol{c}_i \qquad (7)$$

Different algorithms are available to compute the CPD of any given tensor. Jennrich's and Alternating Least Square Algorithm (ALS) are the most popular among them.

Let A, B and C be factor matrices that holds the combination of vectors $(\boldsymbol{a}_i, \boldsymbol{b}_i, \boldsymbol{c}_i)$ forming the rank-1 tensor $\mathcal{A}$ as columns.

$$A = [\boldsymbol{a}_1 \boldsymbol{a}_2 ... \boldsymbol{a}_R]$$

$$B = [\boldsymbol{b}_1 \boldsymbol{b}_2 ... \boldsymbol{b}_R]$$

$$C = [\boldsymbol{c}_1 \boldsymbol{c}_2 ... \boldsymbol{c}_R]$$

Jennrich's algorithm states that if A, B, and C are linearly independent, then the matrix have full rank. We can use this algorithm to compute the factor matrices as the tensor $\mathcal{A} = \sum_{i=1}^{R} \lambda_i \boldsymbol{a}_i \odot \boldsymbol{b}_i \odot \boldsymbol{c}_i$. It is unique up to a trivial permutation of rank and scaling factors. This algorithm works for some problem, but it does not consider all the tensor slices, and it also requires a good difference between two successive eigen values (eigen-gap), absence of which causes numerical instability.

ALS is state of the art for modern tensor decomposition techniques in the CPD family. The key idea is to fix all factor matrices for the tensor except one and then estimating the non-fixed matrix. This step is repeated for all the factor matrices until a specific stopping criterion is achieved. Though the ALS algorithm is straightforward, it takes several steps to converge, and sometimes it may also get stuck at a local optimum.

2.3.2. Tucker Decomposition

In this type of decomposition, a tensor is decomposed in a core tensor and factor matrices. Algorithms like Higher-Order Singular Value Decomposition (HOSVD), Higher-Order Orthogonal Iteration (HOOI) comes under this family of decomposition. However, in contrast to CPD, Tucker decomposition is not unique, and so it is not used for the estimation of latent variables.

2.3.3. Tensor Power Method

This method is a special type that comes under the CPD family. The tensors that can be decomposed by this algorithm should have the following structure:

$$\mathcal{A} = \sum_{i=1}^{R} \lambda_i \boldsymbol{a}_i \odot \boldsymbol{a}_i \odot \boldsymbol{a}_i \qquad (8)$$

In this special case, the factor matrices have to be identical, and $\boldsymbol{a}_i$'s need to be orthogonal to construct vectors from rank-1 tensors. It is very similar to the matrix power method, but this algorithm tries to calculate top singular vectors in a tensor.

The main idea behind the matrix power method is to estimate the eigenvector $\boldsymbol{a}_{i,k+1}$ to $\boldsymbol{a}_i$ as well as the eigenvalue λ_i based on the following recurrence relation:

$$\boldsymbol{a}_{i,k+1} = \frac{A_i(I, \boldsymbol{a}_{i,k})}{\|A_i(I, \boldsymbol{a}_{i,k})\|_2} = \frac{A_i \boldsymbol{a}_{i,k}}{\|A_i \boldsymbol{a}_{i,k}\|_2} \qquad (9)$$

where $\boldsymbol{a}_{i,0}$ will be chosen randomly, or it can be initialized with some correlation to the true eigenvector if possible. This approximation follows the eigenvector/-value relationship $A\boldsymbol{a}_i = A(I, \boldsymbol{a}_i) = \lambda_i \boldsymbol{a}_i$. The top singular value can be computed from the computed eigenvector after convergence. As we have to calculate the first few dominant eigenvalues, this can be computed by the same process after deflating the matrix by the following formulae:

$$A_{i+1} = A_i - \lambda_i \boldsymbol{a}_i \odot \boldsymbol{a}_i \qquad (10)$$

To use this matrix power method in the Tensor approach, we have to incorporate the following changes in Equation (9).

$$\boldsymbol{a}_{i,k+1} = \frac{\mathcal{A}_i(I, \boldsymbol{a}_{i,k}, \boldsymbol{a}_{i,k})}{\|\mathcal{A}_i(I, \boldsymbol{a}_{i,k}, \boldsymbol{a}_{i,k})\|} \qquad (11)$$

$$\mathcal{A}_{i+1} = \mathcal{A}_i - \lambda_i \boldsymbol{a}_i \odot \boldsymbol{a}_i \odot \boldsymbol{a}_i \qquad (12)$$

This tensor Power method was used in the proposed method because of its efficiency in calculating the tensor. In the next section, the approach is explained in detail.

3. Proposed Approach

An uttered sound of a speaker is a collection of feature vectors. Each feature vector is a scaled sum of eigenvectors of that feature vector space. Some of these eigenvectors can be factors that represent age, gender, or other properties about the speakers while some form the content of the speech. If we collect feature vectors of male speaker utterances and construct a feature vector space from those, then that feature vector space gets dominated by the eigenvectors, which are the factors of masculinity. The same goes for females. For any unknown utterances of the speaker, if we find the presence of these eigenvectors, we can infer the gender of the speaker.

The following part consists of feature vector space generation of each gender, computation of dominant eigenvectors using the tensor power method, and finding the presence of these eigenvectors in an unknown utterance.

3.1. Feature Vector Space Generation

We have used MFCCs as feature vectors to generate vector-space for each gender as MFCC is based on the principle of the human's auditory system. Twenty-six MFCCs are collected from each frame of an utterance. Thus each feature vector is of twenty six dimensions ($x \in \mathbb{R}^{26}$). We have a collection of utterances for male and female speakers. We have computed feature vectors from each of the collections and obtained a set of feature vectors for each gender. This set of feature vectors works as a feature space that is used to compute dominant eigenvectors.

3.2. Tensor Formation

Before applying the tensor power method to compute the dominant eigenvectors, we have to form tensor from the feature vectors of each feature-space. A 3rd order tensor is constructed from each set of feature vectors. Method of moments is used to construct the 3rd order tensor. The first raw moment is the mean, which can be computed by the following:

$$m_1 = \mu = E[x] = \frac{1}{N} \sum_{i=1}^{N} x_i \qquad (13)$$

where N is the number of feature vectors in each gender set.

Second ordinal moment can be computed by the following:

$$M_2 = E[x \odot x] - \sigma^2 I \qquad (14)$$

where σ^2 is the smallest eigenvalue of the covarience matrix ($\Sigma = E[x \odot x] - m_1 \odot m_1$) and I is the Identity matrix ($I \in \mathbb{R}^{d \times d}$). Similarly the third ordinal moment can be computed as:

$$\mathcal{M}_3 = E[x \odot x \odot x] - \sigma^2 \sum_{i=1}^{d} (m_1 \odot e_i \odot e_i \\ + e_i \odot m_1 \odot e_i + e_i \odot e_i \odot m_1) \qquad (15)$$

where e_i is the basis vector in i^{th} dimension.

From the work of Hsu and Kakade (Hsu and Kakade, 2013) these moments can be reduced to the following forms:

$$M_2 = \sum_{i=1}^{p} w_i a_i \odot a_i \qquad (16)$$

$$\mathcal{M}_3 = \sum_{i=1}^{p} w_i a_i \odot a_i \odot a_i \qquad (17)$$

Thus $\mathcal{M}_3$ is the scaled sum of p eigenvectors (a_i). We need to find the k dominant eigenvectors that are responsible for the gender property of the speaker. M_2 could have been

used to compute a_is, but due to matrix rotational problem, it can not be computed accurately. Whereas in tensor (3rd order or higher), these can be computed more easily.

These Eigenvectors (a_i) can be computed by the tensor power method only if they are orthogonal in nature. For that, we have to orthogonalize $\mathcal{M}_3$. This has been done using M_2. It is assumed that if a Matrix is found that can orthogonalize M_2 can help to orthogonalize $\mathcal{M}_3$. This orthogonalization of M_2 can be represented as:

$$M_2(W, W) = W^T M_2 W = I \qquad (18)$$

where W is the orthogonalizing matrix, It is also known as the whitening matrix. W can be calculated with the help of eigenvalue decomposition of second-order moment M_2:

$$M_2 = UDU^T \qquad (19)$$

Singular value decomposition has been used to find U, D from Equation (19). W is computed as follows:

$$W = UD^{\dagger \frac{1}{2}} \qquad (20)$$

where $U \in \mathbb{R}^{d \times k}$ is a matrix of orthonormal eigenvectors, $D \in \mathbb{R}^{k \times k}$ is a diagonal matrix of the eigenvalues of M_2 and $A^{\dagger}$ is the Moore-Penrose pseudoinverse of matrix A. By using the following formulae W transforms $\mathcal{M}_3$ into whitened space.

$$\widehat{\mathcal{M}_3} = \mathcal{M}_3(W, W, W)^1 = \sum_{i=1}^{k} \lambda_i v_i \odot v_i \odot v_i \qquad (21)$$

where v_i and λ_i are converted eigenvectors and scaling factors respectively after orthogonalization of $\mathcal{M}_3$.

3.3. Eigenvectors Computation

Now on $\widehat{\mathcal{M}_3}$ we have applied tensor power method to identify dominant eigenvectors (v_i). We shall use Equation (11) and Equation (12) to compute the v_is and deflate the tensor, respectively. This process will be repeated until k dominant eigenvectors are obtained. As v_is are computed from orthogonalized tensor ($\widehat{\mathcal{M}_3}$), so by applying the inversion of the orthogonalization process we transform v_is to a_is of $\mathcal{M}_3$. We shall use the following formulae to do so:

$$A = (W^T)^{\dagger} V Diag(\lambda) \qquad (22)$$

where A is the set of k number of a_is, V is the set of k number of v_i and λ_i are k eigenvalues computed from the tensor power method.

---

[1]

A kth order tensor is denoted by $\mathcal{A} = [\![a_{j_1 \ldots j_k}]\!] \in \mathbb{R}^{d_1 \times \ldots \times d_k}$. Then covariant multi-linear matrix multiplication of $\mathcal{A}$ by $M_1 = [m^{(1)}_{j_1 i_1}] \in \mathbb{R}^{d_1 \times p_1}, \ldots, M_k = [m^{(k)}_{j_1 i_1}] \in \mathbb{R}^{d_k \times p_k}$ can be defined as: $\mathcal{A}(M_1, \ldots, M_k) = [\![\sum_{j_1=1}^{d_1} \cdots \sum_{j_k=1}^{d_k} a_{j_1 \ldots j_k} m^{(1)}_{j_1 i_1} \ldots m^{(k)}_{j_k i_k}]\!] \in \mathbb{R}^{p_1 \times \ldots \times p_k}$

3.4. Model Creation and Evaluation

We have obtained k dominant eigenvectors from each of the feature vector set of male and female speakers. A_m and A_f are the eigenvectors set of male and female speaker, respectively.

For any unknown the feature vector in the feature space, we will calculate distance from the dominating eigenvector (minimum distance). The distance for i^{th} feature vector (x_i) is calculated by using the following formula:

$$D_i = \min_k(\sum_{j=1}^{d}(a_{kj} - x_{ij})^2) \qquad (23)$$

Total distance from A_f and A_m can be computed as follows:

$$\mathcal{D}_m = \sum_{i=1}^{N} D_i \qquad (24)$$

$$\mathcal{D}_f = \sum_{i=1}^{N} D_i \qquad (25)$$

where N is the total number of feature vectors (Number of frames) for a voice sample.

Features vectors collected from male voice will be containing vectors which are affected by male eigenvectors, whereas it will be less affected by the female eigenvectors. Thus $\mathcal{D}_m$ will be less than $\mathcal{D}_f$. For similar reasons, $\mathcal{D}_f$ will be less than $\mathcal{D}_m$ for the female voice.

4. Experimental Setup

Experiments were conducted on two different datasets (TIMIT (S Garofolo et al., 1992) and SHRUTI (Das et al., 2011)). The study can be divided into three different cases, as follows:

1. TIMIT DR1

2. TIMIT Mix

3. SHRUTI dataset

The first dataset is a subset of the TIMIT dataset, which consists of only the New England dialect. TIMIT Mix dataset is the subset that contains eight different dialect regions. The third dataset is a collection of spoken sentences belonging to the Bengali language. Bengali is the predominant language used in West Bengal, a state of the Indian subcontinent. In the present work, a subpart of this database was used. Table 4. gives the complete description of the dataset used in the study. The results obtained using the approach are discussed in the next section.

Dataset Type	Training Set		Testing Set	
	Male	Female	Male	Female
TIMIT (DR1)	246	146	34	25
TIMIT Mix	500	500	150	150
SHRUTI	650	650	150	150

Table 1: Description of datasets.

5. Results and Analysis

The results are presented for different cases, as follows:

1. Different sizes of feature vectors

2. Different number of eigenvectors

3. Comparison on multiple datasets

4. Evaluation of same trained models for different datasets

5. Performance evaluation on noisy data

6. Performance comparison with GMM-EM

At first, feature vectors were used with varying sizes of thirteen, twenty, and twenty-six, while each case considers four dominant eigenvectors. A significant amount of increment in gender detection is observed with the increase of feature vector size. It implies that the proposed approach can capture sufficient characteristics of gender properties successfully. The summary of the results is shown in Table 2.

Size of feature vectors	Dataset Type	Accuracy Type (%)		
		Male	Female	Average
13	**Training**	71.2	98.4	84.7
	Testing	70.4	97.1	83.5
20	**Training**	92.2	76.8	84.5
	Testing	95.2	72.8	84.0
26	**Training**	90.8	92.4	91.2
	Testing	93.36	89.82	91.59

Table 2: Performance with respect to different sizes of feature vector (d).

Next, the performance of the proposed approach with respect to different numbers of dominating eigenvectors was evaluated. In this experiment, the TIMIT Mix dataset was used. The results are shown in Table 3. This experiment also shows that there is an increment in average gender detection accuracy, which denotes that the eigenvectors computed by the proposed approach are relevant to gender detection.

Number of Eigenvectors	Dataset Type	Accuracy Type (%)		
		Male	Female	Average
1	**Training**	46.4	80.2	63.3
	Testing	42.03	76.10	59.06
2	**Training**	72.4	86.4	79.4
	Testing	75.66	84.84	84.75
3	**Training**	90.0	92.4	91.2
	Testing	92.92	91.15	92.03
4	**Training**	90.8	92.4	91.2
	Testing	93.36	89.82	91.59

Table 3: Performance with respect to the number of dominant eigenvectors (k).

We tested the performance of the proposed approach in different datasets: SHRUTI, TIMIT Mix, and TIMIT DR1. Figure 2 shows that the proposed method provides consistent performance across different datasets. To test whether

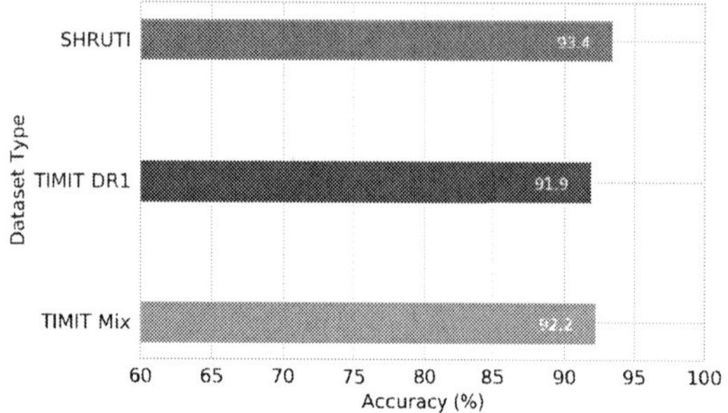

Figure 2: Performance of the proposed approach for different datasets.

the proposed approach is capturing the language-specific or voice-specific gender property, we computed eigenvectors using TIMIT Mix dataset and evaluated with other datasets. We have obtained a comparable accuracy in different datasets (Figure 3), which demonstrates that the proposed approach captures the voice-specific gender property.

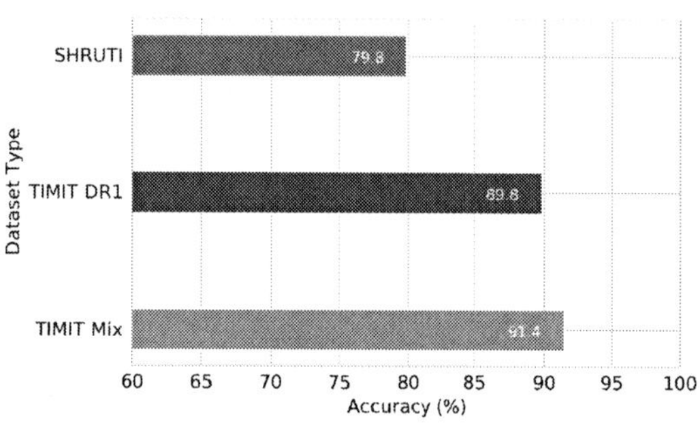

Figure 3: Performance of the proposed approach for different datasets trained using single dataset.

We evaluated its performance with respect to noisy utterances. Figure 4 shows the performance of the proposed approach with different Signal to Noise Ratio (SNR). The proposed method provides a consistent performance where the SNR is more than ten for input utterances.

Size of feature vector	Accuracy (%)	
	GMM - EM	Proposed approach
13	93.2	84.1
26	97.4	91.4

Table 4: Performance comparison of GMM and the proposed approach.

We also compared the performance of our approach with the modern, state-of-the-art GMM-EM on the TIMIT

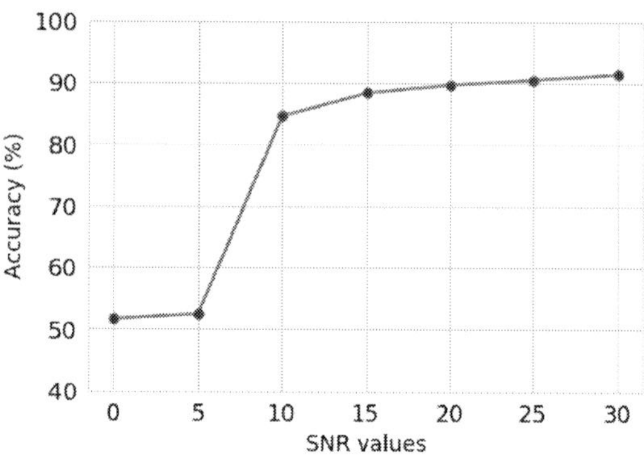

Figure 4: Performance of the proposed approach with respect to noisy data.

dataset. We conducted this experiment on the feature vector of size thirteen and twenty-six. We have presented our results in Table 4.

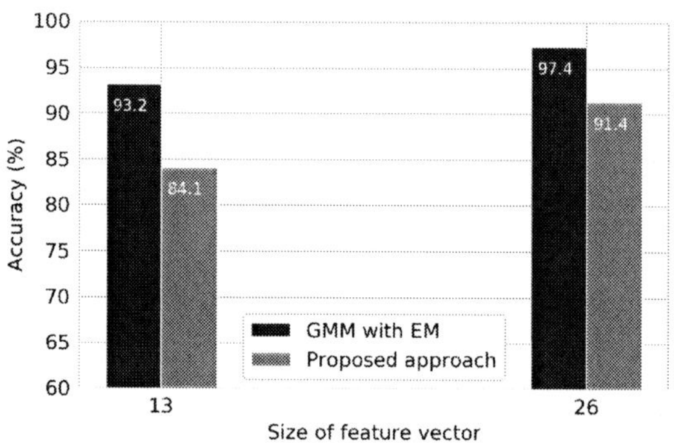

Figure 5: Performance comparison of GMM and the proposed tensor based approach.

Figure 5 provides a comparison between GMM-EM and the proposed method. Even though the detection efficiency of the proposed approach is comparatively less, but the proposed approach does not require multiple restarts like GMM-EM, and the improvement of results with the varying feature vectors is encouraging.

6. Conclusion

In this paper, a simple yet effective tensor-based approach was proposed for gender detection from the human voice. In the approach, we have computed dominant eigenvectors of the feature space of utterances using tensor analysis. It is demonstrated that the proposed method captures the relevant gender properties of the human voice and also provides consistent performance for high dimensional feature vectors. We have evaluated this approach on different datasets and proved that its performance is consistent with an accuracy of 91% in each case. We have also demonstrated its performance on noisy data and concluded that it provides reasonable accuracy for SNR higher than 10. The proposed approach provided comparable performance with respect to

GMM-EM, which ensures that with further improvement, and it can offer better performance without the drawbacks of GMM-EM. This work shows that the eigenvector-based approach using tensor analysis provides consistent performance irrespective of the dataset.

7. Bibliographical References

Anandkumar, A., Ge, R., Hsu, D., Kakade, S. M., and Telgarsky, M. (2014). Tensor decompositions for learning latent variable models. *J. Mach. Learn. Res.*, 15(1):2773–2832, January.

Anandkumar, A., Ge, R., and Janzamin, M. (2017). Analyzing tensor power method dynamics in overcomplete regime. *J. Mach. Learn. Res.*, 18(1):752–791, January.

Das, B., Mandal, S., and Mitra, P. (2011). Bengali speech corpus for continuous auutomatic speech recognition system. In *2011 International Conference on Speech Database and Assessments (Oriental COCOSDA)*, pages 51–55, Oct.

Doukhan, D., Carrive, J., Vallet, F., Larcher, A., and Meignier, S. (2018). An open-source speaker gender detection framework for monitoring gender equality. April.

Hsu, D. and Kakade, S. M. (2013). Learning mixtures of spherical gaussians: Moment methods and spectral decompositions. In *Proceedings of the 4th Conference on Innovations in Theoretical Computer Science*, ITCS '13, pages 11–20, New York, NY, USA. ACM.

Jo, Q., Park, Y., Lee, K., and Chang, J. (2008). A support vector machine-based voice activity detection employing effective feature vectors. *IEICE Transactions*, 91-B(6):2090–2093.

Kolda, T. G. and Bader, B. W. (2009). Tensor decompositions and applications. *SIAM Rev.*, 51(3):455–500, August.

Konig, Y. and Morgan, N. (1992). Gdnn: a gender-dependent neural network for continuous speech recognition. In *[Proceedings 1992] IJCNN International Joint Conference on Neural Networks*, volume 2, pages 332–337 vol.2, June.

Lek-Heng Lim. (2005). Singular values and eigenvalues of tensors: a variational approach. In *1st IEEE International Workshop on Computational Advances in Multi-Sensor Adaptive Processing, 2005.*, pages 129–132, Dec.

Neti, C. and Roukos, S. (1997). Phone-context specific gender-dependent acoustic-models for continuous speech recognition. In *1997 IEEE Workshop on Automatic Speech Recognition and Understanding Proceedings*, pages 192–198, Dec.

Parris, E. S. and Carey, M. J. (1996). Language independent gender identification. In *1996 IEEE International Conference on Acoustics, Speech, and Signal Processing Conference Proceedings*, volume 2, pages 685–688 vol. 2, May.

S Garofolo, J., Lamel, L., M Fisher, W., Fiscus, J., S. Pallett, D., L. Dahlgren, N., and Zue, V. (1992). Timit acoustic-phonetic continuous speech corpus. *Linguistic Data Consortium*, 11.

Sidiropoulos, N. D., De Lathauwer, L., Fu, X., Huang, K., Papalexakis, E. E., and Faloutsos, C. (2017). Tensor decomposition for signal processing and machine learning. *IEEE Transactions on Signal Processing*, 65(13):3551–3582, July.

Tzanetakis, G. and Cook, P. (2002). Musical genre classification of audio signals. *IEEE Transactions on Speech and Audio Processing*, 10:293–302, Jan.

Yücesoy, E. and Nabiyev, V. (2013). Gender identification of a speaker using mfcc and gmm. pages 626–629, Nov.

Proceedings of the 1st Joint SLTU and CCURL Workshop (SLTU-CCURL 2020), pages 218–225
Language Resources and Evaluation Conference (LREC 2020), Marseille, 11–16 May 2020
© European Language Resources Association (ELRA), licensed under CC-BY-NC

Data-Driven Parametric Text Normalization: Rapidly Scaling Finite-State Transduction Verbalizers to New Languages

Sandy Ritchie, Eoin Mahon, Kim Heiligenstein, Nikos Bampounis, Daan van Esch, Christian Schallhart, Jonas Fromseier Mortensen, Benoît Brard

Google

{sandyritchie, emahon, kheiligenstein, nbampounis, dvanesch, schallhart, jfmortensen, benoitb}@google.com

Abstract

This paper presents a methodology for rapidly generating FST-based verbalizers for ASR and TTS systems by efficiently sourcing language-specific data. We describe a questionnaire which collects the necessary data to bootstrap the number grammar induction system and parameterize the verbalizer templates described in Ritchie et al. (2019), and a machine-readable data store which allows the data collected through the questionnaire to be supplemented by additional data from other sources. This system allows us to rapidly scale technologies such as ASR and TTS to more languages, including low-resource languages.

Keywords: verbalization, data collection, linguistic typology

1. Introduction

Written-domain text can be challenging for automatic speech recognition (ASR) and text-to-speech (TTS) systems to process due to the presence of *non-standard words* or *semiotic classes* such as numbers, money expressions and measure expressions (Sproat et al., 2001; Taylor, 2009; van Esch and Sproat, 2017). Before the pronunciation of semiotic classes can be determined, they must be verbalized: expanded into word sequences (see Table 1). Verbalizers are usually a key part of TTS (Ebden and Sproat, 2015) and ASR (Sak et al., 2013a; 2013b) text processing systems, as well as various data preparation modules.

Written domain	Spoken domain
35	thirty five
$1.50	one dollar and fifty cents
5cm	five centimeters

Table 1: Verbalization of semiotic classes

Approaches to the verbalization problem have generally not been favorable to low-resource languages. Manually configured systems based on finite-state transducers (FSTs), such as Ebden and Sproat (2015), require linguistic expertise as well as knowledge of an FST compiler such as Thrax (Roark et al., 2012) or Pynini (Gorman, 2016) to set up in a new language. This makes scaling up to a wide range of languages difficult due to the expense of sourcing and onboarding an expert for each language. Recurrent neural networks (RNNs) with finite-state covering grammars (Sproat and Jaitly, 2017; Zhang et al., 2019) or dual encoder classifiers (Gokcen et al., 2019) propose to solve the scaling problem by collecting annotated training examples instead of encoding the verbalizations directly in FST grammars. Such approaches still require a large amount of annotated data, as well as the development of language-specific output filters. For under-resourced languages, the candidate pool of linguistic experts or annotators diminishes, as does the availability of existing resources. This situation poses difficulties for both types of approaches described above.

Various attempts to address this problem have been presented. Gorman and Sproat (2016) use an algorithm which relies on knowledge about the possible factorizations of numbers across languages to induce an FST from a dataset of 300 examples. Gutkin et al. (2016) develop an FST-based system for Bangla by taking an existing Hindi system and translating all of the strings into Bangla. A more general approach has been to identify language-independent characteristics of each semiotic class and to construct templates exposing a limited number of parameters which capture the possible variation across languages (Ritchie et al., 2019). This approach is in the spirit of Bender (2009; 2011; 2016); Sproat (2016) and Ponti et al. (2019), as the template parameters were selected based on insights from linguistic typology, in particular those relating to word order, morphological concord, and other morphosyntactic features of verbalization.

These approaches all assume certain universal constraints on possible verbalizations and a closed set of data points required to specify a particular language. This offers the potential to turn the development of verbalizers into a data-collection problem where the quantity of data needed is tractable for low-resource languages.

In this paper, we discuss the nature of the data required to develop verbalizers for low-resource languages, and address the operational question of how to rapidly and efficiently obtain the data in the context of the unified verbalizer approach outlined by Ritchie et al. (2019). We also discuss some design features of our data store and potential benefits of our method for low resource languages, in particular the possibility of integration with the Unicode Common Locale Data Repository (CLDR) (Unicode, Inc, 2019) for greater collaboration with community members and other stakeholders in the development of high-quality verbalization data.

This paper is structured as follows. Section 2 recaps the unified verbalizers approach. We discuss and exemplify the types of data required in Section 3, and describe our data collection questionnaire as well as other data sources including CLDR in Section 4. Section 5 describes the format in which the data is stored and how verbalizers can be generated from the data. Section 6 outlines the benefits of this approach for low-resource languages.

2. Unified Verbalizers

Ritchie et al. (2019) describe a system of verbalizer templates with parameters for language-specific features and sub-templates for the different requirements of ASR and TTS verbalizers. In combination with a number names grammar for conversion of cardinal and ordinal numbers, lexical data for the conversion of other written tokens, and parameters for various features of written tokens and their spoken equivalents, these templates can generate verbalizations for a language without the need for hand-written verbalizers.

2.1. Number Names

The most complex aspect of converting non-standard words to their spoken form is the conversion of cardinal and ordinal numbers. We achieve this using a labeled set of 300 examples and an induction algorithm which employs real arithmetic to compute all possible factorizations for numbers up to 999 using addition and multiplication. The algorithm then selects the best parse by analogy with similar parses of smaller numbers (see Ritchie et al. (2019, Section 2.3) for more details). Developers can also manually set certain parameters to handle some more complex aspects of number names systems, such as (weak) vigesimal systems,[1] and 'flop' arithmetic.[2] With an induced number name grammar, the cardinal and ordinal number subcomponents of verbalizations can be handled.

2.2. Verbalizer Templates

While cardinal and ordinal numbers exhibit significant variation across languages, the verbalization of other semiotic classes is more constrained and can often be captured using some lexical content and a few parameters relating to the style and ordering of components in the written and spoken domains. For example, in written money tokens, the currency symbol can only precede or follow the numbers, while in decimal numbers like '1.23', the fractional part can typically only be read as a sequence of digits, as in 'one point two three', or a cardinal number, as in 'one point twenty three', or both.

This parametric nature of verbalization makes it a good candidate for templatization. Rather than supporting near-identical hand-written verbalizers for each language, we have developed verbalization templates which offer options to set parameters like 'currency symbol precedes numbers' and 'decimal fractional part is read as a digit sequence'. Since both ASR and TTS verbalizers convert written tokens to their spoken form, we can also share these templates between the two systems with only minor modifications for each use case.

---

[1]Vigesimal systems use 20 as a base for larger numbers, as in French *quatre-vingts*, 'eighty', lit. 'four twenties'.

[2]Flop arithemetic systems exhibit alternative word orders of addends and multiplicands, e.g. German *einundzwanzig* 'twenty one', lit. 'one and twenty'.

Building on this system, we have developed a suite of data collection and storage methodologies which allow us to capture knowledge of verbalization in a structured and standardized format. In the following sections, we discuss the nature of the data that we need to collect to generate verbalizations, followed by a description of some potential sources for this data, with a particular focus on our questionnaire which covers all the data and parameters required. We then discuss methods for ingesting and storing the data and possibilities for generating FSTs directly from the store.

3. Verbalization Data Types

Data required for verbalizers can be divided into four major categories: written domain, lexical, morphological and syntactic. We will consider these in turn, using examples from high- and medium-resource languages to illustrate each category. We return to the issue of how to gather this data for low-resource languages in Section 4.

3.1. Written Domain Data

Written domain data are details about writing conventions in the target language, such as:

- whether the full stop or the comma is used to separate decimal numbers (e.g. '1.2' or '1,2');
- which symbol is used to separate numbers in dates (e.g. '1.2.2020' or '1/2/2020');
- the order of elements in written dates (e.g. DDMMYYYY or MMDDYYYY);
- which currency symbols are used and whether they precede or follow the numbers (e.g. '$21' or '21€');
- common phone number formats, including the number of digits in a block, and the separator used (e.g. '1-800-234-5678' or '07123 456 789').

This information is used to constrain the possible inputs for a verbalizer so that it will only convert written tokens which follow these conventions. This reduces the potential for some written tokens to be classified and verbalized inappropriately. For example, in writing systems like English where decimals are separated by a full stop, powers of ten in big numbers are typically separated by a comma, and vice versa in other languages. If the decimal verbalizer knows it should only convert numbers with a full stop as the separator, a token like '1,234' will not be inappropriately classified and verbalized as a decimal number.

3.2. Lexical Data

Lexical data primarily consists of spoken equivalents of written tokens. This includes lists of punctuation and other orthographic symbols, emojis and emoticons, currencies, weekdays, months, time zones, etc. Spoken equivalents of written tokens often exhibit variation of two major types. The first is 'free' variation, where a symbol can be verbalized in more than one way in the same context. In US English for example, the hyphen-minus symbol in negative numbers like '-1' can be read as either 'minus' or 'negative'. The more complex kind of variation is the case in which the same written symbol is verbalized differently depending on the context or type of numeric token in which it is used. For example, the hyphen-minus is verbalized in British English in various other ways in different contexts, as shown in Table 2.

Written domain	Spoken domain
-	**hyphen**
-1	**minus** one
1-2	one **to** two
abc-123.com	abc **dash** one two three dot com
3 - 2 = 1	three **take away** two equals one
1-2-2020	first of February twenty twenty

Table 2: British English verbalizations of hyphen-minus in different contexts

We need to capture all contexts in which multi-functional tokens like hyphen-minus are used in order to convert them appropriately.

3.3. Morphological Data

Morphological data can include inherent features of nouns like gender, and inflection of nouns and their dependents for features like number.[3] An example can be found in time verbalizations in Romance languages, where the words for 'hour' and 'minute' have masculine and feminine gender features and exhibit singular/plural number splits. In such cases, some numbers (typically only 1, but also other numbers in some languages like Portuguese) exhibit gender agreement with the hour and minute words, even if the latter are not overtly realized. Examples from Portuguese are shown in (1).

(1)   a.   *uma (hora) e um (minuto)*
      one.F hour.F.SG and one.M minute.M.SG
      'one minute past one'

      b.   *duas (hora-s) e dois (minuto-s)*
      two.F hour.F-PL and two.M minute.M-PL
      'two minutes past two'

Here the hour and minute words exhibit a singular/plural split (marked by a final *-s* on the plural variants) and the cardinal numbers agree with them in gender. In order to generate these verbalizations, we need to know all the relevant inflectional forms that the hour and minute words can take, as well as those of the numbers that agree with them. Another common type of morphological marking is case marking. In languages like Russian, verbalizations of some written tokens can exhibit different marking depending on their grammatical function in the clause, like subject, (indirect) object, etc. See Sproat (2010) for a discussion of the problem in Russian number names.

3.4. Syntactic Data

Syntactic data primarily includes word order parameters. Nearly all semiotic classes exhibit variation in word order. For example, in classes like decimals, percentages, and temperatures, the words for 'minus', 'percent' and 'degree'

can all occur in different orders relative to the numeral. This type of variation can be seen in temperature verbalizations in Malagasy (2a), Bambara (2b) and Swahili (2c), which all exhibit different word orders for the 'minus' and 'degree' words and the numeral.

(2)   a.   *miiba iray degre*
      minus one degree

      b.   *duguma ni degere kelen ye*
      minus   degree one

      c.   *digrii hasi moja*
      degree minus one
      'minus one degree'

Malagasy follows the word order found in English, with the minus word preceding the numeral and the degree word following. In Bambara, the minus word precedes the degree word, and both precede the numeral. In Swahili, both also precede the numeral, but in this case the degree word precedes the minus word.

Another example of this kind of variation in word order can be found in dates. In date verbalizations, most possible orders of day, month and year are attested across languages, and even within a single language, the order in the spoken form doesn't necessarily match the written order. For example, British English speakers may read a date in DDMMYYYY format (e.g. '1/2/2020') as 'February the first twenty twenty' (month-day-year) instead of 'the first of February twenty twenty' (day-month-year). Both are acceptable readings for this date.

4.   Data Sources

In the high-resource scenario, recruiting a skilled worker with expertise in a domain-specific formal language like Thrax or Pynini is a viable option for development of verbalizers. They can use a combination of ad-hoc research and consultation with native speakers (or their own intuitions if they are a native speaker) to create custom grammars which produce naturalistic and comprehensive verbalizations for non-standard words.

One potential solution to the verbalization problem for low-resource languages could be to bypass the written domain altogether, and simply transcribe audio training data for ASR in the spoken domain, for example transcribing times as 'two thirty p m' instead of '2:30pm' and so on. However, there are several issues with this kind of approach. First of all, TTS systems would not be able to convert written tokens in any existing text corpora, and our system covers both ASR and TTS. Second, using spoken-to-written and written-to-spoken conversion makes it easier to build natural language understanding and natural language processing systems on top of ASR and TTS systems for low-resource languages, by using existing technology to classify and otherwise operate on semiotic classes like times in the written domain. Finally, and perhaps most importantly, handling high-, medium- and low-resource languages in the same way is more scalable; it is easier to iterate and improve on existing systems if they are all set up in the same way, and this also allows us to share insights and knowledge from higher-resource languages to other languages.

---

[3]Inflection refers to alternative forms of words depending on their morphological features, for example marking of plural number by the plural suffix *-s* in English 'dollars' versus singular 'dollar'.

This is not to deny the significant issues present in the development of verbalizers for low-resource languages. In general, the resources available in academic literature and online are scarcer, and the pool of potential linguistic consultants with experience in computational linguistics and knowledge of finite-state transducers is significantly smaller. Thus, to produce verbalizations of comparable quality to those in higher-resource languages, we need to turn to other sources of data and linguistic knowledge. The most effective approach appears to be the use of a dedicated questionnaire which asks language consultants with native competence in the target language to transcribe verbalizations of numeric written tokens, as well as answering metalinguistic questions about certain features of these transcriptions.

In addition to such a questionnaire, other potential sources for data include the Unicode Common Locale Data Repository (CLDR), lexical resources like Wiktionary and traditional dictionaries, and typological resources like the World Atlas of Language Structures (WALS) (Dryer and Haspelmath, 2013). Another interesting possibility proposed by Bender et al. (2013) is the use of interlinear glosses in linguistic data to derive lexical and morphosyntactic information. In this section we provide an outline of a questionnaire we have developed for data collection, and briefly discuss CLDR and WALS as potential alternative sources.

4.1. Unified Verbalization Questionnaire

Verbalization questionnaires have been in use at Google for several years (see Sodimana et al. (2018) for a brief discussion in the context of development of TTS systems for low-resource languages). In tandem with the move to shared verbalizers for TTS and ASR, we significantly expanded our existing questionnaire to cover all types of semiotic classes, taking into account insights from the typology literature and the needs of both ASR and TTS.

The unified verbalization questionnaire takes the form of a Google Sheet with machine-readable labels, which is designed such that educated native speakers with some linguistic knowledge (for example translators or educators) can complete it. It typically asks the respondent to transcribe a representative written token like '-1' and provide alternatives alongside the primary or canonical verbalization. Follow-up questions then target sub-parts of the verbalization in order to discern parameters like word order in the spoken form. For example, alongside questions like "How do you say '-1'?" we include follow-up questions like "Which part of this is '-'?". In this way, we can deduce whether the word for hyphen-minus precedes or follows the number in the spoken form, without the need to ask for this piece of information directly.

This indirect method for eliciting data like word order parameters is inspired by data collection methodologies in linguistic fieldwork, where language consultants sometimes do not have any formal linguistic training, so it is necessary to devise elicitation techniques which access this kind of information through other means than direct questions (e.g. Payne (1997); Bowern (2015), among many others). Here we briefly describe how we use this and other techniques to elicit the different types of data described in Section 3.

We elicit written domain data through various means in our questionnaire, including:

- asking for user input in the case of written symbols such as currency symbols;
- asking the respondent to select from a list in the case of ordering of elements in written dates;
- asking respondents to provide examples in the case of phone number formats.

We then dynamically update follow up questions based on initial responses. For example, if a respondent fills out the currency symbol field with the dollar sign '$', and selects the parameter 'currency symbol precedes number', the follow up questions will then be automatically updated to reflect these facts, for example 'How do you say '$1'?'.

To elicit lexical data, we ask for spoken forms of exemplary written tokens for each class, and also ask respondents to provide alternative forms to capture free variation in the spoken form. For example, to gather information about the verbalization of mathematical expressions, we ask the respondents to transcribe an example like '3 - 2 = 1' with any alternatives. Then in follow up questions, we ask them to identify which parts of the verbalization refer to each symbol, for example "Which part of this is '='?".

Using this approach, we elicit both the mapping between written symbols as well as their verbalizations in specific contexts, which also provides us with test cases with which we can evaluate our template verbalizer. In order to capture context-dependent variation of the type demonstrated in Table 2, the questionnaire includes examples of different written contexts in which multi-functional tokens like hyphen-minus occur. This exposes the overlaps and splits in the use of different words for the same symbol in different contexts.

In order to elicit morphological data, we ask respondents to transcribe verbalizations for representative examples of written currencies, times, and the like, which we have selected to ensure that phenomena like gender features, number splits, and morphological concord will be exposed in the transcriptions. Of course it is not possible to predict exactly what we might find in a new language, but we strive to cover as many features as possible by including singular and plural entities to cover potential singular/plural splits, more than one type of currency to cover potential variation in inherent features like gender among currencies, and examples of numbers in combination with currencies, percentages, degrees and so on to cover potential morphological concord between numbers and the nouns which they modify.

We elicit syntactic data by asking respondents to transcribe at least one representative written token for every relevant semiotic class. In the case of more complex classes like cardinals, ordinals and times, we ask them to transcribe more examples in order to capture the character of the word ordering systems and subsystems for these classes. For example, German exhibits addend flops in numbers 21-99. However, above 100, addends occur in the same order as in English, as demonstrated in (3).

(3) a. *ein -und -zwanzig* (1 + 20)
     one and twenty
     'twenty one'

   b. *zwei hundert eins* (200 + 1)
     two hundred one
     'two hundred and one'

In order to elicit splits in word order parameters like this, it is necessary to ask for a larger number of examples. This approach to data collection for number names developed by Gorman and Sproat (2016) has led to refinement of our models of morphosyntactic phenomena in several less well-studied languages. For example, we improved our handling of multiplicand flop arithmetic[4] in the Nigerian languages Hausa and Igbo, and noun class agreement phenomena (as well as multiplicand flops) in Bantu languages like Kinyarwanda and Zulu. Again it is not possible to predict what we might find in less well-studied languages, but requesting more examples allows us to capture at least some of the syntactic complexity present in the target language.

4.2. CLDR

For some languages, CLDR also contains a certain subset of the data described in Section 3. It contains some written domain data (e.g. time and date formats) and some lexical data (day, month, time period and era names; days of the week; time zone names; currency names and measure names). For currency and measure names, it also provides information about morphological concord, indicating how the forms differ when quantified by different amounts. This information can be used to extract e.g. singular/plural number splits in currency and measure words. The machine-readable LDML format of this resource makes it amenable to automated ingestion into a common data store.

A drawback of CLDR is the limited number of languages covered. Nearly all of the languages for which they have significant data are already supported in industry applications. Moreover, many languages that have a lot of new and emerging Internet users, such as those in regions of India, Indonesia, and Africa, are not covered by CLDR. CLDR is also limited in some of the information we require for our purposes; for example it lacks symbols and verbalizations for currency subunits (like '25p' → 'twenty five pence'). Despite these issues, it is currently the most comprehensive open-source resource for verbalization data. In Section 6., we briefly discuss the potential for expanding the data available in CLDR.

4.3. WALS

WALS offers an interesting source of supplementary support for verbalization data, in particular morphological and syntactic data. For example, the chapter on the order of numeral and noun (Dryer, 2013a) contains parameters for 1153 languages (as of 7th February 2020). For languages where no data is yet available from the questionnaire or CLDR, we could use this information in combination with some basic lexical data to provide best-guess verbalizations

for currencies, assuming that the order of the currency word like 'dollar' and the number name follows the stated pattern.

Furthermore, in the case that a language is not listed in that specific chapter, it is also at least theoretically possible to rely on implicational universals of the type introduced by Greenberg (1963) to generate verbalizations. For example, if the chapter on the order of subject, object and verb (Dryer, 2013b) indicates that VSO is the predominant order, even if we do not have information on the order of numeral and noun, it is possible to predict using implicational universals that the numeral will follow the noun. Of course this information will be tenuous at best, but it at least provides some method to localize verbalizations in the absence of any other kind of data.

In this section we identified some possible sources for verbalization data and discussed our data collection methodology via the questionnaire. In the next section we discuss the storage format for the data and briefly touch on the possibility of generating verbalizer FSTs directly from this data store.

5. Data Storage and Verbalizer Generation

While unified verbalizers facilitate verbalizer development, there remains the task of transforming data from different sources into the parameters expected by the templates.

Our solution to this is a data store with a unified data format into which all sources are converted before parameterizing the verbalizers. This means that for any new data source, all that is needed is to convert the data into this format. We use a machine-readable protocol buffer[5] as the data storage format. In its present iteration, the store focuses primarily on lexical (and some basic morphological) data, but our goal is to extend it to all types of data discussed in Section 3.

Entries in the data store take the form of protocol buffers. The data store representation for a particular verbalizable entity provides:

- the data type (e.g. emoji, currency, measure unit, etc.);
- the reference key (typically a written form of the entity);
- possible verbalizations;
- data source;
- time of entry or update;
- any additional entity- and/or language-specific features, such as morphological features like singular/plural number.

Data from each source are imported to the data store when and if they are available, incrementally constructing a gradually more complete set of available data. For example, a record for the verbalization of US dollars in Spanish can be formalized as shown in Figure 1.

In this example, the currency verbalization has been imported from CLDR, while the verbalization for the subunit has been imported from the questionnaire, since CLDR does not provide such information by design. Although the

---

[4]In multiplicand flop systems, the order of multiplicands is reversed with respect to the order found in English, so the equivalent of e.g. 'two hundred' (2 * 100) is 'hundred two' (100 * 2).

[5]See https://developers.google.com/protocol-buffers

```
currencies {
  key: "USD"
  currency_verbalization {
    text: "dólar estadounidense"
    number: SINGULAR
    source: CLDR
    timestamp: 1578813004
  }
  subcurrency_verbalization {
    text: "centavo"
    number: SINGULAR
    source: QUESTIONNAIRE
    timestamp: 1578839575
  }
}
```

Figure 1: Entry for verbalization of US dollars in Spanish

main currency information was available in the questionnaire data, it was not re-imported, as in this case, it was identical to the CLDR data. If needed, manual edits such as importing additional verbalizations obtained from other sources, or corrections can be applied to the collected data. Having data from questionnaires, CLDR, and any other ad-hoc sources in a single data store makes it easier to parameterize verbalizers automatically. It is possible to set up an automatic data pipeline where data from the various sources are ingested into a common data store, and then used to automatically produce ASR and TTS verbalizers (see Figure 2).

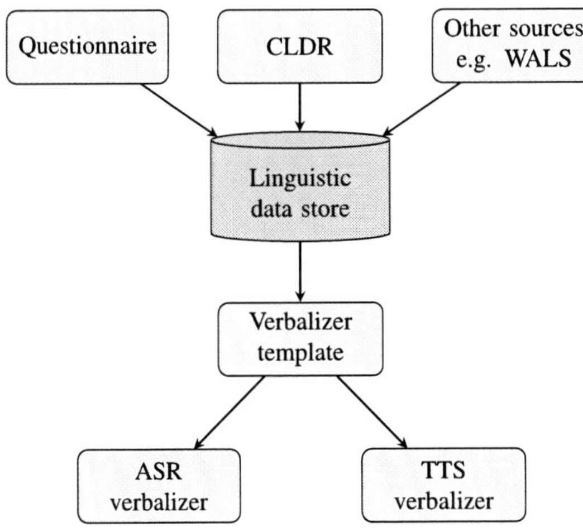

Figure 2: The flow of data from sources to verbalizers

We maintain a source preference hierarchy to reconcile conflicts in the event of competing verbalizations for a given item. All else being equal, a candidate will be selected if its source is preferred according to this hierarchy. For example, a manual correction to a questionnaire entry will eventually take effect and become the default verbalization, since manual entries have been defined as having precedence over any other source. In case of conflicting verbalizations coming from the same source, the newest entry is preferred.

With the above setup, the gradual integration of many sources of data is performed with minimal manual intervention. Having all data in the same place also enables the easy and timely identification of gaps in data coverage. Once all available data have been imported, the data store can be queried for automatic extraction of the necessary data. With further integration of morphological and syntactic information into the store, we can generate verbalization FSTs directly from these specifications, without the need for other intermediate types of representation.

In this section we demonstrated our storage format and preference hierarchy for verbalization data. In the final section we discuss some potential benefits of the system for low resource languages.

6. Benefits for Low-Resource Languages

Producing high-quality verbalizations has long been one of the major bottlenecks in the development of ASR and TTS systems for new languages. Without verbalizers, the quality of text-to-speech and speech-to-text conversion is significantly reduced. Data pipelines like the one we have described in this paper cut down the amount of detailed language-specific work required to set up basic verbalizers for new languages, allowing developers to effectively scale the development of ASR and TTS systems, and to make them available to more language communities faster. Comparing a typical hand-written verbalizer with a configuration file in the new template system, we see a reduction from about 200 lines of custom code to just 25 lines specifying the lexical data, morphological features and syntactic parameters to be used.

A longer-term benefit of our work includes the potential to expand the CLDR data specification based on our analysis of the information needed to set up verbalizers in new languages, so that CLDR can become a central repository of this kind of data. As mentioned above, CLDR already contains a subset of the necessary information, but extending it to cover all relevant information would enable communities and vendors to contribute and share data, paving the way to supporting more languages in more technology platforms. In 2019, we open-sourced part of our number names data for 186 language locales.[6] Open-sourcing verbalization data is more complicated, as it requires further development and refinement of data storage formats and protocols, as well as additional tooling. We are currently working with the CLDR team to explore the options. Our hope is that by including all necessary information in CLDR, everyone would be able to build verbalizers based on data stored in a format which follows well-established protocols from natural language processing as well as insights from linguistic typology.

---

[6]Verbalizations for numbers 1 to 100 along with powers of ten (1000, 10000, etc.) are available at https://github.com/google/UniNum.

7. Summary

In this paper, we discussed the problem of expansion of written tokens to their spoken form. We recapped Ritchie et al. (2019), in which we discussed the development of shared templates for ASR and TTS verbalizers. We then broke down the types of data required for verbalizers according to their linguistic nature, and discussed our methodologies for data collection using a targeted and typologically informed questionnaire, as well as other supplementary data sources. We then described our data storage format and preference hierarchy for data from different sources. Finally we discussed how our system might help to expand the pool of verbalization data, and showed how through better specification and parameterization of the verbalization problem, we can rapidly scale language technologies such as ASR and TTS to more languages around the world.

8. Bibliographical References

Bender, E. M., Goodman, M. W., Crowgey, J., and Xia, F. (2013). Towards creating precision grammars from interlinear glossed text: Inferring large-scale typological properties. In *LaTeCH@ACL*.

Bender, E. M. (2009). Linguistically naïve != language independent: Why NLP needs linguistic typology. In *Proceedings of the EACL 2009 Workshop on the Interaction between Linguistics and Computational Linguistics: Virtuous, Vicious or Vacuous?*, pages 26–32.

Bender, E. M. (2011). On achieving and evaluating language-independence in NLP. *Linguistic Issues in Language Technology*, 6(3):1–26.

Bender, E. M. (2016). Linguistic typology in natural language processing. *Linguistic Typology*, 20(3):645–660.

Bowern, C. (2015). *Linguistic fieldwork: A practical guide*. Springer.

Dryer, M. S. and Haspelmath, M. (2013). *The World Atlas of Language Structures Online*. Max Planck Institute for Evolutionary Anthropology, Leipzig.

Dryer, M. S. (2013a). Order of numeral and noun. In Matthew S. Dryer et al., editors, *The World Atlas of Language Structures Online*. Max Planck Institute for Evolutionary Anthropology, Leipzig.

Dryer, M. S. (2013b). Order of subject, object and verb. In Matthew S. Dryer et al., editors, *The World Atlas of Language Structures Online*. Max Planck Institute for Evolutionary Anthropology, Leipzig.

Ebden, P. and Sproat, R. (2015). The Kestrel TTS text normalization system. *Natural Language Engineering*, 21(3):333–353.

Gokcen, A., Zhang, H., and Sproat, R. (2019). Dual encoder classifier models as constraints in neural text normalization. *Proc. Interspeech 2019*, pages 4489–4493.

Gorman, K. and Sproat, R. (2016). Minimally supervised number normalization. *Transactions of the Association for Computational Linguistics*, 4:507–519.

Gorman, K. (2016). Pynini: A Python library for weighted finite-state grammar compilation. In *Proceedings of the SIGFSM Workshop on Statistical NLP and Weighted Automata*, pages 75–80.

Greenberg, J. (1963). Some universals of grammar with particular reference to the order of meaningful elements. *In J. Greenberg, ed., Universals of Language. 73-113. Cambridge, MA.*

Gutkin, A., Ha, L., Jansche, M., Pipatsrisawat, K., and Sproat, R. (2016). TTS for low resource languages: A Bangla synthesizer. In *Proceedings of the Tenth International Conference on Language Resources and Evaluation (LREC'16)*, pages 2005–2010, Portorož, Slovenia, May. European Language Resources Association (ELRA).

Payne, T. E. (1997). *Describing morphosyntax: A guide for field linguists*. Cambridge University Press.

Ponti, E. M., O'Horan, H., Berzak, Y., Vulić, I., Reichart, R., Poibeau, T., Shutova, E., and Korhonen, A. (2019). Modeling language variation and universals: A survey on typological linguistics for natural language processing. *Computational Linguistics*, 45(3):559–601.

Ritchie, S., Sproat, R., Gorman, K., van Esch, D., Schallhart, C., Bampounis, N., Brard, B., Mortensen, J. F., Holt, M., and Mahon, E. (2019). Unified verbalization for speech recognition & synthesis across languages. In *Proc. Interspeech 2019*, pages 3530–3534.

Roark, B., Sproat, R., Allauzen, C., Riley, M., Sorensen, J., and Tai, T. (2012). The OpenGrm open-source finite-state grammar software libraries. In *Proceedings of the ACL 2012 System Demonstrations*, pages 61–66, Jeju Island, Korea, July. Association for Computational Linguistics.

Sak, H., Beaufays, F., Nakajima, K., and Allauzen, C. (2013a). Language model verbalization for automatic speech recognition. In *ICASSP*, pages 8262–8266.

Sak, H., Beaufays, F., Nakajima, K., and Allauzen, C. (2013b). Written-domain language modeling for automatic speech recognition. In *INTERSPEECH*, pages 675–679.

Sodimana, K., Silva, P. D., Sproat, R., Theeraphol, A., Li, C. F., Gutkin, A., Sarin, S., and Pipatsrisawat, K. (2018). Text normalization for Bangla, Khmer, Nepali, Javanese, Sinhala, and Sundanese TTS systems. In *6th International Workshop on Spoken Language Technologies for Under-Resourced Languages (SLTU-2018)*, pages 147–151, 29-31 August 2018, Gurugram, India.

Sproat, R. and Jaitly, N. (2017). An RNN model of text normalization. In *INTERSPEECH*, pages 754–758. Stockholm.

Sproat, R., Black, A. W., Chen, S., Kumar, S., Ostendorf, M., and Richards, C. (2001). Normalization of non-standard words. *Computer Speech Language*, 15(3):287–333.

Sproat, R. (2010). Lightly supervised learning of text normalization: Russian number names. In *2010 IEEE Spoken Language Technology Workshop*, pages 436–441. IEEE.

Sproat, R. (2016). Language typology in speech and language technology. *Linguistic Typology*, 20(3):635–644.

Taylor, P. (2009). *Text-to-Speech Synthesis*. Cambridge University Press.

Unicode, Inc. (2019). Unicode Common Locale Data Repository. `http://cldr.unicode.org/`.

van Esch, D. and Sproat, R. (2017). An expanded taxonomy of semiotic classes for text normalization. In *INTERSPEECH*, pages 4016–4020. Stockholm.

Zhang, H., Sproat, R., Ng, A. H., Stahlberg, F., Peng, X., Gorman, K., and Roark, B. (2019). Neural models of text normalization for speech applications. *Computational Linguistics*, 45(2):293–337.

Proceedings of the 1st Joint SLTU and CCURL Workshop (SLTU-CCURL 2020), pages 226–234
Language Resources and Evaluation Conference (LREC 2020), Marseille, 11–16 May 2020
© European Language Resources Association (ELRA), licensed under CC-BY-NC

Lenition and Fortition of Stop Codas in Romanian

Mathilde Hutin[1], Oana Niculescu[2], Ioana Vasilescu[1], Lori Lamel[1], Martine Adda-Decker[1,3]

[1] Université Paris-Saclay, CNRS, LIMSI, [2] Romanian Academy Institute of Linguistics "Iorgu Iordan - Al. Rosetti",
[3] Université Paris 3 Sorbonne Nouvelle, CNRS, UMR 7018, LPP
[1] Bât. 507, rue du Belvédère, 91405 Orsay, France [2] Calea 13 Septembrie nr. 13, 050711 București, Romania
[3] 19 rue des Bernardins, 75005 Paris, France
{hutin, ioana, lori.lamel, martine.adda}@limsi.fr, oeniculescu@yahoo.com

Abstract

The present paper aims at providing a first study of lenition- and fortition-type phenomena in coda position in Romanian, a language that can be considered as less-resourced. Our data show that there are two contexts for devoicing in Romanian: before a voiceless obstruent, which means that there is regressive voicelessness assimilation in the language, and before pause, which means that there is a tendency towards final devoicing proper. The data also show that non-canonical voicing is an instance of voicing assimilation, as it is observed mainly before voiced consonants (voiced obstruents and sonorants alike). Two conclusions can be drawn from our analyses. First, from a phonetic point of view, the two devoicing phenomena exhibit the same behavior regarding place of articulation of the coda, while voicing assimilation displays the reverse tendency. In particular, alveolars, which tend to devoice the most, also voice the least. Second, the two assimilation processes have similarities that could distinguish them from final devoicing as such. Final devoicing seems to be sensitive to speech style and gender of the speaker, while assimilation processes do not. This may indicate that the two kinds of processes are phonologized at two different degrees in the language, final devoicing being more sociolinguistically stigmatized than assimilation.

Keywords: Romanian, lenition, fortition, automatic alignment, pronunciation variant

1. Introduction

A segment is considered as undergoing weakening, also known as lenition, if it is subject to a transformation that ultimately ends with segmental deletion. Conversely, a segment can be said to undergo strengthening, also known as fortition, if it follows the reverse path (even though this definition can be debated; Honeybone, 2008). From the observation of diachronic change (Brandão de Carvalho, 2008), it is known that, when a segment gains a voiced feature, for example, it is lenited, and when it loses it, it is fortified. From a synchronic perspective, consonant weakening and strengthening processes may occur at different degrees in several Western Romance languages (Ryant & Liberman, 2016; Vasilescu & al., 2018 on Spanish; Hualde & Prieto, 2014 on Spanish and Catalan; Hualde & Nadeu, 2011 on Italian; Jatteau et al., 2019a,b on French). Eastern Romance languages, on the other hand, have been less investigated. Chitoran et al. (2015), exploring consonant weakening in Romanian in a corpus of 8 native speakers, reported only rare instances of lenition. Niculescu et al. (submitted) reported very few consonant alternations in Romanian, except for codas, which is not surprising since the coda position is famously prone to neutralization processes cross-linguistically.

This is why the present study will focus on voicing and devoicing, i.e. weakening and strengthening processes, in Romanian stops in coda position. Romanian is indeed a good candidate to investigate variable voicing and devoicing in coda position because it has a regular voicing contrast and robustly allows stops to contrast for voicing in word-final position: e.g. /krap/, "I crack" *vs* /krab/, "crab"; /kot/, "elbow" *vs* /kod/, "code"; /fak/, "I do" *vs* /fag/, "beech".

Since substantial amounts of data are the only way linguists have at their disposal to investigate actual linguistic usage in a statistically significant manner (Coleman et al., 2016), large corpora are a promising means to investigate fine variation phenomena such as final voicing and devoicing. Automatic speech recognition (ASR) systems, traditionally trained on very large amounts of carefully transcribed speech data and written texts, can be used to exploit such corpora for linguistic studies. Yet, such quantities of data and material are available in electronic form mainly in the world's dominant languages (e.g. English, Arabic, Chinese, Spanish, French). Since obtaining large volumes of transcribed audio data remains quite costly and requires a substantial investment in time and money as well as an efficient supervision, developing language technologies for less-resourced languages is less common.

Even though it is spoken by 25 million native speakers around the world, Romanian figures among these less-resourced languages (Trandabăţ et al., 2012). As far as we know, corpora of large continuous speech recognition for Romanian are lacking. National oral annotated corpora for Romanian are scarce and rather difficult to access (Mîrzea-Vasile, 2017), needing permission from the coordinator. Either stored on cassette tapes (ROVA, CORV, IVLRA; Dascălu, 2002, 2011; Ionescu-Ruxăndoiu 2002) or magnetic tapes (AFLR; Marin, 1996), there are certain drawbacks which prove harder to overcome such as poor audio quality, vague metadata, unstructured interview making the data challenging to compare, ambiguous policy of data collection and speaker consent. Newer corpora, such as ROMBAC (Ion et al., 2012) or CoRoLa (Barbu Mititelu et al., 2018), are more inclined towards written text data acquisition and processing. During the last decade, however, there have been several attempts to build ASR systems on small corpora (Petrea et al., 2010; Burileanu et al., 2012). As part of the speech technology development in the Quaero program[1], a Romanian ASR system targeting broadcast and web audio was built but the acoustic models were developed in an unsupervised manner similarly to the method employed in Lamel & Vieru (2010), as no detailed annotations were available for the audio training data downloaded from a variety of websites.

A few studies build on these technological advances to investigate linguistic variation and gather information

---

[1] www.quaero.org

about specific trends of spoken Romanian (Vasilescu et al., 2014, 2019; Renwick et al., 2016; Niculescu et al., submitted). The present study follows this emerging body of literature and the methodology therein. Its aims are threefold: (i) to explore consonant voicing and devoicing patterns in Romanian as instances of lenition and fortition respectively, (ii) to contribute to the overall picture of the advent of lenition and fortition phenomena across languages, and (iii) to gain insight into the Romanian language from large corpora. The main premise is to use automatic alignments of speech data with dictionaries containing specific pronunciation variants to investigate non-canonical realizations of stops in coda position in Romanian. After a brief overview of Romanian phonology in Section 2, Section 3 is devoted to the description of our data and methodology. In Section 4, we tackle the question of non-canonical devoicing, especially investigating the difference between final devoicing and voicelessness assimilation. Section 5 is devoted to the issue of non-canonical voicing. In Section 6, we investigate the sociolinguistic factors behind both lenition and fortition-type phenomena. Finally, in Section 7, we conclude and discuss the results.

2. Romanian Phonology

Romanian is the only surviving Eastern-European Romance language (Rosetti, 1986), descending from the vernacular variant of Latin which branched into Daco-Romanian, spoken north of the Danube, and three south Danubian dialects, Aromanian, Megleno-Romanian, and Istro-Romanian. The northern dialect is what is usually referred to as Romanian, while the southern tongues have the status of oral dialects (Vulpe, 1978: 293). Described as a spoken vernacular until the appearance of the first written texts (Maiden et al., 2013), namely the Letter of Neacşu, dated 1521, Romanian stands out from other Romance languages due to the remarkable unity shown by the north-Danubian subdialects despite external influence.

In terms of vowel inventory, Romanian is unique among Romance languages due to the central vowels /i, ə/ and the two unary diphthongs, /e̯a, o̯a/ (Chitoran, 2002). The consonant system inherited from Latin, i.e. /p, t, k, f, s, b, d, g, v, z/ was enriched in Romanian by /tʃ, dʒ, dz, ts, ʃ, ʒ, c, ɟ, h/, without presenting long consonants with phonological function (SOR; Dindelegan, 2016). There are few studies dealing with Romanian phoneme inventory from a statistical viewpoint (see Roceric Alexandrescu (1968) for an in-depth analysis carried out on written texts, and, more recently, Niculescu (2018) for connected speech data).

Romanian is interesting to observe lenition and fortition-type phenomena because, unlike Western Romance languages, Romanian has not undergone lenition diachronically (Brandão de Carvalho & al., 2008; Alkire & Rosen, 2010). It also still displays a voiced/voiceless opposition for all obstruents[2]. Romanian also stands out among Romance languages since it is one of the few, along with French, to include so many codas. From 400 hours of training data and more than 2.5 million tokens[3]

(Adda-Decker, 2019), we know that stops in Romanian have the distribution displayed in Figure 1.

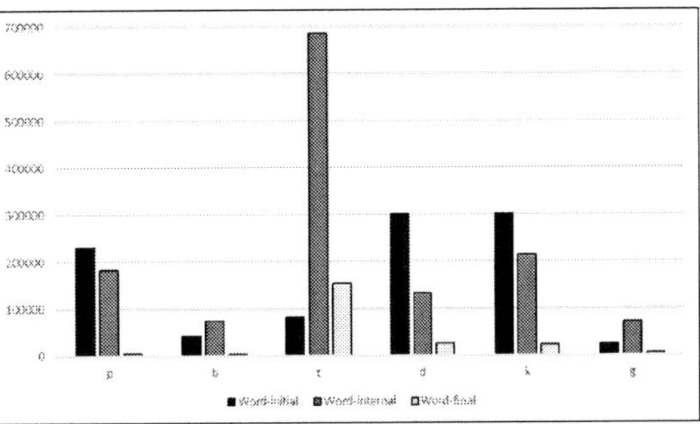

Figure 1. Numbers of stops as a function of position in the word in Romanian.

In this figure, one can see that stops nevertheless tend to appear less in word-final position (8.28%) than in word-initial (38.43%) and word-medial (53.29%) position. Moreover, voiced codas are generally less represented than voiceless ones (26.32% and 73.68% respectively), with a notable dominance, even in coda position, of voiceless alveolars (72.70% of all codas are /t/).

3. Data and Methodology

Consonant alternation in coda position is a very precise issue. Examining this question in large corpora allows the quantification of the variable tendency towards devoicing and voicing under less supervised settings than laboratory recordings, and the larger the corpora, the more precisely the phenomenon can be described (Coleman et al. 2016). Jatteau et al. (2019b) investigated 195,000 items, a substantial amount of data extracted from three large corpora of French. Unfortunately, we do not have access to the same quantity of data for Romanian, which explains why so few large-scale studies on variation have been conducted on this language.

The corpus used for the present study, created by the Quaero program, is representative of Standard Romanian. It is twofold and consists of 3.5 hours of broadcast news, i.e. prepared speech, and 3.5 hours of interviews, i.e. spontaneous speech. More precisely, the first part of the data was gathered from several Romanian radio and television shows (from the RFI Journal and RRA – Radio România Actualități – radio stations and the Euranet news agency) and consists mainly of read and semi-prepared news. Though the number of speakers varies according to the broadcast channel, ranging from 3 to 24, this first part includes a total of 79 different speakers. Broadcasts with significant quantities of overlapping speech and noisy background were excluded. As for the second part, it gathers televised debates recorded from the Romanian national TV channel Antena 3 and includes 50 speakers.

The data have been manually orthographically transcribed and benefited from a speech-to-text alignment with the system described in Vasilescu et al. (2014).

After removing acronymic words followed by the masculine definite marker -*ul* (37 items), the corpus is left

---

[2] Except for the laryngeal fricative /h/ that can only be voiceless.
[3] Unfortunately, this training data were not manually annotated nor the alignment manually verified, meaning that it is not ideal to observe fine phenomena such as voicing alternation.

with a total of 4529 tokens. Of these, 86% are classified as ending in a canonically voiceless stop, and 14% as ending in a canonically voiced stop. The distribution of these codas is given in Table 1.

Voiceless codas			Voiced codas		
p	t	k	b	d	g
110	3288	486	60	487	98

Table 1. Number of occurrences of each coda.

Furthermore, we build here on the method proposed in Hallé & Adda-Decker (2007) to study voicing alternations through automatic forced alignment introducing specific variants in the pronunciation dictionary. Such pronunciation variants are stored in a lexicon which contains both each word's full (also said canonical) pronunciation and potentially altered (also said non-canonical) variants (Adda-Decker & Lamel, 2017), as shown in Figure 2.

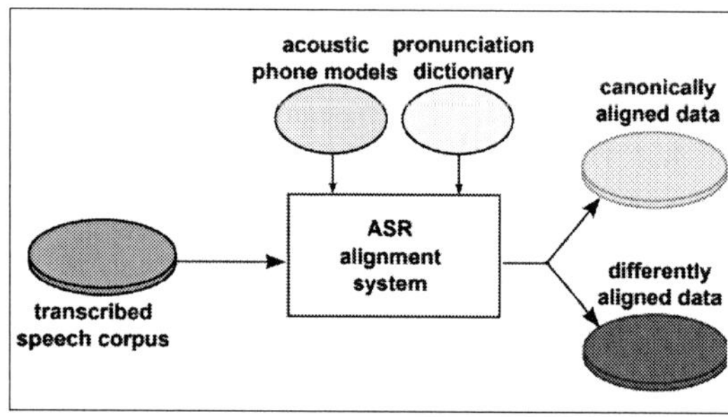

Figure 2. Schema for automatic alignments with
pronunciation variants.

A probability is also associated with each variant (Lamel & Gauvain, 2009) and the system will select the most probable variant given the actual acoustic realization. Although they operate categorically and propose only predefined variants, ASR systems offer an alternative method to human perception, which is known to compensate for the missing acoustic information with other available cues (i.e. speech rate, context and word length; Mitterer, 2011). This variant-based approach has given reliable accounts of lenition and fortition-type consonant variation for Romanian before (Vasilescu & al., 2019), as well as for French (Jatteau & al., 2019a,b) and Spanish (Ryant & Liberman, 2016; Vasilescu & al., 2018). During alignment, voicing and devoicing are decided if the best matching phone model corresponds to the voiced or voiceless variant respectively and not to the original canonical voiceless or voiced phone. Hence, for any occurrence of /b, d, g/, its voiceless counterpart may be selected by the system if the acoustic realization of the consonant best matches the corresponding model. For instance, the Romanian word *dialog*, /dialog/ could be transcribed either as [dialog] or as [dialok] depending on whether the system considered the last consonant to correspond to the voiced or voiceless consonant. Conversely, for any occurrence of /p, t, k/, its voiced counterpart may be selected by the system if the acoustic

realization of the consonant best matches the corresponding model. For instance, the Romanian word *grup*, /grup/ could be transcribed either as [grup] or as [grub] depending on whether the system considered the last consonant to best correspond to the voiceless or voiced consonant.

This data will allow us to observe devoicing and voicing rates according to the stop's right context, point of articulation, speech style and gender of the speaker.

4.   Devoicing Phenomena

Devoicing is a process whereby a canonically voiced consonant such as /b, d, g/ is realized as a devoiced [p, t, k]. It is therefore one manifestation of the wider phenomenon known as fortition.

In the data, 51.78% of /b, d, g/ in coda position are realized as devoiced. Such high rates need to be investigated more finely.

4.1   Voicelessness Assimilation *vs* Final Devoicing

Theoretically, devoicing can be the result of at least two different phenomena: voicelessness assimilation and final devoicing.

Voicelessness assimilation is a process whereby canonically voiced consonants are realized as devoiced due to the presence of a voiceless obstruent in the adjacent left or right context. In the case of codas in synchrony, the assimilation comes from an adjacent right obstruent, such as in French (Snoeren et al., 2006). For instance, Fr. *la soude pue*, "the hold smells bad" can be pronounced /lasutpy/ instead of /lasudpy/ where canonical /d/ is realized as [t] because of the regressive voicelessness assimilation to [p].

Final devoicing is the process whereby canonical contrastive voiced consonants are devoiced in domain-final position, as in Russian *Youtu[p]*. As pointed out by Jatteau et al. (2019a,b), many factors converge to suggest that final devoicing is a "natural" process. It is widely attested cross-linguistically (Blevins, 2006), it appears regularly in L1 and L2 acquisition (Broselow, 2018), and it constitutes a frequent sound change (Kümmel, 2007; pp. 184-186). Several sources for final devoicing have been proposed in the phonetic literature: lack of the consonant-vowel transition and its cues to the voicing contrast (Steriade, 1999), anticipatory glottal opening for breathing (Myers, 2012), utterance-final decrease of subglottal pressure yielding voicing offset prior to the obstruent release (Westbury & Keating, 1986) and failure of production and perception of voicing in utterance-final lengthening (Blevins, 2006; Ohala, 1997). These phonetic sources predict that variable final devoicing could be found in languages which do not present a phonologized process of final neutralization, such as the one observed in contemporary metropolitan French (Jatteau et al., 2019a,b).

To investigate these two devoicing phenomena, this paper studies the voicing alternations of canonically voiced stops in word-final position in a large corpus of Romanian.

4.2 What Kind of Devoicing in Romanian?

As mentioned above, voicelessness assimilation can be shown to happen if a substantial amount of devoicing appears more before a voiceless obstruent than anywhere else. Conversely, final devoicing proper can be shown to happen if a substantial amount of devoicing appears more before pause than in any other environment.

To investigate this question, the data was broken into five categories: whether the consonant appeared before pause (hesitation, breath or silence) or before a word beginning with a vowel, a sonorant, a voiced obstruent or a voiceless obstruent.

Figure 3 shows the rates of devoiced /b, d, g/ in all five possible contexts. The bars indicate the actual numbers of tokens in the data and the rates proportioned on 100%.

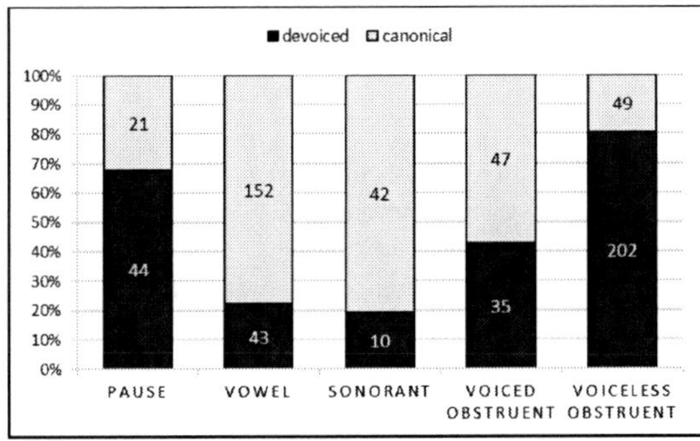

Figure 3: Percentage (and counts) of canonical and devoiced realizations of word-final /b, d, g/ in Romanian as a function of right context.

The data show that there is indeed a high rate of coda devoicing before pause (67.69%), and an even higher rate before voiceless obstruent (80.48%). However, the data also show coda devoicing in contexts where it is not expected, i.e. where devoicing cannot be due to natural devoicing in utterance final position (before pause) nor to assimilation of voiceless segments (before voiceless obstruents). This devoicing before vowel, sonorant or voiced obstruent might be due to the lexical accent, which has not been considered for the present study.

Still, the devoicing rates according to the following context are statistically significant ($\chi^2 = 183.19$, df = 4, p < 2.2e-16). These results indicate that Romanian codas are subject to final devoicing, but most of all are extremely prone to assimilation of the laryngeal feature, in this case of voicelessness.

4.3 Devoicing as a Function of the Coda's Place of Articulation

Since it is more difficult to maintain the pressure differential across the glottis with a smaller vocal tract (Ohala, 1997), we hypothesize that posterior stops will present more devoicing than the anterior ones.

To avoid the bias of the right context and establish the actual part of place of articulation in each type of devoiced codas (the ones undergoing final devoicing *vs* the ones undergoing assimilation), each of them will be investigated separately.

To investigate the role of place of articulation of the coda in final devoicing proper, here we focus on only the canonically voiced codas /b, d, g/ followed by pause (n = 65).

As shown in Figure 4, before pause, the most posterior place of articulation is the one displaying the least final devoicing (63.64%). However, due to the very low number of labial codas in the data, this result is not statistically significant ($\chi^2 = 0.26433$, df = 2, p = 0.8762).

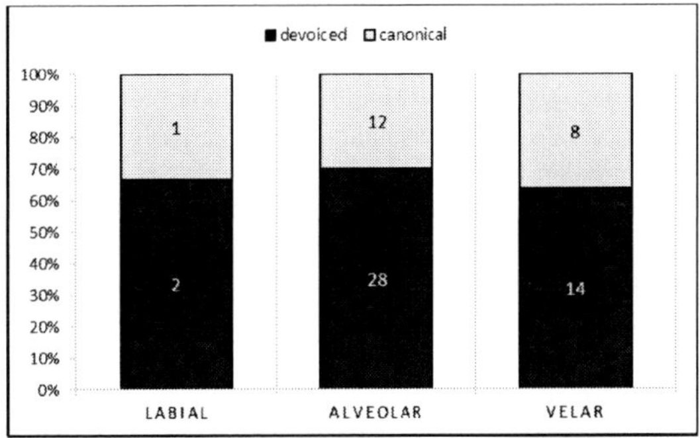

Figure 4: Percentage (and counts) of devoiced codas preceding pause as a function of place of articulation.

To compare those results with the other context favoring devoicing, i.e. the regressive assimilation context, we now focus only on the codas followed by a voiceless obstruent (n = 251), which might provide a better insight on the issue since there are more tokens.

Figure 5 shows the numbers of devoiced codas before voiceless onsets.

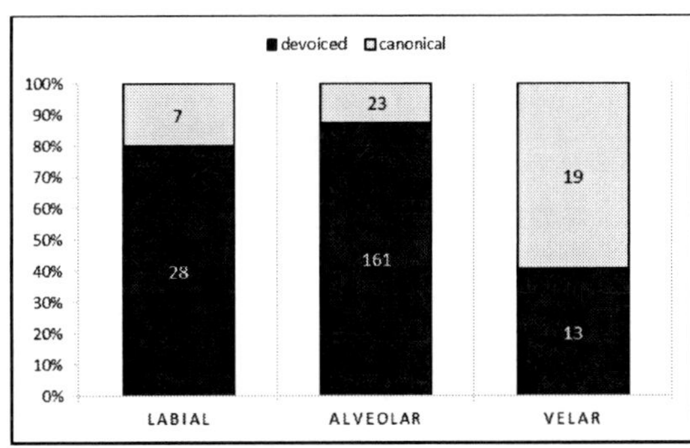

Figure 5: Percentage (and counts) of devoiced codas preceding voiceless obstruent as a function of their place of articulation.

The results here display the same tendencies as for codas before pause: alveolars are the most devoiced (87.50%), followed closely by labials (80.00%), and velars are by far the least devoiced (40.63%). Only in this case, the differences are statistically significant ($\chi^2 = 38.13$, df = 2, p = 5.251e-09).

These results are in line with Jatteau et al. (2019c) who expected more devoicing of velars than of alveolars and labials in French, but found the same results as we do, i.e. more devoicing of labials and alveolars than of velars.

5. Voicing Phenomena

Voicing is the process whereby a canonically voiceless consonant such as /p, t, k/ is realized as a voiced [b, d, g]. It is therefore a manifestation of the wider phenomenon known as lenition.

In the data, 16.47% of /p, t, k/ in coda position are realized as voiced. Although this ratio does not seem as impressive as the one for devoicing, it still represents 639 tokens, which should be enough to gain a valuable insight into voicing patterns in Romanian.

5.1 Regressive Voicing Assimilation

Natural, spontaneous voicing, i.e. in coda position before pause, is controversial, but regressive voicing assimilation, i.e. voicing of codas before voiced obstruent, is well-documented (Snoeren et al. 2006, Hallé & Adda-Decker 2007). This brings us to hypothesize that regressive voicing assimilation can be shown to happen if a substantial amount of voiceless codas are realized as voiced when followed by voiced consonants and not in the other contexts.

To investigate this question, the data was broken into the same five categories: whether the consonant appeared before pause (hesitation, breath or silence) or before a word beginning with a vowel, a sonorant, a voiced obstruent or a voiceless obstruent.

Figure 6 shows the rates of voiced /p, t, k/ in the five possible contexts.

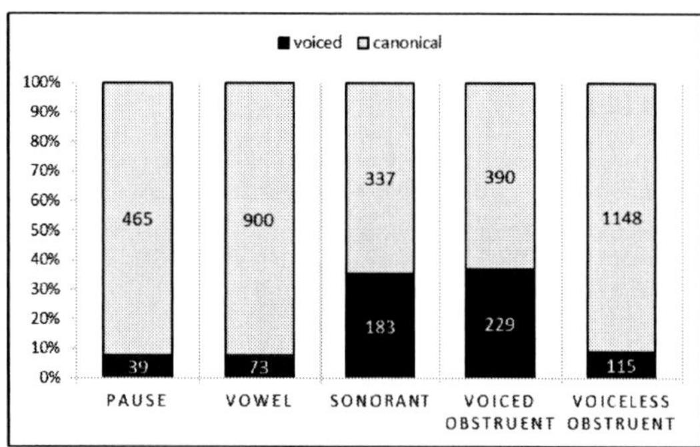

Figure 6: Percentage (and counts) of canonical and voiced realizations of word-final /p, t, k/ in Romanian as a function of right context.

The data show that there are, as expected, rather low rates of voicing before pause (7.74%), vowel (7.50%) or voiceless obstruent (9.11%) and that voicing happens mainly before voiced obstruent (37.00%) or sonorant (35.19%). Since sonorants are voiced by default, they are a possible context for voicing assimilation, and since the differences between our rates are statistically significant (χ^2 = 456.57, df = 4, p < 2.2e-16), we can conclude that non-canonical voicing of codas in Romanian is indeed an instance of regressive voicing assimilation.

5.2 Voicing as a Function of the Coda's Place of Articulation

Since the investigation of place of articulation in devoicing shows unexpected results, it might be interesting to look at the same issue for voicing – especially given the very high number of alveolar voiceless stops in the data.

Figure 7 shows the rates of codas undergoing non-canonical voicing as a function of their place of articulation.

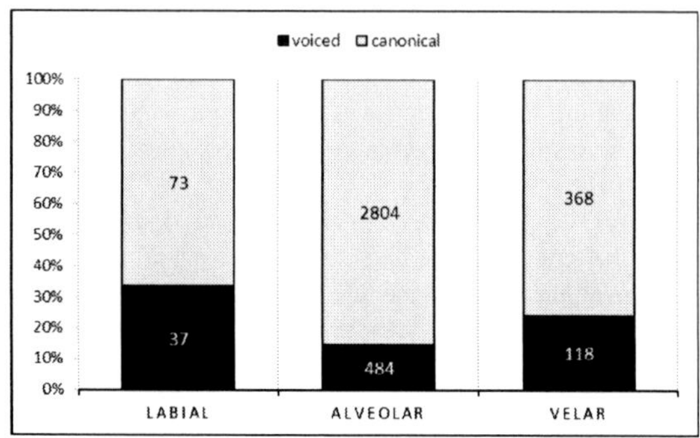

Figure 7: Percentage (and counts) of voiced codas preceding voiced consonants as a function of place of articulation

The results show that labials are more voiced (33.64%) than velars (24.28%) and alveolars (14.72%), the difference between the three places of articulation being statistically significant (χ^2 = 52.471, df = 2, p = 4.036e-12). It is interesting to note that alveolar voiceless stops /t/ are the least voiced when their voiced counterparts /d/ were the most devoiced, and that it could be due to the frequency of /t/ in coda position in Romanian.

6. Sociolinguistic Factors

The data shows that there is a substantial amount of final devoicing proper and of regressive voicelessness and voicing assimilation in Romanian. The strength of such data also resides in the metadata available, which can provide insights into more sociolinguistic questions.

6.1 Non-canonical Realizations Depending on Speech Style

Variation is expected primarily in less formal, spontaneous speech styles (Jatteau et al. 2019a,b; Vasilescu et al. 2019) and we therefore expect more non-canonical realizations in non-prepared rather than in prepared speech. As described in Section 3 about the data and methodology, our data is comprised of two halves: the first can be considered prepared, formal speech in broadcast news (RFI, RRA and Euranet), and the second can be considered as less formal speech in debates and interviews (Antena 3).

For this analysis, we will first consider the effect of speech style on devoicing, then on voicing. In each case, we will only consider consonants in the relevant environment, as to avoid a bias of the right context. We will focus only on canonical /b, d, g/ in contexts of final devoicing (before pause, n = 65) and voicelessness assimilation (before voiceless obstruent, n = 251), and on canonical /p, t, k/ in contexts of voicing assimilation (before voiced obstruent and sonorant, n = 808).

The results for final devoicing as a function of speech style are displayed in Figure 8.

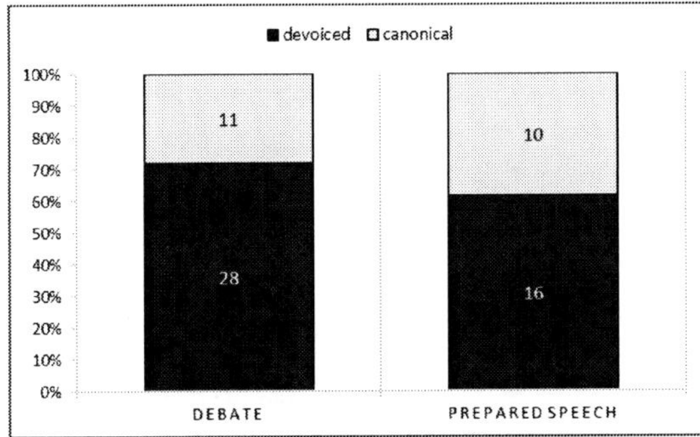

Figure 8: Percentage (and counts) of devoiced codas before pause as a function of speech style.

Figure 8 shows, as expected, more final devoicing in debates (71.79%) than in prepared speech (61.54%). However, the difference between the two speech styles (Δ = 10.26%) is barely significant (χ^2 = 0.35466, df = 1, p = 0.5515).

In the case of voicelessness assimilation however, the results are interesting. There are, overall, more devoiced realizations before voiceless obstruent than before pause, with 82.73% devoicing in debates and 78.72% in prepared speech. However, the difference between speech style is less important (Δ = 4%, χ^2 = 0.40142, df = 1, p = 0.5264). This would indicate that voicelessness assimilation is more generalized across Romanian than final devoicing.

As for voicing, the results of non-canonical realizations of /p, t, k/ before voiced obstruent and sonorant are displayed in Figure 9.

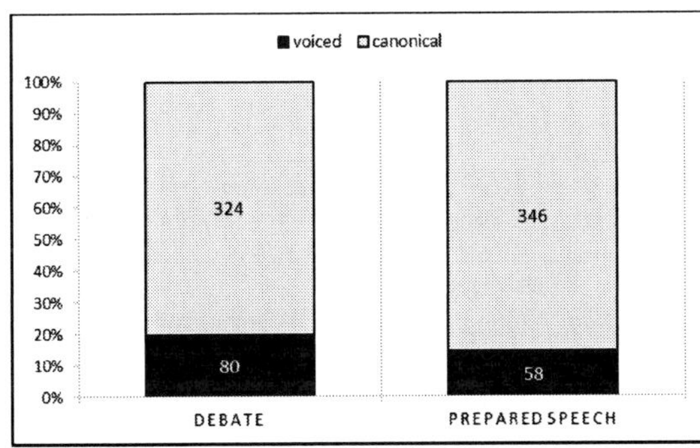

Figure 9: Percentage (and counts) of non-canonically voiced codas preceding voiced consonants as a function of speech style.

Figure 9 shows that there are, as expected, more voicing assimilation in debates (19.80%) than in prepared speech (14.36%), the difference between the two speech styles being statistically significant (χ^2 = 3.8539, df = 1, p = 0.04963).

Overall, then, even though the effect is not significant for final devoicing, non-prepared speech is usually more altered than prepared speech. Interestingly, however, the differences between speech styles are less important for voicelessness assimilation than for voicing assimilation.

6.2 Non-canonical Realizations Depending on Gender of the Speaker

Finally, women tend to avoid speech alterations (Adda-Decker & Lamel 2005). We therefore hypothesize that they would display fewer non-canonical realizations than men.

Again, to avoid the bias of the right context and establish the actual part of gender in final devoicing proper, voicelessness assimilation and voicing assimilation, we focus first only on /b, d, g/ followed by pause (n = 65), then on /b, d, g/ followed by voiceless obstruent (n = 251) and finally on /p, t, k/ followed by voiced obstruents and sonorants (n = 808).

Concerning final devoicing, the numbers displayed in Figure 10 show a higher devoicing rate in male speech (70.00%) than in female speech (60.00%).

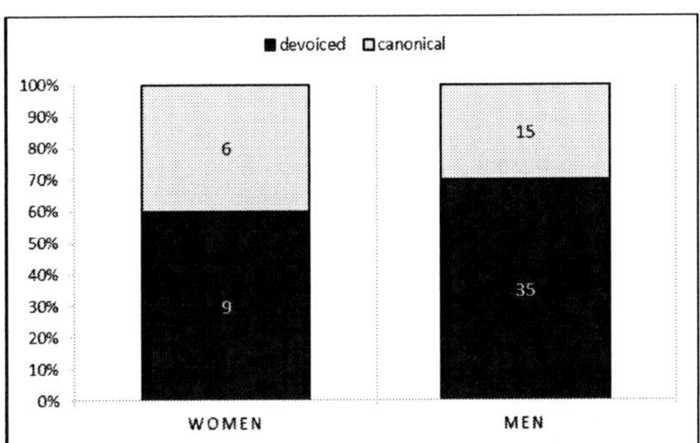

Figure 10: Percentage (and counts) of devoiced codas before pause as a function of gender of the speaker.

Once again, the results are not statistically significant (χ^2=0.16942, df=1, p=0.6806). There are too few female tokens in the data to provide a reliable account of the effect of gender on final devoicing in Romanian. However, this result suggests the tendency we might find with more data.

In the case of voicelessness assimilation, there are no effect of gender whatsoever, with 81.08% of devoicing in female speech and 80.23% in male speech. This again shows that regressive assimilation of voicelessness is not comparable to final devoicing in every case: socio-linguistically, it is more widely used, with no difference between speech styles nor genders, which means that it may be less phonologized than final devoicing.

Finally, Figure 11 displays the results for voicing assimilation. Results show that there is less voicing assimilation in female speech (15.33%) than in male speech (17.92%) but the effect is rather slim (χ^2 = 0.66417, df = 1, p = 0.4151).

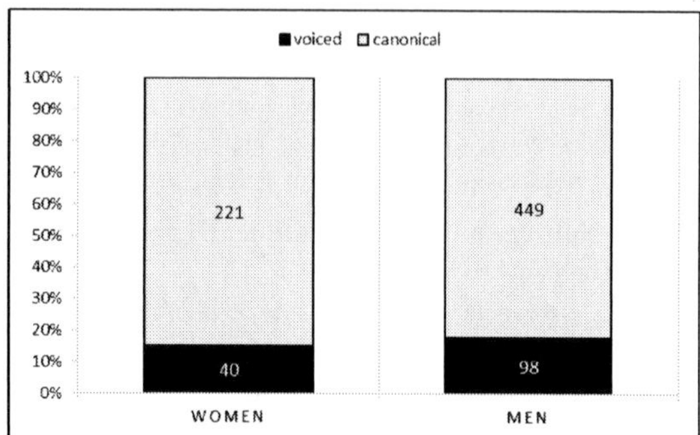

Figure 11: Percentage (and counts) of non-canonically voiced codas preceding voiced consonants as a function of gender of the speaker.

Overall, final devoicing seems to differ more across genders, while assimilation processes seem indifferent to it. This would be an indicator that final devoicing might be more phonologized, to this point, than voicelessness and voicing assimilation in Romanian.

7. Conclusion and Discussion

In conclusion, the present paper aims at providing a first study of lenition- and fortition-type phenomena in coda position in Romanian, a language that can be considered as less-resourced, using several hours of naturalistic speech data.

Our data shows that there are two contexts for devoicing in Romanian: before voiceless obstruent, which means that there is regressive voicelessness assimilation in the language, and before pause, which means that there is a tendency towards final devoicing proper. Data also shows that non-canonical voicing is an instance of voicing assimilation, for it happens mostly before voiced consonants (voiced obstruents and sonorants alike). Although few data were analyzed compared to other Romance languages with stop codas such as French (Jatteau et al. 2019a,b; Hallé & Adda-Decker 2007, Snoeren et al., 2006), trends are consistent with findings in this language, i.e. that there is regressive assimilation of laryngeal feature, that voicelessness assimilates more than voicedness and that final devoicing happens less in velars than hypothesized. However, investigating final devoicing and comparing it to the other two phenomena has proven difficult given the small amount of data available. The limitations of our study show how arduous investigating a less-resourced language can be. To be able to study final devoicing proper, i.e. coda realization before pause, more than 65 tokens in this condition would have been needed, and to study the effect of speech style and gender, more data are needed from more sources and with more varied speakers, especially more women.

Still, two interesting conclusions can be drawn from our analyses. First, from a phonetic point of view, the two devoicing phenomena have the same tendencies regarding place of articulation of the coda, while voicing assimilation displays the reverse tendencies. In particular, alveolars tend to devoice the most, but also to voice the less. Second, an interesting finding is that the two assimilation processes have similarities that could distinguish them from final devoicing as such. Mainly, final devoicing seems sensitive to speech style and gender of the speaker, while assimilation processes do not. This could indicate that the two kinds of processes are phonologized to two different degrees in the language, final devoicing being more sociolinguistically stigmatized than assimilation.

This research is of importance since, although at this stage we don't have enough data to make a decision, previous works point out that including pronunciation variants with model voicing alternation can be helpful (Vasilescu et al., 2018)

8. Acknowledgements

This research was partially supported by the Labex DigiCosme (project ANR-11-LABEX-0045-DIGICOSME) operated by ANR as part of the program "Investissement d'Avenir" Idex Paris-Saclay (ANR-11-IDEX-0003-02).

9. Bibliographical References

Adda-Decker, M. (2006). De la reconnaissance automatique de la parole à l'analyse linguistique des corpus oraux. *Papier présenté aux Journées d'Étude sur la Parole (JEP2006)*, Dinard, France, 12–16 juin

Adda-Decker, M. (2019). Variation in Romance languages: insights from large corpora. *Invited speech at 49th Linguistic Symposium on Romance Languages – LSRL 49.*

Adda-Decker, M. & Lamel, L. (2005) Do speech recognizers prefer female speakers? *Interspeech* 2005: 2205-2208.

Adda-Decker, M. & Lamel, L. (2017). Discovering speech reductions across speaking styles and languages. In Cangemi, F., Clayards M., Niebuhr O., Schuppler B., & Zellers M. *Rethinking reduction: Interdisciplinary perspectives on conditions, mechanisms, and domains for phonetic variation*, De Gruyter Mouton 2017.

Alkire, T. & Rosen, C. (2010). *Romance Languages. A Historical Introduction*, Cambridge University Press, Cambridge.

Barbu Mititelu, V., Tufiş, D. & Irimia, E. (2018). The Reference Corpus of the Contemporary Romanian Language (CoRoLa). *Proceedings of LREC 2018*, Japan, 1178-1185.

Blevins, J. (2006). Theoretical synopsis of Evolutionary Phonology, *Theoretical Linguistics*, vol. 32, 2, 117-166

Brandão de Carvalho, J. (2008). Western Romance. In Brandão de Carvalho, J., Scheer, T. & Ségéral, P. (eds) *Lenition and Fortition*. Berlin: Mouton de Gruyter.

Broselow, E. (2018). Laryngeal contrasts in second language phonology. In L.M. Hymanand & F. Plank, (eds), *Phonological Typology*. Berlin; Boston: De Gruyter Mouton, 312–340.

Burileanu, C., Cucu, H., Besacier, L. & Buzo, A. (2012). ASR domain adaptation methods for low-resourced languages: Application to romanian langage. *European Signal Processing Conference*, 1648– 1652.

Chitoran, I. (2002). *The Phonology of Romanian: A constraint-based approach*. New York, Mouton De Gruyter.

Chitoran, I., Hualde, J. & Niculescu, O. (2015). Gestural undershoot and gestural intrusion – from perceptual errors to historical sound change. *Proceedings of 2nd ERRARE Worskhop* (Sinaia, Romania)

Coleman, J., Renwick, M. E.L. & Temple, R.A.M. (2016). Probabilistic underspecification in nasal place assimilation. *Phonology*, 33(3), 425-458

Dascălu Jinga, L. (2002). *Corpus de română vorbită* (CORV). Eşantioane, Bucureşti, Oscar Print.

Dascălu Jinga, L. (coord.). (2011). Româna vorbită actuală (ROVA). *Corpus şi studii*, Academia Română, Institutul de Lingvistică "Iorgu Iordan – Al. Rosetti".

Dindelegan, G. (ed.). (2016). *The Syntax of Old Romanian*, Oxford, Oxford University Press.

Galliano, S., Geoffrois, E., Mostefa, D., Choukri, K., Bonastre, J.-F. & Gravier, G. (2005). The ESTER phase II evaluation campaign for the rich transcription of French broadcast news. *9th European Conference on Speech Communication and Technology*

Gauvain, J.-L., Lamel, L. & Adda, G. (2002). The LIMSI broadcast news transcription system. *Speech communication* 37 (1-2), 89–108

Gauvain, J.-L., Adda, G., Adda-Decker, M., Allauzen, A., Gendner, V., Lamel, L. & Schwenk, H. (2005). Where Are We in Transcribing French Broadcast News? *Proceedings of ISCA Eurospeech'05*, Lisbon, Sep 2005.

Gravier, G., Adda, G., Paulson, N., Carré, M., Giraudel, A. & Galibert O. (2012). The ETAPE corpus for the evaluation of speech-based TV content processing in the French language. *LREC – 8th International Conference on Language Resources and Evaluation*

Hallé, P. & Adda-Decker, M. (2007).Voicing assimilation in journalistic speech. *16th International Congress of Phonetic Sciences*, 2007, 493–496.

Hallé, P. & Adda-Decker, M. (2011). Voice assimilation in French obstruents: A gradient or a categorical process? *Tones and features: A festschrift for Nick Clements*, De Gruyter, 149–175

Honeybone, P. (2008). Lenition, weakening and consonantal strength: tracing concepts through the history of phonology. In Brandão de Carvalho, J., Scheer, T. & Ségéral, P. (eds) *Lenition and Fortition*. Berlin: Mouton de Gruyter.

Hualde, J. & Nadeu, M. (2011). Lenition and phonemic overlap in Rome Italian. *Phonetica*, 68, 215–242

Hualde, J. & Prieto, P. (2014). Lenition of intervocalic alveolar fricatives in Catalan and Spanish. *Phonetica*, 71, 109–127

Ion, R., Irimia, E., Ştefănescu, D. & Tufiş, D. (2012). ROMBAC: The Romanian Balanced Annotated Corpus. In N. Calzolari, K. Choukri, T. Declerck et al. (ed.), *Proceedings LREC 14*, ELRA, 1235-1239.

Ionescu-Ruxăndoiu, L. (coord.). (2002). Interacţiunea verbală în limba română actuală. Corpus (selectiv). *Schiţă de tipologie*, Bucureşti, Editura Universităţii din Bucureşti.

Jatteau, A., Vasilescu, I., Lamel, L., Adda-Decker, M. & Audibert, N. (2019a). "Gra[f]e!" Word-final devoicing of obstruents in Standard French: An acoustic study based on large corpora. In Proceedings of Interspeech, 1726–1730. Graz, Austria.

Jatteau, A., Vasilescu, I., Lamel, L. & Adda-Decker, M. (2019b). Final devoicing of fricatives in French : Studying variation in large corpora with automatic alignment. *International Congress of Phonetic Sciences*, Melbourne, Australie.

Jatteau, A., Vasilescu, I., Lamel, L. & Adda-Decker, M. (2019c). "Gra[f] ! Le dévoisement final dans les grands corpus de français". Paper presented at the SRPP seminar, Université Sorbonne Nouvelle, Feb. 15th 2019

Keating, P., Linker, P. & Huffmann, M.-K. (1983). Patterns in allophone distribution for voiced and voiceless stops. *Journal of Phonetics* 11(3). 277–290.

Maiden, M., Smith, J. C. & Ledgeway, A. (eds.). (2013). *The Cambridge History of the Romance Languages: Structures*, Cambridge, Cambridge University Press.

Marin, M. (1996). Arhiva fonogramică a limbii romȃne (Dupǎ 40 de ani). *Revista de lingvistică şi ştiinţă literară*, Chişinău, I, 41-46.

Mîrzea-Vasile, C. (2017). Corpusurile de limba română şi importanţa lor în realizarea de materiale didactice pentru limba română ca limbă străină. *Romanian Studies Today*, I, Bucureşti, Editura Universităţii din Bucureşti, 74-95.

Myers, S. (2012). Final devoicing: Production and perception studies. In T. Borowsky, S. Kawahara, T. Shinya, and M. Sugahara (Eds.), *Prosody matters: Essays in honor of Elisabeth Selkirk*, Equinox, 148-180.

Niculescu, O. (2018). *Hiatul intern şi hiatul extern în limba română contemporană. O analiză acustică* [Internal and external hiatus in contemporary standard Romanian. An acoustic analysis], Ph.D. dissertation, University of Bucharest.

Niculescu, O., Vasilescu, I., Chitoran, I., Adda-Decker, M. & Lamel, L. (Submitted). Romanian obstruents still strong after all these years: Obstruent voicing and devoicing in a large corpus study of Romanian. *Proceedings of Labphon 17*, 2020.

Ohala, J. J. (1997). Aerodynamics of phonology. *Proceedings of the Seoul International Conference on Linguistics*. Seoul: Linguistic Society of Korea, 92-97

Petrea, C., Ghelmez-Hanes, D., Burileanu, C., Buzo, A. & Cucu, H. (2010). Romanian spoken language resources and annotation for speaker independent spontaneous speech recognition. *Conference on Digital Telecommunications*, 7–10.

Renwick, M.E.L., Vasilescu, I., Dutrey, C., Lamel, L., Vieru, B. (2016). Marginal contrast among Romanian vowels: evidence from ASR and functional load In Proceedings of Interspeech, San Francisco, USA.

Roceric Alexandrescu, A. (1968). *Fonostatistica limbii romȃne*, Bucureşti, Editura Academiei Romȃne.

Rosetti. A. (1986). *Istoria limbii romȃne. I. De la origini pȃnă la începutul secolului al XVII-lea*, Bucharest, Editura Ştiinţifică si Enciclopedică.

Ryant, N. & Liberman, M. (2016). Large-scale analysis of Spanish /s/-lenition using audiobooks. *Proceedings of the 22nd International Congress on Acoustics* (Buenos Aires, Argentina)

Snoeren, N., Hallé, P. & Segui, J. (2006). A voice for the voiceless: Production and perception of assimilated stops in French. *Journal of Phonetics*, vol.34, 241–268

Torreira, F., Adda-Decker, M. & Ernestus, M. (2010). The Nijmegen corpus of casual French. *Speech Communication*, vol. 52, no. 3, 201–212.

Trandabăţ, D., Irimia, E., Mititelu, V.B., Cristea, D. and Tufiş, D. (2012).The Romanian language in the digital age. In G. Rehm & H. Uszkoreit,(eds.), *META-NET White Paper Studies*, Berlin: Springer, 1–87.

Vasilescu, I., Hernandez, N., Vieru, B. & Lamel, L. (2018). Exploring Temporal Reduction in Dialectal Spanish: A Large-scale Study of Lenition of Voiced Stops and Coda-s. *Proceedings of Interspeech* (Hyderabad, India)

Vasilescu, I., Vieru, B. & Lamel, L. (2014). Exploring Pronunciation Variants for Romanian Speech-to-text Transcription. *Proceedings of SLTU* (St. Petersburg, Russia).

Vasilescu, I., Wu, Y., Jatteau, A., Adda-Decker & Lamel, L. (Submitted). Alternances de voisement et processus de lénition et de fortition : une étude automatisée de grands corpus en cinq langues romanes. *Revue TAL.*

Vulpe, M. (1978). Romanian Dialectology and Sociolinguistics. In A. Rosetti & S. G. Eretescu (eds.), *Revue Roumaine de Linguistique, Current Trends in Romanian Linguistics*, 293-328.

Westbury, J. and Keating, P. (1986). On the naturalness of stop consonant voicing. *Journal of Linguistics*, vol. 22, 145–166.

10. Language Resource References

Quaero Program. (2008-2013). www.quaero.org

Proceedings of the 1st Joint SLTU and CCURL Workshop (SLTU-CCURL 2020), pages 235–239
Language Resources and Evaluation Conference (LREC 2020), Marseille, 11–16 May 2020
© European Language Resources Association (ELRA), licensed under CC-BY-NC

Adapting a Welsh Terminology Tool to Develop a Cornish Dictionary

Delyth Prys
Language Technologies Unit, Bangor University
Bangor, Gwynedd, Wales
{d.prys}@bangor.ac.uk

Abstract

Cornish and Welsh are closely related Celtic languages and this paper provides a brief description of a recent project to publish an online bilingual English/Cornish dictionary, the Gerlyver Kernewek, based on similar work previously undertaken for Welsh. Both languages are endangered, Cornish critically so, but both can benefit from the use of language technology. Welsh has previous experience of using language technologies for language revitalization, and this is now being used to help the Cornish language create new tools and resources, including lexicographical ones, helping a dispersed team of language specialists and editors, many of them in a voluntary capacity, to work collaboratively online. Details are given of the Maes T dictionary writing and publication platform, originally developed for Welsh, and of some of the adaptations that had to be made to accommodate the specific needs of Cornish, including their use of Middle and Late varieties due to its development as a revived language.

Keywords: Cornish, Welsh, lexicography, language revitalization

1. Background

Welsh and Cornish are two closely related languages belonging to the P-Celtic language group. Welsh is a minority language with approximately 562,000 speakers in Wales (Office of National Statistics, 2012), but is the largest of the modern Celtic languages in terms of speaker numbers, with a vibrant youth culture and a strong movement for language revitalization. This is backed by government strategy (Welsh Government, 2017), and an action plan to provide language technologies for Welsh (Welsh Government 2018). Cornish was declared extinct at the end of the eighteenth century, but has been revived and kept alive since then by a small group of adult learners, with a recent upturn in interest in the language and some families now passing on the language to their children. Accurate numbers of speakers are difficult to ascertain, as there is no question on the number of Cornish speakers included in the ten yearly UK census. However, various estimates think that there may be in the region of 300 fluent speakers and 3,000 learners of the language with around 300,000 knowing a few words (Ferdinand, 2013; O'Neill, 2005).

In contrast to the extensive academic support Welsh enjoys, with long-established departments of Welsh language and literature at all Welsh universities, Cornish language scholarship depends to a large degree on the work of a dedicated group of researchers working mainly on a voluntary basis. They are grouped together as the Akademi Kernewek (Cornish Academy)[1], an independent body responsible for the development of the Cornish language and establishing standards for it. The Akademi Kernewek is organized into four panels, responsible for Dictionary Development, Signage and Place-names, Terminology, and Research, and works with Cornwall Council to deliver its agenda. It is recognized by Cornwall Council, the local authority in charge of the Cornish region, as the definitive body responsible for corpus planning for the Cornish language. Another positive development for the Cornish language has been the establishment of a Cornish language office at Cornwall Council, and a small grant from the UK government for Cornish language activities and resources.

Among the Cornish language community's core requirements was the creation of an up-to-date lexical resource, available in an online format, and easily expandable to include new content. Previously there had been various voluntary projects to create lexical resources, but lack of funding meant they were fragmented and difficult to coordinate and publish. There had also been four competing varieties of Cornish, with no generally accepted written standard. This was resolved in 2007 by the creation of a Standard Written Form (Bock and Bruch, 2008) which cleared the way for renewed action on resource creation.

A chance meeting between the Cornish Officer of Cornwall Council and researchers at the Language Technologies Unit, Bangor University, led to a collaboration to adapt an existing Welsh dictionary-writing and publication platform to the needs of the Cornish language and to port existing Cornish dictionary data to it, thus ensuring its speedy publication. It was also intended to aid its further development, future-proofing it so that a dispersed team of editors could continue working on the dictionary, in a way that was compatible with the needs of contributing scholars.

2. Technical Details

The dictionary-writing and publication platform developed at Bangor University was Maes T (Andrews & Prys, 2011). It was originally conceived in order to help terminologists and subject specialists who were geographically distant from each other to collaborate, using a friendly, easy-to-use interface, feeding into a secure and stable master database at its back-end. From this master database it would then be able to easily produce an online version, and if needed, to publish in other formats as well. It had been used to publish over twenty Welsh terminology dictionaries online, some with their own websites in addition to appearing together in a 'one-stop shop' on the Welsh National Terminology Portal (Prys, Jones and Prys, 2012). It had also been adapted to convert The Welsh Academy English-Welsh Dictionary (Griffiths and Jones, 1995), originally published on paper, to an electronic, on-line format (Welsh Language Board, 2012).

---

[1] More information on the Akademi may be found on their website https://www.akademikernewek.org.uk/

Both the terminology panels and the dictionary panels of the Akademi Kernewek share the Maes T system for work, and so a new fork was created from the original terminology orientated version of Maes T, rather than a further adaptation of the first fork created for Welsh Academy Dictionary digitization project. This Maes T interface guides the user through the input and decision making process, with different tabs leading from collecting candidate terms onwards to defining the meaning or concept, then deciding on the standardized form to finally inputting the linguistic information. To date, the Cornish dictionary and the terminology panels have been working on separate projects, but this is catered for within the Maes T system, where different dictionaries can be shown together in the interface for the published dictionary entries. This is similar to the way that the Welsh National Terminology Portal displays records from different dictionaries together on the same results page. Legacy data from work already done to prepare for the Gerlyver Kernewek were ported from other formats, after some initial pre-processing. To date there are 13577 Cornish entries in the main dictionary, with an additional 1400 entries in the terminology one.

Despite the close linguistic relationship between Cornish and Welsh, most of the new fields needed in the Maes T schema for Cornish belong to the Cornish linguistic information stage. The Cornish Dictionary, Gerlyver Kernewek (Akademi Kernewek, 2018) is written in the new Standard Written Form, but requires extra fields to show Middle and Late Cornish forms, as the revived language derives from sources from two different periods, roughly corresponding to the two broad time periods of Middle and Late. This also necessitates further adaptation to show the pronunciation of different forms if needed, as well as different plurals of some forms.

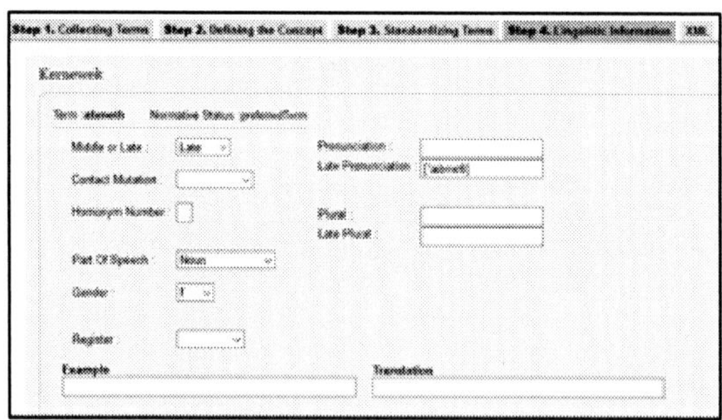

Figure 1: Screenshot of the Linguistic Information screen in Maes T showing fields for Middle or Late forms.

In addition to being able to cope with Middle and Late forms, another new field had to be introduced for a new part of speech, that of Collective Noun. Although this was present in earlier forms of Welsh it is no longer used as a part of speech category in the contemporary language, in contrast to Cornish. This category was therefore added, as well as fields for English glosses, etymology, attestations and example sentences, all requirements requested by our Cornish colleagues in order to capture the different types of information held in their legacy databases and documents.

3. Publishing Online

The publishing interface followed closely the interface already developed for the Welsh dictionaries. This allowed the input of words in either Welsh or English in the Welsh dictionaries, or Cornish or English in the case of the Gerlyver Kernewek, into a simple search box which would then show all relevant entries found. Language direction can be changed at the simple click of a button, and additional information on parts of speech is displayed through using a simple mouse over feature.

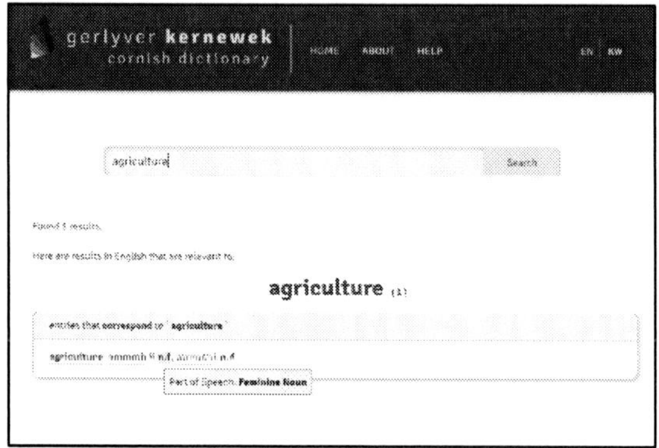

Figure 2: Screenshot of the Gerlyver Kernewek showing a simple search for 'agriculture' showing middle and late Cornish forms and the mouse over for part of speech.

In the Gerlyver, any underlined words can be clicked to show further information in a new view, enabling sophisticated searches with clear layouts.

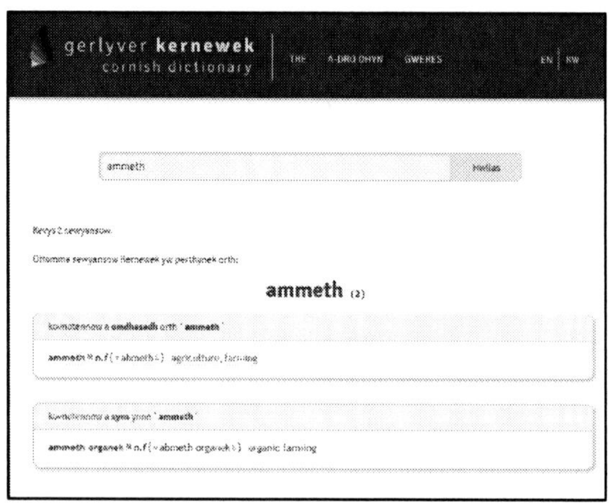

Figure 3: Screenshot of the Gerlyver Kernewek showing the result for 'ammeth' which can be accessed both by typing in 'ammeth' in the search box and by clicking on 'ammeth' underlined in the screenshot in Figure 2.

Electronic dictionary design has become important for many lexicography projects as dictionaries have moved increasingly to the digital sphere, with major languages such as English leading the way (Lew, 2010). However, small language communities are still struggling to provide basic lexicographical resources for their language and may not have access to readily available technical expertise. The Digital Language Survival Kit names dictionary making as a vital, basic resource for language. Whilst acknowledging that building a dictionary is a task for experts, it accepts that this is not always possible, and names several open source platforms, including Wiktionary, as possibilities for collaborative efforts for language communities lacking the infrastructure to make large investments (Berger et al, 2018). Such international platforms are of necessity generic, and designed to be applicable to a broad range of languages.

Where investment or grant aid has been forthcoming, some communities have used it to employ commercial companies to advise or provide technical expertise. Although sustainability and upkeep of legacy data are important topics internationally (Wallnau et al, 2000; Almonaies et al, 2010), they are not always included in project plans for less-resourced languages, resulting in problems at a later date, as discussed in a Round Table on Celtic Language Technologies (Prys and Williams, 2019). Where commercial companies are employed, responsibility must rest with the commissioners of the original work to ensure its sustainability once the project ends. Some have argued that small language communities should insist on open licences for all their tools and resources, as articulated by openlt.org (n.d.) and their manifesto for open language technologies. However, even where free or open source software is used, there still needs to be planning for the long term, and a strategy for the future upkeep and development of the resource. Perhaps the most important element, whatever software is used, is that language communities are empowered to carry out lexicographical and resource development themselves, nurturing expertise within their community without needing high level technical knowledge, at least in the incipient stages. We therefore felt it important to design the Maes T interface to be user friendly to language experts who were unfamiliar with data input in a digital environment. We encouraged the Gerlyver team to take advantage of the more advanced features within Maes T where they were readily available and easy to use.

It is possible that a well-designed, easily navigable dictionary interface, as is true of other well-designed linguistic resources, can help raise the self-esteem of a language community that is used to being in a disadvantaged position in comparison to resources in the majority language. More research is needed to confirm this postulate, but some researchers, e.g. Tsunoda (2013) have argued that improved self-esteem in itself can help with language revitalization.

In the case of Maes T, there was already functionality to support the use of diagrams, scientific symbols, mathematical notations and photographic images within its definitions. These have proved useful to some Welsh terminology dictionaries developed in Maes T, but, to date, the main feature of interest for the Gerlyver Kernewek has been the inclusion of illustrations for some dictionary entries. This is particularly useful for names of plants and animals, and combined with the inclusion of the Latin scientific name, as used by the Akademi Kernewek terminology panel, whose entries also appear in the Gerlyver, have helped enrich them. In some instances the Welsh cognates have also been added, as the information could be shared with existing Welsh dictionaries. This is an on-going process, and other types of information may be added in future.

Although original images can be added by hand, we have found that appropriately licenced photographs from Wikidata Commons[2] are a useful resource of images, and can be imported into our dictionaries without too much trouble. They have been extensively used in the Welsh species dictionary Y Bywiadur (Llên Natur, n.d.), and are now used also in term entries in the Gerlyver. Public reaction since the online publication of the dictionary in June 2019 has been positive, with over 48,000 dictionary searches having been undertaken in it during the first two weeks. It has proved to be particularly popular with language learners both inside and outside of Cornwall, as a free online dictionary, due to the difficulties of distributing Cornish language resources to a wider audience.

Figure 4: Screenshot showing part of the entry for 'sunflower' showing an illustration of the flower together with its Latin scientific name and Welsh cognates.

---

[2] Wikidata Commons is an online repository of free-use images, sounds and other media. https://commons.wikimedia.org/wiki/Commons:Wikidata

4. Further Work

Publishing a comprehensive online dictionary is only one element of the Cornish plan to provide modern language technology tools and resources for their language. The master database that lies behind the Maes T platform needs to be conceived of as a valuable resource in itself, not only as a way to produce an online dictionary. It can be used and reused to produce other lexicographical products, such as a phone or tablet dictionary app, similar to the Welsh Ap Geiriaduron[3], and an online word-by-word translator, similar to the Welsh Vocab (Jones, Prys and Prys, 2016). Other possibilities include using it to produce a Cornish spellchecker and language teaching aids. Teaching aids in particular are of particular interest to Cornish, given that most speakers are second language learners.

Sound files will shortly be added to the Gerlyver, to guide the pronunciation of Cornish. More ambitious plans include developing Cornish speech technology and machine translation, following recent and ongoing similar projects for Welsh (Jones and Cooper, 2016; Prys and Jones, 2019), and extending their corpus resources.

5. Conclusion

Many small language communities find it difficult to source both linguistic and technical expertise from within their own community. Collaboration can help overcome these difficulties, and the exchange of ideas benefits both parties. Building up expertise has wide-ranging benefits, foremost amongst which are a greater confidence and pride in our languages, which can help in revitalization efforts.

The collaborators were initially drawn together by a shared linguistic heritage, but found that other commonalities included a determination to develop sustainable resources and empower their own communities through the use of language technologies.

Building on the success of the Gerlyver Kernewek, we foresee a long-term partnership, where capacity will be built up within Cornwall, and a younger generation of both Cornish linguists and computational experts will be able to undertake their own resource and tool development, and where both Wales and Cornwall can contribute together to wider international projects.

6. Acknowledgements

We wish to thank Cornwall Council for funding the project and for their continued support and encouragement. Special thanks are due to Mark Trevethan, their Cornish Language Officer, and Davydh Trethewey who both provided invaluable help. We wish also to acknowledge the hard work of members of the Akademi Kernewek dictionary and terminology panels and their contribution to the revitalization of the Cornish language.

7. Bibliographical References

Akademi Kernewek. (2018). The Cornish Dictionary / Gerlever Kernewek. Akademi Kernewek, Cornwall. https://www.cornishdictionary.org.uk/ [accessed 13 February 2020].

Almonaies, A. A., Cordy, J. R., and Dean T. R. (2010) Legacy System Evolution towards Service-Oriented Architecture. School of Computing, Queens University Kingston, Ontario.

Andrews, T. and Prys, G. (2011). The Maes T System and its Use in the Welsh-Medium Higher Education Terminology Project. In T. Gornostay & J. Vasil (editors.) Proceedings of CHAT 2011: Creation, Harmonization and Application of Terminology Resources. Riga, Latvia, pp 49-50.

Berger, K.C, Hernaiz, A.G., Baroni, P., Hicks, D., Kruse, E., Quochi, V, Russo I., Salonen T., Sarhimaa, A, Soria, C. (2018) Digital Language Survival Kit: The DLDP Recommendations to Improve Digital Vitality. DLDP.

Bock, A. and Bruch, B. (2008). An Outline of the Standard Written Form of Cornish. Cornish Language Partnership, Cornwall. http://kernowek.net/Specification_Final_Version.pdf [accessed 13 February 2020].

Ferdinand, S. (2013). Brief History of the Cornish language, its Revival and its Current Situation. *E-Keltoi. Vol. 2, 2.* December, pp 199-227.

Griffiths, B. and Jones, D.G. (1995). Geiriadur yr Academi: The Welsh Academy English-Welsh Dictionary. University of Wales Press, Cardiff.

Jones, D.B. and Cooper, S. (2016). *Building Intelligent Digitial Assistants for Speakers of a Lesser-Resourced Language.* In Claudia Soria et al (editors). Proceedings of the LREC 2016 Workshop "CCURL 2016 – Towards an Alliance for Digital Language Diversity". Portorož, Slovenia, May. European Language Resource Association (ELRA), pp 74-79.

Jones, D.B., Prys, G. and Prys, D. (2016). *Vocab: a dictionary plugin for websites. In Teresa Lynn et al (editors).* Proceeding of the Second Celtic Language Technology Workshop. TALN 2016. Paris, pp 93-99.

Lew. R. (2010). Online dictionaries of English. In Fuertes-Olivera, Pedro A. and Henning Bergenholtz (eds), E-Lexicography: The Internet, Digital Initiatives and Lexicography. London/New York: Continuum, p 230–250.

Llên Natur (n.d.). Y Bwyiadur. Llên Natur, Cymdeithas Edward Llwyd, Cymru. https://www.llennatur.cymru/Y-Bywiadur. [accessed 14 February 2020].

Office of National Statistics. (2012). Language in England and Wales : 2011.

openlt.org (n.d). A Manifesto for Open Language Technology. https://openlt.org/ [accessed 23 March 2020].

O'Neill, D. (2005). Rebuilding the Celtic Languages : Reversing Language Shift in the Celtic Countries. Y Lolfa. Talybont, p242.

Prys, D., Jones, D.B. and Prys, G. (2012). The Welsh National Terminology Portal. Bangor University, Bangor. http://termau.cymru/ [accessed 13 February 2020].

Prys, D., and Williams, I. (2019). A roundtable discussion to promote a strategic vision for Celtic Language Technologies. Bangor University, Bangor, pp 4-5. http://techiaith.bangor.ac.uk/wp-content/uploads/2019/08/A-roundtable-discussion-to-

---

[3] The Ap Geiriaduron is available in iOS and Android versions from the App Store and Google Play.

promote-a-strategic-vision-for-Celtic-Language-Technologies.pdf [accessed 323 march 2020].

Prys, M. and Jones, D.B. (2019). Embedding English to Welsh MT in a Private Company. In Teresa Lynn et al (editors). Proceeding of the Celtic Language Technology Workshop. European Association of Machine Translation. Dublin, Ireland, pp 41-47.

Tsunoda, T. (2013) Language Endangerment and Language Revitalization. Mouton de Gruyter, Berlin, p168.

Wallnau, K., Seacord, R. C., and Robert, J. (2000) A Survey of Legacy System Modernization Approaches. Software Engineering Institute, Carnegie Mellon University, Pittsburgh.

Welsh Government. (2017) Cymraeg 2050 : Welsh Language Strategy. Welsh Government. Cardiff.

Welsh Government. (2018). Welsh Language Technology Action Plan. Welsh Government. Cardiff.

Welsh Language Board. (2012). Geiriadur yr Academi : The Welsh Academy English-Welsh Dictionary Online. https://geiriaduracademi.org/ [accessed 13 February 2020].

Proceedings of the 1st Joint SLTU and CCURL Workshop (SLTU-CCURL 2020), pages 240–244
Language Resources and Evaluation Conference (LREC 2020), Marseille, 11–16 May 2020
© European Language Resources Association (ELRA), licensed under CC-BY-NC

Multiple Segmentations of Thai Sentences for Neural Machine Translation

Alberto Poncelas[1], Wichaya Pidchamook[2], Chao-Hong Liu[3], James Hadley[4], Andy Way[1]
[1]ADAPT Centre, School of Computing, Dublin City University, Ireland
[2]SALIS, Dublin City University, Ireland
[3]Iconic Translation Machines
[4]Trinity Centre for Literary and Cultural Translation, Trinity College Dublin, Ireland
{alberto.poncelas, andy.way}@adaptcentre.ie
ch.liu@acm.org, wichaya.pidchamook2@mail.dcu.ie, HADLEYJ@tcd.ie

Abstract

Thai is a low-resource language, so it is often the case that data is not available in sufficient quantities to train an Neural Machine Translation (NMT) model which perform to a high level of quality. In addition, the Thai script does not use white spaces to delimit the boundaries between words, which adds more complexity when building sequence to sequence models. In this work, we explore how to augment a set of English–Thai parallel data by replicating sentence-pairs with different word segmentation methods on Thai, as training data for NMT model training. Using different merge operations of Byte Pair Encoding, different segmentations of Thai sentences can be obtained. The experiments show that combining these datasets, performance is improved for NMT models trained with a dataset that has been split using a supervised splitting tool.

Keywords: Machine Translation, Word Segmentation, Thai Language

In Machine Translation (MT), low-resource languages are especially challenging as the amount of parallel data available to train models may not be enough to achieve high translation quality. One approach to mitigate this problem is to augment the training data with similar languages (Lakew et al., 2018) or artificially-generated text (Sennrich et al., 2016a; Poncelas et al., 2018b).

State-of-the-art Neural Machine Translation (NMT) models are based on the sequence-to-sequence framework (i.e. models are built using pairs of sequences as training data). Therefore, sentences are modeled as a sequence of tokens. As Thai is a *scriptio continua* language (where whitespaces are not used to indicate the boundaries between words) sentences need to be segmented in the preprocessing step in order to be converted into sequences of tokens.

The segmentation of sentences is a well-known problem in Natural Language Processing (NLP), Thai is no exception. How Thai sentences should be split[1] has been discussed at the linguistic level (Aroonmanakun, 2007) and different algorithms have been proposed (Haruechaiyasak et al., 2008) including dictionary-based and machine learning-based approaches.

In this work, we use the problem of segmentation to our advantage. We propose using an unsupervised training method such as Byte Pair Encoding (BPE) to obtain different versions of the same sentence with different segmentations (by using different merge operations).

This leads to different parallel sets (each with different segmentation on the Thai side). These sets can be combined to train NMT models and achieve better translation performance than using one segmentation strategy alone.

1. Combination of Segmented Texts

As the encoder-decoder framework deals with a sequence of tokens, a way to address the Thai language is to split the sentence into words (or tokens). We investigate three splitting strategies: (i) Character-based, using each character as token. This is the simplest approach as there is no need to identify the words; (ii) Supervised word-segmentation: using tokenizers which have been trained on supervised data such as the "Deepcut"[2] library (Kittinaradorn et al., 2018) (trained on the BEST corpus (Kosawat et al., 2009)); and (iii) Language-independent split: useing a language-independent algorithm for spliting such as BPE (Sennrich et al., 2016b). This last method splits the sentence based on the statistics of sequences of letters. Therefore the split is not necessarily word-based. BPE is executed as follows: Initially it considers each character as an independent token; then iteratively the most frequent subsequent pair of tokens x and y are merged into a single token xy. The process is executed iteratively until a given number of merge operation are completed.

Once the sentences of a parallel corpus have been split, they can be used as training data for an NMT engine. Among the three approaches, the supervised word-segmentation strategy is the one that might allow NMT to perform the best, as it encodes the information from the manually-segmented sentences. However, by changing the merge operation parameter of BPE, the set can be split in different ways. Accordingly, in this work we want to explore whether augmenting the training set with the same sentences (but split with BPE using different merge operations) can be beneficial for training an NMT model. By doing this, we artificially increase the vocabulary on the target side. This causes the number of translation candidates of source-side words to be extended, which has been shown to have a positive impact in other approaches such as in statistical

---

[1]In this work, we use interchangeably the term split or segmentation to refer to the process of dividing a word or a sentence into sub-units.

[2]https://github.com/rkcosmos/Deepcut

MT (Poncelas et al., 2016; Poncelas et al., 2017). In addition, we want to explore whether this approach can be followed to augment a dataset split using Deepcut to improve the performance of NMT models.

Note that in this work we are building models in the English-to-Thai direction. The datasets with different splits are only on the target side whereas we keep the same number of merge operations on the source side. The main reason for this is that using several splits on the source side would also mean that NMT models would be evaluated with different versions (different splits) of the test set, which would obviously affect the results.

2. Data and Model Configuration

The models are built in the English to Thai direction using OpenNMT-py (Klein et al., 2017). We keep the default settings of OpenNMT-py: 2-layer LSTM with 500 hidden units and a maximum vocabulary size of 50000 words for each language.

We use the Asian Language Treebank (ALT) Parallel Corpus (Riza et al., 2016) for training and evaluation. We split the corpus so we use 20K sentences for training and 106 sentences for development. We use Tatoeba (Tiedemann, 2012) for evaluating the models (173 sentences).

In order to evaluate the models we translate the test set and measure the quality of the translation using an automatic evaluation metric, which provides an estimation of how good the translation is by comparing it to a human-translated reference. As the evaluation is made in a Thai text (which does not contain n-grams, we use CHRF3 (Popovic, 2015) which is a character-level metric, instead of BLEU (Papineni et al., 2002), which is based on overlap of n-grams.

The English side is tokenized and truecased (applying the proper case of the words) and we apply BPE with 89500 operations (the default explored in Sennrich et al. (2016b)). For the Thai side we explore combinations of different approaches of sentence segmentation:

1. Character-level: Split the sentences character-wise, so each character is a token of the sequence (*character* dataset).

2. Deepcut: Split the sentences using the Deepcut tool.

3. Use BPE with different merge operations. In this work we explore with: 1000, 5000, 10000 and 20000 merge operations (*BPE 1000*, *BPE 5000*, *BPE 10000* and *BPE 20000* datasets, respectively). However, we propose as future work investigating the performance when using BPE with more merge operations.

In total there are six different datasets. Note that they contain the same unique sentences. We train NMT models using these datasets either independently or in combination. The combination is carried out by appending different datasets. In particular we use *character*, *Deepcut* or *BPE 1000* datasets and then accumulatively add *BPE 1000*, *BPE 5000*, *BPE 10000* and *BPE 20000* datasets.

dataset	CHRF3
Deepcut	47.90
character	20.70
BPE 1000	39.88
BPE 5000	45.49
BPE 10000	41.75
BPE 20000	38.77

Table 1: Performance of the NMT model trained with data using different methods for word segmentation on the target-side.

3. Experimental Results

First, we evaluate the performance of the models when different merge operations are used on the Thai side. The performance of the model, evaluated using CHRF3 are presented in Table 1. In the table, each row shows the results (the evaluation of the translation of the test set) of an NMT model built with the training set split following one of the thee chosen approaches. For example, the first row *Deepcut* present the results when the model is built with the set after being split using the Deepcut tool, and in the row *BPE 1000* if the dataset is split with BPE using 1,000 merge operations.

As expected, we see in the table that the best results are obtained when using the Deepcut tool (*Deepcut* row), which splits Thai words grammatically.

Regarding the models in which BPE has been used, we see in Table 1 that the best performance is achieved when 5000 merge operations is used (*BPE 5000* row).

When too many merge operations are performed there is the risk of merging characters of different words into a single token, so the score decreases.

By contrast, if there are too few merge operations, the resulting text is closer to character-split which, as we can see in the *character* row, leads to the worst results.

3.1. Combination of Datasets with Unsupervised Split

dataset	CHRF3
character	20.70
+ 1000	**38.23**
+ 5000	**45.63**
+ 10000	**49.93**
+ 20000	**52.17**
BPE 1000	39.88
+ 5000	**49.54**
+ 10000	**52.33**
+ 20000	**53.45**

Table 2: Performance of the NMT model trained with data combining different unsupervised methods for word segmentation on the target-side. Numbers in bold indicate statistical significant improvement at p=0.01.

The main focus of this paper is to study the impact on the performance when several training sets with different splits are gathered together. We show the results in Table 2. Note that only the training set has been augmented, the development and test set remains the same for all experiments. In the table, each subtable presents the results when the sets are appended. For example, in the first subtable the row *character* indicates the performance of the model trained with the data split by character (the same as in Table 1). The following row, *+1000*, shows the score of the model trained with character-wise split and that split with BPE using 1000 merge operations (so there are two instances of each source sentence). The last row of the subtable (*+20000*) indicates the performance of the model trained with the five datasets concatenated (five instances of each source sentence).

In the table we observe that combining datasets with different segmentations is beneficial. In each subtable of Table 2 we see that the score goes up when we add more datasets with different splits. For example, the performance of the model using data split in a character-wise achieves a score of only 20.70 (first subtable). When we concatenate the same dataset but split using 1000 merge operations, the score increases to 38.23 (85% improvement) and we see that the score increases as we add sentences with different splits. This effect is observed for all three subtables.

The results also show that the lowest scores are achieved in those datasets in which a character-wise split fashion is performed. For example, the performance when using the dataset split with BPE using 1000 operations is 39.88 (*BPE 1000* row in Table 2), whereas when used in combination with character-split set (*+1000* row in the first subtable of Table 2) the score is 38.23. Another indication that character-wise splitting hurts performance is the comparison between the subtables of Table 2. If we compare the rows *+1000*, *+5000*, *+10000* and *+20000* of each subtable, the lower scores are seen in the first subtable

Another research question we want to answer is whether using a combination of splits using BPE can outperform the model trained with a language-independent tool like Deepcut. We see that in the second subtable of Table 2 all of the the combination of BPE-split datasets (*+5000*, *+10000* and *+20000* rows) exceed the 47.90 score achieved by using Deepcut alone.

3.2. Augmenting the Dataset Split with Deepcut

dataset	CHRF3
Deepcut	47.90
+ 1000	47.00
+ 5000	**51.25**
+ 10000	**54.94**
+ 20000	**54.96**

Table 3: Performance of combination of dataset with different split using *Deepcut*. Numbers in bold indicate statistical significant improvement at p=0.01.

As combining different splits can increase the performance of the model, does it also help when used in combination with Deepcut?

In Table 3 we present the results when the dataset split using Deepcut is augmented with datasets split with different

merge operations using BPE. We see that initially, adding the set split with BPE using 1,000 merge operation (*+1000* row) causes the performance to drop slightly. Nonetheless, the performance increases when more data are added (i.e. *+5000*, *+10000*, *+20000* rows). Moreover, it even outperforms the model trained with the Deepcut-split dataset alone.

3.3. Analysis

In Table 4 we show some examples of the output. For each sentence we present the translations produced by the NMT model trained on *Deepcut*, *BPE 20000* and *Deepcut BPE 20000*. We do not include the outputs of the NMT models trained on the *character* dataset as all the translation consisted of the same, meaningless, sequence of characters. In the third column of the table we show the translation of the output of the NMT system after it has been postedited by removing characters (in gray) or replaced (in blue).

In the first sub-table we present how the sentence "the train is here" (meaning that the train is here because it has arrived) has been translated by different models. On the one hand, we see in the *Deepcut* row that the model has not produced an accurate translation. On the other hand, the models trained with data containing sentences of different segmentations (i.e. *BPE 20000* and *Deepcut BPE 20000*) achieve a more accurate translation. Nevertheless, the output is not a perfect translation as it indicates where the train is located instead of expressing that it has arrived.

In the following subtables we observe a similar effect. The models trained with the *Deepcut* dataset produced a translation that is either inaccurate or makes no sense. However, the models trained on *BPE 20000* or *Deepcut BPE 20000* produce a translation closer to the input after some postediting (i.e. removing the characters in gray).

4. Related Work

There are several studies aiming to address the problem of splitting words in Thai. One of the first approaches to segmenting is the *longest-matching* method (Poowarawan, 1986), consisting of identifying the longest sequence of characters that match a word in the dictionary. Another approach is *maximal-matching* method (Sornlertlamvanich, 1993), which consists of generating all possible segmentations and retrieving those containing the smallest amount of words.

Haruechaiyasak and Kongyoung (2009) used conditional random fields to classify each character as either *word-beginning* or *intra-word*. Nararatwong et al. (2018) proposed an improvement to this approach by adding information from POS tags.

The use of several segmentations has also been proposed by Kudo (2018), in which he tries to integrate candidates from different segmentations. This technique has applications in a number of topics such as word-alignment (Xi et al., 2011) or language modeling (Seng et al., 2009; Abate et al., 2010).

The use of multiple instances in the training data, where only one side is modified, has been used by Poncelas et al. (2019), who showed that using multiple instances of the

Dataset	Output	
Source Sentence	the train is here.	
Reference	รถไฟมาแล้ว	
Deepcut	รถไฟนี้เป็นสายพันธุ์	This train is a breed.
BPE 20000	รถไฟอยู่ที่นี่อยู่ที่นี่ด้วย	The train is located here.
Deepcut + BPE 20000	รถไฟนี้อยู่นี่	This train is located here.
Source Sentence	I have a new bicycle.	
Reference	ฉันมีจักรยานใหม่	
Deepcut	ผมได้ทำการทดลองใหม่	I made a new experiment.
BPE 20000	ผมมีรถบรรทุกคนใหม่ๆ	I have a new truck.
Deepcut + BPE 20000	ผมมีรถจักรยานชุดใหม่ขึ้นมาแล้ว	I have a new set of bicycles.
Source Sentence	she does not have many friends in Kyoto.	
Reference	เธอไม่ค่อยมีเพื่อนมากนักที่เกียวโต	
Deepcut	เธอยังไม่มีใครได้รับบาดเจ็บ	She still doesn't have anyone injured.
BPE 20000	เธอไม่ได้มีเพื่อนหลายๆในเกียวโตเกียว	She does not have many friends in Kyoto.
Deepcut + BPE 20000	เธอไม่มีเพื่อนร่วมหลายคนในเกียวโต	She does not have many friends in Kyoto.

Table 4: Examples of translations using different splits

same target sentences, with different source-sides (generated by different MT engines) leads to better results than using a single instance of each sentence.

5. Conclusions and Future Work

In this work we have explored whether the duplication of training sentences with different splits is useful to build NMT models with improved performance. The experiments show that the combination of different splits on the target side does improve NMT models involving a low-resource language such as Thai.

The experiments also reveal that combining the same dataset using different merge operations of BPE not only improves the model trained on the dataset using the single configuration (regardless of the number of merge operations), but also the model trained on data that has been split using a tool trained on supervised data such as Deepcut.

In the future, we plan to conduct more fine-grained experiments to explore which configurations of BPE perform better. For example, would the combination of *BPE 10000* and *BPE 20000* (those with the highest number of operations explored) perform better than the model's original setup? And what would the results be if only *BPE 1000* and *BPE 20000* (those with the lowest and highest number of operation) are combined?

Furthermore, as all the experiments with different splits have been applied on the target side, we plan to investigate NMT models when Thai is on the source side. Similarly, we will also investigate whether these improvements will be achieved using other languages.

Another variation we are interested in exploring is not to replicate all the sentences but to use data-selection algorithms to find a subset of sentences that may boost the performance of the models trained on the subset (Poncelas et al., 2018a; Poncelas et al., 2018c).

Finally, we would like to investigate the applicability of the method of employing several segmentations to other NLP tasks such as text classification (Apichai et al., 2019; Wangpoonsarp et al., 2019).

6. Acknowledgements

The QuantiQual Project, generously funded by the Irish Research Council's COALESCE scheme (COALESCE/2019/117).

This research has been supported by the ADAPT Centre for Digital Content Technology which is funded under the SFI Research Centres Programme (Grant 13/RC/2106).

7. Bibliographical References

Abate, S. T., Besacier, L., and Seng, S. (2010). Boosting n-gram coverage for unsegmented languages using multiple text segmentation approach. In *23rd International Conference on Computational Linguistics*, pages 1–7, Beijing, China.

Apichai, C., Chan, K., and Suzuki, Y. (2019). Classifying short text in social media for extracting valuable ideas. In *20th International Conference on Computational Linguistics and Intelligent Text Processing*, La Rochelle, France.

Aroonmanakun, W. (2007). Thoughts on word and sentence segmentation in thai. In *Proceedings of the Seventh Symposium on Natural language Processing*, pages 85–90, Pattaya, Thailand.

Haruechaiyasak, C. and Kongyoung, S. (2009). Tlex: Thai lexeme analyser based on the conditional random fields. In *Proceedings of 8th International Symposium on Natural Language Processing*, Bangkok, Thailand.

Haruechaiyasak, C., Kongyoung, S., and Dailey, M. (2008). A comparative study on Thai word segmentation approaches. In *2008 5th International Conference on Electrical Engineering/Electronics, Computer,*

Telecommunications and Information Technology, volume 1, pages 125–128.

Kittinaradorn, R., Chaovavanich, K., Achakulvisut, T., and Kaewkasi, C. (2018). A Thai word tokenization library using deep neural network.

Klein, G., Kim, Y., Deng, Y., Senellart, J., and Rush, A. M. (2017). Opennmt: Open-source toolkit for neural machine translation. In *Proceedings of the 55th Annual Meeting of the Association for Computational Linguistics-System Demonstrations*, pages 67–72, Vancouver, Canada.

Kosawat, K., Boriboon, M., Chootrakool, P., Chotimongkol, A., Klaithin, S., Kongyoung, S., Kriengket, K., Phaholphinyo, S., Purodakananda, S., Thanakulwarapas, T., et al. (2009). BEST 2009: Thai word segmentation software contest. In *2009 Eighth International Symposium on Natural Language Processing*, pages 83–88, Bangkok, Thailand.

Kudo, T. (2018). Subword regularization: Improving neural network translation models with multiple subword candidates. In *Proceedings of the 56th Annual Meeting of the Association for Computational Linguistics (Volume 1: Long Papers)*, pages 66–75, Melbourne, Australia.

Lakew, S. M., Erofeeva, A., and Federico, M. (2018). Neural machine translation into language varieties. In *Proceedings of the Third Conference on Machine Translation: Research Papers*, pages 156–164, Brussels, Belgium.

Nararatwong, R., Kertkeidkachorn, N., Cooharojananone, N., and Okada, H. (2018). Improving thai word and sentence segmentation using linguistic knowledge. *IEICE TRANSACTIONS on Information and Systems*, 101(12):3218–3225.

Papineni, K., Roukos, S., Ward, T., and Zhu, W.-J. (2002). Bleu: a method for automatic evaluation of machine translation. In *Proceedings of 40th Annual Meeting of the Association for Computational Linguistics*, pages 311–318, Philadelphia, Pennsylvania, USA.

Poncelas, A., Way, A., and Toral, A. (2016). Extending feature decay algorithms using alignment entropy. In *International Workshop on Future and Emerging Trends in Language Technology*, pages 170–182, Seville, Spain.

Poncelas, A., de Buy Wenniger, G. M., and Way, A. (2017). Applying n-gram alignment entropy to improve feature decay algorithms. *The Prague Bulletin of Mathematical Linguistics*, 108(1):245–256.

Poncelas, A., de Buy Wenniger, G. M., and Way, A. (2018a). Data selection with feature decay algorithms using an approximated target side. In *15th International Workshop on Spoken Language Translation (IWSLT 2018)*, pages 173–180, Bruges, Belgium.

Poncelas, A., Shterionov, D., Way, A., de Buy Wenniger, G. M., and Passban, P. (2018b). Investigating backtranslation in neural machine translation. In *21st Annual Conference of the European Association for Machine Translation*, pages 249–258, Alacant, Spain.

Poncelas, A., Way, A., and Sarasola, K. (2018c). The ADAPT system description for the IWSLT 2018 Basque to English translation task. In *15th International Workshop on Spoken Language Translation*, pages 76–82, Bruges, Belgium.

Poncelas, A., Popovic, M., Shterionov, D., de Buy Wenniger, G. M., and Way, A. (2019). Combining SMT and NMT back-translated data for efficient NMT. In *Proceedings of Recent Advances in Natural Language Processing (RANLP)*, pages 922–931, Varna, Bulgaria.

Poowarawan, Y. (1986). Dictionary-based thai syllable separation. In *Proc. Ninth Electronics Engineering Conference (EECON-86)*, pages 409–418, Bangkok, Thailand.

Popovic, M. (2015). chrF: character n-gram F-score for automatic MT evaluation. In *Proceedings of the Tenth Workshop on Statistical Machine Translation*, pages 392–395, Lisbon, Portugal.

Riza, H., Purwoadi, M., Uliniansyah, T., Ti, A. A., Aljunied, S. M., Mai, L. C., Thang, V. T., Thai, N. P., Chea, V., Sam, S., et al. (2016). Introduction of the asian language treebank. In *2016 Conference of The Oriental Chapter of International Committee for Coordination and Standardization of Speech Databases and Assessment Techniques (O-COCOSDA)*, pages 1–6.

Seng, S., Besacier, L., Bigi, B., and Castelli, E. (2009). Multiple text segmentation for statistical language modeling. In *10th Annual Conference of the International Speech Communication Association (Interspeech)*, pages 2663–2666, Brighton, United Kingdom.

Sennrich, R., Haddow, B., and Birch, A. (2016a). Improving neural machine translation models with monolingual data. In *Proceedings of the 54th Annual Meeting of the Association for Computational Linguistics (Volume 1: Long Papers)*, pages 86–96, Berlin, Germany.

Sennrich, R., Haddow, B., and Birch, A. (2016b). Neural machine translation of rare words with subword units. In *Proceedings of the 54th Annual Meeting of the Association for Computational Linguistics (Volume 1: Long Papers)*, pages 1715–1725, Berlin, Germany.

Sornlertlamvanich, V. (1993). Word segmentation for thai in machine translation system. *Machine Translation*, pages 556–561.

Tiedemann, J. (2012). Parallel data, tools and interfaces in opus. In *Proceedings of the Eighth International conference on on Language Resources and Evaluation (LREC 2012)*, pages 2214–2218, Istanbul, Turkey.

Wangpoonsarp, A., Shimura, K., and Fukumoto, F. (2019). Acquisition of domain-specific senses and its extrinsic evaluation through text categorization. In *20th International Conference on Computational Linguistics and Intelligent Text Processing*, La Rochelle, France.

Xi, N., Tang, G., Li, B., and Zhao, Y. (2011). Word alignment combination over multiple word segmentation. In *Proceedings of the ACL 2011 Student Session*, pages 1–5, Portland, USA.

Proceedings of the 1st Joint SLTU and CCURL Workshop (SLTU-CCURL 2020), pages 245–249
Language Resources and Evaluation Conference (LREC 2020), Marseille, 11–16 May 2020
© European Language Resources Association (ELRA), licensed under CC-BY-NC

Automatic Extraction of Verb Paradigms in Regional Languages:
the case of the Linguistic Crescent varieties

Elena Knyazeva[1], Gilles Adda[1], Philippe Boula de Mareüil[1],
Maximilien Guérin[2], Nicolas Quint[2]

[1] Université Paris-Saclay, CNRS, LIMSI, Orsay, France
[2] LLACAN - UMR 8135 (CNRS/INALCO/USPC) Villejuif, France
{knyazeva, gadda, Mareuil}@limsi.fr
{maximilien.guerin, nicolas.quint}@cnrs.fr

Abstract

Language documentation is crucial for endangered varieties all over the world. Verb conjugation is a key aspect of this documentation for Romance varieties such as those spoken in central France, in the area of the Linguistic Crescent, which extends overs significant portions of the old provinces of Marche and Bourbonnais. We present a first methodological experiment using automatic speech processing tools for the extraction of verbal paradigms collected and recorded during fieldworks sessions made *in situ*. In order to prove the feasibility of the approach, we test it with different protocols, on good quality data, and we offer possible ways of extension for this research.

Keywords: language documentation, speech processing, dialectology, Linguistic Crescent, Romance languages

1. Introduction

An important and costly step in the process of language documentation is the transcription (total or partial transcripts) of speech data collected in the field. Several projects adopt a methodology involving the use of speech transcription systems (Adda et al. 2016; Michaud et al. 2018); in such an approach, it is necessary to adapt the systems so that they can transcribe (at least phonetically) speech collected during fieldwork. However, within the data gathered, some have either an approximate transcription (e.g. in the case of reading), or more or less precise information on its content, for example in the case of verb conjugations: the linguist proposes a verb, and the informant must give all the possible inflections, most often in a fixed order for tenses and persons. The question addressed in this paper is to explore whether it is possible to use a transcription system developed for a given language (here French) without precise adaptation of acoustic models, in order to produce both segmentation and transcription of verbal paradigms of a closely related language (here several Romance varieties spoken in central France), and the conditions under which the system will or will not require post-processing.

Verb conjugation is a major difficulty of the grammar of Romance languages. This holds true for the varieties spoken in the centre of France, in a transition area between *Oïl* and *Oc* varieties called *Croissant* 'Crescent', named after Ronjat (1913) because of its geographical shape, see Figure 1). Knowing that there are about 40 distinct types of verb inflections for a given local Crescent variety, to be multiplied by about 60 forms for different tenses, moods and persons, the descriptivist has to deal with at least 40×60 = 2,400 different verbal inflection for each local variety. Speech processing can facilitate and speed up the analysis of huge amounts of data collected in the field.

Within the framework of an ongoing project described in

Section 2, many fieldwork sessions were done with native speakers in order to record these highly endangered varieties. In this paper, we will present automatic segmentation methods of recordings collected *in situ* in the linguistic Crescent, containing both Crescent and French data in order to extract the targeted content for linguistic studies, namely verb paradigms. The data consist of short recordings (typically less than one minute of speech) where the surveyed speaker conjugates a verb for all possible subjects in a given tense and mood.

In the ideal case, the classical order is followed: 1SG, 2SG, 3SG-M, 3SG-F, 1PL, 2PL, 3PL-M, 3PL-F.[1] An example, much less straightforward than in English (a poorly inflected language), is, in the commune of Dompierre-les-Églises (Guérin 2019:183): [i sori] 'I would know', [tə sorjɑ] 'you (SG) would know', [u sori] 'he would know', [al sori] 'she would know', [nə sorjɑ̃] 'we would know', [u sorjɛ] 'you (PL) would know', [i sorjɑ̃] 'they (M) would know', [al sorjɑ̃] 'they (F) would know'. The actual recordings however, are quite different: they may contain French (from the investigator), digressions (on the part of the interviewee, mainly in French), hesitations, errors (corrected or not), repetitions, a different order from the classical order, gaps, etc. The challenge is therefore to extract what interests us in the presence of these various types of noise and artefact. In the following, solutions are proposed, depending on whether the pronunciation of the searched paradigm is known (through previous descriptive work) or not, in which case we base ourselves on the paradigms already available for neighboring survey points. The two scenarios will be considered successively in Section 3 and will be evaluated in Section 4. Future

---

[1] List of abbreviations used in this paper: AZER = Azerables, CLFR = Cellefrouin, COND = conditional, F = feminine, FUT = future, HYP = hypothesis, M = masculine, PL = plural, SG = singular.

work will be envisioned in Section 5.

2. Background

Field work was carried out in about 30 survey points (or local varieties), 16 of which will be considered here: Archignat, Azerables, Bonnat, Chaillac, Châteauponsac, Cellefrouin, Dompierre-les-Églises, Dunet, Jouac, La Châtre-Langlin, Luchapt, Naves, Oradour-Saint-Genest, Prissac, Saint-Léger-Magnazeix, Saint-Sornin-Leulac (see Figure 1). All the informants are elderly people (mean age > 70) who are also fully proficient in French. With the exception of Naves and Cellefrouin, we have 2 to 5 informants per survey point. Regarding pronunciation, phonological systems may vary from one survey point to another, but in most cases the phonetic realisations hardly differ from (regional) French.[2]

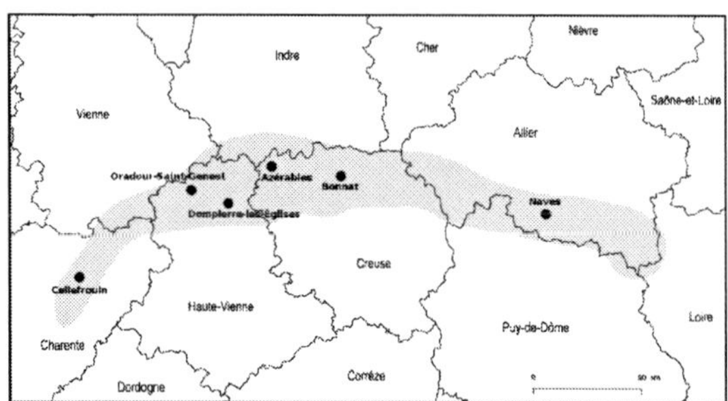

Figure 1: Map of the linguistic Crescent with the localisation of some of the surveyed varieties.

From a dialectological point of view, most of the 16 varieties considered here belong to two different groupings: (1) Archignat and Naves are *Bourbonnais* (i.e. eastern Crescent) varieties, showing closer affinities with Auvergnat Occitan; (2) most of the remaining points belong to the *Marchois* (i.e. western Crescent) group, which shows closer affinities with Limousin Occitan. In addition to Bourbonnais and Marchois, some survey points lying outside but in the close periphery of the Crescent have been taken into account in order to serve as control information. Among our 16-point sample, Châteauponsac represents a Limousin Occitan variety, spoken immediately South to the Crescent, while Dunet and Prissac represent Poitevin-Saintongeais (*Oïl*) varieties spoken immediately North to the Crescent.

All these varieties are being documented and described within the scope of two projects, namely *Les parlers du Croissant*[3] and VC2 - *Central Gallo-Romance: linguistics and ecology of a transitional zone*,[4] respectively funded by the French ANR (National Research Agency) and the

Labex EFL. These two projects regroup a team of researchers — including the authors of the present paper — working in different branches of language sciences and studying the Crescent varieties within various approaches and frameworks.

The descriptivist linguists working in these projects have developed standard questionnaires[5] aiming at providing a set of comparable data for as many varieties as possible. The verbal paradigms considered in this paper have been collected resorting mainly to one of these questionnaires (Brun-Trigaud, Guérin & Quint, 2018) as well as to several monographs devoted to Crescent verbs (e.g. Guérin, 2019; Lavalade, 1987; Quint, 1991; 1996). At least 24 different verbs were administered to the informants for each surveyed variety: regular and irregular patterns (including asyllabic models such as /kwɑ(:)/ 'brood' or /(l)j ɑ(:)/ 'tie together (oxen)'[6]) as well as auxiliaries (the local equivalents of French *avoir* 'have' and *être* 'be'). Each verb paradigm was audio-recorded with a separate file for every tense or mood (see Section 1 above). Note that, in most cases, only one informant was recorded for each variety: as a matter of fact, the Crescent varieties are now on the verge of extinction and it is often not possible to find several active speakers for a given survey point.

3. Methodology

Under the assumption that the inventory of the dialect's phonemes is included in that of French, extracting verb forms pronounced in a Crescent variety could be defined as a task similar to searching for French words. However, adaptations of this technique were felt necessary. A system was consequently implemented, combining two recipes: automatic speech recognition (ASR) in French, provided by a public `git` repository and word spotting provided by the Kaldi distribution (Povey et al., 2011: `egs/babel/s5b/`).

The objective of ASR is to transcribe an audio stream or, more generally, to transform it into a lattice presenting the most likely pronunciation variants in a compact form. Three components are included:

- acoustic models (SGMMs learned from data collected within the framework of the LibriVox project: 13,620 sentences corresponding to 42 hours of read literary works);

---

[2] Some Southern Crescent varieties may exhibit phoneme inventories which happen to be much more at variance with French, including diphthongs such as /aᵉ, aw/ and palatal plosives /c, ɟ/. However, such phonemes are absent from most of the varieties studied herein — or may be equated to French units for an automatic processing.

[3] http://parlersducroissant.huma-num.fr/projet.html

[4] http://www.labex-efl.com/wordpress/2020/01/15/vc2central-gallo-romance-linguistics-and-ecology-of-a-transitional-zone/?lang=en

[5] http://parlersducroissant.huma-num.fr/participer.html

[6] The so-called asyllabic pattern is observed for verbs whose lexical root does not include any vocalic element and therefore cannot be stressed as such. For instance, in most Crescent varieties /kwɑ(:)/ 'brood' has an asyllabic root /kw/, contrasting with the regular verb /ʃɑ'tɑ(:)/, whose root /ʃɑt/ is syllabic and includes a vocalic element /ɑ̃/. When the stress is supposed to lay on the root in a given paradigm (e.g. 1SG present indicative), most syllabic roots remain unchanged (e.g. /i 'ʃɑt/ 'I sing') while asyllabic roots necessarily undergo a change in order to host the stress (e.g. /i 'ku/~/i 'kwe/~/i 'kwø/… 'I brood' according to the variety considered). For more details, see Guérin (2019: 127, 129, 149-150), Quint (forthcoming).

- a language model, trained on the text of the same corpus using the IRST Language Modeling Toolkit (Federico et al., 2008);
- a French pronunciation dictionary provided in the `git` repository (including variants).

The recognition lattices, once they are obtained, are indexed in order to search for keywords. The result of the procedure is a list of hypotheses, each one containing the detected keyword, its start and end point in frames (one frame corresponding to 10 milliseconds), and the associated confidence score, which is the opposite of the posterior probability logarithm (see the examples below). Choosing the hypotheses is the final step of recognition. For all scenarios, French acoustic models are used.

3.1 Scenario 1: the Paradigm is Known

As the paradigm is known, we can supplement the language model and the pronunciation dictionary with this information. The language model is a mere unigram containing the French words as well as the searched verb paradigms, with constant weights (empirically set at 100, 1,000 or 10,000 times the weights of French words, depending on the dataset). The French pronunciation dictionary is supplemented with the searched paradigms, amalgamated with the associated subject personal pronouns, to avoid further confusions. For instance, for the verb *dire* 'say' in the Crescent variety of Cellefrouin (conditional present, singular subject), we added the following entries with their respective pronunciations in the pronunciation dictionary:

- dire-CLFR-COND-1SG   idiri
- dire-CLFR-COND-2SG   tidiri
- dire-CLFR-COND-3SG-M   udiri
- dire-CLFR-COND-3SG-F   adiri

An example of output of the system, for the pronunciation of 6 forms[7] of this verb in the conditional present, is as follows:

```
dire-CLFR-COND-1SG 197 254 0.0
dire-CLFR-COND-2SG 320 395 0.0
dire-CLFR-COND-3SG-F 473 550 0.0
dire-CLFR-COND-1PL 571 648 0.0
dire-CLFR-COND-2PL 678 750 0.0
dire-CLFR-COND-3PL-F 800 851 0.0
```

This example is almost an ideal case, because all paradigms were perfectly detected without any ambiguity. Yet, in other cases, we may have several hypotheses for the same form, as in the following example for the verb *voir* 'see' in the Crescent variety of Naves when inflected in the future tense:

```
voir-NAVES-FUT-1SG 95 169 0.0
voir-NAVES-FUT-2SG 217 302 0.0
voir-NAVES-FUT-3SG-M 324 407 0.0
voir-NAVES-FUT-3SG-F 451 538 3.89
voir-NAVES-FUT-3PL-F 451 544 0.02
voir-NAVES-FUT-1PL 565 648 0.0
voir-NAVES-FUT-2PL 695 783 0.0
voir-NAVES-FUT-1PL 825 913 0.0
voir-NAVES-FUT-3PL-M 957 1044 0.0
voir-NAVES-FUT-3PL-F 1082 1161 0.0
```

There may be three possible sources for these multiple hypotheses: (1) a form is repeated several times, (2) some forms are phonetically similar or identical to each other; (3) for some reason the speech recognition system failed to make accurate detections. To choose among these hypotheses, the confidence score could help us make a correct choice: for instance, the second 3PL-F form (from 1082 to 1161 frame) features a better confidence score (0.0 vs. 0.02). However, this is not always sufficient. In the previous example, the knowledge of the paradigm order allows us to choose the correct 1PL form, given that the two hypotheses have the same confidence score: the first hypothesis (from 565 to 648) is the only one correct with regard to the order, while the second hypothesis (from 825 to 913) results from a confusion with an alternative pronunciation for the 2PL form.

More generally, when selecting from various hypotheses, we added the following two structural constraints. (1) The conjugation is complete: if the 8 forms are not present (the feminine forms are quite often neglected, for instance[8]), this should be specified in a text file associated with the audio. (2) The remaining forms are pronounced in the classical order. These constraints, which are verified in the majority of high-quality recordings significantly contribute to improve the results, as exemplified above.

Technically, for each paradigm, a list of hypotheses with a confidence score greater than a given threshold is built. Then, these hypotheses are organised in a research lattice, where each path leading from the initial state to the final state consists of the hypotheses for the searched conjugation sequences. Only hypotheses compatible with the structural constraints are considered. Finally, the shortest path in this lattice is calculated, which enables the system to determine the best sequence of hypotheses.

3.2 Scenario 2: the Paradigm is Unknown

Scenario 2 represents a difficult task, namely when the verb paradigm of a given local variety is unknown. Yet, work done in nearby varieties may help to segment recordings from a new variety. The excerpt reported in Table 1 below shows that some forms may be repeated from one variety to another.

---

[7] In the Cellefrouin recordings, the speaker systematically omits 3SG-M and 3PL-M forms: therefore, the output contains only 6 persons.

[8] See however the previous note for an opposite case in which the masculine forms are omitted.

Cellefrouin	Dompierre-les-Églises	Oradour-Saint-Genest	Bonnat
i diri	i diri	i diri	i diri
ty diri	tə dirjɑ	tə diri	tə dirjɑ
u/a diri	u/al diri	ø/al diri	u/al diri
nə dirjã	nə dirjã	nə dirjã	nə dirjɛ̃
və dirje	u dirjɛ	u dirjɛ	u dirje
i/a dirjã	i/al dirjã	i/al dirjã	u/al dirjɛ̃

Table 1: Excerpt of known verb paradigms from four local varieties of the Linguistic Crescent.

Technically, for a new local variety (e.g. Azerables), a pronunciation dictionary is completed by combining the personal pronouns specific to this variety (e.g. *i, ti, u, al, n(ə), (v)u, i, al*) with the different verb forms of the surroundings.

- dire-AZER-HYP-COND-1SG idiri
- dire-AZER-HYP-COND-2SG tidiri tidirjɑ
- dire-AZER-HYP-COND-3SG-M udiri
- dire-AZER-HYP-COND-3SG-F aldiri
- dire-AZER-HYP-COND-1PL nədirjã nədirjɛ̃
- dire-AZER-HYP-COND-2PL vudirje vudirjɛ
- dire-AZER-HYP-COND-3PL-M idirjã idirjɛ̃
- dire-AZER-HYP-COND-3PL-F aldirjã aldirjɛ̃

This approach presupposes a certain proximity between the different points, which can lead to errors. For instance, Naves (one of our two only survey points in Bourbonnais, in the East of the Linguistic Crescent), does not have many closely related varieties, as the majority of our sample comprises Marchois varieties (the Western part of the domain, see Section 2 above). This may result in a lower detection quality.

4. Evaluation

The results achieved were manually evaluated on two sets of data by two experts of the corresponding areas. The first one was collected at Azerables; 15 recordings were selected, each containing the 8 persons of the present indicative of different verbs.[9] The pronunciations of these paradigms were approximated by the known pronunciations of the other local varieties spoken in the same region (the set of transcribed varieties reported in Section 2). These data are used in the first evaluation protocol.

The second set of data was collected in Naves. In a similar way, we selected 15 recordings containing the 8 persons of the present indicative of different verbs.[10] As Naves is part of the set of transcribed local varieties, we designed two protocols with this second set of data: for the first one the exact pronunciation is known, while for the second one it is approximated as in the case of Azerables (for this reason, Naves was excluded from the set of varieties used in order to approximate the pronunciations of Naves). Table 2 summarises the three evaluation protocols.

protocol	place	pronunciations
1	Azerables	approximate
2	Naves	exact
3	Naves	approximate

Table 2: The different evaluation protocols.

The quality of the data collected for Azerables is comparable to that of Naves: both provide clean data where all forms[11] are pronounced properly, in the classical order, with few hesitations and unnecessary words.

The results are shown in Table 3. Regarding the correctly recognised paradigms, some happen to be segmented erroneously. The boundary problem may be addressed with appropriate post-processing; detections with imperfect boundaries are also an aid to manual processing by reducing the time required to extract a paradigm.

protocol	# of pronounced paradigms	# and % of paradigms correctly segmented	# and % of paradigms correctly recognised
1	118	80 (67.8%)	101 (85.6%)
2	120	112 (93.3%)	117 (97.5%)
3	120	65 (54.2%)	90 (75.0%)

Table 3: Results of the manual evaluation: (from left to right) the protocol, the total number of paradigms present in the processed recordings, the number and percentage of paradigms segmented correctly, as well as the number and percentage of paradigms which are recognised correctly but whose boundaries may be misplaced.

Here are some remarks regarding these results:

- By comparing the two protocols with approximate pronunciations (1 and 3), we can conclude that the results for Azerables (protocol 1) are better than for Naves (protocol 3). This can be explained by the fact that in the set of transcribed varieties, there are many localities whose varieties are similar to Azerables. Naves, on the other hand, is an atypical example (it is one of the two eastern Crescent varieties contemplated in this study[12]), so its pronunciations are less well approximated.
- By comparing the two protocols of Naves (2 and 3), we notice that knowing the exact paradigm (protocol 2) helps recognition a lot. The effect is further amplified by the fact that, as explained previously, pronunciation approximations for Naves are of poor quality.

---

[9] The first set consists of the following verbs: *acheter* 'buy', *aller* 'go', *avoir* 'have', *blanchir* 'whiten', *chanter* 'sing', *couver* 'brood', *devoir* 'have to', *dire* 'say', *être* 'be', *partir* 'leave', *pouvoir* 'be able to', *prendre* 'take', *savoir* 'know', *venir* 'come', *vouloir* 'want'.

[10] The second set consists of the following verbs: *aller* 'go', *avoir* 'have', *couver* 'brood', *faire* 'do', *lier* 'tie together (oxen)', *partir* 'go away', *pouvoir* 'be able to', *prendre* 'take', *savoir* 'know', *tenir* 'hold', *vendre* 'sell', *venir* 'come', *voir* 'see', *vouloir* 'want'.

---

[11] With a few exceptions (2 paradigms are missing in the Azerables set).

[12] The other one is Archignat, see Section 2 above.

- Finally, a comparison of the last two columns shows that boundary errors are relatively frequent, especially when the pronunciations are of lower quality. In the case of exact pronunciations, we find less than 5% of erroneous boundaries, while this rate rises up to over 15% in the case of better quality approximations (Azerables) and to more than 20% in the case of poorer quality approximations (Naves).

5. Conclusion and Future Work

In summary, we proposed a method for automatically extracting verb paradigms from audio recordings in Romance varieties spoken in France, in the area of the Linguistic Crescent. The searched pronunciations may be known a priori, in which case classical techniques can be improved by taking into account the particular structure of the data. When the verb paradigm is not known a priori, we may benefit from the knowledge of the conjugation in nearby survey points, in which case the quality of the results depends on the degree of similarity of the pronunciations of the varieties that are contemplated.

We can further relax the structural constraint when forms are missing or when the conjugation is not in the classical order. Future work will also combine speaker identification and speech recognition. Indeed, the information we are looking for comes from a native speaker of a given Crescent variety, but the system is sometimes disturbed by the interviewer who can repeat or even suggest verb forms himself. Diarisation can thus filter the speaker who interests us. More powerful neural acoustic models than SGMMs may also be used. Finally, further quantitative assessment of the system performance is highly desirable, as well as the development of a user interface to help linguists exploit the results presented herein.

6. Acknowledgements

This research is part of projects ANR-17-CE27-0001-01 ("The Linguistic Crescent: A Multidisciplinary Approach to a Contact Area between Oc and Oïl varieties") and ANR-10-LABX-0083 (program "Investissements d'Avenir", Labex EFL, Strand 3, Workpackage VC2 – "Central Gallo-Romance: linguistics and ecology of a transitional zone"). It contributes to the IdEx Université de Paris – ANR-18-IDEX-0001.

7. Bibliographical References

Adda, G, Stüker, S., Adda-Decker, M., Ambouroue, O., Besacier, L., Blachon, D., Bonneau-Maynard, H., Godard, P., Hamlaoui, F., Idiatov, D., Kouarata, G.-N., Lamel, L., Makasso, E.-M., Annie Rialland, Van de Velde, M., Yvon, F., Zerbian, S. (2016) Breaking the Unwritten Language Barrier: The BULB Project, *Procedia Computer Science*, 81:8–14.

Brun-Trigaud G., Guérin, M. & Quint, N. (2018). Questionnaire « Parlers du Croissant » — Conjugaison. Projet ANR « Les Parlers du Croissant ». http://parlersducroissant.huma-num.fr/docs/Croissant_Questionnaire_Conjugaison.pdf (last accessed 14/02/2020) or http://tulquest.huma-num.fr/sites/default/files/questionnaires/156/Croissant_Questionnaire_Conjugaison.pdf (last accessed 14/02/2020).

Can, D. & Saraclar, M. (2011). Lattice indexing for spoken term detection. *IEEE Transactions on Audio Speech and Language Processing,* 19(8):2338–2347.

Federico, M.., Bertoldi, N., Cettolo, M. (2008). IRSTLM: an open source toolkit for handling large scale language models. *Proc. 9th Annual Conference of the International Speech Communication Association,* Brisbane, pages 1618–1621.

Guérin, M. (2019). *Grammaire du parler marchois de Dompierre-les-Églises (Haute-Vienne).* Collection « Les Parlers du Croissant ». L'Harmattan, Paris.

Lavalade, Y. (1987). *La Conjugaison occitane (Limousin).* La Clau lemosina, Limoges.

Michaud, A., Adams, O., Cohn, T., Neubig, G., Guillaume, S. (2018) Integrating automatic transcription into the language documentation workflow: Experiments with Na data and the Persephone toolkit, *Language Documentation & Conservation,* University of Hawaii Press, vol. 12, pages 393–429.

Povey, D., Ghoshal, A., Boulianne, G., Burget, L., Glembek, O., Goel, N., Hannemann, M., Motl'ıcek, P., Qian, Y., Schwarz, P., Silovsky, J., Stemmer, G., Vesely, K. (2011). The Kaldi Speech recognition Toolkit. *Proc. IEEE Workshop on Automatic Speech Recognition and Understanding,* Hawaïï, pages 1–4.

Quint, N. (1991). *Le parler marchois de Saint-Priest-la-Feuille (Creuse).* La Clau lemosina, Limoges.

Quint, N. (1996). *Grammaire du parler occitan nord-limousin marchois de Gartempe et de Saint-Sylvain-Montaigut (Creuse).* La Clau lemosina, Limoges.

Quint, N. (forthcoming). *La question des radicaux asyllabiques et des paradigmes verbaux de la 1re conjugaison dans le Croissant limousin et dans d'autres variétés occitanes ou romanes.* In Esher, L., Guérin M., Quint N. & Russo M. (eds), *Le Croissant Linguistique : nouvelles perspectives aux confins oc / oïl.* L'Harmattan, Paris.

Ronjat, J. (1913). *Essai de syntaxe des parlers provençaux modernes.* Imprimerie nationale, Paris.

Proceedings of the 1st Joint SLTU and CCURL Workshop (SLTU-CCURL 2020), pages 250–257
Language Resources and Evaluation Conference (LREC 2020), Marseille, 11–16 May 2020
© European Language Resources Association (ELRA), licensed under CC-BY-NC

FST Morphology for the Endangered Skolt Sami Language

Jack Rueter, Mika Hämäläinen
Department of Digital Humanities
University of Helsinki
{jack.rueter, mika.hamalainen}@helsinki.fi

Abstract

We present advances in the development of a FST-based morphological analyzer and generator for Skolt Sami. Like other minority Uralic languages, Skolt Sami exhibits a rich morphology, on the one hand, and there is little golden standard material for it, on the other. This makes NLP approaches for its study difficult without a solid morphological analysis. The language is severely endangered and the work presented in this paper forms a part of a greater whole in its revitalization efforts. Furthermore, we intersperse our description with facilitation and description practices not well documented in the infrastructure. Currently, the analyzer covers over 30,000 Skolt Sami words in 148 inflectional paradigms and over 12 derivational forms.

Keywords: Skolt Sami, endangered languages, morphology

1. Introduction

Skolt Sami is a minority language belonging to Sami branch of the Uralic language family. With its native speakers at only around 300, it is considered a severely endangered language (Moseley, 2010), which, despite its pluricentric potential, is decidedly focusing on one mutual langauge (Rueter and Hämäläinen, 2019). In this paper, we present our open-source FST morphology for the language, which is a part of the wider context of its on-going revitalization efforts.

The intricacies of Skolt Sami morphology include quality and quantity variation in the word stem as well as suprasegmental palatalization before subsequent affixes. Like Northern Sami and Estonian, Skolt Sami has consonant quantity and quality variation that surpasses that of Finnish, i.e. Skolt Sami has as many as three lengths in the vowel and consonant quantities in a given word.

The finite-state description of Skolt Sami involves developing strategies for reusability of open-source documentation in other minority languages. In other words, the FST description is designed in such a fashion that it can be applied to other languages as well with minimal modifications. Skolt Sami, like many other minority Uralic languages, attests to a fair degree of regular morphology, i.e., its nouns are marked for the categories of number, possession and numerous case forms with regular diminutive derivation, and its verbs are conjugated for tense, mood and person in addition to undergoing several regular derivations. Morphological descriptions have been developed in the *GiellaLT* (Sami Language technology) infrastructure at the Norwegian Arctic University in Tromso, using Helsinki Finite-State Technology (HFST) (Lindén et al., 2013).

Working in the GiellaLT infrastructure, it is possible to apply ready-made solutions to multiple language learning, facilitation and empowerment tasks. Leading into the digital age, there are ongoing implementations, such as keyboards[1] for various platforms, and corpora[2], being expanded to provide developers, researchers and language community

members access to language materials directly. The trick is to find new uses and reuses for data sets and technologies as well as to bring development closer to the language community. If development follows the North Sámi lead, any project can reap from the work already done.

Extensive work has already been done on data and tool development in the GiellaLT infrastructure (Moshagen et al., 2013) and (Moshagen et al., 2014), and previous work also exists for Skolt Sami[3] (Sammallahti and Mosnikoff, 1991; Sammallahti, 2015; Feist, 2015). There are online and click-in-text dictionaries (Rueter, 2017), [4] spell checkers (Morottaja et al., 2018), [5], these are implemented in OpenOffice, but some of the more prominent languages are supported in MS Word, as well as rule-based language learning (Antonsen et al., 2013; Uibo et al., 2015). For languages with extensive description and documentation, there are syntax checkers (Wiechetek et al., 2019), machine translation (Antonsen et al., 2017) and speech synthesis and recognition (Hjortnaes et al., 2020), just to mention the tip of the iceberg (Rueter, 2014). From a language learner and research point of departure, the development and application of these tools points to well-organized morphosyntactic and lexical descriptions of the language in focus. By well-organized descriptions, we mean approaching tasks at hand with applied reusability. Reusability is illustrated in the construction of a morphological analyzer for linguists, which, due to the fact that it is able to recognize and analyze regular morphological forms, can also serve as a morphological spell checker. In fact, this same analyzer can be reversed and used as a generator, which is useful in providing language learners with fixed, analogous and random tasks in morphology. The same morphological an-

---

[3] `http://oahpa.no/sms/useoahpa/background.eng.html/`, read further in this article for subsequent developments in `http://oahpa.no/nuorti/`

[4] The forerunner `https://sanit.oahpa.no/read/`, an online dictionary here, and on analogous pages of other dictionaries, (e.g., `https://saan.oahpa.no/read/`), can be dragged to the tool bar of Firefox and Google Chrome

[5] `http://divvun.no/korrektur/korrektur.html/`

---

[1] `http://divvun.no/keyboards/index.html/`

[2] `http://gtweb.uit.no/korp/`

alyzer, when augmented by glosses, can immediately begin to provide online dictionary and click-in-text analyses.

The development of an optimal morphological analyzer and glossing for a language like Skolt Sami requires concise morphological and lexical work, on the one hand, and access to corpora including language learning materials, on the other. Corpora provide access to language in use, and language learning materials help to establish a received understanding of the language. To this end, the morphological analyzer for Skolt Sami has been constructed to analyze and generate a pedagogically enhanced orthography, for indication of short and long diphthongs preceding geminates as well as mid low front vowels, as might be rendered in a pronouncing dictionary. One such example might be seen in the word *kueʹtt* 'hut' as opposed to the literal norm *kueʹtt*, where the dot below the *e* not only indicates a slightly lowered pronunciation of the vowel but also assists in identifying the paradigm type, *kueʹtt* : *kueʹdid* **'hut+N+Pl+Acc'** versus *kueʹll* : *kuõʹlid* **'fish+N+Pl+Acc'**.

By focusing on the construction of a pedagogical enhanced analyzer-generator, teaching resources can be developed that target randomly generated morphological tasks for the language learner as in the North Sami learning tool **Davvi**[6]. In any given language reader, there are texts with words in various forms and an accompanying vocabulary. While vocabulary translation can readily be utilized as a fixed task in language learning, inflectional tasks, especially in morphologically rich languages, can be developed as random exercises. Although the contextual word forms in the reader are quite limited, it is possible to construct randomized morphological exercises where the student is expected to inflect nouns, adjectives and verbs alike in forms that have been taught but not explicitly given for the random words provided in the reader vocabulary, e.g. in nouns the student may select vocabulary from reader **A** chapters **1–5** with a randomized task for nouns, plural, comitative, third person singular possessive suffix: **+N+Pl+Com+PxSg3**. Essentially all nouns in the selected vocabulary available for this reading are inadvertently presented to the learner.

2. Related Work

In the past, multiple methods have been proposed for automatically learning morphology for a given language. One of these is Morfessor (Creutz and Lagus, 2007), which is a set of tools designed to learn morphology from raw textual data. It has been developed with Finnish in mind, and this means that it is intended to perform well with extensive regular morphology, i.e. morphologically rich languages, too. Bergmanis and Goldwater (Bergmanis and Goldwater, 2017) present another statistical approach that can also take spelling variation into account. Their approach is based on the notion of a morphological chain consisting of child-parent pairs. When analyzing the morphology of a language, the approach takes several features into account such as presence of the parent in the training data, semantic similarity, likely affixes and so on.

Such statistical approaches, however, are data-hungry. This is a problem for various reasons in the case of Skolt Sami.

The scarce quantity of textual data is one limitation, but it is even a greater one given that the language is still being standardized and the users provide a variety of forms and vocabulary when expressing themselves in their native language. This means an even greater variety in morphology that the statistical model should be able capture from a limited dataset.

In the absence of a reasonably sized descriptive corpus of the language, annotated or not, the most accurate way to model the morphology is by using a rule-based methodology.

FSTs (Finite-State Transducers) have been shown in the past to be an effective way to model the morphology even for languages with an abundance of morphological features (cf. (Beesley and Karttunen, 2003)). Perhaps one of the largest-scale FSTs to model the morphology of a language is the one developed for Finnish (Pirinen et al., 2017). This tool, Omorfi, serves as the state-of-the-art morphological analyzer for Finnish.

3. The FST Model Development Pipeline

Developing a morphological description of a language presupposes a language-learning and documentary approach. Other people have learned the language and become proficient in it before you, so extract paradigms from grammars, readers and research to build the language model. If you are the first researcher to describe the language, take hints from the language learners, if there are any, they may be still developing their own understanding of the language morpho-syntax, and, at times, they may provide you with informative interpretations of the language.

Idiosyncrasies of a language can, sometimes, be captured through comparison to those of another. When a description of Skolt Sami, Finnish, Estonian, etc. introduces alien phenomena, such as word-stem quality and quantity variation as well as suprasegmental palatalization, it is a good idea to try describing them both separately and in tandem.

Word-stem quality variation affects both consonants and vowel. In consonants, an analogous English example might be illustrated with the *f:v* variation found in the English words *life*, *lives* and *loaf*, *loaves*. From a historical perspective, the verb *to live* will serve as an instance where long and short vowels accentuate a distinction between nouns and verbs. In a like manner, the English verb paradigm (*sing*, *sang*, *sung*) provides a sample of vowel variation with regular semantic alignment in other verbs, such as *swim* and *drink*. These seemingly peripheral phenomena of English, however, are central to the description of Skolt Sami morphology, where consonant quality and quantity variation permeate the verbal and nominal inflection systems. Suprasegmental palatalization is yet another phenomenon to be dealt with, as it may present its own influence on sound variations in both the consonants and vowels in the same coda of a word stem. These require sound variation modeling in what is referred to as a two-level model, where awareness of underlying hypothetical sound patterns and surface-level reflexes are united to facilitate analysis and generation of paradigmatic stem type variation, e.g. an underlying *sw{iau}m* could be configured with a ^*VowI* trigger to call the form *swim*, ^*VowA* the form *swam*, and

---

[6]http://oanpa.no/davvi/morfas/

^*VowU* the form *swum*.

Theoretically speaking, Skolt Sámi has vowel and consonant quantity variation in three lengths, i.e. monophthongs and diphthongs as well as geminates and consonant clusters are subject to three lengths. One problem with the initial finite-state description of Skolt Sami was that attempts were made to describe Skolt Sami according to the complementary distibution of quantity found in North Sámi[7].

By chance, the author set out to describe vowel and consonant quantity as separate conjoined phenomena, and when the instance of short vowel and shortened consonant in tandem presented itself, only a little extra implementation was required for identifying this new variation. In fact, the phenomenon had been described earlier as allegro versus largo, but it had been ignored in some of the linguistic literature (Koponen and Rueter, 2016).

Preparing the description of a single word is much like writing a terse dictionary entry. The required information consists of a head word form or lemma, a stem form from which to derive all required stems, a continuation lexicon indicating paradigm type (part of speech is also interesting), and finally a gloss or note. The word *radio* 'radio' might be presented as follows:

    radio+N:radio N_RADIO "radio" ;

The LEMMA:STEM CONTINUATION-LEXICON NOTE presentation represents one line of code consisting of four pieces of data. First, comes the index, which consists of the lemma and part-of-speech tag. Second, after a separating colon, comes the stem, which, with the Continuation lexicon (third constituent) make paradigm compilation possible by indicating what base all subsequent concatenated morphology connects to – the loanword 'radio' has no stem-internal variation. Finally, there is the optional NOTE constituent, where a gloss has been provided.

The Continuation lexicon name has been written in uppercase letters to distinguish it from the remainder of the code line. In this language, continuation lexicon names are initially marked for part of speech, hence the initial 'N_'. This part-of-speech increment is more of a mnemonic note to help facilitate faster manual coding. After initial denominal derivation lexica, nouns, adjectives and numerals are directed to mutual handling of case, number and possessive marking.

This initial line of code may encode even more complex data. One such entry might be observed in the noun *ve′rdd* 'stream', which exhibits necessary information for complex stem variation:

    ve′rdd+N:ve^1VOW{′Ø}rdd   N_KAQLBB   "flow, stream";

The index *ve′rdd+N:* (LEMMA constituent and part-of-speech tag), as such, is readily comprehensible. The part-of-speech tag may also be preceded by tags indicating variants in order of preference (+*v1*, +*v2*) and homonymity (+*Hom1*, +*Hom2*), and it may be followed by tags indicating semantics (+*Sem...*) and part-of-speech subtypes (e.g. +*Prop* for proper nouns, +*Dem* as in demonstrative pronoun). Tags, of course, may be inserted at the root or in subsequent continuation lexica – this is simply a matter of taste and the complexity of the continuation lexicon network.

The STEM *ve^1VOW{′Ø}rdd* in combination with the CONTINUATION-LEXICON *N_KAQLBB* is what captures the proliferation of six separate stem forms used in regular inflection: ve′rdd 'SG+NOM', vee′rd 'SG+GEN', verdda 'SG+ILL', vii′rdi 'PL+GEN', ve′rdstes 'SG+LOC+PXSG3', veerdaž 'DIMIN+SG+NOM'. While vowel and consonant variation might be considered peripheral in English, these extensive patterns are wide-spread in Skolt Sami inflection. Some verb types may even have as many as eleven separate stem forms used in regular inflection and derivation. Hence, consonant and vowel quality together with quantity in both provides a challenge for description of the regular inflectional paradigms of Skolt Sámi.

The continuation lexicon *N_KAQLBB* mnemonically points to the Skolt Sámi word *kä′lbb* 'calf (anim.)' as a reference to paradigm type.

Reference to paradigms has traditionally been done using numbers. This entails access to a set of paradigm descriptions, because no one can be expected to memorize large sets of paradigm types by number alone. Using familiar words to allude to paradigm types, however, may be straight forward from a native speaker's perspective, but they too will require documentation in test code. Test codes might be located adjacent to the appropriate affix continuation lexicon or in a separate set of test files (see also the noun *algg* 'beginning' in Figure 1, below). The NOTE section, of course, is open for virtually any type of data.

Development of guidelines helps newcomers join a tradition and construct analogous, parallel descriptions in the same or similar infrastructures. The presupposition of a willingness to adapt new projects to the practices of established analogous work is an important element in open-source FST development at GiellaLT, which has been adopted as the basis for guideline development. At GiellaLT documentation is sometimes sparse, incomplete or difficult to find, and therefore it is imperative that all possible reference be made to shared practices. For maximalized short term achievement (2 to 5 years), the project languages to consult first are North Sami (sme) and South Sami (sma), whereas the experience from the Skolt Sami language project is discussed here.

Skolt Sami specific descriptive materials have been dealt with in the light of work in closely related languages. Here, practice with analogous work in other Sami and Uralic languages has been helpful in learning mnemonic methods that can be applied as well as lexicon code line writing and sound variation modeling. Each language has many of its own requirements, but, where ever possible, we should seek out ways to align all projects.

The tag sets used with various language parsers at GiellaLT are extensive and have been directly adapted to work in the Skolt Sami project to ensure a high usability of tools already implemented and in mutual use in many language

---

[7]In North Sámi, there is a three-way gradation system where grade one has an extra-long vowel and short consonant, grade two has a long vowel with a long consonant, and grade three has a short vowel with an extra-long consonant.

projects. Ordering of tags reflects parsing no later than 2005, e.g. *N+Sg+Nom giehta ...* (Sjur Moshagen and Trosterud, 2005). Inflection types are indicated mnemonically by use of a frequent representative of the type, a strategy also observed in **Omorfi**, e.g. an initial continuation class marking **N_ALGG** (*algg* 'beginning') is given for nouns with a coda structure in $V_{high}C_1C_2C_2$. Inflection type naming of this kind draws the developer's attention to the familiar word and helps to minimize specification consultation required when inflection types are only numerically coded, e.g. 1, 2, 3... Both systems, however, require set specifications for each inflection type.

In order to enable morpho-lexical variation detection, FST description presupposes a degree of wrong form generation. Indeed, wrong form coverage is what facilitates intelligent spell checking suggestions, e.g. generation of a four-year-old's simple past rendition, *swimmed*, with a hint tag +*regular-past-error* could be useful. For extended coverage, more inflection types and extensions are described than would otherwise be assumed from mere phonological descriptions. There is diversity in the spoken language, which has meant that certain stem types or individual forms must be provided with multiple realizations. Here we want to avoid assigning multiple paradigms to individual lemmas where the distinction between the paradigms may lie in only one or two forms (cf. (Iva, 2007)).

In Skolt Sami building a slightly more demanding description of the phonology has meant the inclusion of otherwise pedagogical characters and graphemes. Special filtering is available for converting pedagogic target transducers into normative transducers and spell relaxes extend these in turn to descriptive transducers. These same methods are shared by other language projects in the GiellaLT infrastructure. In the long run, tweeking the description for pedagogic targeting means that even more uses are being made available, and that basic work is almost immediately available for continuation projects already realized or under construction in other language projects, i.e. syntactic disambiguation, text-to-speech, etymology suggestion.

3.1. Development of the two-level description

Skolt Sami Finite-state transducer development reuses descriptive materials for both concatenation strategies and testing. Work in the GiellaLT infrastructure begins with generation-analysis code test files (yaml), with content as in (Figure 1). Each line contains a lemma, subsequent tag set and resulting output word form or forms following a colon, e.g. *algg+N+Sg+Gen: aalg.*

The lines of description in the yaml test file (lemma + tag set + resulting word forms) are readily copied to a lexc affix description file for further editing and implementation as code (Figure 2). Here it can be observed that concatenational morphology is added after the : colon, but at the same time there is a certain amount of further required morphological quality and quantity change.

Editing in the continuation lexica in the affixes/*.lexc files entails stripping the lemma and the part of the target word forms that can serve as the stem. Since Skolt Sami is not a language with entirely simple concatenation strategies, we can make a few observations of the interplay between

```
algg+N+Sg+Nom: algg
algg+N+Sg+Gen: aalg
algg+N+Sg+Acc: aalg
algg+N+Sg+Ill: a'lğğe
algg+N+Sg+Loc: aalgâst
algg+N+Sg+Loc+PxSg1: [algstan, aalgstan]
algg+N+Sg+Com: aalgin
algg+N+Ess: alggân
algg+N+Par: alggâd
algg+N+Sg+Abe: [aalgtaa, aalgtää]
algg+N+Pl+Nom: aalg
algg+N+Pl+Gen: aalgi
algg+N+Pl+Acc: aalgid
algg+N+Pl+Ill: aalgid
algg+N+Pl+Loc: aalgin
algg+N+Pl+Com: aalgivui'm
```

Figure 1: A diagram showing file content for yaml analyzer-generator testing

```
LEXICON N_ALGG ! algg:a%^Vow1{'Ø}lgg
+N+Sg+Nom: ! short vowel + strong consonant cluster
+N+Sg+Gen: ! long vowel + weak consonant cluster
+N+Sg+Acc: ! long vowel + weak consonant cluster
+N+Sg+Ill:%>e ! short vowel + strong consonant cluster
             ! + supra segmental palatalization
+N+Sg+Loc:%>âst ! long vowel + weak consonant cluster
+N+Sg+Loc+PxSg1:%>stan !short vowel + weak consonant cluster
+N+Sg+Loc+PxSg1:%>stan !long vowel + weak consonant cluster
+N+Sg+Com:%>in  ! long vowel + weak consonant cluster
```

Figure 2: A diagram showing LEXICON development for ALGG type nouns

simple morphological concatenation and the complementary two-level model facilitation.

The lemma for the word *algg* 'beginning' is the same as the nominative singular and has no morpho-phonological changes, hence no triggers are present when coding **+N+Sg+Nom**. In the genitive and accusative singular, however, coding **+N+Sg+Acc** co-occurs with coda vowel lengthening indicated with the trigger **V2VV** (lengthening, i.e. one vowel becomes two) and consonant cluster weakening indicated with the trigger **XYY2XY** (i.e. the consonant cluster altenation in *-lgg* and *-lg*) (compare concatenation and phenomena in Figure 2), on the one hand, and the compound of concatenational morphology with accompanying triggers **V2VV** and **XYY2XY**, on the other in (Figure 3).

```
+N+Sg+Nom:                        K ; ! algg
+N+Sg+Gen:%^V2VV%^XYY2XY          K ; ! aalg
+N+Sg+Ill:%^PAL%>e                K ; ! a'lğğe
+N+Sg+Loc:%^V2VV%^XYY2XY%>â K ; ! aalgâst
+N+Sg+Loc+PxSg1:%^XYY2XY          K ; ! algstan
+N+Pl+Loc:%^V2VV%^XYY2XY          K ; ! aalgin
```

Figure 3: A diagram showing some triggers used in description of ALGG type nouns

The .yaml code test content can be further utilized as in-line testing code by simply flipping content left-to-right for analysis reading, as shown in (Figure 4). Implicit in the test data, we can observe five different stems for the monophthong noun *algg*: *algg* 'Sg+Nom', *aalg* 'Sg+Gen', *a'lğğe* 'Sg+Ill', *algstan* 'Sg+Loc+PxSg1', *aa'lje* 'Dimin+N+Sg+Gen'.

```
! Test data:
!!€gt-norm: algg #
!!€ algg:         algg+N+Sg+Nom
!!€ aalg:         algg+N+Sg+Gen
!!€ aalg:         algg+N+Sg+Acc
!!€ a'lğğe:       algg+N+Sg+Ill
!!€ aalgâst:      algg+N+Sg+Loc
!!€ algstan:      algg+N+Sg+Loc+PxSg1
!!€ aalgstan:     algg+N+Sg+Loc+PxSg1
!!€ aalgin:       algg+N+Sg+Com
!!€ alggân:       algg+N+Ess
!!€ alggâd:       algg+N+Par
!!€ algtaa:       algg+N+Sg+Abe
!!€ aalg:         algg+N+Pl+Nom
!!€ aalgi:        algg+N+Pl+Gen
!!€ aalgid:       algg+N+Pl+Acc
!!€ aalgid:       algg+N+Pl+Ill
!!€ aalgin:       algg+N+Pl+Loc
!!€ aalgivui'm:   algg+N+Pl+Com
!!€ aalgitaa:     algg+N+Pl+Abe
!!€ aalgâž:       algg+N+Der+Der/Dimin+N+Sg+Nom
!!€ aa'lje:       algg+N+Der+Der/Dimin+N+Sg+Gen
```

Figure 4: A diagram showing some test data for ALGG type noun analysis

Although there are instances of single stems taking numerous affixes, e.g. *biografia* or *radio*, above, most nominals and verbs require multiple stems. The extensive stem variation observed in the noun *algg*, above, is surpassed in the verb *tie'tted* 'to know'. It uses the following 10 stems in regular inflection: *tie'tt-* 'Inf', *tie'đ-* 'Ind+Prt+Sg3', *tiõt't-* 'Imprt+ConNeg', *tiõd-* 'Deriv', *tiõ't't-* 'Ind+Prt+Pl3', *tiõ'đ-* 'Pot', *teât't-* 'Imprt+Pl3', *teâtt-* 'Ind+Prs+Sg3', *teâd-* 'Cond', *teä't't-* 'Ind+Prs+Pl3'. The vowel quality variation in Skolt Sami and North Sami is analogous to what is observed in Germanic irregular verbs, e.g. *sing, sang, sung*.

Skolt Sami provides a challenge deserving of morpholexical and two-level model descriptions as introduced originally (Koskenniemi, 1983) integration. Integration of concatenation lexicon and morphophonological two-level description has required both intuition and a working knowledge of the target language. Whereas concatenation alludes to simply adding one morpheme to another, morphophonology draws our attention to changes required in the stems; hence the challenge of defining 10 separate stems for a single lemma in Skolt Sami provided above. (More extensive descriptions of quality, quantity and suprasegmental variation are provided in (Feist, 2015; Sammallahti, 2015).) The two-level model utilizes parallel constraints for phonological description. As mentioned above, descriptive grammars of the Skolt Sami language indicate multiple simultaneous, coordinated variation in the stem. Thus work on the two-level model initially opted to provide separate triggers for each individual phenomenon, here ˆ*V2VV* quantity, ˆ*VowRaise* quality and ˆ*PAL* palatalization.

In brief, triggers are an artificial means of replacing the natural phonological features occurring in the morphology. They can be used for causing phenomena subsequent (right-context here) or preceding (left-context). For example, if front-back vowel harmony is highly predictable on the basis of the preceding stem, the individual stems can be marked **{front}** or **{back}** triggers in order to elicit the front or back allomorphs of subsequent suffixes, i.e. triggers are set for right-context phenomena. A trigger provides for manipulation of the harmony reflexes necessary for incorrect morphology, as well, i.e. something needed in recognizing misspellings in intelligent computer-assisted language learning and spell checker suggestions – let us remember the instance of *swimmed*, above.

The two-level model rules facilitate simultaneous variation of many features in the same word. Left and right contexts play an important role in this description, whereas both contexts can contain morpho-phonological phenomena seen to precede or follow the change elicited by a given rule, or they can disregard them. Triggers are used in rule writing, because the actual morphophonology of the words does not necessarily reflect idealconsistant trigger patterning.

Zero-to-surface-entity rules present in the early phases of the project have been corrected by adding multicharacter archiphones to the individual stems. Stem internal change such as matters of vowel quantity and quality are indicated with these symbols. For purposes of phenomenon recognition, curly brackets have been used for displaying arrays of variation, e.g. *{eöâä}* indicates there is a vowel variation of four separate qualities as required in the various stems. Parallel multiple-character symbols have been implemented for suprasegmentals, length markers, etc. Stem variation in the word.

Modeling quantity in Skolt Sami has meant a divorce from the description of other Sami languages. Quantity variation is generally viewed as a coordinated phenomenon affecting vowel and consonant length simultaneously (see reference to North Sámi and complementary distribution of quantity, above). Skolt Sami deviates here: The predictable 'extra long vowel + short consonant'; 'long vowel + long consonant', 'short vowel + extra long consonant' combinations are supplemented by a fourth 'extra short vowel + extra short consonant' pattern. The four-way split required little new coding; original quantity modeling had treated vowel and consonant length as separate phenomena. When the fourth pattern became more apparent after the first half year, all triggers were present, and actually little work was required to implement their use. Since the fourth pattern alternates with the long-vowel-long-consonant pattern *algstan* (allegro) ~ *aalgstan* (largo), respectively 'begin+N+Sg+Loc+PxSg1', more language documentation was required, as this variation was found to permeate the inflection and derivation pattern of the language.

Modeling quality in Skolt Sami has introduced multicharacter symbols in the stem. These multi-character symbols contain arrays of realizations in commented curly brackets, e.g. *t%{ie%}%{eöâä%}%{'Ø%}tt* 'to know', above. Each array indicates a mnemonic list of variables. These lists are easy to interpret and consistent with guesser and cognate search development, where sound change is consistently traceable (Kimmo Koskenniemi and Heiki-Jaan Kaalep, pc.). Moreover, array notations are analogous with inflection group identifying model words as in **N_ALGG** and **N_KAQLBB**, above.

Variation in the multi-character symbols as well as the unmarked consonants is modeled with triggers. Triggers are used to elicit vowel length and height, suprasegmental palatalization (which may affect the realization of both the preceding vowel and subsequent consonantism), as well as consonant length and quality. In the Skolt Sami project, vowel length is triggered with the multi-character symbols *%ˆV2VV* (short to long) and *%ˆVV2V* (long to short).

To avoid balancing problems introduced with flag diacritics and further unexpected complications, triggers are ordered and follow the stem before concatenated suffixes. The *tie′d*-stem required for rendering the form *V+Pot+Sg3: tie′ďež* is elicited with the consecutive triggers: *%ˆVOWRaise, %ˆPALE, %ˆPAL* and *%ˆCC2C*, i.e. vowel raising (which would regularly render *iõ*), suprasegmental coloring (rendering *iõ ⇒ ie*), palatalization (′) and consonant quality change via shortening. The large number of triggers demanded a large memory, and to alleviate the problem a *reversed-intersect* function was implemented in the GiellaLT infrastructure as recommended by a member of the **HFST** team.

3.2. Deviation from Point of Departure on GiellaLT

The Skolt Sami project has seen departure from previous work in the infrastructure but simultaneously adherence to a mnemonic system of description. In the course of the project, the policy of lemma followed by a simple orthographic stem has not been retained. The number of nominal stem types has risen to **308** from the **56** described in (Sammallahti and Mosnikoff, 1991), while the number of verbal stem types is **115** as compared to **30** (ibidem.). Adjectives and numerals share inflection types with nouns. Before the commence of the project in 2013, for instance, only **280** verbs and **828** nouns were partially facilitated by the system, whereas by the end of 2018 the analogous figures were **4844** verb stems with over **40** conjugation forms as well as numerous verbal and nominal derivations and **23683** noun stems with over **98** declensional forms aa well as additional derivations, and the entire lemma count exceeded **36000**.

Multi-character symbol development endears mnemonic forms. Arrays enclosed in curly brackets are used for indicating vowel quality and quantity variation, a practice analogous of inflection type model words that hint at the type of stem variation. Triggers have, in matters of length, been drafted to reflect specific nuances of coda description, e.g. *%ˆ***VV2V** indicates vowel shortening, *%ˆ***CCC2CC** geminate shortening, and *%ˆ***XYY2XY** consonant cluster shortening, respectively.

Triggers have been fashioned for and subsequent affixes. The stem has been filled with multiple-character symbols to indicate which letters and graphemes undergo change and what kind of change. Ordered triggers have been applied to bring about these changes regardless of the orthographic context, which simplifies the generation of incorrect forms, a necessity in the recognition of ill-formed word forms and their alignment with the desired words.

Trigger ordering is aligned with the orthographic realiza-

Word Class	glossed	unglossed	inflections	derivations
Adjectives	4190	166	16	3
Nouns	21640	712	99	3+
Verbs	4845	23	33	6+
total	30675	901	148	12+

Figure 5: morpholexical coverage'

tion of phonological phenomena. Thus, changes in penultimate syllables precede those in ultimate syllables, which is similar to vowel changes preceding suprasegmental marking and subsequent consonants.A special context marker **Pen** is used before each trigger effecting change in the penultimate syllable. The trigger count in a given stem may reach six.

4. Lexical and Morphological Coverage

In the absence of gold annotated data, we do not conduct an evaluation typical to the current mainstream NLP, but rather describe the coverage of forms and lexemes in the transducer. Here we will limit our discussion to the most extensive paradigms, i.e. adjectives, nouns and verbs (see Figure 5). In addition to statistics on glossed and unglossed lexicon, where glossed is a loose term for the presence of at least one single word translation for each Skolt Sámi word in the Akusanat dictionary (Hämäläinen and Rueter, 2018), we will discuss regular inflection and derivation. While inflection refers to conjugation and declension, on the one hand, derivation indicates part-of-speech transformation brought about by morphological means, on the other. As a result of this work, the Skolt Sámi transducer represents a lexicon of over 30,000 lemmas with a coverage of over 2.3 million inflectional forms, not to mention the derivational exponent or compound nouns.

Adjectives in Skolt Sami may have special attribute forms for use in the noun phrase, as is the situation in other Sami languages. Adjectives are also known to decline in the same case forms as nouns, which brings us to a total of approximately 16 paradigmatic forms associated with the declination of each adjective. Regular derivation, it will be noted, is generally limited to comparative and superlative inflection will all cases as well as nominalization, which goes on to feed regular noun inflection.

Nouns, like adjectives, can be declined in seven cases for singular and plural with the addition of the partitive[8]. In contrast to the adjectives, however, number and case can be augmented with possession markers for three persons and two numbers, which brings the number of paradigmatic cells in declination to nearly 100. Nouns can further be derived as regular diminutives (this again feeds regular derivation) and two types of adjectives with the meanings 'without X (privative)' and 'full of X' (both of which can further derived as nouns, and the former is regulary derived as a verb).

The verbal paradigm is also relatively extensive. Each tense and additional mood, with the exception of the imperative, has three categories for person, two for number and an indefinite personal form (7). Thus, in addition to two tenses in the indicative, the subjunctive and potential mood there

---

[8] the partitive has no morphological distinction for number

are five more forms for the imperative, which brings us to a total of 33 forms in a given conjugation paradigm. Non-finite derivation, participles in addition to deverbal nouns and verbs, adds feeders to nominal and verbal derivation alike.

A large percentage of this regular inflection is in place and available in the UralicNLP, a python library for Uralic minority languages (Hämäläinen, 2019). The lexical database for Skolt Sami is also undergoing rigorous scrutiny and development in the editing of the forth-coming Moshnikoff Skolt Sami dictionary in Ve′rdd[9], an open-source dictionary environment for minority language community editor and developer collaboration (Alnajjar et al., 2020). Ve′rdd 'stream, flow' also provides an interface for feedback into the dictionary system.

5. Discussion and Future Work

The FSTs are released in GiellaLT infrastructure as a constantly updating bleeding edge release. Efforts have been made to bring the writing of the FST lexc materials into an easier MediaWiki based framework (Rueter and Hämäläinen, 2017). All edits to the FSTs made in the MediaWiki platform are automatically synchronized with those uploaded to GiellaLT.

According to statistics at GiellaLT for online dictionary usage, the Skolt Sami–Finnish dictionary enjoys a great popularity among the language community. It is only second to North Sami–Norwegian (Trosterud, p.c. 2019–06–04). Statistics provide pointers for where elaboration is needed in definitions as well as the shortcomings of the transducer (analysis of misspelled words).

In order to make the FSTs more accessible for other researchers conducting NLP tasks focused on Skolt Sami, the FSTs have been made available through UralicNLP (Hämäläinen, 2019). This is a specialized Python library for NLP for Uralic languages which makes using FSTs easier by providing a documented programmatic interface. Furthermore, the library uses precompiled models, which further facilitates the reuse of our FSTs.

Modeling diphthongs is still a challenge for Skolt Sami. Future work will attempt to develop separate triggers for the first and second element. Thus, the treatment of diphthongs will be analogous to that of quantity. Especially front and fronted diphthongs still offer unresolved variation in the paradigms of a number of nouns.

FSTs provide a good starting point for development of higher level NLP tools that embrace the new neural network methods. For instance, FSTs can be used to generate parallel sentences out of lexica and abstract syntax descriptions to be used for neural machine translation in scenarios without any real parallel data (Hämäläinen and Alnajjar, 2019). Neural models for morphological tagging can as well benefit from readings provided by FSTs (Ens et al., 2019).

6. Conclusions

We have presented the current state of our on-going project of modeling Skolt Sami morphology. The transducers are

---

made available in a continuously updated fashion in multiple different channels, to promote their use in any tasks that contributes to the revitalization of the language

The highly phonological Skolt Sami orthography has strengthened the notion that one description might be utilized in multiple tools, i.e. text-to-speech, orthographic, pedagogical, etc. This has lead to the addition of two extra characters in the alphabet and the addition of a pedagogic dictionary type generator.

Mnemonic formation of inflection type indicators has been followed by the formulation of mnemonic multiple-character symbols and triggers. Triggers have been ordered, and regular inflection has been modeled to exceed mere finite conjugation and nominal declension. Additional trigger work may be required for the description of diphthong quality change and derivation, but this must be done in collaboration with the language community, language researchers and the normative body.

7. Bibliographical References

Alnajjar, K., Hämäläinen, M., and Rueter, J. (2020). On editing dictionaries for uralic languages in an online environment. In *Proceedings of the Sixth International Workshop on Computational Linguistics of Uralic Languages*.

Antonsen, L., Johnson, R., Trosterud, T., and Uibo, H. (2013). Generating modular grammar exercises with finite-state transducers. In *Proceedings of the second workshop on NLP for computer-assisted language learning at NoDaLiDa 2013*, pages 27–38.

Antonsen, L., Gerstenberger, C., Kappfjell, M., Nystø Rahka, S., Olthuis, M.-L., Trosterud, T., and Tyers, F. M. (2017). Machine translation with north saami as a pivot language. In *Proceedings of the 21st Nordic Conference on Computational Linguistics*, pages 123–131, Gothenburg, Sweden, May. Association for Computational Linguistics.

Beesley, K. R. and Karttunen, L., (2003). *Finite-State Morphology*, pages 451–454. Stanford, CA: CSLI Publications.

Bergmanis, T. and Goldwater, S. (2017). From Segmentation to Analyses: A Probabilistic Model for Unsupervised Morphology Induction. In *Proceedings of the 15th Conference of the European Chapter of the Association for Computational Linguistics: Volume 1, Long Papers*, pages 337–346.

Creutz, M. and Lagus, K. (2007). Unsupervised models for morpheme segmentation and morphology learning. *ACM Transactions on Speech and Language Processing*, 4(1), January.

Ens, J., Hämäläinen, M., Rueter, J., and Pasquier, P. (2019). Morphosyntactic disambiguation in an endangered language setting. In *Proceedings of the 22nd Nordic Conference on Computational Linguistics*, pages 345–349.

Feist, T., (2015). *A Grammar of Skolt Saami*, volume 273, pages 137–216. Helsinki: Suomalais-Ugrilainen Seura.

Hämäläinen, M. and Alnajjar, K. (2019). A template based approach for training nmt for low-resource uralic languages-a pilot with finnish. In *Proceedings of the*

2019 2nd International Conference on Algorithms, Computing and Artificial Intelligence, pages 520–525.

Hämäläinen, M. (2019). UralicNLP: An NLP library for Uralic languages. *Journal of Open Source Software*, 4(37):1345.

Hjortnaes, N., Partanen, N., Rießler, M., and M. Tyers, F. (2020). Towards a speech recognizer for Komi, an endangered and low-resource uralic language. In *Proceedings of the Sixth International Workshop on Computational Linguistics of Uralic Languages*, pages 31–37, Wien, Austria, 10–11 January. Association for Computational Linguistics.

Hämäläinen, M. and Rueter, J. (2018). Advances in Synchronized XML-MediaWiki Dictionary Development in the Context of Endangered Uralic Languages. In *Proceedings of the Eighteenth EURALEX International Congress*, pages 967–978.

Iva, S. (2007). *Võru kirjakeele sõnamuutmissüsteem. [The Inflection System of the Võro Literary Language.] PhD thesis*. University of Tartu.

Koponen, E. and Rueter, J. (2016). The first complete scientific grammar of skolt saami in english. In *Finnisch-Ugrische Forschungen, 2016(63)*, pages 254–266. Suomalais-Ugrilainen Seura.

Koskenniemi, K. (1983). *Two-Level Morphology: A General Computational Model for Word-Form Recognition and Production*. Helsinki: University of Helsinki, Department of General Linguistics.

Lindén, K., Axelson, E., Drobac, S., Hardwick, S., Kuokkala, J., Niemi, J., Pirinen, T. A., and Silfverberg, M. (2013). HFST a system for creating NLP tools. In *International Workshop on Systems and Frameworks for Computational Morphology*, pages 53–71. Springer.

Morottaja, P., Olthuis, M.-L., Trosterud, T., and Antonsen, L. (2018). Anarâškielâ tivvoomohjelm – Kielâ- já ortografiafeeilâi kuorrâm tivvoomohjelmáin. *Dutkansearvvi dieđalaš áigečála*, 1(2):63–259.

Christopher Moseley, editor. (2010). *Atlas of the World's Languages in Danger*. UNESCO Publishing, 3rd edition. Online version: http://www.unesco.org/languages-atlas/.

Moshagen, S. N., Pirinen, T. A., and Trosterud, T. (2013). Building an open-source development infrastructure for language technology projects. In *Proceedings of the 19th Nordic Conference of Computational Linguistics (NODALIDA 2013); May 22-24; 2013; Oslo University; Norway.*, number 85 in 16, pages 343–352. Linköping University Electronic Press; Linköpings universitet.

Moshagen, S., Rueter, J., Pirinen, T., Trosterud, T., and Tyers, F. M. (2014). Open-source infrastructures for collaborative work on under-resourced languages. The LREC 2014 Workshop "CCURL 2014 - Collaboration and Computing for Under-Resourced Languages in the Linked Open Data Era".

Pirinen, T. A., Listenmaa, I., Johnson, R., Tyers, F. M., and Kuokkala, J. (2017). Open morphology of Finnish. LINDAT/CLARIN digital library at the Institute of Formal and Applied Linguistics, Charles University.

Rueter, J. and Hämäläinen, M. (2017). Synchronized Mediawiki Based Analyzer Dictionary Development. In *Proceedings of the Third Workshop on Computational Linguistics for Uralic Languages*, pages 1–7.

Rueter, J. and Hämäläinen, M. (2019). Skolt sami, the makings of a pluricentric language, where does it stand? In Rudolf Muhr, et al., editors, *European Pluricentric Languages in Contact and Conflict*, Bern, Switzerland. Peter Lang.

Rueter, J. (2014). The Livonian-Estonian-Latvian Dictionary as a threshold to the era of language technological applications. *Eesti ja soome-ugri keeleteaduse ajakiri*, 5(1):251–259.

Rueter, J. (2017). DEMO: Giellatekno open-source click-in-text dictionaries for bringing closely related languages into contact. In *Proceedings of the Third Workshop on Computational Linguistics for Uralic Languages*, pages 8–9, St. Petersburg, Russia, January. Association for Computational Linguistics.

Sammallahti, P. and Mosnikoff, J. (1991). *Suomi-Koltansaame sanakirja. Lää'dd-sää'm sää'nneǩe'rjj [Finnish-Skolt Sami Dictionary]*. Ohcejohka: Girjegiisá Oy.

Sammallahti, P., (2015). *Vuõ'lǧǧe jåå'tted ooudâs, De fas johttájedje, Taas mentiin: Sää'mǩiõllsaž lookkâmǩe'rjj, Nuortalašgiel lohkosat, Koltansaamen lukemisto*, volume 14, pages 150–171. Oulu: Oulun Yliopisto.

Sjur Moshagen, P. S. and Trosterud, T. (2005). Twol at work. *CSLI Studies in Computational Linguistics ONLINE*, pages 94–105.

Uibo, H., Pruulmann-Vengerfeldt, J., Rueter, J., and Iva, S. (2015). Oahpa! õpi! opiq! developing free online programs for learning Estonian and võro. In *Proceedings of the fourth workshop on NLP for computer-assisted language learning*, pages 51–64, Vilnius, Lithuania, May. LiU Electronic Press.

Wiechetek, L., Moshagen, S. N., and Omma, T. (2019). Is this the end? two-step tokenization of sentence boundaries. In *Proceedings of the Fifth International Workshop on Computational Linguistics for Uralic Languages*, pages 141–153, Tartu, Estonia, January. Association for Computational Linguistics.

8.   Language Resource References

Sammallahti, P. and Mosnikoff, J., (1991). *Suomi-Koltansaame sanakirja. LÄÄ'DD-SÄÄ'm SÄÄ'NNÊ'RJJ [Finnish-Skolt Sami Dictionary]*, pages 180–202. Ohcejohka: Girjegiisá Oy.

Proceedings of the 1st Joint SLTU and CCURL Workshop (SLTU-CCURL 2020), pages 258–264
Language Resources and Evaluation Conference (LREC 2020), Marseille, 11–16 May 2020
© European Language Resources Association (ELRA), licensed under CC-BY-NC

Voted-Perceptron Approach for Kazakh Morphological Disambiguation

Gulmira Tolegen, Alymzhan Toleu, Rustam Mussabayev
Institute of Information and Computational Technologies
Almaty, Kazakhstan
gulmira.tolegen.cs@gmail.com, alymzhan.toleu@gmail.com, rmusab@gmail.com

Abstract

This paper presents an approach of voted perceptron for morphological disambiguation for the case of Kazakh language. Guided by the intuition that the feature value from the correct path of analyses must be higher than the feature value of non-correct path of analyses, we propose the voted perceptron algorithm with Viterbi decoding manner for disambiguation. The approach can use arbitrary features to learn the feature vector for a sequence of analyses, which plays a vital role for disambiguation. Experimental results show that our approach outperforms other statistical and rule-based models. Moreover, we manually annotated a new morphological disambiguation corpus for Kazakh language.

Keywords: Morphological Disambiguation, Voted Perceptron, Kazakh Language

1. Introduction

Morphological analysis and disambiguation play a vital role in handling the problems of i) reducing the complexity of the word structures and ii) alleviating the data sparsity issue. A morphological analyzer can decompose any raw word into a sequence of morphological tags and it produces more than one analysis per word. An example is given in Table 2, where a simple Kazakh phrase is analyzed and each word has more than one analysis. Morphological disambiguation (MD) is the task of selecting the correct analysis among the candidate analyses by leveraging the context information. Kazakh is an agglutinative language with rich morphology. A root/stem in Kazakh may produce hundreds or thousands of new words. It is apparent from below that Kazakh has large unique tokens than English, which leads to the data sparsity problem.

Corpus size	Kaz uni. tok.	Eng uni. tok.
948,612 (News)	91,495	57,017
25,327,611 (Wikipedia)	873,693	427,980

Table 1: Comparison of Kazakh and English corpora. *uni. tok.* denotes the number of unique tokens.

Developing an accurate disambiguation approach is appealing because it can alleviate the data sparseness problem caused by rich morphology. Most researchers investigating Kazakh MD have utilised Hidden markov model (HMM) (Assylbekov et al., 2016; Makhambetov et al., 2015) as the statistical model. There are several problems with the use of this model: i) the strong assumption of HMM makes it not flexible to use arbitrary features; ii) the complexity of the task itself makes the model not tractable in practice when using a full analysis as labels (breaking-down an analysis into smaller units may work for this case, but the cost may be a loss of accuracy); iii) it cannot capture the long-distance dependency.

In this paper, we present an approach of voted perceptron for MD with a new manually-annotated corpus. We treat an analysis *kala n nom e cop aor p3 pl* as a combination of three main constituents: root, POS, and morpheme chain:

$$\underbrace{kala}_{root} \quad \underbrace{n}_{POS} \quad \underbrace{nom\ e\ cop\ aor\ p3\ pl}_{morpheme\ chain} \tag{1}$$

As we can see that a full analyses have a complex structure, which means the model must correctly predict every single tag in these three parts including the root. The idea behind of these constituents is that we try to represent a sequence analysis with feature vectors. To learn the feature vectors for each sequence of analysis, we present a voted-perceptron approach for MD. The underlying hypothesis is that we need to train the model as follows: the feature vector of the extracted sequence analysis in the correct path should have a large value than those in the non-correct path. In order to improve the model's performance, we use a set of features and assess how these features affect the results. In the experiment, we try to evaluate how the breaking-down technique of analysis affects the model performance and evaluate what is the optimal length of morpheme chain (MC) for disambiguation. The proposed approaches do not need to specify the hand-rules (like constrained grammars (CGs) does), and the approach achieves better results than both the statistical and rule-based models.

2. Related Work

In general, the two tasks morphological disambiguation and morphological tagging are similar to each other. The difference between morphological disambiguation and the morphological tagging is that the latter one only makes prediction through the surface word and it is harder than MD. The former is able to access the possible candidates of analysis, which more designed to solve ambiguity of analysis produced by an analyzer.

2.1. Morphological Disambiguation

Several approaches have been applied for the morphological disambiguation and can be categorized as follows: rule-based, statistical-based model with discrete features, neural network-based and hybrid approaches. Makhambetov et al. (2015) presented a data-driven approach for Kazakh morphological analysis and disambiguation that was based

Kala	Kelbeti	Zhana	...
kala n nom			
kala n attr		zhana adj	
kala n nom e cop aor p3 pl	kelbet n px3sp nom	zhana adv	
kala n nom e cop aor p3 sg	kelbet n px3sp nom e cop aor p3 pl	zhana adj advl	...
kal v iv prc_impf	kelbet n px3sp nom e cop aor p3 sg	zhana adj subst nom	
kala v tv imp p2 sg		...	
kal vaux prc_impf			

Table 2: Example of morphological analysis for a Kazakh sentence: *Kala kelbeti Zhana* (the appearance of the city is new).

on the Hidden Markov Model (HMM). The authors conducted 10 cross-validated evaluations and obtained 86% accuracy on the test data. Kessikbayeva and Cicekli (2016) presented a rule-based morphological disambiguator for Kazakh language and it achieved 87% accuracy on the test data (about 15,000 words). In the same direction, Assylbekov et al. (2016) presented a hybrid approach that applied constrained grammar (CG) with HMM tagger. The authors reported that the HMM tagger achieved 84.55% accuracy and the hybrid approach achieved 90.73% accuracy on the test data.

In recent years, deep learning arguably achieved tremendous success in many research areas such as NLP (Tolegen et al., 2019; Mikolov et al., 2013; Toleu et al., 2017b; Dayanik et al., 2018; Toleu et al., 2019), speech signal processing (Mamyrbayev et al., 2019) and computer vision (Girdhar et al., 2019; Pang et al., 2019). Toleu et al. (2017a) presented a neural network-based disambiguation model, in which the author proposed to measure the distance of the two embeddings: the context and the morphological analyses. In order to measure the distances, the author applies neural networks to learn the context representation from characters and represents the morphological analyses as well. The correct analysis should more similar to the context's embedding; in other words, they are closely arranged in the vector space compared to the other candidate analyses.

2.2. Morphological Tagging

Morphological tagging has been studied extensively for the decade, here we review the work most relevant to this paper Mueller et al. (2013) presented a pruned CRF (PCRF) for morphological tagging and proposed to use coarse-to-fine decoding and early updating to train the higher-order CRF. Experiments on six languages show that the PCRF gives significant improvements in accuracy. Müller and Schütze (2015) compared the performance of the most important representations that can be used for across-domain morphological tagging. One of their findings is that the representations similar to Brown clusters perform best for POS tagging and that word representations based on linguistic morphological analyzers perform best for morphological tagging. Malaviya et al. (2018) combines neural networks and graphical models presented a framework for cross-lingual morphological tagging. Instead of predicting full tag sets, the model predicts single tags separately and modeling the dependencies between tags over time steps. The model is

able to generate tag sets unseen in training data, and share information between similar tag sets. This model is about cross-lingual MT and we do not make comparisons with monolingual morphological tagging models. Tkachenko and Sirts (2018) presented a sequence to sequence model for morphological tagging. The model learns the internal structure of morphological labels by treating them as sequences of morphological feature values and applies a similar strategy of neural sequence-to-sequence models commonly used for machine translation (Sutskever et al., 2014) to do morphological tagging. The authors explored different neural architectures and compare their performance with both PCRF (Mueller et al., 2013). Double layer of biLSTMs were applied in those neural architectures as Encoder (Ling et al., 2015; Labeau et al., 2015; Ma and Hovy, 2016). The encoder uses one biLSTM to compute character embedding and the second biLSTM combine the obtained character embedding along with pre-trained word embedding to generate word context embeddings. The output of those neural networks are different: one of the baselines is to use a single output layer to predict whole morphological labels. As the second baseline, the output layer can be changed to predict the different morphological value of tag with separate output layers. An improved version of the second one is to use a hierarchical separate output layers in order to capture dependencies between tags.

3. HMM-based Disambiguation

Let $\mathbf{w} = w_1, w_2, ..., w_n$ be a sentence of length n words and $\mathbf{t} = t_1, t_2, ...t_n$ be corresponding morphological analysis sequence. $\mathbf{c} = (t_1^{c_1}, t_1^{c_m}), ..., (t_n^{c_1}, t_n^{c_m})$ is the candidate analysis of each word. m is the number of candidates, and it can be vary to each word. Morphological disambiguation is the problem of finding the $\mathbf{t}$ from $\mathbf{c}$ given the $\mathbf{w}$:

$$\underset{\mathbf{t}}{\mathrm{argmax}}\, Pr(\mathbf{t}|\mathbf{w}) = \underset{\mathbf{t}}{\mathrm{argmax}}\, \frac{Pr(\mathbf{t})Pr(\mathbf{w}|\mathbf{t})}{Pr(\mathbf{w})}$$
$$= \underset{\mathbf{t}}{\mathrm{argmax}}\, Pr(\mathbf{t})Pr(\mathbf{w}|\mathbf{t}) \qquad (2)$$

where $Pr(\mathbf{w})$ is a constant and can be ignored.

To compute $Pr(\mathbf{t})$ and $Pr(\mathbf{w}|\mathbf{t})$, the first-order HMM assumptions are applied to simplify the analysis transition probability into that the current analysis depends only on previous analysis.

$$Pr(\mathbf{t}) = \prod_{i=1}^{n} Pr(t_i|t_{i-1}) = \prod_{i=1}^{n} \frac{\alpha + c(t_i, t_{i-1})}{\alpha|T| + c(t_{i-1})} \qquad (3)$$

#	Features	Description
0	w_i	word context
1	r_i	lemma/stem of the word
2	POS_i	POS tags, such as noun, verb etc.
3	mc_i	full morpheme chain
4	ma_i	a full morphological analysis
5	#t	the number of the tags
6	wc_i	word case
7	ps_i	plural and singular tags

Table 3: Feature category.

where $c(t_i, t_{i-1})$ counts the number of occurrences of t_i, t_{i-1} in the corpus. α is smoothing number. T the unique number of tags in the corpus.

$$Pr(\mathbf{w}|\mathbf{t}) = \prod_{i=1}^{n} Pr(w_i|t_i) = \prod_{i=1}^{n} \frac{\alpha + c(w_i, t_i)}{\alpha|V| + c(t_i)} \quad (4)$$

where $c(w_i, t_i)$ is the number of occurrences of word w_i with tag t_i. $|V|$ is the unique word number. Using above transition and emission scores, we could apply Viterbi decoding to find the best path of analysis.

In practice, there are several drawbacks of above approach when applying it on disambiguation task directly: i) if we consider each full analysis as a tag, the unique number of tag become 19,236 (observed in our corpus), then the number of parameters of transition probability will be $19,236^2$, and the number of parameters of emission probability become even more. ii) breaking down analysis into small subtags can definitely decrease the number of tags and it is tractable, but it has an effect on model performance. iii) first-order HMM not able to capture the long-term dependency information.

4. Voted Perceptron-based Disambiguation

In this section, we describe the voted perceptron-based approach for disambiguation. A major advantage of this approach is that it allows us to use arbitrary features and extracts features from both words and the candidate analyses.

4.1. Feature Vectors

In order to generalize the morphological analyses and to train the perceptron algorithm, we use a set of features to generate feature vector as representation of the analyses using global feature function $\Phi(\cdot)$. Table 3 summarizes the feature categories. Let $\phi(\cdot)$ function be the local feature function which is indicator function, it maps the input to an d-dimensional feature vectors. For example, if the template only contains these two: 1) w_0/w_{-1}; 2)$POS_{-1}/POS_0/POS_1$. w_i denotes for word in the position i-th, and POS_i is part-of-speech. $\phi(\cdot)$ extracts the current and previous word with previous, current and next word POS tag as local features through this template at each step to make the disambiguation. The global feature representation is the sum of all local features for input sequence:

$$\Phi(\cdot) = \sum_{n} \phi(\cdot) \quad (5)$$

4.2. Parameter Estimation

To estimate the parameters of the model, we apply the perceptron training algorithms (Collins, 2002) shown in Figure 1. $z_i \in z$ is a predicted path and $\Phi(\cdot)$ is global feature function that generate features. As we can see, it increases the parameter values for features which are extracted from correct morphological analysis's sequence, and down weighting parameter values for features extracted in the non-correct morphological analysis's sequence. The final analyses path is decoded through the Viterbi algorithm.

Data: Training examples (w_i, t_i).
Result: Parameters a.
Initialization: set parameters $a = 0$;
for $e \leftarrow 1$ **to** $Epoch$ **do**
    for $i \leftarrow 1$ **to** n **do**
        Calculate $z_i = argmax_{z \in GEN(x_i)} \Phi(x_i, z) \cdot a$
        if $z_i \neq t_i$ **then**
            $a = a + \Phi(x_i, t_i) - \Phi(x_i, z_i)$
        end
    end
end

Algorithm 1: Voted-Perceptron algorithm.

5. Experiments and Results

5.1. Corpus Construction

One of the aims of this work is to create a manually annotated morphological disambiguation data set as the database for future further research. As known that the task of annotating data is a time-consuming and tedious work. In order to assist the annotation process and to improve the correctness of the annotation, we build an annotation tool with user-friendly interface. Figure 1 shows a screenshot of an annotation process. The annotation process is not trivial and slow, the annotator should annotate every single word appeared in the document. We can briefly illustrate the annotation process as follows: click a word, then the corresponding candidate analyses will show up for annotation; the annotator not only considers the context of that word but also consider the previous/future words' morphological tags to make the decision.

We randomly selected 110 documents from the general news media[1] as the data source for annotation. The annotations have been executed manually by native speaker of Kazakh. The proposed approaches were evaluated on the new morphological disambiguation data set. The corpus consists of 15,466 tokens, and 90% is used as the training set, 10% for the test set. Table 4 shows the statistics about the data set.

	#token	OOV (%)	Avg.
Train	13,849	-	2.97
Test	1,617	27.58	2.93

Table 4: Statistics of the corpus. *OOV* - out-of-vocabulary rate. *Avg.* - the average number of analysis per token.

---

[1]https://www.inform.kz/kz

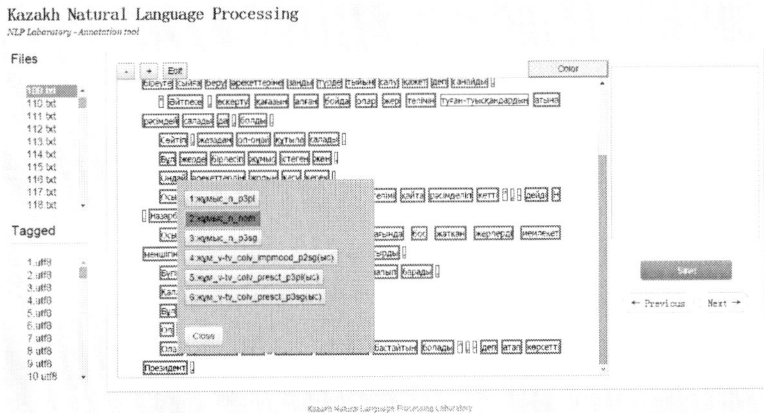

Figure 1: Annotation tool for manually annotating the morphological disambiguation corpus.

5.2. Model Setup

There are 19,236 analysis[2] can be observed in our current corpus, which results in that the number of model's parameters be very large and sparse when training the HMM. In practice, the memory overflow error was raised when we directly use the full analyses as labels. It worth to note that the number of analyses increases with the increase of the corpus volume because each root can produce hundred or thousand new words in Kazakh. To reduce the tag number, we tried to break-down the analysis into smaller units excluding the roots. Because there are 4,050 roots in the corpus, and if we only take the last one tag of the morpheme chain with root as an analysis, the number is still large about 11,167.

Models	Type of tags	#tag
M-1	the last 1 tag of MC	57
M-2	the last 2 tags of MC	241
M-3	the last 3 tags of MC	639
M-4	full morpheme chain	839
M-5	POS + the last 1 tag of MC	216
M-6	POS + the last 2 tags of MC	773
M-7	POS + the last 3 tags of MC	1,453
M-8	POS + full morpheme chain	1,699

Table 5: Various HMM-based models with their tag numbers for disambiguation after breaking down the analysis into a small number of morphological units.

Table 5 provides the summary statistics for HMM model's variations (denoted from M-1 to M-8), which are trained with different morphological units. For instance, model M-1 uses the last single tag of morpheme chain as label to train, and the total number of labels is 57. Models denoted with M-5 to M-8 include the POS combined with thee morpheme tags. We found the max-length and the average length of the morpheme chain in the corpus are 7 and 3.07, respectively. The idea behind such a model setup

is to assess how that breaking-down way affects model's performance and to evaluate what is the optimal length of morpheme chain for disambiguation. The voted-perceptron model trained with features presented in Table 3 with suitable feature template.

5.3. Results

We report the accuracy results for the overall (all tokens), known tokens, and unknown tokens. In terms of strictness, we deem correct only the predictions that match the golden truth completely, i.e. in root, POS and MC (up to a single morpheme tag). Unless stated otherwise we refer to the overall accuracy when comparing model performances.

Table 6 shows the results of HMM models with different tag sets. The top half of the Table 6 shows that the performances are relatively low when the tag from the morpheme chain was used only. The accuracy of models (M-1, M-2, M-3) use the last 1, 2 and 3 tags of morpheme chain are 72.04%, 78.72% and 78.47% respectively. Model M-4 uses full morpheme chain and gives 78.60%. To investigate this further, we take the last 4 tags of morpheme chain as labels and found that the result is 78.6% same with M-4's.

The bottom half of the Table 6 shows the results of all models trained with POS+certain morpheme tags. It is apparent from this table that the models M-6 (POS + last 2 tags) and M-7 (POS + last 3 tags) give same accuracy 84.91% which is the best result among them. No significant differences were found between M-7 and M-8 and the latter one was trained with POS + full morpheme chain, and M-8 shows a little drop over M-7 in terms of unknown tokens accuracy. According to these results, we found that the HMM model achieves the best result when using POS+the last 2/3 morpheme tags. There is no significant improvement when increasing the length of the morpheme tags.

Table 7 presents the results for the voted-perceptron approach and it shows how each feature affects the model. A plus (+) sign before the feature name indicates that these feature combinations are added on top of the rest with suitable feature templates. It can be seen that the proposed model enhanced with the word context ($+w$) only gives 53.68% accuracy. When adding the root feature ($+r$) to

---

[2]Each morphological analysis consists of root, POS, and morpheme chain.

Models	Overall acc.	Known acc.	Unk. acc.
M-1	72.04	77.25	57.24
M-2	78.72	82.19	68.88
M-3	78.47	82.44	67.22
M-4	78.60	82.52	67.45
M-5	79.96	84.86	66.03
M-6	**84.91**	**89.54**	**71.73**
M-7	**84.91**	**89.54**	**71.73**
M-8	84.78	89.54	71.25

Table 6: Accuracy results of HMM-based models. *Unk. acc.* denotes for unknown tokens accuracy.

#	Models	Overall acc.	Known acc.	Unk. acc.
0	+w	53.68	55.51	48.45
1	+r	62.09	65.21	53.21
2	+pos	70.56	75	57.95
3	+mc	**89.11**	**92.39**	**78.81**
4	+ma	89.54	92.47	81.23
5	+#t	89.17	92.47	79.81
6	+wc	90.23	93.39	81.23
7	+ps	**90.53**	**93.39**	**82.42**

Table 7: Accuracy results of the voted-perceptron approach. $+mc$ indicates that the current feature with its feature combinations is added to the model with previous features $+w$, $+r$, $+pos$ accumulatively.

Models	Overall acc.	Known acc.	Unk. acc.
HMM	84.91	89.54	71.73
Voted-Perceptron	90.53	93.39	82.42
Improv.	**5.62**	**3.85**	**10.69**

Table 8: Comparison of the best results from HMM-based models and the voted-perceptron.

the model (trained with $+w$ and $+r$ features), the model performance can be improved to 62.09%, which means that the root feature contributes around 8% improvements. It is apparent that the pos feature ($+pos$) contributes 8.47%, and the model achieves 70.56% accuracy. As we expected, the morpheme chain features ($+mc$) contributes most to model performance. It gives 18.55% improvement over the accumulation of previous features and the model ends up with 89.11% overall accuracy. The feature of full morphological analysis ($+ma$) only gives a minor improvement. Other features like $+t$, $+wc$, and $+ps$ provide positive effect and finally the proposed approach achieves 90.53% overall accuracy.

Table 8 compares the best results obtained from the HMMs and the voted-perceptron. It is apparent from this table that the proposed approach outperforms than HMM by 5.62% overall accuracy, and 10.69% unknown tokens accuracy.

To compare the proposed approach with previous work, we take the two existing models as baselines: i) a statistical

Models	Overal acc.	Unk. acc.
Assylbekov et al. (2016)	84.55	80.90
Constrained Grammar (CG)	87	-
Voted Perceptron	**88.11**	**85.11**

Table 9: Comparison of the best results from HMM-based models and those of voted-perceptron.

model proposed by Assylbekov et al. (2016)[3] and ii) a rule-based constrained grammar tool from the Apertium-kaz CG tagger[4]. These tools cannot applied to our data set directly[5], instead of converting the tools, we evaluate all models on their data set (Assylbekov et al., 2016), and the proposed voted-perceptron was trained on this data with the corresponding features. Since voted-perceptron is a purely statistical model, for the fair comparison, we use the baseline of Assylbekov et al. (2016) of their statistical model based on HMM not the combined model of HMM with CG.

Table 9 shows the comparison results. It is can be seen that voted-perceptron model outperforms the HMM-based disambiguation and also beats the constrained grammar (CG), the rule-based disambiguaton tool.

5.4. Error Analysis

We categorize the errors of model output into three groups: root inconsistency, POS inconsistency and the morpheme chain inconsistency. Table 10 shows error percentages. It can be seen that in models M-1 to M-4 only trained with different length of morpheme chain, the root inconsistency error takes almost half of the total. The POS inconsistency error takes around 25%. After adding the POS to the models (M-5 to M-8), the root and POS inconsistency percentages decreased to around 44% and 20% respectively. It is apparent from this table that for the best HMM-based model, the root inconsistency error accounts for the large part of errors (44.85%). It is reasonable because these models did not include root as a label in training.

Models	root	POS	mc
M-1	48	21.23	30.75
M-2	53.48	25.29	21.22
M-3	52.29	26.43	21.26
M-4	52.31	26.58	21.09
M-5	37.96	16.66	45.37
M-6	44.26	19.67	36.06
M-7	**44.85**	**20.90**	**35.24**
M-8	44.30	21.13	34.55

Table 10: Percentage of root, POS and morpheme chain errors for HMM-based models.

Table 11 shows the error' percentages for voted perceptron.

---

[3]https://svn.code.sf.net/p/apertium/svn/branches/kaz-tagger/
[4]http://wiki.apertium.org/wiki/Apertium-kaz
[5]We used our new developed morphological analyzer to decompose the words, and it has some issue of inconsistency of the name of morphological tags with their analyzer.

It can be seen that the different features affect the model's output error percentage for voted perceptron. The error percentage of the final model for root, POS and morpheme chain inconsistency are 25.49%, 17.64% and 56.86%. It is apparent that a very large portion of error is accounted for morpheme chain inconsistency.

Models	root	POS	mc
+w	37.65	21.76	40.58
+r	11.58	28.87	59.54
+pos	11.34	8.19	80.46
+mc	30.11	18.75	51.13
+ma	30.17	22.48	47.33
+#t	25.14	24	50.85
+wc	27.21	18.98	53.79
+ps	25.49	17.64	56.86

Table 11: Percentage of root, POS and morpheme chain errors for voted perceptron.

Further analysing the output of the models, we found that the models tend to make error prediction for the possessive tags with 3-rd person and tags of tense. Because the possessive tags have the attribute of plural or singular, and these attributes can be determined only after the subject is captured. If there are many words between the subject and the current word with possessive tags or the subject is in hidden form, then the former involves the long-distance dependency problem, and the latter requires the model need certain semantic information of sentences that reflects the subject. Similarly, the corresponding tense tag in also involved to define the sentence tense before tagging the corresponding word with a tense tag. For example, in Kazakh, a verb surface word can have a future or current tense tag simultaneously, and the disambiguation can be done when the sentence tense is determined. As the HMM-based model is the first-order model, these errors cannot be solved. In voted-perceptron, we apply the [-2,-2] window to extract features, and can partially solve the long-distance problem.

6. Conclusion

In this paper, we represent an approach of voted perceptron for morphological disambiguation for the case of Kazakh language. The approach can use arbitrary features in training and testing and can also apply to other languages easily. A new manually annotated corpus for Kazakh morphological disambiguation is presented in this paper for the further research. Experimental results show that voted perceptron outperforms the frequently used HMM-based and the rule-based constrained grammar. One possible future work is to perform transfer learning by using the learned feature vector of this approach for the typologically similar languages. Solving the long-distance dependency problem of morphological disambiguation is the another prior future work.

Acknowledgement

This research has been conducted within the framework of the grant num. BR05236839 "Development of information technologies and systems for stimulation of personalities sustainable development as one of the bases of development of digital Kazakhstan".

7. Bibliographical References

Assylbekov, Z., Washington, J., Tyers, F., Nurkas, A., Sundetova, A., Karibayeva, A., Abduali, B., and Amirova, D. (2016). A free/open-source hybrid morphological disambiguation tool for kazakh. The First International Conference on Turkic Computational Linguistics, Tur-CLing 2016 ; Conference date: 02-04-2016 Through 08-04-2016.

Collins, M. (2002). Discriminative training methods for hidden markov models: Theory and experiments with perceptron algorithms. *EMNLP*.

Dayanik, E., Akyürek, E., and Yuret, D. (2018). Morphnet: A sequence-to-sequence model that combines morphological analysis and disambiguation. *CoRR*, abs/1805.07946.

Girdhar, R., Carreira, J., Doersch, C., and Zisserman, A. (2019). Video action transformer network. In *The IEEE Conference on Computer Vision and Pattern Recognition (CVPR)*, June.

Kessikbayeva, G. and Cicekli, I. (2016). A rule based morphological analyzer and a morphological disambiguator for kazakh language. *Linguistics and Literature Studies*, 4:96–104, 01.

Labeau, M., Löser, K., and Allauzen, A. (2015). Non-lexical neural architecture for fine-grained POS tagging. In *Proceedings of the 2015 Conference on Empirical Methods in Natural Language Processing*, pages 232–237, Lisbon, Portugal, September. Association for Computational Linguistics.

Ling, W., Dyer, C., Black, A. W., Trancoso, I., Fermandez, R., Amir, S., Marujo, L., and Luis, T. (2015). Finding function in form: Compositional character models for open vocabulary word representation. In *Proceedings of the 2015 Conference on Empirical Methods in Natural Language Processing*, pages 1520–1530, Lisbon, Portugal, September. Association for Computational Linguistics.

Ma, X. and Hovy, E. (2016). End-to-end sequence labeling via bi-directional LSTM-CNNs-CRF. In *Proceedings of the 54th Annual Meeting of the Association for Computational Linguistics (Volume 1: Long Papers)*, pages 1064–1074, Berlin, Germany, August. Association for Computational Linguistics.

Makhambetov, O., Makazhanov, A., Sabyrgaliyev, I., and Yessenbayev, Z. (2015). Data-driven morphological analysis and disambiguation for kazakh. In Alexander Gelbukh, editor, *Computational Linguistics and Intelligent Text Processing*, pages 151–163, Cham. Springer International Publishing.

Malaviya, C., Gormley, M. R., and Neubig, G. (2018). Neural factor graph models for cross-lingual morphological tagging. In *ACL*.

Mamyrbayev, , Turdalyuly, M., Mekebayev, N., Mukhsina, K., Alimhan, K., BabaAli, B., Nabieva, G., Duisenbayeva, A., and Akhmetov, B. (2019). Continuous speech recognition of kazakh language. *ITM Web of Conferences*, 24:01012, 01.

Mikolov, T., Sutskever, I., Chen, K., Corrado, G., and
Dean, J. (2013). Distributed representations of words
and phrases and their compositionality. In *Proceedings
of the 26th International Conference on Neural Information Processing Systems - Volume 2*, NIPS'13, pages
3111–3119, USA. Curran Associates Inc.

Mueller, T., Schmid, H., and Schütze, H. (2013). Efficient
higher-order CRFs for morphological tagging. In *Proceedings of the 2013 Conference on Empirical Methods
in Natural Language Processing*, pages 322–332, Seattle, Washington, USA, October. Association for Computational Linguistics.

Müller, T. and Schütze, H. (2015). Robust morphological
tagging with word representations. In *HLT-NAACL*.

Pang, B., Zha, K., Cao, H., Shi, C., and Lu, C. (2019).
Deep rnn framework for visual sequential applications.
In *The IEEE Conference on Computer Vision and Pattern
Recognition (CVPR)*, June.

Sutskever, I., Vinyals, O., and Le, Q. V. (2014). Sequence
to sequence learning with neural networks. In Z. Ghahra-
mani, et al., editors, *Advances in Neural Information
Processing Systems 27*, pages 3104–3112. Curran Associates, Inc.

Tkachenko, A. and Sirts, K. (2018). Modeling composite
labels for neural morphological tagging. In *Proceedings
of the 22nd Conference on Computational Natural Language Learning*, pages 368–379, Brussels, Belgium, October. Association for Computational Linguistics.

Tolegen, G., Toleu, A., Mamyrbayev, O., and Mussabayev,
R. (2019). Neural named entity recognition for kazakh.
In *Proceedings of the 20th International Conference on
Computational Linguistics and Intelligent Text Process-
ing*, CICLing. Springer Lecture Notes in Computer Sci-
ence.

Toleu, A., Tolegen, G., and Makazhanov, A. (2017a).
Character-aware neural morphological disambiguation.
In *Proceedings of the 55th Annual Meeting of the Asso-
ciation for Computational Linguistics (Volume 2: Short
Papers)*, pages 666–671, Vancouver, Canada, July. Asso-
ciation for Computational Linguistics.

Toleu, A., Tolegen, G., and Makazhanov, A. (2017b).
Character-based deep learning models for token and sen-
tence segmentation. In *Proceedings of the 5th Inter-
national Conference on Turkic Languages Processing
(TurkLang 2017)*, Kazan, Tatarstan, Russian Federation,
October.

Toleu, A., Tolegen, G., and Mussabayev, R. (2019).
Keyvector: Unsupervised keyphrase extraction using
weighted topic via semantic relatedness. volume 23,
page 861–869. 10.

Proceedings of the 1st Joint SLTU and CCURL Workshop (SLTU-CCURL 2020), pages 265–270
Language Resources and Evaluation Conference (LREC 2020), Marseille, 11–16 May 2020
© European Language Resources Association (ELRA), licensed under CC-BY-NC

DNN-Based Multilingual Automatic Speech Recognition for Wolaytta using Oromo Speech

Martha Yifiru Tachbelie[1,2], Solomon Teferra Abate[1,2], Tanja Schultz[1]
[1]Cognitive Systems Lab, University of Bremen, Germany
[2]School of Information Science, Addis Ababa University, Ethiopia
abate, marthayifiru, tanja.schultz@uni-bremen.de

Abstract

It is known that Automatic Speech Recognition (ASR) is very useful for human-computer interaction in all the human languages. However, due to its requirement for a big speech corpus, which is very expensive, it has not been developed for most of the languages. Multilingual ASR (MLASR) has been suggested to share existing speech corpora among related languages to develop an ASR for languages which do not have the required speech corpora. Literature shows that phonetic relatedness goes across language families. We have, therefore, conducted experiments on MLASR taking two language families: one as source (Oromo from Cushitic) and the other as target (Wolaytta from Omotic). Using Oromo Deep Neural Network (DNN) based acoustic model, Wolaytta pronunciation dictionary and language model we have achieved Word Error Rate (WER) of 48.34% for Wolaytta. Moreover, our experiments show that adding only 30 minutes of speech data from the target language (Wolaytta) to the whole training data (22.8 hours) of the source language (Oromo) results in a relative WER reduction of 32.77%. Our results show the possibility of developing ASR system for a language, if we have pronunciation dictionary and language model, using an existing speech corpus of another language irrespective of their language family.

Keywords: Multilingual Speech Recognition, Under-resourced language, Oromo, Wolaytta

1. Introduction

Automatic Speech Recognition (ASR) is the automatic recognition and transcription of spoken language into text that can be used as text input for other systems such as information retrieval systems. Since speech is difficult to process directly in the human machine interaction, ASR technologies are important for all the human languages. As a result, a lot of research and development efforts have been exerted and lots of Automatic Speech Recognition Systems (ASRSs) have already been developed in a number of human languages. However, only insignificant number of the 7000 languages are considered.

The main reason for the limited coverage of the human languages in the development of ASRSs is that to develop an ASRS for a new language and improve the performance of the existing ones depend on the availability of speech corpus in that particular language. We do not have such corpora for a significant number of human languages, which are known to be under-resourced languages (Besacier et al., 2014). Almost all Ethiopian languages, such as Wolaytta, are under-resourced and belong to the language groups that are not benefiting from the development of spoken language technologies. To the best of our knowledge, there are only three works (Abate et al., 2020a; Tachbelie et al., 2020b; Abate et al., 2020b) towards the development of an ASRS for Oromo and Wolaytta that use at least a medium-sized speech corpora.

Multilingual Automatic Speech Recognition (MLASR) has been suggested and lots of research is being conducted in this line to solve the problem of speech corpora for under-resourced languages. MLASR system is described as a system that is able to recognize multiple languages which are presented during training(Schultz and Waibel, 2001). (Vu et al., 2014) described MLASR as a system in which at least one of the components (feature extraction, acoustic model,

pronunciation dictionary, or language model) is developed using data from many different languages.

MLASR systems are particularly interesting for under-resourced languages where training data are sparse or not available at all (Schultz and Waibel, 2001). Consequently, various researches in the area of MLASR (Weng et al., 1997; Schultz and Waibel, 1998; Schultz, 2002; Kanthak and Ney, 2003; Vu et al., 2014; Müller and Waibel, 2015; Chuangsuwanich, 2016) have been conducted and a lot others are being conducted for several language groups. Especially the development of artificial neural networks (ANNs) helped to achieve better performance in the development of MLASRSs (Heigold et al., 2013; Li et al., 2019).

In our previous work (Tachbelie et al., 2020a), in which we have analyzed the similarities among GlobalPhone (Schultz et al., 2013) and Ethiopian languages (Amharic and Tigrigna from Semitic, Oromo from Cushitic and Wolaytta from Omotic), we have learned that there is high phonetic overlap among Ethiopian languages. The fact that these languages have shared phonological features is indicated in (Gutman and Avanzati, 2013) as well. From our analysis, we have learned that similarity among languages measured using their phonetic overlap crosses the boundaries of language families. Specifically, we have observed that although Oromo and Wolaytta are from different language families, there exists higher phone overlap between them than the other languages (Amharic and Tigrigna). This may be due to their geographical proximity. (Crass and Meyer, 2009) also indicated that Ethiopian languages, regardless of their language families, display areal patterns by sharing a number of similarities. Our analysis showed that 97.3% of Wolaytta phones are covered by the Oromo language while 92.3% of Oromo phones are covered by Wolaytta. Although both languages are under-resourced, Oromo is in a relatively better position than

Wolaytta. There are also a lot of other Ethiopian languages (more than 70) that are in similar or worse condition than Wolaytta with respect to language and speech resources. We wanted, therefore, to investigate the use of existing language resources to develop ASR for other Ethiopian languages. As a proof of concept, we investigated the development of Wolaytta (target language) ASR using Oromo (source language) training speech.

In this work, we present the results of different experiments we have conducted to explore the benefit we gain from MLASR approach for two languages from two different language families. First, we have conducted a cross-lingual ASR experiment where we decoded Wolaytta test speech using Oromo acoustic model (which is developed using Oromo training speech), Wolaytta language and lexical models. Second, we have developed Wolaytta ASR systems using various sizes of Wolaytta training speech (ranging from 30 minutes to 29 hours) with and without the whole amount of Oromo training speech (22.8). We have also conducted experiments to see if the source language (Oromo) can benefit from sharing training speech of the target language (Wolaytta) to improve the performance of the ASRSs.

In the following section 1.1., we give a brief description on the application of deep neural networks for the development of ASRSs. In section 2., we describe the languages considered in this paper. The speech corpora we used for the research are described in section 3. The development of the monolingual ASR using different sizes of Wolaytta training speech, which are our baseline systems, and the results achieved by the use of MLASR approach for Wolaytta using Oromo training speech are presented in section 4. Finally in section 5., we give conclusions and forward future directions.

1.1. Deep Neural Networks in ASR

Over the last 10 years, DNNs methods for ASR were developed and outperform the traditional Gaussian Mixture Model (HMM-GMM). The major factors for their superior performance are the availability of GPUs and the introduction of different types of neural network architectures such as Convolutional Neural networks (CNN) and more recently Time Delay Neural Networks (TDNN) and Factored TDNN (TDNNf).

Since 2009, DNNs are widely used in automatic speech recognition and they presented dramatic improvement in performance. Numerous studies showed hybrid HMM-DNN systems outperform the dominant HMM-GMM on the same data (Hinton et al., 2012). Currently, TDNNs, also called one-dimensional Convolutional Neural Networks, are an efficient and well-performing neural network architectures for ASR (Peddinti et al., 2015). TDNN has the ability to learn long term temporal contexts. Moreover, by using singular value decomposition (SVD) the number of parameters in TDNN models is reduced which makes them inexpensive compared to RNNs. The factored form of TDNNs (TDNNf)(Povey et al., 2018) has similar structure with TDNN, but is trained from a random start with one of the two factors of each matrix constrained to be semi-orthogonal. TDNNf gives substantial improvement over TDNN and has been shown to be effective in under-resourced scenarios. We have used these state-of-the-art neural network architecture in the development of DNN based ASR systems for the Ethiopian languages.

2. Oromo and Wolaytta

More than 80 languages are spoken in Ethiopia. Ethiopian languages are divided into four major language families: Semitic, Cushitic, Omotic and Nilo-Saharan. The Semitic language family is one of the most widespread language families (with more than 20 languages) in the country. Of which, Amharic (spoken by 29.3% of the total Ethiopian population) and Tigrigna (spoken by 5.9% of the total Ethiopian population) are the most spoken languages. The Cushitic language family has also a long list of (about 22) languages spoken in Ethiopia. Amongst them, Oromo is the most widely spoken language in the country (spoken by 33.8% of the total Ethiopian population). The Omotic family has a large number of (more than 30) languages spoken in Ethiopia, one of which is Wolaytta (spoken by 2.2% of the total Ethiopian population) (CSAE, 2010).

The Cushitic and Omotic language families use Latin script for writing. In both the languages the current writers differentiate the gemminated and the non-gemminated consonants. Similarly, long and short vowels are indicated in their writing system.

Having a newly developed speech corpora (Abate et al., 2020a) for Oromo (a Cushitic language) and Wolaytta (an Omotic language), we have selected these languages to explore the application of MLASR development approach in the ANN framework.

2.1. Phonology

Although they belong to different language families, Oromo and Wolaytta share several phonetic properties including the use of long and short vowels. These languages have five similar vowels and each of the vowels in both languages has long and short variants. Having their own inventory of consonants, Oromo and Wolaytta share a number of them (see Table 1). Of course, each of the languages has its own consonants. For instance, phones ɲ and x are used in Oromo but not in Wolaytta while phone ʒ is used in Wolaytta but not in Oromo.

Almost all the consonants of these languages occur in both single and gemminated forms. The other common phonetic feature of these languages is the use of tones which makes both of them tonal languages. However, in this study we did not differentiate between vowels of different tones since the writing system does not show the tones of the vowels and the pronunciation dictionaries for our study have been generated automatically from the text.

Language	Consonants (IPA)	Vowels (IPA)
Oromo	b d ɗ f g h j k k' l m n ɲ p p' r s ʃ t t' tʃ tʃ' ʤ v w x z ʔ	a e i o u aː eː iː oː uː
Wolaytta	b d ɗ f g h j k k' l m n p p' r s ʃ t t' tʃ tʃ' ʤ w z ʒ ʔ	a e i o u aː eː iː oː uː

Table 1: Oromo and Wolaytta phones

2.2. Morphology

Reflecting the morphological nature of their language families, Oromo and Wolaytta are not as simple as English and not as complex as the Semitic language families. In both Oromo and Wolaytta nominals are inflected for number, gender, case and definiteness and verbs are inflected for person, number, gender, tense, aspect and mood (Griefenow-Mewis, 2001). Unlike the Semitic languages, which allow prefixing, Oromo and Wolaytta are suffixing languages. In these languages words can be generated from stems recursively by adding suffixes only.

3. The Speech Corpora

It is known that the Ethiopian languages, specially Oromo and Wolaytta are under-resourced. As a result, all of the previous works conducted towards the development of ASRSs for these languages are based on limited amounts of speech data. It is only recently that a work on the development of four standard medium-sized read speech corpora (Abate et al., 2020a) has been conducted for four Ethiopian languages including Oromo and Wolaytta. For a country like Ethiopia with more than 80 languages, unless a technological solution is used, it looks hopeless to have equivalent speech corpora for all its languages.

In this work, we have used the existing speech corpora of Oromo (Abate et al., 2020a) to find out a solution for the development of an ASRS for an under-resourced language, Wolaytta. We considered Oromo as a source and Wolaytta as a target language considering the fact that there are more previous works conducted for Oromo, such as (Gelana, 2016; Gutu, 2016) than what we have for Wolaytta. We hope that our findings will be extended to solve the problems of the other Ethiopian languages that fall under four different language families.

4. Multilingual ASR for Wolaytta

4.1. Development of ASR Systems for Wolaytta

Although the aim of our current work is to explore the development of MLASR for Wolaytta as a target language using Oromo training speech (as a source language), we have developed different monolingual GMM- and DNN-based ASRSs for Wolaytta using different sizes of Wolaytta speech corpus for comparison purposes. The description of the procedures we followed is presented in sub-section 4.1.1..

4.1.1. Acoustic, Lexical and Language Models

To build reference AMs that use different sizes of training speech, we have splitted the Wolaytta training speech into 11 clusters: with 30 minutes, 1, 2, 4, 6, 8, 10, 15, 20, 25 and 29 (all) hours of speech length. We have selected roughly equal number of utterances from each speaker randomly for each of these clusters. Each of them has been used to train different AMs.

All the AMs have been built in a similar fashion using Kaldi ASR toolkit (Povey et al., 2011). We have built context dependent HMM-GMM based AM using 39 dimensional mel-frequency cepstral coefficients (MFCCs) to each of which cepstral mean and variance normalization

(CMVN) is applied. The AM uses a fully-continuous 3-state left-to-right HMM. Then we did Linear Discriminant Analysis (LDA) and Maximum Likelihood Linear Transform (MLLT) feature transformation for each of the models. Then Speaker Adaptive Training (SAT) has been done using an offline transform, feature space Maximum Likelihood Linear Regression (fMLLR). We did tuning to find the best number of states and Gaussians for different sizes of the training data.

To train the DNN-based AMs, we have used the best HMM-GMM models to get alignments and the same training speech used to train HMM-GMM models. But we have applied a three-fold data augmentation (Ko et al., 2015) prior to the extraction of 40-dimensional MFCCs without derivatives, 3-dimensional pitch features and 100-dimensional i-vectors for speaker adaptation. The neural network architecture we used is Factored Time Delay Neural Networks with additional Convolutional layers (CNN-TDNNf) according to the standard Kaldi WSJ recipe. The Neural network has 15 hidden layers (6 CNN followed by 9 TDNNf) and a rank reduction layer. The number of units in the TDDNf consists of 1024 and 128 bottleneck units except for the TDNNf layer immediately following the CNN layers which has 256 bottleneck units.

The list of word entries both for training and decoding lexicons have been extracted from the training speech transcription in both the source and target languages. Using the nature of writing system that indicates gemminated and non-gemminated consonants as well as the long and short vowels, we have generated the pronunciation of these words automatically. However, since the tones are not indicated in written form of both languages, we did not consider tones in the current pronunciation dictionaries.

For the development of the LMs we have used the text used in (Abate et al., 2020a). We have developed trigram LMs using the SRILM toolkit (Stolcke, 2002). The LMs are smoothed with unmodified Kneser-Ney smoothing techniques (Chen and Goodman, 1996) and made open by including a special unknown word token. LM probabilities are computed for the lexicon of the training transcription.

4.1.2. Evaluation Results

We have evaluated all AMs trained with different sizes of training speech using the same test set (1:45 hours of speech recorded from four speakers who read a total of 578 utterances), pronunciation dictionary and language model. The performance of the systems is given in Figure 1. These results are our reference points or baselines for the results achieved by using only the source language, and combined with different amounts of target language's training speech. As we can observe from Figure 1, obviously, the WER reduces with the additional training speech in almost all the AMs. The DNN-based systems outperform the HMM-GMM-based ones regardless of the size of the training speech, except for 30 minutes. The DNN-based AMs has brought a relative WER reductions that range from 9.03% (with 1 hour) to 31.45% (with all the training speech). The best system developed using all the available training speech has achieved a WER of 23.23% with the DNN-based AM.

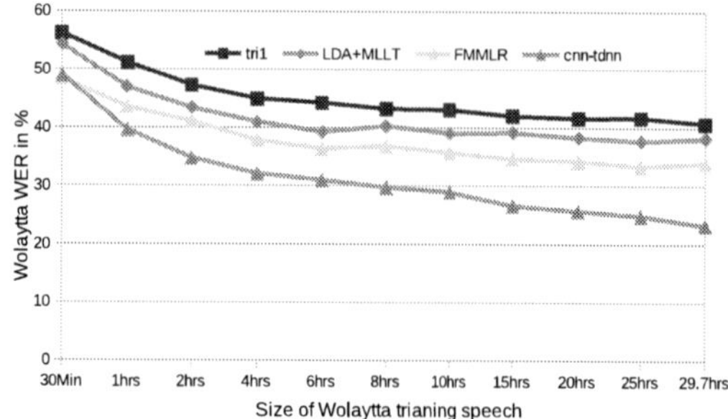

Figure 1: Wolaytta WERs with different sizes of Wolaytta training speech

4.2. Use of Oromo Speech for Wolaytta ASR

First we have decoded the Wolaytta evaluation test speech using a DNN-based Oromo AM (trained using all the training speech of the Oromo corpus), Wolaytta pronunciation dictionary and Wolaytta language model and achieved a WER of 48.34%. For this purpose we needed to map the Wolaytta phones that are not found in Oromo to the nearest possible Oromo phones (see Table 2).

Wolaytta Phones (IPA)	Mapped Oromo Phones(IPA)	Remarks
7 (ʔ)	hh (ʔ)	Same IPA
zh (ʒ)	z (z)	Different IPA
zz (z:)	z (z) z (z)	Double to single mapping
ssh (ʃ:)	sh (ʃ) sh (ʃ)	Double to single mapping
hhhh (ʔ:)	hh (ʔ) hh (ʔ)	Double to single mapping

Table 2: Wolaytta phones mapped to Oromo phones

We have, then, conducted experiments to see the benefits it gets from additional Wolaytta speech incrementally starting from 30 minutes to the whole training speech. The evaluation of all the systems is done using the same evaluation set. The results are presented in Figure 2.

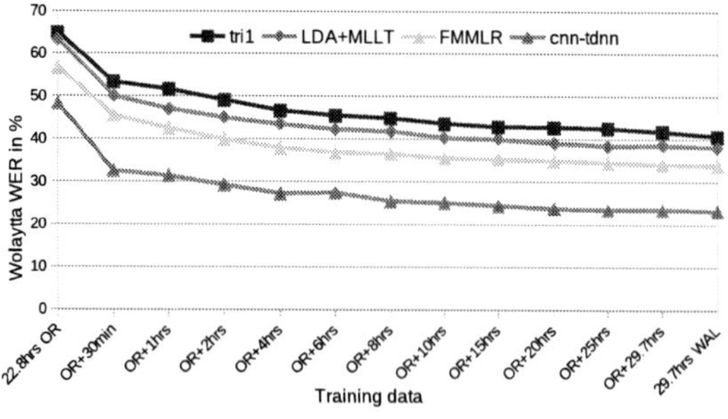

Figure 2: Wolaytta WERs with different sizes of Wolaytta training speech added to the whole training speech of Oromo

The results in Figure 2 show that performance improvement can be obtained by adding training speech from the target language. As we add more and more training speech

from the target language, the improvement in performance reduces. A relative WER reduction of 32.77% has been achieved as a result of adding only 30 minutes of training speech from the target language. That means the WER we could achieve by using only the source language's training speech has been reduced from 48.34% to 32.5% by adding only 30 minutes training speech of the target language that is randomly selected from all the speakers (76) of the target language.

Our results also show that instead of using only small amount of monolingual training speech in the development of an ASRS, specially in the DNN framework, the use of speech data from other related languages bring performance improvement. We have presented this improvement in Figure 3 that shows the comparison of WERs of ASRSs developed using Wolaytta training speech only and that of the ASRSs developed using different sizes of training speech from Wolaytta combined with all (22.8 hours) Oromo training speech. As it can be seen from the Figure, by adding only 30 minutes of Wolaytta training speech to all of the Oromo training speech, we have achieved a relative WER reduction of 33.55% and 5.52% when 25 hours of Wolaytta training speech is added.

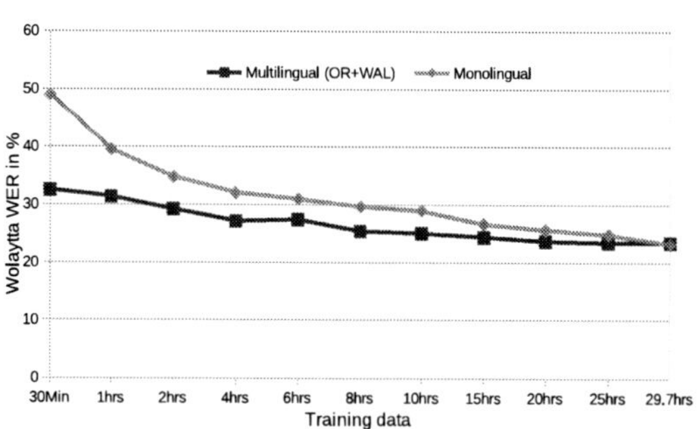

Figure 3: Wolaytta WERs with different sizes of Wolaytta with and without the Oromo speech

4.3. Evaluation of Multilingual Acoustic Models for Oromo

We have decoded Oromo test set using the acoustic models (Wolaytta only AM and MLASR AMs) discussed in the previous sections, Oromo pronunciation dictionary and Oromo language model developed by (Abate et al., 2020a). The results presented in Figure 4 show that we have achieved a WER of 49.25% using the DNN-based AM developed using 29.7 hours of Wolaytta training speech. The performance of MLASR systems on Oromo test set brought slight WER reductions compared to the best WER obtained from a system that is developed using Oromo training speech only. The relative WER reductions we have obtained range from 1.27% (gained from the addition of 10 hours of Wolaytta speech) to 3.31% (gained from the addition of 25 hours of Wolaytta speech). We could observe that adding 30 minutes to 8 hours of Wolaytta training speech has negatively affected Oromo ASR.

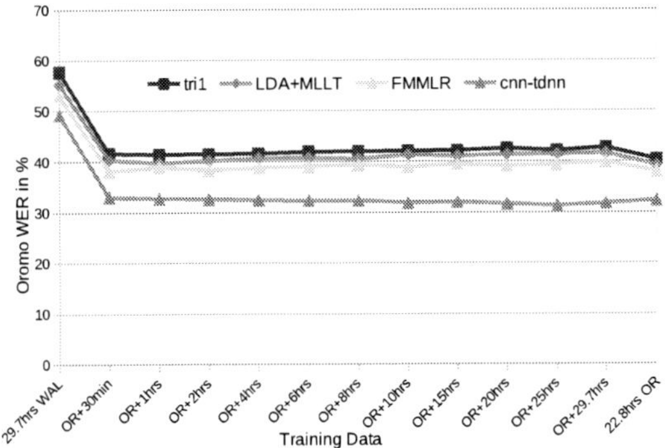

Figure 4: Oromo WERs with different sizes of Wolaytta training speech with and without the Oromo speech

5. Conclusion and Way Forward

In this paper, we have presented the experiments conducted on the development of multilingual ASRs across language families taking Oromo and Wolaytta as source and target languages, respectively. We have achieved a WER of 48.34% for Wolaytta without any training speech from it. By adding only 30 minutes of speech data from Wolaytta to the whole training data of the source language (Oromo) we have achieved a relative WER reduction of 32.77%. The ASRSs developed using all the training speech (22.8 hours) of the source language together with different sizes of training speech from the target language outperformed the ASRSs developed using training speech of the respective size from the target language only. The observed relative WER reductions range from 33.55% (achieved when training speech of Oromo plus only 30 minutes of Wolaytta is used) to 5.52% (achieved when training speech of Oromo plus 25 hours of Wolaytta is used). Based on our results, we conclude that it is possible to develop an ASRS with reasonable performance for a language using speech data of another language, irrespective of its language family, provided that we have a decoding pronunciation dictionary and a language model. We, therefore, recommend the development of a decoding pronunciation dictionary and a language model for the other Ethiopian languages so that they can benefit from the development of MLASRSs using the speech corpora of other languages.

6. Acknowledgment

We would like to express our gratitude to the Alexander von Humboldt Foundation for funding the research stay at the Cognitive Systems Lab (CSL) of the University of Bremen.

7. Bibliographical References

Abate, S. T., Tachbelie, M. Y., Melese, M., Abera, H., Abebe, T., Mulugeta, W., Assabie, Y., Meshesha, M., Atinafu, S., and Ephrem, B. (2020a). Large vocabulary read speech corpora for four ethiopian languages : Amharic, tigrigna, oromo and wolaytta. In *LREC 2020*.

Abate, S. T., Tachbelie, M. Y., and Schultz, T. (2020b). Deep neural networks based automatic speech recognition for four ethiopian languages. In *ICASSP 2020*.

Besacier, L., Barnard, E., Karpov, A., and Schultz, T. (2014). Automatic speech recognition for under-resourced languages: A survey. *Speech Communication*, 56:85–100.

Chen, S. F. and Goodman, J. (1996). An empirical study of smoothing techniques for language modeling. In *34th Annual Meeting of the Association for Computational Linguistics*, pages 310–318, Santa Cruz, California, USA. Association for Computational Linguistics.

Chuangsuwanich, E. (2016). *Multilingual techniques for low resource automatic speech recognition*. Ph.D. thesis.

Crass, J. and Meyer, R. (2009). *Introduction*. Rüdiger Köppe Verlag, Köln.

CSAE. (2010). The 2007 population and housing census.

Gelana, K. (2016). *A Large Vocabulary, Speaker-Independent, Continuous Speech Recognition System for Afaan Oromo: Using Broadcast News Speech Corpus*. Ph.D. thesis, Addis Ababa University.

Griefenow-Mewis, C. (2001). *A Grammatical Sketch of Written Oromo*.

Gutman, A. and Avanzati, B. (2013). Languages of ethiopia and eritrea.

Gutu, Y. G. (2016). *A Continuous, Speaker Independent Speech Recognizer for Afaan Oroomoo: Afaan Oroomoo Speech Recognition Using HMM Model*. Ph.D. thesis, Addis Ababa University.

Heigold, G., Vanhoucke, V., Senior, A., Nguyen, P., Ranzato, M., Devin, M., and Dean, J. (2013). Multilingual acoustic models using distributed deep neural networks. In *2013 IEEE International Conference on Acoustics, Speech and Signal Processing*, pages 8619–8623.

Hinton, G., Deng, L., Yu, D., Dahl, G., Mohamed, A.-r., Jaitly, N., Senior, A., Vanhoucke, V., Nguyen, P., Kingsbury, B., et al. (2012). Deep neural networks for acoustic modeling in speech recognition. *IEEE Signal processing magazine*, 29.

Kanthak, S. and Ney, H. (2003). Multilingual acoustic modeling using graphemes. In *Proceedings of European Conference on Speech Communication and Technology*, pages 1145–1148.

Ko, T., Peddinti, V., Povey, D., and Khudanpur, S. (2015). Audio augmentation for speech recognition. In *INTERSPEECH*.

Li, X., Dalmia, S., Black, A., and Metze, F. (2019). Multilingual speech recognition with corpus relatedness sampling, 08.

Müller, M. and Waibel, A. H. (2015). Using language adaptive deep neural networks for improved multilingual speech recognition.

Peddinti, V., Povey, D., and Khudanpur, S. (2015). A time delay neural network architecture for efficient modeling of long temporal contexts. In *Sixteenth Annual Conference of the International Speech Communication Association*.

Povey, D., Ghoshal, A., Boulianne, G., Burget, L., Glembek, O., Goel, N., Hannemann, M., Motlicek, P., Qian, Y., Schwarz, P., Silovsky, J., Stemmer, G., and Vesely, K. (2011). The kaldi speech recognition toolkit. In *IEEE 2011 Workshop on Automatic Speech Recognition and*

Understanding. IEEE Signal Processing Society, December. IEEE Catalog No.: CFP11SRW-USB.

Povey, D., Cheng, G., Wang, Y., Li, K., Xu, H., Yarmohammadi, M., and Khudanpur, S. (2018). Semi-orthogonal low-rank matrix factorization for deep neural networks. In *Interspeech*, pages 3743–3747.

Schultz, T. and Waibel, A. (1998). Multilingual and crosslingual speech recognition. In *Proc. DARPA Workshop on Broadcast News Transcription and Understanding*, pages 259–262.

Schultz, T. and Waibel, A. (2001). Language-independent and language-adaptive acoustic modeling for speech recognition. *Speech Commun.*, 35(1-2):31–51, August.

Schultz, T., Vu, N. T., and Schlippe, T. (2013). Globalphone: A multilingual text and speech database in 20 languages. In *ICASSP*.

Schultz, T. (2002). Globalphone: a multilingual speech and text database developed at karlsruhe university. In John H. L. Hansen et al., editors, *INTERSPEECH*. ISCA.

Stolcke, A. (2002). Srilm – an extensible language modeling toolkit. In *Proceedings of the 7th International Conference on Spoken Language Processing (ICSLP) 2002*, pages 901–904.

Tachbelie, M. Y., Abate, S. T., and Schultz, T. (2020a). Analysis of globalphone and ethiopian languages speech corpora for multilingual asr. In *LREC 2020*.

Tachbelie, M. Y., Abulimiti, A., Abate, S. T., and Schultz, T. (2020b). Dnn-based speech recognition for globalphone languages. In *ICASSP 2020*.

Vu, N. T., Imseng, D., Povey, D., Motlícek, P., Schultz, T., and Bourlard, H. (2014). Multilingual deep neural network based acoustic modeling for rapid language adaptation. *2014 IEEE International Conference on Acoustics, Speech and Signal Processing (ICASSP)*, pages 7639–7643.

Weng, F., Bratt, H., Neumeyer, L., and Stolcke, A. (1997). A study of multilingual speech recognition. In *EUROSPEECH*.

Proceedings of the 1st Joint SLTU and CCURL Workshop (SLTU-CCURL 2020), pages 271–276
Language Resources and Evaluation Conference (LREC 2020), Marseille, 11–16 May 2020
© European Language Resources Association (ELRA), licensed under CC-BY-NC

Building Language Models for Morphological Rich Low-Resource Languages using Data from Related Donor Languages: the Case of Uyghur

Ayimunishagu Abulimiti, Tanja Schultz

Cognitive Systems Lab, University of Bremen, Germany
{ay.abulimiti, tanja.schultz}@uni-bremen.de

Abstract

Huge amounts of data are needed to build reliable statistical language models. Automatic speech processing tasks in low-resource languages typically suffer from lower performances due to weak or unreliable language models. Furthermore, language modeling for agglutinative languages is very challenging, as the morphological richness results in higher Out Of Vocabulary (OOV) rate. In this work, we show our effort to build word-based as well as morpheme-based language models for Uyghur, a language that combines both challenges, i.e. it is a low-resource and agglutinative language. Fortunately, there exists a closely-related rich-resource language, namely Turkish. Here, we present our work on leveraging Turkish text data to improve Uyghur language models. To maximize the overlap between Uyghur and Turkish words, the Turkish data is pre-processed on the word surface level, which results in 7.76% OOV-rate reduction on the Uyghur development set. To investigate various levels of low-resource conditions, different subsets of Uyghur data are generated. On the smallest subset including only 100 Uyghur utterances, a word-based language model trained with bilingual Uyghur-Turkish data achieved 98.10% relative perplexity reduction over the language models trained with Uyghur data only. Morpheme-based language models trained with bilingual data achieved up to 40.91% relative perplexity reduction over the language models trained only with Uyghur data.

Keywords: Multilingual, Low-resource, Language modeling, Agglutinative languages, GlobalPhone

1. Introduction

A language model is one of the main components of Automatic Speech Recognition (ASR) systems, which significantly impacts the overall recognition performances. To build reliable language models, very large amounts of text data are required. However, even with large corpora, the construction of reliable language models is very challenging for morphological rich languages, since the large vocabulary leads to high Out-Of-Vocabulary (OOV) rates. This problem becomes even more dramatic if only few data resources are available for a language in question. In this paper we address the example of Uyghur, which combines both challenges, i.e. Uyghur has a rich morphology that primarily uses agglutination and Uyghur belongs to the category of low-resource languages.

A common approach in language modeling to overcome high OOV rates in agglutinating languages is the use of sub-words or morphemes as model unit (Hirsimäki et al., 2006; Carki et al., 2000; Arısoy et al., 2009). To build sub-word or morpheme-based language models, text data are usually automatically segmented into sub-units based on morphological analysis and/or statistical segmentation methods. Traditionally, the segmentation methods rely on statistical models, which need reasonable amounts of annotated text data to be reliably trained. While sub-unit based language model approaches may ease the data sparsity problem compared to word-based language models, the lack of data for low-resource languages jeopardizes the training of reliable segmentation models.

In this work, we aim to improve the performance of language models for morphological rich and low-resource language with the example of Uyghur by leveraging data from a resource-rich donor language. As donor language we se-

lected Turkish since it also uses an agglutinative morphology and shares many linguistic features with Uyghur.

To explore the impact of data from the donor language, we compared language models trained on Uyghur data only with language models trained on data from both languages, Uyghur and Turkish. Furthermore, we investigated word-based and morpheme-based language models to address the low-resource and agglutinative features of Uyghur. To study various low-resource conditions, we created different subsets of Uyghur training text data. The resulting language models are evaluated in terms of Perplexity (PPL), n-gram coverage and OOV rates.

This paper is organized as follows: in section 2 we describe the text corpora of Uyghur and Turkish. In Section 3, we introduce some common linguistic properties of Uyghur and Turkish. In Section 4, we describe the experimental set up. In Section 5, we discuss the results of our experiments.

2. Data

Uyghur is an under-resourced language with about 11 million speakers, who are mainly located in western China and Central Asia. Uyghur belongs to the Turkic language family and is closely related to Turkish. Both languages use agglutinative morphology, share features like the order of object-verb constituents, and are in parts mutually intelligible, in particular on the subject of numbers and pronouns. The Uyghur and Turkish text data used in this study were collected by applying the GlobalPhone corpus collection procedures as described in (Schultz, 2002). As of today, the Globalphone corpus comprises of more than 450 hours of high-quality clean speech recorded from more than 2000 native speakers reading newspaper articles (Schultz et al., 2013).

2.1. Uyghur and Turkish Text Data

The Uyghur data collection, partially funded by NSF (award 1519164), comprises of news articles read by 46 speakers, as described in Abulimiti and Schultz (2020). While Uyghur is written in three different writing systems (Arabic, Roman, and Cyrillic alphabet), our corpus consistently uses Roman script.

In this work, we used the transcripts of the Uyghur ASR training data as source for language model training and the ASR development set for evaluating the language models. Table 1 summarizes the statistics of the used Uyghur text data.

	Uyghur		Turkish
	Training	Development	Training
Speakers	37	4	79
Utterances	3380	400	5482
Word tokens	60084	7902	87733

Table 1: Uyghur and Turkish text data

Turkish is used as the donor language and we use the GlobalPhone resources of the Turkish ASR training data to train the morpheme-based segmentation models and language models. The statistics of the used Turkish training text data are given in Table 1.

Since this study is meant to establish a proof-of-concept for bilingual language modeling, we focused on small amounts of Turkish data first. In future steps we plan to use larger available text corpora of Turkish, which have been collected for example within the GlobalPhone project (Carki et al., 2000).

3. Similarity of Uyghur and Turkish

3.1. Morphological Productivity

Uyghur and Turkish are both agglutinative languages, i.e. words consist of morpheme sequences (including stems and affixes) to determine their meaning, but morphemes are not altered in the process of concatenation. Typically, new words in Uyghur and Turkish are generated by adding suffixes to the end of the word. Examples of the morphological productivity are given for Uyghur and Turkish in table 2.

Uyghur words and meaning	
mektep	school
mektep-ler	schools
mektep-ler-i	of schools of third person
mektep-ler-i-de	at schools of third person
Turkish words and meaning	
iş	work
iş-çi	worker
iş-çi-ler	workers
iş-çi-ler-in	of workers

Table 2: Examples of Morphological Productivity

Uyghur and Turkish not only share a similar morphological productivity, but also have a large number of suffixes in common. We thus hope that these similarities may help to improve a morpheme-based Uyghur language model when adding morphologically segmented Turkish text data.

3.2. Mutual Intelligibility

In statistical count-based n-gram language models, every surface form of a word is modeled separately (Goodman, 2001; Tsvetkov et al., 2016). One way to improve the language model of a low-resourced language may be to make use of overlapping words from a closely-related language (Fügen et al., 2003). However, the amount of overlapping words between languages is usually not very large, even when they are closely-related. One reason is that the spelling of words may follow different writing conventions. Uyghur and Turkish share many overlapping words, e.g. *"merhaba (hello), güzel (beautiful), ölum (death), kitap (book)"*, with same meanings and written form. Such overlapping words might be useful when building Uyghur language models with the help of Turkish text data. Overlapping words in Uyghur and Turkish commonly appear mostly in daily communications. In our corpus of speech read from news articles, the rate of overlapping words is thus limited. We observed 9.32% of Uyghur words in the development which appear in the Turkish training data. They corresponds to 90.60% OOV rate in the Uyghur development set.

Nevertheless, the mutual intelligibility of these two languages allows to achieving a fair amount of overlapping words. In addition, there are plenty of words, specially numbers and pronouns, which share the same meaning and similar pronunciations with only slightly different spelling. Table 3 shows some examples.

Uyghur	IPA	Turkish	IPA	in English
we	/vɛ/	ve	/vɛ/	and
ishchi	/iʃt͡ʃi/	işçi	/iʃˈt͡ʃi/	workers
üch	/yt͡ʃ/	üç	/ˈyt͡ʃ/	three
ikki	/ˈiʰt͡ʃːi/	iki	/iˈci/	two
qarar	/qɑrār/	karar	/kɑˈrɑr/	decision
yapon	/japon/	japon	/japon/	japan

Table 3: Words with same meaning but different spelling

From many frequent words in both languages, we noticed joint spelling "patterns". For example, the graphemes in Turkish, *"ç,ş,ı"* correspond to graphemes in Uyghur *"ch, shi, i"*, respectively. After mapping the Turkish graphemes to the corresponding Uyghur graphemes, we gained more overlapping words. The words, such as *"iş (work), üç (three)"* in Turkish were mapped to *"ish, üch"*, respectively and have same spelling form as Uyghur words *"ish (work), üch (three)"* without changing the meaning.

In addition, we know that the numbers contribute to mutual intelligibility of the two languages. Therefore, numbers in Turkish spelling form are mapped to Uyghur spelling form. In this study, 30 mapping rules in total are used on Turkish data to convert the spelling form of words in Turkish to Uyghur. After applying the mapping rules, 17.08% of words in the Uyghur development set were covered by the words in the Turkish training data (82.91% OOV on

Uyghur development data). This corresponds to 7.76% absolute OOV-rate reduction compared to the Turkish data without any pre-processing. After mapping, the 100 most frequent overlapping words along with their frequencies in Uyghur and Turkish data were selected for an exemplary presentation in Figure 1.

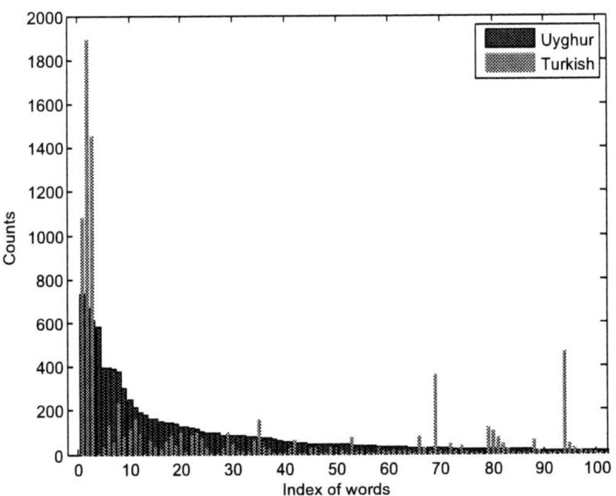

Figure 1: Counts of the 100 most frequent Uyghur words in the training data and overlap with Turkish data

4. Experiments

The main reason for using data from a donor language in a low-resource language modeling is to gain more overlapping words and get more context coverage. For low-resource and morphological rich languages, building more reliable word-based statistical language models with data from a donor language can still be challenging, due to the data sparsity problem and insufficient context coverage. In this work, we investigate how to improve the performance of language models for Uyghur using data from Turkish. We conducted two sets of language modeling experiments, word-based and morpheme-based language modeling. To explore the impact of data from the donor language, we compared language models using Uyghur data only and bilingual data (from Uyghur and Turkish). For building morpheme-based language models, morphological segmentation is done using the open source software Morfessor (Virpioja et al., 2013). It is used for unsupervised morphological segmentation of words into morpheme-like units. For training and evaluating language models, we used the SRILM toolkit (Stolcke, 2002). For word-based and morpheme-based language models, trigram models are trained by applying modified Kneser-Ney discounting (James, 2000) without cut-offs. For all the word-based language models, the words from the full Uyghur training text data (vocabulary size: 8819) is used as vocabulary. For the morpheme-based language models, this vocabulary is segmented applying the segmentation model trained with the data in the training set and then used as vocabulary of the morpheme-based language model.

To investigate various levels of low-resource conditions, we generated subsets by randomly selecting Uyghur utterances from each speaker in Uyghur training text data with varying utterance size. We collected 6 sets of Uyghur training text data for our experiment. The size of utterances, number of words and word tokens in each set are shown in Table 4. In the bilingual data experiments, these data sets are combined with pre-processed Turkish data, as discussed in Section 3.2.

Training set	Utterances	Words	Word tokens
UY_100	100	1234	1841
UY_200	200	2105	3607
UY_1k	1000	5731	17505
UY_2k	2000	7999	35249
UY_3k	3000	8783	53410
UY_all	3380	8819	60084

Table 4: Data sets used for training language models

4.1. Language Modeling on Uyghur Data Only

With the training data from those 6 sets of Uyghur data, word-based trigram language models are trained. To train morpheme-based language models for every set of Uyghur data, a segmentation model is trained with Uyghur data. Then this is used to segment Uyghur training data, Uyghur development data and the language model vocabulary. Finally, a trigram language models is built based on the segmented Uyghur training data.

4.2. Language Modeling on Bilingual Data

Since we use the same Turkish data for each set of Uyghur training data, a word-based trigram language model is trained using Turkish data and Uyghur vocabulary as mentioned above. Afterwards, for each set of Uyghur training data, one word-based trigram language model is built. For each set of Uyghur data, the best interpolation weight of Uyghur language model and Turkish language model is calculated on a held-out set. This weight is then used to interpolate the Uyghur and Turkish language models.

Morpheme-based language models for each set of Uyghur data are built with the following steps. Firstly, the Uyghur training data is merged with Turkish data and the merged data is used for training the segmentation model. After training the segmentation model, Uyghur training data, Uyghur vocabulary, Uyghur development data and Turkish data are segmented with this segmentation model. Then, morpheme-based language models are trained with segmented Uyghur data and segmented Turkish data using the segmented Uyghur vocabulary. Similar to the word-based language models, these language specific morpheme-based languages are interpolated with the best interpolation weight.

5. Evaluation

The trained word-based and morpheme-based language models for each set of Uyghur training data are evaluated on the Uyghur development set. As described in Section 4, the Uyghur development set is segmented into morpheme-like units like Uyghur training data. Evaluation is conducted on the segmented Uyghur development data.

5.1. Word-Based Language Modeling

In Figure 2, the trigram perplexity results of word-based language models trained with Uyghur data only are compared with the interpolated language models trained with bilingual data. As can be seen, the interpolated language models outperform the Uyghur-only language models for all training set conditions. The relative improvements in terms of perplexity range from 98% to 70%. The smaller the Uyghur data in training, the higher is the relative improvement. Considering the findings in Figure 1, we assume that the amount of overlapping words in Turkish contribute to the perplexity improvements. Particularly in the small sets of Uyghur data, the overlapping word tokens of the Uyghur training data get significantly more counts, which might explain why relative reductions are higher on smaller amounts of Uyghur data.

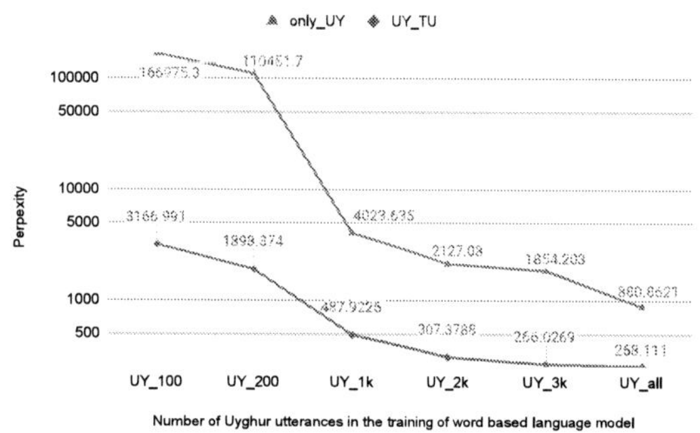

Figure 2: Perplexities of word-based language models trained with Uyghur-only and with bilingual data

Figure 3 presents the bigram coverage of language models on the Uyghur development set. With bilingual data, slightly higher bigram coverages (from 15.71% to 2.39%) are achieved relative to the language models trained with only Uyghur data. For smaller amount of Uyghur training data, the bigram coverage differences are more prominent. For the trigram coverage, we found no big difference between language models trained with Uyghur-only versus bilingual data. However, we achieved about 2% relative OOV-rate reduction on the Uyghur development set with bilingual data compared to Uyghur data only.

5.2. Morpheme-Based Language Modeling

Figure 4) shows the results on the comparisons of interpolated morpheme-based language models in terms of perplexities. As can be observed, the language model trained with bilingual data (red line) outperforms the corresponding language model trained with Uyghur data only (blue line) on all Uyghur data sets. The relative improvements in terms of perplexity range from 40.91% to 1.77%. Furthermore, for the small Uyghur training sets with 100 (UY_100) and 200 (UY_200) utterances only, the relative gains by using bilingual data are larger than for the other sets.

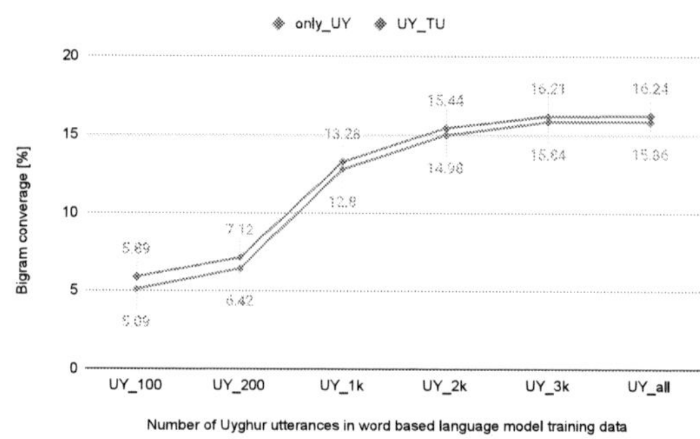

Figure 3: Bigram coverage of word-based language models on Uyghur development set

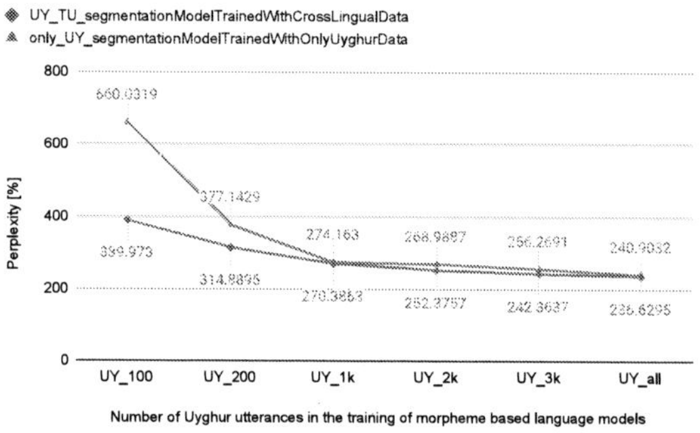

Figure 4: Perplexity of morpheme-based language models trained with only Uyghur data and bilingual data

As shown in Figure 5, the language models with bilingual data have a higher bigram/trigram coverage than the corresponding language models trained with Uyghur data only. Similar to the case of word-based language models, for the smaller data sets language models trained with bilingual data show higher relative improvement in terms of bigram/trigram coverage compared to language models trained with only Uyghur data. For example, on the UY_100 set, the language model with bilingual data has achieved 60.99% with 46.46% relative improvement in terms of bigram and trigram coverage, respectively.

As expected, morpheme-based language models result in much lower perplexities than the corresponding word-based language models. With morpheme-based data, the OOV-rate is significantly reduced compared to the word-based ones. However, regardless of the segmentation level (word- or morpheme-based), the bilingual language models outperform the Uyghur-only language models in all our experiments. Also, we observe that relative improvements are higher in terms of perplexity, n-gram coverage and OOV-rate for smaller Uyghur data sets.

Our experiments were based on the hypothesis that no morpheme-like segmentation model or morphological analysis is available for the low-resourced language. There-

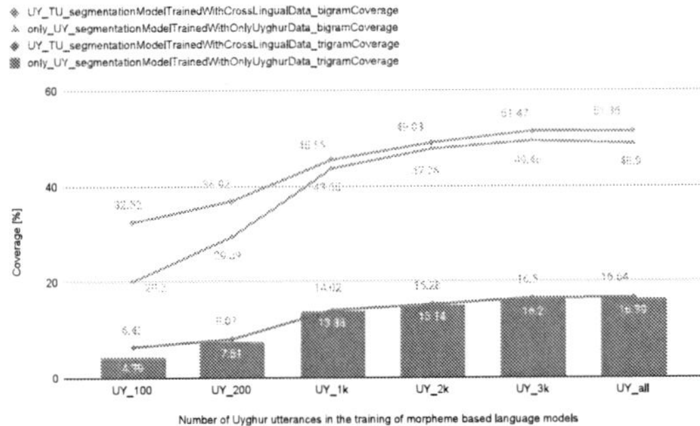

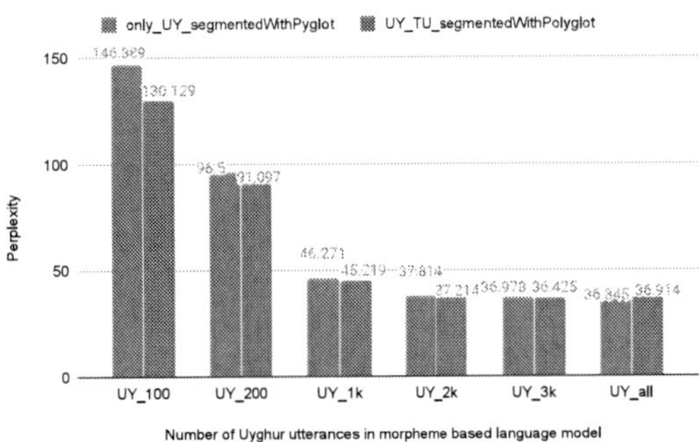

Figure 5: Bigram and trigram coverage of morpheme-based language models on the Uyghur development set

Figure 6: Morpheme-based language models using segmentation model from Polyglot

fore, for each data set, unsupervised statistical segmentation models were trained with the data from each training set. As the training data is limited, the quality of the segmentation model may be sub-optimal. Fortunately, there are software tools like Polyglot (Al-Rfou et al., 2013a; Al-Rfou et al., 2013b), which provide Morfessor models for 135 languages, including Uyghur. To explore the impact of existing and more "reliable" segmentation models, we conducted the morpheme-based language modeling experiments using the segmentation model from Polyglot.

The experiments are conducted in the same fashion as described above. The only difference is that the segmentation model from Polyglot is employed and corresponding data was segmented with that model.

Figure 6 compares the evaluation results of morpheme-based language models using Uyghur data only with bilingual data, which are segmented with Polyglot. Similar to the results from our previous experiments, the relative improvement is higher on small Uyghur data sets when bilingual data are used. On UY_100 and UY_200 set, 11.40% and 5.59% relative improvements in terms of perplexity are achieved by interpolated language models using bilingual data. However, on the sets with larger amount of Uyghur data, i.e., UY_2k and UY_3k, there is only a minor improvement with bilingual data. By the experiments using all Uyghur data (UY_all), the language model using Uyghur data only even has slightly lower perplexity. From these results, we conclude that if there is a reasonable segmentation model, language modeling with bilingual data is more suitable when only very limited data are available in the target language, for instance, under 1000 utterances. In addition, it is noticeable that the perplexity of the language models are much lower (by a factor of ca. 5) than the language models in our previous experiments.

Regarding the bigram and trigram coverage, interpolated language models achieve higher coverage than the language models trained with Uyghur data only (See Figure 7). On smaller set of Uyghur data, the improvement over using Uyghur data only is more significant. On UY_100 set, interpolated language models have relatively higher bigram (32.05%) and trigram (19.18%) coverage. Compared to the results in Figure 5, the corresponding language models have higher bigram coverage (by a factor of 1.7) and tri-

gram coverage (by a factor of 3) in each data set, than the language models, which are trained with morpheme units segmented with the self-trained segmentation model.

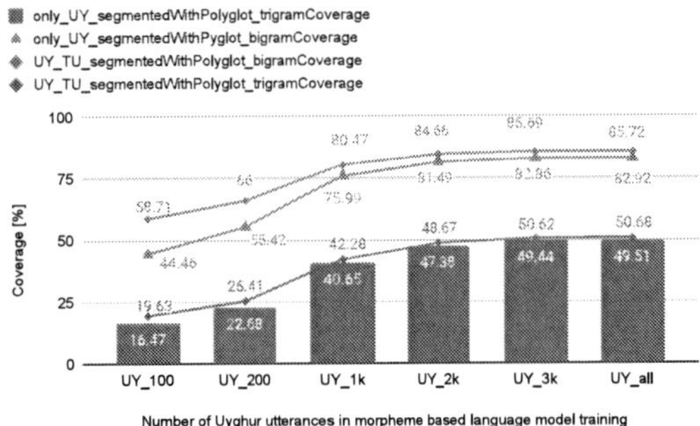

Figure 7: Bigram and trigram coverage of language models using segmentation model from Polyglot

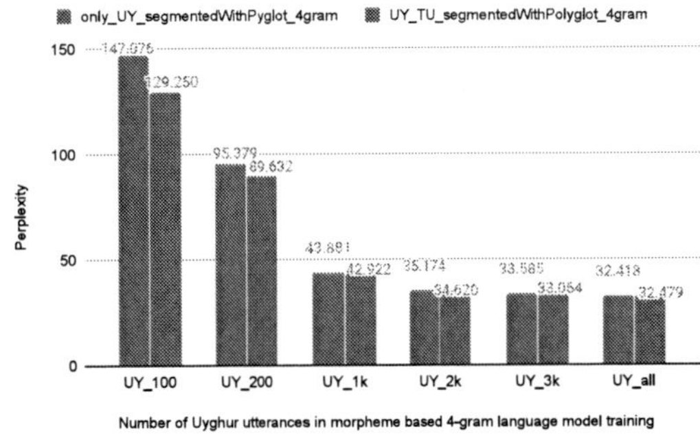

Figure 8: Perplexity of 4-gram language models using segmentation model from Polyglot

In morpheme-based language models, a word may be segmented into several morphemes, e.g. 3 morphemes. In this case, the context of the morpheme-based trigram model

275

may be within a word. Regarding this, we conducted the experiments using Polyglot with same fashion described above but with higher order morpheme-based language models, i.e., 4-grams. The perplexity of the morpheme-based 4-gram language models trained only with Uyghur data and with bilingual data is shown in Figure 8. Similar to the results from our previous experiments, the language models trained with bilingual data showed better performance over the language models trained only with Uyghur data. In each set of the experiments, 4-gram morpheme-based language models showed better performance in terms of perplexity over the corresponding trigram morpheme-based language models.

6. Conclusion

In this paper, we investigated word-based and morpheme-based language models for the low-resource and agglutinative language Uyghur using data from the donor language Turkish. To increase the amount of overlapping words, mapping rules are applied on the Turkish data. With this pre-processing, Turkish data achieves 7.76% of OOV-rate reduction on the Uyghur development set. Subsets of Uyghur data are generated to simulate different levels of low-resource conditions. The results indicate for both word-based and morpheme-based language models that the interpolated language model trained with bilingual data outperform Uyghur-only models in terms of perplexity, n-gram coverage and OOV-rate. Moreover, the smaller the available Uyghur data, the higher relative improvement can be achieved. Furthermore, it can be concluded that a more reliable segmentation model like Polyglot, contributes to a better morpheme-based language model regardless whether it is trained with Uyghur data only or bilingual data.

7. Bibliographical References

Abulimiti, A. and Schultz, T. (2020). Automatic Speech Recognition for Uyghur through Multilingual Acoustic Modelling. In *LREC2020*.

Al-Rfou, R., Perozzi, B., and Skiena, S. (2013a). Polyglot: Distributed Word Representations for Multilingual NLP. *arXiv preprint arXiv:1307.1662*.

Al-Rfou, R., Perozzi, B., and Skiena, S. (2013b). Polyglot: Distributed word representations for multilingual nlp. In *Proceedings of the Seventeenth Conference on Computational Natural Language Learning*, pages 183–192, Sofia, Bulgaria, August. Association for Computational Linguistics.

Arısoy, E., Pellegrini, T., Sraçlar, M., and Lamel, L. (2009). Enhanced Morfessor Algorithm with Phonetic Features: Application to Turkish. In *Proceedings of SPECOM*.

Carki, K., Geutner, P., and Schultz, T. (2000). Turkish LVCSR: Towards better Speech Recognition for Agglutinative Languages. In *2000 IEEE International Conference on Acoustics, Speech, and Signal Processing. Proceedings (Cat. No. 00CH37100)*, volume 3, pages 1563–1566. IEEE.

Fügen, C., Stüker, S., Soltau, H., Metze, F., and Schultz, T. (2003). Efficient handling of multilingual language models. In *2003 IEEE Workshop on Automatic Speech Recognition and Understanding (IEEE Cat. No. 03EX721)*, pages 441–446. IEEE.

Goodman, J. (2001). A bit of progress in language modeling. *arXiv preprint cs/0108005*.

Hirsimäki, T., Creutz, M., Siivola, V., Kurimo, M., Virpioja, S., and Pylkkönen, J. (2006). Unlimited Vocabulary Speech Recognition with morph Language Models applied to Finnish. *Computer Speech & Language*, 20(4):515–541.

James, F. (2000). Modified kneser-ney smoothing of n-gram models.

Schultz, T., Vu, N. T., and Schlippe, T. (2013). Globalphone: A multilingual text & speech database in 20 languages. In *2013 IEEE International Conference on Acoustics, Speech and Signal Processing*, pages 8126–8130. IEEE.

Schultz, T. (2002). Globalphone: a multilingual speech and text database developed at karlsruhe university. In *Seventh International Conference on Spoken Language Processing*.

Stolcke, A. (2002). Srilm-an extensible language modeling toolkit. In *Seventh international conference on spoken language processing*.

Tsvetkov, Y., Sitaram, S., Faruqui, M., Lample, G., Littell, P., Mortensen, D., Black, A. W., Levin, L., and Dyer, C. (2016). Polyglot neural language models: A case study in cross-lingual phonetic representation learning. *arXiv preprint arXiv:1605.03832*.

Virpioja, S., Smit, P., Grönroos, S.-A., Kurimo, M., et al. (2013). Morfessor 2.0: Python implementation and extensions for morfessor baseline.

Proceedings of the 1st Joint SLTU and CCURL Workshop (SLTU-CCURL 2020), pages 277–284
Language Resources and Evaluation Conference (LREC 2020), Marseille, 11–16 May 2020
© European Language Resources Association (ELRA), licensed under CC-BY-NC

Basic Language Resources for 31 Languages (Plus English):
The LORELEI Representative and Incident Language Packs

Jennifer Tracey, Stephanie Strassel

Linguistic Data Consortium, University of Pennsylvania
3600 Market Street, Suite 810, Philadelphia, PA 19104 USA
garjen@ldc.upenn.edu, strassel@ldc.upenn.edu

Abstract

This paper documents and describes the thirty-one basic language resource packs created for the DARPA LORELEI program for use in development and testing of systems capable of providing language-independent situational awareness in emerging scenarios in a low resource language context. Twenty-four Representative Language Packs cover a broad range of language families and typologies, providing large volumes of monolingual and parallel text, smaller volumes of entity and semantic annotations, and a variety of grammatical resources and tools designed to support research into language universals and cross-language transfer. Seven Incident Language Packs provide test data to evaluate system capabilities on a previously unseen low resource language. We discuss the makeup of Representative and Incident Language Packs, the methods used to produce them, and the evolution of their design and implementation over the course of the multi-year LORELEI program. We conclude with a summary of the final language packs including their low-cost publication in the LDC catalog.

Keywords: low resource languages, machine translation, information extraction, situational awareness

1. Introduction

The DARPA Low Resource Languages for Emergent Incidents (LORELEI) Program was a multi-year research program aimed at improving the utility of language technology in the context of rapidly emerging incidents like natural disasters. Language technology has the potential to provide crucial situational awareness to those responding to a crisis. For instance, during a disaster the affected population may turn to social media or use text messaging to report urgent needs and issues. When entity taggers and machine translation systems exist for the language(s) spoken in the disaster zone, this data can be processed to generate "heat maps" showing English-speaking mission planners what kind of help is needed where. Most of the world's languages are considered "low resource" when it comes to language technology (META-NET, 2012), and the unpredictable nature of disasters and other emergent situations means that it is not feasible to make language-specific investments in the development of technologies for every language that might become suddenly important in an emergency. LORELEI was designed to address this challenge by building technologies that can be rapidly transitioned to new languages with little to no new training data, for instance by exploiting language universals and using cross-language projection techniques. Evaluation of LORELEI systems was carried out under the NIST Low Resource HLT (LoReHLT) evaluation program (https://www.nist.gov/itl/iad/mig/lorehlt-evaluations); results of the evaluation are not discussed in this paper.

In order to support the research and evaluation requirements of the LORELEI Program, the Linguistic Data Consortium (LDC) created linguistic resources for text data in 31 languages (plus English)[1]. Corpora created for LORELEI consisted of two types of language packs: representative language packs for system training and development, and incident language packs for system evaluation. This paper describes the completed set of LORELEI language packs across all 31 languages. After presenting the design plan for representative and incident language data, we describe each component of the language packs in detail, including methods used to collect and annotate the data, the evolution of requirements and approaches and over the life of the program, and final results of the data creation effort.

2. Representative and Incident Languages

The 24 Representative Language (RL) Packs created for LORELEI provide basic text resources for system training and development, including large volumes of monolingual and parallel text, several types of annotation designed to support situational awareness, a lexicon, a grammatical sketch, and basic text processing and NLP tools. The seven Incident Language (IL) Packs were created specifically for system evaluation and include very limited amounts of monolingual and parallel text for system adaptation, pointers to known lexical and grammatical resources for the language, and a small set of reference translations and annotations used for scoring.

2.1 RL Pack Content Overview

By design, RLs did not provide training data for specific LORELEI evaluation tasks and languages, Instead, they are intended to enable cross-language and transfer learning methods as well as research into using language universals. The 24 RLs were carefully selected prior to the start of the program, with an eye to covering a broad range of language families, typological characteristics and geographic regions. They include relatively high resource languages (e.g., Spanish, Russian, Mandarin) as well as some very low resource languages (e.g., Wolof, Akan). Due to the need to collect significant amounts of digital text data, languages in which most speakers do not regularly read and write were not selected as either RLs or ILs.

---

[1] A small speech corpus was also created for each LORELEI language by another organization; those resources are not

RL Packs were designed to include the following components[2]:

- At least 2M words of monolingual text
- At least 900K words of parallel text
- 100Kw of English translated into the RL
- 10Kw of noun phrase chunking
- 75K words of named entity annotation
- 25K words of full entity annotation (names, nominals, pronouns and coreference)
- 25K words of simple semantic annotation (light semantic role labeling)
- 25K words of situation frame annotation (an information extraction task aimed at "situational awareness" in disaster settings)
- A lexicon containing at least 10K lemmas
- A grammatical sketch
- Sentence segmenter, tokenizer, named entity tagger, transliterator and other basic tools

Some of the RL Packs also included manual morphological analysis, morphological alignment and/or part of speech tagging, but these were not required elements. Later iterations of the RL language packs dropped the NP chunking task and added entity linking, where labeled entity mentions were linked to an external knowledge base. Three of the RL language packs were produced prior to program kickoff and were made available to performers at the start of LORELEI, while the remaining RLs were distributed incrementally over the course of the program. The types of RL data and annotation are described in more detail below.

2.2   IL Pack Content Overview

LORELEI ILs were selected by DARPA from a set of candidates developed by LDC and were used to test system capabilities. Because the LORELEI use case requires systems to quickly transition to a previously unseen language during an emergent situation, the identity of the incident languages for each year's evaluation were concealed until the start of the evaluation, and results were due at a series of "checkpoints", the first of which was as soon as 24 hours after the release of the evaluation data. In general, ILs were lower resourced than (most of) the RLs, but they still needed to have sufficient volumes of digital text available to support the evaluation requirements, and have a large enough pool of accessible native speakers who could be trained to produce the gold standard annotations used in scoring. ILs also had to have a related RL language pack (e.g. Ilocano IL ~ Tagalog RL). The first LORELEI evaluation included one IL, while all subsequent evaluations included two ILs. IL Packs were designed to contain the following components.

1) Data released to performers at the start of each evaluation for use in for system adaptation and training, consisting of the kinds of found resources that might be discoverable at the outset of an incident, but contains no annotated training data:

- At least 1.3 million words of monolingual text
- At least 300Kw of found parallel text
- Pointer to a 10Kw found IL-English dictionary
- Pointers to at least 5 of the following types of grammatical resources:
    - English Gazetteer for Region
    - Parallel IL-English Gazetteer
    - Monolingual IL Gazetteer
    - 10Kw IL-Non-English Dictionary
    - Monolingual IL Primer
    - Parallel IL-English Grammar
    - Monolingual IL Grammar
    - 10K Monolingual IL Dictionary

2) Test data processed by the LORELEI systems

- 200Kw per IL[3], comprising data from multiple genres focused on one or more real-world incidents in the region where the language is used; incidents were selected based on having sufficient coverage in digital text and giving rise to the types of needs and issues covered by the Situation Frame annotation task (see section 4.3).

3) Reference annotations and translations used in scoring (not released to system developers)

- 75Kw professional quality translation
- 50Kw Simple Named Entity annotation
- 50Kw Situation Frame annotation

IL language packs for year 2 and beyond also contained Entity Linking reference annotation.

Table 1 lists all of the RL and IL languages.

Pre-LORELEI RLs	Hausa, Turkish, Uzbek
RLs	Akan, Amharic, Arabic, Bengali, Farsi, Hindi, Hungarian, Indonesian, Mandarin, Russian, Somali, Spanish, Swahili, Tagalog, Tamil, Thai, Ukrainian, Vietnamese, Wolof, Yoruba, Zulu; English (partial, annotation only)
ILs	Ilocano, Kinyarwanda, Odia, Oromo, Sinhala, Tigrinya, Uyghur

Table 1 : All LORELEI Languages

3.   Monolingual and Parallel Text

The collection approach for monolingual text was the same across both RLs and ILs, while the approaches taken to translation varied slightly between RL and IL packs, due to evaluation requirements for the ILs.

3.1   Monolingual Text

Monolingual text was collected using a combination of manual and automatic methods. Native speakers for each

---

[2] While there are resources available for some of the RLs, for example, through the Universal Dependencies Project at https://universaldependencies.org, LORELEI language packs were designed to have a uniform set of contents across all languages; researchers in the LORELEI program were free to make use of such existing resources, but they were out of scope for inclusion in the language packs produced by LDC for LORELEI.

[3] In the last two LORELEI evaluations, systems also processed a corresponding 50Kw English set for each IL, and were scored against English references in addition to IL references.

language were tasked with finding documents in their language on the web, focusing largely on events in the LORELEI domain (natural disasters and other kinds of emergent situations) in both formal (e.g., news reports) and informal (e.g., blogs, discussion forums, Twitter) genres. For RLs, they searched for a variety of event types and there were no constraints on the date of the material collected. For ILs, target incidents were selected in advance for each language, and searches focused on documents about those specific incidents. During data scouting we also recorded information about individual documents that would help inform data selection for downstream tasks: genre, incident type, incident name, incident Wikipedia page link if available, country/region/location, date, presence of eyewitness accounts, how specific the document was about people/places/organizations/dates and times, and topics (e.g. evacuation, food, shelter).

In addition to collecting individual documents identified by native speakers, wherever possible other documents from the same website were also harvested to provide a pool of background data that was not specifically about LORELEI domain topics. All collected documents were then processed into a uniform tokenized and sentence-segmented xml format to support downstream annotation and evaluation pipelines. LDC acquired rights to use and distribute third party data by a combination of explicit permission from the data provider, a compatible license attached to the data by a data provider, or under the doctrine of fair use which is supported by a fair use analysis commissioned by LDC and conducted by independent counsel. For a handful sources including Twitter, pointers to the source document were provided along with utilities for interacting with the data provider's API to download the documents and convert them into the format used by LDC for annotation.

Because we were collecting tens or even hundreds of millions of words of data in some languages, manual review of every document to ensure that it was in the target language was not possible. Instead, all documents selected for translation and annotation were manually audited for language and other features, while the rest of the monolingual text was subject to automatic language identification using Google CLD2 to filter out documents which were clearly out-of-language.

Monolingual text data volumes included in the corpora vary widely. For ILs, all language packs exceeded the 1.3 million word target. Kinyarwanda included 10 million words of monolingual text, and Uyghur included 27 million words. All of the remaining ILs had between 3 and 7 million words of monolingual text. For RLs, only Wolof fell short of the 2 million word goal. Tagalog, Swahili, Zulu, Akan, Arabic, Yoruba, and Hausa all exceeded the goal but had less than 10 million words of monolingual text. Thai, Tamil, Hindi, Indonesian, Spanish, Somali, Amharic, Mandarin, and Uzbek all exceeded 10 million words, and Bengali, Russian, Vietnamese, Hungarian, Farsi, Ukrainian and Turkish all exceeded 100 million words of monolingual text.

3.2 Parallel Text

Parallel text resources in the LORELEI language packs were produced using three methods: found parallel text, crowd translation, and professional translation. For ILs, found parallel text was provided in the training partition of the language pack, while professional translation was provided in the evaluation references. For RLs each pack contained a mixture of found, crowd, and professional translation, depending on the availability of found parallel text and crowd workers for the language. The goal for RLs was to first maximize the amount of found translations, then use crowdsourcing if viable, and only use professional translation as much as required to make up the remaining amount. Therefore, the RL packs differ considerably in the proportion of professional, crowd and found translation.

3.2.1 Found Parallel Text

Parallel text was harvested from the web using a combination of approaches. When possible, native speaker annotators provided information about sites containing parallel text in their language. We also used Bilingual Internet Text Search (BITS) (Ma and Liberman, 1999) to locate additional data by scanning potential parallel sites and using a translation lexicon to identify pairs of documents that are translations[4]. Champollion (Ma, 2006) was then used to align the documents at the sentence level. In some cases, the amount of parallel text harvested far exceeded the total parallel text target.

3.2.2 Crowdsourced Translation

LDC's goal was to use crowdsourcing wherever possible for RLs. In the first year of the program, 10 of the RLs were scheduled for active collection. We posted hits using Amazon Mechanical Turk (www.mturk.com), but only had good yield for Spanish, Arabic, and Russian. For the second year, we focused our crowdsourcing efforts on Hindi and Bengali, for which we expected to find a reasonable number of crowd workers, and we switched to using CrowdTrans (https://crowdtrans.com/), a platform first developed under LORELEI and designed to allow the workflow to be customized to LORELEI requirements. Sentences that received at least three crowd translations were subjected to a ranking task in which qualified workers gave a best-to-worst ranking of the translations. Sentences with fewer than three translations were included, but did not have the ranking information.

3.2.3 Professional Translation

Professional translation was used to some degree for every language pack. For ILs, translation references used in scoring were all professional quality translations, with 4 independent translations produced for the first year's evaluation, 2 in the second year, and one in the third and fourth years. For the RLs, some data was professionally translated even for languages where the found parallel text was sufficient to meet or exceed the target volume. This was to ensure that an adequate amount of LORELEI domain material was translated for each package and to ensure appropriate genre distribution in the translation data, since the topic content and genre of found parallel text was not necessarily aligned with the targets for the LORELEI language packs. In addition to the data

---

[4] BITS was used rather than more recently developed tools since it was already fully integrated into LDC's collection infrastructure and its results were sufficiently good to satisfy requirements.

translated into English for each language, RL packs also contain a "core" set of English documents that were translated into each RL, so that when all RL packs are combined, these documents form a 25-way parallel corpus (24 RLs plus English). The core English set consists of approximately 80,000 words of news text plus a short phrasebook of conversational sentences and an elicitation corpus designed to highlight various grammatical and morphological features of languages for a total of approximately 100,000 words. A small set of the translated documents from this core set (2000 words) was annotated for each annotation task in every language, so that there is also a small multi-way parallel annotation dataset across all the RLs.

For ILs, two languages (Tigrinya and Oromo) fell short of the goal of 300,000 words of parallel text, and while all other ILs had between 2 and 6 million words of parallel text, much of that was religious text rather than news, informal web text, social media, or other target genres. For RLs, Amharic and Wolof fell below the target volume of 900,000 words of parallel text, while Thai, Bengali, Zulu, Akan, Spanish, Russian, Vietnamese, Hungarian, Uzbek, and Farsi had between 1.3 million and 8.6 million words. All other RLs hit the target volume or exceeded it by 100,000 words or less. These volumes include the combined total of found, crowdsourced, and professional translations; where languages greatly exceeded the target volume, it was due to large amounts of found parallel text.

4. Annotation

In addition to monolingual and parallel text, each language pack contains several types of annotation, described in the following sections.

4.1 Entity Annotation

Three types of entity annotation were performed: simple named entity, full entity and entity linking.

4.1.1 Simple Named Entity and Full Entity

The most basic of the entity annotation tasks for LORELEI is Simple Named Entity (SNE), in which annotators label all the named person, organization, location/facility, and geopolitical entities in a document. All annotations were grounded in text extents. The output of Simple Named Entity annotation serves as input to the subsequent Entity Linking and Situation Frame annotation tasks.

In the Full Entity (FE) task, annotators label entities of the same types labeled for SNE, but in addition to named mentions, all nominal and pronominal mentions are tagged as well. There is also an additional category of title, which is used to capture professional or honorific titles of persons. All annotations were grounded in text extents. FE also includes within document coreference of entity mentions.

All RLs hit the target volume for SNE and FE annotation except for Hausa, which had the full amount of SNE but only 13,000 words of FE due to limited availability of annotators. All ILs met the target volume for SNE annotation.

4.1.2 Entity Linking

In the final entity task, Entity Discovery and Linking (EDL), entity mentions labeled in either SNE or FE[5] are linked to a Knowledge Base (KB) developed especially for use in the LORELEI Program by merging three existing knowledge resources and then performing manual augmentation. Most LORELEI KB entities come from the Geonames[6] database, which contains millions of entries for geographical names, along with information about the places, such as population, latitude and longitude, etc. The CIA World Factbook World Leaders List[7] is the source for person entities, and includes cabinet-level leaders from countries around the world. The CIA World Factbook Appendix B[8] consists of a list of international organizations and groups such as trade organizations, economic development groups, etc. While the Geonames entries cover a huge number of locations and geopolitical entities, the number of persons and organizations covered by the CIA World Factbook sources are quite small, and in order to have better coverage of entities likely to appear in the annotated data, manual augmentation of the KB was performed for each language. New person and organization entities were added to the KB for ILs based on their relevance to the specific incidents selected as the focus of the evaluation. For RLs, since there was no focus on a specific incident, new entities were added to the KB based on frequency of appearance in the annotated SNE data.

During Entity Linking annotation, annotators checked the KB against each entity labeled during the prior SNE (or FE) task. When that entity was found in the KB they created a link by associating the KB ID with the entity ID. In some cases, ambiguity in the labeled data or in the KB itself made it impossible for annotators to determine a single correct KB link; in these cases they created links to all possibly correct KB entries. If no match for the entity was found in the KB, the annotator marked it as a "NIL" entity. After annotation on all documents was complete, the NIL entities were examined to see if any of them were coreferent, and all coreferent entities were clustered together under a new unique KB ID.

Entity linking was added in the second year of the program, and so language packs completed prior to that point (Uzbek, Turkish, Hausa, Somali, Yoruba, Uyghur) do not contain any Entity Linking annotation. All other RLs and ILs have the target volume of annotation.

4.2 Simple Semantic Annotation

In Simple Semantic Annotation (SSA), documents were labeled for predicates (Acts and States) and their basic arguments (Agents, Patients, and Locations). Existing predicate-argument based semantic annotation protocols such as Abstract Meaning Representation (Banarescu et al., 2013) or PropBank (Palmer et al., 2005) are fairly

---

[5]In the year 3 evaluation, EDL was performed on a set of English documents labeled for Full Entity, such that both named and nominal entity mentions were linked to the KB. In all other data sets, EDL used only name mentions from SNE.
[6]www.geonames.org
[7]www.cia.gov/library/publications/world-leaders-1/
[8]www.cia.gov/library/publications/the-world-factbook/appendix/appendix-b.html

complex and require annotators to have a background in linguistics and/or require a substantial amount of annotator training time.

<table>
<tr><td colspan="2">SSA Annotation : Physical Acts</td></tr>
<tr><td colspan="2">Breaking News: Landslide hits Guinsaugon in the south of the Philippine island of Leyte. Reports say village totally flattened and housing destroyed.</td></tr>
</table>

Act : landslide
- Patient : Guinsaugon
- Place : Leyte
- Place : Phillipine
- Place : south

Act : hit
- Agent : landslide
- Patient : Guinsaugon

Act : flattened
- Agent : landslide
- Patient : Guinsaugon

Act : destroyed
- Agent : landslide
- Patient : housing
- Place : Guinsaugon

Figure 1: SSA Annotation Example

In contrast, SSA was designed specifically for LORELEI as a way to get some light semantic role labeling from non-expert annotators with limited time available for training. In order to scope the annotation task (both to constrain the amount of effort and to focus that effort on the most LORELEI-relevant parts of the annotated documents), only physical acts and disaster-relevant states were annotated. Each predicate that falls into one of these categories was first labeled as either an act or state, and then the agent, patient, and location arguments were added.

All annotations were grounded in text extents, and the scope of annotation was the sentence, with the full document available to annotators for context. Figure 1 shows an example of physical acts annotated for SSA.

Ukrainian does not have any SSA, and Hausa has less than the target volume; all other RLs met the target volume for this task. No SSA was performed on any IL.

4.3 Situation Frame

The Situation Frame (SF) annotation was a new task designed specifically for LORELEI; its purpose was to test system capabilities for providing situational awareness about the types and locations of needs (e.g. water, infrastructure) and issues (e.g. civil unrest) present in the source data, as well as the urgency and scope of the situation and any entities involved in reporting or resolving the situation. During Situation Frame annotation native speakers read each document and indicated whether any of needs or issues from a fixed list were present in the document, and when present, they filled in the rest of the situation "frame" with information about location, urgency, status, and so on. Locations and other entities involved in the situation were selected by the annotator from the list of names annotated during SNE. Annotations

for this task are produced at the document level and do not involve anchoring the elements of a situation frame in a text span. Figure 2 shows an example of a labeled need frame.

<table>
<tr><td colspan="2">SF Annotation : Need Frame</td></tr>
<tr><td colspan="2">Breaking News: Landslide hits Guinsaugon in the south of the Philippine island of Leyte. Reports say village totally flattened and housing destroyed.</td></tr>
</table>

Need
- Type(s): Shelter, Infrastructure
- Place : Guinsaugon
- Status : Current
- Scope: Large
- Severity : High
- Reported by : N/A
- Resolved by : N/A

Figure 2: SF Annotation Example

SF Annotation	Y1: Uyghur	Y2: RLs, Tigrinya, Oromo
Reference Annotations	1	RLs: 1 ILs: 3
Types	8 need types 3 issue types	Tweak definitions
Place Values	NAM	NAM
Resolution/ Status Values	3	2
Default Issue Status	None	Currently Relevant
Urgency	Binary	Binary

SF Annotation	Y3: Kinyarwanda, Sinhala	Y4: Odia, Ilocano
Reference Annotations	ILs: 2 Eng: 3	ILs: 2+ Eng: 3
Types	No Change	No Change
Place Values	NAM + NOM (Eng)	NAM
Resolution/ Status Values	No Change	No Change
Default Issue Status	No Change	No Change
Urgency	Scalar: Scope & Severity	No Change

Table 2: SF Task Evolution

The types used for labeling situation frames were developed for LORELEI in consultation with program stakeholders, and were inspired by types used in real-world disaster response projects such as MicroMappers (Imran et al., 2014). Need types include Evacuation,

Infrastructure, Food Supply, Medical Assistance, Search/Rescue, Shelter, Utilities/Energy/Sanitation and Water Supply. Issue types include Civil Unrest/ Widespread Crime, Regime Change and Terrorism or other Extreme Violence.

The SF task evolved significantly over the life of the LORELEI program to address new requirements and to improve the utility of the labeled data for evaluation. For example, initial versions of the task included a binary judgment of whether or not a situation was urgent, but poor inter-annotator agreement on this decision led to a change in which urgency was decomposed into scalar judgments about the scope (size of affected region/population) and severity (low = inconvenience; high = death) of the situation. Table 2 shows the elements of the SF annotation task over the four years of the LORELEI program.

Situation Frame was defined as a task after the LORELEI program was already underway, and so language packs completed prior to that point contain no SF annotation (Turkish, Uzbek, Hausa, Somali, or Yoruba). All other RLs and ILs met the target volumes for Situation Frame annotation.

4.4 Morphosyntactic Annotations

Several types of morphological and syntactic annotations were performed on subsets of the RLs. These annotations were intended to serve as resources for system development and were not directly evaluated, so they only appear in RLs. In response to input from DARPA and LORELEI performers, most morphosyntactic annotation was dropped after the first set of language packs in favor of greater effort elsewhere (e.g. Situation Frame), though one new morphological annotation task was added in subsequent phases of the program.

The first type of morphosyntactic annotation was Noun Phrase Chunking, which was originally planned for all RLs, but was later dropped in favor of additional EDL and SF annotation on the RLs. In this task, annotators identified maximal, non-overlapping noun phrases in the text, following surface syntactic structure and applying constituency tests to determine where to mark the boundaries of the noun phrases. Noun Phrase chunking was performed on Uzbek, Turkish, Hausa, Mandarin, Amharic, Somali, Farsi, Hungarian, Vietnamese, Yoruba, Russian, Spanish, and Arabic (10,000 words per language).

In the three languages for which resources were developed prior to the start of LORELEI (Turkish, Uzbek, and Hausa), morphological analysis and alignment were also performed, tightly coupled with the creation morphological analyzers for each of these languages (Kulick and Bies, 2016). In this task, annotators were presented with a list of possible solutions from the analyzer and were required to select the best one from the list, or choose "unanalyzable" if no correct solution for the token was present. Part-of-speech labels were not directly annotated, but were instead derived from the morphological annotation. For Turkish and Uzbek, morpheme alignment between the Turkish/Uzbek text and an English translation was also performed to identify translational correspondence using the same general approach applied in previous word alignment annotation tasks (e.g., Li et al., 2010) but adapted to align the translations at the morpheme level rather than the word level. These task were dropped from the plan for RLs at the very start of LORELEI and so are not present in any of the subsequent language packs.

However, in collaboration with other LORELEI researchers, some additional morphological segmentation annotation was performed on 9 languages toward the end of the program (Mott et al., 2020). The languages selected for this task include a variety of morphological features of interest such as case marking and noun class systems, infixes, circumfixes, etc. For Akan, Hindi, Hungarian, Indonesian, Russian, Spanish, Swahili, Tagalog, and Tamil, 2000 tokens per language were segmented at morpheme boundaries, and markup was added to indicate substitution (as in *come/came* in English). Due to the difficulty of this type of task for non-expert annotators, the segmentation was performed by a trained linguist working in tandem with a native speaker annotator.

5. Lexical and Grammatical Resources

For each of the RLs, LDC developed a lexicon containing at least 10,000 entries, with part of speech and English glosses. The lexicon was created using a combination of found resources such as existing online dictionaries, and manual effort by native speakers to create new entries. Manual effort focused on adding high frequency tokens that were missing from the found resources, and the amount of manual annotation required varied significantly by language. Lexicons were augmented for several languages by integrating the detailed morphological analysis information in a separate word forms table that is indexed to the entries in the main lexicon. For Arabic, this information was extracted from the Penn Arabic TreeBank (Kulick, et al., 2010); for Amharic, Farsi, Hungarian, Russian, Somali, Spanish and Yoruba, morphological information comes from the Unimorph Project (Kirov, et al., 2018).

Each RL pack also includes a grammatical sketch created specifically for LORELEI. The grammatical sketches provide basic linguistic information including paradigms and brief grammatical descriptions. The sketches were intended to contain the kind of practical information that would be useful in working with the language, rather than the kind of deep theoretical analysis and description of exceptional cases that might be found in a full length academic grammar. A single template was used for all languages so that each sketch includes basic information about the language (e.g., classification, ISO code, word order), orthography, encoding (Unicode chart, etc.), morphology, syntax, and specialized sections for personal names, locations, numbers, and variation, as well as references to in-depth grammars.

For ILs, no LORELEI-specific lexicon or grammatical sketch was produced, but pointers to several types of existing lexical and grammatical resources (monolingual and parallel dictionaries, grammars, and gazetteers) were provided.

6. Tools

Each LORELEI RL pack also includes a set of basic NLP tools and text processing utilities for working with the data. For all RL languages, tokenizers, sentence segmenters and named entity taggers were provided, along with utilities to download and process any data that could not be directly redistributed by LDC. For languages that use whitespace to delimit word boundaries, LDC provided a regular expression-based tokenizer designed to separate words and punctuation while preserving certain kinds of web-text artifacts, such as urls and hashtags, as single tokens. For languages that do not use whitespace at word boundaries, we turned to widely-used existing tokenizers. Sentence segmenters were created using an implementation of the Punkt algorithm based on the version found in NLTK (Kiss and Strunkt., 2006). Custom conditional random field-based named entity taggers were produced for each of the RLs and trained using the SNE annotations described above. For all RLs written in non-Roman scripts, a transliterator was also provided.

7. Quality Control and Validation

Quality control was performed by senior and lead annotators for each stage of collection, translation and annotation. Collection and translation QC involved manual spot checking on individual files, searching for outliers across the corpus, and running a suite of automated sanity checks to identify and correct known issues. Annotation quality control involved formal training and testing of annotators, detailed procedural guidelines for each task, and custom user interfaces for each task that included many types of validation to prevent certain types of error. All annotations were subject to review passes by senior annotators, and corpus-wide checks were conducted at the conclusion of each task. Inter-annotator agreement was measured for tasks/languages with a large enough annotator team, timeline and budget to permit dual annotation. For SNE, agreement for ILs fell within expected ranges given inexperienced annotators working in low resource languages (67-90%). For SF, agreement rates in the first year were poor (under 60%). Analysis of the data revealed that multiple correct answers existed given differences in use of inference and world knowledge, and a decision was made to utilize multiple human references in scoring rather than attempting to redesign the task for better agreement (Strassel et. al., 2017). Other tasks were not subject to IAA analysis given resource constraints. Finally, all RL and IL language packs were subject to independent review by the University of Maryland Center for Advanced Study of Language (CASL) prior to release.

8. Conclusion

We have presented two types of new resources developed by LDC for the DARPA LORELEI Program.

Representative Language Packs and Incident Language Packs are designed to enable creation and evaluation of systems capable of providing language-independent situational awareness in emergent incidents. All language packs have now been completed, covering 31 typologically and geographically diverse languages, plus English. Table 3 summarizes the contents of every final language pack.

KEY — ✓ met target — — fell short — ◎ not done

Incident Languages (Uyghur, Tigrinya, Oromo, Kinyarwanda, Sinhala, Odia, Ilocano); **Pre LORELEX** (Uzbek, Turkish, Hausa); **X** (English)

	Uyghur	Tigrinya	Oromo	Kinyarwanda	Sinhala	Odia	Ilocano	Uzbek	Turkish	Hausa	English
Mono Text	✓	✓	✓	✓	✓	✓	✓	✓	✓	✓	✓
Parallel Text	✓	✓	✓	✓	✓	✓	✓	✓	✓	✓	
POS Tagged								✓	✓	—	
NP Chunking								✓	✓	—	
Morph Analysis								✓	✓	—	
Morph Align								✓	✓	◎	
Morph Seg											
SNE	✓	✓	✓	✓	✓	✓	✓	✓	✓	✓	✓
Full Entity								✓	✓	—	
Entity Linking		✓	✓	✓	✓	✓	✓				✓
SSA								✓	✓	—	✓
Situation Frame	✓	✓	✓	✓	✓	✓	✓				✓

KEY — ✓ met target — — fell short — ◎ not done

Year 1 RLs

	Amharic	Arabic	Farsi	Hungarian	Mandarin	Russian	Somali	Spanish	Ukrainian	Vietnamese	Yoruba
Mono Text	✓	✓	✓	✓	✓	✓	✓	✓	✓	✓	✓
Parallel Text	—	✓	✓	✓	✓	✓	✓	✓	✓	✓	✓
POS Tagged											
NP Chunking	✓	✓	✓	✓	✓	✓	✓	✓		✓	✓
Morph Analysis											
Morph Align											
Morph Seg				✓		✓		✓			
SNE	✓	✓	✓	✓	✓	✓	✓	✓	✓	✓	✓
Full Entity	✓	✓	✓	✓	✓	✓	✓	✓	✓	✓	✓
Entity Linking	✓	✓	✓	✓	✓	✓		✓	✓	✓	
SSA	✓	✓	✓	✓	✓	✓	✓	✓		✓	✓
Situation Frame	✓	✓	✓	✓	✓	✓		✓	✓	✓	

KEY — ✓ met target — — fell short — ◎ not done

Year 2 RLs

	Akan	Bengali	Hindi	Indonesian	Swahili	Tagalog	Tamil	Thai	Wolof	Zulu
Mono Text	✓	✓	✓	✓	✓	✓	✓	✓	—	✓
Parallel Text	✓	✓	✓	✓	✓	✓	✓	✓	—	✓
POS Tagged										
NP Chunking										
Morph Analysis										
Morph Align										
Morph Seg	✓		✓	✓	✓	✓	✓			
SNE	✓	✓	✓	✓	✓	✓	✓	✓	✓	✓
Full Entity	✓	✓	✓	✓	✓	✓	✓	✓	✓	✓
Entity Linking	✓	✓	✓	✓	✓	✓	✓	✓	✓	✓
SSA	✓	✓	✓	✓	✓	✓	✓	✓	✓	✓
Situation Frame	✓	✓	✓	✓	✓	✓	✓	✓	✓	✓

Table 3: Final LORELEI Language Packs

The linguistic resources described here have been distributed to LORELEI performers and to participants in the NIST Open Low Resource Human Language Technologies (LoReHLT) evaluation (NIST, 2019). While some initial LORELEI resources have already been published by LDC, starting in early 2020 the final LORELEI language packs will begin appearing in the LDC catalog at the rate of 1-2 per month. Language packs are available to LDC members at no cost, while non-members pay a minimal fee to defray the costs of data curation, storage and distribution.

Taken as a whole, the LORELEI Language Packs comprise over 2.5 billion words of monolingual text, 60 million words of parallel text, 100 grammatical/lexical resources, and 3 million annotation decisions by over 250 native speakers.

9. Acknowledgements

This material is based upon work supported by the Defense Advanced Research Projects Agency (DARPA) under Contract No. HR0011-15-C-0123. Any opinions, findings and conclusions or recommendations expressed in this material are those of the author(s) and do not necessarily reflect the views of DARPA. The authors gratefully acknowledge Lori Levin, Chris Callison-Burch, Song Chen, Ann Bies, Kira Griffitt, Justin Mott, Dana Delgado, Michael Arrigo, Neil Kuster, Dave Graff, Seth Kulick, Neville Ryant, Jonathan Wright, Brian Gainor, Christopher Caruso, Alex Shelmire, University of Maryland Applied Research Laboratory for Intelligence and Security (ARLIS), formerly UMD Center for Advanced Study of Language (CASL), and the hundreds of LORELEI native speaker annotators for their contributions to this research.

10. Bibliographical References

Banarescu, L., Bonial, C., Cai, S., Georgescu, M., Griffitt, K., Hermjakob, U., Knight, K., Koehn, P., Palmer, M. and Schneider, N. (2013). Abstract Meaning Representation for Sembanking. In Proceedings of the 7th Linguistic Annotation Workshop and Interoperability with Discourse.

Imran, M., Castillo, C., Lucas, J., Meier, P., Vieweg, S. (2014). AIDR: Artificial Intelligence for Disaster Response. In: *WWW'14 Companion*. International World Wide Web Conference Committee (IW3C2)

Kirov, C., Cotterell, R., Sylak-Glassman, J., Walther, G., Vylomova, E., Xia, P., Faruqui, M., Mielke, S., McCarthy, A., Kübler, S., Yarowsky, D., Eisner, J., Hulden, M. (2018). UniMorph 2.0: Universal Morphology. In Nicoletta Calzolari (Conference Chair), et al., editors, Proceedings of the Eleventh International Conference on Language Resources and Evaluation (LREC'18), Miyazaki, Japan, May 7-12. European Language Resource Association (ELRA).

Kiss, T., Strunkt, J. (2006). Unsupervised multilingual sentence boundary detection. *Computational Linguistics* 32: 455-525.

Kulick, S., Bies, A., Maamouri, M. (2010). Consistent and Flexible Integration of Morphological Annotation in the Arabic Treebank. In Nicoletta Calzolari (Conference Chair), et al., editors, Proceedings of the Seventh International Conference on Language Resources and Evaluation (LREC'10), Valetta, Matlta, May 17-23. European Language Resource Association (ELRA).

Kulick, S., Bies, A. (2016). Rapid Development of Morphological Analyzers for Typologically Diverse Languages. In Nicoletta Calzolari (Conference Chair), et al., editors, Proceedings of the Tenth International Conference on Language Resources and Evaluation (LREC'16), Portoroz, Slovenia, May 23-28. European Language Resource Association (ELRA).

Li, X., Ge, N., Grimes, S., Strassel, S., Maeda, K. (2010). Enriching Word Alignment with Linguistic Tags. In Nicoletta Calzolari (Conference Chair), et al., editors, Proceedings of the Seventh International Conference on Language Resources and Evaluation (LREC'10), Valetta, Matlta, May 17-23. European Language Resource Association (ELRA).

Ma, X. (2006). Champollion: A Robust Parallel Text Sentence Aligner. In Nicoletta Calzolari (Conference Chair), ct al., editors, Proceedings of the Fifth International Conference on Language Resources and Evaluation (LREC'06), Genoa, Italy, May 22-28. European Language Resource Association (ELRA).

Ma, X., Liberman, M. (1999). BITS: A Method for Bilingual Text Search over the Web. In Proceedings of Machine Translation Summit VII, Singapore, September 13-17.

META-NET. 2012. META-NET White Paper Series, https://link.springer.com/bookseries/10412, accessed March 20, 2020.

Mott, J., Bies, A., Strassel, S., Kodner, J., Richter, C., Xu, H., Marcus, M. (2020). Morphological Segmentation for Low Resource Languages. To Appear, LREC 2020.

NIST LoReHLT Evaluations Website. https://www.nist.gov/itl/iad/mig/lorehlt-evaluations. Retrieved February 14, 2020.

Palmer, M., Gildea, D., Kingsbury, P. (2005). The Proposition Bank: A Corpus Annotated with Semantic Roles. *Computational Linguistics Journal*, 31:1.

Strassel, S., Bies, A., Tracey, J. (2017). Situational Awareness for Low Resource Languages: the LORELEI Situation Frame Annotation Task. First Workshop on Exploitation of Social Media for Emergency Relief and Preparedness (SMERP), Aberdeen, Scotland, April 8-13.

Strassel, S., Tracey, J. (2016). LORELEI Language Packs: Data, Tools, and Resources for Technology Development in Low Resource Languages. In Nicoletta Calzolari (Conference Chair), et al., editors, Proceedings of the Tenth International Conference on Language Resources and Evaluation (LREC'16), Portoroz, Slovenia, May 23-28. European Language Resource Association (ELRA).

Proceedings of the 1st Joint SLTU and CCURL Workshop (SLTU-CCURL 2020), pages 285–293
Language Resources and Evaluation Conference (LREC 2020), Marseille, 11–16 May 2020
© European Language Resources Association (ELRA), licensed under CC-BY-NC

On the Exploration of English to Urdu Machine Translation

Sadaf Abdul Rauf[1,2]**, Syeda Abida**[1]**, Noor-e-Hira**[1]**, Syeda Zahra**[1]
Dania Parvez[1]**, Javeria Bashir**[1] **and Qurat-ul-ain Majid**[1]
[1] Fatima Jinnah Women University, Pakistan
[2] LIMSI-CNRS, France
{firstName.lastName}@gmail.com

Abstract

Machine Translation is the inevitable technology to reduce communication barriers in today's world. It has made substantial progress in recent years and is being widely used in commercial as well as non-profit sectors. Such is only the case for European and other high resource languages. For English-Urdu language pair, the technology is in its infancy stage due to scarcity of resources. Present research is an important milestone in English-Urdu machine translation, as we present results for four major domains including Biomedical, Religious, Technological and General using Statistical and Neural Machine Translation. We performed series of experiments in attempts to optimize the performance of each system and also to study the impact of data sources on the systems. Finally, we established a comparison of the data sources and the effect of language model size on statistical machine translation performance.

Keywords: English , Urdu, Statistical Machine Translation (SMT), Neural Machine Translation (NMT)

1. Introduction

Machine translation (MT) for low resource languages has been a challenging task (Irvine, 2013; Zoph et al., 2016). The dimensionality of difficulty increases when it comes to translating between a morphologically rich and morphologically poor language (Habash and Sadat, 2006). In this study, we will be presenting one such pair, English to Urdu translation, with English being a morphologically simple language while Urdu is a language with rich inflectional and derivational morphology. In case of Urdu-English translation topological distance between both languages is the biggest hurdle to get best results (Jawaid et al., 2016; Khan et al., 2017).

Findings of WMT 2011 evaluation (Callison-Burch et al., 2011) reported Urdu-English translation to be a relatively difficult problem. With some works on rule based systems (RBMT) (Tafseer and Alvi, 2002; Karamat, 2006; Naila Ata, 2007) and a small cascade of works on phrase based SMT systems (Jawaid and Zeman, 2011; Ali et al., 2013; Jawaid et al., 2014a), hierarchical MT systems (Khan et al., 2013; Jawaid et al., 2014a) and NMT using transfer learning from a high resource language (Zoph et al., 2016), it is still an arena requiring much work. Present study is a consolidated study in this regard.

In this study we present results of some of the unexplored areas with reference to this language pair. Previous works have built general domain translation systems, we present a domain analysis on Technological, Religious and General domain translations (Section 5). This study is also an attempt to initiate the field of MT for Bio-medical domain despite zero resources available for the language pair. Effect of smaller and larger language models on translations are also explored.

We have explored and used all the freely available English-Urdu corpora and also developed various small corpora by using human translations, synthetic corpora by machine translation and Hindi to Urdu transliteration. Starting with a brief review of previous works we describe the resources used in Section 3 followed by detailed results in Section 4 The paper concludes with a brief discussion on results.

2. Related Works

Perhaps, Tafseer and Alvi (2002) presents one of the earliest attempts on English to Urdu translation based on transforming the parse tree of the English sentence to Urdu using transformation rules. Issues relating to translation for verbs in context of English to Urdu RBMT using lexical functional grammar are discussed by (Karamat, 2006). A minimal English to Urdu RBMT system is presented in (Naila Ata, 2007) (Jawaid and Zeman, 2011) used phrase based models to solve the long distance word reordering problem between the two languages. They used Emille (Baker et al., 2002), Treebank (Marcus et al., 1993), Quran and Bible corpora and report improvement in BLEU scores by the proposed reordering scheme. Our general domain systems are built using these above mentioned corpora.

(Jawaid and Zeman, 2011) used phrase based models to solve the long distance word reordering problem between the two languages. They used Emille (Baker et al., 2002), Treebank (Marcus et al., 1993), Quran and bible corpora and report improvement in BLEU scores by the proposed reordering scheme. We also use these corpora in our general domain systems. Building up on previous work (Jawaid et al., 2014a) present a comparison of phrase based versus hierarchical systems. They have added AFRL corpus (not free) to the earlier system and reported the hierarchical systems to outperform phrase based systems. (Ali et al., 2010; Ali et al., 2013) built SMT using parallel ahadith corpus from Sahih bukhari and Sahih Muslim. (Khan et al., 2013) also presented a hierarchical SMT system.

Several other studies have also contributed, for instance (Shahnawaz and Mishra, 2013) and (Khan Jadoon et al., 2017) present neural systems trained on small corpora.

Category	Corpora	Size (Mbs)	Tokens (Millions)		Sentences			
			UR	EN	Train	Dev	Test	Total
General	Emille	1.5	0.12	0.09	5583	176	118	5877
	Treebank	2.3	0.18	0.13	5408	170	115	5693
	Indic	8.8	0.63	0.49	33244	1000	1000	35244
	NLT	3.1	0.22	0.19	10662	336	226	11224
	OPUS	4.7	0.38	0.33	46805	1501	1002	49308
	TDIL	0.42	0.03	0.02	1141	37	25	1203
	Flickr_H	0.42	0.03	0.03	2578	82	55	2715
	Flickr_G	0.41	0.04	0.03	2578	82	55	2715
	Transliterations	0.99	0.08	0.07	3441	516	172	4129
	Total	**22.64**	**1.71**	**1.38**	**111440**	**3990**	**2768**	**118108**
Bio-Medical	Emille	0.92	0.07	0.05	2970	78	77	3125
	Scielo	9.1	0.65	0.60	21680	650	492	22822
	Jang Health News	1.9	0.14	0.12	5450	360	264	6074
	EMEA	14.3	1.03	0.82	51775	1363	1363	54501
	Total	**26.22**	**1.89**	**1.59**	**81875**	**2451**	**2196**	**86522**
Religious	Quran	2.9	0.24	0.03	6000	214	200	6414
	Bible	2.5	0.20	0.21	7400	300	257	7957
	QBJ	55.5	1.13	1.02	47198	1250	1062	49510
	Tanzil	1000	23.1	19.0	710904	22449	14967	748320
	Total	**1060.9**	**24.67**	**20.26**	**771502**	**24213**	**16486**	**812201**
Techno-logy	Gnome	0.85	0.06	0.05	13186	417	278	13881
	Ubuntu	0.16	0.02	0.01	2873	90	62	3025
	Total	**1.01**	**0.08**	**0.06**	**16059**	**507**	**340**	**16906**
Mono-lingual	Jawaid	717.4	95.4	-	-	-	-	5464575
	NLT	5.4	0.63	-	-	-	-	62063
	Jhang	3.3	0.39	-	-	-	-	32984
	All Urdu corpus	199.4	26.2	-	-	-	-	934631
	Total	**925.5**	**122.7**	**-**	**-**	**-**	**-**	**6494253**

Table 1: Corpus Details: Training, development, test and monolingual data used for each domain.

3. Data Collection

Data collection and its cleaning is an important but a challenging part for NLP, including machine translation. Our Data collection scheme included 1) an extensive search of all the freely available parallel corpora. 2) Synthetic parallel corpus creation using a good translation system and 3) transliteration from a highly similar language, Hindi.

We have categorised the corpora in four categories, General, Biomedical, Religious and Technology, each explained in subsections 3.1, 3.2, 3.3, and 3.4 respectively. Corpus details are summarized in table 1.

3.1. General

This section lists the corpora and their details for general category.

1. The Emille[1] corpus (Baker et al., 2002) is a collection of annotated, parallel and monolingual data in written and spoken form. It consists of multi domain corpora (social, legal, educational, health, etc.) in fourteen South Asian languages and is distributed by ELRA (European Language Resource Association). This first crowd sourced corpus enabled initial work on Indian languages. We used English-Urdu part of this dataset consisting of 9000 sentences. Health documents from Emille corpus were separated and used as the BioMedical corpus.

2. CLE[2] released Urdu translations of Wall Street Journal part of The Penn *Treebank* corpus (Marcus et al., 1993). The Urdu corpus was available online and we were able to get English sentences from LDC Treebank.

3. Indic[3] is a freely available multi-domain parallel corpus created by using crowd-sourcing (Post et al., 2012).

4. TDIL[4] is an Indian Language Technology Proliferation and Deployment Center. We were able to get a sample of this corpus in domains of tourism, art, culture and architecture etc.

5. Opus[5] project (Tiedemann, 2012) provides freely

[1]The Emille/CIIL Corpus:ID:ELRA-W0037
[2]http://www.cle.org.pk/software/ling_resources
[3]http://joshua-decoder.org/indian-parallel-corpora/
[4]http://tdil-dc.in/index.php—?lang=en
[5]http://opus.nlpl.eu/

available annotated corpora to the research community. We used their English-Urdu corpus comprising of Tanzil, Tatoeba, OpenSubtitles {2016, 2018}, Ubuntu, GNOME and Global Voices. Tanzil was a religious corpus, whereas Ubuntu and Gnome were technology related corpora. We further sub categorized these according to the domains as shown in table 1.

6. Flickr corpora are the human and automatic translations of the flickr 8[6] Image to text Corpus. The human translations are done from English captions to Urdu by human translators and Google translate was used for automatic translations.

7. National Language Translations (NLT) are the translation documents obtained from a translation agency. We collected translations of various articles, books, survey reports etc. The data collected was in raw form, it was cleaned and sentence aligned.

8. UMC002 Hindi-Urdu transliterations. Hindi and Urdu are almost similar languages having different writing scripts. To overcome data scarceness we experimented with transliterations from Hindi to Urdu. A similar scheme has been used by (Durrani et al., 2014) but in the opposite direction, .i.e they transliterated from Urdu to Hindi.

3.2. Bio-Medical

Since no prior work exists in the Biomedical domain for English-Urdu, consequently there were no separate parallel corpora available. However, *Emille* corpus had a small part comprising of 0.055M English and 0.075 Urdu words respectively in health domain. We used these as Biomedical corpus.

Furthermore, we *developed* Biomedical parallel corpora by using ideas from unsupervised learning techniques successfully used for other language pairs, where translations are used as additional bi-texts to cover up for data scarcity (Lambert et al., 2011) and domain adaptation (Abdul Rauf et al., 2016; Hira et al., 2019). We collected Biomedical parallel corpora from various sources and translated them. We are working on using domain adapted translation and language models for the biomedical domain, however, the translations used in this work are done using google translate. We used the following corpora:

1. Scielo[7] corpus contains documents retrieved from the scielo database comprising of titles and abstracts of published articles in bio-medical domain. Our Scielo corpus comprises of 0.022M sentences. Overall it contains 0.60M English and 0.65M Urdu words.

2. Jang[8] group of news is a Pakistan based media corporation. Their newspapers are published in both Urdu and English independently,but they are not the translations of each other. We cleaned and extracted 6k

English sentences from the *health news* section and translated to Urdu to be used as parallel corpus. We got a corpus of 0.11M words in English and 0.14M words in Urdu.

3. EMEA[9] is a parallel corpus extracted out of documents published by European Medical Agency. The corpus is freely available in a number of language pairs but is not available in Urdu. We downloaded English part of corpus available in plain text and selected data related to medicines, disease, treatment and instructions. We automatically translated the extracted dataset and produced Urdu parallel translations. At the end of translation process we got a parallel dataset comprising of 1.03M words in Urdu and 0.82M words in English.

3.3. Religious

This section lists the corpora and their details for religious category.

1. UMC005 (Jawaid and Zeman, 2011) provides 6414 sentence pairs from Bible and 7957 sentence pairs form Quran corpus.

2. QBJ corpus, which is another collection of Quran+Bible+Joshua was also available online with their own test and dev sets. The data consists of 1.02M English words and 1.13M Urdu words.

3. Tanzil is a collection of online Quranic Translations by different scholars and is a sub part of OPUS corpus. The corpus contains 878 bi-texts with total of 0.75M sentence fragments having 19.0M English tokens and 23.1M Urdu tokens.

3.4. Technology

This consists of English-Urdu Parallel corpus from localization files of Ubuntu and Gnome. Ubuntu contains 3.03k sentences and 0.1M, 0.2M English and Urdu tokens respectively, Gnome has 0.05M English and 0.06M Urdu tokens.

3.5. Monolingual Urdu Corpus

Monolingual corpus is an essential resource for building language models for SMT. We used the corpus developed by (Jawaid et al., 2014b). This corpus consists of 95.4 million Urdu words, representing 5.4 million sentences of various domains including science, news, religion and education.

We also collected Urdu monolingual documents from Jang (0.03M sentences) and other sources comprising of (0.06M sentences) as shown at the end of table 1. Urdu side of all parallel corpora was also used to build the large language model used in the indicated experiments in results.

3.6. Data Preprocessing

Data cleaning and preprocessing is highly important for the performance of MT systems. The corpora provided by Emillie, NLT and Penn Tree-bank were partially parallel

---

[6]https://forms.illinois.edu/sec/1713398

[7]http://www.statmt.org/wmt16/biomedical-translation-task.html

[8]https://jang.com.pk/

[9]http://opus.nlpl.eu/EMEA.php

so we sentence aligned them using LF sentence aligner. [10]
Due to the topological distance between the two languages
we were not able to get fully aligned parallel corpus using
LF aligner, thus manual alignment was done to ensure correctness.

4. Experimental Framework

To demonstrate the performance of MT systems on the corpora collected and generated in this work, we performed a
number of experiments for SMT and a few experiments for
NMT. This section provides the description of the experimental frameworks and settings used for building SMT and
NMT systems.

4.1. Statistical Machine Translation:

The goal of SMT is to produce a target sentence e from
a source sentence f. Among all possible target language
sentences the one with the highest probability is chosen:

$$e^* \quad = \quad \arg \max_e \Pr(e|f) \tag{1}$$

$$= \quad \arg \max_e \Pr(f|e) \Pr(e) \tag{2}$$

where $\Pr(f|e)$ is the translation model and $\Pr(e)$ is the tar-
get language model (LM). This approach is usually referred
to as the *noisy source-channel* approach in SMT (Brown et
al., 1993). Bilingual corpora are needed to train the translation model and monolingual texts to train the target language model.

Common practice is to use phrases as translation units
(Koehn et al., 2003; Och and Ney, 2003a) instead of the
original word-based approach. A phrase is defined as a
group of source words $\tilde{f}$ that should be translated together
into a group of target words $\tilde{e}$. The translation model in
phrase-based systems includes the phrase translation prob-
abilities in both directions, i.e. $P(\tilde{e}|\tilde{f})$ and $P(\tilde{f}|\tilde{e})$. The use
of a maximum entropy approach simplifies the introduction
of several additional models explaining the translation process :

$$e^* \quad = \quad \arg \max Pr(e|f)$$

$$= \quad \arg \max_e \{exp(\sum_i \lambda_i h_i(e, f))\} \tag{3}$$

The feature functions h_i are the system models and the λ_i
weights are typically optimized to maximize a scoring function on a development set. In our system fourteen features
functions were used, namely phrase and lexical translation
probabilities in both directions, seven features for the lexi-
calized distortion model, a word and a phrase penalty, and
a target language model.

To built standard phrase-based SMT systems we used
Moses toolkit (Koehn et al., 2007), with the default settings for all the parameters. A 5-gram KenLM (Heafield,
2011) language model was used. For individual systems
the language models were trained on the target side of the
corpus. For experiments on size of the language model, all
the available monolingual and target side corpus was used
(122.5M Urdu words).

Word-alignment was done using Giza++ (Och and Ney,
2003b) with grow-diag-final-and symmetrization method.
Maximum sentence length was chosen to be 100. A distortion limit of 6 with 100-best list was used. Msd-
bidirectional-fe feature was used for lexical reordering with
the phrase limit of 5. Systems were tuned on the development data using the MERT (Och, 2003). BLEU (Papineni
et al., 2002) scores were computed on dev and test sets of
the corpora, as well as on standard test sets. BLEU scores
were calculated using *multi-bleu.perl*. Scoring is case sensitive and includes punctuation.

4.2. Neural Machine Translation:

We used OpenNMT[11] (Klein et al., 2017) for building Neural MT systems. Two layered encoder-decoder architecture
with global attention (Luong et al., 2015) was used. We
used RNN size of 500 and LSTM for cell structure for both
encoder and decoder, applying dropout of 0.3 for each input cell. Translations were evaluated on BLEU scores to
enable comparison with the corresponding SMT systems.

4.3. Development and Test sets

Most of the corpora available online had their own development (dev) and test sets, so we evaluated the systems according to these *dev* and *test* sets. To be able to compare the
systems in each domain, we created *Standard test set (STS)*
for each domain comprising of 1k sentences. We randomly
selected sentences from test sets of each data source of the
particular domain. This was done on the basis of data set
size and combined these specific sized chunks so that each
data-set is represented on the basis of its size in the standard test set. We also used the test set of CLE^9 which was
used to evaluate the general domain systems and the standard *Scielo* test set for Bio-Medical domain.

5. Results and Discussion

One of the endeavours of our study is to present domain
specific translation results. As is common in machine learning approaches, the domain of the system being built depends on the data used to train the system. MT performance
quickly degrades when the testing domain is different from
the training domain. The reason for this degradation is that
the statistical models closely approximate the empirical distributions of the training data (Abdul Rauf et al., 2016). MT
system trained on parallel data from the news domain may
not give appropriate translations when used to translate articles from the medical domain.

This study intends to build MT systems for four different domains namely Bio-medical, Religious, Technological and General domain. We evaluated our systems on
the development and test data along with the standard test
set for each domain, and the CLE test set as explained in
section 4.3 We will be giving weight-age to Standard test
scores as they are representative of system performance on
the whole domain rather than the test set created from the
data itself (see section 4.3)

---

[10]https://sourceforge.net/projects/aligner/

[11]http://opennmt.net/OpenNMT/

[9]http://www.cle.org.pk/software/ling_ re-
sources/testingcorpusmt.htm

Corpus	Tokens (UR) (millions)	BLEU									
		SMT					largeLM				
		Dev	Test				Dev	Test			
			Self	STS	CLE	Scielo		Self	STS	CLE	Scielo
General											
Emille	0.12	35.38	5.67	2.58	1.97	NA	40.09	8.86	5.34	2.55	NA
Treebank	0.18	18.14	20.90	3.73	5.10	NA	20.66	24.62	6.27	6.13	NA
Indic	0.63	11.67	12.23	8.28	4.41	NA	21.86	22.77	15.39	5.56	NA
NLT	0.22	15.09	8.52	4.80	4.04	NA	20.76	10.96	8.26	4.23	NA
OPUS	0.38	12.27	14.08	4.79	3.06	NA	15.99	18.16	10.15	6.22	NA
TDIL	0.03	5.85	3.01	1.70	1.21	NA	7.93	4.66	2.58	1.51	NA
FlickrHumanTrans	0.03	3.02	2.39	2.04	0.1	NA	3.94	2.78	2.27	0.00	NA
FlickrGooglTrans	0.03	35.71	27.58	0.56	0.1	NA	36.23	28.18	1.98	0.90	NA
Transliteration	0.08	54.30	47.34	2.08	0.95	NA	54.53	48.90	2.21	1.32	NA
Bio-Medical											
Scielo	0.65	39.20	34.33	25.95	NA	27.97	46.59	41.13	37.10	NA	-
Jang	0.14	33.46	49.78	17.78	NA	17.99	40.62	61.76	30.25	NA	-
EMEA	1.03	40.59	48.66	44.45	NA	19.25	54.56	54.43	50.15	NA	-
Emille	0.07	20.88	3.41	12.90	NA	10.81	29.15	3.23	24.25	NA	-
Religious											
Quran	0.24	16.03	12.44	12.54	NA	NA	23.33	20.84	19.63	NA	NA
Bible	0.20	17.69	11.16	11.17	NA	NA	31.07	23.55	23.45	NA	NA
QBJ	1.13	10.37	10.05	9.98	NA	NA	20.29	21.96	22.08	NA	NA
Tanzil	23.1	19.93	17.46	17.08	NA	NA	-	-	-	NA	NA
Technology											
Gnome	0.06	78.58	79.42	79.42	NA	NA	83.25	83.15	12.81	NA	NA
Ubuntu	0.02	10.05	5.36	5.36	NA	NA	13.43	12.60	14.61	NA	NA

Table 2: BLEU Scores of all Standalone corpora on SMT Systems for English to Urdu translation.

5.1. Standalone SMT Systems

To build the best domain specific SMT system, we first explored the performance of each corpora for standalone SMT systems. Table 2 lists the BLEU scores for each system. As already mentioned we are interested in the scores obtained on standard test set, it is observed that *Indic* showed the best performance among the systems built on general domain corpus. Whereas; *Treebank*, *Transliteration* and *FlickrGoogleTranslate*, despite outperforming on self test have shown a decline in performance for standard test set. The standard test set includes part of the test sentences from each corpora basis of data set size. Indic has the most tokens, resultantly the standard test set includes sentences from Indic the most. This explains the best performance on STS.

For the systems built on Bio-medical corpora, *EMEA* showed the best performance on standard set. Interestingly, in this domain we see reasonable BLEU scores on all test sets, including STS. Similar phenomenon of better scores for EMEA on STS is observed, which corresponds to more sentences from *EMEA* test set in STS.SMT system trained on *Jang* shows an abrupt decline in the performance for standard test set while achieving the best BLEU point (49.78) among all the other SMT systems built for this domain, when chosen on test set scores. This is particularly interesting as *Jang* has 0.14M tokens while *EMEA* has 1.03M Urdu tokens.

Tanzil and *Genome* showed the best performance for Religious and technology domains respectively. While over-fitting is observed in these two domains. The performance of the systems, built for these two domains, have shown a uniform trend for both self and standard test sets.

5.1.1. Effect of size of Language Model

Along with, the exploration of best SMT system for each category we also investigated the effect of the size of language model on each standalone SMT system. To explore this dimension, a large language model was also build by concatenating the Urdu text of all the bi-texts and the monolingual corpus mentioned in section 3.5. The scores for large LM are shown in the third column in table 2. It is observed that the BLEU scores of all the standalone systems approximately doubled with large LM. Figure 1 shows these results graphically for each domain. These results highlight the effect of bigger language model on SMT quality, obviously a bigger language model helps improve translation quality by improving the grammar of the output sentences.

5.2. Concatenated SMT Systems

After building standalone systems for each corpus, we selected the corpora which resulted in best BLEU scores, for building systems by concatenating different combinations of corpora. We selected systems on the basis of best score among the standalone systems from each domain (baseline system) and concatenated them with system having second highest BLEU score. Table 3 reports these results.

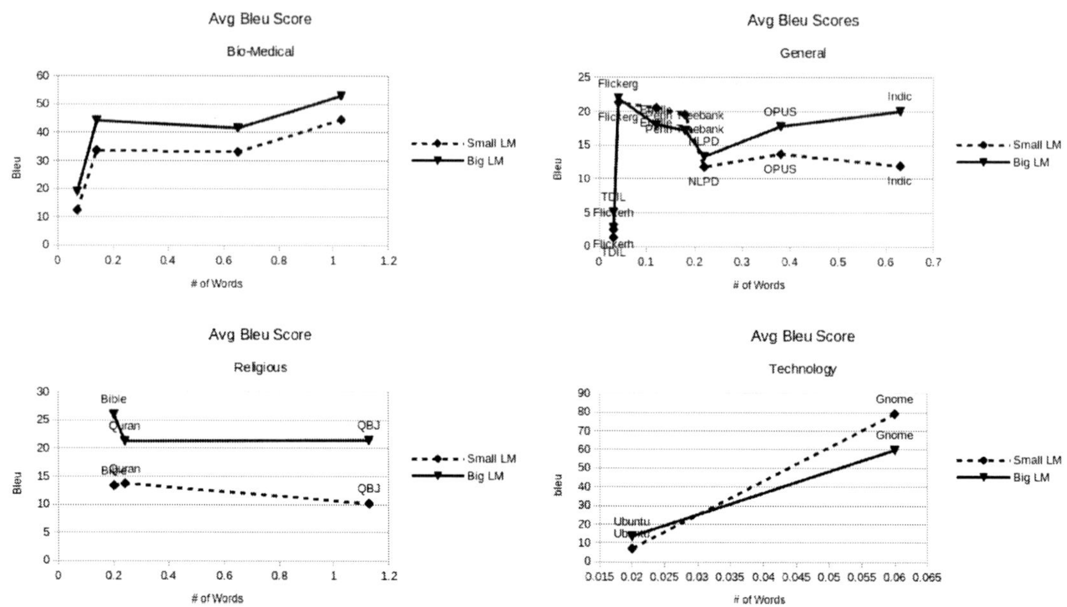

Figure 1: Comparison of systems built on small and large language model (x-axis represents words in millions)

SMT Results on baseline +						
Category	**Baseline**	**Tokens**	**BLEU**			
			Dev	Test	STS	
General	Emille	0.12	35.38	5.67	2.58	
	+Treebank	0.3	23.62	13.32	4.24	
	+Treebank+NLT	0.52	21.08	11.93	6.96	
	+Treebank+NLT+Indic	1.15	15.77	12.06	10.08	
	+Treebank+NLT+Indic+TDIL+OPUS	1.56	15.21	12.53	-	
Bio- Medical	EMEA	1.03	40.59	48.66	44.45	
	+Scielo	1.86	40.09	43.83	50.34	
	+Scielo+jang	1.68	39.91	44.23	49.76	
	+Scileo+jang+Emille	1.89	39.54	44.13	50.71	
Religious	Tanzil	23.1	19.93	17.46	17.08	
	+Bible	23.3	-	-	-	
	+Bible+Quran	23.54	-	-	-	
	+Bible+Quran+QBJ	24.67	19.52	17.18	18.36	
Techno- logy	Gnome	0.06	78.58	79.42	79.42	
	+Ubuntu	0.08	69.38	58.47	58.56	

Table 3: Results of SMT on baselines and addition of bitexts.

5.2.1. Bio-Medical Domain

Bio-medical domain is an interesting domain as the corpora are not of same type. *Emille* are the health domain sentences taken from the *Emille* corpus, *Jang* sentences are taken from a semi-parallel comparable corpus and then sentence aligned and human corrected. Whereas, *EMEA* and *Scielo* are synthetic forward translated corpora.

EMEA was chosen as baseline, for bio-medical domain, having the highest score 44.45 amongst other three standalone systems. Then, we built a system on *EMEA* concatenated with the second best system *Scielo*, having score of 25.95 (table 2). The BLEU score of the resultant system *EMEA+Scielo* is 50.34 (table 3). We can see an improvement in the score after concatenation of these two data-sets. Note that this system is built with only forward translated synthetic corpus, and we get an appreciable BLEU score.

This system $EMEA + Scielo$, is further concatenated with *jang* corpus (standalone score 17.78) and the resultant score of the $EMEA + scielo + jang$ system is 49.76, which is a bit lower than the previous system's score. Contrary to the standard test set scores, addition of bitexts did not improve scores for dev and test, rather resulted in a de-

Corpus	Size(M)	Dev	Test	STS	CLE
FlickrHumanTrans	0.42	3.02	2.39	2.04	0.11
FlickrGooglTrans	0.41	35.71	27.58	0.56	2.35
Transliteration	0.99	54.30	47.34	2.08	0.95
FlickrHumanTrans + Transliteration	1.4	39.23	40.91	2.24	1.44
FlickrGooglTrans + Transliteration	1.4	48.61	45.87	2.66	2.13
Emille	1.5	35.38	5.67	2.58	1.97
Emille + Transliteration	2.5	38.97	30.02	2.36	2.35
Emille + Treebank	3.8	23.62	13.32	4.24	-
Emille + Treebank + FlickrGooglTrans	4.21	24.69	14.28	4.28	6.53

Table 4: Bleu scores using human translations vs machine translations as training data

cline of BLEU score. $EMEA$ and $Scielo$ are translated from standard biomedical corpora as described in data pre-processing section 3.6 The sentences of these corpora specially of EMEA consists of concise short sentences of similar nature (we found certain redundancies in these corpora). That is the reason their concatenation gave a big increase as it mounted to adding more data. On the other hand, we created $Jang$ corpus by automatic translation of news and tips in health section of a national English news paper. This could be a reason that when concatenated with $EMEA + Scielo$ the combined score reduced to 49.76 from 50.34.

Finally, concatenating with $Emille$, having BLEU score 12.90 for standalone model, the score for the resultant system is 50.71 which is highest among all other systems. $Emille$ is again a standard biomedical corpus comprising of health documents from the EMILLE corpus (section 3.6), and its concatenation improved the overall BLEU score. An increase of 6.26 points upon the addition of just 0.86M words of $Scielo + Jang + Emille$ corpora to 1.03M words of EMEA (baseline), has been observed which is a significant gain. These are encouraging results for the development of standard corpora for the Bio-medical domain.

5.2.2. Religious, General and Technology Domain

For the religious domain we have two corpora namely $Tanzil$ and the other is concatenation of $Quran$, $Bible$ and $Joshua(QBJ)$. Firstly we built two standalone systems for both corpora as shown in Table:2, Tanzil having BLEU score of 17.46 on test set and 19.93 on dev set. BLEU score of QBJ is 10.05 on test set and 10.37 on dev set. We did not create standard test set to evaluate these two corpora as there is a huge difference between the size of corpora, if we generate standard corpus out of these by evenly distributing them; the standard test set will mostly consist of bitexts from $Tanzil$. In this case $Tanzil$ will perform well for that specific standard test set but QBJ would not be able to perform well. After standalone evaluation we concatenated both data sets to see the impact of corpora on each other. We got 18.36 BLEU score that is better then the standalone systems. Again the performance of system increases with the increase of the size of corpora.

For the general domain, we considered $Emille$ as a baseline on the basis of higher score 35.38 on dev set and 5.67 on test set so its average BLEU score is higher then the

rest of standalone corpus (table 2). We concatenated it with the $Treebank$ having score 18.14 on dev set and 20.90 on test set,and got 23.63 score on dev set and 13.32 on test set. We further concatenated this system with NLT whose standalone BLEU score are 15.09 on dev and 8.52 on test set, and got scores of 21.08 on dev and 11.93 on test set. Finally we concatenate our last data set $Indic$ having score 11.67 on dev and 12.23 on test set. Following the same trend as seen in the biomedical domain, we see a steady improvement in the standard test scores by the addition of bitexts.

Interestingly, technology domain gave the best results. $Gnome$ being the baseline of the domain achieved 78.58 BLEU score on dev data and 79.42 on both test sets. Whereas, $Ubuntu$ had a standalone BLEU score of 10.05 and 5.36 on dev and test of both test sets (table 2). $Gnome$ corpus had a maximum sentence length of 40 to 50 whereas all other data sets had sentence size of 100 words. A combination of two yields a great improvement with respect to $Ubuntu$ but a decrease for $Gnome$.

5.3. Impact of Various Corpora

We performed series of experiments using transliterations, human and machine translated data to compare the performance of such systems. These results are reported in Table 4. On the standard test set transliterations and human translations were better than google translations having scores on 2.08, 2.04 and 0.56 respectively. When evaluated on dev and test sets of individual corpora, surprisingly $FlickrHumanTrans$ performed worst of all with minimum BLEU scores of 3.02 on dev and 2.39 on test. These are the captions from flickr 8k dataset and often the English side is not grammatically correct. More interestingly, the same corpus when translated using google gave 35.71 on dev, 27.58 on test. $Transliteration$ of Hindi UMC002 corpus to Urdu gave the best scores of 54.30 and 47.34 on dev and test respectively.

$FlickrHumanTrans$ is further combined with the $Transliteration$ data set which is machine transliterated data, to build another system in order to observe the effect of machine transliterated data on the human translations. The performance of the resultant system is far better than the baseline system $FlickrHumanTrans$ yielding 2.24 on standard test set, 39.23 on dev and 40.91 on test. Further, we concatenated transliterations with the baseline

NMT Results on baseline + additional bitexts for Bio-Medical					
Baseline	Tokens	BLEU			
		Dev	Test	STS	Scielo
EMEA	1.03	26.44	40.27	39.81	5.24
+Scielo	1.68	26.96	35.22	45.90	14.37
+Scielo+jang	1.82	27.22	35.01	47.46	16.09
+Scileo+jang+Emille	1.89	27.55	34.62	46.28	16.72

Table 5: Results on NMT on addition of bitexts for Bio-medical domains.

$FlickrGooglTrans$ and a good improvement in scores is observed i.e. 2.66 BLEU on standard test data, 48.61 on dev data, 45.87 on test data.

Now, we address the question of effect on performance by addition of these corpora to the already available resources. $Emille$ is the already available human translated corpus, when combined with our transliterated data set, an improvement of almost 4.00 and 24.35 BLEU points on dev and test is observed, however on standard test a decline of 0.22 points is observed. Similar trend is observed when machine translated data is added to $Emille + Treebank$ yielding improvements on all datasets.

5.4. NMT Systems

We are presenting NMT system performance only for Bio-Medical domain. Table 5 shows the results of our experiments for NMT. We maintained the same baseline and corpus concatenation combination as used in SMT experiments. The results of Bio-Medical NMT are lower than the corresponding SMT systems (Table 3). This is expected as NMT systems don't perform well with small amounts of corpus. A unanimous observation is that addition of bitexts improves the systems across all dev and test sets, a slight deviation to this trend is observed when $Emille$ is added to $EMEA + Scielo + jang$ (last row in Table 5).

6. Conclusion

We presented domain based results on SMT and NMT systems for translation from English to Urdu. This is the first work being reported on several domains for the English-Urdu language pair. We collected corpora for four main domains namely Bio-medical, Religious, Technology and General. We experimented with various methods to reduce data scarcity which include, the use of automatic translations and transliterations. We also collected and compiled human translations from translation agencies as well as produced human translations of Flickr 8k dataset. We performed series of experiments in attempts to optimize the performance of each system and also to study the impact of data sources on the systems. Finally, we established a comparison of the data sources and the effect of Language Model size on statistical machine translation performance.

7. Bibliographical References

Abdul Rauf, S., Schwenk, H., Lambert, P., and Nawaz, M. (2016). Empirical use of information retrieval to build synthetic data for smt domain adaptation. *IEEE Transactions on Audio, Speech and Language Processing*.

Ali, A., Siddiq, S., and Malik, M. K. (2010). Development of Parallel Corpus and English to Urdu Statistical Machine Translation. *International Journal of Engineering*, (05):3–6.

Ali, A., Hussain, A., and Kamran Malik, M. (2013). Model for English-Urdu statistical machine translation. *World Applied Sciences Journal*, 24(10):1362–1367.

Baker, P., Hardie, A., McEnery, T., Cunningham, H., and Gaizauskas, R. J. (2002). Emille, a 67-million word corpus of indic languages: Data collection, mark-up and harmonisation. In *LREC*.

Brown, P., Della Pietra, S., Della Pietra, V. J., and Mercer, R. (1993). The mathematics of statistical machine translation. *Computational Linguistics*, 19(2):263–311.

Callison-Burch, C., Koehn, P., Monz, C., and Zaidan, O. F. (2011). Findings of the 2011 workshop on statistical machine translation. In *Proceedings of the Sixth Workshop on Statistical Machine Translation*, pages 22–64. Association for Computational Linguistics.

Durrani, N., Haddow, B., Koehn, P., and Heafield, K. (2014). Edinburgh's phrase-based machine translation systems for wmt-14. In *Proceedings of the Ninth Workshop on Statistical Machine Translation*, pages 97–104.

Habash, N. and Sadat, F. (2006). Arabic preprocessing schemes for statistical machine translation. In *Proceedings of the Human Language Technology Conference of the NAACL, Companion Volume: Short Papers*, pages 49–52. Association for Computational Linguistics.

Heafield, K. (2011). Kenlm: Faster and smaller language model queries. In *Proceedings of the Sixth Workshop on Statistical Machine Translation*, pages 187–197. Association for Computational Linguistics.

Hira, N.-e., Abdul Rauf, S., Kiani, K., Zafar, A., and Nawaz, R. (2019). Exploring transfer learning and domain data selection for the biomedical translation. In *Proceedings of the Fourth Conference on Machine Translation (Volume 3: Shared Task Papers, Day 2)*, pages 158–165, Florence, Italy, August. Association for Computational Linguistics.

Irvine, A. (2013). Statistical Machine Translation in Low Resource Settings. *Proceedings of the 2013 NAACL HLT Student Research Workshop*, (June):54–61.

Jawaid, B. and Zeman, D. (2011). Word-Order Issues in English-to-Urdu Statistical Machine Translation. *Prague Bulletin of Mathematical Linguistics*, 95(-1):87–106.

Jawaid, B., Kamran, A., and Bojar, O. (2014a). English to Urdu Statistical Machine Translation: Establishing a Baseline. *Proceedings of the Fifth Workshop on South and Southeast Asian Natural Language Processing*, pages 37–42.

Jawaid, B., Kamran, A., and Bojar, O. (2014b). Urdu monolingual corpus. LINDAT/CLARIN digital library at the Institute of Formal and Applied Linguistics ('UFAL), Faculty of Mathematics and Physics, Charles University.

Jawaid, B., Kamran, A., and Bojar, O. (2016). Enriching Source for English-to-Urdu Machine Translation. *Proceedings of the 6th Workshop on South and Southeast Asian Natural Language Processing (WSSANLP2016)*, pages 54–63.

Karamat, N. (2006). *Verb transfer for English to Urdu Machine Translation*. Ph.D. thesis, National University of Computer & Emerging Sciences.

Khan, N., Anwar, M. W., Bajwa, U. I., and Durrani, N. (2013). English to urdu hierarchical phrase-based statistical machine translation. In *Proceedings of the 4th Workshop on South and Southeast Asian Natural Language Processing*, pages 72–76.

Khan, N. J., Anwar, W., and Durrani, N. (2017). Machine Translation Approaches and Survey for Indian Languages. *arXiv preprint arXiv:1701.04290*, 18(1):47–78.

Khan Jadoon, N., Anwar, W., Bajwa, U. I., and Ahmad, F. (2017). Statistical machine translation of Indian languages: a survey. *Neural Computing and Applications*.

Klein, G., Kim, Y., Deng, Y., Senellart, J., and Rush, A. M. (2017). Opennmt: Open-source toolkit for neural machine translation. *CoRR*, abs/1701.02810.

Koehn, P., Och, F. J., and Marcu, D. (2003). Statistical phrased-based machine translation. pages 127–133.

Koehn, P., Hoang, H., Birch, A., Callison-Burch, C., Federico, M., Bertoldi, N., Cowan, B., Shen, W., Moran, C., Zens, R., Dyer, C., Bojar, O., Constantin, A., and Herbst, E. (2007). Moses: Open source toolkit for statistical machine translation. In *Meeting of the Association for Computational Linguistics*, pages 177–180.

Lambert, P., Schwenk, H., Servan, C., and Abdul-Rauf, S. (2011). Investigations on translation model adaptation using monolingual data. In *Proceedings of the Sixth Workshop on Statistical Machine Translation*, pages 284–293, Edinburgh, Scotland, July. Association for Computational Linguistics.

Luong, M.-T., Pham, H., and Manning, C. D. (2015). Effective approaches to attention-based neural machine translation. *arXiv preprint arXiv:1508.04025*.

Marcus, M. P., Santorini, B., and Marcinkiewicz, M. A. (1993). Building a large annotated corpus of English: The Penn Treebank. *Computational Linguistics*, 19(2):313–330.

Naila Ata, Bushra Jawaid, A. K. (2007). Rule based english to urdu machine translation. *In Proceedings of Conference on Language and Technology (CLT'07). 2007*.

Och, F. J. and Ney, H. (2003a). A systematic comparison of various statistical alignement models. *Computational Linguistics*, 29(1):19–51.

Och, F. J. and Ney, H. (2003b). A systematic comparison of various statistical alignment models. *Computational linguistics*, 29(1):19–51.

Och, F. J. (2003). Minimum error rate training in statistical machine translation. In *Proceedings of the 41st Annual Meeting on Association for Computational Linguistics-Volume 1*, pages 160–167. Association for Computational Linguistics.

Papineni, K., Roukos, S., Ward, T., and Zhu, W.-J. (2002). Bleu: a method for automatic evaluation of machine translation. In *Proceedings of the 40th annual meeting on association for computational linguistics*, pages 311–318. Association for Computational Linguistics.

Post, M., Callison-Burch, C., and Osborne, M. (2012). Constructing parallel corpora for six indian languages via crowdsourcing. *Wmt-2012*, pages 401–409.

Shahnawaz and Mishra. (2013). Statistical Machine Translation System for English to Urdu. *Int. J. Adv. Intell. Paradigms*, 5(3):182–203.

Tafseer, A. and Alvi, S. (2002). English to urdu translation system. *manuscript, University of Karachi*.

Tiedemann, J. (2012). Parallel Data, Tools and Interfaces in OPUS. In Nicoletta Calzolari (Conference Chair) and Khalid Choukri and Thierry Declerck and Mehmet Ugur Dogan and Bente Maegaard and Joseph Mariani and Jan Odijk and Stelios Piperidis, editor, *Proceedings of the Eight International Conference on Language Resources and Evaluation (LREC'12)*. European Language Resources Association (ELRA), Istanbul, Turkey.

Zoph, B., Yuret, D., May, J., and Knight, K. (2016). Transfer Learning for Low-Resource Neural Machine Translation.

Proceedings of the 1st Joint SLTU and CCURL Workshop (SLTU-CCURL 2020), pages 294–297
Language Resources and Evaluation Conference (LREC 2020), Marseille, 11–16 May 2020
© European Language Resources Association (ELRA), licensed under CC-BY-NC

Developing a Twi (Asante) Dictionary from Akan Interlinear Glossed Texts

Dorothee Beermann, Lars Hellan, Pavel Mihaylov, Anna Struck

Department of Language and Literature, Norwegian University of Science and Technology, Norway
{lars.hellan, dorothee.beermann}@ntnu.no

Abstract

Traditionally, a lexicographer identifies the lexical items to be added to a dictionary. Here we present a corpus-based approach to dictionary compilation and describe a procedure that derives a Twi dictionary from a TypeCraft corpus of Interlinear Glossed Texts. We first extracted a list of unique words. We excluded words belonging to different dialects of Akan (mostly Fante and Abron). We corrected misspellings and distinguished English loan words to be integrated in our dictionary from instances of code switching. Next to the dictionary itself, one other resource arising from our work is a lexicographical model for Akan which represents the lexical resource itself, and the extended morphological and word class inventories that provide information to be aggregated. We also represent external resources such as the corpus that serves as the source and word level audio files. The Twi dictionary consists at present of 1367 words; it will be available online and from an open mobile app.

Keywords: lexicographical resources, Akan data, Akan lexicographical model, online dictionary

1. Introduction

The availability of lexicographical data is essential for the development of digital applications for less resourced languages. Akan, although a well described language in linguistic terms and a language not without important lexical resources, is still in terms of digital means a lesser resourced language. Here we describe the compilation of a small digital dictionary for Twi (Asante) based on an interlinear glossed corpus of Akan. This being a goal in itself, we at the same time hope to strengthen the development of Interlinear Glossed Text corpora for lesser resourced languages as a resource for the digital deployment of lexicographical data.

Akan is a Kwa language and one of the official languages of Ghana. Foremost among its dictionaries is Christaller (1881) which was the first dictionary of Twi, and still is by far the most comprehensive one. Less comprehensive is Anyidoho et al. 2005. Neither of these two dictionaries is in a format easily amenable to the development of further digital resources.

Online dictionaries for some Ghanaian languages are available from the Ghana Institute of Linguistics Literacy and Bible Translation (GILLBT)[1], including one for Ghanaian Kusaal with over 4000 entries. Its entries may provide information about the part of speech and offer an English translation of the head word. They may give an example in the source language, as exemplified in (1) and (2) below, but entries may also consist just of the head word.

(1) pa'al-1 v teach, *Tinam pa'an biis nɛ yin yɛlsieba amaa asɛɛ pa'annib pa'al ban na niŋ si'em sɔbi li*

(2) pa'al-2 *v* show, *Msaam mɔrimini keŋ pa'al kuob la zɛm si'em*

The present approach describes the compilation of a Twi (Asante) online dictionary from a TypeCraft corpus of Interlinear Glossed Texts. A view of an entry analogous to

the above is shown in Figure 1 and will be described in the main body of the article in more detail.

Figure 1: The word "aboa", in the Twi (Asante) dictionary

Also to be described in the following is the compilation of the dictionary. Our corpus-based approach requires a routine of data cleaning and normalization: we extracted a list of unique words, excluded words belonging to different dialects of Akan (mostly Fante and Abron), corrected misspellings and distinguished English loan words to be integrated in our dictionary from instances of code switching, which is frequently found in spoken Akan also reflected in our corpus.

The paper is structured as follows: Section 2 describes data acquisition and the essential properties of the Akan corpus on which the dictionary is based, together with the basic lexicographical features to be represented in the dictionary. Section 3 presents a lexicographical Language Model for

---

[1] GILLBET's dictionaries like many other dictionaries can be accessed from the Webonary – Dictionaries and Grammars of the World : https://www.webonary.org/

Akan. Section 4 gives a brief evaluation of our present resources and describes the next phase of the development.

2.   The Akan Source Data

2.1 The Corpus

The data used for this dictionary is based on a collection of Akan texts which are stored in TypeCraft - a user-driven

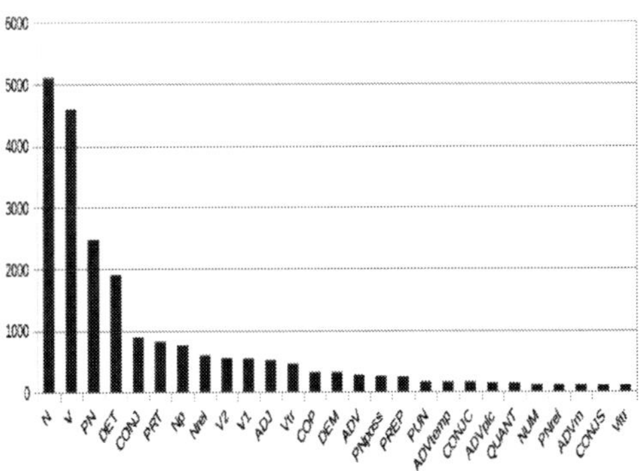

Figure 2 : TC-Akan corpus - Part of Speech labels

online database for Interlinear Glossed Texts. Akan is one of the official languages of Ghana belonging to the Niger-Congo languages of West Africa, Twi (Asante) is one of the main dialects of Akan.

The corpus currently consists of 261 texts, narratives, transcribed dialogue, or linguistic collections, corresponding to 98 000 words. Most of these texts have been annotated for part of speech and are glossed. An entry in the TypeCraft database consists of a sentence, its translation, and several layers of annotation, see Figure 3 below. The most common part of speech tags used for Akan are shown in Figure 2 above.

The largest word class in our corpus are nouns, followed by single main verbs. We distinguish verbs as part of an SVC (V1, V2, V3) from single verbs and copulas. Texts which are fully curated will not contain items labeled as prepositions, which, as Figure 2 shows, still occurs as a label in non-curated parts of the corpus, although it is well-known fact that Akan makes only use of postpositions (relational nouns). We will discuss the morpho/syntactic labeling further in section 4.

Word:	Afua	piaa		Kofi
Morph:	afua	pia	a	kofi
Citation Form:	afua	pia	a	kofi
Meaning:	Afua	push		Kofi
Gloss tags:	SBJ		PAST	OBJ
POS:	Np	V		Np

Figure 3 : Example of an interlinear glossed sentence

2.2 The Lexical Entry

In its present form the entries of our lexicon contain the kind of information instantiated in (3):

```
(3)
[{
"word": "ankaa",
"pos": "N",
"translation": "orange",
"audio": [ "F_9_anka", "M_9_anka" ],
"examples": [ {
"original": "Kofi tɔɔ ankaa firii ankaa-
senasenetɔnfoɔ no hɔ.",
"translation": "Kofi bought an orange from
the peeled orange sellers."
},
...
} ],
"id": 132,
"key": "ankaa"
```

In (3), next to the lemma itself we indicate the part of speech and provide an English translation. Most entries are accompanied by a word level audio file (if available we provide both a female voice and a male voice). Most entries come with a list of examples from the TypeCraft database, as shown in Figure 1.

2.3 Creating the Entries

Akan is a tone language. When creating the audio files for the dictionary, speakers were given sentences to read. In a second round we recorded word level data (for more information, see Van Dommelen and Beermann, 2019). Words written in isolation can correspond to several meanings depending on the lexical tone, but also dependent on the context they appear in. As part of the dictionary compilation, we added new words to the dictionary when an orthographic form corresponded to different tonal patterns and meanings.

The phonetic project that had allowed us to record speakers in phonetic experiments, ended while we still were working on the dictionary compilation. When we finally could revisit the data, some of the links between audio files, words, and the corpus were hard to reconstruct. We therefore used the word's orthographic form, as well as part of speech information and the word's meaning (rendered in English), to extract example sentences from the corpus. The corpus itself does not contain tone marking, which means that not in all cases words and their example sentences may have been aligned correctly.

3.   The Akan Language Model

For the representation of the structure and external resources of the present dictionary, and in order to show the further development that the Twi (Asante) dictionary will take, we present a UML model[2] as shown in Figure 4. The only other African language for which we found a lexicographical language model is Xhosa (Bosch et al.

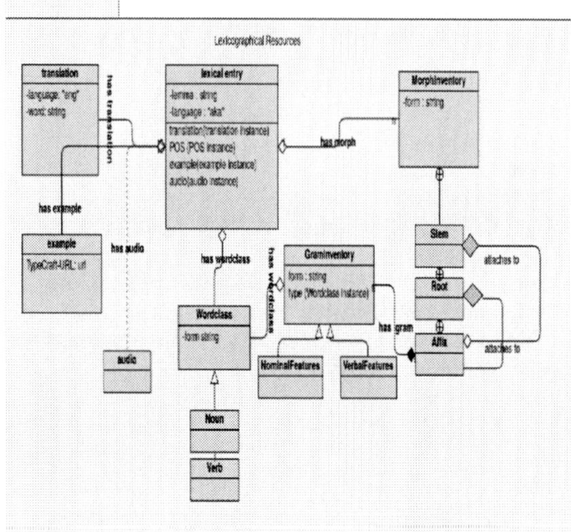

Figure 4: Akan lexicographical model

2018), a Bantu language spoken in South Africa. It is agglutinating in nature, while Akan is a Kwa language and belongs to the Atlantic branch of the Niger-Kongo languages. Like other Kwa languages, Akan does not make use of noun classes and derivational suffixes which is characteristic for Bantu languages. Kwa languages are known for their Serial Verb Constructions (SVC) where

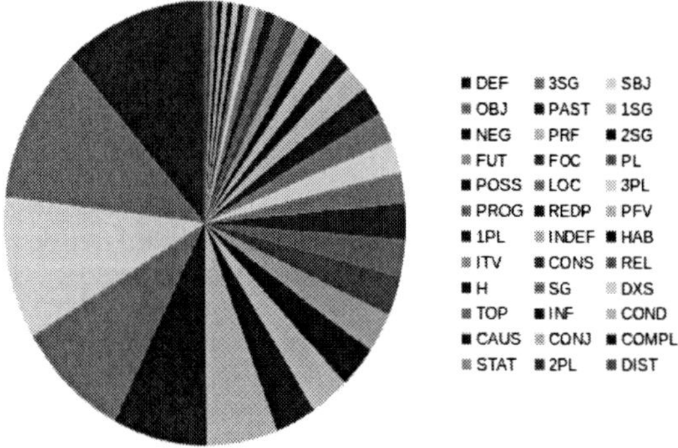

Figure 5: Morpho-functional annotations - TC Akan corpus

several verbs share a subject.[3] When part of an SVC, verbs have an inflection which is sensitive to their position in the cluster as well as to the SVC's temporal-aspectual features. This and other differences between these two language families carry over to their lexicographical models.
Given the present form of the dictionary, only a part of the grammatical information we have stored in our corpus is reflected in the dictionary. On the other hand, additional

external information such as audio and corpus resources in the form of examples have been added to make the dictionary more user friendly.
Morphological information, although available in the corpus, has not yet been included in the dictionary. An overview over the grammatical features annotated in the corpus is given Figure 5. [4]

Interesting in Figure 5 is in this context not so much how frequently a certain label is used as the nature of the information that has been labeled. Especially for languages where a grammar book is not a standard commodity, the inclusion of morphological information in a dictionary is of special interest. The corpus will allow us to use this information as part of the Morph-and-Gram-Inventory which is part of our Akan lexicographical model as shown in Figure 4. Lemmas are shown to be related to the inflectional paradigms they are members of, and this information is stored relative to word class specification.
The *Morph Inventory* as well as the *Gram Inventory* can be populated by morpheme forms and the grammatical features they embody.

Which additional features are available is shown in Figure 5. We find form function pairs for most of the language's Tense-Aspect features, and for some of the grammatical relations. but still very little is known. Although we still lack information about the nominal morphology in our corpus, this information itself is readily available, and can be added to the corpus.

4.   Evaluation and Outlook

The Twi (Asante) dictionary is a small resource which needs to grow in order to be a real resource. At present the dictionary contains word class information, in most cases an audio representation which gives an indication of the tonal properties of a word in its base form. In many cases we provide an extensive list of examples which are glossed and translated into English, which goes beyond what most Akan online dictionaries provide. Already in its present form the dictionary will be useful; especially if new words are added on a regular basis. The resource will be available as an online dictionary and through an open mobile dictionary app (Eckart et al., 2020).

Due to the in-depth annotated TC-Akan corpus we will be able to further extend the dictionary with morphological information. Akan verbs belong to different classes according to which inflectional paradigms unfold (for more information see Dolphyne 1988). We further observe that, when part of an SVC, verbs may be associated with additional inflectional patterns specific to their position in the verb cluster and the nature of the cluster itself. This means that we need to assign Akan verbs to several

---

[2] UML stands for *Unified Modeling Language*

[3] See Beermann and Hellan 2018

[4] SBJ=subject, 3SG=3Person, singular, DEF= definite, 1SG =1Person,singular, PAST=past tense, OBJ=object. A full list of the glosses can be found at TypeCraft: https://typecraft.org/tc2wiki/Special:TypeCraft/GlossTags

inflection paradigms dependent of whether they occur as a single verb or as part of an SVC. Using annotation mining, part of this information may be directly acquired from the Interlinear Glossed Text corpus. In addition, we will make use of the Akan data from the Leipzig Corpus Collection.[5] An LCC corpus contains randomly selected sentences which in the case of the 2018 Akan corpus come from the Wikipedia. Although our corpus resources are small, valuable information can be extracted. The LCC offers a basic language statistic for the corpus, and together with information from word sketches, to show collocational behavior, we hope to arrive at a more accurate and detailed analysis of our lexical data. This then represents the next step in the development of a Twi (Asante) corpus and the Twi dictionary.

5.   Bibliographical References

Anyidoho, Akosua, et al. 2006. *Akan Dictionary*. Pilot project. University of Ghana.

Beermann, Dorothee. 2014. Data management and analysis for less documented languages. In Jones, Marion, and Connolly, C. (eds) *Language Documentation and New Technology*. Cambridge University Press.

Beermann, Dorothee, and Mihaylov, Pavel. 2014. Collaborative databasing and Resource sharing for Linguists. In: *Languages Resources and Evaluation*. Springer. 48. Dordrecht: Springer, 1-23.

Beermann, Dorothee, and Lars Hellan. 2018. West African Serial verb constructions: the case of Akan and Ga. In: Agwuele, Augustine, and Adams Bodomo (eds) *The Routledge Handbook of African Linguistics*. London and New York: Routledge. Pg. 207-221.

Bosch, S., Eckart, T., Klimek, T., Goldhahn, D., and Quasthoff, U. (2018). Preparation and Usage of Xhosa Lexicographical Data for a Multilingual, Federated Environment. In: *Proceedings of the 11th International Conference on Language Resources and Evaluation* (LREC 2018), Miyazaki, Japan.

Christaller, J.G. 1881 (latest edition of 2013). *Dictionary of the Asante and Fante Language*. Basel: Basel Evangelical Missionary Society

Dolphyne, Florence A. 1988. The Akan (Twi-Fante) Language. Accra: Ghana Universities Press.

Eckart, Thomas, Sonja Bosch, Uwe Quasthoff, Erik Körner, Simon Kaleschke, Dirk Goldhahn. Usability and Acessibility of Bantu Language Dictionaries in the Digital Age: Mobile Access in an Open Environment. *Proceedings of LREC 2020, Marseille.*

van Dommelen, Wim A.; Beermann, Dorothee. (2019) Tonal properties of the Akan particle 'na'. *Proceedings of the 19th International Congress of Phonetic Sciences.*

6.   Language Resource References

TypeCraft Akan corpus, Release 1.0: https://www.researchgate.net/publication/323998547_TypeCraft_Akan_Corpus_Release_1.0

Further TypeCraft Akan corpora, non-curated: https://typecraft.org/tc2wiki/Special:TypeCraft/PortalOfLanguages

---

[5] https://wortschatz.uni-leipzig.de/en/download/

Proceedings of the 1st Joint SLTU and CCURL Workshop (SLTU-CCURL 2020), pages 298–305
Language Resources and Evaluation Conference (LREC 2020), Marseille, 11–16 May 2020
© European Language Resources Association (ELRA), licensed under CC-BY-NC

Adapting Language Specific Components of Cross-Media Analysis Frameworks to Less-Resourced Languages: the Case of Amharic

Yonas Woldemariam, Adam Dahlgren

Dept. Computing Science, Umeå University, Sweden
{yonasd, dali}@cs.umu.se

Abstract

We present an ASR based pipeline for Amharic that orchestrates NLP components within a cross media analysis framework (CMAF). One of the major challenges that are inherently associated with CMAFs is effectively addressing multi-lingual issues. As a result, many languages remain under-resourced and fail to leverage out of available media analysis solutions. Although spoken natively by over 22 million people and there is an ever-increasing amount of Amharic multimedia content on the Web, querying them with simple text search is difficult. Searching for, especially audio/video content with simple key words, is even hard as they exist in their raw form. In this study, we introduce a spoken and textual content processing workflow into a CMAF for Amharic. We design an ASR-named entity recognition (NER) pipeline that includes three main components: ASR, a transliterator and NER. We explore various acoustic modeling techniques and develop an OpenNLP-based NER extractor along with a transliterator that interfaces between ASR and NER. The designed ASR-NER pipeline for Amharic promotes the multi-lingual support of CMAFs. Also, the state-of-the art design principles and techniques employed in this study shed light for other less-resourced languages, particularly the Semitic ones.

Keywords: Less-resourced, Amharic, Cross-media analysis, Speech recognition, named entity recognition

1. Introduction and Background

Automatic Speech Recognition (ASR) and Named Entity Recognition (NER) perform information extraction tasks on spoken and textual documents respectively. ASR generates a transcription text from speech data. ASR technologies have been used for many applications such as spoken document indexing and retrieval (Chang et al., 2005; Aichroth et al., 2015; Le et al., 2017), spoken dialogue systems (Ivanov et al., 2015), speech translation (Stüker et al., 2011), and so on. NER is used to identify and extract entity mentions, such as names of people, locations, etc from textual contents. In natural text analysis, NER performs a pre-processing task for downstream annotators (e.g., syntactic parsers (Marneffe et al., 2006)) and identifies proper nouns and classifies them into known categories (e.g., Person, Place, Organization and so on). While both ASR and NER are essential to solve specific problems in isolation, it is also possible to join them systematically to operate on same media (e.g., a webpage containing text and audio tracks), and apply them in succession to add contextual information on the metadata associated with audio/video contents for semantic search (Aichroth et al., 2015; Le et al., 2017).

Depending on the purpose of the application in question, ASR and NER can be combined in various ways. For example, in cross-media analysis frameworks such as EUMSSI[1] (Event Understanding through Multimodal Social Stream Interpretation) and MICO[2] (Media in Context), their combination is defined as an analysis workflow or analysis-chain called an ASR-NER pipeline that basically includes speech transcription and named entity extraction services. Within these frameworks there also exist complex multimedia analysis pipelines designed to meet the requirements of complex information retrieval use cases, for instance,

searching for video shots, where a person (in the shots) says something about a specific political issue using a keywords-driven approach.

Nowadays, there are plenty of multimedia extraction tools used to make searching web contents convenient. However, most of these tools are developed for well researched and resourced languages such as English and Spanish, and specific domains of applications. Due to this reason, many languages including Amharic, remained under-sourced. That severely limits the access of information available in those languages. There are some studies (Abate et al., 2009; Yifiru, 2003; Belay, 2014; Demeke and Hailemariam, 2012) and contributions on building language technologies for Amharic, but most of them are developed as proof-of-concept prototypes with very limited data and resources(Gauthier et al., 2016; ELRA-W0074, 2014; HaBiT, 2016). As a result, it is often challenging to get computational linguistic resources for Amharic required for either NLP studies or commercial use.

Amharic is the official language of Ethiopia, spoken by over 22 million people, also according to the latest census carried out by Central Statistical Agency of Ethiopia[3], the second most spoken Semitic language next to Arabic. The writing system of Amharic is called "fidel"; shared with the other Semitic language of Ethiopia, Tigrinya. Amharic has a unique writing system and its basic alphabet units have a consonant-vowel (CV) syllabic structure, usually vowels are omitted in the written form of CV. There is an ever-increasing amount of Amharic digital contents of various types: text, images, audio, video, etc. on the Web due to emerging information sharing platforms such as social media and video hosting sites. However, querying them with simple text search is difficult, especially audio and video contents, is even very hard as they exist in raw format (not well indexed). Thus, obviously it is very demanding to have

---

[1] https://www.eumssi.eu
[2] https://www.mico-project.eu

[3] https://www.csa.gov.et

linguistically motivated multimedia analysis and extraction tools that could potentially deal with language-related concerns and make Amharic contents more searchable through keywords.

The most reasonable and affordable solution is to use open-source multi-lingual information extraction frameworks that provide media analysis, extraction and indexing, search and retrieval services, though they require language models of certain types. One of existing open-source media analysis solutions, is the MICO platform, though it is at early stage of its release. Ideally, the platform allows extraction of multimedia contents of different languages using the corresponding language models. Within the platform, there are a number of pre-defined analysis pipelines along with their metadata extractors.

The aim of this study is to investigate adapting language specific components of MICO for Amharic. That could potentially be extended to other languages, particularly Semitic ones as they share similar orthography (e.g., Tigrinya) and phonology (e.g., Arabic). Within MICO, there are several natural language dependent multimedia analysis components such as text classification and text language detection including the ASR-NER pipeline. However, we only focus on designing of an ASR-NER pipeline for Amharic using the design principles, the standards and the technologies used in MICO. The pipeline could be considered as the first step to be able to use the MICO platform and for developing other important metadata extractors to analyze Amharic contents. Indeed, the pipeline is useful in itself, at least to index video /audio contents with extracted entities. To completely benefit from the platform more effort is needed in the direction of identifying and adapting other language dependent analysis components, for instance, sentiment analysis. We basically develop Kaldi-based acoustic models, a transliterator and an OpenNLP based NER extractor, to build the **Amharic ASR-NER pipeline**.

We got motivated for this study as we are one the partners of the MICO project and responsible for implementing NLP tools. While most of the implementation is done only for English, the MICO architecture allows for the integration of other language models via its API. Nevertheless, it is challenging to adapt MICO to under-resourced languages due to its requirement of trained language models that strictly satisfy the underlying design principles. This presents an opportunity to investigate the possibilities of adapting relevant language models for Amharic.

We discuss related works in Section 2., the MICO platform in Section 3., the designed ASR-NER pipeline and the discussion in Section 4., the challenges and solutions in Section 5. and, finally, future work and conclusion in Section 6..

2. Related Work

There are a number of papers (Magnini et al., 2013; Hori and Nakamura, 2006) on extraction of named entities on speech transcripts on digital spoken archives for various purposes, though it is hardly possible to get any for Amharic. There are also a few research projects that investigated the introduction of an ASR-NER pipeline in multi-modal cross-media analysis frameworks for different types of languages. We primarily focus on discussing the methods used and the results achieved by these projects, as they probably best put our study into perspective, namely MICO and EUMSSI. In addition to that, although there is no published literature on the task of NER on speech transcription for Amharic, we present a brief review of research works on standalone speech recognition and named entity recognition conducted independently from each other.

During the development of MICO metadata extractors, special attention was given to the ASR component due to the fact that most extractors, particularly text analysis components including NER heavily depend on the result produced by the ASR extractor. In order to achieve high-quality speech transcription, state-of-the-art open-source and proprietary libraries for ASR have been well studied and evaluated against sample video contents, then the respective comparative analysis was carried out beforehand. Consequently, Kaldi[4] was chosen based on the criterion of accuracy and other technical reasons. The other good quality of Kaldi is its multi-lingual support. Most of the experiments that make use of Kaldi within MICO were effectively carried out only for English, though the MICO Showcases were planned for Arabic and Italian as well. The most challenging part of training Kaldi is that preparing a parallel corpus (speech and text) is quite costly.

Within MICO, the ASR is implemented as a speech-to-text pipeline to analyze video content and produce the corresponding text transcription in various formats. The pipeline includes audio-demultiplexing, for extracting and down-sampling the audio signal from video content, speaker diarization (Meignier and Merlin, 2010; Tranter and Reynolds, 2006) for segmenting information along with gender classification and speaker partitioning, speech transcription, for transcribing audio signal into text. The resulting textual content generated from the pipeline is further analyzed by text analysis components including the NER extractor.

The NER extractor provides a named entity extraction service on-demand when requested by other registered extractors requiring (depending) on the output produced by it. NER also takes plain text (with a text/plain MIME type) from other possible sources of textual contents such as forum discussion posts after pre-processing and parsing tasks. The NER extractor is based on the OpenNLP toolkit, that is an open-source library providing a NER service. MICO provides OpenNLP-based NER language models for English, German, Spanish and Italian, and allows an integration of models for other languages.

The ASR-NER pipeline introduced in MICO performs analysis workflows, for instance, detecting a person in a video, by collaborating with image analysis components such as the face detection extractor. Some preliminary showcases have been demonstrated by the use case partners, for instance, InsideOut10 (one of the use case partners of the MICO project) built a showcase application that retrieves video shots containing a specific person talking about a specific title (Kurz et al., 2015).

---

[4]http://kaldi-asr.org

The EUMSSI platform basically provides multimodal analytics and interpretation services for different types of data obtained from various online media sources. (their demo is available on[5]). EUMSSI seems to mainly target journalists as end users, automating their time-consuming tasks of organizing information about various events from different online and traditional data sources providing un/structured contents. The platform allows to search multimedia contents aggregated and filtered from media search engines in an interactive fashion, then enriching, contextualizing the media with extracted metadata and retrieves the result with the multimodal approach.

The NER component of EUMSSI is based on the Stanford NER (Finkel et al., 2005), running on the transcription generated by ASR and text extracted by OCR (Optical character recognition) from video contents, in addition to other types of textual contents from news and social media. The transcription returned from the ASR service is normalized by an auxiliary component beforehand. The ASR-NER pipeline implemented in EUMSSI, is used to annotate the speech segments uttered by each speaker shown in a video with the corresponding transcriptions and mentioned names. The resulting information is intended to get combined with the annotations obtained from the face recognition component, that enables video retrieval applications to support different search options, for instance, retrieving quotations of peoples (Le et al., 2017).

There are also several studies on named entity extraction on speech transcripts for independent NLP systems or audio/video analysis frameworks. For example, in the Evalita (evaluation campaign of NLP and Speech tools for Italian) 2011 workshop (Magnini et al., 2013), one of the tasks was named entity recognition on transcribed broadcast news. The purpose is to investigate the impact of the transcription errors on NLP systems and explore NER approaches that cope with the peculiarities of the resulting transcripts from ASR systems.

There are a number of studies on the design and development of ASR and NER systems for Amharic. Relatively, NER is a less researched area than ASR. The survey in (Abate et al., 2009), summarizes ASR research works attempted for Amharic, ranging from syllable to sentence level detection, from speaker dependent to speaker independent speech recognition. According to the survey most of the works are done using quite similar techniques i.e. HMM (Hidden Markov Model) (Rabiner, 1989) and tools such as HTK (HMM Tool Kit). There is an attempt to develop and integrate an ASR system into the Microsoft Word application to enable it to receive file related commands. The survey also pointed out that the major reasons, why the ASR systems failed to be used in speech applications, to mentions some of them: they are trained on read speech with a limited dataset and fail to handle germination and morphological variations. There are also a few unpublished research works on Amharic NER (Mehamed, 2010; Belay, 2014). The recent work (Gambäck and Sikdar, 2017) introduced deep learning with the skip-gram word-embedding technique by extending the previous works. The authors in (Gambäck and Sikdar, 2017) developed Amharic NER prototypes using the same method i.e., Conditional Random Fields (Sobhana et al., 2010; Finkel et al., 2005) and the same corpus as in (Mehamed, 2010; Belay, 2014) but different subsets, and obtained different results.

3. The MICO Platform

Basically the MICO plaform provides media analysis, metadata publishing, search and recommendation services (described in (Aichroth et al., 2015)). It has three types of metadata extractors, textual extractors for performing linguistic analysis such as parsing, sentiment analysis and text classification, image extractors for performing image analysis for detecting and human faces and animals from images, audio extractors for performing different speech analysis tasks such as detecting whether audio signals contain music or speech, and extracting audio tracks from video content and producing a transcription.

Metadata extractors interact and collaborate with each other in automatic fashion via a service orchestration component (aka broker) to put a media resource in context. Several semantic web technologies such as Apache Marmotta[6] and SPARQL-MM[7] are used for storing the metadata annotation of analysis results in a RDF format and querying the metadata respectively. The Apache Hadoop[8] distributed file system is used for binary data, and Apache Solr[9] for full-text searching.

4. The Amharic ASR-NER Pipeline

The Amharic ASR-NER pipeline designed in this study includes three main components: ASR, a transliterator and NER (see Figure 2). The pipeline performs extracting named mentioned from audio and video contents. Within the MICO architecture, the core ASR component needs to be connected with pre-processing and post-processing components, that forms a speech-to-text sub-pipeline.

There are two pre-processing components, namely audidemux and LIUM diarization. The former does extracting audio tracks from a video input and down-sampling the audio tracks. The later does segmenting the audio tracks into smaller units using gender and speaker information. The post-processing component, namely XML2text transforms the output file (in the text/xml format) generated by the core ASR component to plain text (text/plain) required by the NER component.

4.1. Building the Amharic ASR

We explored and applied three different acoustic modeling techniques, namely GMM-HMMs (Gaussian mixture model-hidden Markov model), DNN (Deep Neural Networks) and SGMM-HMMs (Subspace Gaussian Mixture model) to build the Amharic ASR. The Kaldi (Povey et al., 2011b) framework is used as an open speech recognition toolkit. While DNN-HMM is the state-of-the-art ASR modeling technique, SGMM-HMM (Povey et al., 2011a)

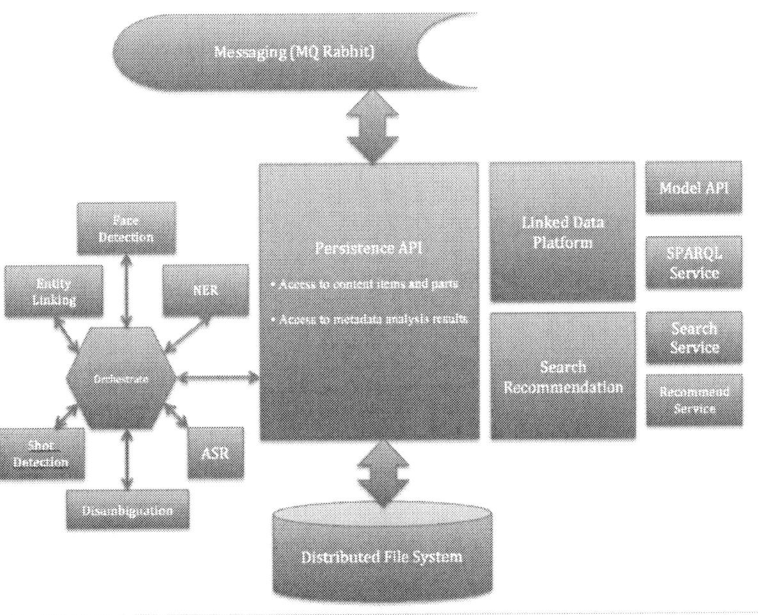

Figure 1: The Architecture of the MICO Platform

is an extension of GMM-HMM that is one of conventional acoustic modeling approaches. In HMM-based ASR systems, (S)GMMs and DNN estimate probability distributions of phonemes over HMM states given observations (acoustic inputs). During training they compute model parameters (e.g, mean vectors and covariance matrices) from training data, (S)GMMs use the expectation maximization algorithm, whereas DNN uses stochastic gradient descent and back-propagation to adjust weights and biases.

As a result, three acoustic models have been built using each technique with a parallel speech-transcription corpus (Gauthier et al., 2016), a pronunciation lexicon and a language model. Originally, the raw corpus was prepared for the study in (Tachbelie et al., 2014), it is about 20 and 2 hours of speech for training and testing respectively. We built a 5-gram language model using the SRILM[10] language modeling toolkit with the Kneser-Ney smoothing method.

All the three acoustic models are trained with 13 Mel-frequency cepstrum coefficients (MFCCs) features, followed by linear discriminant analysis (LDA) and transformation, maximum likelihood transform (MLLT). Also, feature-space maximum likelihood linear regression (fM-LLR) has been used as a speaker adaptation technique. The models are evaluated on the same test set containing 6203 words using the Word Error Rate (WER) metric, and obtained a WER of 50.88%, 38.72%, and 46.25% for GMM-HMM, DNN-HMM, SGMM-HMM respectively.

4.1.1. Discussion of ASR Acoustic Models

The experimental results obtained from the ASR models evaluation show that the DNN-HMM model outperforms than GMM-HMM and SGMM-HMM models, with a WER of 12.16% and 7.53% respectively. The SGMM-HMM model in turn outperforms GMM-HMM with a WER of 4.63%. In our experiments, the GMM-HMM acoustic model gets trained with utterance-level transcriptions, the resulting model is used to generate phone alignments for DNN training. For that reason, the DNN acoustic model appears to have the best performance (regarding WER). DNNs also have the ability to capture larger context (larger window of frames), for example, the DNN in this study, is trained with 5 preceding and 5 following frames. Moreover, the number of model parameters (weights) computed by DNN is extremely larger than (S)GMMs, that potentially help learn the complex relationship between acoustic features extracted from input speech signal and their associated sequence of phonemes. For (S)GMMs, the training data seems to be too small to effectively model the distributions of acoustic units and generalize for new input data. Compared with state-of-the-art ASR systems built for other languages (Wang and Zheng, 2015; Xiong et al., 2018; Ghahremani et al., 2017), for instance, authors in (Xiong et al., 2018) achieved a 5.1% of WER, that suggests more tasks are needed to improve our ASR. Unlike these studies where a large amount of data is used to train acoustic models, in our study the amount of training data is limited to 20 hours. Basically, the results obtained in this study could be improved by increasing the size of the training data, including a large vocabulary to deal with the problem of out-of-vocabulary (OOV) and language models with different size of n-gram (e.g., (n=3 to 7)). However, preparing such resources is quite expensive and time-consuming, especially for less studied and under-resourced languages like Amharic. Therefore, adapting from pre-trained acous-

---

[10]http://www.speech.sri.com/projects/srilm/

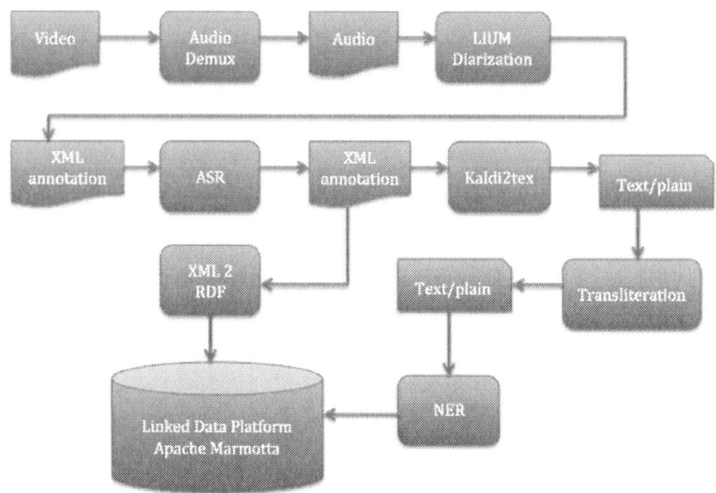

Figure 2: The Amharic ASR-NER Pipeline within a Cross-media Analysis Framework

tic models trained on other languages, particularly well resourced ones, seems to be more reasonable. Besides, multilingual model training (Ghoshal et al., 2013; Wang and Zheng, 2015; Feng and Lee, 2018) could be considered, where under multiple languages (including less-resourced ones) get trained together. Then, the resulting acoustic model can be used to produce speech transcriptions of any of these languages. However, it, in turn, requires a huge amount of multilingual resources including parallel speech-text corpora, language models and pronunciation dictionaries (Besacier et al., 2014; Wang and Zheng, 2015). The languages also need to be related and share the same phone set. In practice, it is too difficult to meet these requirements, especially the problem gets worse when it comes to Amharic and other Semitic languages as they are not yet studied using this approach. The other alternative approach is transfer learning (Wang and Zheng, 2015; Huang et al., 2013; Ghahremani et al., 2017), that allows an acoustic model trained on one language to get adapted to other languages. That is possible via sharing parameters learned during neural net based model training of one language to others.

4.2. The Amharic NER Extractor and Transliterator

Given the very limited alternative choices for Amharic NER models, we used the NER model developed as part of the master thesis by Belay M. (Belay, 2014). As the original model was built in a format which is incompatible with other meta-data extractors within MICO, the data needs to be re-labeled manually to train the OpenNLP name finder models. That is the right format supported by MICO. However, it was possible only to label the small portion of the whole data used in (Belay, 2014) with only the following entities: persons, locations and organizations. The models are trained using machine learning algorithms provided by

OpenNLP: MaxEntropy (Berger et al., 1996) and Perceptron (Kazama and Torisawa, 2007). As shown in **Table 1**, the Perceptron based model outperforms the MaxEntropy based model, regarding all considered metrics. As both the training and testing sets are quite small (compared to the standard requirement, i.e., 15K sentences, but here the models are trained on 420 sentences and evaluated on 45 sentences along with 126 entities) for generalization, the evaluation details are not included in this study. In order to use the models, we then developed a Java-based application that loads the NER models and extracts named mentions from speech transcriptions.

While the NER models are trained on the transliterated form of Amharic text, the ASR acoustic models are trained on transcripts with the actual Amharic orthography. Because it seems to be most open-source NLP research tools are primarily designed for English, Amharic NLP studies tend to use an Amharic-English transliteration scheme (Sebsibe et al., 2004) in their prototype development. In order to support the interfacing of ASR with NER, we implemented a simple rule-based transliteration program that converts Amharic scripts to its corresponding English transliteration form.

5. Challenges and Solutions

Since the main goal of this research is to make less-resourced languages beneficial out of media analysis technologies built for resource rich languages, by dealing with issues related with scarcity of computational linguistic resources, most of the challenges faced in the course of the study is inherently associated with the lack of resources. In addition, we assumed that the resources that have been available can be modified with reasonable amount of configuration tasks and then would fit to the designed experimental settings, but a number of evaluations (compatibility tests) have shown that they turned out to require to get

<table>
<tr><td rowspan="2">Classifier</td><td rowspan="2">Recognized Entity</td><td colspan="3">Metric (in%)</td></tr>
<tr><td>Precision</td><td>Recall</td><td>F-Score</td></tr>
<tr><td rowspan="3">MaxEntropy</td><td>Person</td><td>79.17</td><td>73.08</td><td>76.00</td></tr>
<tr><td>Organization</td><td>84.93</td><td>71.26</td><td>77.50</td></tr>
<tr><td>Location</td><td>16.67</td><td>7.69</td><td>10.53</td></tr>
<tr><td rowspan="3">Perceptron</td><td>Person</td><td>85.71</td><td>92.31</td><td>88.89</td></tr>
<tr><td>Organization</td><td>64.15</td><td>78.16</td><td>70.47</td></tr>
<tr><td>Location</td><td>66.67</td><td>15.38</td><td>25.00</td></tr>
</table>

Table 1: NER Models Evaluation Results

transformed with much amount of works. For example, re-labeling the NER dataset, improving the quality of the acoustic models and so on.

As part of our study, we also observed major important issues that arise from the natural language perspective during the adaptation of MICO for Amharic. The issues are very important for other new languages as well to be considered in advance. That mostly include availability of compatible language dependent analysis components and other pre/post processing auxiliary utilities (e.g., language detection, file format adaptors). In order to effectively meet the compatibility requirements (e.g., data models, file formats), one needs to closely look at the synergies and the dependencies between all meta-data extractors.

Although MICO aims to provide an open data model via its API, at the current stage of its implementation new languages are required to strictly adhere some specifications, for example, while NER models need to be in an OpenNLP based, ASR acoustic models in deep neural net. Among other important language specific components ASR and NER seem to be very foundational and take a high priority, as others downstream extractors such as sentiment analysis, text classification and topic detection rely on the quality provided by the ASR-NER chain.

The other problem is related with computational resources, training the DNN-HMM model has been challenging due to the requirement of GPU processors along with the queue scheduling service configuration. Although it is extremely slow, the training has been done on our CPU machine with a slight job-scheduling configuration task.

Lastly, it concerns the interfacing Amharic ASR with NER. The transcription generated by ASR is in the actual orthographic form of Amharic, where as the NER models are trained on an English-transliteration form. Thus, to support the NER models a simple rule-based transliteration program has been written.

6. Conclusions and Future Work

We identified language dependent analysis components that are viewed as a high priority including ASR and NER, within a cross-media analysis platform. We designed an ASR-NER analysis pipeline for Amharic based on state-of-the art design principles and techniques employed in cross-media solutions, thus promoting the multi-lingual support of the MICO platform. Moreover, this study provides a chance to further explore ASR methods introduced to potentially support under-resourced languages such as transfer learning. Moreover,the quality of both the ASR and

NER models can be enhanced with availability of more data and improve the transliteration phase to reasonable quality in the future. Also, as this study has been done during the early release stages of the MICO platform for English, it has been hard to fully support Amharic for more detailed experiments. However, for future it would be interesting to carry out additional evaluations across other parts of the pipeline. Generally, other languages somehow take advantages of the methods proposed here, especially those that share a similar orthographic structure with Amharic, such as Tigrinya. Also, the method can be easily extended for other Semitic languages such as Arabic and Hebrew.

7. Acknowledgments

We acknowledge the financial support from the EU FP7 MICO project. We also thank Mikyas Belay for providing Amharic NER models used in this study.

8. Bibliographical References

Abate, S., Tachbelie, M., and Menze, W. (2009). Amharic speech recognition: Past, present and future. In *Proceedings of the 16th International Conference of Ethiopian Studies*, pages 1391–1401.

Aichroth, P., Weigel, C., Kurz, T., Stadler, H., Drewes, F., Björklund, J., Schlegel, K., Berndl, E., Perez, A., Bowyer, A., and Volpini, A. (2015). Mico-media in context. In *Proceedings of 2015 IEEE International Conference on Multimedia and Expo Workshops (ICMEW)*, pages 1–4.

Belay, M. (2014). Amharic Named Entity Recognition Using a Hybrid Approach. Master's thesis, School of Information Informatics, Addis Ababa University.

Berger, A. L., Pietra, S. D., and Pietra, V. J. D. (1996). A maximum entropy approach to natural language processing. *Computational Linguistics*, 22:39–71.

Besacier, L., Barnard, E., Karpov, A., and Schultz, T. (2014). Automatic speech recognition for under-resourced languages. *Speech Communication*, 56:85–100.

Chang, S.-F., Manmatha, R., and Chua, T.-S. (2005). Combining text and audio-visible features in video indexing. In *Acoustics, Speech, and Signal Processing*, pages 1005–1008.

Demeke, Y. and Hailemariam, S. (2012). Duration modeling of phonemes for amharic text to speech system. In *Proceedings of the International Conference on Management of Emergent Digital EcoSystems*, pages 1–7.

Feng, S. and Lee, T. (2018). Improving cross-lingual knowledge transferability using multilingual tdnn-blstm with language-dependent pre-final layer. In *Proceedings of Interspeech*, pages 2439–2443.

Finkel, J. R., Grenager, T., and Manning, C. (2005). Incorporating non-local information into information extraction systems by gibbs sampling. In *Proceedings of the 43rd annual meeting on association for computational linguistics*, pages 363–370.

Gambäck, B. and Sikdar, U. K. (2017). Named entity recognition for amharic using deep learning. In *2017 IST-Africa Week Conference (IST-Africa)*, pages 1–8.

Ghahremani, P., Manohar, V., Hadian, H., Povey, D., and Khudanpur, S. (2017). Investigation of transfer learning for asr using lf-mmi trained neural networks. In *Proceedings of 2017 IEEE Automatic Speech Recognition and Understanding Workshop*, pages 279–286.

Ghoshal, A., Swietojanski, P., and Renals, S. (2013). Multilingual training of deep neural networks. In *Proceedings of 2013 IEEE International Conference on Acoustics, Speech and Signal Processing*, pages 7319–7323.

Hori, T. and Nakamura, A. (2006). An extremely large vocabulary approach to named entity extraction from speech. In *2006 IEEE International Conference on Acoustics Speech and Signal Processing Proceedings*, pages 973–976.

Huang, J.-T., Li, J., Yu, D., Deng, L., and Gong, Y. (2013). Cross-language knowledge transfer using multilingual deep neural network with shared hidden layers. In *Proceedings of 2013 IEEE International Conference on Acoustics, Speech and Signal Processing*, pages 7304–7308.

Ivanov, A. V., Ramanarayanan, V., Suendermann-Oeft, D., Lopez, M., Evanini, K., and Tau, J. (2015). Automated speech recognition technology for dialogue interaction with non-native interlocutors. In *Proceedings of the 16th Annual Meeting of the Special Interest Group on Discourse and Dialogue*, pages 134–138.

Kazama, J. and Torisawa, K. (2007). A new perceptron algorithm for sequence labeling with non-local features. In *Proceedings of the 2007 Joint Conference on Empirical Methods in Natural Language Processing and Computational Natural Language Learning (EMNLP-CoNLL)*, pages 315–324.

Kurz, T., Schlegel, K., and Kosch, H. (2015). Enabling access to linked media with sparql-mm. In *Proceedings of the 24th International Conference on World Wide Web*.

Le, N., Bredin, H., Sargent, G., India, M., Lopez-Otero, P., Barras, C., Guinaudeau, C., Gravier, G., da Fonseca, G. B., Freire, I. L., do Patrocínio, Z. K. G., Guimarães, S. J. F., Martí, G., Morros, J. R., Hernando, J., Fernández, L. D., García-Mateo, C., Meignier, S., and Odobez, J.-M. (2017). Towards large scale multimedia indexing: A case study on person discovery in broadcast news. In *Proceedings of International Workshop on Content-Based Multimedia Retrieval*, pages 1–6.

Magnini, B., Cutugno, F., Falcone, M., and Pianta, E. (2013). Evaluation of natural language and speech tools for italian. In *Lecture Notes in Computer Science*, pages 98–106.

Marneffe, M.-C., MacCartney, B., and Manning, C. (2006). Generating typed dependency parses from phrase structure parses. In *InProc. 5th Interna-tional Conference on Language Resources and Evaluation (LREC 2006)*, pages 449–454.

Mehamed, M. (2010). Amharic Named Entity Recognition. Master's thesis, College of Natural Sciences, Addis Ababa University.

Meignier, S. and Merlin, T. (2010). Lium spkdiarization: An open source toolkit for diarization. In *CMU SPUD Workshop*.

Povey, D., Burget, L., Agarwal, M., Akyazi, P., Feng, K., Ghoshal, A., Glembek, O., Goel, N. K., Karafiát, M., Rastrow, A., Rose, R. C., Schwarz, P., and Thomas, S. (2011a). The subspace gaussian mixture model - a structured model for speech recognition. *Computer Speech and Language*, 25(2):404–439.

Povey, D., Ghoshal, A., Boulianne, G., Burget, L., Glembek, O., Goel, N., Hannemann, M., Motlicek, P., Qian, Y., Schwarz, P., Silovsky, J., Stemmer, G., and Vesely, K. (2011b). The Kaldi speech recognition toolkit. In *Proceedings of IEEE 2011 Workshop on Automatic Speech Recognition and Understanding*.

Rabiner, L. R. (1989). A tutorial on hidden Markov models and selected applications in speech recognition. *Proceedings of the IEEE*, 77(2):257–286.

Sebsibe, H., Prahallad, K., Alan, B., Rohit, K., and Rajeev, S. (2004). Unit selection voice for amharic using festvox. In *Fifth ISCA Workshop on Speech Synthesis*, pages 103–107.

Sobhana, N., Mitra, P., and Ghosh, S. (2010). Conditional random field based named entity recognition in geological text. *International Journal of Computer Applications*, 1(3):143–147.

Stüker, S., Kilgour, K., and Niehues, J. (2011). Quaero speech-to-text and text translation evaluation systems. In *High Performance Computing in Science and Engineering'10*, pages 529–542. Springer.

Tachbelie, M., Abate, S., and Besacier, L. (2014). Using different acoustic, lexical and language modeling units for asr of an under-resourced language - amharic. *Speech Communication*, 56:181–194.

Tranter, S. and Reynolds, D. A. (2006). An overview of automatic speaker diarization systems. *IEEE Transactions on Audio, Speech, and Language Processing*, 14:1557–1565.

Wang, D. and Zheng, T. F. (2015). Transfer learning for speech and language processing. In *Proceedings of 2015 Asia-Pacific Signal and Information Processing Association Annual Summit and Conference*, pages 1225–1237.

Xiong, W., Wu, L., Alleva, F., Droppo, J., Huang, X., and Stolcke, A. (2018). The microsoft 2017 conversational speech recognition system. In *Proceedings of 2018 IEEE International Conference on Acoustics, Speech and Signal Processing*, pages 5934–5938.

Yifiru, M. (2003). Automatic Amharic Speech Recognition System to Command and Control Computers. Master's thesis, School of Information Studies for Africa, Addis Ababa University.

9. Language Resource References

ELRA-W0074. (2014). *Amharic-English bilingual corpus, distributed via ELRA,1.0.* distributed via ELRA,1.0, 1.0, ISLRN 590-255-335-719-0.

Elodie Gauthier and Laurent Besacier and Sylvie Voisin and Michael Melese and Uriel Pascal Elingui. (2016). *ALFFA (African Languages in the Field: speech Fundamentals and Automation).* European Language Resources Association (ELRA), Proceedings of the Tenth International Conference on Language Resources and Evaluation (LREC'16), ISLRN SLR25.

HaBiT. (2016). *Harvesting big text data for under-resourced languages.* distributed via Natural Language Processing Centre, Faculty of Informatics, Masaryk University.

Proceedings of the 1st Joint SLTU and CCURL Workshop (SLTU-CCURL 2020), pages 306–315
Language Resources and Evaluation Conference (LREC 2020), Marseille, 11–16 May 2020
© European Language Resources Association (ELRA), licensed under CC-BY-NC

Phonemic Transcription of Low-Resource Languages:
To What Extent can Preprocessing be Automated?

Guillaume Wisniewski[1], Alexis Michaud[2], Séverine Guillaume[2]
(1) Laboratoire de Linguistique Formelle (LLF), CNRS – Université Paris-Diderot, Case 7031,
5 rue Thomas Mann, 75013 Paris, France
(2) Langues et Civilisations à Tradition Orale (LACITO), CNRS – Université Sorbonne Nouvelle – INALCO,
7 rue Guy Môquet, 94800 Villejuif, France
guillaume.wisniewski@u-paris.fr, alexis.michaud@cnrs.fr, severine.guillaume@cnrs.fr

Abstract

Automatic Speech Recognition for low-resource languages has been an active field of research for more than a decade. It holds promise for facilitating the urgent task of documenting the world's dwindling linguistic diversity. Various methodological hurdles are encountered in the course of this exciting development, however. A well-identified difficulty is that data preprocessing is not at all trivial: data collected in classical fieldwork are usually tailored to the needs of the linguist who collects them, and there is baffling diversity in formats and annotation schema, even among fieldworkers who use the same software package (such as ELAN). The tests reported here (on Yongning Na and other languages from the Pangloss Collection, an open archive of endangered languages) explore some possibilities for automating the process of data preprocessing: assessing to what extent it is possible to bypass the involvement of language experts for menial tasks of data preparation for Natural Language Processing (NLP) purposes. What is at stake is the accessibility of language archive data for a range of NLP tasks and beyond.

Keywords: Endangered Languages, Speech Recognition/Understanding, Speech Resource/Database

1. Introduction

1.1. Making Language Archive Data Tractable to Automatic Speech Processing: Why Preprocessing is a Key Issue

Towards Computational Language Documentation
Automatic speech recognition (ASR) tools have potential for facilitating the urgent task of documenting the world's dwindling linguistic diversity (Besacier et al., 2014; Thieberger, 2017; Littell et al., 2018; van Esch et al., 2019). Encouraging results for automatic phoneme recognition for low-resource languages were published two years ago (Adams et al., 2018), and prospects of widespread deployment of the technology look extremely hopeful.

Why Preprocessing is a Major Hurdle Various methodological hurdles are encountered in the course of this exciting development, however. A well-identified difficulty is that data preprocessing is not at all trivial. In classical linguistic fieldwork (Bouquiaux and Thomas, 1971; Newman and Ratliff, 2001; Dixon, 2007), "good corpus production is ongoing, distributed, and opportunistic" (Woodbury, 2003, 47), and thus unlike scenarios in which data acquisition is tailored to meet the requirements of speech processing tasks. Because fieldwork data are not collected specifically for the purpose of ASR, data sets from language archives are highly diverse in a number of respects. Not only is there a wide range of tools for creating linguistic annotations, each with its own format (see the conversion tools TEIconvert `http://ct3.ortolang.fr/teiconvert/` and Multitool `https://github.com/DoReCo/multitool`): there is also diversity in the formats allowed by one and the same software package. Thus, ELAN, a commonly used software package (Brugman and Russel, 2004), allows users to define their own document structures: ELAN supports creation of multiple tiers and tier hierarchies, so that there is, in practice, no such thing as a unique "ELAN format". It would be desirable for a common format to be adopted in the mid run, such as the standard proposed as part of the Text Encoding Initiative (Schmidt, 2011; Liégeois et al., 2016), but convergence is not in sight yet. In the current situation, fieldwork data make up "eclectic data collections" rather than "systematically annotated corpora" (Gerstenberger et al., 2017, 26). Preprocessing typically involves retrieving pieces of information that are not encoded according to widely shared computational standards.

Preprocessing tasks are not just time-consuming: they require familiarity with the target language, and with the specific corpus. This is asking a lot from Natural Language Processing people who wish to try their hand at the data. An example (preprocessing transcriptions of Yongning Na, a Sino-Tibetan language, for training an acoustic model using the `Persephone` toolkit) is documented in some detail in an article that aims to explain to an audience of linguists (i) the way the automatic transcription toolkit `Persephone` operates and (ii) how the process of collaborating with natural language processing specialists was initiated and developed (Michaud et al., 2018). Trying to summarize the 37-page article in one sentence, it seems fair to say that without a sustained dialogue with the linguist who created the transcriptions, the pitfalls of preprocessing would probably have been enough friction to turn computing people off.

Adapting Data Collection Methods for Easier Application of Natural Language Processing Tools? One possible way to go would be to get linguists and Natural Language Processing experts to modify their usual workflows, and to work hand in hand designing and applying tools together. Computer scientists would take the time to find out about the implicit structure of the data sets, and also absorb as much information as possible about the linguistic structure of the target languages. Field linguists would anticipate the requirements of a range of Natural Language Processing tools from the early stages of data collection in the field. It has even been suggested that field linguists should modify their practice so as to assist the task of machine learning: for instance, "making multiple parallel or semi-parallel recordings, so as to have a robust envelope of phonetic variation across speakers that assists in generalizing sound-transcription matching from one speaker to another" (Seifart et al., 2018).

But an issue with this approch is that it adds to the workload of fieldworkers and computer scientists. Speech data acquisition has numerous challenges of its own (Niebuhr and Michaud, 2015), which linguists need to prioritize in their work. Thus, although *respeaking* is known to be a possible way to improve the performance of Automatic Speech Recognition (Sperber et al., 2013), the limited amounts of time that the language consultants and the linguist can spend together are best devoted to recording additional original materials and discussing linguistic issues, rather than to the mechanical task of going through a set of audio files and repeating each sentence. Moreover, tailoring speech data acquisition to cater to the needs of machine learning algorithms is problematic given how rapidly the technology evolves. There is a potential conflict between the traditional perspective of creating a reasonably thorough and balanced record for posterity, on the one hand, and on the other hand, the requirement to put together data sets that lend themselves easily to Natural Language Processing.

From the point of view of Natural Language Processing engineers and computer scientists, the requirement to become familiar with the linguistic structure of the data sets likewise appears too steep, given the number of different languages (and of different data sets) that Natural Language Processing researchers handle in their work. The workflow in the first experiments on the `Persephone` toolkit (Adams et al., 2018) benefited from hands-on participation from the linguists who produced the transcriptions used as input data. Clearly, it is unrealistic to assume that as much 'insider' information will be available for all languages. Seen in this light, it becomes clear that what is at stake in preprocessing is no less than the availability of language archive data for language processing purposes.

The issue of facilitating preprocessing for Natural Language Processing is part of a broader topic which could be referred to as *interdisciplinary user design*: removing hurdles in the way of interdisciplinary collaborations. The expected benefit for language archives is that they can become accessible to an increased number of users, from a wider ranger of backgrounds. To date, data from language archives remain little-used, not only in Natural Language Processing but also in experimental phonetic research, for example (Whalen and McDonough, 2019).

1.2. Goals

The tests reported in the present paper aim at investigating possibilities for automating the process of data preprocess-

ing: assessing to what extent it is possible to bypass the need for thorny and time-consuming expert tasks. We use the same data set from the Yongning Na language as was used in a previous study (Adams et al., 2018) to investigate which properties in the input transcription are conducive to best results in the recognition task. Second, we extend the tests to new languages.

1.3. Relevance to Natural Language Processing Research

In addition to the goal of achieving practical usefulness for field linguists, phonemic transcription for low-resource languages raises several interesting methodological challenges for Natural Language Processing (NLP).

- The amount of training data (transcribed audio) is limited: for data collected in linguistic fieldwork, ten hours counts as a large corpus. Corpus size can be less than one hour.

- Languages differ greatly from one another along various dimensions: phonemic inventories, phonotactic combinations, word structure, not to mention morphology, syntax and pragmatics. As a result, experiments over fieldwork data lead to encounters with a host of linguistic phenomena that differ from those commonly observed in the most widely spoken languages. Designing NLP methods to deal with this diversity of languages is a good way to explore the limits of state-of-the-art models and better understand how (and when) they are working.

- The sheer number of languages to be addressed suggests that attempts at a language-independent acoustic model may be a fruitful avenue to explore. (The world's 30 most widely spoken languages only represent about 1% of the world's linguistic diversity – on the order of 6,000 languages.)

2. Method

2.1. Phonemic Transcription Model

Prediction Model Our work aims at developing a phonemic transcription model which, given an audio signal represented by a sequence of `fbank` vectors,[1] predicts the corresponding sequence of phonemes and tones.

We use the implementation of a long short-term memory (LSTM) recurrent neural network provided by the `Persephone` toolkit (Adams et al., 2018). In all our experiments, we have considered a network made of 3 hidden layers with 250 hidden units. Our experiments show that, as pointed out in Adams et al. (2018), these parameters consistently achieve 'good' performances.

We use the Connectionist Temporal Classification (CTC) loss function (Graves et al., 2006) as a training criterion. This loss function allows us to learn the mapping between an audio signal and a sequence of phonemes without explicitly knowing the alignment between each phoneme and the corresponding audio frames.

---

[1] We consider the 41 usual `fbank` features as well as their first and second derivative.

We trained our model using the `Adam` optimizer (Kingma and Ba, 2015), stopping after 100 epochs or when the loss on the validation set stopped improving for 10 consecutive epochs.

2.2. Extracting Labels

Extracting labels from the training data is a crucial step of the acoustic model creation workflow. The tests carried out here aim at automating the process, with as little reliance as possible on hand-crafted rules based on interactions with the linguist who produced the transcriptions. This is important for wider use of the tool in real-world application.

In the phonemic transcription task we consider, labels are sequences of phonemes. However, when field linguists annotate their recordings, phoneme boundaries are not encoded as such. Linguistic fieldwork data typically consist of transcriptions that are time-aligned with the audio (and, increasingly, video) signal at the level of larger units, such as sentences or intonation units, but rarely at the word level, and even more rarely at the level of the phoneme, which is not even encoded as such. For instance, in the XML format of the Pangloss Collection (Michailovsky et al., 2014),[2] texts are divided into sentences (`S`), themselves divided into words (`W`), divided into morphemes (`M`). Phonemes are not encoded as a level of their own. Instead, there is an implicit convention that transcriptions (the `FORM` at each of the levels) consist of strings of phonemes. Thus, no information about phonemes is readily available.[3] An example is shown in Figure 1.

For the benefit of readers who are not thoroughly familiar with XML, let us spell out explanations on the data structure. (Most readers can safely skip the present paragraph.) The identifier of the sentence (indicating simply that this is the twentieth sentence) is followed by an `AUDIO` element containing the time codes for the entire sentence (in this instance, from the 72nd to the 75th second on the audio recording), then by sentence-level transcriptions, coded as the sentence's `FORM`. There can be different types of transcription: for instance, in this example, there is a phonemic transcription, tagged as `"phono"` (the value assigned to the attribute `kindOf` associated with the transcription), and an orthographic transcription, tagged as `"ortho"`. The choice of using orthographic or phonological (phonemic) transcription is up to the contributor. Differences in performance of automatic transcription for phonological vs. orthographic input will be returned to below. Translations at any level (the sentence, as shown here, or the entire text, or a word or morpheme) appear as `TRANSL` elements, with a tag indicating the translation language using two-letter codes: `"fr"`, `"en"` and `"zh"` for French, English and Chinese, respectively. Word-level information likewise contains `FORM` elements and `TRANSL` elements. Note that orthographic representation and Chinese translations are only offered at the level of the sentence, not for each word. Most pieces of information are optional: word-level glosses are not mandatory, any more than translation into any specific language. Linguists who contribute data to the language archive deposit their documents *as is*, with the levels of annotation that they chose to produce for the sake of their research purposes.

```
<S id="Sister_S020">
 <AUDIO start="72.8482" end="75.6151"/>
 <FORM kindOf="phono">tʰiʌ, | «tse˩ʈʂʰv̩˩-kʰv̩˧, | no˧ | ɑ˩pʰo˩ seʌ!» |
 pi˧-tsɯ˩ ◊ -mv̩˩ |</FORM>
 <FORM kindOf="ortho">Tiq: "Zeichuku, no apo sei!" bi zimu.</FORM>
 <TRANSL xml:lang="fr">alors, [on] a lancé au chien: «Holà, sac à
 puces! tu sors!»</TRANSL>
<TRANSL xml:lang="en">Then, (someone) said, "Get outside, you
fleabag dog!"</TRANSL>
 <TRANSL xml:lang="zh">
 然后，(人家)说了:“狗狗啊，(不欢迎你进来，)你
 出去了吧！”(讲故事的人后来解释:是妹妹自己对
 狗说的一个话)</TRANSL>
 <W>
  <FORM>tʰiʌ</FORM>
  <TRANSL xml:lang="fr">alors</TRANSL>
  <TRANSL xml:lang="en">then</TRANSL>
 </W>
 <W>
  <FORM>tse˩ʈʂʰv̩˩</FORM>
  <TRANSL xml:lang="fr">sac_à_puces</TRANSL>
  <TRANSL xml:lang="en">fleabag</TRANSL>
 </W>
```

Figure 1: Sample of XML code: beginning of sentence 20 of the narrative "The sister's wedding" (`https://doi.org/10.24397/pangloss-0004342#S20`).

Building an automatic phonemic transcription system therefore requires to, first, segment the transcriptions into sequences of phonemes. Transcriptions often contains annotations or comments about the audio content: e.g. to indicate the presence of drum rolls in the transcription of a song, or to point out that the annotator is not sure about what they have heard. See, for instance, the first sentence (`S`-unit) of the epic "Rani Raut 2"[4], whose transcription contains the indication "Dedicatory chant", instead of a transcription of the chant itself. Another example is sentence 24 of the Yongning Na narrative "How the Lake was created",[5] which contains a critical apparatus encoded through conventions (square brackets for additions, and angle brackets for deletions) that are not explained within the XML file itself.

It is also important to 'clean' the transcription to remove information that cannot be directly predicted. This clean-up ensures a direct mapping between the transcription and the audio, therefore making both learning and prediction easier.

In the 2018 LREC paper (Adams et al., 2018), transcrip-

[2]All our experiments are based on corpora freely available from the Pangloss Collection, an open archive of (mostly) endangered languages. See § 2.3. for details.

[3]There are possibilities for adding word-level and phoneme-level time codes to linguistic fieldwork documents using forced alignment (Strunk et al., 2014). In the current state of language archives, phoneme-level alignment remains a rarity, however.

[4]`https://doi.org/10.24397/pangloss-0004315#S1`

[5]`https://doi.org/10.24397/pangloss-0004349#S24`

tions extracted from the Yongning Na documents in the Pangloss Collection were segmented into sequences of phonemes by means of a set of hand-crafted rules. These rules are based on two kinds of information:

- a list of all the phonemes that can appear in Na;

- the explicit knowledge of the convention used by the field linguist that has annotated the data, e.g. that text between square brackets corresponds to additions and comments and should be removed to obtain a direct mapping of the sound signal to the transcription.

The use of these two kinds of information made it possible to extract labels of very high quality in which the sequence of phonemes was a faithful transcription of the audio signal. The process is documented in detail in §3.2 of Michaud et al. (2018). This workflow assumes hands-on participation from the linguist who produced the transcriptions used as input data. By contrast, in the present work, a much simpler approach is chosen to extract the sequence of phonemes from transcriptions.

Tools for Automatic Normalization of Unicode Labels[6] Following the recommendations of the *Unicode Cookbook for Linguists* (Moran and Cysouw, 2018), we carry out a segmentation into *grapheme clusters* in which each letter (as identified by its Unicode category) is grouped with all the modifiers (again identified by their Unicode category). Characters from other Unicode categories (e.g. modifier letter small h, [h]) are considered as 'standard' letters. Table 1 shows an example of a sequence of labels segmented with this method, as compared with the output of the hand-crafted segmentation method of Adams et al. (2018).

①	si˧dzi˩-t͡sʰɯ˩, | t͡ʰææ̃˦ | t͡sʰɯ˦-bɤ˦i̠˦ | dɑ˦-kɤ̠˥-mæ˩! |
②	s i ˦ dz i ˩ t͡sʰ ɯ ˩ t͡ʰ æ æ̃ ˦ t͡sʰ ɯ ˦ b ɤ ˦ i̠ ˦ d ɑ ˦ k ɤ̠ ˥ -m æ ˩
③	s i ˦ d z i ˩ - t̠ s̠ ʰ ɯ ˩ t̠ ʰ æ æ̃ ˦ t̠ s̠ ʰ ɯ ˦ b ɤ ˦ i̠ ˦ d ɑ ˦ - k ɤ̠ ˥ -m æ ˩

Table 1: Example of a transcription of Na (①) and two segmentations into label sequences: in ②, phonemes are separated by whitespaces using the rules of Adams et al. (2018); in ③, whitespaces identify grapheme clusters. Note that, in both segmentations, punctuations marks are removed: in the current setup, no attempts were made at predicting them.

The method used here, ③, has the advantage of being language-independent and of not relying on any knowledge of the data. It also comes with several drawbacks. First, it increases the number of possible labels, which makes both training and prediction slower. More importantly, it places higher demands on the statistical model, which could make prediction less successful. If a phoneme is made of two symbols (e.g. the digraph /d͡z/ for a voiced alveolo-palatal affricate), then these will be considered as two independent symbols and the transcription system will have to learn from the statistical distribution of these symbols that d when followed by z may correspond to fairly different acoustic states than when followed by a vowel (in which case d constitutes a consonant on its own). The difference could have been made explicit by forcing segmentation as /d͡z/ in the one case and /d/ /z/ in the other.

2.3. Workflow for Applying `Persephone` to Data Sets from the Pangloss Collection

A Command Line Interface between `Persephone` and the Pangloss Collection To test the `Persephone` toolkit for various languages, we have developed a simple command line interface between `Persephone` and the Pangloss Collection, a digital library whose objective is to store and facilitate access to audio recordings in endangered languages of the world (Michailovsky et al., 2014). Our tool[7] provides two commands. The first command allows a user to download, from the Pangloss Collection, all the audio recordings matching a language and/or a specific speaker (or set of speakers) and to organize the data so that they can be readily used by the `Persephone` toolkit. The second command can be used to train and test a phonemic transcription system.

The goal of this tool is twofold. First, it aims at allowing NLP practitioners to easily access datasets of great interest (or to say the least, with diverse and unusual characteristics) without having to spend time understanding how the data are organized in the Pangloss Collection. Second, it will (hopefully) help field linguists to train their own transcription models without having to convert their recordings and annotations into yet another format (the format required by `Persephone`).

Choice of Languages Out of the 170 languages currently hosted by the Pangloss Collection, we singled out seven for tests on automatic transcription. We chose data sets that had sentence-level alignment with the audio, a prerequisite for using `Persephone`. We also favoured languages for which substantial amounts of transcribed data are available: earlier tests suggest that when the training set is less than 20 minutes long, the model does not even converge, or error rates are extremely high. This criterion brushes aside no less than 112 languages: twenty minutes or more of transcribed data are currently available for only 58 languages. Table 2 provides the main characteristics of the data sets we used in our experiments: language names, three-letter ISO codes from the Ethnologue inventory of languages (Simons and Fennig, 2017), duration of the training set, nature of the labels, and number of labels. In all our experiments we consider only a single speaker setting.

For the sake of reproducibility (Borgman, 2015; Maurel, 2016; Lust et al., 2019), a preprocessed version of all the data used in our experiments (i.e. the audio file for each sentence and the corresponding sequence of labels) orga-

---

[6]The implementation of this method is freely available in our extension of the `Persephone` toolkit, at `https://github.com/gw17/sltu_corpora`; see § 2.3. for details.

[7]Our tool is freely available in a fork of the `Persephone` toolkit: `https://bitbucket.org/gwisniewski/pangloss-persephone/src/pangloss/`.

nized according to the format expected by `Persephone` is available at `https://github.com/gw17/sltu_corpora`.

3. Experimental Results

We conducted three series of experiments to assess:

- the impact of using the label segmentation method described in Section 2.2. rather than hand-crafted rules tailored to the language at hand;

- the impact of considering different languages.

In all our experiments, we evaluate the performance achieved by our phonemic transcription system by computing the average edit distance between the predicted and gold labels of the test set (i.e. the Label Error Rate). This metric is a crude estimation of the effort required by an annotator to correct the prediction of an automatic transcription system.

3.1. Impact of Label Segmentation

Table 3 reports the performance achieved by `Persephone` when different segmentation methods are applied (see Section 2.2. for details). To start with, it is reassuring to note that we were able to reproduce the results reported in the study that we use as a point of reference (Adams et al., 2018): using the same rules to clean the transcription and identify phonemes, the prediction performance we achieved is very close to the earlier results.

As for segmentation methods, it also appears that using a generic segmentation method rather than a method tailored specifically for the target language hardly impacts prediction performance at all. Our interpretation is that `Persephone` is able to match polygraphs with phonemes (multiple character sequences, such as such as tsʰ, used to denote a phoneme), even when the components of these polygraphs, taken individually, refer to other phonemes (in Na, /t/ and /s/ are phonemes, as are /ts/ and /tsʰ/). This result does not come as a huge surprise, since the machine learning architecture is known to perform well in extracting patterns such as those described by phonotactics. We nonetheless see this as a very important observation from a practical point of view, because it suggests that it is possible to develop transcription systems with no knowledge of the language (in particular, without a list of phonemes drawn up by an expert linguist).

3.2. Evaluation on a Wider Array of Languages

Table 4 reports the performance achieved by `Persephone` on the selection of languages from the Pangloss Collection shown in Table 2. It appears that, for most languages, `Persephone`, when used as a black-box tool, performs very poorly. As shown by the learning curve (Figure 2), for four of the seven languages the system does not even seem to be able to memorize the training data. Increasing the number of parameters (i.e. the number of hidden units and/or of hidden layers) does not improve performance (neither on the validation set nor on the training set).

Several reasons can explain these disappointing results.

Audio Qxuality First, there appears to be a minimum threshold in terms of quality of the audio data. Some recordings may be of insufficient audio quality for automatic transcription given the current state of the art. For instance, the Dotyal data set consists of epics that contain singing, drums and bells: the successive sentences are sung or chanted, rather than spoken. Listening to the data,[8] it does not come as a surprise that automatic transcription as currently offered by `Persephone` does not work. Automatic Speech Recognition for such materials, if possible at all, will have to rely on much more elaborate processing.

Duration of Audio Chunks The upper limit on the duration of audio chunks taken as input by `Persephone` is 10 seconds. This results in exclusion of any longer chunks from the training process. Thus, the document "Roman-mangan, the fairy from the other world"[9] has a duration of 1,890 seconds, and is divided into 212 sentences. The distribution of sentence durations is shown in Figure 3. Seventy sentences, amounting to 1 032 seconds (more than half of the total duration of this substantial story), are above the 10-second limit, and thus not used in training. The total amount of data available for the language is down from 22 minutes to 16. This goes a long way towards explaining why training fails to converge: there is simply not enough data to train a statistical model.

This issue affects the real-life usefulness of `Persephone`, and needs to be addressed so as to make use of all the available data for training. A possibility would be to detect silence and non-silence (by Voice Activity Detection) and then trim the long waveform, removing silences, so as to arrive at a duration below 10 seconds. But removing silences comes at the cost of tampering with the audio signal, removing cues that may well be relevant for training. Pauses are part and parcel of intonational structure, and removing them can create acoustic 'monsters'. Instead, the way to go is to do forced alignment as an initial approach, then split the long sentences based on silence, and finally feed the chunks thus obtained into training. This work is considered as part of future improvements planned for `Persephone`. Within the 10-second limit on audio chunks, it is likely that shorter time-aligned chunks in the training set make for better scores, but this has not been tested empirically yet.[10]

Number of Labels There are large differences in the number of labels and the quantity of training data be-

---

[8]For example: `https://doi.org/10.24397/pangloss-0004091`

[9]`https://doi.org/10.24397/pangloss-0002300`

[10]Remember that the level at which time alignment is generally provided in the Pangloss Collection's XML documents is the S level: the *sentence*, in a sense which contributors can interpret freely. A hypothesis to be tested empirically is that the average duration of the S-level units correlates with the field of specialization of the contributing linguist. Linguists with a strong interest in phonetics and phonology may tend to cut up speech into smaller units, whereas those with a stronger interest in syntax will tend to choose larger chunks, which constitute syntactically complete blocks. The Mwotlap corpus would be a case in point: the texts were collected by a specialist of syntax (François, 2003), and their relatively large chunks make good syntactic sense.

language	duration		IPA	# labels
	total	after filtering		
Dotyal (nep)	1h44mn	44mn	✘	366
Duoxu (ers)	32mn	32mn	✓	35
Mwotlap (mlv)	22mn	16mn	✘	39
Na (nru)	8h35mn	7h49mn	✓	80
Nashta (mkd)	25mn	23mn	✓	39
Limbu (lif)	1h50mn	1h34mn	✓	37
Vatlongos (tvk)	14mn	14mn	✘	20

Table 2: Languages from the Pangloss collection that were used in our experiments. The IPA column indicates whether the transcriptions are phonological (✓) or orthographic (✘). We report the size of each corpus ('total' column) as well as the size after utterances lasting more than 10s have been removing (see §3.2.).

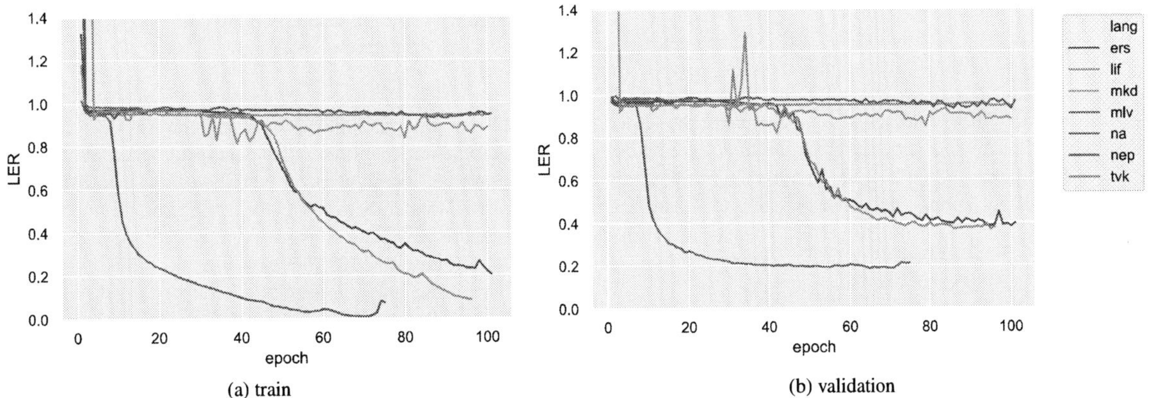

(a) train

(b) validation

Figure 2: Learning curve (train & validation sets) for the different languages considered in our experiments

segmentation method	LER
Adams et al. (2018) (phonemes)	0.130
Adams et al. (2018) (phonemes + tones)	0.172
grapheme cluster (phonemes + tones)	0.186

Table 3: Prediction performance for different segmentation methods. LER = Label Error Rate.

Language	LER on train set	LER on test set
nru	0.016	0.186
lif	0.167	0.368
ers	0.218	0.383
tvk	0.822	0.818
mkd	0.926	0.926
mlv	0.944	0.932
nep	0.98	0.965

Table 4: Results (ordered from best to worse performance) achieved by the `Persephone` toolkit on different languages of the Pangloss collection. LER = Label Error Rate.

tween the different languages and there might not always be enough training data to properly estimate model parameters.

Degree of Phonetic/Phonological Transparency Last but not least, the use of a phonemic representation rather than an orthographic representation seems to result in better performances:[11] the transcriptions of all the languages in our test set for which `Persephone` was actually able to learn something use a phonemic representation in the International Phonetic Alphabet. At the time of creation of an alphabetic writing system, there is usually a good match between graphemes (orthographic units) and phonemes (phonological units). But as languages change, which they do constantly, they gradually diverge from the state reflected in the orthography. As a result, orthographic representations depart from phonemic structure to an extent that varies greatly across orthographic systems, depending partly on their time depth, and partly on features inherited from the orthographic systems that served as a reference when devising them. For instance, Vietnamese orthography contains peculiarities which originate in spelling conventions in various Romance languages (Haudricourt,

---

[11] This point was already noted by Niko Partanen on the basis of tests applying `Persephone` to orthographic data (personal communication, 2018).

Figure 3: Distribution of sentence durations in the Mwotlap narrative "Romanmangan, the fairy from the other world" (https://doi.org/10.24397/pangloss-0002300).

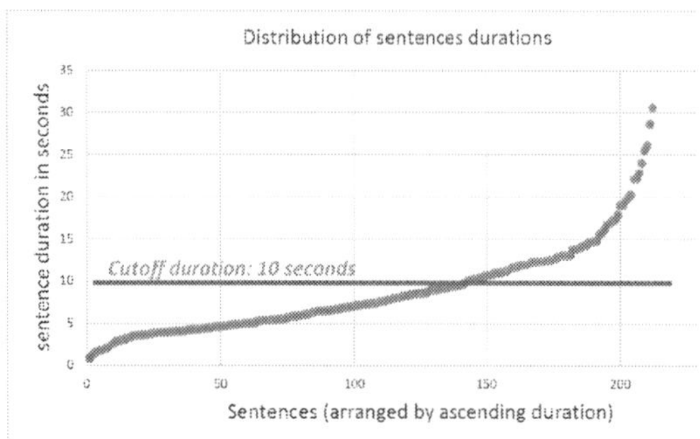

153	mi;mi	165	ni;ni
154	di;ddi	166	ne;ni
155	ɖi;ddei	167	ɲi;ni
156	ti;di	168	li;li
157	ʈi;dei	169	ɬi;lhi
158	tʰi;ti	170	dʑi;jjie
159	ʈʰi;tei	171	tɕi;jie
160	dzi;zzee	172	tɕʰi;qie
161	tsi;zee	173	ɕi;xi
162	tsʰi;cee	174	ʐi;xxi
163	zi;ssee	175	ji;yi
164	si;see	176	gi;ggi

Figure 4: Sample of the syllabic correspondences between IPA and orthography for Yongning Na.

2010), and Na (Narua) orthography follows many conventions of the *Pinyin* romanization system for Standard (Beijing) Mandarin (which young speakers of Na learn at school). There can thus be a large distance between orthography and sound structure as manifested in the audio signal. This makes the training of an automatic transcription system, if not impossible, at least much more complicated.

3.3. Orthographic versus Phonemic Representations

To assess the difficulty of predicting an orthographic rather than a phonological transcription, we again turn to Na data. Roselle Dobbs and Xióng Yàn have developed an orthography for Yongning Na (Dobbs and Yàn, 2018). A complexity is that the orthography was devised as dialect-independent, so as to be an acceptable compromise between the various dialects of this highly diverse language area. As a result, some words are written in the orthography in a way that does not match their pronunciation in the dialect represented in the data set that we use here. For instance, 'pretty' and 'pitiable' are *nuxie* and *niggo*, respectively, in Na orthography, with different vowels in their first syllable, but the first syllable is phonologically identical in the dialect under consideration here. Such mismatches detract from the phonetic transparency of the transcriptions. Phonological transcriptions cannot be converted deterministically into orthographic transcriptions.

But these mismatches are absent from the orthographic transcriptions that we generated from IPA transcriptions. Phonological transcriptions in IPA (as available from the Pangloss Collection) can be readily converted into a simplified Na orthography by means of an algorithm that replaces IPA by orthography on a syllable-by-syllable basis.[12] A sample of the correspondences is shown in Figure 4.[13]

---

[12]The code to convert phonetic transcription of Na into orthographic can be found at https://github.com/alexis-michaud/na.

[13]The syllables in Figure 4 do not carry tone. In view of the fact that tone varies greatly across Na dialects (Dobbs and La, 2016), the choice made in orthography development was to record only very limited tonal information. Automatic (rule-based) conversion currently disregards tone altogether. This topic is not relevant

In the real-life application of generating *bona fide* orthographic transcription for Na documents from IPA transcription, the automatically generated output needs to be improved manually to reflect the orthographic conventions for individual words, as provided in a dictionary of Yongning Na (Michaud, 2018). By contrast, in the tests conducted here, no such adjustments are performed. To distinguish the type of transcription that we generated from *bona fide* orthographic transcription, we will refer to the automatically converted transcriptions as 'quasi-orthographic' transcriptions. 'Quasi-orthographic' transcriptions have a relatively straightforward mapping to IPA – although it is not bijective, because some phonemic distinctions are not reflected in the orthography. For instance, as can be seen from Figure 4, three syllables, /ni/, /ne/ and /ɲi/, all correspond to *ni* in the orthography. The 'quasi-orthographic' transcriptions thus contain slightly fewer distinctions than the IPA notations.

With these caveats in mind, it is possible to compare the performance of a phonemic transcription system trained on the two kinds of transcriptions: phonemic and 'quasi-orthographic'.

The two ways to transcribe data induce two different labels distributions: as shown in Figure 5, there are far more labels in phonological transcriptions, with a long tail. In orthographic transcriptions, the diversity of the phonemes is described by combinations of a small number of symbols and the model must discover and learn the structure of these combinations.

The results are clear: as shown in Table 5, while Persephone achieves very good results when predicting phonological transcriptions with a phoneme error rates of 13.0%, it cannot predict orthographic transcriptions of the same data (the validation error rate is above 90% even after 100 epochs).

These results suggest that orthographies, even with limited

---

to the tests reported in this section, as those focus exclusively on vowels and consonants.

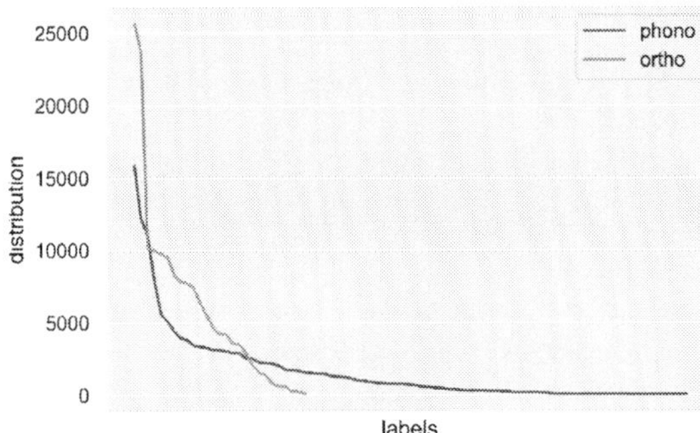

Figure 5: Distribution of the labels for the orthographic (`orth` curve) and phonological (`phono` curve) transcriptions.

labels	tone information	LER (test)
phonetic	✘	0.130
phonetic	✔	0.172
orthographic	✘	0.933

Table 5: Comparison of the performance achieved when using different type of transcriptions.

complexity, offer a less suitable basis for training a tool for automatic transcription. The excellent results reported about Tsuut'ina data transcribed in orthography (Michaud et al., 2019) are certainly due to the high degree of phonemic transparency of Tsuut'ina orthography. To labour the point: orthographic representations can be used: there is no technical gain in using International Phonetic Alphabet symbols rather than any other type of symbols as labels. The issue is not one of writing system *per se*: what matters is the degree of phonemic transparency of the transcription system. Successful application of Persephone in its current state requires a transcription that offers a high degree of phonemic transparency.

4. Conclusion and Perspectives

Towards a *Computational Language Documentation Cookbook* The tests reported here constitute a step towards a *Computational Language Documentation Cookbook* to determine which approaches are most appropriate to make the most of 'small' data sets for Automatic Speech Recognition tasks.

Perspectives for Multi-Speaker Tests and Transfer to other Languages Perspectives for further testing include attempting multi-speaker acoustic models (as against single-speaker setup as mostly studied so far) and model adaptation (pre-training a model on an extensive data set, then adapting it to another speaker, or even another language, on the basis of smaller amounts of data).

User interfaces for Natural Language Processing and Document Editing To empower a greater number of users to carry out tests, an easy-to-use interface is much wanted. Progress in this area is being made at a sustained pace (Foley et al., 2018; Foley et al., 2019). Plans for a general-purpose linguistic annotation backend (LAB) are also being carried out at Carnegie Mellon University (Neubig et al., 2018).

Perspectives for Collaboration with Language Archives: the Issue of Confidential Speaker Metadata One of the issues encountered in the course of the tests reported here is that available metadata are not as rich as one could wish from the point of view of computational tests. For instance, training an acoustic model in single-speaker mode requires knowledge of speaker identity, so as to be able to tease apart recordings from different speakers. But among the documents in the Nashta language available from the Pangloss Collection, seven are by "Anonymous woman" and eight are by "Anonymous man", and there is no telling, from the metadata, whether there is only one "Anonymous woman" or several. Some Romani and Slavic speakers from Greece choose "to remain anonymous due to the complexity of the political context in the country" (Adamou, 2016, v). (Language is a big component of social and ethnic identification, and hence a sensitive topic in many places.) In addition to speaker identity (at the basic level of distinguishing speakers from one another), the language consultants' age, linguistic history (proficiency in languages other than the one(s) that they use during the recording), and even their health record could be relevant parameters in combining documents into a training set. Those are pieces of information to which the investigator is to some extent privy: in the course of immersion fieldwork, one gets to learn a lot about the villages where one is staying. Such personal information must not be disclosed inconsiderately on the open Internet: one owes it to collaborators (language consultants) to protect their data. But destroying private information altogether is also a problem, as it detracts from the usefulness of the data. Use of data from language archives in Natural Language Processing (and in other areas of research) highlights the need for a more elaborate system for metadata management than is currently in place at the Pangloss Collection. In the same way as data can be kept private as long as necessary (the Pangloss Collection's host archive has provisions for keeping data offline for as long as fifty years for reasons of privacy, and as long as a century in the case of state secrets and documents deemed similarly sensitive), it would be a service to research if this archive would curate metadata that go beyond the Dublin Core and the metadata schema of the Open Language Archives Community (and manage the related access rights).

Phonemic Transcription beyond Phonemes: Leveraging the Full Extent of the Linguist's Annotations The research focus was placed here on the recognition of phonemes, but there is, technically, no notion of phoneme in the neural-network architecture, and labels that are not vowels, consonants, tones or other phonemic units can also be fed into the tool at training, and integrated to the acoustic model. Thus, tone-groupe boundaries, an important morpho-phonological landmark in Yongning Na (Michaud, 2017, 321-356), can be recognized by Persephone with good accuracy, and including tone-groupe boundaries improves overall performance.

5. Acknowledgments

We wish to express our gratitude to the language consultants who entrusted their living voices to visiting linguists, and the Pangloss Collection depositors, who generously chose to share the fruit of their hard work.

We are grateful to Oliver Adams, Laurent Besacier, Chris Cox, Hilaria Cruz, Benjamin Galliot, Nathan Hill, Michel Jacobson, Pat Littell, Niko Partanen, and Mandana Seyfeddinipur for useful discussions, to the three reviewers for detailed comments, and to Jesse Gates for proofreading. Errors and shortcomings are the authors' responsibility.

Financial support from grants ANR-10-LABX-0083 (*Laboratoire d'excellence* "Empirical Foundations of Linguistics", 2011-2024) and ANR-19-CE38-0015 ("Computational Language Documentation by 2025", 2019-2024) from *Agence Nationale de la Recherche* (France) is gratefully acknowledged.

6. Bibliographical References

Adamou, E. (2016). *A corpus-driven approach to language contact: Endangered languages in a comparative perspective*. Walter de Gruyter, Berlin.

Adams, O., Cohn, T., Neubig, G., Cruz, H., Bird, S., and Michaud, A. (2018). Evaluation Phonemic Transcription of Low-Resource Tonal Languages for Language Documentation. In Nicoletta Calzolari (Conference chair), et al., editors, *Proceedings of the Eleventh International Conference on Language Resources and Evaluation (LREC 2018)*, Miyazaki, Japan, May 7-12, 2018. European Language Resources Association (ELRA).

Besacier, L., Barnard, E., Karpov, A., and Schultz, T. (2014). Automatic speech recognition for under-resourced languages: A survey. *Speech Communication*, 56:85–100.

Borgman, C. L. (2015). *Big data, little data, no data: scholarship in the networked world*. MIT Press, Cambridge, MA.

Bouquiaux, L. and Thomas, J. (1971). *Enquête et description des langues à tradition orale. Volume I : l'enquête de terrain et l'analyse grammaticale*. Société d'études linguistiques et anthropologiques de France, Paris. 3 volumes.

Brugman, H. and Russel, A. (2004). Annotating multimedia/multi-modal resources with ELAN. In *Proceedings of LREC 2004*.

Dixon, R. M. (2007). Field linguistics: A minor manual. *Sprachtypologie und Universalienforschung*, 60(1):12–31.

Dobbs, R. and La, M. (2016). The two-level tonal system of Lataddi Narua. *Linguistics of the Tibeto-Burman Area*, 39(1):67–104.

Dobbs, R. and Yàn, X. (2018). Yongning Narua orthography: users' guide and developers' notes. https://halshs.archives-ouvertes.fr/halshs-01956606/.

Foley, B., Arnold, J., Coto-Solano, R., Durantin, G., and Ellison, T. M. (2018). Building speech recognition systems for language documentation: the CoEDL Endangered Language Pipeline and Inference System (ELPIS). In *Proceedings of the 6th Intl. Workshop on Spoken Language Technologies for Under-Resourced Languages (SLTU), 29-31 August 2018*, pages 200–204, Gurugram, India. ISCA.

Foley, B., Rakhi, A., Lambourne, N., Buckeridge, N., and Wiles, J. (2019). Elpis, an accessible speech-to-text tool. In *Proceedings of Interspeech 2019*, pages 306–310, Graz.

François, A. (2003). *La sémantique du prédicat en mwotlap, Vanuatu*, volume 84. Peeters, Louvain.

Gerstenberger, C., Partanen, N., Rießler, M., and Wilbur, J. (2017). Instant annotations–Applying NLP methods to the annotation of spoken language documentation corpora. In *Proceedings of the Third Workshop on Computational Linguistics for Uralic Languages*, pages 25–36, St. Petersburg, Russia.

Graves, A., Fernández, S., Gomez, F., and Schmidhuber, J. (2006). Connectionist temporal classification: Labelling unsegmented sequence data with recurrent neural networks. In *Proceedings of the 23rd International Conference on Machine Learning*, ICML '06, page 369–376, New York, NY, USA. Association for Computing Machinery.

Haudricourt, A.-G. (2010). The origin of the peculiarities of the Vietnamese alphabet. *Mon-Khmer Studies*, 39:89–104.

Kingma, D. P. and Ba, J. (2015). Adam: A method for stochastic optimization. In Yoshua Bengio et al., editors, *3rd International Conference on Learning Representations, ICLR 2015, San Diego, CA, USA, May 7-9, 2015, Conference Track Proceedings*.

Littell, P., Kazantseva, A., Kuhn, R., Pine, A., Arppe, A., Cox, C., and Junker, M.-O. (2018). Indigenous language technologies in Canada: Assessment, challenges, and successes. In *Proceedings of the 27th International Conference on Computational Linguistics*, pages 2620–2632.

Liégeois, L., Etienne, C., Parisse, C., Benzitoun, C., and Chanard, C. (2016). Using the TEI as pivot format for oral and multimodal language corpora. *Journal of the Text Encoding Initiative*, 10.

Lust, B. C., Blume, M., Pareja-Lora, A., and Chiarcos, C. (2019). Development of Linguistic Linked Open Data resources for collaborative data-intensive research in the language sciences: An introduction. In *Development of Linguistic Linked Open Data Resources for Collaborative Data-Intensive Research in the Language Sciences*. MIT Press, Cambridge, MA.

Maurel, L. (2016). Quel statut pour les données de la recherche après la loi numérique ? https://scinfolex.com/2016/11/03/quel-statut-pour-les-donnees-de-la-recherche-apres-la-loi-numerique/.

Michailovsky, B., Mazaudon, M., Michaud, A., Guillaume, S., François, A., and Adamou, E. (2014). Documenting and researching endangered languages: The Pangloss Collection. *Language Documentation and Conservation*, 8:119–135.

Michaud, A., Adams, O., Cohn, T., Neubig, G., and Guillaume, S. (2018). Integrating automatic transcription into the language documentation workflow: experiments with Na data and the Persephone toolkit. *Language Documentation and Conservation*, 12:393–429.

Michaud, A., Adams, O., Cox, C., and Guillaume, S. (2019). Phonetic lessons from automatic phonemic transcription: preliminary reflections on Na (Sino-Tibetan) and Tsuut'ina (Dene) data. In *Proceedings of ICPhS XIX (19th International Congress of Phonetic Sciences)*, Melbourne.

Michaud, A. (2017). *Tone in Yongning Na: lexical tones and morphotonology*. Language Science Press, Berlin.

Michaud, A. (2018). *Na (Mosuo)-English-Chinese dictionary*. Lexica, Paris.

Moran, S. and Cysouw, M. (2018). *The Unicode Cookbook for Linguists: Managing writing systems using orthography profiles*. Translation and Multilingual Natural Language Processing. Language Science Press, Feb.

Neubig, G., Littell, P., Chen, C.-Y., Lee, J., Li, Z., Lin, Y.-H., and Zhang, Y. (2018). Towards a general-purpose linguistic annotation backend. *arXiv:1812.05272 [cs]*, December. arXiv: 1812.05272.

Newman, P. and Ratliff, M. (2001). *Linguistic fieldwork*. Cambridge University Press, Cambridge.

Niebuhr, O. and Michaud, A. (2015). Speech data acquisition: The underestimated challenge. *KALIPHO - Kieler Arbeiten zur Linguistik und Phonetik*, 3:1–42.

Schmidt, T. (2011). A TEI-based approach to standardising spoken language transcription. *Journal of the Text Encoding Initiative*, (1).

Seifart, F., Evans, N., Hammarström, H., and Levinson, S. C. (2018). Language documentation twenty-five years on. *Language*, 94(4):e324–e345.

Gary F. Simons et al., editors. (2017). *Ethnologue: languages of the world*. SIL International, Dallas, twentieth edition edition.

Sperber, M., Neubig, G., Fügen, C., Nakamura, S., and Waibel, A. (2013). Efficient speech transcription through respeaking. In *Proceedings of Interspeech 2013*, pages 1087–1091, Lyon.

Strunk, J., Schiel, F., and Seifart, F. (2014). Untrained forced alignment of transcriptions and audio for language documentation corpora using WebMAUS. In *Proceedings of the Ninth International Conference on Language Resources and Evaluation*, pages 3940–3947, Reykjavik. European Language Resources Association (ELRA).

Thieberger, N. (2017). LD&C possibilities for the next decade. *Language Documentation and Conservation*, 11:1–4.

van Esch, D., Foley, B., and San, N. (2019). Future directions in technological support for language documentation. In *Proceedings of the Workshop on Computational Methods for Endangered Languages*, volume 1, page 3, Honolulu, Hawai'i.

Whalen, D. H. and McDonough, J. (2019). Under-resourced languages: Phonetic results from language archives. In William F. Katz et al., editors, *The Routledge Handbook of Phonetics*.

Woodbury, T. (2003). Defining documentary linguistics. In Peter Austin, editor, *Language documentation and description*, volume 1, pages 35–51. School of African and Oriental Studies, London.

Proceedings of the 1st Joint SLTU and CCURL Workshop (SLTU-CCURL 2020), pages 316–320
Language Resources and Evaluation Conference (LREC 2020), Marseille, 11–16 May 2020
© European Language Resources Association (ELRA), licensed under CC-BY-NC

Manual Speech Synthesis Data Acquisition - From Script Design to Recording Speech

Atli Þór Sigurgeirsson, Gunnar Thor Örnólfsson, Jón Guðnason
Reykjavik University, The Árni Magnússon Institute of Icelandic Studies, Reykjavik University
Menntavegur 1 - Reykjavik Iceland, Laugavegur 13 - Reykjavik Iceland, Menntavegur 1 - Reykjavik Iceland
atlithors@ru.is, gunnarthor@hi.is, jg@ru.is

Abstract

In this paper we present the work of collecting a large amount of high quality speech synthesis data for Icelandic. 8 speakers will be recorded for 20 hours each. A script design strategy is proposed and three scripts have been generated to maximize diphone coverage, varying in length. The largest reading script contains 14,400 prompts and includes 87.3% of all Icelandic diphones at least once and 81% of all Icelandic diphones at least twenty times. A recording client was developed to facilitate recording sessions. The client supports easily importing scripts and maintaining multiple collections in parallel. The recorded data can be downloaded straight from the client. Recording sessions are carried out in a professional studio under supervision and started October of 2019. As of writing, 58.7 hours of high quality speech data has been collected. The scripts, the recording software and the speech data will later be released under a CC-BY 4.0 license.

Keywords: Corpus, Acquisition, Tools

1. Introduction

High quality speech data is imperative to the development of good speech synthesis systems. This fact is often a hurdle for under-resourced languages, like Icelandic, since the acquisition of quality speech data is both labor-intensive and a costly process. Meanwhile, as the language technology (LT) community has grown, the development cost of Text-to-speech (TTS) and Automatic Speech recognition (ASR) systems has decreased.

The availability of Icelandic ASR data has increased tremendously in recent years. The Althingi corpus (Helgadóttir et al., 2017) contains over 500 hours of transcribed parliament speeches, the Málrómur corpus (Steingrímsson et al., 2017) includes 152 hours of recorded speech from 563 participants and the Almannarómur corpus which was collected from 563 participants that provided 219 read sentences on average each (Guðnason et al., 2012). All of these datasets are recorded by multiple speakers under different recording environments which is a benefit when training ASR models while it is a hindrance when training natural-sounding TTS models. Speech synthesis datasets for Icelandic remain sparse.

1.1. Related Work

Typically, speech synthesis datasets are recorded professionally by a single speaker in a controlled environment under supervision. The amount of data required for TTS depends on the chosen model. The CMU arctic corpus consists of 1150 phonetically balanced sentences and was designed for unit selection TTS (Kominek et al., 2003). The Merlin toolkit was used to train a statistical parametric speech synthesis (SPSS) model based on neural networks with 2400 training utterances (Wu et al., 2016). Deep voice (Arik et al., 2017), an end-to-end TTS based entirely on neural networks was trained on approximately 20 hours of speech and reached a mean opinion score (MOS) of 3.94 ± 0.26.

The first development of an Icelandic TTS started around the turn of the century. At least three TTS systems for Icelandic exist today and are in use. Most recently, in 2010, the Icelandic association of the visually impaired hired the Polish software company Ivona to develop a unit selection TTS system. These three systems have all had mixed successes. An important downside to these developments is the fact that all three voices were carried out by foreign firms and no open and available TTS datasets for Icelandic exist today (Nikulásdóttir et al., 2020).

A voice recording client is necessary to facilitate the recording sessions. Common Voice [1] is a well known recording client for crowd sourcing ASR data. Google has used a tool referred to as *Datahound* for collecting and building transcribed speech corpora for many languages (Hughes et al., 2010). A speech data acquisition system made in Iceland referred to as *Eyra* was developed in 2016 (Petursson et al., 2016). Eyra was developed as a crowd sourcing tool and was later used to collect about 35 hours ASR data (Guðnason et al., 2017).

1.2. Overview

This paper presents an overview of the speech data acquisition process for a new Icelandic TTS system. The system is being developed as a part of the Icelandic language technology programme (Nikulásdóttir et al., 2020). The programme spans 4 years and many different projects in LT. This paper presents two of the main goals of the TTS project:

- To generate 3 scripts that maximize a diphone coverage. They should be designed for 1 hour, 10 hour and 20 hour collections.

- To record unit selection TTS data from 4 female speakers and 4 male speakers. 20 hours should be collected from each speaker.

---

[1] https://voice.mozilla.org/

The 3 scripts should be suitable for TTS recipe development on a varying scale, from unit-selection models to end-to-end neural speech synthesis models. This work started in autumn 2019 and as of writing, the scripts have been finalized. The twenty hour script contains 14400 unique sentences. The list contains at least one occurrence of 87.3% of all possible diphones and 81% of them appear at least 20 times. Speech recording is an ongoing process and we have collected approximately 59 hours of data as of date. Once all speakers have been recorded, the dataset will be published under a CC-BY 4.0 license.

2. Script Design

Before designing the script, 500,000 sentences were extracted from Risamálheild (Steingrímsson et al., 2018), a large Icelandic text corpus containing more than one billion word tokens. All of these sentences had to pass a naive preprocessing step. To pass, the sentence must:

- be at least 10 letters

- be between 5 and 15 words

- only contain characters from the Icelandic alphabet or any of the Icelandic punctuation symbols

- start with a capital letter

- end with a punctuation symbol

- appear in the database of modern Icelandic inflection (Bjarnadóttir, 2012)

Since Icelandic is a highly inflected language, simply checking if all words in a sentence appear in a dictionary would greatly limit the number of sentences that would pass this preprocessing step. Checking if all words appear in the inflection list does not guarantee grammatical correctness however. The length constraints were enforced to minimize prosodic difference between recordings, which can be an issue for very short sentences (Kominek et al., 2003), and to limit the number of mispronunciations while recording the data.

The phones in a randomly sampled list of sentences will follow an uneven distribution where a small number of phones will appear very frequently. Such a list will therefore likely not contain more than one occurrence of a substantial amount of the possible phonetic combinations in the language. This poses a problem for gathering speech synthesis data since it is critical to train a TTS on most phonetic combinations more than once to generate natural-sounding results. TTS scripts are therefore most often designed to maximize some phonetic coverage. A lot of different metrics have been used for measuring such a coverage. It varies both in terms of the phonetic unit used, e.g. diphones (Kominek et al., 2003) or triphones (Ursin, 2002), and also in terms of the context each unit appears in, where in the sentence the unit appears or where in a word it appears and so on. We decided to maximize diphone coverage while limiting sentence length.

A Sequitur grapheme-to-phoneme (G2P) model (Bisani and Ney, 2008) was trained on the Icelandic Pronunciation Dictionary (IPD) (Nikulásdóttir et al., 2018) To acquire predicted phonetization of the source text. This is needed to analyze the phonetic content of the source text. Icelandic is spoken with six rather similar dialects and IPD contains variants for four of those dialects. A standard dialect in the IPD is used to phonetically transcribe the training data in this work. The training set consists of approximately 40,000 verified word and phonetization pairs. The complete list of Icelandic phones in SAMPA format is given below

```
A,ay,ay:,au,au:,A:,c,c0,ey,ey:,f,h,i,
i:,j,k,k0,l,l0,m,m0,n,n0,ou,ou:,p,p0,r,
r0,s,t,t0,U,U:,v,x,C,D,N,N0,9,9y,9y:,
9:,O,oy,O:,E,E:,G,I,I:,J,J0,Y,yy,Y:,T
```

The trained model achieves a phone error rate (PER) of 3.4%. Using this G2P model, the phonetization for each source sentence was predicted. A special symbol was additionally prepended and appended to each phonetization to denote the start and end of sentences. Using this, a list of diphones was generated for each sentence.

A greedy algorithm was used to order the list by a reward function, R, which was constructed to reward sentences that both improve the phonetic coverage and are short. The final script is initialized as the empty set. Given the large list of sentences, all the sentences are scored by R at every time step and sorted. The sentence with the highest reward is inserted into the final script. The reward function is given by

$$R(s) = \frac{1}{|s|} \sum_{i=1}^{n} \frac{1}{\max(1, [d_i \in \mathbf{D}])}$$

$$s = s_1, \ldots, s_m \quad d(s) = d_1, \ldots, d_n$$

Here, s is the sentence, $d(s)$ is the grapheme-to-diphone mapping of s and $\mathbf{D}$ is the set of all diphones in the script already. We define a complete coverage to include at least 20 occurrences of each possible diphone. After that, a diphone does not count towards the reward. The algorithm runs until complete coverage is achieved or 25,000 sentences have been added to the script.

The coverage at every insertion step is shown In Figure 1. The blue curve shows the actual coverage, that is the coverage with regards to all diphones. It is important to point out that not all diphones are valid diphones in Icelandic and never appear. The red curve shows the coverage with regards to the diphones that appear in the source that the algorithm runs on.

After about 6000 insertions the algorithm reaches the maximum possible coverage. The resulting script contains at least one occurrence of 87.3% of all possible diphones and 81% of them appear at least 20 times.

Figure 2 shows phone-to-phone heat maps of the list generated by the proposed method and the same number of randomly sampled sentences. The heat map for the proposed script demonstrates much greater coverage than that of the randomly sampled list. This underlines the issue of randomly sampling sentences.

After sorting the list by the reward, a number of sentences were added to the script in different categories:

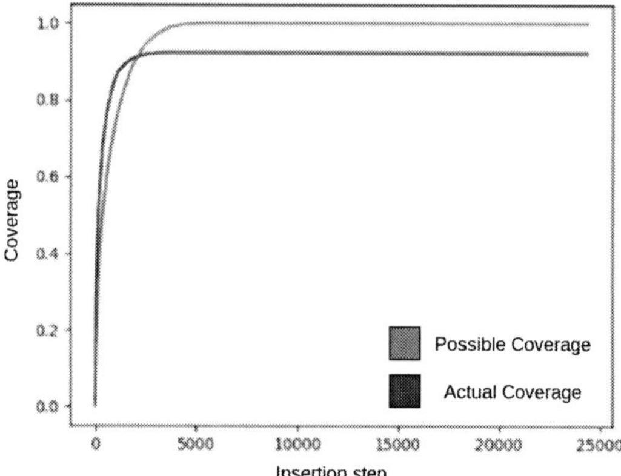

Figure 1: Phonetical coverage at every insertion step of the greedy algorithm.

(a) Randomly sampled script

(b) The proposed script

Figure 2: Heat maps that visualize the diphone distribution of a randomly sampled script and the proposed script. Both axis include all possible phonemes in the same order.

- 2000 sentences between 15-25 words that could be used for learning acoustic alignment for longer sentences.

- 100 sentences containing only digits in written form

- 30 sentences that contain only one word each

To generate the 20 hour script we take the first k sentences from the final list ordered by the reward such that $k = 20 \times 3600s/5s = 14,400$ where we estimate that it takes on average 5 seconds to read a single sentence. The 1 hour and 10 hour scripts are generated in a similar manner.

3. Recording Client

A recording client was developed to facilitate voice recording sessions and we call it *Lobe*. Previously, a speech data acquisition tool called *Eyra* (e. Ear) (Petursson et al., 2016) was developed at Reykjavik University. Eyra was used successfully for gathering ASR data (Guðnason et al., 2017). The ASR focused nature of Eyra did not fit the TTS data acquisition task which prompted the development of Lobe. Lobe is at the core a Python package with a Flask [2] web client. It is hosted on a Reykjavik University server and accessible in the browser. The data is stored in a PostgreSQL database with a weekly backup schedule.

Lobe assigns roles to users, either an administration role or a basic user role. A basic user could be

- A speaker whose voice will be recorded

- A person who controls the prompts while recording speech (*prompt manager*)

- Anyone else that wants to access the data

An administrator starts by creating a collection through Lobe. After selecting a collection name and perhaps assigning a speaker to the collection, the prompts are uploaded through Lobe. Lobe accepts multiple file uploads where each line in a file is treated as a single prompt. As Lobe was designed with the script design in mind it also accepts prompts that include the following in a tab-separated format:

- The prompt itself.

- The source of the prompt (e.g. a certain newspaper).

- An order score. If a score is higher it appears earlier in the prompts.

- The phonetization of the prompt.

In this way, we can start by recording phonetically rich sentences as determined by the reward function.

Next, the administrator creates a new user for the speaker through Lobe. Lobe stores user information such as age, sex and dialect. After that, recording sessions can be carried out. Each recording session contains 50 prompts. The prompt manager presses a key to initialize audio capture and a visual sign prompts the speaker to start speaking. After the speaker reads the prompt the prompt manager

---

[2]https://flask.palletsprojects.com/

presses another key to stop audio capture. At that point the prompt manager can go to the next prompt or download the current audio capture. Since the scripts are not guaranteed to be grammatically correct, the prompt manager also has the option to skip the current prompt and the sentence will be marked as faulty in the database. That sentence will not appear further as a prompt. Lobe has a simple quality con-

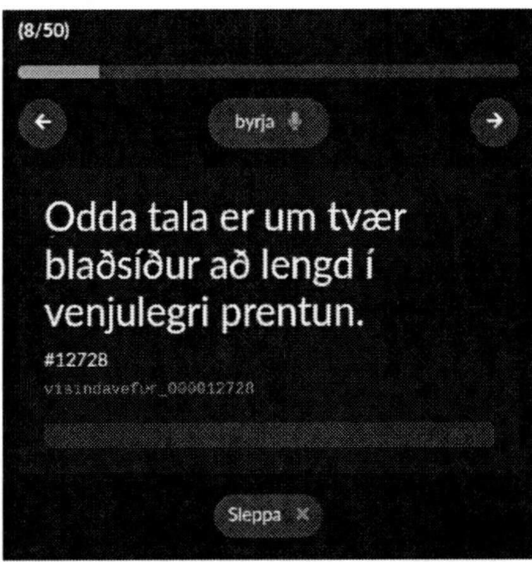

Figure 3: The prompt screen shown to both the speaker and the prompt manager

trol check that runs after each recording. It will prompt the manager if the recording is either too quiet or too loud. For further inspection, the recording can be downloaded and analyzed in any available audio software. We use the Me-diaRecorder[3] interface to record the audio. It is sampled at 41KHz with a 24 bit depth.

After a session is finished, the prompt manager can start a new recording session or log out of Lobe. At any time, the collection can be downloaded as a separate dataset through Lobe. The client creates an archive that includes all prompts and recordings as well as information about each recording session, the speaker and the collection itself.

Since we are using Merlin (Wu et al., 2016) for generating SPSS voice recipes, we made sure that the lobe dataset exports could be easily imported into Merlin.

4. Recording Speech

Eight speakers will be recorded, 20 hours each. As of date we have started recording four of those. One of our goals is to attain diversity in age, dialect and overall speaking style. Four female speakers will be recorded and four male speakers. The first four speakers are in the age range of 49-71 years as shown in Table 1. They also all speak in the same standard dialect. It is therefore important to select the next four speakers with this fact and the goal of attaining diversity in mind. A voice sample of five sentences is recorded and analyzed before a speaker is added to the dataset. We evaluate the speech rate, volume and the overall pleasantness of the voice. Once the speaker has

[3]https://developer.mozilla.org/en-US/docs/Web/API/MediaRecorder

Speaker ID	Age	Sex	Amount recorded
M1	70	Male	20 hours
F1	59	Female	17.3 hours
M2	49	Male	9.8 hours
F2	71	Female	11.6 hours

Table 1: The recording progress for the first 4 speakers

been approved, the speaker is assigned a recording schedule with a prompt manager. A voice recording test is carried out during the first session. This is done to determine the external sound card level that ensures that the recording stays between -18dB and -12dB in playback with 0dB as the distortion threshold. The sound card level is recorded for future reference.

Recording sessions are carried out in a studio at the national broadcaster of Iceland. The studio is separated into a recording space and a monitoring space. The recording space is sound proof and designed to limit resonance. Both prompt managers and the speakers monitor the distance from the pop filter attached to the microphone at the start of each recording session as the distance could affect the recorded results. The speakers are also told not to bring anything else into the recording space and limit movement. The prompt manager sits in the monitor space and communicates with the speaker using a talkback system in the studio. Before starting, the prompt manager starts a voice

Figure 4: The recording environment shown from inside the recording space.

recording test. A single sentence is recorded and then analyzed. If the monitor value is not within the (-18dB;-12dB) range, the prompt manager changes the sound card level accordingly and records a new sound card level. At this point a session can start.

Each session is configured to go through 50 prompts. The speaker never records for more than two hours each day to reduce the risk of vocal strain. Typically eight to twelve such sessions can be completed in a two hour span. The session duration varies between speakers but is normally between seven to 13 minutes with an average duration of about 9 minutes.

5. Conclusions and Future Work

We aim to finish recording 20 hours from the eight speakers each by the 1st of October 2020. The dataset will thereafter be made available. Parallel to this, work on unit selection TTS and SPSS model recipes will be carried out and trained for the speakers that have reached the 20 hour goal.

Work to improve Lobe is ongoing. Most importantly is the work on expanding the built-in quality control. We additionally aim to make Lobe more configurable with regards to the number of prompts in a session, sample rate, bit depth and so on. More features will also soon be added to Lobe to facilitate different types of data collections. Firstly, support for multi-speaker collections will be added. This is necessary as part of the Icelandic language technology programme is to collect 2 hours from 40 speakers each for voice mixing synthesis projects. Secondly, support for video capture will be added to facilitate audio-visual speech recognition data acquisition.

6. Bibliographical References

Arik, S. Ö., Chrzanowski, M., Coates, A., Diamos, G., Gibiansky, A., Kang, Y., Li, X., Miller, J., Ng, A., Raiman, J., et al. (2017). Deep voice: Real-time neural text-to-speech. In *Proceedings of the 34th International Conference on Machine Learning-Volume 70*, pages 195–204. JMLR. org.

Bisani, M. and Ney, H. (2008). Joint-sequence models for grapheme-to-phoneme conversion. *Speech communication*, 50(5):434–451.

Bjarnadóttir, K. (2012). The database of modern icelandic inflection (beygingarlýsing íslensks nútímamáls). *Language Technology for Normalisation of Less-Resourced Languages*, page 13.

Guðnason, J., Kjartansson, O., Jóhannsson, J., Carstensdóttir, E., Vilhjálmsson, H. H., Loftsson, H., Helgadóttir, S., Jóhannsdóttir, K. M., and Rögnvaldsson, E. (2012). Almannaromur: An open icelandic speech corpus. In *Spoken Language Technologies for Under-Resourced Languages*.

Guðnason, J., Pétursson, M., Kjaran, R., Klüpfel, S., and Nikulásdóttir, A. B. (2017). Building ASR corpora using Eyra. In *INTERSPEECH*, pages 2173–2177.

Helgadóttir, I. R., Kjaran, R., Nikulásdóttir, A. B., and Guðnason, J. (2017). Building an ASR corpus using Althingi's parliamentary speeches. In *INTERSPEECH*, pages 2163–2167.

Hughes, T., Nakajima, K., Ha, L., Vasu, A., Moreno, P. J., and LeBeau, M. (2010). Building transcribed speech corpora quickly and cheaply for many languages. In *Eleventh Annual Conference of the International Speech Communication Association*.

Kominek, J., Black, A. W., and Ver, V. (2003). CMU ARCTIC databases for speech synthesis.

Nikulásdóttir, A. B., Guðnason, J., and Rögnvaldsson, E. (2018). An icelandic pronunciation dictionary for tts. In *2018 IEEE Spoken Language Technology Workshop (SLT)*, pages 339–345. IEEE.

Nikulásdóttir, A. B., Guðnason, J., Ingason, A. K., Rögnvaldsson, H., Rögnvaldsson, E., Sigurðsson, E. F., and Steingrímsson, S. (2020). Language technology programme for icelandic 2019-2023. In *LREC*. LREC.

Petursson, M., Klüpfel, S., and Gudnason, J. (2016). Eyra-speech data acquisition system for many languages. *Procedia Computer Science*, 81:53–60.

Steingrímsson, S., Guðnason, J., Helgadóttir, S., and Rögnvaldsson, E. (2017). Málrómur: A manually verified corpus of recorded icelandic speech. In *Proceedings of the 21st Nordic Conference on Computational Linguistics*, pages 237–240.

Steingrímsson, S., Helgadóttir, S., Rögnvaldsson, E., Barkarson, S., and Guðnason, J. (2018). Risamálheild: A very large icelandic text corpus. In *Proceedings of the Eleventh International Conference on Language Resources and Evaluation (LREC 2018)*.

Ursin, M. (2002). Triphone clustering in finnish continuous speech recognition. *Diplomityö, Teknillinen korkeakoulu*.

Wu, Z., Watts, O., and King, S. (2016). Merlin: An open source neural network speech synthesis system. In *SSW*, pages 202–207.

Proceedings of the 1st Joint SLTU and CCURL Workshop (SLTU-CCURL 2020), pages 321–329
Language Resources and Evaluation Conference (LREC 2020), Marseille, 11–16 May 2020
© European Language Resources Association (ELRA), licensed under CC-BY-NC

Owóksape - An Online Language Learning Platform for Lakota

Owóksape Development Team
(Jan Ullrich, Elliot Thornton, Peter Vieira, Logan Swango, Marek Kupiec)
The Language Conservancy
2620 N Walnut St. #810, Bloomington, IN 47404
{juf, elliot, pete.vieira, logan, marek}@languageconservancy.org

Abstract

This paper presents Owóksape, an online language learning platform for the under-resourced language Lakota. The Lakota language (*Lakȟótiyapi*) is a Siouan language native to the United States with fewer than 2000 fluent speakers. Owóksape was developed by The Language Conservancy to support revitalization efforts, including reaching younger generations and providing a tool to complement traditional teaching methods. This project grew out of various multimedia resources in order to combine their most effective aspects into a single, self-paced learning tool. The first section of this paper discusses the motivation for and background of Owóksape. Section two details the linguistic features and language documentation principles that form the backbone of the platform. Section three lays out the unique integration of cultural aspects of the Lakota people into the visual design of the application. Section four explains the pedagogical principles of Owóksape. Application features and exercise types are then discussed in detail with visual examples, followed by an overview of the software design, as well as the effort required to develop the platform. Finally, a description of future features and considerations is presented.

Keywords: Owóksape, Lakota, Lakȟótiyapi, language-learning, under-resourced, The Language Conservancy, Siouan, revitalization, web app, mobile app

1. Introduction

1.1. Background

The Language Conservancy is a non-profit organization which, in collaboration with the Lakota Language Consortium, has produced numerous pedagogical materials for the Lakota language, including an audio series, traditional and speaking dictionaries, a grammar handbook, textbooks, dubbed cartoon series, a vocabulary-building mobile app, print story books, as well as an accompanying augmented reality app. Activity in the community includes summer institutes with language instruction and teacher training. In order to transition to a digital medium, an online learning platform was undertaken, combining aspects of the other pedagogical materials, and resulting in Owóksape, a self-paced digital learning environment (Lakota Languge Consortium Inc, 2019).

This paper first discusses the linguistic and cultural features of the application and its pedagogy. The application features are then described in detail, followed by an overview of the software design. Finally, since Owóksape is an ongoing effort, the intention is to provide a description of the application's current state and end with a description of future improvements.

1.2. General Overview

Owóksape (literally "place of knowledge") contains linear learning paths with exercise types that appeal to various learning styles. It is designed for self-study or to supplement classroom learning. The platform caters to multiple audiences including adult members of the Lakota community who didn't grow up with the language, children in tribal schools in and around the Lakota reservations, and learners of all ages across the U.S. and the world who take an interest in the Lakota language for cultural, linguis-

tic or personal reasons. The platform targets modern web browsers, as well as Android and iOS devices.

2. Linguistic Features

Lakota has provided unique challenges and opportunities in documenting and subsequently creating comprehensive curricula for the language. As with other Siouan languages, Lakota was not written by its speakers prior to the end of the 19th century. Modern Lakota learners generally know English as their first language, so the focus of learning modules has been to bridge the gap between English and Lakota.

2.1. Corpus-based Documentation

Creation of Owóksape's curriculum revolves around analysis of existing corpora, such as the text collected in 1930 by Ella Deloria (Deloria, 1932), unpublished texts in various archives, as well as numerous recordings from native speakers collected by Jan Ullrich from 1992-2020. This approach started with the creation of a consistent phonemic orthography, compilation of a more than 31,000 entry English-Lakota dictionary with more than 53,000 example sentences, and the organization of grammatical analysis in the Lakota Grammar Handbook (Ullrich and Black Bear Jr., 2016).

The importance of this corpus-based approach is two-fold. The collection of texts and recorded stories serve as a lasting accurate reference of the language available to both scholars and lay people, whereas translational elicitation, which has been the prevailing method since the advent of Chomskyan linguistics, results in problematic data more often than not (Chelliah, 2018; Epps et al., 2017). And in the case of Lakota, collections of stories and utterances preserve cultural context and attest to consistencies in the language that become harder to measure as the population of speakers decreases.

2.2. Phonological Treatment

Speaking Lakota requires the pronunciation of aspirated and unaspirated stops, nasals, glottals, velar and uvular fricatives, and other sounds not easily differentiated by English speakers. The voices of fluent speakers are essential in providing accurate models for learners to emulate. Introduction of these sounds is done gradually with emphasis on practice in isolation and within words. Several exercises are designed to help learners distinguish between sounds. One such exercise presents the user with a word that is missing a phoneme. Among the phonemes *k*, *kh*, *kȟ*, and *k'* ([k], [kʰ], [kˣ], and [k'], respectively) the user must select the one that corresponds to the word they hear pronounced by a fluent speaker. Lakota also uses a phonemic pitch accent. Many exercises train the user to distinguish accent placement through listening, typing and multiple choice activities, given differently stressed variations of a word. With accent placement being unpredictable, fluent speakers recognize accent placement, in particular, as a clear sign of experience in the language.

2.3. Learning Vocabulary

The introduction of vocabulary in Owóksape is done first in isolation and eventually in greater context. Teaching vocabulary in semantic groups helps learners solidify associations, therefore it is a primary focus of vocabulary exercise sections. Extra attention is also given to the introduction of verbs, providing the citation form of the verb first, with conjugated forms introduced only after a particular pattern of conjugation is taught in detail. Finally, students are gradually introduced to various types of agglutination.

2.4. Grammatical Treatment

There are many grammatical concepts in Lakota difficult for second language learners. Lakota is a head marking language, which means, among other things, that a verb alone can constitute a clause, and that most word categories can function as predicates. When optional noun phrases are present, they conform to a subject-object-verb word order. The language has no tense. Proper conjugation and use of verbs requires a deeper understanding of modes, person, and the numerous ways to mark aspect. While there are general rules for verb affixes, the position of affixes that express grammatical person or argument cannot always be easily predicted by novice learners, so many verb forms require memorization. This is in addition to word final vowel alternation (ablaut). Where memorization of vocabulary or exceptions is needed, those cases are explained and practiced in exercises designed to contrast those exceptions.

3. Cultural Features

Language is an integral component of any culture. In creating resources for language revitalization, recognizing the audience of these tools is an important aspect both in attracting and supporting users. The visual design of Owóksape seeks to serve the relevance of the oral history of Lakota, but also reflect modern Lakota people.

3.1. Character Design

Modern Lakota people drive cars, use cell phones and wear jeans and sneakers. At the same time, a rich connection to the land and spirituality remains present in everyday life in ways such as hairstyles and adornments. Producing characters that modern Lakota people can relate to involved consultation with numerous tribe members, as well as that of historical and modern photographic references. The end goal is to allow Lakota learners to see themselves in the Lakota language curriculum.

Figure 1: Avatars designed for Lakota people

3.2. Iconography

Icons of Lakota culture are also integrated into the visual style of many aspects of the platform. Eagle feathers are presented to young men and women on important occasions of success like high school graduation or after a feat of bravery. The campfire, tipi, buffalo and other animals also all retain important meaning for modern Lakota people. The integration of these icons serve to again provide context for the language learned and connection to the learner's existing cultural context. These same icons are integrated into curricula relating to traditional dress, items and places of cultural importance, and naturally appear in modules based on texts of traditional stories.

4. Pedagogical Principles of Owóksape

The approach to teaching employed by Owóksape is based primarily in the research on language learning principles, rather than on theoretical concepts of constantly changing methodologies. Thus, Owóksape aims to provide a balanced approach to teaching fluency, accuracy and complexity. Grammatical structures are introduced primarily via guided induction (rather than via explanation) which is combined with input enhancement (such as noticing questions). Deductive activities are provided only in review of the individual previously practiced bottom-up activities.

Another important approach is the attempt to use algorithmization specific to individual learners which provides them with balance in learning and practicing receptive skills (reading, listening), productive skills (speaking, writing), cultural awareness, as well as in learning vocabulary and structure. Additionally there are multiple reward and competition features aimed at keeping learners motivated.

An important characteristic of Owóksape is that all of the learning content is based in authentic (and occasionally semi-authentic) language originating from connected speech recorded from native speakers, rather than in artificially created sentences and text.

4.1. Pattern Based Teaching

Methods and principles used in second language teaching vary across platforms and classrooms. While rote memorization of common conversations may aid a vacationing traveler, the goal of Owóksape is to provide a long-term learning resource for dedicated Lakota learners. Learners gain both a conceptual understanding of the structure of the language and a scaffold of pattern recognition innate in fluent speaking and natural language acquisition (Hakuta, 2006). More advanced units continue to expand on previous patterns. For example, Unit 2 introduces the user to a basic question pattern using colors (e.g. *Sápa he?* 'Is it black?'), then basic patterns of demonstratives are introduced in Unit 12 (e.g. *Hé šiná* 'That blanket near you'), and with this in place, more subtle adverbs in Unit 126 (*Lakȟóta etáŋ hél waŋwíčhalaka he?* 'Did you see any Lakotas there?').

4.2. Spaced-Repetition Algorithm

A number of methods have been used by other platforms in order to maintain varied, but directed learning outside of a linear curriculum sequence. Review is available to learners with both the specificity of a chosen topical category or a global review encompassing all curricula the learner has been exposed to. The organization of this is done via the tracking of the user's previous responses to exercise content segregated by the type of learning exposure (reading, writing, listening, or speaking). Previous correct or incorrect responses are weighed against the number of times the user has been exposed to that content, and the time since the most recent exposure, to create a score for that specific learning content. Each time the user completes an activity, that score is reevaluated and new, more difficult, or less often seen exercises rise to the top of the list. This ensures that as the user continues to review, they are getting pertinent exercises for their learning path and reinforcing core concepts again and again with ample time to reflect and reinforce the learned language (Ebbinghaus, 1885; Kramár et al., 2012).

4.3. Gamification

A varied approach to providing users with feedback on their progress and rewarding persistence is employed. Users may earn badges in three different ways: 1) for completing levels, 2) maintaining a streak of consecutive days of use, or 3) communicating with others in the forum. There is also a public and friend-based leaderboard for comparing a learner's progress with others. The leaderboard shows the user's accrued points. These points not only reflect the user's progress, but also the user's aptitude, as fewer points are awarded when an exercise is repeated after an incorrect response. Points are awarded and celebrated after each exercise with a screen proclaiming a varied set of congratulations in the language (*Taŋyáŋ ečhánuŋ!* 'You did it correctly!', *Áta khilí!* 'Totally Awesome!', *Wašté!* 'Good!'...).

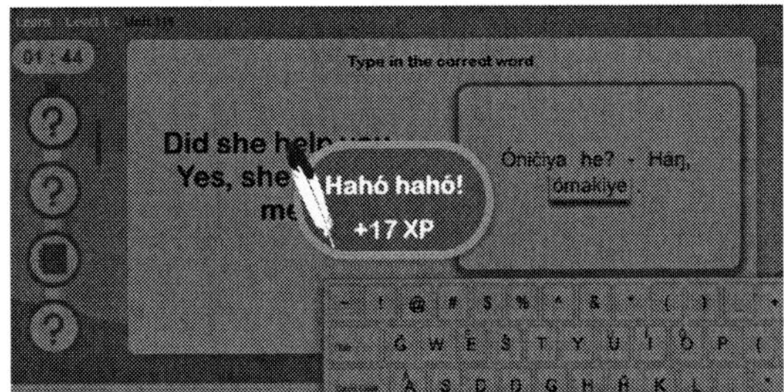

Figure 2: Pop-up rewarding user with points after answering a question correctly

5. Application Features

5.1. Cards

Cards make up the fundamental linguistic data of Owóksape. Each one consists of classes of data known as *components*. Figure 3 shows the required data every card must have, as well as additional optional components that permit creation of more varied activities. On the right is a real example of card data for the Lakota word *tȟó*. Concern-

Card Data	
Required	Card ID
	Card Type (word, pattern)
	Lakota Text
	English Translation
	Lakota Audio
	Grammatical Gender
Optional	Alternate Lakota Text
	Alternate English Glosses
	Image
	Video
	Inflection

Example Card Data	
Card ID	3
Card Type	word
Lakota Text	tȟó
English Text	blue
Lakota Audio	blue.mp3
Grammatical Gender	none
Image	blue.png

Figure 3: Card data components (left) and an example of real card data (right)

ing card types, word cards are used for teaching and learning individual items of vocabulary, whereas pattern cards are intended for teaching and learning phrases and sentence structures. These card data are presented to the user in the form of instructions or quizzes, with different combinations of card components producing unique activity types.

5.2. Learning Paths

At the top of Owóksape's hierarchy are learning paths. Each one is designed to be dedicated to a specific topic or objective such as vocabulary, advanced grammar, fundamentals, etc. Each of these learning paths contains units organized into proficiency levels.

The user progresses through levels by completing sequential units, finishing the current unit to unlock the next one. To finish a learning path the user must complete all the units in each proficiency level until all levels are completed.

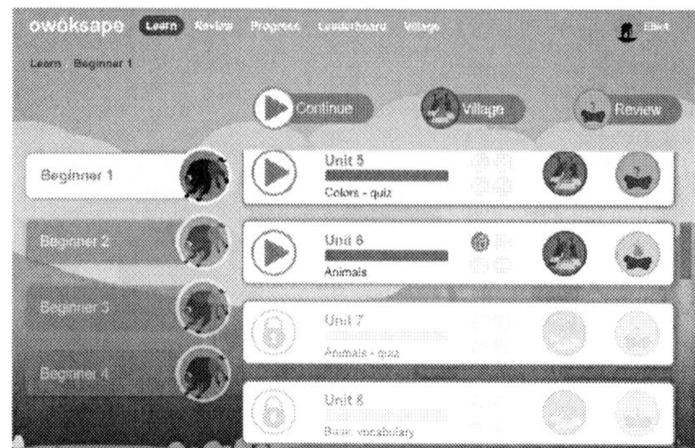

Figure 4: Learning path screen

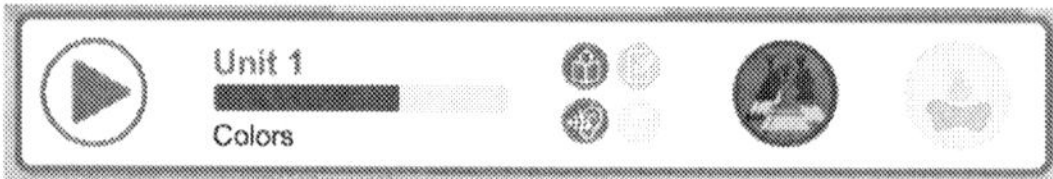

Figure 6: Unit progress bar and four learning skill icons indicating percentage of skills the user has practiced in this unit.

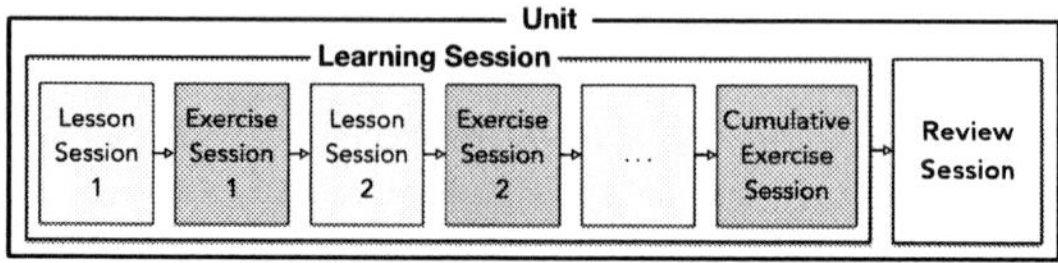

Figure 7: Unit design and user progression through the unit via multiple lesson-exercise session pairs, followed by a cumulative exercise session and finally a review quiz session

5.2.1. Learning Speeds

In a settings menu, a user must select how much time per day they would like to commit to learning Lakota given four possible learning speeds shown in Figure 5. The four settings determine how long a user must use the app before they are rewarded for completing their daily study goal, notified by a pop-up.

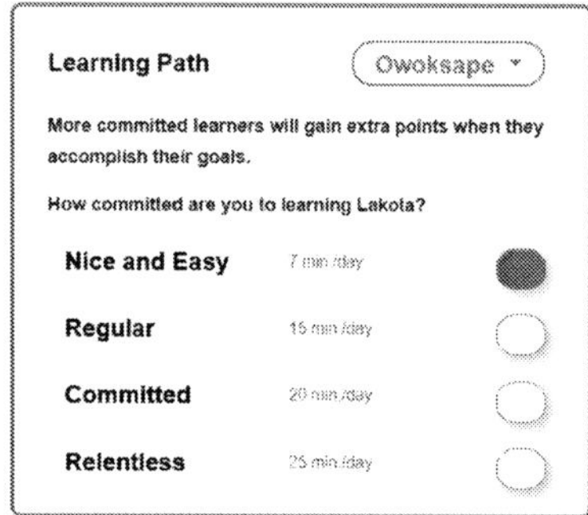

Figure 5: Learning speeds: target minutes per day of study selected by the user

5.3. Proficiency Levels

A learning path contains one or more levels, with the goal of producing content across the seven established Lakota proficiency levels. Each one is represented by a different icon to the left of the list of units (see Figure 4).

5.4. Units

Units are the main activity area for users. The learning page contains a list of units for the current level that the user must progress through sequentially. A unit consists of three major elements: a *learning session*, a *review session*, and a unit-specific forum called the *village* (see Figure 6). The learning session is accessed by pressing the unit's *play* icon, and contains interspersed lessons with associated exercise sessions, ending in a cumulative quiz session. The review session, entered via the *camp fire* icon, comprises unit-specific quiz activities that use the spaced-repetition approach described above.

The progression of unit activities is shown in Figure 7. Completion of the learning session unlocks the review session, for which a predetermined number of activities must be completed before the following unit is unlocked. Once a unit is unlocked a user can always return to that unit. The village, represented by the tipi icon in Figure 6, presents the user with a forum specific to that unit where users can ask and respond to unit-specific questions.

5.4.1. Unit Progress

Certain data pertaining to a user's progress on a unit is displayed on the learning path screen as seen in Figure 6. A progress bar informs the user how much of the unit they have completed, while four small circular blue icons indicating the four different learning skills (reading, writing, listing, and speaking) inform the user of which and how much of each of the skills they have practiced based on the icon's opacity.

5.5. Lessons

Lessons are presentations and explanations of new concepts in the form of multimedia cards with text, images, audio and speech recordings. The concepts range from vocabulary and sentence structure to pronunciation and phoneme distinction. These lessons are carefully designed and unchanging. The order of concepts will always be the same.

5.6. Exercises

To facilitate understanding and retention of the concepts introduced in the lessons, a series of exercises is presented after each set of 4 or 5 cards. Exercises test a user's knowledge of a word or pattern card by displaying one component of the card (the prompt) and requiring them to respond with another specified component of the card (the response).

Correct answers turn green and cause a pop-up to appear that rewards the user with points based on the type of exercise. If the user answers an exercise incorrectly, their answer turns red and a pop-up showing the correct answer

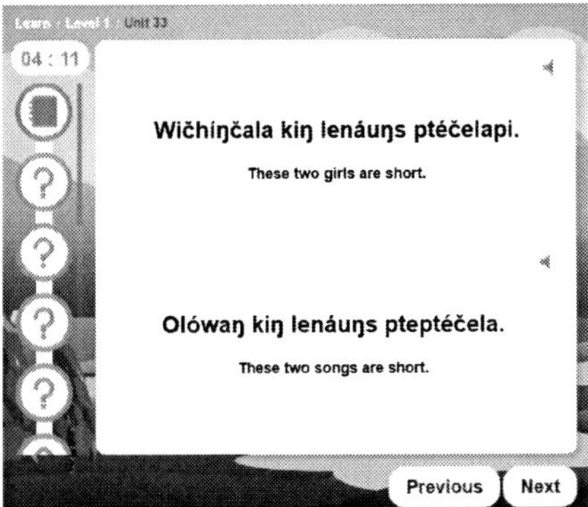

Figure 8: Example lesson concerning the adjective inflections for the word *short*.

appears giving the user time to read and listen to the correct response. That question will then reappear after the other cards in the lesson are quizzed, and will continue to reappear until they respond correctly, or reach a predetermined number of failed attempts. This is done in order to maintain flow and reduce discouragement, with the understanding that all of the concepts will reappear in the review sessions and more advanced units. After every response, the selected cards are colored green or red to indicate to the user that their response was either correct or incorrect, respectively.

5.6.1. Exercise Types Overview

The following are the types of exercises that a user can encounter depending on the unit and type of information presented. Each type of exercise satisfies certain learning skills: reading, listening, writing, and speaking. The listen-

Valid Prompt/Response Pairs by Exercise Type

Multiple-Choice, True/False											
Match-The-Pairs											
Typing, Fill-in-Blanks											
Anagram											
I-L	A-L	E-L	L-L	A-I	L-E	L-I	A-E	E-A	L-A	A-A	I-A

Legend: A: Lakota Audio, E: English text, I: Image, L: Lakota text

Figure 9: Exercise types and their valid types of prompt/response pairs for word cards.

ing skill is divided further into comprehension and phonemic awareness; and within the writing skill a distinction is made between active and passive spelling, where active writing exercises require the user to actively supply the letters or words from their memory, whereas with passive spelling the letters or words are provided to the user and they just have to place them in the correct places to render the word or sentence correct.

Different prompt-response pairs are valid depending on both the type of exercise and whether the prompt card is a word or a pattern. For example, a speaking exercise cannot require the user to type or select something; and a pattern

card can be difficult to represent unambiguously with an image.

5.6.2. True/False

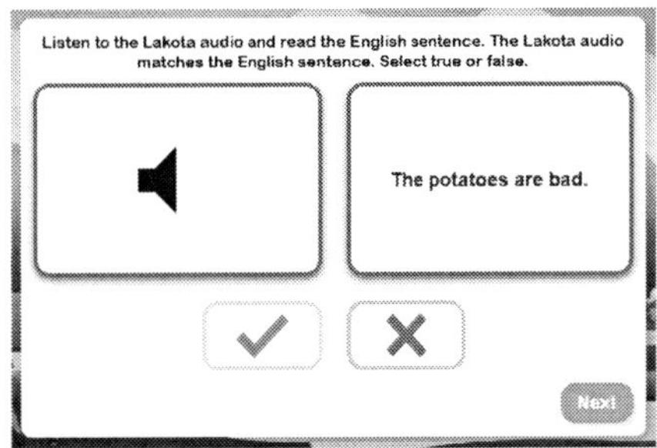

Figure 10: Example of a True/False exercise.

True/False activities are the simplest type of exercise and involve two types of questions. The user may be asked whether the prompt card is equivalent to the response card, or whether the response card correctly answers the prompt card's question.

5.6.3. Multiple Choice

Multiple choice exercises have a single prompt card with up to four options, one of which being the correct answer. For example, in Figure 11 the user listens to the audio prompt of a word card and must select the response among three options that correctly identifies the stressed syllable.

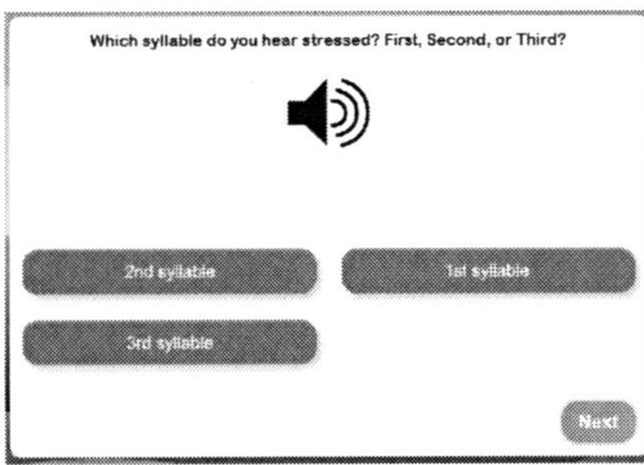

Figure 11: Example multiple-choice exercise.

5.6.4. Match-the-Pairs

Match-the-pairs exercises consist of a group of prompt cards all displaying the same card component and corresponding response cards displaying a different card component. The possible pairs are displayed in Figure 9. The user must first select a prompt card and then select the matching response card. After each attempt to create a pair, a pop-up either rewards the user with points if answered correctly, or displays the correct answer with the ability to listen to the audio version. The user continues making pairs until all prompt cards have been attempted, receiving points after each attempted pair.

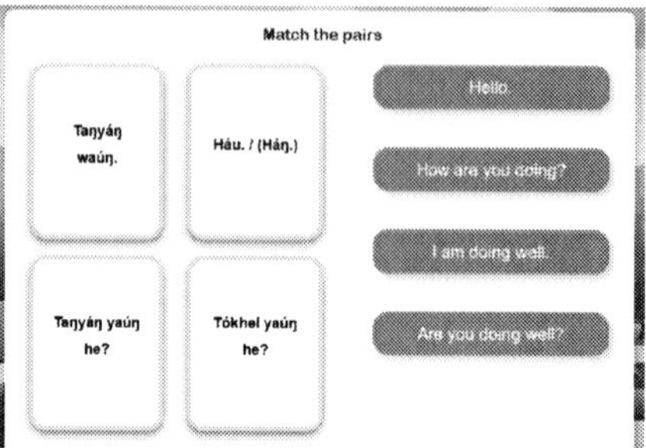

Figure 12: Example match-the-pairs exercise.

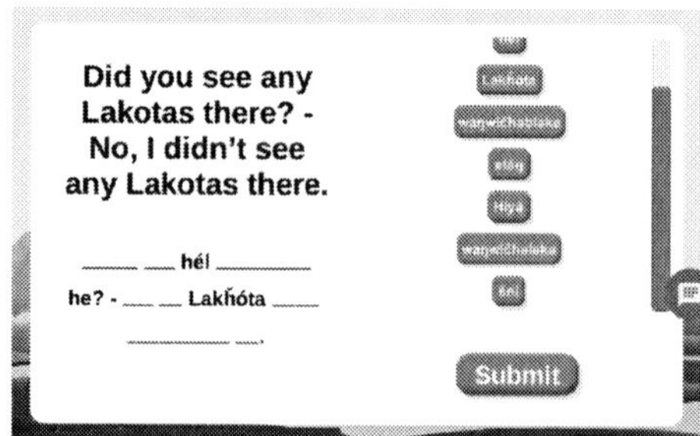

Figure 14: Example building blocks exercise.

5.6.5. Anagram

Anagram activities mark the beginning of the productive exercises with the learner being asked to produce accurate spellings with a constrained letter set. These activities prompt the user with either English text, Lakota audio, or an image, and a jumbled set of letters corresponding to the equivalent Lakota text. The user must drag and drop the letters to put them in the correct order. If any letter is in the wrong place, no points are rewarded.

5.6.6. Fill-in-the-Blanks

Fill-in-the-Blanks exercises present the user with a word or phrase with a missing phoneme or word important to the pattern at hand. Instructions guide the learner in their task, from selecting the correct phoneme based on audio to selecting the missing word in the phrase.

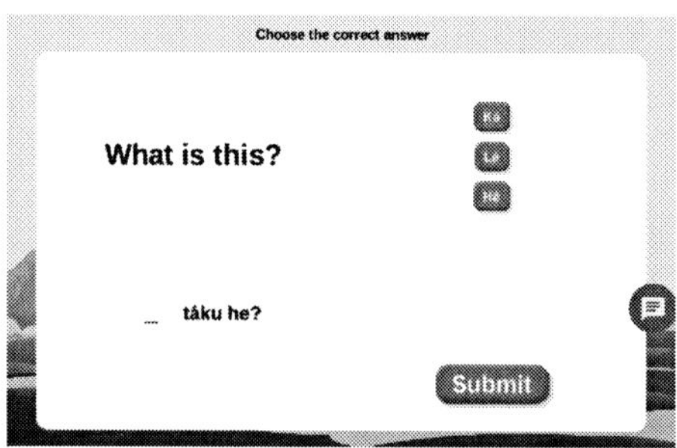

Figure 13: Example Fill-in-the-Blanks exercise.

5.6.7. Building Blocks

Building sentences is a leap in Lakota production. Building blocks exercises are a key first step in this pursuit. These exercises provide a varied prompt asking for a response in the form of rearranging words in the correct order to produce a coherent Lakota sentence.

5.6.8. Typing

As with other pedagogical tools, the computer keyboard and the ability to write with confidence are key components in language fluency in the modern world. The Lakota keyboard layouts for desktop and mobile devices were designed with ease of use and versatility in mind. The integration of the keyboard serves both as an exercise in Lakota typing and as a means to promote the production of full words and sentences from Lakota learners. Since this kind of production suggests a level of advancement in the learner, these exercises are limited to base curricula and later reintroduced as the learner proves excellency in vocabulary and concepts through easier exercises.

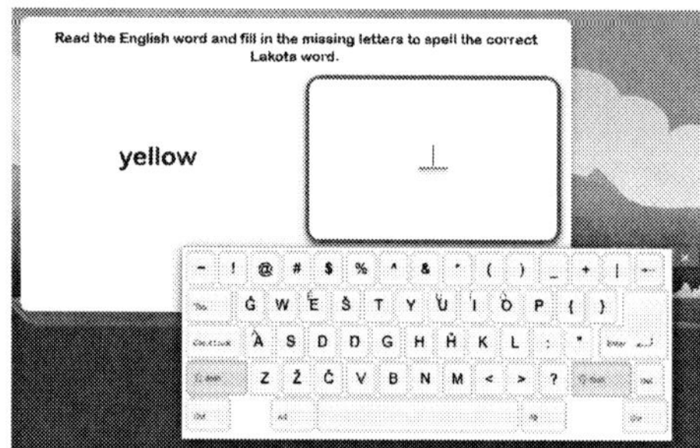

Figure 15: Example typing exercise.

5.6.9. Speaking

While fluency of speaking is still difficult to computationally judge in an environment with limited data and effective tools optimized for more common languages, the importance of eliciting speech from learners remains paramount. During the initial testing and release of Owóksape, existing speaking exercise features were left out for reasons of convenience and complexity, continued work on this aspect of the curriculum is promising. Learners will soon be able to listen to native speech and mimic it with some minor feedback based on pitch and syllable accuracy with greater cost efficient features on the horizon.

5.7. Review

Review sessions are an integral part of Owóksape, exposing the learner to words and patterns they have previously learned in a way that increases retention. A predetermined number of review activities is required at the end of each unit before the next unit is unlocked. There are two types of review sessions, a unit-specific review that tests only the concepts introduced in that unit, and a global review that tests all the cards a user has seen across all units.

The review activities are generated using the aforementioned spaced-repetition algorithm that pulls cards from

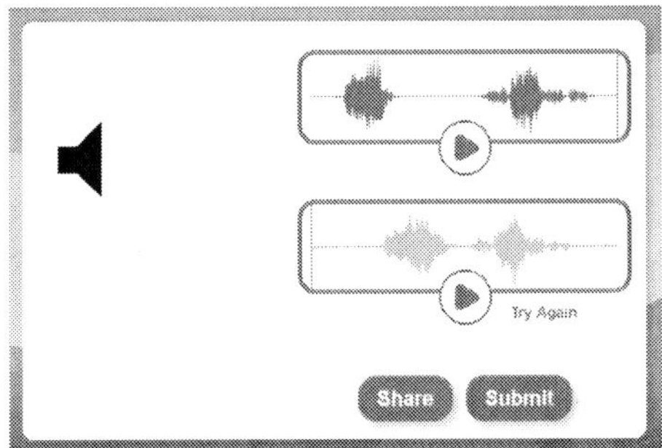

Figure 16: Example speaking exercise.

Activity Types for Word Cards

#	%	Learning Skill	Prompt Type	Response Type	Activity Types
1	25%	Reading	Lakota text	Image, English text	Multiple Choice, Match-The-Pairs
2	25%	Reading	English text, Image	Lakota text	Multiple Choice, Match-The-Pairs
3	50%	Listening	Lakota audio	English text	Multiple Choice, Match-The-Pairs
4	15%	Listening	Lakota audio	Lakota text	
5	2%	Listening	Lakota audio	Lakota text	Fill-in-the-Blanks
6	15%	Listening	Lakota audio	Lakota text	Anagram
7	1%	Listening / Writing	Lakota audio	Lakota text	Typing
8	15%	Writing	English text	Lakota text	Anagram
9	1%	Writing	English text	Lakota text	Typing

Note: "%" signifies percentage of cards presented via exercise of this type

Figure 17: The different activity types within the review session. Percentages are used to probabilistically select the activity type, resulting in an overall percentage of cards in the user's review card list that will be quizzed using that activity type.

four sorted lists corresponding to the four different learning skills. The *repetition_value* is computed for each card and equates to the importance of presenting the card to the user again. The smaller the value, the more important it is to quiz the user on it. Thus, the list is sorted numerically in ascending order. The lists are filled or updated every time a card is presented to the user, either in the form of an exercise or a review activity. Where the card gets placed in a given list is determined by its *repetition_value*, which comes from two calculations: Eq. (1), computes the average score of the last four activities concerning the specific card and the learning skill associated with that list, and Eq. (2), computes the final value that determines its place in the list.

$$\bar{x}_n = \frac{\sum_{i=n-3}^{n} \bar{x}_i}{4} \qquad (1)$$

where $\bar{x}_n$ and $\bar{x}_i$ are the average points awarded for the last four activities and for the ith activity, respectively, related to the current card.

$$repetition\_value = A \cdot \bar{x}_n + B \cdot d + C \cdot n \qquad (2)$$

where *repetition_value* refers to an integer that determines where in the review card list the card will be placed. A, B and C are coefficients that allow for fine adjustment of the parameters in order to optimize the algorithm's efficacy based on user data and statistics. $\bar{x}_n$ is the same as in Eq. (1). d is the time stamp of when the card was last reviewed. The larger the value, the more recently the user was exposed to the card and the less likely it will reappear. Lastly, n is the number of times the card has been presented.

The higher the number, the more practice with it the user has had and therefore the less likely it will be to reappear. The review activities contain a subset of the exercise types found in the quizzes in the learning session. However, instead of being predetermined, the review uses an algorithm to select the activity types, as well as the cards for each activity, in order to create four activities every time the frontend requests more.

This algorithm has three main features: 1) a table of activity types with associated prompt-response pairs and percentages is used to probabilistically select the activity type details, 2) the cards are selected from the user's review card lists to ensure they receive more attention (spaced-repetition), and 3) the combination of activity data and cards selected is used to generate the data for the four activities.

Figure 17 shows the activity types. This table, with its percentages, provides an efficient method of reducing the number of review activities while still testing an effective set of learning skills.

6. Software Overview

Owóksape consists of a web server, a web frontend, and mobile user interfaces. Together these three parts form a whole that provides wide access to the app, as well as an administrator interface for managing language content.

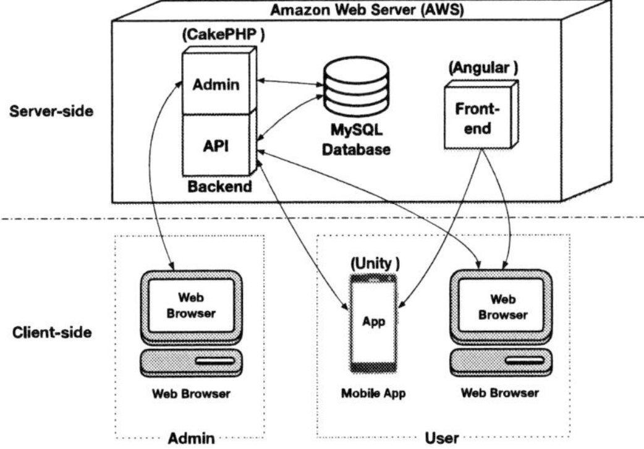

Figure 18: High-level overview of Owóksape's software architecture. Items in parentheses indicate the software development environment.

6.1. Web Server

The server design decisions of Owóksape were made based on two important goals. The first goal was that the app should lend itself well to a rapid development process. With this in mind, the CakePHP framework was chosen.

CakePHP utilizes the Model-View-Controller (MVC) architecture, a common software design pattern found in many web server frameworks. Rapid development is achieved through various command-line function calls allowing the rapid creation of template components.

The second goal was for the app to easily scale as the user base grows. To address this, the web server is situated in the Amazon Web Services (AWS) cloud. Thus, infrastructure and resource allocation that would otherwise be dependent on in-house hardware and network administrators is instead managed in simpler and safer terms through the AWS administration panel.

6.1.1. Application Programming Interface

The Application Programming Interface (API) is written primarily in PHP using the CakePHP framework. This API is used by both the web and mobile applications to obtain data related to users and learning modules. The API interfaces with a MySQL database using CakePHP's built-in Object-relational mapping (ORM) functionality, allowing conversion between the database and object-oriented data structures in PHP.

6.1.2. Admin Interface

Within the web server CakePHP framework is an admin interface enabling the team to create, upload and manage language components, lessons, exercises, images, audio, video, etc. This provides a user-friendly environment for maintaining the MySQL database that stores all information concerning language learning content. Cards containing language data, metadata and references to media can be created and edited individually, or uploaded in bulk from a spreadsheet.

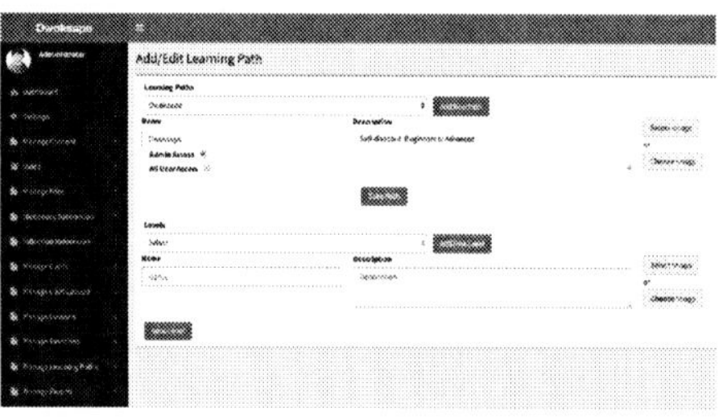

Figure 19: Administrator interface to the web server and database allowing management of language and app data.

6.2. User Platforms

The user applications consist of a web interface for modern desktop browsers and a mobile interface for Android and iOS devices. The web app uses the open-source Typescript-based Angular web application framework, which was selected for various reasons: it has a large community, is open-source, promotes quick development, and is designed for single-page dynamic websites.

The mobile apps are developed using Unity, a cross-platform engine that allows for development of the Android and iOS platforms using a single Integrated Development Environment (IDE). It takes a C# Unity application and outputs versions for Android and iOS.

7.   Project Effort

The Owóksape project started with a grant and design documents in 2016. In late 2017 DreamzTech Solutions, a software development firm from India, was contracted to rapidly build the applications while working closely with the in-house development team until the initial alpha release in 2018. The team consisted of five full-time employees comprising the following roles: linguistics manager, linguistics assistant, software manager, software reviewer, PHP backend developer, Angular frontend developer and a mobile developer. From 2019, the software team was reduced to 2-3 full-time employees. The first official version of Owóksape was released October 10th, 2019.

8.   Future of Owóksape

As Owóksape's user base continues to grow, the development team at The Language Conservancy continues to provide support and develop new features. Near-term additions to the app include a teacher portal, new learning paths, one for vocabulary and another dedicated to the Lakota Grammar Handbook (Ullrich and Black Bear Jr., 2016), and custom review sessions.

8.1. Teacher Portal

Owóksape has provided a complementary learning environment to classrooms. However, what is missing is the ability for Lakota teachers to create customized paths that reflect what they are teaching in their classrooms, as well as the ability to oversee the progress of their students within the app. Teachers will be able to create tracks by selecting and ordering existing units within Owóksape via a teacher administrator interface.

8.2. New Learning Paths

Currently, Owóksape offers a single learning path that is based on the Lakota Audio Series (Lakota Language Consortium, 2014). Soon a new track dedicated to building vocabulary, and another dedicated to the 600-page Lakota Grammar Handbook will be added. Another likely path is the merging of the Lakota dictionary with Owóksape's database, turning the app into a dictionary, with simpler and more reliable unit construction by users and teachers (Lakota Language Consortium Inc, 2018). There is also a plan to offer activities using longer narratives and texts recorded from fluent speakers.

8.3. Supporting Other Languages

While the original goal of Owóksape was to target the Lakota language, its success has predicted viability in extending its support to other under-resourced languages. Dakota is the most viable next language, since it is mutually intelligible with Lakota. The cultural and linguistics milieu of future supported languages would be incorporated after making the main app features language-agnostic. This effort would not be difficult and would largely involve replacing the underlying database and creating a shared core application that would use non-language-specific terms.

9.   Acknowledgments

We thank The Language Conservancy, the Lakota Language Consortium Inc, Ben Black Bear, Jr., Iris Eagle Chasing. The project was also made possible through funding from the Administration for Native Americans, Lush Fresh Made Cosmetics, Santa Fe Natural Tobacco, South Dakota Community Foundation, and San Manuel Band of Mission Indians.

10.   Bibliographical References

Chelliah, S., (2018). *Fieldwork for language description*, pages 51–73. 10.

Deloria, E. C. (1932). *Dakota Texts*, volume 14. G. E. Stechert & Co, New York.

Ebbinghaus, H. (1885). Memory: A contribution to experimental psychology, trans. *HA Ruger & CE Bussenius. Teachers College.[rWvH]*.

Epps, P. L., Webster, A. K., and Woodbury, A. C. (2017). A holistic humanities of speaking: Franz boas and the continuing centrality of texts. *International Journal of American Linguistics*, 83(1):41–78.

Hakuta, K. (2006). Prefabricated patterns and the emergence of structure in second language acquisition. *Language Learning*, 24:287 – 297, 10.

Kramár, E. A., Babayan, A. H., Gavin, C. F., Cox, C. D., Jafari, M., Gall, C. M., Rumbaugh, G., and Lynch, G. (2012). Synaptic evidence for the efficacy of spaced learning. *Proceedings of the National Academy of Sciences*, 109(13):5121–5126.

Ullrich, J. and Black Bear Jr., B. (2016). *Lakota Grammar Handbook*. Lakota Language Consortium, Inc., Bloomington, IN, USA, 1st edition.

11.   Language Resource References

Lakota Language Consortium Inc. (2018). *New Lakota Dictionary. Version 1.1. May 24, 2018. URL: https://lakhota.org*.

Lakota Language Consortium. (2014). *Lakota Audio Series: A Practical Conversation Course Vol 1. 2014. URL: http://www.llcbookstore.com/lakota-audio-series-a-practical-conversation-course-vol-1/*.

Lakota Languge Consortium Inc. (2019). *Owóksape. Version 1.5. Dec. 9, 2019. URL: https://owoksape.com*.

Proceedings of the 1st Joint SLTU and CCURL Workshop (SLTU-CCURL 2020), pages 330–335
Language Resources and Evaluation Conference (LREC 2020), Marseille, 11–16 May 2020
© European Language Resources Association (ELRA), licensed under CC-BY-NC

A Corpus of the Sorani Kurdish Folkloric Lyrics

Sina Ahmadi[1], Hossein Hassani[2], Kamaladdin Abedi[3]
[1]Insight Centre for Data Analytics, National University of Ireland Galway - Ireland
[2]University of Kurdistan Hewlêr, Kurdistan Region - Iraq
[3]Kurdistan University of Medical Sciences, Sanandaj, Iran
[1]sina.ahmadi@insight-centre.org, [2]hosseinh@ukh.edu.krd, [3]kamal.abedi@gmail.com

Abstract

Kurdish poetry and prose narratives were historically transmitted orally and less in a written form. Being an essential medium of oral narration and literature, Kurdish lyrics have had a unique attribute in becoming a vital resource for different types of studies, including Digital Humanities, Computational Folkloristics and Computational Linguistics. As an initial study of its kind for the Kurdish language, this paper presents our efforts in transcribing and collecting Kurdish folk lyrics as a corpus that covers various Kurdish musical genres, in particular *Beyt*, *Goranî*, *Bend*, and *Heyran*. We believe that this corpus contributes to Kurdish language processing in several ways, such as compensation for the lack of a long history of written text by incorporating oral literature, presenting an unexplored realm in Kurdish language processing, and assisting the initiation of Kurdish computational folkloristics. Our corpus contains 49,582 tokens in the Sorani dialect of Kurdish. The corpus is publicly available in the Text Encoding Initiative (TEI) format for non-commercial use under the CC BY-NC-SA 4.0 license at `https://github.com/KurdishBLARK/KurdishLyricsCorpus`.

Keywords: Computational Folkloristics, less-resourced languages, lyrics corpus, Kurdish

1. Introduction

Kurdish is considered a less-resourced language for which general-purpose grammars and raw internet-based corpora are the only existing resources (Hassani, 2018). While the lack of a long history of written text is considered as one of the reasons for this situation, the lack of research and activities on data collection are also counted as other reasons in this regard (Ahmadi et al., 2019).

Folkloric content play a significant role in Kurdish life as a crucial medium in communication between different Kurdish generations (Blum and Hassanpour, 1996). They are also a rich source of vocabulary, as they have mostly been traditionally transferred over generations orally and less in a written form (Kreyenbroek, 2005). A few but crucial efforts have been made to transcribe some products of the Kurdish oral literature in the beginning of the previous century by both western and eastern scholars (Rasul, 1999; Salimi, 2015; Mikailee, 2015). Because these transcripts are mainly available in hard copy and not electronic forms, they are not suitable for computational processes. On the other hand, the lack of optical character recognition systems for Kurdish prevents the automatic conversion of these resources into text formats.

Despite the limited number of resources for Kurdish, there have been various studies to create new corpora. Esmaili et al. (2013) present *Pewan*, a general-purpose corpus based on the news articles in Sorani and Kurmanji dialects of Kurdish. Similarly, Ataman (2018) presents a parallel corpus containing Kurmanji Kurdish news articles. With a particular focus on automatic identification of subdialects, Malmasi (2016) creates a corpus using articles from news sources. In the most recent attempt, Abdulrahman et al. (2019) present the Kurdish Textbooks Corpus (KTC), which is composed of 31 K-12 textbooks in Sorani dialect. Unlike previous resources which are based on news articles, the latter is more domain-specific. However, none of these resources deals with oral material and Kurdish folkloric heritage.

In this paper, we present a corpus of folkloric lyrics and songs in Sorani Kurdish containing 12, 8, 141, and 1 item respectively for four musical genres, namely *Bend*, *Beyt*, *Goranî*, and *Heyran*. The development of the corpus is carried out by transcribing folkloric songs manually from audiovisual materials and transforming the transcription into a structured format in XML according to the Text Encoding Initiative (TEI) (Ide and Véronis, 1995). Moreover, our project could be considered as an initiative to mobilize the Kurdish community to provide further documentations for the Kurdish oral literature.

This corpus can serve various aspects of natural language processing (NLP) for the Kurdish language. While it enriches the diversity of the available datasets and corpora, it also adds a set of folkloric vocabulary which could not be found in the prose and non-poetic Kurdish writing. Furthermore, the computational folkloristics (Abello et al., 2012), which has not been addressed in the context of Kurdish studies yet, can also benefit from the result of this research. As the collected songs are performed by different local singers, this can provide further insights into the subdialectal variations of Sorani Kurdish and therefore, will be beneficial to speech recognition tasks.

The rest of this paper is organized as follows. Section 2 provides an overview of the Kurdish folklore and presents the major types of Kurdish lyrics emphasizing on those that are presented in our corpus. In Section 3, we summarize what has been done with respect to the Kurdish folklore. Section 4 presents the corpus and illustrates some statistics about it. The evaluation of the corpus is given in Section 5. Finally, Section 6 concludes the paper.

2. Kurdish Folklore

The Kurdish folklore has been addressed as the major pillar of the Kurdish literature by eastern and western scholars (Salimi, 2015; Allison, 2001; Abubakir, 2016). Traditionally, this folklore is transmitted orally. They have been influencer of and influenced by other surrounding cultures and folklores (Leezenberg and others, 2011; Rasul, 1999).

Given the diversity of dialects of the Kurdish language, there are many types and genres which are specific to each dialect. Similarly, the content of the transmitted songs might not be identical among these dialects. Furthermore, such a diversity brings a different terminology with itself which might not be similar in all dialects. For instance, the individuals who perform songs are called by different terms, such as *Dengbêj* (bard), *Stranbêj* (minstrel), and *Çirokbêj* (storyteller) in Kurmanji (Broughton et al., 2006) and, *Goranîbêj*, *Heyranbêj*, and *Beytbêj* (and *xoşxwan*) in Sorani. While *Çirokbêj* and *Dengbêj* are used interchangeably in some contexts, they refer to different types of performing (Bocheńska, 2014). In Kurmanji speaking areas, *Dengbêj* is used in a broader context as a person who sings different types of music and also plays certain instruments while singing the song (Reigle, 2014).

According to Mikailee (2015), there has not been significant academic research on the Kurdish lyrics. A survey over the existing literature indicates that there is not a common categorization for the Kurdish lyrics and further discussions about the origin of the lyrics have been ongoing among scholars (Rasul, 1999; Hassanpour, 2005). Hassanpour (2005) discusses the multi-root nature of Kurdish songs. Moreover, a common opinion states that the Kurdish lyrics have been influenced by Turkish, Arabic, Azeri, Persian, and Armenian music during a long interconnection among these ethnics (Rasul, 1999; Leezenberg and others, 2011; Hassanpour, 2005).

Given the diversity of the Kurdish lyrics in form and genres, we only focus on four types of Sorani Kurdish folkloric songs, namely, *Beyt*, *Bend*, *Goranî* and *Heyran*. A few examples of these types are illustrated in Figure 1 for comparison.

2.1. Bend

Bend is a genre of Kurdish secular narrative recital song which is performed by *bendbêj* or *şayîyer*, commonly at rural gatherings and weddings. There is no evidence to indicate when Bend dates back in the history, but a strong element of praise and adoration as one of its most important components, and also a rich structure full of love, village lifestyle, farming work, nature description, local mystics, local lords, rebellions, and warfare stories guide us to assume that it may return to where the first Kurdish local social and political power was formed (Hamelink, 2016; Brenneman, 2016). Another important feature of Bends is the improvisation element which has been evolved over time, dealing with important political and especially social issues of the day. Recently an element of nationalism has been added to Bend, making it much powerful and widespread all over the Sorani-speaking regions and sometimes even in the regions which speak other dialects such as Southern Kurdish and Kurmanji (Christensen, 2007).

2.2. Beyt

Beyt is a term in Sorani dialect for a type of lyric which is usually a long piece of work based on different subjects, such as historical, mythical, legendary, and love figures and events (Merati, 2015; Salimi, 2015). Beyts have different contexts, such as epics, historical battles, mythical tales, fables, and tragic love stories (Rasul, 1999; Sharifi, 2005; Barzegar Khaleghi, 2009; Mikailee, 2015). In some Sorani speaking areas, the term Bend is used interchangeably along with Beyt. However, Bend is usually used with a more popular content . *Beytbêj*, literally meaning Beyt sayer, recites beyt in gatherings (Barzegar Khaleghi, 2009). Although Beyts are poetic, they do not follow any particular standard for their form or size (Barzegar Khaleghi, 2009). The transcription of Beyts in Sorani dates back to the 1900s (Rasul, 1999; Sharifi, 2005). 17 Beyts were transcribed around 1905, which were translated into Sorani Kurdish in 1975 (Rasul, 1999; Sharifi, 2005; Mikailee, 2015). From 1950s onward, other transcriptions started to appear (Mikailee, 2015). According to Sharifi (2005) and Mikailee (2015) during 1960s major transcripts were presented in Sorani Kurdish. In some cases, these transcripts were provided along with the translation into other languages, for instance, Persian (Sharifi, 2005). The transcripts by Qader Fattahi Qazi (also spelled as Ghader Fattahi Ghazi) (Sharifi, 2005; Mikailee, 2015) are examples of the efforts in this area which are also one of the major sources of the Beyts section in our corpus.

2.3. Goranî

In addition to a specific genre, the term *Goranî* is also one of the words for "song" in Sorani Kurdish. It should not be confused with the Goranî dialect[1]. There is a fine line between what is referred to with the term Goranî and with other terms such as *Stran*, *Beste*, and *Meqam* (Salimi, 2015) in different dialects and regions. The terms are observed to be used interchangeably across the Kurdish speaking areas regardless of the dominant dialect.
The themes of *Goranî* come from diverse contexts. This diversity creates different types of *Goranî* for various occasions such as wedding, birth, feasts and funeral, and various feelings, such as love, happiness and hope (Broughton et al., 2006).
A special form of *Goranî* is *Meqam* which has different characteristics among the speakers of different Kurdish dialects. For example, it is essentially used in religious practices in some Kurdish groups (Merati, 2015), while it is a special lyric whose main motif is a love story among other groups. It is usually performed without musical accompaniment.

2.4. Heyran

It is a form of lyric which mostly tells love stories, but it could also be about tragic stories and actions of heroes in the battles (Merati, 2015). The *Heyranbêj*, literally meaning the sayer of Heyran, is the one who performs Heyran. According to Merati (2015), it is a lyric form which is performed in Sorani and mostly in the Iraqi and Iranian Kurdistan. In the Kurdistan Region of Iraq, this type of lyric is

---

[1]also written as Guranî.

Bend		Goranî	
…	…	نۆی کاکی جووتیار، ئەی وەی ڕێم توولانییە	O, the ploughman, my way is long
دیمەن زۆر بە ئەدایە	*Dîmen* is very mischief	یاری هاودەردم، ئەی وەی موکریانییە	My caring companion is from Mokriyan
چیمەن جوان پێدەکەنێ	*Çîmen* smiles beautifully	ئەرێ خاڵۆ ڕێبوار، ئەی وەی ڕێنگام کوێستانە	O, dear traveller, mountain is on my way
کاک خالید سەرکەوتوو بێ	(may) *Kak Xalîd* be successful	دەچم بۆ لای یار، ئەی وەی خاوەن بێستانە	I am going to my companion, (she) owns a garden
هەتا خاکی لەندەنێ	until the land of London	ئامان ئامان...	Aman, Aman…
پڕ بە دڵ دەنگ هەڵدێنم	I scream with full voice	نۆی کاکی جووتیار، ئەی وەی جووتت شاگوڵ بێ	O, the ploughman, (may) your plough (brings) big clusters
هەر وەک کەوی بەندەنێ	just like mountain partridge	تووەکەت ڕازیانە، کاکم خەرمانت گوڵ بێ	(may) your seeds (be) fennel, your harvest (be) flower
ئەگریجەی لوول و خاوت	your frizzy soft hairs	ئەرێ کاکی ڕێبوار، ئەی وەی ڕێم توولانییە	O, dear traveller, my way is long
بخە تۆقی گەردنم	put (them) over my neck	بۆخۆم غەریبم، خاڵۆ یارم بۆکانییە	(I) am a stranger, dear, my companion is from Bokan
مەحاڵە ڕەهاییم بێ	(it) is impossible to get free		
هەتا کاتی مردنم	until my death		
داوێک لە زوڵفی خاوت	a strand of your hair		
بۆم بخە نێو کفنم	put (it) into my shroud		
…	…		

Beyt		Heyran	
…	…	…	…
جیهانپەیما سوڵتانە	*Cîhanpeyma* is Sultan	جا کوتی ئەوجارەکە دەبێ هەموو ڕۆژان بێی بۆ ئێرەکانە	then, (he) said henceforth (you) should come here every day
بۆ ڕۆژی لێ قەومانە	(it) is (made) for the day of catastrophe	کوتی ئاخر بە بێ قسەی ساحێبیم ناتوانم بێم بۆ ئێرە	(she) said, but I cannot come here without my lord's permission
جیهانپەیما بوو سم خڕ	*Cîhanpeyma* had round hooves	ئەورۆش بە بێ ئیجازە هاتووم	even today (I) have come without permission
گوێ مەقەست و مەنزڵ بڕ	Ears (like) scissors and cutter (=sharp)	ئاخیری تینی بۆ هێنا	Finally, (he) got mad
نرکەی دێ وەکوو کوڕکوڕ	(it) neighs like sandgrouse	کوتی ئەگەر بزانم نایەوە	(he) said if I know that you do not come back
لە بۆ خەزای گاور قڕ	(which) ends infidels' destiny	ئەمن ئێستا جەللادان دێنم لە سەرت دەن	(I) will call upon the hangmen
جیهان پەیما بەحرییە	*Cîhanpeyma* is of sea	ئەویش تینی لێ پەیدا بوو وەیزانی ڕاس دەکا	then (she) got mad believing him
قەترێک نێوچاوانی سپییە	A drop between his eyes is white	کوتی بەڵێ شەرت بێ بە شەرتی پیاوان	(she) said alright, I promise solemnly,
کەس وڵاغی وای نییە	No one has such a beast	ئەگەر ئیزنم دەی ئەمن دێمەوە	If you allow me, I will come back
عەسڵە شێر خەزاڵییە	(it) is original, (like a) gazelle	…	…
…	…		

Figure 1: A comparison of the four genres included in our corpus. The translations are literal and additional words are provided in parentheses. Proper names are italicized.

also called by the same name. However, a similar type is called *Lawik* in the Kurmanji-speaking areas of Iraq which is usually longer than Heyran (Merati, 2015). According to Merati (2015), the stanza of Heyran is constructed on three verses with three rhymes in each verse.

2.5. Other Forms of Kurdish Lyrics

As it was mentioned earlier, Kurdish lyrics are not restricted to the forms presented here. They are diverse in their form, colorful in their themes, and varied in their subjects and contexts. Some of these forms are particular to certain dialects, while some are common among the dialects.

One example of these forms is *Hore*. It is particular to Hawramî (Goranî) and the Southern Kurdish dialects, spoken in the Kurdish speaking regions of Iran and Iraq. *Hore* is assumed to be a type of singing with more than several thousand years of history (Merati, 2015). Another example is *Çamary*, which is a song in mourning circumstances, particularly, for the death of socially important individuals (Merati, 2015).

3. Related Work

In this section, we address the related work regarding the collection of folkloric content and lyrics as resources in other Kurdish dialects and also other languages.

Regarding Kurdish, Hamelink and Barış (2014) created a corpus from Kurmanji lyrics. This corpus includes 84 *Kilam*s (or *Kelam*s) (Merati, 2015) which is a title for a type of music mostly in Kurmanji speaking areas, though with different attributes, depending on the geographical position of the community in which the music is performed (Hamelink and Barış, 2014).

Regarding other languages, a famous work on the English song lyrics is The Million Song dataset (Mahieux et al., 2011) which is a freely-available collection of audio features and metadata for a million contemporary popular music tracks. Moreover, Taft (1977) collected over two thousand texts which were performed by about 350 blues (an African-American music genre) singers. Mahedero et al. (2005) presents experiments on lyrics using NLP methods to identify lyrics' language, thematic categorization, structure extraction and to perform similarity searches. This research suggested that information which acoustic and cultural metadata would have been providing could be further improved when they are accompanied by lyrics. McNeil (2018) reports the collection of folklore poetry and popular song lyrics alongside other forms to develop a Tunisian Arabic corpus.

The application of lyric processing in music analysis have been investigated from a variety of perspectives. For example, Hu et al. (2009) conducted research to examine the role that lyric texts could play in the mood classification in audio music. They found the lyric features can outperform audio features in the classification of mood categories in certain cases. They also found that combining lyrics and audio features improve performances on a majority of mood classification categories.

Also, Rodrigues et al. (2019) developed a corpus of English lyrics which they expected that would assist in testing and evaluation of tools pertinent to the language generation in the poetry and lyrics context.

In the same vein, the International Workshop on Folk Music Analysis (FMA)[2] is an annual workshop dedicated to folk music analysis since 2011. The computational folklorisitics has been a repetitive theme in this workshop series wherein many scholars have reported on variety of corpora which have been developed based on various ethnic and national folklore (for example, see (Holzapfel, 2014), (Beauguitte et al., 2016), and (Ali-MacLachlan and Hockman, 2019)). Although the dominant area of these workshops is about musicology, some attempts concerning language processing are observed. For instance, (Strle and Marolt, 2014) reported on the collection of 1,965 variants of Slovenian folk narrative poems to evaluate the effectiveness of two different methods of semantic analysis in NLP.

4. Lyrics Corpus

We transcribed a set of 162 songs in various genres in the four types of Kurdish folkloric materials: *Bend, Beyt, Goranî*, and *Heyran*. Given the wide range of Kurdish dialects and sub-dialects, we only focused on the Sorani dialect of Kurdish which is mostly spoken in the Kurdish regions in Iran and Iraq. As a song may have been performed by many singers, we considered the recording quality and authenticity of the lyrics as the criteria to select one.

4.1. Text Transcription

The transcription process was carried out by native Kurdish speakers by listening to the audiovisual materials. In order to find such content easily and also receive feedback from others regarding our transcription quality, we created a channel on the Telegram Messenger[3] where we regularly published the lyrics along with the audiovisual material over four months. Table 1 provides the statistics of the corpus.

Two main challenges in transcribing the lyrics were the quality of the recording, which was low in some cases, and the way that the singer articulated the words. In many cases, we observed that some words were not pronounced clearly and some parts of the lyrics are left incomplete due to the rhythm. In such cases, we tried to write the lyrics based on various performances of the same song.

Genre	Number of songs	Number of tokens (characters)
Bend	12	6455 (56,723)
Beyt	8	17994 (200,981)
Goranî	141	22588 (212,408)
Heyran	1	2545 (2273)
Total	162	49,582 (472,385)

Table 1: Statistics of the lyrics corpus

4.2. Conversion to TEI

We converted the transcribed songs into TEI format, which is based on XML. The XML format provides a structured form to represent segments in the lyrics and metadata of

---


```
<text id="131">
  <div type="song">
      <head>هەرزاڵێ</head>
      <singer>ناسر ڕەزازی</singer>
      <audio>Audio/Gorani/131.mp3</audio>
      <lg type="Gorani">
          <l>هەرزاڵێ، براکەم هەرزاڵێ</l>
          <l>هەرزاڵ چاترە لە ماڵێ</l>
          <l>ئەو چۆپیکێشە چۆپی ئەکێشێ</l>
          <l>لە خوام گەرەکە، هیچکوێنەی نەیشێ</l>
          <l>هەرزاڵێ، براکەم هەرزاڵێ</l>
          <l>هەرزاڵ چاترە لە ماڵێ</l>
          <l>یان بە گوڵباخی یان بە گوڵەزەردە</l>
          <l>یان بە نازی خۆت بمکە پەروەردە</l>
          <l>هەرزاڵێ، براکەم هەرزاڵێ</l>
          <l>هەرزاڵ چاترە لە ماڵێ</l>
          <l>توخوا چۆپیکێش چۆپیت بە لەنگەر</l>
          <l>هەر وەک پێشمەرگە ڕوو بکە لە سەنگەر</l>
      </lg>
  </div>
```

Figure 2: A transcribed song converted in TEI

each song, including song name, singer's name, URL to the audio file, song ID, and the type of the song. Regarding the name of the songs, we used a title that is most frequently known to the public. We used the refrains to give the title to the songs for which we could not find any title. However, some of the Bends left without a title due to lack of a refrain or a popular title. Figure 2 presents the XML structure of a song of Goranî genre. It should be noted that the attributes are customized and are not defined elsewhere in TEI.

Some of the lyrics are composed of classical Kurdish poems. We use `type="poem"` attribute to distinguish these parts from the folkloric lyrics. In addition, Beyt and Heyran performers usually provide comments in plain language to facilitate the comprehension of the story and guarantee the story flow. We use `type="comment"` to highlight performer's comments.

5. Evaluation

In addition to the statistics of the corpus in Table 1, we evaluate the content by comparing it with two other Sorani Kurdish corpora, Pewan (Esmaili and Salavati, 2013) and KTC (Abdulrahman et al., 2019) which are respectively general-purpose and domain-specific.

Calculating the frequency of words is a measure to understand how they semantically form the resources. Table 2 presents the ten most frequent tokens in our corpus and the two other Sorani Kurdish corpora. Although all these words are function words, i.e., a word whose purpose is to contribute to the syntax rather than the meaning of a sentence, they are not similarly distributed in the lyrics against the two other resources. The frequency of pronouns is observed in the lyrics text, which indicates the narrative nature of the folkloric songs. In addition, punctuation signs, which are commonly used in formal writing in the two other resources, are not frequently used in the lyrics.

In the same vein, Table 3 provides the ten most frequent words excluding the function words. The Pewan corpus has words associated with politics, as it was created based on the news articles. On the other hand, KTC has a more diverse range of words since it contains many domain-specific topics, from geography to linguistics and theology. Regarding the lyrics corpus, the most frequent non-function words are oriented around poetic and literary themes. Moreover, lyrics vocabulary can be used to analyze the semantic change thanks to archaism.

One other evaluation measure is linguistic representativeness (Gray et al., 2017). As the lyrics corpus contains various Sorani sub-dialects, various dialectal differences in the lexical choice and morphology are observed. Among the non-function words, we counted 7,316 tokens in the lyrics which do not exist among the 946,569 unique tokens of a basic Sorani Kurdish dictionary (Ahmadi et al., 2019) and the two other corpora. Having said that, considering lemmatization, which was not possible due to lack of tools for Kurdish, we expect that this number of words decreases to some extent, but still leaving a considerable number of words that could be added to the dictionaries.

Our corpus	KTC (Abdulrahman et al., 2019)	Pewan (Esmaili et al., 2013)
لە (from)	و	لە
بە (to)	لە	و
و (and)	بە	بە
بۆ (for)	که (that)	بۆ
بێ (without)	بۆ	/
ئەو (she/he/it/that)	ئەو	که (that)
من (I/me)	ئەم (this/it)	ئەو
تۆ (you)	.	-
ئەی/ئەوەی/ئانای (O, oh)	:	:
ھەر (only, each)	‘	]

Table 2: The 10 most frequent tokens in our corpus versus two other Sorani Kurdish corpora. The common tokens are highlighted in bold.

Our corpus	KTC (Abdulrahman et al., 2019)	Pewan (Esmaili et al., 2013)
گیان (soul, dear (adjective))	مرۆڤ (human)	کوردستان (Kurdistan)
دەڵێم ((I) say)	گەورە (big)	عێراق (Iraq)
دەکەم ((I) do)	کورد (Kurd, Kurdish)	ھەرێمی (region of)
دەبێ ((it) should)	خودای (god, god of)	سەرۆکی (president of)
وەرە (come (imperative))	کوردستان (Kurdistan)	ھەولێر (Erbil)
کرد ((she/he/it) did)	واتە ((it) means)	حکومەتی (government of)
دڵ (heart)	زمانی (language of)	شاری (city of)
گوڵ (flower)	پێویستە ((it) is needed)	ئێران (Iran)
شەو (night)	مافی (right of)	ئەنجومەنی (parliament of)
خۆم (myself)	وزەی (energy of)	ئەمەریکا (USA)

Table 3: The 10 most frequent tokens, excluding function words, in our corpus versus two other Sorani Kurdish corpora

6. Conclusion

We presented a corpus of folkloric lyrics in the Sorani dialect of Kurdish. The corpus contains lyrics of 162 songs (49,582 tokens) in four Kurdish musical genres: 12, 141, 8 and 1 songs in Bend, Goranî, Beyt and Heyran, respectively. We demonstrated that the current resource provides additional linguistic information, which is not represented in other Sorani Kurdish corpora.

This work is initial in using Sorani lyrics as a source for Kurdish language processing. Therefore, numerous areas could be counted for further developments, such as named-entity recognition, relation extraction, computational musicology and co-reference resolution. Another future work could be the enrichment of this corpus by adding content in other Kurdish dialects and by translating them into other languages, particularly English. We believe that development of such resources will pave the way for further developments in Kurdish language processing, therefore helping it to become a resourceful language. Since the Arabic script of Kurdish has proved to pose challenges in Kurdish text processing (Ahmadi, 2019), we would suggest the transliteration of the corpus into the Latin script, as it is also mostly used in the Kurmanji dialect.

The corpus is publicly available for non-commercial use under the CC BY-NC-SA 4.0 license at `https://github.com/KurdishBLARK/KurdishLyricsCorpus`[4].

7. Acknowledgements

The authors would like to thank the anonymous reviewers for their insightful suggestions and careful reading of the manuscript.

8. Bibliographical References

Abdulrahman, R., Hassani, H., and Ahmadi, S. (2019). Developing a fine-grained corpus for a less-resourced language: the case of Kurdish. *WiNLP ACL 2019*.

Abello, J., Broadwell, P., and Tangherlini, T. R. (2012). Computational folkloristics. *Communications of the ACM*, 55(7):60–70.

Abubakir, N. H. R. (2016). *Bringing Kurdish Music to the West*. Ph.D. thesis, University of Kansas.

Ahmadi, S., Hassani, H., and McCrae, J. P. (2019). Towards Electronic Lexicography for the Kurdish Language. In *Proceedings of the eLex 2019 conference*, pages 881–906, Sintra, Portugal, 1–3 October. Brno: Lexical Computing CZ, s.r.o.

Ahmadi, S. (2019). A rule-based Kurdish text transliteration system. *Asian and Low-Resource Language Information Processing (TALLIP)*, 18(2):18:1–18:8.

Ali-MacLachlan, I. and Hockman, J. (2019). *Proceedings of the 9th International Workshop on Folk Music Analysis (FMA2019), 2-4 July, 2019*. Birmingham City University.

Allison, C. (2001). *The Yezidi Oral Tradition in Iraqi Kurdistan*. Routledge.

Ataman, D. (2018). Bianet: A Parallel News Corpus in Turkish, Kurdish and English. *arXiv preprint arXiv:1805.05095*.

---

[4]`https://creativecommons.org/licenses/by-nc-sa/4.0/`

Barzegar Khaleghi, M. (2009). Kurdish Myths and Legends. *Kavoshnameh - Journal of Research in Persian Language and Literature*, 18:201–223. [In Farsi].

Beauguitte, P., Duggan, B., and Kelleher, J. (2016). *Proceedings of the 6th International Workshop on Folk Music Analysis, 15-17 June, 2016*. Dublin Institute of Technology.

Blum, S. and Hassanpour, A. (1996). 'the morning of freedom rose up': Kurdish popular song and the exigencies of cultural survival. *Popular Music*, 15(3):325–343.

Bocheńska, J. (2014). Kurdish Contemporary Literature in Search for Ordo Amoris-Some Reflections on the Continuity of the Kurdish Literary Tradition and Ethics. *Nûbihar Akademî*, 1(1):35–54.

Brenneman, R. L. (2016). *As strong as the mountains: A Kurdish cultural journey*. Waveland Press.

Broughton, S., Ellingham, M., Lusk, J., and Clark, D. A. (2006). *The Rough Guide to World Music: Africa & Middle East*, volume 1. Rough Guides.

Christensen, D. (2007). Music in Kurdish identity formations. In *Conference on Music in the World of Islam. Assilah*, pages 8–13.

Esmaili, K. S. and Salavati, S. (2013). Sorani Kurdish versus Kurmanji Kurdish: An Empirical Comparison. In *Proceedings of the 51st Annual Meeting of the Association for Computational Linguistics (Volume 2: Short Papers)*, volume 2, pages 300–305.

Esmaili, K. S., Eliassi, D., Salavati, S., Aliabadi, P., Mohammadi, A., Yosefi, S., and Hakimi, S. (2013). Building a test collection for Sorani Kurdish. In *Computer Systems and Applications (AICCSA), 2013 ACS International Conference on*, pages 1–7. IEEE.

Gray, B., Egbert, J., and Biber, D. (2017). Exploring methods for evaluating corpus representativeness. *the Corpus Linguistics International Conference 2017. Birmingham, UK.*

Hamelink, W. and Barış, H. (2014). Dengbêjs on borderlands: Borders and the state as seen through the eyes of Kurdish singer-poets. *Kurdish Studies*, 2(1):34–60.

Hamelink, W. (2016). *The Sung Home. Narrative, Morality, and the Kurdish Nation*. Brill.

Hassani, H. (2018). Blark for multi-dialect languages: towards the Kurdish BLARK. *Language Resources and Evaluation*, 52(2):625–644.

Hassanpour, A. (2005). Wanderings in Adalar Sahilinde. In *Joyce Blau l'éternelle chez les Kurdes*, pages 62–73. Institut français d'études anatoliennes. [Online; accessed 09-Nov-2019].

Holzapfel, A. (2014). *Proceedings of the Fourth International Workshop on Folk Music Analysis, 12 and 13 June, 2014, Istanbul, Turkey: FMA2014*. Boğaziçi University.

Hu, X., Downie, J. S., and Ehmann, A. F. (2009). Lyric text mining in music mood classification. In *Proceedings of the 10th International Society for Music Information Retrieval Conference, ISMIR 2009*, pages 411–416.

Ide, N. and Véronis, J. (1995). *Text encoding initiative: Background and contexts*, volume 29. Springer Science & Business Media.

Kreyenbroek, P. G. (2005). Kurdish written literature. *Encyclopædia Iranica*, page 2.

Leezenberg, M. et al. (2011). Soviet Kurdology and Kurdish Orientalism. *2011). The Heritage of Soviet Oriental Studies*, pages 86–102.

Mahedero, J. P., MartÍnez, Á., Cano, P., Koppenberger, M., and Gouyon, F. (2005). Natural language processing of lyrics. In *Proceedings of the 13th annual ACM international conference on Multimedia*, pages 475–478. ACM.

Mahieux, T. B., Ellis, D. P., Whitman, B., and Lamere, P. (2011). The million song dataset. *ISMIR-11*.

Malmasi, S. (2016). Subdialectal differences in Sorani Kurdish. In *Proceedings of the third workshop on nlp for similar languages, varieties and dialects (vardial3)*, pages 89–96.

McNeil, K. (2018). Tunisian arabic corpus: Creating a written corpus of an 'unwritten'language. *Arabic Corpus Linguistics*, page 30.

Merati, M. A. (2015). *Les formes fondamentales de la musique kurde d'Iran et d'Irak : hore, siâ-çamane, danses, maqâm [In English: The basic forms of Kurdish music from Iran and Iraq]*. Ph.D. thesis, Paris Nanterre University.

Mikailee, H. (2015). "Beyt" in Kurdish Folk Literature. *Journal of Kurdish Literature*, 1(1):57–82. [In Farsi].

Rasul, E. M. (1999). *A Research in the Kurdish Folklore*. Salhaddin Ayyobi. [Farsi translation].

Reigle, R. F. (2014). A brief history of Kurdish music recordings in Turkey. *Hellenic Journal of Music, Education and Culture*, 4(1).

Rodrigues, M. A. G., de Paiva Oliveira, A., and Moreira, A. (2019). Development of a song lyric corpus for the english language. In *International Conference on Applications of Natural Language to Information Systems*, pages 376–383. Springer.

Salimi, H. (2015). Taking a look at Kurdish Folklore. *National Studies Quarterly*, 8(2). [In Farsi].

Sharifi, A. (2005). Kurdish Myths and Legends. *Iranian People's Culture Quarterly*, 7–8. [In Farsi].

Strle, G. and Marolt, M. (2014). Uncovering semantic structures within folk song lyrics. In *Workshop on Folk Music Analysis (FMA2014)*, page 40.

Taft, M. (1977). *The lyrics of race record blues, 1920-1942: a semantic approach to the structural analysis of a formulaic system*. Ph.D. thesis, Memorial University of Newfoundland.

9. Language Resource References

Abdulrahman, Roshna and Hassani, Hossein and Ahmadi, Sina. (2019). *Developing a Fine-grained Corpus for a Less-resourced Language: the case of Kurdish*. Kurdish BLARK.

Proceedings of the 1st Joint SLTU and CCURL Workshop (SLTU-CCURL 2020), pages 336–341
Language Resources and Evaluation Conference (LREC 2020), Marseille, 11–16 May 2020
© European Language Resources Association (ELRA), licensed under CC-BY-NC

Improving the Language Model
for Low-Resource ASR with Online Text Corpora

Nils Hjortnaes[1], Timofey Arkhangelskiy[2], Niko Partanen[3],
Michael Rießler[4], Francis Tyers[1]
[1]Indiana University, [2]University of Hamburg, [3]University of Helsinki, [4]University of Eastern Finland
`nhjortn@iu.edu, timarkh@gmail.com, niko.partanen@helsinki.fi,`
michael.riessler@uef.fi, `ftyers@iu.edu`

Abstract

In this paper, we expand on previous work on automatic speech recognition in a low-resource scenario typical of data collected by field linguists. We train DeepSpeech models on 35 hours of dialectal Komi speech recordings and correct the output using language models constructed from various sources. Previous experiments showed that transfer learning using DeepSpeech can improve the accuracy of a speech recognizer for Komi, though the error rate remained very high. In this paper we present further experiments with language models created using KenLM from text materials available online. These are constructed from two corpora, one containing literary texts, one for social media content, and another combining the two. We then trained the model using each language model to explore the impact of the language model data source on the speech recognition model. Our results show significant improvements of over 25% in character error rate and nearly 20% in word error rate. This offers important methodological insight into how ASR results can be improved under low-resource conditions: transfer learning can be used to compensate the lack of training data in the target language, and online texts are a very useful resource when developing language models in this context.

Keywords: Zyrian Komi (kpv), automatic speech-recognition, documentary linguistics

1. Introduction

Speech recognition has lots of potential to be a highly useful technology while working with the world's various endangered languages. In recent years numerous studies have been conducted on this topic, and especially the recent work on phoneme recognition is reaching very promising results on endangered language corpora (Wisniewski et al., 2020; Michaud et al., 2019). Persephone (Adams et al., 2018) and Elpis (Foley et al., 2018) have been the most widely used systems in the language documentation context, but as the field is rapidly evolving, various methods are available. One of them is Mozilla's DeepSpeech (Hannun et al., 2014). By finding new, more effective ways to use these methods, we can open up their usage to low resource languages. Language documentation is one area in which these methods can be applied. Levow et al. (2017) propose a number of tasks demonstrating the usefulness of natural language processing to language documentation, including speech processing. In this paper we report our latest results using DeepSpeech.

In a recent study we investigated the usefulness of automatic speech-recognition (ASR) in a low-resource scenario, which is generalizable for the fieldwork-based documentation of a medium-size endangered language of Russia (Hjortnaes et al., 2020). We ran various experiments with 35 hours of spoken dialectal Zyrian Komi (Permic < Uralic, henceforth Komi) to optimize the training parameters for DeepSpeech[1] and explored the impact of transfer learning on our corpus. Although the work was a promising start, further research was acutely needed as the reached accuracy

was very low.

In this study, we continue our previous work by exploring new potential methods to improve our results. Specifically, we are looking at how to improve the language model (LM) in order to reach higher accuracy in the ASR. In our earlier experiments, tuning the language model was able to produce slightly better results, though these were very small improvements.

We presume that a domain mismatch may have been involved in our previous low results with the language model despite its relatively large size. The language model we used previously was developed from more formal varieties of written language (literature and Wikipedia), it did not match the domain of the speech data to be recognized, i.e. more informal spoken language recordings. Two obvious differences are the frequent use of discourse particles and code switching to the majority language, Russian, which are atypical of written language. Other differences between written and spoken language are the insertion of dialectal words or word forms and the preference for shorter syntactic units in the latter.

Since written language used in social media tends to be informal (Arkhangelskiy, 2019) we hypothesized that a language model based on a social media corpus would result in significantly higher ASR accuracy. In fact, Komi is actively used in social media today and useful corpus data has recently been published by Timofey Arkhangelskiy. The *Komi-Zyrian corpora*[2] consist of two different sections: a standard written language corpus of 1.76 million words (called the "Main Corpus"), and the "Social Me-

---

[1]`https://github.com/mozilla/DeepSpeech`

[2]`http://komi-zyrian.web-corpora.net`

Corpus	Size
Speech	35 hours
Wiki and Books	1.78M tokens
Literary	1.39M tokens
Social	1.37M tokens
Combined	2.76M tokens

Table 1: Token counts for the corpora used to create the language models. The Wiki and Books corpus also includes the Komi Republic Website and some newspaper articles.

dia Corpus" of 1.85 million words. Since these corpora are of comparable size and are a closer domain match to our speech corpus than the materials used to build the language model in our previous study, the conditions are promising to test how the larger text model influences the results.

Additionally, across these two corpora there are differences in variational sociolinguistic features, which should be taken into account during testing. The Main Corpus contains contemporary on-line press texts. Therefore it matches closely with standard written Komi. The Social Media Corpus, on the other hand, contains posts from the social media platform VKontakte[3] and therefore represents the contemporary language of informal digital communication.

One significant advantage in the use of online texts is that they are available for a considerable number of minority languages and can be harvested relatively easily. Our approach for Komi is therefore generalizable to other languages, although we believe that specific conditions have to be met for endangered languages to have online materials available in sufficient quantity and quality. For online language vitality, see, e.g. Kornai (2015; Gibson (2016). First, internet access is a logical precondition as well as the basic technology for digital use of the written language, especially keyboard layouts for various platforms. Furthermore, the language needs to have a sufficiently large number of speakers and a literary standard vital enough that the speakers are familiar in writing the language (a case of another language, Kildin Saami, which does not have these conditions is described by Rießler (2013)).

Online texts also have an accumulative nature, so that the corpus grows incrementally from day to day. Therefore even a relatively limited amount of online presence can, in few decades, result in a substantially large corpus.

2. Data Acquisition

The speech data used is described more thoroughly in a previous study (Hjortnaes et al., 2020), so we only discuss it here briefly. The corpus itself will be available in the Language Bank of Finland (Blokland et al., 2020) during the spring 2020, and contains 35 hours of aligned transcriptions, primarily from northernmost Komi dialects. The transcription conventions used are close to the written standard. They use Cyrillic script, but include small adaptations to reflect dialectal differences. These adaptations are similar to texts in the recent Komi dialect dictionary by Beznosikova

et al. (2012). Large portions of these materials are also available, and can be studied, via a community-oriented on-line portal (Fedina and Levčenko, 2017; Blokland et al., 2016 2020).[4] This language documentation dataset is used to train the DeepSpeech model itself, but a language model is an essential part of the DeepSpeech architecture, as it is used to adjust the model's output.

The language model used in this study is derived entirely from materials that are online. What it comes to endangered languages spoken in Russia, there is a long tradition of related work. Several corpora based on internet data have been published in in Russia in recent years, e.g. Orekhov et al. (2016) and Krylova et al. (2015), and more recent, similar work has also been conducted in Finland (Jauhiainen et al., 2019). In the future, it could be a promising avenue to combine all these sources, but for our current work we focus on one set of text corpora published last year (Arkhangelskiy, 2019), see above.

The kenlm language model (Heafield, 2011) used by DeepSpeech takes as input a plain-text file with one sentence per line. These were obtained from the annotated corpus files using tsakorpus2kenlm script[5]. Since it is common for social media data to be noisy and contain code switching (Baldwin et al., 2013), automatic language tagging and some text cleaning were performed when building the corpus. The latter included fixing characters with diacritics typed in one of the popular conventions, e.g. replacing *o:* with *ö* or Latin *i* with its identically looking Cyrillic counterpart. Therefore, the social media language model was based on somewhat cleaner data than the original social media posts. The conversion included two additional cleaning stages. First, only sentences with less than one-third OOV words (as determined by a rule-based Komi analyzer[6]) were included, to avoid wrongly tagged Russian sentences. Second, some numerals represented with digits were replaced with text, e.g. *2* was replaced with *кык*. All punctuation was removed. The resulting datasets used with kenlm contain 1.39M words in 153K sentences for the Main Corpus and 1.37M words in 231K sentences for the Social Media Corpus.

Although these preprocessing steps were conducted the social media data in mind, in principle similar adjustments could possibly be useful also in other contexts where noisy text data is used in ASR.

3. Methodology

In our previous work (Hjortnaes et al., 2020), we investigated the benefit of transfer learning and found that the best results were achieved with a learning rate of 0.00001 and dropout of 10% when using transfer learning. Our model, both in the previous work and here, is the DeepSpeech[7] architecture (Hannun et al., 2014; Ardila et al., 2020). DeepSpeech is a relatively simple five layer neural network with one bi-directional LSTM layer. It takes audio as input and outputs a stream of characters, which are then corrected by

---

[3]http://vk.ru

[4]http://videocorpora.ru/
[5]https://bitbucket.org/timarkh/tsakorpus2kenlm/
[6]https://github.com/timarkh/
uniparser-grammar-komi-zyrian
[7]https://github.com/mozilla/DeepSpeech

the language model to produce the final output. The transfer learning branch[8] allows us to reset the last n layers of the network, crucially adjusting for differences in the alphabet size between the source and target language when using transfer learning. We found that resetting the last 2 layers, which does not include the LSTM layer, was most effective. These hyper-parameters are corroborated in Meyer (2019). In this study we continue to examine what kinds of further benefits can be gained by improving the language model. For these experiments, we constructed the language models using kenlm (Heafield, 2011), as described in section 2. We then trained the speech recognition model on the same set of audio data described above, changing only the source of data used for the language model. Finally, we tuned the alpha and beta hyper-parameters of the language model which control how much we weight the LM over the output of the acoustic model and the cost of inserting spaces to separate words respectively.

4. Results

Language model	Size	CER (%)	WER (%)
None	—	70.9	100.0
Wiki	1.78M	72.1	98.1
Literary	1.39M	45.3	80.8
Social Media	1.37M	46.1	81.8
Combined	2.76M	**44.7**	**79.8**

Table 2: The best results for each source of data used to construct the language model. The CER and WER do not necessarily come from the same hyper-parameters used to integrate the language model into the speech recognition system (Hjortnaes et al., 2020).

The previous results are presented alongside our newest results in Table 2 and alone in Table 3. The best word error rate (WER) was achieved with tuned language model parameters using transfer learning (see Table 3). However, the best character error rate (CER) when using the Wikipedia corpus was achieved by disabling the LM entirely. The domain appropriate corpora, however, produced language models which significantly improved upon both the Wikipedia LM and disabling the LM altogether with a CER improvement of over 25% and a WER improvement of nearly 20%.

What is particularly interesting here is that both the literary language model and social media language model resulted in a very similar level of improvement to the performance. The combined model yielded an even greater improvement, though only by about 2%. This goes against the hypothesis that domain would be the most crucial factor here, and calls for further work on various text types.

The hyper-parameters of the language models show many similarities across difference source corpora. In all but the Wikipedia and Book corpus, the best CER was obtained when beta was set to 1, and the best WER in all cases was

with a beta of 1 as well, meaning that the language model favors inserting fewer spaces. When beta becomes large, the predictions tend towards single character words regardless of how long the gold standard is. For all LM corpus sources, as alpha increases, which favors the language model over the output of the acoustic model, the WER goes down, but the CER goes up. This implies that the LM is properly correcting words, but at the cost of other characters.

5. Discussion

It can be observed that many of the remaining errors relate to Russian code-switching within a sentence, and to dialectal forms that do not have corresponding variant in either of the text corpora used. In the following examples the incorrectly recognized words are marked with bold in the Komi sentence, and the Russian parts are marked with italics in both the Komi sentence and Russian translation. The source lines are on top and the system's predictions are below them. Example (1) [CER: 10.0, WER: 55.5][9] shows an almost correctly recognized sentence, where the main problems are in words that contain dialectal morphology. Here we see that the combined model tries to suggest the comitative case form *-көд* from literary Komi, and in the last wordform another dialectal comitative *-кед* goes entirely unrecognized.

(1) тундраын ветлі сизим во керка кари   аслум
тундраын ветлі сизим во керка **каръяс лун**
вокъяскед дядьяскед
вокъяскөд ядъяс ке
'I worked at the tundra for seven years, built a house (in that time) with my brothers and uncles.'

In Example (2) [CER: 15.0, WER: 54.5] an individual borrowed Russian verb *спонсируйтны* 'to sponsor' seems to create conditions where the model fails. It is highly unlikely that such borrowed and loosely adapted items would occur in the language model. The same example, however, displays correctly recognized the Russian noun *страховка* 'insurance'. This illustrates how in this kind of multilingual context drawing an exact line between the languages in contact is very difficult.

(2) никод миян оз   вермы оз мӧд *спонсируйтны*
никод миян **воз веныс по оз нас пони ртны**
пока миян абу *страховка*
пока миян абу страховка
'Nobody is going *to sponsor* us as long we don't have an *insurance*'

The Example (3) [CER: 19.0, WER: 128.5] shows how for an entirely Russian sentence, the language model is not able at all to produce the correct output, but tries to create words in standard Komi. Also here the Russian word *дело* 'thing, issue' is transformed into Komi *делö*, which would be a good approximation of how this word is often pronounced in Komi. However, this shows how finding ways to deal with Russian content is one of the major challenges with

---

[8] https://github.com/mozilla/DeepSpeech/tree/ transfer-learning2

[9] Individual sentences report the number of incorrect characters for CER, not the percentage of incorrect as in WER.

	CER/WER	**beta**				
		1	3	5	7	9
	0.25	76.6/100.0	73.2/100.0	**72.1**/100.0	74.0/100.0	81.8/100.0
alpha	0.5	81.0/99.4	77.0/100.0	74.0/100.0	73.3/100.0	75.8/100.0
	0.75	85.2/**98.1**	80.1/100.0	77.2/100.0	74.8/100.0	74.7/100.0

Table 3: The impact of tuning the language model parameters on Character and Word Error Rates for the Wikipedia dump language model. (Hjortnaes et al., 2020)

	CER/WER	**beta**				
		1	3	5	7	9
	0.25	**45.3**/88.1	45.9/100.0	50.0/100.0	56.8/100.0	67.3/100.0
alpha	0.5	47.6/81.1	46.1/92.6	47.9/100.0	53.0/100.0	61.8/100.0
	0.75	51.6/**80.8**	48.6/85.2	48.3/100.0	51.6/100.0	59.0/100.0

Table 4: The impact of tuning the language model parameters on Character and Word Error Rates for the literary corpus language model.

the language documentation data we are working on. The problems are certainly similar in other highly multilingual contexts.

(3)   *это очень сложное дело не всякому идёт*
та вочис лоны   делӧ не **ся ко мый и де**
'*This is a very difficult issue, it does not fit everyone…*'

In Example (4) [CER: 15.0, WER: 53.8] we see a different issue. Careful listening to the original audio reveals that there truly is a segment like *мый* or *мыйке* (i.e. a pronoun which is not clearly pronounced in the recording), although it is missing from the transcriptions. In this case the model does indeed capture something which the human transcriber didn't. On that note, detecting such mistakes in the original data would generally be a highly useful domain for speech technologies. This example also contains a Russian sequence *мало того что* 'not only, but', which the model, as expected, is not able to analyze.

(4)   сыа бура сёрнитіс *мало того что* сыа бура
сыа бура сёрнитіс **малы тов то са**   бура
сёрнитіс гашке думайтіс коми кывнас
син и мыйкке думайтіс коми кывнас
'He spoke well, *not only* did he speak well, maybe he [even] thought in the Komi language…'

Despite the abundance of Russian confounding our results, there is a very clear difference between the accuracy of the speech recognition as a whole for different corpora. Despite being smaller, both the social media corpus and the literary corpus outperformed the larger Wikipedia corpus. This demonstrates the importance of domain in the choice of corpus for constructing the language model. Size has an impact, as can be seen from the improvement yielded by combining the literary and social media corpus, but it is far less than using a corpus of a more similar domain to the audio data. In this case, online data offers that similarity and improves our results drastically.

6. Conclusion & Future work

As the combined language model was twice as large as the individual models alone, yet offered very little improvement, it remains inconclusive how large the further improvements could be with an even larger language model. We expect that simply increasing the size of the corpus will offer diminishing returns. However, we have demonstrated that creating the language model from available online materials is a very promising and effective way to improve the speech recognition in a low-resource context. By extension, this demonstrates concretely the importance of using quality data of an appropriate domain over simply using as much data as possible. Although the error rates are still relatively high, we are fast approaching a level where the ASR output starts to be sensible and useful for various purposes, primary of which would be to make transcription easier.

It is also noteworthy that the current speech dataset contains over 200 different speakers in very varying recording conditions, which is a realistic scenario for a corpus of fieldwork recordings. There is also a large amount of overlapping speech. Despite these challenges we have been able to produce relatively solid results. Therefore our study is a relevant new contribution in the line of work that attempts to eventually combine ASR systems with the fieldwork-based work of documentary linguistics.

Further experiments in this direction could include even bigger language models, which would firmly establish the role corpus size plays in the effectiveness of the LM. The National Komi Corpus[10] currently contains more than 60 million tokens. This may sound unusually large for a minority language. However, as this body of texts is based on published literature, including printed books and periodicals, which have been printed in a similar, if not higher, magnitude for several other languages of the ethnic Republics of the Soviet Union and Russia, building corpora of comparable size should be possible for various minority languages of Russia as well as other minority languages in similar situations (e.g. in Western Europe). We are aware that printed books and periodicals in endangered languages are not typical of endangered languages globally. How-

---

[10]http://komicorpora.ru/

		beta				
CER/WER		1	3	5	7	9
	0.25	**46.1/88.6**	46.8/100.0	51.2/100.0	58.5/100.0	69.9/100.0
alpha	0.5	48.9/**81.6**	47.2/93.6	49.0/100.0	54.6/100.0	64.2/100.0
	0.75	53.5/81.8	50.1/85.9	49.5/100.0	53.1/100.0	61.3/100.0

Table 5: The impact of tuning the language model parameters on Character and Word Error Rates for the social media language model.

		beta				
CER/WER		1	3	5	7	9
	0.25	**44.7/86.9**	45.5/100.0	49.7/100.0	56.7/100.0	675/100.0
alpha	0.5	47.1/80.0	45.5/91.1	47.5/100.0	52.6/100.0	61.4/100.0
	0.75	51.2/**79.8**	48.1/83.7	47.5/100.0	50.9/100.0	58.2/100.0

Table 6: The impact of tuning the language model parameters on Character and Word Error Rates for the combined corpus language model.

ever, user-generated online communication, through websites and social media, seem to be becoming more and more available, even in contexts where standard literary materials are lacking.

The experiment here used online corpora as a source of spontaneous colloquial data that resembles the spoken transcriptions more than literary standard texts would. Although we have shown there is still some ambiguity in the kind of data we needed to improve the language model, we can experiment more in this direction in the future. For instance, there are numerous text collections available consisting of transcribed dialectal speech similar to those fieldwork-based recordings our ASR system is analysing. For these text collections there is no corresponding audio available. Potential of combining various legacy datasets systematically into language documentation corpora has been discussed before (Blokland et al., 2019), but the benefit for speech recognition may have not been previously recognized. Logically, without audio we can't use these texts in training the ASR system itself, but they could be potentially very useful as a new source of an enriched language model, matching our own speech data perfectly. Apart from simply collecting more data, finding a way to address the Russian which exists in the speech data is a potential avenue for improvement, as the current model essentially ignores it. These language models were constructed exclusively using Komi data, so any Russian which does not exactly match a Komi analogue will be a source of error.

Acknowledgements

This research was supported in part by Lilly Endowment, Inc., through its support for the Indiana University Pervasive Technology Institute. Niko Partanen and Michael Rießler collaborate within the project *Language Documentation meets Language Technology: The Next Step in the Description of Komi*, funded by Kone Foundation, Finland. Timofey Arkhangelskiy was supported by the Alexander von Humboldt foundation.

7. Bibliographical References

Adams, O., Cohn, T., Neubig, G., Cruz, H., Bird, S., and Michaud, A. (2018). Evaluating phonemic transcription of low-resource tonal languages for language documentation. In *Proceedings of LREC 2018*.

Ardila, R., Branson, M., Davis, K., Henretty, M., Kohler, M., Meyer, J., Morais, R., Saunders, L., Tyers, F. M., and Weber, G. (2020). Common Voice. In *Proceedings of the 12th Conference on Language Resources and Evaluation (LREC 2020)*.

Arkhangelskiy, T. (2019). Corpora of social media in minority Uralic languages. In *Proceedings of the Fifth International Workshop on Computational Linguistics for Uralic Languages*, pages 125–140. Tartu.

Baldwin, T., Cook, P., Lui, M., MacKinlay, A., and Wang, L. (2013). How Noisy Social Media Text, How Diffrnt Social Media Sources. In *International Joint Conference on Natural Language Processing*, pages 356–364. Nagoya, Japan.

Beznosikova, L. M., Ajbabina, E. A., Zaboeva, N. K., and Kosnyreva, R. I. (2012). *Komi sërnisikas kyvčykör*. Kola, Syktyvkar.

Blokland, R., Chuprov, V., Levchenko, D., Fedina, M., Fedina, M., Partanen, N., and Rießler, M. (2016-2020). Komi mediateka.

Blokland, R., Partanen, N., Rießler, M., and Wilbur, J. (2019). Using computational approaches to integrate endangered language legacy data into documentation corpora. In *Workshop on the Use of Computational Methods in the Study of Endangered Languages*, pages 24–30.

Blokland, R., Fedina, M., Partanen, N., and Rießler, M. (2020). Spoken Komi Corpus. The Language Bank of Finland.

Fedina, M. S. and Levčenko, Dmitriy, A. (2017). Iz opyta sozdanija komi mediateki. In Marina S. Fedina, editor, *Èlektronnaja pismennost narodov Rossijskoj Federacii*, pages 220–227. Syktyvkar.

Foley, B., Arnold, J. T., Coto-Solano, R., Durantin, G., Ellison, T. M., van Esch, D., Heath, S., Kratochvil, F., Maxwell-Smith, Z., Nash, D., et al. (2018). Building speech recognition systems for language documentation. In *Proceedings of Spoken Language Technologies for Under-resourced Languages (SLTU 2018)*, pages 205–209.

Gibson, M. (2016). Assessing digital vitality. In *Proceedings of the LREC 2016 Workshop, CCURL*, pages 46–51. Portorož.

Hannun, A., Case, C., Casper, J., Catanzaro, B., Diamos, G., Elsen, E., Prenger, R., Satheesh, S., Sengupta, S., Coates, A., and Ng, A. Y. (2014). Deep Speech.

Heafield, K. (2011). Kenlm. In *Proceedings of the sixth workshop on statistical machine translation*, pages 187–197.

Hjortnaes, N., Partanen, N., Rießler, M., and M. Tyers, F. (2020). Towards a speech recognizer for Komi, an endangered and low-resource Uralic language. In *Proceedings of the Sixth International Workshop on Computational Linguistics of Uralic Languages*, pages 31–37. Association for Computational Linguistics, Vienna.

Jauhiainen, H., Jauhiainen, T., and Lindén, K. (2019). Wanca in Korp. In *Data and humanities (RDHUM) 2019 Conference: Data, methods and tools*, page 21.

Kornai, A. (2015). A new method of language vitality assessment. *Linguistic and Cultural Diversity in Cyberspace*, pages 132–138.

Krylova, I., Orekhov, B., Stepanova, E., and Zaydelman, L. (2015). Languages of Russia. In *Russian Summer School in Information Retrieval*, pages 179–185.

Levow, G.-A., Bender, E. M., Littell, P., Howell, K., Chelliah, S., Crowgey, J., Garrette, D., Good, J., Hargus, S., Inman, D., Maxwell, M., Tjalve, M., and Xia, F. (2017). STREAMLInED challenges: Aligning research interests with shared tasks. In *Proceedings of the 2nd Workshop on the Use of Computational Methods in the Study of Endangered Languages*, pages 39–47, Honolulu, March. Association for Computational Linguistics.

Meyer, J. (2019). *Multi-task and transfer learning in low-resource speech recognition*. Ph.D. thesis, University of Arizona.

Michaud, A., Adams, O., Cox, C., and Guillaume, S. (2019). Phonetic lessons from automatic phonemic transcription. In *19th International Congress of Phonetic Sciences (CPhS XIX)*. Melbourne.

Orekhov, B., Krylova, I., Popov, I., Stepanova, L., and Zaydelman, L. (2016). Russian minority languages on the web. In *Computational Linguistics and Intellectual Technologies: Proceedings of the International Conference "Dialogue 2016*, pages 498–508.

Rießler, M. (2013). Towards a digital infrastructure for Kildin Saami. In Erich Kasten et al., editors, *Sustaining indigenous knowledge*, pages 195–218. Kulturstiftung Sibirien.

Wisniewski, G., Guillaume, S., and Michaud, A. (2020). Phonemic transcription of low-resource languages. In *Proceedings of Spoken Language Technologies for Under-resourced Languages (SLTU 2020)*.

Proceedings of the 1st Joint SLTU and CCURL Workshop (SLTU-CCURL 2020), pages 342–351
Language Resources and Evaluation Conference (LREC 2020), Marseille, 11–16 May 2020
© European Language Resources Association (ELRA), licensed under CC-BY-NC

A Summary of the First Workshop on Language Technology for Language Documentation and Revitalization

Graham Neubig[1], Shruti Rijhwani[1], Alexis Palmer[2], Jordan MacKenzie[3], Hilaria Cruz[4],
Xinjian Li[1], Matthew Lee[5], Aditi Chaudhary[1], Luke Gessler[3], Steven Abney[6],
Shirley Anugrah Hayati[1], Antonios Anastasopoulos[1], Olga Zamaraeva[7], Emily Prud'hommeaux[8],
Jennette Child[9], Sara Child[9], Rebecca Knowles[10], Sarah Moeller[11], Jeffrey Micher[1],
Yiyuan Li[1], Sydney Zink[12], Mengzhou Xia[1], Roshan Sharma[1], Patrick Littell[10]

[1]Carnegie Mellon University, Pittsburgh, PA, [2]University of North Texas, Denton, TX,
[3]Georgetown University, Washington, DC,[4]University of Louisville, Louisville, KY,
[5]SIL International, Dallas, TX, [6]University of Michigan, Ann Arbor, MI
[7]University of Washington, Seattle, WA, [8]Boston College, Chestnut Hill, MA,
[9]Sanyak'ola Foundation, Port Hardy, BC, [10]National Research Council Canada, Ottawa, ON,
[11]University of Colorado Boulder, Boulder, CO, [12]Brown University, Providence, RI
neubig@cs.cmu.edu, patrick.littell@nrc-cnrc.gc.ca

Abstract

Despite recent advances in natural language processing and other language technology, the application of such technology to language documentation and conservation has been limited. In August 2019, a workshop was held at Carnegie Mellon University in Pittsburgh to attempt to bring together language community members, documentary linguists, and technologists to discuss how to bridge this gap and create prototypes of novel and practical language revitalization technologies. This paper reports the results of this workshop, including issues discussed, and various conceived and implemented technologies for nine languages: Arapaho, Cayuga, Inuktitut, Irish Gaelic, Kidaw'ida, Kwak'wala, Ojibwe, San Juan Quiahije Chatino, and Seneca.

Keywords: Low-resource languages, language documentation, language revitalization

1. Introduction

Recently there have been large advances in natural language processing and language technology, leading to usable systems for speech recognition (Hinton et al., 2012; Graves et al., 2013; Hannun et al., 2014; Amodei et al., 2016), machine translation (Bahdanau et al., 2015; Luong et al., 2015; Wu et al., 2016), text-to-speech (van den Oord et al., 2016), and question answering (Seo et al., 2017) for a few of the world's most-spoken languages, such as English, German, and Chinese. However, there is an urgent need for similar technology for the rest of the world's languages, particularly those that are threatened or endangered. The rapid documentation and revitalization of these languages is of paramount importance, but all too often language technology plays little role in this process.

In August 2019, the first edition of a 'Workshop on Language Technology for Language Documentation and Revitalization' was held at Carnegie Mellon University in Pittsburgh, PA, USA. The goal of the workshop was to take the recent and rapid advances in language technology (such as speech recognition, speech synthesis, machine translation, automatic analysis of syntax, question answering), and put them in the hands of those on the front lines of language documentation and revitalization, such as language community members or documentary linguists.

The workshop was collaborative, involving language community members, documentary and computational linguists, and computer scientists. These members formed small teams, brainstormed the future of technological support for language documentation and revitalization, and worked on creating prototypes of these technologies. Specifically, the groups focused on spoken technology (§2.), dictionary extraction and management (§3.), supporting education with corpus search (§4.), and supporting language revitalization through social media (§5.). These technologies were applied on nine languages, of various levels of vitality and with varying amounts of available resources:

- **Arapaho** [arap1274], an Algonquian language spoken in the United States.

- **Cayuga** [cayu1261], an Iroquoian language spoken in the US and Canada.

- **Inuktitut** [inui1246], an Inuit-Yupik-Aleut language spoken in Canada.

- **Irish Gaelic** [iris1253], an Indo-European language spoken in Ireland.

- **Kidaw'ida** [tait1250], a Bantu language spoken in Kenya.

- **Kwak'wala** [kwak1269], a Wakashan language spoken in Canada.

- **Ojibwe** [otta1242], an Algonquian language spoken in the US and Canada.

- **San Juan Quiahije Chatino** [sanj1283], an Otomanguean language spoken in Oaxaca, Mexico.

- **Seneca** [sene1264], an Iroquoian language spoken in the US and Canada.

2. Spoken Language Technology

Most spoken language technology assumes a substantial transcribed speech corpus—on the order of hundreds or even thousands of hours of transcribed speech for a typical Automatic Speech Recognition (ASR) system (Hannun et al., 2014, for example). For many languages, however, the only transcribed audio resources that exist are at the scale of minutes or an hour.

The goal of speech technology in a language revitalization setting would be to allow indigenous communities or linguists to gather corpora using up to date technological resources (Michaud et al., 2018). Due to the advancing age of the fluent first-language speakers in many languages, the urgency of this goal is paramount. Thus, it is important to focus on practical, labor-saving speech technologies that are feasible at the data scales that we have currently available, or at least could become feasible with further research. In this workshop, we concentrated on four speech-related tasks, each of which is feasible in low-data (and in some cases zero-data) situations.

2.1. First-Pass Approximate Transcription

The bulk of the speech subgroup's effort concentrated on improving Allosaurus (Li et al., 2020), both improving its performance on new languages, and improving its practical usability for a real-world field context. Allosaurus is intended as an automatic *first-pass transcriber* targeting a narrow IPA representation of the audio, for the purposes of accelerating human transcription efforts or for further processing by downstream systems (e.g. approximate keyword search through an audio corpus).

Unlike a conventional ASR system, Allosaurus does not require pre-existing transcribed speech in its target language; rather, it is trained on a collection of higher-resource languages with typologically diverse phonetic inventories. The system also differs from a conventional ASR system in that it recognizes words at the *phone* level rather than the language-specific phoneme or grapheme.

One important issue that came up was that, although the results of applying the model to a new language like Ojibwe were not unreasonable, it was difficult to imagine practical transcription in cases where the model predicted unfamiliar phones from languages with very different phonological systems. For example, many parts of a speech signal *could* be identified as being voiceless vowels, which Allosaurus predicted due to having been trained on Japanese. However, presenting the user with many voiceless vowels in a language without them makes post-editing a chore.

To mitigate this, we incorporated information from the PHOIBLE database (Moran and McCloy, 2019), a large, manually-curated collection of phone inventories from roughly 2,000 languages. Given the multilingual inventory in Allosaurus (of roughly 190 sounds) and the specific inventory from some target language, as represented in PHOIBLE, we restricted the results to only include phones in the intersection of these two inventories. This both improved recognition (tests after the workshop showed 11-13% improvement) and made human post-editing much more practical. In the screenshot seen in Figure 1, the user has specified that they only want the recognizer to output

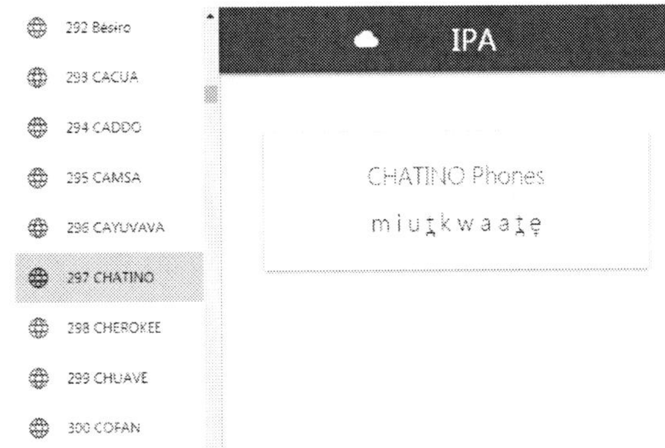

Figure 1: The user can instruct Allosaurus to restrict phone output to a particular PHOIBLE inventory.

phones in PHOIBLE's Chatino inventory.

Additionally, we created an interface to customize the phone inventory if PHOIBLE does not provide inventory for the targeting language (Figure 2). This will also allow easy testing of hypotheses for situations where the phonetic inventory is disputed.

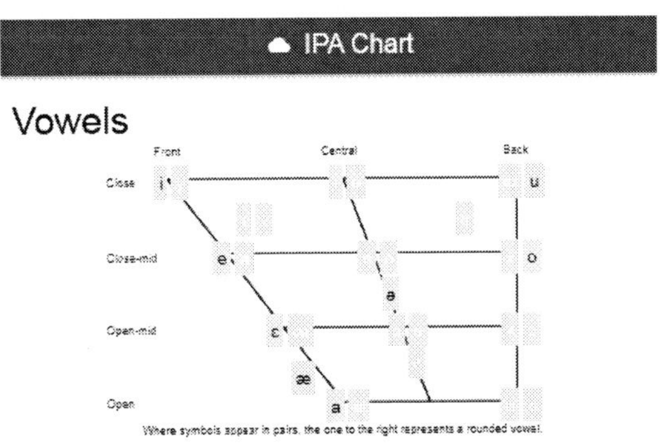

Figure 2: An interface to customize the phone inventory of a language, to restrict Allosaurus output to only those phones desired by the user.

The universal speech recognition method has already been deployed as an app that can be used for documentation at `https://www.dictate.app`, but quantitative testing of its utility in an actual documentation scenario (as in Michaud et al. (2018)) is yet to be performed.

Currently, Allosaurus can currently only output a phone that it has been trained to recognize, but as confused sounds frequently occur at the same place of articulation (Ng, 1998), it should be possible to find links between Allosaurus's inventory and the provided inventory. Future work and possible integration with PanPhon (Mortensen et al., 2016) could allow the tool to adapt the output to the nearest available sound (considering phonological distance) in the language's inventory.

2.2. Phone to Orthography Decoder

Ideally, one would like to convert the phones recognized by Allosaurus to native orthography. If successful, this would provide a speech recognition system that can directly recognize to the native orthography for low-resource languages, with minimal expertise and effort.

Many low-resource languages have fairly new orthographies that are adapted from standard scripts. Because the orthographies are new, the phonetic values of the orthographic symbols are still quite close to their conventional values. We speculate that a phonetician, given no knowledge of the language except a wordlist, could convert the phonetic representation to orthography. We made a first attempt at automating that process, in the form of an Allosaurus-to-orthography decoder called Higgins. Higgins is provided with no information about the language apart from orthographic texts and (optionally) a few pronunciation rules for cases that diverge from conventional usage of the orthography. Importantly, the texts do not include transcriptions of any recordings of interest. For now, we focus only on Latin orthography.

The pronunciation rules used to train Allosaurus were pooled and manually filtered to produce a representation of conventional pronunciation of Latin orthography. The PanPhon system (Mortensen et al., 2016) is used to obtain a similarity metric between phonetic symbols, which we convert to a cost function for matching the phonetic symbols of the Allosaurus representation with the expected sequence for known vocabulary items. Fallback to a 'spelling' mode is provided to accommodate out-of-vocabulary items. Intended, but not yet implemented, is a language model trained from the orthographic texts that the user provides. The decoding algorithm is an adapted form of the Viterbi algorithm, using beam search.

Initial results are mixed, but encouraging enough to warrant further efforts. Orthographic decoding of the output of the current acoustic model does not yield acceptably good results. However, orthographic decoding of a manual phonetic transcription of the recordings is visibly better, suggesting that our goals may be achievable with improvements in both the ASR system and Higgins itself.

2.3. Text-to-Speech

'Unit selection' speech synthesis is another technology that is feasible in a low-data scenario, especially when there is little or no existing transcription but a fluent speaker is available to record prompts. These systems work by identifying short segments of audio as corresponding to particular sounds, then joining these segments together in new sequences to resemble, as much as possible, fluent connected speech. Depending on the size of the target domain (i.e., what range of words/sentences the system is expected to be able to produce), intelligible speech synthesis is possible given only a few hundred or thousand utterances.

Festival (Black et al., 1998) was used to develop an initial TTS system for SJQ Chatino using a 3.8 hour corpus of Eastern Chatino of SJQ with one female speaker

Figure 3: An interactive children's book in SJQ Chatino, that highlights words when spoken in the audio, and speaks words when they are clicked.

(Cavar et al., 2016) from the GORILLA language archive. Some challenges that SJQ Chatino brings for current models of speech synthesis is its complex system of tones. About 70% of the world's languages are tonal, although tones are not represented in most orthographies. Fortunately, Chatino does represent tone on its orthography. The first output (http://tts.speech.cs.cmu.edu/awb/chatino_examples/) yielded excellent results, which is very promising.

2.4. Text/Speech Forced Alignment

Text/speech forced alignment is a mature technology, and is frequently performed cross-lingually (that is, with an acoustic model that was trained on an entirely different language or set of languages), making it an obvious candidate for a technology that will work in a 'no resource' situation. During the workshop, we adapted ReadalongStudio (github.com/dhdaines/ReadAlong-Studio) to align text and speech in SJQ Chatino, and produced a read-along children's book (Figure 3).

ReadalongStudio utilizes a conventional pipeline for cross-linguistic forced alignment, converting the target-language transcription so that it only uses sounds from the model language's phonetic inventory. In this case, we used the pre-trained English model included in PocketSphinx (Huggins-Daines et al., 2006), so the phonetic inventory in question was the English ARPABET inventory. Rather than ask the user to specify this conversion, the cross-linguistic sound-to-sound mapping is performed automatically, using PanPhon (Mortensen et al., 2016) distances between sounds.

While the model performed adequately—a general audience would probably not notice the slight misalignment of some words—the errors revealed the importance of syllable structure to cross-linguistic alignment. When the model erred, it did so on words that had initial nasal-plosive onsets (that is, a prenasalized plosive), aligning the initial word boundary too late (that is, missing the nasal component). This is possibly because the acoustic model, trained solely on English, does not expect these sequences of sounds word-initally. For further work, therefore, we will investigate the incorporation of the multilingually-trained IPA-output model described in §2.1. into our pipeline.

3. Dictionary Management

One major issue identified in the workshop was that most existing materials (dictionaries, pedagogical grammars, etc.) are either not digitized or are not in formats that facilitate non-physical dissemination. Even when these materials are digitized, they are typically in unstructured formats, such as unparsable PDF files, or in outdated or proprietary file formats, which are not conducive to searchability or building automatic language processing tools.

Documentary linguists have long been aware of these problems and have developed best practices for data archiving and management for ongoing language documentation projects (Bird and Simons, 2003; Himmelmann, 2006; Good, 2011), but the task of extracting structure from older resources remains a challenge. During the workshop, we focused on three major avenues:

- Converting dictionary materials from unstructured to structured formats, so that they can be easily used for natural language processing and other computational research, as well as easily presentable in interactive formats online.

- Enhancing the annotations of such dictionaries so that they are tailored to the needs of the language community and to the intricacies of the language.

- Creating a demonstrative website that showcases the created dictionaries along with search functionalities, to retrieve the structured information and annotations extracted from the original PDF files (see Figure 4).

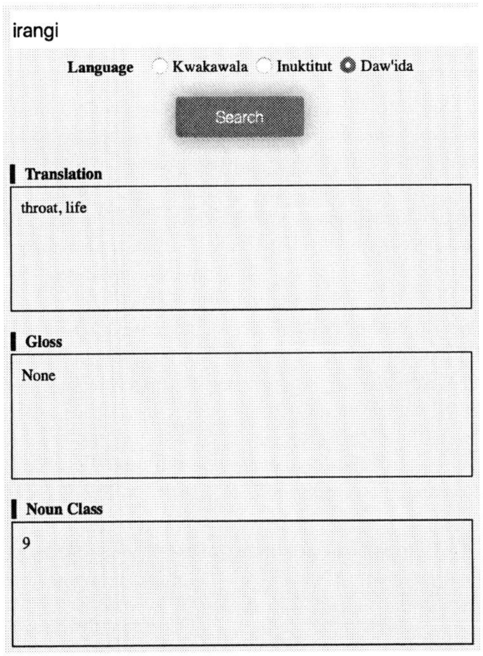

Figure 4: A schematic of the dictionary website interface.

The contents of the original files, in Microsoft Word and PDF format, are not directly accessible by several existing NLP tools. We first converted these into a structured format easily retrieved by our web search service. As a first step, the files are converted to plain text documents. Then, we used regular expressions within Python scripts to extract the relevant information and store them as structured tables.

The website currently supports three languages: Kwak'wala, Inuktitut and Kidaw'ida. Users are able to search for a word in each of these languages, and the website displays its English translation, gloss, noun class, part of speech tag, parallel example sentences, words with the same root and words with the same suffix.

For future work, we plan to expand the annotations of our dictionaries to include morphological information, potentially using automatic segmentation and morphological analysis tools. In addition, as we digitize more materials, we will expand vocabulary coverage and add sentence examples for words in a variety of contexts. Ideally, we will also be able to add audio recordings of example phrases, which is especially important for the growing number of second language learners.

3.1. Kwak'wala

Kwak'wala (previously known as Kwakiutl) is a Wakashan language spoken in Western Canada by the indigenous Kwakwaka'wakw people (which means "those who speak Kwak'wala"). It is considered an endangered language since there are fewer than 200 fluent Kwak'wala speakers today (about 3% of the Kwakwaka'wakw population).

For Kwak'wala, there exist different sources of educational materials in different formats. To make things worse, there are no versions of these materials in easily-searchable digital formats, and as a result the teachers of the language find it difficult to provide language learners with a comprehensive source of information. We processed:

- A dictionary with the original word and its translation
- A file with example sentences for some words
- A file with suffix information for every word

All of the files were in PDF format – these were converted into computer-readable format as described above, and aggregated to be served on our website.

While some dictionaries have morphological information available that will allow for matching queries to stems or suffixes, not all do. One approach to producing automatic alternatives is to use morphological segmentation tools, including unsupervised tools that try to infer morphological boundaries from data. For Kwak'wala, we experimented with two approaches: Morfessor, a probabilistic model for doing unsupervised or semi-supervised morphological segmentation (Virpioja et al., 2013) and byte pair encoding, a compression model that can be applied to automatically segment words (Sennrich et al., 2016). We use these models to split words up into approximate roots and affixes, which are then used for search or to cluster similar words to show to users. Note that there is scope for improvement on this front, including having language speakers determine which automatic systems produce the best segmentations, exploring different ways of visualizing related words, and using these to improve dictionary search.

3.2. Inuktitut

Inuktitut is a polysynthetic language spoken in Northern Canada and is an official language of the Territory of Nunavut. Inuktitut words contain many morphemes, which are realized as different surface forms depending on their context. As such, it is useful for a dictionary to connect different surface forms that share an underlying form, to allow morpheme glossing and comparison with morphemes in other dictionary entries. To do this, we built a prototype system using a morphological analyzer for Inuktitut called Uqailaut (Farley, 2012), which produces a morphological segmentation for an input token along with each morpheme's underlying form. Using dictionary files provided by the analyzer tool, we provide a gloss lookup for each morpheme. Making use of a previously analyzed corpus of parallel Inuktitut-English legislative proceedings (Micher, 2018), we display any parallel sentences containing the input word. Finally, from a database of pre-analyzed words, the website locates additional words containing the same deep form morphemes and displays them to the user.

3.3. Kidaw'ida

Kidaw'ida [dav; E.74] (also Dabida, Taita) is a Bantu language of southeast Kenya. Despite having a robust population of speakers, estimated at 275,000 as of 2009 (Eberhand et al., 2019), Kidaw'ida is highly under-documented. Furthermore, per the hegemony of Kiswahili and English in the region (even in rural areas), extensive asymmetrical borrowings from these languages have occurred, entailing some degree of language shift (Lugano, 2019). The diachronic loss of Kidaw'ida is complicated by the fact no extensive grammatical descriptions have been written of the language, though sketches do exist (Wray, 1894; Sakamoto, 2003). Kidaw'ida lacks a comprehensive mono- or bilingual dictionary. Addressing this shortage of materials is a chief and pressing aim of any documentation effort of Kidaw'ida, with the goal of linguistic preservation and bolstering the status of the language in Kenya.

Kidaw'ida, like any Bantu language, presents a variety of challenges for lexicography because of its complex noun class system—more appropriately deemed a *gender* system (Corbett, 1991)—in which extensive agreement for noun class is realized in prefixes on nouns, verbs, adjectives, prepositions, and determiners (Mdee, 1997). Kidaw'ida has nine genders (following Carstens (2008)), the first six of which contain singular-plural pairs. This means that the language has up to fifteen surface forms of words showing noun class agreement. For instance, the genitive 'of' attests these surface forms: *wa, w'a, ghwa, ya, cha, va, lwa, ra, jha, gha, ya, ra, ghwa, kwa,* and *kwa*. This example highlights a fundamental tension of Bantu lexicography: (redundant) specificity vs. (unclear) simplicity. We are faced with the choice between fifteen distinct and not clearly related entries for genitive 'of' vs. one underspecified entry '-a' that relies on the dictionary user's understanding of the morphological formalism of the hyphen denoting a bound root *and* the noun class agreement system of the language. A main goal in the documentation of Kidaw'ida is to bring current materials in the language "up to date" so they may be processed into dictionaries, grammars, and texts that can be used for pedagogical ends to preserve the language and boost the rate of formal literacy. Our main aim in the context of the workshop was converting extensive yet only semi-organized word lists into a coherent and detailed

spreadsheet that can be fed into a lexicography program, such as TLex[1], which is well suited for Bantu languages. We focused on automating dictionary extraction processing from a word list of Kidaw'ida and English, with definitions, drafted by a native speaker of Kidaw'ida. The original files were in Microsoft Word format and converted using regular expressions as described earlier in this section.

Additionally, we attempted to computationally augment the dictionary with supplementary linguistic information: specifically, part-of-speech tags and noun classes. We used spaCy[2], a natural language processing library, to automatically obtain the part-of-speech tags for the English translation for each dictionary item. These are projected onto the corresponding Kidaw'ida word or phrase. Furthermore, noun classes in Kidaw'ida can be estimated, with reasonable accuracy, by examining the prefix of words that are tagged as nouns. Using a predetermined set of prefixes, we add the predicted noun classes to each word in the dictionary. Although allomorphy is present and noun class marking can occasionally be slightly irregular, in the vast majority of cases this approach greatly reduces annotation effort. The Kidaw'ida dictionary search on our website retrieves the predicted linguistic information in addition to the English translation of the input word. Future work might focus on the creation of platforms to facilitate user-generated data for dictionaries, grammars, and texts, in which users could record pronunciations of words and phrases. This project would also be well served by forum-type interfaces for the generation of meta-linguistic and contextual information furnished by native speakers.

3.4. Chatino

The digitized resource was a collection of complete verb inflection tables in SJQ Chatino. SJQ Chatino verb inflection depends on a rich system of tones (Cruz and Stump, 2019). At the core of this system is an inventory of tone triplets which serve to express person/number distinctions and aspectual/modal distinctions. Each triplet contains a tone expressing first-person singular agreement, another expressing second-person singular agreement, and a third expressing other person-number agreement categories; in addition, each triplet expresses one or another category of aspect/mood. Many triplets are polyfunctional, in the sense that the aspect/mood that they expressed varies according to a verb's inflection class.

The morphological tags were converted to match the Uni-Morph standard (Sylak-Glassman, 2016), with annotations for number, person, and aspect. The result includes a total of 4716 inflection paradigms for more than 200 lemmata, which we used for training automatic morphological inflection systems with promising results.

The development of an SJQ orthography began in 2003 and since then, the system has undergone several changes, especially for tone notation. The current literature employs three different systems for representing tone distinctions: the S-H-M-L system of E. Cruz (2011); the numeral system of H. Cruz (2014); and the alphabetic system of E. Cruz

---

[1] https://tshwanedje.com/tshwanelex/
[2] https://spacy.io

and Woodbury (2013). During the workshop we consolidated two word documents containing 210 paradigm conjugations. Each document had a different tone representation.

4. Teacher-in-the-Loop: Search Tools for Low-Resource Corpora

The goal of this project is to provide an easy-to-use search interface to language corpora, with the specific aim of helping language teachers and other users develop pedagogical materials. In a recent survey of 245 language revitalization projects (Pérez Báez et al., 2019), more than 25% of respondents selected Language Teaching as the most important objective of revitalization efforts. Language Teaching was one of 10 options (including an Other option), and more respondents selected Language Teaching as their top objective than any other option. At the same time, it is not at all clear that the typical products of endangered language documentation projects are inherently useful for language teachers. Much has been written on this issue – here we mention only a handful of the relevant literature. Yamada (2011) takes a positive view of the situation, presenting a successful case study and arguing for new language documentation methods to directly support language teaching. Others (Miyashita and Chatsis, 2013, for example) describe the difficulty of transforming documentation products into language teaching materials. Taylor-Adams (2019) writes that, even when text collections or grammars are available for a language, searching them for materials suitable to a particular lesson can be a daunting task.

Naturalistic language data has been shown to be more effective in language pedagogy than artificially constructed data, since naturalistic examples demonstrate not only how to form a word or phrase correctly but also how the phenomenon is used in real contexts, whether monologue, narrative, or conservation (Reppen, 2010). However, finding naturalistic data can be difficult for rare grammatical phenomena, and while major languages have mature corpus search engines like the Corpus of Contemporary American English (COCA) (Davies, 2008) or the Russian National Corpus (Apresjan et al., 2006), low-resource languages typically lack not only graphical search interfaces, but also the rich annotations (such as morphological and syntactic parses) that are conventionally required to support the function of a search interface. Revitalization programs only rarely have the resources available to enrich a corpus with such expensive annotations, to say nothing of the technical challenge of creating a search interface once the annotation has been completed.

During the workshop, we imagined a corpus search system that would be good enough to let a language teacher find instances of a target grammatical phenomenon without requiring the corpus to be large or richly annotated, and without requiring the user to express the query in technical terms. For example, a teacher may be planning a lesson on transitive verbs and would enter as a query a sentence like *Then my brother carried me down the hill.* The envisioned system, which we call Teacher-in-the-Loop (`https://github.com/lgessler/titl`), allows users to enter a sentence or phrase and uses the input to query an unannotated corpus for syntactically or semantically similar sentences. The system presents several examples to the user, who marks each new result as either relevant or not relevant before completing the loop by submitting their query again. The system returns more sentences, guided by the user's feedback, and the process continues. When the user has amassed enough material for their purposes, the selected sentences can be exported to a file.

This system can be thought of as having two main components: a search engine (§4.1.), and a graphical user interface (§4.2.) that engages users in the feedback cycle (human-in-the-loop). The corpus search will be evaluated as successful if it can retrieve useful examples in any language. The interface must allow users to select candidates as relevant or not, use that feedback to improve the search, and export the best results in an easily accessible format.

During the workshop, we tested our system using a corpus of Arapaho texts (Cowell, nd). Arapaho is a severely endangered Plains Algonquian language, spoken in the western United States of Wyoming and Oklahoma. A finite state transducer model for morphology and an online lexicon and interactive online dictionary exist for Arapaho (Kazeminejad et al., 2017), but we do not exploit these resources for the sake of our experiment that is aimed at languages without such resources.

4.1. Corpus Search Engine

For the corpus search engine, we implemented two different methods: fuzzy string matching, which returns orthographically similar strings, and word embeddings, which are learned numerical representations of words or sentences designed to find semantically, and possibly syntactically, similar tokens/sentences. The two methods have potentially complementary strengths, and they also have dramatically different needs for data and computation.

Fuzzy string matching is a pattern-matching approach for retrieving similar strings. Since it does not involve any training of machine learning models, which can often require a large amount of data, fuzzy matching can be easily applied for low-resource languages. It is appropriate when users are looking for orthographically similar, but not necessarily exactly matched strings.

Word embeddings have also been successful in approximate search, finding semantic similarities between words even across languages. A word embedding is typically a vector representation, trained on large amounts (at least 1M tokens) of monolingual text, whose values reflect syntactic and semantic characteristics of the word, based on the contexts in which the word appears. These embeddings can be obtained using different algorithms, such as GloVe (Pennington et al., 2014), fastText (Bojanowski et al., 2017), or BERT (Devlin et al., 2019), among many others.

4.2. Graphical User Interface (GUI)

A graphical user interface is essential to the system because it makes it easy for our target users (teachers) to query the corpus. Our GUI's design is simple and language-independent. From the user's perspective, the GUI workflow consists of the following steps:

1. An initial query sentence is entered into the interface

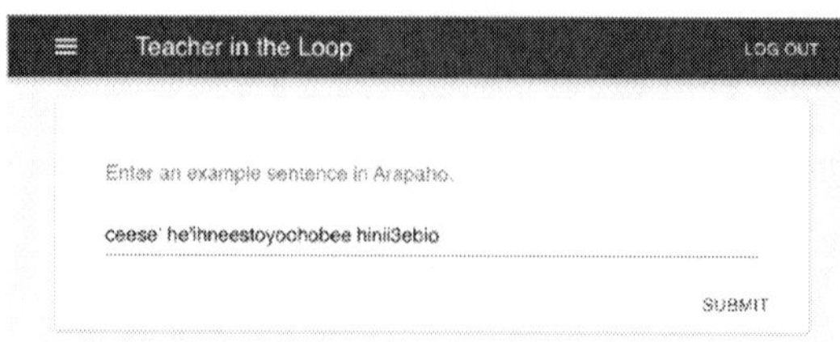

Figure 5: An example of a user entering a sentence into the teacher-in-the-loop system.

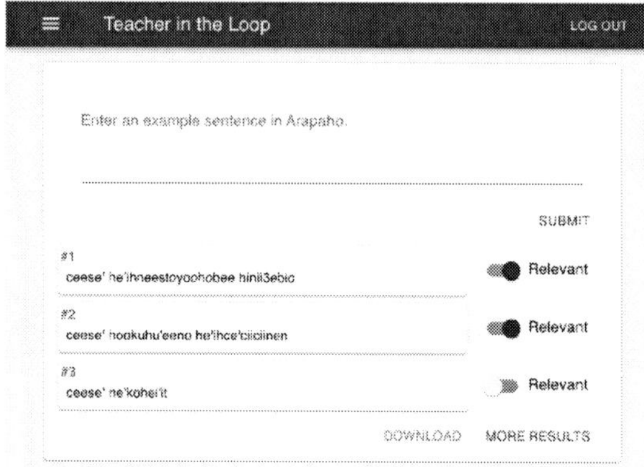

Figure 6: Results from the teacher-in-the-loop system for an example sentence.

2. The system returns a small number of relevant sentences from the corpus

3. The user marks each of the new sentences as either relevant or not relevant

4. The user asks the system for more sentences

5. Steps 2–4 are repeated until the user is satisfied, at which point they may download a file with their relevant examples

The workflow is demonstrated above, with Arapaho as example language. In Fig. 5, we see the user entering the first query sentence. In this example, the user wants to find sentences similar to *ceese' he'ihneestoyoohobee hinii3ebio*, which means 'one remained behind'. The user's intent is to find other sentences with the narrative past affix *he'ih*.

In Fig. 6, we see the state of the system after a user has queried the system for more sentences and has marked the sentences which are relevant. Sentence #1 repeats the query sentence. Sentence #2, *ceese' hookuhu'eeno he'ihce'ciiciinen*, which means 'the skulls were put down again', is marked as relevant by the user since it includes the narrative past affix *he'ih*. Sentence #3 is marked not relevant because, while it does have *ceese'* in common with the query sentence, the *he'ih* affix is not present. Note that this is tied to the query: if the user had instead been looking for sentences with *ceese'* in it, all three sentences would have been relevant.

The user repeats this process, iteratively retrieving more sentences and marking them relevant or irrelevant, until they decide they have enough sentences, at which point they can download all of their sentences.

From the system's perspective, this interaction requires the following steps:

1. We compute an embedding for each sentence in the entire corpus and store it along with the sentence's text.

2. On receiving the user's first query, we convert the query into a vector. The top k sentences that have the highest cosine similarity with the vector are returned.

3. On receipt of the user's relevance judgments on the k sentences that were just presented, the system:

   - discards the irrelevant sentences;
   - computes a new query vector by taking the mean of the vectors for sentences marked as relevant;
   - returns the next k sentences with the highest cosine similarity to the new query vector.

The prototype we developed at the workshop used fastText (Bojanowski et al., 2017) to compute word vectors from an Arapaho corpus of 100,000 tokens. Sentence vectors were derived by taking the arithmetic mean of all word vectors in the sentence. Sentence vectors were stored alongside their text in files, and an HTTP service was created that can take a query and produce the next k nearest sentences. The user interface was developed in JavaScript using the Meteor framework (www.meteor.com) and the UI libraries React (reactjs.org) and Material-UI (material-ui.com).

Embedding algorithms typically assume that a lot of training data is available, and getting good embeddings with a small corpus has been a challenge. Another challenge is that embeddings tend to capture primarily semantic information with some syntactic information, while we want the reverse. Our team has continued to investigate variations on algorithms that might produce the best results. Approaches under consideration include transfer learning with BERT (Devlin et al., 2019), as well as training using skip-grams over part of speech tags or dependency parses (Mikolov et al., 2013; Levy and Goldberg, 2014).

We plan to continue developing embedding strategies that are performant and syntactically rich even when trained with little data, to incorporate fuzzy string matching (possibly augmented with regular expression capabilities) into our system, and to conduct human evaluations that will assess the system's success as a search interface.

5. Social Media

Recently, it has become prevalent for speakers or learners of endangered languages to interact with language on social media (Huaman and Stokes, 2011; Jones and Uribe-Jongbloed, 2012). Previous works on developing extensions for social media include Scannell (2012), who proposed unofficial translation for endangered languages on Facebook, and Arobba et al. (2010) who developed a website called LiveAndTell for sharing, teaching, and learning by, of, and for Lakota speakers and communities interested in preserving Lakota language and culture.

Similarly, the final group in the workshop focused on the potential for use of social media in language documentation or revitalization, specifically focusing on bots for language learning and analysis of social media text.

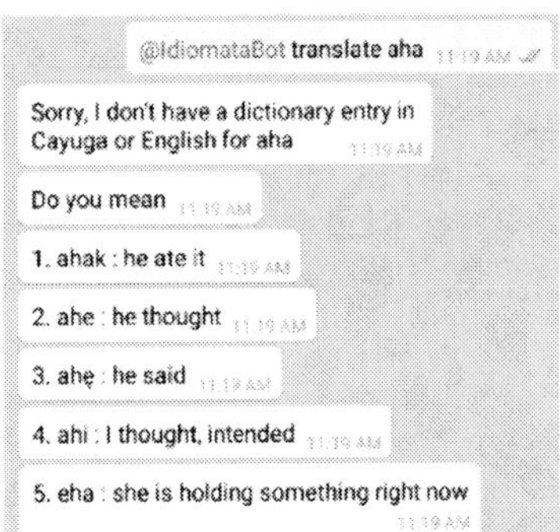

Figure 8: An example of fuzzy dictionary matching.

Figure 7: Usage of the Idiomata bot to search for translations and obtain scores regarding number of words spoken.

5.1. Bots for Language Learning

In discussing potential projects during the workshop, some members of the workshop who are actively learning their ancestral languages noted that they often had trouble coming up with words in the heritage language, and in maintaining their motivation to continue practicing the language. Thus, we created a prototype chatbot, "Idiomata", that users can add to conversations that they would like to have in their language. We implemented this for Seneca and Cayuga, two Haudenosaunee languages indigenous to what is now New York State and Ontario. Idiomata currently has two functionalities:

1. It can be added to a chat between two speakers, and once it is added with the appropriate permissions, it will monitor the number of words the conversants use in each language. The conversants can ask "@Idiomata my score", and the bot will inform the speakers of how many words they used in each language.
2. Second, the bot can propose translations. The speakers can write "@Idiomata translate XXX", and a translation will be provided for the word XXX.

An example of both functionalities is shown in the screenshot in Figure 7. In order to ensure that this functionality is easy to implement even for languages where there is a paucity of resources, both of the above functionalities are based only on a bilingual dictionary between the language the speakers would like to be conversing in, and a language of wider communication such as English.

Importantly for language learners, both functionalities have the capacity for fuzzy matching in case of spelling errors or morphological variation (Figure 8). Specifically, the fuzzy matching is implemented based on edit distance algorithm for string matching. We evaluate the distance between the input of the user and the words in the dictionary of both the low-resourced language and English. If the user input is not in the dictionary, the chatbot will suggest five dictionary words with distances lower than a given threshold.

5.2. Analysis of Social Media Text

A related endeavor of the workshop continued research into temporal codeswitching analyses in the Twitter domain. Focusing on Irish as a relatively well-resourced endangered language under somewhat of a current sociopolitical spotlight, but with the purpose of application to other endangered languages, work continued into more finely identifying features considered Irish versus belonging, lexically or by intent of the user, to some other language—for example, the "Guarda" term semantically situating itself between the "garda" Irish police service and the related English term "guard." Such identifications are important to temporal tracking of endangered language decay (dropout) or shifts within popular multilingual social media platforms where certain languages may feature prominently and pressure shifts on behalf of enabled or sustained engagement.

For these purposes, the continued and future work of the temporal language shift modeling forecasts integration of the aforementioned chatbot project on behalf of both tracking language shifts within individual conversation threads, not just at the level of tracking language shift over a user account lifespan, as well as on behalf of testing models of language shift within social media settings more so under the researchers' control, such as in a chatbot setting involving multiple users or a user and bot.

6. Conclusions

During the workshop teams made significant progress on speech technology, dictionary management, teacher-in-the-loop technology, and social media. Participants responded that they found it quite productive and would like to continue in the following year. Based on this, the organizers are looking to hold the workshop again in the summer of 2020. While there were a variety of participants in the workshop, there was a slant towards technologists given the location of and organization of the workshop, suggesting that perhaps future workshops should be located in a place more conducive to encouraging participation from language community members, either in their territory, or co-located with a conference such as CoLang. Three workshop participants (Anastasopolous, Cruz, and Neubig) are also planning a tutorial on technology for endangered languages at the 2020 edition of the Conference on Computational Linguistics (COLING).

7. Acknowledgments

The authors thank all participants in the workshop. The workshop and this report were supported in part by NSF Award No. 1761548.

8. Bibliographic References

Amodei, D., Ananthanarayanan, S., Anubhai, R., Bai, J., Battenberg, E., Case, C., Casper, J., Catanzaro, B., Cheng, Q., Chen, G., et al. (2016). Deep Speech 2: End-to-end speech recognition in English and Mandarin. In *International conference on machine learning*, pages 173–182.

Apresjan, J., Boguslavsky, I., Iomdin, B., Iomdin, L., Sannikov, A., and Sizov, V. (2006). A Syntactically and Semantically Tagged Corpus of Russian: State of the Art and Prospects. In *Proceedings of LREC 2006*, pages 1378–1381.

Arobba, B., McGrath, R. E., Futrelle, J., and Craig, A. B. (2010). A community-based social media approach for preserving endangered languages and culture.

Bahdanau, D., Cho, K., and Bengio, Y. (2015). Neural machine translation by jointly learning to align and translate. In *3rd International Conference on Learning Representations, ICLR 2015*.

Bird, S. and Simons, G. (2003). Seven dimensions of portability for language documentation and description. *Language*, pages 557–582.

Black, A. W., Taylor, P., and Caley, R. (1998). The Festival speech synthesis system.

Bojanowski, P., Grave, E., Joulin, A., and Mikolov, T. (2017). Enriching word vectors with subword information. *Transactions of the Association for Computational Linguistics*, 5:135–146.

Carstens, V. (2008). DP in Bantu and Romance. In Katherine Demuth et al., editors, *The Bantu Romance Connection*, pages 131–166. John Benjamins.

Corbett, G. G. (1991). *Gender*. Cambridge University Press.

Cruz, H. and Stump, G. (2019). The complex exponence relations of tonal inflection in SJQ Chatino verbs. University of Louisville and University of Kentucky.

Cruz, E. and Woodbury, A. C. (2013). Tonal complexity in San Juan Quiahije Eastern Chatino compound verb inflection. *LSA & SSILA special session: Inflectional classes in the languages of the Americas, Boston MA*.

Cruz, E. (2011). *Phonology, tone and the functions of tone in San Juan Quiahije Chatino*. Ph.D. thesis, The University of Texas at Austin.

Cruz, H. (2014). *Linguistic Poetic and Rhetoric of Eastern Chatino of San Juan Quiahije*. Ph.D. thesis, The University of Texas at Austin.

Devlin, J., Chang, M.-W., Lee, K., and Toutanova, K. (2019). BERT: Pre-training of deep bidirectional transformers for language understanding. In *Proceedings of the 2019 Conference of the North American Chapter of the Association for Computational Linguistics: Human Language Technologies, Volume 1 (Long and Short Papers)*, pages 4171–4186.

Eberhand, D. M., Simons, G. F., and Fennig, C. D. (2019). *Ethnologue: Languages of the World. Twenty-second edition*. SIL International.

Farley, B. (2012). The Uqailaut Project. *URL http://www.inuktitutcomputing.ca*.

Good, J. (2011). Data and language documentation. In Peter Austin et al., editors, *Handbook of Endangered Languages*, pages 212–234. Cambridge University Press.

Graves, A., Mohamed, A.-r., and Hinton, G. (2013). Speech recognition with deep recurrent neural networks. In *2013 IEEE international conference on acoustics, speech and signal processing*, pages 6645–6649. IEEE.

Hannun, A., Case, C., Casper, J., Catanzaro, B., Diamos, G., Elsen, E., Prenger, R., Satheesh, S., Sengupta, S., Coates, A., et al. (2014). Deep Speech: Scaling up end-to-end speech recognition. *arXiv preprint arXiv:1412.5567*.

Himmelmann, N. P. (2006). Language documentation: What is it and what is it good for. *Essentials of language documentation*, 178(1).

Hinton, G., Deng, L., Yu, D., Dahl, G. E., Mohamed, A.-r., Jaitly, N., Senior, A., Vanhoucke, V., Nguyen, P., Sainath, T. N., et al. (2012). Deep neural networks for acoustic modeling in speech recognition: The shared views of four research groups. *IEEE Signal processing magazine*, 29(6):82–97.

Huaman, E. S. and Stokes, P. (2011). Indigenous language revitalization and new media: Postsecondary students as innovators. *Global Media Journal*, 10(18).

Huggins-Daines, D., Kumar, M., Chan, A., Black, A. W., Ravishankar, M., and Rudnicky, A. I. (2006). Pocketsphinx: A free, real-time continuous speech recognition system for hand-held devices. In *2006 IEEE International Conference on Acoustics Speech and Signal Processing Proceedings*, volume 1, pages I–I. IEEE.

Jones, E. H. G. and Uribe-Jongbloed, E. (2012). *Social media and minority languages: Convergence and the creative industries*, volume 152. Multilingual Matters.

Kazeminejad, G., Cowell, A., and Hulden, M. (2017). Creating lexical resources for polysynthetic languages—the case of arapaho.

Levy, O. and Goldberg, Y. (2014). Dependency-based word embeddings. In *Proceedings of the 52nd Annual Meeting of the Association for Computational Linguistics (Volume 2: Short Papers)*, pages 302–308.

Li, X., Dalmia, S., Li, J., Lee, M., Littell, P., Yao, J., Anastasopoulos, A., Mortensen, D. R., Neubig, G., Black, A. W., and Metze, F. (2020). Universal phone recognition with a multilingual allophone system. In *To appear at ICASSP*.

Lugano, R. (2019). Kidawida (Kitaita): A Language Documentation Project. *CAS Research Report 2018-2019*.

Luong, M.-T., Pham, H., and Manning, C. D. (2015). Effective Approaches to Attention-based Neural Machine Translation. In *Proceedings of the 2015 Conference on Empirical Methods in Natural Language Processing*, pages 1412–1421.

Mdee, J. S. (1997). *Nadharia na historia ya leksikografia*. Taasisi ya Uchunguzi wa Kiswahili Chuo Kikuu cha Dar es Salaam, Dar es Salaam, Tanzania.

Michaud, A., Adams, O., Cohn, T. A., Neubig, G., and Guillaume, S. (2018). Integrating automatic transcription into the language documentation workflow: Experiments with Na data and the Persephone toolkit. *Language Documentation & Conservation*, 12:393–429.

Micher, J. C. (2018). Provenance and Processing of an Inuktitut-English Parallel Corpus Part 1: Inuktitut Data Preparation and Factored Data Format. Technical report, US Army Research Laboratory Adelphi United States.

Mikolov, T., Sutskever, I., Chen, K., Corrado, G. S., and Dean, J. (2013). Distributed representations of words and phrases and their compositionality. In *Advances in neural information processing systems*, pages 3111–3119.

Miyashita, M. and Chatsis, A. (2013). Collaborative development of Blackfoot language courses. *Language Documentation & Conservation*, 7:302–330.

Moran, S. and McCloy, D. (2019). PHOIBLE 2.0. *Jena: Max Planck Institute for the Science of Human History. Retrieved*, 2:2019.

Mortensen, D. R., Littell, P., Bharadwaj, A., Goyal, K., Dyer, C., and Levin, L. (2016). Panphon: A resource for mapping IPA segments to articulatory feature vectors. In *Proceedings of COLING 2016, the 26th International Conference on Computational Linguistics: Technical Papers*, pages 3475–3484.

Ng, K. (1998). Towards robust methods for spoken document retrieval. In *Fifth International Conference on Spoken Language Processing*.

Pennington, J., Socher, R., and Manning, C. D. (2014). Glove: Global vectors for word representation. In *Proceedings of the 2014 conference on empirical methods in natural language processing (EMNLP)*, pages 1532–1543.

Pérez Báez, G., Vogel, R., and Patolo, U. (2019). Global Survey of Revitalization Efforts: A mixed methods approach to understanding language revitalization practices. *Language Documentation & Conservation*, 13:446–513.

Reppen, R. (2010). *Using corpora in the language classroom*. Cambridge University Press.

Sakamoto, K. (2003). An Introduction to Kidawida: The Language of the Taita in south-east Kenya, Volume I: Nouns, Adjectives and Numerals. *Bulletin of Policy Studies*, (6).

Scannell, K. (2012). Translating Facebook into endangered languages. In *Proceedings of the 16th Foundation for Endangered Languages Conference*, pages 106–110.

Sennrich, R., Haddow, B., and Birch, A. (2016). Neural Machine Translation of Rare Words with Subword Units. In *Proceedings of the 54th Annual Meeting of the Association for Computational Linguistics (Volume 1: Long Papers)*, pages 1715–1725.

Seo, M., Kembhavi, A., Farhadi, A., and Hajishirzi, H. (2017). Bidirectional attention flow for machine comprehension. *International Conference on Learning Representations*.

Sylak-Glassman, J. (2016). The Composition and Use of the Universal Morphological Feature Scheme (UniMorph Schema). Technical report, Center for Language and Speech Processing, Johns Hopkins University.

Taylor-Adams, A. (2019). Recording to revitalize: Language teachers and documentation design. *Language Documentation & Conservation*, 13:426–445.

van den Oord, A., Dieleman, S., Zen, H., Simonyan, K., Vinyals, O., Graves, A., Kalchbrenner, N., Senior, A., and Kavukcuoglu, K. (2016). Wavenet: A generative model for raw audio. *arXiv preprint arXiv:1609.03499*.

Virpioja, S., Smit, P., Grönroos, S.-A., and Kurimo, M. (2013). Morfessor 2.0: Python implementation and extensions for Morfessor Baseline. *SCIENCE + TECHNOLOGY*.

Wray, J. A. (1894). *An Elementary Introduction to the Taita Language, Eastern Equatorial Africa*. Society for promoting Christian knowledge.

Wu, Y., Schuster, M., Chen, Z., Le, Q. V., Norouzi, M., Macherey, W., Krikun, M., Cao, Y., Gao, Q., Macherey, K., et al. (2016). Google's neural machine translation system: Bridging the gap between human and machine translation. *arXiv preprint arXiv:1609.08144*.

Yamada, R.-M. (2011). Integrating documentation and formal teaching of Kari'nja: Documentary materials as pedagogical materials. *Language Documentation & Conservation*, 5:1–30.

9.   Language Resource References

Cavar, Damir and Cavar, Malgorzata and Cruz, Hilaria. (2016). *Chatino Speech Corpus Archive Dataset*. ELRA, ISLRN 557-415-504-956-6.

Cowell, Andrew. (n.d.). *A Conversational Database of the Arapaho Language in Video Format*. SOAS, Endangered Languages Archive.

Davies, Mark. (2008). *The corpus of contemporary American English (COCA): 520 million words, 1990-present*.

Proceedings of the 1st Joint SLTU and CCURL Workshop (SLTU-CCURL 2020), pages 352–357
Language Resources and Evaluation Conference (LREC 2020), Marseille, 11–16 May 2020
© European Language Resources Association (ELRA), licensed under CC-BY-NC

"A Passage to India": Pre-trained Word Embeddings for Indian Languages

Kumar Saurav[†], Kumar Saunack[†], Diptesh Kanojia[†,♣,⋆], and Pushpak Bhattacharyya[†]

[†]Indian Institute of Technology Bombay, India
[♣]IITB-Monash Research Academy, India
[⋆]Monash University, Australia
{krsrv, krsaunack, diptesh, pb}@cse.iitb.ac.in

Abstract

Dense word vectors or 'word embeddings' which encode semantic properties of words, have now become integral to NLP tasks like Machine Translation (MT), Question Answering (QA), Word Sense Disambiguation (WSD), and Information Retrieval (IR). In this paper, we use various existing approaches to create multiple word embeddings for 14 Indian languages. We place these embeddings for all these languages, *viz.*, Assamese, Bengali, Gujarati, Hindi, Kannada, Konkani, Malayalam, Marathi, Nepali, Odiya, Punjabi, Sanskrit, Tamil, and Telugu in a single repository. Relatively newer approaches that emphasize catering to context (BERT, ELMo, *etc.*) have shown significant improvements, but require a large amount of resources to generate usable models. We release pre-trained embeddings generated using both contextual and non-contextual approaches. We also use MUSE and XLM to train cross-lingual embeddings for all pairs of the aforementioned languages. To show the efficacy of our embeddings, we evaluate our embedding models on XPOS, UPOS and NER tasks for all these languages. We release a total of 436 models using 8 different approaches. We hope they are useful for the resource-constrained Indian language NLP. The title of this paper refers to the famous novel "A Passage to India" by E.M. Forster, published initially in 1924.

Keywords: word embeddings, Indian languages, monolingual embeddings, cross-lingual embeddings, contextual embeddings

1. Introduction

India has a total of 22 scheduled languages with a combined total of more than a billion speakers. Indian language content on the web is accessed by approximately 234 million speakers across the world[1]. Despite the enormous user base, Indian languages are known to be low-resource or resource-constrained languages for NLP. Word embeddings have proven to be important resources, as they provide a dense set of features for downstream NLP tasks like MT, QA, IR, WSD, *etc.* Unlike in classical Machine Learning wherein features have at times to be extracted in a supervised manner, embeddings can be obtained in a completely unsupervised fashion. For Indian languages, there are little corpora and few datasets of appreciable size available for computational tasks. The wikimedia dumps which are used for generating pre-trained models are insufficient. Without sufficient data, it becomes difficult to train embeddings.

NLP tasks that benefit from these pre-trained embeddings are very diverse. Tasks ranging from word analogy and spelling correction to more complex ones like Question Answering (Bordes et al., 2014), Machine Translation (Artetxe et al., 2019), and Information Retrieval (Diaz et al., 2016) have reported improvements with the use of well-trained embeddings models. The recent trend of transformer architecture based neural networks has inspired various language models that help train contextualized embeddings (Devlin et al., 2018; Peters et al., 2018; Melamud et al., 2016; Lample and Conneau, 2019). They report significant improvements over various NLP tasks and release pre-trained embeddings models for many languages. One of the shortcomings of the currently available pre-trained models is the corpora size used for their training. Almost all of these models use Wikimedia corpus to train models which is insufficient

for Indian languages as Wikipedia itself lacks significant number of articles or text in these languages. Although there is no cap or minimum number of documents/lines which define a usable size of a corpus for training such models, it is generally considered that the more input training data, the better the embedding models.

Acquiring raw corpora to be used as input training data has been a perennial problem for NLP researchers who work with low resource languages. Given a raw corpus, monolingual word embeddings can be trained for a given language. Additionally, NLP tasks that rely on utilizing common linguistic properties of more than one language need cross-lingual word embeddings, *i.e.,* embeddings for multiple languages projected into a common vector space. These cross-lingual word embeddings have shown to help the task of cross-lingual information extraction (Levy et al., 2017), False Friends and Cognate detection (Merlo and Rodriguez, 2019), and Unsupervised Neural Machine Translation (Artetxe et al., 2018b). With the recent advent of contextualized embeddings, a significant increase has been observed in the types of word embedding models. It would be convenient if a single repository existed for all such embedding models, especially for low-resource languages. Our work creates such a repository for fourteen Indian languages, keeping this in mind, by training and deploying 436 models with different training algorithms (like word2vec, BERT, etc.) and hyperparameters as detailed further in the paper. *Our key contributions are:*

(1) We acquire raw monolingual corpora for fourteen languages, including Wikimedia dumps. (2) We train various embedding models and evaluate them. (3) We release these embedding models and evaluation data in a single repository[2].

---

[1]Source Link

[2]Repository Link

The roadmap of the paper is as follows: in section 2, we discuss previous work; section 3 discusses the corpora and our evaluation datasets; section 4 briefs on the approaches used for training our models, section 5 discusses the resultant models and their evaluation; section 6 concludes the paper.

2.   Literature Survey

Word embeddings were first introduced in (Y. Bengio, 2003) when it was realised that learning the joint probability of sequences was not feasible due to the *'curse of dimensionality'*, *i.e.,* at that time, the value added by an additional dimension seemed much smaller than the overhead it added in terms of computational time, and space. Since then, several developments have occurred in this field. Word2Vec (Mikolov et al., 2013a) showed the way to train word vectors. The models introduced by them established new state-of-the-art on tasks such as Word Sense Disambiguation (WSD). GloVE (Pennington et al., 2014) and FastText (Bojanowski et al., 2017) further improved on results shown by Mikolov et al. (2013a), where GloVE used a co-occurrence matrix and FastText utilized the sub-word information to generate word vectors. Sent2Vec (Pagliardini et al., 2017) generates sentence vectors inspired by the same idea. Universal Sentence Embeddings (Cer et al., 2018), on the other hand, creates sentence vectors using two variants: transformers and DANs. Doc2Vec (Le and Mikolov, 2014) computes a feature vector for every document in the corpus. Similarly, Context2vec (Melamud et al., 2016) learns embedding for variable length sentential context for target words.

The drawback of earlier models was that the representation for each word was fixed regardless of the context in which it appeared. To alleviate this problem, contextual word embedding models were created. ELMo (Peters et al., 2018) used bidirectional LSTMs to improve on the previous works. Later, BERT(Devlin et al., 2018) used the transformer architecture to establish new a state-of-the-art across different tasks. It was able to learn deep bidirectional context instead of just two unidirectional contexts, which helped it outperform previous models. XLNet (Yang et al., 2019) was a further improvement over BERT. It addressed the issues in BERT by introducing permutation language modelling, which allowed it to surpass BERT on several tasks.

Cross-lingual word embeddings, in contrast with monolingual word embeddings, learn a common projection between two monolingual vector spaces. MUSE (Conneau et al., 2017) was introduced to get cross-lingual embeddings across different languages. VecMap(Artetxe et al., 2018a) introduced unsupervised learning for these embeddings. BERT, which is generally used for monolingual embeddings, can also be trained in a multilingual fashion. XLM(Lample and Conneau, 2019) was introduced as an improvement over BERT in the cross-lingual setting.

The official repository for FastText has several pretrained word embedding for multiple languages, including some Indian languages. The French, Hindi and Polish word embeddings, in particular, have been evaluated on Word Analogy datasets, which were released along with the paper.

Haider (2018) release word embeddings for the Urdu language, which is one of the Indian languages we do not cover with this work. To evaluate the quality of embeddings, they were tested on Urdu translations of English similarity datasets.

3.   Dataset and Experiment Setup

We collect pre-training data for over 14 Indian languages (from a total of 22 scheduled languages in India), including Assamese (as), Bengali (bn), Gujarati (gu), Hindi (hi), Kannada (kn), Konkani (ko), Malayalam (ml), Marathi (mr), Nepali (ne), Odiya (or), Punjabi (pa), Sanskrit (sa), Tamil (ta) and Telugu (te). These languages account for more than 95% of the entire Indian population, with the most widely spoken language, Hindi, alone contributing 43% to the figure[3]. Nonetheless, data that is readily available for computational purposes has been excruciatingly limited, even for these 14 languages.

One of the major contributions of this paper is the accumulation of data in a single repository. This dataset has been collected from various sources, including ILCI corpora (Choudhary and Jha, 2011; Bansal et al., 2013), which contains parallel aligned corpora (including English) with Hindi as the source language in tourism and health domains. As a baseline dataset, we first extract text from Wikipedia dumps[4], and then append the data from other sources onto it. We added the aforementioned ILCI corpus, and then for Hindi, we add the monolingual corpus from HinMonoCorp 0.5 (Bojar et al., 2014), increasing the corpus size by 44 million sentences. For Hindi, Marathi, Nepali, Bengali, Tamil, and Gujarati, we add crawled corpus of film reviews and news websites[5]. For Sanskrit, we download a raw corpus of prose[6] and add it to our corpus. Further, we describe the preprocessing and tokenization of our data.

3.1.   Preprocessing

The corpora collected is intended to be set in general domain instead of being domain-specific, and hence we start by collecting general domain corpora via Wikimedia dumps. We also add corpora from various crawl sources to respective individual language corpus. All the corpora is then cleaned, with the first step being the removal of HTML tags and links which can occur due to the presence of crawled data. Then, foreign language sentences (including English) are removed from each corpus, so that the final pre-training corpus contains words from only its language. Along with foreign languages, numerals written in any language are also removed. Once these steps are completed, paragraphs in the corpus are split into sentences using sentence end markers such as full stop and question mark. Following this, we also remove any special characters which

---

[3]https://en.wikipedia.org/wiki/List_of_languages_by_number_of_native_speakers_in_India

[4]As on 15th August, 2019

[5]https://github.com/goru001

[6]http://sanskrit.jnu.ac.in/currentSanskritProse/

may have included punctuation marks (example - hyphens, commas etc.).

The statistics for the resulting corpus are listed in Table 1.

Language	Abbr.	Sentences	Words
Hindi	hin	48,115,256	3,419,909
Bengali	ben	1,563,137	707,473
Telugu	tel	1,019,430	1,255,086
Tamil	tam	881,429	1,407,646
Nepali	nep	705,503	314,408
Sanskrit	san	553,103	448,784
Marathi	mar	519,506	498,475
Punjabi	pan	503,330	247,835
Malayalam	mal	493,234	1,325,212
Gujarati	guj	468,024	182,566
Konkani	knn	246,722	76,899
Oriya	ori	112,472	55,312
Kannada	kan	51,949	30,031
Assamese	asm	50,470	29,827

Table 1: Corpus statistics for each Indic language with their ISO 639-3 abbreviations (total number of sentences and words)

3.2. Experiment Setup

There is a prevailing scarcity of standardised benchmarks for testing the efficacy of various word embedding models for resource-poor languages. We conducted experiments across some rare standardised datasets that we could find and created new evaluation tasks as well to test the quality of non-contextual word embeddings. The Named Entity Recognition task, collected from (Murthy et al., 2018), and FIRE 2014 workshop for NER, contains NER tagged data for 5 Indian languages, namely Hindi, Tamil, Bengali, Malayalam, and Marathi. We also use a Universal POS (UPOS), as well as an XPOS (language-specific PoS tags) tagged dataset, available from the Universal Dependency (UD) treebank (Nivre et al., 2016), which contains POS tagged data for 4 Indian languages, Hindi, Tamil, Telugu, and Marathi.

For the tasks of NER, UPOS tagging, XPOS tagging, we use the Flair library (Akbik et al., 2018), which embeds our pre-trained embeddings as inputs for training the corresponding tagging models. The tagging models provided by Flair are vanilla BiLSTM-CRF sequence labellers. For the task of word analogy dataset, we simply use the vector addition and subtraction operators to check accuracy (*i.e.*, $v(\text{France}) - v(\text{Paris}) + v(\text{Berlin})$ should be close to $v(\text{Germany})$).

For contextual word embeddings, we collect the statistics provided at the end of the pre-training phase to gauge the quality of the embeddings - perplexity scores for ELMo, masked language model accuracy for BERT, and so on. We report these values in Table 2.

4. Models and Evaluation

In this section, we briefly describe the models created using the approaches mentioned above in the paper.

4.1. Word2Vec (skip-gram and CBOW)

Word2Vec embeddings (Mikolov et al., 2013b) of dimensions {50, 100, 200, 300} for both skip-gram and CBOW architectures are created using the gensim library (Řehůřek and Sojka, 2010) implementation of Word2Vec. Words with a frequency less than 2 in the entire corpus are treated as unknown (out-of-vocabulary) words. For other parameters, default settings of gensim are used. There are no pre-trained Word2Vec word embeddings for any of the 14 languages available publicly.

4.2. FastText

FastText embeddings (Bojanowski et al., 2017) of dimensions {50, 100, 200, 300} (skip-gram architecture) were created using the gensim library (Řehůřek and Sojka, 2010) implementation of FastText. Words with a frequency less than 2 in the entire corpus are treated as unknown (out-of-vocabulary) words. For other parameters, default settings of gensim are used. Except for Konkani and Punjabi, the official repository for FastText provides pre-trained word embeddings for the Indian languages. However, we have trained our word embeddings on a much larger corpus than those used by FastText.

4.3. GloVe

We create GloVe embeddings (Pennington et al., 2014) of dimensions {50, 100, 200, and 300}. Words with occurrence frequency less than 2 are not included in the library. The co-occurrence matrix is created using a symmetric window of size 15. There are no pre-trained word embeddings for any of the 14 languages available with the GloVE embeddings repository[7]. We create these models and provide them with our repository.

4.4. MUSE

MUSE embeddings are cross-lingual embeddings that can be trained using the fastText embeddings, which we had created previously. Due to resource constraints and the fact that cross-lingual representations require a large amount of data, we choose to train 50-dimensional embeddings for each language pair. We train for all the language pairs (14*14) and thus produce 196 models using this approach and provide them in our repository. The training for these models took 2 days over 1 x 2080Ti GPU (12 GB).

4.5. ELMo

We train ELMo embeddings (Peters et al., 2018) of 512 dimensions. These vectors are learned functions of the internal states of a deep bidirectional language model (biLM). The training time for each language corpus was approximately 1 day on a 12 GB Nvidia GeForce GTX TitanX GPU. The batch size is reduced to 64, and the embedding model was trained on a single GPU. The number of training tokens was set to tokens multiplied by 5. We choose this parameter based on the assumption that each sentence contains an average of 4 tokens. There are no pre-trained word embeddings for any of the 14 languages available on the official repository. We provide these models in our repository.

---

[7] https://nlp.stanford.edu/projects/glove/

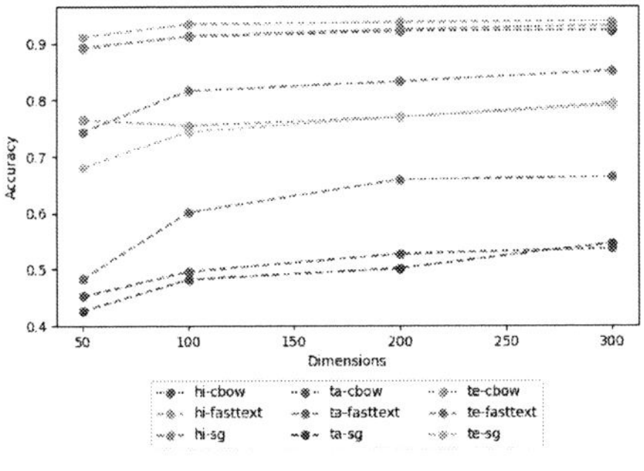

(a) Performance on UPOS tagged dataset

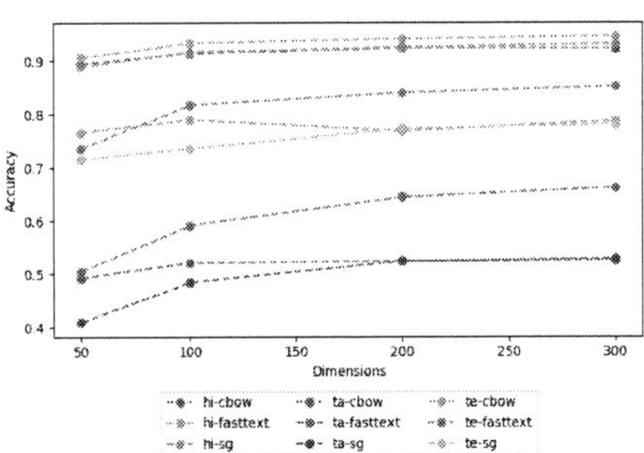

(b) Performance on XPOS tagged dataset

Figure 1: Performance of skip-gram, CBOW, and fasttext models on POS tagging task. Plotted graph is Accuracy vs Dimension. Legend is "language"-"model". Note that FastText is the best performer in each case, and learning saturates around 200 dimensions

Language	as	bn	gu	hi	ml	mr	kn	ko	ne	or	pa	sa	ta	te
Perplexity	455	354	183	518	1689	522	155368	325	253	975	145	399	781	82

Table 2: ELMo prerplexity scores

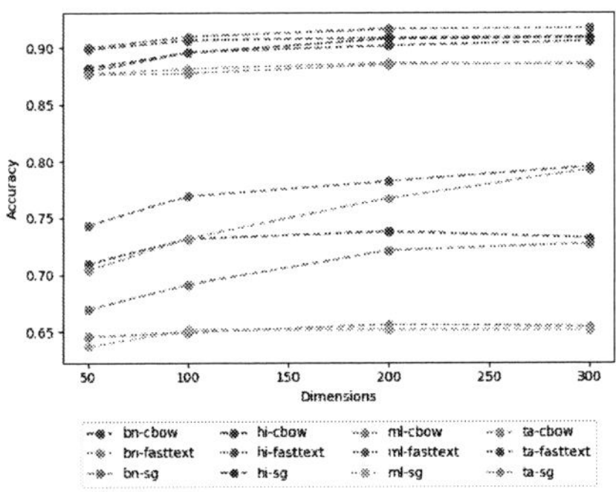

Figure 2: Performance of skip-gram, CBOW, and fasttext models on NER tagged dataset

4.6. BERT

We train BERT (Bidirectional Encoder Representations from Transformers) embeddings (Devlin et al., 2018) of 300 dimensions. Since BERT can be used to train a single multilingual model, we combine and shuffle corpora of all languages into a single corpus and used this as the pre-training data. We use sentence piece embeddings (Google, 2018) that we trained on the corpus with a vocabulary size of 25000. Pre-training this model was completed in less than 1 day using 3 * 12 GB Tesla K80 GPUs. The official repository for BERT provides a multilingual model of 102 languages, which includes all but 4 (Oriya, Assamese, Sanskrit, Konkani) of the 14 languages. We provide a single multilingual BERT model for all the 14 languages, including these 4 languages.

4.7. XLM

We train cross-lingual contextual BERT representation language model using the XLM git repository[8]. We train this model for 300-dimensional embeddings and over the standard hyperparameters as described with their work. The corpus vocabulary size of 25000 was chosen. We use a combined corpus of all 14 Indian languages and shuffle the sentences for data preparation of this model. We use the monolingual model (MLM) method to prepare data as described on their Git repository. This model also required the Byte-pair encoding representations as input and we train them using the standard fastBPE implementation as recommended over their Github. The training for this model took 6 days and 23 hours over 3 x V100 GPUs (16 GB each).

4.8. Evaluation

We evaluate and compare the performance of FastText, Word2Vec, and GloVE embedding models on UPOS and XPOS datasets. The results are shown in the image 1a and in 1b, respectively. The performance of non-contextual word embedding models on NER dataset is shown in image 2. The perplexity scores for ELMo training are listed in table 2. We observe that FastText outperforms both GloVE and Word2Vec models. For Indian languages, the performance of FastText is also an indication of the fact that morphologically rich languages require embedding models with sub-word enriched information. This is clearly depicted in our evaluation.

The overall size of all the aforementioned models was very large to be hosted on a Git repository. We host all of these embeddings in a downloadable ZIP format each on our server, which can be accessed via the link provided above.

---

[8]https://github.com/facebookresearch/XLM

5. Results and Discussion

We have created a comprehensive set of standard word embeddings for multiple Indian languages. We release a total of 422 embedding models for 14 Indic languages. The models contain 4 varying dimensions (50, 100, 200, and 300) each of GloVE, Skipgram, CBOW, and FastText; 1 each of ELMo for every language; a single model each of BERT and XLM of all languages. They also consist of 182 cross-lingual word embedding models for each pair. However, due to the differences in language properties as well as corpora sizes, the quality of the models vary. Table 1 shows the language wise corpus statistics. Evaluation of the models has already been presented in Section 4.8.. An interesting point is that even though Tamil and Telugu have comparable corpora sizes, the evaluations of their word embeddings show different results. Telugu models consistently outperform Tamil models on all common tasks. Note that the NER tagged dataset was not available for Telugu, so they could not be compared on this task.

This also serves to highlight the difference between the properties of these two languages. Even though they belong to the same language family, *Dravidian*, and their dataset size is the same, their evaluations show a marked difference. Each language has 3 non-contextual embeddings (word2vec-skipgram, word2vec-cbow and fasttext-skipgram), and a contextual embedding (ElMo). Along with this, we have created multilingual embeddings via BERT. For BERT pre-training, the masked language model accuracy is 31.8% and next sentence prediction accuracy is 67.9%. Cross-lingual embeddings, on the other hand, have been created using XLM and MUSE.

6. Conclusion and Future Work

The recent past has seen tremendous growth in NLP with ElMo, BERT and XLNet being released in quick succession. All such advances have improved the state-of-the-art in various tasks like NER, Question Answering, Machine Translation, etc. However, most of these results have been presented predominantly for a single language- English. With the potential that Indian languages computing has, it becomes pertinent to perform research in word embeddings for local, low-resource languages as well. In this paper, we present the work done on creating a single repository of corpora for 14 Indian languages. We also discuss the creation of different embedding models in detail. As for our primary contribution, these word embedding models are being publicly released.

In the future, we aim to refine these embeddings and do a more exhaustive evaluation over various tasks such as POS tagging for all these languages, NER for all Indian languages, including a word analogy task. Presently evaluations have been carried out on only a few of these tasks. Also, with newer embedding techniques being released in quick successions, we hope to include them in our repository. The model's parameters can be trained further for specific tasks or improving their performance in general. We hope that our work serves as a stepping stone to better embeddings for low-resource Indian languages.

7. Bibliographical References

Akbik, A., Blythe, D., and Vollgraf, R. (2018). Contextual string embeddings for sequence labeling. In *COLING 2018, 27th International Conference on Computational Linguistics*, pages 1638–1649.

Artetxe, M., Labaka, G., and Agirre, E. (2018a). A robust self-learning method for fully unsupervised cross-lingual mappings of word embeddings. In *Proceedings of the 56th Annual Meeting of the Association for Computational Linguistics (Volume 1: Long Papers)*, pages 789–798.

Artetxe, M., Labaka, G., and Agirre, E. (2018b). Unsupervised statistical machine translation. *arXiv preprint arXiv:1809.01272*.

Artetxe, M., Labaka, G., and Agirre, E. (2019). An effective approach to unsupervised machine translation. *arXiv preprint arXiv:1902.01313*.

Bansal, A., Banerjee, E., and Jha, G. N. (2013). Corpora creation for indian language technologies–the ilci project. In *the sixth Proceedings of Language Technology Conference (LTC '13)*.

Bojanowski, P., Grave, E., Joulin, A., and Mikolov, T. (2017). Enriching word vectors with subword information. *Transactions of the Association for Computational Linguistics*, 5:135–146.

Bojar, O., Diatka, V., Rychlỳ, P., Stranák, P., Suchomel, V., Tamchyna, A., and Zeman, D. (2014). Hindencorp-hindi-english and hindi-only corpus for machine translation. In *LREC*, pages 3550–3555.

Bordes, A., Chopra, S., and Weston, J. (2014). Question answering with subgraph embeddings. *arXiv preprint arXiv:1406.3676*.

Cer, D., Yang, Y., Kong, S.-y., Hua, N., Limtiaco, N., John, R. S., Constant, N., Guajardo-Cespedes, M., Yuan, S., Tar, C., et al. (2018). Universal sentence encoder. *arXiv preprint arXiv:1803.11175*.

Choudhary, N. and Jha, G. N. (2011). Creating multilingual parallel corpora in indian languages. In *Language and Technology Conference*, pages 527–537. Springer.

Conneau, A., Lample, G., Ranzato, M., Denoyer, L., and Jégou, H. (2017). Word translation without parallel data. *arXiv preprint arXiv:1710.04087*.

Devlin, J., Chang, M.-W., Lee, K., and Toutanova, K. (2018). Bert: Pre-training of deep bidirectional transformers for language understanding. *arXiv preprint arXiv:1810.04805*.

Diaz, F., Mitra, B., and Craswell, N. (2016). Query expansion with locally-trained word embeddings. *arXiv preprint arXiv:1605.07891*.

Google. (2018). Sentence piece embeddings. https://github.com/google/sentencepiece.

Haider, S. (2018). Urdu word embeddings. In *Proceedings of the Eleventh International Conference on Language Resources and Evaluation (LREC 2018)*, Miyazaki, Japan, May. European Language Resources Association (ELRA).

Lample, G. and Conneau, A. (2019). Cross-lingual language model pretraining. *arXiv preprint arXiv:1901.07291*.

Le, Q. and Mikolov, T. (2014). Distributed representations of sentences and documents. In *International conference on machine learning*, pages 1188–1196.

Levy, O., Seo, M., Choi, E., and Zettlemoyer, L. (2017). Zero-shot relation extraction via reading comprehension. *arXiv preprint arXiv:1706.04115*.

Melamud, O., Goldberger, J., and Dagan, I. (2016). context2vec: Learning generic context embedding with bidirectional lstm. In *Proceedings of the 20th SIGNLL conference on computational natural language learning*, pages 51–61.

Merlo, P. and Rodriguez, M. A. (2019). Cross-lingual word embeddings and the structure of the human bilingual lexicon. In *Proceedings of the 23rd Conference on Computational Natural Language Learning (CoNLL)*, pages 110–120.

Mikolov, T., Chen, K., Corrado, G., and Dean, J. (2013a). Efficient estimation of word representations in vector space. *arXiv preprint arXiv:1301.3781*.

Mikolov, T., Sutskever, I., Chen, K., Corrado, G. S., and Dean, J. (2013b). Distributed representations of words and phrases and their compositionality. In *Advances in neural information processing systems*, pages 3111–3119.

Murthy, R., Khapra, M. M., and Bhattacharyya, P. (2018). Improving ner tagging performance in low-resource languages via multilingual learning. *ACM Transactions on Asian and Low-Resource Language Information Processing (TALLIP)*, 18(2):9.

Nivre, J., De Marneffe, M.-C., Ginter, F., Goldberg, Y., Hajic, J., Manning, C. D., McDonald, R., Petrov, S., Pyysalo, S., Silveira, N., et al. (2016). Universal dependencies v1: A multilingual treebank collection. In *Proceedings of the Tenth International Conference on Language Resources and Evaluation (LREC'16)*, pages 1659–1666.

Pagliardini, M., Gupta, P., and Jaggi, M. (2017). Unsupervised learning of sentence embeddings using compositional n-gram features. *arXiv preprint arXiv:1703.02507*.

Pennington, J., Socher, R., and Manning, C. (2014). Glove: Global vectors for word representation. In *Proceedings of the 2014 conference on empirical methods in natural language processing (EMNLP)*, pages 1532–1543.

Peters, M. E., Neumann, M., Iyyer, M., Gardner, M., Clark, C., Lee, K., and Zettlemoyer, L. (2018). Deep contextualized word representations. *arXiv preprint arXiv:1802.05365*.

Řehůřek, R. and Sojka, P. (2010). Software Framework for Topic Modelling with Large Corpora. In *Proceedings of the LREC 2010 Workshop on New Challenges for NLP Frameworks*, pages 45–50, Valletta, Malta, May. ELRA. http://is.muni.cz/publication/884893/en.

Y. Bengio, R. Ducharme, P. V. (2003). A neural probabilistic language model. In *Journal of Machine Learning Research*, pages 3:1137–1155.

Yang, Z., Dai, Z., Yang, Y., Carbonell, J., Salakhutdinov, R., and Le, Q. V. (2019). Xlnet: Generalized autoregressive pretraining for language understanding. *arXiv preprint arXiv:1906.08237*.

Proceedings of the 1st Joint SLTU and CCURL Workshop (SLTU-CCURL 2020), pages 358–361
Language Resources and Evaluation Conference (LREC 2020), Marseille, 11–16 May 2020
© European Language Resources Association (ELRA), licensed under CC-BY-NC

A Counselling Corpus in Cantonese

John Lee, Tianyuan Cai, Wenxiu Xie, Lam Xing
Department of Linguistics and Translation
City University of Hong Kong
{jsylee, tianycai, wenxixie, lamxing}@cityu.edu.hk

Abstract

Virtual agents are increasingly used for delivering health information in general, and mental health assistance in particular. This paper presents a corpus designed for training a virtual counsellor in Cantonese, a variety of Chinese. The corpus consists of a domain-independent subcorpus that supports small talk for rapport building with users, and a domain-specific subcorpus that provides material for a particular area of counselling. The former consists of ELIZA style responses, chitchat expressions, and a dataset of general dialog, all of which are reusable across counselling domains. The latter consists of example user inputs and appropriate chatbot replies relevant to the specific domain. In a case study, we created a chatbot with a domain-specific subcorpus that addressed 25 issues in test anxiety, with 436 inputs solicited from native speakers of Cantonese and 150 chatbot replies harvested from mental health websites. Preliminary evaluations show that Word Mover's Distance achieved 56% accuracy in identifying the issue in user input, outperforming a number of baselines.
Keywords: Cantonese, chatbot, counselling, test anxiety

1. Introduction

Virtual agents are increasingly used for delivering health information in general, and mental health assistance in particular. While chatbots may not qualify to replace human counsellors, users have been found to be more willing to disclose information to a chatbot than to a human (Lucas et al., 2014). Woebot, for example, has been shown to be effective in reducing symptoms of depression (Fitzpatrick et al., 2017).

In the "guided conversation" format, virtual counsellors ask pre-determined questions and allow users to choose from suggested responses (Fitzpatrick et al., 2017; Casas et al., 2018). Other chatbots are designed to handle free-form input from users. PAL (Liu et al., 2013) and TeenChat (Huang et al., 2015) are two examples among those operating in Chinese. Targeting teenagers and young adults, these two chatbots offer advice on social topics such as family relations and love affairs. In response to user input, it selects the most relevant answer from a knowledge base, taking into account user characteristics such as gender, marital status and age.

Since no single virtual counsellor can adequately address all mental health issues or serve all user populations, counselling services at schools or mental health organizations may be interested in developing their own bots to provide tailored advice in specialized counselling domains. While existing chatbots contain valuable linguistic and counselling resources, there is often no straightforward way to re-use or adapt them for related counselling tasks.

To facilitate development of virtual counsellors, this paper presents a corpus that is designed to be modifiable and extendable by any counsellor, who will henceforth be referred to as the "administrator". Designed for chatbots in the example-based framework, it contains a *domain-independent* subcorpus with small talk materials for rapport building with users, an essential component in counselling sessions across all domains. It also has a *domain-specific* subcorpus, which is to be populated by the administrator with example user inputs and chatbot replies for the domain concerned.

We developed the corpus in Cantonese, which is considered the "most widely known and influential variety of Chinese other than Mandarin" (Matthews and Yip, 2011). Less frequently used in formal written communication than Mandarin, the dominant variety in mainland China, Cantonese is supported by relatively few resources for natural language processing. Although Cantonese and Mandarin are genetically related, having both developed from Middle Chinese, they are mutually unintelligible in their spoken form and have significant differences in their written form (Wong and Lee, 2018). The differences between the major Chinese varieties have been described as being "at least on the order of the different languages of the Romance family" (Hannas, 1997).

The rest of the paper is organized as follows. After an overview of corpus design in the next section, we describe the content and role of the domain-independent subcorpus (Section 3) and the domain-specific subcorpus (Section 4).[1] We then present a case study on constructing a chatbot for test anxiety (Section 5).

2. Corpus Design

Our corpus, which consists of post-reply sentence pairs, is designed to support the construction of virtual counsellors in any domain. Given a user input, a chatbot can identify the example post in the corpus that is semantically most similar, and then retrieve the corresponding reply.

According to the five-stage framework for counselling sessions adopted by Inoue et al. (2012), the Introduction stage establishes rapport between the therapist and the client. In the Elaboration stage, the therapist explores the client's situation and tries to find clues for a solution. This may be followed by a Resistance stage if the client feels uncomfortable or resists the therapy. The therapist then proposes actions toward a solution in the Intervention stage. Finally, the Solution stage concludes the session.

---

[1] The corpus is available for research purposes on request to the first author.

Category	Description	Example user input	Example chatbot reply
Chitchat	Short social expressions	你好 'hi' 唔該 'thanks' 拜拜 'goodbye'	你好 'hi' 唔洗客氣 'you're welcome' 得閒再搵我啦 'see you later'
	Small talk	你叫咩名？ 'What's your name?'	我叫做... 'My name is ...'
Dialog	General dialog	你的工作是什麼？ 'What's your job?'	陪聊 'Talking to people.'
Encouragers	ELIZA expressions	我覺得 ... 'I feel ...'	點解覺得 ...? 'Why do you feel ... ?'
Advice requests	Explicit request for advice	我想聽下你既建議 'I want to hear your advice'	(To be drawn from the domain-specific subcorpus)

Table 1: Domain-independent subcorpus (Section 3): example post-reply pairs

Category	# post-reply pairs
Chitchat	123
Advice requests	41
Encouragers	103
Dialog	276,000

Table 2: Size of the domain-independent subcorpus (Section 3), with breakdown into the main categories

The *domain-independent* subcorpus (Section 3) provides content for "off-task," social exchanges that are common across many counselling domains, especially during the Introduction stage. In subsequent stages, as users discuss their specific issues, the chatbot is expected to detect the issue types and incorporate appropriate advice in its response. For this purpose, the *domain-specific* subcorpus (Section 4) is to be populated by the administrator with example user inputs and possible advice to address them.

3. Domain-independent Subcorpus

The domain-independent subcorpus targets off-task interactions, such as greetings and chitchat. These interactions are typically dominant in the Introduction stage of a counselling session, but they can also be interweaved with on-task interactions in the subsequent stages. Their purpose is to move the conversation along, while keeping the users engaged and preparing them to disclose their feelings and issues.

Several example post-reply pairs in this subcorpus are shown in Table 1. Expected to be re-usable for most counselling domains and target users, these pairs belong to one of the four categories below. Table 2 shows the size of the domain-independent subcorpus with a breakdown into these categories.

3.1. Chitchat

The chitchat category covers common user expressions such as greetings, thank-you and good-bye, to which formulaic responses from the chatbot is usually sufficient; short yes/no answers (e.g., 係呀 'yes') to the preceding question; as well as small talk such as user enquiries about the chatbot's personal information, including name, age, occupation, family members, favorite food or colors, etc. The chatbot's persona is the only content that is expected to be customized in this subcorpus.

3.2. Encouragers

Encouragers consist of backchannel or empathic replies, mostly defined with ELIZA-like regular expressions (Weizenbaum, 1983).

3.3. Advice Requests

Advice requests are user inputs that explicitly ask the chatbot for counselling advice.

3.4. Dialog

If the user input does not match any of the above categories, the chatbot can backoff to a large-scale dialog database. We compiled a set of over 276,000 Cantonese and Chinese post-reply pairs, to handle general or off-task user input. These pairs are taken from two conversation corpora: the *Xiaohuangji* corpus[2] and the ChatterBot corpus[3].

4. Domain-specific Subcorpus

Following the Introduction stage of the counselling session, the chatbot engages users in discussing their thoughts and experiences, and then gives counselling advice. The domain-specific subcorpus consists of example user inputs and appropriate pieces of advice. Unlike those in the domain-independent subcorpus (Section 3), these post-reply pairs are less likely to be relevant to other domains. The onus is therefore put on the administrators to supply these pairs for their target counselling domain.

Most existing virtual counsellors clearly define their areas of competence. For example, PAL addresses the topics "husband and wife", "family relations", "love affairs", "adolescence", "feeling and mood", and "mental tutors" (Liu et al., 2013), while TeenChat detect stress in the areas of "study", "self-cognition", "interpersonal", "affection" and "general" (Huang et al., 2015). The domain-specific subcorpus likewise expects the administrator to define a set of issues, but at a finer granularity, such that each issue can be mapped to specific pieces of advice.

4.1. Symptom Statements

We will refer to each issue as a "symptom". In the domain of test anxiety, for example, symptoms may include headaches, worries about failure, and worries about parental reaction, which are among the most relevant issues identified in a psychology study (Wren and Benson, 2004).

---

[2] Accessed at https://github.com/skdjfla/dgk_lost_conv
[3] Accessed at https://github.com/gunthercox/chatterbot-corpus

Symptom	Symptom statement	Counselling item
Headache	我頭疼 'I have a headache'	原來係咁, 會唔會係得唔夠? 'I see, did you get enough sleep?'
Worries about failure	如果唔合格咁點算啊？ 'What if I fail?'	依家擔心都冇用順其自然啦 'No need to worry now, let it be!'
Worries about parental reaction	又會被屋企人話 'I'll get critized at home'	只要你盡左力父母一定會明白既 "If you tried hard, your parents would understand'
Severe	想死 'I want to die'	你依家可以打比x 8478搵counsellor傾下先！ 'Call x8478 now to chat with a counsellor'

Table 3: Domain-specific corpus (Section 4): example symptoms, symptom statements and counselling items for the test anxiety domain

For each symptom, the administrator is to provide a set of symptom statements, i.e., typical user inputs that express that symptom. Table 3 shows example symptom statements for the domain of test anxiety (Wren and Benson, 2004).

4.2. Counselling Items

The chatbot should be able to address each symptom with appropriate pieces of advice, which we will refer to as "counselling items". The administrator is to provide these items, which may be practical advice collected from existing mental health materials. They can also be contact information of human counsellors, which would be appropriate for more severe symptoms such as thoughts of suicide.

The administrator can optionally provide a set of sentences for broaching the counselling topic[4], to be deployed when users engage exclusively in small talk for an extended period, to steer them back to on-task discussion.

4.3. Threshold Score

The administrator may adjust the aggressiveness of the chatbot in advice giving by setting the threshold score for symptom detection. The typical system computes a similarity score between the user input and each symptom statement in the subcorpus (Section 5.2). If the score exceeds the threshold, a counselling item for the symptom is returned. A higher threshold leads to a chatbot that is more restrained in giving advice and more inclined to listen. A lower threshold, in contrast, increases its propensity to give counsel.

5. Case Study

To evaluate the proposed chatbot framework, we compiled a domain-specific subcorpus for the domain of test anxiety (Section 5.1) and experimented with a number of semantic similarity measures (Section 5.2). Together with the domain-independent subcorpus, we instantiated a chatbot that addresses test anxiety (Figure 1).

Many websites and pamphlets already offer advice and remedies for test anxiety, an issue that affects many students. Despite the wealth of counselling materials static media, however, there has been little attempt to leverage them for virtual counselling. To the best of our knowledge, the only reported chatbot that specifically deals with test

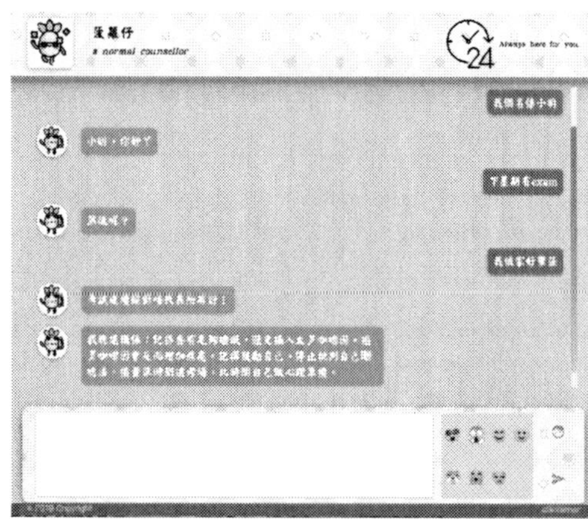

Figure 1: Example conversation in our Cantonese chatbot for test anxiety

anxiety is the *Exam-Stress Counselor and Academic Planner* (Rudra et al., 2012). This system uses a deterministic finite state automaton to analyze user inputs, which are expected to conform to a number of fixed patterns. Our chatbot, in contrast, is designed for interactions with free-form text.

5.1. Compilation of Domain-specific Subcorpus

Our set of symptoms were the 25 most relevant issues in test anxiety identified by Wren and Benson (2004). For symptom statements, we solicited user inputs for each symptom from 12 subjects, all native speakers of Cantonese. After reading the original symptom description in English written by Wren and Benson (2004), the subjects were asked to give paraphrases in Cantonese. They provided a total of 436 sentences, which served as the evaluation dataset.

For counselling items, we collected advice on test anxiety from websites linked to the home page of the counselling department at our university. For severe symptoms requiring human intervention, we supplied the phone number of the department. The subcorpus contained a total of 150 counselling items, with an average of 5.8 items per symptom.

5.2. Semantic Similarity Measures

To determine the symptom in the user input, the chatbot computes semantic similarity scores between the input and

---

[4]e.g., 你有冇有關於學業既野想同我傾下？ 'Do you want to talk about any academic issue?'

Approach	Accuracy
Word Mover's Distance	**56.2%**
ELMo	47.5%
word2vec	47.7%

Table 4: Symptom detection accuracy

the symptom statements in the domain-specific subcorpus. We compared the performance of two semantic similarity measures with the baseline of using word2vec (Mikolov et al., 2013) embeddings alone.

Word Mover's Distance (WMD). We applied this distance metric by representing each word in the sentence with the word2vec vector embeddings. We then used WMD to measure the dissimilarity between two sentences, as expressed by the minimum cumulative distance that the embedded words of one sentence need to travel to match those in the other sentence (Kusner et al., 2015). The symptom statement that yields the shortest distance is returned.

ELMo. Shown to improve the state-of-the-art in a variety of NLP tasks, ELMo is a contextualized word representation that models not only the characteristics of word usage, but also how the usage varies across linguistic contexts, i.e., polysemy (Peters et al., 2018). The word vectors are learned functions of the internal states of a deep bidirectional language model, pre-trained on a large text corpus.

5.3. Symptom Detection Accuracy

We conducted a leave-one-out evaluation on the symptom statements in our domain-specific subcorpus (Section 5.1) to measure accuracy in symptom detection. The chatbot automatically determined the symptom for each of the 436 statements, by retrieving the most similar statement among those in the remainder of the subcorpus, with respect to the similarity measures described in Section 5.2. As shown in Table 4, Word Mover's Distance achieved the best performance in symptom detection, at 56.2% accuracy. It outperformed both ELMo (47.5%) and the word2vec baseline (47.7%).

6. Conclusions

We have presented the first text corpus that is designed for virtual counselling in Cantonese. The corpus consists of a domain-independent subcorpus of chitchat and general dialog materials, which are intended to be re-usable for any counselling domain; and a domain-specific subcorpus, to be populated by administrators with typical user inputs and counselling advice in the domain concerned. We reported a case study on test anxiety, and evaluated the chatbot's accuracy in symptom detection. It is hoped that this corpus will facilitate development of virtual counsellors to serve Cantonese speakers.

7. Acknowledgements

This work was partially supported by CityU Internal Funds for ITF Projects (no. 9678104).

8. Bibliographical References

Casas, J., Mugellini, E., and Khaled, O. A. (2018). Food Diary Coaching Chatbot. In *Proc. ACM International Joint Conference and International Symposium on Pervasive and Ubiquitous Computing and Wearable Computers (UbiComp)*, pages 1676–1680.

Fitzpatrick, K. K., Darcy, A., and Vierhile, M. (2017). Delivering Cognitive Behavior Therapy to Young Adults with Symptoms of Depression and Anxiety using a Fully Automated Conversational Agent (Woebot): A Randomized Controlled Trial. *JMIR Mental Health*, 4(2):e19.

Hannas, W. C. (1997). *Asia's Orthographic Dilemma*. University of Hawaii Press, Honolulu, HI.

Huang, J., Li, Q., Xue, Y., Cheng, T., Xu, S., Jia, J., and Feng, L. (2015). TeenChat: A Chatterbot System for Sensing and Releasing Adolescents' Stress. *LNCS*, 9085:133–145.

Inoue, M., Hanada, R., Furuyama, N., Irino, T., Ichinomiya, T., and Massaki, H. (2012). Multimodal Corpus for Psychotherapeutic Situation. In *Proc. LREC Workshop on Multimodal Corpora for Machine Learning*, pages 18–21.

Kusner, M., Sun, Y., Kolkin, N., and Weinberger, K. (2015). From word embeddings to document distances. In *Proc. International Conference on Machine Learning*, pages 957–966.

Liu, Y., Liu, M., Wang, X., Wang, L., and Li, J. (2013). PAL: A Chatterbot System for Answering Domain-specific Questions. In *Proc. 51st Annual Meeting of the Association for Computational Linguistics (ACL)*, pages 67–72.

Lucas, G. M., Gratch, J., King, A., and Morency, L. P. (2014). It's Only a Computer: Virtual Humans Increase Willingness to Disclose. *Computers in Human Behavior*, 37:94–100.

Matthews, S. and Yip, V. (2011). *Cantonese: A Comprehensive Grammar*. Routledge, New York.

Mikolov, T., Chen, K., Corrado, G., and Dean, J. (2013). Efficient Estimation of Word Representations in Vector Space. In *Proc. International Conference on Learning Representations (ICLR)*.

Peters, M. E., Neumann, M., Iyyer, M., Gardner, M., Clark, C., Lee, K., and Zettlemoyer, L. (2018). Deep Contextualized Word Representations. In *Proc. NAACL-HLT*.

Rudra, T., Li, M., and Kavakli, M. (2012). ESCAP: Towards the Design of an AI Architecture for a Virtual Counselor to Tackle Students' Exam Stress. In *Proc. 45th Hawaii International Conference on System Sciences*.

Weizenbaum, J. (1983). ELIZA–A Computer Program For the Study of Natural Language Communication Between Man and Machine. *Communications of the ACM*, 26(1):23–28.

Wong, T.-S. and Lee, J. (2018). Register-sensitive Translation: A Case Study of Mandarin and Cantonese. In *Proc. Association for Machine Translation in the Americas (AMTA)*.

Wren, D. G. and Benson, J. (2004). Measuring Test Anxiety in Children: Scale Development and Internal Construct Validation. *Anxiety, Stress, & Coping: An international Journal*, 17(3):227–240.

Proceedings of the 1st Joint SLTU and CCURL Workshop (SLTU-CCURL 2020), pages 362–367
Language Resources and Evaluation Conference (LREC 2020), Marseille, 11–16 May 2020

Speech Transcription Challenges for Resource Constrained Indigenous Language Cree

Vishwa Gupta, Gilles Boulianne
Centre de recherche informatique de Montréal (CRIM)
{vishwa.gupta, gilles.boulianne}@crim.ca

Abstract

Cree is one of the most spoken Indigenous languages in Canada. From a speech recognition perspective, it is a low-resource language, since very little data is available for either acoustic or language modeling. This has prevented development of speech technology that could help revitalize the language. We describe our experiments with available Cree data to improve automatic transcription both in speaker- independent and dependent scenarios. While it was difficult to get low speaker-independent word error rates with only six speakers, we were able to get low word and phoneme error rates in the speaker-dependent scenario. We compare our phoneme recognition with two state-of-the-art open-source phoneme recognition toolkits, which use end-to-end training and sequence-to-sequence modeling. Our phoneme error rate (8.7%) is significantly lower than that achieved by the best of these systems (15.1%). With these systems and varying amounts of transcribed and text data, we show that pre-training on other languages is important for speaker-independent recognition, and even small amounts of additional text-only documents are useful. These results can guide practical language documentation work, when deciding how much transcribed and text data is needed to achieve useful phoneme accuracies.

Keywords: Speech recognition/understanding, Endangered Languages, Multimedia Document Processing

1. Introduction

As part of a governmental effort to preserve, revitalize, and promote the more than 70 Indigenous languages being spoken in Canada, we are exploring speech recognition technology for its potential to help transcription in language documentation and to facilitate access to recorded archives. Developing speech models for Indigenous languages is also important for applications valued by communities, such as creation of learning materials with synchronized text and speech, or dictionaries searchable by voice. We report here our work on Cree, one of the most spoken Indigenous languages in Canada, more specifically East Cree, spoken along James Bay coast. We hope to apply similar algorithm to help create speech recognition systems for other Indigenous languages.

From a speech recognition perspective, there is very little audio available in East Cree and even smaller amounts of audio are transcribed. Only a small amount of text (related mostly to the Bible) in Cree can be found for language modeling. We were able to get about 4.5 hours of transcribed audio from the internet: 9 videos from 5 speakers recalling stories, for a total of 1 hour (5939 words), and recordings related to readings of the Bible from one female speaker (3.5 hours, 21205 words). We also have 1247 CBC radio broadcasts in Cree which are not transcribed. Each CBC broadcast is about 1 hour long. We also had access to annual reports and Bible texts (differing from the read Bible audios) for training the language model. We outline here the experiments we have run in order to get good transcription accuracy for Cree with the available data described above.

The low resource transcription and keyword spotting effort received a great impetus from the IARPA Babel program[1]. In this program there were 10 languages with 10 hours (limited language pack or LLP) or 80 hours (full language pack or FLP) of transcribed audio. Many different DNN training algorithms have been experimented within the Babel program (Gales et al., 2014) (Knill et al., 2014) (Huang et al., 2013) (Trmal et al., 2014) (Chen et al., 2013) (Zhang et al., 2014). In (Gales et al., 2014) they experiment with both DNN and tandem systems and achieve token error rates (TER) between 60% and 77% with LLP, depending on the language and training algorithms. They also experiment with data augmentation by automatically labeling untranscribed data. In (Gales et al., 2014) and (Knill et al., 2014), they experiment with zero resource acoustic models where the acoustic models are trained using multiple languages to get good representation of phonemes. However, the language-independent TER is poor (over 80% TER). Another data augmentation method is to jointly train DNNs from multiple languages (Huang et al., 2013) (Trmal et al., 2014). Only the output layer is trained separately for each language.

All the languages in the Babel program are spoken by millions of people. Only the data to train the acoustic and language models was restricted. In contrast, the number of speakers speaking East Cree is estimated to be around 10,000 and very little transcribed audio data is available. The audio data that is available is spoken by only a few speakers. That is why we could only get 4.5 hours of transcribed audio from 6 speakers. For language modeling, written text in Cree was hard to get. There are no large volume publications in Cree. Most of the text is on Bible scriptures or annual community or town reports. Even in these reports, text in Cree is only a very small part of the report. We managed to extract about 260,000 words of text in Cree (written in syllabics) from all sources.

Speaker-dependent word or phoneme error rate (WER or PER) becomes an important issue for resource poor languages (Adams et al., 2018). Generally, we can find audio from a very few speakers, so getting good speaker-independent WER becomes difficult. The question is

---

[1]https://www.iarpa.gov/index.php/research-programs/babel

whether we can transcribe part of the audio from one speaker, train acoustic models, and then recognize the rest with reasonable accuracy. In this case, correcting a transcript with some errors might be much faster than transcribing from scratch.

This was shown in previous work on phoneme recognition for resource-poor languages (Adams et al., 2018). Time-aligned phoneme transcripts can be used to transcribe the audio in a low resource language more efficiently, reducing time and effort. The cited work used Persephone, an open source toolkit for phoneme recognition. We compare our system with Persephone and show that we get significantly lower phoneme error rates both with traditional DNN systems and also with sequence-to-sequence training.

We show here the word error rate and phoneme error rate we can achieve with just 4.5 hours of transcribed audio and 260k words of text for language modeling. We measure both speaker-dependent and speaker-independent WER. With the most advanced algorithms, we can achieve 24.6% WER for speaker-dependent recognition, and 70% WER for speaker-independent recognition. The 24.6% WER is probably good enough to significantly reduce transcription time for one speaker of Cree, for example, for the anchor of the CBC broadcasts in Cree.

2. Acoustic and Language Model Data

The complete data set for training acoustic and language models is outlined in Table 1.

data	amount	source
transcribed video stories	1 hour	beesum
read biblical text	3.5 hours	biblical website
CBC radio broadcasts	1343 hours	CBC radio archives
biblical text	160,000 words	biblical website
text from annual reports	110,000 words	annual reports of Cree organisations

Table 1: Amount of audio and text data in Cree from various sources. The CBC radio broadcasts in Cree are not transcribed. There are 9 transcribed video stories from 5 speakers. The read biblical text is from 1 female speaker.

One male and one female speaker from video data were used for testing (a total of 17 minutes of audio), and the remaining 3 video speakers were used in the training set (a total of 43.6 minutes of audio). The audio from one female speaker reading scriptures was divided into test (17.5 mins) and training (3.1 hours) sets. In order to increase the size of the training set for acoustic modeling, the training audio was speed perturbed, with factors of 0.9 and 1.1 times, before training the deep neural net (DNN) acoustic models. The 4-gram language model was trained on a mix of annual reports and Bible texts downloaded from the internet and different from the read Bible audios described above. The texts were split into 253,245 words for training and 6,737

words for development. Only the words in the LM training set were used as the 4-gram LM vocabulary: a total of 27189 words.

The perplexity of the language model (LM) represents how well the LM represents the word sequences in the text. The lower the perplexity, the better the language model. The 4-gram LM has 82.9 perplexity on the LM dev set, 317 on video transcripts, and 159.7 on Bible transcripts. The weighted out-of- vocabulary (OOV) rate is 7% on LM dev set, 24.9% on video transcripts, and 9.1% on Bible transcripts. So we expect much lower WER on bible transcripts (lower OOV rate and lower perplexity) than on video transcripts using this LM.

We use the same pronunciation dictionary for acoustic model training and decoding: it contains all the words in the LM training set (27189 words) plus the words in the video transcripts for a total of 29598 words. However, during decoding, words not in the language model will be considered as out-of-vocabulary (OOV). All the texts use the Unified Canadian Aboriginal Syllabics character set[2], and all the words are transcribed in X-SAMPA[3] phoneme set, by directly mapping each syllabic character to its phonemic representation.

3. Experiments with Transcribed Data

Since the amount of training data for Cree is very small, we decided to run two separate experiments. In one experiment we train deep neural net (DNN) acoustic models from the training data for Cree only. In the second experiment, we train models from about 4000 hours of transcribed English, and then adapt the resulting models to the Cree training data. Currently, the state-of-the-art DNN models are lattice-free maximum mutual information (LF-MMI) trained factored time delay neural networks (TDNN-F) (Povey et al., 2018)(Povey et al., 2016) and bidirectional long short memory neural networks (BLSTM) (Graves et al., 2013) models. So in the two experiments, we train both BLSTM models and TDNN-F models. In both these experiments, we use the same i-vector extractor trained from a large English dataset with many speakers. I-vectors represent speaker characteristics and adding these i-vector features to the standard mel frequency cepstral coefficients (MFCC) results in significant reduction in word error rates (WER).

For the first experiment, we trained both the GMM/HMM and DNN models from just the Cree training data. We used 40-dimensional MFCC features, and 100 dimensional i-vectors (Gupta et al., 2014) (Saon et al., 2013) (Senior and Lopez-Moreno, 2014) to represent speaker characteristics. For the small TDNN-F models (768-dimensional system with a linear bottleneck dimension of 160), LF-MMI training was followed by two iterations of discriminative training with sMBR (scalable Minimum Bayes Risk) criteria. In each iteration, the alignment between the audio and the audio transcript was created from the previous models followed by 3 epochs of sMBR discriminative training. For the BLSTM models, we did two iterations of back propagation training. In the first iteration, the models were trained

---

[2]https://unicode.org/charts/nameslist/c_1400.html
[3]https://fr.wikipedia.org/wiki/X-SAMPA

by back propagation using 6 epochs of training. In the second iteration models from the first iteration were used for alignment and as the initial models. In second iteration also we did 6 epochs of training.

The various results are shown in Table 2, which shows that BLSTM models give lower WER (74.3%) for video (speaker-independent) test set than either GMM-HMM or TDNN-F models. The TDNN-F models give the lowest WER (25.9%) for the scriptures test set (speaker-dependent). So three hours of audio is enough to give *useful* speaker-dependent results. By *useful* we mean that new audio from the same speaker can be transcribed and time-aligned with these models, and the resulting transcription can be corrected in significantly less time than manually transcribing the whole audio from scratch. Such transcription of large amounts of archived audio from a single speaker at a reasonable cost is of interest for many indigenous languages.

Model architecture	WER video	WER scriptures
GMM-HMM	77.1%	35.0%
BLSTM 1st BP	75.1%	27.9%
(1) BLSTM 2nd BP	74.3%	27.1%
TDNN-F LF-MMI	96.0%	27.0%
TDNN-F LF-MMI + sMBR	89.7%	26.0%
(2) + 2nd sMBR	90.1%	25.9%

Table 2: Word error rates for video (speaker-independent) and scriptures (speaker-dependent) test sets with a total of 3.85 hours of Cree training data. BP refers to back propagation, while sMBR is discriminative training with sMBR criterion.

In the second scenario, we train initial models from a very large dataset, and then adapt these models to the Cree training set. The idea is to have a model with well-trained phoneme set, and then to adapt these phonemes to Cree with the small training set for Cree. Phonemes that occur in the Cree training audio will get trained by Cree data, while other phonemes will still have a somewhat decent representation in these models. For the very large dataset, we used about 4000 hours of transcribed English audio available to us. This audio included Hub4, RT03, RT04, Market, WSJ, Librispeech, Switchboard, and Fisher data. This data is available from LDC. We added Inuktitut data available to us from the same Indigenous languages project, in an effort to cover some of the Cree phonemes missing from English. We used the same X-SAMPA phoneme set for this scenario also.

We then adapt both BLSTM and TDNN-F models trained above to the Cree training set. For training the larger TDNN-F (1536-dimensional system with a linear bottleneck dimension of 160) acoustic models, we ran multiple iterations of discriminative training with sMBR criteria on Cree data starting with the above models. So in the first iteration, the alignments for the Cree data come from the TDNN-F models trained from the 4000 hours of audio, and is followed by three epochs of discriminative training with sMBR criteria using the Cree data only. In the subsequent

iterations, the alignments between Cree training audio and its transcript come from the acoustic models generated in the previous iteration and is followed by three epochs of discriminative training with sMBR criteria using the Cree data only. We ran three such iterations of discriminative training using Cree data only.

For BLSTM adaptation, in the first iteration, we do back propagation starting with alignments from the BLSTM models trained from 4000 hours of audio, followed by 6 epochs of back propagation training. The initial models for this back propagation training are the BLSTM models trained from the 4000 hours of audio. In the subsequent iterations of back propagation, the alignments on Cree training data come from the models generated in the previous iteration and is followed by 6 epochs of back propagation training. In this back propagation training also, the initial BLSTM acoustic models come from the previous iteration. Overall we do four such iterations. The results with this adaptation strategy are shown in Table 3. When we compare Table 2 with Table 3, we see that BLSTM models trained from only Cree training data (first scenario) is only slightly worse than BLSTM acoustic model trained through adaptation from a model trained with large amount of data (74.3% versus 74.1%). However, for TDNN-F models, the speaker-independent WER is much lower with adapted TDNN-F (89.7% versus 78.8%). The speaker-dependent WER is much better when trained using the first scenario for both TDNN-F and BLSTM models. We also tried 40-dimensional filter-bank features instead of 40-dimensional MFCC features, but the WER is a little bit worse. However, since each model is different, we can combine the outputs using ROVER (Fiscus, 1997) to get significantly lower WER for both speaker-independent and speaker-dependent recognition. ROVER combines multiple transcripts obtained from multiple recognizers by first aligning the transcripts, and then taking a majority vote. The last line in Table 3 shows WER after ROVER.

Model specification	WER video	WER scriptures
(3) BLSTM MFCC 4th BP	74.1%	29.5%
(4) BLSTM fbank 4th BP	79.0%	31.2%
(5) TDNN-F 3rd sMBR	78.8%	30.0%
(8) ROVER of 1,2,3,4,5	72.5%	25.1%

Table 3: Word error rates for video and scriptures test sets after adaptation to a total of 3.85 hours of Cree training data. BP refers to back propagation, while sMBR is discriminative training with sMBR criterion.

4. Experiments with Untranscribed Cree

In the MGB-3 challenge, we used closed-captioned audio files for training the acoustic models (Gupta and Boulianne, 2018). JHU also used closed-captioned audio for training the DNNs for Arabic audio (Manohar et al., 2017). The closed-captioned transcripts are not verbatim transcription of the audio. Using the transcripts from closed-captioning as is for training acoustic models will lead to poor acoustic models. So the transcript from the closed-captioning is purified by generating another transcript through recognition, then comparing the two transcripts, and only using segments of the transcripts that match well. This results in acoustic models that give much lower WER. For Cree audio, we do not have a transcript from closed-captioning. So we can fake closed captioning by combining (using ROVER) decoded transcripts from many recognizers as the closed-captioned transcript. This transcript is different from the recognized transcript of the best recognizer, so we can use segments of the transcripts that match well for training new acoustic models.

As a first experiment, we used ROVER of 3 transcripts of 1247 Cree audio files (two best TDNN-F models and the LSTM fbank model). The Cree audio files from CBC radio broadcasts have music, singing, etc. So these portions were removed first by using a DNN-based voice activity detector (Alam et al., 2019). The remaining segments were decoded using the above three acoustic models. The transcripts were then ROVERed to get a final transcript. This transcript was then used as a closed-captioned transcript to find matching segments using the best TDNN-F acoustic model adapted to the Cree audio (item (5) in Table 3). Out of 1247 hours of audio, this process reduced the audio to 221 hours. The 3.85 hours of Cree training audio was then added to these segments. This 224 hours of transcribed audio was then used to adapt the best TDNN-F models to this data by another iteration of discriminative training. The results are shown in Table 4. We have reduced WER for the video test set from 78.8% to 75.1%, and for the scriptures test set from 30.0% to 28.7%. Training BLSTM models with this 224 hours of audio gave 72.5% (video) and 27.6% (scriptures) WER. Note that the WER differences between the TDNN-F and BLSTM models are much smaller after training with the 224 hours of audio. Combining with ROVER the ctm files from all the 7 models (item (9) in Table 4) results in 69.9% WER for the video test set (speaker-independent) and 24.6% WER for the scripture test set (speaker-dependent).

Training	video	scriptures
(6) BLSTM with 224 hours	72.5%	27.6%
(7) TDNN-F with 224 hours	75.1%	28.7%
(9) ROVER 1 thru 7	69.9%	24.6%

Table 4: Word error rates for the video and scriptures test sets after training with untranscribed Cree radio broadcasts.

5. Phoneme Recognition

The work in (Adams et al., 2018) uses a phoneme recognizer to generate time-aligned phoneme and tone sequences for two different low resource languages, Yongning Na and Eastern Chatino. Both training and test audio are from a single speaker. The reason is that recordings from very few speakers are available in a low resource language, and the primary task is to record audio from one speaker and to transcribe it in order to document and preserve the language. The authors claim that as long as phoneme error rate is low, the time-aligned phoneme sequence helps linguists and speeds up the transcription of the audio significantly.

We measure phoneme recognition accuracy on the Cree audio using three different systems: Persephone (Adams et al., 2018), wav2letter++ (Collobert et al., 2016) (Pratap et al., 2019), and the traditional speech recognition system using Kaldi (Povey and others, 2011) as described in the previous section 4. In both wav2letter++ and Kaldi systems, we decode word sequences and translate them to phoneme sequences in order to measure the phoneme error rate (PER). We show that by just training the language model with increasing amounts of text data, we can significantly reduce the PER, even though the language models are trained from a very small amount of additional text. These systems far outperform the Persephone system in this mode.

All three systems are tested with 17.5 minutes of speech from one female speaker reading scriptures. Some of the experiments use additional scripture texts downloaded from the Internet, from scripture books different from training and test sets.

Persephone is the phoneme recognizer used in (Adams et al., 2018), based on Tensorflow and made publicly available. The model is a bidirectional LSTM neural network architecture with the connectionist temporal classification (CTC) loss function. For this system, we tried training the bidirectional LSTM models with and without speed perturbed Cree training data. The Persephone system did not converge when we used both the video and scriptures training data. Long video segments caused training issues, and video speakers are different from the scripture test speaker. So we only used the scripture training set for training the bidirectional LSTM models. Table 5 gives the phoneme error rate for the scriptures test set using the Persephone system with and without speed perturbed training set. The PER goes down from 23.5% to 20.6% with the speed perturbed training set.

Training set	PER
scriptures training set	23.5%
scriptures training set with SP	20.6%

Table 5: Phoneme error rates (PER) with Persephone for the scripture test set after training with the scriptures training set with / without speed perturbation (SP).

Wav2letter++ is an open-source speech recognition toolkit recently released by Facebook for sequence-to-sequence training and decoding. It is entirely written in C++ and is very fast. Wav2letter++ uses convolutional network based acoustic models and a graph decoding. We have used the same architecture as provided in their documentation for Libri-speech data. Since we have much less data, we also tried an acoustic model with dimensions reduced by half. This smaller acoustic model gave slightly better results, so we give results for this acoustic model only. For wav2letter++, the lexicon contained words and their spellings in syllabics. So there were 141 distinct syllabic symbols used in the dictionary as the spelling alphabet (compared to 26 for English). For decoding, wav2letter++ is driven by a language model. For language model, we used the same 4-gram language model as used in the previous section. We also used two different training criteria: Connectionist Temporal Classification (CTC) and AutoSegCriterion (ASG). We ran wav2letter++ on a 32 GB Linux machine with an NVIDIA GPU card inside docker. For wav2letter++ also, training with video data included in the training set failed due to memory allocation failure. So we only trained with the scriptures training set with/without speed perturbation, and with CTC or ASG criterion. Table 6 gives the phoneme error rates for the various training conditions. The phoneme error rate is measured by converting words to phoneme sequences. For wav2letter++ the lowest PER was 15.1% on the scriptures test set when the training used ASG criterion. So wav2letter++ gives lower PER than the Persephone system.

Training set	criterion	PER
scriptures training set	CTC	20.9%
scriptures training set	ASG	15.1%
scriptures training set with SP	ASG	16.0%

Table 6: Phoneme error rates (PER) with wav2letter++ for the scripture test set after training with the scriptures training set with / without speed perturbation (SP).

We also translated the word error rates of different systems from sections 3. and 4. to phoneme error rates shown in Table 7. The system numbers correspond to the numbered systems in Tables 2, 3, 4. The lowest phoneme error rate corresponds to system 1: BLSTM system trained on Cree training data only with 2 iterations of back propagation. The 8.7% PER is significantly lower than 20.6% PER achieved by Persephone and 15.1% PER achieved by wav2letter++.

System	WER for scriptures	PER
(1)	27.1%	8.7%
(2)	25.9%	9.1%
(3)	29.5%	9.6%
(4)	31.2%	11.5%
(5)	30.0%	10.1%
(6)	27.6%	9.0%
(7)	28.7%	10.3%
(8)	25.1%	10.0%
(9)	24.6%	9.3%

Table 7: Phoneme error rates (PER) for the various systems in the previous section for the scripture test set (speaker-dependent error rate).

Both wav2letter++ and Kaldi (TDNN-F and BLSTM models) decoding is driven by a language model, while Persephone does not use any language model. The first two systems have access to additional information from the language modeling text. Are they benefiting from this information, and if so, how much additional text is needed? To answer this question, we ran decoding with several different language models, starting from scripture training transcriptions only, and incrementally added text to the language model training. We only trained 3-gram LMs for this comparison, with the vocabulary found in transcriptions only, to make comparison with Persephone as fair as possible.

Table 8 shows the phoneme error rate for the various LMs, for the best wav2letter++ system (from Table 6) and for the BLSTM system (1). The first entry in the table is when language model training data is limited to transcriptions in the Cree training data only. Then all three systems have access to the same language model information for the Cree language. The phoneme error rate is similar for wav2letter++ (20.7%) and Persephone (20.6%), but is significantly lower for the BLSTM system (1) (14.4%).

As more text data is made available for the LM, in the following lines of the table, PER continues to go down both for wav2letter++ and the BLSTM system (1). This shows that for the best phoneme recognition, we should use all the available text for language modeling.

LM Training set	wav2letter	(1)
scriptures training (20k words)	20.7%	14.4%
scriptures training + 50k words	16.9%	10.1%
scriptures training + 100k words	15.8%	9.4%
scriptures training + 158k words	15.4%	8.7%

Table 8: Phoneme error rates (PER) for wav2letter++ and for the BLSTM system (1) for the scripture test set with increasing LM training set.

6. Implications for Language Documentation and Revitalization

How can speech recognition help in language documentation? There are many aspects to language documentation. One aspect is transcription of audio archives and of audio collected from the elders in the community in order to transcribe and preserve the language. For many native languages, a significant portion of the transcription may be done by linguists and second language learners. For them, displaying time-aligned phoneme sequences and word sequences can be a big help. For speaker independent recognizer for Cree described above, the displays will have too many errors. However, fortunately, significant portion of the audio in general is from a few speakers. So a speaker dependent recognizer can be trained from a few hours of transcribed audio, and the transcription of the remaining audio can be speeded up by displaying time-aligned phoneme and word sequences to the transcriber. As we have shown before, the error rates for the phonemes in speaker-dependent scenario can be well below 10%, and for words, below 30%.

Another issue in language documentation is to have content search capability in native audio archives. Since most of the archives in general are spoken by a few speakers, speaker dependent acoustic models can be used for such a search. Usually, the search looks for a sequence of matching phonemes, and a speech recognizer with less than 10% phoneme error rate can provide reasonable search capability with minimal false alarms.

Automatic transcription in words or phonemes, even with relatively large error rates, opens up new avenues for revitalization that simply bypass the transcription bottleneck. The ability to easily search in an approximate automatic transcription can be used to identify specific phrases in a large audio archive and catalog it by contents. Time-aligned word or phoneme transcriptions make it easy to extract didactic material for language learning, or produce read-along audio books. As our work on East Cree confirms and improves upon previous work on Yongning Na and Eastern Chatino (Adams et al., 2018), we can hope that these methods will apply to many other Indigenous languages.

7. Conclusion

Cree is an Indigenous language spoken in Canada. It is a low-resource language as very little printed text or spoken transcribed audio is available. We could get at most 4.5 hours of transcribed audio, over 1200 hours of untranscribed audio (through CBC radio broadcast archives in Cree) and 260k words of written Cree text. So with this limited data, we estimate word and phoneme error rates in both speaker-independent and speaker-dependent scenario for the best possible speech-to-text systems.

The lowest WER (word error rate) for speaker-independent scenario we achieve is 69.9%. This error rate is too high to accurately transcribe audio from an arbitrary speaker of Cree. However, in the speaker-dependent scenario, we achieved a WER of 24.6% and a PER (phoneme error rate) of 8.7%. These error rates are small enough to help speed up transcription significantly.

We also compare our system with two state-of-the-art end-to-end toolkits. We show that training acoustic deep neural network models in a traditional way still gives significantly lower phoneme error rates, and training language models from additional text (without audio) results in even lower rates. Our experiments also provide quantitative information about minimal amounts of transcription and text documents that lead to useful phoneme recognition accuracies.

8. Acknowledgements

This work was funded in part by National Research Council of Canada (NRC) and the Ministère de l'économie, innovation et exportation (MEIE) of Gouvernement du Québec.

9. Bibliographical References

Adams, O., Cohn, T., Neubig, G., Bird, S., and Michaud, A. (2018). Evaluating Phonemic Transcription of Low-Resource Tonal Languages for Language Documentation. In *Proc. LREC*, pages 3356–3365.

Alam, J., Gupta, V., and Boulianne, G. (2019). Supervised and Unsupervised SAD Algorithms for the 2019 edition of NIST Open Speech Analytic Technologies Evaluation. In *OpenSAT2019 Workshop*, pages 1–21.

Chen, G., Khudanpur, S., Povey, D., Trmal, J., Yarowsky, D., and Yilmaz, O. (2013). Quantifying the value of pronunciation lexicons for keyword search in low resource languages. In *Proc. ICASSP*, pages 8560–8564.

Collobert, R., Puhrsch, C., and Synnaeve, G. (2016). Wav2Letter: an End-to-End ConvNet-based Speech Recognition System. http://arxiv.org/abs/1609.03193.

Fiscus, J. G. (1997). A post-processing system to yield reduced word error rates: Recognizer Output Voting Error Reduction (ROVER). In *Proc. ASRU*, pages 347–352.

Gales, M. J. F., Knill, K. M., Ragni, A., and Rath, S. P. (2014). Speech Recognition and Keyword Spotting for Low Resource Languages: BABEL project research at CUED. In *Proc. SLTU*, pages 14–16.

Graves, A., Jaitly, N., and Mohamed, A. R. (2013). Hybrid speech recognition with Deep Bidirectional LSTM. In *Proc. ASRU*, pages 273–278.

Gupta, V. and Boulianne, G. (2018). CRIM's system for the MGB-3 English multi-genre broadcast media transcription. In *Proc. Interspeech*, pages 2653–2657.

Gupta, V., Kenny, P., Ouellet, P., and Stafylakis, T. (2014). I-vector-based speaker adaptation of deep neural networks for French broadcast audio transcription. In *Proc. ICASSP*, pages 6334–6338.

Huang, J.-T., Li, J., Yu, D., Deng, L., and Gong, Y. (2013). Cross-Language Knowledge Transfer Using Multilingual Deep Neural. In *Proc. ICASSP*, pages 7304–7308.

Knill, K. M., Gales, M. J., Ragni, A., and Rath, S. P. (2014). Language independent and unsupervised acoustic models for speech recognition and keyword spotting. In *Proc. Interspeech*, pages 16–20.

Manohar, V., Povey, D., and Khudanpur, S. (2017). JHU Kaldi system for Arabic MGB-3 ASR challenge using diarization, audio-transcript alignment and transfer learning. In *Proc. ASRU*, pages 346–352.

Povey, D. et al. (2011). The Kaldi speech recognition toolkit. In *Proc. ASRU*.

Povey, D., Peddinti, V., Galvez, D., Ghahremani, P., Manohar, V., Na, X., Wang, Y., and Khudanpur, S. (2016). Purely sequence-trained neural networks for ASR based on lattice-free MMI. In *Proc. Interspeech*, pages 2751–2755.

Povey, D., Cheng, G., Wang, Y., Li, K., Xu, H., Yarmohamadi, M., and Khudanpur, S. (2018). Semi-orthogonal low-rank matrix factorization for deep neural networks. In *Proc. Interspeech*, pages 3743–3747.

Pratap, V., Hannun, A., Xu, Q., Cai, J., Kahn, J., Synnaeve, G., Liptchinsky, V., and Collobert, R. (2019). Wav2letter++: a Fast Open-Source Speech Recognition System. In *Proc. ICASSP*, pages 6460–6464.

Saon, G., Soltau, H., Nahamoo, D., and Picheny, M. (2013). Speaker adaptation of neural network acoustic models using i-vectors. In *Proc. ASRU*, pages 55–59.

Senior, A. and Lopez-Moreno, I. (2014). Improving DNN speaker independence with I-vector inputs. In *Proc. ICASSP*, pages 225–229.

Trmal, J., Chen, G., Povey, D., Khudanpur, S., Ghahremani, P., Zhang, X., Manohar, V., Liu, C., Jansen, A., Klakow, D., Yarowsky, D., and Metze, F. (2014). A keyword search system using open source software. In *Proc. SLT Workshop*, pages 530–535.

Zhang, X., Trmal, J., Povey, D., and Khudanpur, S. (2014). Improving deep neural network acoustic models using generalized maxout networks. In *Proc. ICASSP*, pages 215–219.

Proceedings of the 1st Joint SLTU and CCURL Workshop (SLTU-CCURL 2020), pages 368–375
Language Resources and Evaluation Conference (LREC 2020), Marseille, 11–16 May 2020
© European Language Resources Association (ELRA), licensed under CC-BY-NC

Turkish Emotion-Voice Database (TurEV-DB)

Salih Fırat Canpolat, Zuhal Ormanoğlu, Deniz Zeyrek

Graduate School of Informatics, Cognitive Science Department, Middle East Technical University (METU),

Ankara, Turkey

salih.canpolat@metu.edu.tr, zuhal.ormanoglu@metu.edu.tr, dezeyrek@metu.edu.tr

Abstract

We introduce the Turkish Emotion-Voice Database (TurEV-DB), which involves a corpus of over 1735 tokens based on 82 words uttered by human subjects in four different emotions (*angry, calm, happy, sad*). The speech data were produced by amateur actors, checked by assessors, recorded, and preprocessed by a denoising procedure. An emotion corpus was constructed on the basis of the finalized recordings. The database involves this corpus together with spectrograms, extracted prosodic features, prosodic data graphs overlaid onto spectrograms, and model activations. Three machine learning experiments were run using a convolutional neural network (CNN) and a support vector machine (SVM) model. Frequency-filtering was applied on the validation set, resulting in speech signals in three frequency ranges: 0-8000 Hz, 0-5000 Hz, and 500-8000 Hz. Frequency filtering is motivated by the fact that frequencies up to 8000 Hertz provide adequate information to human beings to detect sounds, frequencies up to 5000 Hz provide the necessary information about speech sounds, and frequencies below 500 Hz lack most of the speech energy. We describe the proposed methodology for constructing the corpus and the database, report the performance of the machine learning models, and for evaluation, compare machine learning results with human judgements.

Keywords: emotion, speech resource, machine learning

1.   Introduction

Emotion is an essential part of interpersonal communication as well as human-machine interaction, and such information can be obtained by processing the features of speech (Rozgić et al., 2012). Emotion recognition can be described as predicting the emotional information, category-wise or factor-wise, from the speech signal (Kim, et al., 2013).

As recording technology and computer processing power improved, the study of emotion has become computerized, and the relation between speech and emotion has been studied in this context extensively. To date, emotion corpora of different languages (encompassing both single languages and multiple languages) have been compiled. For example, Berlin Emotional Speech Database (Burkhardt et al., 2005) consists of a single language, German, and has 800 tokens. INTERFACE (Hozjan et al., 2002) on the other hand, includes English, Slovenian, Spanish, and French, and has 175 to 190 tokens for each language. Each corpus offers different properties regarding emotion.

In the context of Turkish, the link between emotion and voice has recently become quite popular. Among the studies that have been conducted, we can mention (Fidan, 2007) who focused on emotion in prosody. Regarding Turkish emotion resources, Meral et al. (2003) have been one of the first to form a database of four emotions in the Boğaziçi University Emotional database (BUEMDB, cf. Kaya & Karpov (2018)). The resource was based on recorded sentences, which were then analyzed to reveal the F_0 contours of the investigated emotions. Turkish Emotional Speech Database (TurES) (Oflazoglu & Yildirim 2013) offers a database of 5305 Turkish utterances recorded from Turkish movies and tagged with seven emotion categories. The EmoSTAR Database was developed by Parlak, et al. (2014) and includes over 300 spoken samples gathered from the TV or the internet. Korkmaz & Atasoy (2016) used Mel-Frequency Cepstral Coefficients (MFCC) to investigate the emotional content of the speech signal based on the EmoSTAR. Furthermore, Bakir (2017) and Bakır & Yuzkat (2018) gathered a voice-corpus of approximately 3740 Turkish voice samples of words and clauses of differing lengths collected from 25 males and 25 females. The authors developed hybrid machine learning models based on the voice samples. A

Name	Size	# of Actors	Source	Emotions	Emotion Axes	Statistical Features	OpenSmile Package
TurES	5305 tokens	582	Turkish Movies	Afraid, Angry, Neutral, Other, Sad, Surprised	Valence, Arousal, Dominance	Yes	emo_large
EmoSTAR	393 tokens	393	TV and Internet	Angry, Neutral, Happy, Sad	None	Yes	emo_base
BUEMODB	484 files	11	Actors*	Angry, Happy, Sad, Unemotional	None	No	No
Voice Corpus	3740 samples	50	Not known	Afraid, Angry, Sad, Happy, Neutral	None	Yes	No

Table 1: Comparison of overviewed Turkish emotion-voice databases (*non-professional actors).

comparative analysis of the overviewed Turkish emotion voice databases is presented in Table 1.

However, the field still needs more studies. Particularly needed are new databases. The overarching goal of the present study is to introduce Turkish Emotion-Voice Database, or TurEV-DB for short. TurEV is a database of Turkish emotion produced by amateur actors recruited for the sole purpose of the present study.

The specific aims of this study are three-fold: (a) to contribute to the field by compiling a spoken Turkish corpus of words reflecting four emotion categories (*angry, happy, calm, and sad*). These four emotion states were selected as they are generally used in emotion recognition studies such as Eun, et al. (2007), (b) in three experiments, to classify the emotions using two machine learning models; namely, the CNN and the SVM models, and compare the results with human judgements, (c) to form a database that includes the corpus and various peripherals such as spectrograms, continuous and spectral features of the words (e.g. F_0), MFCC, and intermediate activations of the CNN model. In the present study, we describe the corpus and the components of the TurEV database, including how we implemented the two machine learning models. Finally, we compare the performance of the models to each other and to human judgements. Thus, the corpus is evaluated, and the database is validated.

The rest of the paper is arranged as follows: Section 2 describes the data collection process and the database building procedure; Section 3. overviews the machine learning models; Section 4. illustrates the evaluation of the data by human judges; Section 0. presents and discusses the findings, and finally, Section 6. provides a summary and concludes the study.

2. Proposed Methodology

The proposed methodology for TurEV-DB consists of two main parts: The creation of the corpus, and the construction of the database. The creation of the corpus is presented in Section 2.1, and the construction of the database is presented in Section 2.2.

2.1 The Corpus

The creation of the corpus started with selection of words by the authors and proceeded with recording different emotional states by the amateur actors. The steps taken in the corpus creation procedure is presented in Figure 1 and described in the rest of the present section.

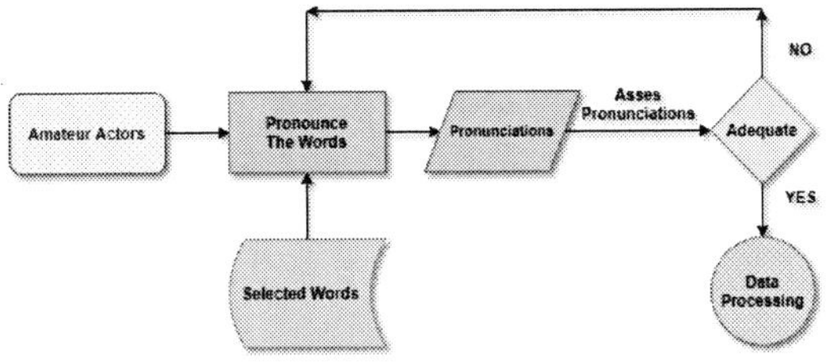

Figure 1: Corpus creation procedure.

2.1.1 Word Selection Procedure

In the literature, there are three types of widely used approaches for constructing an emotion-voice corpus. In the first approach, the desired emotions are induced in the participants by an experimental task; then, emotional speech is collected. The second approach uses the voice of trained or amateur actors who are instructed to speak imitating a specific emotion. The third and the least commonly used method is collecting emotion-induced speech from private recordings and call centers. Since this approach raises ethical concerns and privacy issues, it is not preferred so often. The first method is more natural but less reliable compared to the second approach. We adopted the second approach for our study.

We set out to select the words keeping in mind their phonological profile and selected 82 words from *Türkçenin Ses Dizgesi* (Ergenç & Bekar Uzun, 2017). The selected words involve a range of phonemes, both vowels and consonants, used in various positions in the word. For example, /r/ appears in word-initial and word-final positions as in *rıhtım* /ruhtum/ 'dock' and *demir* /demir/ 'iron', respectively. Such phonological variation allows the machine learning models to be tested for different conditions and increases the robustness of the models. Moreover, these words have already been investigated by Ergenç et al. (2017) in their neutral (calm) emotional state, and their F_0 values, density graphs, and spectrograms up to 5000 Hz are available. In short, this set of words provided the perfect data and the baseline of our experiments. Table 2 presents the number of tokens in the corpus.

Emotion	Actor ID						Total
	7895	1984	1234	1358	1157	6783	
Angry	82	82	82	82	77	82	487
Calm	80	82	82	82	0	82	408
Happy	29	82	82	82	0	82	357
Sad	82	82	82	82	73	82	483
Total	273	328	328	328	150	328	1735

Table 2: Total number of tokens in four emotional states performed by amateur actors.

2.1.2 Amateur Actors

We chose to work with individuals with no previous acting experience to elicit natural speech. From now on, these individuals will be referred to as amateur actors. Using the guidelines, the recruited amateur actors uttered the words and recorded them.

Six amateur actors[1] (three females, three males) produced the selected words. The age of amateur actors was balanced gender-wise to be able to represent the male and the female vocal properties. The ages ranged from the early twenties to mid-thirties. This range enabled us to obtain information from a variety of age groups.

2.1.3 Recording Procedure

The actors followed a set of guidelines prepared by the authors, and conducted their recording sessions on their

---

[1] The amateur actors were volunteering graduate or undergraduate students in Cognitive Science and Psychology departments.

own. They pronounced the words as if they were in each emotional state. They used the Sound Recorder application from Sony Mobile Productions and recorded the words in mono, WAV format, and in 44100-Hz sampling rate. The actors then listened to their own recordings and presented the recordings to an assessor, a third-party individual of their choosing. The pronunciations that lacked any emotional tone according to the actor or the assessor were re-recorded by the amateur actors. In this regard, each pronounced word is considered a token in TurEV-DB. Moreover, each token has relevant data points extracted from it or produced by it, as explained in the following sections.

2.1.4　Preprocessing

The data processing procedure consisted of two stages, namely the denoising stage and the frequency filtering stage for the experiments. In the denoising stage, the tokens were first denoised, and then they were trimmed. The resulting tokens had uniform silence before and after the word and had relatively low noise.

2.1.4.1　Denoising and Preprocessing

We removed the noise from the recordings and preprocessed them using Audacity 2.3.0[2] through the

summarized as the identification of the noise floor for each frequency by analyzing at least 2048 samples, and then removing this noise floor from the entirety of the recording.

2.1.4.2　Frequency Filtering

The data were first split into two, namely, the training and the validation sets. The validation data set consisted of 20% of the tokens and was used in the CNN model, the generation of the activation maps, and in human validation. Frequency filtering was applied to the validation tokens, resulting in speech signals in three frequency ranges: 0-8000 Hz, 0-5000 Hz, and 500-8000 Hz. Machine learning experiments were run on the frequency-filtered data.

Frequencies within 0-8000 Hz contain most of the acoustic features of the human voice. Although a young adult can hear more than 16000 Hz, such high frequencies do not contain useful features for human speech. Also, the 0-8000 Hz range is needed for the optimum amount of information transformation. According to the Nyquist-Shannon theorem (Yadav, 2009; Yao, 2014), in order to describe a signal, it should be sampled at least twice of the Nyquist frequency. In other words, a sine wave with 10 Hz frequency cannot be described by any sampling rate below 20 Hz. However, at 20 Hz, this description yields minimum amount of data. With 22050 Hz Nyquist frequency, we

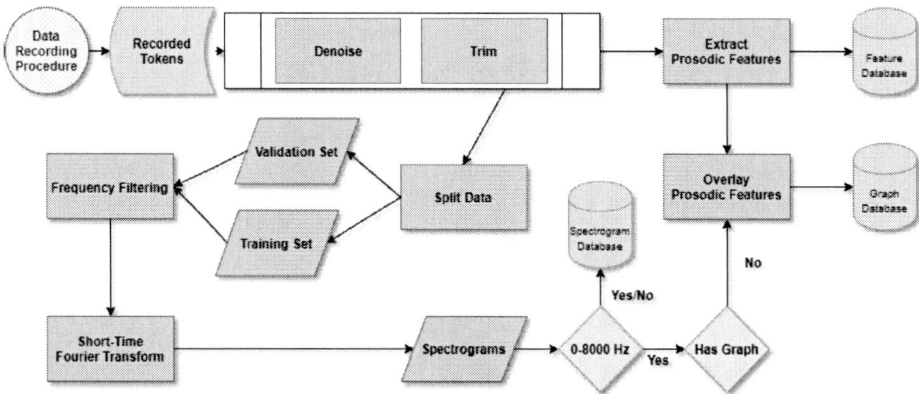

Figure 2: Construction of the database.

following steps:

1. The recording of each word was loaded into Audacity.
2. The signal view was changed from waveform into spectrogram.
3. The part that contained no voice was selected, and a noise profile was generated. The generated profile was used as a base profile in order to remove the noise from the recording.
4. The recording was trimmed leaving 150 milliseconds of silence at the beginning; the end and the rest of the recording were removed.
5. The denoised and preprocessed recording was exported in 32-bit Float Pulse Code Modulation (PCM)[3] WAV format.

In this stage, the statistical noise removal technique was used (Audacity Team, n.d.). The procedure could be

used approximately 1/3 of this maximum value, which is 8000 Hz. This strategy allowed us to be able to work both with a data-rich environment and relatively high frequencies. Thus, for the first experiment, the frequencies over 8000 Hz were trimmed out, and only the frequencies between 0 and 8000 Hz were kept.

Given that frequencies up to 5000 Hz actually contain the most useful features for humans, for the second experiment, the data were filtered trimming frequencies over 5000 Hz and the experiment was run on the 0-5000 Hz range. For the third experiment, the frequencies under 500 Hz were trimmed. This was motivated by the fact that most of the speech energy, as well as F_0 is cut out when the frequencies under this level are blocked. From an empirical perspective, comparing the predictive ability of the CNN model with the humans would be interesting in the third experiment, as it would reveal whether the model and

---

[2] https://www.audacityteam.org/audacity-2-3-0-released/

[3] https://docs.microsoft.com/en-us/windowshardware/drivers/audio/pcm-stream-data-format

humans perform similarly in the absence of low frequencies.

2.2 Construction of the Database

Construction of the database included the process of feature extraction, spectrogram generation, and overlaying the features onto the spectrograms. The construction of the database also overlapped with the creation of the corpus at the data preprocessing stage. A summary of the database construction procedure is presented in Figure 2.

2.2.1 Feature Extraction

Spectral features were extracted from the preprocessed recordings using OpenSmile[4], a freely available application Eyben et al. (2015). Low-level descriptors such as MFCCs and F_0, and the statistical functions applied to them were extracted, amounting to a total of 1582 extracted features. (These features were also used in the SVM model.) Moreover, time-variant acoustic features were also extracted. The procedure is elaborated in Section 2.2.2.

external data, e.g. by means of tokens generated from the same or a different word pool, and even data from different languages.

2.3 Acoustic Information

We extracted further acoustic features using OpenSmile. F_0, voicing probability, and loudness features were extracted with a 50 milliseconds window size and 10 milliseconds step size. These features were projected onto spectrograms for further inspection. The extracted features and spectrograms with acoustic information were added to TurEV-DB. This addition will allow future researchers to inspect the tokens with easy-to-read graphics instead of using hard to read data formats such as CSV. An example of such a spectrogram with projected acoustic features is presented in Figure 3.

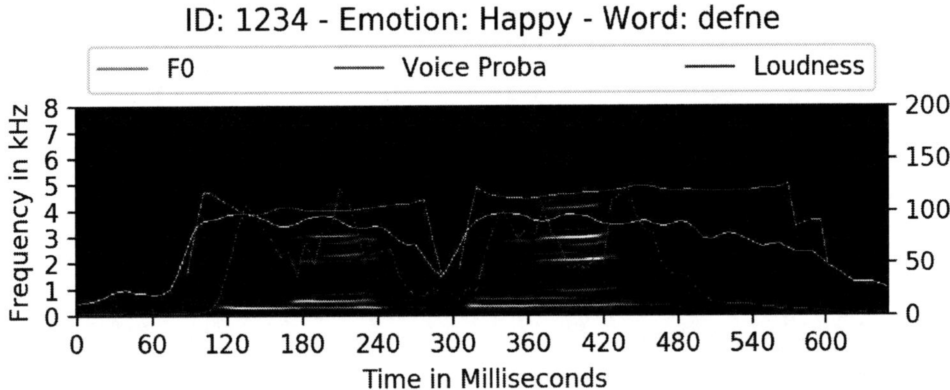

Figure 3: The spectrogram of the token defne 'happy' (uttered in a happy emotional state) and the acoustic features projected on it.

2.2.2 Spectrogram Generation

A spectrogram generation procedure specifically tailored for convolutional neural networks was used in this stage. The script was applied on all of the corpus tokens including the frequency-filtered tokens of the validation set. This procedure consisted of a short-time Fourier transformation (STFT) with Hamming window (Podder, et al., 2014). A 2205- sample long window size, which amounts to 50 milliseconds with 95% overlap was used in the STFT algorithm. In order to determine the optimal spectrogram output, we used different amounts of overlaps and different amounts of sample sizes in our pilot analyses. Each recording was saved as 746x495 pixel PNG image with 32-bit pixel depth in the grayscale colourmap. The spectrograms, as well as the script used for this procedure, were included in the TurEV-DB so that any set of new data could be processed using the script. These components allow the current and future models to be tested using

3. Machine Learning Models

Three experiments were run on frequency-filtered data using a CNN and SVM model. A CNN and an SVM model were constructed since they can be initialized and used on the go with the data included in TurEV-DB. We chose the SVM and the CNN model types because they represent different machine learning paradigms and offer different advantages.

3.1 The SVM Model

The SVM model was initialized with the RBF kernel and one versus rest (OVR) decision function. 10 features were extracted from the initial 1582 features (Section 2.2.1) using principal component analysis (PCA). 80% of the data was selected for training, 10% was used for validation, and 10% for testing. The results of the test set are presented in Table 4.

---

[4] https://www.audeering.com/opensmile/

3.2 The CNN Model

The CNN model was built using a custom set of layers, as shown in Figure 4. It exploits stacked layers of convolution operators without max-pooling in order to produce high-resolution activation maps. The CNN model accepts spectrograms of the words and outputs emotion category probabilities and the activation maps. As we explain briefly below, the activation maps are the result of Grad-CAM operations which allow the model to output its internal state regarding specific data and conditions, e.g. for the pronunciation of *rıhtım* 'dock' in the emotional state *happy*.

The results of the CNN model are also provided in Table 4

3.3 The Gradient-Weighted Class Activation Mapping (Grad-CAM) Model

The Grad-CAM model (Selvaraju et al., 2017) is a sub-part of the CNN model. It uses the final convolutional layer of the CNN model and projects intermediate activations according to an emotional state in this layer. The projections of intermediate activations are then visualized. These visualizations, which are also called heat maps, will allow users to inspect the areas that contribute most to the decision-making process of the CNN model.

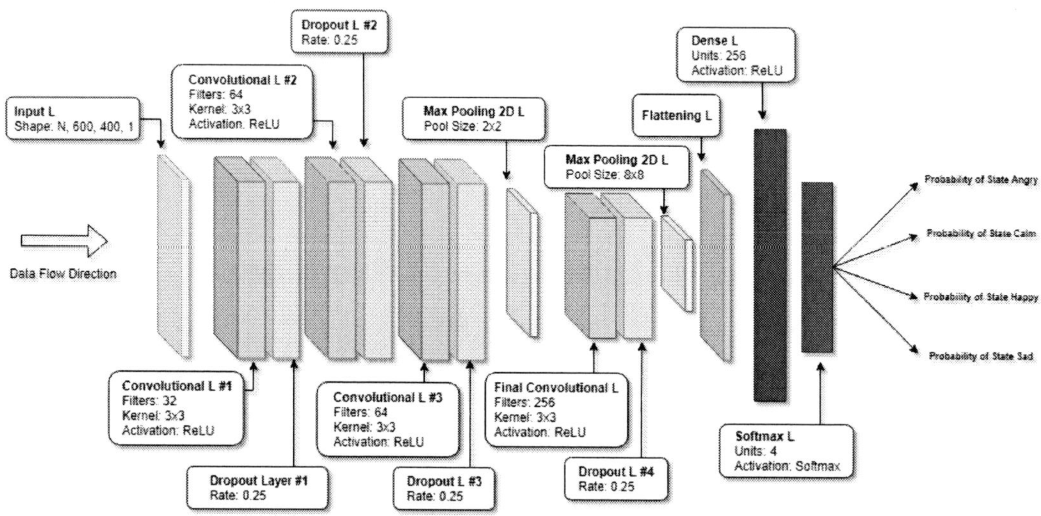

Figure 4: The architecture of the CNN model.

and indicate that with 76% accuracy, the CNN model is the highest performer compared to the SVM model as well as the human judgments for the data in the frequency range between 0-8000 Hz. It performs still well, though with a slightly reduced power (72%) in the frequencies between 0-5000 Hz. However, its accuracy plummets to 49% when it is subjected to spectrograms in the frequency range of 500-8000 Hz. The CNN model required 90 minutes for the 9 epochs of training.

Fold #	Accuracy	
	Maximum	**9th Iteration**
1	0.70	0.65
2	0.74	0.71
3	0.75	0.72
4	0.77	0.77
5	0.75	0.72
6	0.79	0.78

Table 3: Accuracy values for the cross-validation study for the CNN model.

3.4 Validation

The SVM model follows the standard 80% training, 10% validation, and 10% testing splits. The CNN model, on the other hand, uses 6-fold cross-validation. A new CNN model with the same architecture was generated and subjected to training and validation processes for each fold. The final accuracy of the CNN model was found to be within the bounds of the results obtained with the cross-validation study. Therefore, the model can be considered valid within the bounds of TurEV-DB. The results of the cross-validation study are presented in Table 3.

4. Experimental Results and Analysis

4.1 Data Evaluation by Human Judges

For data evaluation, three volunteering human judges were recruited. Each of the three judges was presented with the data of one of the experiments.[5] They were simply asked to listen and group the tokens into one of the four emotional states. They were presented the tokens with pseudo-names and not given any information about their emotional content. The matching decisions were considered correct and mismatching decisions were considered incorrect. The

---

[5] The judges were volunteering graduate students with a Bachelor's degree in psychology.

results of human evaluation are presented in Table 4 and show that they are quite stable across experiments.

4.2 Comparative Analysis of The Results of The CNN Model and The Human Judges

To compare the predictions of the CNN model and the human judgements, contingency tables were created for the frequency ranges investigated in the experiments and presented in Table 5, Table 6, and Table 7. These tables indicate that through different experiments involving different frequency ranges, the model and the judges converge on the categorization of two emotions, namely *happy* and *angry*. The emotion category *happy* is agreed by the CNN model and the judge with a ratio of 68%, 76.47%, and 71.05% in the different frequency ranges, respectively. Similarly, the emotion category *angry* is agreed by the CNN model and the judge with a ratio of 61.90%, 47.06%, and 75.23% in the different frequency ranges, respectively. Regarding the categorization of *angry*, in the frequency range 0-5000 Hz, the power of the model and the judges is lower than the other frequency ranges.

	Frequency Bands (in Hertz)			
	0-8000	0-5000	500-8000	
Judges	0.65	0.64	0.64	**Accuracy Rating**
CNN Model	0.76	0.72	0.49	
SVM Model	0.61	-	-	

Table 4: Classification accuracy of the models compared to human judgments in different frequency ranges.

CNN Model	The Human Judge			
	Angry	**Calm**	**Happy**	**Sad**
Angry	*61.90*	10.69	10.00	6.35
Calm	19.05	*38.17*	14.00	19.05
Happy	14.29	16.79	*68.00*	14.29
Sad	4.76	34.35	8.00	*60.32*

Table 5: Frequency distribution of emotion categorization by CNN and the human judges in the 0-8000 Hertz band.

CNN Model	The Human Judge			
	Angry	**Calm**	**Happy**	**Sad**
Angry	*47.06*	14.73	3.92	1.02
Calm	14.71	*37.21*	13.73	24.49
Happy	32.35	22.48	*76.47*	10.20
Sad	5.88	25.58	5.88	*64.29*

Table 6: Frequency distribution of emotion categorization by CNN and the human judges in the 0-5000 Hertz band.

CNN Model	The Human Judge			
	Angry	**Calm**	**Happy**	**Sad**
Angry	*75.23*	42.98	21.05	43.18
Calm	1.83	*9.65*	2.63	3.41
Happy	16.51	35.96	*71.05*	29.55
Sad	6.42	11.40	5.26	*23.86*

Table 7: Frequency distribution of emotion categorization by CNN and the human judges in the 500-8000 Hertz band.

To reveal the CNN model's and the judges' classification performance, precision, recall and F1 scores were calculated separately using the database labels as the key. The results are presented in Table 8, Table 9 and, Table 10. The metric results presented in Table 8 indicate that the CNN model succeeded in classifying all four emotions when it used the widest frequency band (0-8000 Hz).

According to Table 9, when the CNN model is fed with a signal lacking frequencies above 5000 Hz, it tends to classify *angry* less accurately with a recall of 0.51. However, according to Table 10, when the CNN model is fed with a signal lacking the frequencies below 500 Hz, it outright classifies *angry* with a recall value of 0.84. A similar performance is displayed by the judges for *angry* with a recall of 0.79. In this frequency range, for *calm*, the CNN model yielded a very low recall score of 0.11, and the judges a low recall score of 0.57. The category *sad* also has very low recall score of 0.31, compared to 0.67 of the judges (Table 10).

	The Emotion Categories							
	Angry		Calm		Happy		Sad	
Metrics	M	J	M	J	M	J	M	J
Precision	0.84	0.76	0.69	0.43	0.71	0.80	0.79	0.83
Recall	0.76	0.80	0.74	0.68	0.79	0.56	0.75	0.54
F1	0.80	0.77	0.71	0.53	0.75	0.66	0.77	0.65

Table 8: Metrics for CNN's and the judges' emotion classification for the 0-8000 Hz frequency band.

	The Emotion Categories							
	Angry		Calm		Happy		Sad	
Metrics	M	J	M	J	M	J	M	J
Precision	0.93	0.90	0.67	0.38	0.60	0.84	0.77	0.69
Recall	0.51	0.63	0.73	0.60	0.85	0.61	0.82	0.71
F1	0.66	0.74	0.70	0.46	0.71	0.70	0.80	0.70

Table 9: Metrics for CNN's and the Judges' emotion classification for the 0-5000 Hz frequency band.

	The Emotion Categories							
	Angry		Calm		Happy		Sad	
Metrics	M	J	M	J	M	J	M	J
Precision	0.46	0.71	0.53	0.41	0.41	0.92	0.70	0.74
Recall	0.84	0.79	0.11	0.57	0.64	0.49	0.31	0.67
F1	0.60	0.74	0.18	0.48	0.50	0.64	0.43	0.70

Table 10: Metrics for CNN's and the Judges' emotion classification for the 500-8000 Hz frequency band.

In summary:

- In 0-5000 Hz and 0-8000 Hz frequency ranges, the CNN model has a higher score than the judges as well as the SVM model. In the 500-8000 Hz frequency range, the CNN model underperforms, whereas the judges do not have any performance loss (see Table 4).
- According to Tables 5-7, while the emotion states *happy, angry* have relatively high classification rates both by the CNN model and the judges, the emotion states *calm* and *sad* have low classification scores. In contrast to *sad, calm, angry* and *happy* are high energy emotions with high-frequency outputs.
- Regarding the recall metrics of the human judges and the CNN model, Table 8 shows that the CNN model uses the widest frequency range of 0-8000 Hz to easily differentiate between the emotions *angry* and *happy* well as *calm* and *sad.* Table 10 indicates that the CNN model uses the 500-8000 Hz frequency band to recall the emotion category *angry* with a higher success than the emotion category *happy.*

5. Discussion

Beyond forming a corpus of 1735 tokens in four different emotion states and a database that includes low-level descriptors and acoustic features, the current study has several conclusions and implications. Regarding the machine learning models and the advantages they offer, the CNN model is computationally expensive; therefore, it is slow. On the other hand, the SVM model is computationally cheap, and consequently fast. Both models rely on extracted low-level descriptors and their statistical derivations as features but an SVM model cannot perform in a sample where low frequencies are missing or when there is highly noisy data; in SVM, such features result in the extraction of only noise or blank features. On the other hand, the CNN model can perform over such data. In this regard, the CNN model is more versatile for our purposes. Performance-wise, in frequency ranges 0-8000 Hz, the CNN model outperforms both the human judges and the SVM model, where the SVM model performs the poorest. Another advantage of the CNN model is its ability to produce intermediate activations (heat maps). These intermediate activations can be used both for computational studies and manual inspection. The CNN model is computationally expensive, yet it offers an advantage over SVM by outperforming SVM in the range 0-8000 Hz. Moreover, the CNN model succeeds in the frequency range 0-5000 Hz, where the SVM cannot produce any result. Given that the 0-5000 Hz frequency range involves the frequency band that sufficiently represents human speech, the performance of the CNN model in this frequency range is a good sign that it can be of use in future research.

The low prediction results of CNN in the 500-8000 Hz frequency range may have some implications on human beings' perception of emotion in words. In this frequency range, the CNN model's performance, but not the human judges, substantially decreased. This result may suggest that human beings are not affected by the absence of the missing acoustic properties below 500 Hz in classifying the words into four emotion states, while the CNN model is. In fact, in this frequency range, the CNN performed well in classifying *angry* and to a lesser degree, *happy* (with a recall of 0.64). The overall low performance of CNN in this range is affected by the low recall scores for *calm* (0.11) and *sad* (0.31) (Table 10). Given that *calm* and *sad* are low energy emotional states, we can speculate that when frequencies below 500 Hz are blocked, the CNN model seems affected negatively because, among other acoustic features, speech energy is indeed lost below 500 Hz. Further research is called for to establish what factors precisely led to this result.

6. Conclusion

In this study, we mainly described the development of the Turkish Emotion-Voice Database (TurEV-DB), a database that integrates a core corpus of emotion-laden word pronunciations with peripheries. In this study, we mainly described the development of the Turkish Emotion-Voice Database (TurEV-DB) which resulted a voice corpus and a database package consisting of different features. The corpus component includes 1738 tokens generated from 4 emotions (angry, calm, happy, and sad) and 82 words by 6 amateur actors. The dataset package carries a wide range of components.

- 1582 statistical features extracted using OpenSmile and IS10_paralig configuration.[6]
- 3-time variant prosodic features extracted using OpenSmile and prosodyAcf configuration.
- 1738 spectrograms generated using STFT.
- 1738 spectrograms overplayed with prosodic features.
- An SVM machine learning model.
- A CNN deep learning model.
- 349 heat maps derived from intermediate activations of the CNN model.

The present study was limited by the small number of actors (and therefore tokens) as well as the small number of judges. In the future, we plan to increase the number of tokens and the judges, and develop better evaluation models to increase the quality of the tokens. We also intend to enrich the database by including more recordings from new amateur actors. With the completion of the future work TurEV-DB will be made open to the public.

---

[6] https://www.audeering.com/download/opensmile-book-latest/

7.   Acknowledgements

We would like to thank Şiyar Morsünbül, Kübra Yılmaz, Oğuzcan Ülgen, Cansu Aşıcı, Ayşe Nur Balli, Dilşah Suretli, Gamze Gücenmez Üngörmüş, Mustafa Özaydın, Enis Dönmez, Emre Erçin, Baki Cağdaş, Aydın, Reyyan Baş Ümit Murat, Dilara Uslu, Müge Çelikel, Buşra Gizem Sönmez, and İrem Yıldız for their assistance in data collection, and Cengiz Acartürk and İclal Ergenç for useful comments on an earlier version of the study. We thank three anonymous reviewers for their insightful comments. Any errors are our own.

8.   Bibliographical References

Audacity Team. (n.d.). Audacity Manual. Retrieved February 4, 2019, from https://manual.audacityteam.org/man/noise_reduction.html

Bakir, C. (2017). Speech recognition system for Turkish language with hybrid method. *Global Journal of Computer Sciences: Theory and Research*, 7(1), 48. https://doi.org/10.18844/gjcs.v7i1.2699

Bakır, Ç., & Yuzkat, M. (2018). Speech Emotion Classification and Recognition with different methods for Turkish Language. *Balkan Journal of Electrical and Computer Engineering*, 6(2), 54–60. https://doi.org/10.17694/bajece.419557

Burkhardt, F., Paeschke, A., Rolfes, M., Sendlmeier, W., Weiss, B., Berlin, T. U., Berlin, H. U. (2005). A Database of German Emotional Speech. In *Proc. of INTERSPEECH 2005*.

Ergenç, İ., & Bekar Uzun, İ. P. (2017). *Türkçenin Ses Dizgesi* (1st ed.). Ankara: Seçkin Yayıncılık.

Eun, H. K., Kyung, H. H., Soo, H. K., & Yoon, K. K. (2007). Speech emotion recognition using eigen-FFT in clean and noisy environments. In *Proceedings - IEEE International Workshop on Robot and Human Interactive Communication* (pp. 689–694). https://doi.org/10.1109/ROMAN.2007.4415174

Eyben, F., Wöllmer, M., Schuller, B. B., Weninger, F., Wollmer, M., & Schuller, B. B. (2015). OPENSMILE: open-Source Media Interpretation by Large feature-space Extraction. *MM'10 - Proceedings of the ACM Multimedia 2010 International Conference*. https://doi.org/10.1145/1873951.1874246

Fidan, D. (2007). Türkçe ezgi örüntüsünde duygudurum ve sözedim görünümü [Emotion and speechacts in Turkish intonation pattern] (Unpublished Ph.D. Thesis). Ankara University.

Hozjan, V., Zdravko, K., Asuncion, M., Antonio, B., Albino, N., Moreno, Z., … Nogueiras, A. (2002). Interface Databases: Design and Collection of a Multilingual Emotional Speech Database. In *LREC* (pp. 2019–2023). Las Palmas de Gran Canaria, Spain.

Kaya, H., & Karpov, A. A. (2018). Efficient and effective strategies for cross-corpus acoustic emotion recognition. *Neurocomputing*, *275*, 1028–1034. https://doi.org/10.1016/j.neucom.2017.09.049

Kim, Y., Lee, H., & Provost, E. M. (2013). Deep learning for robust feature generation in audiovisual emotion recognition. In *ICASSP, IEEE International Conference on Acoustics, Speech and Signal Processing - Proceedings*. https://doi.org/10.1109/ICASSP.2013.6638346

Korkmaz, O. E., & Atasoy, A. (2016). Emotion recognition from speech signal using mel-frequency cepstral coefficients. In *ELECO 2015 - 9th International Conference on Electrical and Electronics Engineering* (pp. 1254–1257). Institute of Electrical and Electronics Engineers Inc. https://doi.org/10.1109/ELECO.2015.7394435

Meral, H. M., Ekenek, H. ., & Özsoz, A. (2003). Analysis of emotion in Turkish. In *XVIIth National Conference on Turkish Linguistics*.

Oflazoglu, C., & Yildirim, S. (2013). Recognizing emotion from Turkish speech using acoustic features. *Eurasip Journal on Audio, Speech, and Music Processing*. https://doi.org/10.1186/1687-4722-2013-26

Parlak, C., Diri, B., & Gürgen, F. (2014). A Cross-Corpus Experiment in Speech Emotion Recognition Yildiz Technical University , Turkey. In *2nd Workshop on Speech, Language and Audio in Multimedia (SLAM 2014)* (pp. 11–12). Retrieved from https://www.isca-speech.org/archive/slam_2014/papers/slm4_058.pdf

Podder, P., Zaman Khan, T., Haque Khan, M., & Muktadir Rahman, M. (2014). Comparative Performance Analysis of Hamming, Hanning and Blackman Window. *International Journal of Computer Applications*. https://doi.org/10.5120/16891-6927

Rozgić, V., Ananthakrishnan, S., Saleem, S., Kumar, R., Vembu, A. N., & Prasad, R. (2012). Emotion recognition using acoustic and lexical features. In *13th Annual Conference of the International Speech Communication Association 2012, INTERSPEECH 2012* (Vol. 1, pp. 366–369). Retrieved from http://www.isca-speech.org/archive

Selvaraju, R. R., Cogswell, M., Das, A., Vedantam, R., Parikh, D., & Batra, D. (2017). Grad-CAM: Visual Explanations from Deep Networks via Gradient-Based Localization. In *Proceedings of the IEEE International Conference on Computer Vision*. https://doi.org/10.1109/ICCV.2017.74

Yadav, A. (2009). Nyquist-Shannon Sampling Theorem. In *Digital Communication*.

Yao, Y.-C. (2014). Nyquist Frequency. In *Wiley StatsRef: Statistics Reference Online*. https://doi.org/10.1002/9781118445112.stat03517